Brief Contents

PART 1 **MANAGEMENT CONCEPTS**

1 Management: An Overview 2
2 Management Thought: Past and Present 36
3 Management's Commitments to Quality and Productivity 66
4 The Manager's Environment 98

PART 2 **PLANNING AND DECISION MAKING**

5 Organizational Planning 124
6 Strategic Planning and Strategic Management 158
7 Making Decisions 190

PART 3 **ORGANIZING**

8 Organizing Principles 226
9 Organizational Design 264
10 Organizational Culture and Change 292

PART 4 **STAFFING AND LEADING**

11 Staffing 332
12 Communication: Interpersonal and Organizational 376
13 Human Motivation 408
14 Leadership 450
15 Team Management and Conflict 484

PART 5 **CONTROLLING**

16 Controlling: Purpose and Process 520
17 Control Techniques 546
18 Operations Management 580

PART 6 **SPECIAL CONCERNS**

19 Information Management Systems 614
20 International Management 642
21 Succeeding in Your Organization 680
22 Management Ethics and Social Responsibility 716

Contents

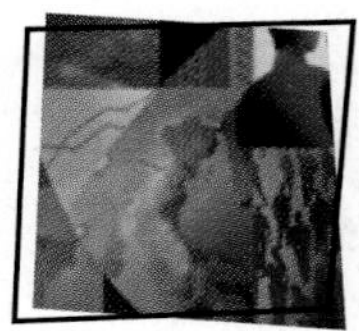

PART 1 MANAGEMENT CONCEPTS

1 Management: An Overview 2

Introduction 4

Management and Managers 5

Organizational Need for Managers 5

The Manager's Universe 6
The Need to Please Customers 7 The Need to Provide Leadership 8 The Need to Act Ethically 9 The Need to Value Diversity in Their Employees 10 The Need to Cope with Global Challenges 12

Levels of Management 13
Top Management 14 Middle Management 14 First-Line Management 15 Functional Managers 16

Management Functions 18
Planning 18 Organizing 19 Staffing 20 Leading 20 Controlling 20 Functions and the Levels of Management 20

Management Roles 22
Interpersonal Roles 22 Informational Roles 22 Decisional Roles 23 Roles and Managerial Functions 24 Roles and the Expectations of Others 24

Management Skills 25
Technical Skills 26 Human Skills 26 Conceptual Skills 26 Skills and Levels of Management 26

Management Myths and Realities 29

Evaluating a Manager's Performance 30

Management in Action
GE—World's Most Respected Company 3

Global Applications
Turnaround at South African Airways 8

Ethical Management
Telemarketing Efforts Raise More Than Money 10

Valuing Diversity
The EDS Approach 11

Managing Technology
The Information Age 27

Application Case
Shake Up at Safecard Services 34

Video Case
Entrepreneurship and Innovation: A Study of Yahoo! 34

2 Management Thought: Past and Present 36

Introduction 38

History and Theory of Management 39
Value of History 39 Ancient History 39 Value of Theory 39

Classical Management Theory 40
Classical Scientific School 41 Classical Administrative School 44

Behavioral Management Theory 46

Quantitative Management Theory 49
Management Science 49

Systems Management Theory 51
Systems School 51 Cumulative Energy of Synergy 52

Contingency Management Theory 54

Management in Action
Deere & Company: Management Trendsetter 37

Valuing Diversity
From Equal Opportunity to Valuing Diversity 43

Ethical Management
How the Pursuit of Quality Can Alienate Customers 56

Managing Technology
Electronic Commerce 58

Global Applications
Government and Industry Cooperation in Japan 59

Quality Management Theory 55
Kaizen Approach 55 Reengineering Approach 56 Major Contributors to Quality Management 57

Application Case
The Norton Company Versus 3M 64

Video Case
Evolution of Management Thought: A Study of Sunshine Cleaning, JIAN, and Archway Cookies 65

3 Management's Commitments to Quality and Productivity 66

Introduction 67

Quality, Productivity, and Profitability 68
Quality Function Deployment 70 Cost-Effective Quality 75 Productivity 75 Quality-Productivity-Profitability Link 76

Improving Quality and Productivity 77
Reengineering Approaches 79 Commitments at the Top 80 Commitments at the Middle 84 Commitments at the Bottom 86 External Commitments 88

Additional Internal and External Influences on Quality and Productivity 90
Internal Influences 90 External Influences 91

Management in Action
Lifelong Customers 67

Global Applications
Hyundai Buys the Quality Message 72

Ethical Management
Rubbermaid's Approach to Reengineering 72

Managing Technology
Computer Literacy 77

Valuing Diversity
Empowerment at Cast-Fab Technologies 84

Application Case
Tenneco's Case Corporation Adopts a Customer Focus 95

Video Case
Wainwright Industries: Completing the Quality Journey 96

4 The Manager's Environment 98

Introduction 100

The Organization as a System 100

Internal Environment 102
Mission, Vision, and Core Values 102 Core Competencies 104 Organizational Culture 104 Organizational Climate 105 Leadership 105 Organizational Structure 105 Resources 106

External Environment 109
Directly Interactive Forces 109 Indirectly Interactive Forces 112

Environments and Management 115
Sensing and Adapting to Environments 116 Influencing Environments 116 Meeting Responsibilities to Stakeholders 116

Management in Action
America OnLine, Inc. Responds to Its Environment 99

Ethical Management
Cola Wars on Campus 111

Global Applications
Britain and the Measure of Things 113

Managing Technology
World Wide Web 115

Valuing Diversity
Diversity at FedEx 117

Application Case
Toys 'R' Us Refocuses 122

Video Case
Burton Snowboards: External Business Environment 122

PART 2 PLANNING AND DECISION MAKING

5 Organizational Planning 124

Management in Action
How Mission Makes the Difference at eBay 125

Managing Technology
Browsers 127

Valuing Diversity
Planning for Diversity 135

Ethical Management
Privacy: Company Policy and the Law 138

Global Applications
Forecasting Leads Mercedes to Alabama 148

Application Case
Mars Clings to Its Plans 155

Video Case
Kropf Fruit Company: A Study in Planning 155

Introduction 126

Planning Defined 126
Mission Statement 126 Goals 129 Plans 130 Strategies and Tactics 131 Determining Resource Requirements 132

Types of Plans 133
Strategic Plans 134 Tactical Plans 135 Operational Plans 136 Unified Hierarchy of Goals 141 Contingency Plans 141

Basic Planning Process 142
Setting Objectives 142 Analyzing and Evaluating the Environment 143 Identifying the Alternatives 145 Evaluating the Alternatives 145 Selecting the Best Solution 145 Implementing the Plan 146 Controlling and Evaluating the Results 146

Making Plans Effective 146
Improving the Quality of Assumptions and Forecasts 147 Planning Tools 149

Barriers to Planning 150
Inability to Plan 150 Lack of Commitment to the Planning Process 150 Inferior Information 151 Lack of Focus on the Long Term 151 Overreliance on the Planning Department 151 Overemphasis on Controllable Variables 151

6 Strategic Planning and Strategic Management 158

Management in Action
Harley-Davidson's Strategic Evolution 159

Managing Technology
URL or Internet Address 169

Ethical Management
Quaker State Leaves Them Crying 173

Global Applications
Interbrew's Springboard for Growth 176

Valuing Diversity
Alpine's Competitive Advantage 185

Application Case
Questionable Strategy at Hallmark 188

Video Case
Hudson's Somerset Store: Planning and Implementing 188

Introduction 161

Nature of Strategic Planning and Strategic Management 161
Elements of Strategic Planning 162 Responsibility for Strategic Planning 164 Strategy Formulation Versus Strategy Implementation 165 Levels of Strategy 165

Strategic Planning Process 167
Creating a Mission Statement and Goals 167 Analyzing the Internal and External Environments 169 Reassessing the Mission Statement and Goals 171 Formulating Strategies 172 Implementing Strategies 172 Monitoring and Evaluating Results 175

Formulating Corporate-Level Strategy 175
Grand Strategies 176 Portfolio Strategy 178

Formulating Business-Level Strategy 180
Adaptive Strategies 180 Competitive Strategies 182

Formulating Functional-Level Strategy 183
Marketing Strategy 184 Production Strategy 184 Human Resources Strategy 184 Financial Strategy 184 Research and Development Strategy 184

7 Making Decisions 190

Management in Action
Microsoft: Life Changing Decisions 191

Introduction 192

What You Need To Know About Decisions 192

Ethical Management
Questionable Decision Making at Food Lion and ABC 196

Managing Technology
Search Engines 199

Global Applications
Making the Right Decisions at Nokia 202

Valuing Diversity
Not Old . . . Wise 215

Application Case
Continental Lite Fails to Fly 223

Video Case
Next Door Food Store: A Study in Decision Making 223

What Decision Making Is 192
Decision Making, Problem Solving, and Opportunity Management 192 Universality of Decision Making 193 Approaches to Decision Making 193 Programmed and Nonprogrammed Decisions 194

Seven-Step Decision-Making Process 196
Defining the Problem or Opportunity 196 Identifying Limiting Factors 198 Developing Potential Alternatives 199 Analyzing the Alternatives 200 Selecting the Best Alternative 201 Implementing the Decision 201 Establishing a Control and Evaluation System 202

Environmental Influence on Decision Making 203
Degree of Certainty 203 Imperfect Resources 205 Internal Environment 205 External Environment 208

Influence of Managerial Style on Decision Making 209
Personal Decision-Making Approaches 209 Ability to Set Priorities 209 Timing of Decisions 210 Tunnel Vision 211 Commitment to Previous Decisions 211 Creativity 211

Group Decision Making 211
Brainstorming 212 Nominal Group Technique 212 Delphi Technique 213 Advantages and Disadvantages of Group Decision Making 214

Quantitative Decision-Making Techniques 215
Decision Trees 215 Payback Analysis 217 Simulations 217

Creating an Environment for Effective Decision Making 219

PART 3 ORGANIZING

8 Organizing Principles 226

Management in Action
Sun Microsystems Masters Outsourcing 227

Global Applications
Reshaping Siemens 232

Valuing Diversity
Reorganizing to Maximize Talent 237

Ethical Management
Payoffs and Kickbacks—Who Pays? 247

Managing Technology
Evaluating Information on the Internet 258

Application Case
Merlin Needs a Magician 262

Video Case
JIAN: A Study in Organizing 262

Introduction 228

The Formal Organization 228

Organizing Process 229
Relationship Between Planning and Organizing 229 Benefits of Organizing 230

Five-Step Organizing Process 230
Reviewing Plans and Goals 230 Determining Work Activities 233 Classifying and Grouping Activities 234 Assigning Work and Delegating Authority 237 Designing a Hierarchy of Relationships 237

Major Organizational Concepts 239
Authority 239 Unity of Command 243 Power 243 Delegation 245 Span of Control 246 Centralization Versus Decentralization 249

The Informal Organization 252
Informal Organization Defined 253 Informal and Formal Organizations Compared 253 Emergence of the Informal Organization 254 Structure of the Informal Organization 255 Impact of the Informal Organization 257

9 Organizational Design 264

Management in Action
Coca-Cola Reformulates Its Business 265

Ethical Management
Profits and Layoffs 268

Introduction 266

Designing Organizational Structures 266
Organizational Design Defined 266 Objectives of Organizational Design 267

Range of Organizational Design Outcomes 269
Mechanistic Organizational Structures 269 Organic Organizational Structures 269

Valuing Diversity
Zales Gets Richer 275

Global Applications
A Quick End to Confusion 283

Managing Technology
Email 287

Application Case
A Great Idea 290

Video Case
Bindco, Inc.: Capacity Planning 290

Contingency Factors Affecting Organizational Design 271
Strategy 271 Environment 272 Size of the Organization 274 Age of the Organization 274 Technology 276

Structural Options in Organizational Design 278
Functional Structure 278 Divisional Structure 279 Matrix Structure 282 Team Structure 284 Network Structure 285

10 Organizational Culture and Change 292

Management in Action
Corning's Cultural Transformation 293

Valuing Diversity
Deloitte & Touche Changes the Culture 296

Managing Technology
Email Addresses 297

Ethical Management
Unhealthy Shared Values and Beliefs 303

Global Applications
South Korea's Bright Star 311

Application Case
A Cultural Mismatch 329

Video Case
Central Michigan Community Hospital: Managing Change 330

Introduction 294

Organizational Culture 294
Organizational Culture Defined 294 Factors Shaping Culture 295

Manifestations of Culture 298
Statements of Principle 298 Stories 299 Slogans 299 Heroes 300 Ceremonies 300 Symbols 301 Climate 301 Physical Environment 302

Creation of Culture 302
Role of Managers 302 Role of Employees 304 Factors Contributing to the Effectiveness of Culture 305

Nature of Change 307
Sources of Change 307 Types of Change 308 Rates of Change 310 Management and Change 313

How to Manage Change 313
Need for Change: Diagnosing and Predicting It 314 Steps in Planned Change 316

Qualities Promoting Change 317
Mutual Trust 317 Organizational Learning 318 Adaptability 318

Implementation of Change 319
Resistance to Change 319 Why Change Efforts Fail 320 Methods of Effecting Change 321

Organizational Development 323
Purposes of Organizational Development 324 Strategies of Organizational Development 324 Evaluating the Effectiveness of Organizational Development 325

PART 4 STAFFING AND LEADING

11 Staffing 332

Management in Action
The Container Store's Intense Employee Commitment 333

Managing Technology
Parts of Email 341

Valuing Diversity
Diversity and Human Resource Managers 343

Ethical Management
Coping with Office Romances 351

Introduction 334

Responsibility for Staffing 334

Staffing Process 335

Staffing Environments 336
Legal Environment 336 Sociocultural Environment 342 Union Environment 345

Human Resource Planning 346
Job Analysis 346 Human Resource Inventory 347 Human Resource Forecasting 348 Inventory and Forecast Comparison 350

Recruitment, Selection, and Orientation 351
Strategies for Recruiting 351 Selection Process 352 Orientation 357

Training and Development 357
Purposes of Training 358 Challenges of Training 358 Techniques of Training 359 Purposes of Development 360 Techniques of Development 360

Performance Appraisal 360
Purposes of Performance Appraisal 361 Components of Appraisal Systems 361 Appraisal Methods 362 Legality of Appraisals 364

Implementation of Employment Decisions 364
Promotions 365 Transfers 365 Demotions 365 Separations 366

Compensation 368
Purposes of Compensation 368 Factors Influencing Compensation 368 Wages and Salaries 368 Benefits 370 Executive Compensation 371

Global Applications
Japan's Lifetime Employment 367

Application Case
Outstanding Business Leader 2000; North American Customer Excellence Award 1998; Black Enterprise's 1995 Auto Dealer of the Year Builds on Diversity 374

Video Case
LaBelle Management: Performance Appraisals 374

12 Communication: Interpersonal and Organizational 376

Introduction 378

Communication Process 378

Mediums of Communication 380
Verbal Communication 380 Nonverbal Communication 382

Interpersonal Communication 384
Communication and Teams 385 Barriers to Interpersonal Communication 386

Organizational Communication 389
Formal Downward Channels 390 Formal Horizontal Channels 391 Formal Upward Channels 392 Formal Communication Networks 393 Informal Communication Channels 394 Barriers to Organizational Communication 395

Improvement of Communication 399
Responsibilities of Senders 399 Responsibilities of Receivers 401 Ten Commandments of Good Communication 403

Management in Action
Dell Connects with Suppliers and Customers 377

Global Applications
The Medium Is the Message 380

Ethical Management
Profits Through Imitation 383

Valuing Diversity
"Discovering" a Market of 25 Million 387

Managing Technology
Email Courtesy (Netiquette) 397

Application Case
Alcoa's Open Work Spaces 406

Video Case
Burke, Inc.: Technology in Business Communication 406

13 Human Motivation 408

Introduction 410

Challenge of Motivation 410
Basics of Motivation 412 Motivation Model 412 Integrated Motivation Model 413

Content Theories: Motivation Theories Focusing on Needs 416
Maslow's Hierarchy of Needs 416 Herzberg's Two-Factor Theory 420 McClelland and the Need for Achievement 423 Alderfer's ERG Theory 424

Process Theories: Motivation Theories Focusing on Behaviors 427
Expectancy Theory 427 Reinforcement Theory 429 Equity Theory 432 Goal-Setting Theory 433

Building a Philosophy of Management 434
Theory X and Theory Y 434 Argyris's Maturity Theory 435 Development of Expectations 436

Managing for Motivation 436
Treating People as Individuals 436 Providing Support 437 Recognizing and Valuing Diversity 438 Empowering Employees 438 Providing an Effective Reward System 440 Redesigning Jobs 440 Promoting Intrapreneurship 442 Creating Flexibility 444

Management in Action
Loyalty Rewarded at Thompson-McCully 409

Global Applications
No More Fear at Semco 412

Ethical Management
A Pink Slip for Structural Dynamics 418

Valuing Diversity
BRW Gets a Wake-up Call 439

Managing Technology
Email Privacy 444

Application Case
Building a Quality Work Environment 447

Video Case
Valassis Communications: Motivating for Performance 447

14 Leadership 450

Management in Action
Participative Leadership at Southwest Airlines 451

Valuing Diversity
"Male" and "Female" Approaches to Leadership 454

Ethical Management
Peer Reviews at Risk International 459

Global Applications
Ford's Jacques A. Nassar 461

Managing Technology
Listservs 466

Application Case
The End of Olds 481

Video Case
Sunshine Cleaning Systems: A Study of Leadership 481

Introduction 452

Leadership Defined 452
Leadership Traits 453 Leadership Skills 454 Leadership Behaviors 455 Management Versus Leadership 457

Power and Leadership 460
Legitimate Power 460 Coercive Power 460 Reward Power 461 Expert Power 461 Referent Power 462

Leadership Styles 463
Positive Versus Negative Motivation 463 Decision-Making Styles 464 Task Orientation Versus People Orientation 466

Theories of Situational Leadership 469
Fiedler's Contingency Model 469 House and Mitchell's Path-Goal Theory 471 Hersy and Blanchard's Life-Cycle Theory 474

Challenges Facing Leaders 475
Leadership Throughout an Organization 475 Leadership and Rapid Response 476 Leadership and Tough Decisions 476

How Managers Can Become Better Leaders 477

15 Team Management and Conflict 484

Management in Action
Boeing Teams to Success 485

Managing Technology
Usenet 491

Global Applications
The Patient Comes First 493

Valuing Diversity
Experience Counts 499

Ethical Management
The Paycheck Counts 506

Application Case
Who Needs Teams? 517

Video Case
Teamwork at GE Medical Systems 517

Introduction 486

Nature of Teams 487
Teams Defined 487 Characteristics of Effective Teams 487 Types of Teams 487

Philosophical Issues of Team Management 489
How to Use Teams 489 How Much Independence to Give Teams 493

Establishment of Team Organization 495
Process of Team Building 495 Team-Building Considerations 498

Management of Team Processes 500
Stages of Team Development 500 Team Cohesiveness 502 Team Norms 502 Team Personality 503

Measurements of Team Effectiveness 504
Benefits of Teams 504 Costs of Teams 505

Team and Individual Conflict 507
Views of Conflict 507 Positive and Negative Aspects of Conflict 508 Sources of Conflict 508

Strategies for Managing Conflict 510
Analysis of the Conflict Situation 510 Development of a Strategy 511 Conflict Stimulation 512

PART 5 CONTROLLING

16 Controlling: Purpose and Process 520

Management in Action
Getting Control at Toshiba 521

Global Applications
Toyota's Camry for 1997: Less Is More 523

Introduction 522

Controlling and the Other Management Functions 524

Control Process 525
Establishing Performance Standards 525 Measuring Performance 528 Comparing Measured Performance to Established Standards 528 Taking Corrective Action 530

Ethical Management
Robinson Helicopter Company—FDA vs. NTSB 529

Valuing Diversity
Latino Boycott Hurts Latinos 531

Managing Technology
Usenet or Newsgroup Courtesy 533

Application Case
New Broom Sweeps Clean 543

Video Case
Organizational Control at Archway Cookies 543

Types of Controls and Control Systems 530
Feedforward Controls 532 Concurrent Controls 533 Feedback Controls 534 Control Systems 534

Characteristics of Effective Controls 535
Focus on Critical Points 535 Integration 535 Acceptability 536 Timeliness 536 Economic Feasibility 536 Accuracy 537 Comprehensibility 537

Control Monitoring 538
Monitoring Organizational Impacts 538 Updating Controls 539

17 Control Techniques 546

Management in Action
Yahoo!s Webvertising 547

Global Applications
Russian Stockholders' Struggles for Control 561

Managing Technology
Chat 566

Valuing Diversity
Valuing Diversity Through Self-Directed Work Teams 572

Ethical Management
Ethics and Secretaries 574

Application Case
Kroch's Cracks, Then Crumbles 578

Video Case
Quality Control at Bindco Corporation 578

Introduction 548

Subsystem Controls 548
Finance Controls 548 Marketing Controls 550 Human Resource Controls 550

Financial Controls 551
Financial Statements 551 Financial Ratio Analysis 555 Financial Responsibility Centers 558 Financial Audits 558

Budget Controls 560
Budget Development Process 561 Operating Budgets 564 Financial Budgets 565

Marketing Controls 565
Marketing Research 566 Test Marketing 567 Marketing Ratios 568 Sales Quotas 568 Stockage 569

Human Resource Controls 569
Statistical Analysis 569 Human Asset Valuation 571 Training and Development 571 Performance Appraisals 572 Attitude Surveys 573 Management Audits 573

Computers and Control 573

18 Operations Management 580

Management in Action
Knitting at a Record Pace 581

Managing Technology
Chatiquette 583

Global Applications
The Newest Assembly Line 591

Valuing Diversity
Training for Quality 597

Ethical Management
Made in the USA? 599

Application Case
Outsourcing Leads to Success 612

Video Case
Operations Management: World Gym 612

Introduction 582

Nature of Operations Management 582
Operations Strategy and Management Defined 582 Importance of Operations Management 583

Operations Planning 584
Product or Service Design Planning 584 Facilities Layout 587 Production Processes and Technology 590 Facilities Location 594 Capacity Planning 595

Management of Operations 595
Aggregate Plan 596 Master Schedule 596 Structure for Implementing Production 597

Controls for Quality and Productivity 597
Design Control 598 Materials Control: Purchasing 598 Inventory Control 600 Scheduling Control 604 Product Control 607

PART 6 SPECIAL CONCERNS

19 Information Management Systems 614

Management in Action
Managing Information at Amazon.com 615

Managing Technology
Downloading Files from the Internet 619

Ethical Management
Staying Close to Customers Can Get You Too Close 629

Valuing Diversity
Meetings and Diversity 632

Global Applications
IT Outsourcing at BP 635

Application Case
Networking at VF Corporation 639

Video Case
Management Information Systems: A Study of Archway Cookies 639

Introduction 616

Information and the Manager 616

Information Management Systems 619
Functions of an Effective Information System (IS) 620 Guidelines for Developing an Information System (IS) 620

Computerized Information Systems 622
Computer Operations 626 Data Processing Models 627 Linking Computer Systems 627 CIS Management Tools 629

Managing Information Systems 632
Overcoming Resistance 632 Enabling Users 633 Outsourcing 634 Evaluating Results 634

20 International Management 642

Management in Action
McDonald's Commitment to Global Expansion 643

Managing Technology
Instant Messaging 645

Global Applications
Daewoo Eyes the World 647

Ethical Management
Beneath the Surface 658

Valuing Diversity
Rockwell Celebrates Its People 668

Application Case
Benetton's International Dilemmas 677

Video Case
Global Strategy: Enforcement Technology 677

Introduction 644

Why Businesses Become International 646

The Multinational Corporation 647

Characteristics of Multinationals 648

International Environment 649
Political Environment 649 Legal Environment 651 Economic Environment 652 Sociocultural Environment 652 Technological Environment 654

Planning and the International Manager 655
Choosing Strategies 655 Assessing the External Variables 656

Organizing and the International Manager 660
Pre-International Division Phase 660 International Division Phase 661 Global Structure Phase 662

Staffing and the International Manager 665
Staffing Problems and Solutions 665 Compensation 666

Leading and the International Manager 667
Employee Attitudes 667 Communication Problems 669 Cross-Cultural Management 670

Controlling and the International Manager 672
Characteristics of Controls 672 Control Problems 673

21 Succeeding in Your Organization 680

Management in Action
Success Unlimited 681

Global Applications
Switching Careers 687

Introduction 682

Managing to Success 682
Nature of Careers 682 Career Perspective 683 New Career Environment 683

Valuing Diversity
Polaroid Supports Careers 699

Managing Technology
Cookies 700

Ethical Management
A Question of Values 710

Application Case
Career Growth Through Feedback 714

Video Case
Career Management: LaBelle Management 714

Career Planning 684
Stages of Career Development 685 Steps in Career Planning 688

Career Management 694
Analyzing and Understanding the Organization 694 Assessment and Alignment 697

Strategies for Career Advancement 697
Committing to Lifelong Learning 697 Creating Visibility 698 Developing Mentor Relationships 701 Developing Networks 702 Understanding Power and Politics 703 Working with the Boss 704 Managing Stress 705

Organizational Dilemmas 709
Conflicts Between Personal and Organizational Values 709 Loyalty Demands 709 Advancement Decisions 710 Independence and Sponsorship 711

Management in Action
Ben & Jerry's: Social Responsibility 717

Global Applications
Thais Run a Sweatshop in Los Angeles 726

Valuing Diversity
Diversity's Link to Social Responsibility: An Open Letter to the Citizens of the Chicago Metropolitan Area 734

Managing Technology
Electronic Commerce Ethics 740

Ethical Management
Bob Holland, Ethical Leader 741

Application Case
Columbia/HCA's Hospitals: Does Getting Lean Mean Getting Mean? 745

Video Case
Social Responsibility: Ben & Jerry's 745

22 Management Ethics and Social Responsibility 716

Introduction 718

Managing Ethically 718
Individuals and Ethical Conduct 720 Leaders' Ethics 721 Organizational Influences on Ethical Conduct 722 Importance of Organizational Controls 723 Legal Constraints 726 Ethical Dilemmas 728 Guidelines for Acting Ethically 730

Nature of Social Responsibility 731
Approaches to Social Responsibility 732 Responsibilities to Stakeholders 733 Government Regulation: Pros and Cons 736

Managing for Social Responsibility 738
Top-Management Commitment 738 Social Audit 741

Recommended Readings 747

References 757

Glossary 779

Index 789

Preface

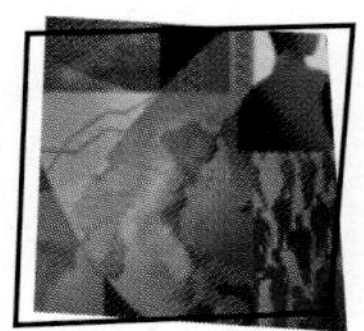

This seventh edition of *Management: Meeting and Exceeding Customer Expectations* is a comprehensive survey of the functions of management as they are currently being applied, in the United States and around the world. The content and features are structured to reinforce two continuing themes that are woven into the chapter narratives: (1) the never-ending effort by managers and organizations to meet or exceed customers' needs, and (2) the need organizations and their people have to be guided by effective leadership.

The authors have made every effort to keep this text objective, timely, and interesting to both the student and the instructor. All case problems, examples, and features portray actual companies and managers in action. Companies have been selected to provide balance between large and small organizations representing service, manufacturing, and retailing industries. Successes as well as failures are included to lend perspective and aid in understanding.

FEATURES

This text is designed to introduce you to terminology, theories, and principles at the core of business management. The book is divided into six comprehensive parts, comprising a variety of examples, applications, exercises, and devices. Each chapter contains the following components:

- A list of specific **Learning Objectives**—concepts to be mastered through chapter content—at the beginning of each chapter. Each learning objective is also highlighted in the page margin to identify where the content addresses the objective.
- A list of **Key Terms** defined within the chapter narrative, highlighted in the page margin, and presented in the glossary at the back of the book.
- A **Management in Action** chapter introductory case involving managers and their organizations—large and small, service, retailing, or manufacturing—engaged in a variety of activities that relate and connect each chapter's essential concepts. The case is regularly referred to throughout the chapter.
- **Figures** designed to illustrate and summarize essential concepts.
- **Photographs** chosen to enrich the chapter content.
- A **Global Applications** feature demonstrating the successful application of one or more of a chapter's concepts from the practice of management in other countries.
- An **Ethical Management** feature reporting on managers facing decisions that contain a variety of issues and consequences for themselves and others.
- A **Valuing Diversity** feature depicting unique ways in which organizations show appreciation for their diverse employees.

- A **Managing Technology** feature highlighting techniques that can make the manager more productive.
- A **Chapter Summary** providing a narrative explanation for each of the chapter's learning objectives.
- **Review Questions** designed to assist in mastery of the chapter's learning objectives.
- **Discussion Questions for Critical Thinking** intended to provide an opportunity to analyze and apply the chapter's concepts to practical situations.
- **Internet Exercises** designed to help in applying one or more of the chapter's key concepts.
- An **Application Case**—found at the end of each chapter—presenting managers and organizations and their attempt to cope with the major issues raised in that chapter.
- A **Video Case** to help bring key management concepts and issues to life in the classroom.

Throughout your study of this text, try to relate what you read and discuss to your own experiences. You have already been practicing—and perhaps violating—many of the principles of management. What you are about to learn is an extension and refinement of what you already know—a blending of it with the experiences of others.

Although you will be reading each chapter as a separate area of study, try to relate it to what you have experienced and read previously. By linking the content of each chapter to that which has preceded it, you will begin to appreciate that management is a tapestry with many threads that run parallel to and across one another. For example, planning relates to all the management functions; it is part of every management activity in much the same way as is communicating. Periodically step back from your study to see the "big picture" of which each chapter is but a part.

Upon completion of this text and course, you will have developed your own philosophy of management and be armed with the essentials necessary for improving your career. You will become a better manager of your own concerns as well as the work of others.

ORGANIZATION OF THE CONTENT

Part 1: Management Concepts. This section provides a basic overview of management, the evolution of management thought, management's commitment to improvement, and the various environments that affect the practice of management.

Chapter 1 explores what management is about, why it is necessary, the needs managers must address, management functions, management roles, management skills, and management myths and realities.

Chapter 2 takes the student on a journey through the past, examining the evolution of management theory from the classical schools through today. It assesses the contributions made by each and explains the links among them.

Chapter 3 focuses on management's commitment to continuous improvement. The link between quality, productivity, and profitability is explained. Factors that affect productivity are examined along with the commitments necessary by top, middle, and first-line management to improve quality and productivity. Key concepts such as core values, reengineering, open-book management, empowerment, and knowledge management are introduced.

Chapter 4 lists and defines the internal and external environments that affect and challenge the practice of management. Business as an open system and the demands of stakeholders are the major focus.

Part 2: Planning and Decision Making. The importance of the first function of management—planning—is examined from several perspectives in Chapters 5 and 6: organizational, contingency, strategic, and operational. The relationship of planning to all other management functions, and ways to make it more effective, are covered. The art of decision making is the focus of Chapter 7.

Chapter 5 explains the importance of planning, the framework for plans, types and uses of plans, and the planning process.

Chapter 6 explores the nature of strategic planning, elements of planning strategies, levels of strategic planning, and the strategic-planning process.

Chapter 7 guides the student through the steps for rational decisions, decision-making climates, quantitative methods, and the various influences on the manager's problem-solving efforts.

Part 3: Organizing. Organizing is examined as a process along with why different organizations adopt different approaches to structuring their operations. Both the formal and informal organization are included in the discussions. Organizing principles are demonstrated with examples.

Chapter 8 looks at the formal organization, the organizing process, its key principles and concepts, and the informal organization.

Chapter 9 covers organizational design, the range of organizational-design outcomes, contingency factors affecting organizational design, and the structures in common use.

Chapter 10 features organizational culture and handling change. The manifestations of cultures and subcultures, creation of cultures, nature of change, managing and implementing change, and the concepts connected with organizational development are covered comprehensively.

Part 4: Staffing and Leading. This section develops the concepts of staffing, communication, motivation, leadership, team management, and conflict. Essential legal concepts are included along with the principles and practices that affect each.

Chapter 11 surveys staffing from human resource planning to employee separations. Sociocultural and legal influences are addressed along with such activities as job analysis, job evaluation, training and development, and the practice of staffing in a union environment.

Chapter 12 focuses on communication—organizational and interpersonal. The communication process and barriers to it are demonstrated along with how managers can improve their communication efforts.

Chapter 13 explores motivation and the applications of the most relevant theories. Special attention is given to how managers can use their insights and principles to get the most from themselves and team members.

Chapter 14 looks at leadership. Its importance and associations with power and authority are detailed. The roles leaders must play with their followers are reviewed along with the theories that govern the practice of leadership and the styles that leaders may adopt.

Chapter 15 examines team management and conflict. The nature and types of teams, philosophical approaches to team management, and how to establish team-based organizations are included. Conflict is defined, and the causes of and methods for managing it are discussed.

Part 5: Controlling. This section examines and applies different aspects of the principles and theories of control.

Chapter 16 focuses on the nature of control, the control process, types of controls, and characteristics of effective controls. Added emphasis is given to the art of making controls effective.

Chapter 17 is an in-depth look at four kinds of controls: financial, budgetary, marketing, and human resource. Financial statement analysis is followed by budget-development processes and types of budgets. Various marketing controls are scrutinized next, followed by popular human resource controls.

Chapter 18 looks at operations management—its nature; its link to planning, processes, and facilities; and how to manage operations. How to control operations for both quality and productivity is included.

Part 6: Special Concerns. This section explores information management systems, international management, succeeding in one's career, and management ethics and social responsibility. Although all chapters include regular features on ethics and international applications, these important subjects merit further exploration.

Chapter 19 focuses on information flow and how it can be managed in organizations. Management information systems and decision support systems are discussed in detail.

Chapter 20 explores the recent trends affecting businesses in global markets, the nature of the international business environment, and the nature of multinational corporations. Each function of management is discussed as it applies to an international operation and environment.

Chapter 21 is concerned with career management. Stages in career development and steps in career planning are analyzed. Discussed next are several strategies managers can take to advance their careers.

Chapter 22 examines ethical issues and the need to be proactive when managing for social responsibility. After defining both concepts, the chapter explores ethical tests, approaches to social responsibility, and the links between them and applicable legal requirements. The issues of responsibilities to stakeholders and of government regulation of business activities are dealt with as well.

SUPPLEMENTS

Thomson Learning is committed to providing you, our educational partners, with the best educational resources available. Because we prepare our instructor resources with a variety of teaching environments in mind, it is likely that you will need only a portion of these for your course. Before you request an item, we ask that you please read thoroughly the description of each resource. If you still need more information about resources, we urge you to contact your local Thomson Learning sales representative or visit our Web site at *http://plunkett.swcollege.com*. Many teaching and learning resources can be downloaded directly from this site.

Student CD-ROM. The student CD-ROM, included with every copy of the text, offers a comprehensive video case that explores the characteristics of learning organizations. It features Yahoo!, the high-tech company that leads the way for more traditional organizations on the Web, learning as it goes. Case questions are programmed to allow students to email their solutions directly to their instructors. Also available on the CD-ROM are additional video cases, interactive quiz questions for each chapter, and a complete management glossary.

Study Guide (0-324-02727-3)—prepared by Harold C. Babson, Columbus State Community College, and Murray S. Brunton, Central Ohio Technical College. Designed from a student's perspective, the value-laden study guide comes with all the tools necessary to maximize results on exams and in class. Chapter outlines are included, as well as pre-tests, post-tests, and numerous self-study questions. Concept applications include skill-builder exercises and a journal for keeping track of observations of concepts presented as they relate to classroom discussion and on-the-job experience. Answers are provided for all self-tests.

Instructor's Resource Guide (0-324-02762-5)—prepared by Thomas Lloyd, Westmoreland County Community College. The Instructor's Manual emphasizes our integrated learning system. Each chapter includes learning objectives; key terms; outlines annotated with additional examples and other lecture-enhancing stories and facts; complete solutions to all end-of-chapter questions, activities, and video cases; and additional cases.

Test Bank (0-324-11683-7)—prepared by Thomas Lloyd, Westmoreland County Community College. Organized around the text's learning objectives, the test bank is available to instructors in print and computerized format. The test bank contains more than 2,900 true/false, multiple-choice, matching, short answer, and essay questions.

Examview (0-324-02731-1). This supplement contains all of the questions in the printed test bank. This program is an easy-to-use test creation software compatible with Microsoft Windows. Instructors can add or edit questions, instructions, and answers, and select questions (randomly or numerically) by previewing them on the screen. Instructors can also create and administer quizzes online, whether over the Internet, a local area network (LAN), or a wide area network (WAN).

PowerPoint—prepared by Stephen M. Peters, Cool Pictures and Multimedia. More than 200 full-color images supplement course content and expand on it through slides drawn from relevant material in the text.

Instructor's Resource CD-ROM (0-324-11652-7). Key instructor ancillaries (instructor's manual, test bank, and PowerPoint slides) are provided on CD-ROM, giving instructors the ultimate tool for customizing lectures and presentations.

Transparency Acetates (0-324-02730-3). A full set of acetate transparencies of all text figures is available to enhance classroom presentations.

Taking the Lead Telecourse Videos—prepared by INTELECOM, a not-for-profit producer of distance learning courseware. An award-winning telecourse that explores the ideas and practices of contemporary management, *Taking the Lead* is a series of 26 half-hour video programs designed by INTELECOM to correlate with *Management: Meeting and Exceeding Customer Expectations*. Related telecourse components include a Telecourse Study Guide, available from South-Western (0-324-02728-1). Designed around the telecourse videos, each lesson in the study guide includes learning objectives; an overview of the lesson's subject material; assignments that link the video lesson with applications in the textbook; a list of key terms and definitions; video viewing questions; a self-test; and expanded analysis of the lesson's concepts.To request a preview or to find out more about this INTELECOM video course, visit *http://www.intelecom.org* or call (626) 796-7300. To license *Taking the Lead* for distance learning, call (800) 576-2988.

Video Cases (0-324-11684-5, 0-324-11685-3, 0-324-11686-1, 0-324-16084-4). Our video package, available on four VHS cassettes, includes twenty-two videos that bring action-based insights right into the classroom. Organizations featured include Yahoo!, Burton Snowboards, and Ben & Jerry's. These videos frame management issues in such a way that students must apply some aspect of chapter content to their analysis of the issues.

CNN Video: Management and Organizations (0-324-13495-9). Forty-five minutes of short segments from CNN, the world's first 24-hour all-news network, are available on VHS cassette to use as lecture launchers, discussion starters, topical introductions, or directed inquiries.

InfoTrac College Edition. With InfoTrac College Edition your students can receive anytime, anywhere online access to a database of full-text articles from hundreds of popular and scholarly periodicals, such as *Newsweek*, *Fortune*, *Entrepreneur*, *Journal of Management*, and *Nation's Business*, among others. Students can use its fast and easy search tools to find relevant news and analytical information among the tens of thousands of articles in the database—updated daily and going back as far as four years—all at a single Web site. InfoTrac is a great way to expose students to online research techniques, with the security that the content is academically based and reliable. An InfoTrac College Edition subscription card is packaged free with new copies of the Plunkett text. For more information, visit *http://www.swcollege.com/infotrac/infotrac.html*.

Web Site (http://plunkett.swcollege.com). A rich Web site at *http://plunkett.swcollege.com* complements the text, providing many extras for students and instructors. Resources include interactive quizzes, downloadable support materials, additional cases and Internet exercises, and links to other useful resources.

WebTutor™ on WebCT and on Blackboard. WebTutor complements *Management: Meeting and Exceeding Customer Expectations* by providing interactive reinforcement. WebTutor's online teaching and learning environment brings together content management, assessment, communication, and collaboration capabilities for enhancing in-class instruction or for delivering distance learning. For more information, including a demo, visit *http://webtutor.swcollege.com*.

Personal WebTutor™. This Web-based study guide reviews critical text material chapter by chapter. Concepts are reinforced through extensive exercises, problems, flashcards, self-tests, and other tools. Access certificates for Personal WebTutor can be bundled with the textbook, or students can preview and purchase the product directly online for subscription periods of one month or four months. Visit *http://pwt.swcollege.com* for more information and to view a demo.

Experiencing Management (0-324-01598-4). An innovative new product, *Experiencing Management* is a totally online collection of Web-based modules that uses the latest Flash technology in its animated scenarios, graphs, and models. Designed to reinforce key management principles in a dynamic learning environment, *Experiencing Management* maintains high motivation through the use of challenging problems. Try it by visiting *http://www.experiencingmanagement.com*. *Experiencing Management* is available for purchase online by each individual module, or as a collection of all fourteen modules. As an alternative to ordering online, higher education academic instructors or curriculum coordinators who wish to place orders for multiple copies to be bundled with *Management: Meeting and Exceeding Customer Expectations* should contact their Thomson Learning/South-Western College Publishing Sales Representative at (800) 876-2350.

Management
POWER

Management Power! PowerPoint Slides (0-324-13380-4). Management Power! is a CD-ROM of PowerPoint slides covering 14 major management and organizational behavior topics: communication, control, decision making, designing organizations, ethics and social responsibility, foundations of management, global management, human resources, innovation and change, leadership, motivation, planning, strategy, and teams. These easy-to-use, multimedia-enriched slides can easily be modified and customized to suit individual preferences.

ACKNOWLEDGMENTS

We would like to thank the following reviewers who were helpful in preparing the previous editions of this text:

Kehinde A. Adesina
Contra Costa College

A. M. Agnello
Solano Community College

Anthony J. Alesi
Passaic County Community College

Douglas Anderson
Ashland College

Doug Ashby
Lewis and Clark Community College

Gary Bacon
North Lake College

Sr. Marian Batho
Aquinas Junior College

Tom Birkenhead
Lane Community College

Rex L. Bishop
Charles County Community College

Donna Bleck
Middlesex Community College

Gus Blomquist
Del Mar College

Allen Bluedorn
University of Missouri, Columbia

John Bohan
Clackamas Community College

Arnold J. Bornfield
Worcester State University

Duane C. Brickner
South Mountain Community College

Bruce E. Bugbee
Glendale Community College

John Carmichael
Union County College

Charles Chanter
Grand Rapids Junior College

Felipe H. Chia
Harrisburg Area Community College

Helen A. Corley
Oxnard College

Linda M. Duckworth
Northeast Mississippi Community College

Jan Feldbauer
Austin Community College

Anthony B. Foster
Cloud County Community College

Don Friis
North Idaho College

Jim Garaventa
Chemeketa Community College

Edward Giermak
College of DuPage

William H. Graham, Jr.
Catawba Valley Community College

David A. Gray
University of Texas, Arlington

Dennis Hansen
Des Moines Area Community College

Theodore L. Hansen, Jr.
Salem State College

Carnella Hardin
Glendale School of Arizona

Dave Harris
Mission College

S. Miller Harrison
Durham Technical Community College

Paul Hegele
Elgin Community College

Ron Herrick
Mesa Community College

Dorothy Hetmerhinds
Trinity Valley Community College

Gene Hilton
Brookhaven College

Linda Hodge
Guilford Technical Community College

Ken Howey
Trident Technical College

Don Hucker
Cypress College

Samir T. Ishak
Grand Valley State University

W. J. Jacobs
Lake City Community College

Scott King
Sinclair Community College

Judith E. Kizzie
Clinton Community College

Gus L. Kotoulas
Morton College

George Labovitz
El Paso Community College

Arthur La Capria, Jr.
El Paso Community College

Clay Lifto
Kirkwood Community College

Norbert Lindskog
Washington College

Robin Livesay
University of Indianapolis

Thomas Lloyd
Westmoreland County Community College

Vladimir G. Marinich
Howard Community College

Leonard Martyns
Chaffey College

John E. McCarty
New Mexico Junior College

Jim Lee Morgan
West Los Angeles College

Joyce P. Moseley
Trident Technical College

David W. Murphy
Madisonville Community College

Tim Nygaard
Madisonville Community College

Sylvia Ong
Scottsdale Community College

George Otto
Truman College

Dennis D. Pappas
Columbus State Community College

C. Richard Paulson
Mankato State University

Pat Plocek
Richland College

Quenton Pulliam
Nashville State Technical Institute

Patricia Mink Rath
The International Academy of Merchandising and Design Ltd.—Chicago Campus

Carol Rowey
Community College of Rhode Island

Joseph C. Santora
Essex County College

Ravi Sarathy
Northeastern University

Tom Shaughnessy
Illinois Central College

Martin St. John
Westmoreland County Community College

Seiji Sugawara
Mendocino College

James B. Thomas
Pennsylvania State University

Bill Tinder
Greenville Tech

Ralph Todd
American River College

Roland Tollefson
Anne Arundel Community College

W. Emory Trainham
Ashland College

Sumner M. White
Massachusetts Bay Community College

Bob Willis
Rogers State College

Larry Wilson
Sandhills Community College

We extend heartfelt thanks to the following reviewers who have been so helpful in preparing this seventh edition:

Joe Ancona
Webster University

Lawrence C. Barry
Cuyamaca College

Anthony Cioffi
Lorain County Community College

Kenneth M. Hadge
Newbury College

David C. Olsen
North Hennepin Community College

Anita Olson
North Hennepin Community College

Daniel Thoren
Atlantic Cape Community College

Larry Wilson
Sandhills Community College

With thanks,

Warren Plunkett
Ray Attner
Gemmy Allen

A Strategic Guide

to the seventh edition of Plunkett, Attner, and Allen's
Management: Meeting and Exceeding Customer Expectations

Good planning and organization are equally essential to successfully operating a business and writing a textbook—and using one! This guide introduces you to the features in the text that are designed to help you master the management concepts fundamental to success in today's business environment.

This text has been organized around the Learning Objectives, to create for you a tightly integrated learning system.

◀ CHAPTER OBJECTIVES

The Learning Objectives listed at the beginning of every chapter briefly state the skills you will acquire from reading the chapter.

NUMBERED ICONS ▶

Each objective, with its numbered icon, then appears in the chapter margin where the objective is fulfilled, so that you can quickly locate the applicable material.

CHAPTER SUMMARIES ▶

The summary at the end of the chapter is organized around the Learning Objectives as well, reinforcing the key points under each objective.

MANAGEMENT ▶ IN ACTION

These cases highlight relevant experiences of actual companies and managers. This example, for instance, offers practical, real-world application of a company's mission.

MANAGEMENT IN ACTION

How Mission Makes the Difference at eBay

Founded in September 1995 by Pierre Omidyar, eBay began as a place for trading Pez dispensers. "Users can find everything from the practical, unique, and interesting on eBay—such as automobiles, chintz china, jewelry, teddy bears, musical instruments, photographic equipment, computers, furniture, and figurines." eBay doesn't actually carry the inventory. It hosts the auctions and charges the sellers a fee for its services. (See "About eBay," http://www.ebay.com.)

By 1998, a headhunter recruited

tomers to express themselves directly to the firm in response to the firm's communications. One of the ways Whitman scans the environment is through the "Voice of the Customer Day." Each month, 10 to 20 customers are brought to eBay's offices to meet new employees, as well as Whitman. "One of the things I'm most focused on is managing something that's growing from a small town to a larger community," says Whitman (Green, 1999).

The eBay user community was sending signals that it was inter-

& Butterfield, which brought higher valued items to the site. She also purchased Cruise International Auctioneers, an automobile auctioneer company, allowing automobiles to be auctioned on the eBay site.

eBay is a multibillion-dollar company and has grown at a phenomenal rate in terms of the number of people who are using eBay, the quantity of items that are being listed for sale, and the dollar amount of transactions that close everyday. It is difficult to forecast this rate of growth, and a lack of forecast caused poor technology planning. Furthermore, eBay had little or no backup strategy in case of an emergency.

For most Web sites, the supporting infrastructure is a fragile ecosystem of software, hardware and wiring. A small weakness in any part can cascade

...d a new market segment for online auctions of higher-

125

Organizational Planning

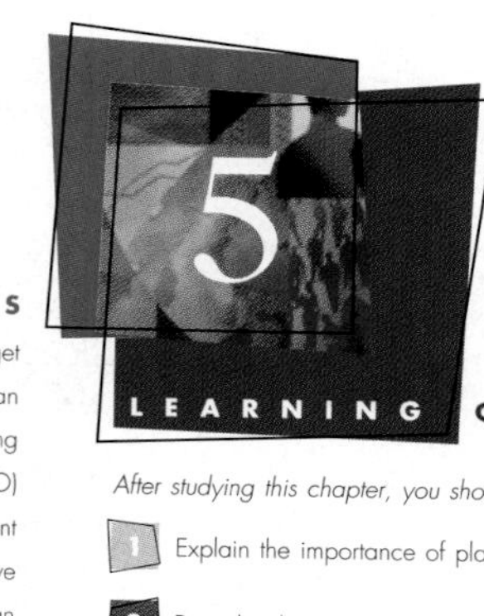

KEY TERMS

budget
contingency plan
forecasting
management by objectives (MBO)
mission statement
operational objective
operational plan
plan
planning
policy
procedure
program
rule
single-use plan
standing plan
strategic goal
strategic plan
strategy
stretch goal
tactic
tactical objective
tactical plan

LEARNING OBJECTIVES

After studying this chapter, you should be able to

1. Explain the importance of planning
2. Describe the importance of an organization's mission statement
3. Discuss the purposes of strategic, tactical, operational, and contingency plans
4. Explain the relationships between strategic, tactical, and operational goals
5. List and explain the steps in a basic planning process
6. Discuss various ways to make plans effective
7. Describe the barriers to planning

◀ KEY TERMS

The terms are your introduction to the vocabulary of management. They are listed at the beginning of each chapter, then defined in context, as well as in a master glossary at the back of the book.

148 Part 2 Planning and Decision Making

forecasting
A planning technique used by an organization's managers to concentrate on developing predictions about the future

In **forecasting**, the organization's managers concentrate on developing predictions about the future. Along with internally generated budgets, managers must develop forecasts that will predict with some degree of certainty the conditions likely to exist in all areas of the internal and external environments. Two examples include forecasts on the availability of labor and raw materials and forecasts on the replacement schedules of capital equipment.

Based on its forecast for the growing profitability of recycled paper businesses, the giant, Chicago-based chemical manufacturer Morton International (now a subsidiary of Rohm and Haas) decided in 1995 to expand into this market by acquiring "the de-inking chemicals line of an Oregon company [Serfax Inc.]" (Bukro, 1995). Before most paper can be effectively recycled, the ink on it must be removed. Morton's acquisition of the assets of Serfax was the result of its forecast for continuing growth in the $100 million de-inking chemicals business.

http://www.rohmhaas.com

In developing forecasts, managers rely on both internal information and outside resources. This chapter's Global Applications feature, which illustrates both, speaks to the assumptions and forecasts behind the expansion of Mercedes-Benz into the U.S. market. Its Alabama facility began supplying some 65,000 all-purpose utility vehicles annually, beginning in 1997.

GLOBAL APPLICATIONS
Forecasting Leads Mercedes to Alabama

The 250,000th Mercedes-Benz M-Class rolled off the production line the week of January 22, 2001. Back in 1993, original projections called for 65,000 M-Class vehicles to be built per year at Mercedes-Benz's Tuscaloosa plant. After two expansions totaling $80 million, the plant produced more than 80,000 vehicles in 2000. According to the original plans, the 250,000th vehicle wouldn't have occurred for another year.

What led giant Mercedes-Benz to build its first U.S. manufacturing facility in Alabama? The answer lies, in part, with its economic and business forecasts for the U.S. market for all-purpose utility vehicles (APUVs), such as the Jeep Cherokee and Ford Explorer. Mercedes researchers estimate that the APUV segment is the fastest growing part of the automotive market. "More than 2.5 million

utility vehicles were sold [in 1994] with about 60 percent ... United States." Mercedes ... saw the United States as ... and fastest growing mark... with 2 million APUVs pro... sales in the United States...

Mercedes planners di... auto analysts who predi... market would be too cro... 1997 to give Mercedes ... 30,000 vehicles sales—... half of its projected prod... remainder of its cars wou... in other countries.) Merce... believed that the compan... selling price of around $3... its quality reputation wou... than adequate to gain th... it sought in the United St... build on it.

Planning by Mercede... newest manufacturing faci... the early 1990s. The Al...

was chosen in 1993 and construc-...

◀ GLOBAL APPLICATIONS

This feature presents a successful application of a chapter concept by an organization from another country. The selection of organizations is varied by country and by industry—service, manufacturing, retail.

138 Part 2 Planning and Decision Making

ETHICAL MANAGEMENT
Privacy: Company Policy and the Law

Federal law allows companies to monitor their employees' behaviors and conversations. As of January, 1996, 45 states had passed laws allowing the monitoring of employee phone calls, "mainly at the request of telemarketers and other businesses that want to record their employees' conversations for quality control, coaching, and training." Many of these laws rule practically nothing out.

Employers are creating policies to keep a tighter rein on employees for a variety of reasons, the least of which determines how they use their time on the job. These policies tell employees that they will be, are being, or can be monitored at work and authorize a variety of monitoring techniques: listening to employees' business-related telephone calls, hiring private investigators to pose as workers, and reading computer-to-computer messages. Some of the specific results follow:

- At the Spears Liquor Store, the owners authorized the monitoring and recording of employee calls from work. The recordings not only revealed business transactions, but also several passion-filled telephone calls between an employee and a customer. The employee was fired.
- Forty Kmart employees at the Manteno, Illinois, store accused management of hiring private investigators to pose as workers. The employees, in a suit for invasion of privacy, charged the investigators with gathering information about everything from employee living arrangements to their recreational plans.
- At Epson American, a computer manufacturer, employees routinely have their email messages monitored by supervisors.

Privacy advocates wo... state laws do not specify...

mation gathered by employers on employees can be used or with whom it can be shared. Although some companies have clearly told their employees about monitoring and have received their consent as a condition for being hired, others have not done so.

What ethical questions are raised when companies create policies authorizing the monitoring of employees? As a manager, under what circumstances would you create a policy authorizing the recording of employee telephone calls?

Sources: Deborah L. Jacobs, "Are You Guilty of Electronic Trespassing?," Management Review (April 1994), pp. 21–25; and Peter Kendall and Christi Parsons, "Listen Up: Bosses May Be on the Line," Chicago Tribune (18 December 1995), sec. 1, pp. 1, 12.

Consider the following six-s... turn of merchandise at a local ...

1. Determine customer's need...
2. Verify that purchase (cash ...
3. Inspect merchandise for da...
4. Consult store return policy...
5. Issue exchange, refund, or ...
6. Deny return and explain re...

Only after performing each step ... exchange, refund, or credit to a...

rule
An ongoing, specific guide for human behavior and conduct at work. Rules are usually "do" and "do not" statements established to promote employee safety, ensure the uniform treatment of employees, and regulate civil behavior.

A **rule** is an ongoing, specif... Rules are usually "do" and "do... safety, ensure the uniform treat... like policies and like procedur... sets of circumstances. A rule th... for no exceptions. Figure 5.7 il...

◀ ETHICAL MANAGEMENT

Focused only on U.S. organizations, you are presented with the ethical dilemma of a company or manager. Selection of firms is balanced between large and small organizations and by industry.

Chapter 5 Organizational Planning 135

VALUING DIVERSITY
Planning for Diversity

Bobbi Gutman, the first and only African-American woman to become a vice president at Motorola, has brought strategic planning to the diversity program. Charged with a mission to develop and oversee strategies to ensure that Motorola attracts, retains, and effectively utilizes the best minds—regardless of race, gender, religion, age, or disability—Gutman began her planning efforts.

First, Gutman gathered the three top executives at Motorola to lay the foundation for planning. Her message: Since diversity is a business initiative and a strategic goal (not merely "nice to do" or "the right thing to do"), it must be embraced by all managers, not just those in human resources. Second, like any business goal, there must be quantifiable measures to gauge the progress being made toward achieving it.

Top management endorsed both elements of the plan. Since all managers plan, organize, lead, and, most importantly, make a variety of staffing decisions, their involvement and cooperation were deemed critical. To help set goals, an internal census was conducted. It detailed what percentage of employees at every level were women, African-American, Hispanic, Asian, and Native American. The census numbers became a baseline for measuring increases.

Has Gutman been successful? When the program began in 1988, there were 1 female and 6 people of color among the ranks of 340 vice presidents. By 1994, out of 400, there were 33 people of color and 23 women vice presidents. Even more impressive results have been achieved at lower management levels.

http://www.motorola.com

Sources: Roberta Gutman, "Changing the Face of Management," Working Woman (November 1994), pp. 21–23. Visit Motorola online at http://www.motorola.com.

ment's strategic plan becomes the foundation for middle-level managers' planning efforts that produce tactical plans. Figure 5.5 illustrates how tactical and then operational objectives evolve from strategic goals.

Tactical Plans

tactical plan
Developed by middle managers, this plan has more details, shorter time frames, and narrower scopes than a strategic plan; it usually spans one year or less.

Developed by middle managers, a **tactical plan** is concerned with what each of the major organizational subsystems must do, how they must do it, when things must be done, where activities will be performed, what resources are to be utilized, and who will have the authority needed to perform each task. Tactical plans have more details, shorter time frames, and narrower scopes than strategic plans; they usually span one year or less.

Strategic and tactical plans are usually but not always related. Every strategy requires a series of tactical and operational plans linked to each other to achieve strategic goals; middle managers, however, do create plans to reach what are uniquely department, division, or team goals, both for the short and long term. The tactical plans discussed in the eBay case are all related to reaching the company's strategic goals. Two such plans involved the following:

- To build a "warm backup," a redundant computer system to take over when the main one failed.
- To build a "hot backup" that could reduce any blackouts to less than an hour.

VALUING DIVERSITY ▶

Designed to illustrate how managers value and utilize diversity, you will see diversity as a business strategy in large and small organizations, balanced by industry.

functions, the behaviors of organizational members, and the shaping of the organization's culture (Jones and Kahaner, 1995). Many companies are placing their mission statements on their Web sites, which can be read with a browser. Browser software is the subject of this chapter's Managing Technology feature.

Figure 5.1 illustrates the mission statements for Starbucks, eBay, and Amgen. Notice the emphasis on quality—meeting customer needs that the organization can meet—in these statements. The mission statement serves as a template against which decisions can be measured. The organization's values should be easily apparent in the mission statement.

While creating a mission statement, management expert Peter Drucker states that two questions must be answered: What is our business? What should it be? (Drucker, 1954). These questions must be raised and answered periodically, not just when forming a business. The answer to the first question is determined in part by the customers an organization currently serves. Meeting their demands and needs has made the organization what it is. The answer to the second question is determined in part by the customers an organization *wishes* to serve. The specific needs of identified customers, along with the firm's experience and expertise, will dictate what products and services it creates and/or sells, what processes it uses, and what their levels of quality will be.

Since the values, beliefs, and wants of an organization's customers keep changing, so too must the organization. Consider the situation eBay has faced since it began in 1995. This virtual auction house (the subject of this chapter's Management in Action case) was growing over 50 percent quarter to quarter, making it a new company every three months. By staying focused on the mission—to help people trade practically anything on earth—CEO Margaret C. Whitman turned eBay from a "quirky idea into an Internet giant capable of handling millions of buyers and sellers. . . . More than that, Whitman has helped legitimize the notion of negotiated pricing—making it one of the most powerful economic forces on the Internet" (Green, 1999).

MANAGING TECHNOLOGY
Browsers

The development of graphical Web browser software, such as Netscape Communicator and Microsoft Internet Explorer, has made it easy to view a Web page. Browsers use hypertext software, which combines sounds, graphic images, video, and text. Across the top of the browser screen are many icons as well as an address line. By typing in an Internet address, called a Uniform Resource Locator (URL), such as http://plunkett.swcollege.com, you go to that page and see its information. From there you can visit other pages simply by clicking on anything that is highlighted or hyperlinked to that page. Hyperlinks link just about everything on the Web to something else, and you can spend hours *surfing*—just moving from place to place seeing what you can find. To visit an Internet site, simply type in the address line and hit the enter key.

◀ MANAGING TECHNOLOGY

Effective management techniques are never static, so each chapter includes an overview of a technology that can increase managers' productivity. Based on emerging technologies, this survey provides insight into the environment that you, as a manager of tomorrow, will face.

APPLICATION CASE

Mars Clings to Its Plans

The brands read like a candy Hall of Fame: Snickers, M&Ms, Milky Way, 3 Musketeers, Twix, and Skittles. With this powerful lineup of familiar brands, Mars has dominated the U.S. and the world candy markets. But for several years, Mars has been quietly, but dramatically, yielding market share in both its U.S. and Western European candy businesses. From 1993 to 1994 in the United States alone, Mars gave up 1.4 market share points in the $10 billion confectionery business. From 1991 to 1994, Mars dropped about three market share points—a lot of Snickers bars.

Yet with all of its success, why has Mars begun to fail? The most basic explanation offered is that Mars has not modified its plans—either strategic or tactical—in the face of changes in its competitive environment.

- The candy industry has experienced dramatic consolidation, with monsters such as Nestlé and Cadbury Schweppes gobbling up smaller competitors. These stronger competitors are bombarding the market with new offerings.
- Innovations in the retail and wholesale distribution chain have shifted power to the hands of big supermarket chains and discount stores. Rather than adjust policy to meet the need for lower costs and more value to the power brokers, Mars eliminated promotional money, that is, special discounts. The action not only enraged the trade giants but also reduced the trade giants' profits.
- Mars has held to its long-term plan, focusing on maximum asset utilization. Quite simply, the plan allows the sales force to sell beyond a manufacturing plant's capacity to produce—even in peak periods.
- Rather than introducing new products, Mars developed plans calling for product line extensions. The result has been additions such as Almond M&Ms, low-fat Milky Way II, and ice cream novelty knockoffs of its candy bars.

http://www.mars.com

Questions

1. How does this case illustrate the importance of flexibility in planning? Cite an example to support your answer.
2. What does this case illustrate about the relationship of the environment to the development of plans? Cite an example to support your answer.
3. Which of the actions by Mars related to a failure to adjust strategic planning? Cite an example to support your answer.
4. Which of the actions by Mars related to a failure to adjust tactical planning? Cite an example to support your answer.

Source: Bill Saporito, "The Eclipse of Mars," *Fortune* (28 November 1994), pp. 82–92.

VIDEO CASE

Kropf Fruit Company: A Study in Planning

Kropf Fruit Company is a family-owned business consisting of orchards, storage, and packing facilities. In the early 1990s, the owners of Kropf faced a critical decision. Changing market conditions favored large fruit processors over medium-sized processors like Kropf. This trend resulted from a consolidation in the grocery store industry. As a result, the owners of Kropf were left with two strategic options: remain a medium-sized processor, or expand and become a major player. Remaining a medium-sized processor meant that the company would continue to face unfavorable market conditions and that some of the young family members might not have a future in the business. Becoming a major player involved risk, but would allow the company to compete with other large growers and processors for major grocery store accounts.

The owners of Kropf decided to expand, but only within the parameters of carefully developed strategic and operational plans and clearly articulated goals. The plans were developed after the owners considered the strengths and weaknesses of the company along with the opportunities and threats in the firm's business environment. During the planning process, the owners also remained open to suggestions from their growers, customers, employees, and other stakeholders. In the end, the company's strategic and operational plans represented a thoughtful analysis of what Kropf needed to do to remain competitive in its business environment today and in the future.

The expansion has been successful, although the owners of Kropf have worked long and hard and the firm has suffered

APPLICATION CASE ▶

Each chapter includes an actual case problem, directly related to the chapter content. Some are success stories; others present unresolved problems. All of these case studies, however, allow you to apply what you have learned. There are no right or wrong answers—just workable solutions, based on underlying principles of informed management decisions.

VIDEO CASE ▶

Each chapter concludes with a video case designed to bring key management concerns and issues to life in the classroom.

Management: An Overview

KEY TERMS

conceptual skills
customer
diversity
ethics
first-line management
functional manager
goal
human skills
leadership
management
management hierarchy
managers
middle management
organization
quality
role
technical skills
top management

LEARNING OBJECTIVES

After studying this chapter, you should be able to

1. Explain why organizations need managers
2. Describe the needs that affect a manager's universe
3. Identify and explain the levels of management
4. List and describe the management functions
5. Describe how management functions apply to each level of management
6. Identify and explain management roles
7. List and describe management skills
8. Contrast the myths with the realities of a manager's job
9. Discuss the criteria used to evaluate a manager's performance

MANAGEMENT IN ACTION

GE—World's Most Respected Company

Most new businesses fail within the first five years of operation, but General Electric (GE) has been in business for over 100 years, and John F. "Jack" Welch was its chairman and chief executive officer (CEO) for over 20 years. (He became GE's eighth chairman and CEO in 1981 and retired in late 2001.) *Financial Times*/Pricewaterhouse Coopers surveyed 720 chief executives from around the world to determine the most respected organizations and leaders. GE was the most respected company in 1998, 1999, and 2000. The chief executives' vote for top chief executive was given to Jack Welch. One of the chief executives polled said: "He took GE from nothing, turned it upside down and made it into what it is today" (Skapinker, 2000).

Founded in 1892, GE operates in more than 100 countries and employs nearly 340,000 people worldwide, including 197,000 in the United States. GE is the only company listed in the Dow Jones Industrial Index today that was also included in the original index in 1896. (See the GE Fact Sheet at http://www.ge.com/factsheet.html.) Jack Welch created more shareholder value than any other manager. "Investors who bought GE stock when Welch assumed control have been well rewarded, earning more than twice the return of the S&P 500 during the same period" (Krames, 2000).

At the beginning of the 1980s, Mr. Welch saw the threat of Japanese competition and moved decisively to build an organization sturdy enough to withstand any competitor. He remade GE into a boundaryless organization that encouraged, and won, participation from employees at all levels. He launched "Six Sigma," a quality initiative that reduces the company's tolerance of production defects, improving the company's products and services. It is the largest corporate quality initiative ever undertaken.

Mr. Welch is known for developing managers. He teaches classes at GE's Crotonville leadership-development center at Ossining, New York. Welch made the center a central part of his mission to transform GE into an informal learning organization. Its courses are directly linked to the strategic priorities of the company, and executives go there to work on issues that perplexed them back at the office. "Jack calls Crotonville the coffee pot," says Steven Kerr, vice president of leadership development. "It doesn't just percolate. It gives off aromas that draw people from all over the company" (Byrne, 1998).

Crotonville is number one in the world in developing top managers. Many former GE executives and officers are now top managers in other companies. Mr. Welch says, "This place runs by its great people. . . . The biggest accomplishment I've had is to find great people. An army of them. They are all better than most CEOs. They are big hitters, and they seem to thrive here" (Byrne, 1998).

All of the executives listed below were at GE as recently as 1997. (List adapted from Graney, 2000.)

Robert Nardelli—president and CEO of Home Depot
James McNerney—chairman and CEO of 3M

For over 100 years, General Electric has thrived under the leadership of top-notch managers and CEOs.

David Cote—president and COO of TRW
Paolo Fresca—chairman of Fiat SpA
Kaj Ahlman—vice chairman of E.W. Blanch
Tom Rogers—chairman and CEO of Primedia
John Trani—chairman and CEO of Stanley Works
Nigel Andrews—managing director of Internet Capital Group
Gary Wendt—chairman and CEO of Conseco
Bruce Albertson—president and CEO of Iomega
Stephen Bennett—president and CEO of Intuit
Warren Jenson—CFO of Amazon .com
Thomas Tiller—president and CEO of Polaris Industries
Dennis Williams—chairman, president, and CEO of IDEX Corp.
Robert Collins—chairman of Scott Technologies ■

For more on GE and Jack Welch, read Michael Skapinker, "Resilience and Flair Triumph," *Financial Times* (13 December 2000), http://specials.ft.com/wmr2000/FT3GX6PUNGC.html; Brian Graney, "GE and Jack Welch's Legacy," *The Motley Fool* (11 December 2000), http://www.fool.com/news/foth/2000/foth001211.htm; Jeffrey A. Krames, "The Price of Heroes," *Barron's Online* (30 October 2000), http://interactive.wsj.com/articles/SB972595546274992381.htm; John A. Byrne, "How Jack Welch Runs GE," *Business Week* (8 June 1998), http://www.ge.com/news/welch/articles/bw0698.htm.

INTRODUCTION

This chapter's Management in Action case discusses key people—the chairman and CEO as well as other managers—creating, overseeing, and expanding the operations of a business organization—General Electric—by coordinating various resources, skills, and activities. In addition to profit-seeking enterprises, key people initiate, oversee, and expand other types of organizations such as service-oriented not-for-profit enterprises, including charities, private schools, and governmental agencies in every country in the world.

> *There are, of course, differences in management between different organizations—mission defines strategy, after all, and strategy defines structure. But the differences between managing a chain of retail stores and managing a Roman Catholic diocese are amazingly fewer than either retail executives or bishops realize. The differences are mainly in application rather than in principles. (Drucker, 1998).*

The paragraphs that follow provide a brief introduction and overview of the ongoing features and themes of this text. They explain what management is and why it is needed and describe the functions, roles, and skills executed by all managers. The following chapters examine the details of what managers do and how they do it.

Each chapter contains six features designed to help you understand and apply its contents:

- *Management in Action:* An introductory case involving American managers and their organizations—large and small, service or manufacturing—engaging in a variety of activities that relate and connect each chapter's essential concepts. It is regularly referred to throughout its chapter.
- *Global Applications:* Successful application of one or more of a chapter's concepts from the practice of management in other countries.
- *Ethical Management:* American managers making or facing decisions that contain a variety of issues and consequences for themselves and others.
- *Valuing Diversity:* Unique ways in which American organizations show appreciation for their diverse employees.
- *Managing Technology:* Ways in which organizations use technology and technology-related concepts to their benefit.

- *Application Case:* Positioned at the end of each chapter, a concluding case of American managers' and organizations' attempts to cope with each chapter's major issues.

Each of these features serves to reinforce two continuing themes that are woven into the following chapters' narratives: (1) The continual effort by managers and organizations to meet or exceed their customers' needs and expectations and (2) the need organizations and their people have to be guided by effective leadership.

MANAGEMENT AND MANAGERS

http://www.ge.com

managers
People who allocate and oversee the use of resources.

management
One or more managers individually and collectively setting and achieving goals by exercising related functions (planning, organizing, staffing, leading, and controlling) and coordinating various resources (information, materials, money, and people).

goal
An outcome to be achieved or a destination to be reached over a period of time through the exercise of management functions and the expenditure of resources.

General Electric (GE) is one of the world's most admired companies. It traces its beginnings to Thomas A. Edison, who established Edison Electric Light Company in 1878. GE has become a diversified services, technology, and manufacturing company operating in over 100 countries. It has great **managers**: people who allocate and oversee the use of resources.

Collectively, GE's managers constitute its **management**: one or more managers individually and collectively setting and achieving goals by exercising related functions (planning, organizing, staffing, leading, and controlling) and coordinating various resources (information, materials, money, and people). A small organization's management may consist of only one person; such is often the case in sole proprietorships. Each management function listed above is briefly defined later in this chapter and examined in great detail in Parts III–V of the text.

A **goal** is an outcome to be achieved or a destination to be reached over a period of time through the exercise of management functions and the expenditure of resources. One long-term goal at GE is its e-Initiative, using the Web internally and externally to conduct business. All of GE's managers must coordinate their efforts with each other to achieve this goal.

A specific kind of goal is called an *objective* and is "characterized by a comparatively short time span and specific, measurable achievements" (Stoner and Freeman, 1992). For GE's business managers, establishing digitization of internal processes is a continuing short-term goal (objective) as is the execution of specific tasks needed to achieve it—Web site creation, hiring information technology (IT) managers, building and equipping each Web site for online sales and auctions, and hiring and training each Web site's staff.

As you have noticed, student learning objectives appear at the beginning of this chapter. These and the ones listed in following chapters can be achieved over the span of this course.

ORGANIZATIONAL NEED FOR MANAGERS

Explain why organizations need managers

organization
An entity managed by one or more persons to achieve stated goals.

Basically, an **organization** is an entity managed by one or more persons to achieve stated goals. GE's businesses are organizations. Renowned management author, professor, and consultant Peter Drucker believes that managers have two basic tasks: "One, running a business, and two, building an organization" (Johnson, 1995). To do both, managers in charge of activities must coordinate what they do with each other while simultaneously accepting "the values [and] the goals . . . of the organization" (Johnson, 1995).

Values constitute beliefs and basic tenets that are important and meaningful to those individuals and organizations that hold them (Erez and Earley, 1993). They must be harmonious and support one another. At GE, all employees contribute in various ways to making one of the company's values—the customer is always the first beneficiary—an everyday reality for its customers.

James C. Collins, business consultant and coauthor of the best-selling book *Built to Last*, reports that companies achieve long-term success by sticking passionately to a set of values and creating systems that encourage employees to act in parallel with those values (Sherman, 1995). The systematic ways in which a company's management selects, trains, evaluates, and rewards its employees demonstrate the values that managers want to promote and their commitment to them.

Organizations exist everywhere and provide the means for individuals, groups, and societies to meet their needs. As at GE, managers create organizations. Once created, organizations need one or more managers to oversee their operations and change/update them as needed. The forces of globalization, and more particularly technology, are driving managers' decisions. The Internet is transforming business. Andrew S. Grove (1999) predicts, "In some period of time, let's say five years, there won't be any Internet companies. There will be companies that use the Internet; all companies that will operate will use the Internet in their business operations, or they will be marginalized out of operations." Integrating the Internet requires managers to redesign basic business processes. For example, in 2000, Chairman and CEO Jack Welch mandated that GE executives weave the Internet into every part of the 122-year-old company's business. Thus, whether a new organization or an old, there is a universal need for managers.

THE MANAGER'S UNIVERSE

Describe the needs that affect a manager's universe

Change is often said to be the only constant in life. Therefore, as we shall note in discussions throughout this text, managers must be able to sense the need for change in themselves, the need for change in their areas of influence and in their organizations, and the need to become the driving force for achieving change.

This section begins the development of the five continuing and evolving themes that are reinforced by each chapter's features. These themes are as follows: The need for managers and their organizations to

- Please customers by meeting or exceeding their needs and expectations
- Provide leadership
- Act ethically
- Value diversity in their employees
- Cope with global challenges

How each need is met is largely affected by each manager's and organization's values, how well each manager executes the five management functions, and the availability of needed resources. We examine each of these needs, beginning with the need to please customers.

The Need to Please Customers

quality
"The totality of features and characteristics of a product or service that bear on its ability to satisfy stated or implied [requirements of those who use or consume them]."

customer
Any person or group, both inside and outside an organization, who uses or consumes outputs from an organization or its members.

Managers know that the survival and profitability of their organization are directly linked to meeting or exceeding customers' needs and expectations. They can satisfy customers by guaranteeing that all individual efforts and their results possess **quality**: "The totality of features and characteristics of a product or service that bear on its ability to satisfy stated or implied [requirements of those who use or consume them]" (Johnson and Winchell, 1989). Quality translates into the ability of some person's, group's, or organization's output to meet or exceed some other person's, group's, or organization's (i.e., a customer's) needs.

Throughout this text, a **customer** includes any person or group, both inside and outside an organization, who uses or consumes outputs from an organization or its members. The *internal* customer is any person or group inside the organization who receives what is needed from others in the organization. Referring back to the Management in Action case, examples include

- Managers at GE's headquarters receiving reports on time from their regional managers
- A GE employee receiving her paycheck on time and in the right amount from the company's payroll clerk
- Each of GE's customers receiving properly prepared orders in a reasonable time

GE's *external* customers—persons or groups outside the organization who expect the organization's outputs to meet their needs—include

- The customer receiving what he ordered in a reasonable period of time and with friendly service
- An outside supplier receiving GE's quality specifications for a GE product it must provide
- A building contractor receiving GE's payments on time and in the proper amounts for services and materials provided

Quality is defined by both internal and external customers' needs, but those needs and expectations are like moving targets—continually and rapidly changing. Customers continue to want things faster, better, and cheaper. Today's external customers can choose from the best that producers anywhere in the world have to offer. As this chapter's Global Applications feature points out, this expectation puts pressure on managers to make the quality of their activities and outputs "world class." Managers and their organizations have "accepted the new dizzying truth: that the only constant in today's world is exponentially increasing change" (Huey, 1994).

All employees are simultaneously customers and the means to satisfy customers. As customers, they must make those who exist to serve them aware of what they need. As the means to satisfy customers, they must determine who their customers are and what they require. Finally, employees must make it both a personal commitment and a primary duty to meet customer needs.

GE's management fully understands that companies are evaluated in the marketplace by both customers and investors on how well they meet *all* their customers' needs. To guarantee that their employees deliver quality outputs, GE employees are

GLOBAL APPLICATIONS
Turnaround at South African Airways

Changes in management attitudes and values underlay the impressive turnaround at South African Airways' (SAA) engine repair division. As with others in its industry, the quality of SAA's operations can mean either satisfied customers arriving safely and on time at their destinations or a disaster resulting in loss of lives and immense human suffering. As SAA management compared the quality of its engine repair division's operations to those of its competitors, it realized that much was lacking. Nearly all its operations were inefficient, and management efforts to make things better seemed to be getting nowhere. Union rules and outdated practices hindered real progress.

According to senior manager Andre Dippenaar, nothing significant happened until management enlisted the commitment and support of all its personnel and brought their talents to bear on the problems. "We had to bring . . . all the mechanics and engineers, including those in three unions, into the process of solving business problems. We began . . . creating teams of real partners."

Management started the division's turnaround by making a commitment to create an open-communications environment. It designed and implemented training programs to transform managers into coaches and team facilitators and to teach the skills workers would need to form and manage self-directed work teams. Thanks in part to a pay-for-knowledge program, the team members gradually took on the activities formerly reserved for managers (such as budgeting), made their own decisions, cross-trained one another, and took on the burden of learning multiple skills required to perform more complicated tasks.

What emerged from the four-year transformation effort was, according to Dippenaar, a shared governance—a workforce that became part of management. Knowledge gained is freely shared. Talents required are quickly brought to bear on a problem to facilitate its rapid solution. People leave their egos at the plant door. Inefficient work rules and plant procedures have been abandoned.

http://www.flysaa.com

For more on South African Airways read Oren Harari, "When Intelligence Rules, the Manager's Job Changes," *Management Review* (July 1994), pp. 33–35.

expected to "live Six Sigma Quality . . . ensure that the customer is always its first beneficiary . . . and use it [quality] to accelerate growth." Chapter 3 examines quality in more detail.

The Need to Provide Leadership

leadership
The ability "to get people to follow voluntarily."

http://www.hp.com

"Today's standard of leadership [is] influencing human behavior in an environment of uncertainty . . ." (Sherman, 1995). The essential characteristic of **leadership** is the ability "to get people to follow voluntarily" (Sherman, 1995). Leadership practitioners (leaders) accomplish this in part by exhibiting sets of values, skills, abilities, and traits that are needed by and are an inspiration to others. Jean Kvasnica, a project manager at the electronics giant Hewlett-Packard, includes these concepts in her description of leaders (Sherman, 1995):

> *They're open-minded, able to joke and laugh at themselves. They can take a volatile situation and stay focused. They bring out the best in me by making me want to be part of their world.*

Leadership involves gaining commitments from organizational members to achieve management's goals and properly equipping them to do so. It involves building personal relationships based on mutual respect and trust, enabling people to do their best, and getting obstacles out of their way (Sherman, 1995).

According to professor and author John Kotter of Harvard University, leaders initiate and facilitate change (Huey, 1994). They face two basic tasks: "First, to develop and articulate exactly what the [organization] is trying to accomplish, and second, to create an environment in which employees can figure out what needs to be done and then do it well" (Huey, 1994). To be successful, companies must have leaders at every level and in every unit, creating and maintaining supportive environments.

GE puts a "premium on integrity." It relies on its partners and suppliers to run their own shows in line with company values and goals. GE leaders "demonstrate . . . always with infectious enthusiasm for the customer . . . the '4-E's' of GE leadership: the personal Energy to welcome and deal with the speed of change . . . the ability to create an atmosphere that Energizes others . . . the Edge to make difficult decisions . . . and the ability to consistently Execute." (See GE's Values at http://www.ge.com/news/podium_papers/ourvalues.htm.) Chapter 14 has more to say about leadership.

The Need to Act Ethically

The daily news is littered with examples of organizations and individuals exercising questionable judgment, ignoring their moral and legal obligations, and taking actions that negatively affect others. What causes underlie these headlines? The answer lies in part with the importance that people and their organizations place on **ethics**: the branch of philosophy concerned with what constitutes right and wrong human conduct, including values and actions, in a given set of circumstances.

ethics
The branch of philosophy concerned with what constitutes right and wrong human conduct, including values and actions, in a given set of circumstances.

When people ignore or act in spite of the negative consequences their actions can yield, they often do needless harm to themselves and others. An individual's previous experiences all combine "to produce a personal moral code of ethical values with associated attitudes" (Dunfee, 1984). Our values dictate to some degree our ethics and moral compass—our conscience. While contemplating or taking action, each one of us can choose to follow or suppress our conscience. And, as this chapter's Ethical Management feature indicates, various pressures exist to drive individuals from an ethical path.

Each employee must have and act on a personal ethical and moral code. Their organization must provide values and support systems to make certain that no person or group is needlessly harmed by the organization's or an employee's actions. Managers cannot be leaders without a strong set of moral and ethical values and a commitment to avoid compromising them. Certainly customers expect no less. Author and researcher Danny Cox has conducted studies on leadership and believes that

> *at the core of any high standard of personal ethics is the declaration of personal responsibility. A person who refuses to accept responsibility lacks the ethical armor to stand against temptation (Cox and Hoover, 1992).*

Chapter 22 explores ethical concepts in more depth.

ETHICAL MANAGEMENT
Telemarketing Efforts Raise More Than Money

About five million telemarketers generate over $500 billion in sales each year in America. Telemarketing efforts sell everything from used books to home repairs; exist at the manufacturing, wholesale, and retail levels in every major industry; and raise millions for charities and not-for-profit institutions. Chicago's Steppenwolf Theater raises the nearly $400,000 it needs annually to supplement its ticket income by year-round telephone solicitation efforts.

The rapid growth of telemarketing (from 80,000 firms in 1985 to 600,000 in 1995 in Chicago alone) is largely due to the productivity and efficiency it offers marketing managers. Telemarketing generates eight to ten times more sales than its direct-mail counterpart and costs far less than putting salespeople on the streets. There is a dark side, however.

Every state's attorney general can testify to the abuses telemarketing efforts bring. "Fraudulent telemarketing schemes, such as phony sweepstakes . . . , bilk Americans, mostly the elderly, out of at least $40 billion a year." More often than not, telemarketing represents an invasion of an individual's and a family's privacy through an unending stream of calls during nearly every hour of the day and evening. Such calls have been known to deny people access to their phones during an emergency.

Those who make the calls pay a psychological price as well. The turnover rate within the industry averages between 60 and 70 percent. "Lots of people have a problem with failures, with people hanging up on them [regularly]," according to Nadji Tehrani, publisher of the magazine *Telemarketing*. Phone solicitors are usually paid the minimum hourly wage and a commission or bonus based on the size or number of orders they generate.

What do you think are the ethical issues relating to telemarketing? How do you respond to unwanted telephone solicitors? Is there an ethical issue involved in the way you respond? How can telemarketers justify the human costs connected with their business?

For more on telemarketing read Barbara Sullivan, "Sure, Telemarketing Grates, But Lots of Folks Are Buying," *Chicago Tribune* (18 February 1995), sec. 1, pp. 1, 6. Federal Trade Commission, "Spread the Word about Telemarketing Fraud," http://www.ftc.gov/bcp/conline/edcams/telemarketing/index.html.

The Need to Value Diversity in Their Employees

Managers no longer manage a homogeneous workforce. Organizations are composed of a heterogeneous mix of people that reflects our nation's population. Data from the U.S. Department of Labor show that "the future racial and ethnic makeup of America will be considerably different than it is today. Trends show that whites will be a declining share of the future total population, while the Hispanic share will grow faster than that of non-Hispanic blacks. By 2050, minorities are projected to rise from one in every four Americans to almost one in every two. The Asian and Pacific Islander population is also expected to increase. Growth rates of both the Hispanic-origin and the Asian and Pacific Islander populations may exceed two percent per year until 2030."

diversity
Includes people from differing age groups, genders, ethnic and racial backgrounds, cultural and national origins, and mental and physical capabilities.

America's **diversity** includes people from differing age groups, genders, ethnic and racial backgrounds, cultural and national origins, and mental and physical capabilities. Our nation's diversity represents three challenges for managers:

1. Integrate the diversity that exists in their communities and in their external customers into their workforces

2. Learn about and understand their employees' differences
3. Find ways for themselves, their employees, and their organizations to utilize and celebrate these differences

http://www.amanet.org

America's equal employment opportunity laws help to guarantee access to organizations for all its citizens. The key issues then become how these differing individuals and groups will be welcomed and managed once inside. In a 1995 survey of 983 managers from many companies in different industries, the American Management Association (AMA) found that minorities were represented at management levels as follows: top management, 10.6 percent; middle management, 15.1 percent; and first-line management, 19.3 percent (Romano, 1995). Each group had increased its minority representation over the levels reported in the AMA's 1992 survey. This chapter's Valuing Diversity feature highlights how Electronic Data Systems Corporation is working to value the diversity of its employees.

VALUING DIVERSITY
The EDS Approach

The Texas-based EDS Corporation is an international leader in computer services. Doing business in over 30 countries places EDS in an enviable position and offers it a specific challenge: How to take full advantage of the enormous pool of talent that its worldwide workforce represents. It has begun a program designed to increase the effectiveness of the ways in which all employees work together. Its central purpose is to create an organization that builds better relationships, creates stronger loyalties, fosters creativity, and understands and shares the same values. EDS's values are

- *Humility.* A recognition that no one has all the answers. Everyone has something of value to teach everyone else.
- *Curiosity.* The active searching of areas one doesn't understand.
- *Trust.* The acceptance of differing points of view and a belief that employees are doing their best, given the ways in which they view the world.
- *Empathy.* The attempt to put oneself in another's place.
- *Self-Esteem.* Respect for the environment, for one's community, and for other individuals and their autonomy.

The company's initial efforts at valuing the diversity of its employees focused solely on race and gender. Management soon realized that this focus would have to be broadened to include the nationalities and customs not only of its employees, but of its suppliers and customers as well. Along with its values, EDS's program is based on the following principles, according to its global diversity director, Dan Leffell:

- A determination of the importance of diversity issues within the framework of EDS's overall long-term business plan.
- Creation of a shared understanding by top management of what diversity is and what it means to EDS.
- Training programs for individuals and EDS as a whole.

Professor Fred Kofman at MIT's Sloan School of Management has helped EDS and many other companies design diversity programs. Here is his assessment of EDS's efforts: "Of all the companies I've worked with I've never felt the openness and permission to explore new areas like I have with EDS. They are really trying to walk their talk."

http://www.eds.com

For more on EDS read Gary Jacobson, "MIT Prof Advocates Love in the Workplace," *The Dallas Morning News* (17 July 1994), p. 2H.

© R.W. JONES/CORBIS

A diverse workforce presents many challenges and opportunities for managers.

The Need to Cope with Global Challenges

http://www.boeing.com

Conducting business internationally is a way of life for many businesses. Most of America's 1,000 largest companies, such as the giant commercial aircraft producer Boeing, make more than half of their sales dollars from foreign customers. Even small businesses that call their customers neighbors cannot escape influences from abroad. Many of their raw materials, supplies, and retail inventories come from growers, producers, and service providers around the world. For example, nearly all the coffee processed and sold in the United States comes from sources outside its borders.

http://www.bmw.com

http://www.bp.com

http://www.michelin.com

http://www.toyota.com

In a global economy, national borders become insignificant. Companies in every industry must locate operations wherever they can serve their customers best and procure needed resources. Organizations including Germany's BMW, England's British Petroleum, France's Michelin, and Japan's Toyota have built production facilities in the United States and in dozens of other nations in order to better serve their customers and lower their production costs. They also obtain needed resources and market their production output in the countries where they have built facilities as well as many other countries.

According to David Fagiano, president and chief executive officer of the American Management Association—a worldwide professional development organization with branches in 30 countries—American managers can learn much from the practice of management by foreigners wherever they do business. "We must stop thinking that the United States has cornered the market on intelligence and realize that innovations in management are happening everywhere" (Fagiano, 1995).

Clearly, integrating the preceding idea into each manager's philosophy and, therefore, into management's approaches to solving problems and making decisions makes the practice of management an awesome challenge. In addition to the above-mentioned needs, however, the manager's universe is made even more complex by several additional international and overlapping factors (Macht, 1995):

- Technological advances that lead to breakthroughs in such areas as virtual reality, telecommunications, robotics, and computer applications require managers to learn new skills, design new training programs, and reexamine operations and procedures.
- Economic changes in levels of interest rates, inflation, taxation, and the onset of a recession in one or more markets require managers to revisit their plans and make adjustments in a variety of areas, including the size of workforces and the spending for resources.
- Natural disasters, such as the 2001 earthquake in Seattle, Washington, and the 2001 flooding in Mozambique, Malwai, require managers in insurance companies, farm cooperatives, utilities, and transportation companies to act immediately and decisively; they must adjust their goals and their timetables.
- Emergencies, such as the bombing of the Federal Building in Oklahoma City in 1995 and tornadoes in the southern United States, activate chains of management decisions in dealing with rescue teams, aid agencies, and the media.
- Social and political changes (for example, widespread drug use discovered in a company's workforce and changes in both laws and population mixes where a company's operations are located) require managers to rethink practices, adjust spending priorities, and implement new training programs.

http://www.xerox.com

In a global economy, managers must adapt their execution of basic functions to unfamiliar cultures, commercial regulations, economic conditions, and climates. Customer demands and preferences, as well as the values and customs of indigenous workforces, must be respected and accommodated. As the head of Fuji Xerox (Xerox's Japanese operations) Yotaro Kobayashi states: "Understanding other people in different parts of the world . . . is very important. That means understanding the factors on which their values and sense of judgment are based" (Sherman, 1995).

http://www.penske.com

All the preceding factors combine to make the real world of management complex, ever changing, exciting, and filled with pressure. As Roger Penske, famous automobile racer and head of the large transportation-focused Penske Corporation, puts it: "The challenges are there every day and stress is a persistent adversary" (Woodruff, 1994). Chapter 20 examines the conduct of business in an international arena in more detail.

LEVELS OF MANAGEMENT

3 Identify and explain the levels of management

management hierarchy *The top, middle, and first-line levels of management.*

Although all managers perform the same set of functions, they actually do so on only three organizational levels. Generically speaking, managers are found at the top, middle, and first-line—sometimes called the supervisory, front-line, and operating—levels of management. Collectively, these levels constitute the **management hierarchy** as shown in Figure 1.1.

FIGURE 1.1 *Pyramid of the management hierarchy*

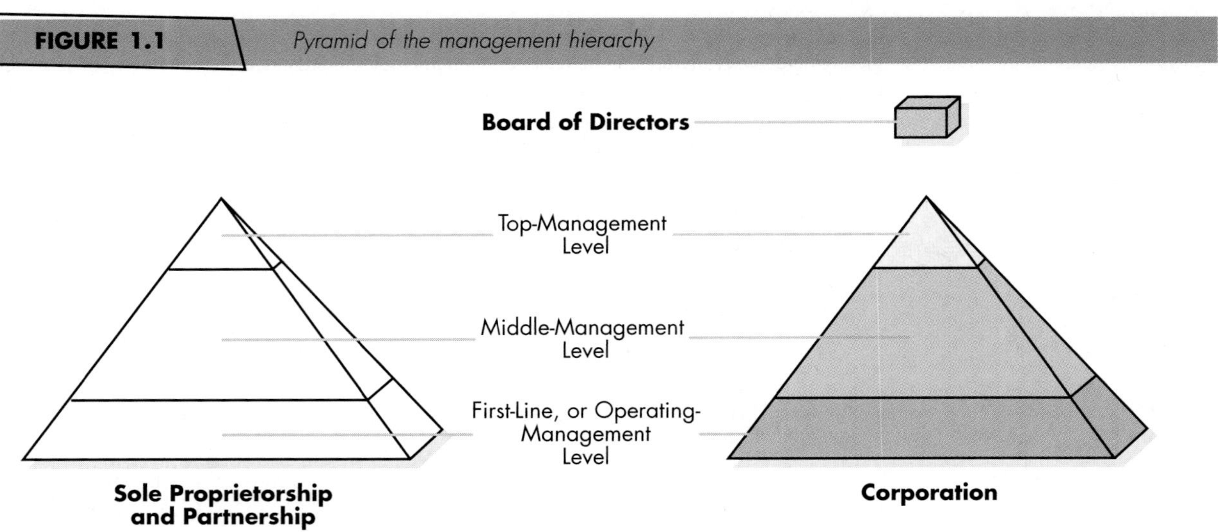

Shown at the left in Figure 1.1 is a pyramid representing management in a medium- or larger-sized sole proprietorship and partnership. On the right is the model of a traditional management structure in a similar-sized corporation. The latter model includes a *board of directors* consisting of members elected by stockholders (the owners of a corporate enterprise) who, in turn, appoint key members of a corporation's top management.

Top Management

top management
The chief executive officer (CEO) and/or president and his, her, or their immediate subordinates, usually called vice presidents.

http://www.ford.com

http://www.nissandriven.com

http://www.outbacksteakhouse.com

The tip of the pyramid consists of the organization's **top management**: The chief executive officer (CEO) and/or president and his, her, or their immediate subordinates, usually called vice presidents (Plunkett, 1996). Top management is responsible for overseeing the entire organization. It establishes long-term, company-wide goals and oversees the work of middle managers. Top management also creates and coordinates alliances and partnerships with outsiders. Ford and Nissan formed an alliance in the late 1980s to develop and produce a front-wheel drive minivan to counter Chrysler's models. Both have benefited from the partnership through lower product-development costs and higher profits.

Outback Steakhouse, Inc. is a company of restaurants that owns and operates "Outback Steakhouse" units throughout the United States as well as Carrabba's Italian Grills, Zazarac, and Lee Roy Selmon's. Robert D. Basham is president of Outback Steakhouse, Chris T. Sullivan is CEO, and J. Timothy Gannon is a senior vice president. Together with a chief financial officer and human resource executive they compose the organization's top management. Expanding the company and keeping it competitive are their primary concerns.

Middle Management

middle management
Includes managers below the rank of vice president but above the supervisory level.

Middle management includes managers below the rank of vice president but above the supervisory level (Plunkett, 1996). The smallest organizations have no middle managers; larger ones have several layers of them. Along with setting their own goals, middle managers typically translate top management's long-term goals into shorter-term objectives that the middle managers will be responsible for achieving. They oversee the work of other middle managers and those on the operating level. Such is the case with Outback's partners or regional managers. Their primary job is to add new restaurants and oversee the performances of their subordinate managers including the restaurant managers in their regions.

According to a variety of management consultants and industry experts, several trends affect middle managers. They are becoming less specialized, they are being trained to become team leaders and facilitators, and their ranks are being thinned or eliminated.

Middle managers are evolving from specialists into generalists. "Ideal candidates have more than one area of expertise and [knowledge of] information technology" (Kunde, 1995). As the American Management Association's director of management studies, Eric Greenberg, states, "a marketing manager . . . knows about manufacturing, a manufacturing manager . . . knows about purchasing. . . . It's the business equivalent of a double major in college" (Kunde, 1995).

http://www.ti.com

Middle managers, like their counterparts at the other levels, are being trained to become team leaders—leading a group as a member of the group—and team facilitators. J. D. Bryant is a team facilitator and a middle manager at a Texas Instrument defense plant in Dallas. He oversees several teams and describes his central purpose as follows: "I'm supposed to teach the teams everything I know and then let them make their own decisions" (Caminiti, 1995).

The continuing trend of the 1990s into the new century in corporate America is to eliminate as many layers of middle managers as possible (thus reducing the height of the management pyramid) in order to reduce costs, become more flexible and responsive to customers, facilitate rapid communication and decision making, and replace the vertical execution of activities with a horizontal one.

One research firm, International Survey Research Corporation, has found that 56 percent of the 300,000 plus managers surveyed over several years in the 1990s believe that their companies "are actually *less* efficient, flexible and competitive than they were before [restructuring] programs were launched" (Yates, 1995). All too often, "most job restructuring involves spreading the same work over fewer workers" (*Chicago Tribune*, "U.S.," 1995). This means that those who remain must devote more time to the job and have the skills necessary to perform the work left behind by departing employees. In many businesses reducing the number of employees has resulted in a greater reliance on overtime, outside suppliers, and temporary employees.

First-Line Management

first-line management *Supervisors, team leaders, and team facilitators who oversee the work of nonmanagement people, often called operating employees, associates, or team members.*

First-line management is the home of supervisors, team leaders, and team facilitators who oversee the work of nonmanagement people, often called operating employees, associates, or team members (Plunkett, 1996). These managers convert middle managers' goals and objectives into their own sets of objectives. Of all the levels, the first-line is most concerned with the day-to-day execution of ongoing operations. It executes the tasks that directly affect most of an organization's external customers each day.

At Outback, the proprietors (restaurant managers) and their assistant managers are its first-line management. They directly interface with restaurant patrons each day, thus affecting, more directly than any other level of management, the company's image and the quality of meals and service experienced by external customers.

Functional Managers

functional managers *Managers whose expertise lies primarily in one or another of the specialty areas.*

Managers may also be identified by the kind of business functions for which they are responsible. Like the functions of management, business functions are universal and apply to every type of business. The most essential business functions are marketing, operations (production of goods and services), finance, and human resource management. Managers whose expertise lies primarily in one or another of the specialty areas are known as **functional managers**. All other managers are usually referred to as *general managers*.

Many businesses, such as Outback Steakhouse, are organized around these functions and execute the varied activities of each function through both individuals and teams, horizontally or vertically, at all three management levels. Figure 1.2 illustrates the three levels of management organized to execute the basic business functions. Note that only the marketing department is shown in the middle and operating levels of management.

Marketing Managers

The marketing function involves identifying current and potential customers' needs and preferences along with developing goods and services that will satisfy them. Working with the other functional managers, marketing managers determine the physical and performance characteristics for three-dimensional products. In addition, they focus on ways to properly price, promote, sell, and distribute an organization's goods and services. In Figure 1.2 the vice president of marketing is the member of top management in charge of this function.

Operations Managers

Managers in operations perform the activities needed to manufacture an item or provide a service. In manufacturing companies, operations managers are concerned about controlling inventory levels and deliveries, determining factory layout, scheduling production, maintaining equipment, and meeting quality requirements for all production activities. Outback's restaurant managers are concerned with delivering both goods and services. They focus on maintaining efficiency and meeting quality requirements in the conduct of kitchen, bar, and dining room activities. In Figure 1.2, the vice president of manufacturing is the member of top management in charge of operations. Chapter 18 examines operations management in more depth.

Finance Managers

Finance managers are most concerned with managing the flow of funds into and out of the organization, and they help to determine how company funds can be used most effectively. Individual managers in this functional area are responsible for granting and using their company's credit, investing company funds, safeguarding the company's assets, keeping track of the company's financial health, and preparing budgets. In Figure 1.2, the vice president of finance oversees the organization's financial activities.

FIGURE 1.2 *Typical titles in the three levels of management*

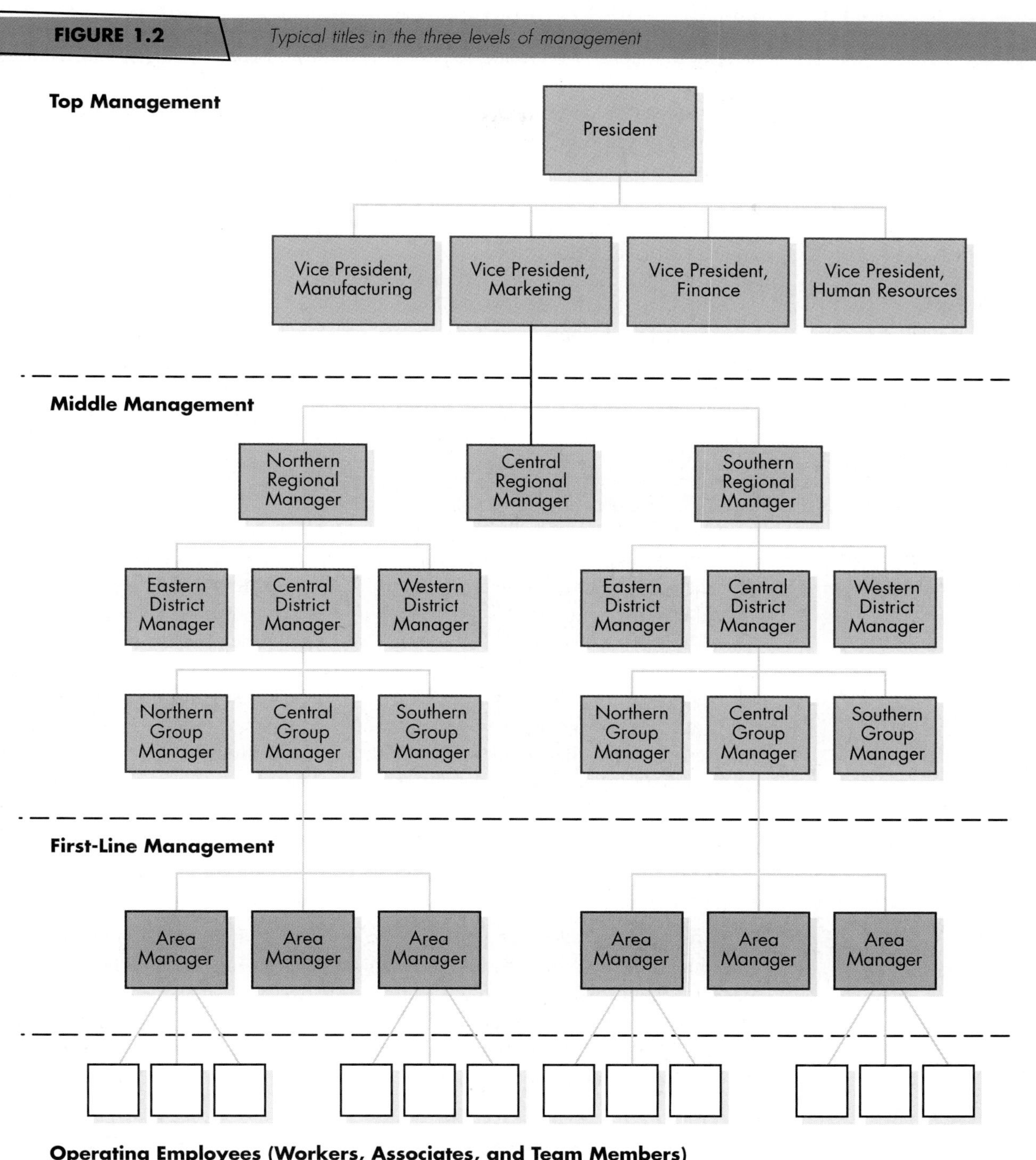

Human Resource Managers

Human resource (HR) managers are responsible for building and maintaining a competent and stable workforce. They execute and assist other managers in executing the activities connected to these tasks to include forecasting the need for recruiting, selecting, and training people; creating performance appraisal and compensation systems; overseeing relations with the company's unions; and handling all these activities within the limits and demands of federal, state, and local laws. In most small organizations, HR activities must usually be performed without the assistance of full-time HR managers. In Figure 1.2, the top-management person who oversees these activities is the vice president of human resources.

Most middle managers and all those at the top should be familiar with more than one of these specialty areas. The higher a person rises in the levels of management, the more knowledge about each of these areas he or she must possess. Chapter 11 focuses on the execution of human resource activities.

We now turn our attention to the major management functions (groups of activities) that all managers perform to set and achieve goals. The objective here is limited to providing a brief explanation of each. Later chapters examine each function in more depth.

MANAGEMENT FUNCTIONS

List and describe the management functions

Part of this chapter's definition of management states that goals are set and achieved "by [the] exercising [of] related functions—planning, organizing, staffing, leading, and controlling. . . ." Managers everywhere perform management functions, but how they are executed is determined in part by organizational influences and the individuals involved.

Although we discuss these functions separately, they are interdependent and must be considered simultaneously. Managers do not plan in the morning, organize before noon, staff between 1:00 P.M. and 2:00 P.M., and control from 2:30 P.M. until the end of the day. Acquiring human resources (staffing), for example, requires planning; the changes that will occur to established work groups must be implemented (organizing); subordinates must be guided as they execute staffing functions (leading); and the progress toward staffing goals and the expenditure of resources in doing so must be monitored and measured (controlling).

Planning

Planning is often called the first function because it lays the groundwork for all other functions and is the first step taken when performing them. When planning, managers begin by identifying goals and alternative ways of achieving them. Managers assign priorities to each goal and determine the resources required to reach each one. Planning determines actions that commit individuals, departments, and the entire organization for days, months, or years to come.

Duration and Scope of Planning

The length of time covered by a manager's plan—its duration—depends on his or her position in management. In general, top managers plan beyond one year and frequently focus on five or more years into the future. Such plans must be continually updated in light of changing circumstances. Top management's plans affect middle management's. Middle managers focus on what they must accomplish each year to guarantee that long-term, company-wide goals will be achieved. At first-line levels, planning is affected by middle managers' plans and spans a day, week, or month.

The scope of plans at each level varies as well. Top management is concerned with the entire organization. Middle managers' plans may be focused on executing and improving a business function like marketing or a process such as purchasing. First-line managers are most concerned with planning their departments' activities and the work of their individual employees and teams.

Influences on Planning

Both internal and external forces influence plans. The most immediate internal influences come from the plans created at higher management levels and the resources they will make available. All managers' plans must adhere to these constraints in order to be both compatible with and supportive of one another. This influence of higher levels on lower ones is known as a *vertical* influence.

Each planner must also consider the impact of a plan on others. Unit managers occupying the same levels must coordinate their plans and planning efforts to prevent confusion and the wasting of resources.

In addition, every manager's plans are continually affected by influences outside the organization (the environmental forces in a manager's universe discussed earlier)—social, legal/political, technological, and so forth. Changes in numerous areas beyond managers' and their organization's abilities to control affect every management and business function. Managers at all levels must continually monitor these external influences to identify trends and changes and adjust their plans as necessary. Chapter 4 examines the manager's environment in greater detail.

Flexibility in Planning

Because of the preceding factors, planning is not a one-time activity. Plans cannot be carved in stone. As time passes and circumstances change, all plans that have not been executed must be reviewed and updated periodically. Also, because many plans do not yield the precise outcomes expected, managers must prepare and be ready to use alternative plans to deal with any deficiencies in their original ones. Chapters 5, 6, and 7 explore planning in greater detail.

Organizing

Organizing creates a structure to facilitate the accomplishment of goals—the management hierarchy—and all the nonmanagement positions that support it. In executing the organizing function, managers determine the tasks that must be accomplished, group these tasks to form positions to be occupied by full- or part-time employees, and decide on the relationships the positions will have to one another.

Organizations are usually a mix of divisions, departments, regions, and individuals or teams within each. Automobile manufacturers may choose to organize by product groups such as General Motors' Chevrolet/Geo, Saturn, Oldsmobile, Pontiac/GMC, Buick, and Cadillac divisions. Each of these in turn can be organized to execute functions either nationwide or by region. FedEx, the international package carrier, is organized to conduct both ground and air delivery services by regions and nations served.

http://www.gm.com

http://www.fedex.com

Like the other functions, organizing is a continuing concern. As a company's situation changes, so, too, will its goals and objectives. This often results in a change to its management structure. As Outback expands into new territories, it must add new regional managers. New restaurant managers must be integrated into each region's management structure. Chapters 8, 9, and 10 explore the organizing function.

Staffing

Staffing—the acquiring and placing of people—breathes life into an organization. Sometimes executed as the final stage of the organizing function, staffing executes the human resource management activities—recruiting, hiring, training, and so on. Planning to staff an organization includes determining what skills and experiences people must possess to hold each position and how many persons will be needed to meet both short- and long-term requirements.

At Outback Steakhouse, staffing is a primary concern of regional and restaurant managers. As new sites are chosen, new first-line managers are hired to run the new facilities. The first-line managers must then hire, train, and help to motivate each restaurant worker and assistant manager. Staffing is the primary focus of Chapter 11.

Leading

Everything stated in this chapter about leadership and leaders applies here as well. Through leadership, managers help their organizations and their employees achieve their goals. They serve as models for expected behaviors. They coach, counsel, inspire, and encourage both individuals and groups. Leaders build and maintain work environments that encourage motivation and construct working relationships based on mutual respect and trust. These activities place a premium on a manager's ability to work with and through people.

To build and maintain a supportive environment a manager must use two-way communication channels to convey values, goals, and expectations; listen to employees; respond to their concerns; and resolve disputes. Chapters 12 through 15 deal with communication and leading.

Controlling

Managers know that the other functions may result in wasted effort unless a mechanism is provided to ensure that things go according to plan. That mechanism is controlling. Basically, controlling attempts to prevent, identify, and correct deviations from guidelines set to evaluate both people and processes. Locks, timing devices, and security guards are examples of prevention controls. Observing ongoing operations and measuring them against maximum and minimum guidelines for acceptable levels of output help workers and managers to identify unacceptable deviations. Finally, identifying and correcting the causes of such deviations must be accomplished to eliminate waste. Chapters 16, 17, and 18 examine controlling.

Functions and the Levels of Management

Describe how management functions apply to each level of management

Regardless of title, position, or management level, all managers execute these five management functions and work through and with others to set and achieve the organization's goals. Figure 1.3 shows the relative amounts of time spent by each management level on each function. Note that although all managers perform the

FIGURE 1.3 *Relative emphasis on each management function at different management levels*

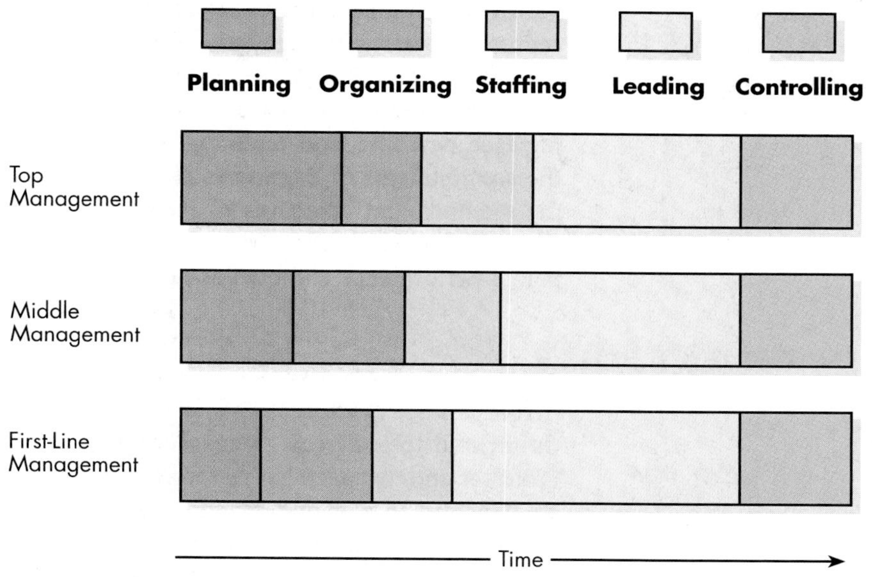

same functions, managers at the various management levels require different amounts of time for each function. The points of emphasis in each function also differ. As you read the following paragraphs, note the differences at each level of management.

Top Management

Top managers plan for the entire organization and the acquisition of needed resources. They develop the organization's values, purpose, long-term goals, and partnerships with outsiders. Their organizing efforts focus on creating and adapting the overall organizational structure to cope with varying challenges and opportunities. Staffing at the top is concerned with determining long-term human resource needs and creating guidelines to govern the staffing practices of managers at all levels. Top management's leadership concerns consist of creating a company-wide management philosophy and putting systems in place to support the development and practice of leadership at all levels. Controlling efforts set guidelines for evaluating overall company performance and determining how efficiently key resources are used and company-wide goals are achieved.

Middle Management

Middle managers develop objectives to implement top-management goals. Organizing and staffing efforts modify the company structure, increasing or decreasing the numbers of positions and people, in line with top-management guidelines, at both the middle- and operating-management levels. Leading focuses on facilitating the work of individual managers and their teams in the middle and operating levels. Controlling consists of monitoring the results of plans and making adjustments as required to ensure that the organization's goals and objectives are achieved.

First-Line Management

First-line managers plan primarily for the short term. For Outback's restaurant manager, planning involves scheduling employees and establishing detailed procedures to perform worker tasks. Organizing may consist of adding additional persons to a shift to handle an unusually large group and reassigning tasks to cover for an absent employee. First-line staffing consists of building an initial staff, training each new hire, and replacing employees as needed. Leading includes gaining the commitments of employees to the values and goals of Outback as well as to the methods and objectives of each restaurant. Controlling focuses on ensuring that individuals and the entire restaurant staff meet the manager's and the company's performance and quality objectives.

MANAGEMENT ROLES

6

Identify and explain management roles

role
A set of expectations for a manager's behavior.

A **role** is a set of expectations for a manager's behavior. Like professional actors throughout their careers, managers play different roles as circumstances dictate. Professor and management researcher Henry Mintzberg defines ten roles managers are expected to play and groups them into three categories: interpersonal, informational, and decisional. Each is examined here. Figure 1.4 describes the roles and provides brief examples of how a typical chief executive officer plays them.

Interpersonal Roles

A manager's interpersonal roles are the result of the position he or she holds in management (Mintzberg, 1975). The three interpersonal roles are

- *Figurehead.* As head of a work unit (division, department, or section), a manager routinely performs certain ceremonial duties. Examples of ceremonial duties include entertaining visitors, attending a subordinate's wedding, and officiating at a group luncheon.
- *Leader.* As a leader, a manager creates the environment, works to improve employees' performances and reduce conflict, provides feedback, and encourages individual growth.
- *Liaison.* In addition to superiors and subordinates, managers interact with others —peer-level managers in other departments, staff specialists, other departments' employees, and suppliers and clients. In this role, the manager builds contacts.

Informational Roles

Partly as a result of contacts inside and outside the organization, a manager normally has more information than do other members of the staff (Mintzberg, 1975). Three key roles derive from the use and dissemination of information:

- *Monitor.* While constantly monitoring the environment to determine what is going on, the manager collects information both directly (by asking questions) and indirectly (by receiving unsolicited information).
- *Disseminator.* As a disseminator, a manager passes on to subordinates some information that would not ordinarily be accessible to them.

FIGURE 1.4 *Mintzberg's ten management roles*

Role	Description	Identifiable Activities from Study of Chief Executives
	INTERPERSONAL	
Figurehead	Performs symbolic routine duties of legal or social nature	Attending ceremonies or other public, legal, or social functions; officiating
Leader	Motivates subordinates, ensures hiring and training of staff	Interacting with subordinates
Liaison	Maintains self-developed network of contacts and informers who provide favors and information	Acknowledging mail and interacting with outsiders
	INFORMATIONAL	
Monitor	Seeks and receives wide variety of special information to develop thorough understanding of the organization and environment	Handling all mail and contacts concerned primarily with receiving information
Disseminator	Transmits information received from outsiders or subordinates to members of the organization (some information is factual, some involves interpretation and integration)	Forwarding mail into the organization for informational purposes, maintaining verbal contacts involving flow to subordinates
Spokesperson	Transmits to outsiders information about organization's plans, policies, actions, results, and so forth; serves as expert on organization's industry	Attending board meetings, handling mail and contacts involving transmission of information to outsiders
	DECISIONAL	
Entrepreneur	Searches organization and its environment for opportunities and initiates projects to bring about change	Implementing strategy and review sessions involving improvement
Disturbance Handler	Initiates corrective action when organization faces important, unexpected disturbances	Implementing strategy to resolve disturbances and crises
Resource Allocator	Fulfills responsibility for the allocation of organizational resources of all kinds—in effect, makes or approves all significant decisions	Scheduling, requesting authorization, budgeting, programming of subordinates' work
Negotiator	Represents the organization in major negotiations	Negotiating

Source: Chart from *The Nature of Managerial Work*, by Henry Mintzberg. Copyright © 1973 by Henry Mintzberg. Reprinted by permission of HarperCollins Publishers, Inc.

- *Spokesperson.* A manager speaks for the work unit to people outside the work unit. Sometimes a spokesperson informs superiors; sometimes he or she communicates with people outside the organization.

Decisional Roles

http://www.henrymintzberg.com

In playing the four decisional roles, managers make choices, alone or with others, or influence the choices of others (Mintzberg, 1975). The decisional roles are

- *Entrepreneur.* In sharing and initiating new ideas or methods that may improve the work unit's operations, a manager assumes the entrepreneur's role.

- *Disturbance handler.* As a disturbance handler, a manager deals with schedule problems, equipment failure, strikes, broken contracts, and any other feature of the work environment that decreases productivity.
- *Resource allocator.* A manager determines who in the work unit gets what resources—money, facilities, equipment, and access to the manager.
- *Negotiator.* A manager must spend a significant portion of time negotiating, because only a manager has the information and authority required to do so. Items to be negotiated include contracts with suppliers, trade-offs for resources inside the organization, and agreements with labor organizations.

Roles and Managerial Functions

By effectively discharging these multiple roles, managers accomplish their managerial functions. In planning and organizing, a manager performs the resource allocator role. In staffing, managers play the leadership role by providing subordinates with feedback on performance. In leading, managers perform as disseminators, entrepreneurs, and disturbance handlers; in controlling, they perform as monitors.

Roles and the Expectations of Others

Simultaneously, managers may be expected to play several roles by several different individuals and groups. Figure 1.5 shows the potentially conflicting role demands on a manager. The ability to meet these multiple role demands makes the difference between a successful manager and an unsuccessful one (Harari, 1995). Any manager who has a problem adjusting to such conflicts will have a work unit that suffers to some extent.

Managers must play the decisional role of disturbance handler when employees go on strike.

© AFP/CORBIS

FIGURE 1.5 *Conflicting role demands on a manager*

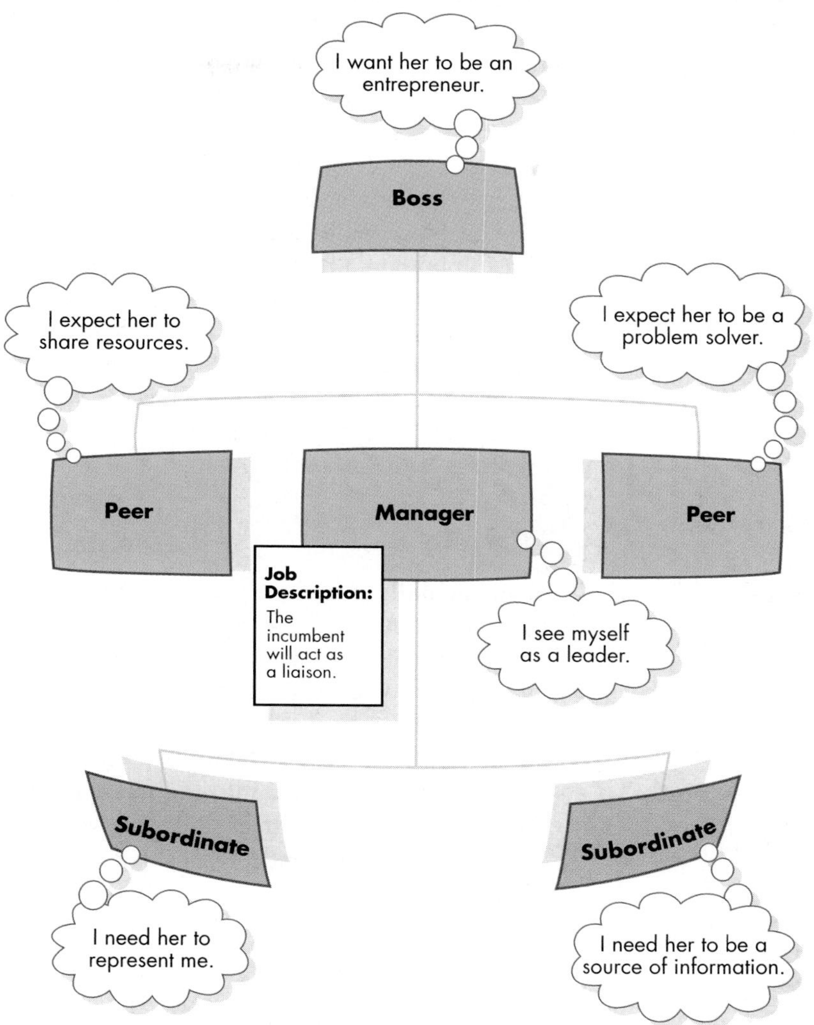

MANAGEMENT SKILLS

List and describe management skills

Skills allow individuals to perform activities and function in society. For instance, everyone needs basic reading, writing, and oral communication skills to grow intellectually and share ideas with others. Communication (the subject of Chapter 12) is at the heart of every human interaction, not just those of managers.

Our focus here is on the three basic sets of skills required of and routinely exercised by managers—technical, human, and conceptual—as identified and described by author and researcher Robert Katz (1974). All are needed to properly execute the five management functions and play the interpersonal, decisional, and informational roles just discussed.

Technical Skills

technical skills
The abilities to use the processes, practices, techniques, and tools of the specialty area a manager supervises.

Technical skills are the abilities to use the processes, practices, techniques, and tools of the specialty area a manager supervises. The manager supervising accountants, for example, must know accounting. Though he or she need not be an expert, the manager must have enough technical knowledge and skill to intelligently direct employees, organize tasks, communicate the work group's needs to others, and solve problems. This chapter's Managing Technology feature emphasizes the importance of technical skills in today's Information Age.

Technical skills are most essential at the first-line level of management and least important at the top. Louis V. Gerstner, Jr., is the chairman and chief executive officer of International Business Machines Corporation. He is not an expert on technology or computers, but he possesses enough technical knowledge to communicate effectively with those among his operating employees who are. Their job is to help corporate customers decide which computers and software to buy to meet their needs. Gerstner's job is to help them to do so by providing needed resources and support.

Human Skills

human skills
The abilities to interact and communicate successfully with other persons.

Human skills (sometimes called human relations) consist of the abilities to interact and communicate successfully with other persons. These skills include leadership of subordinates and facility in intergroup relationships. A manager must be able to understand, work with, and relate to both individuals and groups to build a team environment. The manager's ability to work effectively as a group member and to build cooperative effort within the group depends on human skills (Plunkett, 1992).

As managers move into the international environment and function within a global enterprise, human skills will become even more important. The ability to communicate with and be sensitive to different cultures will be at a premium (Fagiano, 1995).

Conceptual Skills

conceptual skills
The mental capacity to conceive and manipulate ideas and abstract relationships.

Conceptual skills—the mental capacity to conceive and manipulate ideas and abstract relationships—allow the manager to view an organization as a whole and to see how its parts relate to and depend on one another. The conceptually skilled manager can visualize how work units and individuals interrelate, understand the effect of any action throughout the organization, and imaginatively execute the five basic management functions.

Well-developed conceptual skills equip the manager to identify a problem, develop alternative solutions, select the best alternative, and implement the solution. Having conceptual skills ranked #1 in importance in the American Management Association's survey, "Managerial Skills and Competence," March/April 2000. See Figure 1.6 on page 28 for the results of this survey.

Skills and Levels of Management

Figure 1.7 (page 29) shows the importance of each management skill at each of the three levels of management. Note that human skills are required to the same degree

MANAGING TECHNOLOGY
The Information Age

Successful companies have always used technology, the practical application of knowledge, to aid in the conduct of business. The Industrial Revolution began in the eighteenth century and transformed the job of manager from owner-manager to professional, salaried manager. Prior to industrialization, the United States was predominantly an agricultural society. The production of manufactured goods was still in the handicraft stage and consisted of household manufacturing, small shops, and local mills. The inventions, machines, and processes of the Industrial Revolution (such as the use of fossil fuels as sources of energy, the railroad, the improvement of steel and aluminum metallurgical processes, the development of electricity, and the discovery of the internal-combustion engine) transformed business and management. With the industrial innovations in factory-produced goods, transportation, and distribution, big business came into being.

Managers realized that they could profit from immediate knowledge of relevant information. Calculating, sorting, and processing information allowed them to keep pace with the increased speed and complexity of business. The telegraph was the first instrument to transform information into electrical form over long distances. The telephone, radio, television, and computer expanded instant information. Computers store and handle a vast amount of data, automate manufacturing, and enhance modern communication systems. The mainframe in the 1970s, the personal computer (PC) in the 1980s, and the office network in the early 1990s were the platforms that drove massive product development and growth for the technology industry. The modern era is often described as the Information Age which characterizes the general use of technology to transmit information.

Communication and processing technologies are essential tools in almost every field of business. The Internet, with its interconnection of millions of computers, has evolved to potentially become one of the greatest resources available to businesses today. The World Wide Web (WWW) offers access to vast information resources and an immense number of sites on the Internet. The amount of information on the Web continues to grow. By the end of 2000, the Google search engine indexed over 1.3 billion Web pages. Managers can access, store, and move digital information, including voice, sound, text, and numbers. Private corporate intranets provide a universal interface for sharing company-wide information and work group level information. Employees can access information, collaborate, and distribute results anywhere, anytime.

The computer and telecommunications industries continue to converge and have resulted in advances in two-way pagers, digital cellular service, desktop video-conferencing, portable satellite phones, mini-dishes, and high-speed Internet access. Business documents include graphics, text, sound, video, and simultaneous voice communications on computers around the world. Thus, the Information Age implies a time for a revolution in the information environment for business and management. Researchers at the University of California at Berkeley estimated that the world [as of the year 2000] produces somewhere between one and two exabytes of unique information each year, or roughly 250 megabytes for every man, woman, and child on the planet, the vast majority in digital form (Weber, 2000). The changes that are taking place may be more significant to management than were the changes of the Industrial Revolution.

Weber, Thomas E. "Net's Explosive Growth Spurs Need to Build Efficient Links," *The Wall Street Journal* (4 December 2000), http://interactive.wsj.com/archive/retrieve.cgi?id=SB975887242522775859.djm; Google, http://www.google.com.

http://www.iflyswa.com

by all three levels. One reason for this is contained in a quote from Herb Kelleher, chairman and CEO of the super efficient and highly profitable Southwest Airlines:

> *[Recognize] that your own people are absolutely the key to your success. . . . If you serve your own people well, then they will serve the public well. Everybody, be they a producer of products or a producer of services, is in the* Customer Satisfaction *business (Mercado, 1995).*

As one progresses upward in the management ranks, technical skills become less important and conceptual skills become more important. Middle managers need to work within and visualize a larger piece of the organizational "pie" than do first-level managers. Top management must be concerned with the whole pie—its basic ingredients and making it larger.

FIGURE 1.6 *Results of American Management Association Survey*

AMERICAN MANAGEMENT ASSOCIATION SURVEY
MANAGERIAL SKILLS AND COMPETENCE
MARCH/APRIL 2000
921 RESPONDENTS

Respondents rated, on a five-point scale:
—The importance of the listed skills to their organizations; and
—The competence of their managerial corps in the listed skills

CAT	Q#		IMPORTANCE TO ORGANIZATION				MANAGERIAL COMPETENCE				IMPORTANCE/COMPETENCE GAP			
			AVG RTG	RANK	PCT RATING HIGH (5,4)	RANK	AVG RTG	RANK	PCT RATING HIGH (5,4)	RANK	AVG RTG GAP	RANK	PCT GAP	RANK
		CONCEPTUAL SKILLS												
CS	1	Ability to use information to solve business problems	4.64	2	95.0%	2	3.71	2	60.5%	3	0.93	8	34.5%	15
CS	2	Identification of opportunities for innovation	4.33	9	88.7%	8	3.35	14	42.2%	15	0.98	5	46.5%	4
CS	3	Recognizing problem areas and implementing solutions	4.56	3	93.8%	3	3.52	8	50.9%	6	1.04	4	42.9%	7
CS	4	Selecting critical information from masses of data	3.97	19	72.1%	21	3.23	24	37.1%	24	0.74	17	35.0%	14
CS	5	Understanding of business uses of technology	4.15	16	80.3%	16	3.31	21	41.5%	20	0.84	11	38.8%	10
CS	6	Understanding of organization's business model	4.03	18	74.8%	18	3.39	12	45.8%	11	0.64	19	29.0%	21
		CATEGORY AVERAGES AND RANK	4.28	1	84.1%	1	3.42	3	46.3%	3	0.86	1	37.8%	1
		COMMUNICATION SKILLS												
CM	7	Ability to transform ideas into words and actions	4.44	5	91.2%	4	3.55	5	53.3%	5	0.89	10	37.9%	11
CM	8	Credibility among colleagues, peers, & subordinates	4.45	4	91.0%	5	3.69	3	60.6%	2	0.76	16	30.4%	18
CM	9	Listening and asking questions	4.40	6	89.8%	6	3.36	13	43.3%	13	1.04	3	46.5%	3
CM	10	Presentation skills: spoken formats	3.95	21	72.1%	22	3.49	9	47.4%	9	0.46	25	24.7%	24
CM	11	Presentation skills: written and/or graphic formats	3.94	22	72.2%	20	3.45	10	47.2%	10	0.49	24	25.0%	23
		CATEGORY AVERAGES AND RANK	4.24	3	83.3%	3	3.51	1	50.4%	1	0.73	4	32.9%	4
		EFFECTIVENESS SKILLS												
EF	12	Contributing to corporate mission/departmental objectives	4.39	7	88.1%	9	3.57	4	54.6%	4	0.82	14	33.5%	16
EF	13	Customer focus	4.74	1	95.3%	1	3.90	1	68.2%	1	0.84	12	27.1%	22
EF	14	Multitasking: working at multiple tasks in parallel	4.26	13	85.9%	12	3.53	6	50.3%	7	0.73	18	35.6%	13
EF	15	Negotiating skills	3.95	20	73.0%	19	3.33	18	41.0%	21	0.62	20	32.0%	17
EF	16	Project management	4.15	17	79.7%	17	3.33	15	42.6%	14	0.82	13	37.1%	12
EF	17	Reviewing operations and implementing improvements	4.29	11	85.9%	11	3.33	17	41.5%	19	0.96	6	44.4%	5
		Setting & maintaining performance standards:												
EF	18	**Internal**: self & subordinate activities	4.32	10	89.4%	7	3.53	7	49.4%	8	0.79	15	40.0%	9
EF	19	**External**: vendors, suppliers, business partners	3.87	23	69.6%	23	3.29	22	40.0%	22	0.58	22	29.6%	19
EF	20	Setting priorities for attention and activity	4.24	14	85.6%	14	3.32	20	41.6%	18	0.92	9	44.0%	6
EF	21	Time management	4.27	12	85.7%	13	3.19	25	35.0%	25	1.08	2	50.7%	2
		CATEGORY AVERAGES AND RANK	4.25	2	83.8%	2	3.43	2	46.4%	2	0.82	2	37.4%	2
		INTERPERSONAL SKILLS												
IP	22	Coaching & mentoring skills	4.21	15	84.3%	15	2.99	26	28.6%	26	1.22	1	55.7%	1
IP	23	Diversity skills: working with diverse people & cultures	3.85	25	65.1%	25	3.32	19	42.2%	16	0.53	23	22.9%	25
IP	24	Networking within the organization	3.78	26	64.5%	26	3.33	16	41.6%	17	0.45	26	22.9%	26
IP	25	Networking outside of the organization	3.86	24	67.8%	24	3.25	23	38.7%	23	0.61	21	29.1%	20
IP	26	Working in teams (cooperation & commitment)	4.34	8	87.2%	10	3.40	11	45.0%	12	0.94	7	42.2%	8
		CATEGORY AVERAGES AND RANK	4.01	4	73.8%	4	3.26	4	39.2%	4	0.75	3	34.6%	3

Source: http://www.amanet.org/research/pdfs/mankcomp.pdf.

FIGURE 1.7 *Proportions of management skills needed by management level*

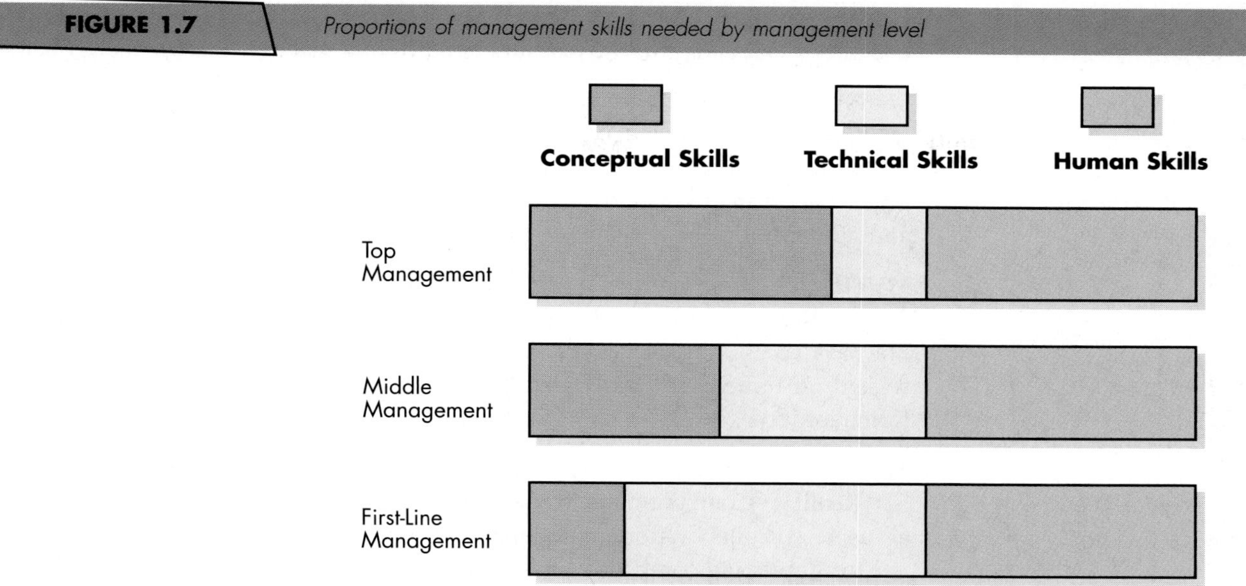

MANAGEMENT MYTHS AND REALITIES

8

Contrast the myths with the realities of a manager's job

People who have not held management jobs and have not studied management often hold perceptions disconnected from reality—that is, myths—about managers' needs and functions. The six myths below and their corresponding realities have been uncovered by the research of several management experts.

Professor and author Henry Mintzberg (1975) examined the effect of multiple demands on managers by studying how managers actually work. His research identified three commonly held beliefs about managers and countered them with the reality of a manager's regular existence:

MYTH #1. Managers are reflective, methodical planners with time to systematically plan and work through a day.

Reality. Typical managers take on so much and encounter such constant interruption that little time remains for reflection. Events range from trivialities to crises; the average time spent on one activity is nine minutes.

MYTH #2. Effective managers have no regular duties to perform. They establish others' responsibilities in advance and then relax to watch others do the work.

Reality. Although their days may be interrupted by crises, managers have regular duties to perform. They must attend meetings, see to visitors from the community and other parts of the organization, and continuously process information. To perform all their duties, managers often extend the day into the night.

MYTH #3. The manager's job is a science; managers work systematically and analytically to determine programs and procedures.

Reality. The manager's job is less a science than an art. Rather than systematic procedures and programs, managers rely heavily on intuition and judgment.

Authors and researchers Clinton Longenecker and Dennis Gioia (1991) have added the following three myths and realities of a manager to Mintzberg's list:

MYTH #4. "Managers are self-starting, self-directing, and autonomous, or they would not be managers."

Reality. "Good managers are self-managing, often to an extraordinary degree. They want, appreciate, and accept autonomy, but they also want input, attention, and guidance that only their superiors can provide."

MYTH #5. "Good managers seek out the information they need."

Reality. "Good managers are [active] information seekers. Yet they often do not have access to the information that their bosses have. Their [efforts are] thus wasted on unnecessary work that their superiors could eliminate with better information flow."

MYTH #6. "Competition among managers is good for . . . business."

Reality. "Competition is effective among businesses but not necessarily within a business. Collaboration and cooperation within the organization are . . . better . . . for improving competitiveness in the business arena."

As you read further in this text, you will discover additional research, principles, and real-world examples that influence the practice of management. They will help you to identify and abandon some of your own myths about management.

EVALUATING A MANAGER'S PERFORMANCE

Discuss the criteria used to evaluate a manager's performance

Managers are evaluated by using a variety of factors, including

- How effectively they play the three sets of management roles listed in this chapter
- Whether they possess and properly apply needed management skills
- How effective they are in setting and achieving goals
- How efficiently they use their talents and resources
- How well they demonstrate leadership
- Whether they act ethically
- How effectively they make use of the diversity in their people
- How effectively they and their people please customers

In short, managers are evaluated in how well they demonstrate through everyday actions the essential ideas in this chapter.

In addition to the preceding factors, consider the findings of an alliance of consulting firms—Manchester Partners International. "About 40 percent of managers and executives who take new positions fail within 18 months" (*Chicago Tribune*, "Rude," 1995). The primary reasons for the failures include

- Being uncertain about the expectations of their bosses
- Being unable to make tough decisions
- Taking too long to learn the job
- Being unable to build partnerships with subordinates and peers
- Lacking political savvy

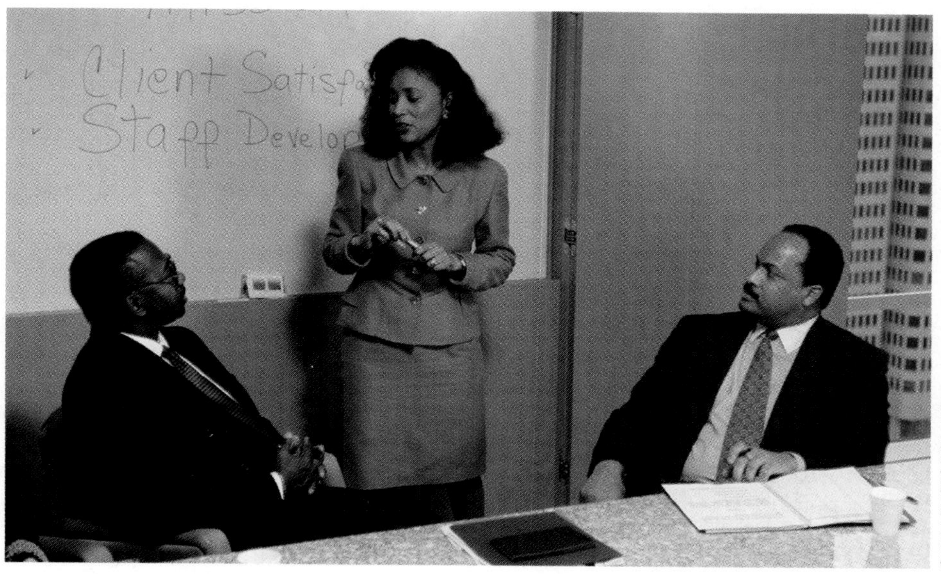

Managers are evaluated on a variety of factors, including how well they demonstrate leadership.

Do you see the link between and among these reasons for failing and the skills, roles, and functions discussed in this chapter? Managers' uncertainty about their boss's expectations may be based on poor communication skills and ignorance of the criteria being used in their organization to evaluate managers. Tough decisions often involve ethical issues and effective and efficient use of resources. Building partnerships requires all the skills and leadership concepts discussed. Political savvy requires partnerships and the practice of human skills.

CHAPTER SUMMARY

1 **Explain why organizations need managers.** Managers—people who set and achieve goals with and through others—are needed to create organizations and oversee their operations and growth. By playing various roles, exercising a variety of skills, and performing five basic functions, they provide the leadership and coordination needed to meet the objectives of every organization.

2 **Describe the needs that affect a manager's universe.** Management's universe is complex, ever-changing, exacting, exciting, and filled with pressure. Managers and their organizations must simultaneously focus on meeting customers' needs, providing leadership, acting ethically, valuing diversity, and coping with international challenges. The manager's universe is shaped by external environmental forces including competition, technological advances, natural phenomena, emergencies, as well as social, cultural, and political factors.

3 **Identify and explain the levels of management.** Most organizations contain the three traditional levels of management: top, middle, and first-line or operating. Top management consists of the chief executive officer and/or president and his or her immediate subordinates—vice presidents. Middle management includes all managers below the rank of vice president but above the first-line level. First-line managers manage workers. Like their counterparts in middle management, they are rapidly being transformed into team leaders and team facilitators.

4 **List and describe the management functions.** The five management functions are planning, organizing, staffing, leading, and controlling. Planning involves identifying goals, alternative ways of achieving them, and the resources required. Organizing includes defining the tasks required to meet goals, grouping these into positions, and creating the manage-

ment hierarchy. Staffing includes determining the organization's need for people and then recruiting, hiring, training, appraising, and compensating the personnel. Leading involves providing guidance and inspiration to individuals and groups, providing a climate in which individuals can deliver motivated behaviors, and communicating and winning commitments to organizational values and goals from employees. Controlling attempts to prevent, identify, and correct deviations from guidelines established to evaluate performances and outputs of both people and processes.

5 **Describe how management functions apply to each level of management.** Managers at every level perform the same functions. They differ in the time spent on each function and the depth of their involvement with each. Top management is most concerned about the long term and the entire organization. Middle managers focus on translating top management's goals into objectives for the execution of both business and management functions. First-line managers take a narrower view. They focus on converting middle managers' objectives into ones of their own, and they concentrate on the execution of operations and functions that directly interact with external customers.

6 **Identify and explain management roles.** To carry out their jobs, managers must be able to perform certain roles. The roles are influenced by a manager's job description and the expectations held by a manager's superiors, subordinates, and peers. The ten management roles are grouped into three categories: interpersonal roles (figurehead, leader, liaison), informational roles (monitor, disseminator, spokesperson), and decisional roles (entrepreneur, disturbance handler, resource allocator, negotiator).

Interpersonal roles require interactions with others on a regular basis. Informational roles require managers to gather information from many sources, share what they discover with the appropriate people, and represent their units to others inside the organization. Decisional roles require managers to acquire, distribute, and safeguard needed resources. Managers must also negotiate with and between competing forces and handle disruptions to their operations.

7 **List and describe management skills.** Managers need three basic skills: technical, human, and conceptual. Technical skills grant the ability to use the processes, practices, techniques, and tools of a specialty area. Human skills consist of the ability to interact and communicate with other persons successfully. Conceptual skills are the ability to (1) view an organization as a whole and see how its parts relate and depend on one another, (2) deal with ideas and abstractions, and (3) diagnose and solve a problem.

8 **Contrast the myths with the realities of a manager's job.** Myths associated with a manager's job and the realities include:

1. *The myth:* The manager is a reflective systematic planner. The reality: The typical manager is so busy there is little time for reflection.
2. *The myth:* The manager has no regular duties to perform. The reality: The manager, although interrupted by crises, has a job description containing regular duties to perform.
3. *The myth:* The manager's job is a science. The reality: The manager's job is less a science than an art.
4. *The myth:* The manager is self-starting, self-directing, and autonomous. The reality: A manager appreciates autonomy, but also wants input, attention, and guidance from superiors.
5. *The myth:* A manager will seek out needed information. The reality: Effective managers are proactive information seekers, but too often managers do not have access to information they need and their bosses possess.
6. *The myth:* Competition among managers is good for managers and the business. The reality: Competition is not effective within a business. Collaboration and cooperation within the organization and among managers is a better approach.

9 **Discuss the criteria used to evaluate a manager's performance.** Managers are evaluated through the use of many criteria including how well they play their roles, exercise their skills, execute the management functions, set and achieve goals, please customers, provide leadership, act ethically, value diversity, and how effectively and efficiently they use their resources.

REVIEW QUESTIONS

1. How do managers assist an organization to achieve its goals and objectives?
2. What factors make the manager's universe complex?
3. Where are managers located within an organization's management hierarchy? How are the different levels similar? How are they different?
4. What are the regular activities that all managers perform? Which of these activities is called the "first" function? Why?
5. How do the functions in question 4 apply to the three levels of management found in most organizations? In what ways is the execution of controlling activities similar on each of the three levels of management? How is it different?

6. What is a management role? Do all managers perform the same roles? Why or why not?
7. What management skills are most essential for a CEO? Why? What skills are required to about the same degree by all managers? Why?
8. Why do people hold the different myths mentioned in this chapter? How do you think people create these myths?
9. If you were a CEO of a small company, what criteria would you use to evaluate your managers' performances? Which criterion do you believe is most essential? Why?

DISCUSSION QUESTIONS FOR CRITICAL THINKING

1. Denzel Jones now holds the job of data entry clerk and is being considered for a promotion into a first-line management position over his coworkers. What additional skills will he need and what types of training should the organization provide to help Jones make the transition to manager?
2. What myths about management have you discovered that you hold and now wish to abandon after having read this chapter?
3. How are the three types of skills related to the execution of the ten management roles and the five management functions?

INTERNET EXERCISES

Check the text Web site at http://plunkett.swcollege.com for updated links to the Internet Exercises.

1. The American Management Association (AMA), a membership-based management development organization, offers a full range of business education and management development programs for individuals and organizations in Europe, the Americas, and Asia. What year did the AMA originate? What is the mission of the AMA?

   American Management Association
   http://www.amanet.org

   AMA's History
   http://www.amanet.org/aboutama/history.htm

   The Power of Management AMA75
   http://www.amanet.org/aboutama/pdfs/ama75yra.pdf

2. The American Institute for Managing Diversity (AIMD) helps organizations understand the business imperative for managing diversity, provides ongoing insights into the strategic implementation of diversity, identifies and categorizes trends in diversity management, and suggests new areas of research critical to successful application. AIMD has links to other Internet resources. List and describe five Internet resources for diversity-related information.
   http://www.aimd.org
3. Faith Popcorn, recognized as a trend expert, has identified such societal concepts as "cocooning," "cashing out," "anchoring," and "pleasure revenge." How does she find trends? Which trends do you believe are most important to management? Why?
   http://www.faithpopcorn.com

APPLICATION CASE

Shake Up at SafeCard Services

In the early 1990s, Florida-based SafeCard Services specialized in offering loss-notification services for credit-card holders. When a client's credit card was lost or stolen, SafeCard notified the issuing company. SafeCard was doing fine until 1993 when it began losing business to more nimble and aggressive competitors. SafeCard's sales performance fell as competitors developed better products and additional services. SafeCard's management had concentrated on controlling costs and had delayed the creation and introduction of new products. Its records were recorded on microfilm rather than in computer data banks.

To boost the company's growth, the board of directors recruited Paul Kahn, a financial services expert and now chairman, to become its new CEO. He "had hoisted AT&T into the bigtime in the U.S. credit-card industry, creating a $1.4 billion business with 16 million cardholders (AT&T's Universal MasterCard)" (Fins and Tanner, 1995). After spending a few weeks observing, talking, and analyzing, Kahn took the following actions:

- A number of top-level executives who had resisted the changes designed by Kahn were dismissed and replaced with experienced people from some top credit-card companies including American Express, AT&T Universal, and MasterCard.
- New products and business partnerships were unveiled such as a co-branded credit card with the Professional Golf Association. The "Partners card lures golfers with Pro-Am clinics and tournaments."
- A program of acquisitions was launched bringing in such operations as Wright Express (a credit-card service for trucking fleet owners) and the National Leisure Group (a company specializing in packaged tours).
- The company's extensive customer data was computerized and the company was renamed the Ideon Group.

Kahn instituted open forums to be held every 90 days, regular breakfast and luncheon meetings, and a daily newsletter. Kahn uses these to announce new products, keep people informed about changes, and allow employees to raise any concerns they might have. Employees soon found that they could raise any issue and get an honest answer from both Kahn and his team.

A gain-sharing program was developed by Kahn to enlist the talents of all employees. Any employee making a suggestion that saves or makes money for the company shares in the results. Top performers are now recognized and rewarded as well. The insecurities created by Kahn's changes have gradually been overcome, and the company has seen its profits reach a record high.

Questions

1. Which management functions did Kahn perform? Cite examples to support your answer.
2. What management roles did Kahn perform in the actions taken? Cite examples to support your answer.
3. Which management skills did Kahn rely on to manage the new environment? Cite examples to support your answer.
4. How did Kahn exercise leadership? Give examples to support your answer.

For more on SafeCard/Ideon Group, see Antonio Fins and Jane Taner, "Has Paul Kahn Lost His Midas Touch?" *Business Week* (12 June 1995), pp. 90–91; and Nancy K. Austin, "The Skills Every Manager Must Master," *Working Woman* (May 1995), pp. 29–30.

VIDEO CASE

Entrepreneurship and Innovation: A Study of Yahoo!

Thousands of people log onto the World Wide Web every day and utilize the services of Yahoo!, the Internet's most popular navigational service engine. Although Yahoo! is a young company, it has quickly evolved into a firm that provides comprehensive Internet services to a global clientele. The story of how Yahoo! started and how the company maintains its leadership position in an extremely competitive industry is quite remarkable.

Yahoo! started as a hobby of its co-founders, David Filo and Jerry Yang, in April 1994. Both individuals were doctoral students at Stanford University and took time off from writing their dissertations to surf the Web, classify the content, and create categories. As the two students classified more and more Web sites, the product they were developing began to attract the attention of other people. This provided Filo and Yang the motivation to expand their efforts, and Yahoo! as a company was soon born.

As a business concept, Yahoo! is free to the user. The company generates revenues by selling advertising space on the Yahoo! search engine. Early on, the company demonstrated a propensity for continuous innovation. To expand its reach, Yahoo! established global search engines to serve the needs of international users and now has sites that are specifically tailored to its users in London, Paris, Tokyo, Toronto, and other international cities. In the same spirit, Yahoo! has also established regional search engines in the United States, and now has specific sites for San Francisco, Chicago, Seattle, and New York, among others. The company has gone beyond this set of innovations to establish sites that are geared to specific clientele. For example, Yahooligans is a search engine that is specifically designed for school-age children.

As a result of its success, Yahoo! has attracted many competitors, such as Excite, Hot Bot, InfoSeek, and Lycos. To maintain its strategy of continuous innovation, Yahoo! has developed into a "learning organization." The company relies upon three principles to remain competitive:

- Rapid response to customer and user feedback.
- Creation of new services that focus on the needs of specific user groups.
- Monitoring of the Internet and other media on a daily basis for new content.

As illustrated in the video, Yahoo! is very diligent in regard to these three principles. Yahoo! is a very fast-paced company that excels through leadership, strategy, culture, organizational design, and information sharing. Unlike many firms, no one at Yahoo! has much time to ponder competitive issues. The average product cycle in the software industry is 14 to 18 months. In comparison, the average product cycle, from beginning to end, on the Internet is three to four months. As a result, the company couples its deliberate management with a type of "seat of the pants enthusiasm" that serves it well in terms of continuous innovation.

Yahoo! is an entrepreneurial company that has remained entrepreneurial and innovative throughout its short corporate life. The company believes that continuous innovation, attention to detail, and management savvy are necessary to sustain its competitiveness in the future.

http://www.yahoo.com

For Discussion:

1. What are your overall impressions of Yahoo!? Do you believe it is a well-managed company? Why or why not?
2. Provide examples of both efficiency and effectiveness in Yahoo!'s current operations. What steps will the managers of Yahoo! need to take to ensure that the company remains both efficient and effective in the future?
3. What environmental trends have made the existence of Yahoo! possible? In what ways is Yahoo! now taking advantage of these trends to build its business?

Management Thought: Past and Present

KEY TERMS

behavioral school
bureaucracy
chaos theory
classical administrative school
classical management theory
classical scientific school
complexity theory
contingency school
kaizen
learning organization
management science
operations management
operations research
OR/MS
quality school
quantitative school
reengineering
synergy
system
systems school
theory

LEARNING OBJECTIVES

After studying this chapter, you should be able to

1 Discuss why knowledge of the evolution of management theories is important to managers

2 Explain the contributions of the following:

a Classical schools of management thought
b Behavioral school of management thought
c Quantitative school of management thought
d Systems school of management thought
e Contingency school of management thought
f Quality school of management thought

MANAGEMENT IN ACTION

Deere & Company: Management Trendsetter

John Deere's steel plow revolutionized farming. He founded his company in 1837, and Deere & Company has grown from a one-man blacksmith shop into the world's largest maker of farm machinery. Today, the company builds equipment for the American agricultural heartland, as well as manufactures, distributes, and finances equipment for "wherever on this planet crops are grown, lawns are tended, or structures built" (http://www.deere.com).

Born during the classical school of management thought, Deere embraced scientific methods for manufacturing. But the use of the scientific method is about the only connection Deere has to that school. John Deere's original values—a commitment to product quality, customer service, business integrity, and a high regard for individual contribution—are as relevant in the twenty-first century as they were in the nineteenth. From its beginnings Deere & Company has been ahead of its time, belonging more to the recent schools of management thought (behavioral, systems, contingency, and quality) than to the classical.

What makes this philosophy so remarkable is that at the turn of the century, most managers at most companies expected workers to do only what they were taught and told to do. Ideas came from the top, not the bottom of organizations. Today, as much as possible, Deere distributes authority to managers and workers by flooding them with information on everything from assembly schedules to quality control. Day-to-day decision making does not come from the top. This has resulted in innovative products, from agricultural tractors and lawn mowers to massive excavators and dump trucks.

Deere remains at the forefront of industrial-process design by pursuing genuine value through continuous improvement and an aggressive business-process excellence initiative. For example, the John Deere Seeding Group in Moline, Illinois, produces seed planters in 45 different models with a total of 1.7 million options—in effect, customizing each planter. Traditional "hand scheduling" does not allow this level of variety, so the company implemented methods from complexity theory to create "perfect" assembly schedules.

Previously confined to science and mathematics, **complexity theory** in its practical application emphasizes the ways in which a factory resembles an ecosystem, responding to natural laws to find the best possible solutions to problems. Complexity theory suggests that organizations need an element of chaos to thrive. **Chaos theory**, a branch of complexity theory, is a name for the mathematical study of complex, unstable systems. There is nonlinearity between cause and effect and tiny causes can lead to big effects. Although it's impossible to predict the exact behavior of such a system, it is possible to make overall models of it. Under the right conditions, large, seemingly chaotic systems will, all by themselves, organize into well-ordered states.

Organizations, like Deere & Company, are interested in extending predictability into realms once thought to be chaotic. The term **learning organization** describes the process whereby groups and

Deere & Company has operated at the forefront of management theories since its inception in 1837.

individuals within the organization challenge existing models of behavior and learn to rapidly and creatively adapt to a changing environment (Senge, 1994). Herbert Spencer, the creator of Social Darwinism, referred to this process of adaptation as "survival of the fittest." In other words, the firm that is most successful in modifying its strategy to adapt to changing conditions in the environment is the firm that is most likely to survive its competitors and thrive in the future. A competitive advantage may be gained by effectively adapting to novel and unpredictable situations faster than the competition.

The Santa Fe Institute (SFI) studies all kinds of complex adaptive systems. It was created by a group of Nobel Prize–winning scientists, economists, mathematicians, and computer scientists who share a conviction that existing scientific and economic orthodoxy can't explain how systems of any type—molecular, economic, and ecological—adapt under conditions of constant change and unpredictability. Santa Fe Institute's Business Network for Complex Systems Research attempts to answer the question, "How do we apply all of this to business?"

An analyst for Deere & Company, Bill Fulkerson, learned about SFI's research on complexity theory and genetic algorithms (GAs). GAs introduce a series of "mutations" in software designed to solve a particular problem and then test each mutant's computational performance with a fitness function. Scheduling is one of many applications of GAs. He believed that algorithms could boost factory productivity and convinced Deere executives to fund development of a prototype system incorporating GAs to schedule the Moline, Illinois, seed-planter manufacturing plant. This would replace the traditional "hand scheduling."

The introduction of the new scheduling system improved productivity. It became the focal point for improving the processing and performance on the assembly-line floor and freed supervisors to focus on strategic issues. Managers are urged to develop an adaptive stance and a preparedness to react to unexpected and unanticipated events. "Before, someone might build the same part over and over again but never know what it did or where it went on the planter," says Janis Atkins, a completed-goods supervisor, who used to schedule the planter assembly line with pencil and paper.

One central idea of complexity theory is that rigorously controlling a complex system is impossible. Managers allow creativity and efficiency to emerge naturally within the organization rather than imposing their own solutions on their employees. They do this by setting some basic ground rules and then encouraging interactions or relationships among their employees so that solutions emerge from the bottom up. For example, if Nelsoandra Cole, an assembler, finds something wrong on a planter as it rolls past her module, she deals with it immediately. "I find the person responsible for the component, and I have it fixed right then and there," Cole says. "And if that person can't get to it in time, I find someone who can." ■

Sources: Graham, Rex. "Evolving Business, with a Santa Fe Institute Twist," *Bulletin of the Santa Fe Institute* (Winter 1998), Vol. 13, No. 1, http://www.santafe.edu/sfi/publications/Bulletins/bulletin-winter98/feature.html; Roberts, Paul. "John Deere Runs on Chaos." *Fast Company* (November 1998), p. 164, http://www.fastcompany.com/online/19/deere.html; Senge, Peter M. *The Fifth Discipline: The Art and Practice of the Learning Organization* (Currency/Doubleday, 1994).

INTRODUCTION

complexity theory
A theory that emphasizes the ways in which a factory resembles an ecosystem, responding to natural laws to find the best possible solutions to problems.

chaos theory
The mathematical study of complex, unstable systems.

For many generations people believed that the earth was flat and the center of the universe. No educated person believes this today. Throughout history one generation's "fact" has become, in part or in total, the next generation's fiction. The conventional wisdom of every era evolves as its cherished beliefs are challenged by the new, leaving behind only those elements that have survived the test of time. So it is with the various schools of thought about the ways in which organizations, their resources, and their processes should be managed. Past pioneers, such as inventors, explorers, and other historic figures, have inspired Doug Burgum, CEO of Great Plains Software. He also reminds his employees about Theodore Judah, an engineer and entrepreneur who 150 years ago laid the groundwork for building a

learning organization
A process whereby groups and individuals within the organization challenge existing models of behavior and learn to rapidly and creatively adapt to a changing environment.

2,000-mile transcontinental railroad. "People said he was crazy but he believed in his idea," Burgum says. Ultimately the railroad transformed the U.S. economy just as the Internet is doing today, "and with the Internet there are no geographic boundaries; all you have to do is make sure you are on it," he adds (Hymowitz, 2000).

Since the Industrial Revolution began in the late 1700s, those in charge of organizations have been alternately creating, testing, embracing, and rejecting multiple theories of management. All have contributed in various ways to how managers currently practice their art. This chapter examines the six major theories or schools of management that have evolved over the past 200 years and assesses them for their relevance to the twenty-first century.

HISTORY AND THEORY OF MANAGEMENT

Discuss why knowledge of the evolution of management theories is important to managers

Each generation of managers needs to understand the lessons learned by its predecessors and build on them. As you shall see throughout this text, preceding generations of managers have much to teach.

Value of History

People who ignore the past are destined to relive it. A person unaware of mistakes made by others is likely to repeat them. The wise person studies the past to avoid its pitfalls and benefit from its achievements.

Ancient History

Graphic records from ancient times—the *Bible*, Egyptian tomb paintings, and Babylonian clay tablets—record how early civilizations thought about management and how they managed their affairs. Management began when the earliest humans banded together in clans and tribes. Their survival depended on effective hunting and gathering. Such activities needed both skilled individuals and cooperative efforts. In time, strong individuals with the ability to manage emerged within each community to take over the management of specialized tasks and of the community as a whole.

Value of Theory

theory
Part of an art or science that attempts to explain the relationships between and among its underlying principles.

A **theory** is a part of an art or science that attempts to explain the relationships between and among its underlying principles. Theories give people a reason for doing things one way rather than another. Various management theories have arisen over past decades; some aspects of each have failed the test of time, others have survived it and are used by managers today.

To summarize the evolution of the six major theories or schools of thought about management see Figure 2.1. It provides a time line showing when each emerged. Notice that all the theories continue into the present, indicating that parts of each are still affecting the ways in which managers practice their art.

FIGURE 2.1 Time line of management thought

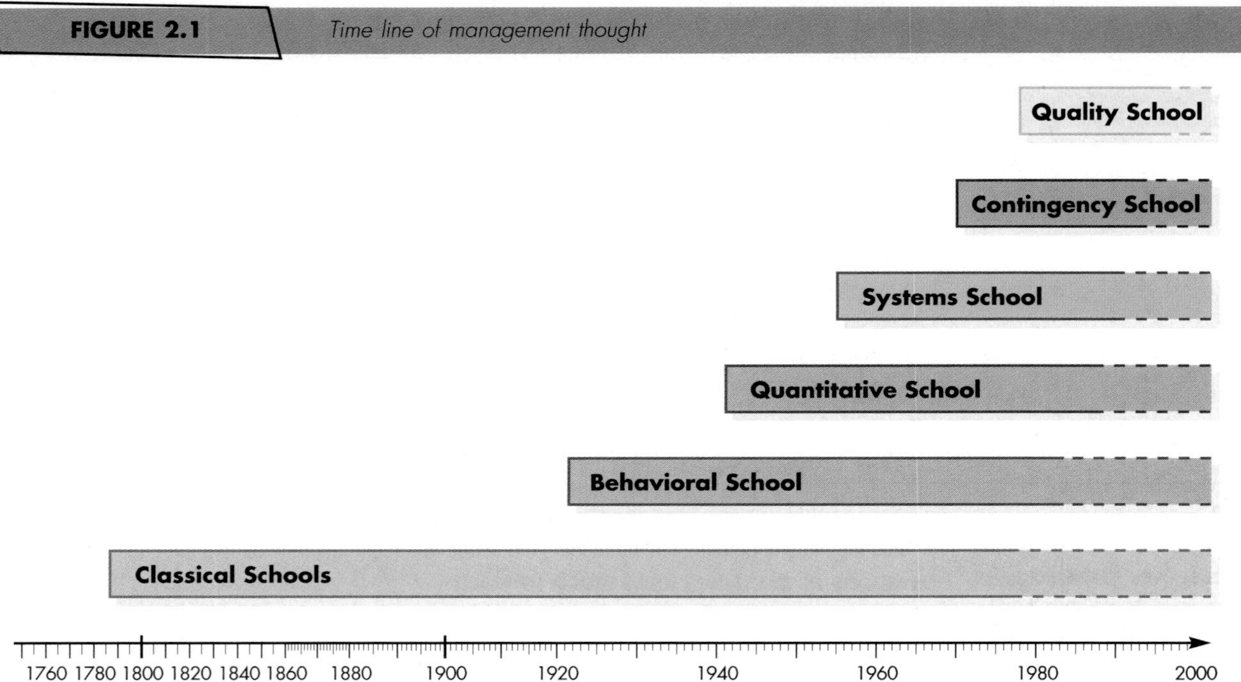

CLASSICAL MANAGEMENT THEORY

Explain the contributions of the classical schools of management thought

classical management theory
A theory that focused on finding the "one best way" to perform and manage tasks.

The **classical management theory** originated during England's Industrial Revolution, which began in the late 1700s with the invention of reliable steam-powered machinery. Steam power freed manufacturers from dependence on running water and wind. For the first time, manufacturers could mass-produce goods in factories that operated year-round. The textile industry was among the first to capitalize on the new technology. Before steam power, an individual working on a home loom wove cotton or woolen cloth. After the Industrial Revolution, weaving was done in urban areas by large groups of semiskilled workers using reliable machines under one roof. The Industrial Revolution allowed manufacturers to make standardized goods for domestic and overseas mass markets.

Early factories depended on a constant flow of labor and materials. Owners needed to plan, organize, lead, control, and staff many different kinds of operations. Writing of the new managerial skills required of successful industrialists, economic historian P. L. Payne observed, "In many cases, better organization contributed almost as much to increased production as the use of the machines themselves" (Haigh, 1990).

The classical management theory focused on finding the "one best way" to perform and manage tasks. As the Industrial Revolution continued, the environment of the early factory gave rise to two separate doctrines of management—two schools of thought linked under the label *classical*.

classical scientific school
Focused on the manufacturing environment and getting work done on the factory floor.

classical administrative school
Emphasized the flow of information and how organizations should operate.

First came the **classical scientific school**, which focused on the manufacturing environment and getting work done on the factory floor. Then came the **classical administrative school**, which emphasized the flow of information and how organizations should operate. Both schools articulated principles and functions of management discussed throughout this text.

Classical Scientific School

http://www.cbi.umn.edu

Among the pioneers of the classical scientific school was British mathematician and inventor Charles Babbage (1792–1871), who in 1832 published *On the Economy of Machinery and Manufactures*, a study that presented the fruit of Babbage's observations of the factory floor. Babbage concluded that definite management principles existed, that they had broad applications, and that they could be determined by experience. He thought that the most important principle was "the division of labor amongst the persons who perform the work." Babbage called for the division of work into discreet processes that could be mastered quickly by one person.

http://attila.stevens-tech.edu/~rdowns/index.html

Other pioneers of the classical scientific school also made theoretical contributions that increased labor efficiency and productivity. Frederick W. Taylor (1856–1915), sometimes called the Father of Scientific Management, applied scientific methods to factory problems and urged the proper use of human labor, tools, and time. In 1909, he published *Principles of Scientific Management*. During a career as executive, consultant, production specialist, and efficiency expert, Taylor pursued four key goals: to develop a science of management, to select workers scientifically, to educate and train workers scientifically, and to create cooperation between management and labor. From his experience at Midvale Steel, Simonds Rolling Machine, and Bethlehem Steel, Taylor developed the core ideas of scientific management. Devising time and motion studies to analyze the movements of workers on the job, he determined the output that individual workers should be able to achieve with specific materials and equipment. From such data he determined the quickest ways to perform tasks. Taylor introduced work breaks and the piece-rate system for worker pay (Merrill, 1970).

http://access.tucson.org/~michael/hm_2.html

Frank Gilbreth (1868–1924) and Lillian Gilbreth (1878–1972) added to Taylor's findings. The Gilbreths used time and motion studies to analyze workers' activities and remove unnecessary movements and causes of fatigue. One of Frank's first studies involved bricklaying. Frank reduced a ten-step process to five steps, thus doubling productivity. His study of hospital operating room functions saved resources and shortened the time patients spent on operating tables. Lillian assisted her husband and expanded on his work after his death.

http://www.accel-team.com/scientific/scientific_04.html

Henry Metcalf, another thinker of the classical scientific school, emphasized the need for scientific administration. The management system he advocated relied on fixed responsibilities for cost control and an effective flow of information. He urged managers to record their experiences for the benefit of others. Henry Gantt's idea represented a move away from authoritarian management. He advocated a bonus system to reward workers for acceptable and superior work, and he invented the Gantt chart, a graphic means of representing and planning production activities and time frames.

Assessment

The theories and principles developed by the early classical scientific thinkers are with us today, although experience and accumulated data have modified the ideas significantly. One of the methods used by the early thinkers, the time and motion study, is still in common use.

Authors, professors, and researchers Christopher A. Bartlett and Sumantra Ghoshal (1995) provide this tight summary of classical thinking:

> *Early in this century, [Frederick] Taylor wrote that management's role was to ensure that workers' tasks were well defined, measured, and controlled. With the objective of making people as consistent, reliable, and efficient as the machines they supported, managers came to regard their subordinates as little more than another factor of production. In that context, managers designed systems, procedures, and policies that would ensure that all employees conformed to the company way. The goal was to make the middle managers' and workers' activities more predictable and thus more controllable. . . . The systems that insured control and conformity also inhibited creativity and initiative. . . . At best, the resulting organizational culture grew passive; with amused resignation employees implemented corporate-led initiatives that they knew would fail. At worst, the tightly controlled environment triggered antagonism and even subversion; people deep in the organization found ways to undermine the system that constrained them.*

The classical school failed to welcome or tap into the great diversity that existed in organizations. Employees with beliefs, values, and customs different from those held by the people in charge—owners and their managers—were told to suppress them and conform to the organization's beliefs, values, and customs. See this chapter's Valuing Diversity feature for the evolution of how diversity has been handled in America. Leadership was expected at the top but suppressed everywhere else; management's primary concern was to meet the organization's needs. People doing the work were taught a precise set of motions for doing it and were not asked about or allowed to deviate from the ways they were taught.

In most industries American companies had little competition from abroad. Whatever they built they could sell. Quality, where concern for it did exist, was the responsibility of a quality control department and depended in large measure on final inspections of finished goods. When defects were spotted, items were reworked or scrapped.

The classical school grew and prospered in a sellers' market with few laws to constrain the conduct of business. The prevailing ethical view among business leaders was that if it was good for business, it was good for the country. Most consumers soon learned to govern their behavior by the motto, "Buyer beware!"

The classical scientific thinkers taught managers to analyze everything, teach effective methods to others, constantly monitor workers, plan responsibly, and organize and control the work and the workers. Their successors—today's managers—realize that, without committed men and women empowered to examine their own output and take responsibility for it, neither productivity nor quality can improve. The idea of specialization, prized in the classical scientific school, has been modified. The aim today is to avoid the physical and psychological hazards of boring, repetitive work, for example. Modern managers emphasize cross training, which allows workers to perform a variety of tasks, many of which require

VALUING DIVERSITY
From Equal Opportunity to Valuing Diversity

Since its very first people arrived, the United States has been populated by diverse groups of immigrants and their descendants. But as history points out, they have not always tolerated one another's existence.

Since the 1964 Civil Rights Act, various federal, state, and local laws have been passed to promote equal employment opportunities for a variety of protected groups: most notably, women and minorities such as African Americans, Hispanic-surnamed Americans, American and Alaskan natives, Asian Americans, the physically and mentally challenged, and people age 40 or over. While equal opportunity laws and the agencies designated to enforce them can help to promote entrance of the above-mentioned groups into organizations, they cannot guarantee their acceptance and effective utilization.

Once diversity is created in an organization's ranks, diverse individuals and groups are usually received with some hostility and a little tolerance (but usually not acceptance and respect) from preexisting personnel. Separateness exists rather than inclusion. To move from these conditions, carefully planned and executed training programs—usually conducted with the aid of outside consultants—are necessary. For these programs to be effective, most organizations must pass through two distinct phases, both of which call for commitment and leadership from top to bottom and for the elimination of biases and stereotypes.

The first phase is an inclusion phase. As diverse individuals and groups are allowed to display their uniqueness, support groups form, often spontaneously, whether encouraged or not by the organization's leadership. The diverse groups and individuals begin to interact, demonstrate their talents, and build respect and appreciation for each other's values, customs, traditions, and contributions.

In the second phase, all organizational members learn to appreciate and value both the need for and the contributions of diverse individuals and groups. Through a variety of company-sponsored programs and activities, employees become active, committed, contributing members, accepted and respected by those who differ from them. All members become full participants individually and in teams. Only in this second phase can the true potential in every employee be developed and effectively utilized. Imagine a company with thousands of employees, most of whom differ from each other in many ways. Imagine further that these people are willing to contribute their talents and energy to solve both the organization's and its customers' problems. You are imagining what is a reality in many of America's most successful large and small organizations. In following chapters, we will use this feature to show you more about how organizations are valuing their diversity.

Managers today act as coaches and mentors, emphasizing cross training to provide workers with the ability to perform a variety of tasks.

high literacy and computational skills. Successful modern factories depend on innovation, imagination, and creativity from dedicated workers who are backed by managers. These managers act not as commanders, but as teachers, coaches, and servants.

Classical Administrative School

As the complexity of organizations grew, managers needed a new theory to help them meet their new challenges. To meet this demand, the classical administrative school grew from classical scientific roots. The administrative branch emphasized efficiency and productivity in running factories and businesses. It provided a theoretical basis for all managers, no matter their area of expertise.

Early Contributors

Frenchman Henri Fayol (1841–1925) believed that management ability was not a personal talent that some had by birth and others did not. From practical experience he knew that management required specific skills that could be learned and taught. As mentioned in Chapter 1, the roots of today's management functions—planning, organizing, staffing, leading, and controlling—can be found in Fayol's universal management functions: planning, organizing, commanding, coordinating, and controlling. (It should be noted here that some authors and managers view staffing as a part of either leading or organizing. Also, coordinating is usually done by all managers while they are executing the other functions.) Fayol also developed fourteen principles (summarized in Figure 2.2) that form the foundation for modern management practice and sound administrative structure (Merrill, 1970).

Another contributor to the administrative school was American political scientist Mary Parker Follett. Her work in the 1920s focused on how organizations cope with conflict and the importance of goal sharing among managers. She emphasized the human element in organizations and the need to discover and enlist individual and group motivation. Believing that the first principle for both individual and group success is the "capacity for organized thinking," Follett urged managers to prepare themselves for their profession as seriously as candidates for any of the traditional learned professions (Matteson and Ivancevich, 1981).

http://www.hbg.psu.edu/Faculty/jxr11/99_4_1_wolf.html

Another American theorist of the administrative school was Chester Barnard, who was president of New Jersey Bell Telephone Company. In his 1938 work, *The Functions of the Executive*, Barnard argued that managers must gain acceptance for their authority. He advocated the use of basic management principles, and he cautioned managers to issue no order that could not or would not be obeyed. To do so, he believed, destroyed authority, discipline, and morale (Matteson and Ivancevich, 1986).

http://www.faculty.rsu.edu/~felwell/Theorists/Weber/Whome.htm

bureaucracies
Rational organizations based on the control of knowledge.

The German theorist Max Weber (1864–1920) was a professor of law and economics who wrote about social, political, and economic issues. Weber was the first to describe the principles of **bureaucracies**—rational organizations based on the control of knowledge. Although Weber's milestone work, *The Theory of Social and Economic Organizations*, appeared in Germany early in the twentieth century, it was not translated into English until 1947. The book describes how bureaucratic organizations operate and how they lend themselves to the administration of ongoing work and functions.

FIGURE 2.2 *Henri Fayol's general principles of management*

1. Division of Work	Specialization allows workers and managers to acquire an ability, sureness, and accuracy that will increase output. More and better work will be produced with the same effort.
2. Authority	The right to give orders and the power to exact obedience are the essence of authority. Its roots are in the person and the position. It cannot be conceived apart from responsibility.
3. Discipline	Discipline comprises obedience, application, energy, behavior, and outward marks of respect between employers and employees. It is essential to any business. Without it, no enterprise can prosper.
4. Unity of Command	For any action whatsoever, an employee should receive orders from one superior only. One person, one boss. In no case can a social organization adapt to a duality of command.
5. Unity of Direction	One head and one plan should lead a group of activities having the same objective.
6. Subordination of the Individual to the General Interest	The interest of one person or group in a business should not prevail over that of the organization.
7. Remuneration of Personnel	The price of services rendered should be fair and satisfactory to both employees and employer. A level of pay depends on an employee's value to the organization and on factors independent of an employee's worth—cost of living, availability of personnel, and general business conditions, for example.
8. Centralization	Everything that serves to reduce the importance of an individual subordinate's role is centralization. Everything that increases the subordinate's importance is decentralization. All situations call for a balance between these two positions.
9. Scalar Chain	The chain formed by managers from the highest to the lowest is called a scalar chain, or chain of command. Managers are the links in the chain. They should communicate to and through the links as they occur in their chains. Links may be skipped only when superiors approve and a real need exists to do so.
10. Order	There should be a place for everyone, and everyone in his or her place; a place for everything, and everything in its place. The objective of order is to avoid loss and waste.
11. Equity	Kindliness and justice should be practiced by persons in authority to extract the best that their subordinates have to give.
12. Stability of Tenure of Personnel	Reducing the turnover of personnel will result in more efficiency and fewer expenses.
13. Initiative	People should be allowed the freedom to propose and execute ideas at all levels of an enterprise. A manager able to permit the exercise of initiative by subordinates is far superior to one unable to do so.
14. Esprit de Corps	In unity there is strength. Managers have the duty to promote harmony and to discourage and avoid those things that disturb harmony.

Source: Adapted from *General Principles of Management* by Henri Fayol. Copyright 1949 by Pitman Learning, Inc., 6 Davis Drive, Belmont, CA 94002.

Weber argued that the bureaucratic organization developed in parallel with the evolving capitalist system. He saw the bureaucratic organization as a superior mechanism for administering businesses, governments, religious orders, universities, and the military. He based his conclusion on his view that technically competent individuals who provide stable, strict, intensive, and continuous administration control bureaucracies. In the typical bureaucratic hierarchy, he said, clearly defined offices (positions) are occupied by qualified career people selected on the basis of their expertise and experience (often on the basis of standardized examinations). By and large, these workers are promoted according to the judgments of superiors, and the workers are subject to the disciplinary system of the organization. A fine example of a classic bureaucracy is the federal government of the United States. Career professionals who hold their positions until retirement age, regardless of political administration, generally are the staff at the Agriculture Department, the Federal Bureau of Investigation, the Bureau of Land Management, the Internal Revenue Service, and the many other federal departments.

Assessment

By 1900 industrial leaders began to recognize that a manager did not have to be the one who owned the business. The flow of authority and paperwork could be governed by scientific principles, and people could be trained to be effective managers. Industrial leaders realized that successful organizations needed unity of purpose, command, and direction. An ordered environment; subordination of individual interests to the survival of the organization; and harmony, equity, and stability of tenure for key personnel all became hallmarks of effective organizations.

Management according to the classical administrative school has limitations, however. The monumental difficulties experienced by the former Soviet Union—possibly the most rigidly bureaucratic system yet attempted—illustrate the downside. Rigid and unresponsive decision making and a lack of commitment among workers given no autonomy led to a strangled economic system.

Within the classical administrative school, the work of Mary Parker Follett most directly discussed the disadvantages of bureaucratic theory. She emphasized for the first time the importance of the individual—both manager and worker. As we briefly discussed previously Follett believed that scientific methods could be applied to human relationships, and she believed that people could reach their potentials only through groups (Matteson and Ivancevich, 1986). Follett and others defined the social context of work and emphasized reliance on skilled, principled, and professional managers.

The classical administrative school opened the door for the next important school: the behavioral, or human relations, school.

BEHAVIORAL MANAGEMENT THEORY

2b

Explain the contributions of the behavioral school of management thought

behavioral school
Recognized employees as individuals with concrete human needs, as parts of work groups, and as members of a larger society.

The **behavioral school** took management thinking one step further. Its proponents recognized employees as individuals with concrete human needs, as parts of work groups, and as members of a larger society. Enlightened managers were to view their subordinates as assets to be developed, not as nameless robots expected to follow orders blindly.

Behavioral School Proponents

The first modern author to address the concern for people in the work environment was Robert Owen, considered by many the father of modern personnel management. In 1813, with the publication of "An Address to the Superintendents of Manufactories," Owen asserted that the quality and quantity of workers' output were influenced by conditions both on and off the job. Owen demonstrated, by referring to the textile mills he managed in Scotland, that devoting attention to the "vital machine" (people) made as much sense as devoting attention to inanimate machines (Merrill, 1970). Owen was far ahead of his time, and not until the work of Mary Parker Follett in the 1920s did the individual worker again receive scholarly attention.

http://www.britannica.com/eb/article?eu=35393

http://www.britannica.com/eb/article?eu=52890

Like Follett, psychologist Elton Mayo emphasized the behavioral aspects of workers. Beginning in 1924 Mayo and the National Academy of Sciences conducted five studies. Each focused on the Western Electric plant in Cicero, Illinois. The studies heightened management's awareness of the social needs of workers and showed how an organization's social environment influenced productivity. He discovered that when employees were treated with dignity, in a way that showed concern for their welfare and individuality, commitment and productivity increased.

Mayo's studies on the effects of piece rates on production led to the discovery that social pressures exerted by coworkers were a significant influence on performance. In the bank-wiring study at Western Electric, workers in teams developed their own production quotas. Mayo found that, rather than release finished pieces, workers kept pieces to help the group meet future quotas, and they pressured coworkers to keep production within the bounds of established quotas (Mayo, 1933). Chapter 13 will examine Mayo's work in more detail.

http://www.maslow.org

http://www.maslow.com

Abraham Maslow—a humanistic psychologist, teacher, and practicing manager—developed a needs-based theory of motivation. Maslow's theory is now considered central to understanding human motivations and behavior. His work paralleled many of the findings of psychology and sociology, social sciences that were then emerging. These sciences affirmed what artists and historians had always known—that people are extraordinarily complex creatures with many motives for behaviors on and off the job. Maslow's seminal work on human behavior in the workplace, *Euspychian Management* published in 1963, was updated with Deborah C. Stephens and Gary Heil in 1998 and entitled *Maslow on Management*.

In a 1943 article for *Psychological Review* entitled "A Theory of Human Motivation," Maslow identified and analyzed five basic needs, which he believed underlay all human behavior. These needs related to physiology (food, water, air, and sex), security (safety, the absence of illness), society or affiliation (friendship, interaction, love), esteem (respect and recognition), and self-actualization (the ability to reach one's potential). Maslow's list of needs provided a radically different perspective for managers; before Maslow, most managers assumed that people were primarily motivated by money. Maslow's work caused many managers to evaluate their own actions, their companies' conduct, and their individual philosophies about people. Chapter 13 will discuss Maslow's hierarchy of needs at length.

http://www.britannica.com/eb/article?eu=115715

In 1960 Douglas McGregor expanded the ideas of his predecessors in management theory by publishing *The Human Side of Enterprise*. In it, McGregor explained his view that all managers operated from one or two basic assumptions about human behavior: Theory X and Theory Y. The first theory, the view traditionally held about labor, portrayed workers in industry as being lazy and needing to be coerced, controlled, and directed. The second described people as McGregor thought them to be: responsible; willing to learn; and, given the proper incentives, inherently motivated to exercise ingenuity and creativity. McGregor believed that the traditional way of treating people—regarding them as unthinking, uncaring robots—must change. Indeed, McGregor stressed that only by changing these assumptions could managers tap into workers' vast talents. What mattered, he emphasized, was how people were treated and valued in their work settings. McGregor told managers that if they gave employees a chance to contribute and to take control and responsibility, they would do so (McGregor, 1960).

Assessment

The behavioral management school brought the human dimension of work firmly into the mainstream of management thought. The results continue today. Many managers work hard to discover what employees want from work; how to enlist their cooperation and commitment; and how to unleash their talents, energy, and creativity. The behaviorists integrated, for the first time, ideas from sociology, anthropology, and psychology with management theory. One result of the behavioral school was the creation of positions for professional human resources managers. Behavioral management theory effectively paved the way for modern-day employee assistance programs, such as substance-abuse intervention and day care for children, and innovations in communication involving subordinates and peers, individually and collectively.

The major limitation of behavioral management theory is its complexity. It does not yield quick or simple conclusions, and it does not conclusively explain or predict the actions of individuals or groups. Most managers, not being trained social scientists, have a difficult time using the vast amount of information provided by the social sciences, as the behavioral school says managers should do. Behavioral theory becomes even more complicated in light of the facts that people are motivated by more than one need at any given time and that they must constantly reconcile conflicting demands. No simple formulas can always motivate all individuals in the workplace. What's more, people's needs change with time, making the same person tough to manage one day and a delight the next. Nevertheless, by considering psychology, managers can prepare themselves to effectively manage their most important and complex resource: people.

Many companies offer on-site day care facilities as a result of the behavioral school of management thought.

The primary difference between one company and another is its people. "To compete in today's market, large corporations need to provide workers an environment in which they can make their own decisions and create their own visions. That means letting go of the old command-and-control model in favor of a looser approach" (Griffith, 1998). This could describe Deere & Company, the subject of this chapter's Management in Action case.

QUANTITATIVE MANAGEMENT THEORY

Explain the contributions of the quantitative school of management thought

quantitative school
Emphasized mathematical approaches to management problems.

The next wave of management thought moved from concern for people to the use of quantitative tools to help plan and control nearly everything in the organization. The emphasis in this new school, the **quantitative school** of management theory, was on mathematical approaches to management problems. This approach was born during World War II with research teams that developed radar, guidance systems, jet engines, information theory, and the atomic bomb. Since then, quantitative tools have been applied to every aspect of business (Campbell, 1982).

Management Science

management science
The study of complex systems of people, money, equipment, and procedures, with the goal of understanding them and improving their effectiveness.

Management science is the study of complex systems of people, money, equipment, and procedures, with the goal of understanding them and improving their effectiveness (Bittel and Ramsey, 1985). Management science is a facet of quantitative management theory. Historians Lester Bittel and Jackson Ramsey presented the following explanation of the management science approach:

> *Such studies are conducted through the use of the scientific method, utilizing tools and knowledge from the physical, mathematical, and behavioral sciences. Its ultimate purpose is to provide the manager with a sound, scientific, and quantitative basis for decision making.*

operations research
An area of management science that commonly uses models, simulations, and games.

Management science enables managers to design specific measures, such as a computer program, to test or evaluate the effects and effectiveness of a process or intended action. Airlines use management science to schedule flights, to schedule maintenance, and to book passenger reservations. An area of management science called **operations research** commonly uses models, simulations, and games. For example, sophisticated computer models and simulations of the interactions between and among atmospheric forces forecast the weather. For another example, through the use of several commercially available software programs, we can predict and understand in advance the impact throughout a business of an expected price increase for vital raw materials.

The techniques and tools of management science are frequently used to plan, organize, staff, lead, and control production operations; this aspect of management science is known as operations management. The management science approach is also used to direct facilities, purchasing, investments, marketing, personnel, and research and development. Management science depends on the participation of a variety of experienced researchers and practitioners to gather and process information, analyze operations, and develop and use the appropriate tools and techniques. Regardless of the methods, tools, and personnel used, however, the ultimate test of management science is whether better decisions are made and more effective processes are developed (Bittel and Ramsey, 1985).

http://www.informs.org

OR/MS
Operations research (OR) and the management sciences (MS) are the professional disciplines that deal with the application of information technology for informed decision making.

operations management
The branch of management science that applies to manufacturing or service industries.

http://www.itaa.org

Today, INFORMS (Institute for Operations Research and the Management Sciences) defines operations research (OR) and the management sciences (MS) as the professional disciplines that deal with the application of information technology for informed decision making.

> ***OR/MS** professionals aim to provide rational bases for decision making by seeking to understand and structure complex situations and to use this understanding to predict system behavior and improve system performance. Much of this work is done using analytical and numerical techniques to develop and manipulate mathematical and computer models of organizational systems composed of people, machines, and procedures. OR/MS draws upon ideas from engineering, management, mathematics, and psychology to contribute to a wide variety of application domains; the field is closely related to several other fields in the "decision sciences"—applied mathematics, computer science, economics, industrial engineering, and systems engineering* (INFORMS, 2000).

Operations Management

The branch of management science that applies to manufacturing or service industries is **operations management**. Some of the most common tools of operations management include

- Inventory models that determine optimum storage levels and reorder points
- Break-even analyses to determine levels of production and sales at which the organization recaptures the total costs of development and manufacturing
- Production scheduling, which determines when operations begin and end
- Production routing, which directs the path followed by parts and products during assembly

Chapter 18 will explore operations management in more detail.

Management Information Systems

A key ingredient in management science is the timely and efficient delivery of up-to-date information. Most organizations utilize information technology to implement, maintain, and oversee their use of computers. A *management information system (MIS)* is a computer-based system that gives managers the information they need to make decisions. Specialists who know what the users of system output need maintain an MIS. The Wal-Mart chain of retail stores implemented a management information system by using computer links to connect headquarters, suppliers, and outlets. The system allowed Wal-Mart to minimize expenses and the time needed to gather and process information about sales and inventory.

Companies that depend on domestic and foreign suppliers and outlets for their goods and services must know promptly and precisely what is happening in all vital operations. Without such information, managers cannot make timely and appropriate decisions. Chapter 19 will examine information technology and management information systems in detail.

Assessment

From the 1950s well into the 1980s, large numbers of American managers became preoccupied with quantitative measurement. The management of business after business was given over to engineers and financial managers dedicated to achieving the lowest possible cost and the highest short-term profits. Symbolic of this view were the substantial bonuses paid to managers according to financial performance in each quarter or year. A decision not based on a quantitative tool or technique was considered a poor decision.

This prolonged, intense focus on immediate results generated significant difficulties. Long-term investment was neglected, especially investment in research and development. Companies ignored trends developing overseas and, as a result, lost market share to innovative competitors. Organizations forgot the humanism of the behavioral approach and the lessons learned from behavioral management theory. Companies produced what they wanted to produce in the way they wanted to produce it; they forgot about quality and their customers. The result was disastrous for many firms and whole industries. Perhaps the most dramatic examples of such industries are the American steel and auto manufacturers. However, examples exist in every industry. The losers run the gamut, from the makers of small appliances and footwear to the manufacturers of textiles and tires.

In hindsight, the lesson of overemphasizing the quantitative management approach is clear. It is not the tools that are important, but the results they bring to the organization and the community. Management science can help managers analyze, develop, and improve operations, but management science techniques cannot substitute for sound, balanced judgment and management experience. Management science cannot be forgotten or ignored, however. Like all phases of management theory, management science contains positive aspects. The wise manager draws upon the best aspects of each management theory and integrates them with insight and imagination.

SYSTEMS MANAGEMENT THEORY

Explain the contributions of the systems school of management thought

system
A set of interrelated parts that work together to achieve stated goals or to function according to a plan or design.

A **system** is a set of interrelated parts that work together to achieve stated goals or to function according to a plan or design. Figure 2.3 shows an organization as a system, with inputs being processed, through operations, into outputs. Outputs go to users who are either inside or outside the organization. An internal user is the person down the line who receives a part or a project when another worker finishes with it. Anyone in the organization who uses or depends on the output of others in the organization is an internal user, or internal customer. Information, products, or services sent outside go to external users (suppliers, customers, or government agencies).

Systems School

systems school
The theory that an organization comprises various parts (subsystems) that must perform tasks necessary for the survival and proper functioning of the system as a whole.

The **systems school** holds that an organization comprises various parts (subsystems) that must perform tasks necessary for the survival and proper functioning of the system as a whole. The functional areas of a business—marketing, finance, and human resources management—are subsystems. So, too, are various processes such as billing and order processing when managed by teams. All managers should understand how each subsystem works, how each interacts with others, and what each contributes to the whole. Changes in any one subsystem usually affect other subsystems and, therefore, the entire system.

FIGURE 2.3 The organization as a system

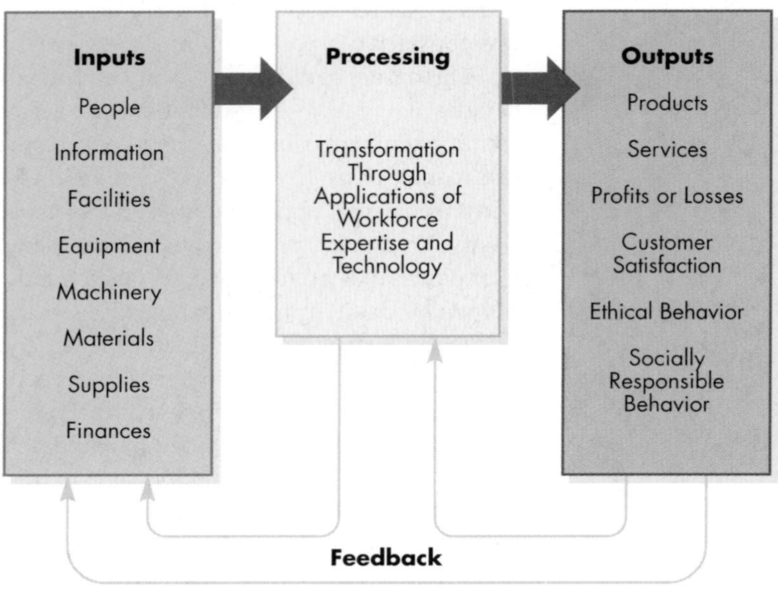

When managers adopt a systems approach, they determine how planned changes will affect others and their operations before they implement them. By keeping the entire system and its subsystems in mind, they hope to ensure that a positive move in one area does not negatively affect another.

A malfunctioning subsystem causes ripple effects that have an impact on other systems. Consider, for example, a United Airlines 777 twin-engine jet carrying 200 passengers from Los Angeles to Chicago. Once serviced and refueled in Chicago, the plane will continue on to New York. Some Los Angeles passengers must make connections in Chicago or New York for other flights, and some passengers boarding in Chicago must make connections in New York. United baggage handlers in Los Angeles fail to properly secure the 777's cargo door. As the plane moves to its takeoff position, a crew member discovers the problem. The plane returns to the loading gate so the door can be secured, thus losing its takeoff position and causing a 30-minute delay. Several Chicago-bound passengers will now miss their connecting flights; many heading for New York are similarly inconvenienced. The delayed departure means a delay in finding an available gate in Chicago. In addition, passengers' families are frustrated and business schedules are affected.

Cumulative Energy of Synergy

Systems and Synergy

synergy
The increased effectiveness that results from combined action or cooperation.

Synergy is the increased effectiveness that results from combined action or cooperation. It is sometimes described as the 2 + 2 = 5 effect, because the result of a synergistic partnership is actually more than the sum of the production of each partner alone. A corporate merger often provides an illustration of a synergistic process. When publishing giant Time, Inc. and entertainment goliath Warner Communications merged in 1991, many experts saw enormous synergistic potential. The combined organization, they believed, offered powerful product and marketing potential unavailable to the separate firms. In such mergers, old identities are lost and a new, stronger combination may be formed. Some combinations produce negative effects, however. A merger may lead to a clash of corporate cultures, as described in Chapter 10, and to the loss of jobs and competition.

Synergy usually occurs when organizations and their subsystems interact with outsiders—subsystems or entire systems. This is one reason why companies form partnerships and invite outsiders to evaluate their operations or products and services. Since its founding, many of 3M's products have been the result of astute salespeople sensing customers' needs and responding to customer recommendations. 3M's employees add synergy to its efforts at new process and product design by sharing the results of their research. Such was the case with Post-it Notes™. A chemist discovered an adhesive with very weak sticking ability. Another employee immediately saw a use for it as a bookmark that would not fall off a page. You know the rest of that product's story.

Assessment

http://pespmc1.vub.ac.be/SYSTHEOR.html

According to systems theory, the components of an enterprise interact to create synergy that can benefit each component and the whole. The systems approach encourages managers to view their organizations holistically—to envision workers, groups, and tasks as interrelated parts of an organic whole. This integrated approach requires information systems that can provide managers at every level with enough accurate and timely input to facilitate sound decisions. Such a situation brings Henri Fayol's principles—unity of command, unity of direction, and harmony—to mind. Keeping people focused on the objectives to be achieved is the manager's most important task. When everyone works together toward a goal to which they are all committed, synergy results.

The systems view (see Chapter 4 for a more detailed examination of systems) has led managers to think about quality (defined in Chapter 1) as a concept affected by each action of every employee and every unit. The result has been a commitment by all employees of an organization, beginning at the top, to focus their energies on meeting or exceeding the organization's internal and external customers' needs. This focus has become so strong and pervasive in so many companies that it has evolved into the most recent school of management thought. It is discussed at the end of this chapter and is the central focus of Chapter 3.

Fear can beset managers when they consider just how complex and connected their organizations' subsystems are. This fear can lead to paralysis. Managers may become overly cautious and refuse to act until they have contacted every possible source, conducted exhaustive analysis, and asked for reviews from upper management. The time constraints and conditions of business seldom allow such luxuries.

CONTINGENCY MANAGEMENT THEORY

Explain the contributions of the contingency school of management thought

contingency school
A theory based on the premise that managers' preferred actions or approaches depend on the variables of the situations they face.

The **contingency school** is based on the premise that managers' preferred actions or approaches depend on the variables of the situations they face. Adherents of the school seek the most effective way to deal with any situation or problem, recognizing that each situation encountered, although possibly similar to others in the past, possesses unique characteristics.

Managers holding the contingency view feel free to draw on all past theories in attempting to analyze and solve problems. The true contingency approach is integrative. During a typical day, a manager may have to use behavioral approaches to soothe a subordinate's hurt feelings, apply management science to program production for a new assembly, and use classical scientific tools to study an assembly operation to determine where it can be improved.

Adherents of the contingency school recognize that a human resources manager at Citibank may need to analyze a job applicant's interview and test results differently than would a human resources manager at First National of Chicago. Both managers have differing systems, needs, and experiences; the contingency school maintains that their choices should reflect those differences as well as the unique characteristics and histories of the job applicants.

The contingency theory can be summarized as an "it all depends" device. Right and proper conduct under one set of circumstances may fail utterly under another set. Since no two problems possess identical details and circumstances, neither should any two solutions. Several solutions and approaches may be possible and might yield equally good results. Supporters of the contingency theory would acknowledge that many roads lead to a city from several directions; they would also stress that the route that appears the shortest may not be the best choice if it is undergoing repairs.

The contingency theory tells managers to look to their experiences and the past and to consider many options before choosing the course of action. It encourages managers to stay flexible and to consider alternatives and fallback positions when defining and attacking problems. The theory also tells them that intelligent choices come only from adequate preliminary research.

Assessment

The contingency theory applies to any organization and to managers who face change. The purchase of one company by another is an example of significant change. By using the contingency approach, top managers of the purchasing company may discover that they need to learn or embrace the methods of the purchased company. If the theory works as its supporters predict, they will make the discovery before imposing inappropriate methods on the acquired firm.

The contingency theory requires managers to know the history of management thought. Managers must be familiar with the tried and true principles and practices that have provided benefits in the past but not be bound to mindlessly repeat them. Contingency thinking tells managers to try the new, to experiment—to think "outside the box" of the past—until they find the right means. It also encourages managers to stay flexible; to consider alternatives and fallback positions when attempting to solve problems, meet challenges, or take advantage of opportunities (regardless of where in the world they arise) within a framework of both the law and ethics. The diversity in most of today's organizations helps to guarantee that additional and unique perspectives and perceptions will be brought to bear on problem solving when it is truly valued. Contingency theory, along with those theories previously discussed, has led managers to the most recent theory of management thought: quality management.

QUALITY MANAGEMENT THEORY

Explain the contributions of the quality school of management thought

During the first 50 years of the last 100, American companies in such major industries as electronics, textiles, automobiles, and steel supplied most of the world's consumer and industrial products. If it wasn't produced by U.S. manufacturers, it either wasn't available or it wasn't as good. After World War I, the United States emerged as the leading industrial power.

Throughout the 1940s and into the 1950s, our major competitors and trading partners today—Great Britain, Germany, France, Italy, Canada, Japan and most of its Asian neighbors—were engaged and recovering from the devastation of World War II. U.S. industries were dominant largely because they had no serious foreign competition and were untouched by both world wars. But challenges came swiftly to most U.S. industries by the 1960s and their impacts were magnified with the oil shortages caused by the major oil-producing nations in the early 1970s. American consumers, along with those in other nations, had discovered alternative products from several foreign nations that better met their needs.

As Chapter 1 pointed out, quality is defined as the ability of a product or service to satisfy the stated or implied goals or requirements of users or customers of that product or service. How managers and organizations can create and nurture this ability is a continuing theme in this book, as its title suggests. You will recall that users/customers exist both inside and outside organizations. Users/customers receive the output generated by people, machines, and processes. The essence of the quality of any output is its ability to meet the needs of the person or group requiring it. This is the heart of the **quality school** of management thought. Quality management is often referred to as total quality management (TQM) or continuous improvement.

quality school
The essence of the quality of any output is its ability to meet the needs of the person or group.

Kaizen Approach

Kaizen is a Japanese term used in business to mean incremental, continuous improvement for people, products, and processes. The kaizen approach to quality means that an individual or organization cannot rest after any achievement. No matter how well things are going, the individual or organization can do better. When defect rates drop from 5 percent to 1 percent, they must continue to drop until no defects occur. Once adopted, the kaizen philosophy commits organizations, their leaders, and their employees to a never-ending journey: to continually strive to improve, learn, and grow.

kaizen
A Japanese term used in business to mean incremental, continuous improvement for people, products, and processes.

http://www.kaizen-institute.com

Increasing sales revenue through better quality products and services that attract more customers and realize better prices can improve profits. However, quality has to be focused on the customers' needs first. This chapter's Ethical Management feature focuses on what can go wrong even when a company becomes obsessed with producing quality products.

ETHICAL MANAGEMENT
How the Pursuit of Quality Can Alienate Customers

Since its founding in 1974, Marmot Mountain (then based in Colorado) has produced what it espoused to be "outdoor clothing and equipment simpler, easier-to-use, more comfortable, more durable, lighter weight, and, at the same time, a better value" than the competition. This small company's products were in high demand by both prestigious retailers and outdoor enthusiasts because of Marmot's high quality as measured by both performance and craftsmanship. But by the end of the 1980s, its fanatical obsession with product quality began to alienate its customers and cause its operations' costs to rise and spin out of control.

Marmot's primary focus—producing quality products—evolved into "its greatest liability." Marmot management prided itself on the fact that the factory looked like one from the nineteenth century: dozens of semiskilled workers, using primarily manual operations, thus foregoing the speed and accuracy of more sophisticated and more efficient machinery. All operations were performed in-house; only raw materials were purchased from outside sources. The slightest flaw—a few crossed stitches in out-of-the-way places—could result in the product's being declared a "second" and not being delivered to a retail customer. Misfortune hit the company in 1989 "when it delivered its entire winter clothing line, due in stores by Labor Day, the following January." Over the early 1990s, Marmot lost a significant amount of business.

While management's attention was focused on factory operations, nearly all other business activities were being ignored. Records were nonexistent or prepared too late to be of use. Marmot's computer-based inventory control system was useless. The cost of manufacturing a sleeping bag exceeded its retail price. Prior to 1993 the company "had never . . . set precise ordering and delivery schedules." By that year the company was facing bankruptcy. Until 1993 the irony of Marmot's commitment to quality was that it did not extend to meeting or exceeding its customers' needs. It had lost sight of the ultimate measure of quality—happy customers, be they internal or external.

What harm can come from producing the finest goods but not having them available to the customer? What additional ethical issues do you note in this feature?

http://www.marmot.com

Source: For more on Marmot and its subsequent recovery, read David Goodman, "One Step at a Time," *Inc.* (August 1995), pp. 64–66, 68, 70.

Reengineering Approach

It has been said that the only constant in business is change. Perhaps the greatest challenges facing managers at every level are to sense the need for change, see change coming, and react effectively to it when it comes. It is precisely for these reasons that a kaizen approach to managing change may not be sufficient. Rapid, radical, and even revolutionary changes may be necessary. In their book, *Reengineering the Corporation* (1993), authors Michael Hammer and James Champy (see Figure 2.4 on page 60) called for such an approach to managing change and efforts to improve quality of products and operations. They define **reengineering** as "the fundamental rethinking and radical redesign of business processes to achieve dramatic improvements in critical, contemporary measures of performance, such as cost, quality, service, and speed." Companies adopting a reengineering approach quickly learn to question everything they do and why they do it. "Reengineering first determines *what* a company must do, then *how* to do it. Reengineering takes nothing for granted. It ignores what *is* and concentrates on what *should be*" (Hammer

reengineering
"The fundamental rethinking and radical redesign of business processes to achieve dramatic improvements in critical, contemporary measures of performance, such as cost, quality, service, and speed."

and Champy, 1993). Reengineering is also known as business process redesign, internal business improvement, or process innovation.

A key concept in reengineering is to determine what a company should be doing, based on its core competencies and experience—that is, what it can do best. The company can then determine if what needs to be done is best done in-house or by some other entity. This approach has led companies to downsize and outsource. Organization owners and managers must continually ask two questions: What are we doing? and What should we be doing?

http://www.brint.com/papers/bpr.htm

> *The most profound lesson of business process reengineering was never reengineering, but business processes. Processes are how we work. Any company that ignores its business processes or fails to improve them risks its future. . . . For technologists, the lesson from reengineering is a reminder of an old truth: information technology is only useful if it helps people do their work better and differently (Davenport, 1995).*

Many companies are achieving impressive savings by reengineering business processes around the Internet. Enterprise resource planning software is used to consolidate accounting, human resources, and manufacturing applications in one integrated package. Software for electronic commerce consolidates online purchasing, supply chain, and sourcing. James Champy, co-author of *Reengineering the Corporation*, says, "The Internet is a catalyst forcing companies to change the way they process orders. Electronic commerce is going to have huge reengineering consequences" (Jones, 1999). This chapter's Managing Technology feature focuses on electronic commerce.

Major Contributors to Quality Management

Beginning in the 1950s, foreign-made goods within several industries began to meet or exceed the requirements of the world's consumers better than did American-made goods. One measure of that is in the chronic, continuing deficit in America's balance of trade with the world. On average for each of the last several years, Americans have spent over $110 billion more on foreign-made goods than the worlds' nations have spent on American-made goods.

As an example, the American auto industry experienced its first serious threat from Volkswagen's Beetle. "Volkswagen sold 330 Beetles in 1950, 32,662 in 1955, and 61,507 in 1959, by which time the Big Three auto marketers were fretting: Who is this contrarian new consumer?" (Sellers, 1995). By the 1960s Japanese cars were gaining a foothold by offering fuel-efficient, low-cost, and high-quality subcompact and compact cars. Their sales really took off with the oil embargo of the 1970s, as Detroit carmakers had few fuel-efficient quality products to meet the domestic demand. By the 1980s import cars had taken more than one-third of the American car market. See this chapter's Global Applications feature for more information on how the Japanese penetrated the U.S. market for cars.

Producers in several nations had discovered the importance of quality. In contrast, most American companies had not, and they waited until the early 1980s to embark on serious efforts to improve the quality of their goods and services. By

MANAGING TECHNOLOGY
Electronic Commerce

Top management has always formulated strategies that dictate how business is conducted. The increasing volume of transactions that take place electronically is a revolution in business practices. Thus, in order to stay competitive, management must formulate an electronic commerce strategy.

Electronic commerce (e-commerce) has grown much faster than anyone anticipated. The word "e-commerce" first appeared in *The New York Times* in an April 24, 1997, Business Day article. By February 2000, the Department of Commerce began tracking retail activity on the Internet, compiling monthly online sales statistics much as it does with economic indicators such as housing starts, gross domestic product, and personal income. A few months after it started tracking retail activity, the Department of Commerce began tracking business-to-business electronic commerce as part of its effort to measure e-commerce's effect on the overall U.S. economy.

Electronic commerce refers to all forms of business transactions involving both organizations and individuals that are based upon the processing and transmission of digitized data, including text, sound, and visual images. The major difference between electronic commerce and traditional commerce is the tools used. Traditional business uses person-to-person contact, as well as mail, faxes, and the telephone as its primary tools. In electronic business, entire transactions —*between businesses and consumers* (known as business-to-consumer, B2C, electronic retailing, or e-tailing) or *among businesses* (known as business-to-business or B2B)—rely on a computer-to-computer exchange of data. Traditionally, many transactions have been handled manually. Electronic commerce automates this process. Customers can go to a Web site to get information about a product, and then they can configure and order products, make payments, and monitor their order status 24 hours a day, 7 days a week (24/7).

Electronic commerce has expanded primarily because of its potential impact on business practices.

- *It reduces costs.* Purchasing online reduces the time and overhead cost associated with processing sales.
- *It reduces inventory.* Storage costs, handling costs, and ordering costs are all associated with holding inventory.
- *It improves customer service*, because customers serve themselves when and where they choose.
- *It develops market opportunities.* An organization can expand its reach, opening markets that would otherwise be inaccessible. Due to the global capacity of the Internet, business conducted over it is automatically international.

http://www.nyt.com
http://www.doc.gov

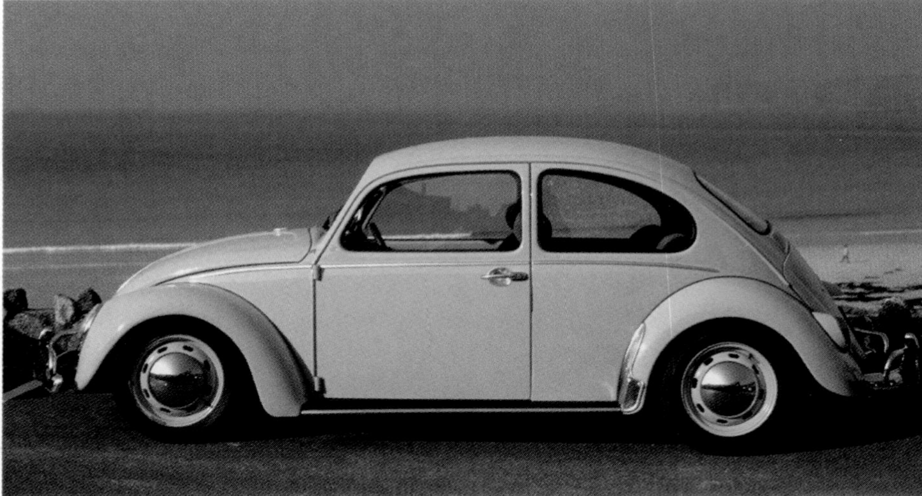

Germany's Volkswagen Beetle was the first foreign car to pose a threat to America's Big Three auto makers.

GLOBAL APPLICATIONS
Government and Industry Cooperation in Japan

With the end of World War II, Japanese policymakers chose to allow government and business to work together to rebuild their nation and its economy. The Japanese created the Ministry of International Trade and Industry (MITI) to work with industrial leaders to determine what direction the country should take. MITI began the rebuilding by concentrating on the creation of a strong infrastructure and the reestablishment of core industries, particularly iron and steel. Next the ministry targeted shipbuilding as the principal industry in which the country should excel. By the 1960s Japan led the world in building seagoing vessels of nearly every type, including oil tankers and bulk freighters.

Through MITI Japan's industrial community cooperates and shares resources. National and industry-wide goals are set, and strong commitments are made to achieve them. The Japanese government protects the industries it determines to be vital to the national interest (farming, steel, communications), and industrial trade associations act to protect individual corporate interests.

A strong network of manufacturers and related suppliers dedicated to the survival of the whole is but one reason why foreign corporations find it difficult to do business in Japan. Industries are targeted by Japanese manufacturers, which make long-term efforts to capture market share. America's consumer electronics industry yielded to Japanese competition by bits and pieces. Zenith remained as the only American producer of consumer electronics until November 1995, when LG Electronics Inc. (LGE) of Korea acquired a majority interest in Zenith.

Similarly, the Japanese targeted the U.S. auto market. They began by offering economy cars at a time when U.S. manufacturers were neither willing nor ready to modify their traditional full-size product lines. By the 1980s Japanese automakers moved upscale, offering luxury cars for a market long dominated by European manufacturers. By 1990 about one in three new cars sold were produced by Japanese auto companies. In the 2000 J. D. Power and Associates' initial quality study of America's new-car purchasers (a poll of 47,000 purchasers and lessees of new 2000 model-year vehicles after three months of ownership), Toyota, Acura, and Lexus models—all Japanese—were judged best in five out of seven car segments.

http://www.zenith.com/about_corphist.html
http://www.lge.com
http://www.jdpower.com/auto/jdpaawards/award-au00.html

that time many domestic markets had fallen entirely or in large part to the dominant foreign producers. The real irony of America's late recognition of the importance of quality is that nearly all of quality's strongest proponents are Americans. Figure 2.4 profiles the major contributors to the evolution of quality management theory. Two of the listed individuals—W. Edwards Deming and Joseph M. Juran—taught Japanese manufacturers most of the major quality concepts and principles the Japanese companies operate under to this day.

http://www.deming.org

http://www.juran.com

Assessment

The quality school of management thought has its roots most directly in the behavioral, quantitative, systems, and contingency schools of management theory. People are the key to both commitments and performance. What is done must be measured and evaluated quantitatively and qualitatively. Systems interact and execute the vast majority of processes. What needs to be done at any given time must be done in the most appropriate manner. Past practices and traditions have many current applications to today's management problems.

FIGURE 2.4 *Major contributors to quality management theory*

G. S. Radford In 1922 Radford published *The Control of Quality in Manufacturing,* in which he advocated inspection as the cornerstone of industrial quality control. In his view, "it was the inspector's job to examine, weigh, and measure every item prior to its being loaded on a truck for shipment" (Hart and Bogan, 1992). Radford believed that maintaining quality was a management responsibility and that quality should be considered during the design stages of a product (Garvin, 1988).

Walter A. Shewhart Shewhart advocated the control of quality through scientific methods and quantitative measures. He and his colleagues at Bell Laboratories, then a division of AT&T, created what is now called statistical quality controls and statistical process controls. Through the use of these tools, any process can be determined to be in control (predictable) or out of control (unpredictable). W. Edwards Deming and Joseph M. Juran, both of whom worked with Shewhart at Bell Labs, adopted and developed Shewhart's ideas (Gabor, 1990).

W. Edwards Deming Deming taught the value of quantitative tools for measuring processes and controlling quality. Following World War II, the Union of Japanese Scientists and Engineers, organized to help in the rebuilding of Japanese industry, contacted Deming and asked for his assistance. Deming, along with Joseph Juran, helped to make Japanese product quality a standard for the world's producers. Japan's most esteemed awards for quality bear Deming's name. In the 1980s he helped Ford and other U.S. companies launch their never-ending journey towards quality improvement.

Joseph M. Juran Juran argues that quality should not be considered merely an expense. It should be viewed, instead, as an investment in a firm's profitability. Juran holds that managers must design quality into products, services, and processes during the planning phase. He urges a systems approach to managing quality, combining three subsystems: quality planning, quality control, and quality improvements. Using Deming's and Juran's teachings, the Japanese developed the kaizen concept.

Armand V. Feigenbaum Following up on Juran's contributions was Armand Feigenbaum, manager of quality control for General Electric headquarters in the 1950s. Feigenbaum believed that "quality was too central to a company's identity to be entrusted to an isolated corps of inspectors. For a total response, every single employee and vendor had to be brought into the process" (Hart and Bogan, 1992; Feigenbaum, 1956). Although quality involved everyone, Feigenbaum believed that managers who were specialists in quality control should take charge of the quality effort. Today the approach differs. Top managers want all employees to be quality control experts and committed to quality in all their undertakings.

Philip B. Crosby Crosby was a 40-year employee of AT&T, a company that has contributed much to management know-how and technological breakthroughs, and a vice president of ITT for 14 years. In his books Crosby asserted that everyone needs to be trained by quality experts in quality control, quality assurance, and total quality management. Crosby has popularized quality through his down-to-earth language and approaches. He and Thomas J. Peters have accelerated national awareness of the importance of quality to our lives, our economy, and the perpetuation of our standard of living.

Thomas J. Peters Author, lecturer, consultant, and professor, Tom Peters has given us a look at companies doing the right things. Peters has sounded alarms and taught average Americans about the need to get better at everything we do, and to become more like our competitors by imitating them, learning from them, and trying to stay ahead of the trends.

Michael Hammer Hammer, author, president of his own consulting firm, and former professor, has added reengineering as a concept related to quality. He calls for giant leaps forward and a continual questioning of what is done, why it is done, and how it is done. Change must sometimes be radical. Managers can tinker with existing systems just so long before they must be replaced or eliminated. Only through a constant rethinking of everything can organizations and their people compete effectively.

James Champy Chairman of a consulting company, Champy, along with his coauthor Michael Hammer, has popularized the reengineering approach in corporate America. Their book, *Reengineering the Corporation* (1993), created a revolution. Their hands-on experiences as consultants allow them to show companies how a horizontal process focus can lead to higher levels of customer satisfaction, greater speed in cycle times, and huge improvements in cutting costs and increasing profits. He rejects gradual (kaizen) improvement in favor of creating new structures and processes.

The quality school is the most current and is embraced worldwide, to varying degrees, by managers and their organizations in every industry. Some adopt a total commitment; others engage in a short-term quest to make substantial improvements in their quality. Once improvements are made, efforts cease. The former is exemplified by companies like Motorola, Xerox, and Ford, and all of their suppliers, both large and small. The latter approach is quite common among smaller enterprises with fewer resources and less enlightened leadership. A company committed to total quality will choose only suppliers and partners who make the same commitment.

http://www.asq.org

The price for not striving for quality and for failing to make a total commitment to the quest is to risk being surpassed and overwhelmed by the competition and to provide products and services that do not meet or exceed customer expectations. In the final analysis, a company exists to help its members and its external customers meet their needs. The company that can do this best will survive and prosper in its industry. Chapter 3 extends our investigation of quality.

CHAPTER SUMMARY

1 **Discuss why a knowledge of the evolution of management theories is important to managers.** People ignorant of the past are destined to repeat it. Knowing what has gone before allows us to avoid mistakes and repeat successes. In order to understand the present you must see its connections to the past. All the theories and schools that make up the history of management thought have some value for today's managers. A manager should use the best and reject the obsolete contributions of each theory.

2a **Explain the contributions of the following: Classical schools of management thought.** Classical management thinkers looked for the "one best way" to do something. Skilled, principled, professional managers continue to search for better ways to do everything, knowing that today's best way will not be tomorrow's. They used time and motion study and a scientific approach to study work and work flow and to solve problems. Many of these tools are used today. Nearly all of Fayol's general principles of management exist in modified form and govern management behavior in today's organizations. Although the following concepts persist, many have fallen from favor: narrow job descriptions; the concept of the one best way; top-down decision making; bureaucratic structures in highly competitive, fast-changing industries; discouraging leadership at lower levels of an organization; and the suppression of diverse groups.

2b **Behavioral school of management thought.** Managers now realize that their most important and complex resource is people. Employees and their contributions are the primary differences between one organization and another. Motivated, satisfied employees perform outstanding work, which leads to satisfying user/customer needs—the central purpose behind any organization. People are viewed as assets, not expenses. Money invested to train and develop talent returns to the business many times over. Only by enlisting the creativity and diverse contributions of all employees can an organization expect to achieve its goals.

2c **Quantitative school of management thought.** Quantitative tools used in decision making proliferate and are made more effective and efficient through a variety of computer software applications and hardware interfaces. They continue to be valuable aids to decision making but are not substitutes for sound, balanced judgment and experience. They continue to be part of problem solving, but they do not rule the process. Without a continuing focus on ethics and customers' needs, even the best of scientifically based, quantitative decisions can lead to disaster. In the diversity of today's organizations, many alternative problem-solving methods and models exist. In the final analysis, a decision is evaluated on the results it achieves, not on the way it is made.

2d **Systems school of management thought.** A systems approach encourages managers to view their organizations holistically—to envision workers, groups, and tasks as interrelated parts of an organic whole. Systems are affected by both internal and external forces, not the least of which are customer demands. Changes in any subsystem can affect other subsystems and the operations of the whole. The systems view has led managers to think about quality as a concept affected by each action of every employee and unit and as customer driven. The result has been a commitment within organizations by all its employees to concentrate their energies on meeting or exceeding all their customers' expectations. The basic tenets of the systems school are very much a part of the contingency and quality schools of management thought.

2e **Contingency school of management thought.** The contingency theory tells managers to experiment and be creative—to try the new and different, to think "outside the box." Although using the best from the past, they are not bound to repeat it in a mindless way. For innovation and creative urges to succeed, managers must develop innovative techniques. This theory also tells managers to stay flexible and to consider alternatives and fallback positions when attempting to solve problems, meet challenges, and take advantage of opportunities. Through contingency thinking, diversity becomes a clear advantage to organizations. Diverse individuals and groups bring differing perspectives and perceptions to bear on every issue. Since no two problems exist in identical circumstances, different approaches allow for tailored solutions.

2f **Quality school of management thought.** The behavioral, quantitative, systems, and contingency schools converge in the quality school of management thought. To determine the quality of products and services, quantitative and qualitative measurements must be used. People are the key, and highly motivated and committed people make quality decisions and deliver quality outputs. Quality depends on everyone's commitment to meet and exceed customers' expectations. The quality commitment must extend beyond an organization's borders to encompass its suppliers' and partners' personnel. Without quality inputs, quality outputs are not possible. Since one size of anything will not fit all, companies must innovate to meet the needs of their customers. Companies must develop and utilize the leadership potential that exists within their employees.

REVIEW QUESTIONS

1. How can knowledge of past schools of management thought benefit today's managers?
2. What are the major contributions of the two schools of classical management thought?
3. How are the contributions of the behavioral school of management thought exhibited where you work? Where you attend school?
4. What areas of business activity can benefit most from the contributions of the quantitative school of management thought? Are there any areas that cannot benefit? Why or why not?
5. In your experience how have the concepts introduced in the systems school of management thought been illustrated?
6. What are the major contributions of the contingency school of management thought?
7. Why is the quality school of management thought so popular?

DISCUSSION QUESTIONS FOR CRITICAL THINKING

1. What evidence can you cite from your experiences to prove the existence of classical school thinking in some of today's organizations?
2. In what specific ways has each of the following contributed to the quality school of management thought?
   a. Behavioral school
   b. Quantitative school
   c. Systems school
   d. Contingency school
3. How does Deere & Company, the subject of this chapter's opening case, exhibit elements from the behavioral school? The systems school? The quality school?
4. What specific examples can you give that demonstrate an application of the kaizen approach to managing organizations? The reengineering approach?

INTERNET EXERCISES

Check the text Web site at http://plunkett.swcollege.com for updated links to the Internet Exercises.

1. Compare the workplace of today with work in the last century. What differences exist? What similarities exist?
   http://www.hrdq.com/content/articles/article2.htm
2. Management theory has evolved based on influences from classical management, behavioral approaches, and quantitative methods. Systems, contingency, and quality have added to management knowledge. Many have contributed to the development of management as a discipline. Research and discuss one of the management pioneers listed below.

Explain how he or she contributed to the development of management.

Chester Barnard
W. Edwards Deming
Peter Drucker
Henri Fayol
Mary Parker Follett
Henry Gantt
Frank Gilbreth
Lillian Gilbreth
Douglas MacGregor
Elton Mayo
Max Weber
Frederick W. Taylor
http://www.britannica.com
http://www.google.com
http://www.altavista.com

3. Compare Mary Parker Follett's thinking of the behavioral school to the contingency school of management thought.
http://www.strategy-business.com/books/96196

APPLICATION CASE

The Norton Company Versus 3M

While its young, small competitor, 3M (originally Minnesota Mining and Manufacturing Company), was struggling for survival in the early 1900s, the Norton Company, a manufacturer of industrial abrasives, was prospering and nearly ten times larger. By the late 1940s, however, the two companies were approximately equal in size. By 1990 3M dominated several industries and had revenues more than ten times greater than Norton's. A large French company, Compagnie de Saint-Gobain, acquired Norton that year.

Born during the classical school of management thought, Norton had built a tall bureaucratic structure to house its product divisions and its many staff managers who churned out detailed reports to aid the company's in-depth controlling and planning efforts. Its upper-level and middle managers built "increasingly sophisticated systems as the lifelines that linked them to their distant . . . operations . . ." (Bartlett and Ghoshal, 1995). Decisions were made at the top (requests for spending of $1,000 or more required the board of directors' approval) and the company became increasingly self-satisfied and inflexible. It had ceased, for all practical purposes, to actively sense the need for or to initiate change.

Beginning in the 1940s and into the 1960s, the quantitative and systems school of management thought were warmly embraced by a number of large and small U.S. firms, Norton among them. "No company participated in the [quantitative] managerial revolution more enthusiastically than the Norton Company . . ." (Bartlett and Ghoshal, 1995). The company adopted a variety of quantitative methods, including computer modeling, to focus on the best ways to expand its existing product lines. It decided to acquire several existing companies in its industry and to continue profit maximization efforts for its several original product divisions. It did little, however, to enter new markets or to develop new product lines.

As the abrasives market began to mature in the 1950s, Norton's response to lagging sales and profits was to focus on reducing costs and becoming more efficient. "During the late 1950s, Norton made a few feeble attempts to branch away from the maturing abrasives industry, but most of these were thwarted by lack of resources and institutional encouragement" (Collins and Porras, 1994). Unlike 3M, its attempts to diversify were concentrated on acquiring companies—to buy its way into new directions.

"Throughout the 1970s and 1980s, 3M continued to evolve into new . . . arenas by encouraging individual initiative. Norton, in contrast, relied primarily on studies and planning models handed down from its consultants" (Collins and Porras, 1994). "If Norton was [a definitive example] of a systems-driven company, 3M [was a definitive example of] a people-centered entrepreneurial model. That model is essential to competing in today's postindustrial [information-centered], global markets" (Bartlett and Ghoshal, 1995).

Questions

1. Which schools of management thought are illustrated in this case?
2. What caused Norton to decline in the very market it dominated for so long?
3. Using this case and 3M's history, what do you think explains 3M's success over its rival, Norton? **http://www.3m.com/profile/looking/history index.html**

Sources: Christopher A. Bartlett and Sumantra Ghoshal, "Changing the Role of Top Management: Beyond Systems to People," *Harvard Business Review* (May–June 1995), pp. 132–135; James C. Collins and Jerry I. Porras, *Built to Last: Successful Habits of Visionary Companies* (New York: HarperBusiness, 1994), pp. 160–163; 3M, http://www.3m.com.

VIDEO CASE

Evolution of Management Thought: A Study of Sunshine Cleaning, JIAN, and Archway Cookies

The Evolution of Management Thought video presents three broad characterizations of management thought, reflecting behavioral tendencies, contingency factors, and quality control issues. To illustrate these perspectives of management thought, we present thumbnail sketches of three companies.

Sunshine Cleaning Systems is a janitorial, pressure-, and window-cleaning business in Florida that puts into practice the behavioral school of management thought. Its management believes that a good employee must first be a happy employee. Therefore, the company not only provides the proper supplies and equipment, but it also has a supportive management style—treating employees with respect and paying relatively good wages. Evidence of its success with this approach is the firm's low employee turnover rate, consistently high customer satisfaction, and profitability.

Headquartered in Silicon Valley, California, JIAN is a software company that illustrates the contingency school of management thought. The company applies modern management techniques to the art of building businesses. It does so by providing expert knowledge and effective, timesaving tools that work with the familiar Windows and Macintosh word processing and spreadsheet software. The industry in which JIAN competes is both rapidly changing and unstable, with a fundamental driving principle of constant innovation. The penalty for an inability to adapt is certain failure. To compete in this environment, JIAN looks for individuals who are entrepreneurial and internally motivated and who respond well to change.

Utilizing a virtual organization design, JIAN has strategic alliances with Bindco for manufacturing and distribution of its products and with Executaff for all its human resource functions. This outsourcing allows JIAN to remain small and flexible and to maintain its ability to emphasize teamwork and collaboration in its primary business, software development. Its founder, Burke Franklin, avoids micromanagement. Instead, he uses a questioning technique of management that allows employees to address key questions and solve problems on their own without having to be told what to do.

Archway Cookie Company exemplifies the quality school of management thought. Archway is currently the third largest cookie manufacturer in the United States and emphasizes product quality. Its cookies are sold fresh, rather than baked and stored in warehouses to be sold later. The company ensures that its employees are well trained through extensive education and gives them the tools they need to bake quality cookies using only the best ingredients. The lifeblood of the business is Archway's ongoing relationships with its suppliers. It inspects suppliers' plants and reviews their policies to ensure that they meet the quality standards to which Archway and its customers are accustomed. Finally, quality control (QC) employees inspect all incoming supplies to the plant with both physical and analytical tests in the company's laboratory. Random samples of finished cookies are also taken, tested, and then kept as references for later comparisons should any problems surface.

http://www.sunshinecleaning.com
http://www.jian.com
http://www.archwaycookies.com

For Discussion:

1. Explain why the management of JIAN selected the contingency school of management thought as its approach.
2. Define total quality management (TQM) and describe which of the three companies is most likely to practice TQM and why.

Management's Commitments to Quality and Productivity

3

KEY TERMS

benchmark
core values
empowerment
intrapreneurs
mission
open-book management
process improvement team
productivity
project improvement team
quality audit
quality circle
quality control audit
quality function deployment (QFD)
quality improvement team
research and development (R&D)
scoreboarding
statistical process control (SPC)
statistical quality control (SQC)
total quality management (TQM)
vision

LEARNING OBJECTIVES

After studying this chapter, you should be able to

1 Discuss how customers influence the quality of goods and services

2 Explain why quality must be cost effective

3 Relate quality, productivity, and profitability to one another

4 Discuss the commitments required to improve quality and productivity at the following:
   a The top of organizations
   b The middle of organizations
   c The bottom of organizations

5 Discuss the external commitments required to improve an organization's quality and productivity

MANAGEMENT IN ACTION

Lifelong Customers

Quality depends on a customer focus throughout an organization, and Carl Sewell's family auto dealerships consistently rank at the top in customer satisfaction. Most people don't associate buying a car or getting a car serviced with a pleasant experience. Yet, by giving customers what they wanted, Sewell grew the business from $10 million in 1967 to more than $500 million in annual sales by 1998. He calculates that the revenue an auto dealer could realize from an average buyer if the dealership keeps the customer for life would be over $300,000.

Sewell applies the works of Deming and Taguchi to his auto dealerships. For example, in his book, *Customers for Life: How to Turn That One-Time Buyer into a Lifelong Customer*, the second commandment on Sewell's list is, "Systems, not smiles. Saying please and thank you doesn't insure you'll do the job right the first time, every time. Only systems guarantee you that."

A benchmark for the Sewell Automotive Company is Disney World. In the chapter "Selling Should Be Theater" Sewell says:

> *I love Disney World. . . . (It's) the image we keep in mind when we're thinking about how our stores should look. We make sure the grass is always cut. I picked out every tree and bush. And we make sure the buildings are freshly painted. . . . (We even bought a street sweeper so that we'd be able to clean the roads in front of our dealerships.) . . . Why devote all this attention to the grounds? Because we're setting a tone. . . . And it tells people what our values are; it's in keeping with the kind of customer we want to attract.*

Each customer is surveyed about how he or she wants to be treated, and the ongoing customer surveys are used to develop a customer satisfaction index (CSI). Several changes have been implemented as a result of what was learned from the surveys. Hours of operations for car servicing include Saturdays and evenings. Customers are given choices while having their cars serviced, such as the availability of loaner cars or someone to pick up their car. The job is done right the first time. ■

Source: Sewell, Carl, and Paul B. Brown. *Customers for Life: How to Turn That One-Time Buyer into a Lifelong Customer* (Pocket Books, 1998); Sewell Automotive Company, http://www.sewell.com; Taguchi Methods, http://akao.larc.nasa.gov/dfc/tm.html; W. Edwards Deming Institute, http://www.deming.org.

Sewell Automotive Company operates on the principles of quality and customer satisfaction.

INTRODUCTION

From the beginning of mass production in America, producing quantity and controlling costs were the major concerns. In early factories a large number of unskilled laborers performed narrowly defined tasks, producing goods composed of interchangeable parts for mass markets under the supervision of engineers. Workers were taught their tasks and expected to perform them exactly; they were not asked for their opinions or suggestions. Since the demand for goods in most industries exceeded supply until the late 1920s, nearly everything produced could be sold.

Until the early 1970s, quality was defined in most companies as the production of goods and services without defects and was primarily the concern of production engineers. "In its early days quality control was a dimension of cost control, with the emphasis on eliminating waste" (Hart and Bogan, 1992). By the early 1900s, inspection and inspectors were standard fixtures in most industrial plants. Inspectors were charged with the duty of weeding out defective parts before the products were shipped to customers (Shewhart, 1939). Often, operations were not inspected until they were out of control and producing defective outputs.

The primary difference between today's managers and their counterparts of the past is their definition of quality and the recognition that quality and efficiency are primary concerns affecting *every* operation and employee, not just those involved with production. Quality is now defined as the ability of a product or service to meet or exceed customer expectations and needs. Consider Sewell Automotive Company, the company in this chapter's Management in Action case. The company's management recognizes that the car ownership experience, not just buying a car, must be satisfying to its customers. At Sewell Automotive Company, concern for quality begins with the customer.

Also, the definition of a customer has been expanded to include those *inside* organizations. Concern for meeting customers' needs now begins with the inception of a new product, service, *and* process. It is linked to how effectively and efficiently each person and process functions.

QUALITY, PRODUCTIVITY, AND PROFITABILITY

Discuss how customers influence the quality of goods and services

http://www.juran.com

Joseph M. Juran (1999), a pioneer thinker on and advocate for quality, advises companies to focus on "product performance [which generates] product satisfaction" and to produce products and services free of deficiencies that create external and internal customers' dissatisfaction. Performance can mean the ability of a machine to deliver flawless output, the capability of a department or team to fill an order quickly and without errors, or the handling characteristics of an automobile. Deficiencies cause users and customers to reject or complain about products and services.

For example, when internal customers' (employees') needs for information are not met, their ability to perform may be adversely affected. They may waste time and other resources while they search for what they need. In turn they may provide inadequate inputs to *their* internal customers. External customers often compare competing products' performance characteristics as one step in their buying decisions. "A product may have no deficiencies and yet be unsalable because some competing product has better product performance" (Juran, 1999). Figure 3.1 shows that product design should begin with consumer research.

Quality features originate with an organization's internal and external designers, producers, users, and customers. Features and characteristics are those aspects of the product, service, process, or project that lead to satisfaction or dissatisfaction.

FIGURE 3.1 *Hypothetical customer satisfaction model*

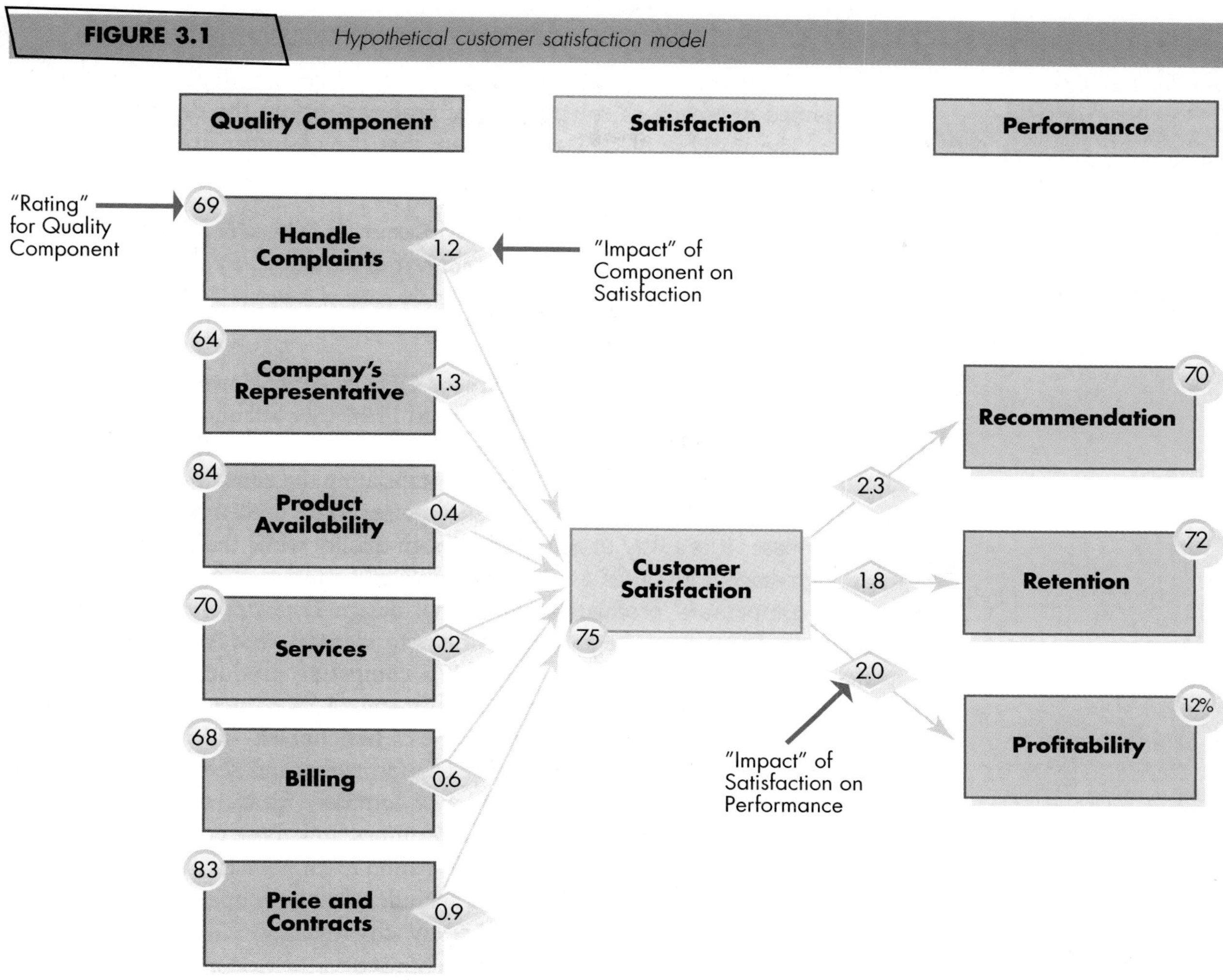

Source: http://www.cfigroup.com/why.html.

http://www.bus.umich.edu/research/nqrc/acsi.html

http://www.cfigroup.com/overview.html

Satisfaction depends on the users'/customers' perceptions that a product or service will meet or exceed their needs or expectations. The American Customer Satisfaction Index (ACSI) was introduced in 1994, and scores for one or two sectors of the U.S. economy have been updated each quarter since. It links customer satisfaction to financial returns. "Firms with the top 50% of ACSI scores generated an average $24 billion in shareholder wealth while firms with the bottom 50% of scores created only $14 billion" (ACSI, 2000). Professor Claes Fornell, key ACSI faculty member at the University of Michigan, said, "If accounting were to incorporate customer satisfaction as an asset on the balance sheet, we would have a better understanding of the relationship between a company's current condition and its future capacity to produce wealth" (CFI, 2000). This chapter's Management in Action case highlights this concept.

Quality Function Deployment

quality function deployment (QFD)
A disciplined approach to solving quality problems before the design phase of a product.

http://akao.larc.nasa.gov/dfc/dfqual.html

http://www.icqfd.org

Designing quality into a product is key to **quality function deployment (QFD)**, a disciplined approach to solving quality problems before the design phase of a product. The purpose of QFD is to assure that the customer obtains high value from a product.

> *To be competitive, we must satisfy the customer. In order to be more competitive, we must delight the customer. Quality is defined here as the measure of customer delightment. Note that customer satisfaction is a region on the scale of customer delightment. To delight the customer, we must design for quality (Dean, 1998).*

Professor Yoji Akao of Japan introduced QFD in 1966. However, the book was not translated from Japanese into English until 1994. (See Mizuno and Akao, 1994.) Professor Akao (1990) defines QFD as a method for developing a design quality aimed at satisfying the consumer and then translating the consumer's demand into design targets and major quality assurance points to be used throughout the production phase. It is a way to assure the design quality while the product is still in the design stage. QFD uses a matrix that relates customer requirements and features of competitors' products to functional design characteristics and customer satisfaction. The process begins with surveys to identify what features and performance characteristics customers value. If a competing product already exists, a sample is purchased and disassembled to determine its particular characteristics. The best of the competing products becomes a **benchmark**—the product to meet or beat in terms of design, manufacture, performance, and service. "Benchmarking is an improvement process in which a company measures its performance against that of best-in-class companies, determines how those companies achieved their performance levels, and uses the information to improve its own performance. The subjects that can be benchmarked include strategies, operations, processes, and procedures" (ASQ "American Society for Quality" Glossary of Terms, http://www.asq.org/info/glossary/definition.html#b).

benchmark
The product to meet or beat in terms of design, manufacture, performance, and service.

http://www.asq.org

http://www.toyota.com

http://www.lexus.com

Toyota used QFD to design and build the Lexus LS 400. In the initial stages of product design, Toyota purchased competing cars from Mercedes, Jaguar, and BMW. Toyota engineers tested the cars rigorously, disassembled them, and studied the parts. The engineers were convinced that Toyota could match or exceed eleven performance goals, including goals relating to weight, fuel economy, aerodynamics, and noise. Toyota continued to refine the design and the manufacturing process that would produce the LS 400. The company spent $500 million in development costs, which included expenditures for new, more precise machine tools and innovative use of materials. The result was a quality product; according to J.D. Power & Associates, a consumer polling service, Lexus models continue to be top-rated for quality and customer satisfaction.

http://www.ups.com

QFD works for services as well. Managers at UPS, a large package delivery company, used to assume that external customers prized on-time delivery of packages above all else. Like its competitors, UPS concentrated on providing on-time delivery. The company was obsessed with time and motion studies, exact scheduling of drivers, and delivery before 10:30 A.M. until its customer surveys revealed

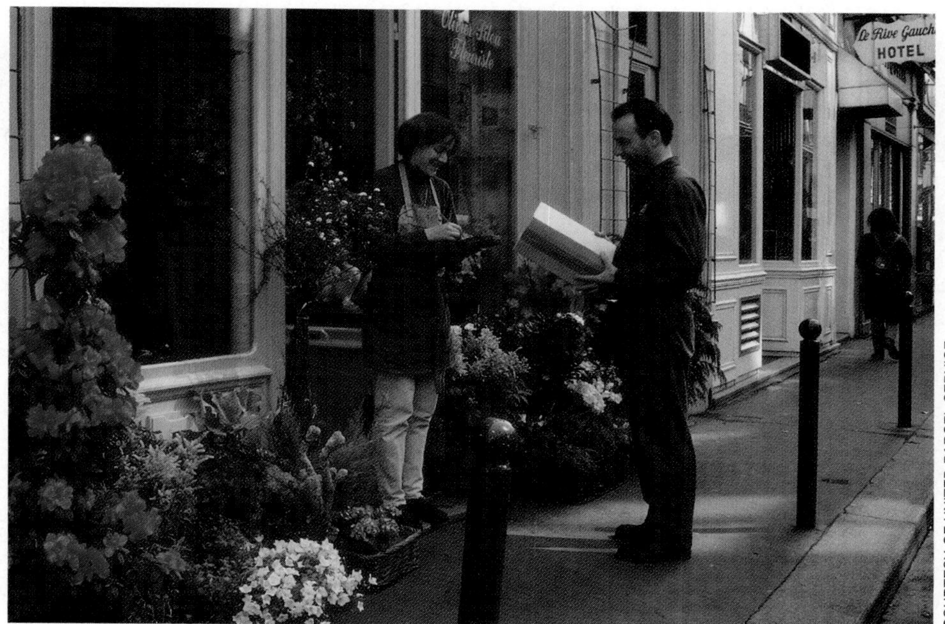

By using quality function deployment (QFD), UPS learned that customers wanted more interaction with drivers in addition to on-time delivery.

COURTESY OF UNITED PARCEL SERVICE

that "Customers wanted more interaction with drivers. . . . If drivers were less [rushed] and more willing to chat, customers could get some practical advice on shipping" (Greising, 1994). As a result, UPS hired more drivers, gave them 30 extra minutes per day to visit with customers, and began paying them a commission on any leads that create sales.

External customers' needs and wants keep changing. "Customers today want more of those things they value. If they value low cost, they want it lower. If they value convenience or speed when they buy, they want it easier and faster" (Treacy and Wiersema, 1997). Customers are "moving targets" who can quickly travel out of sight. Organizations cannot attract and keep customers with thinking rooted in the past—by failing to think "outside the box" of past practices—and products and services that are mere clones of others'. This chapter's Global Applications feature highlights a South Korean automobile company's efforts to change car buyers' perceptions of its quality.

Consultants and authors Michael Treacy and Fred Wiersema (1997) believe that the companies that please their customers best commit to one or a combination of three long-term value disciplines: (1) operational excellence, (2) product leadership, and (3) customer intimacy. PETsMART and Wal-Mart exemplify the first. They provide low prices, inviting environments, and unique and dependable service. Rubbermaid (a maker of household products and subject of this chapter's Ethical Management feature), Nike (the athletic shoes maker), and 3M (the maker of office and consumer products) demonstrate the second discipline. All three thrive on generating vast numbers of cutting-edge products annually that truly delight their users. For example, at Rubbermaid, on average, one new product is made for every day of the year.

http://www.petsmart.com

http://www.walmart.com

http://www.rubbermaid.com

http://www.nike.com

http://www.3M.com

GLOBAL APPLICATIONS
Hyundai Buys the Quality Message

South Korea's Hyundai led the charge of that country's auto producers into the U.S. market in the 1980s. Its models carried low operating costs and sticker prices and gained about 1.4 percent of the U.S. market, but the cars compared poorly to other makes on quality. New-car buyers rated (as measured by J.D. Power & Associates surveys) all of Hyundai's 1994 car models "almost at the bottom of the heap, with an average 193 problems per 100 cars vs. the industry's 110." But Hyundai had more than quality issues to overcome. "Our image got stuck on the cheap, low-level car, and it's very difficult to change," says Chon Sung Won, Hyundai's president.

Hyundai is betting heavily that its new Accent subcompact will help overcome its quality and image difficulties. The 2000 Accent had a suggested retail price around $10,000 (price range of $8,999–$12,500), about $2,000 less than its major competitors, Toyota's Tercel and Chrysler's Neon. To create the new car, the company invested over $437 million and over 50 months. It sent its unions' representatives to the United States to learn just how competitive the market is and what the company's dealers had to say about their cars. It told its engineers to study the competition and to build a car that they themselves would purchase from the perspective of both features and design. According to the company's vice president in charge of exports, Baik Hyo-Whi, Hyundai has sharpened its focus: "Our aim is to meet Japanese quality but at a more competitive price."

Sources: Louis Kraar, "Korea's Automakers Take on the World (Again)," *Fortune* (6 March 1995), pp. 154, 158; Bob Storck, "2000 Hyundai Accent: Accent Proves That Korean Car Industry Has Arrived," *2000 WOMAN MOTORIST*, http://www.womanmotorist.com/review/hyundai/bs-hyundai-accent-2k-01.shtml.

ETHICAL MANAGEMENT
Rubbermaid's Approach to Reengineering

Outsourcing, downsizing, wholesale layoffs, and overburdened workers are all too often connected with reengineering and great leaps forward. However, as Rubbermaid proves, they do not have to be.

Thinking out of the box is a hallmark of Wolfgang Schmitt's and Rubbermaid's approaches to everything. Schmitt gets great ideas by observing his kids at play, communing with nature, trusting his intuition, and looking for unfavorable trends. Schmitt leads Rubbermaid, a company known for introducing a vast array of new low-tech products each year. If you think Honda, Toyota, or Ford makes America's best-selling car you are wrong. It's Rubbermaid's Little Tikes' Cozy Coupe, selling over one-half million toy cars per year.

Rubbermaid's profitability depends on the unleashing of the creativity of all its employees. Twenty-one product teams have the responsibility for creating a large quantity of new ideas, rapidly processing them to obtain a nucleus of the best, and then turning them into product. Rubbermaid overwhelms its competitors by putting so many products out each year that only a few can be copied. To avoid runaway costs, Schmitt keeps his company continually focused on increasing productivity, but not by decreasing people. "Sure, we could take out a lot of our people. But we'd give up our future." Schmitt knows that wholesale layoffs lead to disloyal, demotivated, job-seeking leftover employees. "Instead, Schmitt is hiring. Rubbermaid in the next three or four years will hire 300 'culturally diverse' young managers, mostly from foreign countries." Rubbermaid keeps its competitive edge by carefully nurturing and continually hiring creative people; the product ideas keep flowing in, along with the dollars they generate.

Sources: Marshall Loeb. "How to Grow a New Product Every Day," *Fortune* (14 November 1995), pp. 269–270; Rubbermaid, http://www.rubbermaid.com; Little Tikes, http://www.littletikes.com.

http://www.enterprise.com

An example of the third discipline is a relative newcomer to the car-rental business—the small but growing Enterprise Rent-A-Car Company. Such a company tailors its offerings to meet customers' needs at reasonable costs. "They are adept at giving the customer more than he or she expects. By constantly upgrading offerings, customer-intimate companies stay ahead of customers' rising expectations—expectations that, by the way, they themselves create" (Treacy and Wiersema, 1997).

Total Quality Management

total quality management (TQM) "A strategy for continuously improving performance at every level, and in all areas of responsibility."

Robert Costello, an engineer and former GM executive, was the undersecretary of defense for acquisitions when he built on the work of Deming, Juran, Crosby, and others to create **total quality management (TQM)** for the Department of Defense. The department's TQM Master Plan, issued in August 1988, defined TQM as

> *. . . a strategy for continuously improving performance at every level, and in all areas of responsibility. It combines fundamental management techniques, existing improvement efforts, and specialized technical tools under a disciplined structure focused on continuously improving all processes. Improved performance is directed at satisfying such broad goals as cost, quality, schedule, and mission need and suitability. Increasing user satisfaction is the overriding objective.*

Figure 3.2 is the seven-step model the Department of Defense developed to illustrate TQM. In step 1 the organization establishes the TQM environment. Step 2 defines the mission for each component or subsystem of the organization. Step 3 requires the setting of performance improvement opportunities; it establishes the strategic planning process. In step 4 managers or managers and their subordinates define improvement projects and plans for action. In step 5 the projects are implemented through use of the appropriate tools and techniques. (You will read more about implementation later in this chapter.) Step 6 is the evaluation phase, in which results—cycle times, costs, efficiency, and innovation—are evaluated. Step 7 mandates feedback so that processes can be continuously improved.

TQM Principles

TQM is also known by and practiced under several other labels. At not-for-profit colleges, universities, and hospitals, it is known as "continuous quality improvement" or CQI; at 3M, it is known as "managing total quality"; at Xerox, the large office equipment maker, it is called "leadership through quality." In Japanese companies it is called "total quality control" (TQC). No matter what the name is, its concepts and principles are usually the same (Hunt, 1995):

- Quality improvements create productivity gains.
- Quality is defined as conformance to requirements that satisfy user needs.
- Quality is measured by continual process and product improvement and user satisfaction.
- Quality is determined by product design and achieved by effective process controls.
- Process-control techniques are used to prevent defects.
- Quality is part of every function in all phases of the product life cycle.
- Management is responsible for quality.
- Relationships with suppliers are formed for the long term and are quality-oriented.

FIGURE 3.2 *The seven-step TQM model*

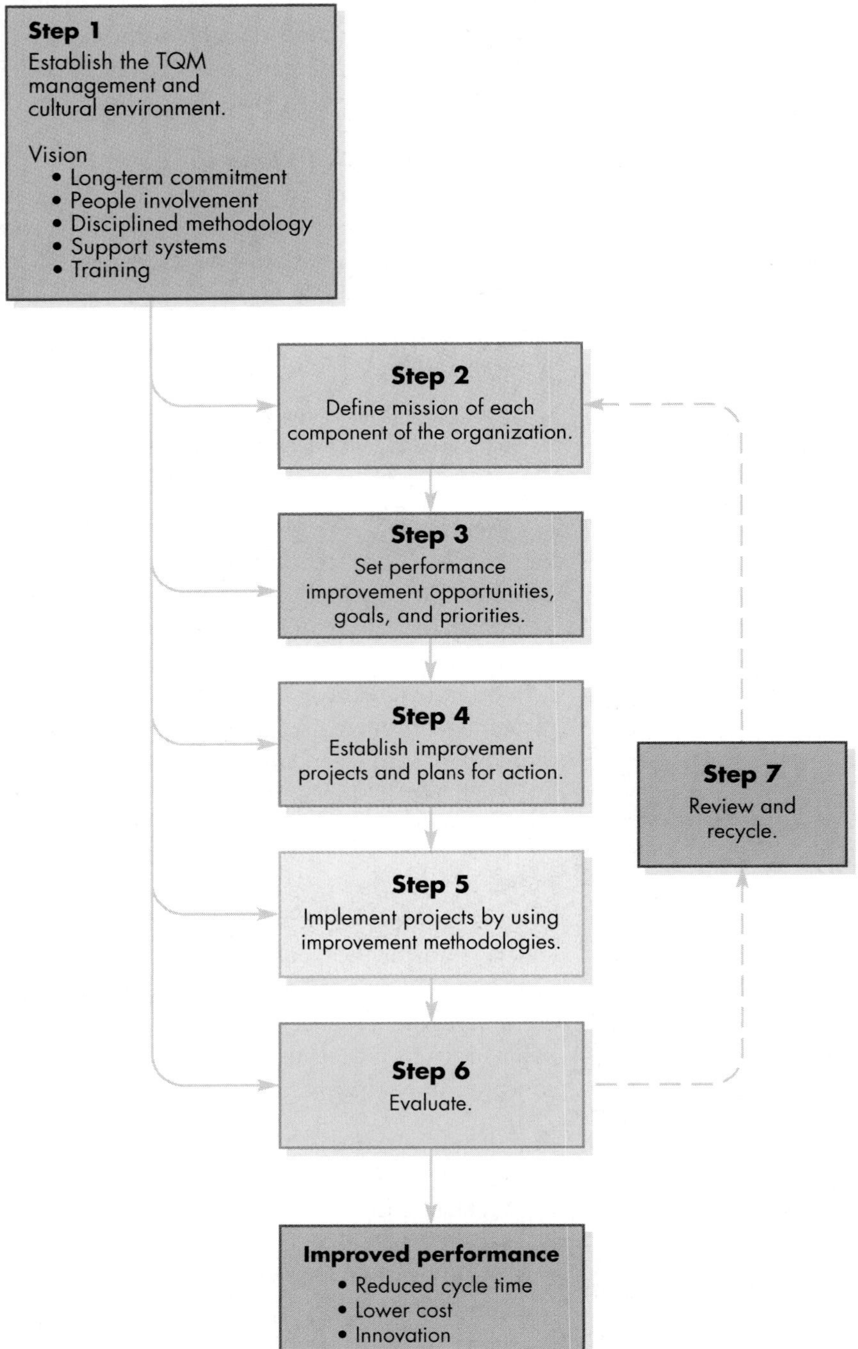
Step 1
Establish the TQM management and cultural environment.
Vision
• Long-term commitment
• People involvement
• Disciplined methodology
• Support systems
• Training
Step 2
Define mission of each component of the organization.
Step 3
Set performance improvement opportunities, goals, and priorities.
Step 4
Establish improvement projects and plans for action.
Step 5
Implement projects by using improvement methodologies.
Step 6
Evaluate.
Step 7
Review and recycle.
Improved performance
• Reduced cycle time
• Lower cost
• Innovation

Source: Department of Defense, *Quality and Productivity Self-Assessment Guide for Defense Organizations* (Washington, D.C.: Department of Defense, 1990).

As Thomas J. Barry (1991) wrote, "TQM/TQC is a journey, not a destination. It is a systematic, strategic process for organizational excellence."

Cost-Effective Quality

2

Explain why quality must be cost effective

http://www.att.com

As the previous two chapters indicate, meeting and exceeding customers' needs and expectations should be a primary aim of any organization. Those that do this both effectively and efficiently will succeed in their markets and surpass their rivals. But organizations and their people must ". . . make sure that the quality they offer is the quality their customers want. . . . [Q]uality that means little to customers doesn't produce a payoff in improved sales, profits, or market share. It's wasted effort and expense" (Greising, 1994). At the nationwide long-distance carrier AT&T, ". . . proponents of any new quality initiative must first demonstrate that the effort will yield at least a 30% drop in defects and a 10% return on investment" (Greising, 1994). Satisfying customers while focusing on the bottom line helps to guarantee that companies will not price products and services out of their markets.

Money spent on quality leads to efficiencies if it saves an organization from having to spend a relatively greater amount on repairing defects. "The cost of quality is the cost of avoiding nonconformance [to company and customer] standards and failure. Maintaining quality helps you avoid compounding costs you would incur from the deviation of not doing the right thing the first time" (Barry, 1991). When quality is viewed as conformance to standards, then lack of quality means a conformance failure has occurred.

http://www.philipcrosby.com

Philip B. Crosby (1984), manager, author, and consultant, wrote, "Quality improvement is built on getting everyone to do it right the first time (DIRFT). But the key to DIRFT is getting requirements clearly understood and then *not* putting things in people's way." Crosby (1979) identified the cost of quality as, basically, inefficiency or ". . . the expense of doing things wrong. It is the scrap, rework, service after service, warranty, inspection, tests, and similar activities made necessary by nonconformance problems."

http://www.xerox.com

At Xerox Corporation, managers take three measurements to determine the cost of quality. They compute the cost of conformance, the cost of nonconformance, and the cost of lost opportunities (Hunt, 1992). Conformance requires continual measurement of work outputs against known customer requirements. Nonconformance costs are those connected with not meeting customer needs and time lost by having to go back and do things over. Lost opportunities are customers and profits lost due to lack of quality.

Productivity

productivity
The relationship between the amount of input needed to produce a given amount of output and the output itself; usually expressed as a ratio.

Productivity, in its most common form, is the relationship between the amount of input needed to produce a given amount of output and the output itself. Productivity is usually expressed as the ratio of inputs to outputs.

$$\frac{\text{Output (units produced)}}{\text{Input (hours of human labor, machining time, or dollars invested)}} = \text{Productivity Index (PI)}$$

Such a ratio is a measure of efficiency that can be used to make comparisons and identify trends.

Productivity can be improved by increasing the amount of output generated by a fixed amount of input, or reducing the amount of input required to generate a fixed amount of output, or a combination of both approaches. Through both kaizen (gradual) and reengineering (revolutionary) approaches, processes and their related activities can be made more efficient or eliminated.

By measuring the productivity of the American automotive industry, a small Michigan-based consulting group, Harbour and Associates, Inc., determined that two of Japan's giant automakers "Nissan . . . and Toyota . . . make the most cars per man-hour in North America, but Chrysler Corp. makes the lowest-cost vehicles . . ." (*Chicago Tribune*, 1995). For both 1994 and 1995, Nissan ran America's "most productive" auto plant in Smyrna, Tennessee. It utilized "2.2 workers for every car made daily." Toyota's Georgetown, Kentucky, plants No. 1 and No. 2 were second and third with 2.42 and 2.49 workers per car produced daily, respectively. (*Chicago Tribune*, 1995). Ford's Atlanta and Chicago Taurus/Sable plants were fourth and fifth on the list with 2.63 workers for each car produced. According to Harbour and Associates, to be as efficient as their Japanese counterparts, GM would need to cut over 51,000 workers, Ford would need to trim nearly 21,000, and Chrysler would have to eliminate nearly 17,000.

In 1994 Andersen Consulting, England's University of Cambridge, and the Cardiff (Wales) Business School conducted the Worldwide Manufacturing Competitiveness Study of "71 automotive components plants in Britain, Canada, France, Germany, Italy, Japan, Mexico, Spain and the U.S." (*Chicago Tribune*, 1994). It measured the relative productivity positions of the plants by country of origin. "Of the thirteen plants classified as 'world class,' five were in Japan, three in France, two in Spain and three in the U.S. . . . Japan's productivity [was] about 35 percent higher than Europe's; U.S. productivity [was] about 15 percent ahead of Europe" (*Chicago Tribune*, 1994).

Efforts to improve productivity must improve product and process quality and vice versa. Improving productivity in an organization paves the way for improvements in its employees' standards of living and quality of life. Computers make workers more productive, resulting in faster, better, and less expensive products and services. This chapter's Managing Technology feature discusses mastering the personal computer. The money saved through increased productivity can be allocated to further improve organizational operations.

Quality-Productivity-Profitability Link

3

Relate quality, productivity, and profitability to one another

http://www.asq.org/join/about/history/ishikawa.html

Profitability results when income received by a firm exceeds the cost of paying its bills. The profitability of a firm depends on its ability to efficiently produce goods and services that please its customers. "No matter how high the quality, if the product is overpriced it cannot gain customer satisfaction" (Ishikawa, 1985).

W. Edwards Deming believed that companies that focused on improving quality would accrue fundamental benefits. Such companies decrease costs by reducing mistakes and waste, reducing the need to rework parts, and improving productivity. Improving quality, said Deming, can also help companies capture markets,

MANAGING TECHNOLOGY
Computer Literacy

The personal computer (PC), a computer used by one person at a time, was introduced by IBM in 1981 and revolutionized communication. It was built over an Intel processor (8088) and fitted to Microsoft's operating system MS-DOS. *Time Magazine* named the computer the Machine of the Year for 1982 (*Time*, 3 January 1983).

In 1991, for the first time ever, companies spent more money on computing and communications gear than the combined monies spent on industrial, mining, farm and construction equipment. This spending pattern offers hard proof that we have entered a new era. The Industrial Age has given way to the Information Age (Pritchett, 1994).

To be considered computer literate, managers must have a basic knowledge of computer terminology, hardware and software components, as well as be able to perform basic computer applications.

The PC user should be able to:

- Describe the basic hardware and software components of the computer.
- Start the computer, run programs, and shut down the computer.
- Control program windows and menus.
- Use dialog boxes.
- Get help in Windows and in programs.
- Create new text documents.
- Name files.
- Copy, cut, and paste text.
- Open and save files.

Sources: History of Computing, http://ei.cs.vt.edu/~history/index.html; Pritchett, Price. *New Work Habits for a Radically Changing World: 13 Ground Rules for Job Success in the Information Age* (Dallas, Tex.: Pritchett & Associates, 1994), pp. 2–6; Pritchett Rummler-Brache, http://www.pritchettnet.com.

http://www.deming.org

ensure their future, and provide more jobs. To Deming, improving quality caused a chain reaction of benefits: "Continual reduction in mistakes, continual improvement of quality, mean lower and lower costs. Less rework in manufacturing. Less waste—less waste of materials, machine time, tools, human effort" (Walton, 1986). Figure 3.3 provides a visual representation of Deming's chain reaction.

IMPROVING QUALITY AND PRODUCTIVITY

To produce significant, ongoing quality and productivity gains requires a 100 percent commitment from everyone involved. As many organizations have discovered, efforts to improve have failed for two main reasons—the changes were neither companywide nor committed and they were too dependent on too few people. As Townsend and Gebhardt (1992), writers who address quality issues, observed,

> *Partial understanding of and involvement in quality can produce only partial success or total failure. The only chance for a quality process to truly succeed is for a company to simultaneously attack all the issues: Leadership, participation, and measurement.*

The same can be said as well for the pursuit of productivity gains.

Commitment to productivity and quality improvements means changes in employee thinking, methods, and approaches to the identification and solution of problems. These modifications mean changes to widely held attitudes, beliefs, values, philosophies, and habits of interacting. For example, an undated publication

FIGURE 3.3 *Deming's chain reaction: the quality-productivity-profitability link*

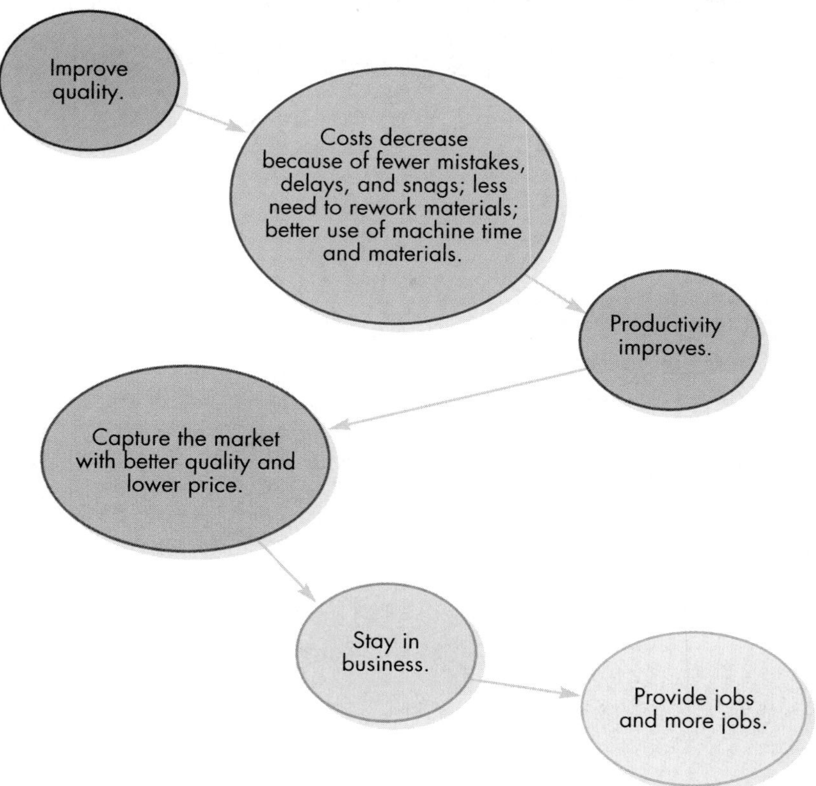

Source: W. Edwards Deming, *Out of the Crisis* (Cambridge, Mass.: Massachusetts Institute of Technology Press, 1988), p. 3.

by Motorola, *The New Truths of Quality*, lists "old truths" and "new truths." The old truth said: "To err is human." The new truth says: "Perfection—total customer satisfaction—is the standard." And companies have discovered a new truth for productivity as well: "Never be satisfied with efficiency improvements."

Joseph Juran (1999) cautions that moving toward improvement means change; change breeds resistance and fear. The existing, usually diverse ways of doing things in an organization provide support and social networks. "Any proposed changes are a potential threat to the stability of the pattern and thereby a potential threat to the well-being of the members. . . ." Juran's list of rules to minimize resistance to change within an organization include

1. Provide participation.
2. Provide enough time.
3. Keep proposals free of excess baggage.
4. Work with the recognized leadership.
5. Treat people with dignity.

6. Take the other person's point of view.
7. Look at the alternatives.

Reengineering Approaches

Defined in Chapter 2, reengineering is an approach for making changes that inevitably affect quality and productivity improvements. Reengineering requires that individuals and organizations "think in terms of processes—order fulfillment, for example—that may extend across many departments, and that they organize their work accordingly. . . . The goal, in addition to reducing costs, must be to . . . respond quickly and effectively to [one's] customers" (Barrier, 1995). But changes in anything and anywhere in a company have ripple effects as Michael Hammer's words indicate: "A sales [representative] has to recognize that his job . . . is acquiring orders, and that's a process in which he is only one player—it's a process that includes the finance people, the marketing people and others" (*Performance*, 1995).

Remember that the kaizen approach to improvement calls for gradual but continual efforts. Reengineering calls for an ongoing questioning of the need to do everything through a continuing investigation of its why and how. The aims are to determine what no longer needs to be done, what must be done, and how to better execute those processes. Says Michael Hammer, "We have to teach everybody in the organization to be creative, out-of-the-box thinkers. They need to think creatively about how they do their work . . ." (*Performance*, 1995). Sewell's innovative customer services indicate that its management thinks "out of the box." So, too, do the managers at 3M by encouraging all their employees to research their own ideas on company time and with company resources.

Reengineering changes fundamental ways in which people and their organizations handle their processes. Typical results of reengineering have been to change organizations' missions, visions, values, activities, and structures. Outsourcing has transferred internal operations to external suppliers, downsizing or rightsizing the organization through the process. Both have led to the loss of thousands of jobs. The results can be increased efficiency, quality, and profitability or the opposite, depending on how top management manages change and its aftermath. Any tool used incorrectly can deliver more harm than good.

A study by consultants at the Wyatt Company examined the results experienced by 531 companies that downsized. "Only 46 percent increased earnings, 34 percent increased productivity, and 33 percent improved customer service" (Longworth, 1995). Some companies have tried to practice reengineering by blindly cutting jobs, not necessarily the work they contained. The result has been more work for fewer people and the resulting insecurity, fear, and stress. James Champy says that this should not happen. "'Reengineering and downsizing are not synonymous. . . . But the two do overlap because in most reengineering, you learn to do work with dramatically fewer people'" (Longworth, 1995). Rubbermaid is an example of a company that reengineers by *adding* jobs! Refer to this chapter's Ethical Management feature on page 72.

The remainder of this section focuses on the essential commitments and elements needed by any organization to improve its quality, productivity, and profitability. We begin with top management's role.

Commitments at the Top

4a

Discuss the commitments required to improve quality and productivity at the top of organizations

Starting with their own commitments, managers at every level must try to obtain every employee's personal commitment to participate in both quality and productivity improvement efforts. Once gained, personal commitments are sustained as long as progress toward improvement continues. Therefore, the need exists to continually carry on the struggle. Leadership begins at the top, but, as Chapter 1 indicates, it must exist at every organizational level, in every unit, and in every team.

Mission

mission
A clear, concise, written declaration of an organization's central and common purpose, its reason for existence.

Every organization needs a clear, concise, written declaration of its central and common purpose. This reason for its existence is called its **mission**. Created by top management, missions act as ". . . the operational, ethical, and financial guiding lights of companies" (Jones and Kahaner, 1995). America's largest software company, Microsoft, began in 1975 with a one-sentence mission statement: "A computer on every desk and in every home" (Microsoft Museum, http://www.microsoft.com/mscorp/museum/musWelcome.asp). Missions unite organizational members and are amplified by both a vision and values. The organization as a whole and all its subsystems need a clear, commonly understood mission and properly funded programs to achieve it. Top management's primary job is to continually reexamine this mission and to plan for the future.

Vision

vision
A clear statement as to where an organization wants to be in the future.

Changing an organization in any significant way is a primary responsibility of top management. Every CEO must sense the need for a change, create a clear statement as to where the organization wants to be in the future (its **vision**), sell that vision to organizational members, create plans to achieve it, commit organizational resources to the effort, lead the effort by removing obstacles, and make certain that the organization's progress is monitored. America's largest aircraft company, Boeing, has a two-sentence vision statement: "People working together as one global company for aerospace leadership. *Boeing—the future of flight*" (Boeing Vision, http://www.boeing.com/companyoffices/aboutus/mission/index.html).

Core Values

core values
Values that should never change, "bedrock principles."

James Collins (1995), consultant and coauthor of *Built to Last: Successful Habits of Visionary Companies*, believes that there are some things organizations should *not* change—their **core values**. "Any great and enduring human institution must have an underpinning of core values . . . that should never change." According to Collins, great companies are great because they have and hold on to, regardless of the costs, their "bedrock principles—[their] 'what we stand for' " cores. One core value for any organization should embrace the continual search for quality and productivity improvement. Ford Motor Company's vision, mission, core values, and the principles underlying them are summarized in Figure 3.4.

http://www.patagonia.com

http://www.hp.com

Along with other companies profiled throughout this text, Patagonia, a small California-based sportswear maker, and Hewlett-Packard, a high-tech giant, have at their cores a deep respect for the individual. Patagonia experienced rapid growth, which brought with it a loss of the sense of family that its owner worked so hard to create. After significant soul-searching, its employees agreed to reduce the size of their company and refuse any new business that would harm this core value. Hewlett-Packard also turns down opportunities for growth if it means hardships

FIGURE 3.4 *Ford's vision, mission, core values, and guiding principles*

Our Vision
To become the world's leading consumer company for automotive products and services.

Our Mission
We are a global, diverse family with a proud heritage passionately committed to providing outstanding products and services that improve people's lives.

Our Values
The customer is Job 1. We do the right thing for our people, our environment and our society. By improving everything we do, we provide superior returns to our shareholders.

for its employees. The company has refused defense contracts because these contracts would mean a cycle of hiring and layoffs. "The decision paid off, though, by fostering greater loyalty among H-P's workers" (Collins, 1995). The same can be said for Patagonia's employees.

http://www.ford.com

Ford Motor Company redesigned itself in the 1980s through the efforts of top management. In 1981 Ford's president, Donald E. Petersen, invited W. Edwards Deming to speak to Ford executives. Refusing to talk about quality as it related to automobiles, Deming insisted on talking about Ford's management philosophy and corporate culture. Deming cross-examined executives to learn their thinking about quality. When asked to define quality, none could. When asked about their roles in quality assurance, managers talked about administration, not what Deming had in mind: commitment from the top to facilitate quality improvement. When asked by managers why America was having trouble competing with the Japanese, Deming answered with rage, "The answer is—MANAGEMENT!" (Gabor, 1990).

Ford was one of the first American companies to embrace Deming's teachings about quality. As Donald E. Petersen wrote, "I agree with Dr. Deming's philosophy of management, and I especially liked the emphasis he placed on the importance of people. In fact, we hired him as a consultant, and I made a point of meeting with him myself roughly once a month" (Petersen and Hillkirk, 1991). Early efforts at implementing TQM at Ford included teaching all employees, not just quality control inspectors, how to use statistical process control (a technique discussed later in the chapter). As Petersen observed, "When something's going wrong, 80 percent of the time there's something wrong with the way your production system or process is functioning" (Petersen and Hillkirk, 1991).

Later, Ford's TQM program dealt with removing fear from the workplace, developing trust in people, and building a supportive structure for the concept of continuous improvement. Ford executives began to ask questions: "What's our culture?" "What do we stand for?" As Petersen put it, "Dr. Deming's philosophy, expressed in his [fourteen points for improving quality], helped many of us zero in on some of the key concepts we wanted to express" (Petersen and Hillkirk, 1991). See Figure 3.5 for Deming's fourteen points. After their many meetings with Deming, Ford's top management rewrote their mission, values, and guiding principles. The current vision, mission, and values are shown in Figure 3.4.

FIGURE 3.5 *Deming's fourteen points for improving quality*

1. **Create a constancy of purpose for improvement of product and service.** Rather than to make money, the purpose of a company is to stay in business and provide jobs through innovation, research, constant improvement, and maintenance.
2. **Adopt the new philosophy.** Americans are too tolerant of poor workmanship and sullen service. We need a new "religion" in which mistakes and negativism are unacceptable.
3. **Cease dependence on mass inspection.** American firms typically inspect a product as it comes off the assembly line or at major stages along the way; defective products are either thrown out or reworked. Both practices are unnecessarily expensive. In effect, a company is paying workers to make defects and then correct them. Quality comes not from inspection but from improvement of the process. With instruction, workers can be enlisted in this improvement.
4. **End the practice of awarding business on the price tag alone.** Purchasing departments customarily operate on orders to seek the lowest-priced vendor. Frequently, this leads to supplies of low quality. Instead, buyers should seek the best quality in a long-term relationship with a single supplier for any one item.
5. **Improve constantly and forever the system of production and service.** Improvement is not a one-time effort. Management is obligated to continually look for ways to reduce waste and improve quality.
6. **Institute training.** Too often, workers have learned their jobs from other workers who were never trained properly. They are forced to follow unintelligible instructions. They cannot do their jobs well because no one tells them how to do so.
7. **Institute leadership.** The job of a supervisor is not to tell people what to do nor to punish them, but to lead. Leading consists of helping people do a better job and of learning by objective methods who is in need of individual help.
8. **Drive out fear.** Many employees are afraid to ask questions or to take a position, even when they do not understand what their job is or what is right or wrong. They will continue to do things the wrong way or not do them at all. The economic losses from fear are appalling. To promote better quality and productivity, people must feel secure.
9. **Break down barriers between staff areas.** Often a company's departments or units are competing with each other or have goals that conflict. They do not work as a team so they can solve or foresee problems. Worse, one department's goals may cause trouble for another.
10. **Eliminate slogans, exhortations, and targets for the workforce.** These never helped anybody do a good job. Let workers formulate their own slogans.
11. **Eliminate numerical quotas.** Quotas take into account only numbers, not quality or methods. They are usually a guarantee of inefficiency and high cost. A person, to hold a job, meets a quota at any cost, without regard to damage to the company.
12. **Remove barriers to pride of workmanship.** People are eager to do a good job and distressed when they cannot. Too often, misguided supervisors, faulty equipment, and defective materials stand in the way of good performance. These barriers must be removed.
13. **Institute a vigorous program of education and retraining.** Both management and the workforce will have to be educated in the new methods these points promote, including teamwork and statistical techniques.
14. **Take action to accomplish the transformation.** It will require a special top-management team with a plan of action to carry out the quality mission. Workers cannot do it on their own, nor can managers.

Source: Based on material in *Deming Management at Work* by Mary Walton (New York: Putnam). Copyright © 1990 Mary Walton.

Open-Book Management

open-book management
Commits organizations and their people to continual learning and requires that well-trained people be allowed to apply, without fear, what they learn.

Open-book management commits organizations and their people to continual learning and requires that well-trained people be allowed to apply, without fear, what they learn. "In an open-book company, employees understand *why* they're being called upon to solve problems, cut costs, reduce defects, and give the customer better service. And they have a reason to do so" (Case, 1995). Through information-sharing techniques and training sessions, employees learn the calcu-

scoreboarding
A technique that routinely keeps employees aware of changes in the critical numbers used to measure a company's processes.

lation methods and meanings of the critical numbers used to measure a company's processes and guarantee their success. The technique of **scoreboarding** routinely keeps employees aware of changes in these numbers as operations progress. Employees are kept informed through meetings, the posting of these numbers in strategic places, and the networking of individuals and groups via computers and other means. "Employees learn that, whatever else they do, part of their job is to move those numbers in the right direction" (Case, 1995). And whatever the savings, employees will receive a share of them.

Says Robert H. Rosen, president of the Healthy Companies research group (Verespej, 1995),

> *You have to link people to organizational performance in an adult context of communication. You must listen to them, and they must have access to information, because sharing more information will lead to trust and an open dialogue that will lead to better solutions. . . . Without that, employees are not able to take responsibility for their behavior because of the differences in power levels between managers and employees. . . . [M]ore and more companies are recognizing that developing a leadership vision and strategy that involves workers is fundamental to achieving changes.*

http://www.srcreman.com

intrapreneurs
Employees who think and act like owners.

Springfield ReManufacturing Corporation, a small Missouri diesel engine rebuilder, practiced open-book management when its owner, Jack Stack, turned employees, individually and in teams, into **intrapreneurs**—employees who think and act like owners—(entrepreneurs), thus changing the ways in which the organization conducted operations. Springfield regularly offers two-day seminars to representatives of dozens of companies who want to learn how they can practice its brand of open-book management in their organizations (Byrne, 1995).

Empowerment

empowerment
The sharing of information and decision making.

An open-book organization fosters continual learning and helps to create committed individuals who, both in and out of teams, perceive themselves to be partners working toward a common purpose. The next step is **empowerment**, the sharing of information *and* decision making. Empowerment gives employees ownership of their tasks and the freedom to experiment and even fail, without fear of reprisals. 3M has built its success on this concept since the early 1900s. Managers must be willing, in James Champy's words, ". . . to let go of control, in terms of letting other people make decisions, particularly when they affect customers. You've got to do that in order to grow" (Barrier, 1995). Empowerment requires managers to develop relationships built on mutual trust and respect, provide needed training and resources, listen to their people, and act on the recommendations they receive.

Empowered individuals and teams give enormous flexibility to organizations. Decisions are made at the lowest level possible, allowing for quick responses to users' and customers' demands. But empowered individuals and teams will only get the most from their autonomy when they represent diverse points of view, value one another, and respect each other's contributions. See this chapter's Valuing Diversity feature for a look at how Cast-Fab Technologies gets the most from its empowered employees.

http://www.cast-fab.com

VALUING DIVERSITY
Empowerment at Cast-Fab Technologies

CEO James E. Bushman has discovered "when employees are empowered, the business gets better results." He has created an environment in which employees have authority to make decisions over their specific work processes to meet customer needs. As a result, costs have been lowered, inventory is turning faster, and employees are happier.

"At the risk of oversimplifying the highly complex practice of empowerment, here are 10 steps manufacturing executives should follow if they want the kind of workplace where employees don't just show up, but bring their hearts, minds, drive, and initiative along with them."

EMPOWER THE PEOPLE

STEP 1: Define the reason for change.
STEP 2: Change senior-management behavior.
STEP 3: Determine what decisions employees can impact.
STEP 4: Establish natural work teams.
STEP 5: Share information.
STEP 6: Select the right people.
STEP 7: Provide training.
STEP 8: Communicate expectations.
STEP 9: Align reward & recognition programs.
STEP 10: Have patience & expect problems.

Sources: http://cast-fab.com and read Shari Caudron, "Ten Steps to Employee Involvement EMPOWER THE PEOPLE," *IW Growing Companies* (June 1998), http://www.cast-fab.com/news/6_98IW.html.

Commitments at the Middle

4b Discuss the commitments required to improve quality and productivity at the middle of organizations

Commitment to improvements must involve midlevel managers, those hardest hit in downsizing, outsourcing, and reengineering efforts. Middle managers are most active in planning and coordinating quality and productivity efforts. They must make certain that any breakthroughs are shared with others to enable any benefits to be shared throughout the organization. Because most processes are horizontal, cross-functional cooperation and communication must take place. Various methods can be used to facilitate this, including rearranging work flow, reassigning tasks, having regular meetings for individuals and teams, developing incentives and rewards for cooperation and breakthroughs (gain-sharing, for example), and teaming.

Teams

Teams may exist at every level, and they all need trained leaders, members with complementary and required skills, a supportive environment, and clear goals and guidelines. Teams create synergy, which makes their efforts more effective than the individual efforts of the team's members would be. Three specific types of empowered teams are used by middle managers to improve *organization-wide* quality and productivity: teams focusing on improving quality, processes, and projects.

quality improvement team *Usually a group of people from all the functional areas of a company. The group meets regularly to assess progress toward goals, identify and solve common problems, and cooperate in planning for the future.*

A **quality improvement team** is usually a group of people from all the functional areas of a company. The group meets regularly to assess progress toward goals, identify and solve common problems, and cooperate in planning for the future. The purpose of such a team is to facilitate operations by providing the support needed and enhancing coordination efforts. Team leaders should enjoy quick and easy access to top managers so that management strategies can be adjusted to meet changing conditions. Members "should represent the company to the outside world, schedule the education program [to bring quality improvement to internal

The synergy created by teams is helpful when trying to improve organizational quality and productivity.

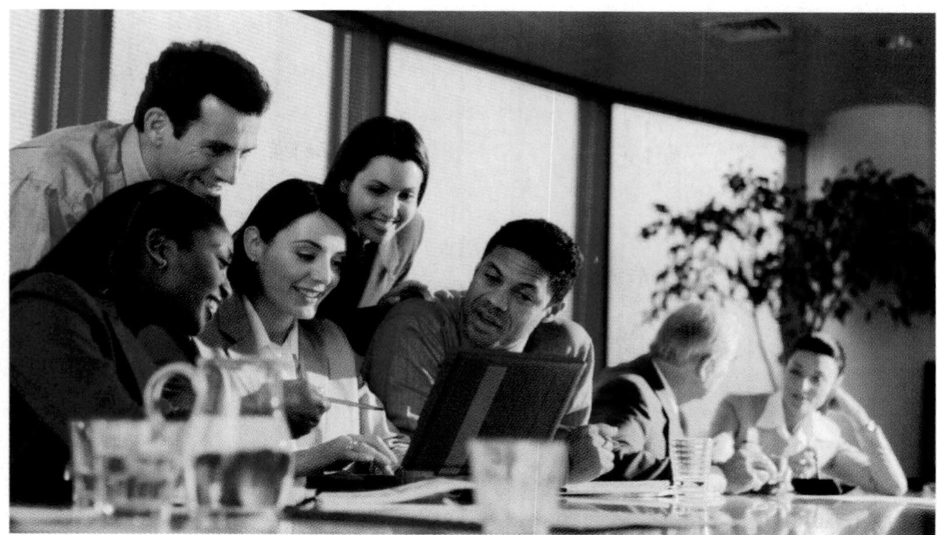

operations], and create company-wide events [to highlight the importance and successes of efforts at quality improvement]" (Crosby, 1984). Large corporations may have several quality improvement teams, one for each operation or operational area. Small companies may have just one.

process improvement team
A team made up of members who are involved with a process. They meet to analyze how they can improve the process.

A **process improvement team** is made up of members who are involved with a process—getting the payroll out, making a part, or sorting the mail, for example. Team members meet to analyze how they can improve the process. They focus on measuring the effectiveness and efficiency of each step, reducing cycle times, and identifying and correcting causes for variations in the quality of inputs and outputs.

project improvement team
A team usually composed of a group of people involved in the same project. They determine how to make the project better.

A **project improvement team** is usually composed of a group of people involved in the same project—installing a new computer system or creating a new product, for example. Members of the team determine how to make the project better. Project improvement teams usually include those who are or will be customers or consumers of the project's output. These users may be insiders or outsiders.

Investigations by all three types of teams may lead to contact with outsiders, especially if they are the source of a problem or its possible solution. Customers and suppliers are two of the likely groups of outsiders.

Audits

The U.S. Army has an old saying: "Don't expect if you don't inspect!" Usually a duty of middle managers, audits monitor progress—or lack of it—toward goals. A **quality audit** determines if customer requirements are being met. If they are not, the auditors discover why not. A quality audit can focus on a particular product, process, or project. A team of insiders or outsiders—a consultant or quality improvement team, for example—can perform the audit.

quality audit
Determines if customer requirements are being met.

quality control audit
A check of quality control efforts that asks two questions: How are we doing? and What are the problems?

A **quality control audit** asks two basic questions: How are we doing? and What are the problems? It focuses on "the way . . . the factory builds quality into a given product, control of subcontracting, the manner in which customer complaints are handled, and the methods of implementing quality assurance at each step of production, starting from . . . new product development" (Ishikawa, 1985).

Measurements

statistical quality control (SQC) and statistical process control (SPC)
SQC is the use of statistical tools and methods to determine the quality of a product or service. SPC is the use of SQC to establish boundaries that determine if a process is in control (predictable) or out of control (unpredictable).

http://akao.larc.nasa.gov/dfc/sqc.html

http://www.nist.gov/itl/div898/handbook/pmc/section3/pmc31.htm

Efforts to improve quality and productivity include various statistical measurements and scientific methods during both audits and when monitoring ongoing operations. As early as the 1930s, Bell Laboratories was using what is now called **statistical quality control (SQC)** and **statistical process control (SPC)**. SQC is the use of statistical tools and methods to determine the quality of a product or service. SPC is the use of SQC to establish boundaries that determine if a process is in control (predictable) or out of control (unpredictable) (Gabor, 1990). Figure 3.6 shows one of these tools—a control chart used to regularly monitor a process that yields frequent outputs. Operations are considered to be in control as long as their outputs fall safely between the upper and lower control limits established for them. Cost accounting uses various types of tools and methods to similarly track and analyze expenses connected to all operations. More will be said about measuring performances in Chapters 11, 16, 17, and 18.

Commitments at the Bottom

Discuss the commitments required to improve quality and productivity at the bottom of organizations

Empowered workers, individually and in teams, feel a dedication and obligation to continually work for improvements, especially when they share in the gains that result. Through process and product teams (cross-functional groupings), they combine talents and energies to identify and solve problems. Such teams may be permanent or temporary. A permanent team is usually in charge of an ongoing process like

FIGURE 3.6 *Control chart used to monitor performance of a process*

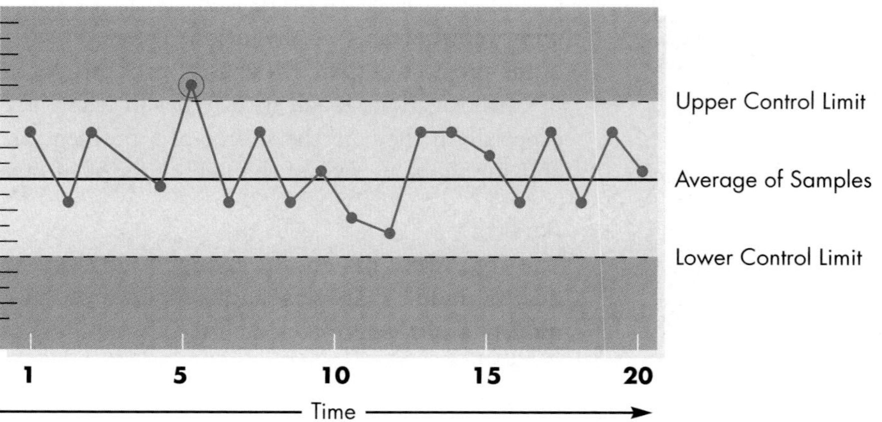

Note: Control limits define the range of expected variations in the normal operations of a process. What is important in control charts is the trends that they indicate toward exceeding the upper or lower limits. Once these trends are spotted, managers must investigate the process to discover the causes of the trends toward defects.

quality circle
A temporary team consisting primarily of workers who share a problem. It meets regularly until the problem is solved.

customer billing or customer service. A **quality circle** is a temporary team. Consisting primarily of workers who share a problem, it meets regularly until the problem is solved. Members of a circle are usually volunteers who agree to use their knowledge and experience to eliminate barriers to both quality and productivity.

http://www.quality.nist.gov

Motorola is a recognized leader in America's quality revolution. Motorola won the first Malcolm Baldrige National Quality Award in 1988 and is committed to aggressive programs for quality and product innovations. The Baldrige Award is presented to U.S. organizations in recognition of their achievements in quality and overall performance. Motorola has developed a "philosophy that allows each employee to contribute insights to the achievement of quality standards. The Participative Management Program (PMP) assumes that under the right conditions, employees will suggest better ways to do their jobs" (Hart and Bogan, 1992). All employees below top managers are members of PMP teams. Each is continuously at work to reduce defects and cycle times, either the time from order receipt to shipment for existing products, or the time from conception to delivery for new products. Targets to reduce defects and cycle times are the basis for rewards (Hart and Bogan, 1992).

Like many forward-looking companies, Motorola sponsors competitions among its teams. They compete in projects designed to raise quality, reduce production time, and improve efficiency. Each year the company showcases the teams' ideas and presents awards to those that created the best innovations (Van, 1991). Such competitions can be an excellent way to foster productivity and continuous improvement.

http://www.cin-made.com

CEO Robert Frey leads a small Ohio-based packaging company, Cin-Made Corporation, and knows the value of empowered worker teams. To overcome union-management strife, poor quality and productivity, and excessive costs, he developed a unique approach to changing his company. When a strike closed one of his plants, Frey discontinued the practice of annual pay increases. Instead,

> *. . . he offered to set aside 30% of all pretax earnings as a bonus pool and delegated to the workers—most of them high-school dropouts—authority to schedule production, control inventories, choose their own team leaders and screen every new hire. Some were sent out to learn such techniques as statistical process control, which they then taught to teammates. Frey also began giving everyone detailed updates on Cin-Made's finances at monthly meetings. Since 1989, workers' bonuses have added 30% to their annual compensation (Richman, 1994).*

Frey knew that nothing would change in any significant way without all workers being committed to seeking a turnaround. Once he had won their trust and respect through open-book management and empowerment, his gamble began to pay off handsomely for both employees and the company. The worldwide appliance maker Whirlpool Corporation experienced similar results in the early 1990s at its Benton Harbor, Michigan, plant.

http://www.whirlpool.com

In the final analysis, company efforts to raise quality and productivity depend on committed workers and associates who do not waste time, steal from their employers, withhold efforts, use forbidden substances on the job, nor resist needed change. Management's best efforts and millions of dollars cannot overcome such barriers. People are both the causes of and the cures for most of a company's productivity and quality problems.

External Commitments

5

Discuss the external commitments required to improve an organization's quality and productivity

Various groups outside an organization have direct and indirect bearing on both the quality of its product or service and its productivity. Companies must continually interact with their customers and various partners. Customers exert by far the greatest influence. Whether an organization has individual consumers or industrial users as its customers, it must develop learning relationships—continuing connections to meet their needs and gain their loyalty (Pine II, Peppers, and Rogers, 1995).

Most companies rely on continuous input from valued customers through surveys (see Figure 3.7), 1–800 numbers, regular sales force interactions, and their involvement in evaluations of those who serve them and of proposed new products or services. These examples of maintaining customer contact help producers keep their best customers and acquire new ones. According to the journalist/editor of *The Marketing Report*, "[W]inning a new customer typically costs a company up to five times as much as keeping a current one and the average business loses 20 percent of its accounts each year" (Stern, 1995).

http://www.varian.com

Customers can also assist producers' search for added efficiency. Varian Medical Systems, Inc., a maker of scientific equipment, has enhanced its productivity, profitability, and customer-service quality by listening to its customers. "When customers complained about the long time that was needed to set up its radiology equipment at hospitals, the company . . . took its time identifying several hundred possible solutions" (Greising, 1994). Its solutions included dozens of changes that made both its customers and the company more efficient. "The changes saved 95 hours in setup time, worth as much as $50,000 per order to hospitals. Varian also saved $1.8 million a year" (Greising, 1994).

http://www.rosscontrols.com

Close connections with suppliers is also essential. Ross Controls, a Michigan-based maker of pneumatic control devices, serves the needs of industrial users such as GM and Reynolds Aluminum. Nearly all of Ross's customers demand specialized, tailored products, necessitating close working relationships. These involve continuous communications and plant visitations. "And once a system is designed to solve the customer's problem, Ross gets feedback from prototypes and encourages the customer to make continuous upgrades to its valve designs, yielding more precisely tailored designs over time" (Pine II, Peppers, and Rogers, 1995). Ross continually learns from its customization efforts and often finds other customers and applications for the designs it has created.

PETsMART and dozens of other companies with hundreds of outside sources of supply must maintain close relationships with their suppliers to guarantee timely arrival of merchandise so as to avoid running out of stock. Factories, retailers, and wholesalers routinely link their operations to those of their suppliers, many by satellite communications linkups.

Partnerships with vendors and suppliers are based on openness and mutual trust. Information flows freely and continuously between the partners. Today, companies are turning increasingly to outside sources for vital materials and services. The primary reason for outsourcing is that others can do what you need done better, faster, cheaper, and with better quality and greater efficiency. Companies are also concentrating on partnering with fewer but more reliable sources for what they need. Both buyer and seller, however, must have the same commitment to quality of output and efficiency of operation for the partnership to last.

FIGURE 3.7 *Excerpts from a typical customer response survey*

We value your opinions! Please take the time to complete this short questionnaire so we can better serve you.

Product name and model number ____________________

Dealer name and city ____________________

How would you rate your satisfaction with	**Very Satisfied**	**Somewhat Satisfied**	**Neither Satisfied nor Dissatisfied**	**Somewhat Dissatisfied**	**Very Dissatisfied**
1. Your overall experience owning our product?	❑	❑	❑	❑	❑
2. The product design and characteristics (appearance, ease of use, etc.)?	❑	❑	❑	❑	❑
3. The overall quality of your purchase (reliability, workmanship, freedom from repair, etc.)?	❑	❑	❑	❑	❑
4. The clarity of the instruction booklet?	❑	❑	❑	❑	❑
5. The overall level of service received from your dealer?	❑	❑	❑	❑	❑
6. Courtesy of the dealer personnel?	❑	❑	❑	❑	❑
7. Convenience of the store hours?	❑	❑	❑	❑	❑
8. Convenience of the store location?	❑	❑	❑	❑	❑
9. Knowledge and expertise of the dealer personnel?	❑	❑	❑	❑	❑
10. Availability of dealer personnel?	❑	❑	❑	❑	❑
11. Explanation of the warranty and the extended service agreement?	❑	❑	❑	❑	❑

	Very Good	**Good**	**Fair**	**Poor**	**Very Poor**
12. Considering your experience, what are the chances that you will return to this dealer for another purchase?	❑	❑	❑	❑	❑

What could we do to improve your purchase, ownership, and service experience?

____

____

____

____

In addition to audits of their own operations, companies that outsource need to continually check on their outsiders' operations. Do they know their costs? Do we know them? Are their costs out of line or in check? Are they working on cost reduction? Can we help them to reduce costs? Companies continually work with their suppliers to reduce costs and, like General Motors, regularly renegotiate contracts on the basis of the savings generated. CommonSense Management's president and management consultant, Gary T. Snyder, adds that outsourcing ". . . can be an effective way to acquire expertise and economies of scale. . . . But remember that you can't just let go of functions that are outsourced: someone in your business must keep tabs on how the [outside source] is performing" (*Nation's Business*, 1995).

ADDITIONAL INTERNAL AND EXTERNAL INFLUENCES ON QUALITY AND PRODUCTIVITY

Systems have a number of internal components or subsystems. (Recall Chapter 2's discussion of the systems school of management thought.) Changes in any one of these can have an impact on one or more of the others. In like manner, significant changes that occur outside a system may have an impact on the system and its subsystems. In addition to the concepts already discussed in this chapter, we must briefly consider several internal elements and external forces and their possible impacts on quality and productivity.

Internal Influences

Nonhuman resources and how they are processed are the primary concerns under the heading of internal influences. These essential resources include information, facilities, machinery and equipment, materials and supplies, and finances. Each has a direct bearing on profitability, productivity, and the quality of outputs.

Information about both internal and external events must be continually gathered, generated, and put to good use by all people of an organization. Knowing the state of things through such mechanisms as audits and regular progress reports keeps people informed and well prepared to plan, organize, staff, lead, and control quality and productivity improvement efforts.

research and development (R&D)
Projects that uncover information useful to create a variety of new materials, processes, and products.

http://www.chrysler.com

Facilities and information are united through **research and development (R&D)** projects, which uncover information useful to create a variety of new materials, processes, and products. They represent a sizable investment of time and money that helps to guarantee an organization's future through a steady stream of customer-pleasing goods and services. Companies can practice R&D in research centers like Chrysler's billion-dollar Technology Center in Michigan or by the unleashing of the creativity of individuals through empowerment and open-book management approaches.

3M chooses to make R&D part of every employee's job. The company encourages each person to become a product champion—to spend part of every working day attempting to create something new and different. The best ideas (those promising the greatest opportunity for financial returns) are given top priority and brought to market as quickly and efficiently as possible.

Machinery and equipment are used in R&D and manufacturing operations. The more efficient the tools and methods, the more quality and productivity will benefit. World-class manufacturing has the following characteristics:

- Direct links to customers and suppliers
- Flexible production lines capable not only of handling large or small runs of specialized products, but also, within minutes, of being reconfigured to produce another product
- Short cycle times
- Horizontal product, project, and process teams
- Just-in-time delivery of vital materials
- Cleanliness
- Empowered teams and individuals performing many varied tasks
- Intense focus on efforts to improve quality and productivity at every level and throughout every process

In addition, manufacturing facilities are becoming showrooms for outsiders and laboratories for insiders as is the case at Springfield ReManufacturing Corporation discussed earlier.

Materials and supplies represent the inputs needed for any process. The quality of outputs is directly related to the quality of inputs. Poor quality materials and supplies used anywhere in a process can cause defects. These, in turn, affect productivity. Careful coordination through regular interactions with suppliers is vital to satisfying internal needs and external customers.

Finally, quality and productivity affect the financial health of organizations and vice versa. Cost-effective quality pleases and attracts customers and generates income. The more inefficient the producer, the less competitive its products and services.

External Influences

Constantly changing external influences on quality and productivity include the economic, legal/political, sociocultural, natural, and technological conditions existing in an organization's domestic and foreign markets. The actions of a business's competitors and the demands of its owners are additional influences.

The levels of prices in any economy affect businesses' plans and internal operations. Falling prices for needed raw materials can translate into lower production costs and higher profits. The reverse is true as well. Rising interest rates can cause a company to postpone borrowing and making the improvements those funds could generate.

Laws can make a company's products more expensive to produce or more difficult to sell. Federal antipollution and safety laws are but two examples. Both have increased production and administrative expenses for many firms; the extra costs are often passed along to the consumers of these products and services in the form of higher prices.

http://www.mcdonalds.com

Sociocultural elements influence product quality because products must contain different features, in line with the requirements of different ethnic groups. McDonald's is one of several fast-food chains that adjust their menus to different

Federal antipollution laws can make a company's products more expensive to produce. These extra costs are often passed on to consumers.

locations and customer preferences. As menu offerings change, so too will some of a company's processes and costs.

Natural forces can make things cheaper or more expensive. Locating manufacturing and distribution facilities close to inexpensive sources of raw materials can greatly reduce a producer's costs. Chicago, with its relatively cheap and plentiful supply of fresh water, is a case in point. And, as many of the residents and owners of businesses on the island of St. Thomas in 1995 can attest, hurricanes can make living in the Virgin Islands and other hurricane-prone areas more expensive.

Technology affects productivity and quality through its proper application. For instance, programmable robots can perform many operations more quickly and efficiently than people can. Fewer defects will usually result. Once the robots are purchased, they can be reprogrammed to meet the demands of changing but similar applications.

As a company's competitors get more efficient, so may the company have to. Outsourcing and downsizing are generally responses to the need of their practitioners to stay efficient and profitable by passing work to those who are more efficient at performing it. A company must continually strive to stay ahead of its competition through innovation and research and development.

Business owners demand a reasonable return on their investments and a share of their companies' profits. Money distributed to owners, however, is not available for other uses, such as improving output quality and productivity or making the investments in training and equipment that will help to guarantee the future of their businesses.

How all the above factors influence managers and their organizations in *additional* ways—beyond their influences on quality and productivity—is the concern of Chapter 4.

CHAPTER SUMMARY

1 **Discuss how customers influence the quality of goods and services.** Customers evaluate goods and services by comparing the quality features and costs of the goods and services against their requirements. Defects cause customers to reject goods and services or complain about them. Customer requirements must be determined and considered in the design phase of product development (QFD). The appropriate features and dimensions can then be designed into goods and services. Often some tailoring is needed to meet specific user requirements. Since customer/user needs and requirements keep changing, so too must products and services. Producers need to stay ahead of customer expectations if their next generation of products and services is to succeed in the market. A product may be defect free but still lose out to others who offer more or different features that better fit the customers' expectations.

2 **Explain why quality must be cost effective.** Quality is cost effective when providers of goods and services deliver the level of quality that satisfies their customers at a reasonable price—one that yields profits as well as customer approval. Delivering quality that isn't desired results in waste and lost revenues. Efforts to produce quality should also lead to efficiency improvements. If they do not, too much is being spent to deliver quality, or the standards being met are too demanding. If efficiency improvements are met, costs are reduced and profits increase accordingly.

3 **Relate quality, productivity, and profitability to one another.** According to Crosby, Juran, Deming, and others, quality must promote efficiency and vice versa. If they do not promote one another, something is wrong. If quality improves, costs decrease; as costs decrease, productivity improves; customers are kept and gained, additional sales take place, company profits increase, and more jobs can be provided (as demonstrated at Rubbermaid).

4a **Discuss the commitments required to improve quality and productivity at the following: The top of organizations.** Top management must sense the need for change, create a vision of it, enlist support for it, and drive the movement to bring change about. Top management must articulate the company's core values, determine the approaches—kaizen or reengineering—it wishes to authorize, and commit the entire organization and all its members to the continual journey toward quality and productivity improvements. To get everyone's commitment, top management must use the tools of open-book management and empowerment.

4b **The middle of organizations.** Midlevel managers usually have the primary monitoring duties and oversee most of a company's projects and functions. They are responsible for creating teams, training their people to function properly in teams, and providing the support both individuals and teams require. They are most responsible for implementing and encouraging open-book management and empowerment initiatives.

4c **The bottom of organizations.** Without committed employees at every level, something less than success will result. People are the key. Their knowledge, experience, skills, ideas, and energy must be given willingly for the best results to occur. When workers are truly empowered and can share in the gains they help create, they usually have the motivation to give their best. To be effective, all employees and their teams must have relationships built on mutual respect and trust.

5 **Discuss the external commitments required to improve an organization's quality and productivity.** A commitment to partners is of great importance. True partners have no secrets. They interact continually and keep working to improve their relationships. A learning relationship must be developed and maintained between companies and their suppliers and customers. Gaining feedback from partners and helping customers to solve their particular problems (as at Varian Medical Systems and Ross Controls) is a learning experience that can lead to both quality and productivity improvements.

REVIEW QUESTIONS

1. What influence over the quality of a product or service do customers really have?
2. How can a company make the quality of its goods and services cost effective?
3. Why must efforts to improve quality lead to improvements in both productivity and profits?
4. What must top management commit to if it wants its organization to improve its productivity and quality and, therefore, its profits?

5. How do middle managers contribute to their organizations' efforts to improve both quality and productivity?
6. In what ways do workers affect productivity and quality? In what way do they affect the efforts to improve both?
7. What external commitments affect quality and productivity improvement efforts?

DISCUSSION QUESTIONS FOR CRITICAL THINKING

1. In what ways does this chapter's Management in Action case illustrate how companies can exceed customers' needs and expectations? What advantages do Sewell Automotive dealerships give car owners that most local auto dealerships do not?
2. How can a company's suppliers affect its quality and productivity? Its profits?
3. A common reengineering approach within many companies today is to outsource any activity that can be done better, cheaper, and faster by an outsider. What changes does this practice create for the outsourcer and those receiving the work?
4. What does this sentence mean to you?—"The effort to improve quality is a continual journey." Can the same be said for improving productivity? Why or why not?

INTERNET EXERCISES

Check the text Web site at http://plunkett.swcollege.com for updated links to the Internet Exercises.

1. The quality requirement is a determining factor of competitiveness and the standard is a unanimously recognized quality reference. World Standards Services Network (WSSN) is a network of publicly accessible World Wide Web servers of standards organizations around the world. One of these is ISO 9000 Standards, created to promote consistent quality practices across international borders and to facilitate the international exchange of goods and services. What is ISO? Is ISO an acronym? What are standards? Why is international standardization needed? For which technologies is international standardization well established?
http://www.wssn.net
http://www.iso.ch
http://www.iso.ch/infoe/intro.htm
http://www.wssn.net/WSSN/gen_inf.htm
2. What is the "Baldrige Index?" Describe who manages it. How does the Baldrige Index prove the link between customer satisfaction and financial returns?
http://www.nist.gov
http://www.nist.gov/public_affairs/releases/stock.htm
3. Unfortunately, there are many more examples of reengineering failures than successes. The Software Engineering Institute (SEI), a federally funded research and development center sponsored by the U.S. Department of Defense and operated by Carnegie Mellon University, was founded in 1984, at least in part to investigate why so many software-intensive systems development efforts failed to meet their stated requirements, were late, and went over their budgets. Read the SEI's report, "Why Reengineering Projects Fail" (April 1999). What are some of the most common reasons for reengineering failures? How can managers avoid the failures represented in this report?
http://www.sei.cmu.edu/publications/documents/99.reports/99tr010/99tr010title.html
http://www.sei.cmu.edu/publications/documents/99.reports/99tr010/99tr010chap01.html
http://www.sei.cmu.edu/publications/documents/99.reports/99tr010/99tr010chap02.html
http://www.sei.cmu.edu/publications/documents/99.reports/99tr010/99tr010chap03.html
http://www.sei.cmu.edu/publications/documents/99.reports/99tr010/99tr010refs.html

APPLICATION CASE

Tenneco's Case Corporation Adopts a Customer Focus

Wisconsin-based Case Corporation was a wholly-owned division within Houston-based Tenneco, Inc., until 1995. Its specialty is the manufacture of farm and construction equipment. From the early 1980s through the early 1990s, "Case made a virtual art of ignoring the market . . ." and found itself with excess manufacturing capacity, products it could not sell, bloated operating costs, and losses of well over $1 billion. During those years its management had made many efforts to fix the things that were wrong, but interference and micromanaging from its parent's (Tenneco's) managers resulted in limited progress.

The problems these managers wrestled with were many. One primary problem was the inward focus of Case's managers. Instead of looking outward and focusing on customers, managers seemed trapped in the past, holding the nineteenth and early twentieth century view that "if we make it, people will buy it." The company had enormous manufacturing capacity. To utilize these facilities to their fullest, Case continued to make products that were not competitive, thus overburdening its company-owned dealerships. For example, its line of tractors was underpowered in relation to its competitors' models and lacked their automobile-like finishes. To move these tractors and other noncompetitive products to users, dealers had to continually cut their retail prices, thus cutting the company's profit margins in the process.

Another problem was one of inefficiency. Case manufactured many of its products' component parts in-house at a cost far higher than outsiders would have charged to make them. This practice carried with it the added burdens of too many people on the payroll and their related overhead costs.

In 1991 Tenneco's board of directors hired a turnaround specialist, Michael H. Walsh, as Tenneco's CEO. He hired an International Paper Company executive, Dana G. Mead, to take over the top-management job at Case. Mead inherited company dealerships "with eleven months of inventory—four months above the industry average—and no customers." Armed with an infusion by Tenneco of much-needed cash and a commitment to avoid the mistakes of the past, Mead assembled a new leadership team. The team created a turnaround plan and was given the power to act on it. Managers' bonuses were linked to achieving the plan's targets, and additional motivation was provided through a promise that, if the company became profitable, it would be sold off and managed as an independent enterprise.

The first of many reforms dealt with the reduction of costs. Excess inventory was sold. Heavy debt incurred in the past was refinanced at lower rates of interest. Unprofitable products were dropped. Some plants were closed immediately and plans were laid to close others by 1997. As payrolls were cut, the manufacture of many components was and continues to be shifted to outside suppliers. Most of Case's 250 dealerships were sold. But Case's management "knows that cost cutting alone won't sell more tractors."

The company's managers are building on reforms begun in 1992. Beginning in that year the company decided that it would be customer driven. It started by seeking customer feedback on its new design for a loader backhoe—a vehicle with entrenching and front-end loading capabilities. While the first test model was being built, "Case sent teams of engineers and marketing managers to talk to 150 key customers and users of rival machines. They quickly got an earful." The company invited valued customers to test its prototype vehicle. Over several days they compared its performance against that of its competitors' machines. Like many who tested the vehicle, Larry Willingham liked some features but not others. One dominant feature was its weight of about 16,000 pounds. It was too heavy for him to use because he would have to buy a new truck to transport it. When he returned a year later to see the proposed final production model of the loader backhoe, Willingham was pleased. Among other things, it weighed only 12,900 pounds. Said Willingham, "I definitely felt they listened to me."

After getting the green light from its customers, Case totally overhauled the Burlington, Iowa, factory that now produces the new vehicle. Ten million dollars was invested just to improve the rust protection and painting operations. When the new model was introduced in 1995, it was an instant success with customers. Production could not keep up with demand. Case is expanding the involvement of its customers in its product design. Profits and sales have steadily increased since 1991, and overhead expenses have fallen. Case's gross profit for 1994 was 23 percent, higher than any of its competitors'. Tenneco delivered on its promise to sell the company to investors. In 1995 Case became Case IH, consolidating International Harvester with Case. Tenneco's decreased ownership in Case resulted in Case becoming 79% publicly owned.

Questions

1. What problems was Case facing before its turnaround team took over?
2. How is each problem you identified in Question 1 related to the quality of Case's products and processes?
3. What did Case's turnaround team do to deal with each problem you have identified?
4. How did Case become customer driven?

Sources: Kevin Kelly, "Case Digs Out from Way Under," *Business Week* (14 August 1995), pp. 62–63; Case Corporation Company History, http://www.caseih.com/corporate/history/index.html; Case Corporation, http://www.caseih.com.

VIDEO CASE

Wainwright Industries: Completing the Quality Journey

In the early 1980s, Wainwright Industries, a manufacturer of precision auto parts, faced nothing less than a crisis. Increased competition on the global level was forcing Wainwright to either increase quality or lose it competitive stature. In the face of this challenge, the employees of the firm decided to make radical changes. It was clear that business as usual with a few minor improvements would not save the company. What Wainwright needed was an entirely new philosophy based on quality and customer satisfaction.

Using the criteria for the Malcolm Baldrige National Quality Award as a road map, Wainwright set out to make a number of changes. First, the company decided to emphasize three principles: employee empowerment, customer satisfaction, and continuous improvement. As a creative way of demonstrating its resolve, the company adopted the duck as a symbol of employee empowerment, based on the fact that ducks fly in formation as a means of supporting one another while in flight. A number of specific employee-oriented initiatives were implemented, ranging from cross training to profit sharing. The culture of the firm also changed in visible ways. The employees of Wainwright now all wear the same uniform (including the CEO), signifying that everyone is working toward the same objective and is on the same team. Office walls have literally been torn down and replaced with glass, based on the premise that if the managers can watch the frontline employees at work, the frontline employees should be able to watch the managers at work too. Changes were also made pertaining to customer satisfaction and continuous improvement. The company implemented just-in-time manufacturing, statistical process control, benchmarking, and quality-minded manufacturing initiatives. The results of the company's activities are linked to five strategic indicators: safety, internal customer satisfaction, external customer satisfaction, six-sigma quality, and business performance. All of the results, including the firm's financial performance, are posted in "Mission Control," a room set aside for activities related to the company's quality initiatives. In addition, all of the firm's employees have access to the data after its accuracy has been verified.

As a result of these initiatives, Wainwright Industries has met the challenge. Its market share, revenues, and profits are at record levels. Remarkably, the company was one of the recipients of the Malcolm Baldridge Award in the mid-1990s, the very award that the company benchmarked itself against in its early days of quality improvements.

http://www.wainwrightindustries.com

For Discussion:

1. What are your overall impressions of Wainwright Industries' approach to quality improvement? What did the company do particularly well in its efforts to improve quality and productivity?

2. Why was it important for Wainwright to focus so intently on its employees (in terms of the uniforms they wear, information they are provided, training they received, etc.) as part of its quality improvement effort? Explain your answer.

3. What other initiatives could Wainwright have pursued in its quality improvement efforts?

The Manager's Environment

KEY TERMS

boundary spanning
boundaryless organization
core competencies
directly interactive forces
economic forces
environmental scanning
external environment
indirectly interactive forces
intellectual capital
internal environment
learning organization
legal/political forces
natural forces
open system
organizational climate
organizational culture
sociocultural forces
stakeholders
technological forces

LEARNING OBJECTIVES

After studying this chapter, you should be able to

1. Discuss why organizations are open systems
2. Identify the elements in an organization's internal environment
3. Describe the directly interactive forces in an organization's external environment
4. Describe the indirectly interactive forces in an organization's external environment
5. Discuss the means available to managers for boundary spanning
6. Explain how managers can influence their external environments
7. Describe the obligations organizations have to their stakeholders

MANAGEMENT IN ACTION

America OnLine, Inc. Responds to Its Environment

Under the leadership of Steve Case since 1991, America OnLine, Inc. (AOL) has experienced phenomenal growth by sensing the power of the Internet and by linking itself to that power by constantly adjusting to the rapidly changing external environment. "It is the concept of AOL anywhere," David Gang, senior vice president for new products at AOL Networks said, "the convenience of AOL anywhere on the Web."

When AOL began, both CompuServe and Prodigy were way ahead in the online market. International Business Machines Corp. (IBM) and Sears, Roebuck and Co. originally backed Prodigy, the first mass-market online service. Computer users soon found AOL's software easy to use and liked the convenience of getting everything they needed to go online—including access, browser software, navigation functions, content, chat rooms and email—from a single source. By 1994, the company's subscriber base had grown to 600,000. By 1995, AOL was the nation's largest online service, with around three million subscribers. Eventually, in 1997, AOL acquired rival CompuServe, which it now operates as a separate service.

Furthermore, AOL withstood the market entry of huge companies, such at AT&T and Microsoft. Today, AOL dominates the home market for Internet users with over 26 million members. AOL's focus on being an online service without "hidden corporate agendas" is the reason behind much of its success, says Case, the company's chief executive, known to subscribers for his monthly letters about the service. "If you're a technology company, you want to sell your technology. If you're a communications company, you want to sell your network," Case said. "With Prodigy, IBM wanted to sell computers and Sears wanted to do retail stuff. AT&T had its ventures. H&R Block with CompuServe—they all had an agenda. For them, the interactive business was an extension. For us, it was the reason we got up every morning. And it still is."

Case said that the company faces "many, many competitors at all levels," including Yahoo! (http://www.yahoo.com), local phone companies, and cable companies. AOL has reacted to the competition by developing a presence on the Web independent of its online service, generating revenue from advertising and electronic commerce. Its Web site (http://www.aol.com) is attracting Internet users who are not AOL subscribers by offering services such as search functions and messaging technology for free. AOL Instant Messenger, a messaging function that alerts Internet users when friends are online and allows them to communicate in real time, has extended AOL's popular Instant Message and Buddy List technology to the Web. Instant Messenger has proven to be a very effective advertising vehicle on the Internet for AOL since the window with the service sits open on the desktop. About 30 percent to 35 percent of the traffic on www.aol.com comes from the Internet at large, rather than from AOL members. AOL operates as a giant system, coordinating the operations of its diverse global subsystems for both the company's prosperity and that of its customers. ■

Sources: Alan Goldstein, "America OnLine Overcomes Obstacles to Outpace Rivals," *The Dallas Morning News* (27 April 1998); Joelle Tessler, "As Imitators Proliferate, AOL Stakes Bigger Claim on the Web," *Dow Jones Newswires* (22 January 1998).

On January 11, 2001, AOL and Time Warner completed their merger to form AOL Time Warner Inc.

INTRODUCTION

Chapter 3 listed the major internal and external influences on customer satisfaction and the efficiency of organizational activities. In this chapter we expand our examination of these major influences and answer two questions: (1) How do both internal and external influences affect organizational activities (other than those affecting quality and productivity)? (2) What can managers do to sense and cope with them?

THE ORGANIZATION AS A SYSTEM

Discuss why organizations are open systems

Chapter 2 introduced the systems school of management thinking. A systems perspective of organizations provides a useful framework for examining the relationship between an organization and its environment. It is the element that integrates the other disciplines together in the learning organization (Senge, 1994a). Managers, like those in this chapter's Management in Action case, think of their organization as systems: interrelated subsystems that process various inputs to generate various outputs, pleasing users and customers as they do so. Systems consist of sets of subsystems (interrelated parts) that act as a whole to generate outputs and function according to a plan or design. Any change in a subsystem can mean change to other subsystems and to the system as a whole. In this context all of an organization's units and personnel affect and are affected by all others to some extent.

An organization must be concerned not only with what happens within and among its subsystems and people, but also with what happens outside of itself. No organization exists or operates in a vacuum. Management decisions must fit within the surrounding environment, which is divided into two components: internal and external. These forces influence conditions of every organization; however, the most influential force in one organization may have little impact on other organizations. Managers must continually scan and monitor the environment. Scanning is the process by which the organization acquires information for decision making. The modes (surveillance and search) of scanning are primarily determined by the external environmental stimuli and by the magnitude and the direction of the discrepancy between the goal and its realization (Schoderbek, Schoderbek, and Kefalas, 1980). While surveillance is useful for the information-gathering process, search is oriented toward finding a satisfactory solution to a specific problem.

environmental scanning *The process of collecting information about the external environment to identify and analyze trends.*

Environmental scanning is the process of collecting information about the external environment to identify and analyze trends. This allows managers to determine their organization's best response to an environmental change. Scanning identifies signals of change and monitoring follows these signals. For example, the onset of lawsuits and legislation surrounding repetitive stress injuries was signaled loud and clear by over 1,200 newspaper and magazine articles on the topic in 1993. Some organizations paid attention and prepared, and others ended up in the courtroom (Ashley and Morrison, 1995).

L. von Bertalanffy (1950) was the first to call systems, which interact with their environments, "open systems." These systems take in inputs from their environments, process them, and return outputs back into the environment. Open sys-

open system
A system that regularly affects and is affected by various and constantly changing forces (elements and components) outside itself.

tems depend on their environments to survive. Even modest environmental shifts can alter the results of management decisions. Figure 4.1 depicts an organization as an **open system**—one that regularly affects and is affected by various and constantly changing forces (elements and components) outside itself. Open systems remain efficient and effective by adapting to shifts in their environments.

FIGURE 4.1 *The organization as an open system*

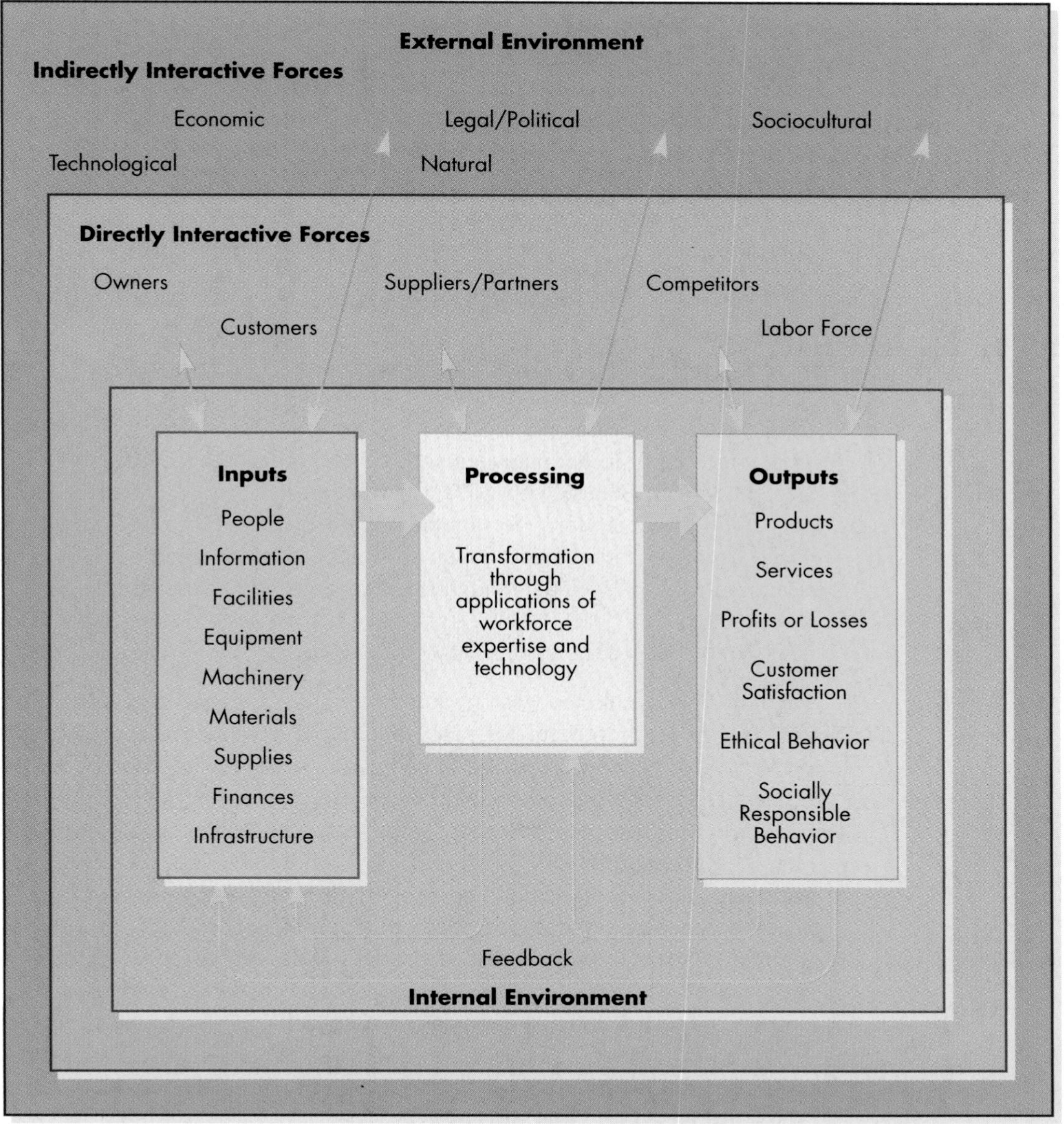

internal environment
Composed of elements within an organization's borders that managers create, acquire, and utilize, including the organization's mission, vision, core values, core competencies, leadership, culture, climate, structure, and available resources.

external environment
Includes all the forces outside an organization's borders that interact directly or indirectly with it.

At the center of Figure 4.1 is an organization consisting of an **internal environment** shown as the basic inputs–processing–outputs model introduced in Chapter 2. Every organization's internal environment is composed of elements within its borders that managers create, acquire, and utilize. These elements include the organization's mission, vision, core values, core competencies, leadership, culture, climate, structure, and available resources.

Notice the two colored bands surrounding the organization. Together these represent any organization's **external environment** and include all the forces outside its borders that interact directly or indirectly with it. Originally, W. Churchman (1968) defined external environment as those factors which not only are outside the system's control but which determine in part how the system performs. In any organization external forces may have a significant impact on the organization but are outside the control of the manager. The boundary that separates the organization from its external environment is not always clear and precise. The two-headed arrows, connecting the external environment to the organization's internal one, represent the influences that an organization exerts on outside forces and the influences they exert on the organization. After an examination of the elements within an organization's internal environment, this chapter explores the forces in any organization's external environment.

INTERNAL ENVIRONMENT

Identify the elements in an organization's internal environment

An organization's internal environment contains elements it acquires and absorbs from outside and elements created by its people. Once inside, these elements are, for the most part, under management's control. Although AOL aligns globally (outside the United States) with a local partner to help run the venture, it demands that the partner conform to company-wide quality, efficiency, and profitability goals. An organization's internal environment makes it unique and is revealed by several tangible as well as intangible expressions. We examine this next.

Mission, Vision, and Core Values

The concepts of mission, vision, and core values were defined in Chapter 3. But clearly they are important for many additional reasons as they affect how every person and process will operate. A company's *mission* is its primary reason for existence. The mission statement is the "touchstone" by which all offerings are judged. In addition to the organization's purpose, other key elements of the mission statement should include whom it serves, how, and why. The most effective mission statements are easily recalled and provide direction and motivation for the organization. Since an organization exists to accomplish something in the larger environment, its specific mission or purpose provides employees with a shared sense of opportunity, direction, significance, and achievement. An explicit mission guides employees to work independently and yet collectively toward the realization of the organization's potential. Thus, a good mission statement gets the emotional bonding and commitment needed. It allows the individual employee to say "I know how I should do my job differently."

Disney's mission is not only to run theme parks, but to provide entertainment.

© AFP/CORBIS

http://disney.go.com

For example, many people might think that The Walt Disney Company's mission is to run theme parks. But, Disney's mission is always moving toward an expanded view. Disney provides entertainment. "Disney's overriding objective is to create shareholder value by continuing to be the world's premier entertainment company from a creative, strategic, and financial standpoint." Also, many people might think that Revlon's mission is to make cosmetics. Yet, Revlon provides glamour, excitement, and innovation. Charles Revson, Revlon's founder, understood the importance of mission. He said "In the factory, we make cosmetics; in the store, we sell hope."

http://www.revlon.com

A company's *vision* states what it wants to evolve into over time. Visionary companies that set a purpose beyond making money were found to have outperformed other companies in the stock market from 1926 to 1990 by more than six to one (Fuchsberg, 1994). Managers require more vision than ever because change is coming faster than ever. Leaders have the ability to make their vision real by engaging the minds, as well as the hearts, of others.

A company's *core values* are the fundamental principles it will not compromise. Values serve as a baseline for actions and decision making and guide employees in the organization's intentions and interests. The values driving behavior define the organizational culture. A strong value system or clearly defined culture turns beliefs into standards such as best quality, best performance, most reliable, most durable, safest, fastest, best value for the money, least expensive, most prestigious, best designed or styled, easiest to use. If asked, "What do we believe in?" or "List our organization's values" all employees in the organization should write down the same values. For example, McDonald's values are captured in its motto of "Q.S.C. & V." which stands for quality, service, cleanliness, and value.

http://www.mcdonalds.com

Core Competencies

core competencies
What an organization knows and does best.

The most significant cause for an organization's success is a continuing focus on what it knows and does best—its **core competencies**. Core competencies are a company's expertise and evolve over time. AOL knows what it does best, and the people working at CompuServe [who shared AOL's passion about the medium] welcomed its leadership and commitment. Conversely, a major cause for company failure is senior management's failure ". . . to ask central questions, such as what precisely is their company's core expertise, what are reasonable long-term and short-term goals, what are the key drivers of profitability in their competitive situation?" (Labich, 1994). Every day senior managers must ask themselves, "What is our business?" and "What should it be?" They must continually assess where they have been, where they are now, and where they wish to go in line with where their expertise lies.

http://www.toysrus.com

As Toys 'R' Us watched its market share shrink, its senior management eventually realized that the company had lost its focus. It had gradually become a company that diverted from its core competency—meeting consumers' needs through the mass retailing of toys. Now Toys 'R' Us is fighting back. It has started a major renovation of its 1,500 stores, developing an easier-to-navigate, brighter layout. It is stepping up its presence on the Internet. The Amazon/Toys 'R' Us Web site is the subject of this chapter's Application Case on page 122.

intellectual capital
An organization's collective experiences, wisdom, knowledge, and expertise.

An organization's core competencies, along with other intangibles, make up its **intellectual capital**—its collective experiences, wisdom, knowledge, and expertise. Intellectual capital is "embedded in the personal skills, brain power, and experience of a company's employees. It's in a company's libraries, its filing cabinets, electronic data bases and patents, copyrights, trademarks, [and] skills . . ." (Yates, 1995). Along with its tangible assets, intellectual capital constitutes the current worth of a company and its future prospects. All organizational members must effectively utilize the intellectual capital if it is to yield the greatest benefits and advantages.

Organizational Culture

organizational culture
Dynamic system of shared values, beliefs, philosophies, experiences, customs, and norms of behavior that give an organization its distinctive character.

http://www.marykay.com

http://www.avon.com

http://www.delta.com

All organizations are dynamic systems of shared values, beliefs, philosophies, experiences, customs, and norms of behavior. The combination of these elements gives an organization a distinctive character called **organizational culture**. Top management provides a primary framework for an organization's culture. Management establishes and articulates the company's values and norms of behavior. Especially in large companies, top management may invest substantially to familiarize employees with these values. McDonald's Hamburger University is an example of such an investment, as are the ritual celebrations for top sellers sponsored by Mary Kay Cosmetics and Avon Corporation.

A firm's culture is also shaped by employees. They shape the culture by bringing their own values and norms to the organization and by the extent to which they accept the management-defined culture. Delta Air Lines' culture thrives on the many and often-told stories about coworkers who go to extraordinary lengths to care for customers. Newsletters, in-flight magazines, and worldwide advertising emphasize the airline's people; and all these communications reinforce the attitude that management and employees prize.

Moreover, within a company's formal and social subsystems, distinctive minicultures usually flourish. Such subcultures develop spontaneously, and management encourages some. The marketing department may have a unique culture (formed in part by past successes as well as failures), separate from and parallel to the organization's culture. Such a subculture influences the corporate culture. Members of ethnic groups bring their cultures with them and often create, within the workplace, subcultures based on their languages, customs, traditions, values, and beliefs. These subcultures contribute to the corporate culture. Sometimes they blend, sometimes they remain distinct. If management values diversity, it will do more than respect such subcultures; management will seek to derive from them benefits for the entire organization.

Organizational Climate

organizational climate
An outgrowth of a corporation's culture showing how employees feel about working there.

http://www.3m.com

An outgrowth of a corporation's culture is its **organizational climate**—how employees feel about working there. Successful organizations often have climates that feel *open*—they foster the individual's creative energies and take advantage of employees' eagerness to participate. Employees are empowered through the practice of open-book management and other means and have the freedom to fail. For example, at 3M everyone "is encouraged to call up any other employee and tap into that person's expertise . . . on the phone, by E-mail, in person, or any other way. . . . The company fosters an environment where happy accidents can happen" (Loeb, 1995). The company stages many celebrations where "peers cheer peers." The 66,000 plus diverse 3M products came from the equally diverse minds of its people whom 3M encourages and rewards for taking risks.

Leadership

Defined in Chapter 1, *leadership* means influencing others to set and achieve goals. Every leader should encourage and enable followers to give their best. The exercise of leadership, however, is influenced by elements both inside and outside an individual. Each person has a set of beliefs, attitudes, and values—acquired through experience—that composes his or her personality, conscience, and philosophy. An organization's mission, vision, core values, culture, and climate also influence those in leadership positions within that organization. Leadership involves setting an example through both words and deeds. Leaders must "walk like they talk." Nothing can derail efforts for change and improvements more effectively than a leader's hypocrisy, according to Peter Scott-Morgan, a business consultant with Arthur D. Little. "They preach the importance of teamwork—then reward individuals who work at standing out from the crowd. They encourage risk taking—then punish good-faith failures" (Labich, 1994). It takes leadership, not necessarily the traditional type, to cultivate learning. Leadership will create a generative shared vision and will provide the catalyst for perpetual learning (Senge, 1994b). Chapter 14 examines leadership in more detail.

Organizational Structure

The formal structure of a company, a component of the company's internal environment, determines how its activities are conducted. Within each of the three management tiers—top, middle, and first-line—teams may be created to execute such basic tasks as design, production, marketing, finance, and human resources management. The formal structure also determines how authority and communications flow from management to employees. Variations in structure are determined by the tasks a company performs, how management wishes to perform them, and external factors. External determinants include customer demands, competitors' strategies, and government regulations.

The trend today is toward less-pyramidal structures, staffed with empowered individuals, empowered teams, and autonomous business units. Such structures facilitate more flexibility and a quicker response to customers. Some companies have gone so far as to depend on loose, temporary collections of freelance experts and consultants to create a specific project; the freelancers and consultants then move on to other jobs once they complete their task. The movie industry creates many of its films by using this model. Others, like Bechtel, a worldwide construction company, function with teams of in-house experts brought together to manage projects. Once each project is completed, team members are reassigned to new project teams. Thus its organizational structure is continually changing.

http://www.bechtel.com

boundaryless organization
An organization not defined or limited by horizontal, vertical, or external boundaries imposed by a predetermined structure.

Boundaryless organizations are not defined or limited by horizontal, vertical, or external boundaries imposed by a predetermined structure. They share many of the characteristics of flat organizations, with a strong emphasis on teams. Cross-functional teams dissolve horizontal barriers and enable the organization to respond quickly to environmental changes and to spearhead innovation. Boundaryless organizations can form relationships (joint ventures, intellectual property, distribution channels, or financial resources) with customers, suppliers, and/or competitors. Telecommuting, strategic alliances, and customer-organization linkages break down external barriers, streamlining work activities. In order to facilitate interactions with customers and suppliers, Jack Welch, CEO of General Electric, first used this un-structure.

learning organization
"An organization skilled at creating, acquiring, and transferring knowledge, and at modifying its behavior to reflect new knowledge and insights."

Organizational adaptability is a function of the ability to learn and to perform according to changes in the environment. A learning organization is one that is able to adapt and respond to change (Senge, 1994a). D. A. Garvin (1993) first defined a **learning organization** as "an organization skilled at creating, acquiring, and transferring knowledge, and at modifying its behavior to reflect new knowledge and insights." A boundaryless environment is required by learning organizations to facilitate team collaboration and the sharing of information. When an organization develops the continuous capacity to adapt and survive in an increasingly competitive environment because all members take an active role in identifying and resolving work-related issues, it has developed a learning culture. This design empowers employees because they acquire and share knowledge and apply this learning to decision making. They are pooling collective intelligence and stimulating creative thought to improve performance. Managers facilitate learning by sharing and aligning the organization's vision for the future and sustaining a sense of community and strong culture. Organizational structure is continually changing. Chapters 8 and 9 explore organizational issues.

Resources

The primary resource of any organization is its people. Chapter 11 focuses on the management of human resources. An organization needs resources in addition to people to continue its mission and reach specific objectives, however. These resources are the inputs to the system—the elements processed, transformed, or used—and they influence the internal environment. Such resources include information, facilities and infrastructure, machinery and equipment, materials and supplies, and finances.

Information

The word *information* refers to the facts and knowledge that provide vital nourishment for all the operations of an organization. Without accurate, timely, up-to-date information, neither employees nor managers can make daily decisions effectively and efficiently, nor can they plan ahead. Information from insiders and outsiders is needed to coordinate and execute tasks at every level. Keeping others informed of problems and progress is every employee's duty. Chapter 19 will deal with information management in depth.

Facilities and Infrastructure

Facilities consist of the physical structures—the work and office spaces and their layouts—required to accomplish the firm's mission and goals. The location, appearance, and condition of an organization's facilities can significantly influence how employees view their company. The term *infrastructure* refers to the surrounding region or community's permanent framework. The framework might include dams, power stations, roads, railways, harbors, and airports.

http://www.nissandriven.com

In 1992 Nissan built the latest in lean and flexible manufacturing facilities on Kyushu, the southernmost of Japan's five main islands. As Clay Chandler and Joseph White (1992) reported, the hospital-clean factory can be used to build a number of different models and types of cars. The key to the flexibility of the plant is that instead of a conveyor belt, the factory uses computer-directed, motor-driven dollies that can move vehicles at various speeds. To make the changes necessary to produce a different kind of car takes minimal retooling.

http://www.bmw.com

Infrastructure resources support not only individual companies but the community at large. Such resources are generally built at public expense or with government support of one kind or another. Their extent and quality are basic to most businesses, especially manufacturing. From freeways and airports to sewage systems and power grids, the operation of modern factories depends on all these and more. BMW, a German automaker, chose in 1992 to build its first American manufacturing facilities in Spartanburg, South Carolina. According to some observers (Ady, 1992), the location was selected due to the qualified workforce, a favorable tax code, and a local willingness to provide significant support for the company's hiring and training efforts. In addition, South Carolina authorities agreed to provide $40 million in improvements to the Greenville-Spartanburg airport, which is adjacent to the new factory's site.

http://www.kpmg.com

In 1992, KPMG Peat Marwick, an international accounting firm, surveyed 617 foreign companies with headquarters in Illinois to determine how they decided on a location for their U.S. facilities (Yates, 1992). Most of the firms—which together offered 41,439 jobs—chose to locate in the suburbs of Chicago because of "proximity to key industries and markets; [proximity] to air transportation; distribution advantages; living conditions and environment; and quality and cost of [the] work force."

Machinery and Equipment

Nissan's computer-directed dollies and all other hardware used to process inputs are part of an organization's machinery and equipment, the tools used in offices, factories, and other workplaces. Furniture, fixtures, telephones, copiers, fax machines, computers, and robots are but a few examples. The quality of machinery and equipment is a function of its maintainability, efficiency, dependability, and speed of operation. Its compatibility with other equipment influences how effectively and efficiently people work together. Current, reliable, and easy-to-use equipment helps to prevent stress to workers. In addition, high-quality equipment encourages people to do their best, freed from interruptions caused by mechanical breakdowns.

Materials and Supplies

Taken together, the services, raw materials, and parts (components and subassemblies) needed to produce goods or services make up an organization's materials and supplies. The division of General Electric that produces home appliances consumes an astounding amount of goods in this category: miles of wiring; tons of sheet metal, nuts, and bolts; motors; coolants and solvents; plastic; and glass. The division needs all of these items to keep production machinery clean and running. At the facility of a service industry—the home office of Aetna Insurance, for example—the materials and supplies list calls for reams of letterhead and multipart forms, printer ribbon cartridges, staples, paper clips, file folders, and cleaning supplies.

http://www.ge.com

http://www.gm.com

Materials and supplies may be acquired outside the company or within. General Motors buys windshields and windows from Pittsburgh Plate Glass and tires from Goodyear. But GM's Chevrolet, Buick, Cadillac, and Pontiac divisions build most of their engines and transmissions in their own facilities. GM assembly plants are the customers for GM engine and transmission factories. The quality of materials and supplies greatly affects the quality of the goods and services a company can produce. The same can be said for the other resources discussed so far.

Finances

The term *finances* means the money available. Finances, which can be generated directly from the sale of the organization's goods and services, can be in the form of cash in bank accounts or a line of credit negotiated with a financial institution (usually a commercial bank). Trade credit is the most significant source of short-term finances. Suppliers grant trade credit whenever they agree to provide materials and supplies in exchange for an organization's promise to pay the invoice, plus interest, within a specified number of weeks.

An important financial resource for U.S. corporations is the sale of stocks and bonds on the open market. Investment brokers and public stock exchanges facilitate such sales. Another source of cash may be the sale of assets. During the last years of Pan Am, the airline was hard pressed to repay massive bank loans. Pan Am managers repeatedly raised needed cash by selling off valuable assets, including its corporate headquarters building in New York and the worldwide routes it had pioneered during better days.

Money is the basis for all of an organization's operations, from acquiring resources to honoring employee paychecks to compensating investors. Money is the lifeblood of an organization. It flows to all operatives and, in turn, allows work to flow. A company's financial health affects its ability to function at every level.

EXTERNAL ENVIRONMENT

External forces exert influences on and are influenced by organizations and their subsystems and present both challenges and opportunities to them. The effects of these influences vary from immediate, constant, and of daily concern to infrequent, modest, and of more long-range concern.

As changes occur in both their internal and external environments, organizations adapt and evolve. In this chapter's Management in Action feature, AOL wanted to enter the Internet market because that market was moving toward its focus—expanding the AOL brand. Its acquisition of CompuServe was a response to changing external economic and market conditions as was transforming its Web site from simply a promotional page to a "destination site" for all to use.

Directly Interactive Forces

3

Describe the directly interactive forces in an organization's external environment

directly interactive forces *An organization's owners, customers, suppliers and partners, competitors, and external labor pool.*

Of most immediate concern to managers are the **directly interactive forces** shown as the closest colored band surrounding the organization in Figure 4.1. Members of these groups regularly make contact with organization members and subsystems, usually on a daily basis. The major directly interactive forces are an organization's owners, customers, suppliers and partners, competitors, and external labor pool.

Owners

Owners may actively participate in managing (as they normally do in sole proprietorships and some kinds of partnerships). In other cases they may play no active role at all. This is the case with stockholders who do not work for the corporations in which they own stock. Both kinds of owners, however, expect a return on their investments and look to all the employees to preserve and advance their interests. From the owners comes the formal authority needed to run the business. In corporations the board of directors is responsible for protecting the owners' investments and ensuring that management earns an adequate return on them.

Customers

The individuals and groups that use or purchase the outputs of an organization are *customers*. Customers can be either internal or external. Internal customers are employees or work units that receive the work of other employees or units. Internal customers process the work further, use it within their work groups, or deliver it outside. The surgeon anxiously awaiting a biopsy report is the customer for a hospital lab. The Delta passenger-service agent checking the computer screen at the airport is a customer of the reservation department. External customers may be manufacturers, wholesalers, retailers, suppliers, or corporate or individual consumers. Ensuring the satisfaction of both internal and external customers is vital in a highly competitive marketplace.

Suppliers and Partners

Suppliers provide a company with many of the resources it needs. These resources range from expertise and raw materials to money and part-time employees. Suppliers may be separate, autonomous parts of a company or unaffiliated organizations. Suppliers may also be independent companies brought together through a joint venture or temporary partnership. IBM, for instance, maintained eleven partnerships with other companies in 1995. Among them was an agreement with Toshiba to build high-resolution color screens for laptop computers.

http://www.ibm.com

http://www.toshiba.com

Several continuing trends in supplier practices emerged during the 1980s. First, companies increased their use of outsourcing. They selected as suppliers small, efficient businesses that could make resources of higher quality at lower cost than the companies could make.

Second, to enhance the effectiveness of working relationships, companies developed close alliances with outside suppliers. To hasten decision making, suppliers were and continue to be brought into projects early, often at the design stage. Chrysler did this to produce its LH models. Many companies have merged with suppliers or have bought them outright to guarantee a reliable source of quality goods and services. To strengthen its capabilities in electronics and computer systems, for example, General Motors acquired Electronic Data Systems (EDS), Texas entrepreneur Ross Perot's original company. EDS was a wholly owned subsidiary of General Motors from 1984 until it split off as an independent company on June 7, 1996.

http://www.chrysler.com

http://www.eds.com

Third, companies are seeking these "deep" alliances with fewer, more dependable suppliers. And fourth, companies are more willing to procure needed supplies from anywhere in the world, turning more frequently to foreign sources to meet their needs for high quality and low price. This chapter's Ethical Management feature highlights a growing arrangement between companies: partnering in order to exclude one's competitors.

Competitors

An organization's *competitors* are those firms that offer similar products and services in the organization's marketplace. Businesses compete on the basis of price, quality, selection, convenience, product features and performance, and customer services. Customer services include delivery, financing, and warranties. Competition is not merely a contest between Toyota and Ford, NBC and CBS, or Delta and Southwest. Instead, competition is an irresistible force at work at every level of commerce in free enterprise systems. Aluminum competes with steel as a manufacturing material; railroads with trucks; network television with cable broadcasters; and long-distance telephone companies with one another.

For most companies, how managers deal with competition determines whether their companies succeed or fail. In the early 1990s IBM was struggling to recover leadership in its industry. Many experts said the company's decline derived from the failure of IBM's management to counter the competition. The experts said IBM clung too long to mainframe computers and did not pursue the PC market as aggressively as did other companies.

ETHICAL MANAGEMENT
Cola Wars on Campus

Coca-Cola and Pepsi have extended their market share war to colleges and universities. "In return for banishing all directly competing soft drink brands from cafeterias, campus stores and dorm vending machines, Coca-Cola and Pepsi-Cola offer schools millions of dollars to be spent wherever needed." The exclusive contracts are the result of bidding wars between the cola giants. In one deal, Coke got a twelve-year exclusive at Penn State for $14 million. In a deal that Pepsi negotiated, "The only soft drinks currently available to 96,000 students on 14 [other] campuses are Pepsi and its brands. . . ."

Such contracts are attractive to many schools. Most have been hit hard by their states' funding cutbacks and are looking for alternate sources of income to help them keep their fees and tuition in check. The cola companies like the school contracts because they create captive markets and help to form the soft-drink habits of thousands of students.

One university vice president in charge of development indicates that his school would not consider such a deal if it were not for state funding cutbacks. He indicated that his school is considering an offer from one of the cola makers to replace lost state funds. One university professor adds that colleges set a bad example when they deprive students of any freedom in selecting soft drinks and that such exclusive contracts actually present state legislators with an additional reason for cutting college funds.

A standard for judging *exclusionary contracts* is that they also must have foreclosed a rival's ability to get to market with its product in some other way. A key to a company's defense is to claim that its rival wasn't foreclosed from the market by the company's exclusive contracts with partners.

What do you think about these exclusive contracts? Are they an attack on the basic consumer right of freedom of choice? Why or why not?

http://www.coca-cola.com

http://www.pepsi.com

Source: Cornell University Law School Legal Information Institute, "Antitrust: An Overview," http://www.law.cornell.edu/topics/antitrust.html, visited 6/13/99. For more on the campus cola wars read Kenneth R. Clark, " 'Cola Wars' Foaming on College Campuses," *Chicago Tribune* (6 November 1994), sec. 1, pp. 23, 25.

Labor Force

The term *labor force* (sometimes used interchangeably with *labor pool* or *workforce*) applies to the people in the community from which an organization can recruit qualified candidates. The key word in the preceding definition is, of course, "qualified."

The needs of businesses are changing. Jobs in the crafts and trades, which traditionally provided work for the members of labor unions, are giving way to jobs that require proficiency in math, verbal communication, and computer sciences. As one business commentator noted (Magnet, 1992): "Though statistics suggest that today's high school student who doesn't go on to college is as literate and numerate as a similar 1950s student, Fifties skills are inadequate to Nineties needs and uncompetitive with the products of foreign school systems."

America's workforce is changing, becoming more culturally segmented and diverse. The notion of cultural diversity applies to communities whose members represent distinctly different ethnic and national backgrounds, language, religious beliefs, lifestyles, and age groups. Patterns of social change and widespread immigration are the principal agents of this change. In recent decades women have entered the U.S. labor force in historic numbers and in every calling from medicine to heavy construction. Since 1970 the number of women as a percentage of the total labor force has doubled.

Organizations must adapt and evolve in response to directly interactive forces, such as the increased number of women in the workforce.

© 2001 PHOTODISC, INC.

. . . the women's labor force will grow more rapidly than the men's, and the women's share of the labor force will increase from 46 percent in 1998 to 48 percent in 2008. . . . The Asian and other share of the labor force will increase from 5 to 6 percent and the Hispanic share from 10 to 13 percent. White non-Hispanics accounted for 74 percent of the labor force in 1998. Their share of the labor force in 2008 will decrease modestly to 71 percent. [Source: Bureau of Labor Statistics New 1998–2008 Employment Projections (30 November 1999), http://stats.bls.gov/emphome.htm.]

Indirectly Interactive Forces

4

Describe the indirectly interactive forces in an organization's external environment

indirectly interactive forces
Domestic and foreign economic, legal/political, sociocultural, technological, and natural forces.

economic forces
Conditions in an economy that influence management decisions and the costs and availability of resources.

http://www.unioncarbide.com

An organization's **indirectly interactive forces** are more remote and generally beyond the ability of managers to control or influence to any great extent. They do, however, affect the execution of all management functions to some degree. The major indirectly interactive forces are both domestic and foreign economic, legal/political, sociocultural, technological, and natural forces.

Economic Forces

The levels of taxes, wages, prices, interest rates, personal spending and saving, business spending and profits, inflation, and the state an entire economy is in at any given time—recession, recovery, boom, and depression—are called **economic forces**. Economic conditions influence management decisions as well as the costs and availability of needed resources. A large chemical producer, Union Carbide (now a subsidiary of The Dow Chemical Corporation), made almost no profits from its core businesses during the 1991–1993 recession. The demand for two of its products—ethyl glycol and polyethylene—was flat until 1994 when it rapidly increased. The company responded by raising prices for the former by 25 percent and raising its prices for the latter by more than 50 percent. This placed the company—the low-cost producer of these chemicals—in an enormously profitable position (Smart, 1995).

Legal/Political Forces

legal/political forces
The general framework of statutes enacted by legislatures; precedents established by court decisions; regulations and rulings created by various federal, state, and local regulatory agencies; and agreements between and among governments and companies from different nations.

The general framework of statutes enacted by legislatures; precedents established by court decisions; regulations and rulings created by various federal, state, and local regulatory agencies; and agreements between and among governments and companies from different nations constitute **legal/political forces**. For American firms, about 122,000 employees in 52 federal regulatory agencies administer tens of thousands of federal regulations at a cost to taxpayers of about $14 billion annually. As one analyst (Warner, 1992) observed,

> *Complying with federal regulations costs small businesses billions of dollars and millions of worker hours each year. It is estimated that the [Americans with Disabilities Act of 1991] will cost taxpayers as much as $20 billion annually, while the [1990 Clean Air Act as amended] will add at least $25.6 billion to the cost of doing business.*

Laws at all levels of government in every country in which a company does business affect all that company's activities. Some regulations, such as antipollution laws, are intended to provide protection for society as a whole; others protect consumers in a variety of ways and preserve or restrict competition in markets. This chapter's Global Applications feature focuses on the impact that Britain's membership in the European Community has had on its traditional means of weighing and measuring.

GLOBAL APPLICATIONS
Britain and the Measure of Things

Since the thirteenth century, Britain has used pounds, gallons, feet, and inches as weights and measures. In 1965, Great Britain, as a condition for becoming a member of the European Common Market, began a transition to the metric system in its trade and commerce. On October 1, 1995, Britain was forced to adopt the metric system's units of weights and measures as a condition of the European Trade Agreement. The metric system is a decimal-based system of measurement units created by the French in the seventeenth century. Like our money system, units for a given quantity (e.g., length) are related by factors of 10. Calculations involve the simple process of moving the decimal point to the right or to the left. (The United States is the only industrialized country in the world not officially using the metric system.)

The changes are a convenience for Britain's European visitors, but they add costs for British shop owners. The costs connected with adjusting labels, scales, packaging, and pricing methods were estimated to be about $316 for each merchant. Shopkeepers who fail to adopt the standards face fines as high as $7,900. British manufacturers and distributors face added costs in similar areas as well, but are spending far more to meet the new standards.

The metric system is not totally foreign to British citizens. In the 1980s Britain converted its money to a decimal system (at the heart of the metric system), abandoning the pounds, shillings, and pence it had used for nearly 700 years. Temperatures have been measured in both Fahrenheit and Celsius (the metric measure) for over a decade. Two bits of tradition will remain, however. Highway signs will continue to measure distances in miles, and taverns will still serve half pints and pints of Britain's favorite ales.

Sources: The United States and the Metric System: A Capsule History, http://ts.nist.gov/ts/htdocs/200/202/lc1136a.htm, visited 12/26/00; and "Measure for Measure, EU Rules Irk British," *Chicago Tribune* (1 October 1995), sec. 1, p. 13.

In support of South Africa's struggle to abolish apartheid, many American companies abandoned their operations there for a number of years and now wish to return. Ironically, they are finding things difficult. McDonald's, Toys 'R' Us, and others have "lost the rights to their trademarks, which have been usurped by local competitors. In other cases, competitors from Europe and Asia took advantage of U.S. departures to entrench themselves . . ." (Menaker, 1995). Coca-Cola never fully left South Africa—it kept a presence through a licensing agreement with a South African company—whereas Pepsi did leave. Coke now has 75 percent of that cola market.

Sociocultural Forces

sociocultural forces
The influences and contributions from diverse groups outside an organization.

The influences and contributions from diverse groups outside an organization constitute **sociocultural forces**. We have already mentioned the value of diverse employees and their subcultures. People don't leave "who they are" at home when they report to work. They bring with them their ethnicity, culture, beliefs, and attitudes. In like fashion, groups of diverse people in an organization's external community influence and react to its plans and actions.

When the Walt Disney Company bought 3,000 acres near the Manassas National Battlefield in Virginia, it intended to spend about $650 million to develop a Civil War theme park and related businesses. Its plans met strong local and national resistance. "Critics, including some historians, argued that the . . . park and adjacent developments would pollute the area and detract from true historic sites only a few miles away" (*Chicago Tribune*, 1995). Rather than fight the public's outrage, Disney announced in September 1995 that it would look for an alternative location.

Technological Forces

technological forces
The combined effects of processes, materials, knowledge, and other discoveries resulting from research and development activities.

Processes, materials, knowledge, and other discoveries resulting from research and development activities sponsored or conducted by governments, private firms, and individuals around the globe give rise to **technological forces**. Research and development have created the technologies that have led to telecommunications, digitizing audio and video, photocopying, and virtual reality, to name but a few. The World Wide Web is a technological breakthrough discussed in the chapter's Managing Technology feature. Breakthroughs in technology influence how efficiently businesses operate as well as the competitiveness and quality of their products and services.

http://crec.bus.utexas.edu

http://www.cisco.com

The Center for Research on Electronic Commerce at the University of Texas in Austin reported that *electronic commerce*—the worldwide purchases across the Internet of books, automobiles, and other goods and services from U.S. companies—generated nearly $102 billion in 1998. The impact of the Internet on the nation's economy exceeded $301 billion in revenues and accounted for more than 1.2 million jobs, growing over the previous four years to a level other industries took decades to reach. Cisco Systems Inc. funded the study. "Internet business, in today's times—it's only in the second or third inning," John Chambers, chairman of Cisco, said. "Think about how long it took other industries to reach $300 billion. Literally, in under a decade, we've reached a level that it took other industries 100 years to reach" (Bridis, 1999). Today more than ever, a business's success can be directly linked to how rapidly and effectively it absorbs and adjusts its operations and outputs to the latest technologies.

MANAGING TECHNOLOGY
World Wide Web

In 1989, Tim Berners-Lee invented the World Wide Web while a computer scientist at CERN, the Geneva-based European Organization for Nuclear Research. He named it World Wide Web (WWW), or "the Web" for short, because the global network had no central server or hub. Computers were connected via a literal web of networks. In 1991 Berners-Lee released a program for browsing and editing to users at CERN, and then to the academic community worldwide by posting it on an Internet newsgroup. The program didn't have the friendly graphical interfaces of today; its users typed in commands.

In 1993, the University of Illinois' National Center for Supercomputing Applications (NCSA) released the Mosaic Web browser for all operating systems. It was the first browser to combine graphics and text on a single page. The benefit of the World Wide Web is that it uses hypertext software, which can combine sounds, graphic images, video, and hypertext on a single page and can link to other pages and other Internet resources. Thus, you can click on highlighted text and be immediately led to another part of the document, a separate document on the same computer, or a document on an entirely different server. Most graphical Web browsers, such as Netscape Communicator and Microsoft Internet Explorer, have been derived from the original Mosaic program developed at the NCSA.

Source: CERN, http://public.web.cern.ch/Public; The Hobbes Internet Timeline puts these developments in greater context. See: http://www.isoc.org/guest/zakon/Internet/History/HIT.html. Tim Berners-Lee founded the World Wide Web Consortium (W3C) in October 1994. http://www.w3.org.

Natural Forces

natural forces
Forces such as climate, weather, geography, and geology that affect how businesses operate and locate their operations.

Forces such as climate, weather, geography, and geology that affect how businesses operate and locate their operations are known collectively as **natural forces**. The climate of a region determines a firm's need for energy for such uses as heating and air conditioning. Storms and other natural disasters can disrupt a firm's production and flow of supplies. The 1995 earthquake that closed Japan's Kobe port killed over 4,000 people, destroyed roads and rail lines, and forced companies in Japan and around the world to seek alternative methods for delivering their goods. Land formations can influence access by rail, road, ship, and air, as well.

The Evans Corporation, a small Chicago-based furrier, knows well the effects of nature on earnings. It reported that the winter of 1994–1995 was the worst in its history for selling its products. With weather warmer in January than it was in April of that year, the company reported weather-related losses of over $6 million in its last quarter (ending in February) and over $12 million for its fiscal year (Buck, 1995).

ENVIRONMENTS AND MANAGEMENT

Environmental forces create challenges, risks, opportunities, and changes for every organization. Managers must remain alert to their internal and external environments, sensing changes or shifts, reacting and adapting quickly and imaginatively. They must forecast and plan for the changes they suspect will come and for the changes they wish to initiate. Managers must cultivate a sensible and controlled reactive behavior toward changes that may affect them with little or no warning, and an imaginative program to manage and capitalize on the changes they can foresee and over which they have some control.

Sensing and Adapting to Environments

Discuss the means available to managers for boundary spanning

boundary spanning
The surveillance of outside areas and factors that can influence plans, forecasts, decisions, and organizations. Sometimes called environmental scanning.

Staying in touch with environments requires that managers monitor events and trends that develop outside their specific areas of influence. The areas could be other departments or divisions within the company, the competition, the economy, and all the other forces that can influence their system or subsystem. This surveillance of outside areas and factors is called **boundary spanning** (Bittel, 1989). Sometimes called environmental scanning, the practice requires current information about what is happening or likely to happen. Boundary spanners look for developments that can influence plans, forecasts, decisions, and organizations. Sources of information include feedback from customers and suppliers, competitors' actions, government statistics, professional and trade publications, industry and trade associations, and colleagues and professional associates inside and outside the organization. Through boundary spanning, managers keep up-to-date, establish networks to facilitate the gathering and dissemination of information, and build personal relationships that can lead to increased power and influence over people and events.

http://www.chevron.com

http://www.unocal.com

Sometimes the challenges posed by the environment are clear to everyone. The key to gaining a competitive advantage is how a firm adapts to the challenges. The intensely competitive field of oil retailing provides an example. In June 1992, Chevron Chemical Company announced the development of a diesel fuel to meet tough new California environmental regulations scheduled to go into effect in October 1993. Chevron was the first company to gain state certification for the fuel. A competitor, Unocal, dropped out of the California diesel-fuel market after company management decided that the required technology was too costly (Rose, 1992).

Influencing Environments

Explain how managers can influence their external environments

Although managers must sense and adapt to environments, they and their organizations can also influence their environments in several ways. In a democratic society, citizens—alone and in groups—have the right to attempt to influence legislation and the rules that determine how the game of business is played. Lobbying allows people to present their points of view to legislators and to push for changes that they see as beneficial. Whether by personal letter to a city alderman or through a paid professional who lobbies legislators, managers and individual citizens' groups will continue to play vital roles in the shaping of our society.

Managers and organizations use the power of the media to influence public opinion and public policy. Their viewpoints and agendas are constantly reported in advertising, public relations announcements, press releases, and in-depth interviews. Industry and trade groups allow businesses to conduct research, build alliances, and raise funds to push their agendas for or against change.

Meeting Responsibilities to Stakeholders

Describe the obligations organizations have to their stakeholders

stakeholders
Groups directly or indirectly affected by the ways in which business is conducted and managers conduct themselves. Stakeholders include owners, employees, customers, suppliers, and society.

Stakeholders are the groups that are directly or indirectly affected by the ways in which business is conducted and managers conduct themselves. Stakeholders include owners, employees, customers, suppliers, and society—people in local communities, our economy, and the world at large. Members of each of these groups lose or gain depending upon how businesses operate. Chapter 22 will examine in detail the responsibilities that managers and businesses have to these groups. A few introductory concepts are needed here, however.

Owners

To owners, businesses owe a fair return on investment. Managers are obligated to make their best effort to use resources effectively and efficiently. Managers must also give an honest accounting of their stewardship over the owners' assets and interests. Most states require by law that corporations give a financial accounting in quarterly and annual reports to their shareholders.

In most sole proprietorships and small partnerships, owners are the managers. In corporations, however, owners depend on elected representatives who sit on the board of directors. One of the board's primary duties is to ensure that managers consider owners' interests when they make corporate decisions.

Employees

As the most important asset of a business, employees need a safe and psychologically rewarding environment. Such an environment supports honest and open communication and shows evidence of real concern for employees' values, goals, and welfare. Employees need nurturing environments that help them grow and become more valuable to themselves and their organizations. FedEx, a large freight and package deliverer, knows how to provide a nurturing environment to employees. This chapter's Valuing Diversity feature takes you inside one of its diversity workshops and indicates some of the changes they can bring.

VALUING DIVERSITY
Diversity at FedEx

The philosophy of FedEx is People–Service–Profit (PSP). So that the workplace reflects the diversity of FedEx customers and the world, training is offered to help its people value the diversity that exists, regardless of where they work in the company. Employees are encouraged to discuss their feelings openly. Some do and others do not. With a person's willingness to do so, however, comes an understanding of that person's beliefs and attitudes as well as insights into one's own feelings. Three of the results for one such encounter follow.

Fred Daniels made a commitment to learn Spanish after his first week working at FedEx. About 75 percent of his workmates are Hispanic. Says Fred, "If I'm going to work with Hispanics, I need to understand them and they need to understand me—and we need to feel comfortable."

Neal Johnson thought he related well to everyone until he completed the course. He discovered that he could be rude and insulting at times without even realizing it—for example, when he communicated with women. "I have a real bad habit of interrupting. . . . I want to jump right in and solve problems. . . . I need to learn to listen."

Sonja Whitemon, an African American, saw subtle changes in herself and her classmates as the course progressed. "People came in generalizing—black about white, white about black. . . . Then at the end . . . I realized that people were talking about individuals . . . I could sense they were trying to understand. And that's a good beginning."

http://www.fedex.com

Source: *Working at FedEx: Work Culture & Diversity*, http://www.federalexpress.com/us/careers/working/culture.html, visited 12/26/00; and Tom Peters, *The Pursuit of Wow!* (New York: Vintage Books, 1994), pp. 219–241.

Employees deserve to know the risks, values, rules, and rewards to which they are exposed. They have the right to ethical treatment, to fairness, and to equity in their relationships with management. Their legal rights must be granted and respected. Businesses that stay focused on the needs of their employees will attract and hold on to them, thus helping to guarantee future success. To most customers, employees *are* the business in the sense that employees are as important as the product or service in establishing the reputation of the business in the customer's mind.

Customers

As stakeholders, customers depend on businesses as places of employment and sources for needed goods and services. By law, they have the right to safe work environments, services, and products. Ethically, they have the right to fair, honest, and equitable treatment.

Suppliers

Suppliers provide the services, materials, and parts needed to carry on the vital operations of business. Quality begins with an understanding of its importance and is designed into products and services from their conception. Most suppliers today are involved in product and service design and determine to a great extent the performance capabilities of the end result. Suppliers need honest and open communication from the managers and organizations they serve. They deserve to be paid for the goods and services rendered and to have the terms of their contracts honored. Reliable sources of dependable supplies are difficult to find; once found, every effort should be made to keep them.

Society

A business's obligations to society begin with its employment base and spread out to the communities in which it does business. A mom-and-pop bakery in Muncie, Indiana, can call the neighborhood in which it operates its piece of society. When the

Businesses, large and small, can call the community in which they operate a part of their society.

parents in the neighborhood call on the bakery to support a Little League baseball team, the bakery owners are expected to respond with some kind of assistance.

http://www.unitedway.org

Every business needs to define the portions of society that it must serve. It can serve society in a variety of ways, from following fair employment practices, to donating funds and equipment, to preventing pollution. The United Way charity program is staffed locally by volunteers from businesses whose salaries are donated by their regular employers. Businesses often adopt a school to assist in a variety of ways. Businesses usually concentrate on serving their communities in ways that enrich both the givers and receivers. In this effort, as in all undertakings, businesses need to be both reactive and proactive. They must sense the needs of their communities and plan to implement the kinds of assistance they are best able to provide.

CHAPTER SUMMARY

1 **Discuss why organizations are open systems.** An open system must interact with its external environments (both directly and indirectly interactive ones) and are regularly influenced by the forces in them. Any organization depends on its directly interactive external environment to obtain needed resources. Customers exist in that external environment and they dictate, in part, quality standards.

2 **Identify the elements in an organization's internal environment.** An organization's internal environment contains the following elements: its mission, vision, core values, core competencies, leadership, culture, climate, structure, and available resources. A mission states an organization's central purpose for existing. Its vision is the destination it chooses to reach in the future. Core values are the key concepts that guide managers and their actions and that do not change in spite of adversity. Core competencies are what a company does best; they rest in part in the organization's intellectual capital. Leadership makes things happen by encouraging and supporting people to give their best and set and achieve goals. The culture of an organization contains its shared values, beliefs, philosophies, experiences, habits, expectations, norms, and behaviors that give it a distinctive character or personality. Structure refers to the formal arrangements between all the organization's members and details who will perform which tasks. Available resources include people, information, intellectual capital, facilities and infrastructure, machinery and equipment, supplies, and finances.

3 **Describe the directly interactive forces in an organization's external environment.** These forces are owners, customers, suppliers and partners, competitors, and the labor force. Owners create businesses and share in their profits. They make demands and contributions. Some are active in management; others are merely investors with a stake in the organization's future. Customers exist inside and outside organizations. Their needs are paramount. Meeting and exceeding their expectations is the primary function of any organization. Suppliers and partners help organizations obtain needed resources. An organization's competitors challenge and threaten; they are after the same customers and resources. The labor force is the source for needed human resources.

4 **Describe the indirectly interactive forces in an organization's external environment.** These domestic and foreign forces are economic, legal/political, sociocultural, technological, and natural. Economic forces include the general state of an economy and levels of spending, saving, taxation, inflation, and interest rates. Economics affects nearly every management decision in some way. Legal/political forces include regulatory agencies, legislatures, courts, and law enforcement groups at the federal, state, and local levels, along with international agreements between companies and governments. Laws govern every aspect of business operations and must be complied with to avoid harming the organization, its people, its customers, and society at large. External sociocultural forces include an organization's diverse customer groups, the communities in which it does business, and society as a whole. Technological forces include the state of the art in manufacturing and methodologies used in any process. To be competitive, one's technology must be competitive. Natural forces include climate, weather, geography, and natural resources, such as oil and coal. Each country and its markets have their own unique history, language, customs, legal and economic system, and culture. All must be understood and considered when operating outside one's native country.

5 Discuss the means available to managers for boundary spanning. The practice of boundary spanning, or scanning one's external environments, is necessary to gather current information about what is happening or is likely to happen. Boundary spanners look for reliable sources of information on customers, suppliers, competitors, government regulators and regulations, and the state of the economies in which they operate. Sources include customers, competitors' actions, government statistics, professional and trade publications, and industry and trade associations. Professional managers also network through a variety of human contacts to keep themselves in touch.

6 Explain how managers can influence their external environments. Managers, like any other individual or groups of individuals, can influence government at every level by letting their voices be heard. They have the right to try to influence legislation through lobbying efforts, either individually or collectively through industry or trade groups. They use public relations and advertising to get their messages to the public. Industry and trade groups allow businesses to conduct research, build alliances, raise funds for worthy causes, and help their communities in various ways.

7 Describe the obligations organizations have to their stakeholders. Several groups, already discussed, compose an organization's stakeholders: its owners, employees, customers, suppliers and partners, and society as a whole. Owners are owed a fair and honest accounting of how the resources are used and of continual efforts to improve productivity and profitability. Employees are owed ethical, legal treatment and a safe, psychologically rewarding environment. Customers are owed safe products and services that meet or exceed their expectations. Suppliers and partners are owed honest and fair dealings, based on continuing and open communications. Bills must be paid in full and on time. Finally, society as a whole is owed compliance with all the laws that protect the environment and ethical behavior toward all those outside the organization.

REVIEW QUESTIONS

1. In what ways does your school or place of employment demonstrate the fact that it is an open system?
2. What are the elements in an organization's internal environment?
3. What is a boundaryless organization?
4. How does a learning organization empower employees?
5. Which forces in an organization's external environments are task or directly interactive? Why are they so?
6. Which forces in an organization's external environments are general or indirectly interactive? Why are they so?
7. How can managers stay in touch with their external environments?
8. What can managers and their organizations do to influence their external environments?
9. What groups compose an organization's stakeholders? What obligations does an organization have to each group?
10. Discuss the importance of customer satisfaction to quality.

DISCUSSION QUESTIONS FOR CRITICAL THINKING

1. What do Toys 'R' Us and AOL have in common?
2. Considering the elements in an organization's internal environment, which ones do you think are most important for an organization to grow and prosper? Why?
3. In terms of their importance to any business, what ranking (first, second, etc.) would you give to each of the groups in the task environment?
4. How would your rankings from Question 3 change for a not-for-profit organization? Why the change?

INTERNET EXERCISES

Check the text Web site at http://plunkett.swcollege.com for updated links to the Internet Exercises.

1. Now that the Internet has opened up the opportunity for borderless business transactions, in your opinion what impact will the Internet have on how organizations compete?

2. Read *Effectiveness Vs. Efficiency* by Ken Blanchard (can be found at Web site listed below). What is the difference between efficiency and effectiveness? Which is more important?
   http://www.smartbiz.com/sbs/arts/exe87.htm

3. The Society of Competitive Intelligence Professionals (SCIP) was founded in 1987 and defines *competitive intelligence* (CI) as the process of monitoring the competitive environment. Visit the society's Web site. How could a manager use competitive intelligence?
   http://www.scip.org

4. Write your representative in Congress and ask, "What current legislation are you supporting to ensure economic growth?"
   http://www.house.gov/writerep

APPLICATION CASE

Toys 'R' Us Refocuses

The business and economic systems are changing profoundly. Electronic commerce is permeating business and management with new ways of thinking about real-time selling of products. Today's managers must understand how the technology and the business models fit together.

A growing number of retailers sell directly to customers via Web sites on the Internet. These organizations operate virtual storefronts, usually maintaining little or no inventory. Instead, they order directly from manufacturers to fill customer orders received via electronic communications. Consumer retail business conducted on the Web was expected to quadruple from $8 billion in 1998 to $33 billion in 2000, according to the Cambridge, Massachusetts-based Forrester Research Inc. Forrester predicted that sales from one business to another would hit $251 billion by 2000 and $1.3 trillion in 2003.

In spite of these forecasts, many traditional retailers have been hesitant to set up virtual storefronts because they fear it will take away from their in-store sales. One such retailer is Toys 'R' Us with over 40 years of experience in the toy business. Most toy sales are made in the short holiday selling season that starts after Thanksgiving. Yet, Toys 'R' Us stores are open and fully stocked all year. Since there are no major toy distributors—buyers have to deal directly with hundreds of different companies, making efficient ordering, warehousing, and delivery difficult—Toys 'R' Us has an established distribution system.

Things are changing at Toys 'R' Us. The company is much more sensitive to its external environment. The largest toy retailer wasn't about to let itself be "Amazoned." That's the industry word for a traditional store chain, such as Barnes & Noble, getting trounced by an Internet startup such as Amazon.com. To better compete with toy retailers, toysrus.com formed a strategic alliance with Amazon.com in August 2000. Amazon is in charge of ordering and shipping, while Toys 'R' Us is handling inventory and will absorb any overstock.

http://www.forrester.com
http://www.toysrus.com
http://www.amazon.com

Questions

1. To which environmental forces is Toys 'R' Us responding?
2. What is appealing to customers about ordering online?
3. What are the advantages to a firm of selling online?

Sources: Wes Conard, "Toys 'R' Us Plans Online Challenge," *Bloomberg News* (9 June 1999); Rachel Beck, "Toys 'R' Us Makes Improvements," *Associated Press*, http://wire.ap.org, (12 June 1999); "Amazon Emphasizes Efficiency," *Associated Press* (26 November 2000).

VIDEO CASE

Burton Snowboards: External Business Environment

In the mid 1960s, Jake Burton was one of the thousands of young people who enjoyed surfing on snow with Sherman Poppen's Snurfers. In 1977, Burton was surprised to discover that, in the intervening years, the industry had not developed, expanded, or innovated much. Noting this lack of development in snowboards, Burton quit the Manhattan business world, moved to Londonderry, Vermont, and started designing and testing his own snowboards. From his recognition of a product need, the possibility of a profitable market niche, and commitment to a quality product came the world's first snowboard factory—Burton Snowboards.

Like most new small businesses, the early years were filled with change and hard work. In just its second year, Burton moved the company into a farmhouse in Manchester, Vermont. Working out of his home, a group of four to five workers produced, sold, and repaired all the Burton snowboard models. The company's toll-free customer service line rang in Burton's bedroom throughout the night. He would often load his car and visit as many as 10 shops a day, pitching the company's boards to shopowners whenever orders were low.

In the 1980s, Jake realized that, for the sport to grow in popularity, it had to become more than just a cult sport in which snowboarders used sledding hills or snow-covered golf courses. Burton lobbied eastern U.S. ski resorts to open their lifts to snowboarders, and one by one they did. As more resorts opened to snowboarders, the demand for the company's snowboards and innovations in them increased rapidly.

For example, edgeless wooden boards that were best suited for powder weren't optimal for the icy conditions of eastern ski resorts. These conditions still drive innovation at Burton

Snowboards. The company's basic policy is that, if a board doesn't work in Vermont, it doesn't get made. As the company continued to grow, Burton moved the company to a modern facility in Burlington, Vermont.

To remain the world's leader in snowboarding and snowboarding accessories, Burton must constantly monitor the company's external environment. He realizes that the environment's most influential factors are snowboarding's social trends. Participants in snowboarding have their own slang, dress, and activities that dominate the industry's culture. It is Burton's responsibility to ensure that the company's products match the changing tastes and preferences of this dynamic group. Although the company produces a product for all ages, its primary target age group is 12 to 35. However, the preferences of this group aren't homogenous, so the company develops different boards for various segments of it.

The company has a strong commitment to technological innovation, annually redesigning and updating its core products. It takes advantage of the latest computer innovations, allowing it to simulate the hills and mountains that its boards will "surf" and improve product design before actually making a prototype.

Burton Snowboards has led the industry by being the innovator and has attracted many competitors who often copy or imitate its earlier designs. The industry also is steadily consolidating small competitors into larger corporations. However, Burton believes that the company's future is secure so long as it remains focused on serving its core consumers. To do so, Burton Snowboards needs to remain committed to producing the highest quality (even if that means higher costs) and most innovative snowboards on the market.

http://www.burton.com

For Discussion:

1. Describe the environmental factors affecting Burton Snowboards.
2. Identify which of the five directly interactive forces have the greatest impact on Burton Snowboards.

Organizational Planning

KEY TERMS

budget
contingency plan
forecasting
management by objectives (MBO)
mission statement
operational objective
operational plan
plan
planning
policy
procedure
program
rule
single-use plan
standing plan
strategic goal
strategic plan
strategy
stretch goal
tactic
tactical objective
tactical plan

LEARNING OBJECTIVES

After studying this chapter, you should be able to

1. Explain the importance of planning
2. Describe the importance of an organization's mission statement
3. Discuss the purposes of strategic, tactical, operational, and contingency plans
4. Explain the relationships between strategic, tactical, and operational goals
5. List and explain the steps in a basic planning process
6. Discuss various ways to make plans effective
7. Describe the barriers to planning

MANAGEMENT IN ACTION

How Mission Makes the Difference at eBay

Founded in September 1995 by Pierre Omidyar, eBay began as a place for trading Pez dispensers. "Users can find everything from the practical, unique, and interesting on eBay—such as automobiles, chintz china, jewelry, teddy bears, musical instruments, photographic equipment, computers, furniture, and figurines." eBay doesn't actually carry the inventory. It hosts the auctions and charges the sellers a fee for its services. (See "About eBay," http://www.ebay.com.)

By 1998, a headhunter recruited Margaret C. Whitman [general manager for Hasbro Inc.'s Preschool Division responsible for global marketing of Playskool and Mr. Potato Head brands], mother of two and holder of an M.B.A. from Harvard Business School and a B.A. in economics from Princeton University, to take over as eBay's CEO and expand the company. She is one of the only women to head a leading electronic commerce site. "As I was talking to Pierre, something he said struck a chord. He said people have met some of their best friends on eBay, and that said there is an emotional connection very few young brands have." Her responsibilities include building a successful business while delivering on customer needs and expectations. She focuses on the user experience, to continue executing and creating a fun, efficient, and safe forum for online person-to-person trading.

Whitman began her tenure at eBay by focusing on the company's mission of personal, online trading and scanning its external environment to uncover opportunities. eBay is an interactive site, allowing customers to express themselves directly to the firm in response to the firm's communications. One of the ways Whitman scans the environment is through the "Voice of the Customer Day." Each month, 10 to 20 customers are brought to eBay's offices to meet new employees, as well as Whitman. "One of the things I'm most focused on is managing something that's growing from a small town to a larger community," says Whitman (Green, 1999).

The eBay user community was sending signals that it was interested in listing additional higher priced items, and this convinced Whitman that a new segment was rapidly developing. Since the eBay name was associated with online auctions, in 1999 Whitman was led by the company's mission (its reason for existing) to purchase Butterfield & Butterfield, which brought higher valued items to the site. She also purchased Cruise International Auctioneers, an automobile auctioneer company, allowing automobiles to be auctioned on the eBay site.

eBay is a multibillion-dollar company and has grown at a phenomenal rate in terms of the number of people who are using eBay, the quantity of items that are being listed for sale, and the dollar amount of transactions that close everyday. It is difficult to forecast this rate of growth, and a lack of forecast caused poor technology planning. Furthermore, eBay had little or no backup strategy in case of an emergency.

For most Web sites, the supporting infrastructure is a fragile ecosystem of software, hardware and wiring. A small weakness in any part can cascade

© MICHELLE GARRETT/CORBIS

Margaret Whitman, CEO of eBay, identified a new market segment for online auctions of higher-priced items.

into a catastrophic event—especially when a Web site has a rapidly growing base of customers and keeps loading on more features to attract still more (Pitta, 1999).

During the Labor Day weekend in 1999, eBay crashed (went dark) for 22 hours. The outage resulted in glaring headlines, cost millions in lost sales, and prompted fed-up customers to buy elsewhere.

Whitman had a contingency plan. She offered Maynard Webb [chief information officer at PC-maker Gateway in San Diego] "$450,000 in salary, a $108,000 sign-on bonus, an extra $300,000 if things went well—and options to buy 500,000 shares of eBay's recently battered stock. His salary is better than Whitman's 1998 paycheck" (Pitta, 1999). Needless to say, Webb became a member of Whitman's management team. His title is President, eBay Technologies, and his responsibilities involve overseeing eBay's technology strategies, engineering, and architecture and site operations.

Webb's first goal was "to reduce downtime rather than tackle the impossibility of eliminating outages altogether." His first tactic was to build a "warm backup," a redundant system to take over when the main one failed. The next tactic was to build a "hot backup"—still more iron that could reduce any blackouts to less than an hour (Pitta, 1999).

eBay couldn't afford another crash, and hiring Webb has paid off. Costly outages have been reduced. By January 2001, the world's leading online trading community had 18.9 million registered users and listed millions of items, in more than 4,500 categories, for sale. ■

Sources: Heather Green, "Margaret C. Whitman," section in Steve Hamm, "The e.biz 25: Masters of the Web Universe," *Businessweek Online* (27 September 1999), http://www.businessweek.com/1999/99_39/b3648001.htm; Julie Pitta, "Webb Master," *Forbes Magazine* (13 December 1999), http://www.forbes.com/forbes/1999/1213/6414322a.html.

INTRODUCTION

This chapter begins our examination of the planning function with an overview. After arriving at definitions of planning and planning terminology, we examine the types of plans managers create, the process used to create plans, commonly used techniques to make planning effective, and barriers to planning. Chapter 6 extends our examination by analyzing the processes and techniques involved in long-term planning for both an organization and its various subsystems.

PLANNING DEFINED

Explain the importance of planning

planning
Preparing for tomorrow, today.

Planning is preparing for tomorrow, today. It provides direction and a unity of purpose for organizations and their subsystems. When planning, managers

1. Construct, review, and/or rewrite their organization's mission
2. Identify and analyze their opportunities
3. Establish the goals they wish to achieve
4. Identify, analyze, and select the course or courses of action required to reach their goals
5. Determine resources they will need to achieve their goals (Lorange, 1993)

Describe the importance of an organization's mission statement

mission statement
When a mission is formalized in writing and communicated to all organizational members.

Mission Statement

As defined in Chapter 3, an organization's *mission* explains its central purpose—its primary reason(s) for existence. When a mission is formalized in writing and communicated to all organizational members, it becomes the organization's **mission statement**. It usually includes references to an organization's core values and principles and serves as an operational and ethical guide. A mission statement should also be the foundation and coordinating device for the execution of management functions, the behaviors of organizational members, and the shaping of the organization's culture (Jones and Kahaner, 1995). Many companies are placing their mission statements on their Web sites, which can be read with a browser. Browser software is the subject of this chapter's Managing Technology feature.

Figure 5.1 illustrates the mission statements for Starbucks, eBay, and Amgen. Notice the emphasis on quality—meeting customer needs that the organization can meet—in these statements. The mission statement serves as a template against which decisions can be measured. The organization's values should be easily apparent in the mission statement.

While creating a mission statement, management expert Peter Drucker states that two questions must be answered: What is our business? What should it be? (Drucker, 1954). These questions must be raised and answered periodically, not just when forming a business. The answer to the first question is determined in part by the customers an organization currently serves. Meeting their demands and needs has made the organization what it is. The answer to the second question is determined in part by the customers an organization *wishes* to serve. The specific needs of identified customers, along with the firm's experience and expertise, will dictate what products and services it creates and/or sells, what processes it uses, and what their levels of quality will be.

Since the values, beliefs, and wants of an organization's customers keep changing, so too must the organization. Consider the situation eBay has faced since it began in 1995. This virtual auction house (the subject of this chapter's Management in Action case) was growing over 50 percent quarter to quarter, making it a new company every three months. By staying focused on the mission—to help people trade practically anything on earth—CEO Margaret C. Whitman turned eBay from a "quirky idea into an Internet giant capable of handling millions of buyers and sellers. . . . More than that, Whitman has helped legitimize the notion of negotiated pricing—making it one of the most powerful economic forces on the Internet" (Green, 1999).

MANAGING TECHNOLOGY
Browsers

The development of graphical Web browser software, such as Netscape Communicator and Microsoft Internet Explorer, has made it easy to view a Web page. Browsers use hypertext software, which combines sounds, graphic images, video, and text. Across the top of the browser screen are many icons as well as an address line. By typing in an Internet address, called a Uniform Resource Locator (URL), such as http://plunkett.swcollege.com, you go to that page and see its information. From there you can visit other pages simply by clicking on anything that is highlighted or hyperlinked to that page. Hyperlinks link just about everything on the Web to something else, and you can spend hours *surfing*—just moving from place to place seeing what you can find. To visit an Internet site, simply type in the address line and hit the enter key.

When computer systems are being serviced and/or updated, or when there are large numbers of users accessing a particular computer system, you may experience occasional periods when you cannot visit a particular Internet site. Make a note of the Internet address and try again later.

http://www.netscape.com

http://www.microsoft.com

FIGURE 5.1 *Examples of mission statements*

http://www.starbucks.com

Starbucks—"Establish Starbucks as the premier purveyor of the finest coffee in the world while maintaining our uncompromising principles as we grow.

The following five guiding principles will help us measure the appropriateness of our decisions:

1) Provide a great work environment and treat each other with respect and dignity.
2) Apply the highest standards of excellence to the purchasing, roasting, and fresh delivery of our coffee.
3) Develop enthusiastically satisfied customers all of the time.
4) Contribute positively to our communities and our environment.
5) Recognize that profitability is essential to our future success."

http://www.ebay.com

eBay—"We help people trade practically anything on earth. eBay was founded with the belief that people are basically good. We believe that each of our customers, whether a buyer or a seller, is an individual who deserves to be treated with respect.

We will continue to enhance the online trading experiences of all—collectors, hobbyists, dealers, small business, unique item seekers, bargain hunters, opportunistic sellers, and browsers. The growth of the eBay community comes from meeting and exceeding the expectations of these special people."

http://www.amgen.com

Amgen—"We aspire to be the best human therapeutics company. We will live the Amgen values and use science and innovation to dramatically improve people's lives.

AMGEN CORPORATE GOALS

- Launch a stream of products that will dramatically improve patients' lives
- Create an environment where the best people choose to work
- Deliver superior shareholder returns compared to our industry peer group
- Be a good corporate citizen in communities where our staff live and work"

http://www.kemper.com

http://www.massmutual.com

Several insurance companies—Kemper and MassMutual, for example—now sell much more than insurance. They have created tax-sheltered retirement accounts, moved into real estate development, and created mutual and money market funds because that is what their competitors were doing and what the insurance companies had to do to keep existing clients and attract new ones.

Once Drucker's two questions are answered, the existing mission statement must be confirmed as valid or rewritten. The challenge for management is to transform its concepts and principles into something that anchors everything an organization does. As you examine Figure 5.2, which highlights the six rules for writing and implementing a mission statement, keep in mind that the leadership challenge for top management is to create a mission that captures the commitment of organizational members (Ward, 1995).

When companies do not ask Drucker's two basic questions regularly or answer them in a less-than-satisfactory manner, they usually experience some rather costly results. Consider what happened to two such companies, Subaru and Jostens, in the following examples (deLosa, 1994):

http://www.subaru.com

- Subaru delighted customers through the late 1970s and early 1980s with inexpensive, sturdy, four-wheel-drive vehicles. Management decided to expand into an already crowded market for midsize family sedans. Subaru's efforts barely penetrated the new market, whereas Jeep, Ford, and Chevrolet vehicles captured much of Subaru's primary four-wheel-drive business. After seven straight years of losses in the United States, Subaru pulled out of the family sedan market, losing nearly $300 million.

http://www.jostens.com

- Jostens—a company with 40 percent of the U.S. market for class rings, yearbooks, and other graduation-related products—lost sight of what its business was and where its expertise resided. Its top management decided to enlarge the business with an expansion into educational software. It launched Jostens Learning Corporation and bought its biggest competitor. Jostens' software was inferior to and required substantially higher initial costs than its competitors' products. The result was a $12 million loss.

Goals

Goals may be long term or short term. Long-term goals require more than one year to achieve. eBay's CEO Margaret C. Whitman began her planning by studying her company's mission statement and determining where its expertise lay. She

FIGURE 5.2 *Six rules for writing and implementing mission statements*

Rule #1: Keep the statement simple; not necessarily short, but simple.

Describe what the company does, not just for the insiders but for outsiders and investors. Tell how the mission will be accomplished.

Rule #2: Allow company-wide input.

Top management should write the mission statement, then send it out for review and comment. Involvement gets commitment.

Rule #3: Involve outsiders. They can bring clarity and a fresh perspective to the statement-writing process.

People inside may be too close to the action to be objective. Outsiders bring a fresh perspective and they can help steer around political swamps.

Rule #4: Develop the wording and the tone to reflect the company's personality or what the company would like to be.

The wording may be proper or colloquial. It may be old-fashioned or fast-moving as long as it represents the company and its image.

Rule #5: Share the mission statement in as many creative ways as possible and in as many languages as necessary. Keep it in front of people constantly.

Many companies place their mission statements on wallet-sized cards and distribute them to all employees and many outsiders. Make the mission statement part of every function and meeting. Place it on the walls and ask each person to restate the company's mission periodically.

Rule #6: Rely on the mission statement for guidance. Challenge it continually, and judge employees by how well they adhere to its tenets. Management must say it and live it.

Make the mission part of employee evaluations to stress its relevance and importance. Since many mission statements have long-term goals in them, they must be revisited periodically and the goals must be updated or replaced as necessary.

Source: From *Say It and Live* It by Patricia Jones and Larry Kahaner. Copyright © 1995 by Kane Associates International Inc. Used by permission Doubleday, a division of Bantam Doubleday Dell Publishing Group Inc.

assessed eBay's strengths and market opportunities. Only then did she establish the long-term goal of eBay becoming "an international phenom where all sorts of things are auctioned—including big-ticket items such as collectible autos" (Green, 1999). This goal capitalized on eBay's experience, expertise, and reputation with existing customers.

Short-term goals can be reached within one year and many are directly connected to long-term goals. Whitman had several such objectives, including launching international auctions in Britain and Germany in 1999, entering five other countries by 2000, and setting up regional auctions in 50 U.S. metropolitan areas so people could sell large items that couldn't easily be mailed. Figure 5.3 defines the characteristics that make goals effective (Green, 1999).

Plans

plan
The end result of the planning effort—commits individuals, departments, entire organizations, and the resources of each to specific courses of action for days, months, and years into the future.

A **plan**—the end result of the planning effort—commits individuals, departments, entire organizations, and the resources of each to specific courses of action for days, months, and years into the future. It provides specific answers to six basic questions in regard to any intended activity—what, when, where, who, how, and how much.

- *What* identifies the specific goals to be accomplished.

FIGURE 5.3 *Characteristics of effective goals and objectives*

Characteristic	Explanation
Specific and measurable	Not all objectives can be expressed in numeric terms, but they should be quantified when possible. Specific outcomes are easier to focus on than general ones, and performance can be more easily measured when the task is defined precisely.
Realistic and challenging	Impossibly difficult objectives demotivate people. Objectives should be challenging but attainable, given the resources and skills available. The best goals require people to stretch their abilities.
Focused on key result areas	It is neither possible nor good practice to set objectives for every detail of an employee's job. Goals should focus on key results—sales, profits, production, or quality, for example—that affect overall performance.
Cover a specific period	A measurable objective is stated in terms of the time in which it is to be completed. Sales objectives, for example, may cover a day, month, quarter, or year. The period should be both realistic (managers should not require ten months of work in five) and productive (a requirement for excessive reporting can be debilitating, for example). Short-term goals should complement long-term goals.
Reward performance	Objectives are meaningless if they are not directly related to rewards for performance. Individuals, work groups, and organizational units should receive prompt rewards for achieving objectives.

- *When* answers a question of timing: each long-term goal may have a series of short-term objectives that must be achieved before the long-term goal can be reached.
- *Where* concerns the place or places where the plan will be executed.
- *Who* identifies specific people who will perform specific tasks essential to a plan's implementation.
- *How* involves the specific actions to be taken to reach the goals.
- *How much* is concerned with the expenditure of resources needed to reach the goals—both short- and long-term.

In setting goals, more businesses are "junking business-as-usual incremental objectives—moving a few grains of sand—and striving instead to hit gigantic, seemingly unreachable milestones called stretch targets" (Tully, 1994). Top managers are recognizing that achieving incremental improvements invites middle- and lower-level managers as well as workers to perform the same comfortable process a little bit better each year. However, even the best-maintained equipment can become obsolete.

stretch goals
Goal that requires great leaps forward on such measures as product development time, return on investment, sales growth, quality improvement, and reduction of manufacturing cycle times.

On the other hand, **stretch goals** (dubbed "Big Hairy Audacious Goals" or BHAGS [pronounced bee-hags] by management analyst James Collins) require great leaps forward on such measures as product development time, return on investment, sales growth, quality improvement, and reduction of manufacturing cycle times (Collins and Porras, 1994). In 1995 the Coca-Cola Company announced its intention "to capture 50 percent of the U.S. market [for soft drinks by the year] 2000, an increase of nearly 9 share points from 1994" (*Chicago Tribune*, "Coke," 1995). This goal would lead the company to over $4 billion in increased sales.

For example, to achieve Starbucks' mission (refer to Figure 5.1), top management developed long-term goals focused on growth. An example is, "Starbucks Coffee Japan, Ltd. plans to have at least 500 stores by the end of March 2004." (http://www.starbucks.com/aboutus/pressdesc.asp?id=156.) The following are two additional examples of BHAGS (Jones and Kahaner, 1995):

http://www.ge.com

1. General Electric's goal is to become No. 1 or No. 2 in every market served and to give the company the speed and agility of a small enterprise. CEO Jack Welch's motto: Fix, close, or sell any business that isn't up to this standard.

http://www.3m.com

2. 3M (Minnesota Mining and Manufacturing) stretched to accelerate product innovation by requiring 30 percent of its sales revenue from products introduced within the past four years. The old target: 25 percent from products introduced in the past five years.

Strategies and Tactics

strategy
A course of action created to achieve a long-term goal.

tactic
A course of action designed to achieve a short-term goal—an objective.

A course of action created to achieve a long-term goal is called a **strategy**. Strategies may exist for an entire organization or for its autonomous units or functional areas (examined in detail in Chapter 6). A course of action designed to achieve a short-term goal—an objective—is called a **tactic**. As with eBay, mission defines strategy. Objectives must be achieved in order to reach a long-term goal. Therefore, strategies influence and often dictate the choice of tactics.

At eBay, creating and successfully managing the company's growth required achieving a sequential set of objectives through a variety of tactics. A strong management team had to be built. People had to be recruited and hired to facilitate allowing people to post items for auction on eBay's Web site and then administering the transaction for a fee. Money had to be raised to finance related activities. New customers' accounts had to be adequately served.

One additional example illustrates the connection between a strategy and tactics. An individual seeking a two- or four-year college degree has a strategy (and goal) that requires two or more years to complete. The strategy requires a sequence of tactics that, semester after semester, will yield the short-term goals—successful completion of courses in their proper sequences—that ultimately lead to the achievement of the strategic goal—a college degree.

Determining Resource Requirements

The best-made plans will not be executed if they lack the resources required. Most plans need various resources, including people, money, facilities, equipment, supplies, and information. Among other things, eBay needed an information technology specialist to accomplish its long-term expansion effort.

In 1995 Amoco, the giant, Illinois-based oil and gas company, made its 1996 capital spending plans; it decided to commit "$4.7 billion, with most of the money budgeted for its worldwide search for oil and natural gas" (*Chicago Tribune*, "Amoco," 1995). This represented a 12 percent increase over its 1995 budget. Amoco planned to obtain the needed funds from retained earnings, 1996 profits, and "the sale of underperforming assets" (*Chicago Tribune*, "Amoco," 1995). (Today, Amoco is part of BP.)

http://www.bp.com

http://www.iflyswa.com

When Southwest Airlines planned its 1995–1996 expansion of low-fare frequent flights to several Florida airports, it had to plan for additional aircraft acquisition (Boeing 737s), the operation of several new airport facilities, and the addition and

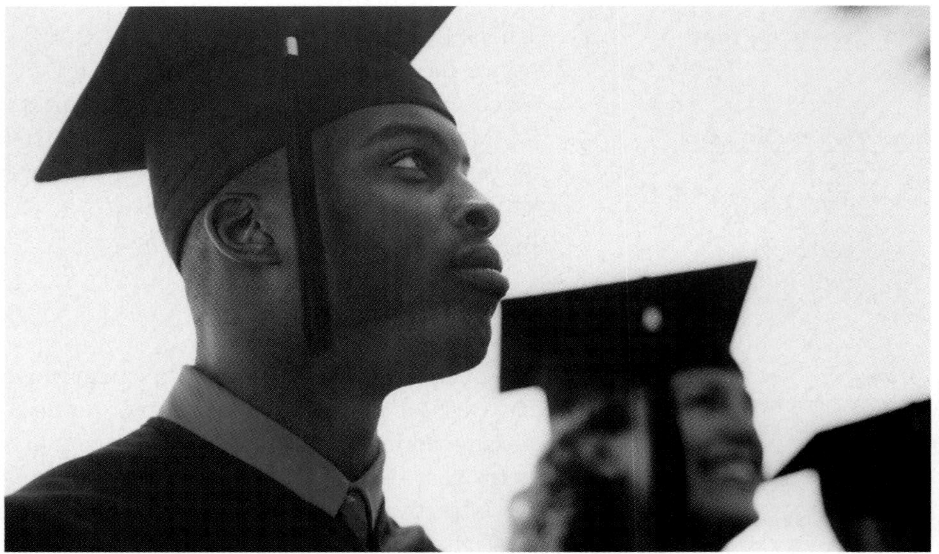

A college student uses tactics over the course of his or her education to achieve the strategic goal of a degree.

http://www.polaroid.com

training of flight crews and ground personnel. When Polaroid Corporation, the Massachusetts-based camera and film producer, announced its plans to "eliminate 1,300 jobs in a restructuring designed to cut costs and refocus some of its operations," it decided to rely on fewer human resources (*Chicago Tribune*, "Polaroid," 1995). The planned reductions were expected to reduce operating costs by as much as $90 million each year, but Polaroid needed to spend $195 million over two years (1995 and 1996) to execute its plans in such categories as early retirement incentives, severance pay and benefit buyouts, and administrative charges connected with the restructuring effort (*Chicago Tribune*, "Polaroid," 1995).

TYPES OF PLANS

3

Discuss the purposes of strategic, tactical, operational, and contingency plans

For an organization to accomplish its goals at all organizational levels—top, middle, and first-line—it must develop three types of mission-based plans: strategic, tactical, and operational (as shown in Figure 5.4). Each must work in harmony with the others if the organization's mission and long-term goals are to become reality.

FIGURE 5.4 *The relationship between goals, objectives, and plans in organizational planning*

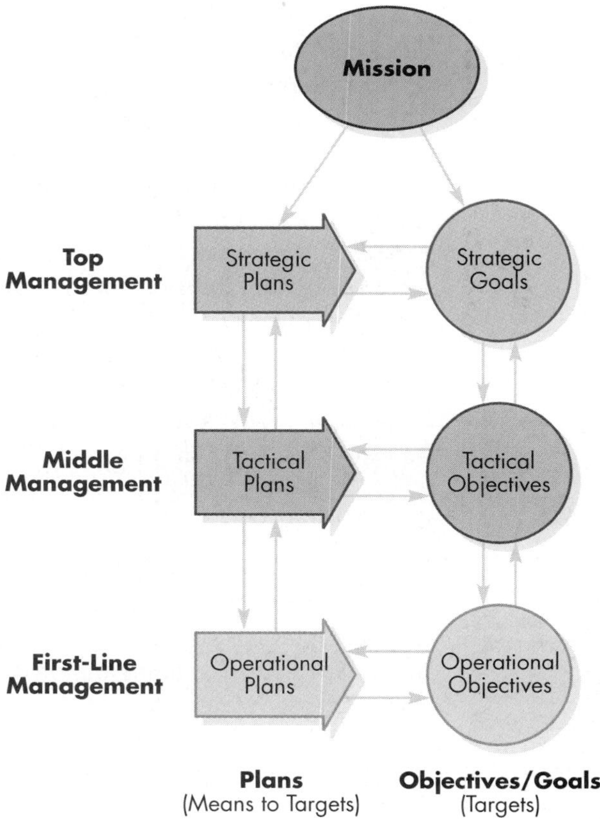

Strategic Plans

strategic plan
Contains the answers to who, what, when, where, how, and how much for achieving strategic goals—long-term, company-wide goals established by top management.

A **strategic plan** contains the answers to who, what, when, where, how, and how much for achieving *strategic goals*—long-term, company-wide goals established by top management. The strategic plan is concerned with the entire organization's direction and purpose—how it intends to grow, compete, and meet its customers' needs—over the next few years.

Strategic planning draws heavily on the leadership abilities of managers. As we have seen at eBay, CEO Margaret C. Whitman's business philosophy has three key ingredients: (1) define your mission, (2) execute, and (3) "Treat people like you would want to be treated yourself, like your mother taught you. That gets you 90 percent there." Regardless of whether a company is large or small, leaders are required to "see"—have vision—where the company needs to go and to design the fabric of actions—organize, staff, lead, and control—so the future becomes a reality. An example of both the importance of leadership and how planning affects the other functions can be seen in actions at Apple Computer while Michael Spindler was CEO.

http://www.apple.com

After Apple "nearly ran itself into a ditch two years ago," Spindler developed plans aimed at regaining Apple's competitiveness and doubling its worldwide market share (Rebello, 1995). The first part of the plan called for new products—Macintoshes and PowerBooks—along with a faster PowerPC chip. Then the company reorganized to capitalize on its traditional strength in the home, education, small business, and entertainment markets. In the process, the need for the so-called customer solution commandos was born. This elite group of employees is charged with combining Apple's technology with products from other companies to solve customers' needs. To create commandos the company hired outsiders and transferred employees from other departments. Said Spindler, "the house is in order. This company is not for sale" (Rebello, 1995).

Just how far into the future a strategic plan will stretch is determined by the degree of certainty managers have about the external environmental conditions and the availability of needed resources. Every strategic plan deals with many hard-to-predict but important future events in their external environments: Will there be a recession? Will inflation continue at its present rates? What will be the situation in our industry with regard to local, state, and federal regulations? What will the competition do? These things are difficult enough to predict over a one-year period, let alone a five-year span. For this reason strategic plans must be regularly reviewed and adjusted for changes that occur over their time frames. They must be viewed as works in progress.

Strategic Goals

strategic goals
Long-term, company-wide goals set by top-management strategic planning efforts. They focus on the changes desired in productivity, product innovation, and responsibilities to stakeholders.

Long-term, company-wide goals set by top-management strategic planning efforts are called **strategic goals**. They focus on the changes desired in such areas as productivity, product innovation, and responsibilities to stakeholders (Drucker, 1954). Motorola has made valuing the diversity of its employees a strategic goal, and as this chapter's Valuing Diversity feature points out, a duty for all its managers.

Just as one person's ceiling can be another person's floor, the completion of one manager's plan marks the beginning of planning efforts by another. Top manage-

VALUING DIVERSITY
Planning for Diversity

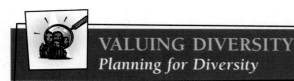

Bobbi Gutman, the first and only African-American woman to become a vice president at Motorola, has brought strategic planning to the diversity program. Charged with a mission to develop and oversee strategies to ensure that Motorola attracts, retains, and effectively utilizes the best minds—regardless of race, gender, religion, age, or disability—Gutman began her planning efforts.

First, Gutman gathered the three top executives at Motorola to lay the foundation for planning. Her message: Since diversity is a business initiative and a strategic goal (not merely "nice to do" or "the right thing to do"), it must be embraced by all managers, not just those in human resources. Second, like any business goal, there must be quantifiable measures to gauge the progress being made toward achieving it.

Top management endorsed both elements of the plan. Since all managers plan, organize, lead, and, most importantly, make a variety of staffing decisions, their involvement and cooperation were deemed critical. To help set goals, an internal census was conducted. It detailed what percentage of employees at every level were women, African-American, Hispanic, Asian, and Native American. The census numbers became a baseline for measuring increases.

Has Gutman been successful? When the program began in 1988, there were 1 female and 6 people of color among the ranks of 340 vice presidents. By 1994, out of 400, there were 33 people of color and 23 women vice presidents. Even more impressive results have been achieved at lower management levels.

http://www.motorola.com

Sources: Roberta Gutman, "Changing the Face of Management," *Working Woman* (November 1994), pp. 21–23. Visit Motorola online at http://www.motorola.com.

ment's strategic plan becomes the foundation for middle-level managers' planning efforts that produce tactical plans. Figure 5.5 illustrates how tactical and then operational objectives evolve from strategic goals.

Tactical Plans

tactical plan
Developed by middle managers, this plan has more details, shorter time frames, and narrower scopes than a strategic plan; it usually spans one year or less.

Developed by middle managers, a **tactical plan** is concerned with what each of the major organizational subsystems must do, how they must do it, when things must be done, where activities will be performed, what resources are to be utilized, and who will have the authority needed to perform each task. Tactical plans have more details, shorter time frames, and narrower scopes than strategic plans; they usually span one year or less.

Strategic and tactical plans are usually but not always related. Every strategy requires a series of tactical and operational plans linked to each other to achieve strategic goals; middle managers, however, do create plans to reach what are uniquely department, division, or team goals, both for the short and long term. The tactical plans discussed in the eBay case are all related to reaching the company's strategic goals. Two such plans involved the following:

- To build a "warm backup," a redundant computer system to take over when the main one failed.
- To build a "hot backup" that could reduce any blackouts to less than an hour.

FIGURE 5.5 An organization's mission and levels of goals

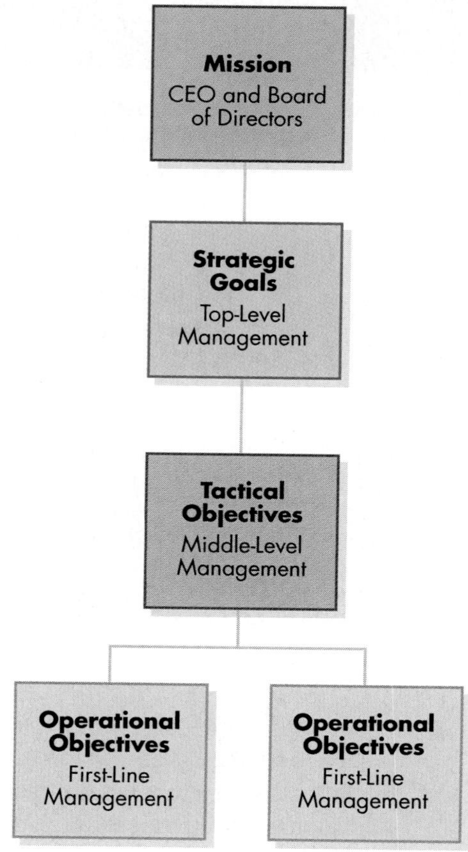

tactical objectives
Short-term goals set by middle managers that must be achieved in order to reach top management's strategic goals and the short- and long-term goals of middle managers.

operational plan
The first-line manager's tool for executing daily, weekly, and monthly activities. Operational plans fall into two major categories: single-use and standing plans.

single-use plan
A plan used for a one-time activity—an activity that does not recur. Two examples of single-use plans are programs and budgets.

Tactical Objectives

Following logically from the strategic goals are **tactical objectives**: short-term goals set by middle managers that must be achieved in order to reach top management's strategic goals and the short- and long-term goals of middle managers. Once eBay devised the tactical plan focused on the infrastructure, it probably formed teams and assigned team members specific duties.

Operational Plans

An **operational plan** is developed by first-line managers—supervisors, team leaders, and team facilitators—in support of tactical plans. It is the first-line manager's tool for executing daily, weekly, and monthly activities. Operational plans fall into two major categories: single-use and standing plans.

Single-Use Plans

A one-time activity—an activity that does not recur—requires a **single-use plan**. Once the activity is completed, the plan is no longer needed. Two examples of single-use plans are programs and budgets. A **program** is a single-use plan for an operation from its beginning to its end. An example would be to gain influential reviews for a company's new line of computers. Once the reviews were obtained, the plan would cease to be of value. In addition, an example would be a program to handle a company's participation in an industry trade show where it could meet the head buyers for the computer superstores.

program
A single-use plan for an operation from its beginning to its end.

Another single-use plan is a **budget**. It is a plan that predicts sources and amounts of income that will be available over a fixed period of time and how those funds will be used. eBay needs several budgets. The company's total operations require a budget each year, and it requires others to back efforts to hire new personnel and to launch new auctions. Budgets prepared at various levels help to control spending in an organization and in its autonomous subsystems. When the specified period for a budget ends, it becomes a historical document and often proves useful for future budgeting efforts.

budget
A single-use plan that predicts sources and amounts of income that will be available over a fixed period of time and how those funds will be used.

Standing Plans

Unlike budgets and programs, a **standing plan** specifies how to handle continuing or recurring activities, such as hiring, granting credit, and maintaining equipment. Once constructed, they continue to be useful over many years but are subject to periodic review and revision. Examples of standing plans include policies, procedures, and rules.

standing plan
Specifies how to handle continuing or recurring activities, such as hiring, granting credit, and maintaining equipment. Examples of standing plans include policies, procedures, and rules.

A **policy** is a broad guide for organizational members to follow when dealing with important and recurring areas of decision making. They set limits and provide boundaries for decision makers. Policies are usually general statements about the ways in which managers and others should attempt to handle their routine responsibilities. Figure 5.6 presents a policy governing the making of hiring and other human resource decisions that was created to conform to federal antidiscrimination guidelines issued by the Equal Employment Opportunity Commission. Policies are not prescriptive. They state a viewpoint the company wants its managers to adopt when conducting ongoing operations. Policies can sometimes be controversial and create ethical issues as this chapter's Ethical Management feature points out.

policy
A broad guide for organizational members to follow when dealing with important and recurring areas of decision making. They set limits and provide boundaries for decision makers.

A **procedure** is a set of step-by-step directions for carrying out activities or tasks. Companies create procedures for such things as preparing budgets, paying employees, preparing business correspondence, and hiring new employees. Like policies, they help to guarantee that recurring, identical activities will be done in a uniform way regardless of who executes them. When followed, procedures give precise methods for completing a task.

procedure
A set of step-by-step directions for carrying out activities or tasks.

FIGURE 5.6 *Human resources policy*

Statement of Policy

There shall be no discrimination for or against any applicant or for or against any current employee because of his or her race, creed, color, national origin, sex, marital status, age, handicap, or membership or lawful participation in the activities of any organization or union, or refusal to join or participate in the activities of any organization or union. Moreover, in each functional division, the company shall adhere to an affirmative action program regarding hiring, promotions, transfers, and other ongoing human resource activities.

ETHICAL MANAGEMENT
Privacy: Company Policy and the Law

Federal law allows companies to monitor their employees' behaviors and conversations. As of January, 1996, 45 states had passed laws allowing the monitoring of employee phone calls, "mainly at the request of telemarketers and other businesses that want to record their employees' conversations for quality control, coaching, and training." Many of these laws rule practically nothing out.

Employers are creating policies to keep a tighter rein on employees for a variety of reasons, the least of which determines how they use their time on the job. These policies tell employees that they will be, are being, or can be monitored at work and authorize a variety of monitoring techniques: listening to employees' business-related telephone calls, hiring private investigators to pose as workers, and reading computer-to-computer messages. Some of the specific results follow:

- At the Spears Liquor Store, the owners authorized the monitoring and recording of employee calls from work. The recordings not only revealed business transactions, but also several passion-filled telephone calls between an employee and a customer. The employee was fired.
- Forty Kmart employees at the Manteno, Illinois, store accused management of hiring private investigators to pose as workers. The employees, in a suit for invasion of privacy, charged the investigators with gathering information about everything from employee living arrangements to their recreational plans.
- At Epson American, a computer manufacturer, employees routinely have their email messages monitored by supervisors.

Privacy advocates worry that most state laws do not specify how information gathered by employers on employees can be used or with whom it can be shared. Although some companies have clearly told their employees about monitoring and have received their consent as a condition for being hired, others have not done so.

What ethical questions are raised when companies create policies authorizing the monitoring of employees? As a manager, under what circumstances would you create a policy authorizing the recording of employee telephone calls?

Sources: Deborah L. Jacobs, "Are You Guilty of Electronic Trespassing?," *Management Review* (April 1994), pp. 21–25; and Peter Kendall and Christi Parsons, "Listen Up: Bosses May Be on the Line," *Chicago Tribune* (18 December 1995), sec. 1, pp. 1, 12.

Consider the following six-step procedure required to process a customer's return of merchandise at a local discount chain store:

1. Determine customer's need: return and refund, or exchange.
2. Verify that purchase (cash or charge) was made at this store.
3. Inspect merchandise for damage.
4. Consult store return policy; apply information obtained in steps 1–3.
5. Issue exchange, refund, or credit as applicable.
6. Deny return and explain reason(s) in line with store policy.

Only after performing each step in the proper sequence can an employee grant an exchange, refund, or credit to a customer.

rule
An ongoing, specific guide for human behavior and conduct at work. Rules are usually "do" and "do not" statements established to promote employee safety, ensure the uniform treatment of employees, and regulate civil behavior.

A **rule** is an ongoing, specific guide for human behavior and conduct at work. Rules are usually "do" and "do not" statements established to promote employee safety, ensure the uniform treatment of employees, and regulate civil behavior. Unlike policies and like procedures, rules tell employees what is expected in given sets of circumstances. A rule that prohibits smoking on company premises allows for no exceptions. Figure 5.7 illustrates some commonly imposed rules at work.

Companies create step-by-step procedures for carrying out certain tasks or activities, such as processing a return of merchandise at a retail store.

FIGURE 5.7 *Common rules in the workplace*

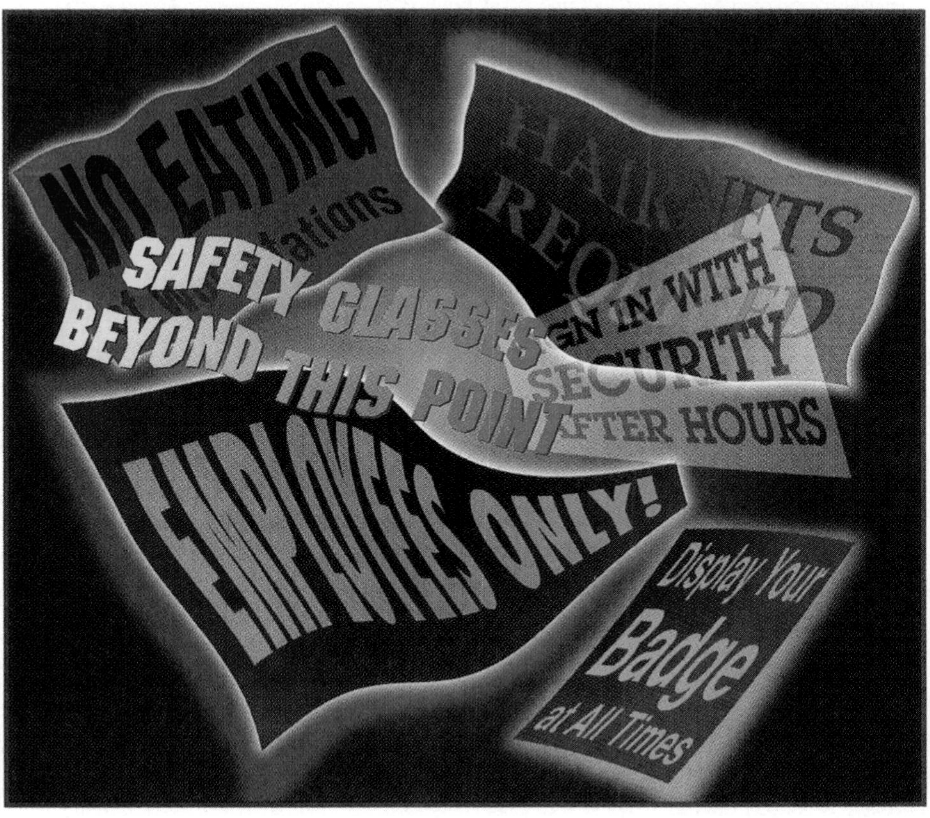

Procedures and rules offer the advantage of standardizing behavior but restrict individual creativity and encourage blind obedience. The more of both that exist, the less freedom employees have to adjust to changing situations. Figure 5.8 offers some additional insights into policies, programs, procedures, and rules.

Operational Objectives

operational objective
The specific results expected from first-level managers, work groups, and individuals.

http://www.boeing.com

First-level managers, work groups, and individuals in these groups have specific results expected from them in the form of **operational objectives**. The Boeing first-line manager in charge of a specific assembly operation has regular daily, weekly, and monthly objectives to achieve in areas such as scheduling overtime, completing work on time and on budget, protecting and allocating various resources, and reducing waste and scrap.

FIGURE 5.8 *The advantages of and the requirements for policies, programs, procedures, and rules*

Policies	Programs	Procedures	Rules
ADVANTAGES			
Promote uniformity	Provide a plan for an operation from beginning to end	Provide the detail for effective performance	Promote safety
Save time	Name participants and detail their duties	Promote uniformity	Promote acceptable conduct
Outline an approach	Coordinate efforts of those seeking the same goal	Save time	Provide security
Set limitations on management conduct		Provide assistance in training	Provide standards for appraising performance and conduct
Promote effectiveness for managers and the organization		Provide security in operations	Save time
		Promote effectiveness and efficiency	Aid in disciplinary situations
REQUIREMENTS			
Should be in writing	Should be in writing in at least an outline format	Should be in writing	Should be in writing
Need to be communicated and understood	Should answer who, when, where, how, and how much	Should be sufficiently detailed	Must be communicated to and understood by all those affected
Should provide some flexibility	Should have clear goals, tactics, and timetables	Should be revised periodically	Should be reviewed and revised periodically
Should be consistent throughout the organization and consistently applied	Need to be communicated to all those affected by them	Should be communicated to and understood by those who need to know them	Should serve needed purposes
Should support the organization's strategy			
Need to be based on the mission			

The President of eBay Technologies, Maynard Webb, had to make certain that his people gave their best and used their resources efficiently to rebuild the computer system. Daily, weekly, and monthly goals had to be established and reached on time to achieve this end result. eBay's new technology people had to create tactics in order for the computer system to serve its millions of users.

Unified Hierarchy of Goals

4

Explain the relationships between strategic, tactical, and operational goals

The result of planning should generate a unified framework for the accomplishment of the organization's purposes. The use of the traditional management pyramid as a model for the planning process results in a hierarchy of objectives in which the work of each subsystem complements that of the next; goals at each level mesh with or fit into each other. In Figure 5.9, for illustrative purposes, a single goal occupies each subunit; in reality, multiple goals are the norm. The figure shows that top management has determined the strategic goal for the entire organization. Middle management has established tactical objectives for the functional areas of marketing and manufacturing. Finally, the first-line managers within each functional area have created objectives for their work groups. The outcome is a coordinated hierarchy of objectives.

But what happens if an individual manager chooses *not* to plan within this framework? If a manager develops a set of objectives based on his or her own ambitions, values, or goals that oppose or contradict top management's goals, conflicting objectives will result. In the example of the shoe company in Figure 5.9, imagine that the marketing manager has misinterpreted top management's objective. Instead of reaching all potential sources of *profitable* sales, the marketing manager asks the operating sales manager to seek out all potential buyers. Thus salespersons will call on and sell to every potential buyer, regardless of the potential size of the order or the cost that the company will incur in servicing that order. The result is bound to be sales to some small or bad-credit accounts that will cause the company losses.

Contingency Plans

Planning should provide the ability to adjust to rapidly changing situations. In most companies, environments change so rapidly that plans must be continually altered as they are being made; at worst, they may actually become useless before they have been totally constructed or fully implemented. To remain as flexible and open to change as possible, managers should create a **contingency plan**: an alternative goal and course or courses of action to reach that goal if and when circumstances and assumptions change so drastically as to make an original plan unusable.

contingency plan
An alternative goal and course or courses of action to reach that goal if and when circumstances and assumptions change so drastically as to make an original plan unusable.

Through contingency planning, managers recognize and prepare for emergencies and other unexpected events that have both positive and negative impacts on their organizations. Examples of contingency plans include those that deal with the need to conduct a product recall, natural and human-made disasters that disrupt normal operations, and rapidly increasing demand for products and services that can outstrip the ability of current facilities to accommodate. A manager who says, "What will I do if . . . ?" and, "If this happens, then I will . . ." is a contingency planner.

FIGURE 5.9 Hierarchy of unified goals and objectives

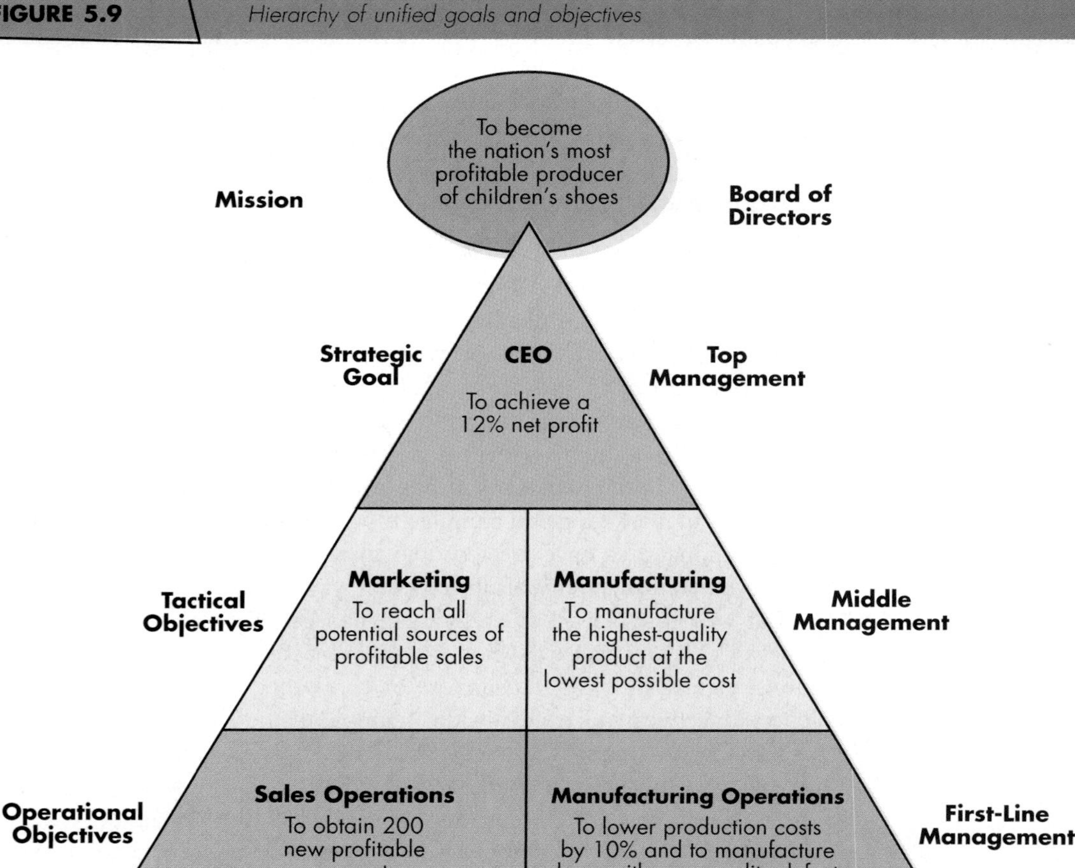

BASIC PLANNING PROCESS

List and explain the steps in a basic planning process

When developing a plan, all managers, regardless of their organizational level, follow some kind of step-by-step process to guide their efforts. Figure 5.10 details a recommended basic planning process that can be used to create tactical and operational plans. As each step is explained, consult Figure 5.11 for applications. The latter highlights how an operating-level manager applied each step in the process to achieve the objective of keeping the office staffed during extended business hours. Chapter 6 examines the strategic planning process.

Setting Objectives

When setting objectives, middle and operating managers focus and commit the attention and energies of their respective personnel, divisions, and departments for several months into the future. The selection of objectives (and the courses of action to achieve them) are influenced in part by the organization's mission and

FIGURE 5.10 *Steps in a basic planning process*

Step 1: *Setting Objectives*
Establishing targets for the short- or long-range future

Step 2: *Analyzing and Evaluating the Environments*
Analyzing the present position, the internal and external environments, and resources available

Step 3: *Identifying the Alternatives*
Constructing a list of possible courses of action that will lead to goal achievement

Step 4: *Evaluating the Alternatives*
Listing and considering the advantages and disadvantages of each possible course of action

Step 5: *Selecting the Best Solution*
Selecting the course of action that possesses the most advantages and the fewest serious disadvantages

Step 6: *Implementing the Plan*
Determining who will be involved, what resources will be assigned, how the plan will be evaluated, and how reporting will be handled

Step 7: *Controlling and Evaluating the Results*
Ensuring that the plan is proceeding according to expectations and making necessary adjustments

values; the strategic plans and goals; the standing plans; the environmental conditions; the availability of resources; and the philosophies, ethics, accumulated experience, and expertise of its managers. Before being finalized, each objective should possess the characteristics outlined in Figure 5.3 on page 130.

Note the first-line manager's objective in Figure 5.11—to ensure that the office is staffed from 8 A.M. to 9 P.M., Monday through Thursday. A date for its achievement has been established. The goal has the characteristics for effective objectives previously listed in Figure 5.3. The objective is specific, measurable, realistic, and probably challenging. It focuses on a key result area, covers a specific time period, and will likely lead to some form of reward for the manager involved.

Analyzing and Evaluating the Environment

Once objectives are established, managers must analyze their present situations and environments to determine what resources they will have available and what other limiting factors such as company policies they must consider as they evaluate possible courses of action or tactics. When assessing the internal environment, managers must consider what human, material, financial, time, and informational resources are available and what the needs of internal customers are. When assessing the external environment, managers must consider such elements as the strengths and weaknesses of suppliers and partners, the availability of additional labor and technology, and the needs of external customers. Choices and commitments made by managers as they plan must not jeopardize efforts to continually improve quality, productivity, or profitability.

FIGURE 5.11 A first-level manager applies the basic planning process

Objective

To ensure that the office is staffed from 8:00 A.M. to 9:00 P.M., Monday through Thursday. Target date: January 1.

Analysis and Evaluation of the Environment

1. *Present staffing situation.* Office is staffed by two full-time hourly employees. One works from 8:00 A.M. to 4:30 P.M. and the other works from 8:00 A.M. to 5:00 P.M.
2. *Financial resources.* Operating budget has sufficient funds to support additional staff at a range of $8 to $10 per hour, but benefits are restricted.
3. *Labor supply.* The potential number of part-time applicants is uncertain based on the rate of pay available.
4. *Company policy.* (1) Severe limits are placed on the use of overtime and compensatory time, and (2) a part-time employee becomes eligible for a limited benefit package when he or she works 15 hours per week.

Alternatives

1. Use present office staff by developing a combination package involving overtime and compensatory time.
2. Use the present office staff by altering the work hours of one or both.
3. Hire a part-time staff member to work 5:00 P.M. to 9:00 P.M. Monday through Thursday.
4. Hire two part-time staff members to work two nights each, from 5:00 P.M. to 9:00 P.M.

Evaluation of Alternatives

Alternative 1 Present staff/combination package. Problems with company pay policy and potential reaction of present staff.

Alternative 2 Present staff/altered work hours. Would provide coverage but would affect daytime productivity. Staff reaction—No!

Alternative 3 One part-time staff member. Would provide office coverage but stretch financial resources because the new employee would be eligible for limited benefits.

Alternative 4 Two part-time staff members/two nights each. Would provide coverage and not exceed financial resources or benefits restriction (neither will work 15 hours). Only question: Can labor supply produce two qualified applicants?

Selection of Best Solution

The alternative with the fewest questions and most promise is Alternative 4. The only problem lies in attracting candidates.

Implementation

1. To overcome the potential limitation (supply of qualified candidates), pay the proposed employees the top authorized rate, $10 per hour.
2. Develop advertising by October 1.
3. Advertise the position internally to attract internal referrals.
4. Advertise the position externally, through newspaper advertisements and job placement offices at colleges, private business schools, and high schools.
5. Establish November 1 as the cutoff date for applications.
6. Complete screening and interviews by November 21.
7. Make hiring offers by December 1.

Control and Evaluation

1. Check daily to determine the number of applications.
2. Extend the advertising deadline until a sufficient number (20 to 30) of applications are received.
3. If two candidates cannot be found, obtain additional funds and implement Alternative 3.

Returning to Figure 5.11, the supervisor has listed the results of an environmental analysis and states limits as well as resources available. The office must be staffed for at least four additional hours, four days per week. Company policies limit overtime and compensatory time and require a limited benefit package for part-time employees working 15 hours per week.

Identifying the Alternatives

Courses of action available to a manager to reach a goal represent alternate paths to a destination. When developing alternatives, a manager should try to create as many roads to each objective as possible. These alternatives may be entirely separate ways to reach a goal as well as variations of one or more separate alternatives. When listing alternatives, managers usually invite any persons who have the relevant knowledge and experience to contribute suggestions. Allowing those who will have to execute a chosen alternative to be part of the process helps to ensure a commitment on their part to make the alternative work.

Notice that in Figure 5.11 the manager has listed four potential alternatives from which to choose. Each alternative represents a possible way to achieve the staffing objective. Which alternative is best, given the situation as outlined, is determined in the next step and should not be determined until then. Attempting to analyze courses of action in this step will only inhibit a free flow of alternatives and thus result in an incomplete listing of possible alternatives.

Evaluating the Alternatives

Each alternative must be evaluated to determine which one or combination is most likely to achieve the objective effectively and efficiently. Most managers begin their evaluation by constructing a list of advantages (benefits) and disadvantages (costs) for each alternative. Managers then return to the second step to make certain that each alternative fits with the resources available and within the identified limits.

Managers need to know the kind and amount of resources, including time, that each alternative will require. They must create an estimate of the costs for each course of action and relate these to the dollar value of the benefits expected. If, for example, $1,000 will be spent to gain an objective valued at a lesser amount, the alternative is inefficient and an unlikely choice.

In addition to financial factors, managers consider the effects each alternative is likely to have on organizational members, the organizational unit, and others outside the area of operations in which the planning is taking place. Possibly, certain side effects, both good and bad, will result from the implementation of an alternative. Managers should determine these effects *before* they finalize the plan.

Notice the evaluation of each alternative in Figure 5.11. All of them have positives and negatives. The manager should choose the one with the greatest number of positives and the fewest or least serious negatives.

Selecting the Best Solution

The analysis of each alternative's benefits and costs should result in determining one course of action that appears better than the others. If no single alternative

CHAPTER SUMMARY

1 **Explain the importance of planning.** Planning helps managers avoid errors, waste, and delays. It provides direction and a common sense of purpose for the organization. Planning sets goals and objectives and selects the means to reach them. It is part of every other management function. Planning allows managers the opportunity of adjusting to, rather than reacting to, expected changes in both their internal and external environments.

2 **Describe the importance of an organization's mission statement.** The planning process for all organizations is built on a framework of an organization's mission, with its accompanying values and principles. An organization's mission statement explains why it exists—what its primary purpose is. Once the mission is defined, all planning efforts must be governed by the mission and not contradict or oppose it in any way. It becomes an anchor for everything a company does or plans to do.

3 **Discuss the purposes of strategic, tactical, operational, and contingency plans.** Plans—the end result of planning—provide answers to the six basic questions: what, when, where, who, how, and how much. Strategic plans establish the steps by which an organization achieves its strategic objectives. They are concerned with the entire organization's direction and the primary responsibility of top management.

Tactical plans are concerned with what the major subsystems within each organization must do, how they must do it, and who will have the responsibility for doing it. As the primary responsibility of middle managers, tactical plans develop the shorter-term activities and goals needed to achieve a strategy.

First-line supervisors develop operational plans as a means to achieve operational objectives in support of tactical as well as strategic plans.

Contingency plans are developed to cope with events that, if they occur, will render primary plans ineffective or obsolete. By planning for changes that have both positive and negative impacts, managers will remain able to deal with worst-case situations and events.

4 **Explain the relationships between strategic, tactical, and operational goals.** There are three levels of goals: strategic, tactical, and operational. Set by top management, strategic goals are achieved over more than one year. They state where the organization as a whole wants to be in the future. Tactical objectives, set by middle managers, establish what the major subsystems must do each year to achieve the organization's strategic goals. Operational objectives are the specific results expected from first-level managers, work groups, and individuals. Many of these flow directly from the tactical goals set by middle managers. All must be anchored by the company's mission, values, and principles.

5 **List and explain the steps in a basic planning process.**

- *Setting objectives.* Establishing targets for the short- or long-range future.
- *Analyzing and evaluating the environments.* Analyzing the present position, analyzing the internal and external environments, and determining the kind of resources that will be available to evaluate courses of action and implement plans.
- *Identifying the alternatives.* Constructing a list of possible courses of action that will lead to goal achievement.
- *Evaluating the alternatives.* Listing and considering the advantages (benefits) and disadvantages (costs) of each possible course of action.
- *Selecting the best solution.* Selecting the course or combination of courses of action that possesses the most advantages and the fewest serious disadvantages.
- *Implementing the plan.* Determining who will be involved, what resources will be assigned, how the plan will be evaluated, and what the reporting structure will be.
- *Controlling and evaluating the results.* Ensuring that the plan is proceeding according to expectations and making necessary adjustments.

6 **Discuss various ways to make plans effective.** Aids to effective planning include improving the quality of assumptions and forecasts through the following:

- *Effective communication.* As managers establish their objectives and begin to flesh out their strategic, tactical, and operational plans to achieve them, it requires constant communication and exchange of information, ideas, and feedback.
- *Quality of information.* A manager increases the probability of success by beginning planning with current, factual, and verifiable information.
- *Involvement of others.* Opening the planning process to others can result in better plans, a higher level of commitment to the plan, and the long-range development of employees who understand planning is a way of life.

Two planning tools can also improve planning efforts:

- *Management by objectives (MBO).* Mutually-agreed-on objectives are set through planning sessions involving a manager and a subordinate. Whether the objectives are achieved, how they are achieved, and what the subordinate learns through his or her achievement efforts become the foundation for evaluating the subordinate's work and for developing the subordinate's skills.
- *Linear programming.* Mathematics, equations, and formulas that factor in the effects of many variables help managers determine an optimum course of action and the best combinations of resources.

Describe the barriers to planning. There are several major barriers to effective planning:

- *Inability to plan.* Some managers lack experience or do not have the skills. These deficiencies can be overcome by training and practice.
- *Lack of commitment to the planning process.* Some managers claim they do not have time to plan; others fear failure. One way to overcome this is to make the attempt. Experience helps.
- *Inferior information.* Information that is out-of-date, of poor quality, or insufficient can be a major barrier to planning. Having an effective organizational management information system as well as prioritizing and promoting the importance of providing reliable information can help to overcome this barrier.
- *Lack of focus on the long term.* Failure to consider the long term because of emphasis on short-term problems can lead to troubles in coordinating plans and preparing for the future. A remedy can be found by including long-term planning as an element of a manager's performance appraisal.
- *Overreliance on the planning department.* Planning specialists often focus on process and lose contact with reality and with line managers. An emphasis needs to be placed on translating the planning department's output into programs for achieving specific goals at defined times.
- *Overemphasis on controllable variables.* Managers can find themselves concentrating on factors within their control and failing to consider outside factors. Variables such as future technology, economic forecasts, and expectations about government restrictions must be considered.

REVIEW QUESTIONS

1. How does planning affect the success of a business?
2. How are mission statements, goals, objectives, and plans related?
3. What are the purposes of strategic, tactical, operational, and contingency planning? In what situation would an organization use each?
4. How are strategic, tactical, and operational goals related?
5. What are the steps in a basic planning process?
6. How can managers make planning efforts more effective?
7. What are the six barriers to effective planning? How does each interfere with effective planning?

DISCUSSION QUESTIONS FOR CRITICAL THINKING

1. What specific examples can you give that demonstrate the importance of a mission statement to the success of a business and a not-for-profit organization?
2. In what ways can you apply strategic, tactical, and operational objectives and plans to your mission of gaining a college education?
3. What are "stretch goals"?
4. What evidence can you cite from your experience to prove the value of contingency planning in today's organizations?
5. Would you like to work in an organization that uses management by objectives? Why or why not?
6. Which of the barriers to successful planning have you encountered while making your plans? What was their impact on your plans?

INTERNET EXERCISES

Check the text Web site at http://plunkett.swcollege.com for updated links to the Internet Exercises.

1. Stephen R. Covey wrote the best seller, "The 7 Habits of Highly Effective People™." Franklin Planner® joined with Covey to become the Franklin Covey Company. Its mission is to inspire change by igniting the power of proven principles so that people and organizations achieve what matters most. As one way to fulfill its mission, Franklin Covey provides a mission formulator so that people can create their own Personal Mission Statement™. Answering the questions helps people to define their values, principles, and what

matters most to them in their lives. Create your Personal Mission Statement.
http://www.franklincovey.com/missionbuilder/index.html

2. Read "Lessons Learned on Tactical Planning: Implications for Procedures and Training" prepared by the U. S. Army Research Institute for the Behavioral and Social Sciences. This information was collected based on combat situations such as Desert Storm and the Arab–Israeli conflict, as well as documented observations from the Combat Training Centers (CTCs), interviews with battalion commanders, and samples of job performance in both laboratories and classrooms. "The review's purpose was to enhance the overall quality of the tactical planning and estimating process by identifying ways to improve its use in training and in practice."

   Use this textbook to explain the purpose of tactical planning. Use "Lessons Learned on Tactical Planning" to explain the most effective way to strengthen the planning and estimating process and to explain the meaning of enhancing planning quality. What did the report find about contingency planning? Compare military and civilian tactical planning.
   http://207.133.209.51/lesslear.htm

3. Read Dun & Bradstreet's "Tips to Help You Create a Planning Roadmap." What are the two most commonly asked questions in business planning? List some helpful hints and guidelines to help you develop a successful strategic plan.
   http://www.dnb.com/planning/hplannin.htm

APPLICATION CASE

Mars Clings to Its Plans

The brands read like a candy Hall of Fame: Snickers, M&Ms, Milky Way, 3 Musketeers, Twix, and Skittles. With this powerful lineup of familiar brands, Mars has dominated the U.S. and the world candy markets. But for several years, Mars has been quietly, but dramatically, yielding market share in both its U.S. and Western European candy businesses. From 1993 to 1994 in the United States alone, Mars gave up 1.4 market share points in the $10 billion confectionery business. From 1991 to 1994, Mars dropped about three market share points—a lot of Snickers bars.

Yet with all of its success, why has Mars begun to fail? The most basic explanation offered is that Mars has not modified its plans—either strategic or tactical—in the face of changes in its competitive environment.

- The candy industry has experienced dramatic consolidation, with monsters such as Nestlé and Cadbury Schweppes gobbling up smaller competitors. These stronger competitors are bombarding the market with new offerings.
- Innovations in the retail and wholesale distribution chain have shifted power to the hands of big supermarket chains and discount stores. Rather than adjust policy to meet the need for lower costs and more value to the power brokers, Mars eliminated promotional money, that is, special discounts. The action not only enraged the trade giants but also reduced the trade giants' profits.
- Mars has held to its long-term plan, focusing on maximum asset utilization. Quite simply, the plan allows the sales force to sell beyond a manufacturing plant's capacity to produce—even in peak periods.
- Rather than introducing new products, Mars developed plans calling for product line extensions. The result has been additions such as Almond M&Ms, low-fat Milky Way II, and ice cream novelty knockoffs of its candy bars. **http://www.mars.com**

Questions

1. How does this case illustrate the importance of flexibility in planning? Cite an example to support your answer.
2. What does this case illustrate about the relationship of the environment to the development of plans? Cite an example to support your answer.
3. Which of the actions by Mars related to a failure to adjust strategic planning? Cite an example to support your answer.
4. Which of the actions by Mars related to a failure to adjust tactical planning? Cite an example to support your answer.

Source: Bill Saporito, "The Eclipse of Mars," *Fortune* (28 November 1994), pp. 82–92.

VIDEO CASE

Kropf Fruit Company: A Study in Planning

Kropf Fruit Company is a family-owned business consisting of orchards, storage, and packing facilities. In the early 1990s, the owners of Kropf faced a critical decision. Changing market conditions favored large fruit processors over medium-sized processors like Kropf. This trend resulted from a consolidation in the grocery store industry. As a result, the owners of Kropf were left with two strategic options: remain a medium-sized processor, or expand and become a major player. Remaining a medium-sized processor meant that the company would continue to face unfavorable market conditions and that some of the young family members might not have a future in the business. Becoming a major player involved risk, but would allow the company to compete with other large growers and processors for major grocery store accounts.

The owners of Kropf decided to expand, but only within the parameters of carefully developed strategic and operational plans and clearly articulated goals. The plans were developed after the owners considered the strengths and weaknesses of the company along with the opportunities and threats in the firm's business environment. During the planning process, the owners also remained open to suggestions from their growers, customers, employees, and other stakeholders. In the end, the company's strategic and operational plans represented a thoughtful analysis of what Kropf needed to do to remain competitive in its business environment today and in the future.

The expansion has been successful, although the owners of Kropf have worked long and hard and the firm has suffered some growing pains. The company has learned that its competitive landscape is in a constant state of change, and that a willingness to adjust to change is a competitive necessity. Growth has provided the company access to some of the country's major grocery store chains and other new markets that are developing. A constant challenge has been developing short-term operational plans that adequately support the longer-term strategic plan. The owners of Kropf have found that communication between the company and its stakeholders is a critical step toward working out any difficulties. At this point, the owners of Kropf are satisfied with their expansion efforts. They are also convinced that both strategic and operational planning have been instrumental in their success.

http://www.kropf-inc.com

For Discussion:

1. For Kropf, has the process of planning forced the company to focus on "forward thinking"? If so, provide an example from the video that illustrates this point.
2. Who initiated the planning process at Kropf? Was planning something that the owners resisted, or did they embrace planning and view it as a potentially vital management technique?
3. Describe how Kropf has used both strategic and operational planning to achieve business success.
4. If the owners of Kropf had not developed strategic and operational plans, do you believe that their expansion effort would have been as successful? Why or why not?

Strategic Planning and Strategic Management

KEY TERMS

analyzer strategy
Boston Consulting Group (BCG) Growth-Share Matrix
business-level strategy
corporate-level strategy
cost-leadership strategy
defender strategy
differentiation strategy
distinctive competitive advantage
diversification strategy
focus strategy
functional-level strategy
grand strategy
growth strategy
horizontal integration
integration strategy
portfolio strategy
prospector strategy
reactor strategy
resource deployment
retrenchment strategy
situation analysis
stability strategy
strategic business unit (SBU)
strategic management
strategic planning
strategy formulation
strategy implementation
vertical integration

LEARNING OBJECTIVES

After studying this chapter, you should be able to

1. Describe the nature of strategic planning and strategic management
2. Distinguish between strategy formulation and strategy implementation
3. Explain the steps involved in the strategic planning process
4. Explain the importance of assessing the internal and external environments as a basis for strategic planning
5. Identify the sources and kinds of information required in the strategic planning process
6. Describe the factors involved in strategy implementation
7. Explain the formulation of corporate-level strategy, business-level strategy, and functional-level strategy

MANAGEMENT IN ACTION

Harley-Davidson's Strategic Evolution

"Harley-Davidson has surpassed the premier franchise elevation and has achieved icon status. After all, how many other brand names will you see tattooed on consumers' bodies? The company is selling much more than motorcycles—it is selling a life experience, freedom, adventure, and the pride of owning an American legend" (Hanks, 2000).

Since it began in 1903 as a producer of motorized bicycles, Milwaukee-based Harley-Davidson has been known for building rugged, durable, and distinctly American motorized two-wheeled transport and has become an American legend in the process. It has worldwide appeal; its largest export markets include Canada, Germany, Australia, and Japan. The company has evolved from a cash-strapped family venture (William Harley and the Davidsons) to a multinational provider of recreational vehicles (campers and golf carts), brand name collectibles and clothing, and motorcycles.

Throughout its almost 100 years, Harley-Davidson has met a number of challenges and taken advantage of many opportunities that have allowed it to survive as the only American manufacturer of motorcycles. Its early years were marked by rapid growth because its products were more rugged and dependable than its competitors'. With little advertising but a strong presence in motor sport events such as races and hill climbs, Harley-Davidson motorcycles outperformed the competition. During the 1920s exports through agents began to Europe and Japan while dealerships grew steadily throughout the United States. By the early 1930s about two-thirds of all motorcycles registered in the United States were Harley-Davidson motorcycles.

The company's first major crisis came during the Great Depression of the 1930s. Production fell steadily because of the decline in demand for its heavy, large, and increasingly expensive models and because of competition provided by the Indian Company's motorcycles, which were faster and lighter. Harley-Davidson was producing what it wanted to, not what a new generation of customers wanted to buy. When it cut production to 9,000 motorcycles in 1932, employees earning $100 or more per week took a 10 percent pay cut and the founding members cut their salaries by 50 percent. Fortunately, the company had invested in research and development for a sportier, faster model, which it did not introduce until 1936. The new model was an instant hit with customers and dealers and was thoroughly up-to-date in engine design and performance characteristics. The company's financial salvation, however, actually came with the beginning of World War II. By the late 1930s it was supplying thousands of motorcycles to Great Britain, Canada, and, by 1942, to the U.S. Army.

Following the war, Harley-Davidson faced a second crisis: the challenge of the sportier, sleeker, cheaper, and faster designs imported from Great Britain and Japan. Harley-Davidson finally started to listen to its dealers, salespeople, and customers. They were telling the company to expand the motorcycle line to include models for the first-time

Evolving since its inception in 1903, Harley-Davidson, Inc., achieved record sales and earning in 2000.

rider, the off-road racer, and the urban commuter. Urgently in need of funds for R&D and more modern production facilities, the families were forced to sell a minority interest in the company to the public. While it constructed a new factory in Wauwatosa, Wisconsin, in 1947, Harley-Davidson was losing market share. By the mid-1950s, foreign imports had captured over 40 percent of the American motorcycle market.

The company's immediate response was to move down-market quickly with the purchase of 50 percent of the Italian motorcycle maker Aeronautica Macchi; Aermacchi Harley-Davidson was born. It placed the Harley-Davidson logo on a variety of inexpensive small and midsize bikes made in Italy; and it bought the time the company needed to develop its own new models. Throughout the 1950s extensive research and development took place, leading to the introduction of a full line of bikes by 1960—from the beginner's moped to full-size, high-speed luxury bikes priced at more than $12,000. In 1962 its growing use of fiberglass prompted Harley-Davidson to purchase a fiberglass company and form its Tomahawk Division. It branched out to making leisure products like golf carts and utility delivery vehicles. By the end of the 1960s, the company faced severe financial problems and had a desperate need for a cash-rich partner. It merged with American Machine and Foundry Company (AMF), which provided the needed capital and new production facilities in York, Pennsylvania. Throughout the 1970s production steadily increased, but the pressures behind the increases led to significant quality problems. The Japanese were offering serious challenges to Harley-Davidson in its dominant market segment—full-size, high-performance bikes.

In 1980 managers from both Harley-Davidson and AMF formed a group and bought the company. Following the U.S. presidential election, Harley managers petitioned the federal government for relief from Japanese competition through tariffs on foreign imports. A sliding scale of tariffs was granted for a period of five years, giving the company time to work out its quality problems and reduce its manufacturing costs. Harley-Davidson's management developed its now-famous triad: just-in-time delivery of needed parts and supplies, employee involvement to improve quality, and statistical process control throughout manufacturing operations. The efforts were so successful that Harley-Davidson requested that the tariffs be discontinued one year early (1987) and took the company public once again through a sale of the company's majority shares.

Major opportunities were spotted and seized during the 1980s. The company created the Harley Owners Groups (HOGS), Ladies of Harley, numerous factory-sponsored events, a museum at its York plant, and a traveling museum. It acquired the Holiday Rambler Corporation, a maker of recreational and light commercial vehicles. It aggressively pursued winning back a market it had lost: motorcycles for the California Highway Patrol (CHP).

It was successful in 1984, 1985, and 1987–1989. Most importantly, it became aware of a relatively untapped market for brand-name merchandise when it discovered a host of products using the Harley-Davidson name without the company's permission. It vigorously prosecuted these companies and began concentrating on developing its own lines and licensing others to use its name.

By 1990 the company was selling 21 models, many of which captured the feel and design elements of its famous classic models of the 1950s, 1960s, and 1970s. It introduced custom and limited edition models to celebrate various company anniversaries as well as the restoration of the Statue of Liberty and of Ellis Island. Beginning in 1991 Harley-Davidson launched successful efforts to make its dealers' showrooms more customer friendly and brighter and to provide better retail outlets for Harley-Davidson merchandise and bike accessories. It opened its first brand-specific store, selling only its own merchandise, in the same year. The Rider's Edge learn-to-ride program was launched in February 2000, aimed at broadening the market and grooming new riders. (http://www.ridersedge.com)

In a survey conducted by Harley-Davidson, 17.6% of U.S. adults, or roughly 30 million people, indicated that they are interested in owning a heavyweight motorcycle. Of those, 43% would choose a Harley and 30% would seriously consider a Harley and may consider a competitor. With a little over 200,000 units expected to ship in 2000, there is considerable room for market expansion (Hanks, 2000).

On January 18, 2000, Harley-Davidson, Inc. reported record sales and earnings. "We pride ourselves in delivering consistent financial performance while fulfilling the dreams of our customers," said Jeffrey L. Bleustein, chairman and chief executive officer of Harley-Davidson, Inc. "For the fourteenth consecutive year, Harley-Davidson's dedicated employees, dealers, and suppliers have once again made this possible." (See "Harley-Davidson Reports 14th Consecutive Record Year and Another Record Fourth Quarter," http://investor.harleydavidson.com/news/20000118-13364.cfm) ■

Sources: Vince Hanks, "Harley-Davidson Rides High," *The Motley Fool* (22 August 2000), http://www.fool.com/dripport/2000/dripport000822.htm; Thomas C. Bolfert, *The Big Book of Harley-Davidson* (Milwaukee: Harley-Davidson, Inc., 1991); Peter Henshaw, *Harley-Davidson* (Stamford, Conn.: Regency House Publishing, 1994); Anita Lienert, "Going Whole HOG," *Chicago Tribune* (31 December 1995), sec. 12, pp. 1, 5; Erick Schonfeld, "Betting on the Boomers," *Fortune* (25 December 1995), pp. 78–80, 84, 86–87.

INTRODUCTION

strategic planning
The process of creating or rewriting an organization's mission, identifying and evaluating the long-term goals and strategies to reach those goals, and determining the required resources.

http://www.harley-davidson.com

Chapter 5 introduced the basics of the planning function, examined types of goals, and defined the kinds of plans created to reach them: strategic, tactical, and operational. This chapter focuses on **strategic planning**—the process of creating or rewriting an organization's mission, identifying and evaluating the long-term goals and strategies to reach those goals, and determining the required resources. Through strategic planning, managers, their organizations, and the autonomous units or divisions of the organization identify and evaluate how they intend to effectively compete in their markets.

As this chapter's opening case points out, Harley-Davidson had to redefine its mission several times. It began as a maker of motorized bicycles. It quickly evolved into a maker of motorcycles—heavier, more powerful means of transport—as the company's capabilities improved and its customers' demands changed. It had to create long-term plans to meet its financial needs (for both survival and expansion) at several stages during its evolution into a producer of motorcycles with world-class quality for users in many different countries. It had to determine a strategy (and create new ones periodically) to expand its product line and diversify its operations.

NATURE OF STRATEGIC PLANNING AND STRATEGIC MANAGEMENT

Describe the nature of strategic planning and strategic management

strategic management
A responsibility of top management, it defines the firm's position, formulates strategies, and guides the execution of long-term organizational functions and processes.

All companies engage in strategic planning as an element of strategic management. **Strategic management** is top management's responsibility; it defines the firm's position, formulates strategies, and guides the execution of long-term organizational functions and processes. The ultimate purpose of strategic planning and strategic management is to help position the organization to achieve a superior competitive fit in its environment in order to achieve its goals (Prescott, 1986).

Companies both large and small undertake strategic planning to respond to competitors, cope with rapidly changing environments, and effectively manage their resources—all within the context of their missions (Holt, 1990). Competitors and environmental changes threatened Harley-Davidson several times. During the 1930s the company experienced a rapid decline for the types of motorcycles it manufactured. Following World War II, the products of both the British and Japanese motorcycle makers took market share away from Harley because it lacked the types of bikes customers demanded. By the 1970s the Japanese threatened Harley-Davidson again by invading its primary market for the larger and more powerful motorcycles. In each case Harley-Davidson's managers had to develop new goals and strategies and acquire additional resources to counter the threats.

With a sharp strategic focus, a company can accomplish all of its goals, a point recognized by Dan Ferguson, CEO of Newell Company. For many years the Newell Company was a tiny, relatively unknown curtain rod maker in Freeport, Illinois. Through strategic planning and management, however, Ferguson shifted the company's focus from selling one line of products to many customers to a focus of selling several different kinds of products to the inner circle of dominant national mass merchandisers—Wal-Mart, Kmart, and Target. Ferguson expanded the company through a strategy of acquiring companies making and selling products that fit within Newell's mission: "Products that are low tech, low in fashion content and low in price but high in value . . . basic products that everyone needs." The company refers to this as "Newellization—a two to three year process that turns newly acquired businesses into streamlined profitable operations." The result: Newell Company sales grew from a few million in the 1960s to nearly $2 billion in the early 1990s (Young, 1994). In March 1999, Newell Company acquired Rubbermaid Inc. and became Newell Rubbermaid.

http://www.newellrubbermaid.com

Elements of Strategic Planning

Strategic planning is designed to help managers answer critical questions in a business. These questions include:

- What is the organization's position in the marketplace?
- What does the organization want its position to be?
- What trends and changes are occurring in the marketplace?
- What are the best alternatives to help the organization achieve its goals?

The processes involved in strategic planning provide the answers through the development of a strategic plan. As Chapter 5 pointed out, a strategic plan provides the course of action (strategy) required to reach a strategic goal and identifies the resources required to do so. The strategy developed should contain four elements: scope, resource deployment, distinctive competitive advantage, and synergy (Hill and Jones, 1989).

Scope

The *scope* of a strategy specifies the position or size (number one in the world or $6 million in profits) the firm wants to achieve, given its environments. It includes the geographical markets it wants to compete in as well as the products and services it will sell. Harley-Davidson wants to compete in every industrialized nation with a variety of products, including brand-name merchandise for motorcycle enthusiasts. The fast-food giant McDonald's made a commitment to be a major retailer worldwide. "In 1988 the company had 2,600 foreign stores and $1.8 billion in overseas revenue. Six years later it [had] 4,700 stores doing $3.4 billion a year" (Serwer, 1994). Future plans call for it to increase its scope of markets until it eventually blankets the earth with golden arches.

http://www.mcdonalds.com

As a counterpoint, Tandy Corporation (now RadioShack Corporation) chose to narrow its scope. The operator of RadioShack and Computer City outlets no longer wanted to manufacture computers or operate the Incredible Universe, Video Concepts, and McDuff chains (Hammonds, 1995).

http://www.radioshackcorporation.com

© EARL & NAZIMA KOWALL/CORBIS

McDonald's strategic plan calls for an increase in the scope of its global markets.

Resource Deployment

resource deployment
Defines how the company intends to allocate its resources—material, financial, and human—to achieve its strategic goals.

Resource deployment defines how the company intends to allocate its resources—material, financial, and human—to achieve its strategic goals. To achieve its diversification and new product development goals, Harley-Davidson had to raise capital, engage in new R&D projects, acquire new companies, and build new factories. It acquired an Italian motorcycle company, a fiberglass company, and a manufacturer of recreational and light commercial vehicles.

Distinctive Competitive Advantage

distinctive competitive advantage
A unique position in relationship to competition.

http://www.hog.com

As discussed in Chapter 4, a firm's core competencies—what it knows and what it does best—gives it a **distinctive competitive advantage**, a unique position in relationship to its competition. As Harley-Davidson pursued its strategic plans, it never lost sight of its core expertise and the reasons for its considerable reputation. What it has always done best is to build the big bikes, those with the look, feel, power, and performance to satisfy the dedicated HOG member, whether on a hill climb, cross-country race, or cross-town joyride. It has maintained several competitive advantages over its rivals. Its primary products are distinctly American—burly, big, rugged—and recognized as classics around the world; its appeals are to freedom, individuality, and nostalgia (Lienert, 1995).

Customer-driven companies find out what customers value, align it with their core competencies, and thrive on it; others don't. For example (Treacy and Wearsema, 1995):

http://www.hertz.com

http://www.fedex.com

- Why does it take only a few minutes and no paperwork to pick up or drop off a rental car at Hertz but three times as long and several forms to check into some hotels?
- Why can FedEx "absolutely, positively" deliver a package overnight but several major airlines can't take off or land on schedule?

http://www.landsend.com

- Why does Lands' End remember your last order and your family members' sizes but after ten years of membership you are still being solicited for membership by your credit-card company?

Instead of trying to be all things to all people, successful companies focus on their competitive edge.

Synergy

As discussed in Chapter 2, *synergy* is the increased effectiveness that results from combined action or cooperation. It is sometimes described as the 2 + 2 = 5 effect because the result of a synergistic partnership actually exceeds the sum of the production each partner can achieve when acting alone. Harley-Davidson's creation of its Italian subsidiary—Aermacchi Harley-Davidson—gave it instant access to R&D and manufacturing facilities for making mopeds, motorbikes, and lightweight motorcycles. Synergy occurs when the parts of a single organization or two separate organizations interact, draw on each other's strengths, and produce a joint effort greater than the sum of the parts acting alone can achieve. With synergy, companies can achieve a special advantage in the areas of market share, technology application, cost reduction, or management skill (Daft, 1994).

http://www.ibm.com

For example, IBM is attempting to develop synergy between computer marketing and software design with its acquisition of Lotus Development Corporation. Although IBM is a large manufacturer of computer software, the bulk of its software sales are for large mainframe computers that are falling out of favor with business customers. Lotus, on the other hand, has a history of developing software products for personal computers that are revolutionary but, because of weak marketing, have had limited commercial success. The hoped-for outcome: a global marketing force behind dynamic product design.

http://www.lotus.com

http://www.conveniencekits.com

Sometimes synergy also can be obtained by creating solid customer-supplier relationships between large and small companies. Convenience Kits International, an eight-employee company in Cedarhurst, New York, designs and produces travel kits that include brand-name health and beauty aids for mass merchants, including Wal-Mart. Synergy is created because Convenience Kits relieves the mass merchandisers from having to design and produce the kits, as well as purchase the health and beauty products from other vendors (Buss, 1994).

Responsibility for Strategic Planning

Just who is responsible for strategic planning depends on the organization. As mentioned in Chapter 5, some companies, like General Motors, hire strategic planning experts and have strategic planning departments. Most often, however, the responsibility for strategic planning belongs to those members of top management who lead the organization's product divisions and regions.

The core group of strategic planners usually includes the senior executives—chief executive officer, division chiefs, and chief financial officer. Increasingly, though, large organizations, such as the pharmaceutical maker SmithKline Beecham, Xerox, the insurer USAA, and Pepsico, want their middle- and lower-level line managers to think and act strategically (Garvin, 1995). They encourage managers at all levels to take the long-term view about where their parts of the organization are going, what major changes will likely occur, and which major decisions will have to be made now to achieve their organization's long-term goals. By encouraging lower-level managers to think and act strategically (it is a significant part of their evaluations), the company not only develops a unified plan but develops its managers (Garvin, 1995). Figure 6.1 presents characteristics of successful strategic managers.

2

Distinguish between strategy formulation and strategy implementation

strategy formulation *The planning and decision making that goes into developing the company's strategic goals and plans, including assessing the environments, analyzing core competencies, and creating goals and plans.*

strategy implementation *The means associated with executing the strategic plan. These include creating teams, adapting new technologies, focusing on processes rather than functions, facilitating communications, offering incentives, and making structural changes.*

Strategy Formulation Versus Strategy Implementation

Another important element in understanding the nature of strategic planning is recognizing the difference between strategy formulation and implementation. **Strategy formulation** includes the planning and decision making that goes into developing the company's strategic goals and plans. It includes assessing the environments, analyzing core competencies, and creating goals and plans. On the other hand, **strategy implementation** refers to means associated with executing the strategic plan. These include creating teams, adapting new technologies, focusing on processes rather than functions, facilitating communications, offering incentives, and making structural changes (Garvin, 1995). Both of these concepts are discussed in more detail later in this chapter.

Levels of Strategy

A final aspect concerned with the nature of strategic planning involves the levels of strategy. As highlighted in Figure 6.2, managers think in terms of three strategy levels: corporate, business, and functional.

Corporate-Level Strategy

corporate-level strategy *Answers the questions: "What business are we in?" and "What business should we be in?"*

The purpose of **corporate-level strategy** is to answer two questions posed earlier: "What business are we in?" and "What business should we be in?" The answers help to chart a long-term course for the entire organization. Harley-Davidson has asked and answered these questions many times. The answers have moved the

FIGURE 6.1 *Characteristics of successful strategic managers*

1. **Well informed.** They use a wide range of information sources to keep in touch with activities throughout the organization, and they use information to make more effective decisions.
2. **Skill at focusing their time and energy.** They delegate effectively and know how to protect their time, yet they know when it is important to make a decision or take action themselves.
3. **Good at building consensus.** They are sensitive to relationships in the organization's hierarchy, and they know how to build consensus for their ideas and form coalitions for getting their plans accomplished.
4. **Good at creating contingency plans.** They know how to adapt their goals to changing conditions and constantly monitor for changes in the environments.
5. **Accomplished at simplifying the process.** They recognize the difficulty in trying to accomplish complex goals, so they try to simplify the process by dividing objectives into smaller, more easily accomplished parts.

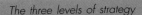

FIGURE 6.2 *The three levels of strategy*

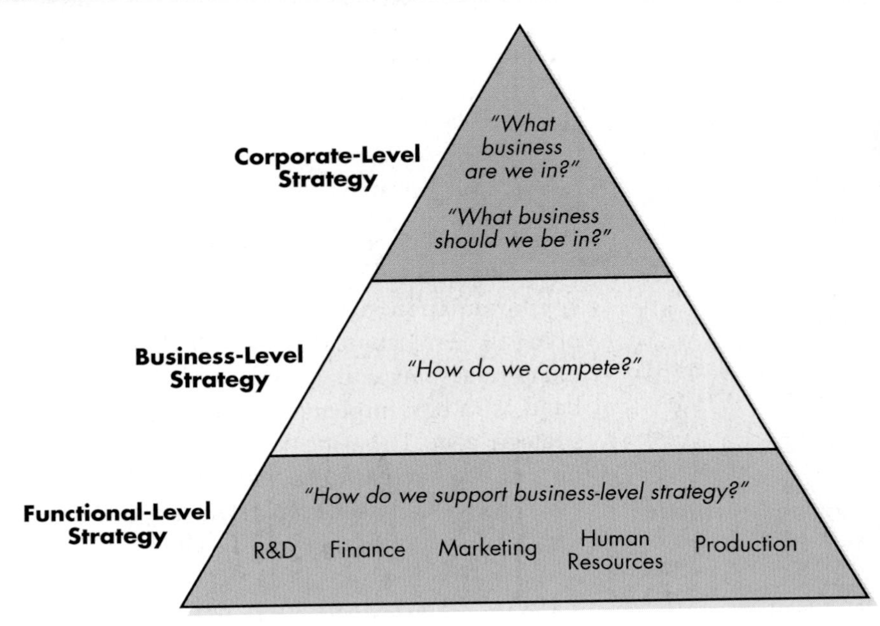

company from motorbikes to motorcycles; expanded product offerings to include recreational, light commercial, and utility vehicles; led the company to create a variety of accessories for bikers, including its MotorClothes line; and established its own brand-specific retail outlets and online store for marketing brand-name merchandise.

http://roadstore.harley-davidson.com

When founded, McDonald's saw itself as a drive-in pioneer, specializing in three main products: hamburgers, fries, and soft drinks. It set out to become the country's biggest and most successful purveyor of these commodities. The next time they asked the questions, top management saw the company differently: "We are in the fast-food business." With this redefinition of its mission, a change in direction took place. McDonald's then saw itself as a purveyor of breakfast, lunch, and dinner and of Egg McMuffins, salads, fish, and chicken. Today McDonald's identifies itself as a service business—a purveyor of smiles; a purveyor of family dining; and a provider of clean, family-friendly, customer-pleasing facilities. As one financial analyst has noted, "McDonald's is arguably the most awesome service machine on the planet" (Serwer, 1994).

Small companies face the same questions as do large ones. Veda International, an Alexandria, Virginia, maker of flight simulators, had focused its energies on serving commercial customers—American Airlines, Southwest, and so on. In exploring the question "What business should we be in?," Veda International decided to branch into the consumer market by developing a flight simulator that could be sold to amusement parks. This decision opened a new market with tremendous growth potential (Gnoffe, 1992). Veda merged with Calspan in 1997 to become Veridian.

http://www.veridian.com

Business-Level Strategy

business-level strategy
Answers the question, "How do we compete?" It focuses on how each product line or business unit within an organization competes for customers.

A **business-level strategy** answers the question, "How do we compete?" It focuses on how each product line or business unit within an organization competes for customers. The decisions at this level determine how much will be spent on such activities as advertising and product research and development, what equipment and facilities will be needed and how they will be used, and whether to expand or contract existing product lines. As Harley-Davidson began to use more fiberglass in the manufacture of its products, it expanded into fiberglass manufacturing with the acquisition of a small company. It decided to make snowmobiles in the 1970s but abandoned the business after several years of disappointing results (Bolfert, 1991).

Functional-Level Strategy

functional-level strategy
Focuses on the major activities of the company: human resources management, research and development, marketing, finance, and production.

http://www.harley-davidson.com/experience/events/daytona_01/index.asp

http://www.iflyswa.com

http://www.littlecaesars.com

The strategy concern for major functional departments is "How can we best support the business-level strategy?" **Functional-level strategy** focuses on the major activities of the company: human resources management, research and development, marketing, finance, and production. At Harley-Davidson, marketing focuses on sponsoring and participating in regular promotional activities—motorcycle racing, hill climbs, HOG and Ladies of Harley events, cross-country runs, and exhibitions such as the annual Daytona Beach, Florida, assembly of bikers and enthusiasts from around the world. It spends more on sponsoring racing and promotional events and activities each year than it does on advertising (Henshaw, 1994).

To compete successfully with frequent-flyer programs at other airlines, Southwest Airlines' functional-level marketing strategy called for a pricing incentive for consumers. In addition to a frequent-flyer program, Southwest created Friends Fly Free: for each round-trip ticket purchased at regular full fare at least one day before departure, a ticket holder's friend flies free (Miller, 1995). Little Caesars Pizza provides another example. As it continues to battle Domino's and Pizza Hut for market share, its marketing strategy evolved to embrace home delivery—not as an innovation, but in an attempt to catch up to its competitors (Zimmerman, 1995).

STRATEGIC PLANNING PROCESS

Explain the steps involved in the strategic planning process

At all levels in an organization, the strategic planning process can be divided into several steps, as shown in Figure 6.3. For new ventures, strategic planning begins with the creation of a mission statement and goals. This is the first step (1) shown in Figure 6.3. For ongoing ventures, strategic planning requires managers to continually (2) analyze the internal and external environments by assessing strengths, weaknesses, opportunities, and threats; (3) reassess the organization's mission statement, goals, and strategies for continued relevance, making adjustments as necessary; (4) formulate a strategic plan containing goals, strategies, and resources; (5) implement the strategy or strategies; and (6) monitor and evaluate the results.

Creating a Mission Statement and Goals

The first step for a new enterprise or one considering a total redefinition of itself is to create a mission statement and strategic goals. When Harley-Davidson began in 1903, it had as its mission the building of rugged, sturdy, and dependable

FIGURE 6.3 The strategic planning process

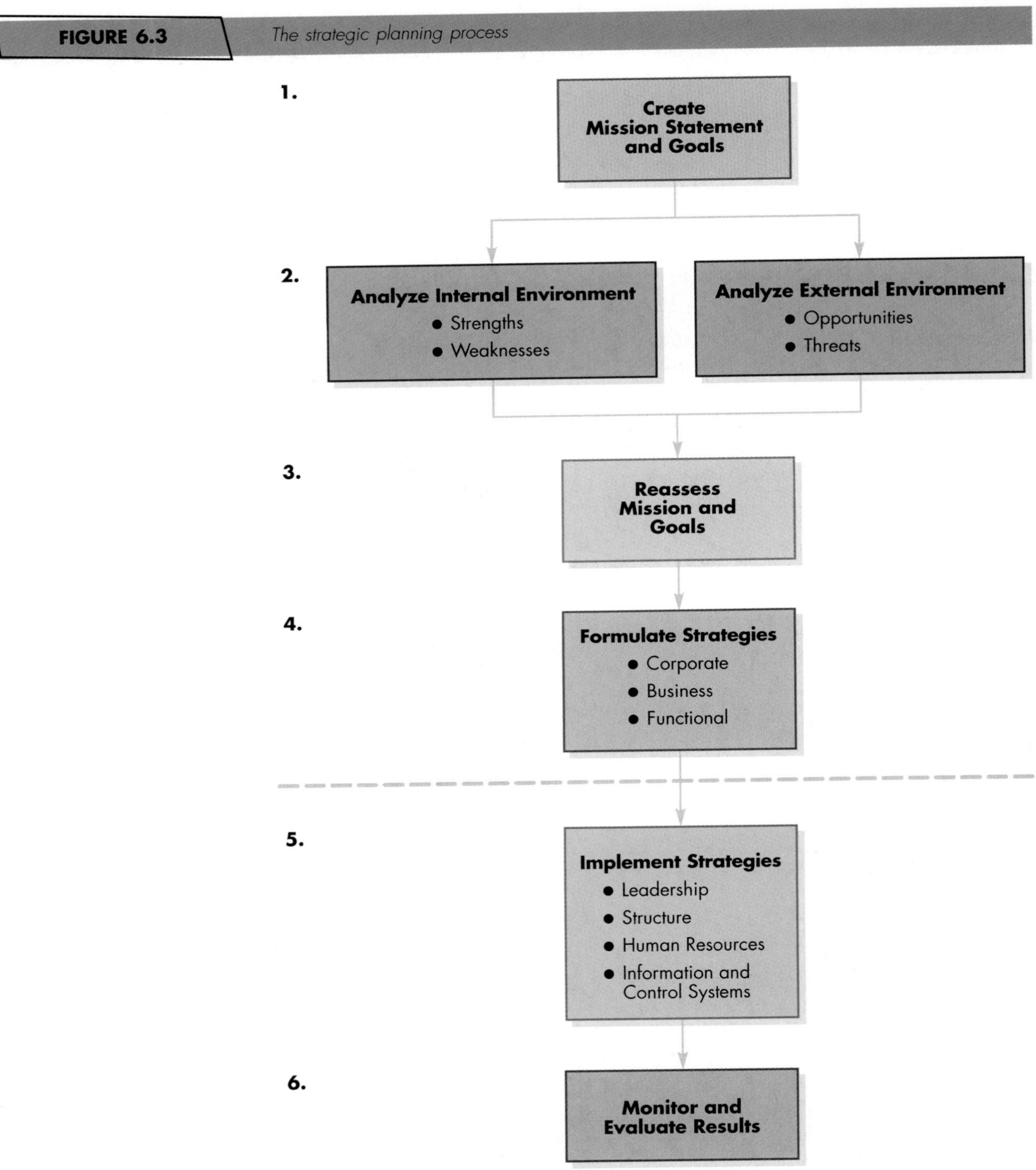

motorized bicycles that could handle rough weather and unpaved roads. As the company developed its engines and had to build progressively heavier and sturdier frames to support them, Harley-Davidson realized that it was moving into a totally different market niche—the one for motorcycles. It rewrote its mission statement to include this move up-market and has done so several times with its moves into recreational vehicles, light utility and commercial vehicles, and retailing of brand-name merchandise.

Explain the importance of assessing the internal and external environments as a basis for strategic planning

situation analysis
A search for strengths and weaknesses and opportunities and threats.

Analyzing the Internal and External Environments

In executing this step, strategic planners in established companies scan their internal and external environments (the subjects of Chapter 4). They perform a **situation analysis**—a search for strengths and weaknesses (primarily the result of the internal environment) and opportunities and threats (primarily due to factors in the external environment). This process is often called a *SWOT* analysis. Planners can use the results obtained to reassess the company's mission statement for its continued relevancy and to develop a strategic plan.

5

Identify the sources and kinds of information required in the strategic planning process

Sources of Information

Planners can gather external information about threats and opportunities from customers, suppliers, partners, government reports, consultants, trade and professional journals, and industry associations. Much of this information is available on the Internet. This chapter's Managing Technology feature explains Internet addresses. Planners can gather information about internal strengths and weaknesses through financial statements and analyses, employee surveys, progress reports on ongoing operations, and statistical analyses of data on such areas as employee turnover and safety. Often by regularly interacting with and observing others, strategic planners can build an adequate assessment of their organization's strengths and weaknesses. Managers often use the expertise of outside consultants to help them obtain as well as analyze the information gathered from both environments.

Internal Strengths and Weaknesses

An organization's internal *strengths*—its core competencies and intellectual capital—are factors the company can build on to reach its goals. *Weaknesses* inhibit performance capabilities; they are gaps in managers' or organizations' experience and

MANAGING TECHNOLOGY
URL or Internet Address

Sites on the Internet can be found either through their Web addresses or by using what are known as search engines, which locate Web sites by using keywords. Surfing is just moving from place to place seeing what you can find. You surf (explore or browse or navigate) the Web (graphical, multimedia portion of the Internet) using software called a "browser" (such as Microsoft Internet Explorer).

Across the top of the browser screen you will find many icons as well as an address line. The address line is where you can type in the address for a Web site you would like to visit. URL, uniform resource locator, is the Internet equivalent of an address. That portion of the URL before the first colon (usually http) specifies the address method. The http, HyperText Transport Protocol, tells the software to expect an http file. The portion following the double forward slashes (//) is the server (host computer) address, or the domain name. It has at least two parts, separated by dots, also known as periods. Following the domain name is a directory containing the resources for a particular topic. The html, HyperText Markup Language, is the language used to create most Web documents. It is found at the end of many URLs and specifies the file that is retrieved from the server.

expertise and the unavailability of needed resources. Plans should be designed to compensate for them if they cannot be eliminated. In determining strengths and weaknesses, a company's strategic planners should consider the following:

- *Management factors*—management structure and managers' philosophies and capabilities
- *Marketing factors*—distribution channels, market share, competitive challenges, levels of customer service and satisfaction
- *Production factors*—manufacturing efficiency, levels of obsolescence for equipment and technology, production capacity, and quality control
- *Research factors*—research and development capabilities, new product development, consumer and market research, and the prospects for technological innovation
- *Human resource factors*—the quality and depth of employee talent and expertise, degrees of employee job satisfaction and morale, turnover rate, and union status
- *Financial factors*—profit margin, return on investment, and various financial ratios

Figure 6.4 shows a sample of a SWOT analysis constructed for Harley-Davidson through the use of references cited in the Management in Action feature. It identifies various threats and opportunities that, when combined with an analysis of strengths and weaknesses, serve as a basis for creating strategic plans. Harley-Davidson experienced threats from new competitors—the British and Japanese—and from changes in economic conditions, similar to those it had experienced in the 1930s. It accurately assessed the opportunities for new markets in areas where it had little or no competition—brand-name merchandise with the Harley logo and sales of products in countries with no domestic motorcycle production. It correctly

FIGURE 6.4 *SWOT analysis chart*

EXTERNAL ENVIRONMENT

OPPORTUNITIES

- Little competition in its strongest market niche
- Many untapped international markets or initial entrance can be significantly expanded

THREATS

- Lack of vehicles can lead consumers to competition
- Intensive competition in secondary markets
- Competition willing to commit significant financial resources to defend and expand markets

INTERNAL ENVIRONMENT

STRENGTHS

- Solid research capabilities in market analysis and consumer behavior
- Superior service and promotional support
- Superior global brand name recognition
- Superior brand marketing support
- Solid managers and management development programs
- Strong supplier/dealer base

WEAKNESSES

- Limited product manufacturing capability
- Inability to support dealers with enough product

addressed its quality problems in the 1970s and 1980s. It met the need for expertise down-market with the acquisition of the Italian motorcycle producer of small and mid-size motorbikes and mopeds.

As shown in Figure 6.4, Harley-Davidson has many strengths and few weaknesses. It has regularly assessed its strengths and weaknesses, building on the former by adding new accessory lines and attacking the latter by acquiring the expertise it lacked through research and development efforts and the acquisition of companies.

External Threats and Opportunities

Management's external assessment focuses on identifying both threats and opportunities. *Threats* are factors that can prevent the organization from achieving its goals. *Opportunities* are the opposite; they can help the organization achieve its goals. The following factors should be assessed:

- The threat of new competitors entering the marketplace
- The threat of substitute products
- The opportunity resulting from entering new marketplaces
- The threat or opportunity created by strategy changes of major competitors
- The threat or opportunity resulting from the potential actions and profitability of customers
- The threat or opportunity created by the actions of suppliers
- The threat or opportunity resulting from new (or abandoned) government regulations
- The threat or opportunity created by new technology
- The threat or opportunity from changes in the state of the economy

As this chapter's Management in Action feature narrates, Harley-Davidson's managers have assessed its external threats and opportunities with varying degrees of success. During its first 50 years, managers accurately predicted and responded to shifting market demand for larger, heavier two-wheeled transportation but failed to foresee the large decline in demand for these vehicles at the onset of the Great Depression of the 1930s and during the years just after World War II (Henshaw, 1994).

Reassessing the Mission Statement and Goals

In this step, management leadership is critical. As noted by management consultant Warren Bennis, "The indispensable first quality of leadership is a strongly defined purpose. When people are aligned behind that purpose, you get a powerful organization" (Loeb, 1994). The analysis of the external opportunities and threats and the internal strengths and weaknesses can produce one of two outcomes: to reaffirm the current mission statement, goals, and strategies or to lead to the formulation of new ones.

As this chapter's Management in Action feature illustrates, Harley-Davidson has repeatedly evaluated its mission over its many years. Its careful assessments have led to periodic adjustments to that mission. It has evolved from a domestic motorbike maker to an international provider of several kinds of vehicles, parts, and service along with various lines of brand-name accessories.

CEO Jan Leschly heads the international pharmaceutical maker and health-care provider SmithKline Beecham. In a 1995 roundtable discussion with other CEOs, conducted by the *Harvard Business Review*, Leschly related how his monitoring of the external environment led him to completely change his company's mission and focus (Garvin, 1995). "The customer completely changed on us," Leschly explained. In the past his business had always been physician driven. In the United States today, however, employers and insurance companies pay the bills; and in Europe, the government pays. The need to satisfy these new customers led Leschly to the powerful realization that the way his company did business had to change completely.

Under Leschly's leadership, the company shifted from autonomous, narrowly defined business units, set up to serve four separate sets of customers, to a focus on three primary areas: care delivery, care management, and care coverage. The company then defined the strategies for each area and looked into what capabilities were necessary for success. It ended up with six critical capabilities: pioneer discovery, product development, low-cost production, customer intimacy, alliance building, and continuous improvement. In January 2000, SmithKline Beecham and Glaxo Wellcome merged to form GlaxoSmithKline.

http://www.gsk.com

Formulating Strategies

Once the mission statement is reaffirmed or rewritten, goals and strategies at the corporate, business, and functional levels can be formulated. In 1999 the president of Microsoft, Steve Ballmer, reviewed its external environment and laid out some general plans to adapt its business model to the Internet age (Goldstein, 1999). He said

http://www.microsoft.com

> *Microsoft expects to evolve from a traditional software company into a service business that lets customers use its programs based on either monthly fees or usage charges. . . . The software is going to have to transform itself from a CD to a service that continually takes care of itself and updates itself.*

As Balmer explained, the transition would affect every aspect of the company. It would offer a closer relationship with Microsoft's customers. Balmer said that Microsoft would facilitate accomplishment of the new goal by becoming a very different company over the next few years.

Implementing Strategies

6 Describe the factors involved in strategy implementation

http://www.xerox.com

Once a new strategy is formulated, it must be implemented. Strategy formulation and strategy implementation are two distinct tasks. If either or both are handled incorrectly, a strategic plan will fail or at least create problems, as seen in this chapter's Ethical Management feature.

According to Xerox CEO Paul Allaire, given leadership from the top, effective implementation of any strategy relies on "a congruence [fit] among strategic direction, organizational design, staff capabilities, and the processes [information and control systems] you use to ensure that people are working together to meet the company's goals" (Garvin, 1995). Figure 6.3 on page 168 lists these in the "Implement Strategies" step as leadership, structure, human resources, and information and control systems (Galbraith and Kazanjian, 1986).

ETHICAL MANAGEMENT
Quaker State Leaves Them Crying

Quaker State Corporation, a Fortune 500 oil producer-retailer, initiated a new strategic plan focused on a number of elements. It launched new marketing and advertising campaigns for its motor oil, sold "noncore services," such as Heritage Insurance Group, and bought Specialty Oil and Slick 50, sellers of specialty oils. The strategic plan also addressed the need to consolidate and centralize its operations when Quaker State's top management "saw [its] center of gravity shifting to the Southwest."

To complete that portion of the plan, Quaker State, the pride of Oil City, Pennsylvania, announced plans to move its headquarters to Dallas. In the last 20 years, Oil City, a town of 12,000 people, has lost hundreds of jobs in almost every industry it had—banking, oil, steel, natural gas, railroad, telephone, glass—but Quaker State was considered the ultimate employer. Most everyone knew someone who worked at Quaker State at one time. Some businesses claimed 40 to 80 percent of their sales came from Quaker State employees.

1. What ethical considerations are involved in this strategic planning?
2. If you had been in Quaker State's position, would you have made the same plan? Why or why not?
3. What should Quaker State do to make its departure less painful for Oil City?

http://www.quakerstate.com

Source: Virginia S. Wiegand, "Quaker State Departure a Bitter Blow to Oil City," *Dallas Morning News* (6 June 1995), pp. 1D, 16D. Note: On 30 December 1998, Quaker State Corporation was merged into Pennzoil Products Group (Pennzoil Company's marketing, manufacturing, and fast oil change businesses) to form Pennzoil-Quaker State Company, a worldwide leader in consumer automotive products and vehicle care, http://www.quakerstate.com/resources/index/aboutqsc_index.html.

Leadership

When implementing strategy, the leadership challenge involves the ability to influence others in the organization to embrace the new strategy and adopt the behaviors needed to put it into action. All managers continually face the challenge of convincing people to accept new goals and strategies. To accomplish this, strategic planners create teams and involve lower-level managers and workers in the strategy-formulation process, thus building coalitions that will support change.

http://www.pepsico.com

President and CEO of Pepsi-Cola North America, Craig Weatherup, rates his managers by three leadership criteria: idea leadership, people leadership, and capability leadership. The first deals with "the ability to find, create, borrow, steal, or reshape ideas, especially big ideas" (Garvin, 1995). People leaders have the ability "to mobilize the troops and energize the organization, to get it moving fast and aggressively" (Garvin, 1995). The third kind of leadership refers to "a manager's ability to build and institutionalize the capabilities of people, the organization, and systems. To do that well requires a focus on core processes" (Garvin, 1995). Figure 6.5 provides managers like Craig Weatherup six principles to follow when implementing strategy.

Organizational Structure

Implementation can be assisted by change in the structure of the organization as reflected in its organizational chart. Managers can greatly facilitate the implementation of new strategies by changing reporting relationships, creating new departments or business units, and providing the opportunity for autonomous decision making. At the small Bread Loaf Construction Company in Middlebury, Vermont,

FIGURE 6.5 *Six strategy implementation principles*

The following six principles contribute to implementing a new strategic plan:

- *Build a fluid, dynamic organization.* Organizations must be able to respond to the needs for geographical flexibility. Central guidance, along with localized decision making, supports the strategic plan.
- *Create mechanisms to respond to revolutionary change.* Typically, organizations are structured to handle routine and evolutionary situations and have a hard time coping with unforeseen competition. Businesses can succeed by opening themselves to major changes and capitalizing on them.
- *Keep specialization to a minimum.* Workforce overspecialization has caused many problems in companies, including organizational inflexibility, lost identity of the end product with the consumer, and the underutilization of the capabilities of the individual. Most people value diversity; companies must find ways to provide it to maximize creativity and productivity
- *Draft the best player.* When hiring, the best all-around candidates should be selected—not necessarily the person who fits the current job requirement, but the person with the best long-term potential.
- *Develop from within; stimulate from without.* Filling positions from within produces higher morale and reinforces the company culture. External hires can be a very effective way of facing the challenge of dramatically changing an environment—bringing in people to accomplish the change when the outcome is totally new to the company
- *Encourage everyone to take full responsibility.* Many firms have failed to properly link the goals of the individual with the goals of the organization. Individual goals are linked to functional areas. Everyone must act as if he or she is responsible for everything.

Source: Reprinted from John Dupuy et al., "Learning to Manage World-Class Strategy," *Management Review*, October 1991. http://www.amanet.org.

CEO Mac McLaughlin has chosen to modify the structural core of the organization to implement new, more customer-responsive strategies. Levels of management are being eliminated and remaining managers are receiving the training necessary to become more empowered (Ehrenfeld, "The Demise," 1995).

Human Resources

http://www.starbucks.com

People are the key to implementing any decision, strategy, or plan. The CEO of Seattle-based Starbucks Corporation, Howard Schultz, has a simple philosophy about the role of human resources in implementing his plans for the gourmet coffee purveyor's expansion both at home and abroad: "I believe in the adage: 'Hire people smarter than you are and get out of their way' " (Yang, 1994). To manage his company-owned outlets, Schultz recruits experienced fast-food managers from such outlets as Taco Bell and Burger King. These store managers in turn receive and give their staffs—recruited from colleges and community groups, not high schools—"24 hours of training in coffee making and lore—key to creating the hip image and quality service that build customer loyalty" (Yang, 1994).

Information and Control Systems

Management needs to create a proper blend of information and control systems that make use of policies, procedures, rules, incentives, budget, and other financial statements to support the implementation phase. Organizational members must be rewarded for adhering to the new system and making it successful (Gupta and

http://www.amgen.com

Govindarajan, 1984). Amgen, a California-based biotechnology firm, designed new reward systems to support the company's implementation of team management that was created to replace the traditional management pyramid. Big rewards await those who perform well in teams and team members whose teams meet objectives (Ehrenfeld, "The Demise," 1995).

To implement its expansion strategies and coordinate operations, Starbucks invested in networking in-store computers. "Each night, store PCs pass information to Seattle headquarters, so planners quickly spot regional buying trends" (Yang, 1994). McDonald's relies heavily on training to get its managers, restaurant workers, and suppliers in line with corporate strategies. Its world-famous Hamburger University at the company's Oak Brook, Illinois, headquarters boasts some 50,000 graduates worldwide. "Fourteen times a year, 200 McDonald's managers with two to five years of experience arrive from 72 countries for the intensive two-week program" (Serwer, 1994). Classes are taught on such topics as team building, increasing market share, retaining staff, and getting closer to customers.

http://www.mcdonalds.com/corporate/careers/hambuniv/index.html

Monitoring and Evaluating Results

http://www.delta.com

Once the strategy is implemented, performance must be monitored and evaluated, and modifications must be made as necessary. In 1994 CEO Ronald W. Allen launched a strategic cost-cutting program—labeled Leadership 7.5—to bring Delta Air Lines, Inc. into a more competitive position against such rivals as Valujet and Southwest Airlines. His goal: "Delta would spend only 7.5 cents per airplane seat per mile of flight by June, 1997" (Greising, 1995). To execute his strategy, Allen created "11 teams and charged each with reaching broad cost-cutting goals. Among them: $400 million from marketing, $300 million from layoffs, and $310 million from onboard services" (Greising, 1995).

To assess his progress, Allen and his teams tracked the numbers related to the cost-cutting initiatives: $201 million in overall savings for the third quarter of 1995, which resulted from the elimination of over 17,000 jobs, restructuring changes, changes in routes, and reengineered processes. Still to come were hoped-for concessions from the pilots' union, which would yield another $340 million in savings. Savings of $2.1 billion were needed overall. By December 1995, Allen was halfway to his destination; he had achieved 8.4 cents per airplane seat per mile of flight (Greising, 1995).

Having examined the strategic planning process, let us take an in-depth look at strategy formulation at all three levels of a traditional organization.

FORMULATING CORPORATE-LEVEL STRATEGY

Explain the formulation of corporate-level strategy, business-level strategy, and functional-level strategy

As discussed earlier, corporate-level strategy involves determining in what business or businesses the firm expects to compete. For companies with a single market or a few closely related markets, the corporate-level strategy involves developing an overall strategy. Most large corporations, however, have complicated organizational structures with stand-alone, often unrelated, business units or divisions, each with different products, markets, and competitors. The corporate-level strategy then involves making decisions on whether to add divisions and product lines—to manage the business's *portfolio* of businesses. A discussion of both types of corporate-level strategy follows.

grand strategy
The overall framework or plan of action developed at the corporate level to achieve an organization's objectives. There are five basic grand strategies—growth, integration, diversification, retrenchment, or stability.

growth strategy
A strategy achieved internally by investing or externally by acquiring additional business units.

integration strategy
A strategy adopted when the business sees a need (1) to stabilize its supply line or reduce costs or (2) to consolidate competition.

vertical integration
Gaining ownership of resources, suppliers, or distribution systems that relate to a company's business.

http://www.tribune.com

horizontal integration
A strategy to consolidate competition by acquiring similar products or services.

Grand Strategies

A **grand strategy** is the overall framework or plan of action developed at the corporate level to achieve an organization's objectives. There are five basic grand strategies—growth, integration, diversification, retrenchment, or stability.

Growth Strategy

A **growth strategy** is adopted when the organization wants to create high levels of growth in one or more of its areas of operations or business units. Growth can be achieved internally by investing or externally by acquiring additional business units. McDonald's has an ambitious program of internal expansion by primarily targeting the international arena for future restaurant sites (Serwer, 1994). Similarly, Starbucks plans to continue its growth and made plans to add 200 new stores each year and increase sales to $1 billion by the year 2000 (Yang, 1994). Interbrew, the subject of this chapter's Global Applications feature, is expanding in leaps and bounds by acquiring brewers all over the world.

Integration Strategy

An **integration strategy** is adopted when the business sees a need (1) to stabilize its supply lines or reduce costs or (2) to consolidate competition. In the first situation the company creates a strategy of **vertical integration**—gaining ownership of resources, suppliers, or distribution systems that relate to a company's business. In 1994 the Chicago-based Tribune Company—a communications giant in newspapers, radio, and television—moved to take over the distribution of its newspapers from private contractors. This move is an example of a vertical integration strategy. **Horizontal integration**, on the other hand, is a strategy to consolidate competition by acquiring similar products or services. Cadbury's purchase of

GLOBAL APPLICATIONS
Interbrew's Springboard for Growth

Interbrew, Belgian's tradition-steeped brewer of 40 beer brands cherished by connoisseurs, faced a mature domestic market. With no room to grow at home, Interbrew's strategic plans focused on the global market. Realizing that it would need years of costly marketing to take its beers worldwide left Interbrew one strategy option—buy growth.

The initial phase of strategy implementation took place in Europe. Interbrew proceeded to buy breweries in Hungary, Croatia, Romania, and Bulgaria. Profits for Interbrew more than doubled in two years.

With cash in hand, Interbrew focused on China, Mexico, and South America. Zhujian Brewery, China's third largest brewery, became a joint venture partner. Mexico's second largest brewer, Femsa Cerveza, became a part of Interbrew's collection of assets. And Interbrew is teaming up with Quilmes Industrial, Argentina's number 1 brewer, to expand into the rapidly growing South American market. One more move turned Interbrew into the world's fourth largest brewer, up from sixteenth. Interbrew bought Canadian brewing giant John Labatt, Ltd. for $2 billion. Labatt will give Interbrew 45 percent of the Canadian market and a rapidly growing U.S. specialty beer business.

http://www.interbrew.com

Source: William C. Symonds and Linda Bernier, "A Belgian Brewer's Plans Come to a Head," *Business Week* (19 June 1995), p. 56.

Cadbury Schweppes' purchase of Dr. Pepper/7-Up and A&W Root Beer is an example of horizontal integration.

http://www.cadburyschweppes.com

Dr. Pepper/7-Up and A&W Root Beer is an example of this strategy. Cadbury decided to compete more effectively against Coca-Cola and Pepsi by concentrating on new beverage lines, the demand for which is growing faster than that for colas (Turner, 1995).

Diversification Strategy

diversification strategy *A strategy adopted if the company wants to move into new products or markets; normally achieved through the acquisition of other businesses and their brands.*

http://www.philipmorris.com

http://www.seagram.com

A **diversification strategy** is adopted if the company wants to move into new products or markets. This strategy is normally achieved through the acquisition of other businesses and their brands. Philip Morris has diversified through the purchase of food companies. Seagram, a worldwide liquor giant, quickly became a key player in the entertainment world with the purchase of MCA, which has business ownership in motion picture productions, music entertainment, television operations and production, movie theaters, theme parks, and publishing (O'Neal, Grover, and Symonds, 1995). "In 1996, MCA INC. was renamed Universal Studios, reclaiming its heritage as one of the industry's oldest and most prestigious movie studios." (See Universal History, http://www.mca.com/homepage/html/about_us.)

Retrenchment Strategy

retrenchment strategy *A strategy used to reduce the size or scope of a firm's activities by cutting back in some areas or eliminating entire businesses.*

http://www.sears.com

A **retrenchment strategy** is used to reduce the size or scope of a firm's activities by cutting back in some areas or eliminating entire businesses. Xerox and Sears have recently pursued retrenchment strategies. Xerox chose to divest itself of its real estate business ventures and focus on its core competencies. Beginning in the early 1990s, Sears has systematically eliminated virtually all of its nonretail business from its corporate family.

Stability Strategy

stability strategy *A strategy adopted when the organization wants to remain the same.*

When the organization wants to remain the same it adopts a **stability strategy**. Sometimes the reason is to have the organization grow slowly; other times such a

http://www.bankofamerica.com

strategy is adopted to recover immediately after a period of sharp growth or retrenchment. Bank of America, formerly NationsBank and North Carolina National Bank, has adopted a strategy of stability after a growth period that saw expansion to Texas and acquisition of banks in Florida and Ohio.

Portfolio Strategy

portfolio strategy
Determines the mix of business units and product lines that will provide a maximum competitive advantage.

strategic business units (SBUs)
Autonomous businesses with their own identities but operating within the framework of one organization.

http://www.fortunebrands.com

Once the managers of a large diversified organization decide on a grand strategy, they develop a portfolio strategy. A **portfolio strategy** determines the mix of business units and product lines that will provide a maximum competitive advantage. Developing a portfolio begins by identifying **strategic business units (SBUs)**, autonomous businesses with their own identities but operating within the framework of one organization. The SBU concept originated at General Electric in the 1970s to provide managers with a framework for directing GE's many diverse businesses. Typically, an SBU has its own product lines, markets, and competitors.

Fortune Brands, formerly known as American Brands, serves as a case in point. Growing from its roots as the American Tobacco Company, Fortune Brands is now a collection of several companies—autonomous divisions totally unrelated to its original business: Jim Beam bourbon, Moen faucets, DeKuyper cordials, Titleist golf equipment, Day-Timer date calendars, and Master Lock's family of security devices. A brand manager runs each under the direction of the chairman and CEO (Oliver, 1995). After a remarkably productive five-year tenure as chairman and chief executive officer, Tom Hays retired at the end of 1999. (See Chairman's Letter, http://www.ambrands.com.) Norm Wesley followed him as chairman of the board and chief executive officer.

Figure 6.6 illustrates another example of a portfolio of strategic business units, MCA's 1995 business portfolio. Notice that each piece of the puzzle represents a part of the total package of business—a broad-based entertainment company—and a part of the grand diversification strategy at Seagrams.

Managing a portfolio of business units is like managing a portfolio of unrelated investments, such as stocks, bonds, and real estate. Each SBU must be continually evaluated as to its performance and relevance to the overall grand strategy. American Brands sold its domestic tobacco business because of threats from the U.S. environment, but kept its European tobacco operations. It sold Franklin Life Insurance because that company was underperforming. A technique often employed by organizations to help them evaluate their portfolios is the **Boston Consulting Group (BCG) Growth-Share Matrix** shown in Figure 6.7.

Boston Consulting Group (BCG) Growth-Share Matrix
A technique often employed by organizations to help them evaluate their portfolios.

http://www.bcg.com

http://www.bcg.com/this_is_bcg/mission/growth_share_matrix.asp

Figure 6.7 shows the location of six SBUs (A to F) in four quadrants of a grid. (To explain each quadrant, one or more of MCA's six 1995 SBUs is used and labeled A through F.) The sales revenue produced by each SBU in relation to the organization's other SBUs is represented by the size of the circle around it. The matrix combines growth rates and market share dimensions to identify four types of strategic business units:

1. *Stars.* Business B (Music Entertainment) is a star because it has a large market share in a rapidly growing industry. The star is important because it has potential to grow and it will generate profits.

FIGURE 6.6 MCA's portfolio of businesses

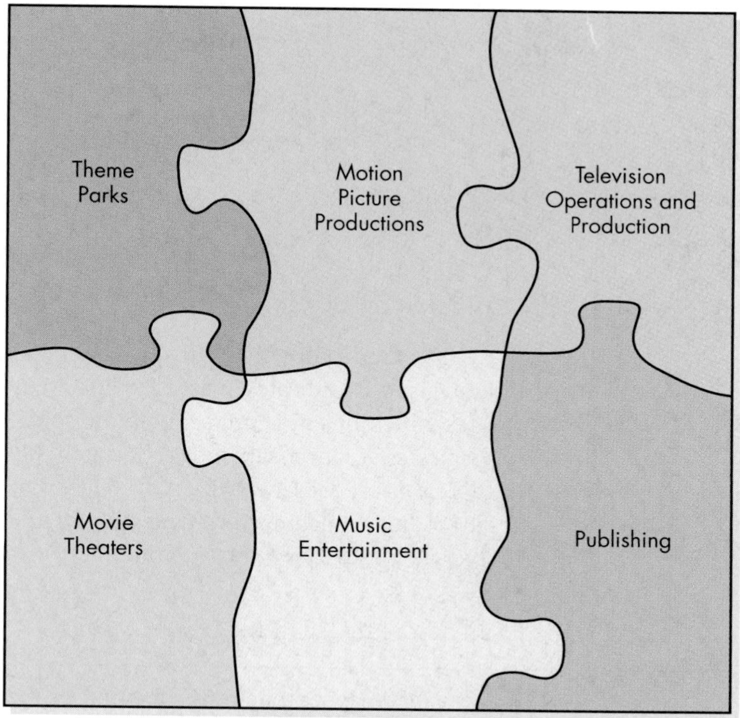

FIGURE 6.7 BCG Growth-Share Matrix

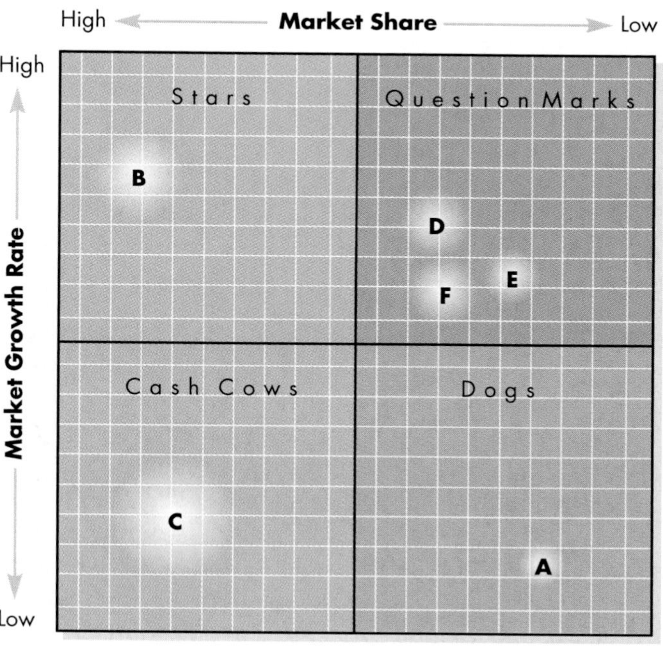

2. *Cash Cows.* The cash cow, Business C (Motion Picture Productions), has a large market share in a stable, slow-growth industry. Because the industry is in slow growth, the business unit can maintain its position with little or no investment. It is in a position to generate cash for the expansion or acquisition of additional SBUs.
3. *Question Marks.* The question marks, Businesses D, E, and F (Television Operations and Production, Theme Parks, and Movie Theaters), have small shares of the market in rapidly expanding industries. Question marks are risky. A business in this category could become a star, but it could also fail.
4. *Dogs.* The dog, Business A (Publishing), is a business with small market shares in a low-growth or declining industry. Notice that A also has the smallest revenue relative to any of the other businesses in the portfolio.

The BCG Growth-Share Matrix provides a valuable tool for corporate-level strategists. It indicates where expansion should and can take place. It also indicates which business units should be sold off. As of January 2001, the portfolio of businesses at Universal Studios (formerly MCA) included Universal Pictures, Universal Television & Networks Group, Universal Studios Recreation Group, and Universal Studios Consumer Products Group. (See About Universal Studios—Company Overview http://www.mca.com/homepage/html/about_us.)

FORMULATING BUSINESS-LEVEL STRATEGY

A business-level strategy is the strategy managers formulate for each SBU (or for the firm itself if it is a single-product business), defining how it intends to compete. The many possible strategies available can be grouped as either adaptive strategies or competitive strategies.

Adaptive Strategies

The philosophy behind the adaptive strategies developed by Raymond Miles and Charles Snow (1978) is that a business's strategy should be a fit between the internal characteristics of the company—its core competencies—and the external environment. The four adaptive strategies include prospector, defender, analyzer, and reactor. Figure 6.8 shows the relationship between the four strategies, the organization's characteristics, and the external environment.

Prospector Strategy

prospector strategy
A strategy based on innovation, taking risks, seeking out opportunities, and expansion.

http://www.3m.com

http://www.zhenbeauty.com

The **prospector strategy** is one based on innovation, taking risks, seeking out opportunities, and expansion. This strategy is appropriate in a dynamic and fast-growing climate, if the organization is flexible, innovative, and creative. The prospector strategy has been a good one for 3M Company, maker of Scotch brand products. It has led to cutting-edge products, new applications of technology, and market leadership. It has also been a good choice for small, aggressive Zhen Corporation. Seeing an opportunity in developing cosmetics for Asian women, Zhen outmaneuvered Revlon and Estée Lauder for contracts with national retail leader Nordstrom's (Berss, 1995). In 1996 Harley-Davidson announced plans for a new motorcycle factory in Missouri to double its production by 2003.

FIGURE 6.8 *Relationship between adaptive strategies, organizational characteristics, and the external environment*

Strategies	External Environment	Organizational Characteristics
Prospector: Innovate. Find new market opportunities. Grow. Take risks.	Dynamic, growing	Creativity, innovation, flexibility, decentralization
Defender: Protect turf. Hold current market. Retrench.	Stable	Tight control, centralization, product efficiency, low overhead
Analyzer: Maintain current market. Innovate moderately.	Moderate change	Tight control, flexibility, efficient production, creativity
Reactor: No clear strategy. React to specific conditions. Drift.	Any condition	No clear organizational approach, depends on current needs

Source: Based on Raymond E. Miles, Charles C. Snow, Alan D. Meyer, and Henry L. Coleman, Jr., "Organizational Strategy, Structure, and Process," *Academy of Management Review* 3 (1978): 546–562. Reproduced with permission of Academy of Management in textbook format via Copyright Clearance Center.

defender strategy
A strategy based on holding current market share or even retrenching.

Defender Strategy

The **defender strategy** is based on holding current market share or even retrenching. It is almost the exact opposite of the prospector strategy. The defender strategy is appropriate in a stable environment if the organization is concerned with internal efficiency to produce reliable products for regular customers. Exxon-Mobil and Royal Dutch/Shell use the defender strategy. Other examples of the defender strategy can be seen in independent hardware, toy, and bookstores as large chains such as Home Depot, Toys "R" Us, and Barnes & Noble invade their territories. The independents are banding together in purchasing and strategy cooperatives to defend their markets (Ehrenfeld, "The New," 1995).

analyzer strategy
An attempt to maintain the current market share while innovating in some markets.

Analyzer Strategy

With the **analyzer strategy** an organization attempts to maintain the current market share while innovating in some markets. It asks managers to perform a kind of balancing act: maintaining the organization in some markets while being aggressive in others. This strategy is appropriate in an environment in which growth is possible, and the organization is both efficient and creative.

Examples of analyzers include Frito Lay and Anheuser-Busch. Each has a reliable product base yet innovatively brings new products to the market. Tecnol Medical Products, a small Texas-based supplier of medical supplies, has used the analyzer strategy successfully. While maintaining its presence in the medical supply market, it seized on a wave of fear over the transmission of the AIDS virus and other diseases to create a line of specialty masks that shield health-care workers from infection. It now has become the top mask supplier to U.S. hospitals—surpassing Johnson and Johnson (Woodruff, 1994).

Reactor Strategy

reactor strategy
An organization adopting this strategy could be said to have no strategy; it responds to environmental threats as they occur and has no clear sense of internal direction.

An organization adopting the **reactor strategy** could be said to have no strategy. Rather than formulating a strategy to fit a specific environment, reactors respond to environmental threats as they occur. With no clear sense of internal direction, a reactor is doomed until it changes strategies—it simply flails away.

Many companies that fail do so because they follow a reactor strategy. Without a strategy, companies fall victim to their competitors and to market changes. They cling to past practices too long, believing that those that worked well in the past will continue to do so. They fail to regularly analyze their environments and reassess their missions, goals, and strategies, until changing customer demands overwhelm them. Northwest Airlines got into financial trouble because it was constantly reacting to its competitors' strategies and had none of its own.

Competitive Strategies

The second set of business-level strategies an organization can initiate—the competitive strategies—were developed by author and management professor Michael Porter (1998). Whereas adaptive strategies are based on fit between the organization and its environment, competitive strategies are dictated by how the organization can best compete based on its core competencies—internal skills, resources, and philosophies. The three potential strategies are differentiation, cost-leadership, and focus (Porter, 1998). Figure 6.9 relates these strategies to the organizational characteristics appropriate for their adoption.

FIGURE 6.9 *Relationship of competitive strategies to organizational characteristics*

Strategy	Commonly Required Skills and Resources	Common Organizational Requirements
Differentiation	Strong marketing abilities. Product engineering. Creative flair. Strong capability in basic research. Corporate reputation for quality or technological leadership.	Strong coordination among functions in R&D, product development, and marketing. Subjective measurement and incentives instead of quantitative measures. Amenities to attract highly skilled labor, scientists, or creative people.
Cost-Leadership	Sustained capital investment and access to capital. Process-engineering skills. Intense supervision of labor. Products designed for ease in manufacture. Low-cost distribution system.	Tight cost control. Frequent, detailed control reports. Structured organization and responsibilities. Incentives based on meeting strict quantitative targets.
Focus	Combination of the above policies directed at a particular strategic target.	Combination of the above policies directed at a particular strategic target.

Source: Reprinted with the permission of The Free Press, a division of Simon & Schuster, from *Competitive Strategy: Techniques for Analyzing Industries and Competitors,* by Michael E. Porter. Copyright © 1980, 1998 by The Free Press.

Target employs a cost-leadership strategy by keeping costs low while maintaining efficient operations and tight controls.

Differentiation Strategy

differentiation strategy
An organization's attempts to set its products or services apart from those of other companies.

With a **differentiation strategy** an organization attempts to set its products or services apart from those of other companies. To accomplish this, an organization focuses on basic, core business processes, such as customer service, product design and development, total quality control, and order processing. Lexus and Rolex focus on quality; FedEx and McDonald's focus on service. Two-Hands, a Los Angeles jewelry design company, specializes in products that appeal to consumers' concerns for social causes (Buss, 1994).

Cost-Leadership Strategy

cost-leadership strategy
A strategy focused on keeping costs as low as possible through efficient operations and tight controls.

A **cost-leadership strategy** is one focused on keeping costs as low as possible through efficient operations and tight controls. In turn, the company can compete by charging lower prices. Target, Pace, and Sam's Wholesale Clubs apply this strategy in the growing discount business. In the motel business, Scottish Inns and Motel 6 provide travelers with low-cost alternatives. Basket Case Gift Services in Detroit won contracts to supply seasonal gift baskets to Kmart with its low-cost strategy (Buss, 1994).

Focus Strategy

focus strategy
When the managers of a firm target a specific market—a particular region or group of potential customers.

When the managers of a firm target a specific market—a particular region or group of potential customers—they are applying a **focus strategy**. Some companies manufacture products for certain buyers. Pro-Line Corporation produces health and beauty aids for African-American markets. Mazda upgraded its sporty RX-7 coupe to target buyers of Nissan's 300ZX model and low-end Porsches.

FORMULATING FUNCTIONAL-LEVEL STRATEGY

The final level of strategy in the organization is the strategy developed by the major functional departments. These action plans support the accomplishment of the business-level strategies. The major functions include marketing, production, human resources, finance, and research and development.

Marketing Strategy

Marketing strategy involves decisions on pricing, promotion, distribution, and the products or services mix of the organization. When taken together, the decisions in each area become a firm's marketing strategy. Nike has committed itself to promote its golf apparel and equipment with Tiger Woods. Frito-Lay's Doritos can be purchased in several flavors, such as ranch, nacho cheese, barbecue, or regular. Celestial Seasonings has multiple distribution channels—through grocery store chains, wholesalers, and health food stores. Wal-Mart has built its inventories around the fastest-moving merchandise in major consumer goods categories.

In the area of marketing services, Kroger Grocery is offering telephone ordering and home delivery. SuperCuts has a low price to attract volume. Banks have placed ATMs on college campuses to better serve their young customers. McDonald's has developed portable ministores for large-scale public events.

Production Strategy

Functional-level strategy for production involves manufacturing goods and providing services. Decisions in this area influence how the organization will compete. Such decisions include choices about plant location, inventory control methods, use of robotics and computer-aided manufacturing techniques, commitments to quality and productivity improvement, and the selection and use of outside suppliers.

Human Resources Strategy

For many businesses, such as hotels, restaurants, health care, and professional sports, the human resources strategy is the fundamental key to survival. These businesses need a specific strategy to execute nearly every employment decision area, such as recruiting, training, and developing human resources. Recruiting must result in attracting people who adequately reflect a firm's customer base and the community's workforce. Once acquired, human resources must be trained and developed in order to take advantage of the potentials they have to offer. This area of strategy is being reshaped as more and more companies recognize the value of diversity to the growth and health of their businesses. This chapter's Valuing Diversity feature illustrates how one company, Alpine Banks, increased the number of its depositors through a diversity recruiting strategy.

Financial Strategy

The financial strategy of a firm involves decisions about the actions to be taken with profits (distribution to stockholders or retention for future investments), how funds will be spent or invested, and how any additional funds will be raised (through borrowing or by attracting new investor capital).

Research and Development Strategy

The functional-level strategy for research and development involves the invention and development of new technologies, or new applications for existing technologies, that

VALUING DIVERSITY
Alpine's Competitive Advantage

By diversifying its workforce, Alpine Banks of Colorado tapped into sources of seasoned talent and broadened its customer base. For some time the Glenwood Springs, Colorado, bank's customer base had been shrinking. The region near Alpine's base had been hard hit by job losses—the most significant caused by the departure of two large employers.

Despite the gloomy outlook, Alpine identified a bright spot. Thousands of Hispanics had arrived in the region in the preceding decade, many of them lured by jobs in area ski resorts. Management determined that Alpine Banks would distinguish itself from competitors by bridging the communications gap with the new residents, many of whom spoke little English.

The bank decided to recruit bilingual employees. Among other actions, Alpine ran help-wanted ads printed in Spanish. Hispanic respondents who were hired then referred names of other Hispanics as potential employees. Ultimately the bank hired 25 bilingual Hispanics and placed them at branches in positions ranging from loan officer to bank teller to receptionist.

The strategy worked. The 200-employee bank attracted hundreds of new depositors. Alpine recognized the value of diversity as a business strategy.

http://www.alpinebank.com

Source: Laura M. Lituan, "Casting a Wider Employment Net," *Nation's Business* (December 1994), p. 49.

lead to new products and services. Each year companies invest millions of dollars in R&D projects, many of which lead to few if any breakthroughs. Investment for the future, however, is critical so that there will be a future for the enterprise.

http://www.chrysler.com

R&D projects by Chrysler and its suppliers have resulted in modular assembly techniques, its newest line of automobiles utilizing team assembly and cab-forward design, and an all-aluminum chassis and frame for Plymouth's new Prowler—a 1990s version of a 1950s customized roadster. R&D has led to such breakthroughs in the auto industry as side-mounted airbags, four-wheel antilock brakes, and dent and chip resistant body panels, found on the Saturn and other GM products. All R&D results from strategic management and strategic planning.

http://www.saturn.com

http://www.gm.com

CHAPTER SUMMARY

1 **Describe the nature of strategic planning and strategic management.** Strategic planning is the decision making and planning processes that chart an organization's long-term course of action. All companies engage in strategic planning as an element of strategic management. Strategic management is top-level management's responsibility for defining the firm's position, formulating strategies, and guiding long-term organizational activities. The ultimate purpose of strategic planning and strategic management is to help position the organization to achieve a superior fit in the environment in order to achieve its objectives.

2 **Distinguish between strategy formulation and strategy implementation.** Strategy formulation includes the planning and decision making that goes into developing the company's strategic goals and strategic plans. It includes assessing the environment—analyzing the internal and external situation—and creating goals and plans. Strategy implementation refers to the processes associated with executing the strategic plan. These processes may include communication, incentives, structural changes, or new technology.

3 Explain the steps involved in the strategic planning process. The strategic planning process involves six steps:

1. *Create mission statement, goals, and strategies.* For new enterprises and those desiring to totally redefine themselves, all planning begins with the creation of a mission statement. It is the anchor for every strategy.
2. *Analyze the environments.* Internal and external environments must be assessed and analyzed. In completing this phase, managers perform a situational analysis and search for internal strengths and weaknesses as well as external opportunities and threats.
3. *Reassess mission statement and goals.* The analysis of the external opportunities and threats and the internal strengths and weaknesses can produce two outcomes: to reestablish the current mission, goals, and strategies or to define a new mission and supporting goals.
4. *Formulate strategies.* Once the mission and goals are reestablished or redefined, strategies at the corporate, business, and functional levels can be formulated.
5. *Implement strategies.* Once strategies are formulated, they must be implemented. Implementation involves the use of four elements: leadership, structure, people, and information.
6. *Monitor and evaluate results.* Once the strategy is implemented, performance must be monitored and evaluated and modifications must be made, if necessary.

4 Explain the importance of assessing the internal and external environments as a basis for strategic planning. The assessment of the internal and external environments identifies factors that shape the development of the strategic plan. The analysis (SWOT) of the external opportunities and threats and the internal strengths and weaknesses can produce two outcomes: to reestablish the current mission, goals, and strategies or to define a new mission and supporting goals.

5 Identify the sources and kinds of information required in the strategic planning process. In the strategic planning process, managers must have information from external as well as internal sources. External information about opportunities and threats can be gained from customers, suppliers, government reports, consultants, professional journals, and meetings. Internal information about strengths and weaknesses may come from profit and loss statements, ratio analysis, employee morale surveys, and budget printouts.

6 Describe the factors involved in strategy implementation. The implementation of a strategy will depend to a great extent on having a good fit between the organizational strategy and culture. The implementation may require changes in the organization's behavior and culture. It achieves implementation through the collaboration of four key elements: leadership, organizational structure, human resources, and information and control systems.

7 Explain the formulation of corporate-level strategy, business-level strategy, and functional-level strategy.

- *Corporate-level strategy.* For companies with a single market or a few closely related markets, the corporate-level strategy involves developing a grand strategy. A grand strategy is the overall framework for the organization. Grand strategies include five types: growth, integration, diversification, retrenchment, and stability. Large companies that have complicated organizational structures with unique business divisions or that have strategic business units, each with different products, markets, and competitors, need a portfolio strategy. After the grand strategy is developed, the portfolio strategy involves determining the power mix of business units and product lines to provide a maximum competitive advantage for the strategic business unit.
- *Business-level strategy.* A business-level strategy is the strategy managers formulate within each SBU (or within the firm itself if it is a single-product business) defining how to compete. Many possible strategies can be chosen; they can be grouped as either adaptive strategies or competitive strategies. Adaptive strategies—prospective, defender, analyzer, and reactor—try to match organizational assets to the external environment. Competitive strategies—differentiation, cost-leadership, and focus—are dictated by how the organization can best compete based on its core competencies—internal skills, resources, and philosophies.
- *Functional-level strategy.* Functional-level strategies are the action plans developed by the major functional departments to support the accomplishment of business-level strategies. The major functions include marketing, production, human resources, finance, and research and development.

REVIEW QUESTIONS

1. What is the purpose of strategic planning?
2. On what issues does strategy formulation focus? What about strategy implementation?
3. What six steps are involved in the strategic planning process? Discuss each one.

4. Why is it important to assess the internal and external environments in strategic planning? What four factors are assessed?
5. What sources and kinds of information are helpful in the strategic planning process?
6. What is the importance of the factors involved in strategy implementation?
7. What is the difference between corporate-level strategies for growth, retrenchment, and stability? What is the purpose of the BCG Matrix in the development of business-level plans? What are three of the five functional-level areas of planning? What needs to be considered in each area?

DISCUSSION QUESTIONS FOR CRITICAL THINKING

1. What specific examples can you give that demonstrate grand strategies? Competitive strategies? Functional-level strategies?
2. How can you apply a SWOT analysis to your strategic plan for gaining a college education?
3. What specific examples can you cite of organizations capitalizing on their distinctive competitive advantage?
4. How have you seen the concept of synergy at work?

INTERNET EXERCISES

Check the text Web site at http://plunkett.swcollege.com for updated links to the Internet Exercises.

1. The Malcolm Baldrige National Quality Award, an annual United States national quality award, is a very prestigious award. It is a form of recognition. The purposes of the award are to promote awareness of quality excellence, to recognize quality achievements of U.S. companies, and to publicize successful quality strategies. Companies want to apply for the Malcolm Baldrige National Quality Award since studies show that quality management can result in impressive returns.

   Explain the relationship between the Baldrige National Quality Program and strategic planning.

   http://www.quality.nist.gov/HTML%20Folder/Business%20Criteria%20HTML/index.html

   http://www.quality.nist.gov/HTML%20Folder/Business%20Criteria%20HTML/2000_criteria_catitemdes.htm

2. How does the Baldrige National Quality Program define *strategic objectives*? Give an example of a strategic objective. What internal and external environmental factors should be considered while writing strategic objectives?
   http://www.quality.nist.gov/HTML%20Folder/Business%20Criteria%20HTML/2000_criteria_glossary.htm
3. Carry out a SWOT analysis to identify your strengths and weaknesses and examine the opportunities and threats you face. Identify the changes you will make.
   http://www.mindtools.com/swot.html

APPLICATION CASE

Questionable Strategy at Hallmark

How can a company with almost 50 percent of the greeting card market be classified as "sagging"? Unfortunately, greeting card giant Hallmark Cards has the answer. Hallmark has seen its market share slip from an estimated 50 percent in 1990 to 45 percent in 1995. Even more troublesome, its return on investment—the return to stockholders—fell dramatically to an estimated 8 percent in 1999—far below its historical 15 to 20 percent.

In searching for the answers to Hallmark's lagging performance, observers identified the following situations:

- Hallmark's cards and merchandise look dated next to hipper upstarts such as Chicago's Recycled Paper Greetings.
- The greeting card business is viewed by Hallmark management as a mature industry with little room for growth. As a result, the company plunged into TV production with a $395 million purchase of RHI Entertainment, best known for Hallmark's Hall of Fame productions. Next came an $80 million investment in Flextech, a European satellite-TV company. Hallmark's management thought synergy would be developed from both decisions.
- Hallmark faces a changing marketplace that now favors mass retailers over the 9,000 independent specialty shops it relies on to sell greeting cards. At one time these specialty card shops accounted for 65 percent of card sales. Now these same independent shops have less than a third of the sales, as discounters, supermarkets, and drugstores dominate the market.

http://www.hallmark.com

Questions

1. Which level of strategy—corporate, business, functional—applies to each of the three situations cited? Explain your answer.
2. What nature of synergy did Hallmark's management expect from uniting greeting cards and television production? How realistic is this expectation?
3. What strategy changes would you recommend to solve each of these three situations? Develop your answer by selecting specific strategies relating to corporate, business, and functional strategy options.

Source: Susan Chandler, "Can Hallmark Get Well Soon?", *Business Week* (19 June 1995), pp. 62–63.

VIDEO CASE

Hudson's Somerset Store: Planning and Implementing

Hudson's Department Stores are part of the fourth largest retailing chain in the United States—the Target Corporation (formerly, Dayton Hudson, Inc.). The retail giant has three major lines of retailing: Mervyn's, Target, and a group of department stores (including Dayton's, Hudson's, and Marshall Field's). The Minnesota-based company decided to develop new upscale stores and first opened one such store—a Hudson's store—in Somerset, Michigan, a wealthy Detroit suburb.

The design of Hudson's Somerset store was heavily influenced by a Marshall Field's store in Northbrook, Illinois (a Chicago suburb), a trendsetter in merchandising and layout design. Both facilities were created by Andrew Markopoulos (Hudson's senior vice president of visual merchandising and design), whose intent was to combine classic department store traditions (e.g., luxurious wood and marble materials) with contemporary layouts to ensure easy and convenient shopping.

The Somerset location features wide aisles that form a simple X shape and branch off a circular atrium like the spokes of a wheel. The store has minimal interior walls, allowing the atrium to be visible from each floor. Each department is wedge-shaped and has contrasting décor to make it easy for customers to tell one department from another.

Despite having the Marshall Field's store as a model, a planning committee of Hudson's employees were involved in making many planning and design decisions for the new store. Committee membership deliberately included employees from various departments and levels of administration. The intent was to keep everyone involved and informed during design and construction so that when overlapping issues arose, they could be attacked head on and resolved quickly.

The committee's role and tasks changed over time. Initially, its members set deadlines and general goals as they discussed all aspects of the new store. However, as work on the store progressed, they began to concentrate on area-specific issues.

The planning process was successful, as evidenced by the store coming in under budget and now being considered the company's benchmark store. The committee kept detailed records and provided timely feedback to headquarters about the process and what the committee members learned from being involved in it. Hudson's management now uses this information in developing other new upscale stores.

http://www.targetcorp.com

For Discussion:

1. What type of planning process did the Hudson's committee utilize at the beginning of the Somerset store's development? Explain.
2. What are some of the recommendations that Hudson's employees offered for future planning projects?
3. The decision by Target's management to develop more upscale department stores is emblematic of which of the following adaptive business-level strategies: prospector strategy, defender strategy, analyzer strategy, or reactor strategy?

Making Decisions

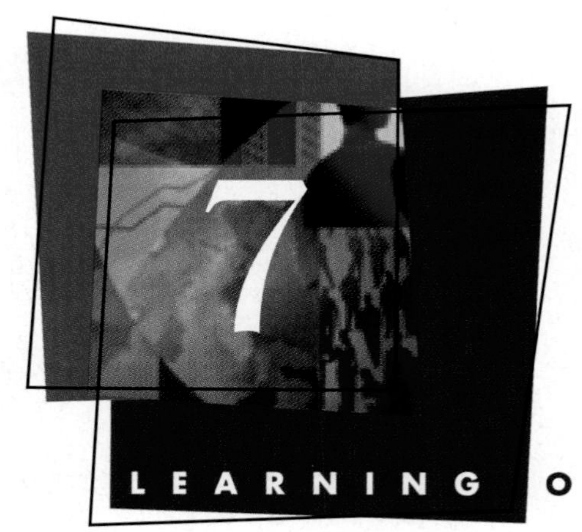

KEY TERMS

alternative
brainstorming
decision
decision making
decision tree
Delphi technique
game theory
groupthink
just-in-time inventory
limiting factors
maximize
nominal group technique
nonprogrammed decision
opportunity
outside-the-box thinking
payback analysis
problem
programmed decision
queueing model
satisfice
simulation
symptom
tunnel vision
Vroom and Yetton decision tree
waiting line model

LEARNING OBJECTIVES

After studying this chapter, you should be able to

1. Recognize that decision making is performed at all management levels
2. Distinguish between formal and informal approaches to decision making
3. List the steps in the decision-making process
4. Describe the environmental factors that influence decision making
5. Describe the personal attributes of a manager that influence decision making
6. Discuss the value of group decision making, and identify three techniques of group decision making
7. Explain three quantitative techniques for decision making, and describe the situations in which each is appropriate
8. Describe strategies a manager can use to create a more effective decision-making environment

MANAGEMENT IN ACTION

Microsoft: Life Changing Decisions

The nation's number one software seller was founded in 1975, when Microsoft's Bill Gates and Paul Allen created and sold the first computer language program for a personal computer—BASIC for the Altaire 8800. At that time, when few people had a personal computer, Microsoft's vision was "A personal computer on every desk and in every home." How did this revolutionary vision come about? The answer can be found in two major decisions and a willingness to follow through on those decisions. These decisions not only changed lives, "but they also made far-reaching economic changes possible for generations to come" (*Bloomberg News*, 1999).

Decision Number One

After developing BASIC, Gates and Allen set up the first software company aimed at personal computers. In order to do this, Bill Gates had to drop out of Harvard. As Gates phrased it, "the industry wasn't going to wait on us while I finished my degree at Harvard." In addition, he said, "I felt the window of opportunity to start a software company might never open again. So I dove into the world of business." (Bill Gates Bio, http://www.microsoft.com/mscorp/museum/BillG.doc)

Decision Number Two

In 1980, Microsoft bought work that had been done on an operating system called SCP-DOS or 8-DOS from Seattle Computer Products, tailored it for the PC market, renamed it MS-DOS, and licensed it to IBM. The new IBM PC was released in August 1981. That same year, Bill Gates became Microsoft's president and chairman of the board. In 1983, an extension of the MS-DOS operating system—Windows—was unveiled. Windows is an operating system, which provides basic functions, such as drawing windows and menus on the screen, managing network communications and accessing disk drives, on which all PC software can draw. Windows resulted in Microsoft's dominance of the PC marketplace.

"Gates' foresight and vision regarding personal computing have been central to the success of Microsoft and the software industry." (Bill Gates Bio, http://www.microsoft.com/mscorp/museum/BillG.doc) In 1999, *Bloomberg News* chose Bill Gates as Wealth creator, one of 20 business leaders of the millennium.

Bill Gates' Microsoft Corp. brought order to chaos to hasten the digital information age. The company's Windows operating system made it vastly easier for hardware and software companies to create mutually compatible products. Sure, Microsoft has famously bullied rivals, seldom invents new ideas and extracts licensing fees from virtually every sector of the economy. This has made Mr. Gates and thousands of others very wealthy. It also has enriched the world. (Bloomberg News, *1999*)

It is fascinating to read Bill Gates' famous memo to Apple, in which he recommended that Apple license its software to other computer companies. Apple decided not to heed his advice. (Jim Carlton, "They Coulda Been a Contender," *Wired*, 11 November 1997.) ■

Sources: Bloomberg News, "Kings of Commerce," 25 December 1999; "Student Information Packet," http://www.microsoft.com/mscorp/museum/musStudent.asp.

© REUTERS NEWMEDIA INC./CORBIS

Bill Gates' decisions to drop out of college to start Microsoft and to license its operating systems to other software companies have made Gates one of the world's most successful businessmen.

INTRODUCTION

http://www.microsoft.com

Microsoft is the world's number one software seller because of solid decision making by Chairman and Chief Software Architect Bill Gates and his management team. As with Microsoft, every organization succeeds or fails based on decisions by its managers. Although many of their critical decisions determine strategic directions (e.g., Microsoft's .NET strategy for Next Generation Internet Services), managers make decisions about all aspects of the organization, including organization structures, staffing, and control systems. This chapter will thoroughly examine managerial decision making—the steps in the decision-making process, the nature of the decision-making environment, influences on decision making, decision-making techniques, and the way managers can create an environment for effective decision making. If you dread decisions, postpone them, or simply feel you could use some extra help on the subject, this chapter is for you. When you finish reading its ideas, examples, and suggestions, your approach to decision making should be more confident.

WHAT YOU NEED TO KNOW ABOUT DECISIONS

For many years you have been making decisions. You are reading these words as a direct result of a decision you made to study management. Your entire life is a result of your decisions and those of others. Many decisions are simple: deciding what to eat or what clothes to wear. Others are much more complex: what school to attend or what area to major in. Regardless of the complexity, a **decision** is a choice made from available alternatives (Daft, 1994).

decision
A choice made from available alternatives.

Managers face the same range of decisions; but unlike our individual decisions, the ones managers make in organizations can affect profitability, the lives of thousands of people, or the location of a company's operations. For example, the decision made by Bill Gates and Paul Allen—licensing its 16-bit operating system, MS-DOS 1.0, to IBM—was the inspiration that set Microsoft apart from its competitors and made it the number one software seller in the country. Similarly, Reid Goldstein made a decision that reversed the fortune of Tustin, California-based Flotool International (now Snapware Corporation). As head of the struggling six-person manufacturer of a variety of consumer-oriented plastic products, ranging from open-and-close motor oil spouts to dry food containers with easily workable lids, Goldstein decided to stop going it alone. Instead, Flotool would become a partner-supplier for big chains. The result: a half dozen big chains, including Target and Wal-Mart, became customers; and its sales are nearly $10 million annually (Buss, 1994).

http://www.flotool.com

WHAT DECISION MAKING IS

Decision Making, Problem Solving, and Opportunity Management

decision making
The process of identifying problems and opportunities, developing alternative solutions, choosing an alternative, and implementing it.

Decision making is the process of identifying problems and opportunities, developing alternative solutions, choosing an alternative, and implementing it (Holt, 1990). Decision making is a process, not a lightning bolt occurrence. In making the decision, a manager is reaching a conclusion—based on considering a number of options or alternatives.

In management the terms *decision making* and *problem solving* are used interchangeably because managers constantly make decisions to solve problems. For example, when an account representative resigns at Verizon, the sales manager has a **problem**—the difference between the current and desired performance or situation (Howard, 1985). Replacing the person requires a decision—promote from within, hire an experienced person, or recruit an inexperienced college graduate. Each alternative could solve the problem.

problem
The difference between the current and desired performance or situation.

But all decision making is not aimed at solving problems; many decisions are made to seize **opportunities**. Managers see a chance, occasion, event, or breakthrough that requires a decision to be made. Such was the case with the Yee sisters of Minneapolis. Susan, the oldest, had been complaining to her sisters about how hard it was to find cosmetics that match the skin tones of many Asian women. Research revealed that some 3.8 million Asian women reside in the United States, and the number is rapidly growing. In addition, the women tend to be affluent: the median Asian-American family income is about 18 percent above the U.S. average. Further research revealed that no cosmetics firm had targeted the Asian-American consumer. Seizing the opportunity and addressing consumer needs, the Yee sisters created Zhen Cosmetics. The Yee sisters developed a strategy for success by landing contracts with prestigious Nordstrom's department stores. They saw an opportunity and took it (Berss, 1995).

opportunity
A chance, occasion, event, or breakthrough that requires a decision to be made.

http://www.zhenbeauty.com

Universality of Decision Making

Recognize that decision making is performed at all management levels

As noted in Chapter 1, decision making is a part of all managers' jobs. A manager constantly makes decisions when performing the functions of planning, organizing, staffing, leading, and controlling. (For example, Bill Gate's 1995 decision to support and enhance the Internet was an element of planning—to respond to what the customer needed and wanted.) Decision making is not a separate, isolated function of management but a common core to the other functions, a fact illustrated by Figure 7.1.

Managers at all levels of the organization engage in decision making. The decisions made by top managers, dealing with the mission of the organization and strategies for achieving it, have an impact on the whole organization. Middle-level managers, in turn, focus their decision making on implementing the strategies, as well as on budgeting and allocating resources. Finally, first-level managers deal with repetitive day-to-day operations. Decision making is indeed universal.

Managers make big and small decisions daily. Whether they realize it or not, they go through a process to make those decisions. Whether planning a budget, organizing a work schedule, interviewing a prospective employee, watching a worker on the assembly line, or making adjustments to a project, the manager is taking part in a decision-making process.

Approaches to Decision Making

Distinguish between formal and informal approaches to decision making

Not all decision-making situations are identical. The nature of the decision often dictates to a manager what approach to take. The more complex or uncertain the problem to be solved, the more effective the manager will be if the formal decision-making process, described in detail later in this chapter, is used. Less complicated problems or those that a manager has a great deal of experience in solving can be

FIGURE 7.1 *Decision making in the five management functions*

Planning	What is the mission of the organization? What should it be? What are the needs of the customers? What are the organization's strengths, weaknesses, threats, and opportunities? What are the strategic, tactical, and operational goals? What strategies will achieve the goals?
Organizing	What organizational option will best achieve the objectives? What type of departmental structure will result in teamwork? How many employees should report to a manager? When should a manager delegate authority? How much?
Staffing	How many employees will we need this year? What skills are necessary to do this job? What type of training will best prepare the employee? How can we improve the quality of the performance appraisal system?
Leading	What can we do to have motivated employees? What style of leadership is the most effective with an individual? What strategies are available to manage conflict? How can we build teams?
Controlling	What tasks in the organization need to be controlled? Which control technique is the most effective for monitoring finances? What is the effect of controls on employee behavior? How do we establish acceptable standards of performance?

handled less formally by following habit or relying on past solutions. Whether the decision is a programmed or nonprogrammed one depends on the nature of the situation.

Programmed and Nonprogrammed Decisions

programmed decisions *Decisions that involve problems or situations that have occurred often enough that both the circumstances and solutions are predictable; made in response to recurring organizational problems.*

Programmed decisions involve problems or situations that have occurred often enough that both the circumstances and solutions are predictable (Simon, 1977). In other words, programmed decisions are made in response to recurring organizational problems. Examples of programmed decisions include the programmed inventory reorder point at Wal-Mart, the paperwork necessary to add a person to payroll, and the handling of routine correspondence. This chapter's Ethical Management feature identifies a situation in which a programmed decision may have solved a large problem for Food Lion. Figure 7.2 presents a model of a programmed decision for processing payroll.

nonprogrammed decisions *Decisions made in response to problems and opportunities that have unique circumstances, unpredictable results, and important consequences for the company.*

Nonprogrammed decisions are made in response to problems and opportunities that have unique circumstances, unpredictable results, and important consequences for the company. Managers often find themselves in situations that have never occurred before or in which the problem is not thoroughly defined. The decisions made by Bill Gates for Microsoft are examples of nonprogrammed decisions. There are no programmed decision steps for making software buying a "shopping experience" or for creating a dazzling marketing strategy. To make these choices, Bill Gates spent hours analyzing the customer, developing and analyzing the alternatives, and making choices. When managers face these difficult, significant choices,

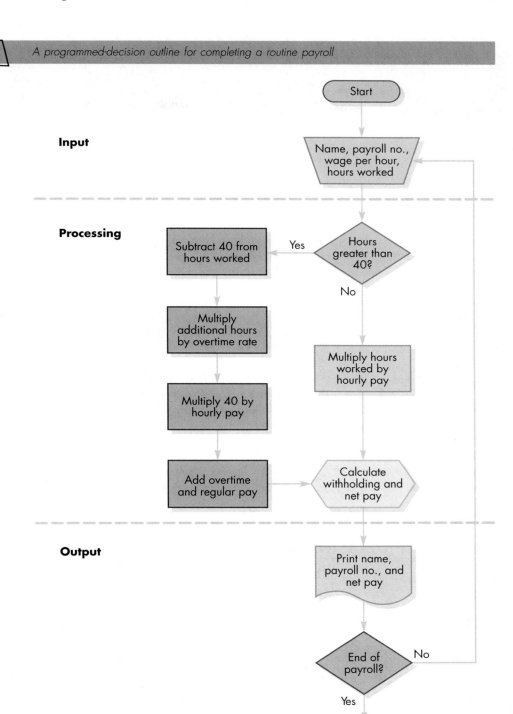

FIGURE 7.2 *A programmed-decision outline for completing a routine payroll*

Input

Start

Name, payroll no., wage per hour, hours worked

Processing

Hours greater than 40?

Yes

Subtract 40 from hours worked

Multiply additional hours by overtime rate

Multiply 40 by hourly pay

Add overtime and regular pay

No

Multiply hours worked by hourly pay

Calculate withholding and net pay

Output

Print name, payroll no., and net pay

End of payroll?

No

Yes

Stop

they must use a sound decision-making process. Furthermore, in these days of turbulent environments and fierce competition, it becomes even more important to make good decisions.

ETHICAL MANAGEMENT
Questionable Decision Making at Food Lion and ABC

In 1995 Food Lion, which operates more than 1,000 stores in fourteen states, was taken to task by consumers for questionable decision making. Washington, D.C.–based Consumers United With Employees reported that members of the organization purchased out-of-date dairy products, meat, and other perishable items at 113 of 116 Food Lion Stores where they shopped. In all, the group found 2,885 outdated perishable products in stores in all fourteen states where the chain operates. Nearly half the items included outdated meat products.

This incident was not Food Lion's first. In November 1992, Food Lion was the subject of an ABC network report alleging the chain engaged in various unsanitary practices, including the selling of outdated meat. In addition, over a six-year period, Consumers United had charged Food Lion with selling expired baby formula and over-the-counter drugs. In all, Consumers United found more than 13,400 out-of-date products at Food Lion over a six-year period. Food Lion's reply to the charges, "We also need to put in context the number of products we are talking about. We sell more than 3 billion products in our stores, so we're talking about less than one in a million."

Also, what about ABC's journalism techniques—use of the hidden camera? Bob Steele, director of the Ethics Program at The Poynter Institute for Media Studies, asks these critical questions: "If ABC News used the threat to public health as a reason for the extensive undercover investigation and the use of deception, why did it take them so long to ring the warning bell? Why did they wait six months after they went undercover before PrimeTime Live aired the report?" In 1997, a North Carolina jury sided with Food Lion against ABC's PrimeTime Live.

1. What ethical questions are raised by Food Lion's response?
2. Is it ethical to knowingly sell one outdated product?
3. As a consumer, what would be your response to Food Lion's ethical practices?
4. Did ABC's journalists respect the rights of others? What ethical questions do ABC's hidden cameras raise?

http://www.foodlion.com

http://abc.go.com

Sources: Del Harkey, "Food Lion Under Attack Once Again," *Dallas Morning News* (4 May 1995), p. 2D. For more on ABC, read Bob Steele, "ABC and Food Lion: The Ethics Questions," *RTNDA Communicator* (April 1997), p. 56, http://www.poynter.org/research/me/me_abc-fl.htm.

SEVEN-STEP DECISION-MAKING PROCESS

3

List the steps in the decision-making process

The decision-making process has seven steps, as shown in Figure 7.3. Each one is essential to the entire process. The sections that follow will examine each step.

Defining the Problem or Opportunity

The initial and most critical step is to define the problem or opportunity. The accuracy of this step affects all the steps that follow. If the problem or opportunity is incorrectly defined, every other step in the decision process will be based on that false start. If a company is losing market share, is the problem poor product quality, technical inferiority, a slow warehouse, or an inadequate sales force? Managers must pinpoint the problem correctly, because each of these problems requires a different solution.

symptom
Signals that something is wrong and draws the manager's attention to finding the cause—that is, the problem.

In problem solving, a manager must differentiate between a problem and a **symptom**. In the example above, the symptom is dwindling market share; the problem may be poor quality. A symptom signals that something is wrong (Bazerman, 1986). It should draw the manager's attention to finding the cause—that is, the problem. To isolate the problem from the symptoms, a manager needs to

FIGURE 7.3 *The decision-making process*

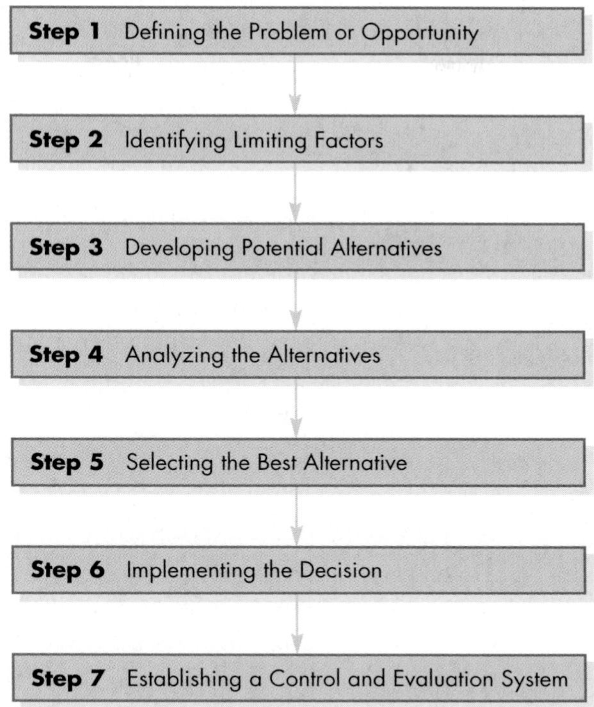

develop a sound questioning process and to ask the right questions. According to Peter Drucker, "The most common source of mistakes in management decisions is the emphasis on finding the right answer rather than asking the right questions" (Drucker, 1954). In the process of asking questions, the manager gathers relevant and timely data about the problem. The best way to get good data is for managers to tune in to the work environment. According to management expert Tom Peters, the source of the most relevant and accurate information for a manager is the people in the workplace (Peters, 1990).

To assist in defining the problem, Charles Kepner and Benjamin Tregoe (1965), who conducted detailed studies of managerial decision making, recommend that managers ask a series of questions using the funnel approach to distinguish between symptoms and problems. Figure 7.4 illustrates how the funnel approach can aid in defining the problem. Initially, a manager notices a problem, such as unmet production quotas. He or she then begins to apply the funnel approach by asking questions to identify the real problem, not just the symptom.

- Are hours worked decreasing? No, absenteeism is normal.
- Is material needed for operations unavailable? No, material is flowing at a normal pace.
- How is employee morale? Are there complaints or concerns? Well, as a matter of fact, there are some rumors of discontent.
- Is it wages? No.

- Is it working conditions? No.
- Is it supervision? Some workers are concerned about the supervision they receive.
- What are their concerns? The supervisor does not answer their questions about technical aspects of the job.

By using the funnel approach, the manager finds out that the supervisor lacks technical skills.

Identifying Limiting Factors

limiting factors
Those constraints that rule out certain alternative solutions. One common limitation is time.

Once the problem is defined, the manager needs to identify the limiting factors of the problem. **Limiting factors** are those constraints that rule out certain alternative solutions. One common limitation is time. If a new product has to be on the dealer's shelves in one month, any alternative that takes more than one month will be eliminated. Resources—personnel, money, facilities, and equipment, as well as

FIGURE 7.4 *The funnel approach to defining a problem*

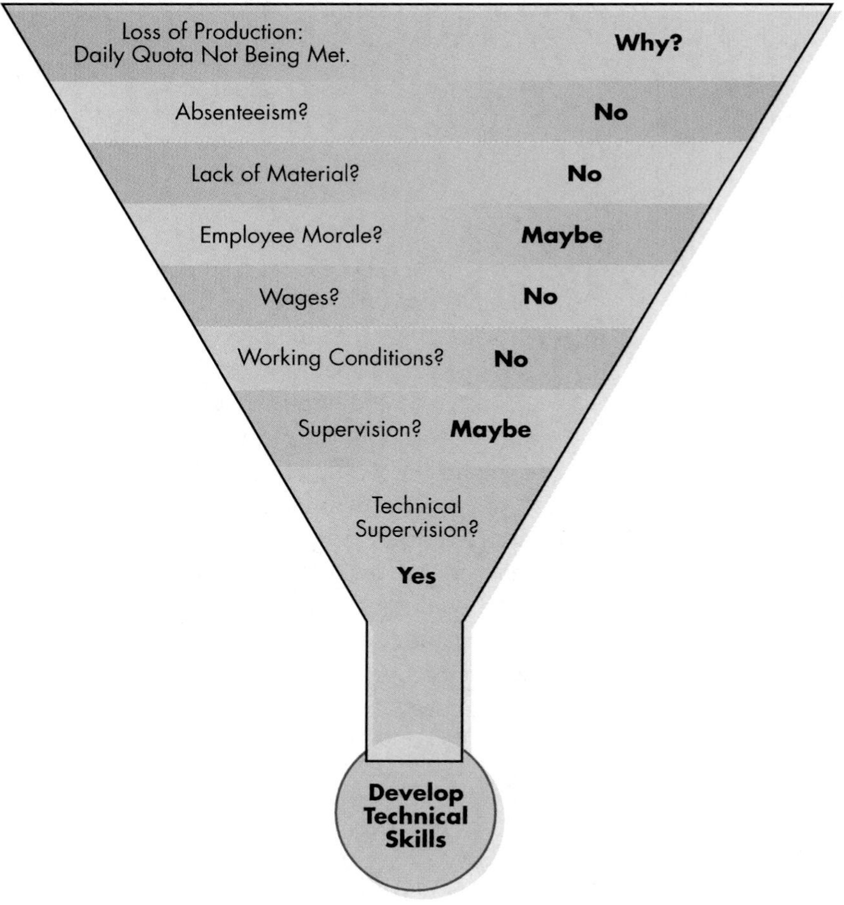

time—are the most common limiting factors that narrow down the range of possible alternatives. In a retailing situation, the limiting factor is that any alternatives or approaches incorporated in the stores should contribute to the total shopping experience. In contrast, at Zhen Cosmetics, the Yee sisters had a more traditional limiting factor: a total of $100,000 in capital to develop and market their cosmetics.

Developing Potential Alternatives

alternatives
Potential solutions to the problem.

At this point, the manager should look for, develop, and list as many possible **alternatives**—potential solutions to the problem. These alternatives should eliminate, correct, or neutralize the problem or maximize the opportunity. Alternative solutions for a manager faced with the problem of trying to maintain scheduled production may be to start an extra work shift, to regularly schedule overtime, to increase the size of the present workforce by hiring employees, or to do nothing. Doing nothing about a problem sometimes is the proper alternative, at least until the situation has been thoroughly analyzed. Occasionally, just the passing of time provides a cure. Of course, the more serious or long term the problem, the less likely that is to be the case.

Sources for alternatives include the manager's own experience; other persons whose opinions and judgments the decision maker respects; group opinions, obtained through the use of task forces and committees; and outside sources, including managers in other organizations. Search engines, the subject of this chapter's Managing Technology feature, can be used to find information on the Internet. (Group decision making will be discussed in detail later in the chapter.)

MANAGING TECHNOLOGY
Search Engines

Since there is no organization in charge of the Internet, no single comprehensive source or index tells you what information is on the Internet or how to find it. People search the Internet using a variety of resource discovery tools called search engines, such as AltaVista, Yahoo, and Google. They are Web sites in and of themselves, accessible through browsers, where you can search for other sites that contain specific keywords. You simply type in the topic, or several key words about what you are looking for, and the search engine will provide Web sites that have information related to that topic. For example, you will get a list of sites by keying in one or more words that best describes what you want.

Different search engines use different commands. Read the online help to find out how a specific search engine's commands operate. Most sites allow use of Boolean language (words that function as commands to help refine a search) in some form, although syntax varies. *AND*, *OR*, and *NOT* are examples of Boolean language. For example, in AltaVista, typing the words *Harvard AND University* would yield pages that contain both the words *Harvard* and *University*. Typing the words *Harvard AND NOT University* would display documents with the word *Harvard* but not the word *University*. If your initial search doesn't produce the desired results, try substituting synonyms for key words. A search covering the word "cars" might miss an important Web page with the word "automobiles." Searching requires patience—and a little detective work—to pay off.

You can keep abreast of more general developments in the field via Search Engine Watch found at http://www.searchenginewatch.com.

http://www.altavista.com

http://www.yahoo.com

http://www.google.com

When building this list of alternatives, a manager should avoid being critical or judgmental about any alternative that arises. Censoring ideas at this stage can needlessly limit the number of alternatives developed (Etzioni, 1989). Initially, each alternative identified should be a separate solution to the problem or a separate strategy for seizing the opportunity. Alternatives that are simply variations of one another provide less choice in the final analysis. After the initial brainstorming process, variations of the listed ideas will begin to crystallize and combinations will emerge.

When developing alternatives, the goal is to be as creative and wide-ranging as possible. Any decision for which a manager cannot identify more than one alternative is by definition not a decision since more than one choice does not exist. Decision makers must always seek out alternatives to ensure that there are choices to be made, and it is to be hoped that the best choice will result in the best decision.

Analyzing the Alternatives

The purpose of this step is to evaluate the relative merits of each alternative, to identify the positives and negatives or the advantages and disadvantages of each. To assist in this process the manager should ask two questions:

1. Does the alternative fit within the limiting factors?
2. What are the consequences of using this alternative?

If any alternatives conflict with the limiting factors identified earlier, they must be automatically discarded or a variation must be found—one that does not conflict with those limiting factors. For example, the department has to produce 1,000 motors by the end of the month—an increase of 500 over the normal quota—and this increased quota needs to be accomplished with a maximum of $10,000 of increased expenditures for employee wages. One alternative is to schedule overtime at night and on Saturdays. When the manager evaluates the suggestion, the calculations reveal that this alternative will result in 1,000 additional units produced—but at a cost of $17,000. As a result, this alternative either needs to be rejected or combined with another alternative. Note the fate of Alternatives 1 and 2 in Figure 7.5.

Second, the manager needs to identify the consequences of using an alternative. Some alternatives, even though they fall within the guidelines established by the limiting factors, have consequences that make them undesirable. For instance, in order to increase the output of one department, an alternative is to hire more employees; to fund that hiring requires taking money from the operating budgets of other departments. Even though the alternative solves the problem, the political and morale problems caused may require it to be eliminated, as is the case with Alternative 3 in Figure 7.5.

Depending on the type of problem, the manager's analysis of the alternatives can be supported by the application of nonquantitative methods—experience and intuition—or quantitative methods—such as payback analysis, decision trees, and simulations. These methods will be discussed in detail later in the chapter.

FIGURE 7.5 *Analyzing alternatives*

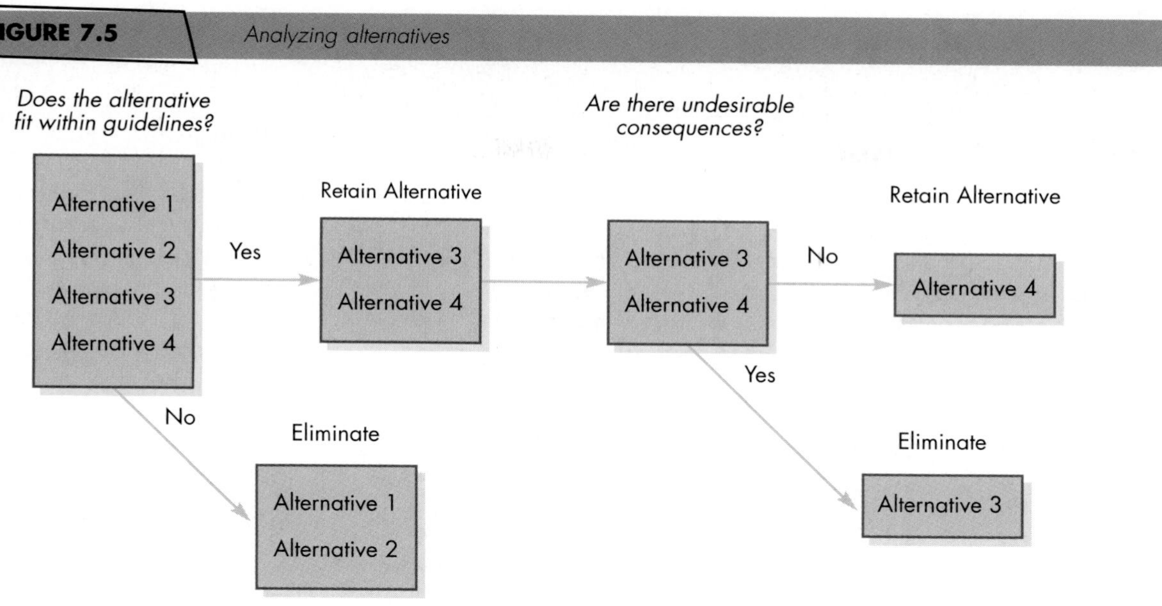

Selecting the Best Alternative

By this step, the remaining alternatives have been listed, along with their corresponding advantages and disadvantages. Which one(s) should be selected?

The best choice is the one that offers the fewest serious disadvantages and the most advantages. Take care not to solve one problem and create another with your choice. Sometimes the optimal solution is a combination of several of the alternatives. A classic example is the actions taken by Richard Stegemeier when he was named president and CEO of Unocal, a Los Angeles-based petroleum company. Faced with a crippling $6.1 billion debt, Stegemeier made some hard decisions. To solve the problem he (1) sold nonessential real estate, including the company headquarters; (2) disposed of Canadian mining operations; (3) closed unprofitable service stations; (4) suspended operations at the money-losing Beaumont Refinery in Nederland, Texas; and (5) signed an agreement to transfer the Chicago refining operations and related marketing assets to a joint venture with Venezuela's national petroleum company.

http://www.unocal.com

Another excellent example is the topic of this chapter's Global Applications feature. Jorma Ollila, faced with a company that had racked up $40 million in losses, made a series of bold decisions that made Nokia the worldwide leader in mobile phones.

Implementing the Decision

Managers are paid to make decisions and to get results from these decisions. A decision that just sits there, hoping someone will put it into effect, may as well never have been made. Everyone involved with carrying out the decision must know what he or she must do, how to do it, and why and when it must be done. Like plans,

GLOBAL APPLICATIONS
Making the Right Decisions at Nokia

In 1992, Nokia, a Helsinki, Finland company, was one of Europe's also-rans. It racked up $40 million in losses, selling everything from television tubes to toilet paper; but when Jorma Ollila took over as CEO, Nokia's fortunes began to change. Ollila made a number of critical decisions that has Nokia grabbing markets from the giants.

Initially, Ollila decided to sell off dozens of product lines and focus in on Nokia's core strength—mobile phone technology. He was convinced that the company had the expertise to become a major player, if it continued to make the right decisions; and Nokia did:

- It made investments in research and development. As a result, Nokia was the first to achieve error-free cellular data transmission.
- It designed phones to be as similar as possible to hold down manufacturing costs. With this, all phones can be made on the same production line, allowing Nokia to shift rapidly from one model to another to meet changes in demand.

Based on these successes, Nokia decided to go global. When the world market for digital phones took off, Nokia's hot products, low-cost manufacturing, and we-try-harder attitude gave it the dominant market share worldwide in mobile phones.

http://www.nokia.com

Sources: Richard McCaffery, "Nokia Grabs Market Share," *The Motley Fool* (24 October 2000), http://www.fool.com/portfolios/rulemaker/2000/rulemaker001024.htm; Gail Edmonson, "Grabbing Markets from the Giants," *Business Week* (9 January 1995), p. 156.

solutions need effective implementation to yield the desired results. Additionally, a good alternative half-heartedly implemented will often create problems, not solve them. People must be convinced of the importance of their roles (Acher, 1986). Finally, programs, procedures, rules, or policies must be thoughtfully put into effect. Figure 7.6 provides some tips on how to translate decisions into actions.

Establishing a Control and Evaluation System

The final step in the decision-making process is to create a control and evaluation system. This system should provide feedback on how well the decision is being implemented, what the positive and negative results are, and what adjustments are necessary to get the results that were desired when the solution was chosen. (And point #6 in Figure 7.6 suggests that the feedback be provided early enough to do something about it.) Often, too, the implementation of a decision produces outcomes that create new problems or opportunities that require new decisions. An evaluation system can help identify those outcomes.

Following these steps gives a manager a greater probability of making successful decisions. Because it provides a step-by-step road map, the manager can move logically through decision making and is unlikely to miss an important point. Also, the care taken in identifying and evaluating alternatives helps ensure that the best choice is made. Finally, the creation of a control system helps ensure that the decision is correctly implemented and subsequent outcomes are handled effectively.

To be successful in decision making, though, the manager must also be aware of the environment in which he or she makes decisions. The following section examines the decision-making environment.

FIGURE 7.6 *How to translate decisions into action*

1. *Persuade the hostile guns and the foot-draggers.*

   From preliminary discussions you know who gave in grudgingly—perhaps after open opposition. Go out of your way to conciliate and persuade.

2. *Determine who needs to be informed and how best to do it.*

   Make sure the list absolutely includes people who "need to know." Be sure to let people know the why of the decision. Select the best method—written or verbal—and tune the vocabulary and tone to the reader or listener.

3. *Check for loose ends.*

   Double-check to make sure clear assignments have been made and that everyone has the resources to perform the task.

4. *Do a good job of selling the decision.*

   Practically none of your decisions will be implemented by you alone. Seek authorization and permission if needed. Provide encouragement to everyone.

5. *Have courage and patience.*

   Stand fast when people say, "it can't be done". . ."it's too costly". . ."it's too soon". . ."it's too late."

6. *Arrange for feedback.*

   Establish a system that will wave red flags when you are heading into trouble—early enough to do something about it.

Source: Reprinted from Carl Heyel, "From Intent to Implement: How to Translate Decisions into Action," *Management Review* (June 1995), p. 63. http://www.amanet.org.

ENVIRONMENTAL INFLUENCES ON DECISION MAKING

Describe the environmental factors that influence decision making

Decision making, like planning, does not take place in a vacuum. Many factors in the environment affect the process and the decision maker.

Degree of Certainty

In some situations, the manager has perfect knowledge of what to do and what the consequences of the action will be. In others, the manager has no such knowledge. Decisions are made under the conditions of certainty, risk, and uncertainty. As Figure 7.7 illustrates, each condition brings degrees of ambiguity and potential for failure.

In conditions of certainty, the manager has what is known as perfect knowledge—he or she knows all the information to make the decision (Eilon, 1987). The manager has made this decision before, knows the alternatives, and fully understands the consequences of each alternative. In this type of situation, the manager simply chooses the alternative known to get the best results. Ambiguity and fear of failure do not exist. As an example, consider a manager at Northern Telecom who has two new employees and has to provide a desk, chair, and related office equipment for each. Only four companies have been approved to bid on the

FIGURE 7.7 *Degrees of ambiguity and potential for failure in decision making*

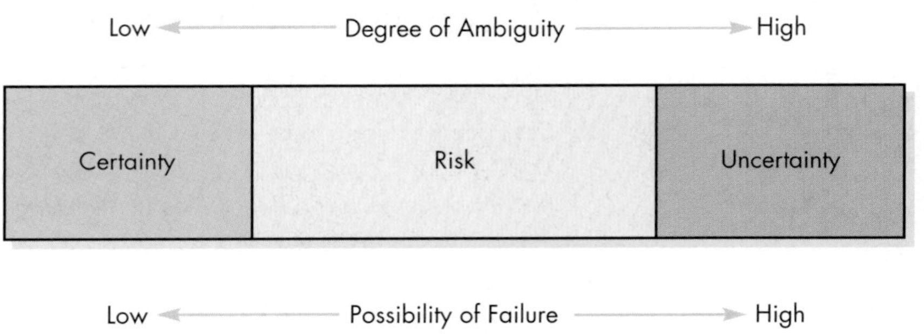

equipment. Each has provided bids in similar situations in the past. The manager knows the product line, quality, price, terms, and service offered by all four vendors. The manager needs only to identify the most important factors to him or her and choose the vendor who best supplies these factors. Under conditions of certainty, the manager can rely on a policy or standing plan; the decisions will be made routinely. In other words, these can be programmed decisions.

Risk provides a more complex environment. In this situation, the manager knows what the problem is and what the alternatives are but cannot be sure of the consequences of each alternative. Therefore, ambiguity and risk are associated with each alternative. For example, a manager has three candidates for a position. All come from inside the company and have known performance histories, but all three worked in other jobs, so their performance in the new position is unknown. After extensive interviewing, the manager must make a decision. The dilemma facing the manager is that each candidate has strengths, but none is a perfect fit for the job. The manager has an idea of the probability that they will succeed, but each one has a degree of risk associated with him or her.

Uncertainty is the most difficult condition for a manager. This situation is like being a pioneer. The manager cannot determine the exact outcomes of the alternatives available either because there are too many variables or too many unknown facts. In addition to the uncertainty associated with the probability of the known alternatives, the manager may not be able to identify all the possible alternatives to be considered (Roussel, 1983). As Figure 7.7 shows, there is high ambiguity and high possibility of failure.

To illustrate this condition, picture a person who has just been promoted into a management position. On the first day an employee reports that a shipment to a highly valued customer has not arrived, and the customer wants the goods—now! The manager can identify some alternatives: send another shipment (but it will take three days) or wait to see if the goods arrive. Unfortunately, the probability of either alternative satisfying the customer is uncertain, and there may be other alternatives the manager has not considered. What can be done? Reliance on experience, judgment, and other people's experiences can assist the manager in assessing the value of the alternatives and identifying others.

Imperfect Resources

maximize
Managers want to make the perfect decisions.

All managers want to **maximize** their decisions: they want to make the perfect ones. To accomplish this, they need ideal resources—information, time, personnel, equipment, and supplies. Managers, however, operate in an environment that normally does not provide ideal resources.

satisfice
To make the best decision possible with the time, resources, and information available.

Managers in the real world do not always have, for example, the time they need to collect all the information they desire about a problem. They may lack the proper budget to buy the printers for every PC or give raises to every employee. Faced with these limits, they choose to do something more realistic: to **satisfice**—that is, to make the best decision possible with the time, resources, and information available. If a manager always tries to maximize decisions, the result may be a great deal of time spent gathering information and not making the decision. In addition, managers in organizations typically cannot justify the time and expense of acquiring complete information (Jackson and Dutton, 1988).

Internal Environment

Decisions cannot solve problems or seize opportunities unless they receive acceptance and support. A manager's decision-making environment is influenced by support (or lack of support) from superiors, subordinates, and organizational systems.

Superiors

A major factor in the manager's decision-making environment is his or her boss. Does the manager's superior have confidence in subordinates, want to be informed on progress, and support logical decisions after receiving the information? If so, then the boss can help create a good decision-making environment for the subordinate manager by providing guidance and ongoing feedback.

In contrast, insecure managers may fear the success of their subordinates and may jealously guard the helpful knowledge they possess. Additionally, some superiors are so afraid of being held accountable for failures that they are reluctant to let their subordinates make any decision of consequence. In such an environment, the subordinate manager faces tough choices. He or she can either work over the long run to create a climate of mutual trust, live with the frustration and be ineffective as a decision maker, or leave the environment to find a more acceptable situation.

Subordinates

Subordinates affect a manager's decision-making environment in important ways. Many of the decisions a manager has to make directly affect employees—when they work, who they work with, how they work. Therefore, without their subordinates' support, input, and understanding of decisions, managers cannot be effective. This situation, in turn, creates a dilemma and thus challenges a manager's leadership ability. When decisions have to be made, what level or degree of involvement should employees have from the range of options shown in Figure 7.8 (Vroom, 1973)?

Which option should the manager use? Two criteria suggested by Norman Maier influence the choice: the objective quality of the decision needed and the degree to which subordinates must accept the decision for it to succeed (Maier,

FIGURE 7.8 *Five levels of subordinate involvement*

1. The manager makes the decision himself or herself, using information available to him or her at that time. Employees provide no input or assistance.
2. The manager obtains the necessary information from subordinates, and then makes the decision. When obtaining information from them, the manager may or may not tell the subordinates what the problem is. The role played by the subordinates is clearly one of providing the necessary information to the manager, rather than generating or evaluating alternative solutions.
3. The manager shares the situation with relevant subordinates individually, getting their ideas and suggestions without bringing them together as a group. Then the manager makes the decision, which may or may not reflect the subordinates' influence.
4. The manager shares the situation with the subordinates as a group; collectively obtains their ideas and suggestions. Then the manager makes the decision, which may or may not reflect the subordinates' influence.
5. The manager shares the situation with the subordinates as a group. Together they generate and evaluate alternatives and attempt to reach agreement (consensus) on a solution. The manager's role is much like that of chairperson. He or she does not try to influence the group to adopt a particular solution and the manager is willing to accept and implement any solution that has the support of the entire group.

Source: Reprinted from *Organizational Dynamics*, Spring 1973, Victor H. Vroom, "A New Look at Managerial Decision Making," p. 67. Copyright 1973 with permission from Elsevier Science.

1963). A decision has a high degree of objective quality if it is made in a logical, rational, step-by-step approach. In other words, a decision made by following the formal decision-making process illustrated in Figure 7.3 on page 197 meets the objective-quality criteria.

A decision has a high degree of acceptance if it has been made with the input of those affected by it. Decisions whose success requires the understanding and support of those affected by them are the kinds of decisions that must meet the acceptance criteria. Examples include decisions about changing procedures, altering the work environment, or scheduling vacations.

How can a manager know which factors are important in a given decision, especially when both acceptance and quality criteria can apply to the same decision? Victor Vroom and Phillip Yetton (1973) have provided managers with a series of questions that guide the manager to the appropriate option. The model is the **Vroom and Yetton decision tree** shown in Figure 7.9. As each question is asked and answered, the manager learns more about the nature of the decision. When the manager reaches the circled number at the end of each series of questions, the most effective decision-making method is identified. Those numbers correspond to the options identifying the levels of subordinate involvement in Figure 7.8.

Vroom and Yetton decision tree
A series of questions that guide the manager to the appropriate option.

http://www.barnesandnoble.com

As an example, suppose Kimberly Holland, Barnes & Noble's store manager in Plano, Texas, is developing work schedules. Holland begins the process by asking these questions:

A. Is there a quality requirement that might make one solution more rational than another? Since the answer is no; Holland moves to D.

D. Is acceptance of the decision by subordinates critical to effective implementation? The answer is yes, the subordinates are very concerned; Holland now moves to E.

E. If Holland makes the decision alone, will subordinates be likely to accept it? Since the answer is no, Holland should use option 5 (from Figure 7.8).

Thus Holland would share the problem with the subordinates as a group. Together they would generate and evaluate alternatives and attempt to reach agreement (consensus) on a solution. Holland should not try to influence the group to

FIGURE 7.9 *Applying the Vroom and Yetton decision tree for choosing a decision-making style*

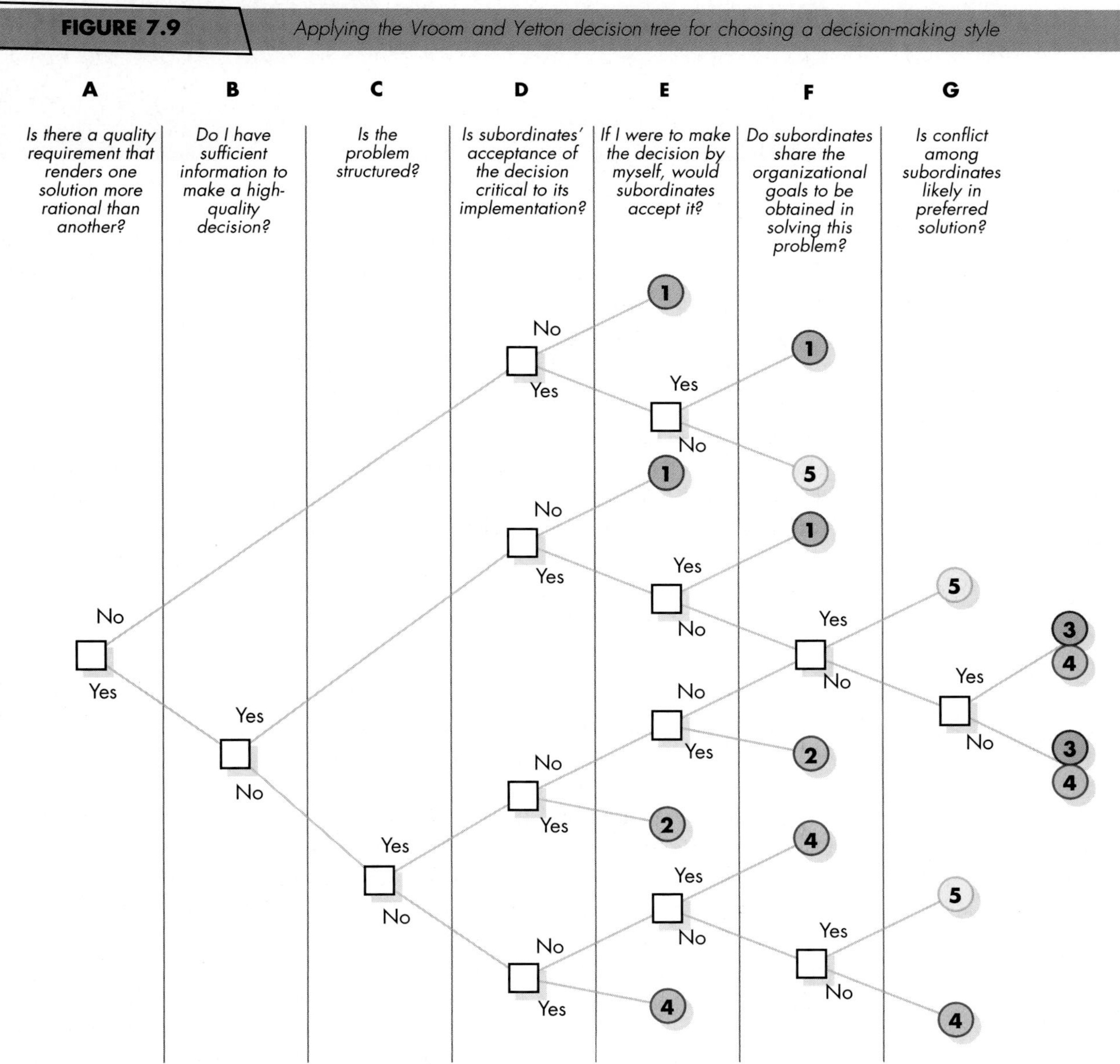

Source: Adapted and reprinted from *Leadership and Decision-Making* by Victor H. Vroom and Philip W. Yetton, by permission of the University of Pittsburgh Press. © 1973 by University of Pittsburgh Press.

Managers need subordinates' support, input, and understanding of decisions in order to be effective leaders.

adopt her solution, and she must be willing to accept and implement any solution that has the support of the entire group, as long as it fits within Barnes & Noble's policies. In this situation, as in most situations in a work environment, working with and cultivating the support of employees for decisions is critical to a manager. Even the highest-quality decisions will not be effectively implemented if employees do not support them.

Organizational Systems

The organizational system is the final element of the internal environment that affects decision making. Every organization has policies, procedures, programs, and rules that serve as boundaries for a manager's decision making. Sometimes these factors may be obsolete or may cause delays—red tape. If they pose major barriers, it may be wise for a manager to delay a decision and try instead to modify the system.

External Environment

As we noted in Chapter 3 and discussed in Chapters 5 and 6, the external environment strongly influences a manager's actions, especially in decision making. Customers, competitors, government agencies, and society in general can and do influence decisions. Customers, as has been consistently noted, are a driving force in decisions. The decisions for new products, improved service, and longer and more accessible hours of operations are all made as companies respond to meet or exceed customer expectation. Competitors force companies to adjust—Coca-Cola and Pepsi; Domino's, Pizza Hut, and Little Caesars; McDonald's, Burger King, and Wendy's. The decisions to improve the quality of products and services have been made in response to customer expectations.

In addition, government actions can alter or even reverse the decisions companies make—as John McDonnell, president of McDonnell Douglas Corporation (now part of The Boeing Company) found out. To strengthen his financially troubled aerospace company, McDonnell decided to sell 40 percent of McDonnell Douglas to Taiwan Aerospace. In turn, McDonnell Douglas would receive $2 billion to develop new planes. When the proposed transaction drew the attention of the United States Senate, pressure was applied to derail the decision (Verespej, 1992).

INFLUENCE OF MANAGERIAL STYLE ON DECISION MAKING

Describe the personal attributes of a manager that influence decision making

In addition to the environment in which decisions take place, other factors influence managerial decision making. These are the manager's personal attributes: his or her decision-making approach, ability to set priorities, timing of decisions, tunnel vision, previous commitments, and degree of creativity.

Personal Decision-Making Approaches

Not all managers approach decisions the same way. Many have a bias for one of the following three approaches.

Rational/Logical Decision Model

This step-by-step approach, illustrated in Figure 7.3 on page 197, is the one recommended in this chapter. This process focuses on facts and logic and minimizes intuitive judgments. The manager using this method tries to thoroughly examine a situation or problem in an orderly fashion. The manager relies on the decision-making steps and on decision tools such as payback analysis, decision trees, and research, which will be discussed later in the chapter.

Intuitive Decision Model

Some managers prefer to avoid statistical analysis and logical processes in making a decision. These gut decision makers rely on their feelings and hunches about the situation. Although it is hard to eliminate all elements of intuition from decision making, the manager who relies on intuition alone for long-range decision making could be courting disaster. The best decisions are often the result of a blend of the decision maker's intuition (based on experience and hindsight) and the rational step-by-step approach.

Predisposed Decision Model

A manager who decides on a solution and then gathers the information to support the decision illustrates this approach. A manager with this tendency is likely to ignore critical information. Such a manager may face the same decision again later (Whyte, 1991).

Another related trait is the tendency of some managers to influence the final solution by favoring specific alternatives. In this way, the manager can distort the value of the preselected alternative.

The critical element is for the manager to know what his or her decision-making tendencies are and to move toward the rational model. A serious problem can result if a manager believes he or she is using one approach but in reality is using a different model.

Ability to Set Priorities

The old saying "When it rains it pours" seems to be true about decisions. They have a tendency to be called for continuously, possibly in bunches. Thus a factor that can influence a manager's success at decision making is the ability to establish priorities. Each manager may have a different set of criteria for prioritizing. Some managers may give priority to the decision having the greatest impact on the organization's goals. Others may assign priorities in terms of what their bosses think is important. A third group of managers may make decisions based on likes and dislikes. No matter what criteria is used, managers need to assign priorities and to know why those were the priorities assigned.

For some managers the ability to set priorities may be limited by procrastination, or putting off, difficult decisions. For a procrastinator, decisions don't have a priority, they are made when the procrastinator gets around to them. Avoiding the difficult decisions creates their own priority system—easy decisions are first and difficult decisions are second. Such a practice is dangerous. Tough decisions often cannot be delayed.

Timing of Decisions

After a decision is made, it must be translated into action. Good timing plays an important part in successfully implementing a decision, and improper timing can harm the best decision. A manager should be sensitive to the influence of timing to increase the possibility of success. One example of the importance of timing is provided by Cadbury's decision to purchase Dr. Pepper/Seven-Up. This decision was timed to outflank Coca-Cola and Pepsi in the cola wars and focus on noncola beverages. The result—Cadbury is now the number one producer of noncola beverages in the United States (Turner, 1995).

http://www.cadburyschweppes.com

Starbucks gourmet coffee chain provides another example. Starbucks decided to grow by adding 200 more stores nationally, by entering new markets like Philadelphia and Las Vegas, and by expanding abroad. The reason was timing. Starbucks' success brought in a host of new competitors each with an eye on Starbucks. In turn Starbucks wanted to beat the competitors to the punch (Steel, 1994).

http://www.starbucks.com

Starbucks got a jump on its competitors by the optimum timing of its decisions to add stores and expand into new markets.

Tunnel Vision

tunnel vision
Having a narrow viewpoint.

http://www.theglassceiling.com

A manager who approaches a problem with an extremely narrow viewpoint will develop a limited choice of alternatives (Mondy and Premeaux, 1995). This narrow view, or **tunnel vision**, can result from bias or limited experience. The "glass ceiling" that continues to prevent women from rising in corporate management may result from the tunnel vision of male managers (Etorre, 1992). In other instances managers can't "see" another way—another alternative—because they have little or no familiarity with a situation.

Commitment to Previous Decisions

Managers must frequently make decisions that relate to previous decisions. Consider the CEO who has committed substantial financial resources to the development of a product that could revolutionize the marketplace. He or she may be strongly influenced to commit additional resources, even if the decision seems not to be working. It is difficult to undo a decision, especially with reputations and personal pride at stake. In such instances the implementation of a control mechanism, with benchmarks for follow-up actions, may be helpful.

Creativity

Being innovative and able to see new ways of doing things aid the manager's decision making. Most people possess creativity, but they don't always apply it, often because of situational factors. For example, a shift manager at McDonald's has specific policies, procedures, and systems that dictate how and when tasks will be completed. In addition, this same manager works in an environment that can best be described as chaotic during peak times. Neither of the characteristics of the environment provides opportunity for reflection and innovation.

outside-the-box thinking
To adopt a new perspective and see it work; not get caught up in the old ways.

http://www.pwcglobal.com

To counter the lack of innovation and creativity, organizations like PricewaterhouseCoopers, Motorola, and 3M promote **outside-the-box thinking**. Instead of approaching a problem with preconceived ideas and limitations managers at these progressive firms are encouraged to "get outside the box, adopt a new perspective, and see it work" says Paul Pederson, a partner at Price Waterhouse (now PricewaterhouseCoopers). "What we need to do as managers is not get caught up in the old ways, rather we need to tap our corporate brainpower" (Stewart, 1995).

GROUP DECISION MAKING

6

Discuss the value of group decision making, and identify three techniques of group decision making

Earlier in the chapter we noted how subordinates influence a manager's decision-making process. Workers who participate in making decisions are likely to support them. As more organizations and managers accept that real participation in decision making produces ownership of the job and better quality products, the concept of group decision making will become an increasingly important part of the work environment. Many management experts feel that such involvement is not a maybe, but a must. Front-line employees must become partners with the manager in the decision-making process (Ettling and Jago, 1988). Such partnerships are a primary goal of team management, the topic of Chapter 15. But for now, the next section will examine three proven techniques for involving groups in the decision-making process: brainstorming, the nominal group technique, and the Delphi technique.

Brainstorming

brainstorming
A group effort at generating ideas and alternatives that can help a manager solve a problem or seize an opportunity.

Brainstorming is a group effort at generating ideas and alternatives that can help a manager solve a problem or seize an opportunity (Grover, 1988). It helps overcome tunnel vision by encouraging any and all ideas while withholding criticism. The following elements are part of a successful brainstorming session:

- A half dozen to a dozen people are gathered in a comfortable setting for a specified time—free from outside interruptions.
- Participants are given the problem (barriers to advancement in the company) or opportunity (new products or new markets) and told that no idea or suggestion is too ridiculous to be voiced.
- The facilitator encourages the free flow of ideas until all opinions have been presented.
- A person acting as the designated scribe records the ideas on a chalkboard or flipchart. After the session, the ideas are sorted and examined in more detail by the manager or another group.

http://www.us.deloitte.com

An example of using brainstorming to generate problem-solving ideas can be seen at Deloitte & Touche, the national accounting firm. Top management discovered a sudden and rapid decrease in the number of women who were seeking employment in the company. Women were leaving because there were barriers to career advancement. After a series of brainstorming sessions, the company developed a separate career program for women. In addition, it created a company-wide task force to recommend policies to support the advancement of women (Briggins, 1995).

Brainstorming works well when the problem is straightforward and well defined and the atmosphere is supportive of a solution; but it is only a process for generating ideas. The next two techniques offer ways to arrive at a solution.

Nominal Group Technique

nominal group technique
Creating a structure to provide for equal—but independent—participation by all members.

Group discussion sessions can be ineffective when only a few people talk and dominate the discussion. The **nominal group technique** eliminates this problem by creating a structure to provide for equal—but independent—participation by all members (Fox, 1989). As shown in Figure 7.10, the process involves seven steps:

1. *Problem definition.* When the nominal group is assembled, the group leader defines the problem. No discussion is permitted, although questions to clarify the problem may be asked.
2. *Development of ideas.* Each participant writes down his or her ideas about the problem. Once again, there is no discussion.
3. *Round-robin presentation.* Each member of the group presents his or her ideas to the group. The group leader records the ideas on a flipchart or blackboard. The process continues without discussion until all ideas are recorded.

FIGURE 7.10 *Steps in the nominal group technique*

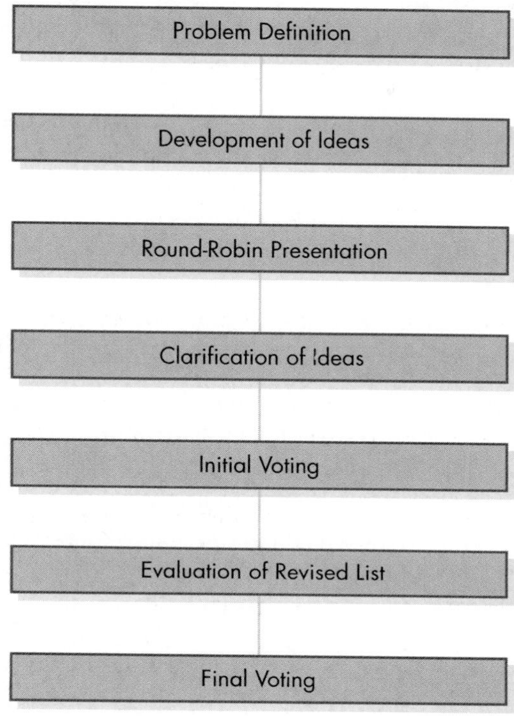

4. *Clarification of ideas.* The group conducts an open discussion of the ideas with members providing explanations when needed.
5. *Initial voting.* In a secret ballot, each member independently ranks what he or she thinks are the best solutions. The solutions with the lowest average ranking are eliminated.
6. *Evaluation of revised list.* The group members question each other on the remaining solutions.
7. *Final voting.* In another secret ballot, all the ideas are ranked. The idea receiving the highest vote total is adopted.

In addition to providing a structure for equal participation, the nominal group technique encourages individual creativity. The environment created by the structure provides the opportunity to have an idea developed and presented without interference. The negative associated with this process is that it is time-consuming.

Delphi technique
Group decision making conducted by a group leader through the use of written questionnaires; it provides a structure, leads to consensus, and emphasizes equal participation.

Delphi Technique

Similar to the nominal group technique is the **Delphi technique**. It too provides a structure, leads to consensus, and emphasizes equal participation—but the Delphi participants never meet. Rather, the decision making is conducted by a group leader through the use of written questionnaires. The process works as follows:

1. The problem is stated to a group of experts through a questionnaire. Each person is asked to provide solutions. The experts do not interact.
2. Each participant completes the questionnaire and returns it.
3. A summary of opinions is developed from the answers received. The summary is distributed to the experts along with a second questionnaire.
4. The experts complete the second questionnaire. In this stage participants have the benefit of other people's opinions and can change their suggestions to reflect this.
5. The process continues until the experts reach consensus.

http://www.sheraton.com

Although it is expensive and time-consuming, the Delphi technique works well. It also provides for a thorough, unrushed analysis of information, a factor that aided ITT Sheraton (now part of Starwood Hotels & Resorts Worldwide, Inc.) in solving a problem—lower sales caused by a sales force that wasn't viewed as helpful or as knowledgeable as its competitors. To address the problem, ITT Sheraton used its Meetings Advisory Board. By following the Delphi process, the board's experts identified that the major difference between Sheraton and its competitors was that Sheraton was a generalist, whereas the competitors were specialists. The competitors broke business down according to corporate transient, corporate group, and association group travel, each of which has different needs. The solution dealt with refining general categories into specific market segments. Now sales have increased by 31 percent (Shermach, 1995).

Advantages and Disadvantages of Group Decision Making

Regardless of what group techniques a manager chooses to use for decision making, the manager should be aware of the advantages and disadvantages.

Advantages

Groups bring a broader perspective to the decision-making process. The rich diversity found in today's organizations broadens the views on any topic. The differences in cultures, ethnicity, national origin, gender, and age found within provide valuable perspectives in defining a problem and in developing alternatives (a factor emphasized at Blue Cross Blue Shield in this chapter's Valuing Diversity feature). When people participate in decision making they are more likely to be satisfied with the decision and to support it, thus facilitating its implementation. Group decision making provides the opportunity for discussion to help answer questions and reduce uncertainty for decision makers who may not be willing to take risks alone.

Disadvantages

groupthink
Group members becoming so committed to the group that they become reluctant to disagree.

A disadvantage—besides the fact that group decision making is time-consuming—is the possibility that the decision reached will be a compromise rather than the optimal outcome. At times individuals can become guilty of **groupthink**. The members become so committed to the group that they become reluctant to disagree with other members. Additionally, groups have difficulty in performing certain tasks. Specifically groups struggle when assigned to draft policies and procedures; they do much better at editing or commenting on documents. Also, most groups

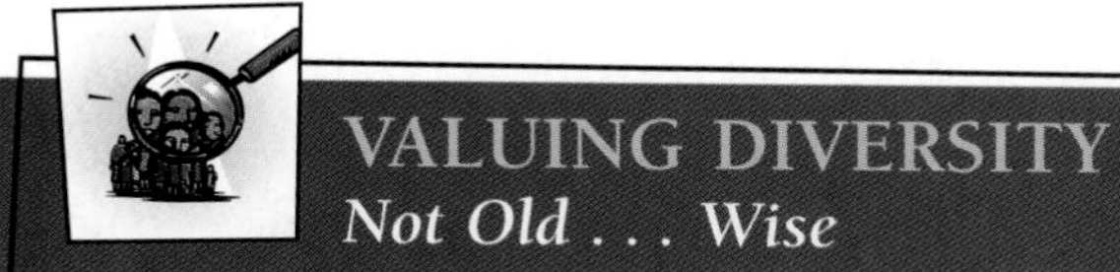

VALUING DIVERSITY
Not Old . . . Wise

Michelle Gaggini will be the first to admit she hasn't always done the right thing when it comes to managing older workers. As a twenty-three-year-old supervisor, the people who reported to Gaggini were mainly workers who had been with the company for ten or fifteen years. In many cases they were old enough to be her parents. Admittedly, Gaggini made plenty of mistakes—assuming that everyone thought as she did.

After eighteen years as a supervisor, Gaggini has a different perspective. As the vice president for national benefit delivery services at Blue Cross Blue Shield of Michigan, Gaggini values the diversity. "We all have different ways of looking at things, regardless of age, culture, or race." Older workers are particularly valuable in the operation. They can sometimes point out land mines that are obvious to them from their many years on the job. In full agreement Gaggini adds, "I think I might have a solution, and then an older worker with more experience says, 'we tried that back in 1984 and here's why it didn't work.' That helps me identify pitfalls and rethink my decision. Even though I am the boss, someone on my team may have more knowledge, and I think whoever is the most knowledgeable should be listened to the most."

http://www.bcbsm.com

Source: Charles E. Cohen, "Managing Older Workers," *Working Woman* (November 1994), pp. 61–62.

have difficulty in taking the initiative, instead they tend to react rather than initiate action. A final disadvantage is that in group decision making, no one person has responsibility for the decision (Whyte, 1989).

QUANTITATIVE DECISION-MAKING TECHNIQUES

7

Explain three quantitative techniques for decision making, and describe the situations in which each is appropriate

A manager has several quantitative tools available to help improve the overall quality of decisions. Depending on the type of problem, the application of decision trees, payback analysis, and simulations provide several choices.

Decision Trees

decision tree
A graphical representation of the actions a manager can take and how these actions relate to other events.

http://www.pizzahut.com

Earlier in the chapter, Barnes & Noble store manager Kimberly Holland used a version of a decision tree (Figure 7.9, page 207) to help her decide to what degree her employees needed to be involved in developing a new work schedule. Kimberly chose this tool because a **decision tree** shows a complete picture of a potential decision. It allows a manager to graph alternative decision paths, observe the outcomes of the decisions, and see how the decisions relate to future events.

To illustrate the value and flexibility of this tool, a decision tree has been developed to help Lisa, a marketing manager for Pizza Hut. She must decide whether to spend money either test marketing in a new market or improving the company's marketing performance in an existing market—the kind of situation that McDonald's, Taco Bell, and TGI Fridays face constantly. If the venture into the new market succeeds, Pizza Hut will have a competitive edge. If it fails, competitors (Little Caesars, Domino's) may enter the market and gain so much momentum that Pizza Hut may lose its overall position. The danger stems from the potential lack of success in the new market and the vulnerability created in the old market by diverting funds and attention away from it.

Lisa's decision tree comprises branches from decision points (squares) and chance or competitive moves (circles). In Figure 7.11 the decision path starts with Lisa's initial decision: to test market or not to test market. If the outcome of the decision (shown to the right of the decision point) is to authorize the project, point B is the second point for a decision. At point B the test market has been successful. Then Lisa must decide between entering the market with a full-scale advertising program or waiting until a later date. With each alternative she will face competitive actions by Little Caesars and Domino's.

Decision trees require a manager to include only important decisions and events or results—that is, ones having consequences that need to be compared. Note that Figure 7.11 also projects an outcome if Lisa chooses not to begin test marketing at all.

FIGURE 7.11 *Decision tree with chains of activities and events*

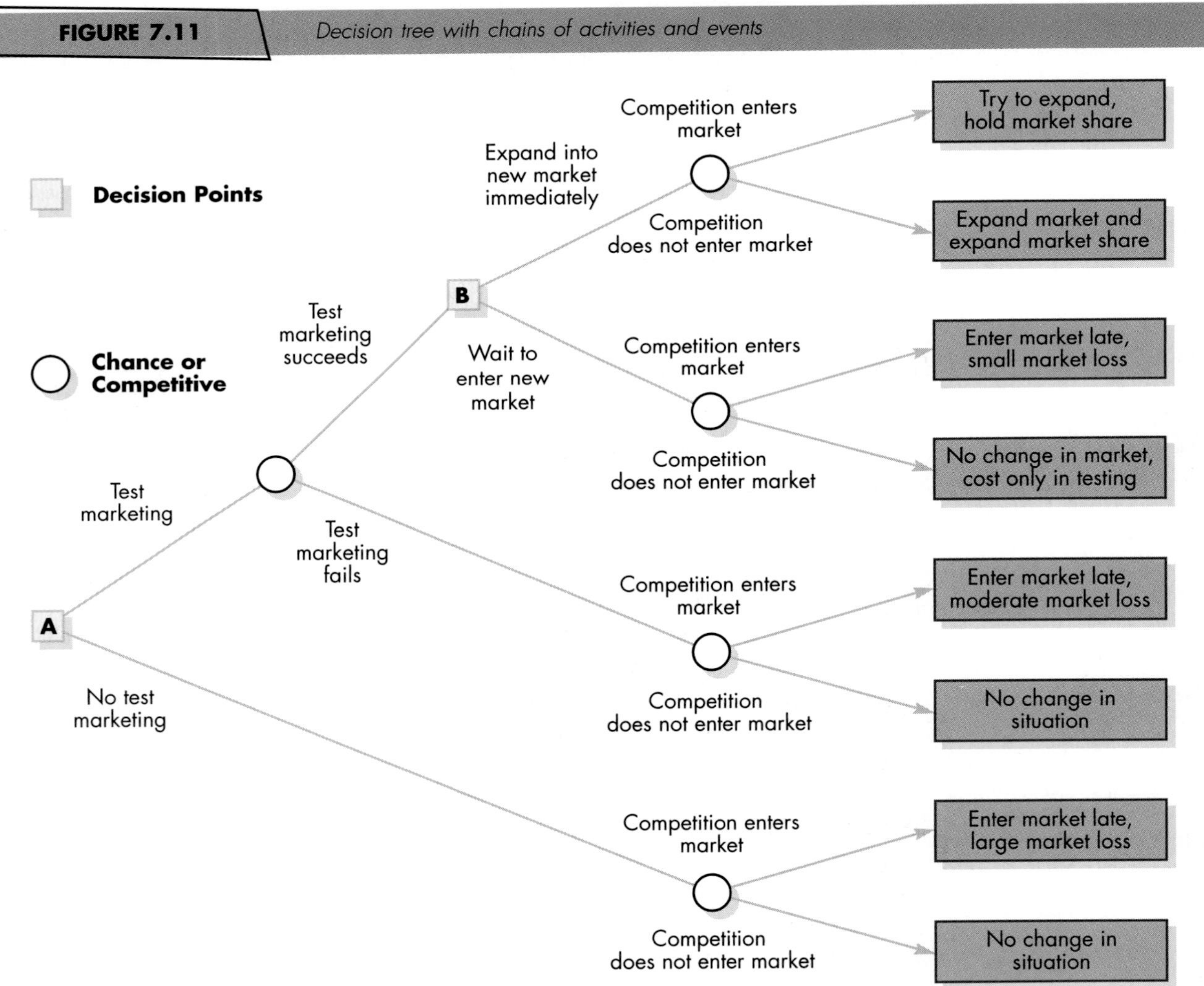

Source: Reprinted by permission of *Harvard Business Review*. An exhibit from "Decision Trees for Decision Making" by John F. Magee (July/August 1964).

Payback Analysis

payback analysis
A technique that ranks alternatives according to how long each takes to pay back its initial cost.

"Out of these three models, which one should I buy? They all have different prices and features. How do you compare apples and oranges?" Sometimes managers face a dilemma in making capital-purchasing decisions. To evaluate alternatives, an excellent strategy is **payback analysis**, a technique that ranks alternatives according to how long each takes to pay back its initial cost. The strategy involves choosing the alternative that has the quickest payback.

Quick Copy owner Tim Collins plans to purchase a computerized printing system. Three suppliers have given him prices for three different systems. Each system has unique features that will affect the revenue to be earned. Which one should Collins choose? To be able to compare systems, Collins prepares a payback analysis as shown in Figure 7.12. For each system, Collins lists the initial cost along with the projected annual revenues derived from the system until that cost is paid back. As Figure 7.12 shows, System A takes seven years to recover Collins's investment; System B takes six years. In this case System C's four-year payback makes it the best investment—even though it has the highest initial cost.

Simulations

Chapter 2 described the quantitative school of management theory. It focused on the development of mathematical techniques to solve management problems and aid decision making. These techniques are generally referred to as simulations and include the specific applications of queuing models or waiting line models and game theory. Initially this section examines the general concept of simulations and then explores queuing and game theory.

simulation
A model of a real activity or process.

A **simulation** is a model of a real activity or process. When a process is simulated, a model is created that will behave like that process. For example, the federal government and many private corporations and universities have computer

FIGURE 7.12 *An example of a payback analysis*

		Computerized Printing System		
		A	B	C
Initial Cost		$14,000	$12,000	$17,000
Revenues	Year 1	0	500	2,000
	Year 2	1,000	1,000	3,000
	Year 3	1,500	1,500	5,000
	Year 4	2,000	2,500	7,000
	Year 5	2,500	3,000	
	Year 6	3,000	3,500	
	Year 7	4,000		
Payback Period		$\frac{\$14,000}{\$\ 2,000} = 7.0$	$\frac{\$12,000}{\$\ 2,000} = 6.0$	$\frac{\$17,000}{\$\ 4,250} = 4.0$

simulations to tell how the economy might respond when various changes are introduced into it. Data on a proposed tax cut or increases in the interest rates can be fed into a computer; what will emerge is a view of the areas of the economy that will be affected and how they will change.

Models may be physical or abstract. The computer model just mentioned is an example of an abstract model, as are a designer's drawings or mathematical or chemical equations. Most of us are more familiar with physical models, because they are tangible and three-dimensional. Manufacturers' prototypes (one-of-a-kind, handmade models), architectural models of finished structures, and Detroit's dream cars are just a few examples. As you will soon see when queuing and game theory are discussed, a simulation or model is used in decision making because it allows managers to

- See the results much more quickly than would be the case if actual changes were made in the real world.
- Anticipate competitive responses to strategy decisions.
- Make decisions under a wide variety of changing conditions.
- Avoid the interruptions of normal business operations that real-life experimentation can cause.
- Avoid the time loss and expense associated with experimenting with actual company assets.
- Avoid annoying the customers and taking facilities out of service while training or experimentation is being conducted.

queueing models or waiting line models
Models that help managers decide what length of waiting line or queue would be optimal.

http://www.walmart.com

If you have ever stood in line at a restaurant, movie theater, grocery store, or discount store, you will appreciate the value of **queueing models** or **waiting line models**. These help managers decide what length of waiting line or queue would be optimal. At Wal-Mart, managers have a continuing concern about the length of the checkout line at the cash register and the subsequent time customers must wait in that line. Customers forced to wait too long may take their business to Target or Kmart. Management must weigh the cost of opening other checkout areas to provide faster service against the risk of losing customers. They must decide what balance between customer dissatisfaction and operating costs is the best.

To help achieve the proper balance, managers can create a model simulating the bottlenecks that form in checkout lines. The neighborhood supermarket opens additional checkout counters when two to three customers are in line. Most movie theaters have created a ticket window where tickets may be purchased hours before a show.

just-in-time inventory
Delivery of raw materials or other kinds of normal inventories to correspond to production schedules, leading to the elimination of the need to warehouse items.

http://www.ti.com

Queues also form in manufacturing, as goods are funneled through a production run. To help solve the problem, companies have devised the **just-in-time inventory** approach. At Texas Instruments parts used in manufacturing are delivered several times each day, and the goods are sent immediately to where they are needed in the production line. This just-in-time (JIT) delivery of raw materials or other kinds of normal inventories to correspond to production schedules has led to the elimination of the need to warehouse items.

game theory
Attempts to predict how people or organizations will behave in competitive situations.

Game theory attempts to predict how people or organizations will behave in competitive situations. It allows managers to devise strategies to counter the behavior of competitors. Managers apply game theory in situations in which organizations

Queuing models can help alleviate long lines and customer frustrations.

http://www.pg.com

compete against one another in regard to price, product development, advertising, and distribution systems. If managers at Procter & Gamble were able to predict with a degree of accuracy whether and within what time frame Lever Brothers would initiate a price decrease, the managers at Procter & Gamble could decide whether or not to decrease their own price.

http://www.merck.com

http://www.merck-medco.com

The use of game theory has been exploding in the last few years in corporate takeovers, negotiations, and competitive bidding. Before moving to acquire Medco, a mail-order distributor of low-priced generic drugs, drug maker Merck hired a game theorist to study the impact of health reform on Merck's drug prices—both with and without Medco. In another situation General Re-Insurance, worried that it was being used to extract a higher price from a rival, was advised by a game theorist to change the rules—that is, refuse to participate unless there was only a single round of bids. Then General Re-Insurance was advised to make unconditional bids that forced the seller to make quick responses. It also gave its rival, General Electric, little time to come up with counteroffers. The rules gave an equal chance to the smaller bidder, and General Re-Insurance won the contest in a quick, one-week decision (Helm, 1994).

CREATING AN ENVIRONMENT FOR EFFECTIVE DECISION MAKING

8

Describe strategies a manager can use to create a more effective decision-making environment

Because managers in today's organizations face complex, challenging, and stressful decision-making demands, it is critical that they create an effective decision-making environment for themselves. The following hints can help them do so (Ireland, Hill, and Williams, 1992):

1. *Provide time for decisions to be made.* Don't be pushed—or push others—into making a decision too rapidly. If necessary, negotiate for more time to make a quality decision.

2. *Have self-confidence.* Courage and self-confidence are required for a manager to make the risk-laden decisions called for in today's rapidly changing business environment.
3. *Encourage others to make decisions.* Trust subordinates and allow them the freedom to act.
4. *Learn from past decisions.* The confidence of others is gained by not making the same mistake. Study decisions to see why they worked—and why they didn't.
5. *Recognize the difference in decision-making situations.* All decisions do not have the same degree of risk or priority, nor should all decisions be approached the same way.
6. *Recognize the importance of quality information.* Assume that quality information is available and insist that subordinates support their decisions with data.
7. *Make the tough decisions.* Don't procrastinate or avoid dealing with decisions that could be unpopular. Once the decision is made—whether yes or no—provide an explanation to everyone.
8. *Know when to hold off.* Recognize that sometimes the best decision is no decision; it may be necessary for events to play themselves out or for more information to be gathered.
9. *Be ready to try things.* Today's excellent companies are those that act—that try things. Rather than debating a new product idea, they test market it. Managers who change the status quo, even on a small scale, can learn more about their market or workforce by watching the effects of those changes than can those who simply observe the status quo.
10. *Be ready to ask for help.* Everyone needs help at some time or another; it isn't a sign of weakness to ask for assistance. In fact, knowing when to ask for help is a sign of wisdom.

CHAPTER SUMMARY

1 **Recognize that decision making is performed at all management levels.** Decision making is a part of all managers' jobs. At all levels of the organization, managers are engaged in decision making. Top managers make decisions dealing with the mission of the organization and strategies for achieving it. Middle-level managers focus their decision making on implementing the strategies, as well as budgeting and allocating resources. First-level managers deal with repetitive day-to-day operations.

2 **Distinguish between formal and informal approaches to decision making.** Not all decision-making situations are identical. The nature of the decision often dictates what approach to take. Complex problems or situations require the use of a formal decision-making process. Less complicated problems or those that a manager has had a great deal of experience in solving can be handled less formally by following habit or relying on past situations.

3 **List the steps in the decision-making process.** There are seven steps in the formal decision-making process: (1) defining the problem or opportunity, (2) identifying limiting factors, (3) developing potential alternatives, (4) analyzing the alternatives, (5) selecting the best alternative, (6) implementing the decision, (7) establishing a control and evaluation system.

4 **Describe the environmental factors that influence decision making.** Decision making is influenced by the following environmental factors:

- *Degree of certainty.* Managers make decisions under three conditions of knowledge and ambiguity—certainty, risk, and uncertainty.
- *Imperfect resources.* Managers do not make decisions with ideal resources—information, time, personnel, equipment, and supplies.
- *Internal environment.* A manager's decision is influenced by superiors, subordinates, and organizational systems.

- *External environment.* Customers, competitors, government agencies, and society in general are forces that can and do influence decisions.

5 Describe the personal attributes of a manager that influence decision making. The personal attributes of a manager that influence decision making are

- *Personal decision-making approaches.* Managers may prefer to use the rational/logical decision model, the nonrational/intuitive model, or the predisposed decision model.
- *Ability to set priorities.* Each manager may have a different set of criteria for prioritizing—greatest impact on organizational goals, what the boss wants, likes or dislikes.
- *Timing of decisions.* Timing plays an important part in successfully implementing a decision, and improper timing can harm the best decision.
- *Tunnel vision.* A manager who approaches a problem with an extremely narrow viewpoint will develop a limited choice of alternatives. This tunnel vision may be caused by bias or limited experience.
- *Commitment to previous decisions.* Managers must frequently make decisions that relate to previous decisions. In such situations the manager may be strongly influenced to commit additional resources even if the decision seems not to be working.
- *Creativity.* Although most people possess creativity, they don't always apply it.

6 Discuss the value of group decision making, and identify three techniques of group decision making. Groups bring a broader perspective to the decision-making process. In addition, people who participate in decision making are more likely to be satisfied with it and support it, thus facilitating implementation. Group decision making provides the opportunity for discussion, which helps answer questions and reduces uncertainty for decision makers who may not be willing to take risks alone. Group decision-making techniques include brainstorming, the nominal group technique, and the Delphi technique.

7 Explain three quantitative techniques for decision making, and describe the situations in which each is appropriate.

- A decision tree shows a complete picture of a potential decision. It allows a manager to graph alternative decision paths, observe the outcomes of the decision, and see how the decision relates to future events. Decision trees help the manager think carefully through situations.
- Payback analysis can be used in making capital purchasing decisions. It helps the manager rank each alternative according to how long each takes to pay back its initial cost.
- Simulations develop models of a real activity. They allow managers to see results much more quickly than would be the case if actual changes were made in the real world. Types of situations include queueing models or waiting line models, used to help managers decide what length of waiting line is optimal. A second type of simulation, game theory, attempts to predict how people or organizations will behave in competitive situations. It then allows managers to devise strategies to counter the behavior of competitors.

8 Describe strategies a manager can use to create a more effective decision-making environment. To create a more effective learning environment a manager can

- Provide time for decisions to be made.
- Have confidence.
- Encourage others to make decisions.
- Learn from past decisions.
- Recognize the difference in decision-making situations.
- Recognize the importance of quality information.
- Make the tough decisions.
- Know when to hold off.
- Be ready to try things.
- Be willing to ask for help.

REVIEW QUESTIONS

1. For each managerial level, provide examples of the kinds of decisions that managers make at that level.
2. What factors influence whether a manager should use a formal or informal approach to decision making?
3. Identify each step in the decision-making process, and describe briefly what should happen in each step.
4. What four factors in the decision-making environment influence the decision-making process and the decision maker?
5. What are the three personal decision-making approaches a manager may use? What are the characteristics of each?
6. What are three group decision-making techniques? What is the value of each?
7. Under what circumstances would you use payback analysis? What purpose does payback analysis serve?
8. What are three strategies a manager can use to create a more effective decision-making environment?

DISCUSSION QUESTIONS FOR CRITICAL THINKING

1. What example can you provide to demonstrate the application of the seven-step decision-making process? Take a problem or opportunity you have had and apply the seven-step process.
2. Provide evidence that shows which personal decision-making approach or approaches you use.
3. How do you set priorities for making decisions? What rationale can you give to support your priority setting?
4. What specific applications can you give where organizations have applied queueing models? What examples can you give of companies that need to apply queueing models?

INTERNET EXERCISES

Check the text Web site at http://plunkett.swcollege.com for updated links to the Internet Exercises.

1. Briefly describe a decision you need to make. Use Plus/Minus/Interesting (PMI), a development by Edward de Bono discussed at the Web site listed below. Did it help you make your decision? Why or why not?
   http://www.mindtools.com/pmi.html
2. Skill in decision making is enhanced by creativity. What does it mean to be creative? What are some obstacles to creativity? What action steps will you take to improve your creativity?
   http://www.ozemail.com.au/~caveman/Creative/Basics/definitions.htm

   http://www.ozemail.com.au/~caveman/Creative/Basics/obstacles.htm

   http://www.ozemail.com.au/~caveman/Creative/Basics/increase.htm
3. Many decisions are made that treat a symptom, not the problem. List some guiding principles that will improve problem identification. Discuss a time you have seen one or more of these guiding principles affect a decision.
   http://www.innovnet.com/change3.htm

APPLICATION CASE

Continental Lite Fails to Fly

Shadowed by questionable decision making, Continental Airlines CEO Robert Ferguson resigned. Ferguson had been the main architect of Continental's attempt to mimic Southwest Airlines with its own Continental Lite. Ferguson had expected the no-frills operation, which made up about 35 percent of the airline's domestic capacity, to be a major revenue producer. Sadly, costs remained too high and revenues fell far below projections, with 20 percent of Continental Lite's routes losing money.

Ferguson made three major decisions at the outset that presented hurdles for Continental Lite.

- Continental Lite decided to copy the tactics of Southwest Airlines, known for dominating its markets and driving out competition with its lower prices. Some of Continental's routes, however, simply were not traveled heavily enough to support frequent Southwest-style flights. In addition, Continental Lite relied more heavily on one-stop and connecting flights than did Southwest, thus forcing more late flights and other operating problems.
- Continental Lite decided it would face limited competition; but rivals such as USAir and Delta responded more aggressively to Lite fares than expected. Also, given a choice, consumers were less likely to choose Continental, which had a higher rate of customer complaints.
- When Continental decided to launch its no-frills service, it lacked a distinct name or identity, thus missing its chance to make a splash. Then, to compound the problem, Continental tried to sell consumers three "brands" at once—Lite, a premium international service, and its more traditional long-haul domestic flights. The result was confusion. Continental tried to be all things to all people, failed, and then decided to discontinue the Continental Lite concept.

http://www.continental.com

Questions

1. How would you classify each of Continental's three decisions—programmed or nonprogrammed? Explain your answer.
2. What type of decision-making environment—certainty, risk, uncertainty—did Continental Lite have for each decision? Explain your answer.
3. What internal and external factors might have influenced the success of each decision?
4. What quantitative decision techniques might have helped Continental Lite in making each of the three decisions? Explain your answer.

For more on Continental Lite, see Wendy Zellner, "Why Continental's CEO Fell to Earth," *Business Week*, November 7, 1994, p. 32.

VIDEO CASE

Next Door Food Store: A Study in Decision Making

The Next Door Food Store convenience chain is headquartered in Mt. Pleasant, Michigan, and has more than 30 locations throughout the state. The company's stores have evolved since their creation in 1920 into "a whole lot more than the corner gas station," according to company President David C. Johnson. The company's management has a strong commitment to innovation and has never been afraid of change or making difficult decisions. This willingness to change is illustrated by the company's decision to create the first combination gas station and convenience store in northern Michigan (in Charlevoix) in 1978. The remodeled gas station was so successful that management quickly converted all its locations to the new layout, a decision that led to a doubling of the company's size by 1989. In 1994, the chain decided to add Subway sandwich shops to its stores, which in turn attracted other food service franchises to Next Door store locations.

Early on, executives at Next Door realized that consumers' wishes and concerns should guide their decision making. To satisfy consumers, yet make rational decisions in the interests of the chain, management had to determine which items each store should carry and how to distribute these items to the stores. To address these fundamental product and distribution issues, management first considered the goals of the company and the constraints facing it. The goals of Next Door Food Store cover four main areas: (1) to maintain a variety of products that meet customer demands; (2) to keep distribution costs as low as possible; (3) to minimize inventory levels; and (4) to utilize just-in-time (JIT) inventory systems in cooperation with suppliers.

Decisions regarding product and distribution issues were also influenced by several constraints. First, the sales volume of each small store was quite low relative to that of large supermarkets. Second, each location has relatively small shelf and storage space. Third, the limited number of convenience stores meant that the company would not enjoy economies of scale in purchasing. Fourth, the company's more than 30 stores were scattered throughout the state. Finally, the company did not have its own trucks for shipping goods to its stores.

Based on these goals and constraints, Next Door's management considered two options: (1) build and operate its own warehouse and distribution network or (2) rely on other wholesalers and distributors to supply its stores.

Next Door's management realized that the first option would be a tremendous drain on the firm's financial and human capital. The company would have to build and operate a facility and then hire and train a large number of additional employees. The second option would not impose such a large financial burden on the firm and would place these responsibilities on existing wholesalers and distributors that had the experience, modes of transportation, and warehousing capabilities needed to serve the needs of all the company's stores. Considering all the factors involved, management determined that option two was the best approach for the firm to take.

http://www.nextdoor1.com

For Discussion:

1. In what ways does Next Door Food Store rely on its wholesalers and distributors?
2. What fundamental mistake did Next Door Food Store commit when it decided to enter into an exclusive agreement with Coca-Cola?

Organizing Principles

KEY TERMS

accountability
authority
centralization
chain of command
coercive power
cohesion
customer departmentalization
decentralization
delegation
departmentalization
division of labor
downsizing
expert power
formal organization
functional authority
functional definition
functional departmentalization
geographical departmentalization
informal organization
interaction chart
legitimate power
line authority
line department
norm
organization chart
organizing
power
product departmentalization
referent power
responsibility
reward power
rightsizing
sanctions
span of control
specialization of labor
staff authority
staff department
unity of command
unity of direction

LEARNING OBJECTIVES

After studying this chapter, you should be able to

1. Explain the relationship between planning and organizing
2. Explain the importance of the organizing process
3. List and discuss the five steps in the organizing process
4. Describe and give an example of the four approaches to departmentalization
5. Define authority, and explain how line, staff, and functional authority differ
6. Explain the concept of power and its sources
7. Discuss the following major organizing concepts and how they influence organizing decisions
   - Unity of direction
   - Chain of command
   - Line and staff departments
   - Unity of command
   - Delegation
   - Responsibility
   - Accountability
   - Span of control
   - Centralization and decentralization
8. Explain the term "informal organization"
9. Compare the informal organization to the formal organization

MANAGEMENT IN ACTION

Sun Microsystems Masters Outsourcing

The Internet is transforming organizations. It extends the organization's relationship with customers, employees, and suppliers; it is being used to make sales, delight customers, empower employees, cut costs, and grow businesses. Business processes are moving to the Internet. Sun Microsystems, the leading global supplier of network computing solutions, has been a part of the Internet revolution right from the start.

The architect of the organization structure at Sun Microsystems is chairman and chief executive officer Scott McNealy. He cofounded Sun Microsystems in 1982 and became chief executive officer (CEO) in 1984. McNealy is a proponent of outsourcing, the use of outside resources to perform a business process. He tells businesses, "In fact, you ought to be taking a close look at your organization right now and deciding what to outsource. Resources that should be going into making your company more competitive are being wasted on routine stuff that someone else could do better and cheaper. . . . What you want to handle in-house is the stuff that gives you an edge over your competition—your core competencies" (McNealy, 1999).

With its size, Sun Microsystems' top brass could make a case for tightly controlling everything from headquarters in Palo Alto, California; but they don't. Instead they focus on outsourcing as a core competency in the pursuit of Sun Microsystems' belief that "The Network Is The Computer™." Sun Microsystems may have mastered the art of outsourcing better than any other company in the world. They outsource all work that is "support" rather than revenue producing.

> *At Sun Microsystems we are leading the charge to outsource everything that's not a core competency. Our customers don't care who cooks the food in our cafeteria, cleans our buildings or waters the shrubs. Nor will they care who runs our e-mail systems or accounting applications. But our shareholders care if our overhead is too high because we're not outsourcing the things we should be. Industry analysts estimate the cost savings from outsourcing of computing functions as anywhere from 10% to 30%, depending on a variety of factors, including how efficiently your shop is running now. . . . The best thing about outsourcing is that it frees you to concentrate on your business. (McNealy, 1999)*

Outsourcing works for Sun Microsystems. As technology companies are scrambling to cope with a dynamic environment, Sun Microsystems' methods have enabled it to perform well. Investors have made money; Sun's revenues have grown an average of 20% annually over the past decade [1990–2000]. ■

Sources: Scott McNealy, "The Future of the Net—Why We Don't Want You to Buy Our Software," *The Wall Street Journal* (1 September 1999); Scott McNealy, "Executive Perspectives," http://www.sun.com/dot-com/perspectives/mcnealy.html; Visit Sun Microsystems at http://www.sun.com. For more on outsourcing visit The Outsourcing Institute at http://www.outsourcing.com.

Scott McNealy, chairman and CEO of Sun Microsystems, is the mastermind behind Sun's skillful use of outsourcing.

INTRODUCTION

"You can't tell me what to do; only Larry can—he's my boss!"

"When did the research and development department start reporting to marketing? I thought it was part of the production group."

"All I want is a decision on this engineering drawing. Can't anyone make a decision? Who's in charge here, anyway?"

The second managerial function is organizing. Every enterprise continually wrestles with the problem of how to organize or reorganize to pursue a new strategy, to respond to changing market conditions, or to successfully respond to customer expectations. It wants to achieve systematic, continuing improvement—what the Japanese call kaizen (Chapter 2).

In Chapters 5, 6, and 7 you learned that an organization's success begins with thorough and integrated planning and decision making—mission, goals, objectives, strategy, tactics. Planning provides the beginning. Organizing converts plans into reality; it makes things happen.

A company that has taken the time, energy, and money to develop quality plans needs to organize its employees to attain these objectives and needs managers who understand the importance of organizing. Organizing, like planning, is a process that must be carefully worked out and applied. This process involves deciding what work is needed, assigning those tasks, and arranging them into a decision-making framework (an organizational structure). This framework provides a structure for all jobs, making clear who has responsibility for what tasks and who reports to whom. An organization without structure can result in confusion, frustration, loss of efficiency, and limited effectiveness.

This chapter will examine the fundamental organizing concepts, to include the organizing steps, the types of departmentalization, authority, delegation, the span of control, and the decentralization that managers use to organize. Chapter 9 will apply the concepts to the problem of organizational design.

THE FORMAL ORGANIZATION

http://www.sun.com

Remember that a business is an organization. As with Sun Microsystems, owners and managers create businesses to achieve specific goals and objectives: to provide a quality product or service to a customer at a profit. When managers create an organization, then, they are actually developing a framework in which to create the desired product or service and provide a profit. This framework establishes the operating relationships among people: who supervises whom, who reports to whom, what departments are formed, and what kind of work each department performs. This framework is known as a **formal organization**—the official organizational structure that top management conceives and builds. A formal organization does not just happen; managers develop it through the organizing function of management.

formal organization
The official organizational structure that top management conceives and builds.

ORGANIZING PROCESS

organizing
The management function that establishes relationships between activity and authority.

Organizing is the management function that establishes relationships between activity and authority. It has five distinct steps that will be examined later in the chapter. The result of the organizing process is an organization—a whole consisting of unified parts (a system) acting in harmony to execute tasks that achieve goals effectively and efficiently and accomplish the company's mission (Child, 1984).

Relationship Between Planning and Organizing

Explain the relationship between planning and organizing

The managerial functions of planning and organizing are intimately related. Organizing begins with and is governed by plans that state where the organization is going and how it will get there. An organization must be built or an existing one modified to ensure that those plans are executed and objectives achieved. The organization must be able to concentrate its resources in a unified way to translate plans from intentions to realities.

An organizational structure is a tool of management to achieve plans. As the plans change, the structure should be responsive. The ability to change and keep up with the global society is the way to profits and existence. Examples of the relationship between planning and organizing—more specifically, how changes in plans affect the organization—can be seen in the changes taking place through business and industry.

downsizing
Also known as ***rightsizing****, it calls for shrinking both the size of the company and the number of employees.*

http://www.ge.com

http://www.lockheedmartin.com

Although these plans and organizational changes are primarily aimed at growth strategies, sometimes plans call for **downsizing**. Also known as **rightsizing**, downsizing calls for shrinking both the size of the company and the number of employees. Companies like General Electric used this strategy to fuel strategic turnarounds. GE literally restructured—it pulled layers of middle management out of the organization, eliminated jobs, and changed reporting relationships (Evans, 1995). Also, Lockheed Martin Corporation, the nation's largest aerospace and defense company, downsized to save $1.8 billion annually and refashion a leaner company. The restructuring shaved 12,000 jobs, closed a dozen plants, and eliminated 26 duplicative field offices. Of the restructuring, Daniel Tellep, then Lockheed chairman and CEO, stated, "We have great concerns for employees who will be impacted by the consolidation plan, but the remaining employees deserve to work in a company which is competitive and is positioned to succeed—not just today but well into the 21st century" (Saul, 1995).

http://www.ingersoll-rand.com

Also, as companies focus on reengineering efforts to best create value for customers (Chapter 2), organizational changes often result. When companies like Ingersoll-Rand rethink and redesign business processes to achieve customer-driven improvements in cost, quality, service, and speed, they make decisions to eliminate or prevent barriers that create a distance between employees and the people they should be serving. The result: they may eliminate business units, create teams, and empower groups (Etorre, 1995).

Before we move on to examine the benefits of the organizing process, remember that changes in organizing influence the staffing, leading, and controlling functions. Hiring and training plans are quite different when a structure is expanding and when it is downsizing. The same is true for leading, if the company reorganizes into teams. Control systems, too, will need to be created to monitor effectiveness.

Benefits of Organizing

Explain the importance of the organizing process

7

Discuss the following major organizing concepts and how they influence organizing decisions

- Unity of direction
- Chain of command

unity of direction *The establishment of one authority figure for each designated task of the organization.*

chain of command *The unbroken line of reporting relationships from the bottom to the top of the organization.*

As noted, the organizing process is important as a way to help the organization attain its mission. In addition, it does the following (Lawrence and Lorsch, 1967):

1. *Clarifies the work environment.* Everyone understands what to do. The tasks and responsibilities of all individuals, departments, and major organizational divisions are clear. The type and limits of authority are determined.
2. *Creates a coordinated environment.* Confusion is minimized and obstacles to performance are removed because it defines the interrelationships of the various work units and establishes guidelines for interaction among personnel.
3. *Achieves the principle of unity of direction.* The principle of **unity of direction** calls for the establishment of one authority figure for each designated task of the organization; this person has the authority to coordinate all plans concerning that task. The importance of this principle can be illustrated by the following example of its absence: various government agencies develop separate plans on the same topic because no one agency or person is in control of the task or can coordinate plans.
4. *Establishes the chain of command.* The **chain of command** is the unbroken line of reporting relationships from the bottom to the top of the organization. It defines the formal decision-making structure and provides for the orderly progression up and down the hierarchy for both decision making and decision-making communication. As a result, the confusion highlighted by the question, "Who's in charge here, anyway?" should not occur.

By applying the organizing process, management will improve the possibilities of achieving a functioning work environment.

FIVE-STEP ORGANIZING PROCESS

List and discuss the five steps in the organizing process

Figure 8.1 illustrates the organizing process at the Excelsior Table Saw Corporation. At Excelsior—as in all organizations—organizing includes five steps:

1. Reviewing plans and goals
2. Determining work activities
3. Classifying and grouping activities
4. Assigning work and delegating authority
5. Designing a hierarchy of relationships

As you read and study the following description of the five-step process, refer to Figure 8.1 to see an example of how you build an organizational structure.

Reviewing Plans and Goals

A company's goals and its plans to achieve them dictate its activities. Excelsior Table Saw plans to make and sell a top-quality table saw, which will dictate its activities. Some purposes, and thus some activities, are likely to remain fairly constant once a business is established. For example, the business will continue to seek a profit and it will continue to employ people and other resources. In time

FIGURE 8.1 *The organizing process in action*

Step 1
Reviewing Plans and Goals

Excelsior Table Saw Corporation
Our aim: To manufacture and market the Mark IV Table Saw at a 10% return on investment

Step 2
Determining Work Activities

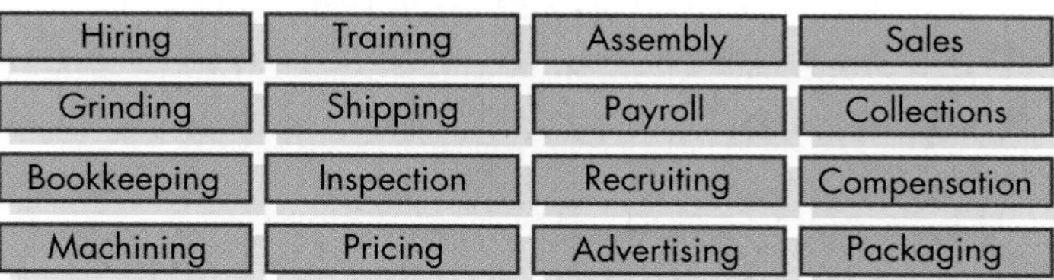

Step 3
Classifying and Grouping Activities

Marketing
Sales
Advertising
Packaging
Shipping

Finance
Pricing
Payroll
Bookkeeping
Collections

Human Res.
Recruiting
Hiring
Training
Compensation

Production
Machining
Grinding
Assembly
Inspection

Step 4
Assigning Work and Delegating Authority

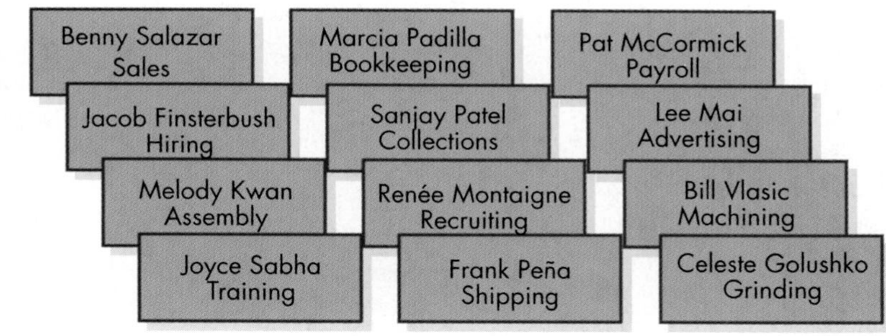

Step 5
Designing a Hierarchy of Relationships

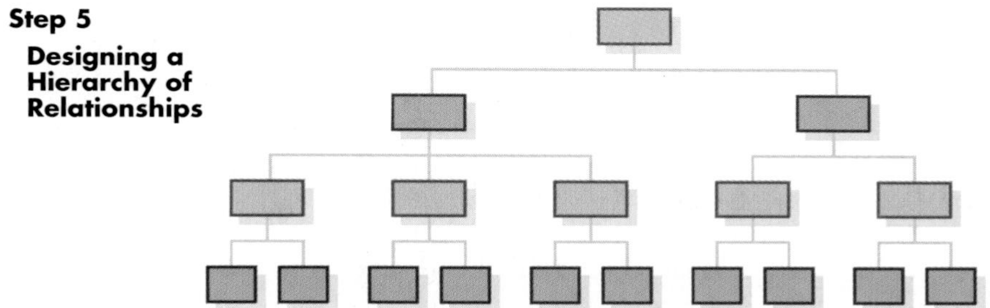

and with new plans, however, the ways in which it carries out basic activities will change. The company may create new departments; it may give old ones additional responsibilities; some departments may cease to exist. New relationships between groups of decision makers may come into being as well. Organizing will create the new structure and relationships and modify the existing ones.

Businesses adjust their organizational structures in response to new plans. When Sun Microsystems seeks new opportunities, it does so as well. Business magazines and daily newspapers frequently carry announcements about companies making structural changes. Previous chapters have provided examples at IBM, Cadbury, and McDonald's. Each company is adjusting structures to mesh with plans aimed at helping it compete in the world economy. Another example is Siemens AG, the subject of this chapter's Global Applications (Smart, 1995).

GLOBAL APPLICATIONS
Reshaping Siemens

Step inside the new Siemens. After nearly a decade of hit-or-miss efforts to speed product development, Siemens, a gigantic electronics manufacturer, has finally shed its plodding perfectionism and bureaucracy. Gone are the endless meetings, the aimless research, and the fear of taking risks. Now a new generation of managers is fostering cooperation across the company: setting up new organizational structures, creating teams to develop products and attack new markets, and thriving on accountability. The new emphasis is on revving up innovation and pleasing the customer.

The man responsible for the organizational rebirth and restructuring is Siemens's Chief Executive Officer Heinrich Von Pierer. Since taking the helm in 1992, Von Pierer has

- Replaced the hierarchical structure with new emphasis on customer service and innovation
- Slashed two layers of middle management
- Given managers in local markets authority to cut costs and bid for projects
- Sold $2 billion in noncore businesses
- Set up facilities in Asia and Eastern Europe to lower costs and reach new customers

In the process of restructuring, Von Pierer found his most critical challenge to be breaking with entrenched management practices. By trying to change the Siemens's mind-set, he has gone beyond the cost cutting common to most of corporate Germany and Siemens's European rivals. Immediately after assuming the leadership position, Von Pierer opened up Siemens for a financial airing. He began disclosing profits for Siemens's eight divisions, making management accountable for the bottom line. In addition, Von Pierer adopted radical measures to force managers to adapt to stern market demands. The company called in blue-ribbon customers such as Opel, Ford, and Sony to provide feedback on Siemens's performance. At one workshop, Sony Corporation "blasted chip managers for rotten service and erratic delivery." A Siemens manager remembers that "it was brutal"; but the unit got the message.

Even with all the restructuring and organizational changes, Von Pierer is not finished. "We have to keep asking ourselves: Are we flexible enough? Are we changing enough? It is a completely different way of thinking. People are no longer afraid to speak out with an idea." The observable results: a totally different way of producing everything from hearing aids to power plants, a 20 percent increase in corporate earnings, and a 10.3 percent share price increase.

http://www.siemens.com

Source: Karen Lowrey Miller, "Siemens Shapes Up," *Business Week* (1 May 1995), pp. 52–53.

Determining Work Activities

In the second step, managers ask what work activities are necessary to accomplish these goals. Creating a list of tasks to be accomplished begins with identifying ongoing tasks and ends with considering the tasks unique to this business. Hiring, training, and record keeping are part of the regular routine for running any business. What, in addition, are the unique needs of this organization? Do they include assembling, machining, shipping, storing, inspecting, selling, and advertising? Identifying all necessary activities (as Figure 8.1 illustrates for Excelsior Table Saw) is important.

Specialization or Division of Labor

specialization of labor or division of labor *Breaks a potentially complex job down into simpler tasks or activities.*

An important concept in specifying tasks is **specialization of labor** or **division of labor**. Both terms refer to the degree to which organizational tasks are subdivided into separate jobs (Daft, 1994). When using specialization of labor, a manager breaks a potentially complex job down into simpler tasks or activities. The result is that one person or group may complete only that activity or a related group of activities. Figure 8.2 shows three different degrees of work specialization in the job of producing a VCR—low, moderate, or high specialization. The shaded bars at the side, top, and bottom of Figure 8.2 illustrate the relationship of specialization, efficiency, and job satisfaction.

FIGURE 8.2 *Degrees of specialization in producing a VCR*

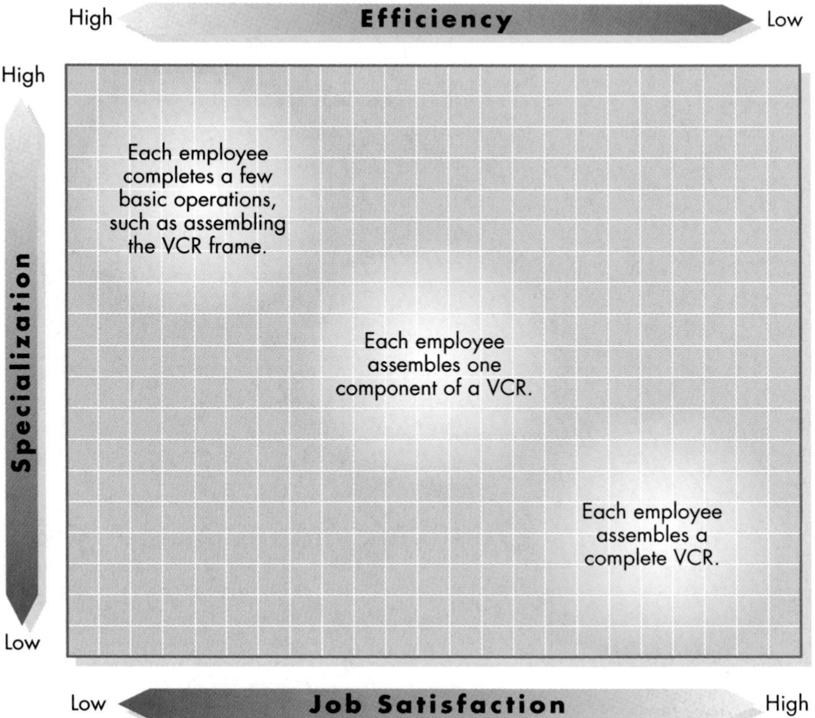

While work specialization allows a job to be performed more skillfully and efficiently, it can also become boring for the worker.

An advantage of work specialization is that work can be performed more efficiently if employees are allowed to specialize (Smith, 1937). In addition, because employees are allowed to specialize in one area, they can gain skill and expertise. Specialization facilitates the process of selecting employees as well as decreasing training requirements. Finally, it allows managers to supervise more employees. Because each job is simplified, managers know what performance standard to expect and can detect job-related performance problems quickly.

Disadvantages of Work Specialization

Despite its advantages, specialization can create problems. When specialization is overdone, jobs can become too simplified. When employees do one simple task—for example, tightening a nut—for eight hours a day, five days a week, they become bored and tired. In turn, when employees become bored and tired, safety problems and accident rates increase, absenteeism rises, and the quality of work may suffer (Miner, 1987). Some companies have tried to overcome this disadvantage by job redesign (Chapter 13 describes this approach). Other companies have moved to the development of teams responsible for an entire product (Chapter 15 describes teams).

The process of specialization leads to designing a job. This job and the abilities required of a person to do the job are clearly stated in a *job description* and a *job specification*. These documents serve as the basis for staffing the organization (see Chapter 11).

Classifying and Grouping Activities

4

Describe and give an example of the four approaches to departmentalization

Once managers know what tasks must be done, they classify and group these activities into manageable work units. This third step takes the jumble of Excelsior's tasks and creates four related and identifiable groups of like activities (Figure 8.1). When managers group tasks that are similar in terms of tasks, processes, or skills, they are grouping them by the principle of functional similarity or similarity of activity. This guideline is simple to apply and logical.

Managers apply the principle in three steps:

1. They examine each activity identified to determine its general nature. Normally, identifiable areas include marketing, production, finance, and human resources.
2. They group the activities into these related areas.
3. They establish the basic department design for the organizational structure.

In practice, the first two steps occur simultaneously. Sales, advertising, packaging, and shipping can be considered marketing-related activities. Thus they are grouped under the marketing heading. Machining, grinding, assembly, and inspection are manufacturing processes; they can be grouped under production. Personnel-related activities include recruiting, hiring, training, and compensation; they are grouped under human resources.

departmentalization
The basic organizational format or departmental structure for the company.

As the tasks are classified and grouped into related work units (production, marketing, finance, and human resources), the third step, **departmentalization**, is being finalized; that is, a decision is being made on the basic organizational format or departmental structure. Groups, departments, and divisions are being formed on the basis of the organization's objectives. Management can choose one of four departmental types. Although Chapter 9 will describe these in detail, we will briefly discuss the options here.

functional departmentalization
Creating departments on the basis of the specialized activities of the business—finance, production, marketing, human resources.

Functional departmentalization involves creating departments on the basis of the specialized activities of the business—finance, production, marketing, human resources. Note in Figure 8.1, Step 3, that the managers at Excelsior Table Saw used this type of departmentalization. For most businesses the functional approach is the logical way to organize departments. It is simple, groups the same or similar activities, simplifies training, allows specialization, and minimizes costs (Twomey, Scherr, and Hunt, 1988).

geographical departmentalization
Grouping activities and responsibilities according to territory.

http://disney.go.com

http://www.fedex.com

Geographical departmentalization groups activities and responsibilities according to territory. To be near customers, expanding companies often locate production plants, sales offices, and repair facilities in their market areas. This grouping allows the company to serve customers quickly and efficiently and helps the company stay abreast of the changing needs and tastes of the customer. Disney—with theme parks in Anaheim, Orlando, France, and Japan—uses geographical departmentalization for that aspect of its business. FedEx pursues its mission by using a geographic design, as shown in Figure 8.3.

FIGURE 8.3 *Geographical departmentalization*

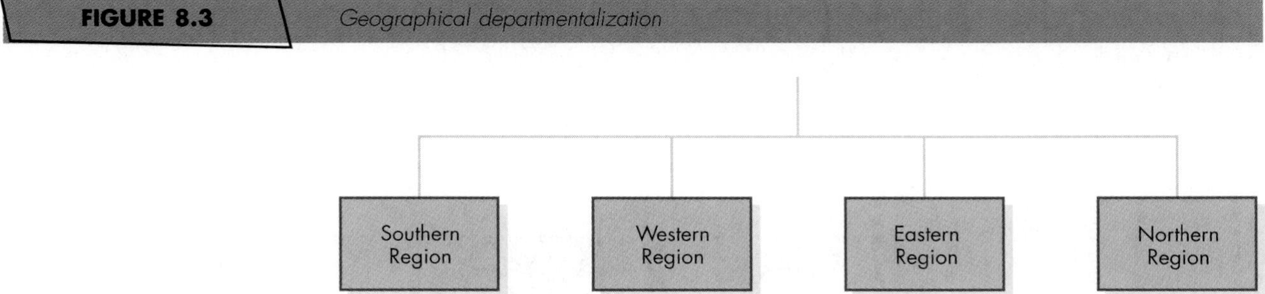

product departmentalization *Assembling the activities of creating, producing, and marketing each product into a separate department.*

http://www.utc.com

customer departmentalization *Grouping activities and responsibilities in departments based on the needs of specific customer groups.*

http://www.jnj.com

Product departmentalization assembles the activities of creating, producing, and marketing each product into a separate department. This option is adopted when each product of a company requires a unique marketing strategy, production process, distribution system, or financial resources. As shown in Figure 8.4, United Technologies has six product categories and capitalizes on this approach.

Customer departmentalization groups activities and responsibilities in departments based on the needs of specific customer groups. As shown in Figure 8.5, a company like Johnson & Johnson that markets products to three different customer groups—pharmaceutical, professional, and final consumer—faces an extremely difficult task. Because each customer group has its own demands, needs, and preferences, Johnson & Johnson must use tailored strategies that are not necessarily compatible. Another example can be found at the Hoffman Agency, a small public relations firm that is the subject of this chapter's Valuing Diversity feature. By using customer departmentalization, Hoffman was better able to focus on customer needs and eliminate problems caused by functional departmentalization.

Although these department types have been presented individually, in reality most companies use a combination of types to meet their needs.

> *There is no such thing as the one right organization. There are only organizations, each of which has distinct strengths, distinct limitations and specific applications. It has become clear that organization is not an absolute. It is a tool for making people productive in working together. As such, a given organizational structure fits certain tasks in certain conditions and at certain times. . . . In any enterprise . . . there is need for a number of different organizational structures coexisting side by side.* (Drucker, 1998)

http://www.gm.com

http://www.att.com

http://www.compaq.com

Companies like General Motors, AT&T, and Compaq incorporate departments arranged by function, geography, product, and customer to meet their objectives.

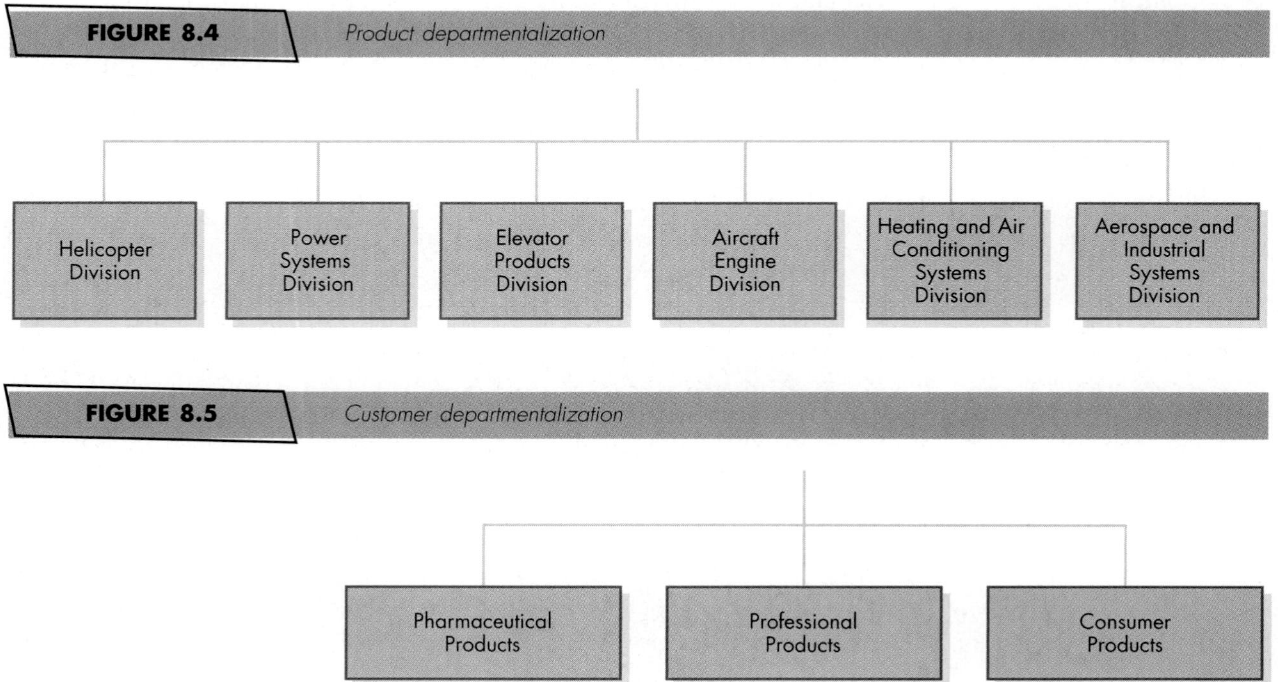

FIGURE 8.4 *Product departmentalization*

FIGURE 8.5 *Customer departmentalization*

VALUING DIVERSITY
Reorganizing to Maximize Talent

"Delegation and empowerment are great words," states Lou Hoffman, "but they don't have much meaning if people don't know one another well enough to resolve things on their own." That was the problem at Hoffman's San Jose public relations firm. The number of employees at the Hoffman Agency had doubled in two years, and Hoffman found himself dealing with issues that were a direct by-product of two factors—the departmental structure and the increasing ethnic diversity of the staff. If someone from the accounting department was dissatisfied with something coming out of the editing group, it wound up on Hoffman's desk. All the talent brought by the diverse staff was being short-circuited by the departmental structure.

Hoffman's solution: He restructured his departments to mesh the different functions and the staff's diversity. The new departmental design, focused on the customer base, not only combined accounting, editing, and creative elements but also captured the diversity in each former functional department. The teams were purposely designed to incorporate young and old, as well as different genders, ethnicities, and cultures. To nudge the new structure along and help develop camaraderie and cooperation, Hoffman offered to pick up the tab for any two employees on the team who dined at the restaurant down the road. Moreover, he offered a special prize to anyone who lunched with every other person on the team. Over a two-month period, Hoffman spent $2,100. The results: Delegated authority was used more effectively, all employees developed a better understanding of the workings of the agency, and the diverse backgrounds were combined to meet customer needs.

http://www.hoffman.com

Source: Donna Fenn, "Out to Lunch," *Inc.* (June, 1995), p. 89.

Assigning Work and Delegating Authority

functional definition
The activities to be performed determine the type and quantity of authority necessary.

After identifying the activities necessary to achieve objectives and classifying and grouping them departmentally, managers must assign these activities to individuals and give these employees the appropriate authority to accomplish the task. This step, critical to the success of organizing, is based on the principle of **functional definition**—in establishing a department, its nature, purpose, tasks, and performance must first be determined as a basis for authority. This principle means that the activities to be performed determine the type and quantity of authority necessary. How much is needed to accomplish the tasks?

The step of assigning work and delegating authority is as necessary in a reorganization as it is in the structuring of a new company. In our Global Applications, when Siemens slashed two layers of middle management from its management structure, it created new activities and gave managers local market authority (Miller, 1995).

Designing a Hierarchy of Relationships

The last step requires managers to determine the vertical and horizontal operating relationships of the organization as a whole. In effect, this step puts together all the parts of the organizing puzzle.

The vertical structuring of the organization results in a decision-making hierarchy that shows who is in charge of each task, each specialty area, and the organization as a whole. Levels of management are established from bottom to top in the organization. These levels create the chain of command, or hierarchy of decision-making levels, in the company.

span of control
The number of subordinates under the direction of a manager.

organization chart
The complete organizational structure shown visually.

The horizontal structuring has two important effects: (1) It defines the working relationships between operating departments, and (2) it makes the final decision on the span of control of each manager. **Span of control** is the number of subordinates under the direction of a manager.

The result of this step is a complete organizational structure. An **organization chart** shows this structure visually. Look closely at Excelsior Table Saw's organization chart (Figure 8.6). As do all organization charts, it tells us the following:

1. Who reports to whom—that is, the chain of command.
2. How many subordinates work for each manager—that is, the span of control.
3. The channels of official communication—as shown by the solid lines that connect each job.
4. How the company is departmentalized—by function, customer, or product, for example.
5. The work being done in each position—The labels in the boxes describe each person's activities.

FIGURE 8.6 *Organization chart of Excelsior Table Saw Corporation*

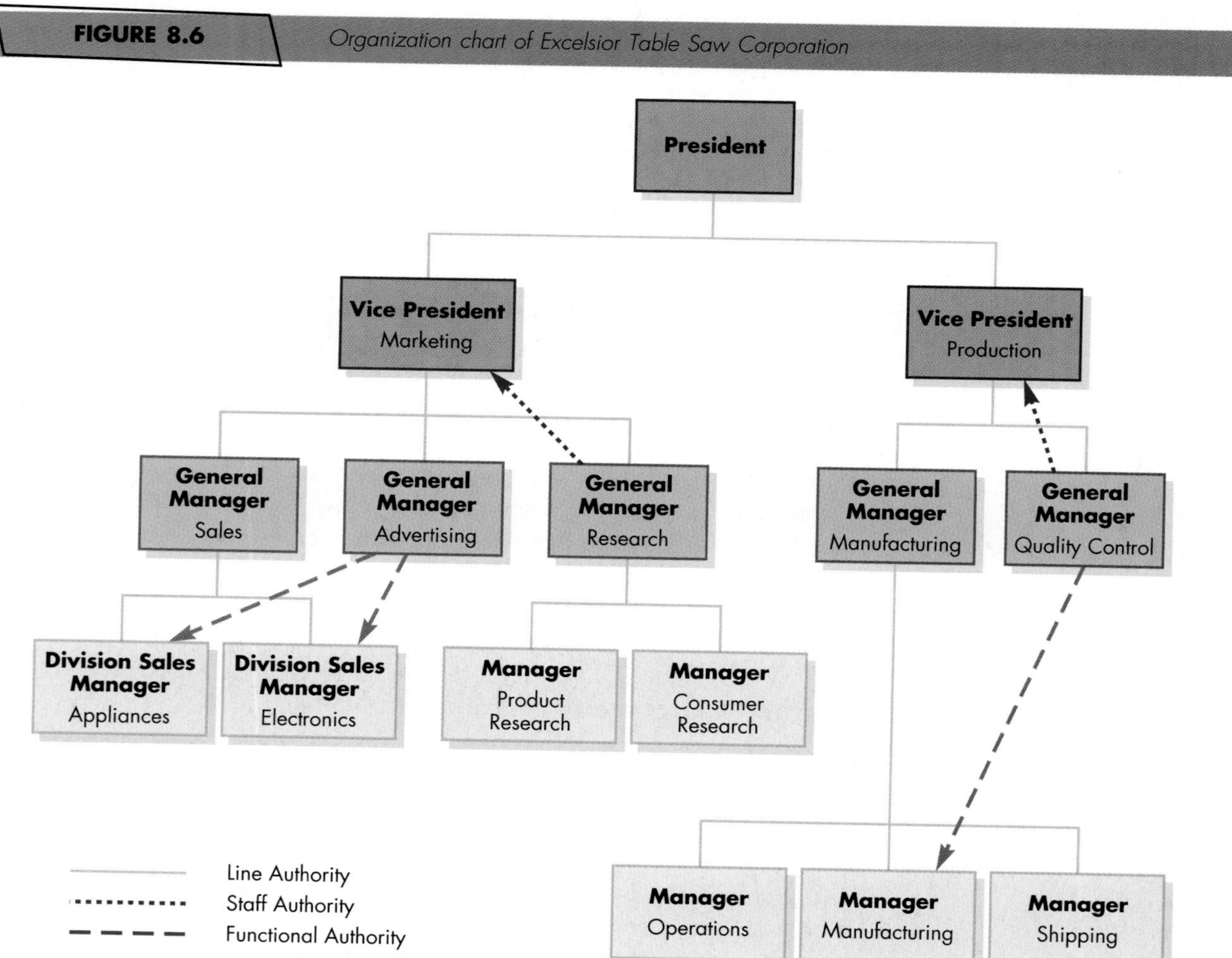

6. The hierarchy of decision making—where the ultimate decision maker for a request, problem, appeal, or grievance is located.
7. The types of authority relationships—Solid connections between boxes illustrate line authority, dotted lines show staff authority, and broken lines trace functional authority. These types of authority will be explained in the next section.

In addition, the chart serves as a troubleshooting tool. In the design (or redesign) stage, managers can create alternative structures to study their effectiveness and spot difficulties. In the operational stage, it can help managers locate duplications and conflicts that result from awkward arrangements. The chart does not, however, show the degrees of authority, informal communication channels, and informal relationships—all keys in managing successfully. We will discuss these later in the chapter.

The organizing process draws heavily on the leadership skills of the management group. Very much like building a ship to carry the company across the ocean, the initial application of the process results in the company's first organizational structure and organization chart. Then, like a launched ship, the organization begins its journey in pursuit of its goals. Management is called on to monitor and control its actions, successes, or failures. Leadership will also be necessary—as was the case at Lockheed Martin, United Technologies, and Hoffman Agency—to realign or redesign the structure in a new application of the organizing process. Recall the words of Lockheed Martin CEO Daniel Tellep, ". . . the remaining employees deserve to work in a company which is competitive and is positioned to succeed—not just today but well into the 21st century" (Saul, 1995).

MAJOR ORGANIZATIONAL CONCEPTS

Define authority, and explain how line, staff, and functional authority differ

The organizing process requires managers to draw on and integrate a number of major organizational concepts. To organize effectively, leaders/managers need to master concepts, including authority, power, delegation, span of control, and centralization/decentralization.

Authority

> *One hears a great deal today about "the end of hierarchy." This is blatant nonsense. In any institution there has to be a final authority, that is, a "boss"—someone who can make the final decision and who can then expect to be obeyed in a situation of common peril—and every institution is likely to encounter it sooner or later. If the ship founders, the captain does not call a meeting; the captain gives an order. And if the ship is to be saved, everyone must obey the order, must know exactly where to go and what to do and do it without "participation" or argument. Hierarchy, and the unquestioning acceptance of it by everyone in the organization, is the only hope in a crisis. (Drucker, 1998)*

Because authority plays so central a role in organizations, managers should fully understand its nature, sources, importance, variations and relationship to power.

authority
The formal and legitimate right of a manager to make decisions, give orders, and allocate resources.

Nature, Sources, and Importance of Authority

All managers in an organization have authority in different degrees, based on the level of management they occupy. **Authority** is the formal and legitimate right of a manager to make decisions, give orders, and allocate resources. It holds the organization together, because it provides the means of command. How does a manager acquire authority?

It has been said that "authority comes with the territory," meaning that authority is vested in a manager because of the position he or she occupies in the organization. Thus authority is defined in each manager's job description or job charter. The person who occupies a position has its formal authority as long as he or she remains in that position. As the job changes in scope and complexity, so should the amount and kind of formal authority possessed. As Albert Bersticker, former CEO of Ferro Corporation, a diversified organization composed of 100 SBUs, noted, "The Ivory Tower isn't dictating all corporate moves. What I stress from my management team is that they make the decisions. I won't tell a divisional manager what to do—I want him to decide how to fix it, tweak it, or get rid of it. The authority for decisions is theirs—that's what their job is" (Moskal, 1992).

http://www.ferro.com

Johnson & Johnson CEO Ralph Larsen sings the same tune. When Robert Croce took over the reins at Ethicon Endo-Surgery, a Johnson & Johnson SBU, Larsen did not tell Croce what the latter's growth and earnings targets should be but let Croce decide instead. Croce was far more ambitious than Larsen expected, claiming he would control half of the world's staple and endosurgery business and be profitable in three years (O'Reilly, 1994).

http://www.ethicon.com

Types of Authority

In an organization, three different types of authority are created by the relationships between individuals and departments.

line authority *The relationship between superior and subordinate. Any manager who supervises operating employees—or other managers—has line authority.*

Line authority defines the relationship between superior and subordinate. Any manager who supervises operating employees—or other managers—has line authority, allowing the manager to give direct orders to those subordinates, evaluate their actions, and reward or punish them. At Johnson & Johnson, Ralph Larsen has line authority over the CEOs of the 168 SBUs, who in turn have line authority over their vice presidents. In an organization, line authority, shown by solid lines with arrows in Figure 8.7, flows downward directly from superior to subordinate.

FIGURE 8.7 *Line authority: the relationship between superior and subordinate*

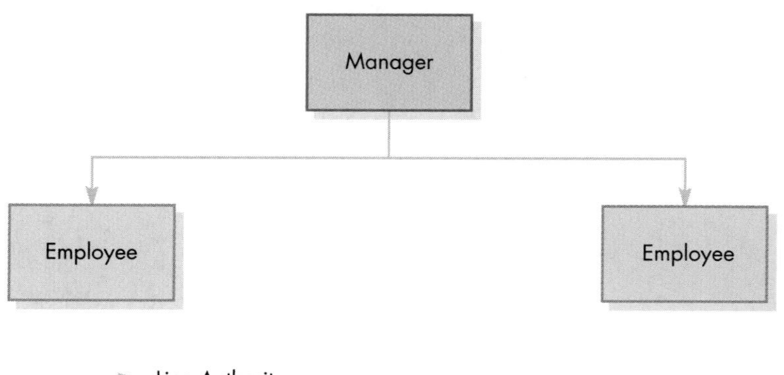

staff authority
The authority to serve in an advisory capacity; it flows upward to the decision maker.

Staff authority is the authority to serve in an advisory capacity. Managers who provide advice or technical assistance are granted advisory authority. This staff or advisory authority provides no basis for direct control over the subordinates or activities of other departments with which the person holding staff authority consults; however, within the staff manager's own department, he or she can exercise line authority over subordinates. Staff authority—in the form of advice or assistance—flows upward to the decision maker. In Figure 8.8 both the legal department and the research and development department provide advice to the president, as shown by the dotted lines.

functional authority
The authority that permits staff managers to make decisions about specific activities performed by employees within other departments.

Functional authority permits staff managers to make decisions about specific activities performed by employees within other departments. Staff departments often use functional authority to control their procedures in other departments. For example, as Figure 8.9 illustrates, the human resources manager monitors and reviews compliance of recruiting, selecting, and evaluation systems in operating departments. Functional authority, however, applies only to those systems; the human resources manager does not have the authority to tell the advertising manager which products to promote or the manufacturing manager which products to manufacture. At Johnson & Johnson, the chief financial officer has functional authority over all of the SBUs for budgeting and financial reporting.

Discuss the following major organizing concept and how it influences organizing decisions

- Line and staff departments

Line and Staff Departments

Line and staff authority describe the authority granted to managers; line and staff departments are terms for different roles or positions for various functions in the organizational structure.

FIGURE 8.8 *Staff authority: advice and information flow upward*

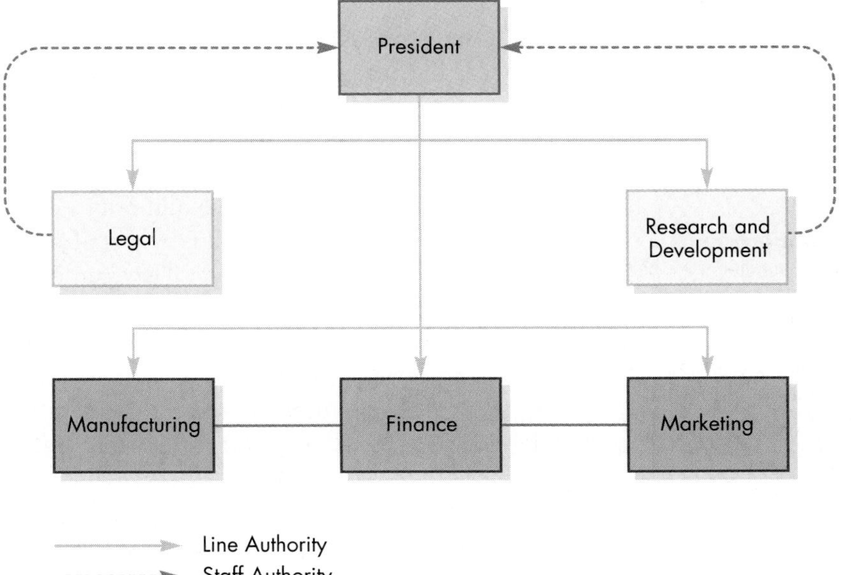

FIGURE 8.9 *Functional authority: managers make decisions about activities performed by personnel in other departments*

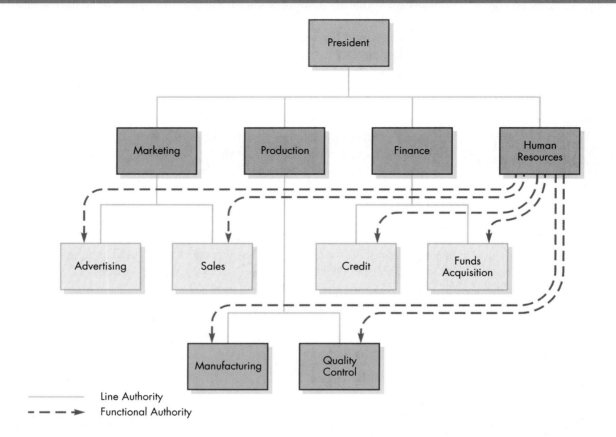

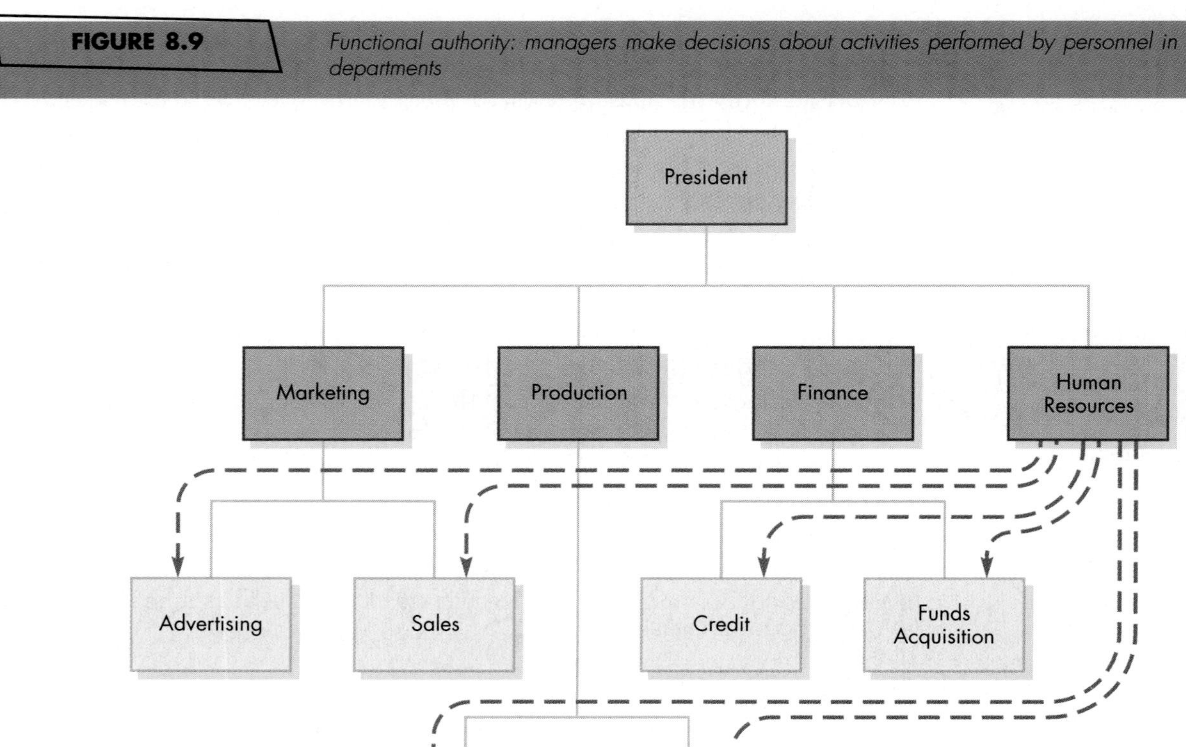

line departments
The departments established to meet the major objectives of the business and directly influence the success (profitability) of a business.

staff departments
The departments—including legal, human resources, computer services, and public relations—that provide assistance to the line departments and to each other, making money indirectly for the company through advice, service, and assistance.

Line departments, headed by a line manager, are the departments established to meet the major objectives of the business and directly influence the success (profitability) of a business. Examples include production (of goods and services for sale to a market), marketing (to include sales, advertising, and physical distribution), and finance (acquiring capital resources). The line managers who head such departments exercise line authority.

Staff departments, headed by a staff manager, provide assistance to the line departments and to each other. They can be viewed as making money indirectly for the company—through advice, service, and assistance—rather than directly contributing to achieving the company's major objectives. Traditional staff departments include legal, human resources, computer services, and public relations. Staff departments meet the special needs of the organization. As an organization develops, its need for expert, timely, and ongoing advice becomes critical. If the organization's resources can support the existence of a staff department, one can be created to fill the special needs gap. Staff departments can play a vital role in the success of a company. Staff department heads have line authority over their subordinates but staff authority in relation to other departments.

Line–staff interactions offer some real dangers of which all managers should be aware. Because staff people must sell their ideas, line personnel may view them as pushy or, in extreme cases, as undermining the line managers. Staff managers need to develop tact and persuasive skills along with ideas. They also need to foster credibility for their ideas to be accepted. Bad advice can result in no audience the next time. Another problem is that line managers are inclined to feel that "the buck stops" with them. In other words, because staff personnel are not responsible for the performance results of the line managers' unit and the line managers ultimately make the decisions, they don't have to take staff advice seriously.

Unity of Command

Discuss the following major organizing concept and how it influences organizing decisions

- Unity of command

unity of command
The organizing principle that states that each person within an organization should take orders from and report to only one person.

A concern of all managers in applying staff and functional authority is violation of the principle of **unity of command**, one of Henri Fayol's (1949) management principles (Chapter 2). The principle requires that each person within the organization take orders from and report to only one person.

Unity of command should guide any attempt to develop operating relationships. Although each person should have only one boss, the operating relationships developed through staff departments mean that workers may have more than one supervisor in a given situation—or at least perceive that they do from the style with which advice is given. A departmental manager or subordinate may receive guidance or directives on a given day from human resources on employment practices, from finance on budget time frames, and from data processing concerning computer procedures. If possible, these situations should be minimized, or at least clarified, for the sake of all affected.

> *It is a sound general principle for all kinds of organizations that any member of the organization should have only one "master." There is wisdom in the old proverb of the Roman law that a slave who has three masters is a free man. It is a very old principle of human relations that no one should be put into a conflict of loyalties—and having more than one master creates such a conflict (Drucker, 1998).*

Power

Explain the concept of power and its sources

power
The ability to exert influence in the organization. Power is personal.

Two managers could occupy positions of equal formal authority, with the same degree of acceptance of this authority by their employees, and still not be equally effective in the organization. Why? Because one manager possesses more power than the other.

Power is the ability to exert influence in the organization. As Figure 8.10 shows, having power can multiply managers' effectiveness to influence people beyond what they can attain through formal authority alone. Authority is positional—it will be there when the incumbent leaves; and, as Figure 8.10 shows, it is part of the larger concept of power. Power is personal; it exists because of the person. A person does not need to be a manager to have power. Some administrative assistants of top managers have considerable power, but no authority. Managers can acquire power from several different sources.

FIGURE 8.10 *Power increases a manager's ability to influence*

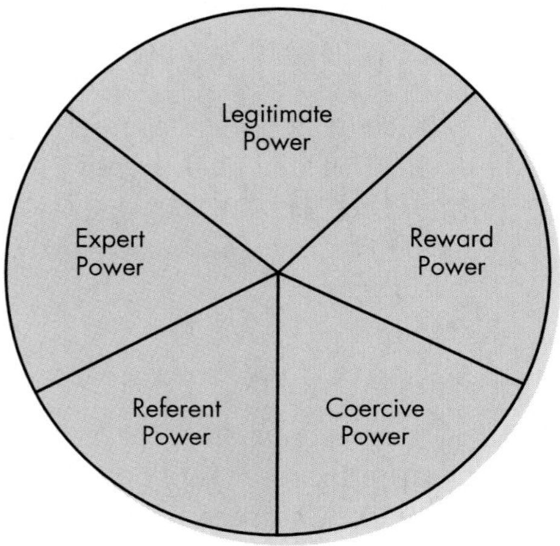

Legitimate or Position Power

legitimate power
The power possessed by managers and derived from the positions they occupy in the formal organization.

Holding a managerial position with its accompanying authority provides a manager with a power base. The manager has the right to use this **legitimate power** because of the position. The higher a manager sits in the organization hierarchy, the greater is the "perceived power," that power thought by the subordinates to exist (whether or not it really does). Vice presidents wield or can wield a lot of power.

Reward Power

reward power
The power that comes from the ability to promise or grant rewards.

The opposite of coercive power, **reward power** comes from the ability to promise or grant rewards. Managers have the ability to decide on raises, promotions, favorable performance appraisals, and preferred work shifts.

Coercive Power

coercive power
The power dependent on fear of the negative results that may happen if one fails to comply.

Coercive power is dependent on fear. A person reacts to this power out of the fear of the negative results that may happen if one fails to comply. Managers, because of their position, have the ability to punish by assigning unpleasant or boring work, withholding raises or promotions, and suspending or dismissing an employee.

Referent Power

referent power
The power that is based on the kind of personality or charisma an individual has and how others perceive it.

Referent power is based on the kind of personality or charisma an individual has and how others perceive it. A manager who is admired by others—the latter perhaps demonstrating this admiration by their desire to identify with or emulate the manager—has referent power. The manager can use this power effectively to motivate and lead others.

Expert Power

expert power
Influence due to abilities, skills, knowledge, or experience.

Persons who have demonstrated their superior skills and knowledge possess **expert power**. They know what to do and how to do it. Others hope to stay on this expert's good side to be able to benefit from his or her expertise. A seasoned manager exercises power with newcomers. Knowledge of budgets, systems, or company culture that others need provides a basis for the manager's power. Later in the chapter, in our discussion of the informal organization, the concept of power will be discussed. Chapter 13 also provides a discussion on power as a basis of leadership.

Delegation

Discuss the following major organizing concept and how it influences organizing decisions

- Delegation

delegation
The downward transfer of formal authority from one person to another.

Delegating authority takes place as a company grows and more demands are placed on a manager or because a manager wishes to develop subordinates' skills. **Delegation** is the downward transfer of formal authority from one person to another. Superiors delegate, or pass, authority to subordinates to facilitate the accomplishment of work.

Importance of Delegation

No person can do it all in an organization. Therefore, managers should delegate authority to free themselves from some management areas to be able to focus better on more critical concerns. Having capable subordinates can increase the ability of a manager. Delegation is also a valuable tool in training subordinates.

When authority is truly shifted to the hands of nonmanagers and is accompanied by shared information, needed training, and relationships based on mutual trust and respect, delegation becomes empowerment. Employees are given ownership of their tasks, along with the freedom to experiment and even fail, without fear of reprisal. As noted in Chapter 3, empowerment is a key to quality and customer service.

http://www.armstrong.com

Armstrong World Industries empowered employees in steps. "The first steps were taken in the 1960s and 1970s when they began recognizing and rewarding employees through pay-for-knowledge or pay-for-skills systems. The 1980s shifted the focus from individual workers to high-performance work teams. The 1990s pushed empowerment even further by emphasizing the work, or output, itself rather than the job" (Kent, 1997).

http://www.7-eleven.com

Bob Price, a 7-Eleven store manager in The Colony, Texas, now tracks daily orders and leftovers of fresh sandwiches and pastries; then he figures in weather reports, special events in the area, and other factors that could affect demand. Using the information he has gathered, he maps out future orders. "Before this, we had no say about what we needed in our store. Either you had a field consultant come in and say we need to have more of something, or else they'd automatically ship the stuff. Now we have to make the decisions" (Hammonds, 1994).

Fear of Delegation

"When you fail to delegate, the monkey on your back gets fatter and fatter until it squashes you," says Paul Maguire, a senior partner of a management consulting firm (Ayers-Williams, 1992). Even when they know the potential of empowerment, some managers still do not delegate. Some managers fear giving up authority or lack confidence in subordinates. Others worry that the employee may perform the job better than they can, are impatient, or are too detail oriented to let go. Some managers simply don't know how to delegate. Learning how to delegate is like learning to ride a bicycle—you have to learn to let go (Hellman, 1992). Delegation is not only a tool for survival, it is recognized as one of the key factors in a manager's success or failure (Taylor, 1992). The process itself involves two of the most critical concepts in management: responsibility and accountability.

Delegation Process

7

Discuss the following major organizing concepts and how they influence organizing decisions

- Responsibility
- Accountability

When managers choose to delegate authority, they create a sequence of events.

- *Assignment of tasks.* The manager identifies specific tasks or duties to assign to the subordinate, then approaches him or her with those tasks. As an example, at Grimpen Advertising, Sharon's manager assigns her the task of designing an advertising campaign for the company's new client, a styling salon called The Hair Connection.
- *Delegation of authority.* For the subordinate to complete the duties or tasks, the manager should delegate to the subordinate the authority necessary to do them. A guideline for the amount of authority to be delegated is that it be adequate to complete the task—no more and no less. In Sharon's case, she receives the authority to spend $10,000 on the campaign and to hire a graphic designer.
- *Acceptance of responsibility.* **Responsibility** is the obligation to carry out one's assigned duties to the best of one's ability. A manager does not delegate responsibility to an employee; rather, the employee's acceptance of an assignment creates an obligation to do his or her best. When Sharon takes on The Hair Connection account and agrees to complete it by the deadline and within the budget, she becomes responsible to her boss for the project.
- *Creation of accountability.* **Accountability** is having to answer to someone for your actions. It means accepting the consequences—either credit or blame—of these actions. When a subordinate accepts an assignment and the authority to carry out that assignment, he or she is accountable, or answerable, for his or her actions.

responsibility
The obligation to carry out one's assigned duties to the best of one's ability.

accountability
The need to answer to someone for your actions. It means accepting the consequences—either credit or blame—of these actions.

Delegation does not relieve managers of responsibility and accountability. Managers are responsible and accountable for the use of their authority and for their personal performance as well as for the performance of subordinates. If Sharon goes beyond the deadline, spends more than the budgeted amount, or does not develop an acceptable advertising campaign, she must answer to her boss. Her boss, in turn, is accountable to his or her boss for assigning the project to Sharon. On the positive side, if Sharon completes the project as designed, she will receive the credit and the praise and so will Sharon's boss for having delegated authority well. This chapter's Ethical Management feature focuses on the nature of responsibility and accountability for companies involved in payoffs and kickbacks.

The sequence of events outlined here should ensure that the process of delegation produces clear understanding on the part of the manager and the subordinate. The manager should take the time to think through what is being assigned and to confer the authority necessary to achieve results. The subordinate, in accepting the assignment, becomes obligated (responsible) to perform, knowing that he or she is accountable (answerable) for the results. Figure 8.11 provides some quick tips for successful delegation of authority.

Span of Control

7

Discuss the following major organizing concept and how it influences organizing decisions

- Span of control

As managers design the organizational structure, they are concerned with the *span of control*—the number of subordinates a manager directly supervises.

ETHICAL MANAGEMENT
Payoffs and Kickbacks—Who Pays?

Caremark Rx, Inc., a Northbrook, Illinois, home health-care company, and American Honda Motor Company, based in Torrance, California, have something in common. They got caught.

- Caremark has been on the losing side of a battle with federal investigators probing charges that the company paid kickbacks to physicians in return for referrals within its home-infusion, oncology, hemophilia, and human-growth-hormone businesses. The battle ended when Caremark agreed to plead guilty and pay $159 million in civil damages and criminal fines.
- American Honda has been embroiled in the controversy surrounding dealer payoffs. The company management refused to stop dealer payoffs to executives because top management considered the payments compensation for poor salaries. In return for the payoffs, the dealers were given preferential treatment.

1. How do these two situations relate to the concept of responsibility?
2. Who—middle-level or top-level management—will be held accountable?
3. How could these actions be known but go uncorrected by management?

http://www.caremark.com

http://www.honda.com

Sources: Ron Stodghill, "A Mea Culpa—And a Comeback?" *Business Week* (3 July 1995), p. 33; John Dilley, "Honda Tacitly Ok'd Payoffs," *Dallas Morning News* (13 May 1995), p. 3F.

FIGURE 8.11 *Quick tips for successful delegation of authority*

- **Develop a good attitude.**
  Give up some control.
  Trust your employees.
  Stay calm and patient.
- **Decide what to delegate.**
  Delegate whenever possible.
  Consider skill, motivation, and work load.
- **Select the right person.**
  Match skills and interests with tasks.
  Motivate your employees.
- **Communicate responsibility.**
  Set and prioritize clear goals.
  Share possible pitfalls.
  Develop performance standards.
  Develop reasonable deadlines for progress reports and project completion.
- **Provide support.**
  Let everyone know how and when you can help.
  Share your resources.
  Don't overrule decisions.
- **Monitor the delegation.**
  Record progress.
  Ask for feedback on how well you are delegating.
- **Evaluate the delegation.**
  Compare results with goals.
  Evaluate the employee's role.
  Discuss and give feedback.

Source: Reprinted from Gerald Williams et al., "Quick Tips: The Sweet Success of Delegation," *Supervisory Management*, November 1993. http://www.amanet.org.

Wide and Narrow Spans of Control

As a general rule, the more complex a subordinate's job, the fewer subordinates with those jobs should report to a manager. The more routine the work of subordinates, the greater the number of subordinates that can be effectively directed and controlled by one manager. Because of these general rules, organizations always seem to have narrow spans at their tops and wider spans at lower levels (Davis, 1951). The higher one goes in the organization's hierarchy, the fewer subordinates, as Figure 8.12 illustrates.

Finding a factory production supervisor with fifteen or more subordinates is not uncommon. Workers who can be well trained to follow procedures will, once they master their tasks, require less of their supervisor's time and energies. They will know what they must do and exactly how to do it to meet their performance standards.

FIGURE 8.12 *Narrow and wide spans of control*

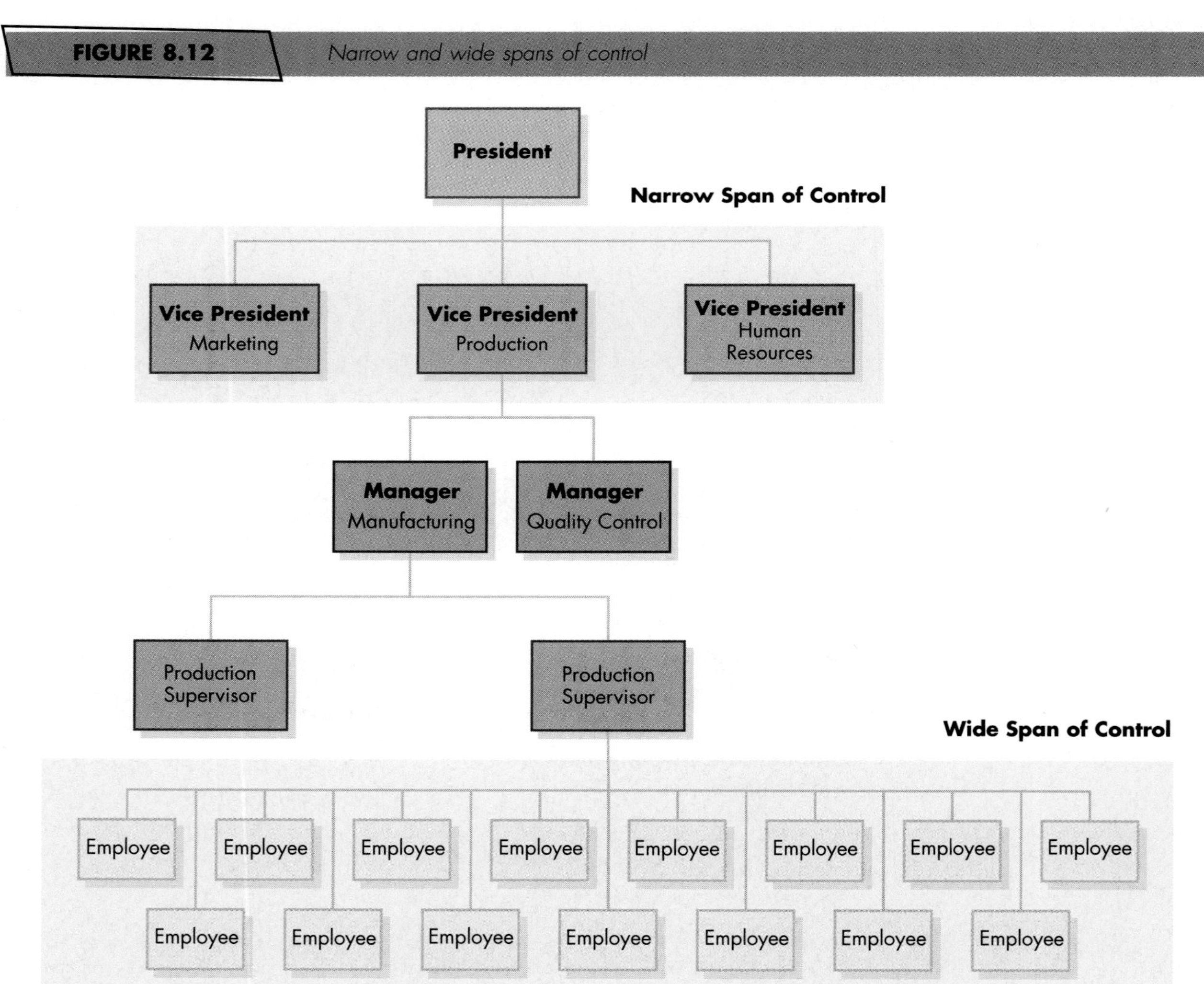

Conversely, looking again at Figure 8.12, finding a corporate vice president with more than three or four subordinates is uncommon (Urwick, 1938). Middle and upper managers perform little that is routine. Their tasks usually require ingenuity and creativity; and, because the problems are more complex, they are more difficult to resolve. Managers at these levels require more time to plan and organize their efforts. When they turn to their bosses for help, those bosses need to have the time available to render the assistance required. The only way to ensure having that time is to limit the number of people who will approach that boss for help—thus creating a narrow span of control (Van Fleet, 1983).

Proper Span of Control

Given these general rules, how many subordinates should any one manager have? The answer depends on many factors and must be determined in terms of a specific manager:

- The complexity and variety of the subordinates' work
- The ability of the manager
- The ability and training of the subordinates themselves
- The supervisor's willingness to delegate authority
- The company's philosophy for centralization or decentralization of decision making

Setting an effective span of control for each manager is crucial to effectiveness. If a manager has too many people to supervise, his or her subordinates will be frustrated by their inability to get immediate assistance from or access to their boss. Time and other resources could be wasted. Plans, decisions, and actions might be delayed or made without proper controls or safeguards. On the other hand, if a manager has too few people to supervise, the subordinates might be either overworked or oversupervised and could become frustrated and dissatisfied.

Two managers who hold jobs at the same level in the organization should not automatically be assigned identical spans of control because their abilities and those of their subordinates will differ. Managers' and subordinates' qualifications and experience must be considered when spans of control are created. The more capable and experienced the subordinates, the greater the number who can be effectively supervised by one competent manager. The less time needed to train and acclimate employees, the more time is available to devote to producing output. In general, spans can be widened as the experience and competence of personnel grow—thus the continuing need for training and development. Of course, this generalization applies only up to the middle-management level of the organization; once there, the need for limited spans of control due to complexity becomes paramount.

The company's philosophy toward centralization or decentralization for decision making can also influence the span of control of a manager. We will next examine the concept of centralization and then explain how it relates to span of control.

Discuss the following major organizing concept and how it influences organizing decisions

- Centralization and decentralization

Centralization Versus Decentralization

The terms **centralization** and **decentralization** refer to a philosophy of organization and management that focuses on either systematically retaining authority in the hands of higher level managers (centralization) or systematically delegating

centralization
A philosophy of organization and management that focuses on systematically retaining authority in the hands of higher level managers.

decentralization
A philosophy of organization and management that focuses on systematically delegating authority throughout the organization to middle- and lower-level managers.

authority throughout the organization to middle- and lower-level managers (decentralization) (Kountz and O'Donnel, 1976). Management's operating philosophy determines where authority resides. Management can decide either to concentrate authority for decision making in the hands of one or a few or to force it down the organization structure into the hands of many. Johnson & Johnson's extraordinary success is attributed to the art of decentralized management. Behind the art is the philosophy held by CEO Ralph Larsen and his two predecessors, Jim Burke and Robert Wood Johnson. Decentralized decision making is a core value and a core competency at Johnson & Johnson.

Centralization and decentralization are relative concepts when applied to organizations. Top management may decide to centralize all decision making: purchasing, staffing, and operations. Or it may decide to decentralize in part—setting limits on what can be purchased at each level by dollar amounts, giving first-level managers authority to hire clerical workers, and letting operational decisions be made where appropriate (Jones, 1988).

Why Decentralize?

To be effective, authority should be decentralized to the management level best suited to make the decision in question. A company president should not decide when to overhaul the engine in a forklift. Authority for that decision should be decentralized to the lowest possible level, in this case the plant maintenance manager or, if the company believes in empowerment, to the worker. Empowerment is the maximum expression of a decentralized philosophy. More companies are decentralizing authority to the people who know the jobs the best—the workers. This is especially true with team management, the topic of Chapter 15.

More and more organizations see decentralization as a means to achieving greater productivity and rebuilding the organization. Decentralization allows managers to be closer to the action and get closer to the consumer. As more organizations move toward "flatter" organizational structures, with fewer levels of management, decentralization and accountability are becoming watchwords for management success (Spertus, 1992). For example, Staples, an office-supply retailer, has committed to the principle of decentralization to develop "customer intimacy." Staples already provides great prices on papers, pens, fax machines, and other office supplies; however, it plans to grow by providing customers with the best solutions to their problems. With a level of management removed, Staples encourages and empowers store managers and employees to solve customers' problems (Jacob, 1995). For example, when a customer wanted to buy an unusual variety of map pin, a salesclerk was empowered to

http://www.staples.com

- Telephone the manufacturer of a similar pin
- Fax the information on the pins to the customer after the customer returned to his own place of business
- Deliver the $20 order of pins to the customer

Guidelines for Judging Decentralization

Research and experience have developed guidelines to follow in determining the degree to which a company is decentralized:

1. The greater the number of decisions made at the lower levels of management, the more the company is decentralized.

Staples uses decentralization to encourage and empower employees to better serve its customers.

2. The more important the decisions made at lower levels, the greater the decentralization. Purchasing decisions are a good measure. A company with a purchasing limit of $100,000 at the first level is more decentralized than another company in the same industry with a first-level limit of $1,000.
3. The more flexible the interpretation of company policy at the lower levels, the greater the degree of decentralization.
4. The more widely dispersed the operations of the company geographically, the greater the degree of decentralization.
5. The less a subordinate has to refer to his or her manager prior to making a decision, the greater the decentralization.

Relationship of Centralization to Span of Control

A company's philosophy of centralization or decentralization in decision making can influence the span of control of lower and middle managers. It also can influence the number of levels in an organization. Centralized decision making produces narrow spans of control and more levels of management. With centralized management, top-level managers delegate little authority and must closely supervise those who report to them. Recall from our discussion on span of control, if a manager closely supervises subordinates, the manager has committed his or her time to a limited few. Given the philosophy of centralization, successive levels of managers will follow the same practice. Thus, there will always be narrow spans of control and the company will need many levels of management to reach first-line supervisors (see Figure 8.13).

Conversely, a philosophy of decentralized decision making generally means that the company will have wider spans of control and fewer levels of management. Such firms delegate authority and decision making down the organization to lower levels of management. Decentralization relieves managers of time commitments and allows them to spend time with more subordinates. As managers at each successive level follow this philosophy, two outcomes should be predictable: (1) A manager can supervise more subordinates and thus can have a wider span

FIGURE 8.13 *Structures of centralized and decentralized organizations*

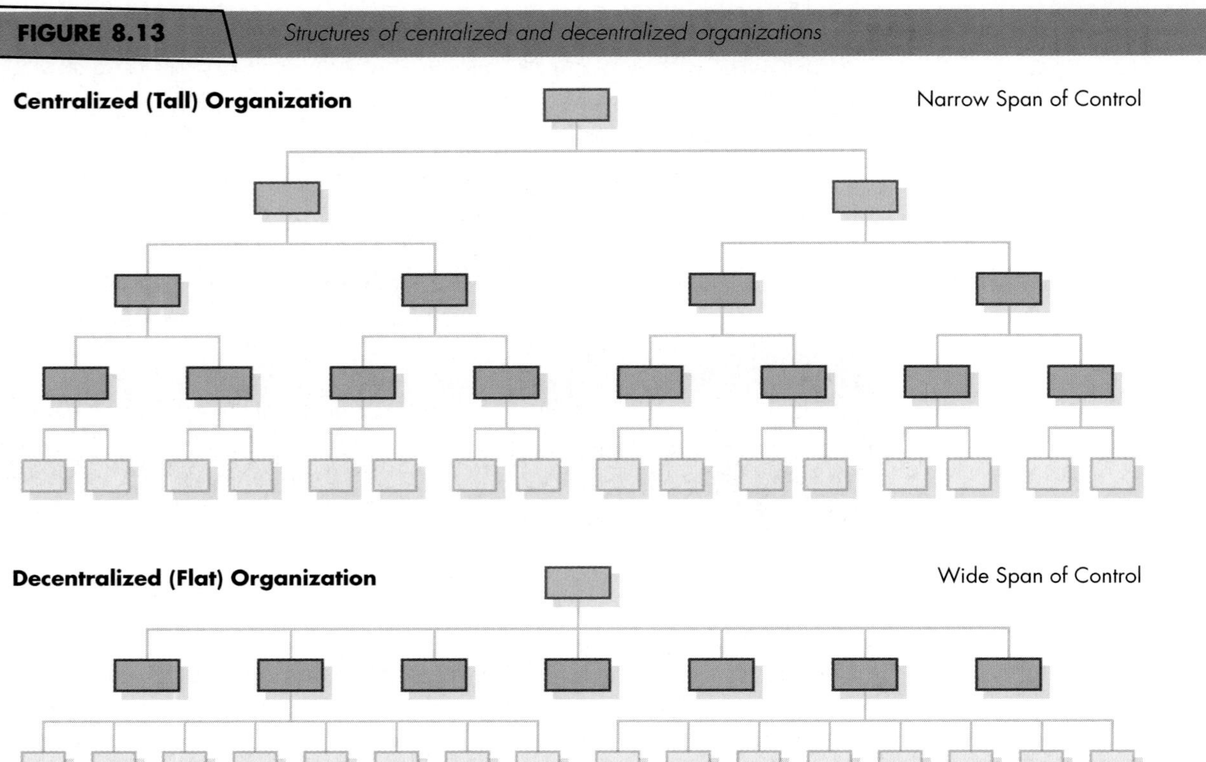

of control, and (2) a company needs fewer management levels to do the same job because people operate more independently. Review Figure 8.13 to examine an organization chart of a decentralized organization.

Despite the logic of this interrelationship of decision making and span of control, it does not often happen in practice. Managers with wide spans of control may choose not to delegate authority, and they are frequently not as effective as they could be if they did delegate. Another problem with this generalization is that other factors, as noted in the discussion on span of control, can influence how many subordinates report to a manager.

THE INFORMAL ORGANIZATION

Explain the term "informal organization"

Functioning within the formal organization designed by management—the organization of departmental structure, designated leaders (managers), decision-making guidelines, policies, procedures, and rules—is a system of social relationships. These relationships, collectively, constitute the informal organization. Managers need to understand this informal organization because it influences the productivity and job satisfaction of all members of the organization—managers as well as nonmanagers. Managers find out through experience that not everything in an organization takes place within the squares on the organization chart. People by nature refuse to "stay in the boxes" as drawn. They choose to operate within the confines of and with the support of the informal organization.

Informal Organization Defined

informal organization
A network of personal and social relationships that arise spontaneously as people associate with one another in a work environment.

The **informal organization** is a network of personal and social relationships that arise spontaneously as people associate with one another in a work environment (Davis and Newstrom, 1989). It consists of all the informal groupings of people within a formal organization. Memberships in most informal organizations change with time. Members join together through the need for or enjoyment of one another's company; they find membership beneficial to them in one or more ways.

The informal organization challenges a manager because it consists of actual relationships that have real consequences on workers' behavior but that are not prescribed by the formal organization and, therefore, not shown on the company's organization chart.

The informal organization knows no boundaries. It cuts across the organization because it results from personal and social relationships, not prescribed roles. When two workers, at break or after work, gossip and share their perceptions of company affairs and fellow workers, their action is an example of the informal organization. Another example is an employee's assisting someone in another department in solving a work problem. The informal organization should not be thought of as the domain of only workers. Managers form informal groups that cut across departmental lines. In addition, they actively participate in other groups with nonmanagers. The informal organization exists everywhere. The lunch bunch, the coffee break group, and the employees who run, jog, or walk together at lunch are other examples of informal groups.

Informal and Formal Organizations Compared

Compare the informal organization to the formal organization

The informal organization puts emphasis on people and their relationships; the formal organization puts emphasis on official organizational positions. The leverage or clout in the informal organization is informal power that attaches to the individual. In the formal organization, the formal authority comes directly from the

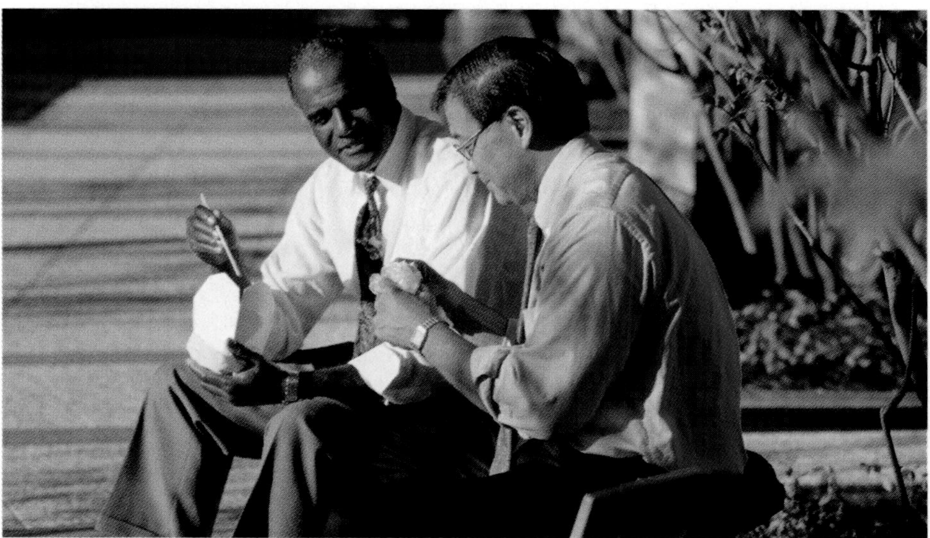

It is important for managers to be aware of and understand the informal organization—a network of personal and social relationships—in addition to the formal organization.

position; and the person has it only when occupying that position. Informal power is personal and authority is organizational, as noted in Figure 8.14.

Informal power does not come from within a person but is, instead, given by group members; informal power does not follow the official chain of command. Authority, in contrast, is delegated by management and creates a chain of command. Workers may grant power to a coworker at the same level or to someone in another department. Power is much less stable than authority; it comes from how people feel about each other and may change rapidly.

A manager probably has some informal power along with his or her formal authority, but the manager does not necessarily have more informal power than does anyone else in the group. The manager and the informal leader can be—and often are—two different individuals.

Formal organizations may grow to be extremely large, but informal organizations tend to remain smaller in order to maintain the personal relationships. As a result, large corporations like Johnson & Johnson tend to have hundreds of informal organizations operating within them (Davis and Newstrom, 1989).

Emergence of the Informal Organization

The informal organization emerges within the formal organization. Because of the relationships and alliances in the informal group, workers' behavior differs from what managers may have expected based on the reporting relationships, procedures, and rules established in the formal organization. Several factors contribute to these differences. First, employees sometimes act differently than anticipated. They may work faster or slower than expected, or they may modify a work procedure based on their experience and knowledge. Second, employees often interact with people other than those the formal organization specifies or with specified people more or less often than their job requires. Gene may seek advice from Joy instead of Larry, for example. Cindy may spend more time helping Buddy than she does helping Maceo. Third, workers may adopt a whole set of beliefs and attitudes that differ from those the organization expects of them. The company may

FIGURE 8.14 *Comparison of informal and formal organizations*

Informal Organization	Formal Organization
Unofficial organization created by relationships	Official organization created by management
Primary area of emphasis is on people and their relationships	Primary area of emphasis is official organization positions
Leverage is provided by power	Leverage is provided by authority
Source of power: given by the group	Source of authority: delegated by management
Functions with power and politics	Functions with authority and responsibility
Behavior guidelines provided by group norms	Behavior guidelines provided by rules, policies, and procedures
Sources of control over the individual are positive or negative sanctions	Sources of control over the individual are rewards and penalties

expect loyalty, commitment, and enthusiasm, but some employees may become totally unenthusiastic whereas others may act rebellious and alienated. Values or attitudes that employees as a group accept as standards of behavior are known as **norms**. A norm serves as a guideline of behavior and an internal control device on members. Fourth, the groups of workers that form begin to display cohesion. **Cohesion** is a strong attachment to the group and a closeness measured by a singleness of purpose and a high degree of cooperation. As a result, a manager has dual sets of behavior to monitor—the activities, interactions, and beliefs required by the formal organization and the ones that develop as people interact (Davis and Newstrom, 1989).

norms
Values or attitudes that employees as a group accept as standards of behavior and that serve as a guideline of behavior and an internal control device on members.

cohesion
A strong attachment to the group and a closeness measured by a singleness of purpose and a high degree of cooperation.

Structure of the Informal Organization

Because individuals constantly enter and exit an informal organization, it continually changes. Its structure can be identified through the communication and contact people have with each other. Figure 8.15, an **interaction chart**, aids in identifying the informal organization structure by spotlighting the informal interactions people have with one another. Notice that the contacts don't always follow the formal organizational chart. The arrows indicate which person initiates contact with others.

interaction chart
A diagram that aids in identifying the informal organization structure by spotlighting the informal interactions people have with one another.

Leadership of the Group

As in a formal organization, the informal group develops leader–follower relationships. Because of the number of informal groups in an organization, a person may be a leader in one group and a follower in another. To determine why a person assumes the leadership role, you have to look at the groups and the individual members.

When you look at a group, each member has identifiable characteristics that distinguish him or her from the others—for example, age, seniority, level of earnings, and technical ability. Each of these elements can provide status to its holder,

FIGURE 8.15 *Interaction chart indicating interaction of informal communication*

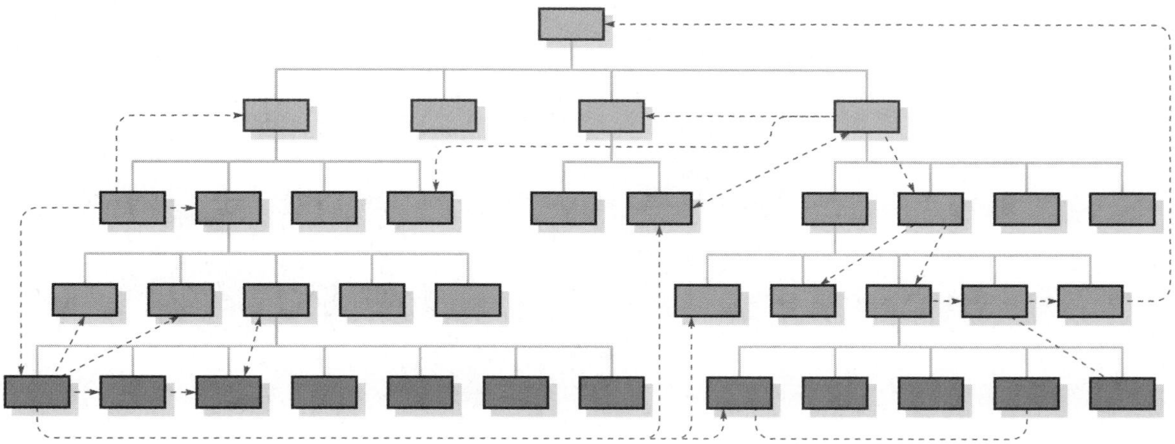

based on what the group members value. The employee with the most status in the informal organization emerges as its informal leader. This person possesses great informal power. In some groups, charismatic leadership (leadership based on the person's personality) is common. In others, the leader may be the most senior person or the person holding the highest position in the formal organization.

A group may have several leaders of varying importance to perform different functions. The group may look to one person as the expert on organizational matters and to another as its social leader. A third may be consulted on technical questions. Even in a situation of multiple leaders, however, one leader usually exerts more influence on the group than do the others.

Nonleader Roles for Members

Members of an informal group play other roles besides leader. As Figure 8.16 illustrates, an informal group normally has an inner core, or primary group; a fringe group, which functions within and outside of the larger group; and an out-status group, which, although identified with the larger group, does not actively participate in the larger group's activities (Harmon and Scott, 1970).

FIGURE 8.16 *Composition of an informal group*

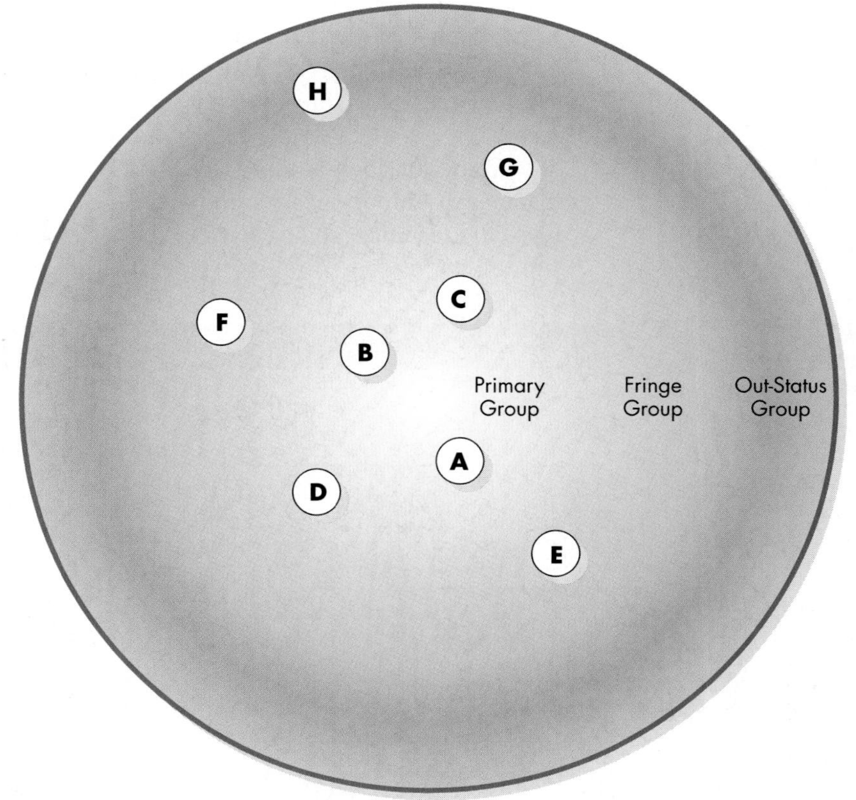

Working with the Informal Organization

The three steps a manager must take in order to work with the informal organization are as follows:

1. Recognize that informal groups exist.
2. Identify the roles members play within those groups.
3. Use that information to work with the informal groups.

Managers need to understand the personality, values, and culture of each group. They need to know how the groups' values and norms differ from those of the formal organization—if, indeed, they do. Managers also need to be able to identify the leaders of these groups and work with them to influence the total group. Trying to influence a group by appealing to a fringe member will fail. Managers need to approach the leaders at the core of decision making. Managers can also use the communication network of the informal organization to spread the word about a new company policy or to learn about how workers perceive a new company head. If the information is on the Internet, the manager can help employees evaluate it. See this chapter's Managing Technology feature.

Impact of the Informal Organization

The informal organization can affect the formal organization positively and negatively, as shown in Figure 8.17.

Positive Impact

The informal organization has the potential to be helpful to managers in the following ways (Davis and Newstrom, 1989):

- *Makes the total system effective.* If the informal organization blends well with the formal system, the organization can function more effectively. The ability of the informal group to provide flexibility and instantaneous reactions can enhance the plans and procedures developed through the formal organization.
- *Provides support to management.* The informal organization can provide support to the individual manager. If the manager will accept assistance, the informal organization can fill in gaps in the manager's knowledge through advice or through actually doing the needed work. When the group performs effectively and positively, it builds a cooperative environment. This, in turn, can lead the manager to delegate more tasks to the employees.

FIGURE 8.17 *Positive and negative potential of informal organizations*

Positives	Negatives
+ Makes the total system effective	– Develops pressure for conformity
+ Provides support to management	– Creates conflicts
+ Provides stability in the workplace	– Resists change
+ Provides a useful communication channel	– Initiates rumors and processes false information
+ Encourages better management	– Exposes weak management

MANAGING TECHNOLOGY
Evaluating Information on the Internet

Just about anyone can put up a Web page. By January 2001, the Google search engine had found 1,326,920,000 Web pages. Largely unchecked and unregulated, the Internet contains some information that isn't what it seems. How do you separate good information from bad?

Look carefully through a Web site for information on who has produced it.

- Who are the authors?
- Where do the authors work?
- Is the information current?
- Who owns the Web site? (In other words, who stands to profit from the site? For example, the maker of a brand of zinc lozenges might have a study at its site saying that the product will reduce the symptoms of the common cold. However, after carefully studying the site, you discover that the company funded the research!)

Look for industry affiliations, company background, and contact information, which should include a physical address and phone number as well as email address. Does the site include an area for reader feedback? If not, check what others are saying about it by running its name through http://groups.google.com, a search engine of newsgroups or discussions.

http://www.google.com

- *Provides stability in the workplace.* The informal organization provides acceptance and a sense of belonging. These feelings of being wanted and part of the group can encourage employees to remain in the workplace environment, reducing turnover. Additionally, the informal organization provides a place for the person to vent frustrations. Being able to discuss them in a supportive environment may relieve emotional pressures.
- *Provides a useful communication channel.* The informal organization provides employees with the opportunities for interacting socially, for discussing their work, and for understanding what is happening in the work environment.
- *Encourages better management.* Managers should be aware of the power of the informal organization in what is actually a checks-and-balance system. Planned changes should be made with an awareness of the ability of the informal group to make the plan successful or unsuccessful.

Negative Impact

There are potential problem areas associated with the informal organization (Davis and Newstrom, 1989):

- *Develops pressure for conformity.* The norms of informal groups strongly pressure group members to conform. The more cohesive the group, the more accepted are the behavioral standards. An informal group often uses rewards or penalties, called **sanctions**, to persuade its members to conform to its norms. Nonconforming can result in gentle verbal reminders from the group, but such a situation can escalate to outright harassment—ostracism, hiding supplies, or sabotaging computer files.
- *Creates conflict.* The informal group can create two masters for an employee. In an attempt to satisfy the informal group, the employee may come in conflict with the formal organization. The lunch bunch enjoys going together as

sanctions
Rewards or penalties used by an informal group to persuade its members to conform to its norms.

a group, eating a leisurely meal, and analyzing the company. The lunch bunch enjoys its 60-minute lunch each day even though management has authorized only a 30-minute lunchtime. The employees' social satisfaction conflicts with the employer's need for productivity.

- *Resists change.* The informal organization can resist change. In an effort to protect its values and beliefs, the informal group can place roadblocks in the path of any work modifications. Establishing a four-day workweek or hiring younger workers could infringe on the values of the informal group, resulting in resistance to the change.
- *Initiates rumors and processes false information.* The informal communication system—the grapevine—can create and process false information or rumors. Rumors can upset the balance of the work environment.
- *Exposes weak management.* Although skilled managers can see the relationships of the informal organization, less practiced managers can be stymied by them. The result may be a work group that does not perform and a manager who does not last.

CHAPTER SUMMARY

1 Explain the relationship between planning and organizing. Planning and organizing are intimately related. Organizing begins with and is governed by plans that state where the organization is going and how it will get there. An organization must be built, or an existing one modified, to ensure that those plans are executed and objectives achieved.

2 Explain the importance of the organizing process. The organizing process results in the creation of an organization—a whole consisting of unified parts (a system) acting in harmony to execute tasks that achieve goals effectively and efficiently and accomplish the company's mission. Additionally, the organizing process clarifies the work environment, creates a coordinated environment, achieves the principle of unity of direction, and establishes the chain of command.

3 List and discuss the five steps in the organizing process. The steps are:

1. *Reviewing plans and goals.* A company's goals and its plans to achieve them dictate its work activities.
2. *Determining work activities.* Managers need to ask what work activities are necessary to accomplish the objectives. Both ongoing and unique tasks need to be determined.
3. *Classifying and grouping activities.* Once managers know what tasks must be done, they classify and group these activities into manageable work units—departments. Grouping tasks is accomplished by applying the principle of functional similarity. Departmentalization may be functional, geographical, product, or customer.
4. *Assigning work and delegating authority.* After grouping the activities into departments, managers must assign the units to individuals and give them the appropriate authority to accomplish the task.
5. *Designing a hierarchy of relationships.* The last step requires managers to determine the vertical and horizontal operating relationships of the organization as a whole. Vertical structuring results in a decision-making hierarchy. Horizontal structuring defines working relationships between operating departments and makes the final decision on the span of control of each manager.

4 Describe and give an example of the four approaches to departmentalization. Approaches to departmentalization:

- Functional departmentalization is logical and simple; it involves creating departments on the basis of specialized activities of the business—finance, production, marketing, human resources.
- Geographical departmentalization groups activities and responsibilities according to territory—for example, northern region, southern region. It allows companies to be close to, and adapt to, the needs of customers.
- Product departmentalization assembles the activities of creating, producing, and marketing each product into a separate department—for example, elevator products division, aircraft products division. It is adopted when each product requires unique marketing strategies, production processes, distribution systems, or financial resources.
- Customer departmentalization groups activities and responsibilities in departments organized on the needs of specific customer groups—for example, pharmaceutical, professional, or final consumer.

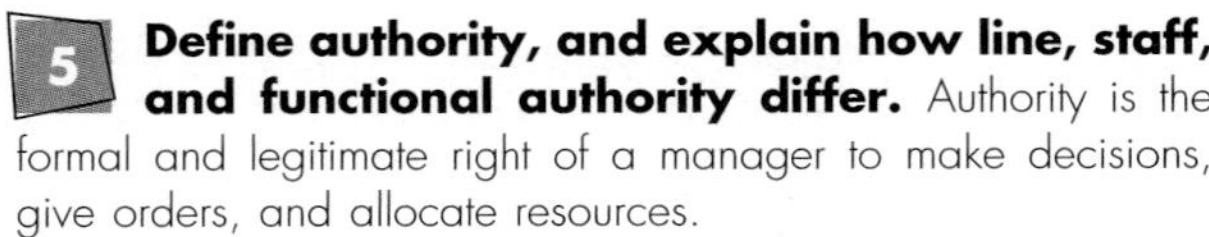

5 Define authority, and explain how line, staff, and functional authority differ. Authority is the formal and legitimate right of a manager to make decisions, give orders, and allocate resources.

- Line authority is supervisory authority. It allows managers to give direct orders to subordinates, evaluate their actions, and reward or punish them.
- Staff authority is the authority to serve in an advisory capacity. Managers who provide advice or technical assistance are granted advisory authority.
- Functional authority permits staff managers to make decisions on specific activities performed by personnel within other departments.

6 Explain the concept of power and its sources. Power is the ability to exert influence in the organization. Whereas authority is positional, power is personal—it exists because of the person. There are five sources of power: legitimate or position power, coercive power, reward power, referent power, and expert power.

7 Discuss the major organizing concepts and how they influence organizing decisions. The major organizational concepts include

- *Unity of direction:* A principle of organizing that calls for the establishment of one authority figure for each designated task of the organization. This person has the authority to coordinate all plans concerning that task.
- *Chain of command:* The unbroken line of reporting relationships from the bottom to the top of the organization. It defines the formal decision-making structure and provides for the orderly progression up and down the hierarchy for both decision making and communications.
- *Line and staff departments:* Organizations operate with line and staff departments. Line departments meet the major objectives of an organization and directly influence its success. Staff departments contribute indirectly—through advice, service, and assistance.
- *Unity of command:* Each person within the organization takes orders and reports to only one person. It should guide any attempt to develop operating relationships.
- *Delegation:* The downward transfer of formal authority from one person to another. It involves assignment of tasks, delegation of authority, acceptance of responsibility, and creation of accountability. Delegation frees managers from some management areas to be able to focus on more critical concerns. It can increase the ability of a manager.
- *Responsibility:* The obligation to carry out one's assigned duties to the best of one's abilities. Responsibility cannot be delegated to an employee; rather, the employee's acceptance of an assignment creates an obligation to do his or her best. Responsibility is a step in the delegation process.
- *Accountability:* Having to answer to someone for your actions. Accountability means accepting the consequences—either credit or blame—for these actions. Accountability is a step in the delegation process.
- *Span of control:* Refers to the number of employees a manager directly supervises. There is no correct number for the span of control, but it is normally narrower at the top of the organization than at the bottom. Generally, the more complex a subordinate's job, the fewer such subordinates should report to a manager. The more routine the work, the greater the number to be supervised.
- *Centralization and decentralization:* A philosophy of organization and management that focuses on either the concentration (centralization) or disposal (decentralization) of authority within the organization. Management determines where authority resides in an organization—either to concentrate authority for decision making in the hands of the few or to force it down the organization structure into the hands of many.

8 Explain the term "informal organization." The informal organization is a network of personal and social relationships that arise spontaneously as people associate in a work environment. It consists of all the informal groupings of people within a formal organization.

9 Compare the informal organization to the formal organization. The informal organization puts emphasis on people and their relationships; the formal organization puts emphasis on official organizational positions. The leverage or clout in the informal organization is informal power—it attaches to the person. In the formal organization, the formal authority comes directly from the position, and the person has it only when occupying that position. Informal power is given by group members; management delegates authority. Informal power does not follow the chain of command; authority does. Power is much less stable than authority. Formal organizations may grow to be extremely large, but informal organizations tend to remain smaller. As a result, large corporations tend to have hundreds of informal organizations operating throughout them.

REVIEW QUESTIONS

1. How do the functions of planning and organizing relate to each other (a) in the initial development of a company and (b) during the modification of the company's structure?
2. Identify and explain three important benefits of the organizing process.

3. List the five steps in the organizing process. Draft a one-sentence description of each.
4. Identify the four popular approaches to departmentalizing. Specify which approach you would recommend for each of the following organizations and defend your choices:
   a. A retail hardware store
   b. A company that manufactures and markets one product
   c. A company with sales offices in forty states
   d. A retail department store
5. Identify and explain the three types of authority.
6. What is power? What are its sources? How does it differ from authority?
7. Explain the importance to managers of each of these organizing concepts or principles:
   a. Unity of direction
   b. Chain of command
   c. Line and staff departments
   d. Unity of command
   e. Delegation of authority
   f. Responsibility
   g. Accountability
   h. Span of control
   i. Centralization/decentralization
8. What does the term *informal organization* mean? Of what does the informal organization consist?
9. How does the formal organization differ from the informal organization?

DISCUSSION QUESTIONS FOR CRITICAL THINKING

1. What type of departmentalization does your company or school use in its organizational structure? Diagram the structure and explain your answer.
2. Develop a different way to departmentalize your company or school. What are the specific advantages of your form of departmentalization over the present departmentalization design?
3. Which type of department (line or staff) is most important to an organization? Why? Could an organization function without either of them? Why or why not?
4. At your company or school, what is the span of control for the president? A vice president? A first-line supervisor or chair of a department? Why do different spans of control exist among these managers?

INTERNET EXERCISES

Check the text Web site at http://plunkett.swcollege.com for updated links to the Internet Exercises.

1. Driven by a set of radical changes in their internal and external environments, large global corporations are innovating a new organizational form. Premised on knowledge and expertise rather than capital or scale as the key strategic resources, this new form is fundamentally different from the multidivisional organization that emerged in the 1920s and became the dominant corporate model in the post-war years. Read "Beyond the M-Form: Toward a Managerial Theory of the Firm" by Christopher A. Bartlett, professor of business administration, Harvard Business School, and Sumantra Ghoshal, professor of strategy and management, INSEAD. Describe this new organization and highlight its differences from the classic M-form by contrasting its structure, processes, and decision-making mechanisms.
   http://www.gsia.cmu.edu/bosch/bart.html
2. "Span of Effective Command and Control: Implications of New Research for Organizing the Force" examines span of control in the military. What factors were used to develop a preliminary model of effective span of command and control? Discuss which factors make command and control easier. Do these differ from those used in business?
   http://207.133.209.51/socc.htm
3. Read "The Why, What and To Whom of Delegating" by Andrew E. Schwartz. What are the benefits of effective delegation? What are the obstacles to delegation? What work should be delegated? What are four essential rules that enhance the probabilities of successful delegation?
   http://www.aeschwartz.com/delegate.html

APPLICATION CASE

Merlin Needs a Magician

After getting a master's degree in business, spending time as a stockbroker on Wall Street, and working as a manager in a traditionally organized manufacturing company, Ashley Korenblat was hired as president of Merlin Metalworks. Korenblat, fresh from her experience at a large company, was anxious to try out her own theories at the small, Albany, New York–based producer of bicycles. In short order Korenblat had to contend with the following organizational problems:

- Two welders, unable to get a decision from their supervisor, requested time off. One welder had a dentist appointment and the other needed to leave early to pick up an anniversary present.
- A review of the previous day's shipping log revealed that nothing had been shipped. The reason: a customer had called about a problem bottom bracket—the place where the bicycle pedals attach—which made the customer's $4,000 bike useless. The customer service department had the authority to stop everything to solve a customer's problem. In this case it meant turning off the final threading machine for a day, which brought the shipments to a halt.
- After little discussion, Korenblat made a decision to redesign the brakes on road bikes, believing it would be less expensive. Shortly after the first production run began, the person in charge of purchasing insisted on rehashing the decision. It turned out that the new design would lead to a series of new expenses—adding up to more than the expected savings.
- In an effort to have the employees make decisions and be more independent, the machine department was organized into teams. The teams were responsible for developing the production schedule, determining the size of the production runs, and coordinating the 35 operations in any given production run—some of which were linear, others which proceeded simultaneously. All went well until the company approached a six-month backlog in a seasonal business. To respond, Korenblat kept increasing the size of the runs—"I know you made 200 57-centimeter road bikes last week, but this week we need 250 58-centimeter bikes." The result: the machine shop came to a standstill, waiting for the next command.

http://www.merlinbike.com

Questions

1. For each of the four situations noted, what organizational concepts apply? Identify the concept and explain the related problem.
2. As an adviser to President Ashley Korenblat, how would you resolve each problem?

VIDEO CASE

JIAN: A Study in Organizing

Founded in Silicon Valley by CEO Burke Franklin in 1988, JIAN, Inc., has become a leader in the provider of time-saving business software templates. One of the company's key contributions in this area is the Biz Plan Builder software that provides a complete business plan. This software allows users to edit the standardized business plan and tailor it to their unique needs, rather than having to write a business plan from scratch. Editing the generic plan that his company provides, Franklin argues, is much easier than writing an entirely new business plan.

Making things easier for managers is also consistent with Franklin's decisions regarding the organization of JIAN. Started as a small business in Franklin's home, JIAN soon experienced rapid growth and thus needed to change its organization radically in order to continue that growth. At the time, most software companies tended to produce, develop, market, and distribute their products themselves and thus had organizations reflecting that business strategy. Franklin chose not to follow suit, but instead to focus on what he considered to be the strengths of JIAN.

Rather than "doing it all" like other software companies, Franklin decided to outsource the production and distribution functions in order to concentrate on software development and marketing. Initially, the company selected a number of producers and distributors to provide specific process components. This approach led to a lot of "finger pointing" among producers and distributors when quality or distribution problems arose. Desiring to avoid such problems in the future but to continue outsourcing, Franklin changed JIAN's organizational structure to that of a virtual corporation.

Franklin consolidated the various functions that were being outsourced. He also decided not only to outsource production and distribution, but also the human resources function. To do so, he selected Bindco to handle all the production and distribution functions that had previously been divided among various firms and Execustaff to handle all aspects of JIAN's human resources function. Bindco manufacturers the boxes, duplicates the disks, publishes the manuals, and performs a host of distribution tasks (e.g., processing orders over the Internet) to name just a few. Execustaff acts as a complete human resources department, doing all the recruiting, hiring, and firing of employees, and implementing JIAN's employee policies and procedures. These two companies, in essence, provide "one-stop shopping" to handle all of JIAN's outsourcing needs, allowing the company to focus on its core business-software development and marketing. JIAN's virtual organization has enabled it to continue to grow, increased its flexibility, and allowed it to gain a competitive advantage in the marketplace.

http://www.jian.com

For Discussion:

1. What is the "secret" to the success of virtual corporations according to Burke Franklin, CEO of JIAN?
2. What types of relationships or what characteristics should exist to enable partners to succeed in a virtual corporation?
3. What type of departmentalization does JIAN use in its method of outsourcing?

Organizational Design

KEY TERMS

continuous-process production
divisional structure
flexible manufacturing systems (FMS)
functional structure
large batch technology
mass production technology
matrix structure
mechanistic structure
network structure
organic structure
organizational design
organizational life cycle
small batch technology
team structure
technology
unit production technology

LEARNING OBJECTIVES

After studying this chapter, you should be able to

1. Explain the meaning of organizational design
2. Describe the four objectives of organizational design
3. Distinguish between mechanistic and organic organizational structures
4. Discuss the influence that contingency factors—organizational strategy, environment, size, age, and technology—have on organizational design
5. Describe the characteristics, advantages, and disadvantages of functional, divisional, matrix, team, and network structural designs

MANAGEMENT IN ACTION

Coca-Cola Reformulates Its Business

Coca-Cola's products are sold in more than 200 countries and account for a billion servings of beverages consumed every day. Frustrated with the slumping market share of its flagship brand, Douglas Daft's first decision [after being elected CEO of Coca-Cola in February 2000] was to restructure the company—"a plan requiring the layoff of 6,000 workers, including nearly half of those at Coke headquarters in Atlanta. . . . The huge layoffs are meant to clear the way for Coke to become a quicker company, a marketer better attuned to customers and other constituents" (Hays, 2000). He summed up the strategy as "think local, act local."

The twenty-first century offers new challenges, and Coca-Cola's goal is to become the world's premier consumer relationship organization. This vision requires focusing on consumers and connecting with them, as well as building relationships with other parties: the bottlers, distributors, and retailers. Coca-Cola is giving local managers the autonomy to make decisions so regional flavors and marketing campaigns can more accurately match local customer preferences around the world.

This is not the first time that Coca-Cola's business has been reformulated. Cuban émigré Roberto Goizueta was chosen as Coca-Cola's CEO in 1981. At that time, Coca-Cola "was a hodgepodge of businesses, including shrimp farming and industrial water treatment, as well as soft drinks. . . . Goizueta sold poorly profitable businesses steadily, keeping only soft drinks and focusing on overseas markets. He emphasized stock market increases, rewarded top performers with rich stock options, and borrowed heavily to buy independent Coke bottlers around the world" (Connor, 1997). He oversaw the successful introduction of Diet Coke in 1982.

Goizueta's most well known mistake was New Coke. In the mid 1980s Pepsi outsold Coke in supermarkets with its highly successful "Take the Pepsi Challenge" advertising campaign. The challenge was to choose the preferred cola in a blind taste test, where respondents did not know which brand they were testing. Then, Coca-Cola searched for a new flavor to beat Pepsi in blind taste tests. After 200,000 taste tests, it settled on New Coke, a sweeter, smoother flavor that beat Pepsi and old Coke in the blind taste tests. In 1985 New Coke replaced Classic Coke. Coke customers were angry. Coca-Cola brought back Classic Coke alongside New Coke. Customers continued to reject New Coke. Five years after being introduced, New Coke was finished.

Roberto Goizueta . . . taught his executives that when they set goals for market share, they needed to focus on the share of stomach, not the share of carbonated beverages. His adversary was water, not soda. By this definition, Coke's 40%-plus market share became 3%, changing the company's view of growth. He then redefined the term global for a company that was already seemingly everywhere. By 1997 he pushed Coke's overseas profits up to nearly 80% of total earnings, from 65%. This global view was reflected in people too. Goizueta gave real meaning to the word diversity, developing a multinational talent pool. He also became an avid disciple of the idea of economic value creation—a gauge of success that eliminates accounting gimmicks. He

Coca-Cola's recent restructuring and decentralization support its goal to become the world's premier consumer relationship organization.

used it to create more value in less time than almost anyone else (Charan, 1998).

Roberto Goizueta has become a CEO legend. "From the time he became chief executive until his death in 1997, Coke's sales more than quadrupled, from $4 billion to $18 billion, while its market capitalization ballooned from $4.3 billion to $180 billion, a staggering 3,500% increase" (Greising, 1998). His vision and drive transformed the giant company into a global power. But after his death in 1997, the company floundered. Douglas Ivester, chief financial officer under Goizueta, was put in charge. He retired and Douglas Daft, an Australian overseeing operations in the Middle East and Asia, was elected CEO.

In the spring of 1999 [when Ivester was CEO] children in Belgium said they felt sick after drinking Coke products. Coca-Cola was slow to respond and was perceived as arrogant and uncaring. Asked about that situation, Daft said, "Maybe there was no one there who understood the environment. Or, if we had people who understood the environment, we didn't listen to them" (Hays, 2000).

Daft's restructured and decentralized Coca-Cola will let local managers make decisions about products, advertising, and other functions that previously were controlled from Atlanta. They will be more responsive to political and social concerns. "To me it was so natural and logical," Daft said. "It's something I've always lived by" (Hays, 2000). ■

Sources: David Greising, "I'd Like the World To Buy a Coke: The Life and Leadership of Roberto Goizueta," *Business Week Online* (13 April 1998), http://www.businessweek.com/1998/15/b3573108.htm; "Doug Daft Speaks at Atlanta's Commerce Club," *New @ Coke* (29 November 2000), http://www.thecoca-colacompany.com/news/index.html, and listen to the Audio Archives of Management Insights, http://www.thecoca-colacompany.com/investors/index.html; Michael Connor, "Coke Chairman Robert Goizueta Hospitalized," *Reuters* (14 October 1997), http://198.62.75.1/www2/fcf/cokechairhospitalized101497.html; Constance L. Hays, "Learning to Think Smaller at Coke," *The New York Times* (6 February 2000), http://www.lincoln.ac.nz/comm/subjects/bmkt326/coke.htm; Ram Charan, "Managing To Be the Best: The Century's Smartest Bosses Have Influence Beyond Their Companies," *Time* (7 December 1998), http://www.ge.com/news/welch/articles/t1298.htm.

INTRODUCTION

http://www.coca-cola.com

Managers in companies like Coca-Cola frequently must rethink and reorganize to pursue their mission and strategic goals. As companies focus or refocus their attention on the customer—whether in manufacturing or marketing a product or providing a service—it becomes necessary to modify structures or, as in the case of Coca-Cola, drastically overhaul the organization.

Chapter 8 identified and examined the concepts and process of organizing. This chapter will focus on organizational structure as a tool. It will examine how managers integrate departmentalization, decentralization, and span of control into an organizational design to achieve specific objectives. Initially the chapter will examine the nature of organizational design and its objectives and then introduce potential design outcomes. The chapter will conclude with a discussion of the organizational structure options available to a designer.

DESIGNING ORGANIZATIONAL STRUCTURES

Organizational Design Defined

1 Explain the meaning of organizational design

organizational design *The creation of or change to an organization's structure.*

What is organizational design? Quite simply, when managers create or change an organization's structure, they engage in **organizational design** (Robbins, 1994). They develop the overall layout of the positions and departments as well as the interrelationships of the departments. Most importantly, these managers create the means to implement plans, achieve goals and objectives, and ultimately accomplish the organization's mission—to satisfy the customer. Designers make decisions critical to success. As management consultant Frank Ostroff rightly noted, "The right organizational structure can take you from 100 horsepower to 500 horsepower" (Jacob, 1995).

For organizational designers at Coca-Cola, organizational design is like putting together a giant jigsaw puzzle, with two differences. Unlike a jigsaw puzzle, an organization offers no picture to tell the designer what the final outcome should look like; and organizational design involves billions of dollars for putting the correct pieces together.

Objectives of Organizational Design

2

Describe the four objectives of organizational design

http://www.ppg.com

http://www.nortel.com

http://www.sears.com

http://www.honda.com

http://www.aa.com

http://www.exxonmobil.com

http://www.campbellsoup.com

Organizations have certain common elements: they operate with authority, they have departments, and they use line and staff positions. As alike as they may seem, however, no two organizations are exactly the same. Some, like PPG Industries, rely on functional departmentalization; others, like Northern Telecom (now Nortel Networks), choose product groups (Verespej, 1992). Some, like Sears, centralize decision making; others, like Honda, decentralize. Some, like Matsushita, have narrow spans of control; others, like American Airlines, have developed wide spans. The decisions made by managers on the various elements determine the organizational design; and organizations continually evolve to suit their operational requirements.

Regardless of whether managers responsible for organizational design work for ExxonMobil or Campbell's Soup, they have the same objectives: respond to change, integrate new elements, coordinate the components, and encourage flexibility.

Responding to Change

"Nothing lasts forever" could be the slogan of organizational designers. For a firm to stay competitive, it must respond to changes in the environment—competition, technology, the global economy, and consumer needs—as well as to changes that emerge from the company's evolutionary development. To remain static in the face of warning signals could eventually result in making change an arduous process. General Motors continues to face such a situation.

http://www.gm.com

In the early 1990s, GM had become a bloated, slow-moving bureaucracy, marked by overcentralization and a cultural disdain for ideas from anywhere else (Reese, 1992). With losses totaling more than $7 billion in three years, GM was described by auto industry observers as, "Living in a dreamworld for years. . . . Change may be hard, but not changing could be fatal" (*Newsweek*, 1992). GM had ignored warning signals. The competition now included foreign producers, not just Chrysler and Ford. Technological changes integrating computers throughout the manufacturing process gave Japanese manufacturers the edge. GM could not respond to changes in consumer wants and needs as quickly as the marketplace demanded.

Then, when GM realized it had to change, overcoming inertia made the process more difficult. New CEO Jack Smith struggled to overcome an overstaffed, rigid, and slow-moving organization. He trimmed jobs, eliminated some levels of middle management, and invested in technology. Although GM has become profitable, more efficient, and competitive, it still has not restructured itself to be responsive. Much of the bureaucracy still exists. Multiple levels of management and a rigid structure hinder decision making. Jobs are still narrowly defined and specialized.

Customer needs do not always reach the appropriate decision makers. As Smith notes, "The next round of improvements must come from within our own four walls—we have to be responsive to the customer" (Kerwin, 1994). Another company that needed to trim down to be competitive in a changing environment was Lockheed Martin. Sometimes meeting the objective, however, creates consequences for employers, as this chapter's Ethical Management feature illustrates.

Integrating New Elements

As organizations grow, evolve, and respond to changes, they add new positions and new departments to deal with factors in the external environment or with new strategic needs. The objective of organizational design is "seamlessness"—that is, integrating these new elements into the overall fabric of the organization. Accomplishing this objective may mean adding a department to a level in the organization or virtually restructuring the company, as at Coca-Cola. The strategic need to provide quality customer service required the dismantling of functional departments, creating teams, and redelegating authority.

Coordinating the Components

Simply placing a department in a structure is not enough. Managers need to find a way to tie all the departments together to ensure coordination and collaboration across the departments. If this objective is not accomplished, the departments may not work together. Whether through reporting relationships, teams, or task forces, departments must collaborate to avoid conflict and problems and to meet customer needs. Ford Motor Company uses field teams to provide dealer support. By creating the three-person teams, Ford achieved collaboration to solve customer problems. Notes Dick Strauss, a Ford Motor dealer in Richmond, "It removes several

http://www.ford.com

ETHICAL MANAGEMENT
Profits and Layoffs

The nation's largest aerospace and defense company unveiled a mammoth restructuring that shaved 12,000 jobs and shuttered a dozen plants to maintain profitability. Lockheed Martin, a $23 billion giant based in Bethesda, Maryland, projected that the downsizing would eliminate enough fat to save $1.8 billion annually and fashion a leaner company.

Even in an industry plagued by massive cutbacks since the end of the Cold War, Lockheed Martin's downsizing appeared drastic. In total, 26 duplicative field offices and 12 manufacturing plants in Texas, Maryland, California, Arizona, Pennsylvania, New Jersey, and Ottawa, Canada, closed, sending thousands to the ranks of the unemployed. In addition to the nature of the reshaping, the speedy decision caught many people, both inside and outside the company, off guard. The company's board of directors approved the restructuring plan 100 days after the $10 billion merger between Martin Marietta Corporation and Lockheed Corporation.

1. Are layoffs used as a management tool a matter of ethical concern?
2. Does Lockheed Martin's management owe a greater duty to its stockholders than to its employees?
3. What ethical guidelines would you recommend to Lockheed Martin's management to use when determining which operations, offices, and jobs to eliminate?

http://www.lockheedmartin.com

Source: Michael Saul, "Lockheed Martin to Trim 12,000 Jobs, Close Plants," *Dallas Morning News* (27 June 1995), pp. 1D, 15D.

layers of hierarchy we had to go through for official recognition of a customer problem. Now we make decisions on the spot in out-of-warranty situations, and the customer service rep backs us up" (Jacob, 1995).

Encouraging Flexibility

The final objective of organizational designers is flexibility. Designers want to build into the organization—with all its authority, chains of command, and bases of departmentalization—flexibility for decision making, for responding and redirecting energies, and for spotlighting people's talents. This goal differs from the aim of responding to change. One of former CEO Edgar Woolard's goals in restructuring DuPont was to change the image of DuPont from giant sloth to gazelle. With its layers of bureaucracy, DuPont "studied" over decisions; it was the way of life. With an eye on getting "the company to understand that customers pay our bills," Woolard slashed thousands of middle-management posts, sold $2.8 billion in ill-fitting businesses, and cut 37,000 jobs (Weber, 1995).

http://www.dupont.com

RANGE OF ORGANIZATIONAL DESIGN OUTCOMES

Remember that the organizational designer creates a structure to accomplish the company's objectives and mission. The elements that a designer has to work with—chain of command, centralization/decentralization, formal authority, types of departments, and span of control—fit together to form an overall structural approach. Depending on the balance of the elements, the design outcome can be very different. Some organizations see the need to use the formal, vertical hierarchy as a means of control and coordination. Other organizations decentralize decision making, create teams, and provide managers with loosely structured jobs. The range of options can be described as tight (mechanistic) structures or loose (organic) structures.

Mechanistic Organizational Structures

3 Distinguish between mechanistic and organic organizational structures

mechanistic structure *A tight organizational structure characterized by rigidly defined tasks, formalization, many rules and regulations, and centralized decision making.*

A tight, or **mechanistic, structure** is characterized by rigidly defined tasks, formalization, many rules and regulations, and centralized decision making (Figure 9.1 shows the characteristics of a mechanistic structure). In an organization with a mechanistic structure, the vertical structure is very tight, with emphasis on control from top levels down. Tasks are broken down into rigidly defined, routine jobs. Many rules exist, and the hierarchy of authority is the major form of control. Decision making is centralized, and communication is vertical—it follows the chain of command (Burns and Stalker, 1961). The most vivid example of a mechanistic structure is the military. In the private sector, Sears with its tight controls, rigidly defined tasks, and numerous rules and regulations is mechanistic.

Organic Organizational Structures

organic structure *A flexible, free-flowing organizational structure that has few rules and regulations and decentralizes decision making right down to the employees performing the job.*

A flexible, or **organic, structure** is free flowing, has few rules and regulations, and decentralizes decision making right down to the employees performing the job. Often referred to as the horizontal structure, the organic structure is a highly adaptive form that is as loose and workable as the mechanistic organization structure

FIGURE 9.1 *Mechanistic structures versus organic structures*

Vertical Structure Dominant	Horizontal Structure Dominant
• Fixed and Specialized Tasks	• Adaptable and Shared Tasks
• Centralized Decision Making	• Decentralized Decision Making
• Formal Vertical Communication	• Informal Horizontal Communication
• Rigid Hierarchical Relationships	• Vertical and Horizontal Collaboration
• Many Rules	• Few Rules
• Strict Hierarchy of Authority	• Relaxed Hierarchy; Authority by Expertise
Mechanistic Structure	**Organic Structure**

is rigid and stable. Rather than having standardized jobs and regulations, the organic structure allows changes to be made rapidly as the needs require. Organic structures have a division of labor, but the jobs people do are not standardized. Organizations with organic structures frequently redefine tasks to fit employee and environmental needs (Robbins, 1994). They have few rules, and base authority on expertise rather than on the hierarchical position of the person. Decision making is decentralized and communication is horizontal, rather than being vertical up and down the chain of command. They empower employees to make decisions, as is the case, for example, at GE Medical Systems, a manufacturer of X rays. Here CEO Frank Waltz confesses that he cannot evaluate his three immediate subordinates because he sees too little of them. In the X-ray facility only a production manager stands between Waltz and 170 people on the factory floor. The company has few rules, procedures, or policies. The company is flexible and adaptive to changes in customer needs (Jacob, 1995). Figure 9.1 contrasts the characteristics of organic organizations with those of mechanistic structures.

http://www.gemedicalsystems.com

These Army recruits, in their first day of boot camp, will quickly learn about the military's rigid rules and mechanistic structure.

Although the companies we have identified represent mechanistic and organic organizations, it is difficult to categorize an organization as purely mechanistic or organic. In actuality, organizations favor one or the other depending on how designers have integrated contingency factors, the topic of our next section.

CONTINGENCY FACTORS AFFECTING ORGANIZATIONAL DESIGN

Discuss the influence that contingency factors—organizational strategy, environment, size, age, and technology—have on organizational design

The dilemma facing managers charged with the responsibility for organizational design is to determine how mechanistic or organic the structure should be, for either may be successful. Studying the contingency factors that affect organizational design provides the solution: strategy, environment, size of the organization, age of the organization, and technology. The manager designs a structure to fit these contingency factors, as illustrated in Figure 9.2. If the organization structure is incorrect, problems occur (Lammers, 1992).

Strategy

Managers build organizational structures to achieve objectives. Logically then, structure follows strategy; and when strategy changes, structure must change. Coca-Cola serves as an example. At the corporate level, the foundation for strategy is the mission and strategic goals. In Roberto Goizueto's "Strategy for the 1980s" he stated, "I happen not to like the term 'strategic planning,' because it can lead to

FIGURE 9.2 *Contingency factors that affect organizational design*

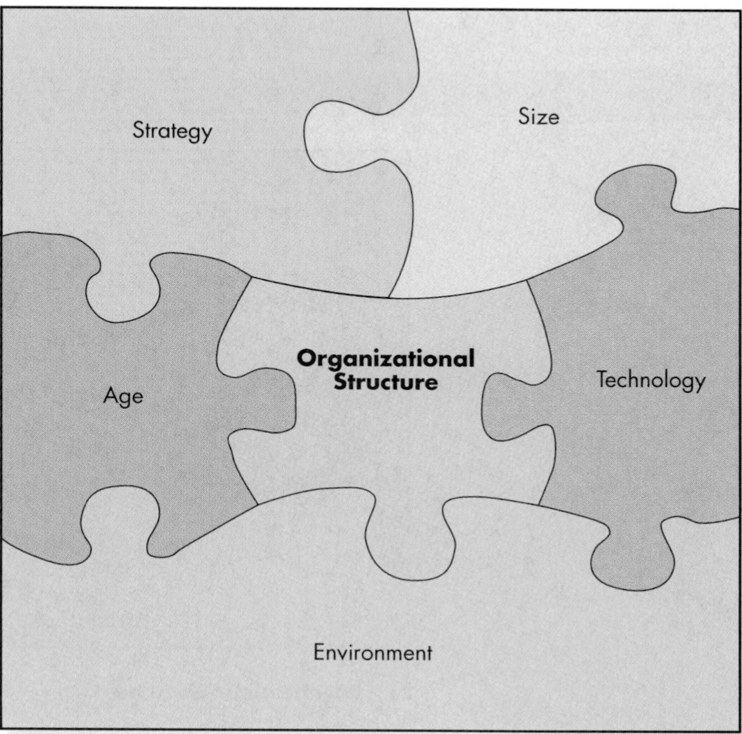

misinterpretations. To my mind, corporate strategy deals with what we want to be as a company, and planning, and specifically long-range planning, deals with how we become what we want to be" (Greising, 1998).

http://www.dell.com

Then to carry out strategic goals, a company develops a business-level strategy. Chapter 6 introduced different business-level strategies that companies can adopt to achieve their goals. For example, if Dell Computers chooses to pursue a prospector strategy, it must innovate, seek new markets, grow, and take risks. An organic structure providing for flexibility and decentralization matches best with this strategy (Simnacher, 1992). In contrast, if a top manager at ExxonMobil adopts a defender strategy—holding on to its current market and protecting its turf—a mechanistic structure providing for tight control, stability, efficiency, and centralization would be the best fit (Miles and Snow, 1978).

http://www.jnj.com

Firms can also select differentiation or cost-leadership strategies (Porter, 1980). With a differentiation strategy, the company attempts to develop new products for the market. Internally, it requires coordination, flexibility, and communication. The proper fit is an organic structure, like the one at Johnson & Johnson. A strategy of cost leadership, in contrast, focuses on internal efficiency. A mechanistic structure is appropriate to achieve these objectives because it provides structured organization and responsibilities. Figure 9.3 provides a comparison of strategy–structure alternatives.

Environment

Chapter 7 showed the impact of environment on decision making—specifically, the difficulty of making decisions in an uncertain or unpredictable environment. As in decision making, the organizational environment provides a major influence

FIGURE 9.3 *Influence of strategy on structure*

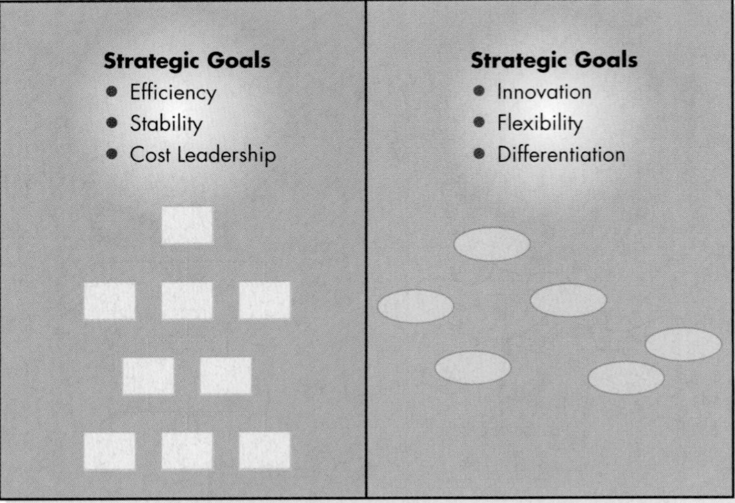

on the design of organizational structure. The stability and predictability of the environment have a direct bearing on the ability of the organization to function effectively. An unstable environment that changes rapidly and is less predictable raises two requirements:

- The organization must be able to adapt to change. It needs to be flexible and responsive.
- The organization needs greater coordination between departments. The individual departments cannot become isolated, creating their own goals and ignoring each other. In fact, departments tend to work more autonomously during periods of instability, which creates barriers.

As seen in Figure 9.4, the organizational structure must fit the environment for the organization to succeed. In a stable and predictable environment, the organization should have a mechanistic structure. Centralized decision making, wide spans of control, and specialization "fit" in such an atmosphere. An uncertain environment calls for an organic structure that emphasizes flexibility, coordination, and less formal procedures (Lawrence and Lorsch, 1969).

General Motors provides a good historical example of the influence of the environment. During the 1950s and 1960s, GM, with its mechanistic structure, succeeded in a stable environment. During that time, competition was limited to Chrysler, Ford, American Motors, and a few foreign imports. GM sold cars regardless of styling, repair record, or fuel economy. Its market share was 50 percent.

FIGURE 9.4 *Relationship between environment and structure*

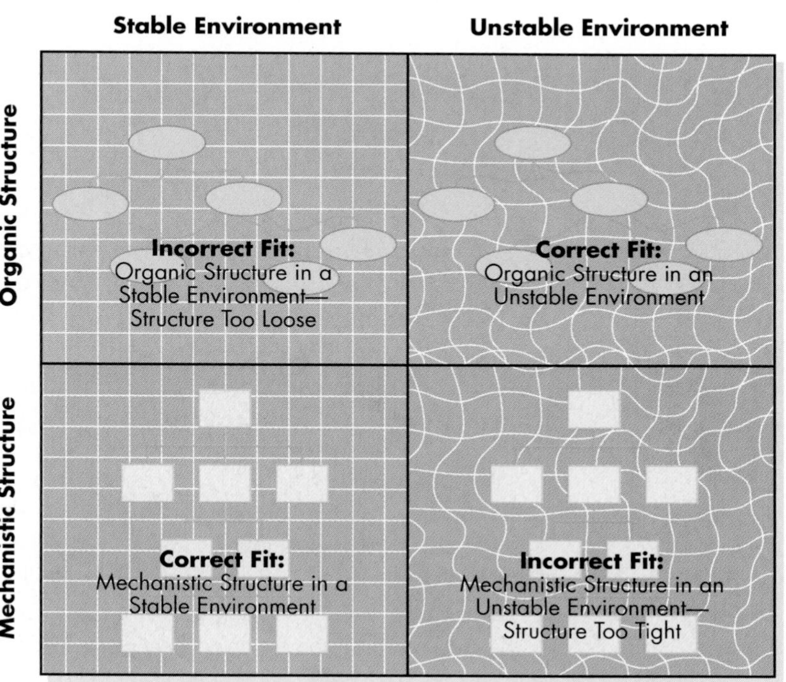

In the 1990s an unstable environment rocked GM. Its U.S. market share fell to 34 percent. Japanese manufacturers and the resurgence of Ford and Chrysler-AMC strengthened competition. Strong competition also came from car manufacturers in Germany, Sweden, and South Korea. As the rumblings from GM attested, the mechanistic structure was no longer functioning (Taylor, 1992). To help turn the fortunes of GM around, President Jack Smith took steps to make GM less mechanistic. Plans focused on slashing 10,000 of its 13,500-employee corporate staff in an attempt "to oust GM's hierarchical and fiefdom clogged bureaucracy" (Kerwin and Treece, 1992). As noted earlier, even though changes have been made, GM has still not regained its position of leadership.

Size of the Organization

http://www.zhenbeauty.com

The size of an organization is normally measured by the number of employees. Research has found that large organizations differ structurally from small ones. Small organizations—for example, De Mar Plumbing, Zhen Cosmetics, and Tony's Café—have little division of labor, few rules and regulations, and informal performance appraisals and budget development procedures. These characteristics describe an organic system. Large organizations, with tens of thousands of employees—for example, ExxonMobil and American Airlines—are mechanistic. They have a greater division of labor, more rules and regulations, and more elaborate internal systems to control performance appraisals, rewards, and creativity (Astley, 1985). These large organizations—including Ford Customer Service Division and DuPont—have, however, begun to recognize the limitations of mechanistic structures and are moving toward more organic structures. In some cases they accomplish change by shifting structures; but more often, by downsizing. Although downsizing normally results in helping the organization in the long run, it does cost employees' jobs. Sometimes both the company and the employees benefit from downsizing and restructuring. Such is the case at Zale Corporation, the subject of this chapter's Valuing Diversity feature.

Age of the Organization

The longer an organization operates, the more formalized it is likely to become. With age come standardized systems, procedures, and regulations. Therefore, older companies take on characteristics of mechanistic structures.

organizational life cycle *The stages an organization goes through: birth, youth, midlife, and maturity. Each stage involves changes in overall structure.*

Organizations, like people, evolve through stages of a life cycle. Within this **organizational life cycle**, businesses follow observable and predictable patterns. Figure 9.5 presents the four stages: birth, youth, midlife, and maturity. Each stage involves changes in the overall structure (Quinn and Cameron, 1983).

Birth Stage

http://www.fritolay.com

In the birth stage, an entrepreneur creates the organization. The informal organization has no professional staff, no rules, and no regulations. Decision making is centralized with the owner, and tasks are not specialized. Frito-Lay was in the birth stage when Elmer Lay, making corn chips in the kitchen from an old family recipe, began to sell to the neighborhood grocery store.

VALUING DIVERSITY
Zales Gets Richer

Although restructuring often means loss of jobs and lost opportunities for employees, it is not always the outcome. For Zale Corporation, the Dallas-based owner and operator of retail jewelry stores, reorganization provided the opportunity to enrich the diversity of its executive officers and line managers. Prior to the reorganization, Zales had no women among the thirteen top management group identified as executive officers.

While realigning its operating store divisions—Zales Jewelry, Gordon Jewelry, and Corrigan's Jewelry—Zales management accomplished another corporate objective, gender diversity. As part of the sweeping management changes, Zales recruited women to head two of its major divisions and promoted another to senior vice president.

With an eye toward broadening the skills and experience base of the executive group, Zales named Macy's East Senior Vice President Beryl Raff president of its 519-store Zales Division. Moving from a post as senior vice president of QVC/Home Shopping Network, Mary Forte became the president of Zale's Gordon Jewelry Division. And, Jo Ann Connelly—with ten years at Zales—was promoted to senior vice president of corporate merchandising. As noted by a Zales spokesperson, "The diverse views and talents we put in place today will help drive us into the twenty-first century."

http://www.zales.com

Source: Diana Kunde, "Minorities and Women: Steps to the Top," *Dallas Morning News* (7 May 1995), pp. 1H–2H.

FIGURE 9.5 *Relationship between organizational life cycle and structural characteristics*

Structural Characteristics	Birth Stage	Youth Stage	Midlife Stage	Maturity Stage
Division of labor	Overlapping tasks	Some departments	Many departments, well-defined tasks, organization chart	Extensive—small jobs, written job descriptions
Centralization	One-person rule	Top leaders rule	Decentralization to department heads	Enforced decentralization (top management overloaded)
Degree of formal control	No written rules	Few rules	Policy and procedures manuals	Extensive—most activities covered by written manuals
Administrative staff	Secretary, no professional staff	Increasing clerical and maintenance, few professional staff members	Increasing size of professional support staff	Large—multiple professional and clerical staff departments
Internal systems (information, budget, planning, performance)	Nonexistent	Crude budget and information system	Control systems in place—budget, performance, operational reports	Extensive—planning, financial, and personnel systems added

Source: Based on Robert E. Quinn and Kim Cameron, "Organizational Life Cycles and Shifting Criteria of Effectiveness: Some Preliminary Evidence," *Management Science* 29 (1983), pp. 33–51.

Youth Stage

In the youth stage, the organization is growing—its product succeeds, and it hires more employees. A division of labor begins to emerge, as do a few formal rules and policies. Decision making is still centralized with the owner, although it is shared with an inner circle. Frito-Lay was in the youth stage when Elmer Lay began a partnership with John Gantry. They combined their resources, opened two plants, and began regional distribution.

Midlife Stage

In the midlife stage, the company has done well and grown quite large. It now has an extensive set of rules, regulations, policies, and systems to guide specialized employees. Control systems are put in place. Professional and clerical staff are hired to undertake specialized support activities. Top management decentralizes many tasks and assigns authority to functional departments; but in the process, it loses flexibility and innovation. Frito-Lay moved into this stage when it was purchased by PepsiCo and became one of its SBUs. PepsiCo, in turn, provided professional management to expand the product line, perk up promotions, and expand national distribution.

http://www.pepsico.com

Maturity Stage

In the maturity stage, the organization is large and mechanistic. The vertical control structure becomes overwhelming. Rules, regulations, specialized staffs, budgets, a refined division of labor, and control systems are in place. The company—as happened with GM and DuPont—faces stagnation. Innovation and aggressiveness can only come with moves to decentralize and increase flexibility through reorganization. When Frito-Lay entered the maturity stage, it had layers of management and specialists and was not responding to competitors. Under CEO Roger Enrico, the company underwent a major downsizing and restructuring, which reshaped its fortunes and competitiveness.

The critical point of these discussions is for managers to shape and adjust the structure to minimize or eliminate the mechanistic outcome of the maturity stage. As we have seen, Coca-Cola reached this stage but was able to restructure to gain flexibility and responsiveness.

Technology

Every organization uses some form of technology to convert its resources into outcomes. **Technology** includes the knowledge, machinery, work procedures, and materials that transform the inputs into outputs (Daft, 1994). The technology required by ExxonMobil to produce oil differs from the technology employed by Zhen to produce cosmetics, but both use some kind of technology. Production technology directly influences organizational structure. The structure must fit the technology, as well as work with an organization's strategy, external environment, age, and size.

technology
The knowledge, machinery, work procedures, and materials that transform the inputs into outputs.

British industrial sociologist Joan Woodward related the three basic types of work flow technology (Woodward, 1965) to elements of structure (small batch, mass production, or continuous process). Firms that produce goods in small quan-

small batch technology or unit production technology
A type of technology that produces goods in small quantities designed to customer specifications.

large batch technology or mass production technology
A type of technology that produces a large volume of standardized products.

continuous-process production
A technology in which the entire conversion process is completed through a series of mechanical or chemical processes.

http://www.coors.com

flexible manufacturing systems (FMS)
The automating and integrating of manufacturing elements such as product design, production equipment, robotics, and performance analysis.

tities to customer specifications use **small batch technology**, or **unit production technology**. Human labor plays a large part in small batch technology. Examples of this technology include making custom clothing or space satellites or doing the work of a small print shop.

When a company produces a large volume of standardized products, it employs **large batch technology** or **mass production technology**. Such technology makes greater use of machines than does small batch production. Some automakers' assembly lines use mass production. In **continuous-process production**, as at an ExxonMobil refinery or Coors brewery, the entire conversion process is completed through a series of mechanical or chemical processes. Employees' primary roles are to fix equipment and oversee the process.

In general, the form of organizational design appropriate for a company depends on its dominant technology. As shown in Figure 9.6, organizations that rely on small batch or unit production should employ an organic structure. A large batch or mass production system works more readily with a mechanistic structure, where centralized decision making and well-defined rules exist. A continuous-process production calls for organic structure because it needs flexibility to oversee the complex technology (Nemetz and Fry, 1988).

Since Woodward conducted her studies, manufacturing technology has changed significantly. Computer systems allow for the automating and integrating of manufacturing elements such as product design, production equipment, robotics, and performance analysis. These systems, known as **flexible manufacturing systems (FMS)** (discussed in detail in Chapter 18), are revolutionizing the traditional perception of mass assembly line operations and small batch production—both can now be done simultaneously in the same facility.

The technology associated with flexible manufacturing places this system in a higher position of complexity than any of the three technologies Woodward studied. Because of this complexity, the approach associated with it focuses on low formal control, high decentralization of decision making, a very narrow span of control, and an organic structure (Womack, Jones, and Roos, 1991).

FIGURE 9.6 *Relationship between production technology and organizational structure*

Elements of Structure	Production Technology		
	Small Batch	**Mass Production**	**Continuous Process**
Complexity of technology	Low	Medium	High
Organizational structure:			
Degree of formal control	Low	High	Low
Centralization	Low	High	Low
Typical span of control	23	48	15
Overall structure	Organic	Mechanistic	Organic

Source: Based on Joan Woodward, *Industrial Oganization: Theory and Practice* (London: Oxford University Press, 1965). Reprinted by permission of Oxford University Press.

STRUCTURAL OPTIONS IN ORGANIZATIONAL DESIGN

Describe the characteristics, advantages, and disadvantages of functional, divisional, matrix, team, and network structural designs

Because no single organizational design suits all circumstances, managers must carefully consider their company's situation—strategy, environment, age, size, and technology—before designing a structure for it. When the contingency factors favor a more mechanistic design, there are options from which to choose. If the need is for an organic design, there are other viable choices.

Before discussing the options, we must make one other point. Some options are more clearly mechanistic or organic in practice, but the majority of them are not purely one way or the other. Figure 9.7 arranges the five options—functional, divisional, matrix, team, and network—on a continuum from mechanistic to organic. As you can see, most fall in the middle rather than reflecting either extreme.

Functional Structure

functional structure
An organizational design that groups positions into departments based on similar skills, expertise, and resources.

http://www.usx.com

The **functional structure** groups positions into departments based on similar skills, expertise, and resources. Functional structure is an expanded version of functional departmentalization, introduced in Chapter 8. In an organization with functional structure, activities are grouped under headings common to nearly every business—headings such as finance, production, marketing, and human resources. The entire organization is then divided into areas such as the one shown in Figure 9.8. American Airlines, PPG, and USX use this type of structure (Mitchell and Files, 1992).

Advantages of the Functional Structure

Putting specialties together results in economies of scale and minimizes duplication of personnel and equipment. Employees tend to feel comfortable in a functional structure because it gives them the opportunity to talk the same language with their peers. Because the structure acknowledges occupational specialization, it also simplifies training.

Organizationally, the functional structure offers a way to centralize decision making and provide unified direction from the top. Within each department, communication and coordination are excellent. Finally, the functional structure increases the quality of technical problem solving because it gives workers quick access to those with technical expertise.

FIGURE 9.7 *Structural options on the mechanistic–organic continuum*

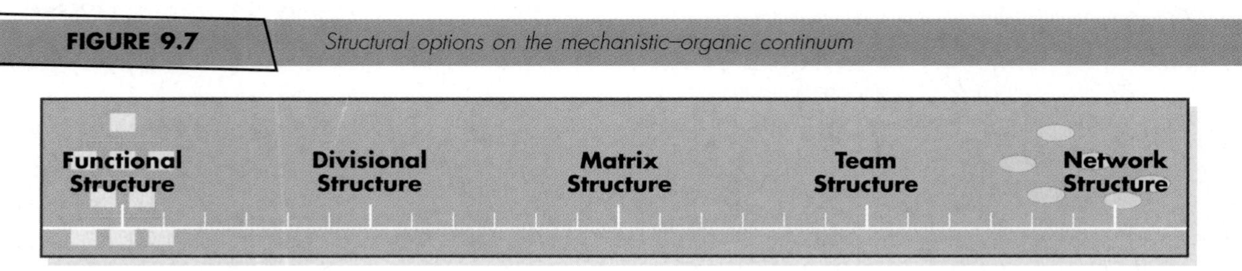

FIGURE 9.8 Functional organizational structure

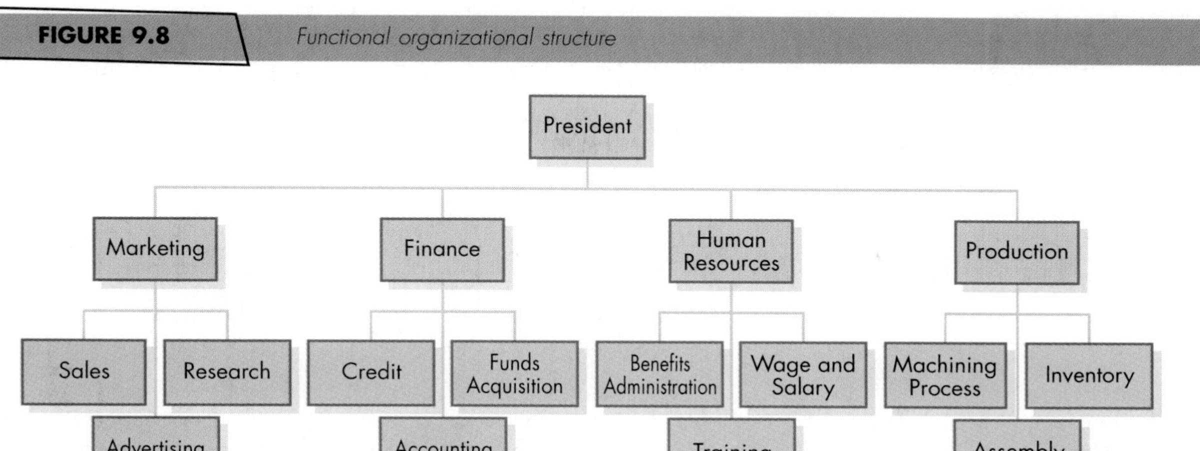

Disadvantages of the Functional Structure

The functional structure also has inherent disadvantages. Because functions are separate from one another, employees may have little understanding of and concern for the specialty areas outside their own functional area. This narrowness can lead to barriers in communication, cooperation, and coordination. Departments may develop their own focus rather than a company focus. Also, because a functional structure has rigid and separate chains of command, response time to changes in the environment may be slow.

Managers in a functional structure also become focused on their functional area, both long and short range. Problems are seen from one perspective and individuals become isolated. In addition, this narrowness carries over to long-range development. The specialization does not give managers a broad perspective on the company or other functional areas. This lack of a broad general perspective minimizes the training for future chief executives.

At DuPont, introduced earlier in the discussion of design objectives, these disadvantages had pyramided to such a point that the company faced a crisis of competitiveness. Former CEO Edgar Woolard realized that the functional specialties, with their layers of middle managers, had created a bureaucracy. As Woolard noted, "We had to face reality. Our costs were too high and we had become too slow to respond. I had to get people in the company to understand that customers pay our bills" (Weber, 1995). With that said, Woolard then redesigned the company, using a divisional structure.

Divisional Structure

divisional structure
An organizational design that groups departments based on organizational outputs; these divisions are self-contained strategic business units that produce a single product.

An alternative to the functional structure is the **divisional structure**, which groups departments based on organizational outputs. As shown in Figure 9.9, divisions are self-contained strategic business units that produce a single product. As we noted in Chapter 6, each SBU or division is responsible for the management of a given product or product family. Within each division, diverse departments—for example, production and marketing—are brought together to accomplish the division's objective.

FIGURE 9.9 *Divisional organizational structure*

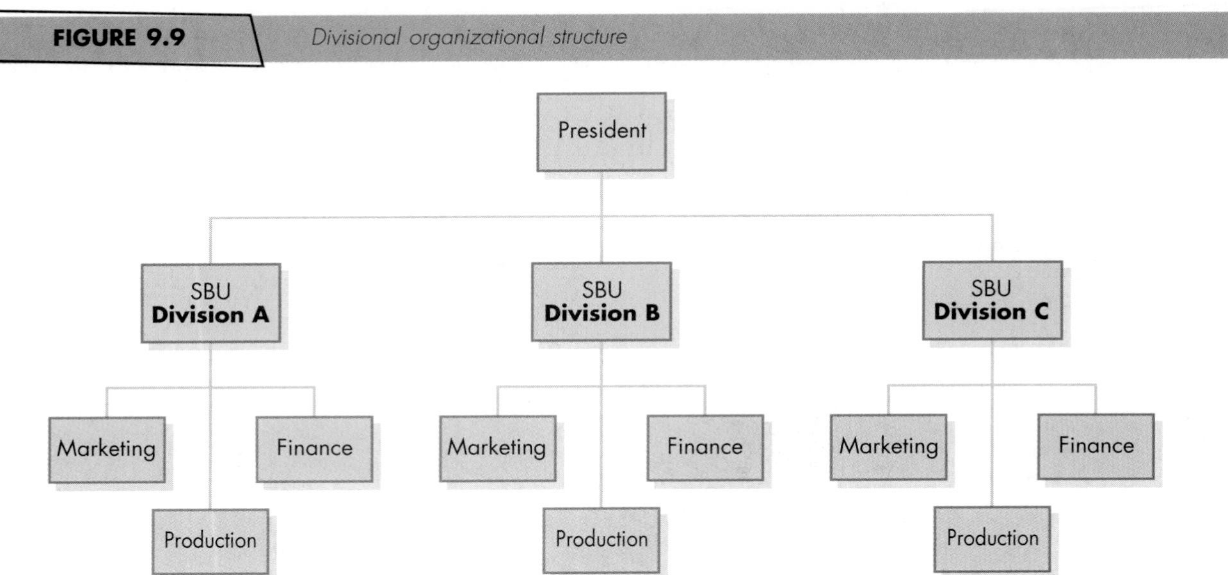

http://www.tropicana.com

The divisional structure creates a set of autonomous minicompanies. In a large company such as PepsiCo, each division has its own market, competitors, and technologies. At PepsiCo the divisions include Frito-Lay, Pepsi-Cola, and Tropicana. In addition to organizing by product, a company can organize divisions by customer or geography. A customer divisional structure is called for when customers are distinct enough in their demands, preferences, and needs to justify it. For large customers—say, state and federal governments—as well as for commercial accounts with a certain line of products, the company can group all the skills necessary and establish divisions to serve those customers full time. The structure provides a company focus for the employees. Chapter 8's discussion on Johnson & Johnson

PepsiCo uses a divisional structure for its Frito-Lay, Pepsi-Cola, and Tropicana divisions, since each division has its own market, competitors, and technologies.

provides an example of customer divisions. To better serve the distinct customer groups, three divisions were established at Johnson & Johnson. One focuses on final consumers, a second on professionals, and the third on pharmaceutical buyers (O'Reilly, 1994).

Managers create geographic divisions when a company needs to group functional skills for a specific region—international, national, or regional. This structure tries to capitalize on situations in which the geography dictates differences in such factors as laws, currencies, languages, and taxation. Department stores such as J. C. Penney and Sears have created regional divisions. On an international scale, McDonald's has structured geographically based on continent—European, North American, and Asian divisions.

http://www.jcpenney.com

http://www.mcdonalds.com

Advantages of the Divisional Structure

The divisional structure focuses the attention of employees and managers on results for the product, the customer, or the geographical area. Divisional structure is flexible and responsive to change, because each unit focuses on its own environment. Coordination among different functions within the division benefits from singleness of purpose. Because each division is a self-contained unit, responsibility and accountability for performance are easier to target. When Edgar Woolard split DuPont into 21 SBUs, he reaped all these benefits. Each SBU operates as a free-standing unit, and managers report directly to the CEO or to a handful of top aides. DuPont eliminated the complex hierarchy in which a half dozen middle managers stood between the CEO and the operating business heads and another six between them and their operating employees. The SBUs are focused and coordinated (Weber, 1995).

Finally, the divisional structure is also an excellent vehicle for developing senior executives, a factor identified as one of the strengths of Johnson & Johnson's organizational structure (O'Reilly, 1994). Division managers gain a broad range of experience in running their autonomous units, which are, in essence, companies. An organization that has a large number of divisions is developing a number of generalists for the company's top positions.

Disadvantages of the Divisional Structure

The major disadvantage of divisional structure is duplication of activities and resources. Instead of a single marketing or research department, each division maintains its own. The structure loses efficiency and economies of scale; and a lack of technical specialization, expertise, and training can result. Interdivisional coordination may suffer, and employees in different divisions may feel they are competing with one another—a mixed blessing.

Historically, General Motors has operated with a divisional product structure, and its inherent limitations. For each automobile division—Buick, Chevrolet—a separate marketing, manufacturing, and research area exists. The duplicate activities lose overall corporate efficiency. Divisions compete with each other with almost identical car designs. Intercompany teamwork is almost nonexistent. Although GM has "slashed its blue collar ranks by 20 percent," the company's productivity still does not match Ford's and DaimlerChrysler's. In addition, because of coordination problems between engineering and manufacturing, product development time still takes four years. DaimlerChrysler and Japanese carmakers spend only three years (Kerwin, 1994).

Matrix Structure

matrix structure
An organizational design that utilizes functional and divisional chains of command simultaneously in the same part of the organization.

The **matrix structure** combines the advantages of functional specialization with the focus and accountability of the divisional structure. A matrix utilizes functional and divisional chains of command simultaneously in the same part of the organization (Burns, 1989). To achieve this combination, the matrix structure employs dual lines of authority. As Figure 9.10 shows, the functional hierarchy of authority runs vertically from the functional departments—production, materials purchasing, human resources, and so on—and project authority runs laterally from group to group. This combination of function and project authority creates a grid, or matrix. As a result each employee has two bosses, with a dual chain of command based on both the department and individual projects (Koloday, 1981).

FIGURE 9.10 *Matrix organizational structure*

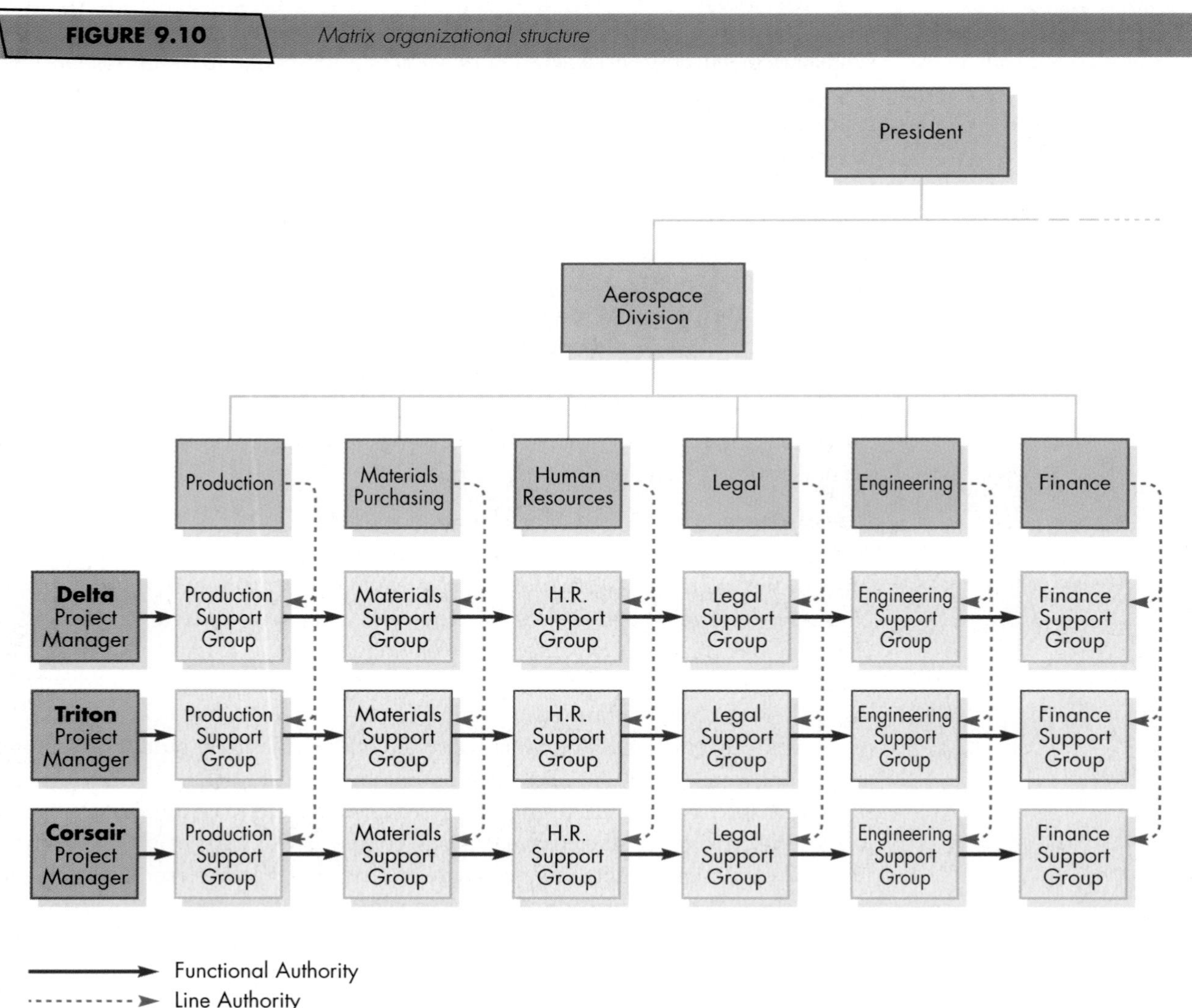

A matrix structure can be created when any division established for a specific product, program, or project is combined with a functional structure. In general, a matrix design will most likely be used in one of two situations (Van Fleet, 1991). First, it is used when a firm offers a diverse set of products, has a complex environment, and requires functional expertise. With a matrix, the company can bring important functional skills to bear on each product while simultaneously responding to the changing environment.

Second, the matrix organization is used when managers want to maximize economies of scale and shared resources. Resource duplication is minimized by having employees work for more than one division or by transferring employees among divisions as requirements change. The manager in charge of the engineering department shown in Figure 9.10 can assign engineers as the needs of each project demand.

Advantages of the Matrix Structure

http://www.monsanto.com

http://www.dow.com

http://www.abb.com

Monsanto, Dow Chemical, and Asea-Brown Boveri (ABB) have used the matrix structure successfully. It has proven to be flexible; teams can be created, changed, and dissolved without a major problem. Communication and coordination are increased. Lars Ramquist, the subject of this chapter's Global Applications feature, was so impressed with the advantages of the matrix structure that his first move as CEO of Sweden's L. M. Ericsson Corporation was to solve organizational problems by installing a matrix structure.

The matrix structure increases the motivation of individual employees. The achievement of goals can bring a sense of commitment and satisfaction. The structure also provides training in functional and general management skills. People within functional departments receive technical training, and team coordination provides the opportunity to develop a general perspective.

GLOBAL APPLICATIONS
A Quick End to Confusion

Lars Ramquist's first move as CEO was to figure out how to get L. M. Ericsson's business units to work as a team. The Swedish maker of optical lenses had a real problem. "We behaved like seven different companies, each calling on the same accounts. Our customers were confused."

Ramquist decided on a radical overhaul that would bind together a sprawling, research-intensive empire and bring better customer service. First, he centralized decision making for sales of all products in each country unit. Then he introduced a matrix system with the unit managers reporting to both product divisions and corporate headquarters.

While top managers have to put more time into consensus building, the matrix has been very effective for sharing information among the 40 research and development labs around the globe and for getting products to market fast. For example, when it was moving into advanced laser technology, Ericsson designed the units and set up the manufacturing and service networks simultaneously. That put the company way ahead of its competitors.

http://www.ericsson.com

Source: Julia Flynn, "An Ever-Quicker Trip from R & D to Customer," *Business Week* (10 January 1995), p. 88.

Disadvantages of the Matrix Structure

The most obvious disadvantage is the potential conflict, confusion, and frustration created by the dual chain of command. Employees have two bosses—the functional manager and the project manager. Also, the matrix often pits divisional objectives against functional objectives, creating conflict. Another disadvantage directly relates to the previous one: the productive time lost to meetings and discussions to resolve this conflict. The structure places a premium on interpersonal skills and human relations training—conflict management, working with two bosses, and open communication. Finally, the matrix structure may create a problem with a balance of power between the functional and divisional sides of the matrix. If one side has more power, the advantages of the matrix—coordination and cooperation—will be lost. These problems persuaded Mercedes-Benz CEO Helmut Werner to abandon the matrix structure in favor of a team structure (Templeman and Woodruff, 1994).

http://www.mercedes-benz.com

Team Structure

team structure
An organizational design that places separate functions or processes into a group according to one overall objective.

The newest and most potentially powerful approach to organizational structure has been the attempt by organizations to implement a team structure. The **team structure**—organizing separate functions or processes into a group based on one overall objective—takes direct aim at the traditional organization hierarchy, whether functional, divisional, or matrix, and flattens it. Although the vertical chain of command is a powerful control device, it requires passing decisions up the hierarchy and takes too long. Such an approach also keeps responsibility at the top. Companies adopting the team structure are pushing authority down to lower levels through empowerment and holding the team accountable.

Rather than departments being structured by functional specialty, team departments are created. Team members representing different functions or processes are grouped together: a number of such teams report to the same supervisor. Although variations of the team concept occur—some teams are responsible for a product, others, such as Ford Customer Service Division, for a process—the result is the same. The traditional functions are reorganized, layers of management are removed, and the company becomes decentralized. Figure 9.11 illustrates the reorganization of a vertical functional structure to a horizontal team product structure.

http://www.pg.com

http://www.ge.com

Although Procter & Gamble and Ford Customer Service Division provide good examples, the team structure at General Electric's factory at Bayamon, Puerto Rico, is an even better example. The facility employs a factory manager, 172 hourly workers, and just 15 salaried supervisors who act as advisers. (A conventional plant would have twice as many salaried supervisors.) That translates to three layers of organization. Each hourly worker is on a ten-person team. The team is responsible—"owns" in team terms—part of the factory's overall work—assembly, shipping and receiving, and so on. Team members come from all areas of the plant; thus each group has representation from operations in the process. A supervisor-adviser sits in the back of the room and speaks up only if the team needs help (Stewart, 1992). Teams will be discussed in detail in Chapter 15.

FIGURE 9.11 Development of a team structure

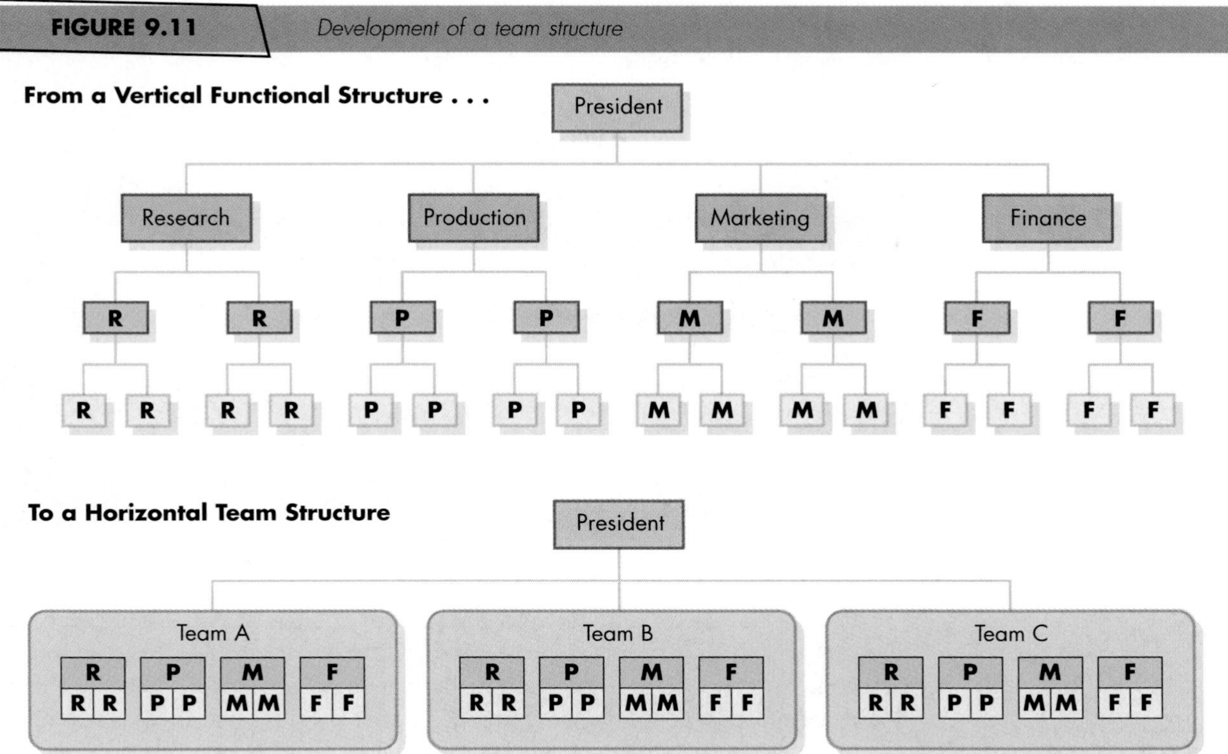

Advantages of the Team Structure

The team concept breaks down barriers across departments because people who know one another are more likely to compromise than would strangers. The team structure also speeds up decision making and response time. Decisions no longer need to go to the top of a hierarchy for approval. Employees are strongly motivated. They take responsibility for a project rather than for a narrowly defined task, and the result is enthusiasm and commitment. Decentralization of authority is accompanied by the elimination of levels of managers, which results in lower administrative costs. Finally, team structure is an improvement over the matrix structure in that it does not involve the problem of double reporting. Each worker believes he or she is part of a team rather than an individual who performs a designated function.

Disadvantages of the Team Structure

The team structure depends on employees who learn and train for success. If the company won't provide training, performance suffers. Also, a large amount of time may be required for team meetings, thus increasing coordination time.

network structure
An organizational design option in which a small central organization relies on other organizations to perform manufacturing, marketing, engineering, or other critical functions on a contract basis.

Network Structure

The final approach to structure is known as the "dynamic network" organization. In the **network structure** a small central organization relies on other organizations

The team structure can speed up decision making and motivate employees, but the amount of time needed for meetings can increase coordination time.

http://www.nike.com

http://www.esprit.com

to perform manufacturing, marketing, engineering, or other critical functions on a contract basis (Miles, 1989). In other words, rather than these functions being performed under one roof, they are really free-standing services. Nike and Esprit Apparel, both of whom have booming businesses even though they own no manufacturing facilities and employ only a few hundred people, use the network structure concept (see Figure 9.12). Rather than create the functions internally,

FIGURE 9.12 *Network organizational structure*

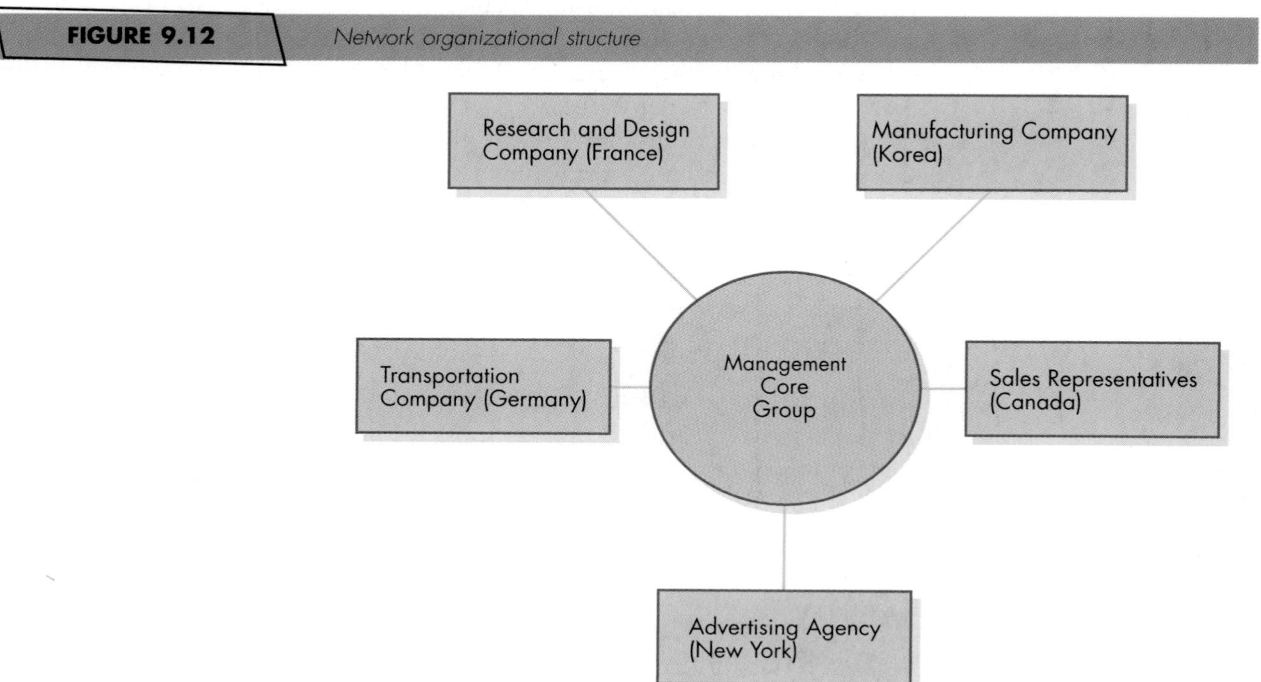

they connect independent designers, manufacturers, and sales representatives to perform needed functions on a contract basis (Rammrath, 1992).

Rickard Associates has also capitalized on the network structure. At the Hopewell, New Jersey–based producer of magazines and marketing materials, only two people show up for work each day—the owner Wendy Rickard and her assistant. The company contracts with an art director in Arizona; editors in Florida, Georgia, and Michigan; and production houses "all over" the country (Verity, 1994).

Advantages of the Network Structure

The network structure provides flexibility because a company purchases only the specific services needed. Administrative overhead remains low because large teams of staff specialists and other administrative personnel are not needed. Email, the subject of this chapter's Managing Technology feature, is a common method used by a network to communicate.

Disadvantages of the Network Structure

The major shortcoming of this type of structure is lack of control. The management core must rely on contractors. This limitation can be minimized if management is willing and able to work closely with the suppliers. The reliability of supply, however, is less predictable than it would be if the company owned the means of supply. If a supplier fails to deliver, goes out of business, or suffers a plant breakdown, the central hub of the network is endangered. Also, if an organization relies on contract work, central managers may lack technical expertise to resolve problems effectively.

MANAGING TECHNOLOGY
Email

Electronic mail (email) enables a computer user to send a message automatically to another computer user anywhere in the world. Email is the most popular activity on the Internet. It allows people to send messages and files around the world in seconds. Hundreds of millions of people are interacting at the speed of light! In addition to one-on-one communication, other Internet resources can be tapped through email. These resources include receiving electronic publications; searching for and retrieving files; and participating in discussion groups.

Some organizations have email systems that are not part of the Internet. Most computer networks, even if not directly connected to the Internet, can send and receive Internet email through a "gateway" or a computer that passes information between networks. This means you don't have to have a direct Internet connection to use Internet email, but you must have a computerized mailbox that can be reached by other computers on the Internet.

To use email, you need an electronic mailbox from where your mail can be sent. Also, you must know the exact electronic mailing address of the person to whom you are sending the message. If you aren't exact, your email will "bounce" back to you with a "User Unknown" error.

CHAPTER SUMMARY

1 **Explain the meaning of organizational design.** Organizational design is the creation of or change to an organization's structure. It involves developing the overall layout of the positions and departments as well as establishing the interrelationships among the positions and departments.

2 **Describe the four objectives of organizational design.** The managers responsible for organizational design have four objectives in creating organizational structures. They design structure to

1. *Respond to change.* To stay competitive the company must respond to changes in the environment as well as to changes that emerge from its evolutionary development.
2. *Integrate new elements.* As organizations grow, evolve, and respond, new positions and new departments must be integrated into the fabric of the organization.
3. *Coordinate the components.* Managers need to find a way to tie all departments together to ensure coordination and collaboration across the departments.
4. *Encourage flexibility.* Designers need to institutionalize the ability to respond to change.

3 **Distinguish between mechanistic and organic organizational structures.** Depending on how organizational concepts are balanced, the design produced can be a tight, or mechanistic, structure, or a flexible, or organic, structure. A mechanistic structure is characterized by rigidly defined tasks, formalization, many rules and regulations, and centralized decision making. An organic structure is free flowing, has few rules and regulations, and decentralizes decision making right down to the employees performing the job.

4 **Discuss the influences that contingency factors—organizational strategy, environment, size, age, and technology—have on organizational design.** Whether an organization will be mechanistic or organic is influenced by the meshing of five factors.

1. *Organization strategy.* The mission, corporate-level strategy, and business-level strategy influence design. Structure is a tool to accomplish strategy.
2. *Organization environment.* Whether a company operates in a stable or in a dynamically changing environment influences structure. A mechanistic structure functions well in a stable environment; an organic structure functions better in a changing environment.
3. *Organization size.* Large companies tend to have mechanistic structures. Small companies have organic structures.
4. *Organization age.* Older, mature companies tend to have mechanistic structures. New or young organizations tend to have organic structures.
5. *Organization technology.* Every organization uses some form of technology to convert resources to outputs. The type of technology—small batch, mass production, or continuous process—influences the type of structure. Small batch and continuous process favor organic structures. Mass production technology favors a mechanistic structure.

5 **Describe the characteristics, advantages, and disadvantages of functional, divisional, matrix, team, and network structural designs.** The organizational design alternatives include a functional structure, divisional structure, matrix structure, team structure, and network structure.

- The functional structure groups positions into departments based on similar skills, expertise, and resources used. The functional structure has the advantages of economies of scale, minimizes duplication of personnel and equipment, makes employees comfortable, and simplifies training. Disadvantages include the lack of understanding and concern for other specialty areas, communication barriers, lack of cooperation and coordination, and slow response time to changes in the environment.
- The divisional structure groups departments based on organizational outputs. Divisions become self-contained strategic business units (SBUs). The divisional structure focuses the attention of the employees and managers on the results for the product, customer, or geographical area. It is flexible and responsive to change, performance is easier to target, and it aids in developing senior executives. Disadvantages include duplication of activities and resources; lack of technical specialization, expertise, and training; lack of coordination across positions; and competition among divisions.
- The matrix structure combines the advantages of functional specialization with the focus and accountability of the divisional structure. It utilizes the functional and divisional chains of command simultaneously in the same part of the organization. To achieve this, the matrix structure uses dual lines of authority. The matrix organization is flexible, communication and coordination are increased, motivation is increased for the individual employee, and technical training is provided for both functional and general management skills. Disadvantages include potential conflict, confusion, and frustration created by the dual chain of command, the danger of creating conflict by pitting divisional objectives against functional objectives, time lost in meetings to resolve conflicts, and the problem of balance of power between the functional and divisional sides of the matrix.
- The team structure organizes separate functions or processes into a group based on one overall objective. The team concept breaks down barriers across departments; speeds up decision making and response time; motivates employees by developing employee responsibility; eliminates levels of managers, resulting in lower administrative costs; and eliminates the double reporting problem associated with the

matrix structure. Disadvantages include the dependence on employee learning and training for the system to succeed and the large amount of time required for meetings.

- The network organization structure features a small central organization that relies on other organizations to perform critical functions on a contract basis. The network structure provides flexibility and reduces administrative overhead. Disadvantages include the lack of control, the unpredictability of supply, and the lack of internal managerial technical expertise to effectively resolve technical problems.

REVIEW QUESTIONS

1. When managers are engaged in organizational design, what are they developing?
2. Identify and discuss the four objectives of organizational design.
3. What are the characteristics of a mechanistic organization? What are the characteristics of an organic organization?
4. Name factors that influence organizational design. How does an organization's strategy influence organizational design? What types of structure are appropriate for the three types of technology? What two needs in organizational design result from a volatile environment?
5. What are the characteristics of a functional organization structure? What are the advantages of a divisional structure? What are the characteristics of a matrix organizational structure? What are the characteristics of teams? What are the advantages and disadvantages of networks?

DISCUSSION QUESTIONS FOR CRITICAL THINKING

1. In which structural design options—functional, divisional, or matrix—would you prefer to work? Least prefer? Explain your answers.
2. What examples can you provide to demonstrate the application of the team structure? Was the team organized by process or by function?
3. The discussion on contingency factors affecting organizational design states that organizational structure follows strategy. Other observers suggest that strategy should fit the organization's structure. With which position do you agree? Why?
4. Based on the experience of AC International in this chapter's Application Case on page 290, would you use this type of organizational structure? Why or why not?

INTERNET EXERCISES

Check the text Web site at http://plunkett.swcollege.com for updated links to the Internet Exercises.

1. Team structure breaks down barriers across departments, speeds up decision making and response time, motivates employees, and lowers administrative costs by eliminating levels of managers. Understanding different personality types is important to understanding team dynamics and interactions. Read the background on the Keirsey Temperament Sorter at the Web site below, then take and score the test. What is your personality profile? Describe how you might make use of what you have learned from your personality test to work better with a team. Describe ways in which you might be able to use information about the personality test results of others on your team.
http://www.advisorteam.com/user/kts.asp
2. Organizational structure refers to who reports to whom in an organization and is depicted in the organization chart. Use a search engine to find an organization chart. How does the structure of the organization you chose meet the four objectives of organizational design? Explain thoroughly.
http://www.altavista.com
http://www.google.com
3. Read "21st Century Organizational Trends" by Stephen P. Borgatti at the Web site below. Briefly discuss the key trends affecting organizational structures today.
http://www.analytictech.com/mb021/trendsin.htm

APPLICATION CASE

A Great Idea

AC International's organizational structure was the brainchild of its cofounders, Randy Kirk and Terry Brown. The company was created to manufacture and distribute a patented product called Mr. Tuffy, a bicycle-tire liner that stops puncture flats. AC International would be different. Kirk and Brown would supply the finances and brains; manufacturing would be contracted to a job shop; a distribution company specializing in bike accessories would handle packaging and distribution; and a manufacturer's rep company would handle sales and billing. The idea was born.

AC International grew by adding other products from domestic or foreign manufacturers. It controlled packaging, marketing, advertising, and product development, all through contract companies. What seemed like perfection, however, began to cause problems. Customers were constantly on the phone complaining about late shipments and back orders. In turn, AC International was constantly screaming at suppliers for not keeping promises. Then began a series of events that reshaped AC International.

- Just as AC was introducing a new bicycle helmet, the contractor's factory was hit by a major fire. It was out of production for six weeks. Then, within three weeks of resuming operations, the factory was completely destroyed by a second fire.
- Soon after, AC's most important job shop—responsible for manufacturing, packaging, and shipping Mr. Tuffy—went bankrupt. AC quickly devised a plan to have the owner of the shop become a contract laborer. The owner would supply the equipment and oversee the operations. AC would supply the labor and facilities. Almost immediately, shipping improved, and costs went down by more than 25 percent.
- Later, AC purchased a patent for a bicycle tire-changing tool from the company that had been making it. The cost dropped by more than 75 percent when AC began making it.
- Finally, the contractor in charge of blow molding, cap molding, as well as silk-screening of advertising on the outside of bicycle water bottles, could not meet production schedules. Within three months of starting production, AC decided to buy its own blow-molding equipment. Within 60 days from the decision, production was on schedule and costs were halved. Molding the bottle caps saved 80 percent on the process. The decision to bring printing—photo labs and silk screening equipment—inside the company saved 80 percent in film costs and 90 percent in silk screening.

AC was now in control of quality, delivery, and cost—with all operations occurring inside the company.

http://www.mrtuffy.com

Questions

1. When AC International began operations, what kind of organizational structure did it choose? Explain your answer.
2. Draw AC International's initial organization chart.
3. Draw AC International's final organization chart.
4. If you were a consultant, what advice would you have given Kirk and Brown on how to make their original organization successful?

Source: Randy W. Kirk, "It's About Control," *Inc.* (August 1994), pp. 25–26.

VIDEO CASE

Bindco, Inc.: Capacity Planning

Bindco, Inc., is a leading manufacturer and distributor of computer software and related products for firms such as Sun Microsystems and McCaffee. Bindco has evolved from a simple three-ring binding company (hence the name Bindco) to a firm engaged in providing virtually all the production and distribution services required of its software clients.

The company basically offers "turnkey manufacturing" to its clients by providing services such as printing instructional manuals; manufacturing floppy disks and compact disks; storing materials; designing, producing, and assembling kit boxes; handling all returned software; and operating an information system to facilitate all these activities. Bindco began providing production and distribution services after monitoring its external environment and anticipating the future needs of its clients. Management actively continues to monitor and anticipate trends in the software industry to gauge their impact on the company's capacity planning and decision-making process.

Bindco's emphasis on capacity planning is reflected in its continual forecasting of trends. The company utilizes a variety of forecasting methods, the basis for which is an aggressive information gathering process. It listens to the ideas, suggestions, and complaints of the ultimate consumers of its products. It surveys software resellers to get their opinions regarding the future of the market. And, it actively seeks the opinions of industry experts about the future of the computer software industry and monitors its competitors' activities. This approach has uncovered a number of trends regarding software demand (e.g., less use of diskettes and more use of CDs and emergence of the Internet). All have some impact on the company's capacity planning and decision making, and some even pose potential threats to the existence of Bindco and other software providers if they fail to adapt.

In response to the industry's risky and uncertain environment, Bindco's management faced three options. First, it could take the lead and anticipate demand for software development, marketing, and distribution and lead the competition. Second, it could closely follow demand for software products rather than lead, mimicking the actions of its competitors. Third, it could lag far behind demand by waiting for the next generation of software to be developed and new marketing and distribution methods to be put in place before acting.

The company's management chose to follow closely the demand for software development, marketing, and distribution, rather than to lead it or lag far behind it. Management concedes that there is a "fine line" between keeping abreast of the latest technologies and innovations and having the ability to implement these changes quickly enough to capture a reasonable market share. The risks involve being either too late in responding to the changes in the industry or too early in committing to a technology that the industry and its customers won't embrace.

By adopting a strategy of closely monitoring its external environment, Bindco will constantly face many new problems and opportunities that will significantly affect its organizational design, capacity planning, and operating decisions in the future.

http://www.bindco.com

For Discussion:

1. Describe the main trends facing Bindco and the software industry. Then describe the impact they may have on the firm.
2. Would an organic or a mechanistic organizational structure favor Bindco in its current environment? Explain.
3. Explain Bindco management's decision to follow demand closely in its industry.

Organizational Culture and Change

KEY TERMS

change
change agent
evolutionary change
force field analysis
management by reaction
mutual trust
organizational development (OD)
organizational learning
planned change
revolutionary change
subculture
three-step approach

LEARNING OBJECTIVES

After studying this chapter, you should be able to

1. Define organizational culture and the factors that influence it
2. List and describe the ways that culture is manifested
3. Explain the role of managers and employees in creating culture
4. Explain what factors make a culture effective
5. Define change and identify the kinds of change that can occur in an organization
6. Distinguish between evolutionary change and revolutionary change
7. Distinguish between planned and unplanned change
8. Explain the steps managers can follow to implement planned change
9. Identify the organizational qualities that promote change
10. Explain why people resist change and what managers can do to overcome that resistance
11. Explain why change efforts fail
12. Explain the purpose of an organizational development program

MANAGEMENT IN ACTION

Corning's Cultural Transformation

Chief executive officer John Loose says that when he looks at Corning today, he thinks of Alice in Wonderland, when the caterpillar said to Alice, "Who are you?" She said, "I know who I was when I got up this morning, but I must have been changed several times since then" (http://www.corning.com/inside_corning).

Corning has a history of innovation, even though many people associate it only with Corningware and Pyrex. "Corning produced the glass that enabled Thomas Edison to realize his invention of the light bulb, as well as the equipment for its mass production. It invented optical fiber 30 years ago and previously helped develop the all-glass television tube" (*Financial Times*, 2000). In 1998, it sold its consumer businesses. Today Corning's products—such as optical fiber, photonics, and network components—are marketed to the telecommunications industry. Thus, the company's focus has shifted from housewares to high-technology products and services. Corning has rebuilt itself around its strengths to meet opportunities in the marketplace.

The cultural changes are harder to spot, but easy to feel. For nearly 149 of its 150 years, Corning was the epitome of a technology-driven company. Its credo was this: Make what you can and stick with it for as long as it takes to turn a profit. And, the corollary: If Corning did not discover it, Corning would not sell it—or even buy another company that had made the breakthrough first. Other technology-driven companies—Hewlett-Packard and I.B.M. were once classic examples—abandoned that model years ago. They recognized that investors and customers prefer companies that use the market-driven approach: identify a customer need, then design a product or service to fill it. Corning was one of the last holdouts (Deutsch, 2001).

"We used to be like a casino—invent something and then roll the dice," said Roger G. Ackerman, Corning's affable chairman. "But now we realize that, if you don't understand market dynamics, you'll crash" (Deutsch, 2001). Hence, before Corning turns an idea into a product, it makes sure that its target market demands it. Furthermore, Corning seeks partners to help it get its products to market as quickly as possible. "We're still geeks, nerds, wonks, researchers at heart, but there's just too much to do for anyone to do it all," said Gerald J. Fine, Corning's vice president for photonics technologies—Corning's term for the many devices that blast signals down the fiber optic pipelines (Deutsch, 2001). In order to respond more quickly to changing customer needs with technology that already has been developed, Corning might acquire a company to increase manufacturing capacity, make a long-term technology investment, or fill some other business need.

Mr. Ackerman says the new Corning is as close to invulnerable as it can get. "Everything we've done is in the business books," he said. "But the thing is, this time, we've learned to execute, execute, execute." At last (Deutsch, 2001). ■

Sources: Claudia H. Deutsch, "At Corning, Ideas Now Match Markets," *The New York Times* (7 January 2001); Charles Fishman, "Creative Tension," *Fast Company* (November 2000), http://www.fastcompany.com/online/40/corning.html; "Veteran US Manufacturer Is Still A Nimble Operator," *Financial Times* (November 2000), FT.com, http://specials.ft.com/telecoms/nov00/FT3N2YOXGFC.html.

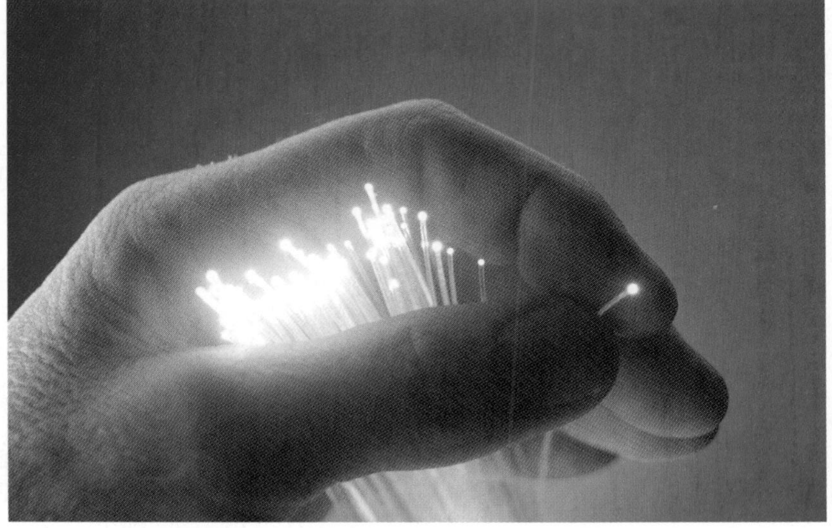

Corning has shifted its business from its familiar housewares products to high-technology products and services, such as optical fiber, photonics, and network components.

INTRODUCTION

3M, Boeing, Johnson & Johnson, Nordstrom, Motorola, Walt Disney, and Wal-Mart have already accomplished what James Collins, consultant and coauthor of *Built To Last*, described as a visionary company—one with core values, a drive to stimulate progress, and a cultlike culture (Collins and Porras, 1994).

This chapter will focus on two of those key ingredients—culture and change. Initially the chapter explores the nature of organizational culture, manifestations of culture, and how culture is created. Then the chapter discussion turns to the nature of change—sources of change, types of change, rates of change, and how to successfully manage and implement change.

ORGANIZATIONAL CULTURE

Organizational Culture Defined

1

Define organizational culture and the factors that influence it

Chapter 4's discussion of the manager's environments introduced a critical concept in the successful management of a company—organizational culture. *Organizational culture* is a dynamic system of shared values, beliefs, philosophies, experiences, habits, expectations, norms, and behaviors that give an organization its distinctive character. More importantly that system—the organizational culture—defines what is important to the organization, the way decisions are made, the methods of communication, the degree of structure, the freedom to function independently, how people should behave, how they should interact with each other, and for what they should be striving. Sharing these beliefs, values, and norms helps employees develop a sense of group identity and pride—both valuable contributors to organizational effectiveness. The norms for behavior develop around a set of values and create an "invisible hand"—a consensus and driving force for goal accomplishment.

http://store.nordstrom.com

http://www.pg.com

Because each organization has its own beliefs, values, and norms, each has a unique culture. At Nordstrom, the department store chain, the organizational culture makes a crusade of providing customer service. Procter & Gamble's culture stresses quality and competitive marketing. Although organizational culture may seem suspiciously like a company's mission, there is more to it than that. The organizational culture provides a means through which each employee can translate the core values of the mission into his or her own guiding passion.

http://www.mcdonalds.com

Management writers Tom Peters and Robert Waterman (1982) related the words of a business executive who had worked at McDonald's as a seventeen-year-old. In describing his experience at McDonald's, the exec pointed out the importance of the company credo of quality: "If French fries were overdone, we threw them out." Though they were young, inexperienced workers on the burger assembly line, he and his coworkers had fully absorbed the company's chief value—quality—and the norms for defect handling.

The young workers absorbed those values and norms because McDonald's has a strong culture. The more a culture's values are intensely held and widely shared throughout the organization, the stronger the culture. McDonald's culture is also highly functional. The factors that influence culture are all consistent with and supportive of the organization's strategy.

Factors Shaping Culture

Although each company's special blend of elements develops a unique culture, a comparison of many organizations identifies seven culture-shaping factors:

- Key organizational processes
- Dominant coalition
- Employees and other tangible assets
- Formal organizational arrangements
- Social system
- Technology
- External environment

As shown in Figure 10.1, these factors interact with each other. In fact, no single ingredient is independent of the others. Let us examine each of these factors (Kotter, 1978).

Key Organizational Processes

At the core of every organization, and fundamental to it, are the processes people follow to gather information, communicate, make decisions, manage work flow, and produce a good or service. How managers communicate to employees, how they share decision making, and how they structure the flow of work define the

FIGURE 10.1 *Factors that shape organizational culture*

organization. These processes affect and are affected by the other six factors that influence organizational culture.

Dominant Coalition

An organization's culture is greatly affected by the objectives, strategies, personal characteristics, and interrelationships of its managers, who form the dominant coalition. Managers' leadership styles determine how employees are treated and how they feel about themselves and their work. The dynamic energy and vision of Bill Gates at Microsoft have made his company the world leader in computer software. Herb Kelleher of Southwest Airlines created a culture that values having fun at work and that stresses the importance of the contribution of each employee. At Deloitte & Touche, the subject of this chapter's Valuing Diversity feature, CEO Michael Cook changed a culture that spurned women to one that valued and retained them.

http://www.microsoft.com

http://www.iflyswa.com

Employees and Other Tangible Assets

An organization uses its resources—employee population, plant and offices, equipment, tools, land, inventory, and money—to carry out its activities. These assets are the most visible and complex of the factors that influence organizational culture. Their quantity and quality have a major impact on organizational culture and performance. For example, Procter & Gamble attributes much of its success to the quality of its people—who in turn are proud to be part of an organization that describes itself as "special," "great," "excellent," and "unique among the world's business institutions." As one Procter & Gamble manager commented at the conclusion of a

VALUING DIVERSITY
Deloitte & Touche Changes the Culture

For ten years Cynthia Turk inched her way up the ladder at the accounting firm of Deloitte & Touche. Eventually she became a partner—when fewer than 10 percent of the partners were women—but she wasn't welcomed openly. "I walked into a culture that wasn't used to having women in very senior positions. It wasn't warm, welcoming, or nurturing." Three years later, Turk left, still feeling unaccepted.

Since Turk, together with many other women, left, few firms have made a more public commitment to top-to-bottom cultural change than has Deloitte & Touche. Following a fact-finding study to determine why, after years of hiring women for 50 percent of the entry-level jobs, fewer than 10 percent of those promoted to partner were female, a task force was formed. A strategic plan with top-down accountability was developed.

To change a culture where women, once they had a family, were perceived as less committed, Deloitte & Touche embarked on an ambitious program. Focused at all parts of the culture, the program included gender-awareness training for 5,000 partners and managers, formal career planning for all female partners and senior managers, and succession planning for senior women. The 1992 program also involved more flexible work arrangements, including the possibility of becoming a partner on a part-time basis. Partners are also monitored to ensure they give their female managers challenging, growth-oriented assignments, rather than clerical work.

"Deloitte's gender gap in turnover has now nearly vanished, and the number of women partners and directors is the highest among the Big Five. These cultural changes weren't easy, but they've enabled Deloitte to grow faster than any of its competitors" (McCracken, 2000).

http://www.us.deloitte.com

Sources: Douglas M. McCracken, "Best Practice—Winning the Talent War for Women: Sometimes It Takes a Revolution," *Harvard Business Review* (November-December, 2000), http://www.us.deloitte.com/us/news/00Dec/hbr.htm; Angela Briggins, "Win-Win Initiatives for Women," *Management Review* (June 1995), p. 6; Julia Lawlor, "Executive Exodus," *Working Woman* (November 1994), pp. 39–41, 80–87.

particularly difficult project, "If there was one characteristic I saw demonstrated by everyone it was the pride of being the best" (Collins and Porras, 1994).

Formal Organizational Arrangements

The formal arrangements that organize tasks and individuals constitute another factor that affects organizational culture. These arrangements include the structure of the organization and its procedures and rules. Specific mandated behaviors are also a part of organizational arrangements. A firm called Atmospheric Processing, for instance, invests its major efforts not in manufacturing but in heat-treating auto parts. For this organization, the prime challenge is rapid response to marketplace changes. The firm's skilled and creative employees function better with no traditional formal hierarchy, few rules, and decentralized decision making (Lammers, 1992). Email is an example of a formal organizational arrangement. It is a formal means of communicating throughout the organization. See this chapter's Managing Technology feature for an explanation of email addresses.

Social System

The social system, which contributes norms and values to organizational culture, includes the set of employee relationships that relate to power, affiliation, and trust. It also includes the grapevine and the informal organization, thus helping render it one of the most important factors of organizational culture. Because people are the organization, their relationships are crucial to defining what the organization is like—a factor well recognized at Procter & Gamble. New hires—especially those in brand management—immediately find nearly all of their time spent working or socializing with other members of "the family." From this interaction they learn more about the values and practices at Procter & Gamble. They learn about performance expectations and what it takes to succeed at Procter & Gamble (Collins and Porras, 1994).

MANAGING TECHNOLOGY
Email Addresses

The first part of a computer user's email address is the user's identification. The next part of the address is the "@" symbol, followed by the name of the computer server. The computer server name typically includes an extension indicating the type of operation, such as "com" (commercial businesses), "edu" (educational institutions), "gov" (government bodies), "org" (nonprofit organizations), "net" (network), and "mil" (military). In addition to indicating the type of operation, the extension to the server name can include the country where the computer resides (ca for Canada, il for Israel, uk for United Kingdom, and so forth). The "where" is often omitted for U.S. networks.

For example, here is the email address for the Webmaster at South-Western College Publishing.

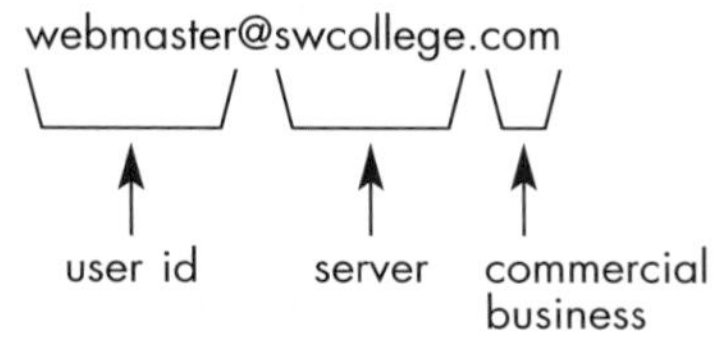

A great place to find email addresses for prospective employers or trade associations is at that particular organization's Web site. In addition, at some Web sites you can automatically send an email message to the organization without typing in the email address. Look for specific instructions at each Web site.

Technology

http://www.volvo.com

The major technological processes and equipment that employees use and how they use them also affect organizational culture. Is a machine or process intended to replace human labor or enhance workers' skills and productivity? The answer sends a message about the values of employees in the organization. Assembly-line technology promotes an impersonal, uninvolved culture. Many years ago, Volvo of Sweden embraced quality and worker satisfaction as corporate values. As a result, Volvo managers adopted team organizations and unconventional layouts in Volvo facilities. These changes helped shift the organizational culture away from the mechanistic values of the assembly line.

External Environment

http://www.robodoc.com

The discussions on the external environment in Chapters 4, 5, 6, and 7 related how suppliers, markets, competitors, the economy, regulators, and other factors outside an organization affect its goals, resources, and processes. Clearly these factors influence a firm's culture in many ways. For example, a change made by the FDA altered the organizational culture and operations at Integrated Surgical Systems, a 33-employee medical-device developer in Davis, California. ISS initially focused its new product development strategy with a U.S. perspective. ISS developed products over a three-year period and introduced them nationally. With a change in FDA review and approval processes, ISS was forced to alter its operations to a six-year development process and an introduction of these products overseas. ISS became an international company overnight, with a division in the Netherlands, international employees, and a more complex decision-making system. International employees brought their values, beliefs, and attitudes to the organization. This infusion of diversity altered the culture of ISS. In addition, extending the period for product development to six years had its effect on the culture. Initially the company environment nurtured rapidly moving entrepreneurial developers, while the new environment fostered and valued systematic and patient employees (Musits, 1994).

MANIFESTATIONS OF CULTURE

An organization's culture is nurtured and becomes apparent to its members in various ways. Some aspects of culture are explicit; some must be inferred. The chief evidences of culture include statements of principle, stories, slogans, heroes, ceremonies, symbols, climate, and the physical environment.

Statements of Principle

2

List and describe the ways that culture is manifested

http://www.mars.com

Some corporations have developed written expressions of basic principles central to organizational culture. Many years ago Forrest Mars developed the "Five Principles of Mars," which established fundamental beliefs for the company (Brenner, 1992). Mars's principles, which still guide the company today, are

- *Quality.* No one at Mars has the word *quality* in his or her job title; quality control is everywhere and everyone is responsible for it.
- *Responsibility.* All employees are expected to take on direct and total responsibility for results, exercising initiative and making decisions.

- *Mutuality.* In all dealings—with the consumer, other employees, a supplier or distributor, or the community at large—employees are to act so that everyone can win.
- *Efficiency.* Almost all of the company's 41 factories operate 24 hours a day, 7 days a week. As a whole, the company uses 30 percent fewer employees than its competitors do.
- *Freedom.* The company provides freedom to allow employees to shape their futures, and profits that allow employees to remain free.

Stories

http://www.corning.com

Shared stories illustrate the culture. "Corning scientists transmit and reinterpret their own culture by constantly telling each other stories of their successes and failures. People at Corning know the legendary story of the company's first dramatic innovation, which involved railroad signal lanterns, a primitive form of communication using glass and light that foreshadowed fiber optics" (Fishman, 2000). Telling stories acquaints new employees with the culture's values and reaffirms those values for existing employees. For example, all new employees at Nordstrom learn the importance of being a "customer service hero" through the story told by Nordstrom veteran employees (Collins and Porras, 1994).

> *At Nordstrom, everybody starts at the bottom. Bruce, Jim, and John—the three Nordstrom brothers that make up the chairman's office—all started on the floor. Bruce likes to remind us that he and his brothers were all raised sitting on a shoe sales stool in front of the customer; it is a literal and figurative posture that we all keep in mind. You get a lot of operational freedom here; no one will be directing your every move, and you're only limited by your ability to perform. But, if you're not willing to do whatever it takes to make a customer happy—to personally deliver a suit to his hotel room, get down on your knees to fit a shoe, force yourself to smile when a customer is a real jerk—then you don't belong here, period. Nobody tells you to be a customer service hero, it's just sort of expected.*

Slogans

http://www.walmart.com

http://www.dana.com

A slogan is a phrase or saying that clearly expresses a key organizational value. The late Sam Walton's slogan, "The customer is the boss," keeps the culture of Wal-Mart focused on providing high-quality customer service. A slogan, however, should not be confused with a company's advertising campaign, as two experts on corporate culture point out, unless the slogan is genuinely backed by the actions of the company and becomes a company value. In discussing Dana Corporation, with its former slogan "productivity through people," Terrence Deal and Allan Kennedy (1982) explain how a slogan that expresses an important cultural value can be made to live in the organization:

> *[Dana] has virtually doubled its productivity over the past seven years, a period when the overall growth of American productivity has been slowing. . . . [To achieve this growth, Dana] relied on its people, right down to the shop-floor level. . . . It put this value into action by creating a multitude of task forces and other special activities; by giving its people practical opportunities to generate productivity; by listening to ideas and then implementing them; and by consistently, visibly, and frequently rewarding success.*

Heroes

A hero is a person in the organization who exemplifies the values of the culture, as Southwest Airlines CEO Herb Kelleher does. To his 16,000 employees, Kelleher embodies what Southwest stands for—customers first, quality service, and have fun while doing it. A true hero? All of Southwest's 16,000 employees secretly contributed to buying a full-page ad in *USA Today* (14 October 1994) for Bosses Day. The message included these tributes:

> *For remembering every one of our names.*
> *For supporting the Ronald McDonald House.*
> *For helping load baggage on Thanksgiving.*
> *For giving everyone a kiss (and we mean everyone).*
> *For listening.*
> *For letting us wear shorts and sneakers to work.*
> *For golfing the LUV Classic with only one club.*
> *For running the only profitable major airline.*
> *For singing at our holiday party.*
> *For singing only once a year.*
> *For riding your Harley-Davidson into Southwest's headquarters.*
> *For being a friend, not just a boss.*

http://www.graniterock.com

Although heroes are often the company's founder or an executive who spurred the organization's initial success, as with Herb Kelleher, an organization can benefit when heroes are drawn from employees at all levels. At Granite Rock, a rock-and-asphalt business in Watsonville, California, and the recipient of the 1992 Baldrige National Quality Award, the employees are the heroes. Here, heroes are "Granite Rock People," not "employees." To become one, "you have to live the ideology—quality, service, and fairness" (Collins, "Building," 1995).

Ceremonies

http://www.marykay.com

http://www.manco.com

Managers hold ceremonies to exemplify and reinforce company values. Awards ceremonies for outstanding service, top producers, or high-performance teams promote the values of the culture and allow recipients and colleagues to share the experience of achievement. Awards ceremonies at Mary Kay Cosmetics are legendary in the cosmetics industry. At these lavish affairs, high-achieving sales representatives receive furs, pins, and cars. Whereas ceremonies at Mary Kay are simmering with sophistication, the same could hardly be said at Cleveland's Manco Duct Tape. Manco's celebrations are raucous and fast moving. To celebrate successes, people in yellow duck outfits ("duct" sounds like "duck") waddle through the halls; and top salespeople yell the Manco cheer and plunge into an ice cold pond (Collins, "Building," 1995). Also, visit Manco's Web site and read about their culture at http://www.manco.com/AboutUs/culture/culture.asp.

Many companies use a ceremony to mark the advancement of a new hire from trainee to full-fledged employee. Ceremonies also include rituals that honor promotions. These events increase the employee's identification with the organization's values.

Symbols

An object or image that conveys meaning to others is a symbol. Some organizations use symbols to embody their core values. At Nordstrom each employee receives a copy of the employee handbook, which consists of a single five-by-eight-inch card. As shown in Figure 10.2, the symbolic handbook embodies the core values of customer service and autonomy. Walt Disney created an entire symbolic language to reinforce his company's core values. At the Disney theme parks (Collins, "Building," 1995):

http://disney.go.com

- Employees are "cast members."
- Customers are "guests."
- A crowd is an "audience."
- A work shift is a "performance."
- A job is a "part."
- A uniform is a "costume."
- The personnel department is "casting."
- Being on duty is "on stage."
- Being off duty is "off stage."

Symbols may include job titles and perks, such as the location of a reserved parking space, the size and location of the office, or the size of the desk.

Climate

As defined in Chapter 4, organizational climate is the quality of the work environment experienced by employees—that is, how it feels to work there. Climate is largely a function of how workers feel about the organization. Do they work

FIGURE 10.2 *Nordstrom's handbook symbolizes its core values*

WELCOME TO NORDSTROM

We're glad to have you with our Company.
Our number one goal is to provide
outstanding customer service.
Set both your personal and professional goals high.
We have great confidence in your ability to achieve them.

Nordstrom Rules:
Rule #1: **Use your good judgment in all situations.**
There will be no additional rules.

Please feel free to ask your department manager,
store manager or division general manager
any questions at any time.

hard and apply themselves to the task, cooperating with management goals and directives; or do they drag their feet, resenting management instructions and resisting demands for output?

> *Dana Bookbinder, a scientist at Corning, says, "I can work on things that I think are important without being needled about it. They trust me, and they know that I won't embarrass them, wasting a lot of money and effort. If a project isn't working, I tell them. If I'm out of ideas, if I can't find the right person, I'll tell them. They know I will go figure stuff out that will make money and create jobs. This company has a 140-year history of inventors. This company realizes that invention is its whole lifeblood. I can see through a bad boss or two. There are a lot of neat people here. And I have a tremendous amount of fun at what I do."* (Fishman, 2000).

http://www.3m.com

3M's climate is an example of a healthy one. The company encourages everyone to tap into the other person's expertise, empowers people and rewards them for taking risks, and provides lots of celebrations where peers cheer peers (Loeb, 1995). An unhealthy climate is found in enterprises where management has different values, is in conflict, and has widely divergent goals.

Physical Environment

http://www.sears.com

Last but not least in the discussion of culture-shaping factors is a simple but powerful force: the physical environment of an organization. It is no coincidence that Sears & Roebuck, a hierarchical organization, built the world's tallest building. The Sears Tower dominates the Chicago skyline and reflects the multilayered structure and centralized culture of the organization that it built. A software developer or computer maker, on the other hand, may create a campuslike environment to promote the free exchange of ideas. Such enclaves are common in California's Silicon Valley.

CREATION OF CULTURE

The efforts of managers and employees create organizational culture. Managers like Walt Disney deliberately set out to instill certain values. In other cases the culture simply emerges from a pattern of behaviors that may not be consciously planned.

Role of Managers

3

Explain the role of managers and employees in creating culture

Managers at all levels in an organization help develop the culture. Quite simply, managers set the tone, control the resources, and have the means to influence the results. Management helps create culture in the following ways:

- Clearly defining the company's mission and goals
- Identifying the core values
- Determining the amount of individual autonomy and the degree to which people work separately or in groups
- Structuring the work in accordance with the corporation's values to achieve its goals
- Developing reward systems that reinforce the values and goals
- Creating methods of socialization that will bring new workers inside the culture and reinforce the culture for existing workers

If applied correctly, these factors will result in a healthy, dynamic culture; but if based on questionable values, a culture similar to the one illustrated by this chapter's Ethical Management can be the outcome.

The task of defining the culture often begins with the organization's founder. Both Walt Disney and Sam Walton created and put their stamp on strong organizational cultures. Sometimes, though, managers in charge of existing organizations wish to change that organization's culture. For example, when George Fisher moved to the position of chairman and CEO at Eastman Kodak in 1993 from the top spot at visionary Motorola, he found a culture that venerated authority and frowned on confrontation. Said Fisher, "It was so hierarchically oriented that everybody looked to the guy above him for what needed to be done. Decisions were too slow. People didn't take risks." Looking for the reason, Fisher observed that no one would take risks because decisions were overridden so frequently. Kodak had developed a custodial mentality geared to protecting current businesses rather than seeking new frontiers. As Fisher noted, ". . . Kodak is in such a state of doldrums and Motorola is vibrant. You have a different mental attitude when you drive for growth" (Maremont, 1995).

http://www.kodak.com

http://www.motorola.com

Fisher focused on bringing a new spirit to the company and establishing a willingness to compete. To begin the transformation, Fisher established a new mission focusing on photography and imaging—rather than on household and health products. Fisher cited five core values on which to build the culture:

- Respect for the individual
- Uncompromising integrity in everything Kodak does

ETHICAL MANAGEMENT
Unhealthy Shared Values and Beliefs

John Kotter, professor of leadership at Harvard Business School and coauthor of *Corporate Culture and Performance*, notes that the culture of many Fortune 500 companies has historically expected male executives to give them total dedication—even at the expense of the family—in exchange for job security and rewards. Such is the culture at MacAndrews and Forbes Group, Inc.

MacAndrews and Forbes Group is a holding company whose businesses include Revlon Cosmetics, Sunbeam small appliances, and Coleman Company, an outdoor equipment maker. The shared values and beliefs at MacAndrews include a traditional executive breakfast meeting. Every morning the CEO would have breakfast with his closest aides and plot corporate strategy. For seven years MacAndrews' CFO was a partner in those meetings. His commitment and loyalty were unquestioned. For example, in addition to maintaining a house in Scarsdale, New York, he spent $30,000 a year to keep an apartment within walking distance of the company's Manhattan headquarters to assure meeting attendance.

Then the CFO began missing these and other meetings to bathe and dress his wife who had been stricken with Alzheimer's disease. He contended that with a car phone and other advanced technology, he could conduct business away from the office while caring for his wife. By the end of the year, the CFO, who could no longer live up to his contract to devote "complete attention" to business, had been fired.

1. What is the proper balance between company and family?
2. At what point do a company's demands and expectations create an unhealthy culture? What would you have done if you had been the CFO? Why? What would you have done if you had been the CEO? Why?

Source: "Executive Fired after Caring for Ill Wife Sues Perelman," *Dallas Morning News* (6 July 1995), p. 2D.

- Trust
- Credibility
- Continuous improvement

Said Fisher, "These values are the operating principles we will use with our customers, employees, shareholders, suppliers, and the communities in which we live and work. We will rebuild this corporation based on these five values . . . without those values you don't have a company. . . . If you don't get a value system well established and well communicated to employees, you end up with a company that is schizoid" (Jacobson, 1995).

Regardless of whether the manager is the organization's founder, a second generation CEO, or a newly positioned chief executive, James Collins and Jerry Porras (1994) point out that truly visionary managers and companies "translate their core values into tangible mechanisms aligned to send a consistent set of reinforcing signals. They indoctrinate people, impose tightness of fit, and create a sense of belonging to something special." Figure 10.3 presents a summary of practical ways Collins recommends for building culture.

Role of Employees

Employees contribute to organizational culture to the extent that they accept and adopt the culture. Workers at Disney theme parks are renowned for their sunny disposition and friendliness to patrons. The training they receive after hiring clearly succeeds in making them see themselves as performers who give enjoyment.

FIGURE 10.3 *Practical ways to build a culture*

- Create orientation and ongoing training programs that have ideological as well as practical content, teaching such things as values, norms, and traditions.
- Promote on-the-job socialization by peers and immediate supervisors.
- Initiate rigorous up-through-the-ranks policies—hiring young, promoting from within, and shaping the employee's mind-set from a young age.
- Ensure exposure to pervasive methodology of "heroic deeds" and corporate exemplars (for example, customer heroic letters, marble statues).
- Create unique language and terminology (such as *cast members, Motorolans*) that reinforce a frame of reference and sense of belonging to an elite group.
- Develop corporate songs, cheers, affirmations, or pledges that reinforce psychological commitment.
- Initiate tight screening processes, either during hiring or within the first few years of employment.
- Provide incentive and advancement criteria explicitly linked to fit with the corporate ideology.
- Furnish awards, contests, and public recognition that reward those who display great effort consistent with the ideology; assure tangible and physical penalties for those who break ideological boundaries.
- Have tolerance for honest mistakes that do not breach the company's ideology ("nonsins"); provide severe penalties or termination for breaching the ideology ("sins").
- Create buy-in mechanisms (financial, time, investment).
- Design plant and office layouts that reinforce norms and values.
- Place constant verbal and written emphasis on corporate values, heritage, and the sense of something special.

Source: James C. Collins and Jerry I. Pooras, *Built to Last* (New York: HarperBusiness, 1993), p. 136. Copyright © 1994 by James C. Collins and Jerry I. Porras. Reprinted by permission of HarperCollins Publishers, Inc.

Disney employees, known as "cast members," are trained to provide enjoyable experiences for theme-park visitors.

© KELLY-MOONEY PHOTOGRAPHY/CORBIS

Also, workers contribute to organizational culture by helping to shape the values it embodies. Employees who shirk the tasks at hand—and influence newcomers to do the same—have a significant effect on quality, regardless of what top managers may say about quality as a value. Employees who give each other a hand to meet a deadline create a feeling of teamwork that exists regardless of management's decisions about structuring work.

subculture
A unit within an organization that is based on the shared values, norms, and beliefs of its members.

Finally, workers play a role in influencing organizational culture by forming subcultures. A **subculture** is a unit within an organization that is based on the shared values, norms, and beliefs of its members. The values of the subculture may or may not complement those of the dominant organizational culture. Unionized employees constitute a subculture. Groups of workers who share a common background or interest or who work in the same department may also form subcultures. When workers form a subculture, their shared experiences take on a deeper meaning because they also share values, norms, and beliefs. Subcultures influence their members' behavior; managers should, therefore, consider them important. If a subculture's values and norms conflict with those of the dominant culture, managers must take action.

Factors Contributing to the Effectiveness of Culture

4

Explain what factors make a culture effective

Culture affects performance. In a recent study of hundreds of firms, John P. Kotter and James Heskett (1992) found a dramatic difference between effective and ineffective cultures.

> *We found that firms with cultures that emphasized all the key managerial constituencies (customers, stockholders, and employees) and leadership from managers at all levels outperformed firms that did not have those cultural traits by a huge margin. Over an eleven-year period, the former increased revenues by an average of 682 percent versus 166 percent for the latter, expanded their work forces by 282 percent versus 36 percent, grew their stock prices by 901 percent versus 74 percent, and improved their net incomes by 756 percent versus 1 percent.*

Kotter and Heskett went on to warn that managers must do more than promote an effective culture; they must be constantly on the lookout for the signs of an ineffective culture.

> *Corporate cultures that inhibit strong long-term financial performance are not rare; they develop easily, even in firms that are full of reasonable and intelligent people. Cultures that encourage inappropriate behavior and inhibit change to more appropriate strategies tend to emerge slowly and quietly over a period of years, usually when firms are performing well.*

Three factors help determine the effectiveness of an organizational culture: (1) coherence, (2) pervasiveness and depth, and (3) adaptability to environment.

Coherence

In discussions of organizational culture, *coherence* refers to how well the culture fits the mission and other organizational elements. A culture like the one at Wal-Mart, which values customer service and a low-cost strategy, must train employees to recognize customer needs. It must also empower them to make decisions to meet those needs, create processes and structures that will achieve the goals of low inventory cost and low overhead, and employ technology to meet those goals. If decision-making authority at Wal-Mart were centralized, the culture would be less coherent, because such a design does not mesh with other aspects of the culture.

Pervasiveness and Depth

The phrase *pervasiveness and depth* refers to the extent to which employees adopt the culture of an organization. The greater the acceptance of and commitment to organizational values, the stronger the culture (Dubrin, 1974). By insisting that all employees take responsibility for quality, Mars ensures that quality, as a value, is pervasive. By training theme-park employees extensively, Disney helps guarantee that employees deeply hold its values.

Adaptability to the External Environment

http://www.att.com

If organizational culture fits the external environment, managers and employees have the mind-set they need to compete. For decades American Telephone & Telegraph (AT&T) enjoyed a monopoly on long-distance telephone service. In the 1980s, when long-distance service was deregulated, AT&T employees found they did not have the mind-set to compete in their new environment; their organizational culture had a poor degree of fit in terms of the real world. The new external environment had created new demands, and it required a new way of thinking—a new culture.

http://www.ibm.com

http://www.gm.com

Of the three factors that determine the effectiveness of organizational culture, the degree of fit with the external environment is perhaps the most critical. Its importance lies in the fact that the environment changes. Just ask managers at Sears, IBM, or General Motors about the importance of change in the external environment. These three organizations fell on hard times because they were not adaptable enough. Each organization possessed an effective culture. Indeed, IBM provided a model of strong corporate culture. The true measure of the effectiveness of a culture, then, is its ability to adapt. Managers must achieve the difficult task of building a culture strong enough to compel commitment and unwavering support but flexible enough to allow change in the face of emerging external demands.

Meeting that challenge will likely become even more important to organizational survival in the future. In the current volatile business world, environmental change is a constant. We now turn to understanding change and learning how to manage change.

NATURE OF CHANGE

Define change and identify the kinds of change that can occur in an organization

Not since the Industrial Revolution has U.S. business experienced so much change. In the past decade almost every industry has been rocked by change. Telecommunications has been changed by divestitures. Pharmaceuticals and banking have undergone consolidation. The banking and transportation industries have had to adjust to deregulation as investment brokers and health-care providers have had to adjust to increasing regulation. Manufacturers battle an increase in foreign competition, and the computer industry must constantly accommodate technological innovation. The Internet has affected every single industry. The increasing volume of transactions that take place electronically is a revolution in business practices. Managers are assaulted by change. Furthermore, as soon as they adjust to one change, they must readjust to accommodate another.

change
Any alteration in the current work environment.

Change is any alteration in the current work environment. The shift may be in the way things are perceived or in how they are organized, processed, created, or maintained. Every individual and organization experiences change. Sometimes change results from external events beyond the control of a person or an organization. For example, previously we noted how Integrated Surgical Systems, suddenly confronted with new FDA requirements, experienced change beyond its control. Sometimes the change results from planning. When a company lowers its prices to increase market penetration, for example, the change in price is purposeful.

The example about lowering prices indicates how complex a change can be. Lowering prices may seem to be a simple matter, but it involves more than just printing a new price list. A company lowers prices to increase sales. If sales increase, the company may need additional staff or equipment (phone lines or computers) to handle the volume of orders. It may need more production capacity to fill the orders, a more efficient technology to meet the needs, and so on. Furthermore, the information system must communicate the new price throughout the organization, and employees must receive briefings so they will know how to handle the increase. Even an apparently mechanical change calls for adjustments throughout an organization.

This section explores change by discussing its sources and types. The sections that follow will examine the kinds of changes that confront an organization during its typical life span and how change affects managers at each level.

Sources of Change

Change originates in either the external or internal environments of the organization.

External Sources

Change may come from the political, social, technological, or economic environment. Externally motivated change may involve government action, technology, competition, social values, and economic variables. Developments in the external environment require managers to make adjustments. New government regulations, for example, can require that a manufacturer install pollution-control devices or that a restaurant raise the wages of its workers to meet a new minimum. The actions of competitors certainly put demands on a business. When one U.S. airline launches new low fares, other domestic airlines in the same markets feel compelled to follow suit. Companies successful at coping with change take advantage of new technologies earlier rather than later. "Corning has work that needs to be done, and fast. The 'clock times' in the telecommunications businesses where Corning makes the most money are so short that the company often forms three or four teams to attack technical problems simultaneously from different angles. It can't wait to fail and start again; it needs to fail and succeed at the same time" (Fishman, 2000).

Internal Sources

Internal sources of change include managerial policies or styles; systems and procedures; technology; and employee attitudes. When managers change the standards by which they measure job performance or when a new manager takes over a department or company, employees must adapt their behavior to fit the new situation. When Corning sold its consumer-products business [dishes], it initiated a cultural transformation that was "emotionally difficult" for employees and managers alike. "But by 1998, the business accounted for less than 10% of Corning's revenues, and the company was becoming an optical-networking firm focused on high technology" (Fishman, 2000).

New conditions in the external environment clearly can bring about changes within the organization; internal change can also cause external change. Whether internal change affects the external environment depends on the extent of the internal change and on whether the change affects a part of the organization that has impact on the environment. New internal policies requiring employees to check their email at least once each day will unlikely have any impact on the external environment.

Types of Change

Change can also be understood on the basis of its focus, which can be strategic, structural, process oriented, or people centered. Such changes can have dramatic impact on the organizational culture.

Strategic Change

As discussed in Chapter 6, sometimes managers find it necessary to change the strategy or the mission of the organization. Organizations that decide to focus on a single mission often need to divest themselves of unrelated businesses, as Kodak did when it sold off its household and health products. Managers who want to expand operations to new areas may move to acquire another company, as Seagram did in its purchase of MCA.

http://www.seagram.com

http://www.mca.com

http://www.ford.com

Achieving strategic changes can require, in turn, a change in organizational culture or other elements. When Ford adopted quality as a key to its competitive strategy, it had to adopt quality work as a corporate value.

Structural Change

Managers often find it necessary to change the structure of their organizations, as has been the case in recent years, with the prevalence of team building and downsizing. These changes have usually been made to make operations run more smoothly, improve overall coordination and control, or empower individuals to make their own decisions. Because structural change has a major impact on an organization's social system and climate, it greatly affects organizational culture.

Process-Oriented Change

Many changes aim at processes, such as using new technology, shifting from human to mechanical labor in plants that employ robotics for manufacturing, or adopting new procedures. If process-oriented change takes the form of reengineering, it may have dramatic effects on the organization and its culture. As defined in Chapter 2 and discussed in Chapter 3, *reengineering* is the fundamental rethinking and radical redesign of business processes to achieve dramatic improvements in critical, traditional measures of performance, such as cost, quality, service, and speed. Reengineering first determines what process is necessary, then how to do it (Hammer and Champy, 1993).

As illustrated in Figure 10.4, most business processes involve activities in more than one department. When the steps have been completed in one department, the process continues as additional activities are undertaken in the next department. In most instances the result is an inefficient and ineffective process (Manganelli and Klein, August 1994). Reengineering takes aim at these processes to optimize the workflow and productivity. Changing or reengineering the processes may change the entire organization (Manganelli and Klein, June 1994).

FIGURE 10.4 *Processes wind throughout the organization*

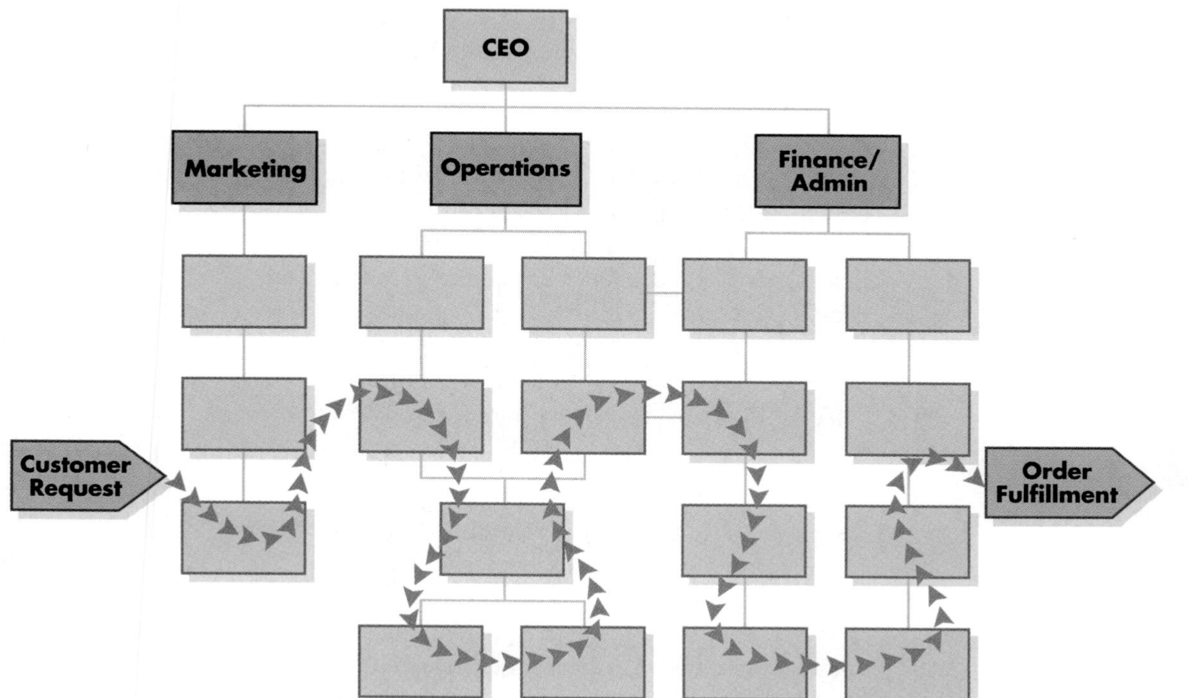

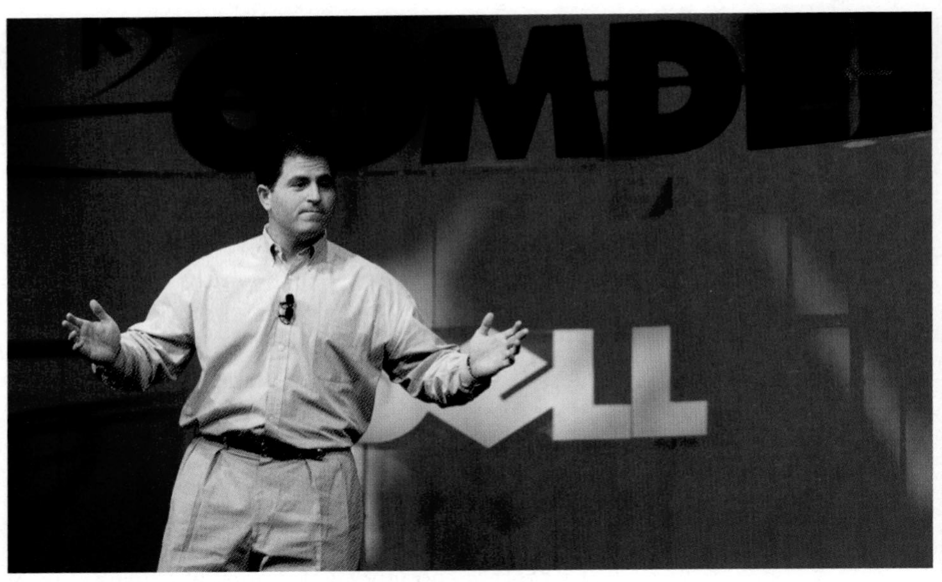

Michael Dell is considered a catalyst for digitally based e-commerce.

http://www.dell.com

Businesses processes are becoming integrated electronically, as technology is used to aid in the conduct of business. Early adopters of the Internet were those businesses willing to innovate and to take some risks. Michael Dell of Dell Computer Corporation is considered the leading architect of the Internet-enabled, thoroughly digital business enterprise. Dell helped pioneer the end-to-end use of digital networks to communicate with its customer, take orders, and then pull together products from suppliers. Dell did this by surpassing traditional distribution channels (middlemen) and going directly to customers. By September 2000, Dell was selling more than $50 million worth of computer equipment from its Web site every day.

People-Centered Change

Many changes are directed at the attitudes, behaviors, skills, or performance of the company's employees. At Goldstar Company (now LG Electronics, Inc.), in this chapter's Global Applications feature, former CEO Lee Hun-Jo began his program of change by focusing on people. As Hun-Jo noted, "You have to transform human beings. If you can't change your people, you can't change your organization." These changes can be achieved through retraining, replacing current employees, or increasing the performance expectations of new employees. The task of changing attitudes and behaviors falls into the domain of behavioral training. As an aspect of organizational development, behavioral training will be discussed later in this chapter.

Distinguish between evolutionary change and revolutionary change

Rates of Change

evolutionary change
The incremental steps taken to bring about progress and change.

http://www.jnj.com

Change can also be viewed based on its pace—that is, either evolutionary or revolutionary. **Evolutionary change** focuses on the incremental steps taken to bring about progress and change. Organizations like Johnson & Johnson and Motorola show a strategy for incremental change. These visionary companies have a philosophical commitment to constant change, but at a measured pace (Collins and Porras, 1994). Motorola and Johnson & Johnson were among the first to commit to incremental change techniques defined and discussed in Chapter 3: kaizen, total

GLOBAL APPLICATIONS
South Korea's Bright Star

In 1990 Goldstar Company (now LG Electronics, Inc.) was in deep trouble. The largest South Korean maker of electrical appliances and consumer electronics had seen its market share slip as product quality plummeted, losses piled up, margins fell, and costs rose.

Today, however, the healthy and vibrant company has regained its sales position in South Korea for color televisions, refrigerators, and washing machines. Former Chairman Lee Hun-Jo is responsible for this transformation; he shifted Goldstar from a family-managed business to one employing the skills and training of professional managers.

To initiate the change, Hun-Jo focused on people first. "You have to transform human beings. If you can't change your people, you can't change your organization." He won workers' confidence by closing the communication gap. He revealed as much financial information about the company as he could. He opened his doors to visits by employees at any time.

Having won employee support, Hun-Jo began to restructure. He reorganized Goldstar into nine SBUs that include 29 operational groups, each with a multidisciplinary team of designers, engineers, factory workers, and marketing people. The plan called for decentralizing management as far down as possible, thereby encouraging line managers, workers, and salespeople to open up the lines of communication among themselves.

Hun-Jo then changed the product development process. In the past Goldstar concentrated on bringing in a foreign product and reverse-engineering it. Although it allowed for some technology gains, it also kept the company permanently behind the cutting edge. Hun-Jo changed the focus. He sent engineers out to see for themselves what customers wanted. It resulted in the development of a refrigerator that helped Goldstar regain the number one position in its domestic market.

http://www.lgeus.com

Sources: Laxmi Nakarami, "Goldstar Is Burning Bright," *Business Week* (26 September 1994), pp. 129–130; Laxmi Nakarami, "Will Lucky Goldstar Reach Its Peak with Zenith?" *Business Week* (7 August 1994), p. 40.

quality management, quality circles, and benchmarking. Each technique has at its core a belief in continuous, gradual change.

Kodak's CEO, George Fisher, is a practitioner of evolutionary change. His "go-slow approach stands in sharp contrast to the rapid-fire cuts and reorganizations practiced by many other CEOs who parachute into troubled companies." In contrast to many of the latter, "Fisher thinks cost-cutting edicts from on high don't work well. He prefers to set tough goals, then let his managers decide how to achieve them. Moreover, he fears drastic action could cause harm to morale" (Maremont, 1995). Since assuming his position, Fisher's approach has been to initiate change in core values, strategy, and culture. Fisher's goal is to mold and shape Kodak to compete, to have energy, and to have spirit—incrementally. Figure 10.5 illustrates Fisher's evolutionary changes at Kodak (Maremont, 1995).

revolutionary change *Bold, discontinuous advances that bring about dramatic transformations in organizational strategies and structure.*

http://www.ge.com

Revolutionary change focuses on bold, discontinuous advances. To the observer, these "leaps" bring about dramatic transformations in organizational strategies and structure. Organizations and managers involved in revolutionary change push the envelope and practice outside-of-the-box thinking. By his actions, Jack Welch, CEO of General Electric, is a supporter of revolutionary change. In transforming General Electric, Welch opted for immediate rather than incremental change. Welch, using a tool of revolutionary change, challenged the company by setting a BHAG (as described in Chapter 5, a BHAG is a Big Hairy Audacious Goal). GE was "to become #1 or #2 in every market [they] serve and revolutionize the company to have the speed and ability of a small enterprise" (Tichy and Sherman, 1993).

FIGURE 10.5 *Examples of evolutionary and revolutionary change*

Factors	Evolutionary Change at Eastman Kodak	Revolutionary Change at Scott Paper Company
Time Period	One year	One year
Strategy	Strategy refocused on core business	Strategy focused on downsizing
	Noncore businesses sold	Older plants in United States and Europe closed
		11,200 jobs eliminated
Structure	Digital Imaging Unit created	70 percent of headquarters staff eliminated
	Digital imaging talent organized into one unit	50 percent of management eliminated
	Experienced computer marketer hired to lead new unit	20 percent of nonmanagerial employees eliminated
Culture	Five core values identified	Organization focused on cost cutting
	Culture reshaped to stress accountability, quality, and cycle time	Cultural change bypassed
People	Morale positive	Morale negative
	Future bright	Future uncertain
	Communication open	Communication sporadic
Finance	Debt reduced from $7.5 to $1.5 billion by sale of noncore businesses	Debt of $2.3 billion eliminated by the streamlining of operations and the selling of assets
	Growth now funded by photography cash cow, not debt	Assets worth $2.4 billion sold

Source: Based on Mark Maremont, "Kodak's New Focus," *Business Week* (30 January 1995) pp. 62–68, and Jim Mitchell, "Dunlap's Math 1 + 1 = 3," *Dallas Morning News* (18 July 1995), pp. 1D, 4D.

As previously discussed, reengineering, another tool of revolutionary change, takes nothing for granted. It ignores what is and concentrates on what should be. It calls everything into questioning—what no longer needs to be done, what must be done, and how better to execute the latter. Reengineering changes the fundamental ways in which people and their organization handle their processes. Typical results of reengineering have been to dramatically change organization's missions, visions, values, activities, and structures.

http://www.scottbrand.com

http://www.kimberly-clark.com

As strongly as George Fisher supported evolutionary change, former Scott Paper Chairman and CEO, Albert Dunlap, championed revolutionary change and reengineering. Referred to as "Rambo in pinstripes" and "Chainsaw Dunlap," the CEO, in one year, eliminated one-third of Scott's workforce, including 70 percent of its headquarters staff, half its managers, and 20 percent of the workers. In the process he more than doubled the value of Scott's shares and made the company more profitable. Figure 10.5 illustrates Dunlap's revolutionary changes at Scott Paper Company (Mitchell, 1995).

Management and Change

Each level of management faces change in a different way. As we have seen with George Fisher and Albert Dunlap, top-level managers are involved in change in terms of the organization as a whole. They tend not to address minute details; instead they focus on the broad outlines of the desired change. Top-level managers are more likely to be involved in changes of strategy, structure, and process. Because such changes have a major impact on culture and on the way an organization does business, the effects of change decisions made by top managers ripple throughout an organization. Top managers must be sensitive to the external environment; that is, they need to stay attuned to changes in that environment. By scanning the external environment, they may be able to see when internal changes are needed to fit new circumstances and meet new opportunities.

Middle managers will likely face structural, process-oriented, or people-centered changes, although they may well have some input into decisions about strategic change. To achieve greater efficiency or higher quality, they may reorganize staff or work flow. They may develop training programs to introduce new technology. In any case, the changes implemented by middle managers are likely to have a wide impact. They may affect all members of a division.

Although first-line managers may participate in discussions about strategic or structural changes, they are unlikely to make decisions about these issues. First-line managers institute process-oriented and people-centered change. They implement all types of changes developed higher in the hierarchy. Because they come into close contact with their employees, these managers must understand how to manage change.

HOW TO MANAGE CHANGE

Distinguish between planned and unplanned change

planned change
Trying to anticipate what changes will occur in both the external and internal environments and then developing a response that will maximize the organization's success.

management by reaction
A management method that does not anticipate change but merely reacts to it.

http://www.kmart.com

A company can deal with change by trying to anticipate the need for it and plan for it. A company and its managers can adopt a philosophy of **planned change**, which involves trying to anticipate what changes will occur in both the external and internal environments and then developing a response that will maximize the organization's success. When managers plan for change—whether employing George Fisher's evolutionary approach or Albert Dunlap's revolutionary style—they more likely can predict the results and control events. The alternative—**management by reaction**—can invite disaster, as we saw in the actions and reactions of Kmart. Steamrolled by Wal-Mart and Target, Kmart had no plan. Steeped in a culture that discouraged risk taking and innovation, Kmart lost market share and, in the process, its CEO. Now Kmart's store managers and senior executives are trying new approaches to sell more merchandise and increase profitability. Rather than having one plan, "the company is experimenting with many changes in its stores"—new concepts, new departments, and new merchandise. "Some of the approaches are borrowed from Wal-Mart, some patterned after Target, and some come from Kmart itself." According to Michael Crosson of John Greenberg & Associates, which designs store layouts and interiors, "The key is for Kmart to develop its own identity and approach. The goal needs to be: We need to be the store of first choice for customers in specific (merchandise) areas" (Elmer, 1995).

change agent
A person who implements planned change.

The **change agent** implements planned change. The change agent could be the manager who conceived of the need to change, as was Corning's Roger Ackerman; it could be another manager within the organization who is delegated the task; it could be an outsider, a consultant brought in specifically to help an organization adopt a new way of doing things; or it could be someone other than a consultant, hired from the outside to change the organization. George Fisher at Kodak, Albert Dunlap at Scott Paper, and Lou Gerstner at IBM fall into this last category. An outside change agent is considered to be more objective, less influenced by existing politics and people, and committed to the goals agreed to upon hiring. Inside change agents often cannot see the correct actions to take or are reluctant initiators (Sherman, 1994).

The next section will examine planned change by looking at the kinds of changes that managers can expect throughout the life of the organization, the steps involved in planned change, and the attitudes that underlie an effective approach to change.

Need for Change: Diagnosing and Predicting It

Managers can diagnose and predict the need for organizational change by studying the typical phases of change. Recall the organizational life cycle of birth, youth, midlife, and maturity (see Chapter 9) and some of the crises commonly experienced by organizations at each stage. Management consultant Larry Greiner (1972) has graphed these predictable phases of organizational evolution (see Figure 10.6). Anticipating these phases can help managers prepare for change rather than simply reacting to it. Greiner has identified five phases of growth.

Phase 1: Creativity

This birth stage of the organization is marked by concerns for product and market, by an informal social system, and by an entrepreneurial style of management. Soon the need for capital, new products, new markets, and new employees forces the organization to change. A crisis of leadership occurs when management becomes incapable of reacting to the growing organization's need for structure. The organization enters a new phase.

Phase 2: Direction

The second phase is characterized by the implementation of rules, regulations, and procedures. A functional organizational structure is introduced; an accounting system is created; incentives, budgets, and work standards are established; and formal, impersonal communications begin. Eventually, lower-level managers demand greater decision-making authority, which brings on another crisis and launches the organization into the next phase.

Phase 3: Delegation

Decentralization is the key to the third phase, in which top management creates profit centers under territorial managers who are given leeway to act and held

FIGURE 10.6 *Model of organizational growth and change*

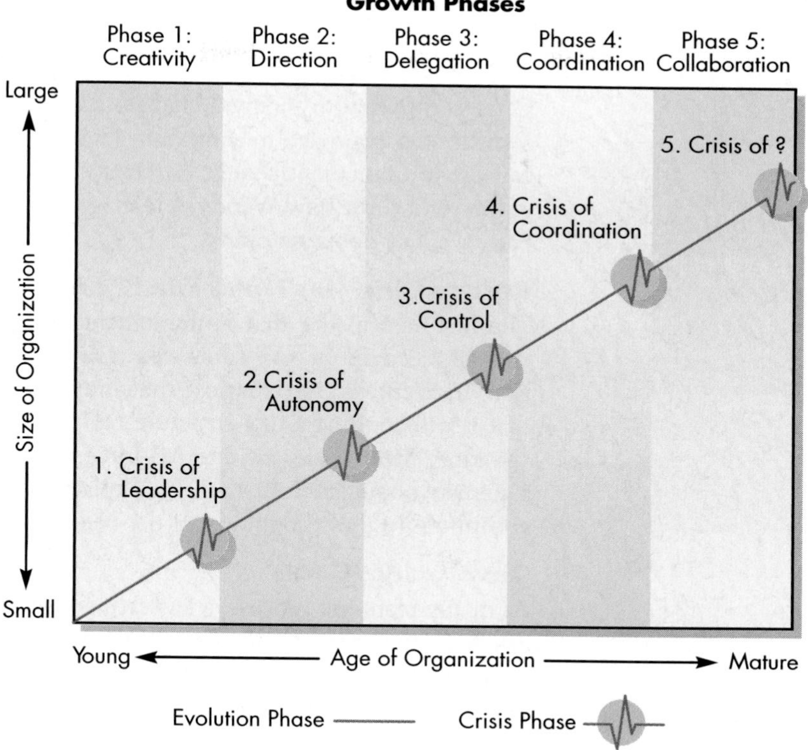

Source: Reprinted and adpated by permission of *Harvard Business Review* from "Evolution and Revolution as Organizations Grow," by Larry E. Greiner, *Harvard Business Review* (July–August 1972), pp. 55–64. Copyright © 1972 by the Harvard Business School Publishing Corporation; all rights reserved.

accountable for the results. Communication from the top becomes less frequent. Eventually, top managers sense that they have lost control of the organization. This realization brings on another crisis and another major change.

Phase 4: Coordination

Responding to their sense of loss of control, managers attempt to seize control by emphasizing coordination. Decentralized work units are merged, formal organization-wide planning is introduced, capital expenditures are restricted, and staff personnel begin to wield greater power. The price of this phase: Red tape and interpersonal distance between line and staff and between headquarters and the field develop. A new crisis takes place.

Phase 5: Collaboration

The final phase introduces a new people-oriented and flexible system, with managers exhibiting more spontaneity. Characteristics of this phase include problem solving by teams, reductions in headquarters staff, simplification of formal systems, and encouragement of an attitude of risk taking and innovation.

The heart of Greiner's model shows a key point about change. The solution to one set of problems eventually creates another set of problems that require solving. In other words, the need for change is constant.

Steps in Planned Change

8

Explain the steps managers can follow to implement planned change

Once committed to planned change, a manager or an organization must create a step-by-step approach to achieve it. Figure 10.7 presents the steps that a manager can use to implement change (Greiner, 1967). As an example, the following paragraphs will show how Wendy, a manager, can use this process to change her company's policy about smoking.

Recognizing the Need for Change

The first step in the change-implementation process is to identify the need for a change. Recognition can come as a result of factors inside or outside an organization. In Wendy's case, suppose the company's health insurance carrier notifies her that it will conduct a rate-structure review in light of research about the effects of smoking. Meanwhile, an internal force, a group of employees, requests a policy statement about smoking in the workplace. In this case, external and internal forces contribute to the recognition of the need for change.

Developing Goals

As in any planning process, a key step is the identification of goals. Managers must ask what they wish to achieve. In Wendy's case, the manager's goals become (1) to develop a smoking policy for the organization that will be widely accepted and (2) to prevent insurance costs from rising.

Selecting a Change Agent

With goals in mind, the next issue is to determine who will manage the change. Wendy asks the leader of the group concerned about smoking to assist her as a change agent.

FIGURE 10.7 *Nine steps for implementing planned change*

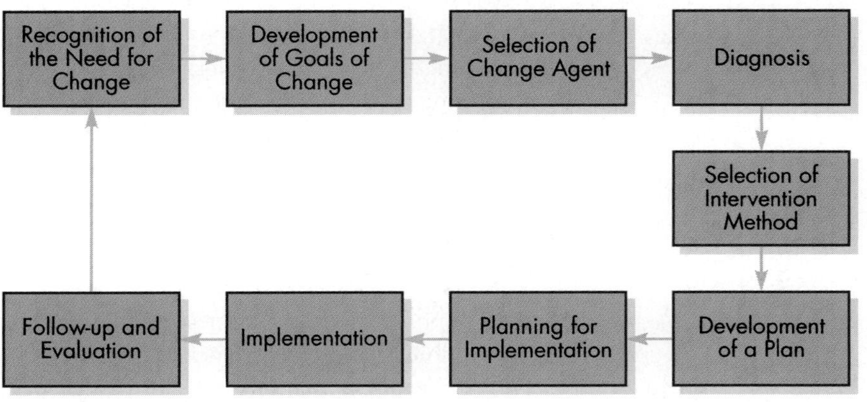

Diagnosing the Problem

In the next step, the manager gathers data about the problem and analyzes the data to identify the key issues. The two change agents in the current example find that other companies control health insurance costs by instituting smoking restrictions. They also learn that whether employees support or oppose smoking in the workplace, smoking is an emotional issue.

Selecting the Intervention Method

In the fifth step, the manager must decide how to achieve the change. Because smoking is such an emotionally charged issue, the change agents in the current example decide not to create the needed policy themselves. Instead, they form a task force that includes representatives from all departments. They believe that large-scale participation will help ensure the facilitation of the change.

Developing a Plan

This step involves actually putting together the "what" of the change. The task force must decide if the company will have a no smoking policy or will designate areas that permit smoking.

Planning for Implementation

In this phase, the decision maker must decide the "when," "where," and "how" of the plan. The task force in Wendy's case must decide when the policy will go into effect, how it will be communicated, and how its impact will be monitored and evaluated.

Implementing the Plan

After a plan is created, it must be put into effect. Implementing the plan requires notifying the employees who will be affected by the change. Notification may consist of written messages, briefings, or training sessions. The choice depends on the depth of the change and the impact it will have on people. With a major change, such as the adoption of work teams, training may be necessary for some time. In Wendy's case, the task force decides to settle the smoking issue by announcing the plan and holding briefings.

Following Up and Evaluating

Once a change has been implemented, the manager must follow up by evaluating it. Evaluation consists of comparing actual results to goals. If the new smoking policy receives widespread employee acceptance and holds the line on insurance costs, then the change was worthwhile.

QUALITIES PROMOTING CHANGE

Identify the organizational qualities that promote change

Managers can help create a climate that promotes change by developing a philosophy toward change that includes three elements: mutual trust, organizational learning, and adaptability.

Mutual Trust

Creating an environment of mutual trust between managers and employees is vital for managers who wish to implement change. Many research studies indicate that trust is the most important factor in creating an effective, well-run organization (Barnes, 1981). In this context, **mutual trust** is the ability of individuals to rely on each other based on their character, ability, and truthfulness. In a period of uncertainty and hard times, mutual trust allows individuals to continue to function while maintaining a hope that things will improve.

mutual trust
The ability of individuals to rely on each other based on their character, ability, and truthfulness.

Mutual trust includes two essential ingredients: sense of adequacy and personal security. Adequacy means that each employee feels that he or she counts for something in the organization and that his or her presence makes a difference in the overall performance of the firm. Personal security is the degree to which each person feels safe when speaking honestly and candidly.

Mutual trust can lessen fear of change, which can help managers implement change. When trust is present, employees will feel comfortable as the organization moves through change even though change is threatening. A report from the collective experiences of 50 global CEOs cites the importance of trust in today's corporations. "When employees are being asked to stretch, to act like owners, to take risks, or to commit themselves, they need assurance that if they go the extra mile, their employers will do so too. In the wrong setting, with the wrong players, employees know that pursuing such goals can work against self-interest" (Executive Management Forum, 1995).

Organizational Learning

organizational learning
The ability to integrate new ideas into an organization's established systems to produce better ways of doing things.

The term **organizational learning** refers to the ability to integrate new ideas into an organization's established systems to produce better ways of doing things. A manager can view organizational learning as either single looped or double looped (Argyris and Schon, 1978).

A single-looped learning situation is one in which only one way of making adjustments exists. An organization with single-looped learning has a prescribed way of doing things. When actions do not follow the prescription, the actions are adjusted to meet the standards. An organization with this belief is inflexible; it does not change its attitude, only its responses.

Double-looped learning, on the other hand, is based on the realization that more than one alternative exists. Double-looped learning facilitates change because it allows for more than one way to do something. If a manager believes there are numerous ways of reaching a goal, each employee can freely share ideas and the assumptions underlying the ideas. Double-looped learning provides for a change in both attitude and behavior.

3M's organizational climate is one that recognizes and encourages double-looped learning. At 3M everyone "is encouraged to call up any other employee and tap into that person's expertise . . . on the phone, by e-mail, in person, or any other way" (Loeb, 1995).

Adaptability

Managers can either plan for change or react to it. Being adaptive takes energy, commitment, and caring, but the wear and tear of the reactive approach is far worse. Adaptiveness means being open to new and different ways of doing things; it means being flexible rather than rigid.

According to James C. Collins, adaptiveness means changing without losing the company's core values. Companies have done so by grasping the differences between timeless principles and daily practices. For example, Disney has almost religiously preserved central core values of wholesomeness and bringing happiness to people, yet it has continually changed its product strategy from cartoons to feature films, to the Mickey Mouse Club, to Disneyland, to videos (Collins, "Change," 1995).

IMPLEMENTATION OF CHANGE

To implement a program of change, a manager must be aware of why people resist change, why change efforts fail, and what techniques can be used to modify behavior.

Resistance to Change

10 Explain why people resist change and what managers can do to overcome that resistance

One of the greatest difficulties faced by managers trying to institute change involves overcoming the resistance of those who must change. In his book, *The Reengineering Revolution*, MIT professor-consultant Michael Hammer calls people's innate resistance to change "the most perplexing, annoying, distressing, and confusing part" of the change process (Fisher, 1995). Nevertheless, resistance must be overcome or the change cannot take place.

Sources of Resistance

People resist changes for many reasons. The following list includes some of them (Hodgetts and Altman, 1979):

- *Loss of security.* Change scares people. Individuals tend to find security in traditional methods; the familiar is comfortable. New technology, new systems, new procedures, and new managers can threaten that security and thus cause resistance.
- *Fear of economic loss.* Sometimes people resist change because they foresee, or fear, an economic loss. Workers may disapprove of new processes because they feel that the result will be layoffs or reduced wages.
- *Loss of power and control.* Change often poses problems of power and control. "Will my influence still exist?" "Where will I end up in the pecking order?" These questions reflect the anxiety caused by change (Nadler, 1987). Some reorganizations clearly indicate that specific people will lose power. These people are likely to wish to preserve the status quo.
- *Reluctance to change old habits.* Habits provided a programmed method for decision making and performing. Someone who needs no initiative to solve problems may think, "I can do this job blindfolded." Learning new processes requires rethinking or learning to think again; it's hard work.
- *Selective perception.* A person who has a biased interpretation of reality is guilty of selective perception. To someone with selective perception, reality is what the person thinks it is. Employees prone to selective perception tend to think in terms of stereotypes, and these stereotypes can permeate their logic. Faced with a change at work, a person with selective perception might think, "It's a

management plot to do away with us." An employee with such an attitude is difficult for a manager to deal with. If the employee's views are extreme, he or she regards all actions of management as suspect.

- *Awareness of weaknesses in the proposed change.* Sometimes employees resist change because they see that the change may cause problems. This type of resistance can be constructive. By listening to the objections of these employees, managers can help the organization avoid problems and save time, money, and energy. For employees to have a constructive effect, however, they must communicate their concerns effectively and early.

Techniques for Overcoming Resistance

Managers can use five techniques to overcome resistance to change:

- *Participation.* Participation can be as simple as saying "we changed" instead of "they changed." A person involved in the process of change understands the goals and feels more strongly committed to the change than someone who did not participate. Organizations have recognized and have responded by implementing cross-functional teams (one of the topics in Chapter 15).
- *Open communication.* Uncertainty breeds fear, which creates rumors, which causes more uncertainty. Managers can reduce the likelihood of this unsettling cycle by providing timely, complete, and accurate information. Holding back information destroys trust.
- *Advance warning.* Sudden change can have the same effect as an earthquake. People adapt better to change if they are prepared for it. As managers sense a need for change or know that change is imminent, they should inform the employees who will be affected. Continuous education and training help people prepare for change. Continuous learning seems to enhance adaptability.
- *Sensitivity.* When implementing change, managers must work with those affected to learn each employee's concerns and respond to them. In other words, managers must be sensitive to the effects the change has on each person. Sensitivity minimizes resistance to the change.
- *Security.* People are much more willing to accept change if the fear of dire consequences can be removed. In many cases, managers can reassure workers simply by explaining that the change will not affect income and job security. Of course, such a commitment is meaningful only if it's true. When managers break promises, they are taking the first step to employee discontent.

Why Change Efforts Fail

11
Explain why change efforts fail

Not all change efforts are successful. Even when they undertake change for the best of reasons, managers cannot always bring about desired changes. Normally, failure can be traced to one of the following causes.

Faulty Thinking

Managers can fail to achieve change by not analyzing the situation properly. John Loose describes Corning as "a company that has rebuilt itself around our strengths and the opportunities of the marketplace." If they didn't think this way, they'd still be manufacturing cookware.

Inadequate Process

Sometimes change efforts fail because of the process used to bring them about. A change may fail because the manager did not follow the steps for change shown in Figure 10.7 or because he or she did not follow the steps properly. Perhaps the manager chose an inappropriate change agent or neglected a step in the process. In any case, an incomplete approach usually leads to failure.

Lack of Resources

Some changes require a significant expenditure of time and money. If those resources aren't available, the change effort may be doomed from the beginning.

Lack of Acceptance and Commitment

If individuals, both managers and employees, do not accept the need for change and commit to it, change will not occur. Lack of commitment typically occurs in an organization whose managers frequently announce change but do not follow through to implement it. In such a situation employees begin to see each new announcement as merely a program of the month—entertaining perhaps, but nothing to be taken seriously.

Michael Hammer refers to this as the flavor-of-the-month approach and sees it as the change agent's greatest enemy. "You foster an attitude in people that says, 'Oh yeah, been there, done that, got the T-shirt, coffee mug, ho hum.' Meanwhile they haven't taken a fresh look at their job in years, if ever, and aren't likely to do so no matter what anybody says." Hammer's prescription is to create a "sense of inevitability," which he compares to a moving train. "A lot of people will stand in front of a train that isn't moving and trust or assume that it won't start rolling toward them. Very few people will jump out in front of a train that is already barreling along at 80 or 100 miles an hour. In a lot of companies now, the thing is to get the train rolling" (Fisher, 1995).

Lack of Time and Poor Timing

Some situations do not allow enough time for people to think about the change, accept it, and implement it. In other instances the timing is poor—for example, an economic downturn may lower revenue, employees may be occupied with other commitments, or a competitor may release a new product. A company may invest years and millions of dollars into a change only to find that the environment has evolved so much that the plan devised for success no longer applies.

A Resistant Culture

In some cases the cultural climate of an organization needs to be changed before anything else can be.

Methods of Effecting Change

This section will explore how to change behavior on the individual level. Most first-line managers need to understand this kind of change, because their change efforts will be directed at modifying or altering their subordinates' behavior. Change in individuals usually relates to a change in skills, knowledge, or attitude. The paragraphs that follow explore two approaches: the three-step approach and force field analysis.

Three-Step Approach

Many psychologists and educators have observed that different people react differently to pressures to change. Most will accept the need to learn new skills and update their knowledge, but most resent efforts to change their attitudes. Accordingly, workplace efforts to change attitudes meet the least success of any change efforts. Yet if attitudes are not changed, the behaviors that grow out of attitudes cannot change. Kurt Lewin (1947) provided a useful approach to changing attitudes in a lasting way. His method, called the **three-step approach**, consists of three phases: unfreezing, change, and refreezing.

three-step approach
A technique of behavior modification to change attitudes in a lasting way; it consists of three phases: unfreezing, change, and refreezing.

In the first step, unfreezing, managers who spot deficiencies in a subordinate's behavior must identify the causes of that behavior. They confront the individual with the behavior and the problem it causes; they then begin trying to convince him or her to change by suggesting methods and offering incentives. This step may include pressure on the individual that makes him or her uncomfortable and dissatisfied. When the person is upset enough, step two may begin.

For example, say that Jessica wants to improve the productivity of Jane, a staff member in the Information Center. By spending too much time on her work, Jane increases the workload of others in the department. To resolve the problem, Jessica must first explain to Jane that her work is inadequate and that her coworkers must unfairly carry her burden. She may mention that the others are starting to complain about Jane. Having reviewed Jane's work, Jessica thinks that the basic problem is lack of training. As a result, she suggests that Jane undertake a special weeklong training course offered by the company. She could offer an incentive; too, pointing out that the higher productivity could mean a better chance at a salary increase.

In the second step, change, the individual's discomfort level rises. When it rises high enough, he or she will look for ways to reduce the tension. This leads the employee to question his or her motives for the current behavior, and this questioning provides the manager with the opening to present new role models that promote the desired behavior. As the individual adopts that behavior, performance will improve; but the manager must support and reinforce that behavior if it is to last.

In our example Jane might begin to notice the disapproving looks or whispered comments from coworkers. Uncomfortable in this unfriendly atmosphere, she might decide she will undertake the needed training.

In step three, refreezing, the manager recognizes and rewards new and approved attitudes and behaviors. If any new problems arise, the manager must identify and discourage them; in other words, the process begins again. After Jane takes the training, Jessica should closely monitor Jane's productivity. When Jessica sees output increase, she must be sure to congratulate Jane on the improvement. For the desired behavior to continue, positive reinforcement should come fairly frequently, especially at first. If a salary increase was promised, that promise must be kept.

The three-step process is continuous. Managers must watch that the new behaviors do not become counterproductive. If they do, the behaviors must be unfrozen and replaced by a new, more desirable behavior.

force field analysis
A technique to implement change by determining which forces drive change and which forces resist it.

Force Field Analysis

Kurt Lewin also developed **force field analysis**, another useful tool for managing change. As Figure 10.8 shows, to achieve change a manager must overcome the

FIGURE 10.8 *Forces that contribute to a force field*

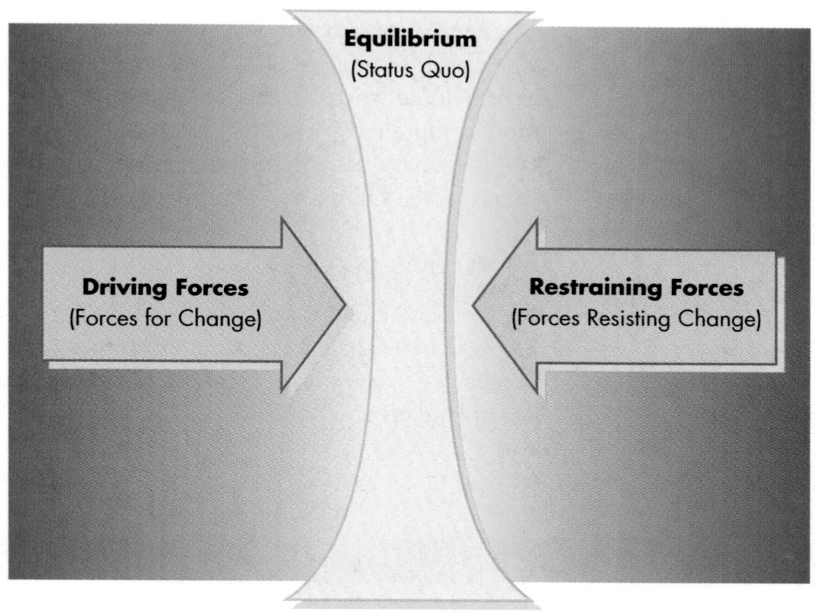

status quo—the balance between forces that favor change and forces that resist change. The change forces are known as *driving forces*, and the resisting forces are known as *restraining forces*. Managers trying to implement a change must analyze the balance of driving and restraining forces, then attempt to tip that balance by selectively removing or weakening the restraining forces. The driving forces will then become strong enough to enable the change to be made.

To see how force field analysis works, return to the example of Jane, the worker in the Information Center. To convince Jane to change, Jessica must first identify the driving forces: self-esteem, the regard of peers, and increased monetary compensation. The key restraining forces might be Jane's lack of desire to expend the effort to improve and discomfort with the computer. Jessica can weaken the restraining forces by having one of Jane's coworkers tell Jane how the training program helped the coworker. This information may strengthen the driving forces and alter the balance of the forces, leading Jane to accept the change.

ORGANIZATIONAL DEVELOPMENT

organizational development (OD)
A process of conducting a thorough analysis of an organization's problems and then implementing long-term solutions to solve them.

Managing change is an ongoing process. If a manager does it well, he or she can maintain a positive organizational climate. Some organizations make thorough analyses of their problems and then implement long-term solutions to solve them. Such an approach is called **organizational development (OD)**.

Purposes of Organizational Development

12

Explain the purpose of an organizational development program

The main purpose of OD, according to one management writer, is "to bring about a system of organizational renewal that can effectively cope with environmental changes. In doing so, OD strives to maximize organizational effectiveness as well as individual work satisfaction" (Burton, 1976). Organizational development is the most comprehensive strategy for intervention. It involves all the activities and levels of management in ongoing problems that respond to external and internal sources. The OD process is cyclical, as Figure 10.9 shows.

Strategies of Organizational Development

Managers may choose one or more of the tools and strategies of OD described in Figure 10.10. The choice depends on the circumstances. Restrictions the managers may have to take into account include limits on time and money and lack of skill at implementing a strategy.

FIGURE 10.9 *Model of the organizational developmental process*

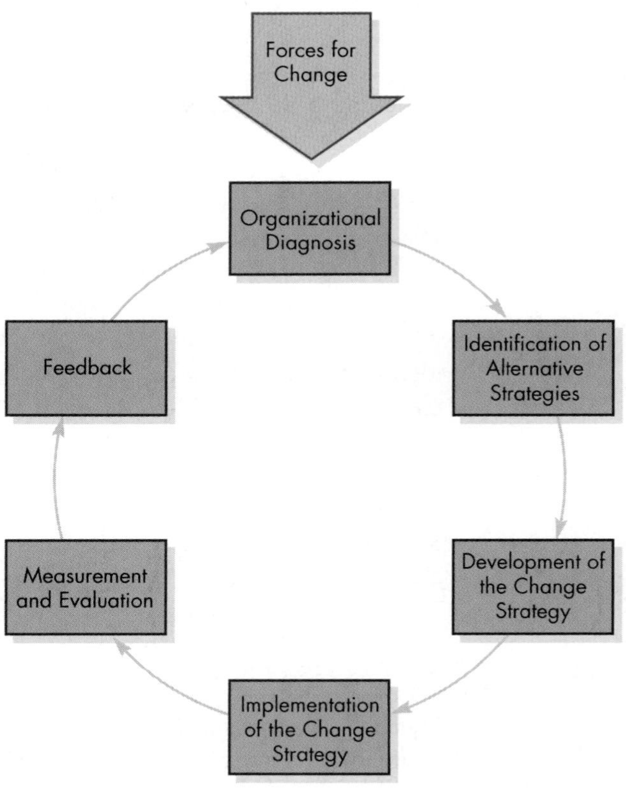

Source: Gene F. Burton, "Organizational Development—A Systematic Process," *Management World* (March 1975), Reprinted with permission from the Administration Management Society, Willow Grove, PA. Copyright 1976 AMS.

FIGURE 10.10 *Tools and methods for applying organizational development strategies*

	DIAGNOSTIC STRATEGIES
Consultants	This strategy consists of bringing in objective outsiders (consultants) to analyze and conduct audits of existing policies, procedures, and problems. Consultants can be individuals or groups and may act as change agents as well.
Surveys	Surveys consist of interviews or questionnaires used to assess the attitudes, complaints, problems, and unmet needs of employees. Surveys are usually conducted by outsiders and guarantee anonymity to participants.
Group discussions	Group discussions are periodic meetings conducted by managers to uncover problems and sources of their subordinates' discomfort and dissatisfaction.
	CHANGE STRATEGIES
Training programs	Training programs are ongoing or special efforts to improve or increase skill levels, change or instill attitudes, or increase the knowledge needed to perform present jobs more effectively and efficiently.
Meetings and seminars	As change strategies, meetings or seminars are gatherings held to explore mutual problems and seek mutually agreeable solutions. Such group sessions may be chaired by insiders or outsiders and may be used to prepare people for changes in advance of implementation.
Grid OD	Grid OD is a six-phase program based on the leadership grid. Its purpose is management and organizational development. The first two phases focus on management development. The last four phases are devoted to organizational development. The six phases are laboratory training, team development, intergroup development, organizational goal setting, goal attainment, and stabilization.

The choice of a strategy usually results from conferences and discussions involving those who will be most directly affected. The experiences, feelings, and perceptions of conference participants help determine if their parts of the organization are ready for change and for OD techniques. The success of OD depends on a high level of receptiveness to change.

Evaluating the Effectiveness of Organizational Development

Since OD requires an ongoing, long-term effort to bring about lasting change in an organization's technology, structure, and people, a successful OD program takes a significant investment of money and time. Both are needed for managers to adequately diagnose the problem, select the strategy, and evaluate the effectiveness of the program.

Managers can measure the effectiveness by comparing the results of the program to the goals before it was implemented. Were the goals met? If not, why not? Perhaps they were too rigid and too hard to achieve. Perhaps the problems were inadequately defined, and the inadequate definition resulted in the choice of an inappropriate solution. Perhaps managers tried to institute changes before people were prepared for them. Regardless of the cause, the results of the OD analysis will provide feedback needed for later changes.

In the final analysis, as is the case with any other management effort, the effectiveness of OD depends on the quality of its inputs and the skills of those making the analysis. Successful OD depends on solid research, clear goals, and implementation by effective change agents who use appropriate methods.

OD is an expression of managers' efforts to stay flexible. Managers recognize that events inside and outside the organization can happen quite suddenly and can create pressure for change. OD provides the personnel and mechanisms to deal with change; control its evolution; and direct its impact on organizational structure, technology, and people.

CHAPTER SUMMARY

1 Define organizational culture and the factors that influence it. Organizational culture is the distinctive character of an organization comprising its shared values, beliefs, philosophies, experiences, habits, expectations, norms, and behaviors. Seven factors influence organizational culture: key organizational processes, the dominant coalition, employees and other tangible assets, formal organizational arrangements, the social system, technology, and the external environment.

2 List and describe the ways culture is manifested. The culture becomes apparent through the following manifestations:

- *Statements of principle*—written expressions of basic principles central to the organizational culture
- *Stories*—illustrations of the culture used to acquaint new employees with the cultural values and to reaffirm those values to existing employees
- *Slogans*—a phrase or saying clearly expressing a key organizational value
- *Heroes*—people in the organization who exemplify the values of the culture
- *Ceremonies*—presentation of awards to provide examples of and reinforce company values
- *Symbols*—objects or images that convey meaning to others
- *Climate*—the quality of the work environment experienced by employees
- *Physical environment*—the structure of the work setting, which often reflects the cultural values

3 Explain the role of managers and employees in creating culture. Managers help develop culture by identifying core values, defining the company's mission, determining the amount of individual autonomy and the degree to which people work separately or in groups, structuring the work in accordance with the corporation's values, developing reward systems that reinforce values, and creating methods of socialization that will bring new workers inside the culture and reinforce the culture for existing workers. Employees contribute to defining the culture by the extent to which they accept and adopt it, by shaping the organization's norms and values, and by forming subcultures.

4 Explain what factors make a culture effective. The three factors that make a culture effective include

1. *Coherence*—how well the culture fits the organization's mission and other organizational elements
2. *Pervasiveness and depth*—the extent to which employees adopt the culture of an organization
3. *Adaptability to the external environment*—the degree to which a culture is flexible enough to allow change in the face of emerging external demands.

5 Define change and identify the kinds of change that can occur in an organization. Change is any alternative in the present work environment. Change can occur in strategy, structure, process, and people.

6 **Distinguish between evolutionary change and revolutionary change.** Evolutionary change focuses on incremental steps to bring about progress. Its techniques include kaizen, total quality management, quality circles, and benchmarking. Revolutionary change focuses on bold, discontinuous advances. Its techniques include BHAGS and reengineering.

7 **Distinguish between planned and unplanned change.** Planned change involves trying to anticipate what changes will occur in both external and internal environments and then developing a response that will maximize the organization's success. Unplanned change involves reacting to events rather than anticipating them.

8 **Explain the steps managers can follow to implement planned change.** To implement planned change, managers should follow these steps: recognize the need for change, develop goals, select a change agent, diagnose the problem, select the intervention method, develop a plan, plan for implementation, implement the plan, and follow up and evaluate.

9 **Identify the organizational qualities that promote change.** The organizational qualities that promote change include mutual trust, organizational learning, and adaptiveness.

10 **Explain why people resist change and what managers can do to overcome that resistance.** People resist change because of loss of security, fear of economic loss, loss of power and control, reluctance to change old habits, selective perception, and awareness of weaknesses in the proposed change. To overcome resistance, managers might develop techniques including participation, open communication, advance warning, sensitivity, and security.

11 **Explain why change efforts fail.** Change efforts fail for a number of reasons, including faulty thinking or an inadequate process, lack of resources or commitment, poor timing, or a resistant cultural climate.

12 **Explain the purpose of an organizational development program.** The purpose of an organizational development program is to bring about a system of organizational renewal that can effectively cope with environmental changes. In doing so, OD strives to maximize organizational effectiveness as well as individual work satisfaction.

REVIEW QUESTIONS

1. What are the seven factors that influence culture? Use specific examples to explain how they interact.
2. How is culture evidenced?
3. What is the role of managers in creating culture? What is the role of employees in creating culture?
4. How does culture influence organizational effectiveness? What factors contribute to an effective culture?
5. What are the four kinds of change that can occur in an organization?
6. What are the differences between evolutionary change and revolutionary change?
7. What are the differences between planned and unplanned change?
8. What are the steps of planned change?
9. What organizational qualities promote change?
10. Describe three reasons that people resist change, and explain what managers can do to overcome that resistance.
11. What are three reasons that change efforts fail?
12. Why do organizations adopt an organizational development program?

DISCUSSION QUESTIONS FOR CRITICAL THINKING

1. What specific examples can you give to demonstrate the manifestations of culture (statements of principle, stories, slogans, symbols, heroes, etc.) in an organization with which you have been involved?
2. Can a change made in one area of a company—in strategy, for instance—lead to a change in other areas? Why or why not?

3. If appointed CEO of your company, would you adopt a revolutionary or evolutionary change agent style? Why? Which would be more effective?

4. Demonstrate your understanding of force field analysis by applying it to a change with which you have been involved.

INTERNET EXERCISES

Check the text Web site at http://plunkett.swcollege.com for updated links to the Internet Exercises.

1. In order to be proactive, instead of reacting to change, managers must anticipate and make change happen. List some rules for leading change.
   http://www.innovnet.com/change4.htm

2. Read Johnson & Johnson's credo. What manifestations of culture (stories, slogans, heroes, ceremonies, symbols, climate, statements of principle, the physical environment) does it make and how does it convey the company's culture?
   http://www.jnj.com/who_is_jnj/cr_usa.html

3. Use a search engine to find a situation where a company made a strategic change, a structural change, a process-oriented change, or a people-centered change. Give a thorough description of the change.
   http://www.altavista.com
   http://www.google.com

APPLICATION CASE

A Cultural Mismatch

Harty Press operates out of a complex of one-story cinder-block buildings in the industrial section of New Haven, Connecticut. A commercial printer of everything from local advertising to slick annual reports, Harty has stood unfailing since its founding in 1911. Inside the plant the air is ripe with the smell of ink and the hum of presses. Harty's CEO George R. Platt grew up working in the company, first during summers, and then full time after college to work alongside his father and founder, George E. Platt.

When George R. Platt took over Harty Press, the business had 20 employees and $1 million in sales. With a keen eye for assessing Harty's strengths and weaknesses—and with a drive to grow—Platt beefed up quality and customer service. He found higher-margin market niches. The rapid technological changes overtaking the industry, however, limited future growth. Printing was moving quickly from the world of film, type, and light to the computer-driven, digitized world of the desktop. Platt tried to solve the problem by hiring a specialist to computerize Harty's prepress process. But Platt soon learned that building digital desktop capability from scratch would cost more than a million dollars.

The solution to that problem—and to growth—came in the form of Pre-Press Graphics. Based in nearby Branford, Connecticut, Pre-Press Graphics had been one of the first in the state to aggressively use advanced desktop technology. It had already done much of the costly research and development work Platt knew he would have to undertake. In addition, because the owner of Pre-Press had been spending a lot of time, money, and energy on the development of technology, the business had plateaued. The owner was looking for a buyer.

Harty Press bought Pre-Press Graphics for $500,000; and the merging of the two companies began. Platt immediately had major problems with the change:

- It was hard to imagine two more different cultures than those of Harty Press and Pre-Press Graphics.
- Harty is based in the heart of an industrial neighborhood. Pre-Press sits twelve miles away, out in the bustling world of office parks and fast-food joints.
- Harty's workers, many with 10 to 20 years of service, wear smudged aprons, have ink under their fingernails, and carry union cards. At Pre-Press, people in running shoes and jeans sit in front of computer screens.
- Harty's management is low key, loose, and creates autonomy. The management at Pre-Press was intense, precise, and controlling.
- The move of Harty's twelve-person prepress department to consolidate with Pre-Press created chaos. The firms' procedures and systems did not dovetail. Neither group had been given enough notice to plan for and comprehend the effects of the merger.
- Although Harty had bought Pre-Press specifically for its knowledge of desktop publishing, Pre-Press employees who knew how to operate the computers saw that Harty workers lacked those skills. They became protective of their knowledge and their jobs.
- A key Harty employee was sent to Pre-Press to work on the transition. He was sent with no job description and no defined role; an immediate hassle resulted with former Pre-Press managers.
- Training courses on computer technology lasted for only one session. Then "familiarization training" on the computer was announced. No one knew what that meant, and no one ever figured it out because it never took place.

http://www.hartypress.com

Questions

1. Based on the experiences of Harty Press and Pre-Press Graphics, what is the importance of culture in the change process?
2. What specific cultural factors caused problems in the change process? Cite examples to support your answer.
3. What specific mistakes did Harty and Pre-Press make in the change process? Cite examples to support your answer.
4. Using as your guide the nine steps for planned change discussed in this chapter, construct a change process to successfully merge Harty Press with Pre-Press Graphics.

Source: Edward O. Welles, "Mis-Match," *Inc.* (June 1994), pp. 70–79.

VIDEO CASE

Central Michigan Community Hospital: Managing Change

Central Michigan Community Hospital (CMCH) has provided the residents of Isabella County with high-quality health-care services since 1943. It is a 151-bed, nonsectarian, nonprofit, acute care hospital, which now grants practice privileges to more than 120 doctors and renders a wide variety of health-care services. The hospital is committed to quality and was rewarded for that commitment in 1994 by being named one of the top 100 hospitals in the United States. The award cited CMCH as a benchmark institution among rural hospitals. The following year, the hospital was one of 75 (of the previous 100) to exceed the median industry performance, gaining an honorable mention.

Despite past success CMCH's board, administration, and medical staff are confronting a great deal of uncertainty and must change to meet the challenges of today and the future. Patients, employees, insurance companies, and state and federal governments—all are demanding an ever-higher quality of services while containing costs. The hospital and its leaders, like many others, are involved in a fundamental shift in emphasis in the health-care industry—from a complete focus on care toward a more balanced focus on care and business concerns. This shift reflects, in part, the proliferation of managed care and health maintenance organizations (HMOs). One concern at CMCH is that hospitals in nearby larger cities (within a 30-mile radius) can offer more attractive health-care packages and lure better paying customers away, leaving CMCH with poorer patients and those who are uninsured or underinsured. Another concern is that an increasingly older population will require more time for diagnosis and treatment, which might impede the hospital's ability to expand its emergency care. Also, the hospital recognizes a need to serve the rapidly increasing number of tourists in the area (some 30,000 visitors a day) who might need medical care while there.

The board, administration, and medical staff have responded to the changing needs of CMCH's constituencies and expressed its commitment to them in a variety of ways by (1) continuing to provide basic inpatient and outpatient health-care services; (2) beginning to collaborate with other health-care providers, employers, and consumers to provide access to a wide range of health-care products and services; (3) striving to improve the health of the community at large and its patients; and (4) seeking to develop better methods of meeting consumer needs for quality and value in an integrated health-care delivery system. Evidence of this commitment can be found throughout the hospital. For example, a major renovation to accommodate new equipment at CMCH recognizes the trend toward greater use of outpatient services, including diagnostic, therapeutic, behavioral, and surgical procedures.

Change is difficult for most individuals and organizations, but the problem is particularly salient in large health-care facilities. The culture promotes autonomy of doctors, nurses, and other professionals in their decision making, and thus, they are often reluctant to take direction (or even suggestions) from others. Disputes over issues are often heated and sometimes result in even more resistance to change. To be successful, CMCH will have to overcome resistance to change and implement decisions that will best position it to meet the demands of the rapidly changing health-care environment and remain a leader in its industry.

http://www.cmhs.org

For Discussion:

1. What types of changes should CMCH implement in order to respond to its environment and compete with other health-care providers in the region?
2. What are some of the recommendations for handling change that CMCH employees and administrators submitted?
3. How would you describe the types of organizational change being implemented at CMCH?

Staffing

KEY TERMS

affirmative action
assessment center
benefit
collective bargaining
compensation
demotion
development
discrimination
disparate impact
equal employment opportunity
human resource manager
job analysis
job evaluation
orientation
performance appraisal
perk
personnel manager
promotion
recruiting
selection
separation
sexual harassment
staffing
test
training
transfer

LEARNING OBJECTIVES

After studying this chapter, you should be able to

1. Explain the importance of the staffing function
2. List and explain the eight elements of the staffing process
3. Describe the three primary staffing environments
4. Describe the four activities related to human resource planning
5. List and describe the primary screening devices used in the selection process
6. Explain the differences and similarities between training and development
7. Explain the purpose of a performance appraisal
8. Describe the four primary employment decisions
9. Explain the purposes and components of compensation

MANAGEMENT IN ACTION

The Container Store's Intense Employee Commitment

The Container Store, originator of the storage and organizational retail concept, was the first company to repeat at the top of *Fortune*'s annual list of 100 Best Companies to Work For. It did it by earning high marks from enthusiastic employees, with 97 percent saying "People care about each other here." To develop the list, *Fortune* asked 36,106 employees at 234 candidate companies to complete The Great Place to Work Trust Index (an employee survey that evaluates trust in management, pride in work and the company, and camaraderie). The companies provided *Fortune* with the entry-level salary for both professional and production or service workers and the number of workers in each category.

The Container Store operates retail, mail order, and online business devoted to storage products such as closet organization systems, decorative shelving, and wire and plastic bins. Garrett Boone, chief executive officer, and Kip Tindell, president, opened their first store in Dallas, Texas, in 1978. By 2000, the company had grown from a 1,600-square-foot space to 20 stores across the country ranging in size from 22,000 to 25,000 square feet. The Container Store's philosophy is centered on strict merchandising, superior customer service, and intense employee commitment. The passion for the company that employees at The Container Store feel comes from the top. Garrett and Kip can be found selling, dusting shelves, and helping with customer carry-outs.

One of The Container Store's core business philosophies is that three good people equal one great person. Elizabeth Barrett, vice president of operations, describes the characteristics of an indispensable employee as "One who has tremendous vision and relentless dedication to The Container Store's philosophy, culture and customer service level. That employee has a great enthusiasm for his or her job and a work ethic that is equally enthusiastic and comes from loving the job that they do."

Most employees at The Container Store were customers first. Barrett is an example. "I moved to Dallas from New York immediately after graduation from college. In September of 1981, I went into one of our original stores . . . looking for some part-time work that would keep me busy until my 'real' career began. I figured that I would put my liberal arts degree and my French major to use at a later time. I fell in love with the way The Container Store treats its customers and its employees, and here I am, 19 years later!" ■

Sources: "America's Top Employers," *Fortune* (January 2001), http://www.fortune.com/bestcompanies; "Employment: Success Story," *The Dallas Morning News* (3 September 2000); The Container Store at http://www.containerstore.com.

Employees' passion and commitment make The Container Store one of the 100 Best Companies to Work For.

INTRODUCTION

Explain the importance of the staffing function

staffing
Efforts designed to attract, hire, train, develop, reward, and retain the people needed to accomplish an organization's goals and promote job satisfaction.

The primary purposes of **staffing** are to attract, hire, train, develop, reward, and retain the required number of good people, helping them meet their needs while they help the organization meet its needs. Texas entrepreneur Courtland L. Logue has created or managed 28 companies—running them for a time, then selling some and acquiring others. Here is what he thinks about the importance of finding and hiring the right number of good people (Nulty, 1995):

> *First, get good people. If you don't have good people, that's your fault. Remember, .200 hitters don't win championships. Overpay and get .300 hitters. Just don't hire more of them than you need.*

"Good" people are those with proven performance records or potential that demonstrates they will or do fit into the organization's culture and climate. Frank Sonnenberg, business author and consultant, adds this insight: "The point is, you don't just hire bodies, but seek employees that you value enough to invest in" (Brown, 1995). Since most job applicants have some deficiencies, the key issue is the employer's willingness and ability to help applicants remedy their deficiencies. Providing needed investments (training, for example) makes good people even better, making them more confident and capable and more valuable to their organizations.

Once good people are on board, organizations must retain them. This goal leads to the second part of staffing: helping employees meet their needs while they help the organization to meet its needs. Lorry Lokey, founder and CEO of Business Wire, a wireless news provider, believes the following: "My people spend a fourth of their lives—or more—working for this company, so they deserve to have their needs taken care of. . . ." His financial chief, Constance Cummings, adds, "There's no fear here because we believe in doing everything we can to hold on to good employees and to improve the quality of their lives." These few words sum up the essence of the company's staffing philosophy" (Fraser, 1995).

http://www.businesswire.com

Staffing, which follows organizing, links people and processes. People create an organization's intellectual capital—that which makes the organization unique and separates it from its competition. Without dedicated, knowledgeable, and motivated employees, the best-laid plans cannot bear fruit. Empowered people working in a diverse and open climate—one based on mutual trust and respect—can make bad plans work and good plans better.

This chapter examines many major investments that organizations make in their human resources, along with the laws, principles, and processes that affect staffing in the United States. Chapter 20 includes staffing concerns for organizations operating in an international environment.

RESPONSIBILITY FOR STAFFING

In small organizations, every manager is responsible for the staffing function; even worker teams can participate. A large firm usually establishes a separate department dedicated to staffing. A subunit that focuses on staffing is usually called a personnel or human resource department. Managers of such a department—

human resource manager or personnel manager
A manager who fulfills one or more personnel, or human resource, functions.

human resource managers, or **personnel managers**—assist others by planning, organizing, staffing, coordinating, controlling, and sometimes executing specific personnel and human resource (P/HR) management functions.

Some human resource managers and practitioners are specialists who focus on a specific aspect of P/HR management—compensation, training, or recruiting, for example. Others are generalists who are responsible for several functions. This book will use the terms *human resource manager* and *human resource specialist* to refer to both groups.

STAFFING PROCESS

List and explain the eight elements of the staffing process

Figure 11.1 summarizes the eight elements of the staffing process. The list that follows briefly describes each element:

1. *Human resource planning.* This aspect of staffing involves assessing current employees, forecasting future needs, and making plans to add or remove workers. To adapt to changing strategies and changing needs, managers must continually update their plans.
2. *Recruiting.* In this step, managers with positions to fill look for qualified people inside or outside the company.
3. *Selection.* This step involves testing and interviewing candidates and hiring the best available.
4. *Orientation.* In this phase of staffing, new employees learn about their surroundings, meet their coworkers, and learn about the rules, regulations, and benefits of the company.
5. *Training and development.* To train and develop employees, employers establish programs to help workers learn their jobs and improve their skills.
6. *Performance appraisal.* As part of the controlling function of management, managers must establish the criteria for evaluating work, schedule formal sessions to discuss evaluations with employees, and determine how to reward high achievers and motivate others to become high achievers. All these tasks are part of the performance-appraisal element of staffing.
7. *Compensation.* This aspect of staffing relates to establishing pay and, in some cases, benefits.
8. *Employment decisions.* Workers' careers involve transfers, promotions, demotions, layoffs, and firings. Making decisions about these career developments is part of the staffing process.

FIGURE 11.1 *Eight elements of the staffing process*

1. Human Resource Planning
2. Recruiting
3. Selection
4. Orientation
5. Training and Development
6. Performance Appraisal
7. Compensation
8. Employment Decisions—Transfers, Promotions, Demotions, Layoffs, and Firings

Not all the elements of the staffing process are components of every staffing problem. Recruiting, for example, is not necessary unless new employees are needed. Some elements are constants, however. Planning, training, and appraisal accompany the primary management functions. Therefore, every manager must be concerned about staffing.

STAFFING ENVIRONMENTS

Staffing, like other managerial functions, is subject to outside influences. Events and pressures from many sources in an organization's external environment—customers, suppliers, and competitors, for example—influence staffing and dictate the human resource plans and strategies necessary to carry them out.

Legal Environment

Describe the three primary staffing environments

The laws and principles that govern a community inevitably affect the way companies do business. Consider just a few of the legal issues that pertain to even the smallest company: contracts, criminal law, negligence, and equity. A legal concept that has a great impact on organizations today is the idea that the law is a tool to correct and prevent wrongs to individuals and groups. Laws and legal principles act as controls on managers who discharge staffing responsibilities.

Executive orders and laws generated by federal, state, county, and city agencies regulate how companies, usually those with fifteen or more employees, must conduct staffing. So complex are these regulations, and so great is the potential for harm due to noncompliance, that many large companies and institutions hire attorneys and specialists to deal with reporting and disclosure requirements.

Figure 11.2 highlights federal laws regarding three topics: equal employment opportunity, affirmative action, and sexual harassment. The paragraphs that follow will review each topic.

Equal Employment Opportunity

discrimination
Using illegal criteria when making employment decisions. Discrimination results in an adverse impact on members of protected groups.

equal employment opportunity
Legislation designed to protect individuals and groups from discrimination.

Federal laws prohibit discrimination in employment decisions. **Discrimination** means using illegal criteria in staffing. Laws that prohibit discrimination are designed to guarantee **equal employment opportunity**. The Equal Employment Opportunity Commission (EEOC) enforces antidiscrimination laws. In 1998 alone, more than 12,500 claims of discrimination filed with the U.S. Equal Employment Opportunity Commission based on race/color, national origin, gender, religion, age, or disability were found to be meritorious allegations or were resolved in favor of the complaining party (U.S. Equal Employment Opportunity Commission, Enforcement Statistics, http://www.eeoc.gov/stats/all.html).

According to the United States Senate (1972), it is unlawful for an employer to do either of the following:

1. To fail or refuse to hire or to discharge an individual solely on the basis of race, color, religion, sex, age, national origin, or handicap
2. To limit, segregate, or classify employees or applicants for employment in any way that would tend to deprive the individual of employment opportunities solely on the basis of race, color, religion, sex, age, national origin, or handicap

FIGURE 11.2 *U.S. federal legislation related to staffing*

Federal Legislation	Description of Provisions
Equal Pay Act of 1963	Prohibits paying employees of one sex less than employees of the opposite sex for doing roughly equivalent work. Applies to private employers.
Title VI 1964 Civil Rights Act	In staffing decisions, prohibits discrimination based on race, color, religion, sex, or national origin. Applies to employers receiving federal financial assistance.
Title VII 1964 Civil Rights Act (amended 1972)	Prohibits discrimination based on race, color, religion, sex, or national origin. Applies to private employers of fifteen or more employees; federal, state, and local governments; unions; and employment agencies.
Executive Orders 11246 and 11375 (1965)	In staffing decisions, prohibits discrimination based on race, color, religion, sex, or national origin. Establishes requirements for affirmative action plans. Applies to federal contractors and subcontractors.
Age Discrimination in Employment Act of 1967 (amended 1978)	Prohibits age discrimination in staffing decisions against people over 40 years of age. Applies to all employers of 20 or more employees.
Title I 1968 Civil Rights Act	Prohibits interference with a person's exercise of rights with respect to race, color, religion, sex, or national origin.
Rehabilitation Act of 1973	In staffing decisions, prohibits discrimination based on certain physical and mental handicaps. Applies to employers doing business with or for the federal government.
Vietnam Era Veterans Readjustment Act of 1974	In staffing decisions, prohibits discrimination against disabled veterans and Vietnam-era veterans.
Privacy Act of 1974	Establishes the right of employees to examine letters of reference concerning them unless the right is waived.
Revised Guidelines on Employee Selection (1976, 1978, and 1979)	Establishes a single set of guidelines that define discrimination on the basis of race, color, religion, sex, and national origin. The guidelines provide a framework for making legal employment decisions about hiring, promoting, and demoting and for the proper use of tests and other selection procedures.
Pregnancy Discrimination Act of 1978	Prohibits discrimination in employment based on pregnancy, childbirth, or related medical conditions.
Equal Employment Opportunity Guidelines of 1981—Sexual Harassment	Prohibits sexual harassment when such conduct is an explicit or implicit condition of employment, if the employee's response becomes a basis for employment or promotion decisions, or if it interferes with an employee's performance. The guidelines protect men and women.
Equal Employment Opportunity Guidelines of 1981—National Origin	Identifies potential national-origin discrimination to include fluency-in-English job requirements and disqualification due to foreign training or education. Identifies national-origin harassment in the work environment to include ethnic slurs and physical conduct with the purpose of creating an intimidating or hostile environment or unreasonable interference with work.
Equal Employment Opportunity Guidelines of 1981—Religion	Determines that employers have an obligation to accommodate religious practices of employees unless they can demonstrate that doing so would result in undue hardship. Accommodation may be achieved through voluntary substitutes, flexible scheduling, lateral transfer, and change of job assignment.

(continued)

FIGURE 11.2 *(Concluded)*

Federal Legislation	Description of Provisions
Mandatory Retirement Act (amended 1987)	Determines that employees may not be forced to retire before age 70.
Americans with Disabilities Act of 1990	Prohibits discrimination on the basis of physical or mental handicap.
Civil Rights Act of 1991	Permits women, persons with disabilities, and persons who are religious minorities to have a jury trial and sue for punitive damages if they can prove intentional hiring and workplace discrimination. Also requires companies to provide evidence that the business practice that led to the discrimination was not discriminatory but was job related for the position in question and consistent with business necessity.

A company's best defense against accusations of discrimination or bias in hiring is to be certain that any employment practice or device adheres to the following (Schuler, 1995):

- It is job related—that is, it is predictive of success or failure on a specific job.
- It is a business necessity—that is, the company must do what it does to provide for its continued existence.
- It acknowledges a bona fide occupational qualification (BFOQ)—for example, a licensing or age requirement.
- It honors a bona fide seniority system (BFSS)—that is, a seniority system established and maintained that does not have the intent to illegally discriminate.

Protected Groups

The federal government has created several protected groups—people against whom it is illegal to discriminate. These groups are women, the disabled or differently abled, and minorities. Federal guidelines list minorities as follows:

- Hispanic-surnamed Americans
- Asians and Pacific Islanders
- African Americans not of Hispanic origin
- Native Americans
- Native Alaskans

As defined under federal law, the differently abled in America are those who:

- Have a physical or mental impairment that substantially limits one or more major life activities
- Have a record of such impairment
- Are regarded as having such an impairment

Two major laws govern the protection of people with such disabilities: the Rehabilitation Act of 1973 (covering firms doing business with the federal government) and the Americans with Disabilities Act of 1990 (covering nearly every firm with fifteen or more employees). Protection is extended to people with current or past physical and mental conditions. Examples of those protected are people with dependency on legal drugs whose dependency does not impair work performance; people with a history of cancer, heart trouble, or a contagious disease, providing that their conditions do not pose a significant risk to coworkers or render them unable to perform their work; and people who have undergone or who now are undergoing rehabilitation for their drug dependencies.

Under both laws employers must make reasonable accommodations (that cause no "undue hardship") for the disabled. Jobs may have to be redefined, removing those tasks that the person with a disability cannot perform. Prerequisites such as passing a physical exam may have to be waived when parts of that exam are not job related. Physical facilities may have to be altered to accommodate access by persons with disabilities. Signs in Braille and wheelchair ramps are but two examples. According to the Job Accommodation Network, a federal agency (Kleiman, "In Brief," 1994):

http://janweb.icdi.wvu.edu

> *For every dollar spent by businesses to accommodate workers with disabilities, employers are realizing a gain of $30 in benefits. . . . Among the benefits: the ability to hire or retain a qualified employee; elimination of the cost of training a new employee; savings in worker's compensation and other insurance costs; and increased productivity. Nationwide, 261 companies reported the average cost of making adjustments for workers with disabilities is $735. The average benefit is $22,065.*

In 1998, the U.S. Supreme Court ruled that Title VII covers claims of same-sex sexual harassment but does not include claims of "sexual orientation discrimination" (*Bibby v. The Philadelphia Coca-Cola Bottling Co.*). Several states, counties, and muncipalities have added the category of sexual orientation to fair housing, employment, public accommodations, and credit laws that already protect people in the preceding categories from discrimination. The ten states with laws protecting lesbians and gay men against workplace discrimination are California, Connecticut, Hawaii, Massachusetts, Minnesota, New Hampshire, New Jersey, Rhode Island, Vermont, and Wisconsin; the District of Columbia also has these protection laws in place. In addition, many companies, including Microsoft, Levi Strauss, Hewlett-Packard, Fox Inc., Ben & Jerry's, and Disney, have adopted nondiscrimination policies with regard to sexual orientation. A few states and cities, however, specifically exclude protecting people from discrimination on the basis of their sexual orientation.

http://www.aclu.org/issues/gay/gaylaws.html

By law, managers must refrain from employment decisions that produce a disparate impact on these protected groups. A **disparate impact** is any result that harms one group more than another. Not hiring an applicant because she is a woman causes a disparate impact. Using an employment test that eliminates a significantly greater percentage of protected groups than unprotected groups also causes a disparate impact. The actions in both these cases are considered discriminatory under law. The organization and the managers involved in the discriminatory decisions would be subject to criminal penalties.

disparate impact
The result of using employment criteria that have a significantly greater negative effect on some groups than on others.

Title VII of the 1964 Civil Rights Act requires parties who file discrimination complaints to do so within 180 days of the alleged violation. It provides two basic remedies when discrimination is proved: reinstatement and recovery of lost pay. The Civil Rights Act of 1991 amended the 1964 Civil Rights Act to allow for the recovery of *punitive* damages if it can be proved that a company engaged in a discriminatory practice with malice or with reckless indifference to the law. Limits placed on these damages are as follows:

- Between 15 and 100 employees: $50,000
- Between 101 and 200 employees: $100,000
- Between 201 and 500 employees: $200,000
- Over 500 employees: $300,000

Affirmative Action

affirmative action
A plan to give members of specific groups priority in hiring or promotion.

Some laws go beyond prohibiting discrimination. Laws that mandate **affirmative action** require employers to make an extra effort to employ protected groups. Affirmative action laws apply to employers that have, in the past, practiced discrimination or failed to develop a workforce that is representative of the whole population of their community. (Under current laws, affirmative action is not required with regard to disabled Americans.) The fact that an organization has an affirmative action plan does not necessarily mean that the organization practiced unfair employment practices in the past, however. Managers of many organizations choose to develop affirmative action plans even when the law does not require them to do so. Affirmative action plans must include goals and timetables for achieving greater representation of and equity for protected groups.

Sexual Harassment

sexual harassment
Unwelcome verbal or physical conduct of a sexual nature that implies, directly or indirectly, that sexual compliance is a condition of employment or advancement or that interferes with an employee's work performance.

Title VII of the 1964 Civil Rights Act and guidelines established by the EEOC prohibit sexual harassment (Moskal, 1989). **Sexual harassment** includes unwelcome sexual advances, requests for sexual favors, and other verbal or physical conduct of a sexual nature when

1. Submission to such conduct is an explicit or implicit term or condition of employment
2. Submission to or rejection of such conduct is used as a basis for any employment decision
3. Such conduct has the purpose of unreasonably interfering with the individual's work performance or creating an intimidating, hostile, or offensive working environment

Sexual harassment creates anger, suspicion, fear, stress, mistrust, victims, and costs in a workplace. Costs are both psychological and financial. Companies experience losses in employee morale, loyalty, company reputation, and, correspondingly, reductions in quality and productivity. According to research by Ellen Bravo and Ellen Cassedy (1992):

- In general, men and women have different views of what constitutes harassment.
- Most harassers are men, but most men are not harassers.
- Intentional harassment is an exercise of power, not romantic attraction.
- Ninety percent of harassment cases involve men harassing women; 9 percent involve same-sex harassment; 1 percent involve women harassing men.

Preventing sexual harassment is no easy task; efforts to do so begin with top management. They must create a clear policy and communicate to everyone that sexual harassment will not be tolerated. Every employee must be made aware of

http://www.9to5.org

what sexual harassment is and is not. In most organizations creating awareness means bringing in outside experts who will conduct training. The National Association of Working Women, 9 to 5, offers these guidelines for creating a meaningful policy (Bravo and Cassedy, 1992):

- Involve all employees.
- Clearly define procedures to protect the complainant and the accused.
- Investigate promptly, using a team of impartial investigators.
- Give several options for reporting, including informal channels.
- Indicate appropriate discipline, including counseling.

An option for reporting sexual harassment is email, the subject of this chapter's Managing Technology feature. Email flattens hierarchies within the bounds of an office. Many employees find it far easier to communicate to their supervisor and colleagues via email than in a pressure-filled meeting room. Whenever an employee has something difficult to say, email can make it easier.

MANAGING TECHNOLOGY
Parts of Email

Email messages can be broken up into four parts: the header, the subject line, the body, and the signature. The header provides useful information about who sent you the message and from where. The subject line is the theme of the message. The body is the message itself. The signature is a personalized closing.

One advantage of email is being able to prioritize messages, whereas with voice mail or answering machine messages you must listen to them in sequence no matter how unimportant. When you check email messages, a list of senders and topics is displayed on your computer screen. You can use the subject lines to prioritize messages and select which message to read first, then reply immediately by clicking a reply button, typing a response, and clicking "send." Delete junk mail and other mail that does not pertain to you without opening it. If you don't want to be on someone's group mailing list, tell him or her. Make sure all the people on your group mailing list want to be there. Software packages such as Microsoft Outlook can help you filter and categorize your email.

Make the subject line in your email as detailed as possible. Readers of your email should sense from the subject line how urgent the message is and why it pertains to them. For example, assume you need to reschedule tomorrow morning's group meeting. The boss wants the meeting to begin at 9:00 A.M. rather than 8:00 A.M. You need to advise six people of the change in schedule quickly. By using email, you can immediately broadcast the message to the six people and request that they reply via email to confirm that they received your message. Instead of typing in "meeting" as the subject, type, "meeting postponed to 9:00 A.M."

Begin your message with a friendly greeting. Use the person's first name, if you know him or her on a first-name basis. If not, you can be more formal and use a courtesy title and last name, such as Dr. Jones. If your message is going to a group, use a generic greeting, such as "Greetings."

Messages should be concise. When you do not know the person, identify yourself in the first line of your message. If you are replying to another email, copy pertinent parts of the original message into your own message. For all messages, briefly state why you are writing and what you need from the recipient. Limit your paragraphs to around three sentences, and separate the paragraphs by a blank line. (This makes it easier to read a screen of text.)

Include a simple closing such as "Thanks" or "Regards." On a separate line, put two hyphens. On another line put your name. Or, you can use a signature file, a feature of some email programs. A signature file automatically inserts text of your choosing at the end of all your messages. You might consider including your name, title, work address, and telephone number(s) in your signature file.

Sociocultural Environment

http://www.census.gov

http://www.dol.gov

http://www.bls.gov

The U.S. labor force is becoming larger and more diverse. In 1999, according to the U.S. Census Bureau, the civilian labor force, those 16 years old and over, numbered 139.4 million. Former Secretary of Labor, Alexis M. Herman, delivered a report on Labor Day 1999 entitled "*Futurework*—Trends and Challenges for Work in the 21st Century." This report examined where the United States has been, where the United States is, and where the country is going.

> *In 1995, the United States was estimated to be 83 percent white, 13 percent black, 1 percent American Indian, Eskimo, and Aleut, and 4 percent Asian and Pacific Islander. Ten percent of Americans, mostly blacks and whites, were also of Hispanic origin. Nearly one in eleven Americans was foreign born. . . . Trends show that whites will be a declining share of the future total population while the Hispanic share will grow faster than that of non-Hispanic blacks. By 2050, minorities are projected to rise from one in every four Americans to almost one in every two. The Asian and Pacific Islander population is also expected to increase ("The changing face of the workforce,"* Futurework, *http://www.dol.gov/dol/asp/public/futurework/report/chapter1/main.htm#2b.).*
>
> *Nearly 83 percent of all adults ages 25 and over have completed high school, and 24 percent have obtained a bachelor's degree or more ("Educational Attainment Is Rising,"* Futurework, *http://www.dol.gov/dol/asp/public/futurework/report/chapter1/main.htm#3b).*
>
> *Since 1950, the proportion of men in the labor force has declined from 86 percent to 75 percent. In contrast, the trend for women is on the rise. In 1950, one-third of women worked outside the home. Almost 50 years later, 60 percent of women are in the labor force ("Women Are Working More; Men Are Working Less,"* Futurework, *http://www.dol.gov/dol/asp/public/futurework/report/chapter1/main.htm#4b).*

Cultural Diversity

Differing sociocultural groups both inside and outside organizations make demands on and contribute to those organizations. They constitute any organization's stakeholders, help shape its culture and climate, and must have adequate representation in all staffing activities.

In the past most managers tried to create a homogeneous workforce—to treat everyone in the same way and make people fit the dominant corporate culture. These efforts did not always build a stable, committed group of employees. What was needed—and what is rapidly appearing in enlightened corporations—is respect for what workers from different backgrounds bring to the workplace. Across America managers are participating in workshops designed to facilitate understanding among diverse groups, not just tolerance of one another's existence.

Glass Ceilings and Glass Walls

The terms *glass ceiling* and *glass wall* refer to invisible barriers of discrimination that block the careers of women and other protected groups (Kleiman, "Some," 1992). A glass ceiling is discrimination that keeps individuals from protected groups out of upper-level management jobs; a glass wall prevents them from pursuing fast-track career paths. Do these invisible barriers really exist? The data indicate that *something* is keeping protected groups out of the top jobs.

> *According to the 1995 report of the Glass Ceiling Commission, only six-tenths of one percent of senior management positions in the nation's largest companies were held by blacks,*

four-tenths of a percent by Hispanics, and three-tenths of a percent by Asian Americans. Women held between three and five percent of these positions. White males made up 43 percent of the work force but held 95 percent of the senior management jobs ("Discrimination, Though Diminishing, Persists," Futurework, *http://www.dol.gov/dol/asp/public/futurework/report/chapter5/main.htm#6b).*

http://www.catalystwomen.org

In 1992 Catalyst, a nonprofit research organization that focuses on women's issues in the workplace, conducted another survey about job discrimination. The survey revealed that human resource managers often steer women away from jobs in marketing and production. Stereotyped as support providers, women end up in staff positions. One reason for the perpetuation of the stereotype is that many men, especially those in the upper ranks of management, feel uncomfortable dealing with women. The Catalyst study suggested that women should "find out what type of experience companies require of their executives and then seek to get it." The report also suggested that "companies should create programs to encourage mentoring and career development and to discourage gender stereotyping" (Fuchsberg, 1992). See this chapter's Valuing Diversity feature.

http://www.statefarm.com

The cost of discrimination against women can be high in terms of lost morale, commitment, and productivity. Penalties can be high as well. In 1992 State Farm Insurance paid $157 million to settle a case filed by 814 women. The women claimed that because of their sex, State Farm had refused to give them lucrative sales jobs. In addition to the settlement, the women's claims led to changes in the recruiting and hiring of State Farm agents in California. An affirmative action plan, in place since 1988, required the company to hire women for 50 percent of the sales agent jobs to be filled through 1998.

VALUING DIVERSITY

Diversity and Human Resource Managers

A primary responsibility for human resource managers is to manage diversity—that is, to see that individuals from diverse groups are attracted, hired, and valued. But the ethnic composition of 785 human resource executives surveyed in 1994 indicates that the majority of top HR officials are white (91.3 percent) and about evenly split between male and female. The remainder breaks down as follows: 5 percent African American, 1.7 percent Hispanic, and 1.6 percent Asian.

The Society for Human Resource Management, an association of HR professionals in Virginia, has about 53,000 members active in 44 different nations. It is currently working to diversify its leadership and membership. According to its president, Michael R. Losey, the society's typical member "is a white member who works at a firm with 1,000 or fewer employees. Almost half are younger than 40 and have an average annual salary of $50,000." About 83 percent of current members are nonminorities.

The above seems to justify the fear of minorities that predominantly white human resource managers will have trouble managing diversity. But the 1994 survey (conducted by the Society for Human Resource Management and the Chicago-based Commerce Clearing House) results should allay such fear. "Between 1983 and 1993, the number of women in their work forces increased an average of 69.1 percent; African Americans, 59.1 percent; Hispanics, 49.4 percent; and Asians, 44.4 percent."

Sources: Carol Kleiman, "Making Diversity Work," *Chicago Tribune* (1 May 1994), sec. 8, p. 1; Diversity Today, http://www.shrm.org/diversity.

http://www.aa.com

http://www.anheuser-busch.com

http://www.jnj.com

Many companies recognize that glass ceilings and glass walls exist and have worked hard to eliminate them. American Airlines requires corporate officers to submit detailed, cross-functional plans regarding the development of all high-potential women in middle management and above (Fuchsberg, 1992). Anheuser-Busch has a management-development program that moves women and minorities from jobs in inventory to jobs as coordinators and then to supervisory positions. Johnson & Johnson, the pharmaceutical giant, operates workshops to sensitize managers and supervisors to the problems of those striving for the top. The company has a significant number of women and minorities in high positions (Kleiman, "Some," 1992).

AIDS and Drug Testing

Acquired immune deficiency syndrome (AIDS) is a frightening condition that—until medical progress can prevent it—eventually leads to death. HIV, the virus that causes AIDS, cannot be casually transmitted; but fear of AIDS is a reality in the workplace. Companies need policies telling employees and managers how to deal with the issue. Federal law prohibits discrimination against employees suffering from AIDS and any other contagious diseases (Stodghill, 1993). Will a company accommodate the employee who does not want to work with an employee who has HIV? What will management do when an employee's routine physical reveals that he or she is HIV positive?

Most of America's largest companies have had experience with employees who are suffering from some sort of drug addiction. Less than half of these companies have drug policies. Employees with drug or alcohol dependencies can and do cause losses to their companies, themselves, and others. Workers with drug problems compromise safety, quality, and productivity.

According to the 1990 Americans with Disabilities Act, drug-addicted employees are protected from discrimination if they are currently enrolled in legitimate drug-intervention programs or have completed such programs and are drug free. Testing for drugs raises issues about employee privacy, because most drug tests involve blood and urine analysis. These tests can reveal conditions that an employer has no business knowing about. In addition, drug tests can produce false positive results. Many companies require drug testing for all applicants, and some require random testing of current employees involved in work that is potentially hazardous to themselves or others. Where a workforce is unionized, it is wise to involve the union in any drug-testing efforts before they are instituted.

Genetic Screening

Medical tests of a person's genetic makeup can identify his or her predisposition to diseases like heart disease and certain types of cancer. Such tests can be used to deny employment, insurance, and advancement (Hoerr, 1988). Few bans on genetic screening currently exist. Those that do are state and local efforts; no federal laws address the issue. To prevent confusion and injustice, however, employers must develop policies about the use of genetic screening.

In the American Medical Association's "Use of Genetic Testing by Employers," the Council on Ethical and Judicial Affairs points out that employers, insurers, and law enforcement agencies all have uses for genetic information and techniques. It concludes that generally it is inappropriate to exclude workers because of risk, but a limited testing might be done (1) if a disease were so rapidly serious and irreversible that monitoring could not prevent harm; (2) if data demonstrate that abnormality results in many susceptible persons; or (3) if the cost of lowering the toxic substance to protect the susceptible is too high. Testing must be done only with the informed consent of the employee or applicant for employment (JAMA, 1991; JAMA, 1992).

Union Environment

According to the U.S. Bureau of Labor Statistics, 16 million workers were union members in 1998—16 percent of employed men and 12 percent of employed women. That figure represented a significant decrease; 22.6 percent of American workers had union representation in 1977. From 1977 to 1992, union representation in the private sector fell from 23.3 percent to 11.9 percent. With the decline of manufacturing jobs in America, unions have turned to recruiting white-collar and service workers. In 1999, union membership rose by more than 265,000—the largest annual increase in 20 years, according to a federal Bureau of Labor Standards report released January 19, 2000. The percentage of U.S. workers who belong to unions remained steady at 13.9 percent, reversing a trend of decline. Most union members belong to unions affiliated with the American Federation of Labor/Congress of Industrial Organizations (AFL/CIO). The AFL/CIO had 13 million members in 2001.

http://www.aflcio.org

Companies that employ unionized workers must bargain collectively to create a contract, to enforce that contract, and to process complaints (called grievances) about how the contract is enforced. Unions typically bargain for their members' wages, hours, and working conditions. Whether the issue is employment, work methods, equipment, safety, or productivity improvement, a union can impede or support changes that managers want to make.

Collective Bargaining

collective bargaining
Negotiation between a union and an employer in regard to wages, benefits, hours, rules, and working conditions.

In **collective bargaining**, negotiators from management and a union sit down together and try to agree on the terms of a contract that will apply to the union's members for a fixed period of time. Both parties prepare for these negotiations by analyzing past problems and agreements, polling their constituents, building a list of demands, and creating strategies. Both want what they perceive to be the best deal for themselves, given their respective needs and priorities. Negotiations usually begin before an existing contract expires, and negotiators try to reach a new agreement while the contract is still in effect.

Grievance Processing

A labor agreement (contract) provides a process by which managers and workers can file grievances: complaints alleging that a contract violation has taken place. The process of filing a grievance usually begins at the lowest level. If no settlement can be reached at that level, the complaint is brought before those at successively higher levels. A grievance can progress to the point that it becomes a focus for top managers and union officials. When these parties cannot agree, a third party may be called in. Third parties are usually neutral professionals hired to recommend or enforce a settlement. A third party can be a mediator or an arbitrator. Mediators make recommendations. Arbitrators suggest settlements that are enforced. Arbitrators have the power to hold hearings, gather evidence, and render a decision to which both parties agree in advance to adhere.

HUMAN RESOURCE PLANNING

In planning to meet staffing needs, managers must know their organization's plans and what human resources are available. They study existing jobs by performing job analyses. They review their firm's past staffing needs, inventory current human resources, forecast personnel needs in light of strategic plans, and compare their human resource inventory to the forecast. Then, with line managers, they construct plans to expand the company's employee roster, maintain the status quo, or reduce the number of jobs. Figure 11.3 illustrates this process.

Job Analysis

Describe the four activities related to human resource planning

job analysis
A study that determines the duties associated with a job and the human qualities needed to perform it.

Before managers can determine personnel needs, they must perform a **job analysis** for each job. The first step in a job analysis is to prepare up-to-date descriptions that list the duties and skills required of each jobholder. Then managers must compare all the analyses to ensure that some jobholders are not duplicating the efforts of others. This comparison enhances effectiveness and efficiency in the organization.

To prepare an in-depth study of jobs, some companies employ job analysts. To do their work, job analysts (1) observe the job holder executing his or her duties; (2) review questionnaires completed by the job holder and supervisor; (3) conduct interviews with both; or (4) form a committee to analyze, review, and summarize the results. Job analysts may study more than one jobholder in a job category over several months.

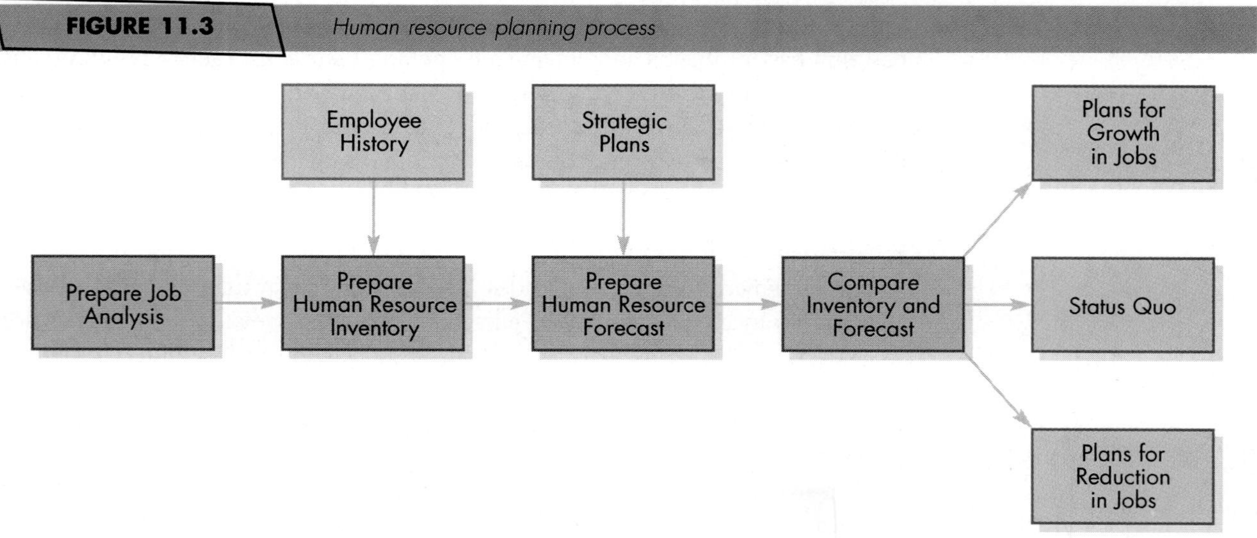

A job description details an employee's major work activities, levels of authority, equipment and materials used, and any physical demands or hazardous conditions.

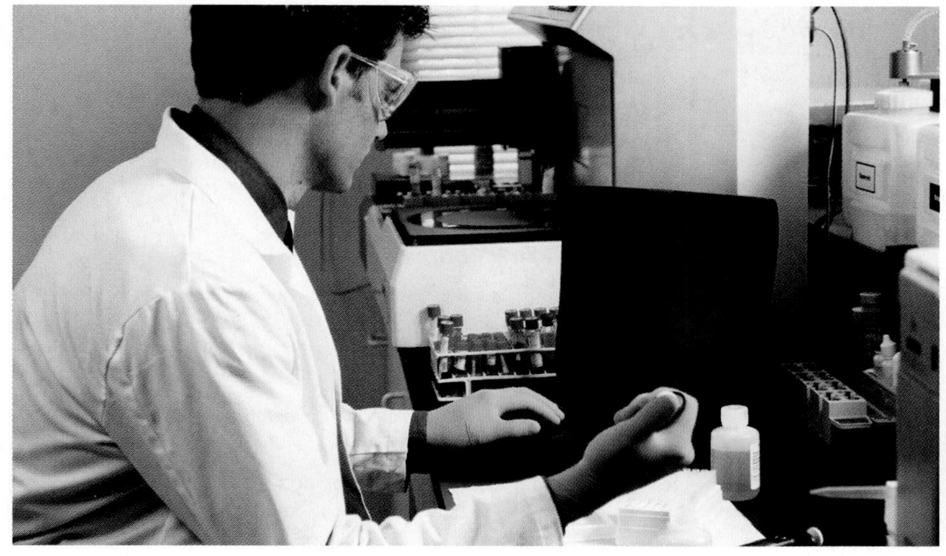

© 2001 PHOTODISC, INC.

The job analysis produces two coordinated documents: a *job description* and a *job specification*. Figure 11.4 presents an example of a job description. A job description cites the job title and the purpose of the job. It lists major work activities, the levels of authority above and below the jobholder, the equipment and materials the jobholder must use, and any physical demands or hazardous conditions the job may involve.

Figure 11.5 presents an example of a job specification. A job specification lists the human dimensions that a position requires. These include education, experience, skills, training, and knowledge. To avoid even the appearance of discrimination, those who create job specifications must take care to list only those factors directly linked to successful work performance.

Managers should review job descriptions and specifications regularly (usually each year) to ensure that they continue to reflect the positions to which they refer. Jobs evolve with time as changes in duties, knowledge bases, and equipment take place; the documents should reflect that evolution. When new positions are added to the organization, job descriptions and specifications must be created.

Human Resource Inventory

The human resource inventory provides information about an organization's present personnel. The inventory is a catalog of the skills, abilities, interests, training, experience, and qualifications of each member of its current workforce. A human resource inventory tells managers the qualifications, length of service, responsibilities, experiences, and promotion potential of each person in the firm. This information is updated periodically and supplemented by the most recent appraisals given to jobholders. What emerges is something similar to Figure 11.6 (page 350), a plan for staffing changes in management ranks. Developing such a chart makes managers aware of strengths and weaknesses in the current personnel base and allows them to develop a managerial succession plan.

FIGURE 11.4 *Example of a job description*

I Job Identification

Position Title: Customer-Service Representative

Department: Policyholders' Service

Effective Date:

II Function

To resolve policyholders' questions and make corresponding adjustments to policies if necessary after the policy is issued

III Scope

(a) Internal (within department)
Interacts with other members of the department in researching answers to problems

(b) External (within company)
Interacts with Policy Issue in regard to policy cancellations, Premium Accounting in regard to accounting procedures, and Accounting in regard to processing checks

(c) External (outside company)
Interacts with policyholders, to answer policy-related questions; client-company payroll departments, to resolve billing questions; and carriers, to modify policies

IV Responsibilities

The job holder will be responsible for

(a) Resolving policyholder inquiries about policies and coverage

(b) Initiating changes in policies with carriers (at the request of the insured)

(c) Adjusting in-house records as a result of approved changes

(d) Corresponding with policyholders regarding changes requested

(e) Reporting to the department manager any problems he or she is unable to resolve

V Authority Relationships

(a) Reporting relationships: Reports to the manager of Policyholders' Service

(b) Supervisory relationship: None

VI Equipment, Materials, and Machines

Personal computer, calculator, and video display terminal

VII Physical Conditions or Hazards

95 percent of the duties are performed sitting at either a desk or video display terminal

VIII Other

Other duties as assigned

Human Resource Forecasting

When forecasting an organization's personnel requirements, managers need to consider the strategic plans of the company and its normal level of attrition. Strategic

FIGURE 11.5 *Example of a job specification*

I Job Identification

Position: File/Mail Clerk

Department: Policyholders' Service

Effective Date:

II Education

Minimum: High school or equivalent

III Experience

Minimum: Six months of experience developing, monitoring, and maintaining a file system

IV Skills

Keyboarding skills: Must be able to set up own work and operate an IBM-compatible computer. No minimum WPM.

V Special Requirements

(a) Must be flexible to the demands of the organization for overtime and change in work load

(b) Must be able to comply with previously established procedures

(c) Must be tolerant of work requiring detailed accuracy (the work of monitoring file signouts and filing files, for example)

(d) Must be able to apply systems knowledge (to anticipate the new procedures that a system change will require, for example)

VI Behavioral Characteristics

(a) Must have high level of initiative as demonstrated by the ability to recognize a problem, resolve it, and report it to the supervisor

(b) Must have interpersonal skills as demonstrated by the ability to work as a team member and cooperate with other departments

plans determine the company's direction and its need for people. A long-term plan to stabilize the company at its present employment level will mean the need to replace those who leave.

Consider how a fictional furniture-making company translates strategic plans into actual personnel requirements. Suppose managers decide to increase production by 30 percent to meet a forecast increase in long-term demand. They analyze present capabilities, reject the use of overtime, and decide to add a third shift within three months. Using up-to-date job descriptions and specifications for the jobs to be added, managers determine how many and what kinds of employees to hire: nine production workers. Then the managers look at anticipated turnover in the existing shifts and support personnel. They decide to hire two new employees over the next three months to replace retiring employees. Therefore, the managers must acquire eleven new hires over the next three months.

FIGURE 11.6 Abbreviated human resource inventory

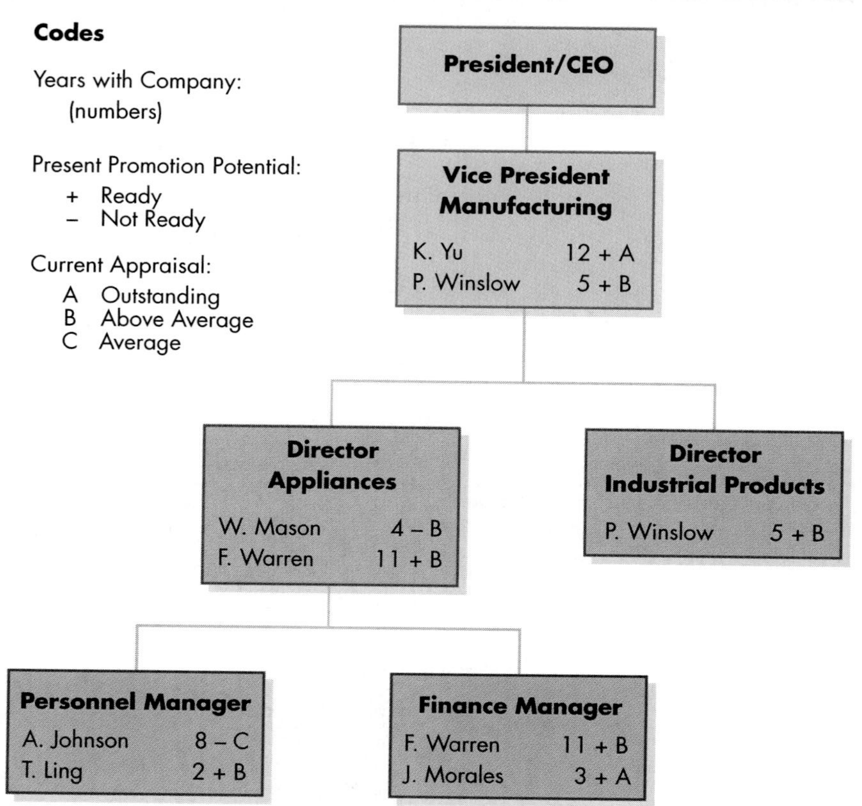

Inventory and Forecast Comparison

By comparing the inventory and the forecast, managers determine who in the organization is qualified to fill the projected openings and which personnel needs must be met externally. At the furniture company, managers decide that most of the needed personnel must come from outside, because many of the positions are entry-level jobs and members of the existing workforce will be needed to replace retiring workers.

If the managers decide to try to fill some of the vacancies from within, the first question is whether present employees qualify. If so, the managers must advertise the jobs within the company and encourage employees to apply for them. If current employees do not qualify, the next question is whether, through training and development, they can achieve the qualifications. If so, and if the company can afford the money and time, managers should prepare a plan to provide the needed training and development.

RECRUITMENT, SELECTION, AND ORIENTATION

recruiting
Efforts to find qualified people and encourage them to apply for positions that need to be filled.

With the forecast and inventory complete and job descriptions and specifications in hand, managers begin **recruiting**—the process of locating and soliciting a sufficient number of qualified candidates. Sources of applicants should include employed and unemployed prospects and temporary-help services. Managers may also want to investigate the option of leasing employees. This option involves working with a company that hires workers to lease to a client firm. The lease company hires, fires, complies with all government regulations, pays the leased employees, and is responsible for all human relations functions.

Company policies define strategies for and limits on filling vacancies. Among the concerns many companies have are the issues of *nepotism*—employing spouses or other relatives of existing employees—and of employing friends of employees. See this chapter's Ethical Management feature for some recent research in this area.

Strategies for Recruiting

At our fictitious furniture-making company, managers decide to look outside for the needed applicants. This decision presents several options. They can call private or state-operated employment services. They can run ads on the Internet, in

ETHICAL MANAGEMENT
Coping with Office Romances

Many organizations have policies that prevent the hiring of an existing employee's spouse. Others forbid two employees, once they marry, from continuing to work; one of them must quit or be fired. But Microsoft, like a growing number of companies, sees advantages to employing married couples. "The company's Seattle headquarters has at least a dozen married couples who met and courted during their 18-hour workdays. People who work together have, almost by definition, similar backgrounds, talents, and aspirations." Microsoft ought to know. Its billionaire CEO, Bill Gates, married one of his executives in 1993.

A 1994 survey by *Fortune* found that 70 percent or more of executives surveyed believed that office romances are "none of the company's business" and they "expose the company to the danger of sexual harassment suits." According to *Fortune*, "A growing body of academic research suggests that sexual attraction between co-workers, whether or not it is acted upon, may boost people's productivity on the job." One study comparing all-male teams with teams of both sexes discovered "that, without exception, the mixed-sex teams were faster and more imaginative at problem solving than the single-sex teams."

A Society for Human Resource Management (SHRM) 1998 Workplace Romance Survey of more than 600 human resource professionals found that while most companies do not have formal written policies, businesses have reported undesirable consequences due to office romances. The most likely outcome, according to 55 percent of the survey respondents, is marriage of the people involved in the office romance. Other outcomes had less favorable results, including complaints of favoritism by workers outside of the relationship (28 percent), claims of sexual harassment (24 percent), and decreased productivity of those involved in the office romance (24 percent).

- What experiences that relate to this ethical issue can you share with your classmates?

Sources: Anne B. Fisher, "Getting Comfortable with Couples in the Workplace," *Fortune* (3 October 1994), pp. 138–142, 144; SHRM Survey Finds Office Romances Are Often Frowned Upon By Employers (28 January 1998), http://www.shrm.org/press/releases/980128-3.htm.

newspapers and other publications, including trade journals and papers that appeal to racial and ethnic minorities. They can ask current employees to recommend qualified friends and relatives. (Many companies offer bonuses to employees who refer people who are eventually hired.) They can contact schools and offer a training program, and they can participate in job fairs. The managers can ask neighborhood and community groups to help them reach minorities and other protected groups and encourage them to apply for the jobs. If the company employs union labor, managers can contact trade unions in their search for skilled workers.

Many companies like to recruit for entry-level positions through internship programs. These offer a person, usually a student, a chance to gain some full- or part-time experience in his or her specialty area while assisting an employer. Networking with associates in various professional groups and trade associations often leads to referrals of likely prospects. Another option involves the use of public and private employment agencies. "Indeed, search firms that are industry-specific can help you locate the best in the field and could well be worth the price . . ." (Klimas, 1995).

Fees for hiring through private search firms can run as high as a new hire's first year's salary. According to an Employment Management Association survey of 36 firms, "the average cost for [hourly workers] and internal hires in 1993 was $3,207. . . . The average cost to hire [salaried] employees was $6,504 . . . which equals 14.1 percent of the average salaries [for that year]" (Kleiman, "In Brief," 1994).

Selection Process

List and describe the primary screening devices used in the selection process

selection
Evaluating applicants and finding those best qualified to perform a job and most likely to fit into the culture of the organization.

Selection is the process of deciding which candidate out of the pool of applicants possesses the qualifications for the job to be filled. Selection begins where recruiting ends. Its goal is to eliminate unqualified candidates through use of the screening devices shown in Figure 11.7.

Application Form

Usually, a prospective employee must fill out an application form as part of the selection process. An application form summarizes the candidate's education, skills, and experiences relating to the job for which he or she is applying. To avoid discrimination in the selection process, employers must not ask for information that is unrelated to the candidate's ability to perform the job successfully. Questions regarding home ownership, marital status, age, ethnic or racial background, and place of birth are usually irrelevant. When used properly, the completed application yields needed information. In addition, it indicates a person's ability to follow simple instructions and use basic language skills.

Preliminary Interview

In small firms a job candidate's first interview at a firm may be conducted by the very manager for whom the person hired will work. In large companies someone from the human resource staff may be the designated screening interviewer. In very large or sophisticated firms, a human relations specialist may conduct the preliminary interview. If a team has authority to hire, several team members may question each applicant. This procedure is usually the case if the team is self-managing.

FIGURE 11.7 *Screening devices of the selection process*

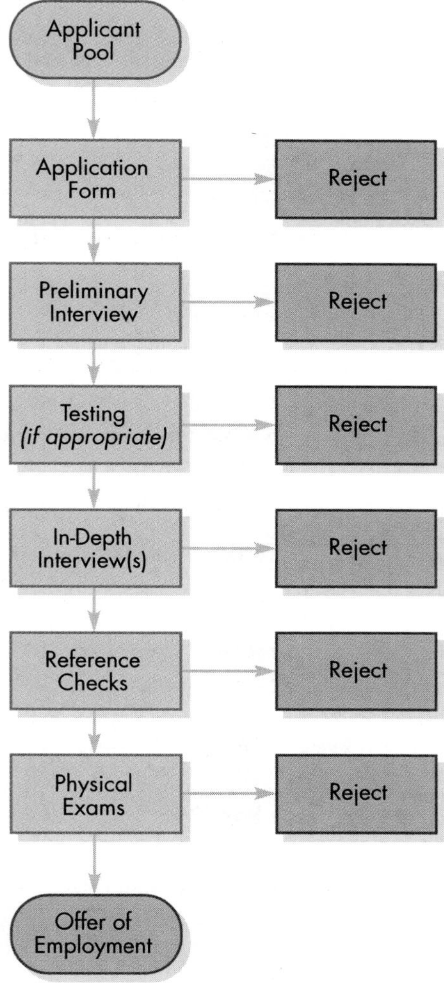

A preliminary interview may be structured—scripted with specific questions—or unstructured. An unstructured format allows an applicant relative freedom to express thoughts and feelings. An interviewer uses the preliminary meeting to verify details from the application form and to obtain information needed to continue the selection process. Interviewers must avoid topics that are not related to the applicant's abilities to perform successfully on the job. An ability necessary to perform a job is called a bona fide occupational qualification. For example, if a job involves work in a men's locker room, a question about the gender of the applicant is probably not discriminatory because it asks about a bona fide occupational qualification.

Employers and job candidates must be particularly sensitive to the potential for discrimination in interviews. Both parties must avoid sensitive issues; Figure 11.8 presents some interviewing guidelines prepared by one state employment agency.

FIGURE 11.8 *Employment application forms and interviews: potentially discriminatory inquiries*

The best general guideline to follow on employment application forms and in interviews is to ensure that information elicited relates to qualifications for effective performance on the job. The topics listed in bold in this figure are especially sensitive.

Age? Date of birth? In general, asking whether a candidate is under 18 or over 70 is permissible.

Arrests? Since an arrest is no indication of guilt and because, proportionally, minorities are arrested more than those in other segments of the population, questions about arrests are probably discriminatory. Such an inquiry is prohibited by the Illinois Department of Human Rights.

Convictions (other than traffic violations)? Military record? Questions about convictions are generally inadvisable, though they may be appropriate for screening candidates who have been convicted of certain offenses and are under consideration for certain kinds of jobs. Questions about less-than-honorable military discharges are likewise inappropriate unless the job involves security issues. In general, a candidate can be asked what branch of service he or she served in and what kind of work the candidate did. If information about convictions or military discharge is necessary, exercise care in how it is used; avoid possible discrimination.

Available for Saturday or Sunday work? Although knowing when employees are available to work is important, a question about availability on certain days may discourage applicants from certain religious groups. If business requirements necessitate such a question, indicate that the employer will make an effort to accommodate the religious needs of employees.

Age and number of children? Arrangements for child care? Although the intent of these questions may be to explore a source of absenteeism or tardiness, the effect can be to discriminate against women. Do not ask questions about children or their care.

Credit record? Own a car? Own a home? Unless the person hired must use personal credit, a personal car, or do business from a home he or she owns, avoid these questions. They could discriminate against minorities and women.

Eyes? Hair color? Eye and hair color are not related to job performance and may serve to indicate an applicant's race or national origin.

Fidelity bond? Since a bond may have been denied for an arbitrary or discriminatory reason, use other screening considerations.

Friends or relatives? This question implies a preference for friends or relatives of employees and is potentially discriminatory because such people are likely to reflect the demography of the company's present workforce.

Garnishment record? Federal courts have held that wage garnishments do not normally affect a worker's ability to perform effectively on the job.

Height? Weight? Unless height or weight relates directly to job performance, do not ask about it on an application form or in an interview.

Maiden name? Prior married name? Widowed, divorced, separated? These questions are not related to job performance and may be an indication of religion or national origin. These inquiries may be appropriate, however, if the information gained is needed for a preemployment investigation or security check.

Marital status? A federal court has held that refusal to employ a married woman when married men occupy similar jobs is unlawful sex discrimination. Do not ask about an applicant's marital status.

Sex? State and federal laws prohibit discrimination on the basis of sex except where sex is a bona fide occupational qualification necessary to the normal operation of business.

NOTE: *If certain information is needed for postemployment purposes, such as in the administration of affirmative action plans, the employer can obtain it after the applicant has been hired. Keep this data separate from data used in career advancement decisions.*

Source: Illinois Department of Employment Security

Testing

test
Any criterion or performance measure used as a basis for an employment decision.

http://www.access.gpo.gov/su_docs/aces/aces140.html

According to Equal Employment Opportunity Commission guidelines, a **test** is any criterion or performance measure used as a basis for any employment decision. Such measures include interviews, application forms, psychological and performance exams, physical requirements for a job, and any other device that is scored and used as a basis for selecting an applicant (*Federal Register*, 1978). All tests used for screening should attempt to measure only performance capabilities that have been or can be proven to be essential to successful performance of the job (Kleiman, "From," 1992).

Regardless of the tests used, employers must avoid producing a disparate impact—that is, creating a test that one demographic group is more likely to perform better on than another. Employers must also ensure that each test has validity. A test with validity is a predictor of future performance on a specific job. A person receiving a high score on a valid test will be able to perform the related job successfully. Those who perform poorly on the test would perform poorly on the job. If test performance does not correlate to job performance, the test is probably invalid.

assessment center
A place where candidates are screened for managerial positions, which usually involves extensive testing and hands-on exercises.

Assessment centers specialize in screening candidates for managerial positions. Tests administered at assessment centers attempt to analyze a person's ability to communicate, decide, plan, organize, lead, and solve problems. The testing techniques used include interviews, in-basket exercises (tests that present a person with limited time to decide how to handle a variety of problems), group exercises intended to uncover leadership potential and the ability to work with others, and a variety of hands-on tasks. The assessments usually last several days and take place away from the usual job site. Many large companies, especially Japanese employers, use assessment centers to determine who will make it into a company or up its corporate ladder. The results from assessment centers are usually more accurately predictive than paper-and-pencil exercises that assess managerial ability.

In-Depth Interview

http://www.eaton.com

An in-depth interview is almost always conducted by the person or persons for or with whom the applicant will work if hired. The goal of an in-depth interview is to determine how well the applicant will fit into the organization's culture and the subsystem in which he or she would work. Eaton Corporation, for example, screens its applicants to be certain they will be willing to share authority. In-depth interviews may or may not be structured. They can be used to relay information specifically related to the job and its environment as well as to talk about benefits, hours, and working conditions. Applicants who have passed through the initial screenings and progress to in-depth interviews need the endorsement of the person for whom they will work. Without this person's commitment to the success of the new hire, the applicant's future at that firm is in doubt. As is the case with application forms and preliminary interviews, interviewers must take care to avoid topics that could lead to accusations of employment discrimination.

Reference Checks

A *Chicago Tribune* article (Kleiman, "From," 1992) reported that most employers conduct fairly extensive background checks:

- 84 percent verify education and past-employment claims
- 60 percent contact persons listed as references
- 63 percent review school transcripts

Checking an applicant's past can present problems. First, employers must avoid background checks that could be discriminatory. Checks of credit history and arrest records, for example, are discriminatory. Second, checking references can be difficult because most former employers refuse to cooperate. They may avoid saying anything negative for fear of a defamation-of-character lawsuit by the ex-employee. According to one survey (Amend, 1990), 41 percent of companies surveyed prohibited current employees from giving references about ex-employees.

http://www.flashcreative.com

David Blumenthal, who owns Flash Creative Management, a small company focused on information technology, provides an interesting twist to reference checking. He requires applicants to "call *his* references (most of whom are customers) in order to really understand what kind of company they are trying to enter." Why? Blumenthal believes that by doing so, job candidates will truly "understand his commitment to customer service and what he expects of employees. . . . Blumenthal asks his customers for their opinions of prospective hires. . . . Would the customer feel comfortable working with that applicant?" (Fenn, 1995).

Physical Exam

According to one article (Kleiman, "From," 1992), 52 percent of employers surveyed asked applicants to take a preemployment physical exam as part of the selection process; 19 percent asked for a medical history without a physical exam. Employers use physical exams and medical histories to prevent insurance claims for illnesses and injuries that occurred prior to employment. Physical exams also detect communicable diseases and certify that an applicant is physically capable of performing his or her job. If the job description cites physical demands, they must be valid. According to the Americans with Disabilities Act, employers must make reasonable accommodations for the physically impaired and not use physical barriers as an excuse for not hiring.

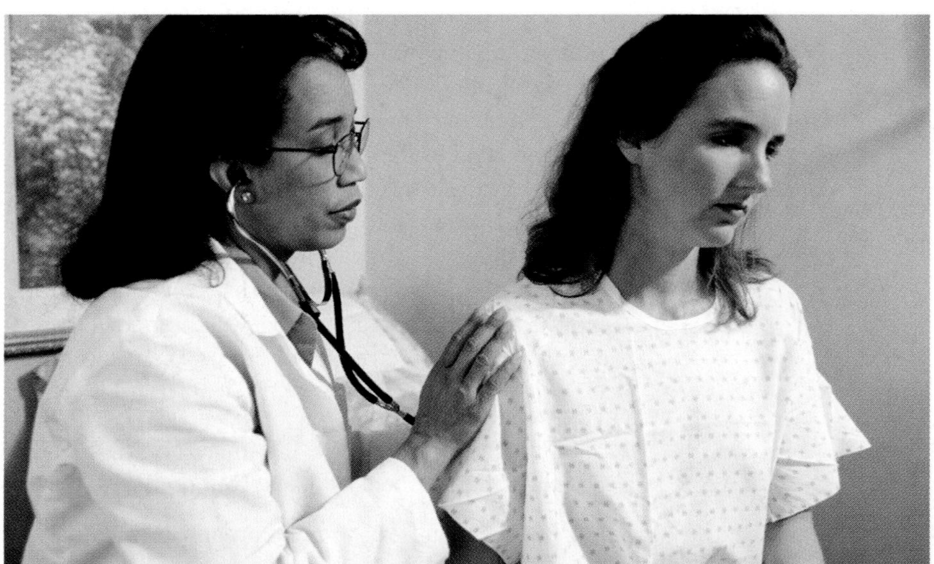

Many employers require physical exams to ensure that employees are physically capable of performing their jobs.

Offer of Employment

At this point in the selection process, the manager or team offers the job to the top-rated applicant. This step may involve a series of negotiations about salary or wages, work schedule, vacation time, types of benefits desired, and other special considerations. With the diversity of the workforce of today, an employer may have to accommodate an employee's disability, make time for him or her to get children off to school or be at home when they return, or to arrange for day care. Federal law requires that within 24 hours from the time of hiring, the new employee must furnish proof of U.S. citizenship or the proper authorization needed to work in the United States as a legal alien.

Orientation

The previous steps in the selection process have done much to familiarize the newcomer with the company and the job. What the new hire needs now is a warm welcome so he or she can begin contributing as soon as possible. The newcomer needs to be introduced to his or her workstation, team, and coworkers. Managers and coworkers should answer the new employee's questions promptly and openly. Someone should explain work rules, company policies, benefits, and procedures and fill out the paperwork necessary to get the new person on the payroll. All employee assistance programs should be explained, and the new hire should be told how to take advantage of them.

All this can be done in stages and by several different people. Human resource specialists may handle the paperwork; team members or a supervisor may take charge of introductions to the work area and coworkers. All equipment, tools, and supplies that the newcomer needs should be in place when he or she reports for work.

orientation
Introducing new employees to the organization by explaining their duties, helping them meet their coworkers, and acclimating them to their work environment.

A new employee's first impressions and early experiences should be realistic and as positive as possible. **Orientation** is the beginning of a continuing socialization process that builds and cements employees' relationships, attitudes, and commitment to the company. Orientation should be thoroughly planned and skillfully executed.

TRAINING AND DEVELOPMENT

Explain the differences and similarities between training and development

training
Giving employees the knowledge, skills, and attitudes needed to perform their jobs.

Training teaches skills for use in the present and near future. Development focuses on the future. Both involve teaching the particular attitudes, knowledge, and skills a person needs. Both are designed to give people something new, and both have three prerequisites for success: (1) Those who design training or development programs must create needs assessments to determine what the content and objectives of the programs should be; (2) the people who execute the programs must know how to teach, how people learn, and what individuals need to be taught; and (3) all participants—trainers, developers, and those receiving the training or development—must be willing participants.

American employers spend in excess of $210 billion each year to provide training and development for their employees (Kleiman, "Employer-Based," 1992). In most U.S. businesses, training and development are continual processes. The American

http://www.astd.org

http://www.xerox.com

Society for Training and Development named the Xerox Corporation as one of several businesses with the best training systems. Xerox spends about 4 percent of its payroll (between $250 million and $300 million per year) for training its 110,000 employees. Xerox has its own training center in Leesburg, Virginia, and the corporation employs 120 trainers who train 12,000 employees annually. An additional 21,000 employees receive at least 40 hours of training each year at a district headquarters (Kleiman, "Employer-Based," 1992).

Purposes of Training

http://www.nsbe.org

Training has five major aims: to increase knowledge and skills, to increase motivation to succeed, to improve chances for advancement, to improve morale and the sense of competence and pride in performance, and to increase quality and productivity. To understand just how important training is and will be, consider the following quote from Anita Womack, editor for the Virginia-based National Society of Black Engineers (Kleiman, "Are," 1995):

> *The next 10 years will present the [greatest number of] technological changes and challenges the world has faced since the advent of machinery. Millions of jobs will be created and millions will become obsolete. The primary factors that will determine whether we are ably employed are education, technical training, and the willingness to change and learn something new.*

Today's corporate emphasis on downsizing and flattening hierarchies only leads to greater efficiency and customer satisfaction when it is accompanied by reengineering organizational processes. If it is otherwise, all that will happen is that the same amount of work must be done by fewer people who will quickly become stressed out and overburdened.

Reengineering the right way inevitably means "better technology, better processes, and fewer, better workers. The ideal: technology that actually helps workers make decisions, in organizations that encourage them to do so" (Hammonds, Kelly, and Thurston, 1994). Moving to open-book management and empowering workers, however, means preparing people for these changes through training. Also, since technology keeps changing, both workers and managers need to continually train to become and remain technically competent.

Technically competent, multiskilled workers are the nucleus of both temporary and permanent, empowered cross-functional teams that are so pervasive today. Before people can function effectively in team environments, however, team members, team leaders, and team facilitators need various types of training to gain the skills, knowledge, and attitudes necessary for teaming.

Challenges of Training

According to the Southport Institute for Policy Analysis, half of America's businesses that employ fewer than 50 people report that 40 percent of their workforces (some 10 million employees) have serious problems with reading, writing, and math. For this reason, many firms need to conduct remedial training so that workers can cope with job demands and prepare themselves for positions of greater responsibility (*Chicago Tribune*, 1992).

One answer to language and illiteracy problems is job redesign. The redesigned jobs avoid, as much as possible, the need to rely on English and math. "Some warehouses use computers with speech capability to tell forklift operators who cannot read where they should go in the warehouse. Some construction firms rely on portable computers with touch-activated display screens that allow workers to record their reports by touching appropriate pictures on the screens" (Bulkeley, 1992).

Another challenge is America's increasingly diverse workforce, which by the year 2000, was 25 percent. In the culturally diverse workforce of today, employees often need to improve their ability to handle English, to gain an appreciation of the organization's diverse cultures, and to learn how to cope with the many changes that occur on the job, such as new technologies, methods, and duties.

Immigrants, many highly educated in their home countries, bring motivation and skills to the workplace. They also bring cultural values and norms that may make it difficult for them to find well-paying jobs. Aside from their language difficulties, their views about the value of time, the relative importance of work and family, and how people should interact at work may not mesh with those of the dominant culture or the current mix of cultures.

Techniques of Training

A company can train employees in various places. A trainee can be sent to a job site, a corporate training center, a college classroom, or various workshops, seminars, and professional gatherings. When the employer does training in house, it commonly takes the following forms:

- *On-the-job training (OJT).* In this approach, an employee learns while performing the job. Training proceeds through coaching or by the trainee observing proficient performers and then doing the work. Apprenticeships and internships are on-the-job training programs.
- *Machine-based training.* In this technique, trainees interact with a computer, simulator, or other type of machine. The environment is usually controlled and the interaction is one-on-one. The trainees proceed at their own pace or at a pace set by the training equipment.
- *Vestibule training.* This system simulates the work environment by providing actual equipment and tools in a laboratory setting. The noise and distractions of a real work area and the pressure of meeting production goals are absent, so the trainee can concentrate on learning.
- *Job rotation.* In a job-rotation program, trainees move from one job to another. The temporary assignments allow them to learn various skills and acquire an awareness of how each job relates to others. In the process, trainees become more valuable because they develop the flexibility to perform many tasks. Internships utilize this form of training. (Job rotation is also used as a development technique.)
- *Internet-based training.* In this technique, training is delivered over the Internet. The trainees proceed at their own pace or at a pace set by the instructor.

Regardless of the techniques used, training must be realistic. It must teach what is necessary in ways that can be applied directly to the work setting once training ends. Progress must be monitored to determine how well trainees are mastering the material.

Purposes of Development

development
Efforts to acquire the knowledge, skills, and attitudes needed to move to a job with greater authority and responsibility.

Development is a way of preparing someone for the new and greater challenges he or she will encounter in another, more demanding job. Workers seek development opportunities to prepare for management positions; supervisors need development to prepare to move into middle management. All development is really self-development. Without a personal commitment, development cannot occur. People can be pressured into training just to keep their jobs, but development, when offered, can be rejected. Employees cannot depend on their employers for development opportunities. Small companies cannot afford it, and many large employers will not pay for development when it is not directly related to an employee's current job or career track. In 1994 American companies employing over 100 people spent about $50 billion or 1.4 percent of their payrolls on developing their people (Hammonds, Kelly, and Thurston, 1994).

Techniques of Development

Development techniques include job rotation, sending people to professional workshops or seminars, sponsoring memberships in professional associations, paying for an employee's formal education courses, and granting a person a sabbatical (leave of absence) to pursue further education or engage in community service. An employee should regard a company-sponsored program as a reward and as a clear statement about his or her worth to the company. Such programs are conduits through which workers can gain prestige, confidence, and competence.

Development efforts should never end; indeed, they can be part of a daily routine. By reading professional journals and business publications regularly and by interacting with experts at professional meetings, employees can help keep themselves up-to-date. Another approach to development involves volunteering for difficult assignments. Meeting tough challenges encourages a person to expand his or her abilities.

Mentoring is another form of development that can be extremely significant. Mentors are professionals who are one or two steps above a person in his or her profession. Mentors can come from a person's present environment or from another organization. Whatever their affiliation, mentors are willing to share experiences and give competent advice about handling advancement opportunities, company politics, and self-development.

PERFORMANCE APPRAISAL

performance appraisal
A formal, structured comparison between employee performance and established quantity and quality standards.

In most organizations some assessment of job performance takes place every day, at least informally. When results for a given period are summarized and shared with those being reviewed, **performance appraisal** becomes a formal, structured system designed (in line with legal limits) to measure the actual job performance of an employee by comparing it to designated standards. These standards are introduced and reinforced in the selection and training processes.

Purposes of Performance Appraisal

7

Explain the purpose of a performance appraisal

Most organizations use appraisals to

- Provide feedback about the success of previous training and disclose the need for additional training
- Develop individuals' plans for improving their performance and assist them in making such plans
- Determine whether rewards such as pay increases, promotions, transfers, or commendations are due or whether warning or termination is required
- Identify areas for additional growth and the methods that can be utilized to achieve it
- Develop and enhance the relationship between the person being evaluated and the supervisor doing the evaluation
- Give the employee a clear understanding of where he or she stands in relation to the supervisor's expectations and in relation to the achievement of specific goals

Company policy establishes the frequency and form of the appraisal. Whatever form evaluations take, managers should provide daily feedback to an employee about performance. The employee's team members should do the same. If feedback is continual, the formal annual or semiannual performance appraisal will contain no surprises.

Components of Appraisal Systems

Performance appraisal systems include three major components:

- The criteria (factors and standards) against which the employee's performance is measured. Criteria could include quality of work, efforts at improvement, specific attitudes, and quantity of output.

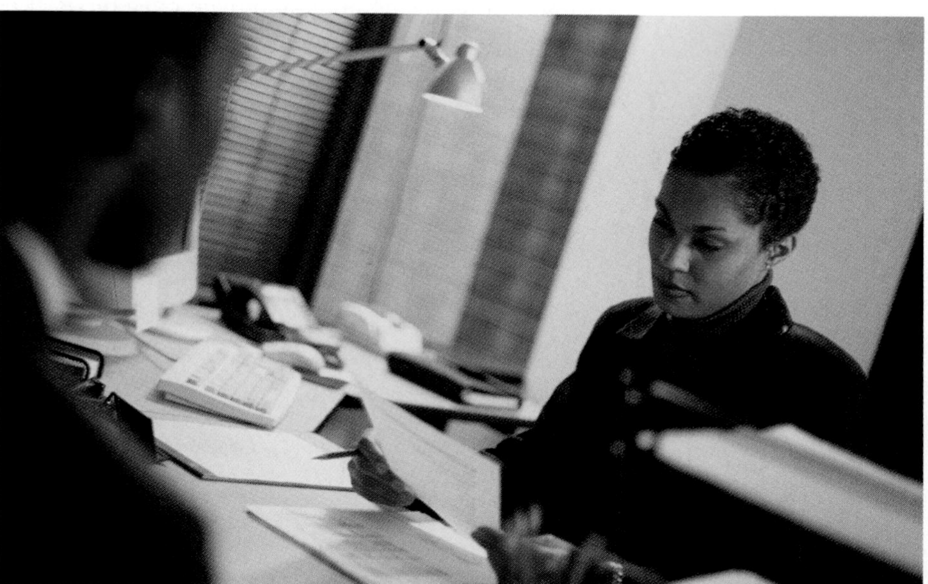

Performance appraisals should focus not only on past performance, but also on the setting and achieving of future goals.

- The rating that summarizes how well the employee is doing.
- The methods used to determine the ratings. Methods could involve specific forms, people, and procedures.

Different personalities, jobs, organizations, and subsystems call for different criteria, ratings, and methods. According to Susan Resnick-West, coauthor of *Designing Performance Appraisal Systems*, the major predictor of the effectiveness of a performance system is whether it is tailored for individuals. Factors that system designers should consider include task competency, previous experience, educational levels, and individual preferences (Mohrman, Resnick-West, and Lawler, 1989).

Appraisal systems can be classified as subjective or objective. Subjective systems allow raters to operate from their own personal points of view. Raters may be allowed the freedom to create factors, define what each factor means, and determine the employee's proficiency in each category. Figure 11.9 shows how one rater uses a simple matrix of four categories—Time Management, Attitude, Knowledge of Job, and Communication—and the proficiency categories Excellent, Good, Fair, and Poor. What do these words mean? How is the rater defining each? In comparison to another person or to an ideal? Definitions used by one rater using this form may vary from those of another. Worse, the evaluator's stereotypes of and prejudices against an employee may become factors in the evaluation. Subjective methods and forms are difficult to justify when faced with accusations of discrimination. An employer should make every effort to keep subjectivity out of ratings.

Objective performance appraisals attempt to remove rater biases. Criteria are clearly defined and shared with the employee well in advance of the actual rating. Figure 11.10 shows just how concrete standards can be. An objective approach causes little confusion about the factors used for evaluation.

Appraisal Methods

Four appraisal methods dominate current practice: management by objectives, behaviorally anchored rating scales, computer monitoring, and 360-degree feedback. After a brief look at each type, this chapter will examine the legal constraints on all rating methods.

FIGURE 11.9 *Subjective performance appraisal system*

	Excellent	Good	Fair	Poor
Time Management		✔		
Attitude		✔		
Knowledge of Job	✔			
Communication			✔	

FIGURE 11.10 *Portion of an objective performance appraisal system*

Performance Aspect	Rating 1	2	3	4	5
1. Self-Improvement Consider the desire to expand present capabilities in both depth and breadth. ❑ *No opportunity to observe.*	Has no interest in learning additional duties.	Has limited interest in expanding job assignments. Has little interest in preparing for advancement.	Has demonstrated interest in additional assignments. Has shown some interest in and preparation for advancement.	Has shown extra effort to learn additional duties. Has undertaken advancement preparation.	Is very inquisitive concerning all phases of job-related assignments. Has undertaken advancement preparation.
2. Attendance Consider the regularity with which the employee reports to work.	Excessively absent.	Frequently absent.	Occasionally absent.	Rarely absent.	Almost never absent.
3. Punctuality Consider number of occasions late. ❑ *Punctuality is not essential to this job.*	Excessively tardy.	Frequently tardy.	Occasionally tardy.	Rarely tardy.	Almost never tardy.
4. Work Planning Consider how the work load is planned and organized for maximum efficiency. ❑ *No opportunity to observe.*	Unsystematic, unable to organize work load.	Fair on routine but unable to organize variations effectively.	Efficient under normal conditions. Gives priority to important jobs.	Skillful in organizing and planning work. Meets emergencies promptly.	Exceptional efficiency. Keeps priority items in proper perspective.

Management by Objectives

Recall from Chapter 5 that a management by objectives (MBO) system requires a manager and subordinate to meet periodically to agree on specific performance goals for the subordinate over a fixed period. At the end of that period, an employee working under MBO is evaluated in regard to the number of goals met, how effectively and efficiently each one was achieved, and the growth that took place during the effort. Evaluators take into account the difficulties that the employee had to overcome to reach those goals.

Behaviorally Anchored Rating Scales

BARS, or behaviorally anchored rating scales, identify specific behaviors that correspond to different levels of performance. Each behavior corresponds to a numeric rating. Figure 11.10 illustrated a behaviorally anchored rating scale. The employee's overall rating is the sum of the points earned in each category.

Computer Monitoring

A computer monitoring system tracks an employee's performance as it is taking place. The performance of those who work with computers or computerized equipment can be evaluated in terms of the amount of time their machines are operating productively, the number of keystrokes per minute, or total output. Managers can compare the ratings of various employees in similar jobs and rank workers according to productivity. Managers can use performance averages to set or confirm existing standards. Retailers, banks, insurance companies, telephone companies, and transport firms use computer monitoring as one objective measure of employee performance.

360-Degree Feedback

Feedback is sought from all or most of the constituencies with which an employee has contact, particularly coworkers and customers. The goal of 360-degree feedback is to increase employees' self-awareness so that they can improve their work performance. This is also known as multi-rater feedback, multi-source feedback, full-circle appraisal, and group performance review.

Legality of Appraisals

An analysis of U.S. Supreme Court rulings over the past 25 years reveals that performance appraisals are likely to be illegal if

- The instruments used are invalid
- Standards are not job related and objective (quantifiable and observable)
- The results of the process have a disparate impact on women, the disabled, or minorities
- The scoring method is not standardized
- People who are performing similar jobs are evaluated differently, using different forms, factors, or processes
- Evaluative criteria are not developed according to EEOC guidelines
- Employees are not warned of declining or substandard performance
- The evaluation is not based on the employee's current duties

Also, women, disabled people, and minorities in a proportion that is representative of the community at large should fill the ranks of performance appraisers.

Raters must be trained to carry out performance appraisals consistently and in accordance with legal requirements. Lawrence H. Peters, professor of management at Texas Christian University, gave practical advice to raters and ratees: "It's hard to remember what the employee did 12, 11, or 10 months ago. It's important for managers to keep information as it occurs, and if you don't, stop and take time to collect your thoughts before the performance review. Employees should do the same" (Kleiman, "Employee," 1992). In addition, raters need to reserve adequate facilities and time to review appraisals with subordinates.

IMPLEMENTATION OF EMPLOYMENT DECISIONS

Describe the four primary employment decisions

As you recall, employment decisions include decisions about promotions, transfers, demotions, and separations (voluntary or involuntary). These changes are influenced by appraisals and by how an organization recruits, hires, orients, and trains. All employment decisions mean change—change that has a ripple effect throughout an organization's subsystems and its ability to interact with the external environment.

Promotions

promotion
A job change that results in increased status, compensation, and responsibility.

Promotions are job changes that lead to higher pay and greater authority and that reward devoted, outstanding effort. They serve as incentives, as well, offering the promise of greater personal growth and challenges to those who seek them. Employees usually earn a promotion by exhibiting superior performance and going beyond that which is expected.

Sometimes past performance is not the sole criterion for a promotion. Affirmative action requires that underrepresented groups such as women and minorities be better represented at all levels within an organization. Therefore, affirmative action goals may dictate that members of these groups be given special status in hiring and promoting decisions. In many union agreements, seniority is the most significant factor influencing promotion decisions.

Transfers

transfer
Moving an employee to a job with similar levels of status, compensation, and responsibility.

http://www.moatskennedy.com

Opportunities for promotion are not as available now as they were only a few years ago. The leaner, flatter management structures of today and the trend toward teams mean there simply are not a large number of openings. According to Marilyn M. Kennedy, editor of the newsletter *Kennedy's Career Strategist*, **transfers**—lateral moves that require new skills—may be a company's only means of retaining talent (Rigdon, 1992):

> *Companies that have restructured have taken steps to make sideways moves more palatable. RJR-Nabisco's Nabisco Foods Group (in New Jersey) recently added tiers to its pay scales so that workers who move sideways have a better chance of getting pay raises instead of cuts. Corning Inc., which has long wooed recruits by promising them they can "change careers without changing companies," recently began offering five percent raises to managers who make lateral moves. The policy comes on the heels of restructuring.*

For years companies have used lateral moves in attempts to train and develop employees. Job rotation is one way of exposing people to different aspects of an operation and helping them see the big corporate picture. Transfers can help people advance by moving them from an area where few opportunities exist to an area that offers a less congested career track.

Demotions

demotion
A reduction in an employee's status, pay, and responsibility.

A **demotion** is a reassignment to a lower rank in an organization's hierarchy. In the business climate of today, demotions are rarely used as punishment. (Ineffective performers are fired, not retained.) Demotions are used to retain employees who lose their positions through no fault of their own. Some people prefer taking a lower-status, lower-paying job to the alternative of being laid off. Others choose a demotion to decrease stress, allow them more freedom to pursue outside interests, or meet challenges such as having to care for children or an elderly parent.

Some companies have established what have become known as "mommy tracks"—temporary career interruptions for parents. Mommy tracks allow a parent to take care of children from pregnancy through the preschool years. By offering adjustments such as part-time work, a mix of telecommuting and in-house office hours, and flexible work schedules, companies help valued employees cope with new interests and demands on their time. As Joan Beck (1992) notes, however, some of these arrangements have drawbacks:

> *Unfortunately, many employers still exact a steep price for non-standard work arrangements. Part-time work typically pays low wages and usually includes few if any benefits. Even women at middle-management levels or on fast professional tracks find that cutting back on work hours and trying other strategies to eke out more time for family cuts chances for promotion.*

Separations

separation
The voluntary or involuntary departure of employees from a company.

http://www.dec.com

A **separation**, the departure of an employee from an organization, may be voluntary or involuntary. Voluntary separations include resignations and retirements. Involuntary separations include layoffs and firings. Employers sometimes encourage voluntary separation by offering incentives to encourage employees to retire early. In May 1992 Digital Equipment Corporation (now part of Compaq) offered 7,000 employees an early-retirement buyout; 3,000 accepted (Wilke, 1992). Involuntary separations seem to be on the rise in U.S. business. Layoffs due to declining business, personal performance, or company bankruptcies (as in the cases of Pan Am and Eastern Airlines) have cost millions of Americans their jobs. See this chapter's Global Applications feature for a discussion of Japan's custom of lifetime employment.

Layoffs

Although downsizing can make companies more competitive, it can also undermine the loyalty of employees threatened with layoffs. According to Sanford M. Sherizen, a Massachusetts-based computer security consultant, downsizing leads to more responsibility for fewer people, which means less time to devote to the security of information systems. An insecure system practically invites a disgruntled employee to destroy data or leave behind a computer virus that will sabotage the system after the employee has left (Steinert-Threlkeld, 1992). An information security consultant, William H. Murray, says that the best way to protect a company against sabotage is to take steps to prevent employee disaffection—to treat those who must leave as well as possible before the layoff and compensate remaining employees fairly. According to Murray, most revenge comes from those who conclude that their contributions are unrecognized. People need to know they are appreciated day by day (Steinert-Threlkeld, 1992).

As alternatives to layoffs, many companies are implementing other strategies. Some have enacted hiring freezes, which allow normal attrition to reduce the workforce. Other strategies include job sharing, restricting the use of overtime, retraining and redeploying workers, reducing hours, and converting managers to paid consultants. Managers at Unarco, a manufacturer of shopping carts, pride themselves on the company's no-layoff policy. Unarco managers find useful employment for displaced workers by relying on retraining and normal attrition.

http://www.unarco.com

GLOBAL APPLICATIONS
Japan's Lifetime Employment

Three principles dominate Japan's employment system: company unions, pay for seniority, and lifetime employment. The latter is a result of informal industry agreements formed after World War II, which restricted competition for labor by companies in the same industry. One could not hire another's employees. It is not so much company loyalty that keeps Japanese workers from job-hopping; it is the lack of opportunity for another job in their industries.

Advantages of lifetime employment outweigh its disadvantages. Japanese workers and managers do not fear innovation and efforts to improve their employer's quality and productivity as many Western employees do. "In fact, they embrace new technology because they know it will enhance their company's future and their own jobs." Japan's employers are more willing than Western ones to make considerable investments both in employees' training and in research and development because their employees are less likely to share newly acquired skills and knowledge with competitors through job changes. Finally, Japanese managers also realize that decisions they make must be made with a view toward the future. "A Japanese executive knows that the decisions he makes today will remain permanently on his record, and he may be asked to account for them many years from now."

Technology and the global economy are changing Japan's system. The Internet is allowing manufacturers worldwide to click directly onto supply routes that are fast, cheap, and eliminate middlemen. Foreigners are now allowed to invest in long-shielded sectors of the Japanese economy. General Electric Co. chairman Jack Welch gave a clue as to what he has in mind for Japanese investments: "It's an abuse of management rights to try to keep a weak business going in the name of lifetime employment. It's better for the employees to leave the weak business and have it merged with a stronger company." By 1999 unemployment in Japan reached a post-war high of 5%.

Sources: Eamonn Fingleton, "Jobs for Life: Why Japan Won't Give Them Up," *Fortune* (20 March 1995), pp. 119–120, 122–123, 125; Tim Larimer, "Great News: No More Jobs for Life," *Time Asia* (1 November 1999), http://www.time.com/time/asia/magazine/99/1101/japan.nissan.html.

Unarco managers and managers everywhere have good reasons to avoid layoffs. Layoffs can be extremely expensive. Processing paperwork, closing facilities, and paying severance costs and higher unemployment-insurance premiums can cost thousands of dollars. The psychological costs are high as well. Those left behind after layoffs are fearful and insecure; those laid off are more likely than employed people to experience family problems, suffer divorce, or commit suicide.

Exit Interviews

Exit interviews are voluntary discussions between managers and employees who are being laid off or who are leaving voluntarily. A recent survey found that 96 percent of companies responding to the survey conducted exit interviews. The subjects discussed in the interviews included job satisfaction, working conditions, and compensation (Kleiman, "Worker," 1991). Because the costs of laying off and replacing workers are high, a manager should use exit interviews to find out about factors that could cause employees to leave. Once the manager identifies a problem, he or she should fix it. Managers should realize, however, that exit interviews have a limitation. Because department employees may not wish to leave a negative impression, they may not be totally open and honest. The fact that exit interviews do not reveal a cause for employee dissatisfaction does not necessarily mean that a cause does not exist.

COMPENSATION

9

Explain the purposes and components of compensation

compensation
All forms of financial payments to employees. Compensation includes salaries, wages, and benefits.

Compensation includes all forms of financial payments to employees: salaries and wages, benefits, bonuses, gain sharing, profit sharing, and awards of goods or services. The trend today is to offer increases in compensation in response to increases in performance that add value to the organization, its services, or its products. Increasing compensation is a way of retaining employees who have proved themselves valuable. This response makes sense. As employees become more valuable, losing them becomes more costly.

Purposes of Compensation

Compensation has three primary purposes: to attract, help develop, and retain talented performers. The level of compensation offered by a firm can either increase or decrease a company's attractiveness to job seekers. Compensation should encourage workers to continually improve their performance and to make themselves more valuable both to themselves and to their employers. Compensation must also anchor valued employees to the company, discouraging them from leaving to find other employment. People who consider their compensation fair and adequate feel that they are being treated with recognition and respect. They feel that the organization is giving them a fair return on their investment of time, energy, and commitment. Finally, compensation should give employees a sense of security, freeing them to unleash their full energies without the distraction that comes with the inability to meet financial needs. This has certainly become the case at The Container Store (see Management in Action at the beginning of the chapter).

Factors Influencing Compensation

When designing a compensation package for employees, managers should be concerned about being equitable, meeting legal and strategic requirements, and linking compensation philosophy to various market factors. When certain types of workers are in short supply, managers may have to offer premium compensation to attract or hold them. Similarly, managers who decide to make their organization a leader in terms of the compensation it offers will probably be able to attract and keep the best employees.

The U.S. Fair Labor Standards Act, passed in 1938 and amended many times, relates to the payment of wages and overtime to workers under eighteen years of age. Other federal laws address the level of wages that must be paid to workers in companies doing business with the federal government. Some local and state laws affect compensation systems, and union contracts set wages and restrict compensation decisions in the organizations that are party to them.

Wages and Salaries

job evaluation
A study that determines the worth of a job in terms of its value to an organization.

To determine the worth of each job and establish a compensation package for each that is fair in relation to all jobs, organizations use a process called **job evaluation**. Human resource compensation specialists usually do job evaluations. To complete the evaluation process, the specialist works with a manager with firsthand knowledge of the job and the employee or employees who hold the job.

One common job evaluation method involves grouping jobs by type and then choosing factors common to each type. For example, two groups of jobs that job evaluation specialists often define are manufacturing jobs (wage jobs) and sales jobs (salary jobs). An evaluation might involve examining each type of job in light of the responsibility, education, skills, training, experience, and working conditions that are common to it. Then the evaluator assigns various levels within each factor and assigns point values to each level as measures of achievement.

To illustrate this process, suppose the job being analyzed is that of an industrial products sales professional. The evaluator chooses experience as an evaluation factor and defines experience as number of years in the selling profession. The levels for this factor might be one year or less of experience, one to three years of experience, three to five years of experience, and more than five years of experience. By assigning points to each level, the specialist shows the relative value the organization places on each. If the top level is worth ten points and the previous one is worth five points, the organization is saying that more than five years of experience is twice as valuable as three to five years of experience.

Once all jobs have been evaluated, they can be grouped by total points into what are usually called job grades, or classifications. Evaluators then rank, by point total, jobs within each grade. For example, all jobs with point totals between 0 and 200 might be in the same grade. What emerges is a "job ladder" that shows jobs with the fewest total points at the bottom. At the top are the jobs with the most points. Evaluators assign a salary range to jobs in the same grade. Figure 11.11 shows the result of a typical job evaluation.

FIGURE 11.11 *Result of a typical job evaluation*

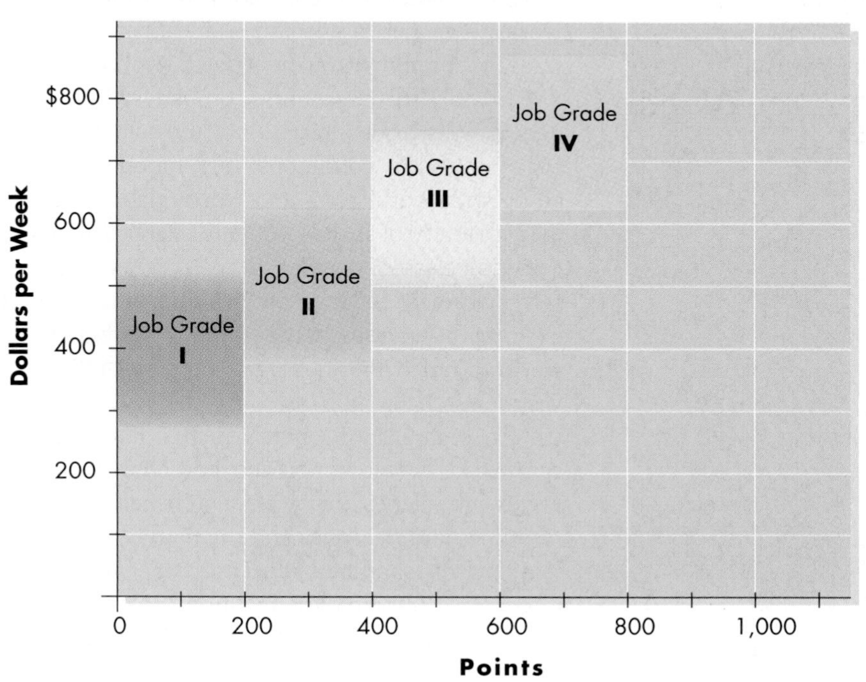

Job evaluation requires skill, up-to-date job descriptions and specifications, knowledge, and ample time. Many companies conduct pay surveys within their industries as a base for beginning the job evaluation process or as a substitute for it. Pay surveys show what competitors pay for comparable jobs. These rates of pay may be available through industry and trade associations as well as from the federal government. Not all jobs must be compared with the survey results; the evaluator compares only those that are representative of their grades or classes. Compensation for the other jobs is established in relation to the jobs that are compared.

In the final analysis, the minimum and maximum compensation assigned to a job are determined by an organization's ability to pay, market conditions for specific types of jobs, and the organization's strategies and philosophy about employee compensation.

Benefits

benefit
Legally required or voluntary compensation provided to employees in addition to their salaries or wages.

Each year employers spend about an additional 40 percent of their payroll costs on employee **benefits**—the additional or indirect compensation employees receive beyond their direct compensation (wages and salaries). Benefits can be divided into two general types: legally required and voluntary. The first type includes Social Security, unemployment compensation, and worker's compensation insurance. The second type includes variable work schedules, life and health insurance, pension and savings plans, payment for hours not worked (sick days), leaves of absence, profit-sharing and bonus plans (usually one-time payments), and employee assistance programs (EAPs). Business Wire provides its employees with most of these.

EAPs have gained in popularity over the years. Most can be classified as health and wellness programs that deal with either prevention of health-related problems or coping with chronic work-related problems. Stop-smoking clinics, weight-loss programs, and exercise facilities are examples of prevention efforts. Stress-reduction workshops, day-care facilities, and financial and psychological counseling concentrate on coping with work-related problems.

http://www.highsmith.com

In 1991 the Highsmith Company, a Wisconsin-based provider of library products, saw its health-related expenses climbing. Its 240 employees exhibited a variety of unhealthy conditions (high blood pressure, smoking, high cholesterol levels) along with work stress and work-related injuries. In the 1990s the company created a variety of EAPs—"on-site exercise, weight control, nutrition, and smoking-cessation classes"—under its "Wellpower Plus program," which have paid for themselves through savings on health insurance premiums and other health-related expenses. According to the company's president, Duncan Highsmith, "Qualitatively, we have much more energetic and self-reliant employees, and that's the best investment" (*Inc.*, 1995).

An organization offers benefits, like other forms of compensation, so that it can attract, develop, motivate, and retain talented and committed workers. As with wages and salaries, managers plan benefits according to their organizations' financial resources and strategies and the market conditions the organization faces. Business Wire provides tailored benefits to appeal to a variety of needs for its diverse workforce. CEO Lorry Lokey instituted them after carefully weighing his options and their costs. They have achieved many of the goals he set; among them developing a core of committed managers and workers. As with wages and salaries, however, benefits must be constantly reviewed for their relevance and economic feasibility, as Lokey does at Business Wire.

Executive Compensation

perk
A payment or benefit received in addition to a regular wage or salary.

In addition to salaries and the benefits all other employees in their firm receive, executives—members of top management—may also receive benefits unique to their status. These benefits are called perquisites, commonly known as **perks** (Bennett, 1992). Most perks are financial—actual cash or goods and services that have a measurable cash value. Such items include shares of the company's stock, stock options (rights to purchase a company's stock at a discount), bonuses based on overall company performance, use of a company's airplane and regional residential suites, generous travel and lodging allowances, paid-for housing, no-interest loans, and memberships in various clubs and associations. A Conference Board study found that median total compensation for chief executives in fourteen surveyed industries surpassed $1 million in 1999 (Gill, 2000).

> *According to* Business Week's *annual survey, the average CEO of a major corporation made $12.4 million in 1999, up 17 percent from the previous year. That's 475 times more than an average blue-collar worker and six times the average CEO paycheck in 1990. . . . According to Towers Perrin's 1999 Worldwide Total Remuneration report, German CEOs make 13 times what the average manufacturing employee makes. In Japan, the CEO-to-worker pay ratio is just 11-to-1 ("Runaway CEO Pay—A Global View," http://www.aflcio.org/paywatch/ceopay.htm).*

In recent years, however, discussion of "excessive" executive compensation has appeared in popular periodicals and the business press.

CHAPTER SUMMARY

1 Explain the importance of the staffing function. Staffing breathes life into an organization. It acquires and nurtures the human resources needed to execute tasks and functions. People are the key to everything in organizations. They are the organization's most valuable resources. As such, they must be selected, trained, developed, rewarded, and retained for effective and efficient use of the organization's other resources. Staffing is every manager's concern.

2 List and explain the eight elements of the staffing process.

1. Human resource planning begins with job analysis. Performing a job analysis involves creating descriptions and specifications of all jobs and their human qualifications. Next an inventory of people on hand and their abilities to meet current and future needs is determined. Planning also includes forecasting—attempting to predict the future human resource needs. Finally, forecasts are compared to the inventory and needs to recruit or reduce personnel are determined.
2. Recruiting brings enough qualified people into a hiring pool. Care must be taken to find sufficient numbers of people from all ethnic and racial groups. Existing employees must be trained and developed to become eligible for future openings.
3. Selection involves a series of preemployment screening devices used to determine each candidate's ability to provide the organization what it needs. Care must be taken to determine a fit with the company's cultures and to avoid discrimination.
4. Orientation includes a set of activities designed to introduce and welcome newcomers to their new company and working environments. Rights and duties are explained along with the introduction of existing personnel to the new ones.
5. Training and development increase and change employee knowledge, skills, and attitudes. Training is focused on the near term; development focuses on the future. Both help companies to meet their needs and make employees more valuable to both themselves and their organizations.

6. Performance appraisal measures outcomes and behaviors of employees against established and taught standards. Appraisals become the basis for rewards, punishments, promotions, and terminations, and affect nearly every employment decision made by managers. They provide necessary feedback, helping to keep people motivated and focused on their most essential duties.
7. Compensation includes all financial and psychological rewards and incentives provided to employees. Direct compensation is largely composed of wages and salaries. Indirect compensation includes financial and nonfinancial rewards and incentives such as benefits, bonuses, gain and profit sharing, leaves of absence, and employee assistance programs.
8. Employment decisions include transfers, promotions, demotions, layoffs, and firings. All have their specific appropriate applications and must be performed without discrimination.

3 **Describe the three primary staffing environments.** The environments are legal, sociocultural, and union. The legal environment sets limits and provides guidelines for conducting all staffing activities. Specifically, it attempts to provide protection for employees and groups from discrimination and in the areas of health and safety. The sociocultural environment is a collection of diverse individuals and groups, both inside and outside an organization, that make demands on and contribute to it. The union environment affects some companies more than others. Union contracts govern work rules, wages, and conditions of employment. Wages and benefits established in some industries are often duplicated or exceeded by nonunion organizations.

4 **Describe the four activities related to human resource planning.** In job analysis, groups of jobs are studied to determine their basic duties and the human qualities needed to perform them. A human resource inventory determines who are on board along with their present qualifications and future prospects. The human resource forecast is based on both short- and long-term plans and strategies for the company and its various parts. Finally, a comparison is made between the inventory and the forecasted needs to determine if contraction, expansion, or keeping the status quo is the correct plan to follow.

5 **List and describe the primary screening devices used in the selection process.** All selection devices must be job related and validated in order to avoid discrimination. The application provides essential personal data—job history, education, aspirations—about a person's suitability for a particular job. Preliminary interviews verify the data on applications and provide an initial face-to-face encounter for both applicant and employer. Testing may include any paper-and-pencil exercise or performance that will be used to make a hiring decision. In-depth interviews are usually conducted by the person or persons for whom and with whom the new person, if hired, will work. Reference checks provide verification of key facts about a job applicant such as work history, compensation earned, and successes in various positions. Physical exams help to avoid bringing newcomers into an environment that could be injurious to their health.

6 **Explain the differences and similarities between training and development.** Training increases knowledge and skills, motivation to succeed, chances for advancement, morale, pride in performance, and quality and productivity. It is usually provided to keep people current in the present jobs and to prepare them for changes to those jobs. Development focuses on preparing people for new and different positions, challenges, and opportunities. It also imparts skills, knowledge, and attitudes. Training is usually provided by organizations. Development is each person's individual responsibility and may or may not be aided by one's organization.

7 **Explain the purpose of a performance appraisal.** The primary purpose is to provide feedback on one's performances and outputs, enabling rewards and needed improvement efforts to take place. It helps to evaluate the results of previous training and to determine any additional training needs. It helps individuals and teams plan for their improvement and choose the methods they will utilize. Appraisals also help to improve the relationships between the evaluator and the evaluated. People know how they are doing—what's right and wrong—and the expectations for their future performances.

8 **Describe the four primary employment decisions.** Promotions lead individuals to higher levels of responsibility, greater demands on their talents, and improvements in earnings. They are often earned rewards for present performance and development efforts undertaken to qualify them for a new, more demanding position. Transfers are often temporary lateral movements to crosstrain and provide additional experiences. Demotions are the opposite of promotions and are primarily used to save good people until more appropriate positions become available. Separations are voluntary and involuntary. Resignations and retirements are examples of the first; layoffs and firings are examples of the latter.

9 **Explain the purposes and components of compensation.** Compensation in all its forms is intended to help organizations attract, train, develop, reward, and retain good people. Compensation is direct and indirect. Wages, commissions, piece rates, and salaries are direct because they link directly to hours or days worked or outputs achieved. Indirect compensation includes financial and psychological rewards beyond the preceding. Benefits include the largest segment. These include such items as insurance, pay for time not worked, gain sharing, profit sharing, pensions, and employee assistance programs such as wellness programs. Psychological rewards include satisfaction achieved through work and various alterations to one's working schedule.

REVIEW QUESTIONS

1. Why is staffing so important to organizations?
2. What are the components of staffing and in what order do they occur?
3. Which external environments affect the staffing process most directly? How do they affect it?
4. What takes place under the heading of "human resource planning"?
5. What are the primary screening devices used in staffing?
6. How are training and development similar? How are they different?
7. What are the primary purposes of appraising employees?
8. Under what circumstances would an organization perform each of the following: promotion, transfer, demotion, and separation?
9. What purposes do organizations try to achieve through compensation? What forms can compensation take?

DISCUSSION QUESTIONS FOR CRITICAL THINKING

1. Why are the concepts of equal employment opportunity and affirmative action so important to organizations today?
2. How would an organization recruit if it is looking for electrical engineers with a knowledge of the latest technologies? If it is looking for medical technicians with at least three years of experience?
3. What kind of compensation do you think is most important to each of the following: people five years away from retirement? Single people in their twenties? Young marrieds with their first child on the way?
4. How are you appraised in your classes? At work? What value do you find in such appraisals?

INTERNET EXERCISES

Check the text Web site at http://plunkett.swcollege.com for updated links to the Internet Exercises.

1. The *Occupational Outlook Handbook*, published by the U.S. Bureau of Labor Statistics, is a source of career information. Each job description includes Nature of the Work, Working Conditions, Employment, Training, Other Qualifications, Advancement, Job Outlook, Earnings, Related Occupations, and Sources of Additional Information. Look at the description for Human Resources, Training, and Labor Relations Specialists and Managers. Which of these jobs interest you? Why?
   http://www.bls.gov/oco/ocos021.htm
2. What are the benefits of using the Internet for recruiting? Do you recommend that managers use the Internet for recruiting? Justify your recommendations.
   http://www.google.com
   [benefits of online recruiting] Google Search

   http://www.altavista.com
   ["benefits of online recruiting"] Search
3. Discussions of "excessive" executive compensation have appeared in popular periodicals and the business press. Identify a company for which you have worked or for which you would like to work. What did the CEO of your company make last year? How does his/her pay package compare with that of the average worker, a minimum-wage earner, and the president of the United States? Briefly explain why you think the CEO deserves or doesn't deserve that level of compensation.
   http://www.aflcio.org/cgi-bin/aflcio.pl

APPLICATION CASE

Outstanding Business Leader 2000; North American Customer Excellence Award 1998; Black Enterprise's 1995 Auto Dealer of the Year Builds on Diversity

Riverside Ford is the oldest African-American-owned Ford dealership in the country. On February 4, 2000, Northwood University recognized Nathan G. Conyers, president and founder of Conyers-Riverside Ford in Detroit, as one of America's "Outstanding Business Leaders." Also in 2000, Conyers was awarded a Jaguar Motorcar Franchise, only the second black-owned Jaguar franchise in the company's history. In 1998, Ford Motor Company recognized Nathan G. Conyers with the coveted North American Customer Excellence Award.

In the late 1960s major metropolitan areas such as Chicago, Los Angeles, and Detroit were racked with violence and racial unrest. Businesses were fleeing black neighborhoods. At this time Ford Motor Company made a decision to "get more black auto dealers on board."

Enter the Conyers family. With financing support from Ford, John Conyers, Sr., along with his sons John, Jr. and Nathan, was able to fulfill a lifelong dream of owning a family business by investing in a Ford franchise. John Conyers, Sr. had worked for Chrysler for many years. Nathan was a partner in a law firm but left it to join his father as president of Conyers Riverside Ford in 1970. Eventually John, Sr.'s five children joined the dealership, holding a variety of jobs. (The dealership is located near the Detroit River, close to the center of the city.) John, Jr. remains an investor and is a congressman in the U.S. House of Representatives.

After 30 years of riding the peaks and valleys of auto sales, Conyers Riverside Ford now has 91 employees and sales of over $30 million annually. It hasn't been easy. Many black-owned businesses in black neighborhoods have failed. A Ford spokesperson believes that "Conyers endured by knowing his market, being a hands-on manager, and changing with the times."

Initially his customers were African Americans who knew the Conyers family members. Whites would visit the dealership, look around, and buy their Fords elsewhere. Nathan's response? "He hired more white sales staff and managers to 'create a comfort level for any customer that comes in.' He aggressively marketed his service department to downtown office workers, figuring that if they trusted him to fix their cars, they'd eventually trust him to sell them a new one." More than half of the dealership's managers are white—eight of thirteen. All Conyers employees are constantly focused on customer satisfaction and cost control and are appraised accordingly. Both have been driving forces behind change since the dealership began.

Nathan Conyers has resisted the temptation of moving the dealership to the wealthier suburbs. Born and raised in Detroit (a city of about 70 percent African Americans), Nathan has a strong commitment to his community, the city's economic viability, and "to doing the right thing because it's the right thing to do." He helped establish the National Association of Minority Automobile dealers and served as its first president.

http://www.riverford.com

Questions

1. Why did Conyers initially diversify its staff?
2. What possible problems may arise in a family-owned business that provides employment for a father and his children?
3. How is Detroit's sociocultural environment affecting Conyers' management decisions?

Sources: Dan Holly, "Heads, We Win," *Black Enterprise* (June 1995), pp. 134–136, 140; "Conyers-Riverside Ford Auto Dealer Receives National Business Award," *The Auto Channel* (11 February 2000), http://www.theautochannel.com/news/press/date/20000211/press007745.html; "Conyers Honored by Ford Motor," *The Detroit News* (15 May 1998), http://detnews.com/1998/biz/9805/15/05150126.htm; Conyers Riverside Ford, http://www.riverford.com.

VIDEO CASE

LaBelle Management: Performance Appraisals

In 1948, the late Norman LaBelle opened the Pixie Hamburger Drive-In Restaurant, complete with carhops and inexpensive food. The Pixie quickly became a popular place with both the local population and the fast-growing enrollment of Central Michigan University. Little did he know at the time that his two sons would later run the business and that it would eventually grow to more than 30 restaurants and hotels employing some 2,000 people.

LaBelle's growth has included both expansion and diversification into other types of restaurants. In 1972, the first Sweet Onion opened, followed eight years later by a second. The Mt. Pleasant Big Boy Restaurants were started in 1982, and three more locations in Michigan were eventually added. Next came the Ponderosa Steakhouses, with three locations. By 1987, the company had assumed operation of the Michigan Division of Cafeteria at Dow Chemical and had added eight more Ponderosa's in Indiana (since then, nine more Ponderosa's have opened). By May 1995, LaBelle Management opened the Italian Oven Restaurant and a Bennigan's Irish Pub in Mt. Pleasant.

But restaurants comprised only part of the company's diversification efforts and its emergence as LaBelle Management. LaBelle started Comfort Inns in 1989. Then, in 1998, it acquired the Grand Beach Resort Hotel. In all, LaBelle Management now owns and operates 30 properties in Indiana and Michigan. They include hotels, resorts, conference centers, and freestanding restaurants located in resorts, major cities, small cities, suburbs, and small towns.

A common element in all its operations is the company's commitment to use of a comprehensive performance appraisal system. LaBelle's management views its system for employee appraisal as a two-way exchange between superior and subordinate whereby both benefit from the exchange of information and learn what each expects of the other. Formal performance appraisals are scheduled for each employee twice a year, but management believes in an open feedback system, whereby feedback is given to employees on an ongoing basis (when they need it, not as long as 6 months later).

LaBelle uses different methods and criteria by which to evaluate its crew members and managers. Crew evaluations include such things as attitude, job performance, attendance, customer service, and teamwork. Manager appraisals focus on their human resource skills, leadership abilities, profitability of the operation, and degree of customer service.

LaBelle Management utilizes its performance appraisals for various administrative and developmental purposes. Its top management believes that managers should tell employees where they stand so that they know what they're doing right and what they're doing wrong. Top management views the performance appraisal system as a key to the company's continued success.

http://www.labellemgt.com

For Discussion:

1. LaBelle Management uses different methods and criteria to evaluate personnel at different organizational levels, but all are evaluated in the same general way. How are they all evaluated?
2. For what specific purposes does LaBelle Management utilize performance appraisals?
3. Why does LaBelle Management believe that feedback must be directed to the superior from the subordinate, as well as to the subordinate from the superior?

Communication: Interpersonal and Organizational

KEY TERMS

communication
diction
feedback
formal communication channels
formal communication network
grapevine
informal communication channels
information
interpersonal communication
jargon
medium
message
noise
nonverbal communication
perceptions
receiver
semantics
sender
stereotype
understanding

LEARNING OBJECTIVES

After studying this chapter, you should be able to

1. Discuss the importance of communication in organizations
2. Diagram the communication process and label all its parts
3. List and explain the barriers to interpersonal communication and suggest remedies to overcome them
4. Describe the uses of downward, horizontal, and upward communication channels
5. Describe the informal communication channel known as the grapevine
6. List and explain the barriers to organizational communication and suggest remedies to overcome them
7. Describe the responsibilities of senders and receivers during the communication process

MANAGEMENT IN ACTION

Dell Connects with Suppliers and Customers

Dell Computer Corporation makes computer systems and supplies technology for the Internet infrastructure. It was founded in 1984 by Michael Dell, the computer industry's longest-tenured chief executive officer, on a simple concept: that by selling personal computer systems directly to customers, Dell could best understand their needs and efficiently provide the most effective computing solutions to meet those needs. Through the direct business model, Dell offers in-person relationships with consumer, corporate, and institutional customers; telephone and Internet purchasing; customized computer systems; online and phone technical support; and next-day, on-site product service. For maximum efficiency and effectiveness, the company has linked itself electronically to suppliers and customers.

Early adopters of the Internet were those businesses willing to innovate and to take some risks. Michael Dell is considered the leading architect of the Internet-enabled, thoroughly digital business enterprise. Dell helped pioneer the end-to-end use of digital networks to communicate with its customer, take orders, and then pull together products from suppliers. Dell did this by surpassing traditional distribution channels (middlemen) and going directly to customers. First, Dell built its internal operations for Internet integration; then, its partners were tied to the operations; and finally, customers were linked through the Internet. The company launched www.dell.com in 1994 and added electronic commerce capability in 1996. By September 2000, Dell was selling more than $50 million worth of computer equipment from its Web site every day.

Every system is built-to-order so that customers get exactly what they want. As soon as the customer places his or her order, Dell shares production data with suppliers online. A survey of 1,200 companies conducted by McCombs School of Business at the University of Texas [sponsored by Dell], found a strong relationship between financial performance and companies that have invested heavily using technology to redesign businesses' processes and cultivate electronic business relationships with suppliers. The survey found only one in seven companies shares production data with suppliers online.

To provide superior service to its customers, Dell uses knowledge gained from direct customer contact before and after the sale to provide award-winning reliability and tailored customer service. When an order enters the system, the material availability is confirmed and all parts are released to complete the system. Customers can use the Dell Order Status to follow their order through Dell's build-to-order model from the time the order was taken, to the time Dell ships it to them. Delivery preparation is normally completed within one day of the date production is complete. Dell recognizes that a large part of customer service and business success rests in cutting the time it takes to design, build, and place the product in the customer's hands. ■

Sources: John Dodge, "Dell's Internet-Based Plant Keeps Production Efficient," *The Wall Street Journal* (26 September 2000), http://www.wsj.com; Anitesh Barua, Prabhudev Konana, Andrew Whinston, and Fang Yin, "Making E-Business Pay: Eight Key Drivers for Operational Success," (in *IEEE IT Professional*, November/December, 2000), http://crec.bus.utexas.edu. Find more details at http://www.dell.com.

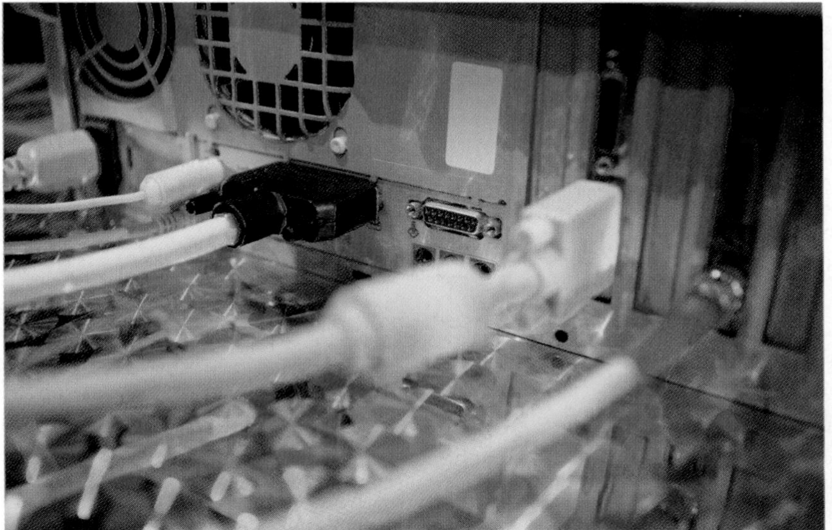

Dell Computer has succeeded on the simple concept of selling directly to customers in order to meet and exceed their needs.

INTRODUCTION

Discuss the importance of communication in organizations

http://www.walmart.com

http://www.dell.com

Communication is the process through which people and organizations accomplish objectives. By communicating with others we share attitudes, values, emotions, ambitions, wants, and needs. Behind most successes is effective communication—that which is well planned and thoughtfully executed. The process of communication, however, is difficult. Failed plans are often the result of failed attempts at communicating.

Successful managers effectively communicate their vision for a work unit or the company as a whole. At Wal-Mart, Sam Walton's vision to make the customer number one led his company to its place as the most successful retailer in American history. The late Sam Walton (1992) stated his thoughts about the importance of communication:

> *Communicate everything you possibly can to your partners. The more they know, the more they'll understand. The more they understand, the more they'll care. Once they care, there is no stopping them. If you don't trust your associates to know what's going on, they'll know you don't really consider them partners. Information is power, and the gain you get from empowering your associates more than offsets the risk of informing your competitors.*
>
> *Listen to everyone in your company. And figure out ways to get them talking. The folks on the front lines—the ones who actually talk to the customer—are the only ones who really know what's going on out there. You'd better find out what they know. This really is what total quality is all about. To push responsibility down in your organization, and to force good ideas to bubble up within it, you must listen to what your associates are trying to tell you.*

Dell's electronic communication links to its customers and partners (dealers and suppliers) allow it to respond instantly in real time to their needs. Web-site-driven systems provide an important means for effective and efficient customer service. Internet integration is but one manifestation of the importance placed on communication by Dell's leaders.

People in organizations need each other. They must coordinate and pool their efforts to achieve their goals and avoid waste and confusion. They must focus on the needs of the customers, those inside as well as outside the company. They must be able to articulate their needs so that they can work cooperatively. They must be free to express what they know and believe in order to capitalize on opportunities for meaningful change. Managers who really believe that their people are the organization's most valuable resource will make communicating with those people their most vital process.

COMMUNICATION PROCESS

Diagram the communication process and label all its parts

communication
The transmission of information and understanding from one person or group to another.

Communication is the transmission of **information**—data in a coherent, usable form—from one person or group to another. Rational communicators strive to achieve a common **understanding**—agreement about the meaning and intent of the message—among all parties to each communication. Although much of the information that managers rely on is in numeric form, the greatest portion of managerial activity depends on verbal communication and competent use of language. Able communicators respect the conventions of language—spelling, grammar, and punctuation. They know precisely what they wish to say and thoughtfully select

information
Processed data that is useful to the receiver.

understanding
The situation that exists when all senders and receivers agree about the meaning and intent of a message.

sender
The person or group that initiates the communication process.

receiver
The person or group for whom a communication effort is intended.

message
The information that the sender wants to transmit.

medium
The means by which a sender transmits a message.

feedback
Information about the receiver's perception of the sender's message.

the best way to say it. In addition, the communicator needs to be certain that the person who receives the information actually understands the message.

Communication is a process—a set of steps usually taken in a definite sequence. The initiator of communication is called a **sender**; the person or group that gets the communication is the **receiver**. The information that the sender wants to transmit is the **message**. The means chosen by the sender to transmit the message is the **medium**, or channel. Finally, the process must provide mechanisms through which both sender and receiver can determine if the intended communication has taken place and mutual understanding achieved. That mechanism provides **feedback**—information the receiver provides to show how he or she perceived the sender's message. In providing feedback the receiver becomes a sender and the original sender becomes a receiver; the process of sending and receiving messages proceeds until both communicators believe that understanding has taken place. The more carefully crafted and unambiguous the message is, the less the feedback will be required to achieve understanding. Figure 12.1 provides a model of the communication process.

To illustrate the communication process, consider an example involving Harry Trent, a manufacturing director. Harry calls Anita Raton, the human resource manager for his company, and says, "I need a replacement employee." In response to the message, Anita says, "What kind of skills do you need? For which department?" The receiver is seeking clarification of the original message and becomes a sender in doing so. Harry now shifts to being a receiver and must clarify his original message before responding and becoming a sender again. Many conversations flow in this manner because the sender transmits an incomplete message—one that requires the receiver to ask for additional information so that understanding can take place. Harry failed to refine his message before he initiated the communication process.

FIGURE 12.1 *Model of the communication process*

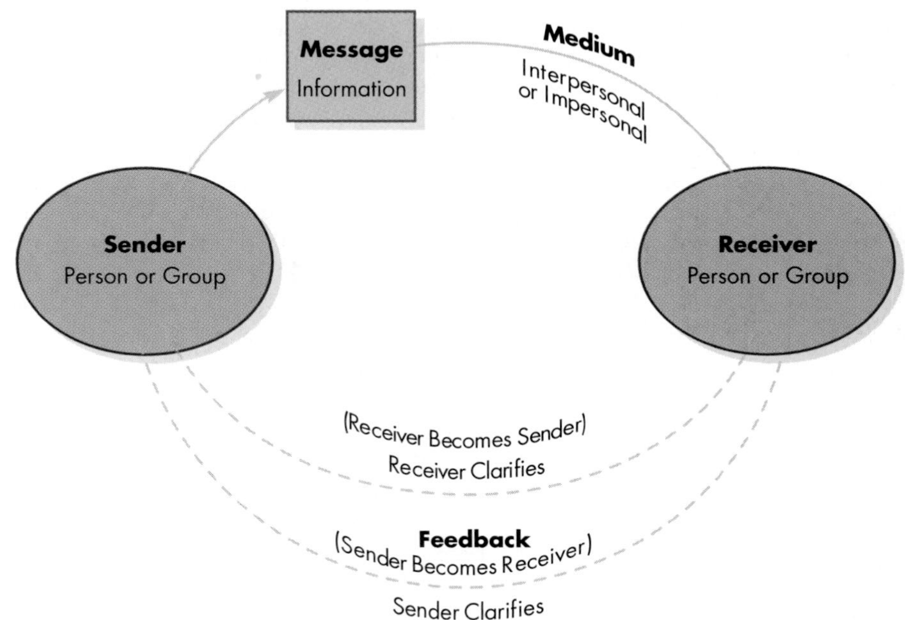

MEDIUMS OF COMMUNICATION

Communication mediums are verbal (spoken or written words) and nonverbal (images, facial expressions, gestures, and body language). Sometimes the medium is the message. See this chapter's Global Applications feature.

Verbal Communication

Spoken verbal messages can be delivered face-to-face or by electronic means such as telephone, voice mail, and voice messaging. Written verbal mediums include traditional printed matter, such as memos, letters, manuals, newsletters, and reports, and electronic delivery systems, including email, facsimiles (faxes), pagers, computer networking, and groupware—software that allows simultaneous group-member interactions by networked computers. "Since 1987 we've added over 130 million information receptacles. Americans now possess 146.6 million email addresses, cellular phones, pagers, fax machines, voice mailboxes, and answering machines—up 365% from . . . 1987" (Tetzeli, 1994).

> *The top 20 percent of workers surveyed [in the 2000 study, Managing Communication in the 21st Century Workplace, commissioned by Pitney Bowes in partnership with The Institute for the Future] manage an average of 363 messages (44 percent more) per day, as compared to 204 messages for the average worker, with high incoming volume in e-mail,*

GLOBAL APPLICATIONS
The Medium Is the Message

Nicolas Hayek, Swiss by birth and CEO of the Swiss Corporation for Microelectronics and Watchmaking (SMH), almost singlehandedly revitalized Swiss watchmaking with a personal vision. Why couldn't, he asked, Swiss watchmakers make a profit creating and selling low-cost, high-quality watches? His company answered that question with the "brash and playful Swatch . . . [which] has become a popular culture phenomenon." It took the company about nine years to celebrate the making of its 100 millionth Swatch!

Says Hayek, "We are not just offering people a style. We are offering them a message. . . . Fashion is about image. Emotional products are about message—a strong, exciting, distinct, authentic message that tells people who you are and why you do what you do." Swatch watches send several nonverbal messages: quality, fun, a tug on one's emotions, a celebration of one's culture, and reasonable cost.

People collect as well as wear Swatches. The average Italian customer owns six. Out-of-production models are sold for ever-increasing prices at Sotheby's international auctions. Hayek believes the Swatch appeal "rests on four pillars: design, communication in the widest sense, quality, and price." Since its introduction, each Swatch has sold for $40 or its equivalent around the world and no dealers are allowed to change that price.

Swatch designs originate in a Milan, Italy, workshop with a constantly changing population of about 20 designers under the direction of Alessandro Mendini, art director. Two collections of 70 designs each are created per year. Only the designs on the watch face and wristband change. "We are looking for an immediate emotional reaction—spontaneity. . . . We want arresting images but we also wink at the consumer," says Mendini.

http://www.swatch.com

Sources: William Taylor, "Message and Muscle: An Interview with Swatch Titan Nicolas Hayek," *Harvard Business Review* (March-April 1993); "The Swiss Watch Industry—History and Today," http://www.fhs.ch/Ehistory.htm; "Markets in Time: The Rise, Fall, and Revival of Swiss Watchmaking" by Anthony Young, http://www.libertyhaven.com/countriesandregions/swiss/marketstime.shtml.

Popular technologies, such as cell phones and palm computers, allow people to communicate virtually anywhere, anytime.

> *postal mail, fax, pager and USPS Express Mail. Receiving approximately 40 more messages per day than they send out, 94 percent of high-volume messagers filter and prioritize their messages in order to manage their high-volume of communications and workflow (Pitney Bowes Workplace Study, 2000).*

The sender's choice of medium is influenced by several factors: the content of the message, the importance of feedback, the number of intended receivers, the receiver's and sender's preferences and characteristics, the sender's and receiver's locations and environments, and the technologies available. Communication requiring immediate, two-way feedback and a personal touch should be oral and in person. If the message is complicated and requires a considered response, communication should be written. In this chapter's opening case, Dell chose electronic mediums for their obvious advantages of speed and accuracy. No human can keep records of suppliers and parts in so many locations, keep them current, search through them, and then schedule shipments as swiftly as computers can.

Conversation, perhaps the most common communication medium for managers, takes place on the shop floor, in the office, over the telephone, at lunch, on the way to meetings, and in group settings. Conversation should be used when the message is for one person and requires personal contact, or when give-and-take is vital. Henry Mintzberg (1973) studied five CEOs and found that they spent 78 percent of their time talking with others. These conversations were generally short—49 percent of their daily encounters lasted less than nine minutes; only 10 percent lasted longer than an hour.

John Kotter found virtually the same results. The fifteen executive general managers he studied spent 76 percent of their time talking with others (Deutschman, 1992). As Suzanne Rinfret Moore, who directs three companies, reported (Deutschman, 1992):

> *Someone can say to me in 30 seconds what it might take 15 minutes to write in a memo—and it generates the ability to think on your feet. . . . [Oral communication] fosters creativity*

for yourself and the people you work with. Access is critical. I want people who can come to my door. They're not time bandits.

Oral communication cannot always substitute for the written word, however. The process of preparing a written document allows careful consideration. The initiator can precisely determine and control the content, organization, complexity, tone, and style of the message. Receivers can digest such communications according to their own schedule and at their own pace. They can prepare considered responses. A written message can be enriched with graphics and other illustrations. In addition, writing tends to support confidentiality. Among the countless variations of written communications are emails, letters, memos, outlines, reports, procedures manuals, press releases, contracts, advertisements, and forms. Figure 12.2 suggests conventional applications for common written communication tools.

Written forms of communication have disadvantages. They are impersonal, do not provide the immediacy of face-to-face contact, and do not elicit immediate feedback.

Some forms of written communication—such as notices on bulletin boards, handbooks, and newsletters—are by their nature impersonal. Do not rely on these tools when timely feedback or elaboration is needed or when the message is critical. Receivers read these communications casually. If communication is vital, use tools of this nature as supplements to immediate tools.

Nonverbal Communication

nonverbal communication
Images, actions, and behaviors that transmit messages.

Nonverbal communication consists of messages transmitted without the use of words. Nonverbal transmitters include facial expressions, gestures, and body language (posture, placement of limbs, and proximity to others). Photographs, charts, and videos also convey information nonverbally. Visual transmitters are powerful and persuasive tools that enable senders to send messages that are nearly impossible to communicate verbally. For example, a product's distinctive name, appearance, and packaging communicate messages to consumers. (See this chapter's Ethical Management feature.) To further understand how valuable images can be, try to convey the drawing in Figure 12.3 using words alone.

FIGURE 12.2 *Four written forms of communication*

Letters	For correspondence with persons or groups outside an organization. Usually produced in a format—a form letter or block-style letter, for example.
Memos	For routine correspondence with superiors, subordinates, and peers. Memos should contain the date, the names of intended receivers and their titles, the subject of the correspondence (ideally only one subject per memo), the message, and the name and title of the sender. The ideal memo is no more than one page long.
Outlines	For indicating the structure of a lecture, report, or agenda and to order major and minor points. Outlines are useful in developing tables of contents and summaries.
Reports	For reporting the results of an investigation or routine and ongoing activities. Report formats range from fill-in-the-blank styles to manuscripts with or without statistical data. The format is often prescribed.

FIGURE 12.3 *Exercise in nonverbal communication*

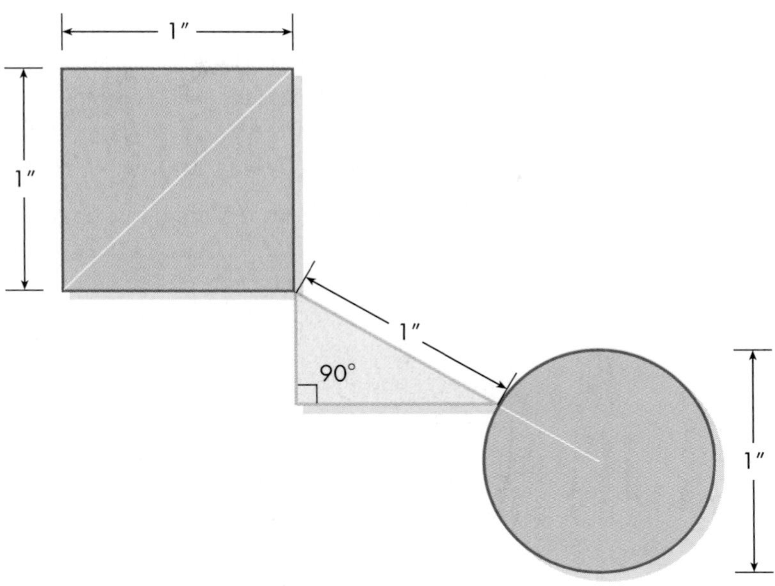

ETHICAL MANAGEMENT
Profits Through Imitation

How would you like to work for a company that makes most of its profits by imitating the best that name-brand cereal makers can create? That's what Ralcorp Holdings, Inc., a leader in private label or store brand foods, does to earn about 70 percent of its profits.

Compared to name-brand cereals, private-label cereals have only 6 percent of the market, but things are changing. In 1994 "private-label cereal growth averaged 8% while branded cereals grew 3%. And [industry] analysts expect even more private-label growth as the aggressive Ralcorp pours on new products." Compared with the high cost of national brands, Ralcorp's knockoffs sell for about $1 less per box at retail while delivering more profit per box to retailers, who get their names on the box as well. Another positive result of private-label growth has been virtual wholesale price freezes on name-brand cereals.

Ralcorp works hard to simulate the look, taste, and packaging of the name brands it mimics. "To make his imitations even more sincere forms of flattery, [former] CEO Richard A. Pearce invest[ed] in new plant technology that will help Ralcorp more exactly copy the brands." Ralcorp's names mimic originals: Tasteeos for Cheerios, Fruit Rings for Froot Loops, and Apple Dapples for Apple Jacks. Because cereals are made with routine manufacturing methods, the legality of copying most types of cereals is not an issue.

- Is what Ralcorp does a form of "legalized" theft?
- Why does Ralcorp try to imitate the packaging of name-brand cereals?
- What additional ethical issues do you see in this case?

http://www.ralcorp.com

Sources: Greg Burns, "A Froot Loop by Any Other Name . . ." *Business Week* (26 June 1995), pp. 72, 76. Ralcorp Holdings, Inc.'s http://www.ralcorp.com business units include Ralston Foods (cereals), http://www.ralstonfoods.com; Bremner (cookies and crackers), http://www.bremnerbiscuit.com; Nutcracker/Flavor House (snack nuts), http://www.nutcrackerbrands.com; and Carriage House, formerly Red Wing/Martin Gillet (sauces and dressings), http://www.carriagehousecos.com.

http://www.boeing.com

A picture can communicate more effectively than words. Boeing uses computer graphics to aid its workers (Sprout, 1994):

> *Researchers are developing head-mounted displays that put computer graphics to uses that are . . . helping workers do complex wiring or place the perfect rivet. . . . Cables connect the headset to a computer, which generates the image and changes it when the worker turns or proceeds to a new task; a magnetic or ultrasonic receiver on the helmet helps the system track its position . . . so the wearer sees a diagram superimposed on whatever he's working.*

Like pictures, gestures and body language convey messages. Research and your own experiences indicate that a sender's body language and other nonverbal expressions help a receiver to understand the sender's feelings and intent. The upset boss communicates emotions through facial expressions, clenched fists, aggressive gestures, a louder-than-normal voice, closer-than-normal physical presence, and eye-to-eye contact—expressions that are all direct and intense.

Suppose a manager remains seated behind the desk when a visitor arrives, refuses to look at the person, and grunts an acknowledgment of the visitor's presence. These behaviors transmit one or more of the following messages to the visitor: "This person is not pleased to see me," "I have done something to annoy this person," "This person does not respect me," or "Maybe this is not a good time to visit with this person." The manager sends quite a different set of messages if he or she rises and extends a hand, seeks eye contact, smiles broadly, and says, "It's great to see you. Have a seat!"

Senders and receivers must be aware of the messages inherent in nonverbal communication. When nonverbal cues seem to contradict the sender's verbal messages, the receiver tends to believe the nonverbal message.

INTERPERSONAL COMMUNICATION

interpersonal communication
Face-to-face or voice-to-voice (telephone) conversations that take place in real time and allow instant feedback.

http://www.net2phone.com

Interpersonal communication involves real-time face-to-face or voice-to-voice (telephone) conversation that allows instant feedback. Transmitting voice and fax over the Internet has become a catalyst in the continuing drop in international telecommunications rates. Net2Phone was the first company to bridge the Internet with telephone networks. Internet Telephony known as VoIP, or Voice over Internet Protocol, is the technology that enables the real-time transmission of voice signals over the IP network. Net2Phone transmits voice and fax over the Internet by using public telephone switching networks for the minimum portion of the call and the Internet to carry the call over the widest distance.

http://www.kmart.com

A number of companies now use satellite-transmitted videoconferences for interpersonal communication. Kmart, for example, regularly runs videoconferences involving managers at its Michigan headquarters and those in its stores nationwide. The managers at headquarters make a presentation, and the store managers are invited to ask questions (Comins, 1992).

Interpersonal communications are appropriate for discussing matters that require give-and-take between participants. Applications include discussions about a performance appraisal; MBO sessions; conversations in which praise or criticism is given; and coaching, counseling, or training sessions. Meetings and conferences are useful forms of interpersonal communication when the issues affect others or require input from more than one or two parties. Brainstorming sessions, quality circles, committee meetings, and contract negotiations are but a few uses for interpersonal communication (Plunkett and Fournier, 1991).

Communication and Teams

Teams are taking an increasingly large role in organizations. Managers find that by putting workers together, they can get better work. Chapter 15 will explore team dynamics in detail; this chapter will focus on the management of team communication.

Team members generally engage in four kinds of communication. They exchange views, discuss work, deliberate on a problem or issue, and transmit information.

Whether a team is a permanent work group or temporarily gathered to address an issue, team members share a leader, a goal or goals, related activities (though each member may have a distinct role), and mutual dependency. Each individual possesses unique traits, of course, but the shared characteristics build group identity. In fact, group members often develop common perspectives about management and the organization. These shared viewpoints arise first from the fact that group members affect each other and also from the fact that communications within the group transmit and reinforce similar attitudes. One key to managing intergroup communication, then, is to ensure that the viewpoints being shared are positive and match the organization's culture and goals.

Often disputes arise between group members and must be competently handled. Ellen Lord leads a team at Textron's Davidson Interiors plant in New Hampshire. She has "found that to keep teams happy, managers must have the patience and presence of mind to act like a parent, teacher, and referee all at once" (Dumaine, 1994). As her team was forming, its members found a variety of issues to argue over. "A neatnik sitting next to a slob lost his cool. People were becoming emotional about what kind of coffee was brewing in the pot. . . . No matter how bad it gets you must keep people together and talking until they feel comfortable, a process that can take months" (Dumaine, 1994). See Figure 12.4 for a checklist dealing with productive group and team communication.

FIGURE 12.4 *Checklist for ensuring effective communications between groups and among group members*

1. Are members clear about the group's purposes and goals? ____
2. Is each group member clear about his or her roles? ____
3. Does mutual trust and respect exist between group members? ____
4. Do all members have access to the information they need? ____
5. Are formal discussions properly led and their results recorded? ____
6. Do groups and their members receive prompt feedback on the results of their efforts? ____
7. Do members periodically evaluate the effectiveness of their group and individual members' contributions? ____
8. Are groups and their members given recognition and rewards for their valuable contributions? ____

Much team communication revolves around getting the job done—copywriters talk to product managers about a product's features and target market, and designers discuss page layouts with copywriters. A manager's main concerns with this kind of communication are to ensure that people send and receive accurate information, that all team members get the information they need when they need it, and that team members show sensitivity to one another's ideas and concerns.

The third kind of team communication takes place when a group meets to explore an issue, determine how to implement a procedure, solve a technical problem, or make a pricing decision. Group decision making offers many benefits. Hearing multiple perspectives can help a person generate more ideas than he or she could generate alone; the interaction of people can create a powerful synergy. In addition, participation increases commitment to the decision (see Chapter 7). Group deliberations, however, must be carefully managed to ensure that they are effective. Managers must set a clear agenda for the meeting and keep the discussion to the point. They need to ensure that all group members participate by channeling discussion to avoid domination by a few. They must keep an eye on the clock so the meeting does not waste time.

The fourth type of intrateam communication involves the transmission of information. Whether a manager is informing team members about a new organizational policy or a team member is passing on the findings of a telephone conversation with a consultant, a team meeting is ideal for this kind of communication. Telling five people at once is far more efficient than seeking out and telling each one individually. Also, when information is transmitted to several people at a time, the chance of each team member receiving the same information increases. Finally, having the team assembled to hear this kind of message provides the opportunity for team members to discuss its implications (Plunkett and Fournier, 1991).

Barriers to Interpersonal Communication

List and explain the barriers to interpersonal communication and suggest remedies to overcome them

Leonard R. Sayles and George Strauss (1966) identified common barriers to interpersonal, or face-to-face, communication; the paragraphs that follow summarize the barriers they defined. These barriers can be overcome in large measure by following the guidelines for improving communication that appear toward the end of this chapter.

Diction and Semantics

diction
The choice and use of words in speech and writing.

semantics
The study of the meanings of words.

Diction—the choice and use of words in speech and writing—significantly affects communication. **Semantics**, the study of the meanings of words, confirms that words may possess different meanings for different people. In everyday usage, abstract words such as *liberal*, *conservative*, and *motivate* create different images for senders and receivers. Business terms can cause the same problems. Terms such as *discipline* and *grievance* usually convey both negative and positive connotations and may have a strong emotional impact. The effective communicator is sensitive to such effects.

In today's culturally diverse workplaces, English is a second language to many. To overcome problems related to this situation, companies are providing basic English courses. They are also capitalizing on America's bilingual population by catering to its needs. (See this chapter's Valuing Diversity feature.)

VALUING DIVERSITY
"Discovering" a Market of 25 Million

Just who is your customer? If you are a large national bookstore chain like Borders, your answer will be: American readers. Since this answer now includes millions of people who use English as a second language, Borders has adjusted its inventories to accommodate them. Among the largest segment in this market are Hispanics, numbering over 31 million (http://www.census.gov, March 1999). From its beginning in the 1970s, the company has stocked Spanish-language books. Its Miami-area stores' volume is second only to the Washington, D.C., market. Its primary Chicago outlet has the largest inventory of Spanish-language books of any chain in that city. Finding enough and the right mix of titles, however, is not easy.

Raquel Roque, a distributor of Spanish-language books, says, "There are titles that cross borders, but many others that do not. . . . You want the customer to come in for his [Spanish-language] how-to books on speaking English. . . . Hopefully he'll . . . come back for his books on . . . how to open a small business, as well as literature." Hispanic consumers and authors, like many others, have varying dialects, tastes, and national origins. One Hispanic author may sell well in California but not in Florida. Many books that are popular in English do not translate well into Spanish, for example, comedian Tim Allen's 1994 best-seller, *Don't Stand Too Close to a Naked Man*.

Spanish-language publishers and their publications are growing along with their counterparts in broadcasting—both radio and television. This growth testifies to the growing importance of Latin cultures and bilingual capabilities in America.

http://www.borders.com

Sources: Melita Marie Garza, "Language Barrier," *Chicago Tribune* (15 June 1995), sec. 5, pp. 1–2; Roberto R. Ramirez, "The Hispanic Population in the United States," March 1999, http://www.census.gov/prod/2000pubs/p20-527.pdf.

jargon
The specialized or technical language of a trade, profession, subculture, or other group.

Jargon—the specialized or technical language that develops in trades, professions, subcultures, and other groups—poses its own set of hazards. Each corporate culture, subculture, unit, and division has its own unique terminology and slang expressions. Computer experts talk about bits, bytes, and boilerplate. Financial managers use terms like *leverage*, *equity*, and *depreciation*. When members of these subcultures attempt to communicate with those outside their group by using these expressions, confusion can result.

The lesson for communicators is clear. Strive for language that means the same thing to receiver and sender. The sender who has any doubt about the possible interpretation of unusual, specialized, or vague words should take extra care to ask receivers if they understand the terms. Communication with newcomers to American culture and language deserves special attention. Local English is treacherous to speakers who tend to take things literally and may be unaware of slang and jargon. For example, the meaning of *chewing the fat* differs significantly in Cleveland and Nome.

Expectations of Familiarity

How many times have you been in a conversation and tuned out the speaker because you absolutely knew what he or she was going to say? People do this because they are familiar with a speaker's thoughts on particular topics. The speaker begins with a statement and tone that sounds similar to openings used in the past. At that moment, listening stops. When a parent begins by saying "When I was your age . . . ," the child tunes out. When the boss begins with "When I did your job, I . . . ," the subordinate tunes out. Failure to listen because of the listener's expectation of familiarity is a factor that inhibits communication.

When addressing people on familiar topics, senders should engage their receivers by asking questions about their understanding and current knowledge of the topic. If receivers already know what a sender wants to communicate, no further effort is needed. If what is about to be sent is new, senders should state that fact and proceed to convey the new data.

Source's Lack of Credibility

If a sender has credibility in the receiver's mind, the message will be received more readily than if the sender lacks credibility. When a person proven to have knowledge and a successful track record speaks about his or her specialty, people tend to listen. The finance manager is presumed to have more expertise in budgetary matters than the marketing manager. The experienced plant manager's ideas about how to handle a maintenance problem should prevail over those of his or her new apprentice. New and inexperienced employees, however, often bring an unbiased and fresh approach to problems. They may spot more effective or efficient ways to get things done. Their ideas deserve a hearing. Empowering employees means giving them the freedom and authority to offer suggestions and devise new solutions.

Preconceived Notions

If the new and different viewpoint the receivers hear contradicts what they "know" to be true, the receivers do not accept it. In reacting this way, the receivers close their minds and inhibit growth and change. They shut others out even though the others could be the means of the receivers' own growth and development.

Differing Perceptions

Most organizations include people from different social, economic, and cultural backgrounds. These people may hold different values, beliefs, expectations, and goals. Many do not even share a common language. These differences contribute to differing **perceptions**—ways of observing and the bases for making judgments. Predetermined sets of conventional and oversimplified beliefs about groups of people—**stereotypes**—cause positive or negative reactions to those groups. "He's Hispanic, so he must be . . . ," "Women just don't . . . ," and "Germans always . . ." are expressions of stereotypes. Stereotypes can inhibit interaction and communication. Everyone needs to keep an open mind.

perceptions
Ways in which people observe and the bases for their judgments about the stimuli they experience.

stereotype
Predetermined belief about a group of people.

Conflicting Nonverbal Communication

A person who frowns while saying "I feel great" is sending conflicting messages. The manager who squirms in her seat and keeps checking her watch while telling us to continue a conversation is really telling us to stop.

A person's physical appearance and behavior send messages. Suppose a manager urges employees to strive for thoroughness. The urgings are likely to go unheeded if the manager always looks sloppy. Whatever a manager says about the need for continual improvement may be mitigated if he or she is never on time for meetings. Tardiness says that other things are more important, that the meeting is unnecessary, or that other peoples' time has no value.

Emotions

Tempers interfere with reason and understanding; therefore, they inhibit communication. Sender and receiver become opponent and adversary. When the head coach of the Chicago Bears lost his temper on the sidelines during a football game, sports commentators and some team members claimed that it turned the momentum in favor of the opposing team. The Bears had a fourteen-point lead at the time but scored no more points and lost the game. Attempts at achieving a meeting of the minds dissolved into name calling and offensive remarks and behaviors. Messages communicated in anger can be damaging to people and their relationships for some time to come. Once offensive words are spoken, they cannot be unsaid. Apologies will not erase the hurt that receivers felt.

The best way to overcome the barriers to communication that emotions can pose is to develop a sense of timing. A sense of timing helps a sender know the best time to initiate a communication. Sam shows sensitivity to timing when he says, "I wouldn't see the boss today. He's just heard that his new budget was rejected." Similarly, the end of a tiring workday is not the best time to attempt to communicate complex messages. People are usually not in the proper condition to make communication successful.

Noise

noise
Anything in the environment of a communication that interferes with the sending and receiving of messages.

Anything in the environment that interferes with the sending and receiving of messages is **noise**. If you have ever tried to speak over the roar of machinery or over a telephone with a bad connection, you know how noise interferes with communication. When people have to shout to be heard or are overburdened with irrelevant messages, they are experiencing noise.

ORGANIZATIONAL COMMUNICATION

formal communication channels
Management-designated pipelines—running up, down, and across the organizational structure—used for official communication efforts.

Now that we understand how people communicate on an interpersonal level, we are ready to explore organizational communication. This section will begin by discussing the **formal communication channels**, the channels that result from a company's organizational structure. These designated pipelines for messages run in three directions: upward, downward, and horizontally. Managers are charged with the responsibility of creating, using, and keeping these channels open and available to organization members. The channels act as connections between members and outsiders and as paths through which official communications flow.

One look at a company's formal organization chart will reveal who is connected to whom and, therefore, in which directions communications will flow. Figure 12.5 shows a formal organization chart and the communication links between line and staff managers. Remember that communication is a two-way effort, so these channels carry messages from, as well as to, the persons they link.

In the not-too-distant past, formal communication flowed down from the top and rarely in any other direction. A strict chain of command existed at each level in every work unit or subsystem. Feedback efforts were difficult and time-consuming. A great dependence on paper and written communication was the norm. Orders were given, procedures were written, and those who received them obeyed them.

FIGURE 12.5 Organization's formal channels for communication

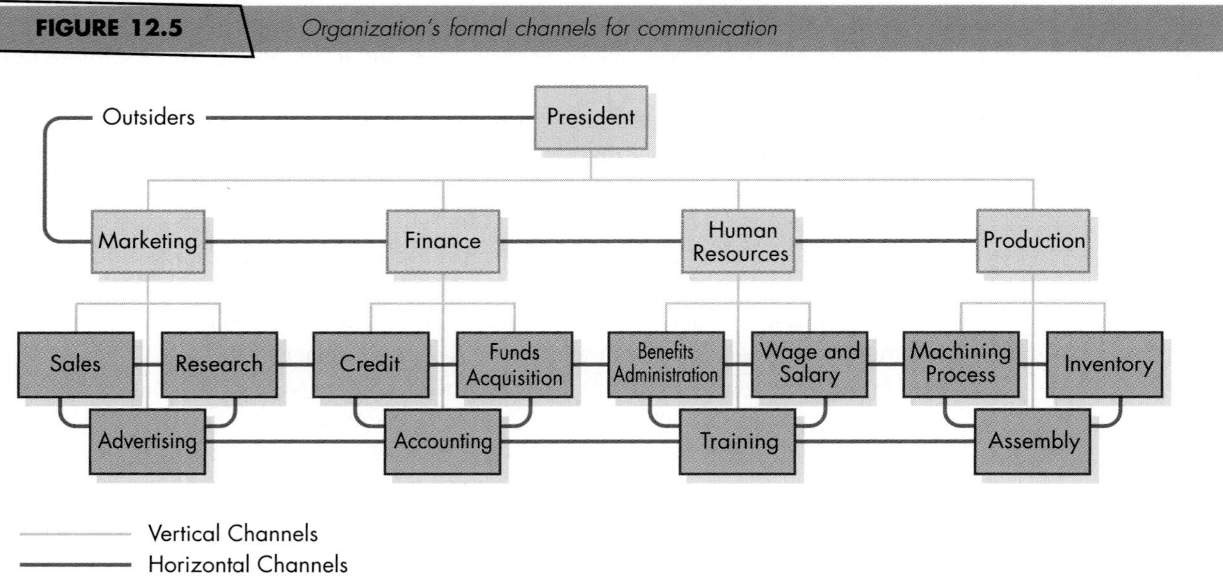

Today, organizations emphasize electronic means of communicating, empowerment of employees, flexibility, and integrated teams. Therefore, compared to the past, more communication flows from the bottom up and from side to side.

Because layers of middle management have been removed, communications today are faster, more direct, and subject to less filtering than in the past. Computer networks, fax machines, satellite communications, and teleconferencing link those who must work together—even if they are in another part of town or in another country. With a computer and a connection to the Internet an employee is never out of touch. Today, managers and workers occupy offices that are, in effect, without walls.

Formal Downward Channels

4 Describe the uses of downward, horizontal, and upward communication channels

Downward communication conveys the kinds of information shown in Figure 12.6. Along with the messages themselves, managers should communicate the reasoning behind the messages—why things are being done and the advantages and disadvantages that may result to all concerned. Sharing reasons has the effect of bringing others into the decision-making process. As Chapter 7 reported, the results can be extremely beneficial.

Downward communication takes place daily, in on-the-job conversations and interactions between managers or team leaders and their subordinates. Downward communication can be one-on-one or take place in large meetings. Dell's efforts at communication began with top management explaining the company's position to suppliers. Typical devices used to carry downward communication are company procedures manuals, newsletters, public relations announcements, annual statements, and various types of memos, reports, letters, and directives.

FIGURE 12.6 *Subjects for downward, horizontal, and upward communication*

DOWNWARD COMMUNICATION

CEO's vision	Job designs
Changes in rules or procedures	Performance appraisals
Company mission	Policies
Delegation of authority	Solutions
Development	Staff managers' advice
Feedback	Strategic goals
Incentives	Training

HORIZONTAL COMMUNICATION

Coordination efforts	Information to and about customers
Efforts to seek assistance	Information to and about suppliers
Feedback	Group-member interactions

UPWARD COMMUNICATION

Complaints	Requests for assistance
Feedback	Status reports
Recommended solutions	Research results

http://www.zingermans.com

The cofounders of Zingerman's Deli in Ann Arbor, Michigan, began their company newsletter when the deli got too large for them to talk to all 130 employees. The cofounders justify the cost of the newsletter, $2,000 a year, because it gives them a way to communicate with their workers. As Ellen Spragins reported (1992), the cofounders give three reasons for the newsletter's positive reception:

- Nothing gets published that is offensive or a put-down.
- The editor receives extra pay for producing the newsletter. Therefore, the editor has an incentive for producing a quality communication that will appeal to the workers.
- Some 30 percent of the newsletter's content is created by the front-line employees (the remainder comes from the managers and cofounders).

Zingerman's writes newsletters and catalogs, teaches classes, offers tastes, and, since September 2000, went online with the zingermans.com Web site. It uses its network to get more and better information about great food out there where people can use it.

Formal Horizontal Channels

As Figure 12.6 implies, horizontal channels connect people of similar rank and status within an organization, such as engineers and team members, and outside stakeholders, such as dealers and customers, with those insiders who can best meet their needs. Dell's links are but one example of such horizontal interpersonal electronic communications. Through horizontal channels, workers and managers provide feedback, keep teammates informed, coordinate activities, seek assistance, and stay in contact with customers. Staying close to customers can mean literally staying close.

http://www.ussurg.com

United States Surgical Corporation (USSC) has had a long history of listening to its customers and responding to their needs with innovative products and services. For many years, members of the company's technically trained sales organization have instructed surgeons in the use of USSC's instruments and have provided technical assistance in the operating room. Today, with an increased focus on cost containment, this group's responsibilities, as well as its customer base, have expanded. In addition to surgeons, the salesperson also works with hospital administrators, financial managers, and materials managers to identify ways of reducing systemwide costs, improving quality and efficiency, and effectively marketing the hospital's services. USSC currently has approximately 60 percent share of the surgical stapler market and more than 50 percent share of the market for single-use laparoscopic instruments.

http://www.corel.com

Toll-free long-distance telephone lines for customers are horizontal channels that connect consumers with those in the company, no matter what level, who can best answer their questions or meet their needs. WordPerfect (Corel Corporation) is renowned in the PC world for the rapid and exhaustive telephone support it supplies for consumers of many of its software products.

Horizontal communication channels are used to set goals; define roles; create, examine, and improve methods; improve working relationships; define, investigate, and solve problems; and gather, process, and distribute information.

http://www.kodak.com

Horizontal communication is becoming increasingly important as managers institute more and more work teams. One observer pointed out the advantages of horizontal communication and the team approach: "Information moves straight to where it's needed, unfiltered by a hierarchy. If you have a problem with people upstream from you, you deal with them directly, rather than asking your boss to talk to theirs'." Workers at Kodak's black-and-white film operations, called zebras, have worked in teams for several years. The teams work closely with the customers, communicating constantly about schedules, new products, and other customer needs.

Professor Shoshana Zuboff of Harvard University calls for all companies to "informate" employees by placing the corporation at their fingertips—giving them real-time access to all the information and experts in the system (Peters, 1991).

Formal Upward Channels

Upward communication provides the feedback required by downward communication. It allows workers to request assistance in solving some problems, and it provides a means for workers to recommend solutions to others. Workers also use upward communication to provide status reports and inform higher authorities about employee complaints. The tools of upward communication are employee surveys; newsletters; regular meetings between managers and their subordinates; suggestion systems; team meetings; and an open-door policy, which provides employee access to managers.

When asked what their companies had done to improve communication and productivity, CEOs responding to a survey cited several actions that related to upward communication. These included meeting regularly with employees, delayering the organization, broadening participation in decision making, and instituting grievance panels and hotlines (Fisher, 1991).

Sometimes outside consultants are asked to provide information vital to organizational matters, such as feedback from customers on their levels of satisfaction with products and services. All automakers subscribe to reports compiled by J. D. Power and Associates, a firm specializing in gathering and selling data on automobile owners' satisfaction with their new cars. Its most celebrated survey deals with how well new-car buyers like their choices after owning them for 90 days. The company measures the owners' satisfaction by mailing thousands of questionnaires each year and summarizing the respondents' answers.

http://www.jdpa.com

When Chrysler vehicles did not rate well in J. D. Power and Associates' surveys, Chrysler hired another consultant—Detroit-based Process Development Corporation (PDC)—to help the company improve its ratings. According to Tom Kowaleski, a Chrysler spokesperson, PDC's job is to study the survey's questions—what they rate and how—and "what we should look at when we build a car" (Mateja, 1994). Chrysler has learned that such things as the "feel" of a knob, switch, or dial and the "location" of cup holders and ashtrays are as important as smooth-running engines and transmissions. As a result, the company "is considering removing equipment that prompts complaints from those interviewed by J. D. Power" (Mateja, 1994).

http://www.chrysler.com

Formal Communication Networks

formal communication network
An electronic link between people and their equipment and between people and databases.

Formal communication networks are electronic links between people and their equipment and between people and databases that store information. Organizations have linked their desktop computers for years. Since the 1970s, supermarkets and other large retailers have maintained computer links between their stores, headquarters, distribution centers, and suppliers. Xerox Corporation's research operations in Palo Alto, California, have videoconferencing links between employee lounges and various departments and buildings. The links allow researchers to confer easily (Ryan, 1992).

http://www.xerox.com

At Boeing, employees engage in brainstorming sessions by computer. Using special software called groupware, which tracks all brainstormers' contributions, Boeing has slashed the team size for most projects by 90 percent. One team designed a control system for machine tools in 35 days—a task that would have taken a year in the precomputer days (Kirkpatrick, 1992).

According to one observer, electronic links help forge a sense of belonging. "Researchers find that electronic-mail users are more likely to feel committed to their jobs than do the unplugged. No similar data yet exist for groupware, but anecdotal evidence so far suggests it creates an even more powerful sense of belonging" (Kirkpatrick, 1992). Carl Di Pietro, a human resource executive at Marriott, has used groupware to run meetings. In describing the experience, he reported: "In my 30 years, it's the most revolutionary thing I've seen for improving the quality and productivity of meetings. It gets you closer to the truth." He adds

http://www.marriott.com

that it enables a group to come to a consensus and the members to become more committed to decisions of the group. In addition, Di Pietro reported that groupware could overcome the difficulties that cultural diversity sometimes presents. "You don't know if that idea you're reading comes from a woman or a man, part of the minority or majority, or a senior or junior person. People begin to say 'Hey, we've got a lot in common with each other'" (Kirkpatrick, 1992).

Informal Communication Channels

Describe the informal communication channel known as the grapevine

informal communication channels
The informal networks, existing outside the formal channels, that are used to transmit casual, personal, and social messages at work.

grapevine
An informal communication channel.

The formal communication channels designed by management are not the only means of communication in an organization. **Informal communication channels** carry casual, social, and personal messages on a regular basis in or around the workplace. These channels are often called, collectively, the **grapevine**. Informal communication channels disseminate rumors, gossip, accurate as well as inaccurate information, and, on occasion, official messages. Anyone inside or outside an organization can originate a grapevine message. Grapevine messages are transmitted in many ways—face-to-face and by telephone, email, or fax.

Messages transmitted through informal channels usually result from incomplete information from official sources, environmental influences in the organization or outside it, and the basic human needs to socialize and stay informed. When changes occur, people like to speculate about what they will mean. When people feel insecure or fearful because of cutbacks and layoffs, rumors fly about what will happen next. When Jill is absent from her job, friends and coworkers want to know why. People who are the first to know something special usually want to share their new knowledge with others. Figure 12.7 shows how messages might travel through the grapevine. The grapevine has a number of characteristics:

- It can penetrate the tightest security.
- It is fast (with or without electronic links).
- It tends to carry messages from anonymous sources.
- Its messages are difficult to stop or counter once they get started.
- It is accessible to every person in an organization.
- It can be supportive of or an obstacle to management's efforts.

In most organizations, relatively few individuals disseminate most of the grapevine messages. These people create networks through which the messages are carried. Managers need to be attuned to the grapevine—that is, they should be aware of the messages it carries and the people who control it. They should not, however, use it as a formal communication channel. Inaccurate messages must be countered with the truth as soon as possible.

Figure 12.8 illustrates four common grapevine configurations. The most common is the cluster chain. Through it, an initiator—A, in this case—sends a message to a cluster, or group, that consists of B, E, and L. Through their own connections these three send the message to others. Each party involved usually distorts the message. Not all recipients carry the message to others. If a recipient has no interest in a grapevine communication or disagrees with it, he or she probably does not repeat it.

FIGURE 12.7 Grapevine in action

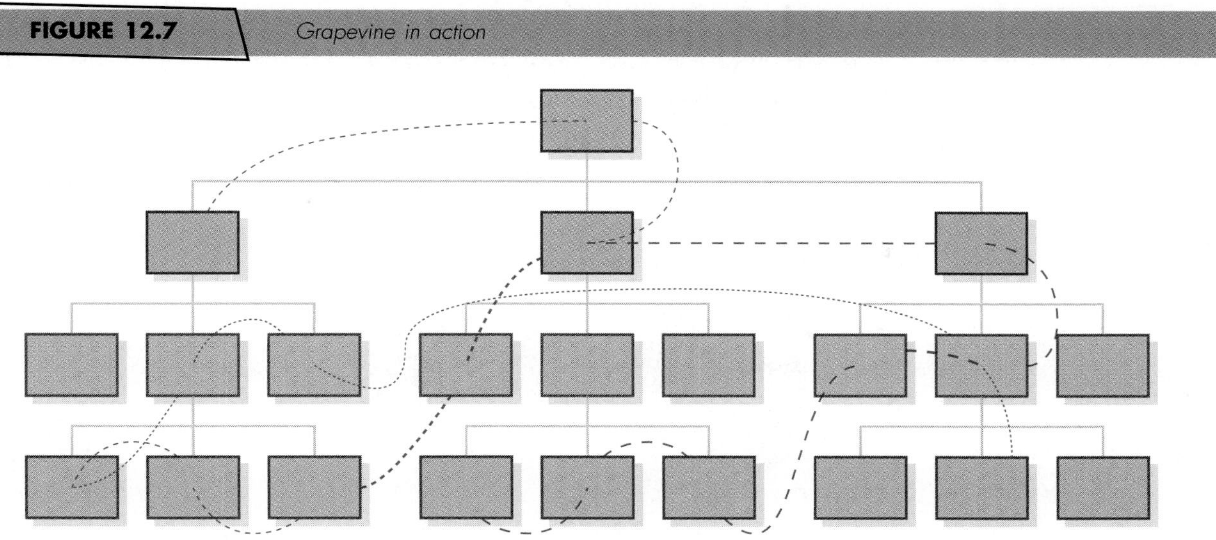

Barriers to Organizational Communication

List and explain the barriers to organizational communication and suggest remedies to overcome them

Communication in organizations can be blocked by interpersonal barriers and by barriers that are part of the organizational environment. The way workstations are positioned in an office or factory can enhance or hinder communication, for example. People who cannot see each other or who are not physically close to one another may find it difficult to stay in touch, although telephones, email, and fax machines can diminish the difficulty. Some managers have found that people seek each other out more often in a building equipped with escalators than in one with stairways or elevators. Escalators, they believe, offer relative privacy and allow senders and receivers to pay more attention to each other when communicating on an escalator.

The paragraphs that follow will review several barriers to organizational communication.

Overload

In the context of communication, the term *overload* means too much information. Everyone receives dozens of pieces of junk mail at home each week. The same thing occurs in plants and offices every day. People receive information they do not need. This overload is a type of noise, and employees must waste time trying to sort through it. One job for a company's management information system specialist is to make certain that people receive only what they need and that they receive it in the form that is most useful to them.

Filtering by Levels

The management levels in a company can become barriers to communication. According to Keith Davis (1989), the more levels that information has to pass through, the more it can be embellished or filtered. The message the last receiver receives may bear little resemblance to the original communication. The current trend toward flattened organizational structures should help to prevent such distortion.

FIGURE 12.8 *Four common grapevine configurations*

Single Chain

Gossip

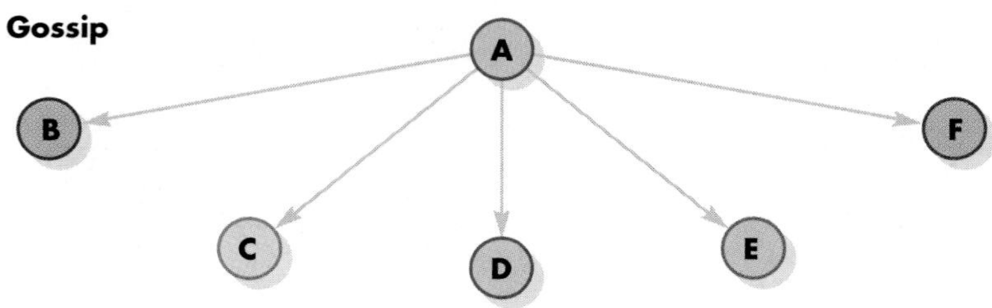

Random

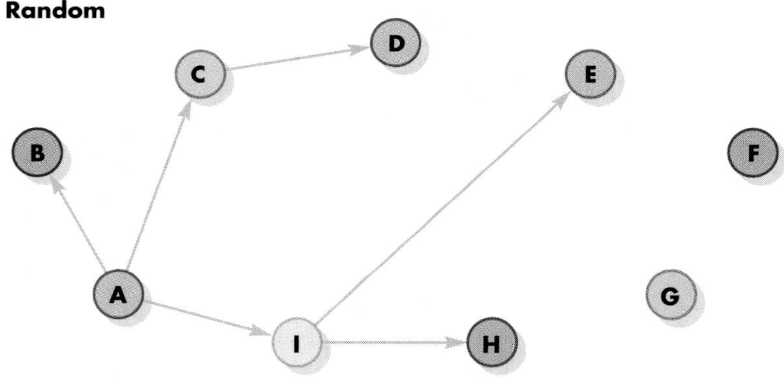

Cluster

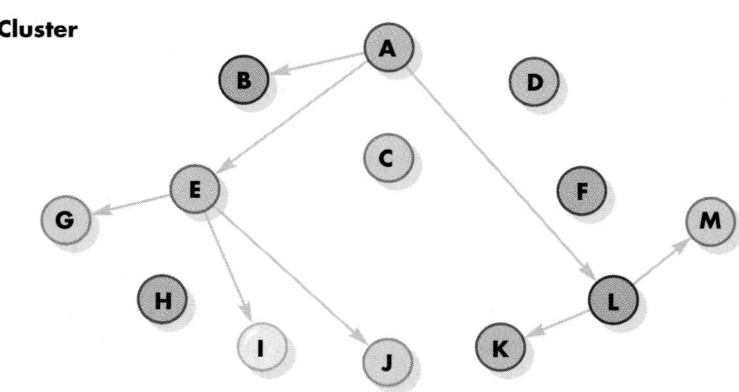

Alcoa, the subject of this chapter's Application Case on page 406, reengineered its organizational structure and working relationships from the mechanistic to the organic. One reason for this action was to remove physical and structural barriers that delayed decision making and responses to rapidly changing customer needs. By reducing levels of management and grouping people together in open workspace, Alcoa greatly improved communications and coordination.

Timing

Communications that must pass through several hands can be delayed in the process. Anything in an organization that prevents the free and quick flow of needed information impedes communication. The spread of high-speed communication technologies (such as email) and the growing use of teams (whose members are trained to recognize the need to share information) are expected to reduce barriers to prompt communication. Email courtesy, known as netiquette, is the subject of this chapter's Managing Technology feature.

Lack of Trust and Openness

http://www.callbell.com

Companies that are secretive about sharing vital information with employees lack openness; such behavior says that they do not trust their employees. A lack of openness in organizational communications derives from a lack of trust or from the fear that wrongdoing will be exposed. Workers and managers at Bell Atlantic (now part of Verizon Long Distance) play games to develop good working relationships and mutual trust. Each year, in a two and one-half day seminar, everyone from the chairman of the board to the customer-service representatives undergoes the same training program. The session consists of games such as blindfolded dart throwing. Blindfolded throwers have little chance of hitting the target unless others coach them. "It's just a silly dart game," said former CEO Raymond Smith, "but people never forget it" (Huber, 1992).

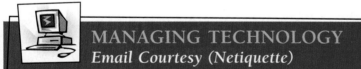

MANAGING TECHNOLOGY
Email Courtesy (Netiquette)

When sending email messages, practice email etiquette by following these guidelines.

- Use a descriptive subject line in your mail header.
- DON'T PUT YOUR MESSAGES IN ALL UPPER CASE LETTERS. Readers will think you are shouting.
- Use the * (asterisk) before and after a word for emphasis. Avoid bold and underline.
- Remember, anything you send could become common knowledge. Reread your message before sending.
- Use common acronyms: BTW (by the way), OTOH (on the other hand), WYSIWYG (what you see is what you get), IMHO (in my humble opinion).
- Use "emoticon" symbols to express emotions.
  Use a smiley face for humor, laughter, and friendliness.
  Use a frowney face for sadness, anger, and upset feelings.
- Include your name, position, and affiliation at the bottom of email messages.

Inappropriate Span of Control

If a manager supervises more people than time and energy permit, communication suffers. The manager who has too few people to oversee may become overbearing and attempt to communicate too much. The more that leaders empower their people by delegating authority and providing quick access to needed information, the less they need to worry about keeping communication effective. Well-trained, self-managing work teams know that when they need help, all they have to do is seek it. Until then, the manager should observe, track, and facilitate as needed.

Change

http://www.sdlcg.com

Changes anywhere in a company can hurt or hinder communication. When a new manager takes over, he or she invariably introduces changes in goals, methods, and communication style. What matters is how well people are prepared to cope with the changes. Larry Senn, head of Senn-Delaney Leadership Consulting Group in California, had this advice: "Take the time to describe your expectations to people. In a small organization, one person who's not open to change and not a team player can really gum up the works" (Huber, 1992).

Rank or Status in the Company

Unfortunately, in too many organizations the higher a manager is in the hierarchy, the less available he or she seems to be to others. Rank or status can make others timid and hesitant to communicate, or willing to communicate good news only. Some people in high positions begin to imagine that they are something special, an attitude that leads them to avoid listening to what subordinates have to offer.

In *Riding the Runaway Horse*, Charles C. Kenney (1992) examined the fall of Wang Laboratories. He attributed the company's decline to, among other things, an unwillingness to respect diverse opinions and stay close to customers. An Wang, the founder, created two classes of stock to avoid stockholder influences on his decisions. He delayed moving into the personal computer field until that field fell to others. He announced the development of new products when the products were nothing but ideas on paper. And, on his deathbed in 1989, he fired his son and president, Fred Wang, so that Fred would be blamed for the company's failures. In the words of a former president at Wang, John Cunningham, An Wang had become "a humble egomaniac."

Managers' Interpretations

Managers, like everyone else, are people with biases, stereotypes, values, needs, morals, and ethics. How they perceive their world determines how they will react to it. Managers will communicate where, when, what, and to whom they believe they must. As an example, consider the manager who is facing a crisis and asks for emergency funding for additional overtime. He needs the approval quickly, but the finance manager who receives the request is in no hurry. She wants to defer the request until next year's budget kicks in, a wait of about two months. When pressured for a decision, she responds: "You'll get the money you requested when I decide to give it." Both managers have different needs and agendas. Both have differing perspectives, priorities—and levels of courtesy.

Electronic Noise

Modern electronics have added yet more noise to the work environment. Breakdowns, overloads, static on the line, and ill-trained operators are barriers to organizational communication. Voice-mail systems can be barriers to communication, especially for people unaccustomed to using them. Dell managers recognized the potential electronic noise it might experience and, before initiating Internet integration, both domestically and internationally, made certain that its users received the proper training on the appropriate uses of its hardware and software.

IMPROVEMENT OF COMMUNICATION

Describe the responsibilities of senders and receivers during the communication process

Being adept at communicating involves individual skills as well as organizational frameworks and aids. Both the sender and the receiver have distinct responsibilities in the communication process. Meeting those responsibilities can help both parties avoid or overcome barriers to communication.

Responsibilities of Senders

Those who send messages must shape them and be aware of how they are received. The paragraphs that follow discuss the sender's responsibilities.

Being Certain of Intent

The sender's first task is to be clear about the intent of the message. Figure 12.9 lists some typical goals of communication. As the exhibit shows, the goals often vary according to the receiver. One goal common to all messages is that the receiver understands them.

FIGURE 12.9 *Typical communication goals*

When Communicating with Superiors
- To provide responses to requests
- To keep them informed of progress
- To solicit help in solving problems
- To sell ideas and suggestions for improvement
- To seek clarification of instructions

When Communicating with Peers
- To share ideas for improvement
- To coordinate activities
- To provide assistance
- To get to know them as individuals

When Communicating with Subordinates
- To issue instructions
- To persuade and sell
- To appraise performance
- To compliment, reward, and discipline
- To clarify intentions and instructions
- To get to know them as individuals

Knowing the Receiver and Constructing the Message Accordingly

The sender should acquire as much information as possible about the individual or group that is to receive the message. Senders need to know the receiver's job, experience, personality, perceptions, and needs. If the sender and receiver use different native languages, are from different cultures, or have had significantly different experiences, the sender must be aware of the barriers these differences could pose. For instance, pictures and charts may be the best way to communicate when senders and receivers do not speak the same native languages.

Senders must choose words with receivers' vocabularies in mind, not their own. While composing a message, senders should try to imagine themselves as the receiver and ask themselves if they would understand it. One basic goal of all communication is to help the receiver view the content of the message as the sender does. The sender should emphasize aspects of the message that relate to the receiver. If the message announces a change, the sender should point out the advantages that will result for the receiver. If the purpose is to ask for assistance, the sender should cite what the receiver will gain by providing it.

Selecting the Proper Medium

The choice of a medium to carry the message depends in part on the content of the message. Confidentialities and praise always call for a personal touch. If the receiver is in a remote location or if the matter is complex and lengthy, putting it in writing might be the best choice. If the receiver prefers a given medium, the sender should try to use that method. A sightless person may prefer a voice message or one encoded in Braille. A person who has a hearing difficulty may prefer a visual presentation. Finally, the sender must consider the physical and emotional environment to be faced when attempting to communicate. What kind of noise will there be?

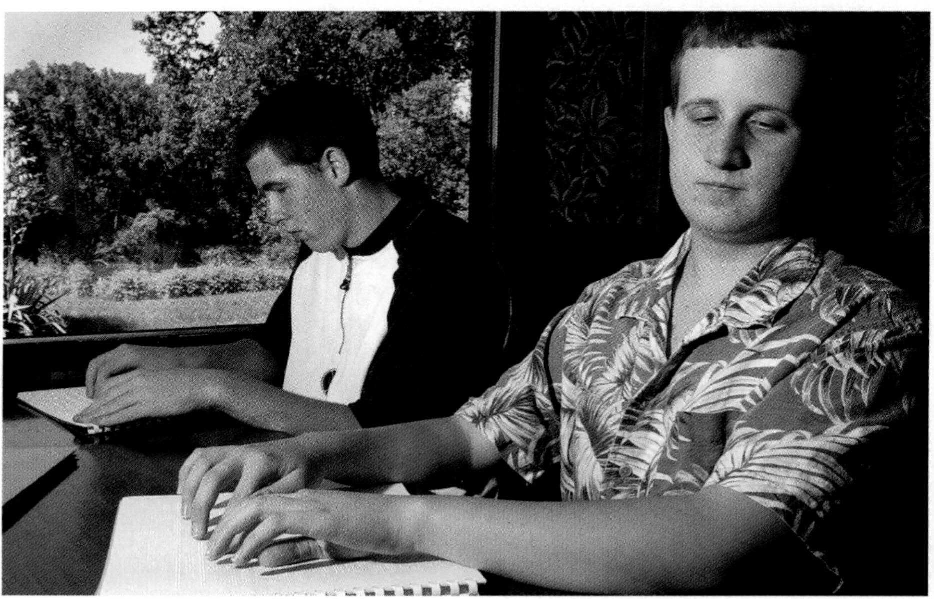

The sender must consider the receiver's needs when selecting the proper medium for a message. For example, a sightless person may require that a message be encoded in Braille.

Timing the Transmission

The timing of the communication affects its success. The sender's needs along with the receiver's must be considered in determining the best time. A supervisor may want to talk with a subordinate at 4:00 P.M., but if the worker leaves at 3:30 P.M., 4:00 is an inappropriate time. Business communications should be delivered to people who are in a receptive mood and under the proper circumstances. Important discussions about a new budget would be inappropriate at a company picnic or when people are on their breaks. People who are clearly overwhelmed with work when a message sender contacts them cannot give their full attention to the message.

Seeking and Giving Feedback

Senders have the primary responsibility to make certain that their messages have been received and understood. The only way to make certain is to get feedback. The sender cannot settle for the response, "I understand." If receivers have no questions, the sender should have some. One technique to assess understanding is to ask the receiver to restate the message using his or her own words. Another approach is to ask questions to check on the receiver's grasp of specifics.

As the receiver engages in feedback, he or she may ask questions that require responses from the sender. At this time the sender must understand how the receiver has interpreted the message and then take the actions needed to clear up any misunderstandings.

Responsibilities of Receivers

Just as senders have specific obligations, so do receivers. The paragraphs that follow discuss these responsibilities.

Listening Actively

A receiver must listen attentively to the message being sent. Listening attentively requires that receivers block out distractions that can interfere with communication. Because people speak more slowly than listeners can process words, listeners' minds are often tempted to wander. Receivers must not attempt to pass judgment on the sender or the message until the message has been completely transmitted. Being critical distracts from listening. According to John J. Gabarro (1991), a professor of human resource management at the Harvard Business School, "The greatest barrier to effective communication is the tendency to evaluate what another person is saying and therefore to misunderstand or to not really 'hear.'"

Active listeners take notes and list any areas where a sender's meanings are unclear. Good listeners ask questions to clarify messages. They observe gestures, tone of voice, facial expressions, and body language and note contradictions between them. If necessary, they seek explanations for the contradictions.

Being Sensitive to the Sender

Senders communicate because they believe they must. They pick a certain medium, time, and receiver because they see these elements of communication as appropriate. Receivers should approach every communication with the assumption that the message is important to the sender. They should try to discover why that is so and what value the message has for them as receivers. Being sensitive means not interrupting or distracting the speaker. If a sender has difficulties in making the message clear, the receiver must try to help or act to postpone communication until the sender is better prepared.

Indicating an Appropriate Medium

Receivers can often facilitate communication by stating a preference for a certain medium. Many managers want to receive important messages in writing so that they can study and store them. Email, faxes, letters, memos, and reports can meet these requirements. Sometimes the request is for a face-to-face meeting so that two or more people can interact. Expressing a preference speeds up a communication effort and removes possible guesswork by the sender. Both parties, therefore, should be more comfortable. Of course, company rules and procedures or a union contract often specify various mediums as appropriate for handling routine communications.

Initiating Feedback

Receivers bear the primary responsibility for providing feedback. Until the receiver states his or her interpretation of the message, the sender will never know if it was understood. Similarly, the receiver cannot be certain that he or she has understood the sender's intentions until the receiver summarizes the message and receives confirmation that the summary was correct. When a receiver cannot restate a message, it is a sure sign that he or she did not understand it.

Ten Commandments of Good Communication

http://www.amanet.org

The American Management Association International has prepared guidelines for effective communication that serve as a useful summary of, and offer additional insights into, much of what we have examined in this chapter. Figure 12.10 presents these guidelines.

FIGURE 12.10 *The American Management Association International's ten commandments of good communication*

1. Clarify your ideas before communicating. The more systematically you analyze the problem or idea to be communicated, the clearer it becomes. This is the first step toward effective communication.
2. Examine the true purpose of each communication. Before you communicate, ask yourself what you really want to accomplish with your message—obtain information, initiate action, change another person's attitude? Identify your most important goal and then adapt your language, tone, and total approach to serve that specific objective.
3. Consider the total physical and human setting whenever you communicate. Meaning and intent are conveyed by more than words alone.
4. Consult with others, when appropriate. Frequently, it is desirable or necessary to seek the participation of others in planning a communication or developing the facts on which to base it.
5. Be mindful, while you communicate, of the overtones as well as the basic content of your message. Your tone of voice, expression, and apparent receptiveness to the responses of others have tremendous impact on those you wish to reach.

(continued)

FIGURE 12.10 (Concluded)

6. Take the opportunity, when it arises, to convey something of help or value to the receiver. Consideration of the other person's interests and needs will frequently highlight opportunities to convey something of immediate benefit or long-range value to the receiver.
7. Follow up your communication. Unless you follow up, your best efforts at communication may be wasted and you may never know whether you have succeeded in expressing your meaning and intent.
8. Communicate for yesterday and tomorrow as well as today. Although a message may be aimed primarily at meeting the demands of an immediate situation, you must plan it with the past in mind if it is to maintain consistency in the receiver's view. More important, it must be consistent with long-range interests and goals.
9. Be sure your actions support your communications. In the final analysis, the most persuasive kind of communication is not what you say but what you do. When a person's actions or attitudes contradict his or her words, we tend to discount what that person has said.
10. Seek not only to be understood but to understand—be a good listener. When we start talking, we often cease to listen in that larger sense of being attuned to the other person's unspoken reactions and attitudes.

Source: Adapted from "Ten Commandments of Good Communication," *Management Review*, October 1955. http://www.amanet.org.

CHAPTER SUMMARY

1 **Discuss the importance of communication in organizations.** Communication is the process through which people and organizations accomplish objectives. By communicating with others, we share a common understanding of one another's attitudes, values, emotions, ambitions, wants, and needs. People must coordinate and pool their efforts, electronically or otherwise, to please their customers. Prompt communication of and about problems is essential for adapting to and creating change. Quality, productivity, and profitability depend on accurate and timely communications on a variety of issues. All employees must have feedback during their communication efforts and work performance.

2 **Diagram the communication process and label all its parts.** Figure 12.1 illustrates the process. It begins with the sender (a person or group) planning the effort. The sender's ideas are formulated into a message. An appropriate medium is chosen and used to deliver the message to the intended receiver. Finally, efforts to ensure mutual understanding and seek clarification (feedback) are engaged in by both sender and receiver.

3 **List and explain the barriers to interpersonal communication and suggest remedies to overcome them.** The major barriers and remedies to overcome them are

1. *Diction and semantics:* The use of words, terms, and symbols that are abstract or have multiple meanings and emotional impacts.
   Remedy: Choose clear and precise language, keeping your receiver's understanding in mind.
2. *Expectations of familiarity:* The assumption that you know what the sender is sending before you receive the entire message.
   Remedy: Don't draw any conclusions until the entire message has been delivered and received. Read and listen with an open mind.
3. *Source's lack of credibility:* The receiver's perception that the sender lacks sufficient credibility in the subject area.
   Remedy: Hear the sender out; fresh perspectives often bring new and better suggestions and solutions.
4. *Preconceived notions:* The negative reaction to ideas that differ from your own.
   Remedy: Try to keep an open mind on every subject, especially those most familiar.
5. *Differing perceptions:* The different way each person observes and makes judgments. Most people hold good and bad stereotypes that prejudge people and their motives.
   Remedy: Judge people on their individual merits. What matters is who they are as individuals.
6. *Conflicting nonverbal communication:* The noncorrelation of body language, expressions, and gestures with other messages being sent.
   Remedy: Actions speak louder than words. At the very least, try to determine what might explain the contradiction; stress and emotions can cloud the process.

7. *Emotions:* The clouding of logic and judgment by emotion. Sender and receiver may become adversaries rather than partners in a process.
Remedy: Avoid the communication process when either the sender or receiver is in an emotional and perhaps irrational state.

8. *Noise:* Anything in the communication environment that can interfere with the sending and receiving of messages.
Remedy: Avoid the process until you can eliminate or avoid the sources of noise. Don't try to compete with those sources for a receiver's attention.

4 **Describe the uses of downward, horizontal, and upward communication channels.** Downward channels send messages from managers to nonmanagers and from top management to all others in the company. Mission, vision, feedback to requests from below, policies, solutions, goals, and appraisals are typical subject areas.

Horizontal channels connect people of similar rank and status, insiders connect with outsiders, and team members interact with one another.

Upward channels provide feedback required by downward communication. They provide input for decisions at higher levels and status reports on the conditions throughout the organization.

5 **Describe the informal communication channel known as the grapevine.** The grapevine arises spontaneously through social interactions and carries all nonofficial messages between and among organization members. It is usually word of mouth and can penetrate the tightest security. It is fast, difficult to stop, and may be a support for or an obstruction to management efforts.

6 **List and explain the barriers to organizational communication and suggest remedies to overcome them.** The major barriers and remedies to overcome them are

1. *Overload:* The sending and receiving of too much information, given the circumstances surrounding the communication.
Remedy: As a sender, send only what your best judgment and observations during the effort suggest your receiver can handle. As a receiver, inform the sender when too much occurs.

2. *Filtering by levels:* The increased embellishment and filtering of information as it passes through successive levels.
Remedy: Try to deliver messages in the most direct way possible; avoid nonessential handling. Use written forms that can pass unaltered through several layers or hands.

3. *Timing:* The sending of information too late to be of use; the receiver is not receptive.
Remedy: Use technology to speed the flow and store the message until the receiver is receptive.

4. *Lack of trust and openness:* The guarding and control of information and access to it by key people, resulting in a closed culture and climate. Such cultures and climates ignore individuals and operate on fear and suspicion.
Remedy: Training to create trust, ethical behavior, and "walking your talk" are cures for this barrier.

5. *Inappropriate span of control:* Too many subordinates or team members to lead.
Remedy: Reorganize and reassign personnel to more appropriate groupings.

6. *Change:* Change in processes, systems, or leadership creating new demands for communication; fear causes resistance.
Remedy: Remove fear through forewarning and by making standards and requirements clear. Point out the positives and similarities to what is, before communicating the differences.

7. *Rank or status in the company:* Differences in rank and status inhibiting communications by one party's being intimidated by the other of higher position. Self-image can become distorted if a person is surrounded by yes-men and no opposition.
Remedy: Instituting appraisals by one's subordinates and peers using objective, measurable standards is helpful. Hold people accountable for how well they serve their particular customers' needs. Downplay and eliminate artificial barriers.

8. *Managers' interpretations:* The perhaps flawed judgment of managers. Managers are most often the initiators of the communication process. Like those they manage, they have their virtues and vices. Their judgment about the when, where, how, and why of the process is not flawless.
Remedy: Provide training in how to communicate in all the various media.

9. *Electronic noise:* Breakdowns, overloads, static on the lines, and poorly trained operators, resulting in miscommunication. Electronic media both help and hinder communication efforts.
Remedy: Provide training for all in the proper use and maintenance of various pieces of equipment and software programs before people are authorized to use them.

7 **Describe the responsibilities of senders and receivers during the communication process.** Senders have the following responsibilities:

- Being certain of intent before attempting communication
- Knowing the receiver and constructing the message accordingly
- Selecting the proper medium, given the particular circumstances
- Timing the transmission for maximum effect
- Seeking and giving feedback

Receivers have the following responsibilities:

- Listening actively
- Being sensitive to the sender
- Indicating an appropriate medium
- Initiating feedback

REVIEW QUESTIONS

1. Why is communication so important in organizations?
2. What are the essential elements in any effort to communicate?
3. What are the barriers that can interfere with interpersonal communication efforts?
4. What are the major uses for downward, horizontal, and upward communications?
5. How does the grapevine work in organizations?
6. What are the barriers that can interfere with organizational communication efforts?
7. What must a sender do before attempting to communicate?
8. What must a receiver do when entering into the communication process?

DISCUSSION QUESTIONS FOR CRITICAL THINKING

1. What barriers exist in your working or school environment that inhibit your ability to get information you need on a timely basis? Are these organizational, interpersonal, or both?
2. Referring to this chapter's Management in Action case, what kind of barriers to communication is Dell likely to experience with its heavy reliance on electronic linkages to customers and suppliers?
3. Find individuals in class or at work who own a Swatch. Ask them why they purchased their Swatch and whether or not their motivations match up with those stated in this chapter's Global Applications feature.

INTERNET EXERCISES

Check the text Web site at http://plunkett.swcollege.com for updated links to the Internet Exercises.

1. In your new position, you will manage a team selling to the Japanese. To be effective, you must understand the manners and customs of the Japanese. Make a list of Japanese manners and customs that differ from those of Westerners. **http://mothra.rerf.or.jp/ENG/Hiroshima/DidYouKnow/106.html**
2. Use the speech recipe found at this Web site to organize a speech explaining several instances in which you have personally encountered some of the barriers to interpersonal communication and how you overcame them. **http://www.casaa-resources.net/resources/sourcebook/acquiring-leadership-skills/public-speaking.html**
3. Follow the guidelines from Toastmasters and Korbel Champagne found at the Web site below to prepare a toast. **http://homearts.com/gh/betterw/12bwtof1.htm**

APPLICATION CASE

Alcoa's Open Work Spaces

More managers are working in open work spaces. According to a report from the International Facility Management Association, "In offices across the country, 58 percent feature open floor plans, 36 percent have offices with doors that shut and 6 percent are "bullpens," areas where many people work closely together" (Freeman, 1998).

Alcoa's Corporate Center is an example of a building with open work spaces. Alcoa is the world's leading producer of primary aluminum, fabricated aluminum, and alumina. The corporate center in Pittsburgh is located on the Allegheny River and houses 400 people in a unique open environment. "The building contains 800,000 pounds of Alcoa aluminum and 70,000 square feet of exterior glass. Its look is profoundly medium gray and glassily metallic." Office floors have desk-storage areas and small conference tables with ports (for easy connections between employees' laptop computers and the company's customers and suppliers). Also, it is possible for employees to plug in laptop computers randomly at meeting tables and elsewhere, even on the deck near the cafeteria. There are at least two paneled work spaces on each floor for employees to improve their computer skills away from their desk tops or to view videos.

No one has an office. There are practically no walls or doors. "A main reason why this unique building works, with its open floor office arrangements, full-height central atrium, metal and glass escalators and nine-foot-square work spaces, is because of the philosophy of Paul O'Neill, [former] Alcoa chairman of the board and chief executive officer. O'Neill [was] a low-key team player in a white shirt and tie with his eye trained not just on profits, but on an improved environment as well—for the city, the world and Alcoans."

O'Neill disliked corporate pretentiousness or imposing too much on the environment. He did away with hierarchic attitudes and substituted open work spaces, not offices, even for the top executives. The new organic environment allows employees to meet and form problem-solving groups anywhere within the facility at any time.

http://www.alcoa.com

Questions

1. What barriers to organizational communication are overcome by this type of working situation?
2. What problems can arise in such an open environment?
3. What kind of workers or work might experience problems in such an environment?

Sources: Donald Miller, "Alcoa Corporate Center: A Triumph over Pretension," *Post-Gazette* (18 September 1998), http://www.post-gazette.com/regionstate/19980918alcoa5.asp; Alcoa Inc., http://www.alcoa.com.

VIDEO CASE

Burke, Inc.: Technology in Business Communication

Based in Cincinnati, Ohio, Burke, Inc., is a leading international firm in marketing research that has been providing its services to blue chip companies since 1931. Because of its long and successful history, the company believes that it has researched virtually every category of products and services and business and marketing topics on behalf of its clients.

The company provides full-service custom marketing research, analysis, and consulting for consumer and business-to-business goods and services companies to help them understand marketplace dynamics worldwide. The services that Burke offers include product testing, brand equity research, pricing research, market segmentation, image and positioning studies, and a wide range of marketing research protocols targeted at both tactical and strategic business issues.

Burke describes itself as being in the knowledge business and being uniquely qualified to uncover insights into marketplace dynamics anywhere in the world. In large measure, the success that this company has enjoyed during the past 70 years is in large measure a result of effectively communicating the knowledge gleaned from its research to its clients.

To do so successfully, the company has embraced several technologies that have changed the face of business communication. For instance, Burke researchers and analysts make extensive use of electronic mail (email) to improve written internal (within the organization) and external (with clients) communication. In fact, with some clients (e.g., Sun Microsystems), the company relies entirely on electronically communicated data with no paper being physically sent to them.

Another technology that Burke utilizes is teleconferencing to increase the efficiency of its oral communications. Teleconferences are held with both the company's clients and members of its own organization (many of whom are often dispersed geographically). Burke's management believes that videoconferencing has not yet achieved the potential that many thought it would quickly attain. This technology is currently limited by each group of participants having to meet physically in central teleconferencing rooms. This restriction can be inconvenient at least or untenable at most for many organizations and their clients. Teleconferencing, however, does not have this limitation and allows for diverse groups of individuals to meet literally from their own desks.

Finally, Burke is a strong advocate for the increased use of Internet technology as means of both collecting data and transferring results of its data analysis. The Internet allows Burke and many other organizations to collect and disseminate information quickly, both within an office and throughout the world.

Burke's extensive utilization of these three technologies illustrates their increasing use by organizations in improving business communication.

http://www.burke.com

For Discussion:

1. What should managers consider when deciding whether to use each of the three communication technologies (email, teleconferencing or videoconferencing, and the Internet) presented in this video?
2. In what ways can the use of email and the Internet improve written communication?
3. With regard to the communication process and the receiver in particular, what potential problems do the Internet and email present to the sender, as opposed to other technologies such as teleconferencing?

Human Motivation

KEY TERMS

compressed workweek
content theories
equity theory
ERG theory
expectancy theory
flextime
goal-setting theory
hygiene factors
intrapreneurship
job depth
job enlargement
job enrichment
job redesign
job rotation
job scope
job sharing
morale
motivation
motivation factors
needs
philosophy of management
process theories
quality of work life (QWL)
reinforcement theory
Theory X
Theory Y

LEARNING OBJECTIVES

After studying this chapter, you should be able to

1. Discuss the factors that stimulate and influence motivation
2. Differentiate between content and process theories of motivation
3. List the five levels of needs according to Maslow and give an example of each
4. Discuss the impact of hygiene and motivation factors in the work environment
5. Explain the characteristics of a person with high-achievement needs
6. Identify the needs associated with ERG theory
7. Discuss the relationship between expectations and motivation
8. Explain the relationship between reinforcement and motivation
9. Explain how equity influences motivation
10. Explain how goals influence motivation
11. Discuss the importance of a manager's philosophy of management in creating a positive work environment
12. Describe how managers can structure the environment to provide motivation

MANAGEMENT IN ACTION

Loyalty Rewarded at Thompson-McCully

Many workers fantasize about what they would do if they were millionaires—but few ever have the opportunity. Ninety individuals who worked for Robert M. Thompson, founder and president of Michigan's largest asphalt paving contractor, Thompson-McCully Company, saw that dream become a reality. Several hundred others found a big windfall as well. When Bob Thompson sold his company in 1999 for $422 million to Oldcastle Materials, a subsidiary of Ireland's CRH plc, he recognized his employees' contributions to his success by giving the 550 company employees and retirees a "special bonus" of $128 million total. Also, he paid the taxes on the bonuses. He chose Oldcastle Materials because of its record of not dismantling companies or firing workers. Thompson said "It's sharing good times, that's really all it is," he says. "I don't think you can read more into it. I'm a proud person. I wanted to go out a winner and I wanted to go out doing the right thing" (Cohen, 1999).

Business owners rarely are this generous with their profits. "These people have helped me live a life I never dreamed possible," said Thompson, 67. "I have employees who will work seven days a week. And they've adjusted their schedules to work at night these past few years. Now that I can, I want to give back to them." Thompson-McCully's employees work very hard. The job takes place outside in the scorching heat, the workday can be fourteen hours long, and the workweek can be six days long. "There is a kind of inherent brutality in asphalt paving because of the huge amounts of material and work that must be done almost around the clock during the 140-day paving season in Michigan" (Krizan, 2000).

Thompson started the company in 1959 when he was 27 years old with his uncle, Wilford McCully. His wife, Ellen, had saved $3,500 from her teaching job, and they invested it in the business. "Since 1959, they've bought about 12 smaller paving companies in Michigan, and now own 18 offices, plants and quarries across the state" (Hall, 1999). Today, he is one of the most influential men in the Michigan road industry. "You can't travel to any region of the state without driving on roads that have been made better by Bob Thompson," said Gary Naeyaert, director of communications for the Michigan Department of Transportation (Hall, 1999).

Thompson describes the success of his company, "We all have certain talents and we have to know what we don't do well. The narrower the focus, the better. We narrowed the focus to finding rock, crushing it, transporting it, making asphalt and either selling it or laying it" (Krizan, 2000).

The editors of *Engineering News-Record* gave humanitarian Robert M. Thompson ENR's Award of Excellence for 2000. The following quotes come from their editorial (enr.com, 2000).

Bob Thompson and Thompson-McCully Co. can serve as a model for many firms. Although it works in a low-bid, hard-money contract environment, Thompson has had a standing policy that any employee who wanted to go to school could do it at company expense. The reasoning is that these people are not only making themselves better, but more effective. 'The more

© KEVIN FLEMING/CORBIS

When Bob Thompson sold Thompson-McCully, Michigan's largest asphalt paving contractor, in 1999, he rewarded loyal employees with a $128 million bonus from the proceeds of the sale.

you learn, the more important you are to the company,' says one manager.

But the biggest company core philosophy and practice is the constant measurement of just about everything to set those stretch volume, financial, reliability or quality goals. The more you measure and benchmark, the easier it is to quantify the business return from investing in people. 'It is terrible to manage without information,' says Dennis Rickard, who is taking over as Thompson-McCully president. There is a daily financial accounting and the financial performance of key managers is posted, leading to brisk internal competition, say managers.

That performance is tied to annual bonuses, and the company has an unusual compensation system in that bonuses are unlimited. 'We reward people handsomely if they perform. It is a simple process,' says Rickard. 'In the end, they are the ones that determine the limit.' ■

Sources: Krizan, William G. "Award of Excellence," *Engineering News-Record*, April 17, 2000, http://www.enr.com/new/c41700.asp; *ABC News 20/20*, "Making Millionaires," May 26, 2000, http://more.abcnews.go.com/onair/2020/2020_000526_millionaires.html; Hall, Sheri. "Shrewdness, Humanity Blend to Make Corporate Benefactor," *The Detroit News*, July 25, 1999, http://detnews.com/1999/biz/9907/25/07250046.htm; *Engineering News-Record*, "Taking Care of People Can Be Done at All Levels," April 17, 2000, http://www.enr.com/new/e41700.asp; Cohen, Sharon. "One in a Million; Boss Rewards Workers by Splitting 9-Figure Fortune," Associated Press, September 12, 1999, http://www.dallasnews.com/national/0912nat2thanks.htm.

INTRODUCTION

When you ask people what motivates them at work, most will tell you, in a tone usually reserved for children and in-laws, that they do it for money. But if that were entirely true, how do you explain people like Warren Buffet or Bill Gates, whose combined net worth is greater than the GDP of Luxembourg and yet who throw themselves into their jobs as if their next meal depended on it? So, if it's not only the money, what is it? Today, as more and more companies reengineer, restructure, and reshape organizational culture, they are looking for the answers to employee motivation (Dumaine, 1994).

This chapter will assist in providing the answers. Initially, the chapter presents the basics of motivation. Then it continues with an analysis of motivation theories that focus on employee needs and ones that focus on behaviors. The chapter concludes with a description of how managers can structure the environment to provide motivation.

CHALLENGE OF MOTIVATION

http://www.iflyswa.com

http://www.chilis.com

http://store.nordstrom.com

http://www.thompsonmccully.com

morale
The attitude or feelings workers have about the organization and their total work life.

What do Southwest Airlines, Chili's restaurants, Nordstrom, and Thompson-McCully have in common? One answer is success. If you entered each workplace, you would notice another similarity. In each organization the morale is excellent. **Morale** is the attitude or feelings the workers have about the organization and their total work life (Straub and Attner, 1994). The CEOs of each company and their management teams have created a positive work environment. In their own unique ways, each has taken steps to enhance the **quality of work life (QWL)** (Case, 1992). QWL efforts focus on enhancing workers' dignity, improving their physical and emotional well-being, and enhancing the satisfaction individuals achieve in the workplace. By developing a positive work environment, managers can capture the commitment of their employees. The result is employees who are truly motivated—they

quality of work life (QWL)
Factors in the work environment contributing positively or negatively to workers' physical and emotional well-being and job satisfaction.

want to do their jobs well. "His [Bob Thompson of Thompson-McCully] workers describe him as a no-nonsense boss who is down to earth, very demanding, driven, but fair and willing to listen" (Cohen, 1999). Such commitment, combined with the skill to do the job, creates an energetic, highly competent labor force to work in partnership with management. Figure 13.1 shows the factors that contribute to the quality of work life.

The managers at Southwest Airlines, Chili's, Nordstrom, Thompson-McCully, and Semco (the latter the subject of this chapter's Global Applications feature) have met one of the great management challenges. They have discovered how to motivate employees. These managers recognize that motivation is not magic, but it is a set of processes that influences behavioral choices (Steers and Porter, 1987).

FIGURE 13.1 *Factors that enhance the quality of work life*

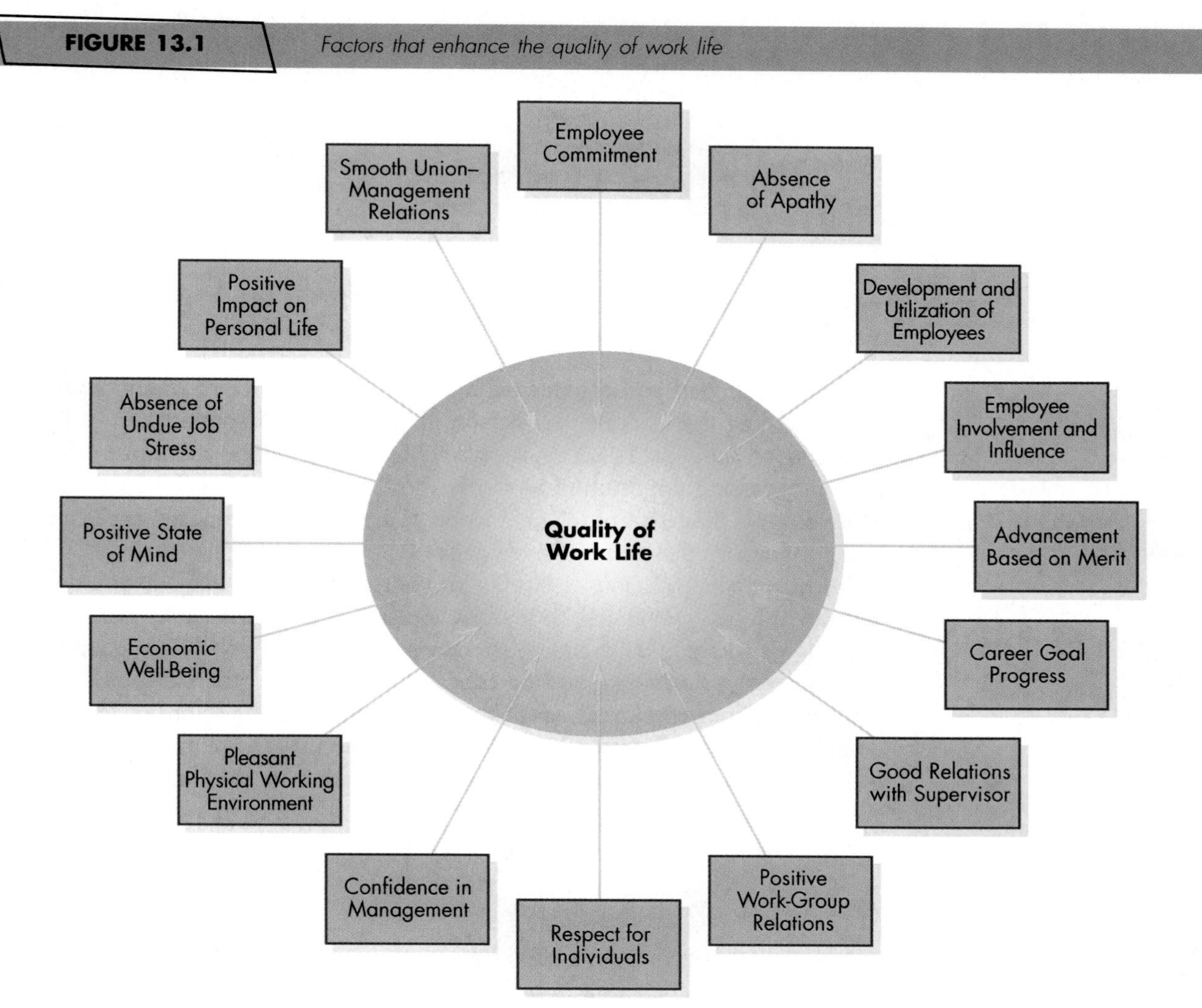

GLOBAL APPLICATIONS
No More Fear at Semco

When Ricardo Semler took over the family business, Semco, which makes industrial pumps, propellers, and rocket fuel propellant mixers for satellites, among other products, looked much like any other old-line Brazilian company. Fear was the governing principle. Guards patrolled the factory floor, timed people's trips to the bathroom, and frisked workers who left the plant. Anyone who was unlucky enough to break a piece of equipment had to replace it out of his or her own pocket.

Semler initially carried on in this style but soon revolted, vowing to remake his company into a "true democracy, a place run on trust and freedom, not fear." He has created an environment where people want to work—Semco gets 1,000 applications for every job opening.

Now employees are empowered to run the company. They wear what they want, choose their own bosses, and come and go as they please. A third of them actually set their own salaries, with one crucial "hitch." They have to reapply for their jobs every six months. Production workers evaluate their managers once a year and post the score. If a manager's grade is consistently low, he or she steps down.

Semler also shares company profits. He regularly distributes 23 percent of profits to the employees—in 1995 that amounted to $278,000. He also shares his title. Six people, including a woman, rotate as CEO, each putting in six-month tours. In addition, even though Semler owns the company, his vote carries no more weight than anyone else's.

In a country that barely blinks at 3,000 percent inflation, mere survival is a feat; but Semco has done much better than that. Sales per employee are $135,000, more than four times the average for Semco's competitors.

http://www.semcomaq.com.br

Source: Semler, Ricardo. *Maverick: The Success Story Behind the World's Most Unusual Workplace*, Warner Books, 1995. For more on Ricardo Semler, see Fierman, Jaclyn. "Winning Ideas from Maverick Managers," Fortune, February 6, 1995, pp. 66–80.

Basics of Motivation

1

Discuss the factors that stimulate and influence motivation

motivation
The result of the interaction of a person's internal needs and external influences—involving perceptions of equity, expectancy, previous conditioning, and goal setting—that determine behavior.

Modern researchers and enlightened managers have discovered that motivation is not something that is done to a person. It results from a combination of factors, including an individual's needs, the ability to make choices, and an environment that provides the opportunity to satisfy those needs and to make those choices. **Motivation** is the result of the interaction of a person's internalized needs and external influences that determine behavior.

People make conscious decisions for their own welfare. Why do you do what you do? Why do you choose to go to school and someone else does not? Why do you choose to study hard and someone else does not? Why do some employees at Southwest Airlines take outside education classes and others do not? Why do some Nordstrom employees adopt the culture and become "Nordies" and others do not (Collins and Porras, 1993)? The study of motivation is concerned with what prompts people to act, what influences their choice of action, and why they persist in acting in a certain way. The starting point is to look at a person's needs by using a motivation model.

Motivation Model

needs
Physiological or psychological conditions in humans that act as stimuli for behavior.

A person's needs provide the basis for a motivation model. **Needs** are deficiencies that a person experiences at a particular time. They can be physiological or psychological. Physiological needs relate to the body and include the needs for air, water, and food. Psychological needs include the needs for affiliation and self-esteem. Needs create a tension (stimulus) that results in wants. The person then develops a behavior or set of behaviors to satisfy the wants. The behavior results in action toward goal achievement (Davis and Newstrom, 1992).

Figure 13.2 offers a rudimentary example of the motivation model. A person feels hunger (a need). Recognition of the need triggers a want (food). The person chooses to cook a hamburger (behavior) and then he eats it (he takes action to achieve the goal). Satisfied, he feels no hunger (feedback). When the model is modified to reflect the fact that behavior is subject to many influences, it grows more complex. Why did the person in the example choose a hamburger, not cereal? Why did he prepare the hamburger himself instead of buying it? Has the person previously practiced the behavior? If so, did it satisfy the need? The integrated motivation model—by addressing more complex influences on motivational choices—provides these explanations.

Integrated Motivation Model

Unsatisfied needs stimulate wants and behaviors. In choosing a behavior to satisfy a need, a person must evaluate several factors:

1. *Past experiences.* All the person's past experiences with the situation at hand enter into the motivation model. These include the satisfaction derived from acting in a certain way, any frustration felt, the amount of effort required, and the relationship of performance to rewards.
2. *Environmental influences.* The choices of behaviors are affected by the environment, which in a business setting comprises the organization's values as well as the expectations and actions of management.
3. *Perceptions.* The individual is influenced by perceptions of the expected effort required to achieve performance and the value of the reward both absolutely and in relation to what peers have received for the same effort.

In addition to these three variables, two other factors are at work: skills and incentives. *Skills* are a person's performance capabilities; they result from training. *Incentives* are factors created by managers to encourage workers to perform a task.

Look at the motivation process again, but this time from a business perspective:

- Unsatisfied needs stimulate wants. In this situation a first-level manager feels a need to be respected. She wants to be recognized by top management as an outstanding employee.
- Behavior is identified to satisfy the want. The first-level manager identifies two behaviors that can satisfy the want: volunteering to write a report or seeking a special project. To consider which behavior to choose, she consciously evaluates the rewards or punishments associated with the performance (incentives); her abilities to accomplish the activities identified (skills); and past experiences, environmental influences, and perceptions.
- The individual takes action. Based on her analysis, the first-level manager selects what she considers the best option (behavior) and then takes action.
- The individual receives feedback. The response the manager gets from top management constitutes the feedback in this case. If the response is positive,

FIGURE 13.2 *Basic motivation model*

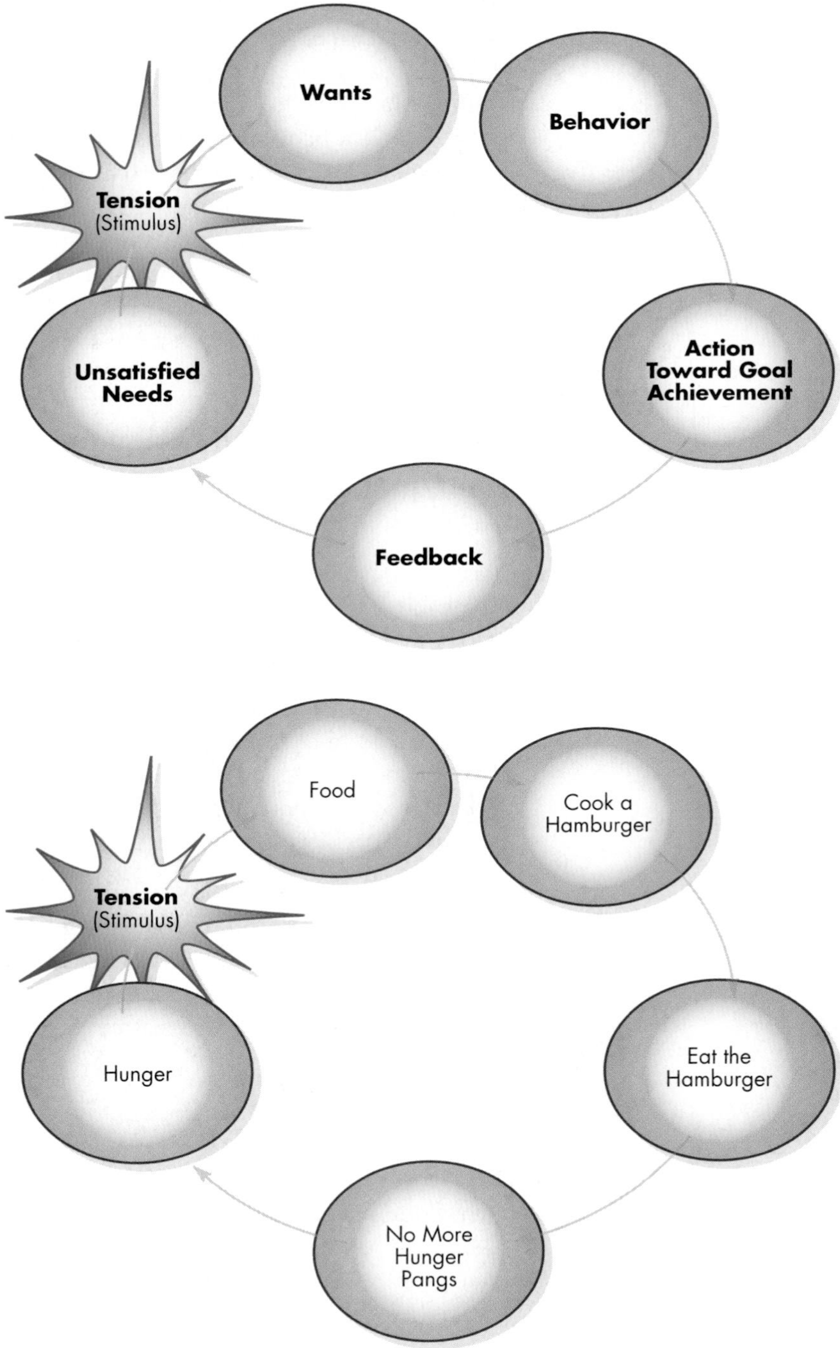

Differentiate between content and process theories of motivation

the top manager has done more than help the first-level manager meet her need. The top manager has increased the likelihood that the first-level manager will behave similarly in the future.

content theories
A group of motivation theories emphasizing the needs that motivate people.

process theories
A group of theories that explain how employees choose behaviors to meet their needs and how they determine whether their choices were successful.

Figure 13.3 presents the integrated motivation model, which shows how experience, environment, and perceptions influence decision making.

The integrated motivation model is useful in exploring theories of motivation in two categories: content theories and process theories. **Content theories** emphasize the needs that motivate people. If managers understand workers' needs, they can include factors in the work environment to meet them, thereby helping to direct employees' energies toward the organization's goals. **Process theories** explain how employees choose behaviors to meet their needs and how they determine whether their choices were successful (Daft, 1994).

FIGURE 13.3 *Integrated motivation model*

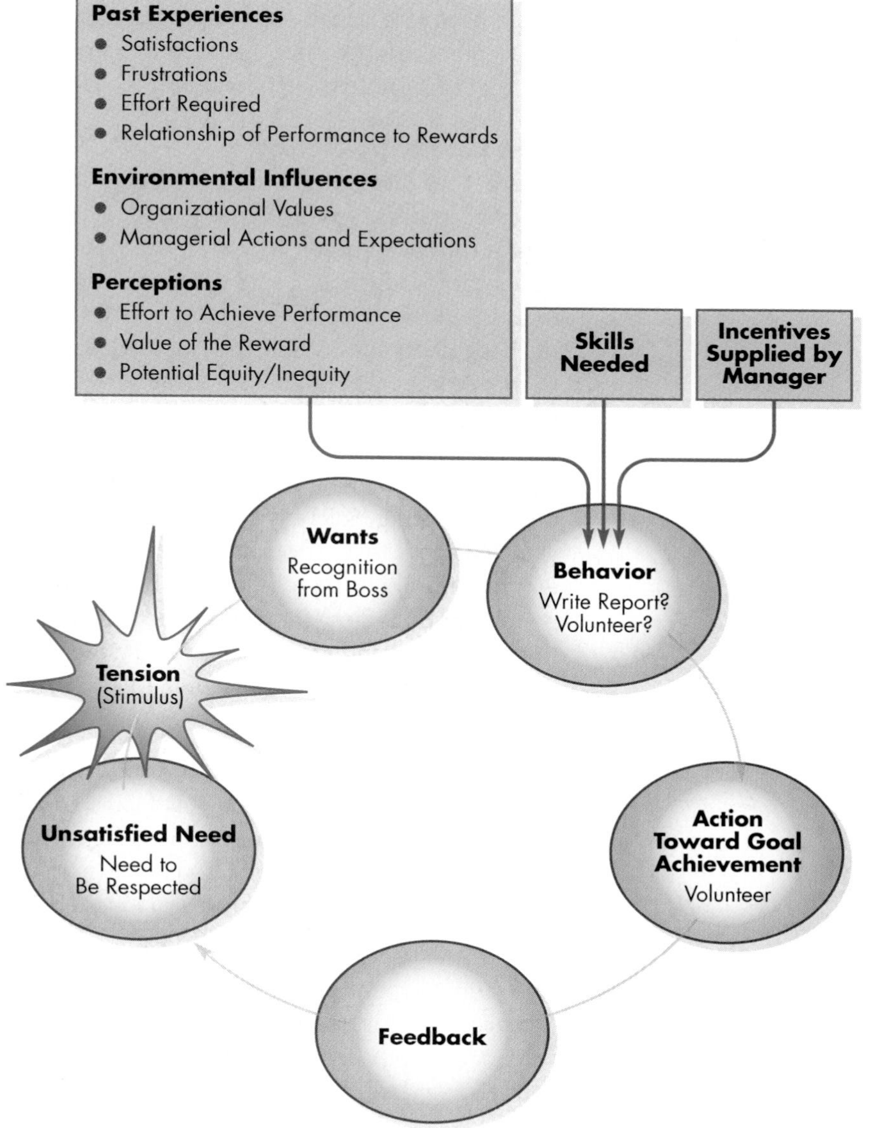

CONTENT THEORIES: MOTIVATION THEORIES FOCUSING ON NEEDS

Maslow's Hierarchy of Needs

3

List the five levels of needs according to Maslow and give an example of each

http://www.maslow.org

http://www.maslow.com

Psychologist Abraham H. Maslow (1943) based his study of motivation on a hierarchy of needs. His theory is based on four premises:

1. Only an unsatisfied need can influence behavior; a satisfied need is not a motivator. Thus, someone who has just eaten is unlikely to want food until the hunger need arises again.
2. A person's needs are arranged in a priority order of importance. The hierarchy goes from the most basic needs (such as water or shelter) to the most complex (esteem and self-actualization).
3. A person will at least minimally satisfy each level of need before feeling the need at the next level. Someone must feel companionship before desiring recognition.
4. If need satisfaction is not maintained at any level, the unsatisfied need will become a priority once again. For example, for a person who is presently feeling social needs, safety will become a priority once again if he or she is fired.

Five Levels of Needs

Figure 13.4 displays Maslow's hierarchy of needs. The exhibit lists the needs in order of priority, from bottom to top. The first category is composed of physiological (physical) needs. These are the primary, or basic-level, needs: the needs for water, air, food, shelter, and comfort. In the working environment, managers try to satisfy these needs by providing salaries and wages that allow employees to buy the basic necessities. While the employee is at work, the manager meets these needs by providing water fountains, clean air, no objectionable odors or noises, comfortable temperatures, and lunch breaks.

When physiological needs are met to the individual's satisfaction, the next priority becomes safety—the need to avoid bodily harm and uncertainty about one's well-being. Safety is closely allied to security, the freedom from risk or danger. Behaviors that reflect safety needs include joining unions, seeking jobs with tenure, and choosing jobs on the basis of health insurance and retirement programs. All of us desire a work environment in which we can be free from threats to our physical and emotional sense of security (Maslow, 1943). Managers attempt to satisfy safety needs by providing salary, benefits, safe work conditions, and job security.

> *"It was unbelievable. It is hard to tell you how I felt," says Frank Azzopardi, quarry manager [of Thompson-McCully] in Newport, Mich., who received an annuity that kicks in at 55. He says he now has a "secure feeling" because retirement funding "was always a big worry." Azzopardi says he "started on the end of a shovel as a laborer" and worked his way up. "I never thought 14 years ago that I would be a manager in this company or that I would share in the proceeds" (Krizan, 2000).*

Unfortunately, not all companies treat employees as well, as this chapter's Ethical Management feature illustrates.

Social needs become dominant when safety needs have been minimally gratified. People desire friendship, companionship, and a place in a group. Love needs

FIGURE 13.4 *Abraham Maslow's hierarchy of human needs*

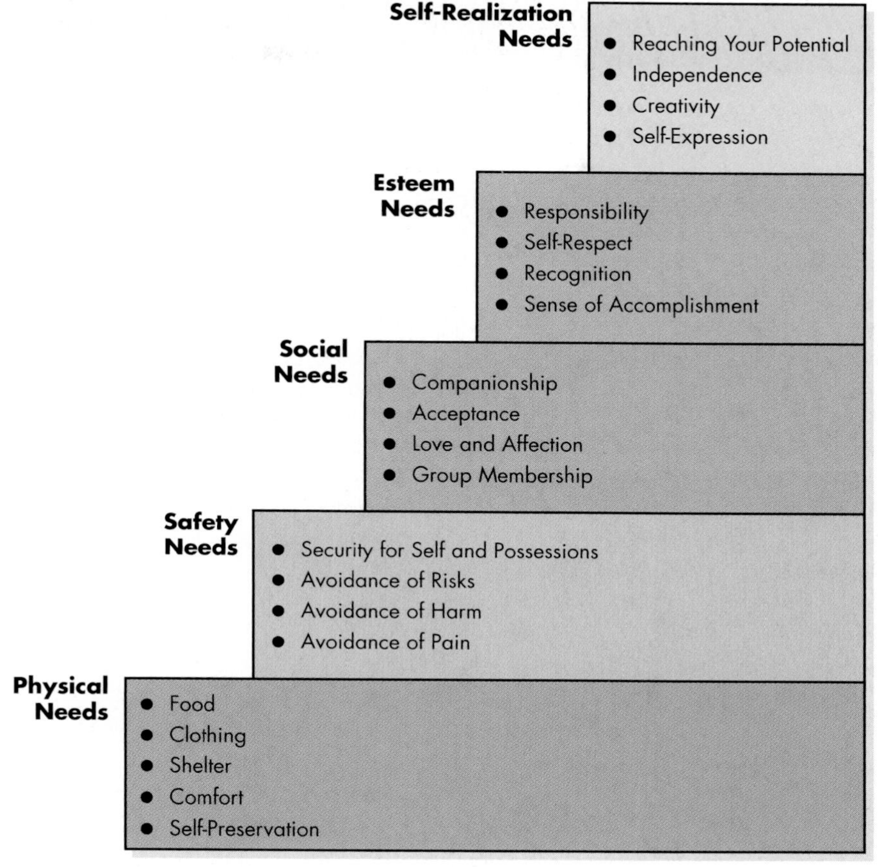

include the needs for giving and receiving love (Maslow, 1943). At work employees meet social needs by interacting frequently with fellow workers and through acceptance by others. The typical conversation at the water cooler reflects employees' needs to interact socially as well as in their official business roles. The groups that employees form at lunchtime are also a result of their need to be social. Managers can meet these needs by supporting employee get-togethers—birthday parties, lunches, and sports teams.

The next level in the hierarchy, esteem needs, includes the desire for self-respect and for the recognition of one's abilities by others. Satisfaction of these needs gives one pride, self-confidence, and a genuine sense of importance. Lack of satisfaction of these needs can result in feelings of inferiority, weakness, and helplessness. Work-related activities and outcomes that help meet individual esteem needs include successfully completing projects, being recognized by peers and superiors as someone who makes valuable contributions, and acquiring organizational titles. Sam Walton of Wal-Mart recognized the importance of this need in creating Sam's Rules for Building a Business. In Walton's words: "Rule 5:

http://www.walmart.com

ETHICAL MANAGEMENT
A Pink Slip for Structural Dynamics

Companies pay management consultants hundreds of thousands of dollars to help them create work environments in which employees can be productive. One of the basic themes promoted by consultants is to value and respect the individual. For most it is a lesson quietly internalized, but evidently not at Structural Dynamics Research Corporation.

In Milford, Ohio, home of Structural Dynamics, Marisa Means hoped to observe her father doing his job on "Take Our Daughters to Work Day." Instead, the eight-year-old and her father were escorted from the building when he was fired.

Marisa's father, a systems engineering manager for two years at Structural Dynamics, had no idea of his fate when he was called to talk with his supervisor early in the morning. He asked a colleague to watch his daughter when he left her in his office for what he thought would be a routine meeting. Shortly, Marisa was escorted from the office to be reunited with her father, and they were sent home before lunch.

This action took place despite the fact that company employees had been sent an electronic mail reminder in advance that they were free to bring their children for the day. In response to the situation, a company spokesperson stated, "The timing of the dismissal was regrettable."

1. What does this situation say about the company's value system?
2. If you were an employee, what effect would this action have on your morale?
3. What is your reaction to the company's statement?

http://www.sdrc.com
http://www.takeourdaughterstowork.org

Source: Dallas Morning News. "They Didn't Expect a Pink Slip for Daughter's Day at Work," May 5, 1995, p. 1D.

Appreciate everything your associates do for the business . . . nothing else can substitute for a few well-chosen, well-timed, sincere words of praise" (Trimble, 1992).

Maslow's highest need level, self-realization, relates to the desire for fulfillment. Self-realization (also called self-actualization) represents the need to maximize the use of one's skills, abilities, and potential.

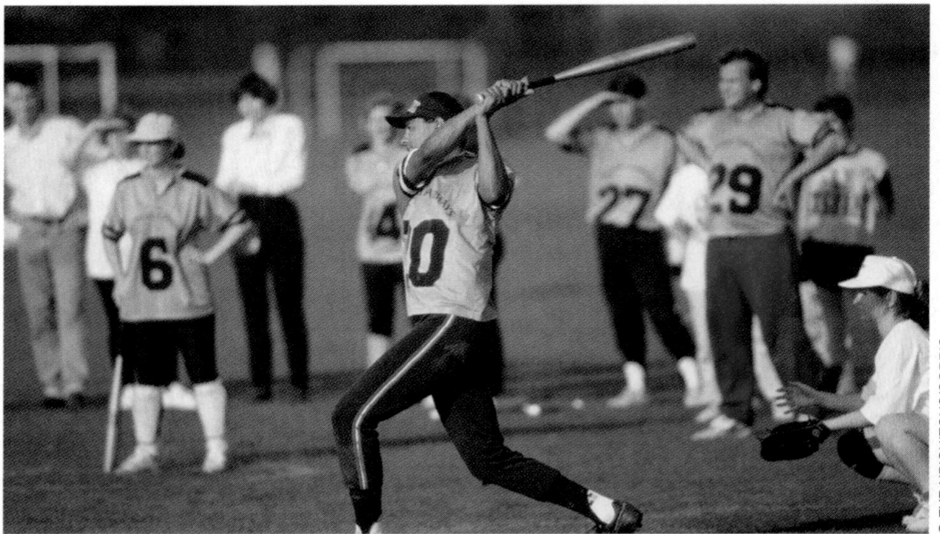

Group outings and functions, such as company sports teams, can help employees meet their social needs.

Implications for Managers

Maslow's needs theory applies to all environments, not specifically to the workplace. Nevertheless, it presents a workable motivation framework for managers. By analyzing employees' comments, attitudes, quality and quantity of work, and personal circumstances, the manager can try to identify the particular need level that individual workers are attempting to satisfy. Then the manager can attempt to build into the work environment the opportunities that will allow individuals to satisfy their needs. To see how a manager applies Maslow's theory and the needs that are likely to accompany them, review Figure 13.5. The figure also lists ways the manager can facilitate need satisfaction.

Because people are unique in their perceptions and personalities, applying the needs theory poses some difficulties. Just as one motive may lead to different behaviors, similar behavior in individuals can spring from different motives. The act of working hard on a new project, for instance, can arise from many needs. Some people apply themselves in order to grow and develop; others do so to be liked; still others wish to earn more money to enhance their sense of security; and yet others want the recognition that success will bring. For this reason, managers must use care when assessing motives simply by observing behavior.

An unmet need can frustrate an employee. It will continue to influence his or her behavior until it is satisfied, either on the job or off. The means of satisfaction might mesh with the organization's goals and processes. On the other hand, it could

FIGURE 13.5 *Five common worker needs and appropriate managerial responses*

Workers' Circumstances	Levels of Need Demanding Satisfaction	Need-Satisfying Actions
Employee has two children entering college next year	Physiological/safety	Increase pay or train and promote employee to higher-paying job if justified; confirm job security.
Worker feels concern about a competitor's purchase of the firm	Safety	If possible, reassure worker that jobs will not be eliminated; otherwise, frankly admit that certain jobs will be abolished. Encourage and assist those affected to seek employment elsewhere.
Worker feels uncomfortable as a new addition in a closely knit work group	Social	Invite subordinates to a social evening at your home, creating an opportunity for the newcomer to meet peers in an informal setting. Encourage the new worker to participate in company recreational activities. Sponsor the new worker for membership in professional organizations.
Employee feels unappreciated	Ego/self-esteem	Examine the employee's job performance and find reasons for praise. Accept the employee's suggestions where applicable. Build closer rapport.
Worker wants to get ahead in the organization and has a general idea of an ultimate employment goal in the company	Self-realization/ self-actualization	Provide specific guidance in pinpointing ultimate goal; help chart career path. Facilitate educational improvement. Provide opportunities for job experience and company recognition.

compete or even conflict with them. The esteem need, for example, can be satisfied by involvement with work-related groups or groups outside the work environment.

The level of need satisfaction constantly fluctuates. Once a need is satisfied, it ceases to influence behavior, but only for a time. Needs do not remain satisfied over the long term.

Herzberg's Two-Factor Theory

4

Discuss the impact of hygiene and motivation factors in the work environment

Psychologist Frederick Herzberg (1975) and his associates developed a needs theory called the two-factor, or hygiene-motivator, theory. Herzberg's theory defines one set of factors that lead to job dissatisfaction; these factors are called hygiene factors. The theory also defines a set of factors that produce job satisfaction and motivation; these factors are called motivators.

Hygiene Factors

hygiene factors
Maintenance factors (such as salary, status, working conditions) that do not relate directly to a person's actual work activity, but when of low quality are the cause of unhappiness on the job.

According to Herzberg, a manager's poor handling of **hygiene factors** (often referred to as maintenance factors) is the primary cause of unhappiness on the job. Hygiene factors are extrinsic to the job—that is, they do not relate directly to a person's actual work activity. Hygiene factors are part of a job's environment; they are part of the context of the job, not its content. When the hygiene factors that an employer provides are of low quality, employees feel job dissatisfaction. When the factors are of sufficient quality, they do not necessarily act as motivators. High-quality hygiene factors are not necessarily stimuli for growth or greater effort. They lead only to employees' lack of job dissatisfaction (Herzberg, 1975). Hygiene factors include

- *Salary*. To prevent job dissatisfaction, a manager should provide adequate wages, salaries, and fringe benefits.
- *Job security*. Company grievance procedures and seniority privileges contribute to high-quality hygiene.
- *Working conditions*. Managers ensure adequate heat, light, ventilation, and hours of work to prevent dissatisfaction.
- *Status*. Managers who are mindful of the importance of hygiene factors provide privileges, job titles, and other symbols of rank and position.
- *Company policies*. To prevent job dissatisfaction, managers should provide policies as guidelines for behavior and administer the policies fairly.
- *Quality of technical supervision*. When employees are not able to receive answers to job-related questions, they become frustrated. Providing high-quality technical supervision for employees prevents frustration.
- *Quality of interpersonal relations among peers, supervisors, and subordinates*. In an organization with high-quality hygiene factors, the workplace provides social opportunities as well as the chance to enjoy comfortable work-related relationships.

Motivation Factors

motivation factors
The conditions, intrinsic to the job, that can lead to an individual's job satisfaction.

According to Herzberg, **motivation factors** are the primary cause of job satisfaction. They are intrinsic to a job and relate directly to the real nature of the work people perform. In other words, motivation factors relate to job content. When an employer fails to provide motivation factors, employees experience no job satisfaction. With motivation factors, employees enjoy job satisfaction and provide high performance. Different people require different kinds and degrees of motivation factors—what stimulates one worker may not affect another. Motivation factors also act as stimuli for psychological and personal growth. These factors include

- *Achievement.* The opportunity to accomplish something or contribute something of value can serve as a source of job satisfaction.
- *Recognition.* Wise managers let employees know that their efforts have been worthwhile and that management notes and appreciates them.
- *Responsibility.* The potential for acquiring new duties and responsibilities, either through job expansion or delegation, can be a powerful motivator for some workers.
- *Advancement.* The opportunity to improve one's position as a result of job performance gives employees a clear reason for high performance.
- *The work itself.* When a task offers an opportunity for self-expression, personal satisfaction, and meaningful challenge, employees are likely to undertake the task with enthusiasm.
- *Possibility of growth.* The opportunity to increase knowledge and personal development is likely to lead to job satisfaction.

Figure 13.6 illustrates the hygiene and motivation factors. The hygiene factors relate to responses that range from no dissatisfaction to high dissatisfaction. The motivators, if present in the work environment, can provide low to high satisfaction. If not present, no satisfaction can result.

FIGURE 13.6 *Results of hygiene factors and motivation factors*

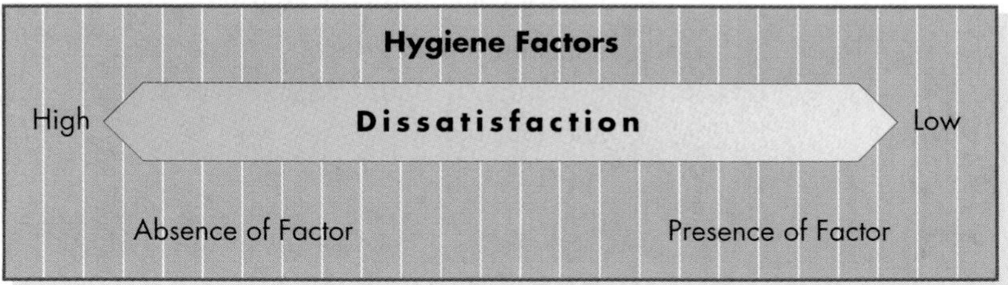

The quality of each factor present influences each employee's level of satisfaction or dissatisfaction

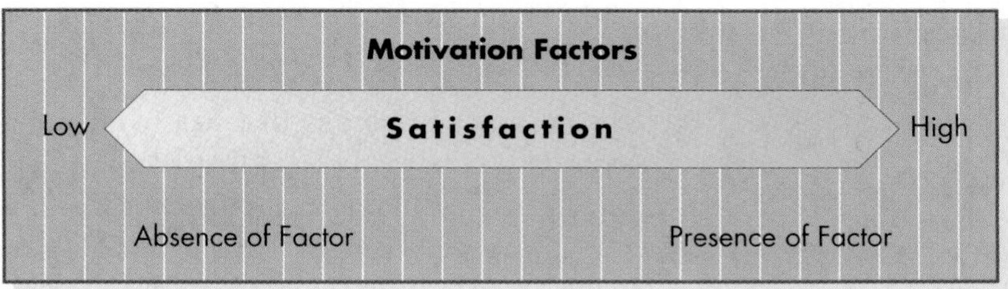

Implications for Managers

Herzberg's theory relates specifically to the work environment. Managers can use their knowledge to ensure that hygiene factors are in place in the environment as a foundation on which to build motivation. The absence of quality hygiene factors can lead to dissatisfaction for the workforce—a lesson quickly learned by Chuck Mitchell at GTO, Inc., a deteriorating five-year-old maker of automatic gate openers in Tallahassee, Florida. When Mitchell replaced the founder, who had suffered a fatal heart attack, he inherited greatly disillusioned workers in a work environment where hygiene factors had been neglected. It had been common practice for the founder to

http://www.gtoinc.com

- Harangue employees for filing claims on the company's health insurance policy
- Begrudge employees ten-minute breaks every two hours
- Have no budget funds available for machine repairs
- Insist that hourly workers work overtime without premium pay
- Direct employees to repair antique cars, install basketball backboards, and build fences for the owner on company time
- Require employees to bring their own coffee and supplies for the break room

After Mitchell gained a sense of some of the higher-priority items among the employees, there were certain hygiene factors he knew he could improve immediately. As Mitchell notes, "The little things often mean more to people, and they show that management cares about everybody." So, for starters, Mitchell

- Bought coffee and supplies for the break room
- Hired a roofer to patch the leaking building
- Encouraged employees to bring in their personal cars so they could use some of GTO's tools to repair them over the weekend
- Changed the health insurance policy from one with a $300 employee deductible to one featuring a $5 copayment
- Introduced company-paid employee disability insurance
- Gave employees keys to the building
- Provided a "blank check" when employees needed money for machine parts and repairs
- Instituted a profit-sharing program (Hyatt, 1995)

Once top management has provided satisfactory hygiene factors, they can focus on motivation factors.

> *Bob Thompson "challenges people to achieve more by giving them more responsibility," says office manager Marlene Van Patten, an annuity recipient who joined Thompson-McCully when it purchased Spartan Asphalt in 1985. "He is a demanding person, but extremely fair. He always has wanted to be the best and he has wanted his people to be the best" (Krizan, 2000).*

A critical point to note is that nearly all supervisors have the power to increase motivation in the workplaces they manage by granting more responsibility to employees, praising their accomplishments, and making them feel that they are succeeding. Top managers at DuPont or Southwest Airlines have come to the same conclusion. Motivated employees believe they have control over their jobs and

http://www.dupont.com

can make a contribution (Wilson, 1992). This belief provides the basis for team management, empowerment, and intrapreneurship—to be discussed later in this chapter.

McClelland and the Need for Achievement

David McClelland (1971) developed a needs theory that holds that certain types of needs are learned during a lifetime of interaction with the environment. McClelland's three needs relate to

- Achievement, or the desire to excel or achieve in relation to a set of standards
- Power, or the desire to control others or have influence over them
- Affiliation, the desire for friendship, cooperation, and close interpersonal relationships

Achievement relates to individual performance. Power and affiliation, on the other hand, involve interpersonal relationships.

Studies of achievement motivation have produced two important ideas: (1) A strong achievement need relates to how well individuals are motivated to perform their work, and (2) the achievement need can be strengthened by training.

McClelland's needs theory recognizes that people may have different mixtures or combinations of the needs; an individual could be described as a high achiever, a power-motivated person, or an affiliator.

High Achiever

Explain the characteristics of a person with high-achievement needs

McClelland and an associate, David Burnham (1976), defined the characteristics of the high achiever. They believed the high achiever

- Performs a task because of a compelling need for personal achievement, not necessarily for the rewards associated with accomplishing the task. The desire to excel applies to both means and end; the high achiever wants to do the job more efficiently than it has been done before as well as do a good job.
- Prefers to take personal responsibility for solving problems rather than leaving the outcome to others. Achievers may be viewed as loners. At times they may appear to have difficulty delegating authority.
- Prefers to set moderate goals that, with stretching, are achievable. For the achiever, easy goals with a high probability of success provide no challenge and thus no satisfaction. Difficult goals with a low probability of success would require an achiever to gamble on success. Because the achiever likes to be in control, an outcome that depends on chance is unacceptable.
- Prefers immediate and concrete feedback about performance, which assists in measuring progress toward the goal. The feedback needs to be in terms of goal performance (rather than personality variables) so the achiever can determine what needs to be done to improve performance.

Power-Motivated Person

The person with a strong desire for power needs to acquire, exercise, and maintain influence over others. Such persons compete with others if success will allow them to be dominant. The power-motivated person does not avoid confrontations.

Affiliator

The person with a high need for affiliation wants to be liked by other people, attempts to establish friendships, and seeks to avoid conflict. The affiliator prefers conciliation.

Implications for Managers

Based on McClelland's theory, managers should work to identify and encourage the development of high achievers. Managers should capitalize on the latter's ability to set goals and on their desire for responsibility by providing them with opportunities for participation, by delegating authority to them, and by using management by objectives (discussed in Chapter 5). To work effectively with high achievers, managers should provide immediate, concrete feedback. For example, Tom Warner, president of Warner Corporation, a Washington, D.C.–based plumbing, heating, ventilation, and air-conditioning contractor, structured a unique program to capitalize on his high achievers (Hyatt, 1995). Considered revolutionary in the mundane world of stopped-up sinks and balky furnaces, Warner has 80 area technical directors (ATD) in his 260-person business. ATDs have their own business to manage within their assigned zip codes. Warner prepares the ATD with training in sales and marketing, budgeting, negotiating, cost estimating, and customer services. Then he empowers them to build up the business in their assigned locations. Says Warner, "The guys who gravitate to the ATD program want more, with more effort. If you want a 9-to-5 job, it's not for you. Last year ATDs averaged 63 hours a week." The program is not for everyone, only for the high achievers. Eight out of the first twelve ATDs decided the program wasn't for them; they wanted to remain ordinary mechanics.

When dealing with the power-motivated person of McClelland's theory, managers should recognize that the use of power is a necessary part of corporate life and that those who are motivated by power can serve as necessary and useful members of the organization. Managers should be aware, however, of the negative aspect of power as a motivator. Many individuals seek power solely for personal benefit. The power-motivated person may not, therefore, have the organization's best interests at heart.

In working with employees whom McClelland labeled affiliators, managers must be aware that these employees desire to avoid conflict, which may prevent them from handling organizational conflict effectively.

Figure 13.7 shows how the three needs theories relate. Each theory provides the manager with a different viewpoint from which to understand the cause of behavior. Herzberg's hygiene factors relate to Maslow's lower-level needs; Herzberg's motivation factors relate to the higher-level needs, as do McClelland's needs for power and achievement.

Alderfer's ERG Theory

6
Identify the needs associated with ERG theory

Clayton Alderfer (1972) proposed a needs theory that compressed Maslow's five need levels into three:

- *Existence.* Existence needs relate to a person's physical well-being. (In terms of Maslow's model, existence needs include physiological and safety needs.)

FIGURE 13.7 *Comparison of the theories of Maslow, Herzberg, and McClelland*

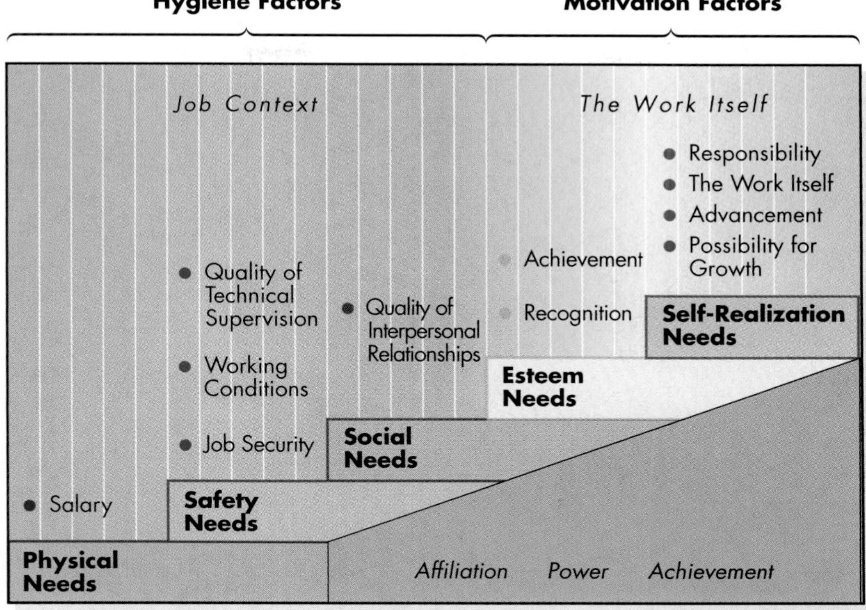

- *Relatedness.* This level includes needs for satisfactory relationships with others. (Relatedness needs correspond, in terms of Maslow's model, to social needs.)
- *Growth.* Growth needs call for the realization of potential and the achievement of competence. (In terms of Maslow's model, growth needs include esteem and self-realization needs.)

ERG theory
A motivation theory establishing three categories of human needs: existence needs, relatedness needs, and growth needs.

The name of Alderfer's theory is the **ERG theory**. The name derives from the first three letters of each of the needs Alderfer defined.

Maslow and Alderfer agreed that an unsatisfied need is a motivator, and that as lower-level needs are satisfied they become less important. Alderfer believed, however, that higher-level needs become more important as they are satisfied. If a person is frustrated at attaining more of a need, the individual might return to a lower-level need. For example, the employee frustrated in an attempt to achieve more growth could redirect energies to, say, becoming part of a group. When high-tech computer-related businesses in the Silicon Valley began to retrench after a period of expansion, managers who had been focusing on furthering their growth needs began to seek new organizations to meet their existence needs. Figure 13.8 illustrates the relationship between the theories of Maslow and Alderfer.

Implications for Managers

According to Alderfer, managers should realize that a person can voluntarily move down the needs hierarchy if attempts to achieve needs are frustrated. To maintain high levels of performance, managers should provide opportunities for

FIGURE 13.8 *Comparison of the theories of Maslow and Alderfer*

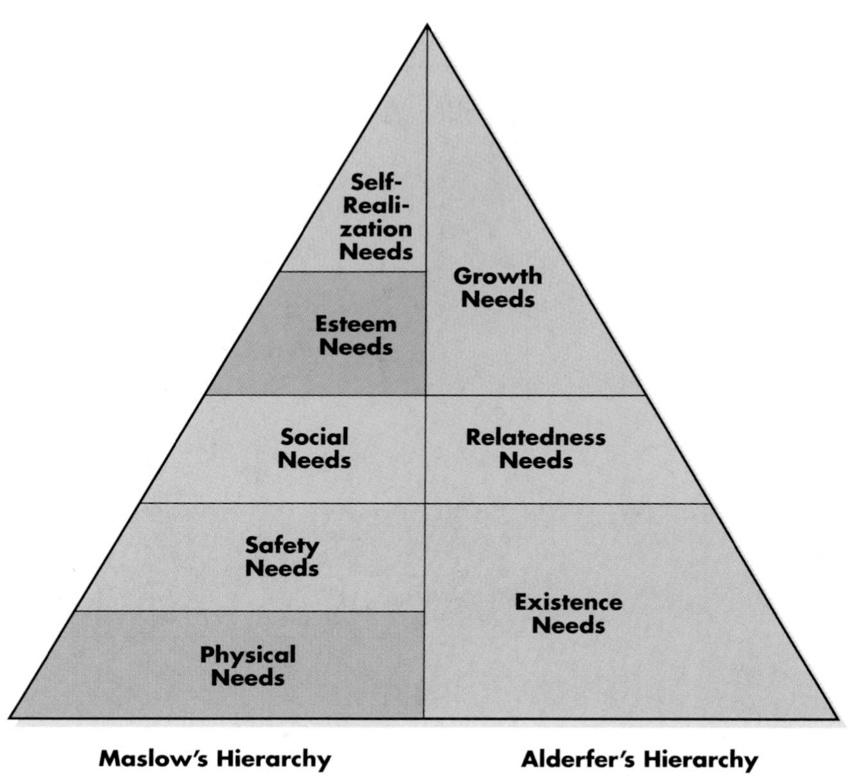

employees to capitalize on the increased importance of higher-order needs by recognizing employees and encouraging participation in decision making. For example, at Silicon Graphics, Inc., 40 people are chosen each year by their peers as the employees who best represent the culture and spirit of the company. The winners are announced with great fanfare, and each receives a trip for two to Hawaii. At least equally important to the trip is the recognition by peers, which meets esteem needs.

http://www.sgi.com

The importance of fulfilling growth and self-realization needs is illustrated by the comments of Ocelia Williams, an hourly worker at Cincinnati's Cin-Made, a small manufacturer of mailing tubes and other cardboard-and-metal containers and a practitioner of open-book management. "I couldn't see how the company could make it unless we all took our share of responsibility. I now know what is going on, and where I fit. What I do does make a difference." What Ocelia and other employees do is share responsibility. Hourly workers now do all of Cin-Made's purchasing and have a voice in every hiring decision. They schedule their own hours, hire and supervise all temporary employees, oversee the company's safety program, and administer its skill-based pay system (Case, 1995).

http://www.cin-made.com

PROCESS THEORIES: MOTIVATION THEORIES FOCUSING ON BEHAVIORS

Now that we have examined four motivation theories relating to the individual's needs, we can explore four theories about why people choose a particular behavior to satisfy their needs. This section will discuss four behavior-oriented theories: expectancy theory, reinforcement theory, equity theory, and goal-setting theory. Each derives from the factors summarized in Figure 13.3: past experiences, environmental influences, and perceptions.

Expectancy Theory

Discuss the relationship between expectations and motivation

expectancy theory
A motivation theory stating that three factors influence behavior: the value of rewards, the relationship of rewards to the necessary performance, and the effort required for performance.

Developed by Victor Vroom (1964), **expectancy theory** states that, before choosing a behavior, an individual will evaluate various possibilities on the basis of anticipated work and reward. Motivation—the spur to act—is a function of how badly we want something and how likely we think we are to get it. Its intensity functions in direct proportion to perceived or expected rewards. Expectancy theory includes three variables:

- *Effort-performance link.* Will the effort achieve performance? How much effort will performance require? How probable is success?
- *Performance-reward link.* What is the possibility that a certain performance will produce the desired reward or outcome?
- *Attractiveness.* How attractive is the reward? This factor relates to the strength or importance of the reward to the individual and deals with his or her unsatisfied needs.

To see how expectancy theory can be applied, consider an example. Suppose that, late one Friday afternoon, John Friedman's boss asks him to develop a presentation of the six-month budget results. The presentation is due the following Monday. John realizes he can complete the four-hour project in one of two ways. He can stay at the office and do the work, or he can take the work home over the weekend.

John evaluates the first option, staying at work for the needed four hours. He realizes that staying will result in a completed presentation by Monday (effort-performance link). He knows from past experience that a completed project will result in recognition by his boss (performance-reward link). John has a high regard for this recognition, because it will eventually lead to a promotion. Working late on Friday will, however, interfere with existing plans and may cause domestic problems. (The domestic problems affect the attractiveness of the reward.)

As John evaluates the second option, taking work home, he realizes that the effort-performance link and the performance-reward link will be the same as in option 1. By taking the work home, however, John can avoid the negative consequences of interfering with social plans. (This makes the reward seem more attractive.) John chooses the second option.

In this decision making, John asked himself a series of questions: "Can I accomplish the task?" Yes, it will take four hours, but I can do it. "What's in it for me?" When I do the task it can bring both positive and negative results (option 1) or just positive results (option 2). "Is it worth it?" The positive is, but the negative isn't. Study Figure 13.9 and determine the stage of the expectancy theory to which each question pertains.

Implications for Managers

According to expectancy theory, behavior is heavily influenced by perceptions of the outcomes of behavior. The individual who expects an outcome, possesses the competence to achieve it, and wants it badly enough will exhibit the behavior required by the organization. The person who expects that a specific behavior will produce an outcome perceived as undesirable will be less inclined to exhibit that behavior. A manager who knows each subordinate's expectations and desires can tailor outcomes associated with specific behaviors to produce motivation (Vroom, 1964; Porter and Lawler, 1968). To motivate behavior, managers must

- Understand that employees measure the value associated with the assignment. As a manager, you get from your people what you reward, not what you ask for.
- Find out what outcomes are perceived as desirable by employees and provide them. Outcomes may be intrinsic (experienced directly by the individual) or extrinsic (provided by the company). A feeling of self-worth after doing a good job is intrinsic; the promotion that the job produces is extrinsic. For an outcome to be satisfying to an employee the employee must recognize it as an outcome that relates to his or her needs and one that is consistent with his or her expectations of what is due (Schuler, 1987).
- Make the job intrinsically rewarding. If this is a valued outcome, it is critical for managers to provide experiences that enhance an employee's feeling of self-worth.
- Effectively and clearly communicate desired behaviors and their outcomes. Employees need to know what is acceptable and what is unacceptable to the organization.
- Link rewards to performance. Once the acceptable performance level is attained, rewards should quickly follow.

FIGURE 13.9 *Model of expectancy theory*

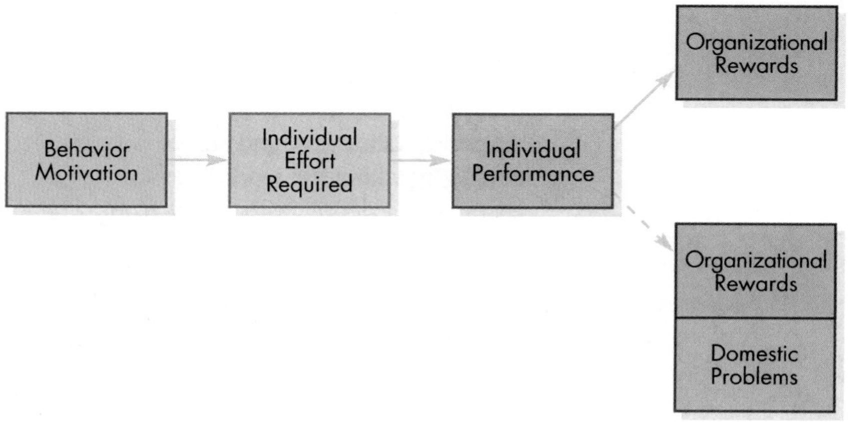

- Be aware that people and their goals, needs, desires, and levels of performance differ. The manager must set a level of performance for each employee that is attainable by that person.
- Strengthen each individual's perceptions of his or her ability to execute desired behaviors and achieve outcomes by providing guidance and direction.

http://www.blackbox.com

With these guidelines in mind, some companies incorporate expectancy theory principles in designing incentive pay systems that focus on organizational goals. The key factor for successful programs is the effort-performance link. Incentive pay works when workers feel they can meet targets. Therefore, company-wide goals must be translated and pushed down to the employee level. For example, at Black Box Corporation, a Pittsburgh-based marketer of computer network and other communication devices, the corporate goal is to increase customer satisfaction. Workers can help attain the goal by increasing their skill levels—and substantially increasing their pay in the same job. For instance, Black Box pays starting order takers about $17,000 per year. As they boost their product knowledge and customer skills, their pay can increase to $28,000. Those who improve their skills even more, such as improving their sales skills, or learning another language to handle international sales, can make over $40,000 and hence receive a larger profit-sharing bonus in addition because it is based on annual earnings (Gleckman, 1994).

Reinforcement Theory

Explain the relationship between reinforcement and motivation

http://www.bfskinner.org

reinforcement theory
A motivation theory that states a supervisor's reactions and past rewards and penalties affect employees' behavior.

Another theory that examines the reasons for behavior has its foundation in B. F. Skinner's work regarding operant conditioning (Skinner, 1969). **Reinforcement theory** holds that a person's behavior in a situation is influenced by the rewards or penalties experienced in similar situations in the past. John, the employee who was faced with the task of preparing a budget presentation, received praise from his boss for expending extra effort in the past. This positive reinforcement influenced John's behavior when the boss had another last-minute request.

Reinforcement theory introduces a major point that managers should understand. Much of motivated behavior is learned behavior (Tarpy, 1974). The employee learns over time what type of performance is acceptable and what is unacceptable. This learning influences future behavior. Figure 13.10 shows how reinforcement affects behavior.

Types of Reinforcement

Managers can choose from four main types of reinforcement: positive reinforcement, avoidance, extinction, and punishment. Of these four approaches, positive reinforcement most often leads to long-range growth in individuals by producing lasting and positive behavioral changes.

- To increase the probability that an individual will repeat a desired behavior, a manager provides positive reinforcement as soon as possible after the desired behavior occurs. Positive reinforcers can be praise, pay, or promotions—elements normally regarded as favorable by employees.
- Avoidance attempts to increase the probability that a positive behavior will be repeated by showing the consequences of behavior the manager does not desire. The employee is allowed to avoid those consequences by displaying

FIGURE 13.10 *How the reinforcement process affects behavior*

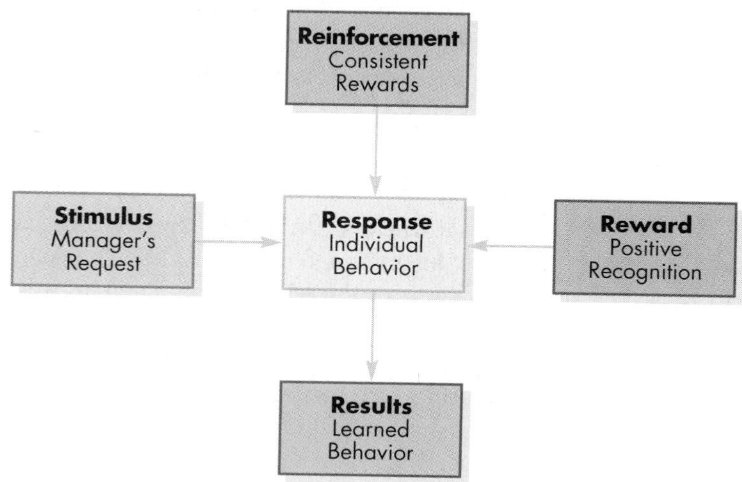

the desired behavior. For example, a manager has a policy of penalizing all employees who do not turn in reports on time. As long as the threat of punishment is there, employees will be motivated to turn in the reports on time.

- Extinction consists of ignoring the behavior of subordinates in order to weaken the behavior. Managers can use this approach when behavior is temporary, atypical, and not serious in its negative consequences. The supervisor's hope is that the behavior will soon go away or disappear if it is ignored. Extinction might also be appropriate in a situation of changed circumstances. Say a manager and an employee have developed the habit of talking during working hours about off-the-job topics. After the manager is promoted to another job

A manager should use positive reinforcement as soon as possible after a desired behavior occurs to increase the likelihood of the employee repeating the behavior.

in another area, the employee continues to drop by, a practice that makes the manager uncomfortable. If the manager continues to work while the employee is there, the employee will eventually get the message and the behavior will be extinguished.

- Punishment is an attempt to decrease the recurrence of a behavior by applying negative consequences. Loss of privileges, docked pay, and suspension are forms of punishment. The trouble with punishment as a response to behavior is that the person will learn what not to do but will not necessarily learn the desired behavior.

Reinforcement is affected by time. The closer the reinforcement is to the behavior, the greater the impact it will have on future behavior.

Implications for Managers

Reinforcement theory has several implications for managers. First, managers should bear in mind that motivated behavior is influenced by the employee's learning what is acceptable and unacceptable to the organization (Hamner, 1974). In addition, in working with employees to develop motivated behavior, managers should

- Tell individuals what they can do to get positive reinforcement. The establishment of a work standard lets all individuals know what behavior is acceptable.
- Tell individuals what they are doing wrong. The person who does not know why rewards are not forthcoming may be confused. Information allows a person to improve motivated behavior.
- Base rewards on performance. Managers should not reward all individuals in the same way. If the manager gives the same rewards to all employees for all degrees of performance, poor or average performance is reinforced and high performance may be ignored.
- Administer the reinforcement as close in time to the related behavior as possible. To achieve maximum impact, the appropriate reinforcement should immediately follow performance.
- Recognize that failure to reward can also modify behavior. If a manager does not praise a subordinate for meritorious behavior, the subordinate can become confused about the behavior the manager wants.

By applying these guidelines, managers can help employees focus on organizational objectives and can modify employee behavior at the same time. For example, CEO Steve Wilson of Mid-States Technical Staffing Services in Davenport, Iowa, used positive reinforcement to develop teamwork, follow-through, and initiative. After teaching everyone to understand company financial statements and to take responsibility for budget items, Wilson told employees, "Every time you hit $75,000 in net earnings, I'll pay a bonus." As Wilson notes, "The light dawned slowly. At first employees thought, 'Great, I don't have to wait 'til Christmas for my bonus,' but when we paid out the second one two months after the first, that's when they changed." Now, employees watch weekly budget and income numbers like hawks, and move heaven and earth if they think they are falling behind plans or have a chance to reach the target. Salespeople help one another out instead of hoarding customers. Office workers, each of whom has responsibility for certain expenses, find other departments eager to cooperate in cutting spending (Case, 1995).

Equity Theory

Explain how equity influences motivation

equity theory
A motivation theory stating that comparisons of relative input-outcome ratios influence behavior choices.

Another view of motivation, **equity theory**, states that people's behavior relates to their perception of the fairness of treatment they receive. Most professional athletes use equity arguments to support their salary demands. They point to publicized salaries received by peers as justification for their negotiating stands. Equity theory also involves the fairness that an individual perceives in the relationship between effort expended and reward.

People determine equity by calculating a simple ratio: the effort they are expected to invest on the job (their input) in relation to what they expect to receive after investing that effort (their outcome or reward). As Figure 13.11 shows, this input-outcome ratio should provide a means of comparison with the ratios of other individuals or groups. Equity exists when the ratios are equivalent. Inequity exists when, in the employee's mind, inputs exceed the relative or perceived values of outcomes (Adams, 1963).

Consider an example: Ellen McCann has been working as a salesperson for ten months. In this time, she has gone to sales school three times (achieving superior ratings in all categories), consistently achieved 125 percent of sales quota, and has won two local sales contests. In recognition of this achievement, Ellen's boss gave her a $150 per month raise. Ellen's motivation has dropped noticeably in the past month, however. Why? She learned that a salesperson with no prior experience had been hired at $2,550 per month—$50 more than Ellen is making! As Ellen said, "It's not fair! If they can do that, I'm going to start to look around for an employer who will appreciate me."

This example leads to two points about equity theory. First, when an individual perceives himself or herself as the victim of inequity, one of three responses occurs. The person can decide to escape the situation ("I quit"), put the input-outcome ratios in balance ("I'll do less" or "I want a raise"), or attempt to change perceptions ("It's really fair because . . .").

The second important point about equity theory concerns the referent the person selects for comparison. There are two categories: other and system. In the example of professional athletes, the "other" category includes those persons in the same job, same team, or same league or those with similar backgrounds or in the

FIGURE 13.11 *Equity theory in action*

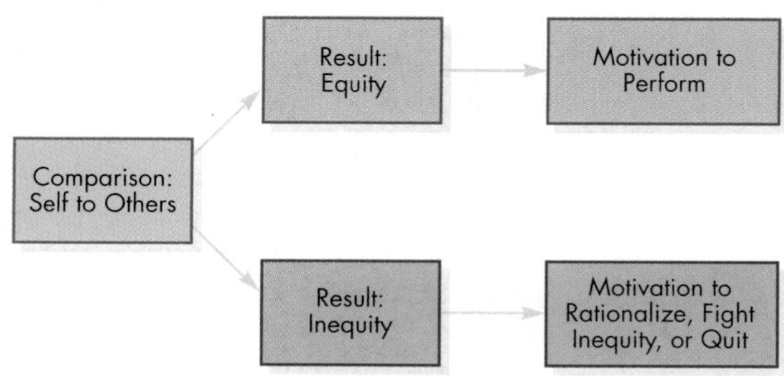

same circle of friends. The system is the referent when the individual recognizes the presence of organization-wide policies and procedures: "If those people are allowed overtime, I should have overtime when I need it to complete my work" (Goodman and Fredman, 1971).

Implications for Managers

Equity theory emphasizes that employees are motivated by absolute rewards and the relative rewards available in the system. More importantly, employees make conscious comparisons of equity that influence their motivation levels. Therefore, managers must make conscious efforts to establish and maintain equity in the work environment. In addition, managers need to recognize that perceptions of equity are not a one-time occurrence. Present perceptions are affected by past perceptions. By bearing this in mind, a manager may be able to identify the incident that served as the straw that broke the camel's back.

http://www.intel.com

http://www.gene.com

Organizations like Intel and Genentech have applied equity theory in the work environment. At Intel everyone has a small, open cubicle, including chairman Andy Grove; and no one gets a reserved parking spot. At Genentech everyone gets three weeks of vacation, regardless of position or seniority; and everyone gets stock options (Deutschman, 1994).

Goal-Setting Theory

10

Explain how goals influence motivation

goal-setting theory
A motivation theory stating that behavior is influenced by goals, which tell employees what they need to do and how much effort they need to expend.

The fourth behavior-oriented theory, **goal-setting theory**, states that people's behavior is influenced by the goals that are established. In essence, goals tell an employee what needs to be done and how much effort will need to be expended (Robbins, 1991). "Other practices that Thompson tends to endorse include promoting from within and setting achievable stretch goals for managers and workers alike. When you think that you are doing the best you can do, 'he can get a little more out of you,' says CFO Gregg Campbell" (enr.com, 2000).

Goal-setting theory is similar to the concepts associated with expectancy theory in that it focuses on the conscious choices a person makes. According to the theory, there are two approaches to goal setting: (1) managers may set goals for the employees or (2) employees and managers develop employee goals together.

Implications for Managers

According to goal-setting theory, managers should

- Work with employees in setting goals to provide targets for motivation.
- Make goals specific rather than general. The goal of "Doing your best" is not as effective as "Complete the project by June 15 with no budget overruns."
- Provide feedback on performance. Feedback acts as a guide to behavior. It helps identify shortcomings in performance and provides the means for corrective action.

http://www.ncr.com

Jere Stead, former CEO of AT&T's Global Information Solutions (now NCR Corporation), has led business transformations five times by relying on goal setting theory. Notes Stead, "At GIS all objectives must clearly link to key results: customer or shareholder satisfaction and profitable growth. The goal setting links the organization, provides a basis for gauging progress, and gives specific measures for rewards" (Stewart, 1994).

BUILDING A PHILOSOPHY OF MANAGEMENT

Discuss the importance of a manager's philosophy of management in creating a positive work environment

The theories of Maslow, Herzberg, McClelland, and Alderfer offer valuable insight into the needs that trigger motivated behavior. The theories of expectancy, reinforcement, equity, and goal setting reveal the why of motivation—why employees display different types of motivated behavior. Each theory makes an important contribution to understanding the motivation of an employee, and each provides input for the motivation model. Familiarity with theories of motivation allows a manager an educated viewpoint from which to consider how to foster motivation in workers, capture commitment, and develop a positive work environment.

philosophy of management
A manager's attitude about work and the people who perform it, which influences the motivation approaches he or she selects.

One significant factor that sets the foundation for creating a positive work environment is a manager's **philosophy of management**, or attitude about work and the people who do the work. A manager's philosophy of management incorporates and reflects personal beliefs about human nature in the work setting—about worker attitudes and characteristics, employee maturity, and the influence of management expectations on behavior. Ed Armatis, an operator and mechanic at the oil blending facility at Thompson-McGully, describes Bob Thompson this way, "He is a fair guy, but very demanding. You don't see him around much if you do your job" (Krizan, 2000). A manager's philosophy influences the motivation approaches he or she will select. Managers who think subordinates are ambitious and eager, wish to do work well, want to be independent, and enjoy work will take far different actions than managers who think subordinates are lazy and work only to attain security.

To develop a philosophy of management, there are three concepts describing human nature that should be incorporated: Theory X and Theory Y, Argyris's maturity theory, and the development of management expectations.

Theory X and Theory Y

Theory X
A philosophy of management with a negative perception of subordinates' potential for and attitudes toward work.

Theory Y
A philosophy of management with a positive perception of subordinates' potential for and attitudes toward work.

Douglas McGregor (1960), a professor of industrial management, said that an individual's management philosophy reflects one of two sets of assumptions about workers. He called the two sets Theory X and Theory Y. **Theory X** is a philosophy of management with a negative perception of subordinates' potential for work and attitudes toward work. It assumes that subordinates dislike work, are poorly motivated, and require close supervision. A manager with these beliefs tends to control the group, use negative motivation, and refuse to delegate decision making. Figure 13.12 lists the components of Theory X.

Theory Y is a philosophy of management with a positive perception of subordinates' potential for and attitudes toward work. It assumes, as Figure 13.12 shows, that subordinates can be self-directing, will seek responsibility, and find work as natural as play or rest. The outcome of this belief is a manager who encourages people to seek responsibility, involves people in decision making, and works with people to achieve their goals.

The important point about Theory X and Theory Y is that a management philosophy influences the type of work climate the manager endeavors to create and, ultimately, how the manager treats people.

FIGURE 13.12 *Assumptions about workers according to Theory X and Theory Y*

Theory X	Theory Y
People basically dislike work and avoid it whenever possible.	Most people find work as natural as play or rest and develop an attitude toward work based on their experience with it.
Because most people dislike work, they have to be closely supervised and threatened with punishment to reach objectives.	People do not need to be threatened with punishment; they will work voluntarily toward organizational objectives to which they are committed.
Most people prefer to be told what to do, have little ambition, want to avoid responsibility, and want security above all else.	The average person working in an environment with good human relations will accept and seek responsibility.
Most people have little creativity. They are not capable of solving problems. Rather, they must be directed.	Most people possess a high degree of imagination, ingenuity, and creativity with which to solve organizational problems.
Most people have limited intellectual potential. Contributions above basic job performance should not be expected.	Although people have intellectual potential, modern industrial life utilizes only part of it.

Argyris's Maturity Theory

http://www.strategy-business.com/thoughtleaders/98109

A manager's philosophy incorporates his or her attitude toward employee maturity. The work of Chris Argyris (1957) summarized these attitudes. Argyris related the development of individual maturity to the structure of organizations. Argyris believed that people develop along a continuum from immaturity to maturity. People who have reached maturity

- Tend to be active rather than passive.
- Are independent rather than dependent.
- Are self-aware rather than unaware.
- Are self-controlled rather than controlled by others.

Argyris's concern was that a mature personality conflicts with typical organizations in four ways:

- The formal chain of command limits self-determination, making individuals passive and manager dependent.
- The span of control decreases a person's self-determination.
- Unity of direction places objectives under the control of one manager. It limits the employee's ability to define objectives.
- Specialization of labor limits initiative and self-determination.

Managers who create work environments that are obstacles to mature employees set up themselves and their organizations for failure. Mature people confronted with rigid, limiting circumstances become passive and dependent. They cannot grow, and they can rarely see long-term implications. Recognition of these realities in recent years has fueled the growth of the movement to employee empowerment, which this chapter will discuss later.

Development of Expectations

In developing a philosophy of management, a manager must consider the importance of expectations.

> *Bob Thompson "challenges people to achieve more by giving them more responsibility," says office manager Marlene Van Patten, an annuity recipient who joined Thompson-McCully when it purchased Spartan Asphalt in 1985. "He is a demanding person, but extremely fair. He always has wanted to be the best and he has wanted his people to be the best"* (Krizan, 2000).

A manager must communicate his or her expectations directly to employees. John L. Single (1980) reports that

- Subordinates do what they believe they are expected to do.
- Ineffective managers fail to develop high expectations for performance.
- Managers perceived as excellent create high performance expectations that their employees can fulfill.

The last point, that employees fulfill their manager's expectations, is often referred to as the self-fulfilling prophecy. It is a key management concept. Sam Walton believed in it so much that it became "Rule 3 of Sam's Rules for Building a Business: Motivate your partners. Money and ownership aren't enough. . . . Set high goals, encourage competition, and then keep score" (Trimble, 1992).

Incorporating expectations into management requires two phases. The first consists of developing and communicating expectations of performance, group citizenship, individual initiative, and job creativity. The second involves consistency. The manager must be consistent in his or her expectations and in communicating them. Consistency will produce reinforcement and, in the end, promote stability and reduce anxiety. Employees will know what the boss expects.

MANAGING FOR MOTIVATION

Describe how managers can structure the environment to provide motivation

With a well-rounded, people-centered philosophy in place, a manager is ready to motivate by creating a positive, supportive work environment. In the next few pages we will discuss how to manage for motivation: how to treat people as individuals, provide support, recognize and value diversity, empower employees, provide an effective reward system, redesign jobs, promote intrapreneurship, and create flexibility in work.

Treating People as Individuals

All of us are different. We think differently; we have different needs and wants; and we cherish different values, expectations, and goals. Each wants to be treated as a special person because each of us is a special person. What is more, we change. Today, a person's link to others may be paramount; a year from now, recognition for accomplishment may be the driving passion.

Good managers treat employees as individuals, regardless of age, race, or gender.

Looking at today's workforce brings the concept of individuality into sharp focus. Baby-boomers, senior citizens, ethnic and racial group members, women, and working mothers bring their own needs, goals, and values to the workplace (Mills and Cannon, 1992).

Successful managers recognize people as individuals and work with their particular differences. Such recognition goes further. The successful manager knows that, because each of us is an individual, each of us is motivated differently. The more managers know about motivation, the more successful they will be in working with people.

Providing Support

To develop motivated employees, a manager must provide a climate in which each employee's needs can be met. A starting point is to facilitate attainment of the employee's goals. The manager does this by removing barriers, developing mutual goal-setting opportunities, initiating training and education programs, encouraging risk taking, and providing stability.

Two other actions can provide support and enhance the environment. First, openly appreciate the contributions of the employee. According to Jill Barad, former president of Mattel USA (Oliver, 1992):

http://www.mattel.com

> *Taking time to tell people how good they are is one of the best ways management can reward people for their efforts. We in management tend to focus on what's* not *being done, how people are not performing instead of recognizing that our people* are *performing. We must constantly remind people of their strengths so they can make the most of those behaviors.*

Barad's point is echoed by AT&T Global Information Solution's former CEO, Jere Stead: "Even middle managers, who often have little money and few promotions to dispense, have plenty they can give: Attaboys, letters, notes, trips, cash—really pound out rewards" (Stewart, 1994).

Second, show sensitivity to employees' need for equity. Each employee must feel that she or he is receiving a fair exchange for his or her input into the company and in comparison to other employees. This point is supported by Norman Brinker, former CEO of Chili's and Macaroni Grill restaurants (Hall, 1992): "Compensation has to be equitable. From the top to the bottom of the organization, the program must recognize the value of inputs into the company. Everyone is aware of everyone else."

http://www.macaronigrill.com

Recognizing and Valuing Diversity

As we have discussed throughout the text, part of working with people as individuals is the ability to recognize and incorporate the value of diversity within the workplace. The composition of the workforce is changing—and with it, workers' needs, goals, and values. As noted in Chapter 1, managers are no longer managing a homogeneous workforce. Rather, the workforce of present-day organizations manifests a kaleidoscope of diversity: young and old; of all races, colors, ethnicities, cultures, national origins; male and female—all with differing mental and physical capabilities—as well as full time, part time, and temporary (Schlossberg, 1991).

Managers need to respond to this diversity by understanding, appreciating, and utilizing the differences. If they do not, according to Xerox Regional Vice President Tracy Whitaker, ". . . 30 percent of your intellectual capital is not participating in your organization" (Files, 1995).

http://www.xerox.com

As the diversity in the workforce continues to change, traditional programs for training, monitoring, and compensation may have to be modified (Ettorre, 1992). One example of an organization that has recognized the need to modify its policies and practices is BRW, the subject of this chapter's Valuing Diversity feature. Another is Umanoff & Parsons, a New York City bakery. Umanoff & Parson's senior management team is composed of three women and three men from five diverse cultures: Jamaican, American, Haitian, Hispanic, and Russian. Half the workforce of the bakery is foreign born; the workers come from Haiti, Trinidad, Grenada, the Dominican Republic, and Russia. The diversity brings contrasting viewpoints, experiences, and needs to the work environment. With these in mind, the company has devised innovative training programs, mentoring programs, and cross-cultural teams.

http://www.umanoffparsons.com

Empowering Employees

"You want motivated workers?" asks Peter C. Fleming (1992), vice president of Prudential Insurance Company. "Just empower them and you will see what motivation and ownership means." As discussed in Chapter 3, leaders empower employees by sharing authority and information, providing needed training, listening to employees, developing relationships based on mutual trust and respect, and acting on employee recommendations. "The greatest thing he [Bob Thompson] gave me was opportunity," says Dean Agozino, division manager for the oil-blending facility [at Thompson-McCully] in Monroe. "I plan on staying and making this place successful" (Krizan, 2000). As noted management consultant Tom Peters (1990) states, empowerment occurs when individuals in an organization are "given autonomy, authority, trusted, and encouraged to break the rules in order to get on with the job."

http://www.prudential.com

VALUING DIVERSITY
BRW Gets a Wake-up Call

A diversity audit set off big changes at BRW, a $38 million architecture and engineering firm with 400 employees. The internal audit revealed that BRW's rates of promotion and attrition for minorities and women were not good. The finding caused top management to take a closer look at itself and to think about the consequences to the company—that is, whether it would be better or worse off—if top management didn't take diversity into consideration. The managers realized that there was a stark contrast with regard to diversity between BRW managers (96 percent were white males) and the companies to whom they were pitching their services (a much more diverse group). They felt that the company would be far less competitive if it continued to be a white male–dominated firm.

As a result, BRW's transformation began. A diversity committee of 35 employees evaluated BRW's personnel system. Based on the committee's recommendations, BRW took the following actions:

- All employees attended a diversity training session led by a consulting firm. The session revealed to managers how and why their preconceived notions about race, gender, and national origin were affecting hiring and retention.
- Human resources rewrote the company handbook to reflect BRW's more aggressive commitment to diversity.
- BRW enhanced its benefits package to include flexible scheduling and health benefits for all workers.

The actions had the desired effect. By 1995, white males occupied 81 percent of BRW's management positions—a 15 percent drop in less than five years. (BRW is now part of URS Corporation.)

http://www.urscorp.com

Source: Fenn, Donna. "More Than Just Affirmative Action," *Inc.* (July 1995), p. 93.

Empowerment is designed to unshackle the worker and make the job—not just part of the job—the worker's. In the words of James Champy (Barrier, 1995), managers must be willing "to let go of control, in terms of letting people make decisions, particularly when they affect customers." An example of this approach is Chesapeake Packaging Co.'s Baltimore box plant, which created eight employee-managed, so-called internal companies. Customer service is the providence of a "company" called Boxbusters. A "company" called Bob's Big Boys runs the flexigraphic-printing department. Like any business, the internal companies manage their own affairs. Employees track and measure output and figure how to improve it. They watch costs. If they need new equipment, they order it. They get involved in the annual plantwide planning and budgeting process. The members of each "company" review one another's performance and take part in hiring and disciplinary decisions (Case, 1995).

http://www.cskcorp.com

Employees, by being empowered, make decisions that formerly were made by the manager. Empowerment results in greater responsibility and innovation and a willingness to take risks. Ownership and trust, along with autonomy and authority, become a motivational package.

http://www.reflexite.com

Another company that is reaping the benefits of empowered workers is Reflexite Corporation of Avon, Connecticut. CEO Cecil Ursprung says of the employees, "They wanted more than money—they wanted to be committed to something, and they wanted power over the decisions affecting their work lives. Give them that and they would repay the company a thousand times over" (Case, 1992). Empowerment, in the form of work teams responsible for production and quality, has given employees control over the decisions affecting their work lives. The teams plan the production operation, work with suppliers, respond to customer questions, and are accountable for bottom-line decisions. The quality team, composed of members from all production operations, has established individual responsibility for quality assurance as an organizational value. At Reflexite the results can be seen in increased productivity, attainment of quality goals, and a committed workforce.

Providing an Effective Reward System

To motivate behavior, an organization must provide an effective reward system. Given the belief that all people are individuals with different needs, values, expectations, and goals, the reward system must accommodate many variables.

According to David Van Fleet (1991), an effective reward system has the following characteristics:

- Rewards must satisfy the basic needs of all employees. Pay, for example, must be adequate, benefits reasonable, and vacations and holidays appropriate.
- Rewards must be comparable to those offered by competitive organizations in the same area. For example, the pay offered for the same job should be equal to that offered by a competitive company. In addition, benefit packages and other programs should be equal to those provided by a competing company.
- Rewards must be equally available to people in the same positions and be distributed fairly and equitably. People performing the same job need to have the same options for rewards and also be involved in the decision governing which rewards they receive. When employees are asked to complete a special task or project, the employees should have the opportunity to determine the reward they value—a day off or extra pay.
- The reward system must be multifaceted. Because all people are different, managers must provide a range of rewards that focus on different aspects—pay, time off, recognition, or promotion. In addition, managers should provide several different ways to earn these rewards.

http://www.pg.com

http://www.monsanto.com

This last point is worth noting. With the widely developing trend toward empowerment in American industry, many are beginning to view traditional pay systems as inadequate. In a traditional system, people are paid according to the positions they hold, not the contributions they make. As organizations adopt approaches built on teams, customer satisfaction, and empowerment, workers need to be paid differently. Companies like Procter & Gamble and Monsanto have already responded to this change in perspective. P & G has a pay system that provides rewards based on skill levels. Monsanto has more than 60 pay plans at various operations around the world. "Each is different," says Barry Bingham, the company's director of compensation. "All have been built from the bottom up by employee design teams" (Gleckman, 1994).

Redesigning Jobs

job redesign
The application of motivational theories to the structure of work, to increase output and satisfaction.

Jobs are important motivational tools because what they contain may provide a means to meet an employee's needs. Managers need to know what elements of a job provide motivation and then apply the concepts of **job redesign**, the application of motivational theories to the structure of work, to increase output and satisfaction.

Principles of Job Redesign

Recent trends in management have attempted to increase output and satisfaction in several ways. Jobs and organizations have been reexamined with the aim of putting challenge and other psychological rewards back into work. To this end, managers have assigned many repetitive tasks to robots and other kinds of computer-assisted machinery. Training and development programs have been devised that enable people to perform more demanding tasks and jobs.

Job redesign requires a knowledge of and concern for the human qualities that people bring with them to the organization—such things as their needs and expectations, perceptions and values, and level of skills and abilities. Job redesign also requires knowledge of the qualities of jobs—the physical and mental demands made on those performing the job and the environment in which the job is performed. Job redesign usually tailors a job to fit the person who must perform it. The beginner who holds a redesigned job gets pieces of the work in measured increments until he or she masters the tasks required to complete the whole job. Workers who have more experience and who are becoming bored with their jobs may be given more challenging tasks and more flexibility or autonomy in dealing with them.

job scope
An element of job redesign that refers to the variety of tasks incorporated into a job.

job depth
An element of job redesign referring to the degree of discretion an employee has to alter the job.

The two approaches to job redesign relate to job scope and job depth. **Job scope** refers to the variety of tasks incorporated into a job. **Job depth** refers to the degree of discretion the person possesses to alter the job. Job redesign alternatives include job enlargement, job rotation, and job enrichment.

job enlargement
Increasing the variety or the number of tasks a job includes, not the quality or the challenge of those tasks.

Job Enlargement

To increase the number of tasks a job includes, not the quality or the challenge, is to implement **job enlargement**. Often called horizontal loading, job enlargement may attempt to demand more of the same from an employee or to add other tasks containing an equal or lesser amount of meaning or challenge. Underworked employees can benefit from job enlargement. These people need to be kept constantly busy and occupied with routine tasks that they understand and have mastered. Their sense of competence improves as their volume of output does. Some people, however, seek more variety, not more tasks; job enlargement is not an appropriate strategy for the latter.

job rotation
Temporarily assigning people to different jobs, or tasks, on a rotating basis.

Job Rotation

Temporarily assigning people to different jobs or tasks to different people is **job rotation**. The idea is to add variety and to emphasize the interdependence of a group of jobs. Managers involved in job rotation gain knowledge about the operations of specific departments. Assembly-line workers may be assigned one set of tasks one month and another set the following month. Office workers may swap jobs for a time to learn additional dimensions of the office's responsibilities, to gain additional insights, and to enable them to substitute for one another in times of need.

http://www.tonylama.com

At the Tony Lama Company—a boot manufacturer in El Paso, Texas—customer-service department employees work in the store for one week. Similarly, salespeople work a week in the shipping department. The experiences broaden employees' perspectives. Job rotation can be used to cross-train or to facilitate permanent job transfers or promotions. Workers who can benefit from job rotation are those who are interested in or ready for promotion and those who need variety.

Job Enrichment

job enrichment
Designing a job to provide more responsibility, control, feedback, and authority for decision making.

Frederick Herzberg (1975) pointed out that jobs can allow workers to satisfy some of their psychological needs. **Job enrichment** is the result of designing jobs that can enhance psychological satisfaction. (Herzberg referred to job enrichment as vertical job loading.) Job enrichment should include the following elements:

- *Variety of tasks.* An enriched job introduces an employee to new and more difficult tasks he or she has not previously handled.
- *Task importance.* An employee with an enriched job handles a complete natural unit of work and also handles specific or specialized tasks that enable him or her to become an expert.
- *Task responsibility.* An employee with an enriched job is accountable for his or her own work and can exercise authority in the course of job activities.
- *Feedback.* Workers in enriched jobs receive periodic and specialized reports that are delivered directly to them.

http://www.volvo.com

Experiments with job enrichment vary widely in their approach, scope, and content. Most efforts at job enrichment increase the workers' control over work. For example, Volvo pioneered the concept of having a team of workers work on the entire auto-assembly operation to produce a single car. The result was increased employee commitment, increased productivity, and fewer quality defects. Many manufacturers have allowed skilled machine operators to set up their machines, maintain the machines, plan their own work flow and pace, and inspect their own output. In some companies like Cin-Made, which practice open-book management, employees are given the knowledge to help them shape and control their jobs. As discussed in Chapter 3, in an open-book company employees understand why they are being called on to solve problems, cut costs, reduce defects, and give the customer better service. Furthermore, employees

- See—and learn to understand—the company's financial reports, along with all the other numbers that are critical to tracking the business's performance.
- Learn that, whatever else they do, part of their job is to move the numbers in the right direction.
- Have a direct stake in the company's success. If the business is profitable, they get a cut of the action; if it's not, they don't (Case, 1995).

Regardless of the approach selected, for job enrichment to be successful, participation must be voluntary and management must be competent in its day-to-day operations as well as in its efforts at job enrichment. However, managers and workers can be expected to resist some efforts at job enrichment. (See Chapter 10 for an analysis of resistance to change.) Also, once introduced, changes do not yield improvements overnight; mistakes can be made in the implementation of job enrichment programs and setbacks can occur. Nevertheless, companies that undertake job enrichment find higher morale and improved productivity.

Promoting Intrapreneurship

As an organization grows, it has a tendency to establish rules, policies, and procedures—to become mechanistic in nature. The formal control systems that become established along with bureaucratic procedures cause it to lose innovative energy. The corporate environment can stifle the creative energy of entrepreneurial employees. To meet their need for creativity, these employees often leave and create their own organizations.

intrapreneurship
Entrepreneurship within an organization, allowing employees flexibility and authority in pursuing and developing new ideas.

Recognizing this problem—and the losses their organizations suffer as a result—the top managers of many large corporations are trying to foster environments that promote corporate entrepreneurship, or intrapreneurship (Winters and Murfin, 1988). **Intrapreneurship** occurs when entrepreneurship exists within the boundaries of a formal organization. It is, in essence, a process whereby an individual pursues an idea and has the authority to develop and promote it within the boundaries of the formal organization. As discussed in Chapter 3, these individuals become intrapreneurs—employees who think and act like owners. They take responsibility for an idea or project and are empowered to make it successful. According to Donald Kuratko and Richard Hodgetts (1989), a manager can foster intrapreneurship by following these guidelines:

- Encourage action.
- Use informal meetings whenever possible.
- Tolerate—do not punish—failure and use it as a learning experience.
- Be persistent.
- Reward innovation for innovation's sake.
- Plan the physical layout to encourage informal communication.
- Reward and/or promote innovative personnel.
- Encourage people to go around red tape.
- Eliminate rigid procedures.
- Organize people into small teams to pursue future-oriented projects.

Managers who really want a climate of intrapreneurship cannot be timid. True intrapreneurs are not comfortable with structure—they will figure a way around orders that block their dreams. They will do any job that will make the project successful, always being true to their goals (Pinchot, 1985).

http://www.3m.com

3M is a company that thrives on intrapreneurship. Its first president, William McKnight, "Wanted to create an organization that would continually self-mutate from within, impelled forward by employees exercising their individual initiative." McKnight's approach is captured in these phrases that are a part of 3M's culture (Collins and Porras, 1993):

- "Listen to anyone with an original idea, no matter how absurd it might sound at first."
- "Encourage; don't nitpick. Let people run with an idea."
- "Encourage experimental doodling."
- "If you put fences around people, you get sheep. Give people the room they need."

This philosophy created a climate for intrapreneurs to dabble, take chances, and make mistakes. Spurred along by such traditions as the 15 percent rule (technical people are encouraged to spend up to 15 percent of their time on projects of their own choosing) and Genesis Grants (an internal venture capital fund that distributes parcels up to $50,000 for researchers to develop prototypes and market tests), 3M-ers have brought wide-ranging products to the market—reflective highway signs, electrical connectors, air filters, stethoscopes, surgical drapes and tape, and Post-it® Notes.

Creating Flexibility

Another way managers can motivate workers is to provide them with flexibility in work through flextime, a compressed workweek, or job sharing. Flexibility in work is facilitated through the use of email communication. Managers need to share the organization's policy on email privacy with employees. See this chapter's Managing Technology feature.

flextime
An employment alternative allowing employees to decide, within a certain range, when to begin and end each workday.

http://www.nu.com

Flextime allows employees to decide, within a certain range, when to begin and end each workday. It thus allows them to take care of personal business before or after work, vary their daily schedules, and enjoy more control over their lives. Companies that have adopted this approach—Northeast Utilities, a Hartford, Connecticut, power company, for example—have reported decreases in absenteeism, lower turnover, less tardiness, and higher morale. Employees caught in the work-family pressure cooker, which makes juggling conflicting demands their daily fare, are virtually unanimous in choosing flexibility as the chief means of relief from this dilemma (Executive Management Forum, 1995).

compressed workweek
A schedule that allows employees to fulfill weekly time obligations in fewer days than the traditional five-day workweek.

A **compressed workweek** allows employees to fulfill their work obligation in fewer days than the traditional five-day workweek. The most often used model is four ten-hour days. The approach—like flextime—provides more time for personal business and recreation. Employees who adopt it report job satisfaction. Nevertheless, not all managers are supportive of the idea. Some managers think compressed workweeks make scheduling more difficult. They fear that providing employee coverage at all times may be impossible if people are in and out. Other managers fear loss of control (Austin, 1994).

job sharing
A technique to provide flexibility by permitting two part-time workers to divide one full-time job.

Job sharing, or twinning, permits two part-time workers to divide one full-time job. Such an occupational buddy system is ideal for parents who are raising school-aged children or those who prefer part-time employment. The benefit from an employer's standpoint is that the employer gets the advantage of ideas from two sources but has to pay one salary and only one set of benefits.

MANAGING TECHNOLOGY
Email Privacy

Many organizations have policies that say employees' email is not private and can be read at any time by the employer. Consider setting up a separate personal email account for personal messages. Anyone can get free email (such as Hotmail and Yahoo!), which is accessible from the Internet. However, your privacy may be jeopardized when you use free email addresses. Be aware that profiles you complete when applying for a free email account may be accessible to others. Always assume that any information you provide could be made public.

Email accounts are vulnerable to hackers, who have tricks for learning your password. Change your password frequently and never reveal your password to anyone. It is best to use a combination of letters and numbers for your password. This makes it harder for someone to learn your password. Also, be sure to "log off" or exit your email anytime you will be leaving your computer. You do not want someone to come in and send emails from your account—recipients will think that it is you. It could be quite damaging to your reputation.

http://www.hotmail.com

http://www.yahoo.com

CHAPTER SUMMARY

1 **Discuss the factors that stimulate and influence motivation.** Motivation results from a combination of factors, including the individual's needs, the ability to make choices, and an environment that provides the opportunity to satisfy those needs and make those choices. In choosing behavior to satisfy a need, a person evaluates past experiences, environmental influences, perceptions, skills, and incentives.

2 **Differentiate between content and process theories of motivation.** Content theories emphasize the needs that motivate people. Process theories explain how employees choose behaviors to meet their work needs and how they determine whether their choices were successful.

3 **List the five levels of needs according to Maslow and give an example of each.** The five levels of needs are physiological (water, food); safety (avoiding bodily harm); social (friendship); esteem (recognition); and self-realization (maximizing abilities).

4 **Discuss the impact of hygiene and motivation factors in the work environment.** Hygiene factors (salary; job security; working conditions; status; company policies; quality of technical supervision; and quality of interpersonal relationships among peers, supervisors, and subordinates) are the primary elements involved in job dissatisfaction. When present in sufficient quality, they have no effect; when absent, they can lead to job dissatisfaction. Motivation factors (achievement, recognition, responsibility, advancement, the work itself, and possibility of growth) are the primary elements involved in job satisfaction. When present, they can stimulate personal and psychological growth.

5 **Explain the characteristics of a person with high-achievement needs.** A person with high-achievement needs

- Performs a task because of a compelling need for personal achievement, not necessarily for the rewards associated with accomplishing the task.
- Prefers to take personal responsibility for solving problems rather than leaving the outcome to others.
- Prefers to set moderate goals, that with stretching are achievable.
- Prefers immediate and concrete feedback on performance, which assists in measuring progress toward the goal.

6 **Identify the needs associated with ERG theory.** The ERG theory identifies three categories of needs: existence, relatedness, and growth. Existence needs relate to a person's well-being. Relatedness needs include needs for satisfactory relationships with others. Growth needs call for realization of potential and the achievement of competence.

7 **Discuss the relationship between expectations and motivation.** Motivation is a function of how badly a person wants something and how likely the person thinks he or she will get it. The intensity of motivation functions in direct proportion to perceived or expected rewards.

8 **Explain the relationship between reinforcement and motivation.** Much of motivated behavior is learned behavior. Learning in turn is influenced by the rewards or penalties individuals have experienced in similar situations in the past. Employees learn over time what type of performance is acceptable and what is unacceptable. This learning then influences employees' subsequent behavior.

9 **Explain how equity influences motivation.** Employees' behavior relates to their perception of the fairness of treatment they receive. Employees make conscious comparisons of rewards they receive to the amount of effort they expend and to the rewards of other employees. These comparisons influence their levels of motivation.

10 **Explain how goals influence motivation.** A person's behavior is influenced by the goals that are set. The goals tell an employee what needs to be done and how much effort will need to be expended.

11 **Discuss the importance of a manager's philosophy of management in creating a positive work environment.** A manager's philosophy of management can set the foundation for a positive work environment. Because a manager's philosophy incorporates and reflects personal beliefs about human nature in the work setting—about worker attitudes and characteristics, employee maturity, and the influence of management expectations on behavior—it influences the motivation choices he or she will select.

12 **Describe how managers can structure the environment to provide motivation.** Managers can structure the environment to provide motivation by treating people as individuals, providing support, recognizing and valuing diversity, empowering employees, providing an effective reward system, redesigning jobs, promoting intrapreneurship, and creating flexibility at work.

REVIEW QUESTIONS

1. What stimulates motivation? What three factors influence the behavior an individual will choose to satisfy a stimulus?
2. On what do content theories of motivation focus? What theories are included in this category? On what do process theories of motivation focus? What theories belong in this category?
3. List and explain the five categories of human needs identified by Abraham Maslow. Why are the needs arranged in a hierarchy?
4. Define Frederick Herzberg's hygiene and motivation factors and give three examples of each. What is the importance of each set of factors to a manager?
5. Why is a high achiever likely to focus on goal setting, feedback, individual responsibility, and rewards?
6. What three needs does Clayton Alderfer's ERG theory identify?
7. What is the relationship between expectancy and motivation? What is the relationship among effort-performance link, performance-reward link, and attractiveness?
8. List and explain the four main types of reinforcement.
9. Describe the two factors a person uses to determine equity in a work situation.
10. What influence on behavior and motivation is the result of employee goal setting?
11. What is the importance of a manager's philosophy of management in creating a positive work environment?
12. How can a manager influence motivation through empowerment, intrapreneurship, and recognition of diversity?

DISCUSSION QUESTIONS FOR CRITICAL THINKING

1. Would a person with high achievement needs be a good manager? Why or why not?
2. How does expectancy theory apply to your classroom experience? Discuss your motivation for grades in relationship to the value of the reward (grade), the relationship of the reward to performance (tests, papers), and the amount of effort required to receive the grade (time spent in class and studying).
3. What two experiences can you cite to demonstrate the influence of reinforcement theory on your behavior (motivation)?
4. Which of the eight motivational concepts discussed in this chapter's Managing for Motivation section would be your first priority as manager? Which would be your last priority? Why?

INTERNET EXERCISES

Check the text Web site at http://plunkett.swcollege.com for updated links to the Internet Exercises.

1. In reinforcement theory, the rules of consequences are used in a three-step sequence that defines the process of reinforcement. Apply these steps [When-Do-Get] as found at the site below to a management situation.
http://www.as.wvu.edu/~sbb/comm221/chapters/rf.htm
2. In an interview about her book, *On the Frontiers of Management*, Rosabeth Moss Kanter sees traditional sources of power eroding and the old motivational tools losing their magic. What are the five new motivational tools mentioned by Kanter?
http://www.managementfirst.com/practical_management/kanter_interview.htm
3. Good managers are often compared to coaches. What makes a good coach? Relate this to management and motivation.
http://www.ltf.com/coach.htm

APPLICATION CASE

Building a Quality Work Environment

Harry Clark, the founder, owner, and CEO of Muni Financial Services (MFS), had a successful business. Having begun MFS as a consulting firm specializing in software design to help cities, counties, and special districts administer bond issues, Clark took the organization one step further. MFS's business expanded into handling everything: plotting the districts, collecting the payments, pursuing the deadbeats, year after year and decade after decade, for as long as the bonds were out there. Harry Clark had hit a gold mine—signing clients to 25-year contracts.

To Clark, however, that wasn't all there was to success. "A lot of business owners, all they care about is running the business. They don't care about the values and principles and environments that their employees are in. They're doing it as a transaction. Well for me it isn't a transaction. It's a lifestyle. It's a belief. It's a community." For Clark, building an environment meant first of all providing employees with benefits: three weeks' vacation to start; health insurance; dollar-for-dollar matching contributions on 401K plans, up to 4 percent; profit sharing at 7 percent; a generous bonus plan; an on-site workout room; and periodic surprises, like the holiday bus trip to the mall, where he passed out two $50 bills to all of his employees and ordered them to spend it on themselves.

Building an environment also meant keeping everyone in the communications loop. For that, Clark relied on a Yes Meeting. Anyone could call one by pushing the page button on the phone. Attendance was mandatory. Yes Meetings could be about almost everything—strategy, financial results—but typically the purpose was to announce a new client. Clark had created a culture that required credit for success to be shared as widely as possible. Thus at the end of a Yes Meeting whose purpose was to announce a new client, it was tradition for everyone to stand up and cheer "One-two-three, yes!"

In addition, to Harry Clark, building an environment meant providing his employees with plenty of room to grow. "It's absolutely phenomenal how you can take someone who is just a staff person and, if you put him in the right position with the right circumstances, the limits on his performance can be so high," Clark says. Indeed, MFS is full of success stories of people who were hired as support staff and are now team leaders. Clark seems to be able to identify people who have their own internal goals and then he "stretches" them.

Questions

1. Using Figure 13.1 on page 411 as a guide, evaluate the quality of work life at MFS. Provide examples from the case that relate to specific factors contributing to the quality of work life.
2. Which motivation theories did Harry Clark apply in developing his overall motivation strategy? Provide examples of specific elements of each theory to support your answer.
3. Did Clark focus on content theories, process theories, or both? Explain your answer.

Source: Whitford, David. "The Trouble with Harry," *Inc.* (April 1995), pp. 64–73.

VIDEO CASE

Valassis Communications: Motivating for Performance

As one of the nation's leading marketing services companies, Valassis Communications offers a variety of door-to-door marketing services for consumer package goods companies and franchise retailers. Accounting for roughly more than 75 percent of the company's revenues is its flagship product, Free-Standing Inserts (FSIs). These are four-color booklets containing coupons and other promotional offers from leading consumer package goods companies. Through its FSIs, Valassis reaches almost 60 million households each week via Sunday newspapers and distributes nearly 90 percent of all coupons in the United States.

The Valassis Impact Promotions (VIP) division provides franchise retailers with a variety of specialty promotions that can be customized in unique shapes and sizes, highly targeted, and distributed by a variety of methods (e.g., zoned newspapers and direct mail). The VIP customer base is growing to include food services, telecommunications, and retail franchises.

Through its Targeted Marketing Services division, Valassis provides newspaper-delivered product samples and advertising, geo-demographic targeting capabilities, run-of-press advertising, and targeted solo print promotions. Valassis is now expanding its database and Internet services through its 50 percent ownership in an online coupon site (Save.com) and a stake in the Relationship Marketing Group.

According to *Fortune* magazine, Valassis is also one of the "Best 100 Companies To Work For" in the United States. This achievement is due largely to the company's policies and actions to motivate its employees, both individually and in groups. Valassis management views its key to success as having a culture that is fun—and where goal-oriented individuals are rewarded for achieving their goals—and an environment that embraces flexibility and change.

Valassis has a performance-driven culture. Its executives want all employees to feel and behave like they are owners of the company and to believe that they will share in the rewards of the company. The company's pay-for-performance plan includes (1) base salary, (2) fringe benefits, (3) profit sharing, (4) stock purchases, and (5) "champion pay."

Pay is not the only motivation used at Valassis. Others include celebration of past achievements, comfortable employee facilities, various types of recognition awards, and many other programs that together help make employees enjoy coming to work and brag about their employer in their community.

http://www.valassis.com

For Discussion:

1. Describe "champion pay" and explain why it is used as a motivator at Valassis Communications.
2. In addition to champion pay, what other actions has Valassis taken to motivate its employees?
3. Does Valassis engage more in goal-setting or reinforcement motivational strategies?

Leadership

KEY TERMS

autocratic style
contingency model
free-rein style
influence
leadership
Leadership Grid®
leadership style
life-cycle theory
participative style
path-goal theory

LEARNING OBJECTIVES

After studying this chapter, you should be able to

1. Discuss leadership traits, skills, and behaviors
2. Differentiate between management and leadership
3. Describe the five sources of power leaders may possess
4. Differentiate between positive and negative motivation
5. Describe the three decision-making styles used by leaders
6. Explain the two primary approaches leaders can take: task centered and people centered
7. Describe the three theories of situational leadership
8. Discuss the three challenges facing leaders

MANAGEMENT IN ACTION

Participative Leadership at Southwest Airlines

In 1999, *Chief Executive* magazine named Herb Kelleher CEO of the Year. He has been CEO of Southwest Airlines since 1978. The company is famous for its high productivity and customer service. When asked, Kelleher will tell you that Southwest's biggest competitive advantage is its culture. Since the airline's founding in 1971, Herb Kelleher has led a culture of caring for people. He is known for his great sense of humor, and Southwest Airlines' "familial environment prizes creativity, independence and a sense of humor" (Yung, 1999). The company so prizes its esprit de corps that it has had a "culture committee" for over ten years. Employees serve two-year terms as committee members. "The culture committee has spawned everything from 'Hokey Days,' where some committee members clean up an airplane to give flight attendants a break, to company cookouts to 'Heroes of the Heart,' a tribute to behind-the-scenes employees" (Yung, 1999).

A participative leader rewards, motivates, empowers, values, is creative, has vision, proposes change, connects, networks, is flexible, facilitates, teaches, nourishes growth, reaches out, and provides information. An example of a participative leader is Southwest Airline's Herb Kelleher. Herb Kelleher cofounded the airline with the notion: "If you get your passengers to their destinations when they want to get there, on time, at the lowest possible fares, and make darn sure they have a good time doing it, people will fly your airline." Southwest Airlines started with three planes serving three Texas cities. By January 2000, it had over 300 airplanes in 55 cities. Results for 1999 marked Southwest Airlines' 27th consecutive year of profitability. (See "About SWA" at http://www.iflyswa.com.)

Southwest Airlines has a flat organizational structure, and Kelleher combats bureaucracy by constantly questioning the need for additions of documents and personnel. "Do we really need this rule? Does this manual have to be so long? Is this really the best way to get this done?" When he wants to know how well anything works, he asks the workers on the line who have to live with the process daily. Herb Kelleher has always encouraged Southwest employees to contribute new ideas that might cut costs. And Southwest implements employees' ideas! When asked how he motivates employees, Kelleher said:

> *I don't think I'm the primary motivator. I give people license to be themselves and motivate others in that way. We give people the opportunity to be a maverick. You don't have to fit into a constraining mold at work—you can have a good time. People respond to that. We also try to show that what they do matters. That's why we share with employees the letters we get from passengers. We got one from a divorced dad who said that if it wasn't for our low fares, he wouldn't be able to visit his son as often as he does (Lancaster, 1999).*

Herb Kelleher stepped down as CEO of Southwest Airlines on June 19, 2001, but will continue as chairman of the board of directors.

Sources: Yung, Katherine. "From David to Goliath," *The Dallas Morning News*, December 26, 1999; Lancaster, Hal. "Kelleher's Main Strategy: Treat All Employees Well," *The Wall Street Journal*, August 31, 1999; *Chief Executive*, http://www.chiefexecutive.net; and visit Southwest Airlines, http://www.iflyswa.com.

Herb Kelleher, CEO of Southwest Airlines, is known for his personal and nurturing management style.

INTRODUCTION

Leading is one of five functions of management. It is vital to the execution of the other four. Leading people and their organizations requires the ability to do many of the activities we have discussed so far in this text. The principles governing communication, decision making, and motivation form the foundation of leading. At the top of any organization, leading is most concerned with

- Establishing values, culture, and climate
- Defining a mission
- Identifying core competencies
- Scanning environments
- Sensing the need for change
- Creating a vision for the future
- Enlisting cooperation and support for that vision
- Keeping people and processes focused on satisfying various customers
- Unleashing the full potential in and soliciting contributions from all the organization's human resources through training, development, and empowerment

People with the ability to lead, however, must exist at *all* organizational levels and within each of its units and teams.

http://www.iflyswa.com

In our opening case, Herb Kelleher encourages participation from his employees. He says that people are the secret to Southwest Airlines' success. His company is the United States' only major short haul, low-fare, high frequency, and point-to-point carrier. Kelleher provides top-level leadership and treats his employees as his heroes. "How you treat them determines how they treat people on the outside. We have people going around the company all the time doing other people's jobs, but not for cross-utilization. We just want everybody to understand what everybody else's problems are" (Lancaster, 1999).

LEADERSHIP DEFINED

leadership
The process of influencing individuals and groups to set and achieve goals.

influence
The power to sway people to one's will or views.

Leadership, in its management application, is the process of influencing individuals and groups to set and achieve goals. **Influence** is the power to sway other people to one's will or views. Leaders—those who practice leadership—guide, direct, persuade, coach, counsel, and inspire others. How well they do this depends on several variables.

Leadership involves three sets of variables: the leader, those being led, and the circumstances and situations they find themselves facing. All three are constantly changing. The leader, like those being led, is a human being with various skills, traits, knowledge, and attitudes developed through experience that shape his or her personality, personal philosophies, and ethical beliefs—that is, his or her moral compass. These factors can contribute to or detract from the leader's ability to influence others. They are the sources of the individual's strengths or weaknesses.

What qualities must a leader have? As Carol Kleiman (1992) reported, Jeffrey Christian, president and chief executive officer of a Cleveland-based executive search firm, looks for managers

> *who are high impact players, change agents, drivers and winners—people who are extremely flexible, bright, tactical and strategic, who can handle a lot of information, make*

decisions quickly, motivate others, chase a moving target and shake things up. Previously, corporate recruiting emphasized credentials [schooling] and experience, which are still important, but . . . you can't teach good leadership or how to be excited about life.

Robert Greenleaf, former director of management research at AT&T and founding director of the Center for Applied Ethics, said: "The leader exists to serve those whom he nominally leads, those who supposedly follow him. He (or she) takes *their* fulfillment as his (or her) principal aim" (Kiechell, 1992). The servant-leader takes people and their work seriously, listens to and takes the lead from the troops, heals, is self-effacing, and sees himself or herself as a steward (Kiechell, 1992).

Leadership Traits

1 Discuss leadership traits, skills, and behaviors

Early theories about leadership suggested that excellent leaders possessed certain traits, or personal characteristics, that lay at the root of their ability to lead. Following World War II, the U.S. Army surveyed soldiers in an attempt to compile a list of traits shared by commanders whom soldiers perceived as leaders. The resulting list, which included fourteen traits, was clearly inadequate to describe leadership. No two commanders displayed all the traits, and many famous commanders lacked several.

More recently, Gary Yukl (1981) constructed a list of traits and skills commonly associated with effective leaders. Figure 14.1 presents these traits. Yukl's list suggests that a leader is strongly motivated to excel and succeed.

No list of leadership traits and skills can be definitive, however, because no two leaders are exactly alike. Different leaders working with different people in different situations need different traits. If people in charge possess what is needed when it is needed, they should be able to exercise effective leadership.

FIGURE 14.1 *Traits and skills commonly associated with effective leadership*

Traits	Skills
Adaptable	Cleverness (intelligence)
Alert to social environment	Conceptual ability
Ambitious and achievement-oriented	Creativity
Assertive	Diplomacy and tact
Cooperative	Fluency in speaking
Decisive	Knowledge about the group task
Dependable	Organizational (administrative) ability
Dominant (desires to influence others)	Persuasiveness
Energetic (high activity level)	Social ability
Persistent	
Self-confident	
Tolerant of stress	
Willing to assume responsibility	

Source: Leadership in Organizations, p. 70, by Gary Yukl. © 1981 by Prentice-Hall, Inc. Adapted with permission of Pearson Education, Inc., Upper Saddle River, N.J. 97458.

William Peace, a former executive with Westinghouse and United Technologies, is currently director and executive consultant with Doctus Management Consultancy of Chester, England. In the course of his career, Peace learned that certain traits serve him well in management jobs. In an article for *Harvard Business Review*, Peace (1991) noted the importance of intelligence, energy, confidence, and responsibility. He differed from some observers in his emphasis on candor, sensitivity, and a "certain willingness to suffer the painful consequences of unpopular decisions." Peace called using these traits in management "soft management." As this chapter's Valuing Diversity feature points out, personal traits are often perceived as masculine, feminine, or gender neutral.

Leadership Skills

A person's skills are the competencies and capabilities he or she possesses. Look again at Figure 14.1 and notice that many of the skills Yukl identified are primarily useful in dealing with others. These skills include diplomacy, fluency in speech (communication skills), persuasiveness, and social ability. Some of the traits listed imply the existence of skills. For example, being decisive means that one has skill in making decisions by both rational and intuitive means.

VALUING DIVERSITY
"Male" and "Female" Approaches to Leadership

According to the National Foundation for Women Business Owners, as of 1999, there were 9.1 million women-owned businesses in the United States, employing over 27.5 million people and generating over $3.6 trillion in sales.

A recent survey of 456 executives (355 women and 101 men) revealed some interesting differences between the ways in which men and women approach their leadership roles. Women respondents favored being interactive—encouraging others to participate and making subordinates feel good about themselves and their organizations. Interactive leaders attempt to create a group identity, encouraging others to have a say in almost every aspect of work from setting performance goals to determining strategy. To facilitate inclusion, interactive leaders create mechanisms to encourage people to participate.

The majority of male respondents described their styles of leadership as a set of "transactions with subordinates—exchanging rewards for services rendered or punishment for inadequate performance." More men than women reported that they use the power that comes from their formal authority.

Both male and female respondents report having an equal mix of traits generally considered to be feminine, masculine, or gender neutral. So-called feminine traits include understanding, compassion, sensitivity, and dependency. So-called masculine traits include dominance, toughness, assertiveness, and competitiveness. Gender-neutral traits are integrity, adaptiveness, tactfulness, sincerity, efficiency, and reliability. Some men lead with feminine traits; some women lead with masculine traits; both sexes often lead with a combination of all three sets of traits. Both men and women must vary their approaches as circumstances dictate. What mix is "best" depends on organizational context. A detrimental trait under one set of circumstances becomes a beneficial trait under another set.

http://www.nfwbo.org

Sources: Sullivan, Barbara. "Despite New, Expanded Horizons, Women's Businesses Face Old Boundaries," *Chicago Tribune*, July 5, 1995, sec. 3, pp. 1, 2; *Nation's Business*. "Women Entrepreneurs: A Pretty Big Game," (August 1992), p. 53; Kleiman, Carol. "Male, Female Leadership: A Study in Contrasts," *Chicago Tribune*, July 20, 1992, sec. 4, p. 3.; Rosener, Judy B. "Ways Women Lead," *Harvard Business Review* (November–December 1990), pp. 119–125; National Foundation for Women Business Owners. "Key Facts," http://www.nfwbo.org.

http://www.datatec.com

Chris Carey, former president of Datatec Industries, which makes in-store computer systems, believes that subordinates should evaluate their bosses in what he calls reverse performance reviews. He had his 318 employees score their managers' skills in areas such as coaching, listening, praising, and responsiveness. Employees rated upper managers in terms of support of employees, articulation of goals, attention to employee ideas, and fairness. The surveys were anonymous and the results were shared. Formal, top-down appraisals followed within a month. "Scheduling the reviews back-to-back underscores the fact that everyone can perform better and everyone has a chance to say how that will happen" (*Inc.*, 1992).

Leadership Behaviors

Gary Yukl (1981) and his colleagues determined nineteen categories of "meaningful and measurable" leadership behavior. Figure 14.2 presents the Yukl group's categories along with definitions and examples. As you examine these behaviors—the things leaders do in the everyday exercise of leadership—relate them to the traits and skills discussed earlier. Then link the concepts to what you know about human behavior and motivation as described in Chapter 13.

FIGURE 14.2 *The Yukl group's nineteen categories of leadership behavior*

1. **Performance emphasis:** The extent to which a leader emphasizes the importance of subordinate performance, tries to improve productivity and efficiency, tries to keep subordinates working up to their capacity, and checks on their performance.

   Example: My supervisor urged us to be careful not to let orders go out with defective components.

2. **Consideration:** The extent to which a leader is friendly, supportive, and considerate toward subordinates and strives to be fair and objective.

   Example: When a subordinate was upset about something, the supervisor was sympathetic and tried to console him.

3. **Inspiration:** The extent to which a leader stimulates subordinates' enthusiasm for the work of the group and says things to build subordinates' confidence in their ability to perform assignments successfully and attain group objectives.

   Example: My boss told us we were the best design group he had ever worked with, and he was sure that our new product was going to break every sales record in the company.

4. **Praise-recognition:** The extent to which a leader provides praise and recognition to subordinates with effective performance, shows appreciation for their special efforts and contributions, and makes sure they get credit for their helpful ideas and suggestions.

   Example: In a meeting, the supervisor told us she was satisfied with our work and that she appreciated the extra effort we had made this month.

5. **Structuring reward contingencies:** The extent to which a leader rewards effective subordinate performance with tangible benefits. Such benefits include pay increases, promotions, preferred assignments, a better work schedule, and time off.

   Example: My supervisor established a new policy that any subordinate who brought in a new client would earn 10% of the contracted fee.

6. **Decision participation:** The extent to which a leader consults with subordinates and otherwise allows them to influence decisions.

   Example: My supervisor asked me to attend a meeting with him and his boss to develop a new production schedule. He was very receptive to my ideas on the subject.

(continued)

FIGURE 14.2 *(Continued)*

7. **Autonomy-delegation:** The extent to which a leader delegates authority and responsibility to subordinates and allows them to determine how to do their work.

   Example: My boss gave me a new project and encouraged me to handle it as I think best.

8. **Role clarification:** The extent to which a leader informs subordinates about their duties and responsibilities, specifies the rules and policies that must be observed, and lets subordinates know what is expected of them.

   Example: My boss called me in to inform me about a rush project that must be given top priority, and she gave me some specific assignments related to this project.

9. **Goal setting:** The extent to which a leader emphasizes the importance of setting specific performance goals for each important aspect of a subordinate's job, measures progress toward the goals, and provides concrete feedback.

   Example: The supervisor held a meeting to discuss the sales quota for next month.

10. **Training-coaching:** The extent to which a leader determines training needs for subordinates and provides any necessary training and coaching.

    Example: My boss asked me to attend an outside course at the company's expense and said I could leave the office early on the days classes were to be held.

11. **Information dissemination:** The extent to which a leader keeps subordinates informed about developments that affect their work, including events in other work units or outside the organization; decisions made by higher management; and progress in meetings with superiors or outsiders.

    Example: The supervisor briefed us about some high-level changes in policy.

12. **Problem solving:** The extent to which a leader takes the initiative in proposing solutions to serious work-related problems and acts decisively to deal with such problems when a prompt solution is needed.

    Example: The unit was short-handed due to illness, and we had an important deadline to meet. My supervisor arranged to borrow two people from other units, so we could finish the job today.

13. **Planning:** The extent to which a leader decides how to organize and schedule work efficiently, plans how to attain work-unit objectives, and makes contingency plans for potential problems.

    Example: My supervisor suggested a shortcut that allows us to prepare our financial statements in three days instead of the four days it used to take.

14. **Coordinating:** The extent to which a leader coordinates the work of subordinates, emphasizes the importance of coordination, and encourages subordinates to coordinate their activities.

    Example: My supervisor encouraged subordinates who were ahead in their work to help those who were behind. By helping each other, all the different parts of the project will be ready at the same time.

15. **Work facilitation:** The extent to which a leader obtains for subordinates any necessary supplies, equipment, support services, or other resources; eliminates problems in the work environment; and removes other obstacles that interfere with the work.

    Example: I asked my boss to order some supplies, and he arranged to get them right away.

16. **Representation:** The extent to which a leader establishes contacts with other groups and important people in the organization, persuades them to appreciate and support the leader's work unit, and influences superiors and outsiders to promote and defend the interests of the work unit.

    Example: My supervisor met with the data processing manager to ask for revisions to the computer programs. The revised programs will meet our needs more effectively.

17. **Interaction facilitation:** The extent to which a leader tries to get subordinates to be friendly with each other, cooperate, share information and ideas, and help each other.

    Example: The sales manager took the group out to lunch to give everybody a chance to get to know the new sales representative.

FIGURE 14.2 *(Concluded)*

18. **Conflict management:** The extent to which a leader restrains subordinates from fighting and arguing, encourages them to resolve conflicts in a constructive manner, and helps settle disagreements between subordinates.

    Example: Two members of the department who were working together on a project had a dispute about it. The manager met with them to help resolve the matter.

19. **Criticism-discipline:** The extent to which a leader criticizes or disciplines a subordinate who shows consistently poor performance, violates a rule, or disobeys an order. Disciplinary actions include official warnings, reprimands, suspensions, and dismissals.

    Example: The supervisor, concerned that a subordinate repeatedly made the same kinds of errors, made sure that the subordinate was aware of expectations concerning quality.

Source: Leadership in Organizations, p. 70, by Gary Yukl. © 1981 by Prentice Hall, Inc. Adapted with permission of Pearson Education, Inc., Upper Saddle River, N.J. 97458.

http://www.lyondell.com

The first behavior Yukl listed, performance emphasis, remains a popular focus for managers and business writers. The movement in business today is to pay people for what they learn and to reward them for their individual and group performance. At Lyondell Petrochemical, "Managers and workers tackle new undertakings in teams, which get bonuses if their ideas fly" (Nulty, 1992). By putting their emphasis and money where their words are, company managers emphasize performance and productivity.

Management Versus Leadership

2

Differentiate between management and leadership

Management and *leadership* are not synonyms. Managers plan, organize, staff, lead, and control. They may or may not be effective in influencing their subordinates or team members to set and achieve goals. Ideally, leadership and management skills combine to allow a manager to function as a leader, as Figure 14.3 suggests. The manager who gives orders and explicit instructions to experienced people, for instance, is not leading but actually impeding productivity. Planning effectively helps one to become a manager; enabling others to plan effectively is leading. Leaders empower—they give people the things they need to grow, to change, and to cope with change. Leaders create and share visions, generating strategies to bring the visions to reality.

According to Datatec's Chris Carey, empowering people requires a corporate culture that makes empowerment a core value. His company worked hard to create a culture that has as "its core values: honesty, openness, empowerment, and acceptance of failure" (*Inc.*, 1992).

John Kotter and James Heskett (1992), in *Corporate Culture and Performance*, listed organizations that had made major cultural changes. The leaders of these organizations first had to realize that change was needed. Then they had to communicate to employees the facts that pointed to a crisis or potential crisis so the employees would perceive the need to change. Finally, as Kotter and Heskett described, these leaders

> *developed or clarified their visions of what changes were needed. . . . After perceiving some minimum readiness on the part of their managers, the leaders then began communicating their visions of what changes were necessary. These visions always carried some general message about key constituencies, especially customers. . . . [Also] included was information*

FIGURE 14.3 Relationship between management and leadership

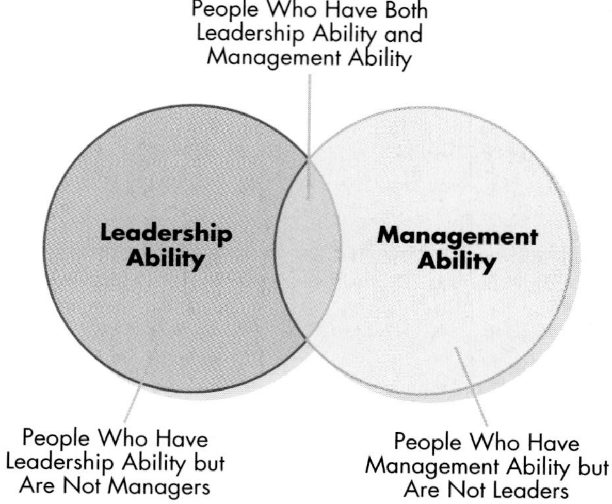

about more specific strategies and practices that were seen as needed to deal with the current business climate or competitive situation.

As the leaders' visions and strategies were conveyed, they won allies and became role models for other managers. "Their ability to change and play a useful leadership role signaled that others could also" (Kotter and Heskett, 1992). Such leaders are often called transformational leaders, because they are able to create fundamental changes in their organizations' values, missions, and cultures. Figure 14.4, which is based on John Kotter's work, further differentiates between management and leadership. Notice how Kotter's list of leadership behaviors emphasizes people skills and motivational connections.

Kotter (1995) notes that "A few . . . corporate change efforts have been very successful. A few have been utter failures. Most fall somewhere in between, with a distinct tilt toward the lower end of the scale." Why so few big successes? Management can get stuck in the planning phase or be trapped with a culture, a decision structure, practices, and people who resist change. "A paralyzed senior management often comes from having too many managers and not enough leaders" (Kotter, 1995).

To enlist support for change and gain progress toward it, consultant Peter Scott-Morgan at Arthur D. Little believes that although "humans are amazingly adaptable, you have to make it logical for them to want to change" (Fisher, 1995). Integra Financial, a Pennsylvania-based holding company, wanted to shift from a superstar culture to one based on teamwork. It "developed a carefully crafted system of evaluations and rewards to discourage hot-dogging, grandstanding, filibustering, and other ego games. The best team players get the goodies; the worst get a gentle dressing down. . . . One thing that you can count on: Whatever gets rewarded will get done" (Fisher, 1995). (See this chapter's Ethical Management feature for a discussion on how peer reviews can be used to identify true leaders in an organization.)

FIGURE 14.4 *Differences between management and leadership*

Management	Leadership
Planning and budgeting. Establishing detailed steps and timetables for achieving needed results and then allocating the resources necessary to make them happen.	**Establishing direction.** Developing a vision of the future, often the distant future, and strategies for producing the changes needed to achieve that vision.
Organizing and staffing. Establishing a structure for accomplishing plan requirements, staffing that structure with individuals, delegating responsibility and authority for carrying out the plan, providing policies and procedures to help guide people, and creating methods or systems to monitor implementation.	**Aligning people.** Communicating the direction by words and deeds to all those whose cooperation may be needed to influence the creation of teams and coalitions that understand the vision and strategies and accept their validity.
Controlling and problem solving. Close monitoring of results in terms of the plan, identifying deviations, and then planning and organizing to solve these problems.	**Motivating and inspiring.** Energizing people to overcome major political, bureaucratic, and resource barriers by satisfying basic, but often unfulfilled, human needs.
Produces a degree of predictability and order and consistently achieves the key results expected by various stakeholders (for customers, being on time; for stockholders, being on budget).	*Produces change, often to a dramatic degree, that has the potential of being extremely useful (for example, developing new products that customers want or new approaches to labor relations that help make a firm more competitive).*

Source: Reprinted with the permission of The Free Press, a division of Simon & Schuster from *A Force for Change: How Leadership Differs from Management*, p. 6, by John P. Kotter. Copyright © 1990 by John P. Kotter, Inc.

ETHICAL MANAGEMENT
Peer Reviews at Risk International

Peers rating peers (workers rating workers and managers rating other managers of equal rank) is a relatively new approach to appraising employees in industry. Many employees fear receiving such ratings and having the responsibility for rating workmates. Among their ethical concerns are confidentiality and privacy.

Ohio-based Risk International believes it has discovered a way to make such reviews pay off and is pleased with the results. The risk-management company has 47 employees who rate "only those [peers] they work with directly" once each year through a standardized form. Eleven specific, equally weighted areas are evaluated on a scale of 1 (the highest rating) through 4 (unacceptable) along with an "unknown." A 3 means improvements are needed; a 2 is a satisfactory rating; a 1 denotes a strength. The first item on the form asks how well a peer "demonstrates high ethical standards and personal integrity." The other areas deal with how well an employee deals with quality and customer service, solves problems and makes judgments, gets his or her work out, conducts him- or herself on the job, manages resources, communicates, teams, markets company services, exhibits personal excellence, and understands the company and its operations.

The results are tabulated by a temporary employee who receives the forms in sealed envelopes. Who said what is not disclosed. The results are shared with rated persons through meetings with their supervisors, at which time plans are made for improvements. Risk International has discovered its "quietly competent workers" who are no longer ignored; it has identified superstars and those who exhibit true leadership traits and behaviors.

- What do you think about evaluating and being evaluated by your peers?
- What additional ethical issues can you identify with such a process?

http://www.riskinternational.com

Sources: Gruner, Stephanie. "The Team-Building Peer Review," *Inc.* (July 1995), pp. 63–65; Risk International, http://www.riskinternational.com.

As is the case at Southwest Airlines, corporate culture begins with a leader that leads by example ("walks like they talk") and creates a vision, a strategy to achieve it, and a coalition consisting of empowered people at every level committed to change. Leadership is the ability to articulate a vision and to inspire the best efforts of followers in the service of that vision. Herb Kelleher focuses on social interactions with the people of Southwest Airlines, fostering an atmosphere of mutual trust and mutual commitment to the interests of the organization as a whole.

POWER AND LEADERSHIP

Describe the five sources of power leaders may possess

Power gives people the ability to exert influence over others, to get them to follow; it makes leadership possible. Leaders possess power, as do all managers whether or not they are leaders. Possessing power can increase the effectiveness of managers by enabling them to inspire people—to get them to perform willingly, without relying solely on formal managerial authority. Formal authority grants a manager legitimate power; but as Chapter 8 has pointed out, coercive, reward, expert, and referent power exist as well. A brief review of these five foundation stones of leadership is in order here.

Legitimate Power

Managers' formal authority derives from their positions in their organizations, which each position's job description usually specifies. A manager's formal authority grants power or influence because it enables the holder to use organizational resources, including other employees. An employee's instructor, manager, or team leader has the right to assign work, establish standards for its execution, and apply those standards to both outcomes and behaviors of subordinates. All employees recognize that they have a fundamental duty to comply with lawful and ethical orders, rules, and standards established by those in formal positions of authority.

The employees under Jacques Nasser at several of Ford's overseas operations respected and feared him because of the legitimate power he possessed. He was charged with making those facilities more effective and efficient. He did so in many different ways, using the power of his formal management position. (See this chapter's Global Applications feature.)

Coercive Power

One result of the exercise of legitimate power—a person's formal authority—is punishment for a subordinate's unacceptable outcomes and performances. People with authority and, therefore, influence over others usually have the right to punish or withhold rewards from them. A few of the possible results from the exercise of coercive powers include oral and written warnings, suspension, and firing. If these punishments are to act as deterrents for inappropriate behaviors, however, people subjected to them must believe that they will be administered in a timely and appropriate manner.

GLOBAL APPLICATIONS
Ford's Jacques A. Nasser

Ford's president and chief executive officer, Jacques A. Nasser, was born in Lebanon in 1947 but became an Australian citizen after his family emigrated to Australia in 1950. He has an Australian college degree and can communicate in four languages. He has served Ford's overseas operations in several leadership positions in both Australia and Europe. Previously, he was executive vice president for Ford's Automotive Operations. From 1994–1996, his job was to "merge the company's . . . design and engineering organizations to create a new generation of vehicles that can be tailored for any of the world's markets." The result will be one product development office and world-car program for one market—the world. The first tangible result of the reorganization was the company's 1996 Taurus; it was sold in seven countries, with more to come.

His familiarity with tough decisions has earned him several promotions and the nickname of "Jac the knife." As a reengineering specialist, he has overhauled several Ford operations and cut about 17,000 jobs in the process. This restructuring was but a small part of "Ford 2000," Ford's grand strategy for redefining how it manages. The strategy's three primary aims were "[One,] to make sure that [global] perspective is in all of our markets. Two, product excellence. [Three,] . . . productivity and efficiency." To achieve these ends, Ford benchmarked the best of the best in many industries. Nasser believes that Ford's leadership has the global outlook and global mind-set needed to succeed around the globe.

http://www.ford.com

Sources: Ford 1999 Proxy Statement "Board of Directors"; Lienert, Paul. "Jac the Knife," *Automobile* (April 1995), pp. 87–88, 92–93; Ford Motor Company, http://www.ford.com.

Reward Power

The opposite of coercive power is reward power—the right to promise or grant rewards, such as raises, praise, promotions, and so on. It, too, is often the result of exercising legitimate power. As Chapter 13 has pointed out, people usually work hard to please those who can reward or punish them. The attractiveness of the reward is important; it must have a strong appeal to the person being influenced or it may have little impact on that person's motivation. When rewards are promised and not granted in a timely manner, however, they can actually have a negative impact on an individual's motivation. Finally, rewards must be earned before being granted; to do otherwise is to lessen their value and importance to the individual.

Expert Power

A person's abilities, skills, knowledge, and experience can exert influence when others value them. A seasoned practitioner exercises expert power with newcomers and apprentices. A trainer or coach uses it to impart his or her knowledge, skills, and attitudes to trainees. Physicians, lawyers, and other licensed professionals earn their living by selling their expertise. A person in need of legal advice, however, may find a production manager's expertise to be of little value. Unlike legitimate, coercive, and reward power, expert power may reside in and be exercised by nearly everyone, whether inside or outside an organization.

© REUTERS NEWMEDIA INC./CORBIS

New York Knicks' coach Jeff Van Gundy uses expert power to lead his players to a winning season.

Referent Power

Power that comes to people because of the kind of personality or personal attractiveness they have to others is known as referent, or charismatic, power; it creates in people a desire to associate with or emulate the person who has it. Your personality, sense of humor, openness, honesty, and other endearing traits can draw others to you. Many of this chapter's leadership traits generate referent power in those who possess them. Like expert power, referent power is possessed by nearly everyone to some degree; but not all people are attracted to the same personalities or traits. Another may consider what one admires unappealing.

In this chapter's Management in Action case, CEO Herb Kelleher understands the people he is leading. He gets to know his followers, and the followers see him as their leader. In other words, they trust him and he trusts them. Kelleher is accepted because he possesses legitimate, referent, and expert power.

Managers can become leaders when they couple their formal authority (legitimate power) with the other types of power. As the foregoing indicates, it is possible to be a leader without being a manager and a manager without being a leader. A major goal for many organizations is to develop and tap into the leadership potential that exists in nearly every employee.

Possessing power and using it wisely are two different things. Power gives individuals and groups the means to influence for both good and evil, as Chapter 22, entitled "Management Ethics and Social Responsibility," points out. Leaders without moral and ethical values or who disregard the law can do others, themselves, and their organizations great harm. The use of power in any organization must not contradict its core values. Mickey Mantle, a baseball great, held a press conference following his liver transplant in 1995. He admitted to long abuse of alcohol, a primary cause for his liver's failure. He cautioned all his fans and admirers to *not* emulate him, fearful that his behavior had or would become a model for others.

LEADERSHIP STYLES

leadership style
The perceived approaches and behaviors a manager uses to influence others.

From the discussion of leadership and its power bases, we turn now to the dynamic interaction between a leader and other people. The perceived approaches and behaviors a manager uses to influence others constitute the manager's **leadership style** (Davis and Newstrom, 1989). Managers' leadership styles result from their philosophies about motivation, their choices of decision-making styles, and their areas of emphasis in the work environment—whether they focus on tasks or people.

Positive Versus Negative Motivation

4

Differentiate between positive and negative motivation

Leaders influence others to achieve goals through their approach to motivation. Depending on the style of the manager, the motivation can take the form of rewards or penalties (Davis and Newstrom, 1989). Figure 14.5 presents a continuum containing positive and negative motivations. Leaders with positive styles use positive motivators. They motivate by using praise, recognition, or monetary rewards or by increasing security or granting additional responsibilities.

A negative leadership style incorporates coercion known as *sanctions*—fines, suspensions, termination, and the like. The manager who says "Do it my way or else" employs negative motivation. Implied in the statement is the manager's willingness to exercise disciplinary powers; the subordinate's failure to comply would be an act of insubordination.

FIGURE 14.5 *Motivation continuum*

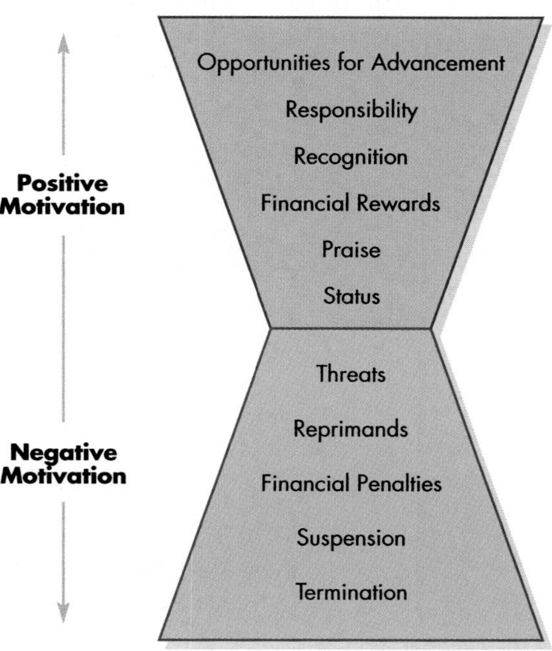

Positive leadership styles encourage development of employees and result in higher levels of job satisfaction (Keller and Szilagyi, 1978). Negative leadership styles are based on the manager's ability to withhold items of value from employees. The result of negative leadership may be an environment of fear, where managers are viewed with distrust and seen as dictators rather than leaders or team players.

Decision-Making Styles

Describe the three decision-making styles used by leaders

Another element in a manager's leadership style is the degree to which he or she shares decision-making authority with subordinates. Managers' styles range from not sharing at all to completely delegating decision-making authority. Figure 14.6 shows the degrees of sharing as a continuum, with the range of styles categorized in three groups: autocratic style, participative style, and free-rein style. Which style a manager chooses should relate to the situation encountered.

Autocratic Style

autocratic style
A leadership approach in which a manager does not share decision-making authority with subordinates.

A manager who uses the **autocratic style** does not share decision-making authority with subordinates. The manager makes the decision and then announces it. Autocratic managers may ask for subordinates' ideas and feedback about the decision, but the input does not usually change the decision unless it indicates that something vital has been overlooked. The hallmark of this style is that the manager, who retains all the authority, executes the entire process. Consequently, the autocratic style is sometimes called the "I" approach.

Under certain conditions, the autocratic style is appropriate. When a manager is training a subordinate, for instance, the content, objectives, pacing, and execution of decisions properly remain in the hands of the trainer. (The manager should elicit feedback from the trainee, however.) During a crisis—a hazardous-materials spill or bomb threat, say—leaders are expected to take charge, issue orders, and make decisions. When a subordinate directly challenges a manager's authority, an autocratic response may be needed to preclude acts of insubordination. In circumstances in which employees have not been empowered to make decisions, supervisors must make them. Some subordinates do not want to share authority or

FIGURE 14.6 *Leadership styles and the distribution of decision-making authority*

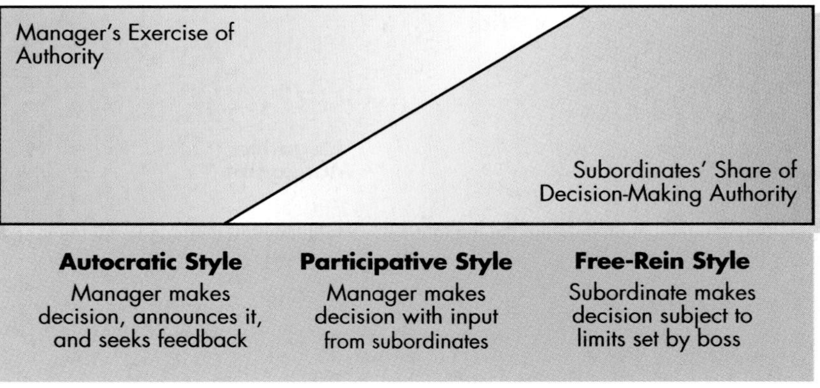

become involved in any way beyond the performance of their routine duties. Managers should respect these preferences but also make incentives and growth opportunities available.

To use the autocratic style effectively, managers must know what needs to be done, and they must possess expert power. The autocratic style is effective when managers face issues that they are best equipped to solve, create solutions whose implementation does not depend on others, and desire to communicate through orders and instructions. If these conditions do not exist, one of the other two leadership styles is probably more appropriate.

Participative Style

participative style *A leadership approach in which a manager shares decision-making authority with subordinates.*

Managers who use the **participative style** share decision-making authority with subordinates. The degree of sharing can range from the manager's presenting a tentative decision that is subject to change, to letting the group or subordinate participate in making the decision. Sometimes called the "we" approach, participative management involves others and lets them bring their unique viewpoints, talents, and experiences to bear on an issue. This style is strongly emphasized today because of the trends toward downsizing, employee empowerment, and worker teams.

A consultative and democratic approach works best for resolving issues that affect more than just the manager or decision maker. People affected by decisions support them more enthusiastically when they participate in the decision making than when decisions are imposed on them. Also, if others in a manager's unit know more than the manager does about an issue, common sense urges their inclusion in decisions concerning it.

Before subordinates can be brought into the process, mutual trust and respect must exist between them and their managers. The subordinates must be willing to participate and be trained to do so. People need training in rational decision making. They must also possess the related skills and knowledge needed to cope with the problems they are expected to solve. It takes time to give people the confidence and competence needed to make decisions. Managers must have the time, means, and patience to prepare subordinates to participate. When employees participate, they devise solutions they feel they own. This sense of ownership increases their commitment to making the solutions work.

Inc. magazine (1992) reported that the participation of Datatec employees is encouraged even in the matter of their bosses' appraisals. Datatec managers believe that

> *giving employees the chance to appraise their bosses forces a company to live up to its commitment to participative management. [Managers are asked] to conduct one-on-one reverse appraisals with subordinates. Employees who find appraising their bosses simply too discomforting may choose to talk to another manager. [President] Carey wants to make sure that problems don't get buried just because they're prickly ones.*

Limits on subordinates' participation must be clearly spelled out beforehand; there should be no misunderstandings about who holds authority to do what. Mistakes will be made and some waste will occur, but the power of the participative style to motivate and energize people is great. In many organizations, such as Datatec, managers must use this style; corporate culture and policies demand it.

free-rein style
A leadership approach in which a manager shares decision-making authority with subordinates, empowering them to function without direct involvement from managers to whom they report.

Free-Rein Style

Often called the "they" approach, or spectator style, the **free-rein style** empowers individuals or groups to function on their own, without direct involvement from the managers to whom they report. The style relies heavily on delegation of authority and works best when the parties have expert power, when participants have and know how to use the tools and techniques needed for their tasks. Under this style, managers set limits and remain available for consultation. The managers also hold participants accountable for their actions by reviewing and evaluating performance. Listservs, the subject of this chapter's Managing Technology feature, are used by many free-rein leaders.

Free-rein leadership works particularly well with managers and experienced professionals in engineering, design, research, and sales. Such people generally resist other kinds of supervision.

In most organizations managers must be able to use the decision-making style that circumstances dictate. Lee is new, so his manager needs to use an autocratic approach until he develops the confidence and knowledge to perform independently or until he joins a team. Kim, experienced in her job and better at it than anyone else, will probably do well under a participative or free-rein approach. Because people and circumstances constantly change and because subordinates must be prepared for change, the effective manager switches from one leadership style to another as appropriate.

Explain the two primary approaches leaders can take: task centered and people centered

Task Orientation Versus People Orientation

Yet another element of leadership style is the manager's philosophy about the most effective way to get work done. Leaders can adopt a focus on task (a work, or task, orientation) or a focus on employees (a relationship, or people-centered, approach). Depending on the manager's perspective and situation, these two approaches can be used separately or in combination.

MANAGING TECHNOLOGY
Listservs

A listserv is an email discussion group that focuses on a particular topic. Joining a listserv is a terrific way to exchange information with people on topics of interest. Here are some helpful tips when using a listserv:

- When you join a listserv, you will receive important information about the list, known as frequently asked questions (FAQ), including how to unsubscribe to that list. Do not delete that information. The email address that you use to subscribe and unsubscribe to a list is not the same address to which you post.
- Once you join a listserv, "lurk" and observe for a few days before posting a message. You need to get a feel for the level of formality and focus of discussion before you join the conversation.
- The listserv is a community to which you belong. Never flame (give someone a public, verbal lashing).
- Take private conversations off the list and continue them via regular email.
- If the list is very active, follow your FAQ instructions and set your mail to digest. Digest allows you to receive multiple messages in one file delivered once or twice a day to your inbox.

A task focus emphasizes technology, methods, plans, programs, deadlines, goals, and getting the work out. Typically, the manager who focuses on a task uses the autocratic style of leadership and issues guidelines and instructions to subordinates. A task focus works well in the short run, especially with tight schedules or under crisis conditions. Used over the long term, however, a task focus can create personnel problems. It may cause the best performers, who desire flexibility and freedom to be creative, to leave the group; and it may increase absenteeism and decrease job satisfaction (Likert, 1976).

The manager who focuses on employees emphasizes workers' needs. He or she treats employees as valuable assets and respects their views. Building teamwork, positive relationships, and mutual trust are important activities of the people-centered leader. By focusing on employees, a manager can increase job satisfaction and decrease absenteeism (Likert, 1976).

University of Michigan Studies

In the 1970s researchers at the University of Michigan compared the behaviors of effective and ineffective supervisors. The researchers' findings indicated that supervisors who focused on their subordinates' needs (employee-centered leaders) were the most effective, building high-performance teams that reached their goals. The less-effective supervisors (job-centered leaders) tended to focus on tasks and were more concerned with efficiency and meeting schedules (Likert, 1979).

The Ohio State University Studies

Researchers at The Ohio State University surveyed hundreds of leaders in the 1970s. The researchers studied their behavior in terms of two factors: consideration and initiating structure. *Consideration* was defined as concern for subordinates' ideas and feelings (what the University of Michigan studies referred to as an employee focus). Leaders who rated high in consideration communicated openly, developed teams, and focused on subordinates' needs. *Initiating structure* was defined as concern for goal achievement and task orientation (what the Michigan studies called job focus). Leaders who rated high in initiating structure were concerned with deadlines, planning work, and meeting schedules (Schriesheim and Bird, 1979).

The researchers found that leaders had one of four combinations of the two behaviors: high consideration and low initiating structure, low consideration and high initiating structure, low consideration and low initiating structure, and high consideration and high initiating structure. The researchers concluded that the last combination resulted in the greatest job satisfaction and performance by subordinates (Schriesheim and Bird, 1979).

Since the Ohio State studies, additional research suggests that the approach a manager takes should vary, depending on the people involved and the situation. In a crisis, managers should focus on task. When training people to become a self-managing work team, managers should focus on people—their needs to cooperate, get to know one another, and develop relationships. Managers, these studies suggest, must be flexible and provide the kind of leadership their people and situations require.

The Leadership Grid®

Leadership Grid®
Blake and Mouton's two-dimensional model for visualizing the extent to which a manager focuses on tasks, employees, or both.

In its original version, Figure 14.7 was published as the Managerial Grid by Robert R. Blake and Jane S. Mouton. Along with the Grid theory itself, the figure has evolved through the years to its present configuration and is now referred to as **The Leadership Grid®**. It presents two axes: the vertical axis measures concern for people; the horizontal axis measures concern for production. (The axes correspond to employee- and job-centeredness in the University of Michigan studies and to consideration and initiating structure in the Ohio State studies.) The positions on the grid are stated in terms of a 9-point scale, with 1 representing a low concern and 9 representing a high concern. The grid effectively summarizes posi-

FIGURE 14.7 *The Leadership Grid®*

9,1 Grid Style: CONTROLLING (Direct & Dominate)
I expect results and take control by clearly stating a course of action. I enforce rules that sustain high results and do not permit deviation.

1,9 Grid Style: ACCOMMODATING (Yield & Comply)
I support results that establish and reinforce harmony. I generate enthusiasm by focusing on positive and pleasing aspects of work.

5,5 Grid Style: STATUS QUO (Balance & Compromise)
I endorse results that are popular but caution against taking unnecessary risk. I test my opinions with others involved to assure ongoing acceptability.

1,1 Grid Style: INDIFFERENT (Evade & Elude)
I distance myself from taking active responsibility for results to avoid getting entangled in problems. If forced, I take a passive or supportive position.

PATERNALISTIC Grid Style (Prescribe & Guide)
I provide leadership by defining initaives for myself and others. I offer praise and appreciation for support, and discourage challenges to my thinking.

OPPORTUNISTIC Grid Style (Exploit & Manipulate)
I persuade others to support results that offer me private benefit. If they also benefit, that's even better in gaining support. I rely on whatever approach is needed to secure an advantage.

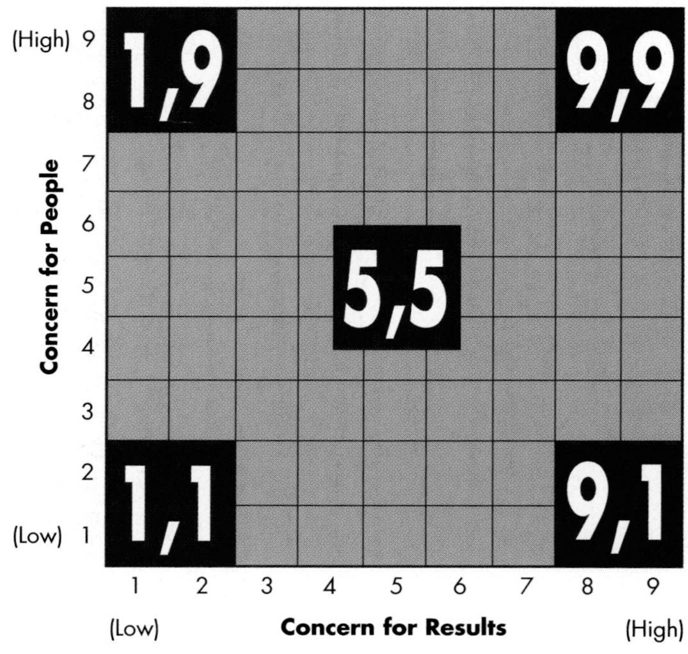

9,9 Grid Style: SOUND (Contribute & Commit)
I initiate team action in a way that invites involvement and commitment. I explore all facts and alternative views to reach a shared understanding of the best solution.

Source: This image is a black and white adaptation of The Leadership Grid® figure as it appears in *The Power to Change*, Rachel McKee and Bruce Carlson (Austin: Grid International, Inc.), p. 16. Copyright © 1999 by Grid International, Inc. Reproduced by permission of the owners.

tions that managers and leaders can take under a variety of circumstances and with different employees.

http://www.grid-intl.com

The Leadership Grid® provides a framework for understanding leadership. Karen McCormick of Grid International, Inc., gives the following explanation:

> *The premise behind Grid theory is that there is one basic set of principles by which to manage that is appropriate to* all situations. *The different "styles" in the theory are behavioral generalizations that manifest themselves as a result of the axes of "concern" and depict how a person characterized by that style of behavior would react (positively or negatively) given that same set of basic management principles. Grid theory does not recommend the use of any particular style but holds up fundamental principles as a yardstick against which the behavior styles are measured. When a person is characterized as a certain "style" on the Grid, this is a characterization of his or her behavior in relation to this ideal set of principles that remain unchanged.*
>
> *For example, when faced with conflict in the workplace, a 1,9-oriented person would tend to smooth over conflict and ease feelings and hope it just "goes away." (But as anyone who has ever experienced workplace conflict knows, it never does—it just festers.) The 9,9-oriented leader, on the other hand, would confront the conflict, determine the root causes, and create ways to eliminate the* source *of the conflict. This represents management by a basic, unchanging set of principles across the board, rather than situational management where the very foundation on which one manages is subject to change at the whim of external circumstances.*

The next section will examine three theories of leadership that incorporate situational elements: the contingency model, the path-goal theory, and the life-cycle theory.

THEORIES OF SITUATIONAL LEADERSHIP

Describe the three theories of situational leadership

Three general theories of leadership address adaptation of leadership to situations. All have strong roots in the motivational theories discussed in Chapter 13.

Fiedler's Contingency Model

contingency model
A leadership theory stating that a manager should focus on either tasks or employees, depending on the interaction of three variables—leader-member relations, task structure, and leader position power.

Fred Fiedler (1974) holds that the most appropriate style of leadership for a manager depends on the manager's situation. Fiedler's model of management, the **contingency model**, suggests that a manager should choose task or employee focus according to the interaction of three situational variables: leader-member relations, task structure, and leader position power. Because Fiedler's model emphasizes the importance of the situation, Fiedler's work is sometimes called the theory of situational leadership. Figure 14.8 shows Fiedler's contingency model.

The solid line plotted at the top of Figure 14.8 reveals the recommended focus for specific situations. To understand the recommendations and how they were reached, we must understand the variables the model uses.

The scale of leader-member relations refers to the degree to which the leader is or feels accepted by the group. Measured by the observed degree of mutual respect, trust, and confidence, this acceptance is rated as good or poor. In a good

FIGURE 14.8 *Fiedler's contingency model, depicting the interaction of leadership orientations with situational variables*

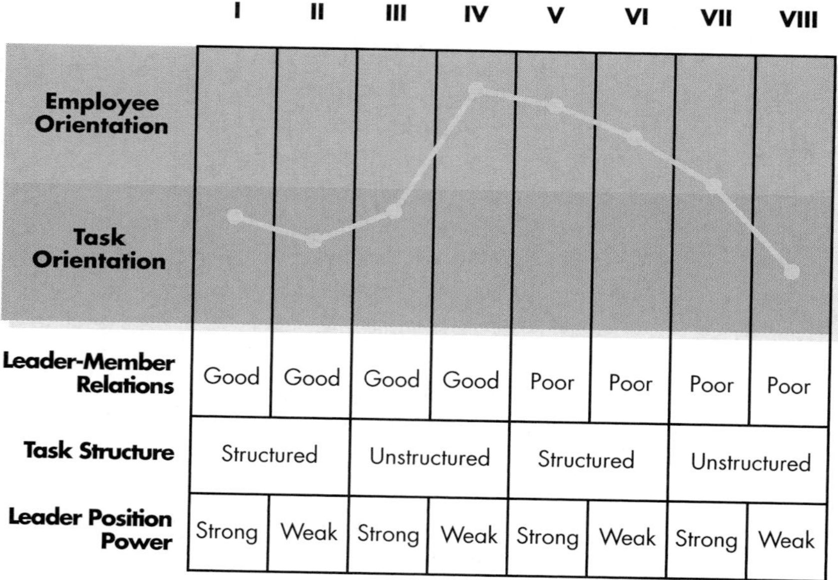

Source: Reprinted by permission of the *Harvard Business Review*. Adapted from "Engineer the Job to Fit the Manager" by Fred E. Fiedler, September–October 1965. Copyright © 1965 by the Harvard Business School Publishing Corporation; all rights reserved.

relationship, the leader should be able to inspire and influence subordinates. If the relationship is poor, the manager may have to resort to negotiating or to promising favors to get performance.

The task structure ratings relate to the nature of subordinates' jobs or tasks. A structured task is or can be broken into procedures. It is narrowly defined and may be machine-paced, and it tends to be full of routines that are repeated regularly. Data entry clerks, file clerks, and supermarket checkers hold structured jobs. An unstructured job includes complexities, variety, and latitude for creative expression. Researchers, managers, design engineers, and most professionals hold unstructured jobs.

The ratings for leader position power describe the organizational power base from which the leader operates. To what degree can the leader reward and punish? With whom is the leader allied? The leader's connections, legitimate power, expert power, and referent power determine weakness or strength—the ability to exercise a little influence or a great deal of influence inside the organization.

Note position I in Figure 14.8. In a situation displaying good leader-member relations, structured tasks, and strong leader position power, the contingency model tells the leader to adopt a task orientation. At position VII, a nearly equal blend of employee and task orientation is best. Employee-oriented leaders perform best under conditions associated with positions IV, V, and VI. When a manager is promoted or given a temporary assignment—as project leader or product design team leader,

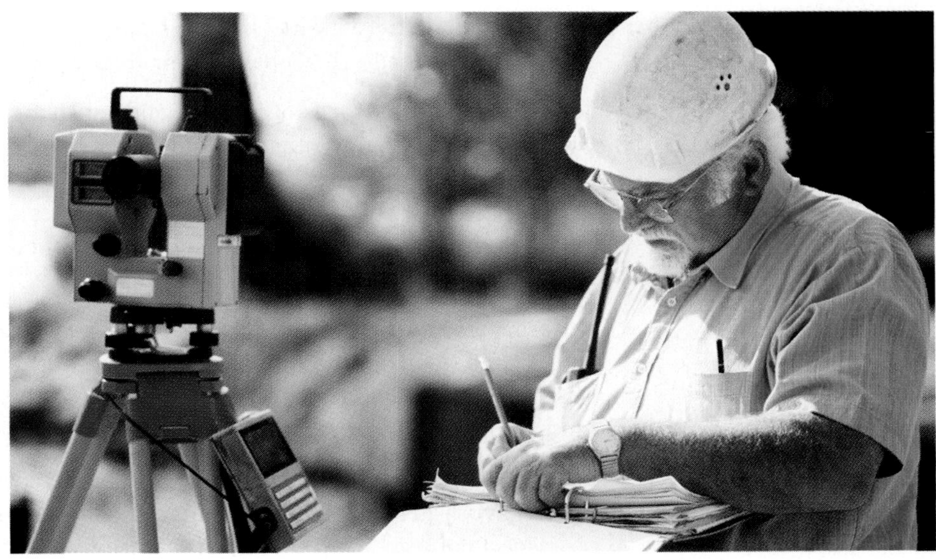

A survey engineer's job is unstructured. It includes complexities, variety, and latitude for creative expression.

for example—he or she will find a new combination of people and circumstances. Each combination calls for a fresh assessment of Fiedler's three variables.

House and Mitchell's Path-Goal Theory

path-goal theory
A view of management asserting that subordinates' behaviors and motivations are influenced by the behaviors managers exhibit toward them.

Robert House and Terrence Mitchell (1974) developed the **path-goal theory** of leadership. Their theory relates to the behaviors a leader can use to stimulate subordinates' motivation to achieve both personal and organizational goals and rewards (House, 1971). The path-goal theory suggests that a leadership style is effective or ineffective on the basis of how successfully leaders influence and support their subordinates' perceptions of

- Goals that need to be achieved
- Rewards for successful performance
- Behaviors that lead to successful performance

According to the path-goal theory, leaders can influence subordinates' motivation by (1) teaching employees the competencies they will need to perform successfully and gain rewards, (2) tailoring rewards to meet employees' needs, and (3) acting to support subordinates' efforts. Teaching (coaching, development, and training) builds confidence and competencies. Adapting rewards to the specific needs of individual employees makes them more appealing. Supportive behaviors assist subordinates as necessary, enabling them to achieve both personal and organizational goals.

The path-goal theory has its basis in the expectancy theory of motivation. In that theory employees' motivations are influenced by their perceptions of what a task requires, their confidence in their abilities to perform, the attractiveness of the reward being offered, and the relationship of the reward to the accomplishment of the task. The more self-confidence and the greater the desire for the reward, the more willing employees will be to perform as required. According to the path-goal theory, leadership behaviors and situational factors influence the motivational process.

Leadership Behaviors

House and Mitchell (1974) based their theory on the following two assumptions:

1. A leader's behavior is acceptable and satisfying to subordinates to the extent that they view it as either an immediate source of satisfaction or as an instrument to some future satisfaction.
2. A leader's behavior will increase subordinates' efforts if it links satisfaction of their needs to effective performance and supports their efforts to achieve goals.

These two assumptions tell managers to increase the number of ways in which performance can be deemed successful, to clear away barriers to successful outcomes, and to help subordinates see these outcomes as desirable (House and Mitchell, 1974). To enable leaders to do these things, the theory provides four kinds of leadership behavior:

- *Instrumental behavior* (task-oriented). This behavior, sometimes called directive behavior, involves the planning, directing, monitoring, and task-assignment aspects of leadership. It can be prescriptive. A manager who uses instrumental behavior establishes precise procedures, goals, and timetables and utilizes the autocratic style of leadership. This behavior can be used to increase an employee's work effort or to clarify outcomes.
- *Supportive behavior* (employee-oriented). This behavior creates a climate of mutual trust and respect between leaders and followers. It involves the coaching, counseling, and mentoring aspects of leadership. Supportive behavior requires open communication and a leader's honest concern for subordinates' needs. This type of behavior builds teams.
- *Participative behavior* (employee-oriented). In this behavior a leader solicits and uses subordinates' ideas and contributions and involves subordinates in decision making. During the planning and execution phases of an operation, the manager tries to obtain input from everyone concerned. Supportive behavior promotes participative behavior. The reverse is true as well. Participative behavior builds team spirit, values individuals and their contributions, and encourages development through exposure to others' points of view and experience.
- *Achievement-oriented behavior* (employee-oriented). A leader who shows this type of behavior helps subordinates grow and increases their competencies through training and development. The leader's primary aim is to improve subordinates' abilities and performance, thus making the employees more valuable to themselves and their organization. Instrumental behavior, supportive behavior, and participative behavior increase a leader's ability to engage in achievement-oriented behavior, which paves the way for subordinates' advancement.

http://www.pepsico.com

As CEO, Wayne Calloway headed up the 480,000 employees of PepsiCo's worldwide operations. His regular routines included all four types of behavior that House and Mitchell described. He used instrumental behavior in his hands-on approach to hiring, strategic planning, and executive appraisals. He interviewed all job candidates for positions at the vice-presidential level or above, and some 75 executives each year. Twice a year Calloway was personally involved in evaluating some 600 managers (Konrad and Rothman, 1992).

Calloway used supportive behavior in a company-wide drive to build on past decentralization with renewed efforts at empowerment. His participative behavior included encouraging employees—everyone from route salespeople to restaurant workers—to recommend ways to improve the business. In 1991, for example, Calloway introduced the Great PepsiCo Brainstorm, in which employees won prizes for contributing ideas. His achievement-oriented behavior included encouraging people to take risks and rewarding them for their initiative, whether it leads to success or failure (Konrad and Rothman, 1992). [In 1996, Roger Enrico succeeded Wayne Calloway as chief executive officer.]

Situational Factors

Two situational factors are important components in the path-goal theory: the personal characteristics of subordinates and the work environment. These two factors influence the behavior a leader should choose.

The personal characteristics of subordinates include their abilities, self-confidence, personal needs and motivations, and perceptions of their leaders. When subordinates exhibit low levels of performance, leaders must be ready to provide coaching, training, and direction. The leader must ensure that the rewards offered for outstanding performance are rewards that appeal to employees.

Factors in the work environment include the organization's culture and subcultures, the philosophy of management, how power is exercised, policies and rules, and the extent to which tasks are structured. These factors are environmental pressures beyond the abilities of employees to control, but they affect employees' abilities to accomplish tasks and achieve goals.

Leaders must know what their people want from work, what their motivations are, and what stands between them and successful performance. Leaders must provide to each person the appropriate leadership, depending on the employees and the environmental conditions. Where skills are weak, instrumental behavior is called for; when subordinates lack motivation, achievement-oriented behavior may be appropriate.

http://www.powerbond.com

Managers at Collins & Aikman, a floor coverings manufacturer, decided to give their employees what they needed: new technology. Instead of opting for cheap labor overseas as a means to stay competitive, the company chose to invest in its U.S. workforce and operations and install state-of-the-art equipment. In their Georgia plant, the primary tufting and shearing machines were to be linked to computers. But the prospect of working with computers terrified many of the firm's 560 employees. Almost one-third of the workers had not finished high school; some could not read or write (Cooper, 1992).

A needs assessment revealed that only 8 percent of the workers possessed the skills needed to adjust to the new high-tech environment. Collins & Aikman provided basic literacy training at a cost of about $1,200 per worker, and the employer implemented other in-house training programs as well. Productivity and employee self-confidence rose, and so did a flood of workers' suggestions about how to improve just about every phase of the operation. Production rejects fell by 50 percent, and workers needed less assistance from supervisors (Cooper, 1992).

Hersey and Blanchard's Life-Cycle Theory

life-cycle theory
A view of management that asserts that a leader's behavior toward a subordinate should relate to the subordinate's maturity level. The focus on tasks and relationships should vary as the subordinate matures.

http://www.blanchardtraining.com

http://www.situational.com

Paul Hersey and Kenneth Blanchard (1982) developed the **life-cycle theory** of leadership. As Figure 14.9 shows, the life-cycle theory relates leadership behavior to subordinates' maturity levels. Immature employees (new and inexperienced) require leadership with a high task–low relationship focus (the lower-right quadrant in the exhibit). As people learn and mature in their jobs, they become increasingly able to direct themselves and participate in decision making. Employees develop relationships with their coworkers, team members, and superiors that lead to mutual respect and trust. New skills and knowledge make employees more valuable to themselves and their organizations. As they progress in their organizational lives, employees require from their leaders first a high task–high relationship focus, followed by a high relationship–low task approach, and finally a low task–low relationship focus.

For employees described in quadrant 1 of Figure 14.9, an autocratic leadership style would be appropriate. For employees described in quadrants 2 and 3, the manager should move to a participative style. For those described in quadrant 4, the free-rein style is appropriate. Stated in terms of path-goal theory behaviors, quadrant 1 calls for instrumental behavior. Quadrants 2 and 3 call for supportive, participative, and achievement-oriented behaviors. By the time employees attain the characteristics described in quadrant 4, they should be operating in a relatively autonomous way, turning to the manager or higher authority on an as-needed basis.

FIGURE 14.9 *Adaptation of Hersey and Blanchard's life-cycle theory of leadership*

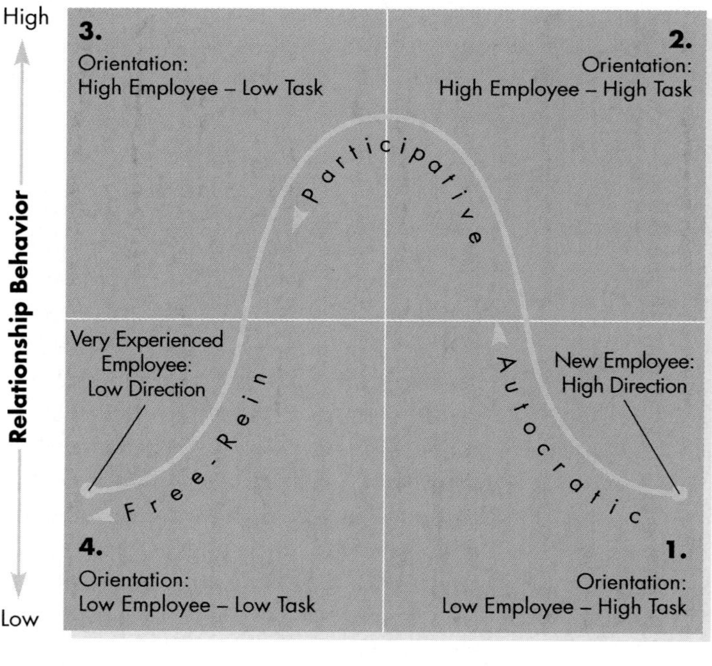

Hersey and Blanchard built on and combined ideas from the managerial grid and path-goal theory. Their theory does not allow for changes in situations, however, and it assumes that leaders are capable and mature.

CHALLENGES FACING LEADERS

Discuss the three challenges facing leaders

Leaders provide vision. They also supply incentives that enlist the support of others in making the vision a reality. Leaders keep people focused on what is important and what must be done. They set examples and foster values that become part of their organizations' cultures. Leaders are change agents, sensing the need for change and creating strategies that will help to initiate it.

http://www.amp.com

An example of a leader who takes his role as a change agent seriously is Harold McInnes, the former CEO of AMP, a business that supplies electronic and electrical connectors. From its headquarters in Pennsylvania, AMP does business through its companies located in 45 countries around the globe. While he was CEO, McInnes's vision was to build on his company's position by devoting 11–12 percent of sales dollars to R&D each year. He believed this investment would allow the company to move from being a supplier of connectors to being a provider of larger, more complete subsystems. McInnes called the process "moving up the food chain." One strategy for achieving McInnes's vision was to couple AMP's sales engineers with product-design teams at customers' locations. "That way, when computer whizzes sit down to formulate next-generation products, AMP people are right there determining which AMP subsystems can be designed into them." Harold McInnes developed plans to ensure that his company would thrive in the future (Erdman, 1992).

Leadership Throughout an Organization

It is not enough to have a leader at the top of an organization. Leadership must be exerted at all levels, or change will be resisted and blocked. Leaders must occupy top, middle, and supervisory ranks. Workers in self-directed teams need leaders too. Staff development and training efforts (see Chapter 11) should encourage and empower people to become leaders at every level.

http://www.harley-davidson.com

If one story illustrates the value of leadership at all levels of a company, it is the dramatic turnaround of Harley-Davidson, the motorcycle maker. Harley-Davidson tried various approaches to improving the quality and dependability of its motorcycles. Results were insignificant until managers discovered the power within their own workforce.

In the 1980s Harley-Davidson managers decided to replace the obsolete manufacturing system in its Pennsylvania plant and introduce a just-in-time inventory system. To implement the new system, the company took a step that was unusual for that time. Managers involved employees in deciding how to handle the changeover. Instead of having managers and engineers make all the decisions and announce them to workers, managers spent several months discussing the desired changes with everyone. After all parties helped decide on the changes, everyone cooperated to make them work (Boyett and Conn, 1991).

Employee involvement worked so well that management decided to enlist employees in solving quality problems. Employees learned how to use statistical tools for monitoring and controlling the quality of their own work; managers and supervisors were trained as team leaders. Both quality and morale improved. Employee involvement, just-in-time inventory, and statistical operator control became part of what Harley-Davidson came to call its productivity triad (Boyett and Conn, 1991). Employees were empowered to monitor their own work, resolve problems, and implement their own solutions. Managers worked with teams, sharing authority and supporting team efforts in every way possible.

Leadership and Rapid Response

Constantly changing demands challenge a leader's effectiveness. As culturally diverse organizations evolve, the leader's constituencies grow increasingly complex. Different circumstances and demands call for different kinds of direction, change, and strategies. In a business world based on high technology, speed is essential. In Sam Walton's (1992) words, a company must be able to "turn on a dime."

http://www.marriott.com

Marriott Hotels have gained customer loyalty by empowering their front-line employees—those who have direct contact with guests. Their primary concern is to delight their guests and turn them into repeat customers. Through careful screening of new hires, investments in training, sharing of management authority, and reengineering its processes, the hotel giant has lowered its turnover and costs; increased employee commitment, enthusiasm, and efficiency; and provided superior service to its guests (Henkoff, 1994).

The company's First Ten program concentrated on making each guest's first ten minutes pleasurable and memorable. Marriott guests can preregister by using a credit card. When they arrive a "guest service associate," or GSA, greets them at the door. His or her responsibility is to pick "up your key and paperwork from a rack in the lobby and then [escort] you directly to your room" (Henkoff, 1994). No hassles, no waiting in line, no confusion about your reservations. Each GSA can do what it takes to make a guest happy without clearance from on high.

Leadership and Tough Decisions

Anyone can lead when decisions are easy and please constituencies. Leaders must often, however, make unpopular, difficult decisions that adversely affect people inside and outside an organization. Leaders need the courage to see their decisions through and to face the consequences. Leaders must have the ability to do—within legal, moral, and ethical boundaries—what is best for their organizations.

http://www.nimo.com

In a crisis a company may turn to an outsider for guidance. Niagara Mohawk Power of Syracuse, New York, turned to an insider, Bill Donlon. Maintenance problems had caused the shutdown of a nuclear power station, forcing the company to buy electricity from rival producers. Cost overruns from the construction of a second nuclear plant were also hurting the bottom line. Donlon turned the company around by bringing in 20 new senior officers, reassigning key staff, terminating poor performers, reassessing the functions of all 11,000 employees, and enlisting everyone's help in establishing changes and productivity savings. "The whole system just wasn't working any longer," said Donlon. "It was apparent to me that we had to change" (Losee, 1992).

Making tough decisions is how Jacques Nasser, the subject of this chapter's Global Application feature and Ford's president and CEO, earned his reputation (he's called "Jac the knife") and promotions. The Lebanese-born Australian had to make a number of hard decisions at several Ford facilities in both Europe and Australia. His overriding concern has always been to do what's best for the company, given the people and circumstances. He is responsible for having increased efficiency, improved products, and eliminated about 17,000 jobs over the last few years. Says Nasser (Lienert, 1995)

> *I've been in some difficult jobs, probably as difficult as they come in the automotive industry. Not only in terms of political and economic environment, but also in terms of the business conditions that existed at the time. When you look at each one, the operation has come out of it a little stronger. What I'm particularly proud of is that in every one the product has improved dramatically.*

http://www.admworld.com

On October 15, 1996, the multibillion-dollar Archer Daniels Midland Company (ADM) agreed to pay $100 million in fines for participating in price fixing of three agricultural products: high-fructose corn syrup, citric acid, and lysine. In 1992, Mark Whitacre, president of the company's bioproducts division, had gone to the FBI with allegations of price fixing. He was given a briefcase equipped with a recorder, which he used to tape dozens of management conversations from 1992 into 1995. (ADM is known to do business through face-to-face discussions; as one industry analyst put it: "They don't have committee meetings, and they don't have memos . . ." [Franklin, 1995].) Speculation in the press suggested, "that he was more of a technical expert rather than a business strategist and was shocked by what he considered unethical behavior" (Gunset and Tackett, 1995).

HOW MANAGERS CAN BECOME BETTER LEADERS

Becoming a better leader begins with efforts to know oneself. Each manager has diverse values, needs, goals, ethics, strengths, and weaknesses; these determine how he or she will use the arts of management and leadership. An individual's philosophy about work and about the people who perform it will influence approaches to leadership. Managers who respect individuals will value diversity and treat each person with dignity. Managers who value security above all else may be too cautious, unwilling to make tough decisions and take the consequences of those decisions. Conversely, managers who value growth and challenge will seek new approaches, take on tough assignments, and willingly endure personal sacrifice to improve themselves, their subordinates, and their organizations. Such managers will encourage others to do the same.

Because leadership is situational, leaders must be adaptable. They must build teams and work with them. Leaders must willingly and ably exercise different leadership styles and utilize the behaviors discussed in this chapter. Only by doing so will their businesses be able to turn on a dime—a capability that the business environment of today requires. Managers must provide a vision and "sell" it to their constituents. They need to sense the need for change, prepare themselves and their team members for change, and articulate what is needed for change. Then they must act as change agents. They can do all these things only by staying current in their fields, remaining open to what is new and different, and committing themselves to constant efforts at self-improvement through the adoption of the kaizen philosophy.

Leaders must be willing to suppress what may seem best for themselves and implement what is best for others—subordinates, customers, and their organizations. As a servant who tailors leadership style and behavior to fit others' needs, the true leader excels by doing what is best for others. Being a manager is tough; being a leader-manager is tougher still.

CHAPTER SUMMARY

1 **Discuss leadership traits, skills, and behaviors.** Leadership traits are specific personal characteristics possessed by individuals that can both help or hinder their ability to lead and manage. Being dependable, for example, is a must for building mutual trust and respect between oneself and others. Without it, people discount or ignore a person and his or her contributions. With a proper mix of traits, given the circumstances and the available resources, a leader can be a source of influence over others.

Skills are a person's ability to demonstrate knowledge and competencies. They are capabilities to perform some process or task. Communicating effectively requires many skills such as critical thinking, listening actively, and fluency with one or more languages. Skills represent employment security, provided they are not obsolete and are in demand. Skills move people from knowing to doing. As such, certain types of skills are essential to leading people and are a source of power over others.

Behaviors for leaders are detailed in Figure 14.2. Each requires specific knowledge, traits, and skills. Praise-recognition, for example, requires such traits as decisiveness, willingness to assume responsibility, and dominance. Skills required are diplomacy and tact, fluency in speaking and writing, and knowledge about individual and group task performances. The key concept is: if what is needed in any situation is available in an individual or team, leadership can take place.

2 **Differentiate between management and leadership.** Some managers may be leaders, some leaders may be managers, and leadership can be exhibited by other than management personnel. Leading may be done in or out of a leadership or management position. Leading is a management function that can be exercised by any employee. Leadership is based on five sources of power (discussed in Learning Objective 3), and may be exercised by people regardless of their job descriptions. The key difference between these two concepts is the willingness of a person's subordinates to follow that person's direction. Leaders persuade, guide, direct, counsel, coach, and inspire others. They do so because they possess more than one source of power.

3 **Describe the five sources of power leaders may possess.** The five kinds of power are legitimate, coercive, reward, expert, and referent. Legitimate power flows from a person's formal authority, as denoted in his or her job description. Coercive power is defined as the ability to punish or deny rewards. It rests in both managers' job descriptions and in various group members who can exert peer pressure. Reward power, the opposite of coercive power, is the ability to bestow rewards. Like coercive power, it is held by managers and nonmanagers. Expert power is based on a person's knowledge and expertise—what one is able to do or knows. Anyone with skills, knowledge, or capabilities needed by others can exercise this kind of power. Finally, a person's traits, characteristics, and personality are a source of influence over others. A person with referent power is attractive to others—those attracted want to associate with or emulate the person possessing it. Referent power is the basis for friendships.

4 **Differentiate between positive and negative motivation.** Positive motivation is practiced by true leaders. Using Herzberg's (Chapter 13) motivational factors, leaders engineer jobs and offer the kinds of rewards desired by individuals to bring out their best and keep them motivated. Challenges and opportunities are offered and supports provided to meet or exceed those challenges. People are encouraged to take risks, to welcome responsibilities, and to develop their talents.

Negative motivation relies primarily on fear. It uses coercive power to threaten and punish. It tends to work in a crisis or for the short run but cannot stimulate lasting motivated behaviors. It becomes too stressful and eventually leads to employee dissatisfaction and loss of commitment. What behavior is not acceptable is made clear; but what behavior is necessary is often vague and uncertain.

5 **Describe the three decision-making styles used by leaders.** The three styles are the autocratic, the participative, and the free rein. The autocratic style is an "I" approach to leadership. The leader keeps the decision-making authority but may consult with followers when making decisions. This style

is appropriate when handling crises, instructing others, and exerting maximum focus on the task.

The participative style shares decision-making authority to some degree. Followers are involved in one or more of the decision-making steps (Chapter 7). Sharing authority through this style helps to teach and develop subordinates and begins the empowerment process. It seeks the unique contributions of others. Often those closest to a problem know most about it and have suggestions for solving it. In addition, those who must implement a decision will do so more willingly if they have had a say in its creation. The participative style is an expression of the leader's confidence in his or her followers and elicits stronger motivation and commitment than does the autocratic style.

The free-rein style asks subordinates and followers to take over the decision-making process—to solve and resolve the problem. It is the ultimate expression of empowerment. Experienced experts desire and usually must have such a style. It treats people as though they were self-employed—giving them the ultimate authority and responsibility for solving problems. Leaders know they must be able to use all three styles as circumstances and individuals dictate. Using the wrong style with an individual can inhibit his or her motivation.

6 Explain the two primary approaches leaders can take: task centered and people centered. When leading, leaders and managers can take a task-centered approach, a people-centered approach, or an approach that blends the two. Which one they choose is usually dictated to them by what their followers or subordinates need and what the situation requires. Task orientation is usually practiced when people must focus on getting their work or the job done, as is the case in a crisis. People orientation helps build teams and cooperation between and among individuals and within groups. In most situations leaders must give some emphasis to both people and tasks.

7 Describe the three theories of situational leadership. The three theories are Fiedler's contingency model, House and Mitchell's path-goal theory, and Hersey and Blanchard's life-cycle theory. Fiedler links focus on task or people to conditions in three variables: leader-member relations (good or poor), task structure (structured or unstructured), and leader position power (weak or strong). All three relate to a leader's situation at any given time and underscore the need to be flexible in adopting any orientation.

House and Mitchell's path-goal theory holds that leaders can influence subordinates' motivation by (1) teaching employees the competencies they need to perform to standards and gain rewards, (2) tailoring rewards to meet employees' needs, and (3) acting to support subordinates' efforts. This theory is the basis for the expectancy theory of motivation (Chapter 13). It links subordinates' success to examples and supports provided by their leaders.

Hersey and Blanchard's life-cycle theory states that throughout one's career, the style of leadership he or she requires will change and evolve from the autocratic to the free rein. When employees are new to a job or task, autocratic supervision is appropriate. When they gain experience, employees become more able to contribute and participate in those decisions affecting them and the work. Finally, experienced old-timers and professionals need a free rein to function most effectively.

8 Discuss the three challenges facing leaders. The first challenge has to do with the traditional way of running an organization—few leaders, many followers, and a hierarchy of decision makers. Today's fast-moving markets and business climates call for a much more rapid response to challenges and opportunities. This response cannot take place without empowered individuals at every layer and in every function and process. As companies downsize and outsource, fewer people are left to do the work; and that work is becoming increasingly more technical and demanding.

The second challenge is one of gaining a rapid-response capability. Time is the enemy in most situations. Competitors and markets do not remain static. Customers must be accommodated and their demands met. Empowering employees through open-book management, training, authority sharing, and selective hiring is the key. This allows the frontline to respond rapidly to both challenges and opportunities.

The third challenge leaders face is to make tough, unpleasant decisions; they must often bite the bullet and sublimate their egos. Leaders must have the courage to do what is right in line with the company's core values and their personal moral and ethical codes. When taking these difficult actions, they must obey the law. To do otherwise is to put the future of the organization and its members at risk.

REVIEW QUESTIONS

1. In what ways do a person's traits and skills give them influence over others?
2. How are management and leadership similar? Different?
3. What are the five sources of influence over others in organizations?
4. Do you think it is better to lead through positive or negative motivational means? Why? What are the advantages and disadvantages of each approach?
5. What set of circumstances can you give that would require a leader to use an autocratic style? A participative one? A free-rein style?

6. Under what circumstances should a leader be task centered? People centered? Use a blend of both approaches?
7. What are the basic components of Fiedler's contingency model of leadership? How do they affect a leader's choice to focus on task or people?
8. What does the path-goal theory of leadership tell a leader to do?
9. What does the life-cycle theory of leadership say about the use of the three styles of decision making?
10. What are the three challenges facing leaders today? How can leaders deal with each?

DISCUSSION QUESTIONS FOR CRITICAL THINKING

1. Who is currently a leader to you and why is he or she a leader?
2. Can a manager be a leader by simply relying on his or her positional or formal authority? Why or why not?
3. Is it essential for a manager to have a "moral compass"? Why or why not?

INTERNET EXERCISES

Check the text Web site at http://plunkett.swcollege.com for updated links to the Internet Exercises.

1. What is your leadership style? Blake and Mouton's Managerial Grid is famous for determining leadership style. Did it describe your style accurately? Now that you have a description of your style, what do you plan to do with this information?
http://www.nwlink.com/~donclark/leader/bm_model.html
2. *Transformative Leadership*, a presentation given by Dr. Elizabeth Lolly at the 1996 Ohio Literacy Resource Center Leadership Institute, can help you assess your strength in the Leadership Empowerment Principles. Read the statements that describe some of the key skills and actions needed to apply each principle and then indicate whether this principle is an area of strength for you or one in which you would like to improve.
http://archon.educ.kent.edu/Oasis/Leadership/over2.htm
3. Assess your leadership potential at work by taking the Leadership Test by Cyberia Shrink and Lily Ink. What is your score? What are your general leadership qualities and potential?
http://www.queendom.com/tests/leadership.html

APPLICATION CASE

The End of Olds

"Oldsmobile is the only American automobile more than 100 years old" (Wright, 2000). Yet, on December 12, 2000, General Motors' CEO Rick Wagoner announced that the Oldsmobile Division would be phased out over several years. "It is the oldest automotive brand in America with a history that is rich with innovation and success stories, including dozens of legendary cars, and over the years it was one of the jewels in the General Motors' crown," he said (*Oldsmobile News*, 2000). "Oldsmobile's demise has been a matter of speculation since the early 1990s when its annual sales plummeted" (Miller, 2000). Long branded as an "old man's car" and a "Buick clone," the Oldsmobile was rumored in the automotive press to be headed down the road taken by Packard, Hudson, and Nash.

In 1992 John Rock became Olds' new chief executive. He was previously head of GMC trucks. Given a sense of urgency by the press reports, Rock swung into action. Within one month he had assembled the Olds dealers at the Oldsmobile design center. He showed them the new models that were in the pipeline and asked for their help in creating a strategy to revitalize the Olds division. After several meetings and changes in the mix of members at each, a consensus was reached. "In January 1993, we went to GM's North American Automotive Operations with that plan, to throw out old brands and create new ones . . . ," says Rock (Mateja, 1995).

Another goal in Rock's strategy was to become more "Saturn-like." He moved the division toward "value pricing—offering a particular car with certain options at a specific discounted price" and getting that price without "haggling" with customers. Much of Rock's strategy rested on the success of emerging product lines. Since 1992 new models, such as Aurora, have sold well. In 1996 the Bravada sport utility model returned to the lineup after being absent for one year. In 1997 both the new Ciera—a replacement for the 98—and a redesigned, steel-clad mini-van entered Oldsmobile dealers' showrooms. In 1998 a whole new Achieva arrived, along with a totally redone Cutlass. By that time Rock hoped to reach the final goal in his plan: his retirement to the wilds of Montana.

This strategy did bring in younger buyers, but not in the numbers that Oldsmobile had hoped. "Despite attempts to resurrect Olds with a new lineup and aggressive retail incentives, it sold only 265,878 vehicles during the first eleven months of 2000, putting it on pace for its worst sales year since 1952" (Miller, 2000).

http://www.oldsmobile.com

Questions

1. What kind of leadership style did Rock use with his division's dealers? What kind of leadership style did Rock's boss probably use with him? Was it appropriate?
2. Which leadership traits did Rock exhibit? Which skills?
3. Which of Yukl's leadership behaviors did Rock exhibit?
4. How did Rock's planned retirement help him to make some tough decisions?

Sources: Miller, Joe. "It's the End of the Road for Olds," *The Detroit News*, December 12, 2000, http://detnews.com/2000/autos/0012/12/a01-161212.htm; Wright, Richard A. "Oldsmobile Was America's Oldest Surviving Nameplate," *The Detroit News*, November 6, 2000, http://detnews.com/joyrides/2000/oldsmobile/oldsmobile.htm; Mateja, Jim. "Scary Wakeup Calls Worked for Olds," *Chicago Tribune*, July 10, 1995, sec. 4, p. 5; *Oldsmobile News*. "GM to Restructure Oldsmobile Division," http://www.oldsmobile.com.

VIDEO CASE

Sunshine Cleaning Systems: A Study of Leadership

Sunshine Cleaning Systems is a privately held company headquartered in Florida. The company employs approximately 1,000 people and offers janitorial, pressure cleaning, and window cleaning services. The CEO is Larry Calufetti, a former catcher for the New York Mets, and a former coach in minor league and college baseball. Sunshine Cleaning Systems has some interesting clients, including the Miami Dolphin's Training Center, the Orlando Arena (home of the Orlando Magic), the Florida Citrus Bowl, the Orlando Convention Center, the Florida Turnpike, and the Smithsonian Institute in Washington, D.C.

What makes Sunshine Cleaning Systems unique is the company's coaching leadership style, which is heavily influenced by Larry Calufetti's baseball experiences. The company has implemented a leadership philosophy that encourages the managers at Sunshine to act as "coaches" rather than traditional managers in their relationships with their employees. This approach to leadership is based on the following set of principles, which is well understood by both the managers and rank-and-file employees:

- supportive management
- access to training (and cross-training)
- providing employees with the tools they need to do quality work
- asking employees to accept responsibility
- encouraging innovation
- providing rewards
- promoting from within

In addition, employees are encouraged to feel good about their work and are reinforced by their managers on a continual basis. For instance, the company has an employee-of-the-month program, which is designed to reinforce outstanding work habits. In addition, Larry Calufetti's strong commitment to the coaching leadership style led him to develop Larry's Dream Team, a formal statement that outlines Sunshine's commitment to its employees. This statement is posted throughout the company and provides direction for all managers in their relations with employees. Sunshine's efforts are paying off. The company has very little turnover, which is unusual for a firm in the janitorial industry. Firm sales and profitability are also on solid ground.

By working together, the Sunshine team will continue to grow and provide quality service to its customers. The managers and employees at Sunshine believe that the company's coaching leadership style is an important part of their collective success.

For Discussion:

1. At Sunshine Cleaning Systems, how does "coaching" differ from "managing"? What are the attributes of a good "coach" (in an organizational setting)?
2. Do you believe that Sunshine's low turnover rate is due to its coaching leadership style? If so, how?
3. Think about your own strengths and weaknesses and how you relate to people. Would you fit in as a leader at Sunshine Cleaning Systems? Why or why not?

Team Management and Conflict

KEY TERMS

avoidance
collaboration
committee
compromise
conflict
confrontation
cross-functional team
dysfunctional conflict
executive team
formal team
forming stage
free rider
functional conflict
horizontal team
norming stage
performing stage
process team
product development team
project team
quality assurance team
self-managed work team
smoothing
storming stage
superordinate objective
task force
team
vertical team
virtual team
work team

LEARNING OBJECTIVES

After studying this chapter, you should be able to

1. Discuss the nature of teams and the characteristics of effective teams
2. Identify the types of teams that organizations use
3. Discuss potential uses of teams
4. Use decision-making authority as a characteristic by which to distinguish team type
5. Identify and discuss steps in establishing teams
6. Identify and discuss the roles of team members and team leaders
7. Describe the four stages of team development
8. Discuss team cohesiveness and team norms and their relationship to team performance
9. Evaluate the benefits and costs of teams
10. Discuss the positive and negative aspects of conflict in an organization
11. Identify the sources of conflict in an organization
12. Describe a manager's role in conflict management and potential strategies to manage conflict

MANAGEMENT IN ACTION

Boeing Teams to Success

The Boeing Company is the largest aerospace company in the world, and the 777 jetliner is the most sophisticated product ever made. Since acquiring Rockwell International's space and defense units in 1996 and merging with McDonnell Douglas in 1997, the Boeing Company has grown to 198,000 employees in 60 countries and 26 states. Boeing is NASA's leading contractor and leads the U.S. industry team for the International Space Station (Boeing Overview, January 2001, http://www.boeing.com/companyoffices/aboutus/brief.html).

Boeing Chairman and Chief Executive Officer Phil Condit "led the team that launched the wide-body Boeing 777 airplane. He pioneered management concepts that integrated design/build teams of customers, suppliers and employees to design and produce the 21st-century jet. The 777 'Working Together' team has received numerous aeronautical awards, including the prestigious Collier Award" (Philip M. Condit Executive Biography, January 2001, http://www.boeing.com/companyoffices/aboutus/execprofiles/condit.html).

When Boeing set out to design the 777, a massive project eventually involving 10,000 employees and more than 500 suppliers, top managers knew they wanted an entirely team-based organization; but they weren't sure how to make it all work. After much discussion, Boeing created a hierarchy of teams, a structure meant to get all Boeing work teams pulling in the same direction. "Our goal," said Boeing president, Philip Condit, "is a barrier-free enterprise where all are working to satisfy the customer."

Boeing's 777 project looked like the traditional organizational pyramid; but instead of layers of management, it had three layers of teams. In all there were over 200 cross-functional teams, each made up of people from departments like engineering, manufacturing, and finance. At the top of the pyramid was a management team of the five or six top managers from each discipline, who, as a group, had ultimate responsibility for building the 777 correctly and on time. Underneath this management team was a group of 50 leaders—half each from engineering and operations, set up in 25 to 30 two-person teams—who supervised the 200-plus work teams that had responsibility for specific parts of the plane. These work teams were cross-functional groups of five to fifteen workers—a wing team, a flap team, a tail team.

To manage this project, the top management team held a weekly meeting. The members of the second tier team communicated with the top team through their leaders in engineering and operations and also held meetings in which they handled major issues like schedule delays or quality problems with suppliers. The team of 50 then returned to the work teams with solutions.

While this team structure worked well to move information quickly up the organization, the top management team realized near the end of the 777 project that information wasn't moving well horizontally. In other words, the wing teams were not necessarily communicating as well with the cockpit team as the management team would have liked, causing design glitches. To solve the

Boeing's 777 was designed and built through the expertise and cooperation of over 200 cross-functional work teams.

problem, the management team added a fourth layer of what it called airplane integration teams—five teams, each with twelve to fifteen people drawn from work teams.

The integration teams served as problem solvers and communicators; for example, as the final stages of the project neared, two work teams came into conflict. One team had designed the passenger oxygen system in the same spot that the other had put the system for the gasper, the little nozzle that directs air toward the passenger. One of the teams called in an integration team, which prompted everyone to think about what was best for the airplane. Within three hours the three teams, working together, had developed an ingenious solution: a special clamp that holds both systems.

At the old Boeing—before teams—a similar problem likely would not have been caught until the plane was manufactured. In contrast, the new team structure not only solved the problem, it cut the number of engineering hang-ups on the 777-passenger project by more than half. Boeing spokesman Robert Jorgensen (Anderson, 1997) said, "The way we design and build planes has forever changed because of the 777. And the people element of working in teams forever will change the way we work together and with our customers." ■

Source: Anderson, K. Jackson. "The Best of Times," *HeraldNet*, March 9, 1997, http://www.heraldnet.com/Stories/97/3/9/boeing.htm; Labich, Kenneth. "Boeing's New Dream Machine," *Fortune*, February 19, 1996, http://www.fortune.com/fortune/magazine/1996/960219/boeing.html; Dumaine, Brian. "The Trouble with Teams," *Fortune*, September 5, 1994, pp. 86–92.

INTRODUCTION

http://www.apple.com

http://www.cypress.com

http://www.levistrauss.com

http://www.xerox.com

http://www.ge.com

http://www.fedex.com

http://www.ids.net

http://www.verizon.com

http://www.boeing.com

http://www.marshall.usc.edu/ceo

http://www.marshall.usc.edu/ceo/bios/bio_lawler.html

A not so quiet revolution is taking place in American business. At companies such as Apple Computer, Cypress Semiconductor, Levi Strauss, Xerox, and General Electric, teams are emerging as an organizational force. Companies are realizing that the team approach can ignite superior performance. Scores of service companies, like Federal Express and IDS, have boosted productivity as much as 40 percent by adopting self-managed work teams; Nynex, which merged with Bell Atlantic and is now part of Verizon, used teams to make the difficult transition from a bureaucratic Baby Bell to a high-speed cruiser on the information highway; and Boeing used teams to cut the number of engineering hang-ups on its 777 passenger jet by more than half (Dumaine, 1994). Teams in all their various forms—self-managed work teams, task forces, and project teams are but a few—are changing organizational structures, the way work is approached, the role of managers, and the involvement of workers (Cox, 1992).

Despite all their successes, the use of high performance teams has not spread as fast as some experts expected. A survey conducted by the Center for Effective Organizations at the University of Southern California (USC) revealed that, although 68 percent of Fortune 1,000 companies use self-managed work teams, only 10 percent of the workers are in such teams. Notes USC's Edward Lawler (Dumaine, 1994), "People are very naive about how easy it is to create a team. Teams are the Ferraris of work design. They're high performance, but high maintenance and expensive."

With Professor Lawler's comments in mind, we will discuss how to maximize the potential of teams in this chapter. We will examine types of teams, how teams are created and managed, and their benefits and costs. We will also see how to keep teams functioning effectively through the management of conflict.

NATURE OF TEAMS

Teams Defined

Discuss the nature of teams and the characteristics of effective teams

team
A group of two or more people who interact regularly and coordinate their work to accomplish a common objective.

In an organization a **team** is a group of two or more people who interact regularly and coordinate their work to accomplish a common objective (Larson and La Fasto, 1989). Three points characterize a team:

- First, at least two people must be involved. The ultimate size of the group can vary depending on the nature of the assignment.
- Second, the members must interact regularly and coordinate their work. People who are in the same department but do not interact regularly are not a team; nor are people who have lunch together every day but never actually coordinate their work.
- Third, members of a team must share a common objective. Regardless of the objective—ensuring service quality, designing a new product, or reducing costs—each member works toward a common, shared objective.

Characteristics of Effective Teams

Teams can and do function throughout organizations. Their effectiveness relates directly to how well managers engineer team structure and how team members behave. For example, Boeing's teams share technical and operational information across international borders, time zones, and cultural differences. As Edgar Schein (1969) reported, the characteristics of effective teams include the following:

- Team members are committed to and involved in clear, shared goals.
- All team members feel free to express themselves and participate in discussions and decisions. Each member is valued and heard.
- Members trust each other. In discussions they openly disagree without fear of negative consequences.
- When needs for leadership arise, any member feels free to volunteer. Team leadership varies with the situation.
- Decisions are made by consensus. All team members support final decisions.
- As problems occur, the team focuses on causes, not symptoms. Likewise, when members develop solutions, they direct them at the causes of the problem.
- Team members are flexible in terms of work processes and problem solving. They search for new ways of acting.
- Team members change and grow. All members encourage and support growth.

Types of Teams

Identify the types of teams that organizations use

formal team
A team created by managers to function as part of the organizational structure.

Many different types of teams are emerging in business organizations. These are **formal teams** created by management as a functioning part of the organizational structure. They are not informal nor are they created by social interaction. (For a discussion of informal groups, see Chapter 8.) In terms of origin, not function, we can identify two types of teams: vertical teams and horizontal teams.

Vertical Teams

vertical team
A team composed of a manager and subordinates.

http://www.citicorp.com

http://www.admworld.com

A **vertical team**—sometimes called a *command team* or a *functional team*—is composed of a manager and his or her subordinates in the formal chain of command. A vertical team may include as many as three or four levels of management. Examples include the human resources department at Citicorp, the accounting department at Archer Daniels Midland, and the "wing team" at Boeing. Each fits the definition of *team*: two or more people interacting and coordinating their work for the purpose of achieving a common shared objective. The marketing department illustrated in Figure 15.1 is a vertical team, as are the finance, production, and engineering departments.

Horizontal Teams

horizontal team
A team composed of members drawn from different departments.

A **horizontal team** is made up of members drawn from different departments in an organization (Owens, 1989). In most cases such a team is created to address a specific task or objective. The team may disband after the objective is achieved. Three common kinds of horizontal teams are task forces, cross-functional teams, and committees.

FIGURE 15.1 *Vertical and horizontal teams*

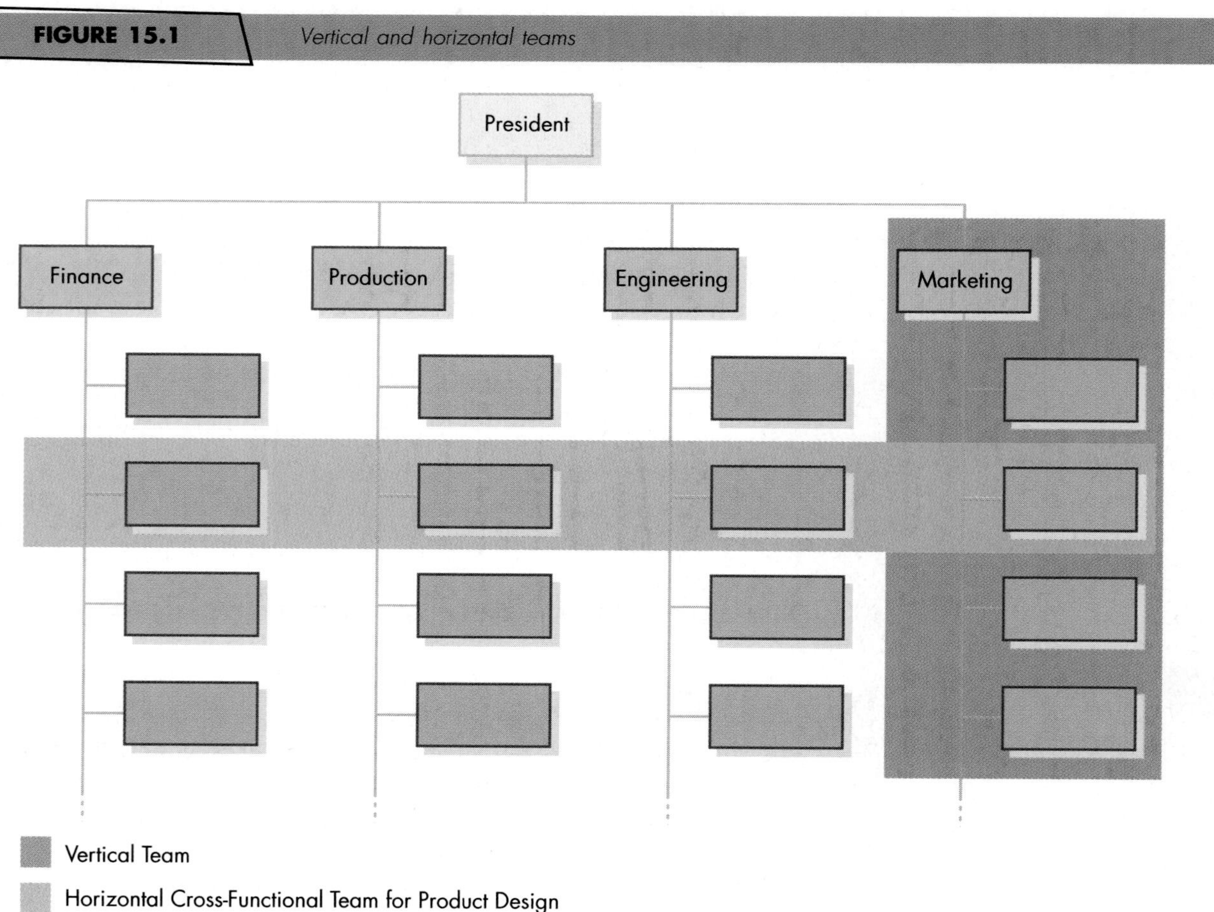

task force
A horizontal team composed of employees from different departments designed to accomplish a limited number of objectives and existing only until it has met the objectives.

http://www.master-ind.com

A **task force** is designed to accomplish a limited number of objectives or tasks, and it is composed of employees from different departments. A task force exists only until it meets its objectives. Master Industries, an injection-molding company in Ohio, formed a task force to implement a smoke-free policy in the workplace within eighteen months. When this objective was attained, the task force disbanded (McKee, 1992).

cross-functional team
A team with an undefined life span designed to bring together the knowledge of various functional areas to work on solutions to operational problems.

http://www.sequins.com

A **cross-functional team** harnesses the knowledge of people from various functional areas to solve problems. Like task forces, cross-functional teams focus on objectives, but they have a continuous life. At Sequins International, a New York-based manufacturer of sequins, two cross-functional teams—one for product satisfaction, the other for customer support—have been created. Composed of representatives from manpower, machines, methods, and material they pursue their ongoing goal to improve product satisfaction or customer service (Ettorre, 1995). Figure 15.1 includes a cross-functional product design team.

committee
A horizontal team—either ad hoc or permanent—designed to focus on one objective; members represent functional areas of expertise.

A **committee** may be ad hoc (set up to do a job and then disbanded) or standing (permanent). The work of a standing committee—handling grievances, for instance—is ongoing. Committee representation may be chosen by functional area to reflect department views. Individuals are not necessarily chosen for specific technical ability, as members of a task force are. Thus, to ensure participation from all areas, a budget committee may have a representative from each of the major functional areas (Dumaine, 1992).

PHILOSOPHICAL ISSUES OF TEAM MANAGEMENT

Given the current trend toward the team approach in American business—and reflecting on Professor Lawler's words earlier in the chapter—many managers are asking, "What can teams do?" and "How do they function within the organization?"

How to Use Teams

3

Discuss potential uses of teams

The purpose of a team is to accomplish one or more objectives. A team provides a vehicle for combining skills, securing commitment and involvement, and sharing expertise and opinions in pursuit of a specific objective. The objective could be to improve quality, design a product, solve a problem, or carry out departmental work. Although managers may choose from unlimited team options, as Figure 15.2 shows, there are five main categories of teams: product development teams, project teams, quality teams, process teams, and work teams.

Product Development Teams

product development team
A team organized to create new products.

http://www.ibm.com

Whether they are task forces or cross-functional teams, **product development teams** are organized to create new products. At Berrios Manufacturing Company, CEO Willis Berrios has created teams that combine people from different areas of expertise with the objective of smoothly bringing a new product to market. The teams include representatives from quality control, engineering, production, systems design, marketing, and manufacturing. IBM used a product development team to create the Think-Pad 701 C laptop PC, code-named Butterfly, that became the first on-time product from the PC group in years. The Butterfly, with

FIGURE 15.2 Potential uses for teams

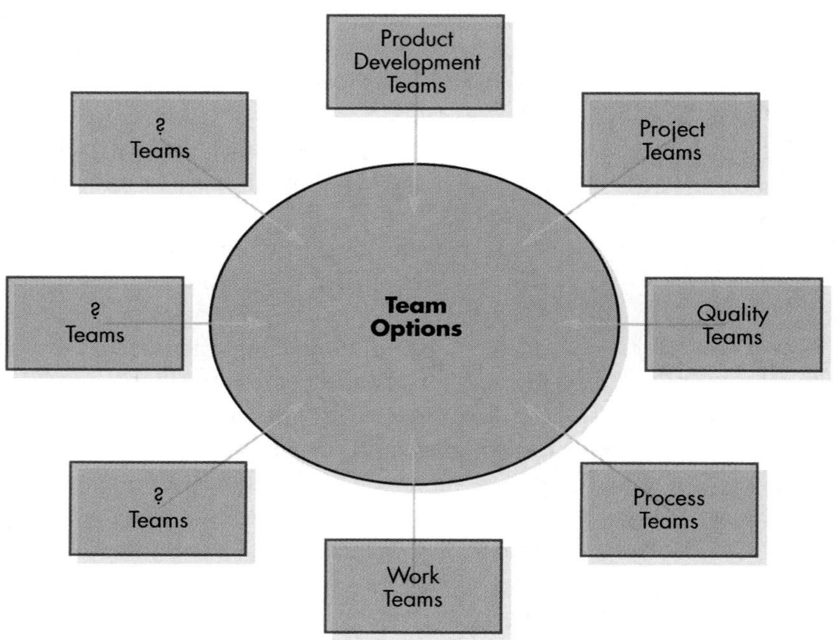

two keyboard halves that come together on a single plane, was designed in one year. In the old system, product developers, working independently, took years to build a prototype. For example, it took six years for an earlier IBM innovation—an eraserlike pointing device for portables—to hit the market (Sager, 1995).

Project Teams

project team
A team organized to complete a specific task in the organization.

http://www.ti.com

http://www.gd.com

Instead of focusing on development of a single product, managers often assemble **project teams** (sometimes called *problem-solving teams*) to complete a specific task in an organization. Project teams flourish at Xerox, Apple Computer, Texas Instruments, General Dynamics, and as we have seen at Boeing. Teams of engineers and operations specialists move in to work out operating problems in systems and apply their creativity to develop strategic delivery systems (Dumaine, 1994).

http://www.chrysler.com

Sometimes, to address an important project, teams operate outside the scope of the organizational structure. Although part of the formal organization, such teams maintain their own reporting structures. In these cases members perceive their team as an independent and separate entity with plenty of "corporate breathing room" (Daft, 1994). For example, when Chrysler Corporation sets out to create a new model or revamp an old model, it creates a self-contained multidisciplinary project team from engineering, design, manufacturing, marketing, and finance. CEO Robert Eaton and a dozen senior managers act with the team to sketch a vision for the vehicle and set aggressive goals: for design, performance, fuel economy, and cost. The goals are transferred into a contract with the team, after which the team is turned loose. Explains Eaton, "The contract simply sets out all the objectives we hope to achieve. Then they go away and do it, and they don't get back to us unless they have a major problem. And so far they aren't having any major problems" (Gunn, 1995).

virtual team
A team where members primarily interact electronically because they are physically separated (by time and/or space).

Team members do not always have to be in the same place at the same time. One type of project team is a **virtual team** where team members primarily interact electronically. This is a result of computers and the Internet, global competition, and travel time and expenses. Virtual teams have three defining characteristics that separate them from traditional teams (Fisher, 1997):

- Members are distributed across multiple locations
- Membership can be extremely diverse in skills and culture
- Team members can join or depart the team in midstream

An example of a very successful virtual team was Boeing's 777 development project that included United Airlines engineers as well as a horizontal cross-section of the Boeing organization. Virtual teams may use Usenet or newsgroups, the subject of this chapter's Managing Technology feature, to share information.

MANAGING TECHNOLOGY
Usenet

Usenet is a text-only section of the Internet made up of newsgroups, which are electronic bulletin boards organized by topic and subtopic. It started in 1979 when a pair of Duke University graduate students thought of a way to link up computers at Duke with machines at the University of North Carolina so that Unix operating-system devotees could exchange information. From there, Usenet's network has grown steadily. It contains thousands upon thousands of newsgroups containing millions of posted messages about every subject imaginable. To comprehend the possible audience of a newsgroup—imagine if one of the bulletin boards on campus could be read by millions of people all over the world, and if millions of people all over the world could post messages to the bulletin board—that is the scope of a newsgroup.

Usenet is arranged in hierarchies of newsgroups, with general categories broken down into narrower subcategories. For example, rec.sport is divided into 34 groups from rec.sport.archery to rec.sport.waterski, and those groups are themselves subdivided. The distinctions between groups may seem arbitrary to an outsider, but it's of considerable importance to the regulars in those groups. Such fine distinctions mean that many newsgroups are actually fairly small communities where reputations matter.

Participants post "articles" or "messages." Some newsgroups are "moderated." The messages are first sent to a moderator for approval before appearing in the newsgroup. The experts of the boards are well known—and given great respect—while newcomers must earn their place by proving their worth. In the most highly trafficked newsgroups, there may be one to at most a dozen experts, and hundreds of people interacting with those experts.

Information travels from database to database as robots and spider technology are used to acquire and distribute information. Steer away from posting personal information in Internet newsgroups. They are open to everyone to read. Once something is posted on a newsgroup, it's basically available forever, thanks to Deja.com and other archives of newsgroup postings. However, authors can remove their own postings from Deja.com's archive. Home addresses, telephone numbers, and other personal data are best left to emails with individuals you know rather than in public postings, or within public replies to other newsgroup messages. You wouldn't give your personal information to anyone who asked for it on the street, so why post it on the Internet?

Quality Teams

As we have emphasized throughout the text, quality and quality assurance have become driving forces in American industry. Many firms have established *quality improvement teams* that monitor and ensure quality. An early quality assurance tool was the quality circle. As discussed in Chapter 3, a quality circle is a group of volunteers from the same or related work areas who meet regularly to identify the quality issues facing the company or department and offer suggestions for improvement. Other organizations have developed **quality assurance teams**, whose mission it is to guarantee the quality of services and products by contacting customers and working with vendors. For example, customer service teams consisting of seven to ten AT&T Global Information Solutions employees are being assembled in the United States and abroad and are being given team training with customer participation. The teams number several hundred, are in 110 countries, and are made up of representatives throughout the organization. Once the training is completed, members stay in contact with the customer through regularly scheduled meetings and customer calls. "In the past you may have had sales and marketing people working together with specific customers, but what we are talking about here are representatives from throughout the corporation focused on individual customers. This transformation represents a total restructuring of how a corporation does business. Customer-focused teams have access to local and global resources in order to speed decisions, increase our responsiveness, and provide world class solutions," says Des Randall, vice president of the global sales program for AT&T Global Information Systems (Executive Management Forum, "Customer . . . ," 1994). AT&T Global Information Systems is now part of NCR Corporation.

quality assurance team
A team created to guarantee the quality of services and products, contact customers, and work with vendors.

http://www.att.com

http://www.ncr.com

Process Teams

The stimulus provided by companies who have reengineered has led to process teams. A **process team** groups members who perform the organization's major processes into teams. A process team not only performs the processes but also refines them. Most organizations like Karolinska Hospital, this chapter's Global Applications feature, develop process teams as they restructure from a functional organization design. The process teams remove departmental barriers and emphasize coordination. For example, Olin Industries transformed fourteen functional departments into eight process teams with names like "fulfillment," "new products," and "sources." Similarly, Zeneca Agricultural Products (now known as Syngenta) CEO, Bob Wood, took apart every business process from product development to order fulfillment to create a dozen process teams structured to satisfy the customer (Stewart, 1994).

process team
A team that groups members who perform and refine the organization's major processes.

http://www.olin.com

http://www.syngenta-us.com

Work Teams

When a company creates a small multiskilled team that does all the tasks previously performed by the individual members of a functional department or departments, the group is known as a **work team**. Work team members assume responsibility for the function or tasks, sharing skills and complementing each other. Since adopting work teams, Frito-Lay's plant in Lubbock, Texas, has logged double-digit cost cuts and seen its quality jump from the bottom 20 to the top 6 of Frito's 48 U.S. factories. The eleven-member work teams are responsible for everything

work team
A team, composed of multiskilled workers, that does all the tasks previously done by individual members in a functional department or departments.

http://www.fritolay.com

GLOBAL APPLICATIONS
The Patient Comes First

In 1992 Karolinska Hospital in Stockholm faced financial difficulties. Chief executive Jan Lindsten, knowing that any budgetary cuts would impair the quality of patient care, recruited the services of the Boston Consulting Group. Its recommendation was to reorganize the structure of the hospital around patient flow. Instead of bouncing a patient around from department to department, BCG advised Karolinska to look at a patient's illness to recovery journey as a process, with pit stops in admission, surgery, and recovery. Karolinska began the conversion to process teams.

What this meant in practice for Karolinska was that it had to restructure itself along patient dimensions, rather than operating in terms of specializations as before. With process teams, for instance, a patient meets with a surgeon and a doctor of internal medicine together rather than separately. The result: better care and fewer hospital visits.

By focusing on the patient, Karolinska moved from 47 departments to 11 process teams. To provide coordination and manage patient flow, the hospital created a new position—sort of a "process doctor"—titled nurse coordinator. The responsibilities of the nurse coordinator focus on guaranteeing "smooth baton handoffs" between or within process teams. In a radical departure from practice, the doctors report to the nurse coordinator.

http://www.ks.se/english

Source: Jacob, Rahul. "The Struggle to Create an Organization for the 21st Century," *Fortune*, April 3, 1995, pp. 98–99.

from product processing (potatoes for the potato chip team, for example) to equipment maintenance, to team scheduling. The team even interviews potential employees for the team. To help them devise ways to produce and ship products more efficiently, teammates receive weekly reports on cost, quality, and service performance (Zellner, 1994).

4 Use decision-making authority as a characteristic by which to distinguish team type

How Much Independence to Give Teams

How much authority and operating freedom should teams have? The continuum in Figure 15.3 shows the independence that various types of teams have in day-to-day operations.

FIGURE 15.3 *Continuum of autonomy*

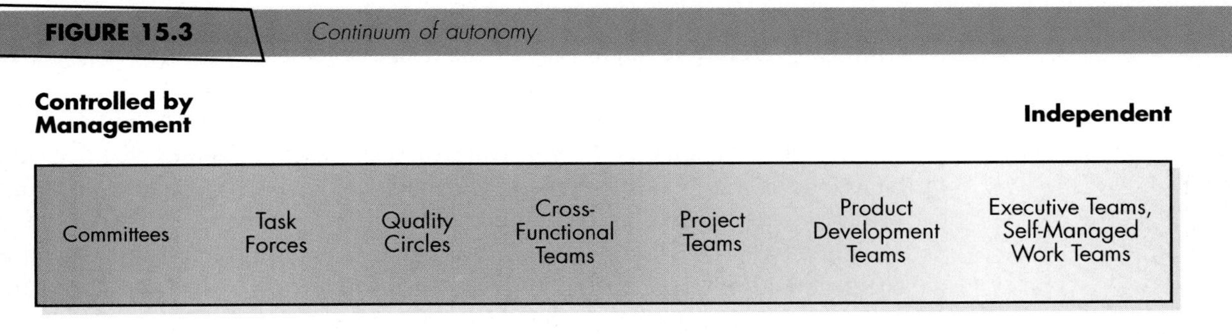

Teams Closely Controlled by Management

Teams holding the least authority for decision making are committees, task forces, and quality circles. Although some task forces may make decisions within a normally defined charge, most operating committees and task forces are not decision-making bodies; they make recommendations to management. Quality circles, with greater latitude in defining quality, still have little authority. Like other closely controlled teams, quality circles make recommendations to management. They usually work in a setting in which the circle facilitator is either a manager or a trained worker-facilitator, and they rely on management to implement their recommendations (Reynolds, 1992).

Teams with Moderate Independence

Cross-functional, project, and product development teams have more decision-making authority than closely controlled teams. Although empowered to make many decisions about the work at hand, management appoints the leaders of moderately independent teams. Therefore, the leaders of these teams tend to make decisions that support management. In addition, management controls budgetary decisions as well as team membership (Greenwald, 1992).

Independent Work Teams

Self-managed, or self-directed, work teams and executive teams are independent. Each controls day-to-day decision making.

self-managed work team
A team, fully responsible for its own work, that sets goals, creates its own schedules, prepares its own budgets, and coordinates its work with other departments.

A **self-managed work team** assumes complete responsibility for its work. The team manages itself, sets goals, takes responsibility for the quality of the output, creates its own schedules, reviews its own performance as a group, prepares its own budgets, and coordinates its work with that done by the company's other departments or divisions. These teams plan, control, and improve operations independent of formal management supervision (Byham, 1992).

Self-managed teams are used anywhere in an organization where work units exist—in production, customer service, engineering, or design, for example. If a company has created process teams, they too may be self-managed. Companies using self-management teams report that team membership gives workers control over their jobs and a bigger stake in the company, resulting in the blossoming of creativity (Case, 1992). Two examples support these points. First, at Taco Bell managers discarded an outmoded command-and-control management style that kept a tight reign on employees. Managers replaced it with team-managed units in which frontline crews run the day-to-day operations without supervision. Taco Bell top managers report an increased sense of ownership and responsibility for customer service and overall unit performance (Executive Management Forum, 1994).

http://www.tacobell.com

http://www.pubimage.com

A second example is the self-managed work teams at Published Image, a financial newsletter publisher in Boston. Founder and CEO Eric Gresham, frustrated with newsletters-in-process hitting bottlenecks from edit to art to production, created "little Published Images"—self-managed work teams responsible for their own client newsletters, start to finish. Today, teams with names like Quality Matters run their own businesses. Each team has its own editor, art director, and salesperson, and a couple of junior staffers. As a self-contained business, teams line up clients and negotiate prices. They take responsibility for producing their client

Since implementing team-managed units, Taco Bell managers report an increased sense of ownership and responsibility for customer satisfaction.

newsletters, collect their own accounts receivable, and keep their own books. Since the changeover, earnings are up 35 percent and the company's own customer satisfaction measures are up 78 percent (Case, 1995).

http://store.nordstrom.com

executive team
A team consisting of two or more people to do the job traditionally held by one upper-level manager.

In the executive suites at Xerox and Nordstrom, managers decided that the jobs of *chair* and *president* were too complex for one person to handle. As a result, these responsibilities were put into the hands of **executive teams**. At Seattle-based Nordstrom, three Nordstrom brothers shared the chair and four managers shared the president's position. In the case of the chairpersons, the decisions were made by committee, but were generally limited to the control of strategic direction. Day-to-day management was left to the four presidents. "Like the cochairmen, the presidents have ample debate, they say, and resolve most disagreements by focusing on what would be best for the customer . . . '(we) leave our egos at the doorstop.'" Each of the copresidents concentrated on his or her own specialty area and acted with great autonomy (Yang, 1992).

ESTABLISHMENT OF TEAM ORGANIZATION

5

Identify and discuss steps in establishing teams

Team management represents a fundamental change from conventional ways of doing business, thinking, and managing. Consequently, the decision to adopt team management requires a philosophical commitment by top executives and careful, systematic implementation. The task of setting up work teams among employees must begin at the top (Brown, 1992).

Process of Team Building

Successful team building requires a fresh assessment of the organization's basics. Figure 15.4 lists the steps involved (McKee, 1992). The paragraphs that follow will describe each step in turn.

FIGURE 15.4 *Steps in the process of team building*

Step 1: Assessing feasibility. Will team building work? How long will it take? Is there a commitment to teams?
Step 2: Identifying priorities. What are the critical needs of the organization? Where can teams make an impact?
Step 3: Defining mission and objectives. What is the organization trying to achieve? How can teams help attain those goals?
Step 4: Uncovering and eliminating barriers to team building. What lack of skills, cultural peculiarities, and process specifics might limit teams?
Step 5: Starting with small teams. Where can the team approach begin? Which priorities will most benefit from teams?
Step 6: Planning for training needs. What training or guidance is needed to make teams effective?
Step 7: Planning to empower. Can managers let go? Are they willing to let people make mistakes?
Step 8: Planning for feedback and development time. What type and frequency of feedback is needed? Can management be patient?

Assessing Feasibility

Will the team approach work? For the organization new to teams, a feasibility study should be the starting point. The study should be a thorough, penetrating review of mission, resources (especially personnel), and current and projected circumstances. The study should provide reasonable estimates of how long it might take to institute teams and what kind of commitment is required.

Identifying Priorities

An assessment of concerns by order of urgency should reveal the points where teams may be effective. The concerns could include customer needs, production processes and capacity, and delivery systems. This step should eliminate the most common trouble with teams. According to USC's Edward Lawler, most companies rush out and form the wrong kind of team for the wrong job (Dumaine, 1994).

Defining Mission and Objectives

Before an organization begins to build teams, managers should take care that the company's mission and objectives are solid, well defined, and accepted throughout the organization.

Uncovering and Eliminating Barriers to Team Building

Three kinds of barriers impede teams: subject matter barriers, process barriers, and cultural barriers.

- Subject matter barriers arise when employees and managers are not sufficiently knowledgeable or technically proficient. Without adequate expertise, teams fail.
- Process barriers stem from unwieldy procedural approaches that limit teams' ability to do their work. Cumbersome approval processes and communication channels that follow the chain of command are incompatible with effective team operation.

- Cultural barriers are ways of thinking that run counter to the team approach. Especially in long-established firms, powerful departments may be unwilling to relinquish authority or to change cherished habits.

Such barriers must be identified and overcome; any one of these can stop teams cold.

Starting with Small Teams

Begin team projects and planning in a pocket of the company—one of the clear priority areas. A sound idea is to begin by creating a design team that represents a cross section of the company. The purpose of the team is not to design a product, but to create other teams.

Planning for Training Needs

At the outset, top or middle managers should offer their unreserved help and guidance to teams as those groups refine their objectives and boundaries (as Chrysler's top managers do with project teams when they are in their formative stages). Team members will probably need training in planning, the effective use of meetings, and team dynamics. Members of cross-functional teams will need skills training. Recognizing this, when XEL, a manufacturer of communications equipment, committed to teams, CEO Bill Sanko set up "XEL University." The curriculum includes 30 classes on topics from soldering to problem solving. On average each worker spends five hours a month in class (Cronin, 1994).

http://www.xel.com

Planning to Empower

Executives and other managers must empower workers when creating teams. Senior people need to step back and let the team members make decisions, including making mistakes and failing. Empowering involves giving team members the opportunities to fail as well as to succeed.

Planning for Feedback and Development Time

Teams require feedback. Eventually, teams develop their own feedback mechanisms. Initially, however, it is vital that the team builders provide one. Simultaneously, in the team environment, individuals must have ample opportunity to grow and develop. Managers must be patient.

Launching teams often raises unfamiliar issues and procedures. The process can be intimidating as well as confusing. Companies that are beginning a team program can smooth the process by using consultants who specialize in team building. Skilled and experienced consultants can design a process, assist the organization in the implementation, train workers and managers in new roles and in new ways of thinking, and identify potential barriers. Even with this assistance, however, team building takes time and patience. As management guru Peter Drucker notes, "You can't rush teams. It takes five years just to learn to build a team and decide what kind you want." The team system requires massive changes of habits (Executive Management Forum, 1995):

- Individuals who used to compete against each other for recognition, raises, and resources will have to learn to collaborate with each other.

- Workers who used to be paid for their individual efforts will be rewarded based on their own efforts plus the efforts of coworkers.
- Supervisors who used to be directive in their style will have to become facilitative: coaching workers instead of giving orders.

Team-Building Considerations

Once top managers have decided to create teams and have prepared a comprehensive blueprint of the team-building process, they must make decisions about the details of specific teams. They must make decisions about team size, member roles, and team leadership, for example.

Team Size

As previously noted, it is best to begin a team program with small teams—that is, teams having fewer than twelve members. Small teams tend to reach consensus more readily than do large teams. In addition, small teams allow more opportunity for interaction and self-expression, and they tend not to break into subgroups. Small size allows members to use their diverse skills, to cross train, and to solve problems aggressively.

If possible, small teams should be maintained after the start-up phase. As teams become larger, team members have more difficulty interacting, becoming a cohesive unit, and communicating. In large teams subgroups may form with their own agendas, and conflict occurs more readily than it does in small teams (Shaw, 1985). Nathan Myhrvold, Microsoft's senior vice president for advanced technology, echoes this point. "Although the temptation is there to throw bodies at a project, 8 people is right for our teams." Myhrvold observes that as teams get larger, employees must spend more time communicating what's already inside their heads and less time actually applying knowledge to accomplish their work. The productivity of each employee diminishes quickly (Deutschman, 1994).

http://www.microsoft.com

Small teams—those with fewer than twelve members—seem to be most successful.

Member Roles

Identify and discuss the roles of team members and team leaders

As GB Tech, the subject of this chapter's Valuing Diversity feature, knows, effective teams display balance. To achieve balance requires people with diverse technical abilities and those with complementing interpersonal skills. Some members play task-oriented roles and others meet team needs for encouragement and harmony (Prince, 1989). Glenn Parker (1990) reported that the typical team includes roles for task specialists and social specialists. Roles for task specialists include the following:

- The *contributor*, a data-driven person who supplies needed information and pushes for high team performance standards
- The *challenger*, a team player who constantly questions the goals, methods, and even the ethics of the team
- The *initiator*, the person who proposes new solutions, new methods, and new systems for team problems

Roles for the social specialists include the following:

- The *collaborator*, the "big picture" person who urges the team to stay with its vision and to achieve it
- The *communicator*, the person who listens well, facilitates well, and humanizes the work of the team
- The *cheerleader*, the person on the team who encourages and praises individual and team efforts
- The *compromiser*, the team member who will shift opinions to maintain harmony

Having individuals in a team who can perform two or more of these roles is quite possible—even desirable. Regardless, the objective is to achieve balance. For sustained effectiveness, each team's task environments and interpersonal environments must sustain and energize members.

VALUING DIVERSITY
Experience Counts

GB Tech Inc., a Houston-based information systems company, needed help in writing bid proposals for subcontracts from the National Aeronautics and Space Administration. GB Tech managers believed the solution was to team company staff with experienced retirees. The retirees would bring much needed technical expertise to the job of completing the complex paperwork. The experienced retirees, who used to work for aerospace corporations, could also help enhance the reputation of GB Tech, a relative newcomer. As Gale Burkett, the company's chairman and CEO, noted, "We were concerned about whether we would be accepted because we were still a fairly new company."

The company began advertising for candidates in several high-tech disciplines. Respondents were carefully screened for technical as well as team skills. Ten retired technical team members were eventually hired. Each functioned effectively within teams as an internal consultant.

GB Tech, in turn, has prospered from the experience diversity brought. The company's revenues have grown from $160,000—before recruiting began—to $7.8 million today. Employment skyrocketed from 14 workers to 415. CEO Burkett attributed much of that growth to the efforts and advice of the retirees.

http://www.gbtech.net

Source: Litvan, Laura M. "Casting a Wider Employment Net," *Nation's Business* (December 1994), pp. 49–51.

Team Leadership

http://www.gore.com

A key consideration in effective teams is team leadership. In self-managed teams, the team members provide leadership. For example, at W. L. Gore & Associates, famous for Gore-Tex waterproof fabric, the leader evolves from within the team. The leader is not appointed; he or she achieves the position by assuming leadership, which must be approved in a consensus reached through discussion—not a vote (Huey, 1994).

Team leaders appointed by management require a special set of skills. The role must be filled by someone with values oriented toward teamwork and cooperation. Effective team leaders create a noncompetitive atmosphere, renew trust, think reasonably, share leadership, encourage members to assume as much responsibility as they can handle, and positively reinforce even the slightest contributions. At the same time team leaders need to keep their teams focused on results (Executive Management Forum, 1995).

http://www.northgrum.com

As an effective team leader for a data storage system team on Northrop Grumman's B2 bomber project, Eric Doremus embodies these abilities. The first time he met with the 40 members of the B2 bomber team, he admitted he would not be much help with technical problems. "My most important task was not trying to figure out everybody's job. It was to help this team feel as if they owned the project by getting them whatever information, financial or otherwise, they needed. I knew that if we could charge up the hill together, we would be successful." Doremus was right. His team shaped the first prototype of the data storage unit in two years and delivered a fully functional unit in less than three (Caminiti, 1995). Doremus and other successful team leaders provide these tips:

- Don't be afraid to admit ignorance.
- Know when to intervene.
- Learn to truly share power.
- Worry about what you take on, not what you give up.
- Get used to learning the job.

MANAGEMENT OF TEAM PROCESSES

Once teams are in place, managers need to address special concerns regarding the management of internal team processes. The specific processes, which relate to the changing dynamics resulting from the team structure, include the stages of team development, team cohesiveness, team norms, and team personality.

Stages of Team Development

7

Describe the four stages of team development

When a team is created, its members do not come together instantly; rather, the team goes through distinct stages (Tuckman, 1965; Gersick, 1989). Figure 15.5 shows the four stages of development: forming, storming, norming, and performing.

Forming

forming stage
The phase of team development in which team members are becoming acquainted.

During the **forming stage**, individual members become acquainted. Members test behaviors to determine which are acceptable and which are unacceptable to individuals in the group. This stage is marked by a high degree of uncertainty. As a

FIGURE 15.5 *Stages of team development*

result, the individuals accept the power and authority of both formal and informal leaders. An important task for the team leader in this stage is to provide sufficient time and a suitable atmosphere for team members to get to know each other.

Storming

storming stage
The phase of team development characterized by disagreement and conflict as individual roles and personalities emerge.

In the **storming stage**, disagreement and conflict occur. Individual personalities emerge and team members assert their opinions. Disagreements may arise over priorities, immediate goals, or methods. Coalitions or subgroups may emerge as a means to resolve disagreements. The team is not yet unified; some unsuccessful teams never get beyond this stage. The team leader's role during this stage is to openly encourage the necessary interaction. With sound leadership, the group can work through its disagreements and enter the next stage.

Norming

norming stage
The phase of team development in which disagreement and conflict have been resolved and team members enjoy unity and focus.

As the pattern in Figure 15.5 suggests, the team comes together in the **norming stage**. With disagreements and conflicts resolved, the team achieves unity, consensus about who holds the power, and an understanding of the roles members will play. The team is now focused; it has oneness—a sense of team cohesion. The team leader builds on this newfound unity and helps to clarify the team's values and norms.

Performing

performing stage
The phase of team development in which team members progress toward team objectives, handle problems, coordinate work, and confront each other if necessary.

http://www.textron.com

In the **performing stage**, the team begins to function and moves toward accomplishing its objectives. Having accepted the oneness achieved during the norming stage, team members interact well with each other. They deal with problems, coordinate work, and confront each other if necessary. During this stage the team leader's role is to provide and maintain the balance between various members' requirements.

As Ellen Lord, a team leader at Davidson Interior's, a division of Textron, found, it takes a good team leader to help teams through the stages. According to Lord, team leaders "must have patience and presence of mind to act like a parent, teacher, and referee all at once." When forming her product development team, Lord carefully screened workers before inviting them to join; but this careful selection did not ease the team's forming process. "We put all the people in one room and they had to work with each other. The people from different functions didn't know each other, they couldn't ask favors, and infighting was pretty intense." The storming stage brought even more intensity and conflict. Team members sometimes got into fights. "A neatnik sitting next to a slob lost his cool. People were emotional about what kind of coffee was brewing in the pot. The manufacturing types thought the engineering members were focused on trivia and bluntly let them know" (Dumaine, 1994).

Eventually, according to Lord, the team came together; it reached the norming stage. The team members realized that all of them were doers who had a depth of knowledge they could apply. The team then began to perform; and perform it did. Lord's product development team created a high-tech coating that makes plastic for cars look exactly like chrome, but it won't rust, scratch, or crack. The grills of Ford's Lincoln cars contain the new material; and the automaker plans to use it on other lines.

http://www.ford.com

Team Cohesiveness

Discuss team cohesiveness and team norms and their relationship to team performance

An important dimension of team dynamics is cohesiveness. As discussed in Chapter 8, cohesiveness, or cohesion, is the extent to which members are attracted to the team and motivated to remain together. In a highly cohesive team, members are committed to team activities, pull together to accomplish the activities, are happy with the success of the team, and are committed to staying in the team. In contrast, members of less cohesive teams are not team focused, are less concerned about team objectives, and are more ready to leave the team.

Factors Determining Team Cohesiveness

Teams with few members, frequent interaction, clear objectives, and identifiable success tend to be cohesive. Teams are less cohesive when groups are large, when team size or members' location prevents frequent interaction, when objectives are ambiguous, and when team efforts do not achieve success (Shaw, 1985). Figure 15.6 illustrates the factors that determine cohesiveness.

Results of Team Cohesiveness

Figure 15.6 also shows the outcome of team cohesiveness. High cohesiveness contributes to effectiveness and high morale. If cohesiveness is low, the team is less likely to achieve its objectives and morale will be low (Cartright and Zandler, 1968).

Cohesiveness and success result from each other. High cohesiveness contributes to high achievement, which makes the team more cohesive. Knowing this, team leaders should foster cohesiveness by establishing clear direction, providing for frequent interaction (in regard to work and nonwork topics), and designing small groups.

Team Norms

As discussed in Chapter 8, a team norm is a standard of behavior that all team members accept. Norms are the ground rules, or guidelines, that tell team members what they can or cannot do under certain circumstances; they provide boundaries of acceptable behavior. Individuals conform to these norms.

The team itself sets team norms. Through an informal process, the key values, role expectations, and performance expectations emerge as norms. At Boeing, team members developed a set of values and expectations. The teams believed in open communication and collaborative problem solving. These norms set the ground rules and were vital to the success of the teams.

FIGURE 15.6 Determinants and results of team cohesiveness

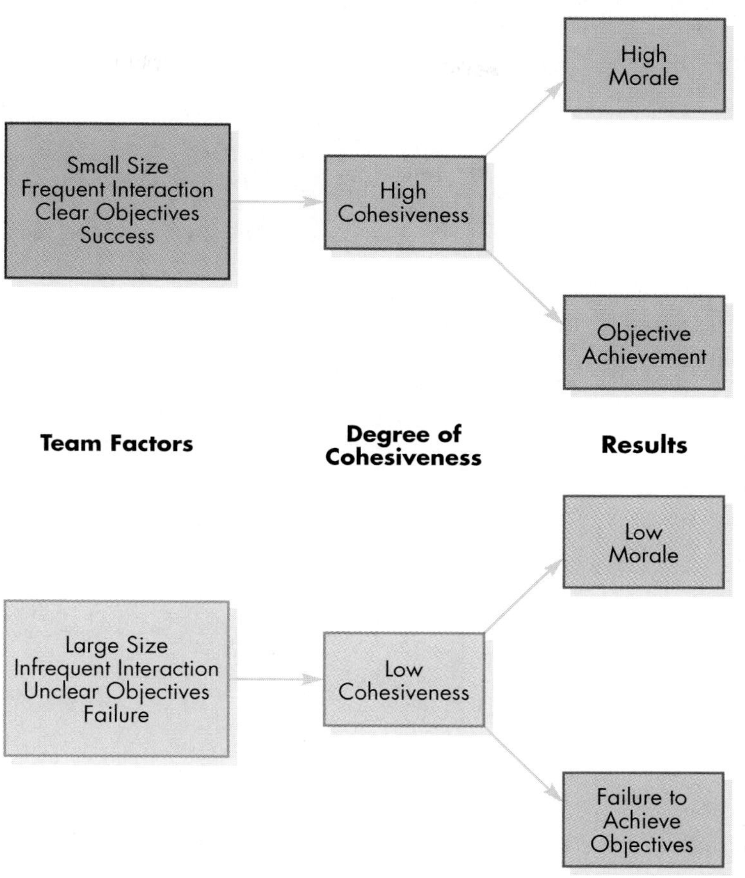

A key norm for teams is one that identifies the acceptable level of performance—high, low, or moderate. Together with team cohesiveness, this norm is a critical determinant of team productivity. As Figure 15.7 shows, productivity is highest when the team is highly cohesive and has a high performance norm (quadrant A). Moderate productivity occurs when cohesiveness is low, because team members are less committed to performance norms (quadrant B). Low-to-moderate productivity occurs when cohesiveness is low and the performance norm is low (quadrant C). The lowest productivity occurs when the team members are highly cohesive in their commitment *not* to perform (quadrant D).

Team Personality

A team's personality is closely related to its norms (Uris, 1964). A personality for a team results from team members' cohesiveness and norms, the pressures they face, their experiences, and their successes and failures. The team can be enthusiastic, energetic, and cooperative—or just the reverse. A team leader must monitor the personality of the team, identify its strengths and weaknesses, and then supply the leadership to remedy weaknesses and build on strengths.

FIGURE 15.7 *Effects of cohesiveness and performance norms on productivity*

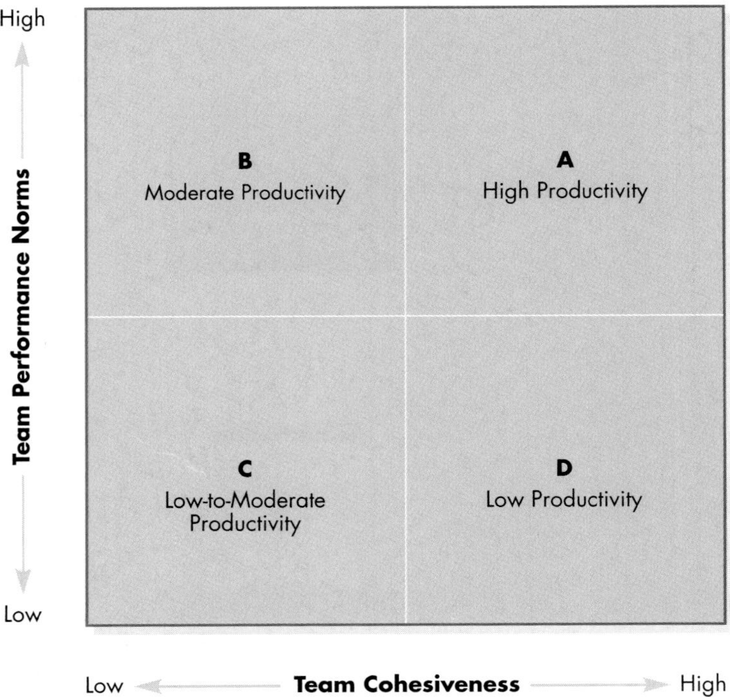

MEASUREMENTS OF TEAM EFFECTIVENESS

Evaluate the benefits and costs of teams

The decision to create teams, like every management decision, generates benefits and costs. Team effectiveness is measured by weighing these benefits and costs.

Benefits of Teams

If sound processes and techniques underlie team building and management, an organization can harness the benefits of a team. These benefits include synergy, increased skills and knowledge, flexibility, and commitment.

Synergy

A team of employees working together develops synergy; it produces more and has more creativity and energy than do the same number of individuals working alone. Working in the team environment provides camaraderie and sharing that is often absent in normal structures. When using productivity as a measure of synergy, we find that increases ranging from 30 to 50 percent are not uncommon, especially in manufacturing and services (Executive Management Forum, 1995). As noted earlier, companies like Chrysler and IBM report significant improvement in product development cycles; and, as Sequins International and Published Images can attest, customer service significantly improves.

Increased Skills and Knowledge

In a team the skills and knowledge of the members increase. This increase is due, in part, to training. In addition to formal training, when individuals are exposed to jobs other than their own, they naturally pick up skills and knowledge from other workers. The result is their increasing worth to themselves and to the company.

Flexibility

As team workers become more adaptable in their attitudes and capacity to perform, the organization gains flexibility. The broader knowledge base of team members allows them to adjust to changes in work demands and work flow and to respond positively to emergencies. Moreover, the enhanced skill of individual team members permits improved response to organizational demands.

Commitment

http://www.goodyear.com

In an era highlighted by employee demotivation and lack of commitment, teams provide the opportunity for workers to "own" their work. As more companies move toward self-managed work teams and empowerment, the satisfaction and commitment level of employees increases. At Goodyear, former CEO Stanley Gault proudly boasted, "The teams at Goodyear are now telling the boss how to run things—and I must say, I'm not doing a half-bad job because of it" (Greenwald, 1992).

Costs of Teams

The major costs associated with implementing a team concept include power-realignment costs, training expenses, lost productivity, free-riding costs, and loss of productive workers.

Power-Realignment Costs

Implementing a team-centered approach results in loss of power by lower- and middle-level managers. The power in the organization shifts from central management to the team and team worker. If adjustment is difficult and resistance occurs, the cost in time and money can be high. This situation is especially true if former managers who become new team leaders embrace the job in words only. J. D. Bryant of Texas Instruments knows because that's what he did. Says Bryant, "I didn't buy into teams . . . I never let the operators do any scheduling or any ordering of parts because that was mine. I figured as long as I had that, I had a job" (Caminiti, 1995).

Team-Training Costs

Employees most likely will need retraining to be able to function in teams. The financial costs associated with the retraining fall into two areas: costs for technical cross training and costs for training individuals to function as part of a team. Of the two, the technical component is usually easier to accomplish. Training in team dynamics is often hampered by the fact that many employees do not know they need it. Recall from Chapter 7 some of the potential pitfalls associated with group decision making: groupthink, excessive compromise, lost time, and lack of individual accountability. Team members need to be trained to avoid these problems through programs like those offered at XEL by "XEL University."

Lost Productivity

Developing teams takes time, and time spent in team development is lost to production. The time spent selecting and retraining team members also lowers output of the product or service. In addition, team members need time to adjust to their new environments and roles. They will not reach peak performance overnight.

Free-Riding Costs

free rider
A person who receives the benefit of team membership but does not do a proportionate share of work.

Free riders are team members who receive the benefits of team membership but do not do a proportionate share of the work. Free riding occurs because not all people are equally committed to the team goals or exert the same amount of effort (Albanese and Van Fleet, 1985). Compounding the problem is the dilemma associated with team compensation, the subject of this chapter's Ethical Management feature. Free riders can be compensated for others' work.

Loss of Productive Workers

When companies move to a team system, some workers will not fit in. They do not want to think about their jobs, and they do not want increased responsibility. These workers may be forced out or resign voluntarily. Either way, the organization loses skilled employees (Verespej, 1992).

ETHICAL MANAGEMENT
The Paycheck Counts

As more companies embrace teams, team concepts, and empowerment, the rules of work are evolving. Managers are no longer just managers; they have become facilitators. Employees are transformed from being directed workers into being full-fledged decision-making partners.

The roles of managers and employees are being defined in the new work environment, but one area lacks consistency: team compensation. Companies are struggling with creating programs that measure performances accurately.

At a manufacturing facility, accurate performance measures are easier to determine—output, quality, and safety, for example. But for service companies like GTE Corporation, figuring performance can be tough. GTE, like other services, made customer satisfaction a key component of its incentive plan.

GTE devised a dual-bonus system, which applied to about 25,000 telephone operations workers in Texas, California, and Florida. A key component was surveys that measured customer approval; but, customers can be fickle and their attitudes can be highly subjective. As a result, work teams questioned the measures. "I don't know how fair that is, you can work very hard and a customer may not like what you do or the way you do it," noted one installer. "I want to be paid for what I do, not what someone thinks I do."

In 1998, GTE and Bell Atlantic merged and formed Verizon.

http://www.verizon.com

1. Is it ethical to base team compensation on a subjective performance criterion? Why or why not?
2. Should a company convert to a team structure if an appropriate compensation system has not been created?
3. If you were a team member, what would be your response in this situation?

Source: Gleckman, Howard. "Bonus Pay: Buzzword or Bonanza?" *Business Week*, November 14, 1994, pp. 62–64.

TEAM AND INDIVIDUAL CONFLICT

conflict
A disagreement between two or more organizational members or teams.

Whether a manager is working with teams or individuals, conflict inevitably occurs. Whenever people work together, the potential for conflict exists. **Conflict** is disagreement between two or more organizational members or teams (Stoner, 1986). Conflict occurs because people do not always agree—on goals, issues, perceptions, and the like—and because people inevitably compete.

Views of Conflict

What does a manager do when conflict arises? The answer depends on the manager's views and beliefs about conflict (Thomas, 1976). Figure 15.8 shows three basic philosophical approaches to conflict.

Traditional View

The manager who views conflict as unnecessary and harmful to an organization fears conflict and eliminates all evidence of it. Such a manager holds the traditional view of conflict. If conflict does occur, the manager perceives it as a personal failure.

Behavioral View

The behaviorist recognizes that conflict frequently occurs because of human nature, the need to allocate resources, and organizational life. A manager who holds the

FIGURE 15.8 *Philosophical approaches to conflict*

Beliefs	Reactions
TRADITIONAL VIEW	
• Conflict is unnecessary. • Conflict is to be feared. • Conflict is harmful. • Conflict is a personal failure.	• Immediately stop conflict. • Remove all evidence of conflict, including people.
BEHAVIORAL VIEW	
• Conflict occurs frequently in organizations. • Conflict is to be expected. • Conflict can be positive but, more likely, it is harmful.	• Immediately move to resolve or eliminate conflict.
INTERACTIONIST VIEW	
• Conflict is inevitable in organizations. • Conflict is necessary for organizational health. • Conflict is neither inherently good nor bad.	• Manage conflict to maximize the positive. • Manage conflict to minimize the negative.

behavioral view expects conflict. He or she believes that, on occasion, conflict can produce positive results. In general, however, a manager with a behavioral view believes that conflict is usually harmful. With this philosophical foundation, the manager's reaction to conflict is to resolve conflict or eliminate it as soon as it occurs.

Interactionist View

A more current philosophy, the interactionist view, holds that conflict is not only inevitable but also necessary for organizational health. Furthermore, this view maintains that conflict can be good or bad, depending on how it is managed. A manager with an interactionist view attempts to harness conflict to maximize its positive potential for organizational growth and to minimize its negative effects.

10

Discuss the positive and negative aspects of conflict in an organization

dysfunctional conflict
Conflict that limits the organization's ability to achieve its objectives.

functional conflict
Conflict that supports the objectives of the organization.

Positive and Negative Aspects of Conflict

A manager with an interactionist philosophy is able to identify the positive and negative aspects of conflict. The manager sees **dysfunctional conflict** as that which limits the organization's ability to achieve its objectives. **Functional conflict**, however, can support the objectives of the organization, especially when performance is low. People can be motivated to improve performance by competition—a kind of conflict—if they think their way is better than someone else's (Stoner, 1986).

Sources of Conflict

Identify the sources of conflict in an organization

Competition is but one of many sources of conflict. Others include differences in objectives, values, attitudes, and perceptions; disagreements about role requirements, work activities, and individual approaches; and breakdowns in communication.

Competition

Competition can take the form of two individuals trying to outperform each other. Competition can also erupt over a struggle for limited resources. The manager of each work unit depends on the allocation of money, personnel, equipment, materials, and physical facilities to accomplish his or her objectives. Some managers inevitably receive fewer resources than others. This can lead not only to a lack of cooperation but to open conflict as well.

Conflict can also arise from competition for rewards associated with performance. Managed correctly, such conflict generates positive results.

Differences in Objectives

Individual employees' objectives may differ from those of the organization. An individual may aim to advance within an organization over a three-year period, whereas the organization may have a tradition of seasoning an employee over a longer period. There may be conflict in this situation.

http://www.rainbowprinting.com

Individuals may have conflict with each other. For example, at Rainbow Printing, the two owners do not see eye-to-eye. "We just don't agree on what direction the company should take and how it should be run." In addition, each interferes with the other's work (Singer and Lazar, 1995).

Departments within the organization may also develop conflicting objectives. For example, if the production department focuses its energies on manufacturing a product at the lowest possible cost and the sales department wishes to promote high quality, conflict may arise.

Differences in Values, Attitudes, and Perceptions

The value systems and perceptions of each individual differ from those of others. These differences can lead to conflict. For instance, an employee may place a high value on time with family. A manager may request frequent overtime or late hours, not understanding the employee's need for family time. An obvious value-system conflict arises.

Groups as well as individuals can have conflicting values, attitudes, and perceptions. Upper-level managers may perceive reports and procedures as valuable control devices designed to provide information. Line workers may view such paperwork as needless drudgery.

Disagreements About Role Requirements

When employees begin working in teams, their roles must change. Suppose, for example, that an employee who has received numerous rewards for individual performance must now play the unaccustomed role of team player. Conflict is likely to arise between the team and the individual.

Line and staff employees may find their new roles uncomfortable at first. In team interaction of line and staff personnel, the line manager may expect the staff person to give advice, be supportive of the organization, and be action oriented. The staff person may see himself or herself as one who provides answers, not advice. The staff person may be analytical (and sometimes critical) of the organization, and he or she may be reflective in reviewing potential alternatives. In such a case, conflict between the line and staff employees is almost certain.

An employee's need for family time may be a source of conflict with a manager who expects frequent overtime or late hours.

Disagreements About Work Activities

Conflict between individuals and groups can arise over the quantity of work assigned or the relationship among the work units. In the first situation, the cause of conflict can be resentment because one group or individual believes the work load is inequitable.

Conflict over the relationships of work groups can take two forms. One group or individual may depend on another to complete work before starting its own. If the work is late or is of poor quality, conflict can result. The other conflict situation arises when two work groups or individuals are purposely placed in competition with each other.

Disagreements About Individual Approaches

People exhibit diverse styles and approaches in dealing with others and with situations. One person may be reflective, speaking little until ready and then speaking wisely. Another person may be combative, often taking an argumentative approach, giving immediate responses with little thought, and pressuring for agreement.

Breakdowns in Communication

Communication is seldom perfect, and imperfect communication may result in misperception and misunderstanding. Sometimes a communication breakdown is inadvertent. Because the receiver is not listening actively, the receiver may simply misunderstand the sender. The result can be a disagreement about goals, roles, or intentions. Sometimes information is withheld intentionally, for personal gain or to embarrass a colleague.

STRATEGIES FOR MANAGING CONFLICT

Describe a manager's role in conflict management and potential strategies to manage conflict

A manager must recognize potential sources of conflict and be prepared to manage it. A viable strategy for conflict management begins with an analysis of the conflict situation and then moves to the development of strategy options.

Analysis of the Conflict Situation

By answering three key questions, managers can analyze a conflict situation.

- *Who is in conflict?* The conflict may be between individuals, between individuals and teams, or between departments.
- *What is the source of conflict?* The conflict may arise from competition, personal differences, or organizational roles. Answering this question requires trying to view each situation through the eyes of the parties involved.
- *What is the level of conflict?* The situation may be at a stage where the manager must deal with it immediately; or the conflict may be at a moderate level of intensity. If the goals of the work group are threatened or sabotage is occurring, the manager must take action immediately. If individuals or groups are simply in disagreement, a less immediate response is required.

Development of a Strategy

When the situation requires action, what options are available? A manager can consider seven possibilities: avoidance, smoothing, compromise, collaboration, confrontation, appeals to superordinate objectives, and decisions by a third party.

Avoidance

avoidance
A conflict strategy in which a manager ignores the conflict situation.

Sometimes **avoidance** is the best solution. The manager can withdraw or ignore the conflict, letting the participants resolve it themselves. Avoidance is best when the conflict is trivial. The manager should use it simply because he or she does not want to deal with the problem. Letting the parties disagree may be the best course if disagreement results in no consequences.

Smoothing

smoothing
A conflict strategy in which the manager diplomatically acknowledges that conflict exists but downplays its importance.

When using the option called **smoothing**, a manager diplomatically acknowledges conflict but downplays its importance. If there are no real issues to resolve, the approach may succeed in calming the parties. If there are real issues, however, this option will not work.

Compromise

compromise
A conflict-resolution strategy in which each party gives up something.

With **compromise**, each party is required to give up something in order to get something. Each party moves to find a middle ground. Compromise can be effective when the parties in conflict are about equal in power, when major values are not involved, when a temporary solution to a complex issue is desirable, or if time pressures force a quick resolution.

Collaboration

collaboration
A conflict strategy in which the manager focuses on mutual problem solving by both parties.

In attempting **collaboration**, the manager promotes mutual problem solving by both parties. Each party seeks to satisfy his or her interests by openly discussing the issues, understanding differences, and developing a full range of alternatives. From this, the outcome sought is consensus—mutual agreement—about the best alternative.

Confrontation

confrontation
A conflict strategy that forces parties to verbalize their positions and area of disagreement.

If **confrontation** is used, the conflicting parties are forced to verbalize their positions and disagreements. Although this approach can produce stress, it can also be effective. The goal is to identify a reason to favor one solution or another and thus resolve the conflict. Many times, however, confrontation ends in hurt feelings and no resolution.

Appeals to Superordinate Objectives

superordinate objective
An objective that overshadows personal interests, to which a manager can appeal as a strategy for resolving conflict.

Sometimes a manager can identify superordinate objectives that will allow the disputing parties to rise above their conflict. A **superordinate objective** is a goal that overshadows each party's individual interest. As an example, suppose individual work groups are vying for budget allocations in the face of an organizational downturn. If the two parties agree that the reductions are in the best interest of the organization, each will move beyond the conflict.

Decisions by a Third Party

At times, the manager may turn to a third party and ask him or her to resolve a conflict. The third party can be another supervisor, an upper-level manager, or someone from the human resource department. If the conflict is between two subordinates, the manager may be the third party.

http://www.fordvehicles.com/cars/taurus

Perhaps of all the conflict strategy options, collaboration, an appeal to superordinate objectives, and decisions by a third party are the most difficult to visualize. Applications of these strategies played a significant role in the successful redesign of the Ford Taurus by Team Taurus. Richard Landraff, project team leader, was given a clear mandate. The new Taurus was to be the first American car that truly matched the quality and engineering of Japanese rivals—specifically the Honda Accord and Toyota Camry. Landraff had to harness the creative energies of Team Taurus' 700 engineers, designers, marketers, accountants, factory-floor workers, and suppliers (Kerwin, Updike, and Naughton, 1995). For example, Landraff did the following:

- He encouraged the designers in charge of the interior and exterior of the Taurus to collaborate rather than compete. The two, sitting side by side, constantly exchanged drawings and critiqued each other's work. As a result, the new Taurus avoids the mix-and-match dissonance of many American cars.
- He forced designers and manufacturing engineers to focus on a superordinate objective when quality issues kept bumping up against costs. The designers argued that each side of the Taurus body should be fashioned from a single piece of steel rather than from two panels welded together. The engineers countered that costs were prohibitive and resisted simply because this idea was different. Landraff brought the conflicting parties together, restated the Team Taurus objective, and pointed to a banner that read, "*Beat Accord*." The issue was resolved—the body would be fashioned from one piece of steel.
- He appealed to a third party when cost issues conflicted with manufacturing performance. Manufacturing engineers lobbied for a new, $90 million stamping press that would replace six body presses from the 1950s and result in much higher quality. With Ford in the thick of a cost-cutting frenzy brought on by slumping car sales, finance managers argued against the purchase. Landraff took the conflict to Ford chairman, Alexander Trotman. After a lengthy debate, Trotman surprised everyone by approving the purchase. "The quality argument was so persuasive that we all agreed we had to do it," he said.

Conflict Stimulation

At times a manager may wish to increase the level of conflict and competition in a work situation. The circumstances in which a manager might wish to stimulate conflict are these:

- When team members exhibit and accept minimal performance
- When people appear to be afraid to do anything other than the norm
- When team members passively accept events or behavior that should motivate action

Stephen Robbins (1986) reported that managers can choose among five strategies to stimulate conflict:

- *Bring in an outsider.* A person from outside the organization or team—someone who does not have the same background, attitudes, or values—may serve to establish the desired characteristics. Chapter 10 noted how Kodak, Scott Paper Company, and Chase Manhattan Bank relied on CEOs from outside the organization to stimulate the environment.
- *Change the rules.* In some instances, a manager may choose to either involve people who are not ordinarily included or exclude those who are usually involved. This alteration stimulates the work environment. For example, a manager who is attempting to open up the environment may ask an informal leader to attend management-only meetings as a full participant. The result may be that both workers and manager gain new knowledge and change their actions.
- *Change the organization.* Another approach is to realign work groups and departments. A change in reporting relationships and the composition of work teams can allow individuals to have new experiences with people and perceptions. When a company names a new CEO, either from inside or outside the company, one of the first actions the new CEO often takes to stimulate the environment is the realigning of work groups.
- *Change managers.* Inserting a manager into a work group that can benefit from his or her style of leadership can be an appropriate response. The practice of rotating managers of work teams on a regular schedule can also stimulate groups.
- *Encourage competition.* Managers can encourage competition between groups or individuals by offering bonuses, travel, time off, or certificates of merit to employees who perform best.

Edgar Schein (1970) reported that the manager who chooses to encourage competition may reap one of the following benefits:

- An increase in cohesion within the competitive group
- An increased focus on task accomplishment
- An increase in organization and efficiency

If he or she doesn't manage the situation correctly, however, the competition can produce negative consequences:

- Communication between competitors can decrease or cease to exist.
- The competition may be perceived as an enemy.
- Open hostility may develop between competitors.
- One competitor can sabotage the efforts of another.

The emphasis on competition at Spectrum Associates produced all these negative consequences. The little software service company founders' strategy is designed to ". . . make sure no one gets comfortable" (Murphy, 1994). Spectrum is organized into competitive business groups. The groups compete for customers by presenting proposals to founders Tony Baudanza and John Nugent. "Whoever comes up with the best proposal and best quote wins," a practice which gives competitors the license to poach. The competition exacts a toll. As one manager states, "If you put four, five, or six Type-A personalities with an entrepreneurial bent in the same tank, they can end up killing each other." Not quite, but the group managers have withheld information from each other and have negotiated behind the scenes to gain advantage.

CHAPTER SUMMARY

1 Describe the nature of teams and the characteristics of effective teams. For a group to be considered a team, at least two people must be involved, the members must interact regularly and coordinate their work, and members must share a common objective.

Effective teams have the following characteristics:

- Team members are committed to and involved in clear, shared goals.
- All team members feel free to express themselves and participate in discussions and decisions.
- Members trust each other.
- When needs for leadership arise, any member feels free to volunteer.
- Decisions are made by consensus.
- As problems occur, the team focuses on causes, not symptoms.
- Team members are flexible in terms of work processes and problem solving.
- Team members change and grow.

2 Identify the types of teams that organizations use. The two basic types of teams are vertical teams and horizontal teams. A vertical team is composed of a manager and his or her subordinates in the formal chain of command. A horizontal team is made up of members drawn from different departments in the organization.

3 Distinguish potential uses of teams. Although managers may choose from unlimited team options, five main categories of teams are common:

- Product development teams are organized to create new products.
- Project teams are designed to complete a specific task in an organization.
- Quality teams focus on quality products and services. Quality circles identify quality issues facing the company or department and offer suggestions for improvement. Quality assurance teams guarantee the quality of service and products by contacting customers and working with vendors.
- Process teams group members who perform the organization's major processes. The team not only performs the processes but also refines them.
- Work teams perform all the tasks previously performed by the individual members of a functional department or departments.

4 Use decision-making authority as a characteristic by which to distinguish team type. Teams may be characterized as teams closely controlled by management, teams that have moderate independence, and independent work teams.

- Teams closely controlled by management include committees, task forces, and quality circles.
- Teams that have moderate independence include cross-functional teams, project teams, and product development teams.
- Independent work teams include self-directed work teams and executive work teams.

5 Identify and discuss steps in establishing teams. There are eight steps in building teams:

1. *Assessing feasibility.* A feasibility study should help determine if the team approach will work as well as how long it will take to initiate teams and the type of commitment it will require.
2. *Identifying priorities.* An assessment should determine the critical needs of the organization and where teams can make an impact.
3. *Defining mission and objectives.* Before an organization begins to build teams, managers should determine that the company's mission and objectives are solid, well defined, and accepted throughout the organization.
4. *Uncovering and eliminating barriers to team building.* Three kinds of barriers impede teams: subject matter barriers, process barriers, and cultural barriers. Such barriers must be identified and overcome.
5. *Starting with small teams.* Begin team projects and planning in a pocket of the company.

6. *Planning for training needs.* Team members will probably need training in planning, the effective use of meetings, and team dynamics.
7. *Planning to empower.* Executives and other managers must empower workers when creating teams. Top managers need to step back and let team members make decisions, including making mistakes and failing.
8. *Planning for feedback and development time.* Teams require feedback. Initially team builders should provide a mechanism to provide feedback.

6 **Identify and discuss the roles of team members and team leaders.** Effective teams display balance. Balance requires some people to play task-oriented roles and others to play social roles. Task specialists include the contributor, challenger, and initiator. Social specialists include the collaborator, communicator, cheerleader, and compromiser.

A key consideration in effective teams is team leadership. In self-managed teams, leadership is provided by team members. Team leaders appointed by management focus on teamwork, cooperation, and results. Effective team leaders create a noncompetitive atmosphere, renew trust, think reasonably, share leadership, encourage members to assume as much responsibility as they can handle, and positively reinforce even the slightest contributions.

7 **Describe the four stages of team development.** The four stages of team development are

- *Forming.* During the forming stage individual members become acquainted. Members test behaviors to determine which are acceptable and which are unacceptable.
- *Storming.* In the storming stage disagreement and conflict occur. Individual personalities emerge and team members assert their opinions. Disagreements may arise over priorities, goals, or methods.
- *Norming.* In the norming stage the team comes together. With disagreements and conflicts resolved, the team achieves unity, consensus about who holds power, and an understanding of the roles members will play.
- *Performing.* In the performing stage the team begins to function and moves toward accomplishing its objectives.

8 **Discuss team cohesiveness and team norms and their relationship to team performance.** Cohesiveness is the extent to which members are attracted to the team and motivated to remain together. Teams with few members, frequent interaction, clear objectives, and identifiable success tend to be cohesive. High cohesiveness contributes to effectiveness and high morale.

A team norm is a standard of behavior that all team members accept. Norms are guidelines that tell members what they can or cannot do under certain circumstances. Team norms are set by the team itself.

A key norm for teams is one that identifies the acceptable level of performance—high, low, or moderate. Together with team cohesiveness, this norm is a critical determinant of team productivity. Productivity is highest when the team is highly cohesive and has a high performance norm. The lowest productivity occurs when the team members are highly cohesive in their commitment *not* to perform.

9 **Evaluate the benefits and costs of teams.** The benefits of teams include synergy, increased skills and knowledge, flexibility, and commitment. The costs of teams include power-realignment costs, team-training costs, lost productivity, free-riding costs, and loss of productive workers.

10 **Discuss the positive and negative aspects of conflict in an organization.** Dysfunctional (negative) conflict limits the organization's ability to achieve its objectives. Functional (positive) conflict can support the objectives of the organization.

11 **Identify the sources of conflict in an organization.** The sources of conflict include competition, differences in objectives, values, attitudes, and perceptions; disagreements about role requirements, work activities, and individual approaches; and breakdowns in communication.

12 **Describe a manager's role in conflict management and potential strategies to manage conflict.** A manager's role in conflict management begins with an analysis of the conflict situation and then moves to the development of strategy options. By answering the following three key questions, managers can analyze a conflict situation: (1) Who is in conflict? (2) What is the source of conflict? (3) What is the level of conflict?

The potential strategies to manage conflict include

- *Avoidance.* This strategy calls for a manager to withdraw or ignore the conflict, letting the participants resolve it themselves.
- *Smoothing.* When using this option, a manager diplomatically acknowledges conflict but downplays its importance.
- *Compromise.* With compromise, each party is required to give up something in order to get something.
- *Collaboration.* In attempting collaboration, the manager promotes mutual problem solving by both parties.
- *Confrontation.* If confrontation is used, the conflicting parties are forced to verbalize their positions and disagreements.
- *Appeals to superordinate objectives.* When managers identify goals that overshadow each party's individual interests, they appeal to superordinate objectives.
- *Decisions by a third party.* At times the manager may turn to a third party and ask him or her to resolve a conflict.

REVIEW QUESTIONS

1. What elements are needed for a group to be considered a team? What are the characteristics of effective teams?
2. What are vertical teams? What three types of teams are considered horizontal teams?
3. What is the purpose of a project team? How does it differ from a work team?
4. In terms of authority for day-to-day decisions, what is the difference between a self-managed work team and a product development team?
5. What are the eight steps involved in the process of establishing teams?
6. What two major kinds of roles do team members play within a team? What is the importance of each role?
7. What are the four stages of team development? What occurs in each stage?
8. What is team cohesiveness? What factors contribute to high team cohesiveness?
9. What are the benefits associated with teams?
10. What are the positive and negative effects of conflict in an organization?
11. What are four potential sources of conflict in an organization? Explain each.
12. What strategies are available for conflict management? Explain each.

DISCUSSION QUESTIONS FOR CRITICAL THINKING

1. In what situations do you think individuals, operating independently, outperform teams in an organization? Why?
2. In your work experience have you ever been a member of a vertical team? A committee? A task force? A work team? How did your experience differ in each type of team?
3. If you were a member of a student project team and one member was not doing his or her share, which conflict management strategy would you adopt? Why?
4. When you are a member of a team at work or school, do you adopt a task specialist or social specialist role? In your opinion, which role is more important to the team's success? Why?

INTERNET EXERCISES

Check the text Web site at http://plunkett.swcollege.com for updated links to the Internet Exercises.

1. Explain five issues to be considered in teambuilding. Which teambuilding exercises would you use? Why or why not? **http://www.public.asu.edu/~ledlow/sledlow/teambuilding.htm**
2. What should you consider before selecting a successful teambuilding activity for your team? Which "Great Event" found at the Web site below interests you? Describe what you think might happen at this event. **http://www.greateventsinc.com/teambuilding.htm**
3. What is your conflict management style? Which styles do you use? **http://www.queendom.com/tests/conflict.html**

APPLICATION CASE

Who Needs Teams?

Inside Motorola's glistening walkie-talkie plant in Penang, Malaysia, the atmosphere resembles a high school sports department. Group shots of exuberant Malaysian production workers, charts with performance statistics, and morale-boosting slogans line the walls. A trophy case is filled with awards hauled back from quality competitions across the United States and Asia by teams with names like Orient Express and Road Runners. The messages are hammered home: We are a family. This is your company. "Here," says Managing Director Ko Soek King, "everyone marches in the same direction."

In productivity, quality, and innovation, the Penang plant is regarded as one of the best within Motorola's Land Mobile Division. The plant's quality-centered program relies in part on recommendations received from workers. In a recent year, employees submitted 41,000 suggestions for improving operations, which resulted in $2 million in savings.

Motorola is struggling to duplicate Penang's success at its 2,300-worker factory in Plantation, Florida. At the Plantation plant, which makes products similar to those in Penang, managers are trying to get employees at all levels to forget narrow job titles and work together in teams to identify and act on problems that hinder quality and productivity.

To facilitate the team concept, managers screen new applicants on the basis of their attitude toward teamwork. In addition, the Plantation plant now displays lists of star teams; and managers hand out rewards ranging from "golden attitude" pins to cash bonuses for good ideas.

Nevertheless, getting the Plantation workers to match the Malaysians' enthusiasm has not been easy. "The whole plant in Penang had this craving for learning," says Jerry Mysliwiec, director of manufacturing in Plantation, who spent three years in Penang. "People in the U.S. are less trusting and believing." For example, when a Plantation team member shut down a production line because of defective radio parts, workers watched to see what would happen. To their surprise, she was handed a $50 reward and an "attitude" pin. Despite this response from management, one ten-year Motorola veteran was not impressed. "I view this all as a headache," she said, "I don't even want to come to work."

http://www.motorola.com

Questions

1. What reasons can you cite for the differences in team success at the Penang and Plantation plants?
2. What causes of conflict between Motorola and the workers at the Plantation plant can you identify? Explain your answer.
3. What recommendations to resolve the conflict and help the transition would you make to managers at the Plantation plant? Explain your answer.

VIDEO CASE

Teamwork at GE Medical Systems

In late 1986, GE Medical Systems began forming work teams (called GEMS Teams) at its Florence, South Carolina, factory. Initially, some of the employees were skeptical. Teamwork meant a shift in responsibility from management to employee-directed work teams. The skepticism resulted from disbelief on the part of many rank-and-file employees that management would give up any of its power. However, from the beginning, the teams were successful, and the employees could see that management had a genuine interest in seeing the teams succeed. By 1988, all of the employees at the plant were involved at some level in a work team. This was not accomplished at a small cost. To provide employees with skills that complement teamwork, a high level of training was required, particularly in the areas of communications and feedback skills. The move from traditional management to employee-directed work teams also demanded a change in the culture of the factory.

Today, there are 26 employee-directed work teams in the factory. The teams are involved in a wide variety of activities, ranging from routine production to problem solving and special projects. The video case provides samples of interviews with managers and rank-and-file employees about the success of teamwork at the Florence factory. Most employees see teamwork as a positive development, which has increased their output and the pride that they have in their work. The employees also feel that the shift from traditional management to employee-directed work teams has had a positive effect on the culture of the factory. Because the managers of the plant often work closely with the teams, the traditional walls that separate management and rank-and-file employees are coming down. One employee remarked that she is no longer nervous when a manager walks through the factory. She said that she is now more nervous about disappointing a team member than a manager. Another employee remarked that for the first time she believes everyone in the plant is working toward the same goals.

For the managers at the Florence plant, the movement toward employee-directed work teams has placed them in a coaching role rather than a traditional management role. An example of how this works was illustrated in one of the interviews. A manager indicated that when he had a problem to solve, prior to the implementation of employee-directed work teams, he would have simply found a solution to the problem and told the workers what to do. Now, he indicated that he would take the problem to the team that would most likely be affected, and act as a coach in helping the team arrive at a solution. Once a solution was agreed upon, the team would then be implementing its solution, rather than his idea, in making the change.

Clearly, the implementation of employee-directed work teams at GE Medical Systems in Florence has been a success. Hopefully, the experience of this organization will serve as a model for other firms interested in improving organizational effectiveness through employee-directed work teams.

http://www.gemedicalsystems.com

For Discussion:

1. In what ways has the implementation of employee-directed work teams at GE Medical Systems in Florence increased employee job satisfaction? What positive outcomes can an increase in job satisfaction have?
2. In your judgment, have the GEMS teams at GE Medical Systems been effective? Why or why not?
3. Would you enjoy being a part of an employee-directed work team? Why or why not?

Controlling: Purpose and Process

KEY TERMS

concurrent control

control process

control system

controlling

critical control point

feedback control

feedforward control

risk manager

Six Sigma

standard

LEARNING OBJECTIVES

After studying this chapter, you should be able to

1. Describe the relationship between controlling and the other four functions of management
2. List and describe the four steps in the control process
3. Describe the nature and importance of feedforward, concurrent, and feedback controls
4. Describe the importance of a control system
5. Explain the characteristics of effective controls
6. Explain the steps managers can take to make controls more effective

MANAGEMENT IN ACTION

Getting Control at Toshiba

After decades of leading the world in productivity, Japan's giant companies began to lose momentum. The 1990s brought cost-consciousness, recession, and fierce competition. For years, Taizo Nishimuro, director and chairman of the board of Toshiba, knew that Toshiba needed to remake itself. "But he had to wage a subtle, four-year battle—just to persuade recalcitrant managers that change was needed. . . . In the end, he offered the ultimate corporate sacrifice: He stepped down from running Toshiba's day-to-day operations, in part as a way of persuading several top anti-reformists to retire" (Guth, 2000).

In 2000, the Toshiba Corporation celebrated its 125th anniversary. Hisashige Tanaka, a well-known Japanese inventor, founded the company in 1875 as Tanaka Seizo-sho (Tanaka Engineering Works), Japan's first manufacturer of telegraphic equipment. Under the name Shibaura Seisaku-sho (Shibaura Engineering Works), his company became one of Japan's largest manufacturers of heavy electrical apparatus. In 1890, Hakunetsu-sha & Co., Ltd., was established as Japan's first plant for electric incandescent lamps. Subsequent diversification saw the company evolve as a manufacturer of consumer products. In 1899, the company was renamed Tokyo Denki (Tokyo Electric Co.). In 1939, these two companies merged to form an integrated electric equipment manufacturer, Tokyo Shibaura Denki (Tokyo Shibaura Electric Co. Ltd.). Toshiba became its official name in 1978 (Toshiba History).

The company continued to diversify and by "the 1990s Toshiba ballooned to a universe of nearly 200,000 employees, hundreds of subsidiaries and myriad products whose common trait was little more than that they either generated or used electricity. On one side are heavy electronics, things like power plants and control systems for steel mills. On the information technology end are comparatively new areas like semiconductors and PCs, including Toshiba's best-selling line of Portégé laptops" (Guth, 2000).

Nishimuro was faced with the challenge of getting control of Toshiba without reducing quality. In 1997 he proposed that Toshiba adopt the "Six Sigma" methods of measuring performance, declared that Toshiba needed to focus on a few core businesses, and spin the rest into joint ventures with competitors or fold them into other Toshiba units. "If we do not change, the final destination is the collapse of the company," he told management and employees.

Some managers in the company argued that Six Sigma was a "U.S. version of Japanese quality control." Gradually, managers began to believe his warning. "In March 1998, Toshiba reported an 89% plunge in net income for the fiscal year" (Guth, 2000). Tadashi Okamura, president and chief executive officer of Toshiba Corporation, resolved to meet the challenges of borderless operations and mega-competition so that Toshiba could remain at the cutting-edge of the world's electronics industry. He is taking the lead in strongly promoting "Management Innovation 2001," a company-wide initiative that promotes maximized customer satisfaction and provides an effective tool for promoting market-centric management. The market or

A Toshiba employee displays the world's first portable DVD player enabling to play back DVD without any loss of resolution.

customer is at the center of all of Toshiba's activities, so that they can provide the utmost satisfaction to their customers.

Efforts at gaining control began by the reexamination of everything. The relative performances of Toshiba's businesses were assessed. After careful analysis of each business, some were kept, and others were modified or eliminated. Toshiba's most valuable sectors included information and Internet services, semiconductors, electronic components, and information-technology goods like PCs and DVDs.

In late 1998, all upper management personnel began training in Six Sigma methodology, with a directive for all employees to apply Six Sigma to their everyday job functions. Toshiba has cut costs and boosted productivity and profits by introducing Six Sigma into its culture. The measures have contributed to saving Toshiba 130 billion yen in 2000 (*Industry Search*, 2000). In 2001, Toshiba was the world's seventh largest integrated manufacturer of electric and electronic equipment, with over 198,000 employees worldwide and annual sales over $40 billion on a consolidated basis. ■

Sources: Guth, Rob. "Restructuring a Behemoth: How Mr. Nishimuro Reinvented Toshiba," *The Wall Street Journal*, December 27, 2000; *Industry Search*. "Quality Control Plan Hoped to Save Toshiba 130 Billion Yen in FY 2000," July 11, 2000, http://www.industrysearch.com.au/news/viewrecord.asp?ID=3921; About Toshiba, http://www.toshiba.co.jp/worldwide/about/about_message.html.

INTRODUCTION

Of all the management functions, this book discusses the function of controlling last because it applies to each of the others. Without some way to monitor the execution of plans, managers would not know whether their work was effective or efficient. People and processes must be monitored to prevent, detect, and correct unacceptable differences between managers' expectations and actual results. In this chapter's Management in Action case, Toshiba Chairman Taizo Nishimuro (in 1997) proposed that Toshiba adopt the "Six Sigma" method of measuring performance that Jack Welch had used to reinvigorate GE; Toshiba's ability to compete efficiently was at risk.

http://www.toshiba.com

http://www.ge.com

Six Sigma
A highly disciplined process that helps companies focus on developing and delivering near-perfect products and services.

http://www.motorola.com

Six Sigma is a process quality goal. It is a highly disciplined process that helps companies focus on developing and delivering near-perfect products and services. The statistical goal is to operate with only 3.4 defects per million transactions. Motorola and other industrial companies developed the quality management method in an effort to cut costs, build revenues, and eliminate manufacturing errors. Jack Welch's GE applied it to financial services. "One of Motorola's most significant contributions was to change the discussion of quality from one where quality levels were measured in percentages (parts per hundred) to a discussion of parts per million or even parts per billion. Motorola correctly pointed out that modern technology was so complex that old ideas about acceptable quality levels were no longer acceptable" (Pyzdek, 1997).

controlling
The process through which standards for the performance of people and processes are set, communicated, and applied.

standard
Any established rule or basis of comparison used to measure capacity, quantity, content, value, cost, quality, or performance.

In its most basic form, **controlling** is the management function in which managers set and communicate performance standards for people, processes, and devices. A **standard** is any guideline or benchmark established as the basis for the measurement of capacity, quantity, content, value, cost, quality, or performance. Whether quantitative or qualitative, standards must be precise, explicit, and formal statements of the expected result. Once those who must abide by standards understand and can apply them, standards serve as mechanisms to prevent and detect unacceptable deviations from plans. Standards may be applied to people and a process before, during, and after work is performed.

Controlling is about managing risks. Since companies regularly face a variety of risks, they are moving toward "the development of comprehensive, company wide programs that target the entire array of a company's risks" (Zweig et al., 1994). In many companies these programs are formulated by and make use of a relatively new, high-level management position, that of **risk manager**. This person must monitor people and processes and help transform functional managers (such as those who oversee finance) into advisers and consultants, enabling them to teach others how to deal with the risks that haunt their areas of expertise. "Internal auditors, once regarded as moles who ferreted out waste and fraud, are enjoying expanded roles as monitors of such 'soft' items as ethical standards, which, if violated, can increase a company's vulnerability" (Zweig et al., 1994).

risk manager
A high-level person in charge of planning for and overseeing efforts to control the management of all the risks an organization faces.

Regarding risk, consider the decision made by Eckhard Pfeiffer, former president of Compaq Computer. He took a huge risk in 1992 when he increased his company's inventory to "$2.3 billion worth of PCs, two or three times as many as any competitor. When Christmas sales took off as Compaq had expected, other companies were caught short" (Loeb, 1995). See this chapter's Global Applications feature for Toyota's approach to managing the risk of a rising yen and its impact on costs to American consumers.

http://www.compaq.com

This chapter examines the need for controls, the control process, general types and characteristics of controls, and methods for making controls effective. Chapter 17 will examine specific kinds of controls that nearly every business organization can use.

GLOBAL APPLICATIONS
Toyota's Camry for 1997: Less Is More

Some things are beyond a manager's control. One of these is the ever-changing exchange rates of national currencies. As the U.S. dollar fell relative to the yen, Toyota watched its average sticker price for a Camry rise out of control to over $20,000, placing two-thirds of its sales (the U.S. share) in jeopardy. To regain control over pricing, a stretch goal was set: "to trim the cost of developing and building the Camry by up to 20%, to an estimated $500 million." With this savings, the company could make about a 5 percent gross profit and cut its suggested retail-selling price by $1,000.

Toyota's efforts centered on reducing about one-third of the parts and many of the operations needed to build its restyled 1997 Camry. Toyota wanted to trim costs while sustaining high quality and pleasing customers. A case in point: At a time when cost control is vital, Ford made power windows standard equipment on its totally redesigned 1996 Taurus; Toyota's Camry (one of Taurus's benchmarks) has kept the manual option. Ford's decision added costs and risked alienating customers (those who do not mind rolling down their windows and do not want to pay for the power equipment to do so); Toyota's does not.

The result? The Camry sedan became the top-selling car in America in 1997. In his 2000 review of the Toyota Camry, Daniel Heraud wrote, "Overtaking the Ford Taurus and the Honda Accord, the Toyota Camry has taken the lead in automobile sales in North America with more than 450,000 units finding buyers in the United States and Canada alone. Its success is nothing accidental, nor is it the result of clever marketing. It's mainly due to this model's intrinsic qualities and its builder's solid reputation, which is recognized throughout the world."

http://www.toyota.com

Sources: Heraud, Daniel. "Test Drive," *MSN CarPoint Reviews*, http://carpoint.msn.com/Vip/Heraud/Toyota/Camry/2000O.asp; Naughton, Keith, and Edith Hill Updike. "Will Less Be More for Toyota's Camry?" *Business Week*, July 24, 1995, p. 66.

CONTROLLING AND THE OTHER MANAGEMENT FUNCTIONS

Describe the relationship between controlling and the other four functions of management

As Lester Bittel (1989) noted, "Controlling is the function that brings the management cycle full circle. It is the steering mechanism that links all the preceding functions of organizing, staffing, and [leading] to the goals of planning." The planning process determines the goals and objectives that eventually become the foundation of controls. As the first function, planning is at the heart of all the others. The strategic goals and plans made at the top level in an organization are derived from the organization's purpose and mission. From these plans flow the objectives to be achieved by successively lower levels of management.

As these plans and goals are developed, managers must establish controls to monitor progress toward them. The feedback from these controls should tell managers how each level of the organization—indeed, each individual—is progressing toward the relevant goals and objectives. The feedback may indicate that progress is proceeding as planned. If progress falls short of the plan, however, the feedback should indicate that managers need to change the plan (Odiorne, Weihrich, and Mendleson, 1980).

http://www.hyatt.com

By looking at Hyatt Hotels Corporation, we can briefly examine how controlling affects and is affected by the other four management functions. After two decades spent piling on services regardless of cost, Hyatt risked losing many management contracts in the early 1990s. During the 1970s and 1980s, more was better in the hospitality industry. Costs seemed to be unimportant; what mattered then was pleasing, even wowing customers with luxury surroundings and accommodations. It was a boom time and the era of huge, expansive spaces and elegant fixtures. The bubble burst, however, with the arrival of the cost-conscious 1990s and their value-conscious consumers. Recession and fierce competition began to drive prices down (Melcher, 1995).

- *Planning and Controlling.* Hyatt could not act responsibly when making its needed changes without adequate feedback from guests and the owners of the properties it manages. Both sources helped to provide the company with the data it needed to decide which services should be kept and which could be modified or eliminated without compromising service quality. In addition, Hyatt reexamined every operation; it calculated costs and brought them into line with the new standards set to guarantee efficiency. The company needed plans to eliminate the superfluous employees. Those remaining had to be taught the new and modified procedures, thus necessitating the creation of training programs. Managers had to design controls to make certain that all of the changes took place effectively and efficiently. Once properly positioned financially, the company was ready to continue planning its expansion efforts.
- *Organizing and Controlling.* Hyatt's new president, Douglas Geoga, had to create his own top-management team to help him reorganize and reevaluate all Hyatt operations. Top management had to delegate authority and define reporting relationships. The decision to centralize purchasing activities resulted in the cutting of about 1,000 mid-level management jobs and the redefining of the remaining jobs. Additional reorganization efforts placed Hyatt salespeople into national teams.

- *Staffing and Controlling.* The reorganization of purchasing and salespeople caused Hyatt to make many personnel changes, starting with the naming of a new president. Along with eliminating nearly 1,000 positions, Hyatt had to equip people to handle change efforts. It had to create teams to analyze costs and decide what to do in each area under scrutiny. The company had to combine numerous duties and reassign them to people and teams, probably necessitating a reevaluation of compensation levels. Hyatt also had to staff and execute additional training efforts so employees with new duties and new employees could be taught the standards that would govern their behaviors and outputs.
- *Leading and Controlling.* Geoga was chosen by Hyatt's controlling family's members to lead the change effort at Hyatt. New leadership was also required in the purchasing area because of its reorganization. Leadership changes took place throughout the Hyatt properties due to the elimination of nearly 1,000 positions. Sales teams required new leadership as well. In short, each organizational unit impacted by changes underwent some kind of leadership change. Leadership needed to handle the change efforts and conduct the required training to develop and enforce new standards and controls for both people and processes.

In addition to its relationship to the other four functions, controlling meets a very practical need. Organizations have limited resources. The successful acquisition and use of these resources determine a firm's survival. No person or organization should expend resources to achieve a goal without arranging to monitor their use.

CONTROL PROCESS

List and describe the four steps in the control process

control process
A four-step process that consists of establishing performance standards, measuring performance, comparing measured performance to established standards, and taking corrective action.

We are now ready to examine the four steps of the **control process**. As Figure 16.1 shows, the steps are (1) establishing performance standards, (2) measuring performance, (3) comparing measured performance to established standards, and (4) taking corrective action.

Establishing Performance Standards

As you know, a standard is a quantitative or qualitative measuring device designed to monitor people, money, capital goods, or processes. The exact nature of a standard depends on

- Who designs, works with, and receives the output from controls
- What is being monitored
- What is to be achieved through monitoring
- Where monitoring efforts will take place (location and functional area)
- When controls will be used (before, during, or after operations)
- What resources are available to expend on the controls

Standards and the controls they are part of usually focus on measuring and monitoring productivity (cost control through effective resource management) and

FIGURE 16.1 Steps in the control process

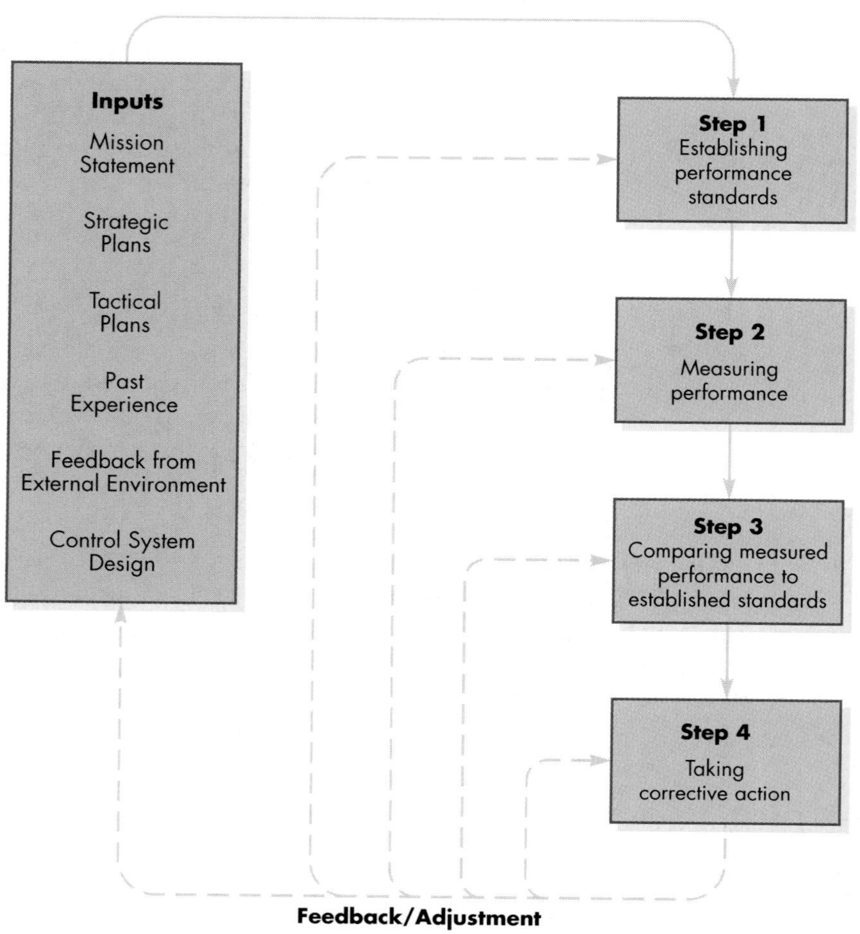

http://www.asq.org

quality (internal and external customer/user satisfaction). Thomas Barry (1991) of the American Society for Quality stresses the importance of measurement and standards:

> *Measurement is the springboard to involvement, allowing the organization to initiate corrective action, set priorities, and evaluate progress. Standards and measures should reflect customer requirements and expectations. Each employee must be a partner in achieving quality goals. Teamwork involves managers, supervisors, and employees in improving service delivery, solving systemic problems, and correcting errors in all parts of work processes.*

All standards and their controls must be continually reexamined to ensure that they are still required and operating effectively and efficiently. Also, as Chapter 3 points out, efforts to improve quality and productivity must not interfere with each other and must enhance profitability.

Productivity

Productivity is the amount of output achieved from the use of a given amount of inputs. Productivity can be measured quantitatively and qualitatively. Examples of quantitative measures include the number of customers served per hour and the total units produced per machine hour of operation. Qualitative measures incorporate such factors as customer/user feedback—feedback about how well a product or service meets their needs or how a service provider treats them. Deere & Company uses both measures.

http://www.deere.com

The experiences of Deere & Company, an Illinois-based farm-equipment maker, illustrate the efforts an organization can make to set standards for productivity and quality. During the first half of the 1980s, Deere & Company was experiencing runaway costs for its employees' health care. In 1985 it created its own health maintenance organization (HMO), the Heritage National Healthplan, to gain control of health-care costs. After 10 years the HMO was so successful in controlling costs that more than 75 percent of its members work for other companies "including Chrysler, Eastman Chemical, and Woolworth" (Kelly, 1994).

http://www.mayoclinic.com

Building on this success, Deere created a joint venture with the Mayo Clinic from Minnesota in 1993 to treat employees through on-site clinics near its various manufacturing facilities in Illinois and Iowa. Clinic staffers developed cost-efficient treatment standards "to treat 20 common illnesses, including heart disease, lower-back problems, and depression. By standardizing patient care, Deere hopes to eliminate duplicate tests and treatments" (Kelly, 1994).

http://www.johndeerehealth.com

Deere set up John Deere Health Care, Inc. as a strategic business unit to oversee its health-care ventures. It is profitable and growing increasingly so. The health-care unit's employees are encouraged "to meet regularly to come up with ways to save money, just as [Deere] calls on hourly workers at its factories to review assembly-line methods" (Kelly, 1994). Deere's efforts to improve productivity have enhanced its efforts to improve both profits and the quality of health care for its and others' employees. Says one union official and member of Heritage's board of directors, "saving dollars on health care translates into higher wages" (Kelly, 1994).

Quality

Concern for quality, that is, customer satisfaction, begins with the standards and methods used to recruit, hire, train, evaluate, and reward employees. Concern for quality must exist within every person and process. It must be a core value within an organization's culture and within the cultures of its suppliers and partners.

To control quality, companies create standards and quality assurance (QA) systems—"a validation process to ensure measurement accuracy and standardization. The QA system focuses on constant incremental quality improvement [kaizen] measurements and results" (Barry, 1991). At times, QA is promoted by such reengineering approaches as empowered individuals and teams, stretch goals, and process redesign. Deere employs both approaches.

Deere's HMO "was a hit with Deere employees" (Kelly, 1994). It also became popular with those employees of other companies that were enrolled in it. The Mayo-Deere on-site clinics made immediate care convenient for Deere employees. Clinic employees are concentrating on getting patients, such as expectant mothers and diabetics, to be more concerned with preventive care. "If we screen people up front, we can improve people's health status before things get serious," says Richard Van Bell, Deere's health-care unit's president (Kelly, 1994).

Along with the standard that no patient should have to wait longer than fifteen minutes, Deere's health-care providers are evaluated four times each year by their patients. "Their performance reviews are detailed to the point that they include feedback from patients about their [physician's] bedside manner" (Kelly, 1994). Says the benefits manager at Eastman Chemical Company, "They try to manage health care, not just costs" (Kelly, 1994).

http://www.eastman.com

Measuring Performance

After standards are established, managers must measure actual performance to determine variation from standard. The mechanisms for this purpose can be extremely sensitive, particularly in high-tech environments. Building modern airliners, for example, requires extraordinarily refined measurement and control systems. Along with visual inspections, technicians induce electric current in the metal surfaces to create magnetic fields. Any distortion in the fields indicates a problem (*Business Week*, 1991).

Computers are becoming increasingly important as tools for measuring performance. They can monitor people and operations as they occur, and they can store data to be used later. Many retail stores use computerized scanning equipment that simultaneously accesses prices and tallies sales and then tracks inventory by department, vendor, and branch store. The computerized scanning systems can also track the sales personnel, recording transactions and salesclerk activity. The displays and reports these systems produce often show current standards and actual performance measurements. Computerized systems of all kinds give managers the up-to-the-minute information they need to make sound decisions.

Comparing Measured Performance to Established Standards

The next step in the control process is to compare actual performance to the standards set for that performance. If deviations from the standards exist, the evaluator must decide if they are significant—if they require corrective action. If so, the evaluator must determine what is causing the variance.

To understand variance in regard to manufacturing, consider an operation that mills a billet of titanium into a complex shape to be used as an engine part. The established tolerance, or standard of variance, for the part is plus or minus 1/1000 inch from the specified dimensions. Periodically throughout the milling process, the machinist measures the part to be sure that it remains within tolerance. Any part milled beyond the tolerance must be rejected. A search for the cause of the unacceptable variance begins.

The source of a deviation may lie beyond the employee who first discovers it. (See this chapter's Ethical Management feature for a look at how well two government agencies are controlling the aviation industry.) Suppliers may have shipped faulty materials. Previous operators may have been poorly trained, dishonest about results, or misinformed about applicable standards. If equipment is in poor condition, it may be incapable of producing output that meets the standards—no matter how hard the operator tries. Determining the cause of substandard performance involves going beyond an examination of task performance, however. It involves examining the standards being applied and the accuracy of the measurement and comparison processes. As Lester Bittel and Jackson Ramsey (1985) explained, the control may be too loose or too tight:

> *If control is too loose, a deviation between actual and planned performance may result in poor coordination among organizational subunits and the failure to respond in time to unforeseen problems or opportunities. Loose control may also reduce some of the incentives for managers to meet their plans. On the other hand, tighter control generally calls for additional data collection, information processing, and management reporting. The cost and inconvenience of the "red tape" associated with tight control is likely to be resented by the persons being controlled. Tight control may restrict the ability of lower-level managers to exercise imagination and initiative in response to changed conditions.*

In the productivity- and quality-centered environment of today, workers and managers are often empowered to evaluate their own work for quality, productivity, and cost improvements. Individuals and groups throughout organizations are being given the responsibility to control their own behaviors and operations. By putting the authority to make decisions in the hands of those who are best equipped to make them, employees can respond almost instantly to substandard performance.

ETHICAL MANAGEMENT
Robinson Helicopter Company—FAA vs. NTSB

The Federal Aviation Administration (FAA) and the National Transportation Safety Board (NTSB) were created by Congress to exercise control over the aviation industry. The NTSB investigates crashes and airplane mishaps and makes recommendations to the FAA. The FAA formulates standards, issues directives and orders to pilots and flight schools, oversees air traffic control, and mandates recalls to fix defective aircraft.

Frank D. Robinson heads Robinson Helicopter, a company he founded in California. It specializes in providing top-selling, relatively inexpensive ($110,000) civilian-use helicopters (R-22s and R-44s) to flight schools, police and emergency services, and traffic-tracking radio and television stations around the world. "From 1983 to 1994, the NTSB says . . . 32 [Robinson] choppers broke up in flight after the helicopters' rotor blades hit the fuselage or tail."

While the NTSB has repeatedly urged the recall of the company's models, claiming a design flaw, Robinson and the FAA claim that pilot error is behind the breakups and crashes. Robinson believes the FAA should issue further restrictions on flight instructors and that aviation schools should provide additional training for pilots. In 1995 the FAA issued several rules. One tells pilots to avoid flying "in severe turbulence," another calls for "special pilot training for R-22 and R-44 fliers," and a third bans pilots from "performing a tricky flying maneuver in Robinson copters." The FAA is currently "working with Robinson on engineering changes to prevent the speed of the rotor blades from slowing—a cause of many of the accidents."

- Do you think the FAA has done its job? Why or why not? Why do you suppose the FAA ignores the NTSB's repeated calls for recall?

http://www.robinsonheli.com

http://www.faa.gov

http://www.ntsb.gov

Source: Del Valle, Christina, and Larry Armstrong. "33 Crashes: Design Flaw or Pilot Error?" *Business Week,* June 12, 1995, p. 40.

Taking Corrective Action

When an employee determines the cause, or causes, of a significant deviation from a standard, he or she must take corrective action to avoid repetition of the problem or defect. Policies and procedures may prescribe the actions. Such guidelines help shorten the time needed to react to deviations. Policies and procedures cannot be employed in all instances, however.

http://www.equifax.com

In some cases, pressures and controls imposed from outside an organization dictate the nature of corrective action. Equifax, a company that provides consumer credit reports, had to take action as a result of legal challenges. *Business Week* (1992) reported the extent to which Equifax executives decided to change company practices:

> *Equifax successfully avoided being sued when it agreed on June 30 [1992] to revamp its methods. After talks with attorneys general of 18 states, Equifax announced it would go beyond federal law to ensure the accuracy of its credit reports and correct errors promptly. Equifax said it would continue with many of the steps it had already taken, including installing new software, providing a toll-free number for consumer questions, looking into disputes within 30 days, and providing free copies of reports to consumers denied requests for credit. The state attorneys extracted a similar agreement last year from TRW, another leading credit report company.*

Some corrective actions are automatic. Just as a thermostat can activate a heating or cooling system automatically, assembly operations with computer-guided equipment can sense deviations and take corrective actions without the need for human involvement. Managers must not overlook automatic controls when searching for the causes of substandard performance. Even automatic controls can malfunction on occasion.

Some corrective actions call for exceptions to prescribed modes of behavior. To retain the goodwill of a valued customer, for example, a manager may authorize an exception to the firm's refund policy. Some hotel and restaurant chains empower customer-service employees to "do whatever it takes" to guarantee customer satisfaction. If managers direct employees to do whatever it takes, the managers must allow the employees to use their discretion and judgment. The employees will face problems for which no guidelines exist—problems that will demand unique and creative solutions. Procedures, rules, and policies should not be substitutes for good judgment and employee initiative.

This chapter's Valuing Diversity feature points out a conflict between opposing groups of Latino-Americans over control of California's political climate.

TYPES OF CONTROLS AND CONTROL SYSTEMS

Describe the nature and importance of feedforward, concurrent, and feedback controls

This section will begin by discussing three types of controls: feedforward controls, concurrent controls, and feedback controls. Each focuses on a different point of a process—before the process begins, during the process, or after it ceases. Most experts agree that controls "are most economic and effective when applied selectively at the crucial points most likely to determine the success or failure of an operation or activity" (Bittel, 1989). A restaurant must focus on controlling the quality of its

VALUING DIVERSITY
Latino Boycott Hurts Latinos

The Latino community has a long and successful history of effective boycotts. "The growing Latino political presence in California was noticed in 1994 when Latinos registered to vote and earned citizenship in record numbers. Experts called it a backlash against Wilson and state anti-immigrant initiatives, which some viewed as anti-Latino. As a result, Latinos voted overwhelmingly for Democrat Gray Davis in the last gubernatorial election, experts said" (Garcia, 2000). In 1994 Governor Pete Wilson of California backed the state's Proposition 187 that denies state services to illegal immigrants. In response, Latinos organized a boycott against those companies that financially supported the governor's reelection campaign. These included such giants as Chevron, the Walt Disney Company, and RJR Nabisco. Roberto L. Martinez, director of the US/Mexico Border Project and a boycott organizer, believes that since Wilson is responsible for some of the "immigrant-bashing going on in California . . . [w]e intend to hurt these companies in their pocketbooks."

Although the Walt Disney Company says it was neutral on the proposition, the company became a focus for the statewide boycott that is threatening to expand nationwide. Mickey Mouse was displayed as an Immigration and Naturalization Service officer. One day after a Latino group began its boycott of Disneyland, another Latino group opposed it. This latter and larger group was composed "of Latino hotel and restaurant workers" who may be badly hurt by the boycott. Analysis of voting by Latinos shows that 22 percent voted for Proposition 187.

Sources: Garcia, Olivia Reyes. "Powerful Latino Bloc to be Heard," *The Bakersfield Californian*, November 5, 2000, http://www.bakersfield.com/top/Story/243499p-232175c.html; Schine, Eric. "California's Latino Backlash," *Business Week*, December 26, 1994, p. 67.

ingredients, their preparation, and their presentation. All these control points are critical to the restaurant's safe and effective operation. Poor ingredients will yield a bad meal, as will poorly cooked food. Poor customer service will alienate diners. Figure 16.2 shows how the three types of controls apply to restaurant operations.

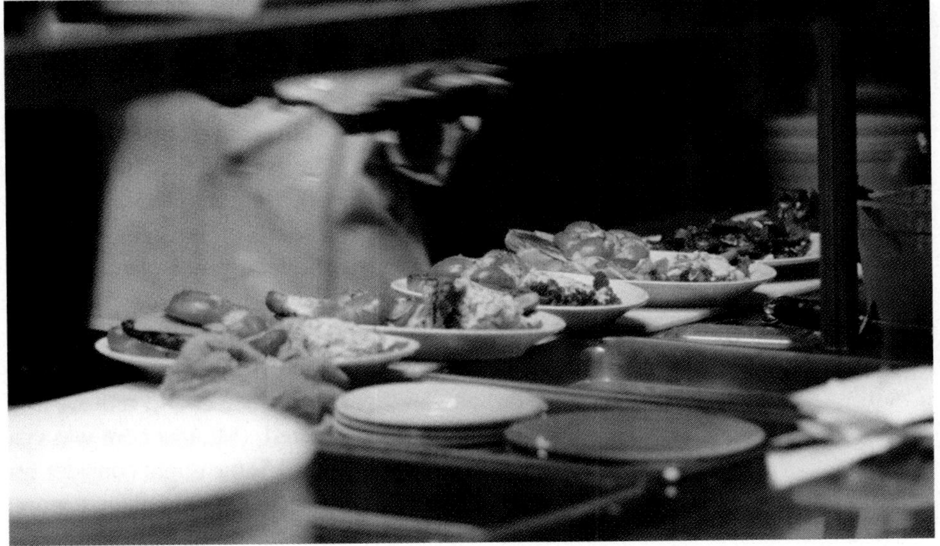

Control points such as high-quality ingredients, proper preparation, and appealing presentation are critical to a restaurant's operations.

FIGURE 16.2 Three types of controls applied to restaurant operations

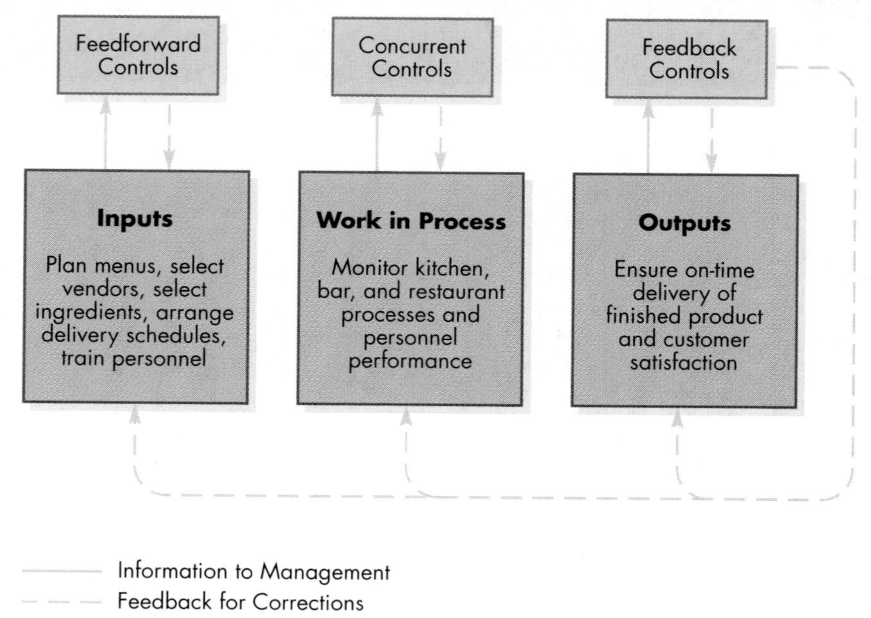

Feedforward Controls

feedforward control *A control that prevents defects and deviations from standards.*

Controls that focus on operations before they begin are called **feedforward controls**. (These controls are sometimes called preliminary, screening, or prevention controls.) Feedforward controls are intended to prevent defects and deviations from standards. Locks on doors and bars on windows, safety equipment and guidelines, employee-selection procedures, employee-training programs, and budgets are all feedforward controls. When a manufacturer works closely with its suppliers to ensure that the suppliers deliver goods and services that meet standards, the manufacturer is implementing a feedforward control. A maintenance procedure that keeps equipment in top-notch shape is also a feedforward control.

Deere & Company's clinics are physical manifestations of prevention controls; they emphasize preventive care for their patients and are located near the facilities where their patients work. In this chapter's Application Case on page 543, the Chicago School Reform Board of Trustees, once installed in July 1995, took several actions to prevent the recurrence of the many abuses that had been plaguing the city's schools for years. It froze expenditures, created and initiated new policies, and required all expenditures to be board approved (Haynes, 1995).

http://www.mcafee.com

McAfee Anti-Virus computer software is another example of feedforward control. The software, which can detect and remove 50,000 known viruses from computers, is continually updated. (McAfee.com was visited in February 2001 at http://www.mcafee.com/anti-virus.) Some might consider usenet or newsgroup courtesy, the subject of this chapter's Managing Technology feature, a form of feedforward control.

MANAGING TECHNOLOGY
Usenet or Newsgroup Courtesy

When posting messages to newsgroups, be considerate by following these guidelines.

- Read first, then post. Take time to read past messages that have been posted so you do not post a question that has already been discussed. If there is a special posting marked FAQ (frequently asked questions), be sure to read it before posting a new message.
- Use a descriptive subject in your posting header.
- Be polite. Respect that others may not share your opinion. Do not post a flaming message. [Flaming is giving someone a verbal lashing in public.] Send thank-you messages to people who take the time to respond to your question.
- Target your posting. When responding to a question, send an email directly to the person asking the question if the answer would not be of interest to the entire discussion group. When posting a message to "ALL," remember that it is being posted worldwide. Do not spam. [Spam are unsolicited messages on the Internet.]

Concurrent Controls

concurrent control
A control that applies to processes as they are happening.

Controls that apply to processes as they are happening are called **concurrent controls**, or steering controls. Consider word processing software, which allows a writer to change a document before storing or printing it. The software provides concurrent control. A word processor's spelling checker also provides concurrent control.

Some concurrent controls are designed to provide readouts or audible warnings. Most photocopiers and computer printers, for example, have display panels that alert their users to malfunctions during operation. Many of the devices on the dashboard of an automobile are concurrent controls. The odometer keeps track of miles traveled; the speedometer tracks the speed of the vehicle. Various warning lights alert the driver to impending or actual problems, such as low levels of fuel or oil and problems with the brakes or computerized systems. The steering wheel is a concurrent control that allows a driver to make adjustments in the course of the vehicle. If you try to exit a newly built automobile without turning off the headlights, a warning device, perhaps even a gently scolding electronic voice, may concurrently control you.

The most important concurrent control in any undertaking is often the skilled and experienced operator, whose eyes, ears, and "feel" for the operation give timely warnings that things are not as they should be. Recognizing the importance of experienced employees as control mechanisms, many companies are enhancing workers' power to affect operations.

http://www.prudential.com

For example, at the Prudential Insurance Company of America in 1994, former Chairman Robert C. Winters asked Martha Clark Goss, a senior vice president, to "install a top-to-bottom system of integrated internal controls in every unit and, along the way overhaul the corporate culture" (Zweig, 1994). Winters assured

Goss that he was committed to exerting his influence to make it happen. Along with considering the creation of a top-management risk-management unit, Goss worked on getting employees to recognize that they hold the key to controlling risks: "[T]hey have not only a right but also a responsibility to ask questions if they are instructed to do something they don't think is right or don't fully understand" (Zweig, 1994).

Feedback Controls

feedback control
A control that focuses on the outputs or results of operations.

Controls that focus on the results of operations are called **feedback controls**. They are after-the-fact, or postperformance, controls. They are called feedback controls because the information they provide is fed back into the process or to the controller, who must then make any necessary adjustments. "On a larger scale, however, measurements and comparisons made after an operation has been concluded (postperformance) serve to guide future planning, goals, inputs, and process designs" (Bittel, 1989). At the end of the year, for example, a manager should carefully review the budget control report. Which accounts were overdrawn? Which accounts retained a surplus? Were priorities established through the budget proper and in line with organizational demands? Why or why not? Lessons learned from historical information can be used to perform every task more effectively and efficiently. Everyone can learn from past performance.

http://www.lifetimetv.com/onair/shows/chicago/frameset.shtml

TV shows, such as *Chicago Hope*, could not be produced on schedule without the benefit of high-tech, computerized feedback controls. Editing is almost instantaneous once a scene is shot. Says David E. Kelley, creator and executive producer of this show, "Everything's on computer, so you can change scenes with the push of a button. No longer do you have to take out film and cut it and wait an hour before you can see the same scene again. Now you can see the scene within minutes" (Macht, 1995).

Control Systems

4

Describe the importance of a control system

control system
A system in which feedforward, concurrent, and feedback controls operate in harmony to ensure that standards are enforced, goals are reached, and resources are used effectively and efficiently.

Feedforward, concurrent, and feedback controls should be viewed as part of an overall **control system**. Able managers integrate suitable control combinations to enforce standards, make sure elements function smoothly with one another, and ensure that resources are used effectively and efficiently. Today companies are emphasizing feedforward and concurrent controls. They are avoiding dependence on feedback controls, which often provide information when it is too late to avoid losses.

Toshiba instituted a variety of controls through its change agent and head designer of the control system, Taizo Nishimuro. Feedforward, or prevention, controls include surveying of customers before making changes. Its emphasis on feedback, or postperformance, controls included return on investment, cash-flow management, and a form of economic value added. Toshiba managers and employees at all corporate levels use a variety of concurrent controls including scrutinizing processes, analyzing and rectifying errors, and putting measures in place to ensure errors do not reoccur.

CHARACTERISTICS OF EFFECTIVE CONTROLS

Explain the characteristics of effective controls

Controls at every level focus on inputs, processes, and outputs; but what characteristics make controls effective? Effective controls are focused on critical points and integrated into the corporate culture. They are timely and accepted by those who use them or abide by them. In addition, effective controls are economically feasible, accurate, and comprehensible.

Focus on Critical Points

critical control point
An area of operations that directly affects the survival of a firm and the success of its most essential activities.

Critical control points are all the operations that directly affect the survival of an organization and the success of its most essential activities. Critical control points exist in many areas of business activity—production, sales, customer service, and finance, for example. Controls should focus on those points at which failures cannot be tolerated and where time and money costs are greatest.

The objective is to apply controls to the essential aspects of a business, not the peripheral ones. Having a salesperson report on all the activities undertaken during a long sales trip would be one way to control. The resulting report would probably obscure the important issues, however, and the task of writing it would burden the salesperson. A simple report of actual sales calls and sales revenues would be far more relevant and effective.

The organizations in this chapter's opening and closing cases focused on gaining control over costs—an area critical to an organization's success. Toshiba eliminated some costs and reduced others through careful analysis and comprehensive actions, such as realigning itself around a few core areas and spinning nonessential business units into joint ventures. The Chicago School Reform Board of Trustees focused on controlling spending and on instituting preventive measures, such as its new policies on conflict of interest and on hiring or conducting business with relatives.

Integration

Controls exhibit integration when the corporate culture supports and enforces them and when they work in harmony, not at cross-purposes. When controls and the need for them are consonant with the organization's values, the controls will be effective. Coordinated controls do not impede work; they function harmoniously to give people what they need to make informed judgments.

At Prudential, both Goss and Winters realized that risk management/controlling would mean more than rules. It would require reforming the company's culture and instilling in individuals the commitment to act ethically and responsibly in all their undertakings.

When managers and employees trust each other and workers at all levels believe that the controls are necessary, employees can be relied on to implement the controls. When everyone accepts the organization's mission and culture, the corporate climate nourishes self-discipline and commitment. Work teams are self-policing and share values that are consistent with those of the organization. As workers enter these supportive environments, managers and coworkers take care to ensure that the newcomers "buy into" the culture (Walton, 1985).

Acceptability

People must agree that controls are necessary, that the particular kinds of controls in use are appropriate, and that the controls will not have negative impacts on individuals or their efforts to achieve personal goals. Controls that appear to be arbitrary, subjective, or an invasion of privacy will not elicit the support of those they affect. Likewise, controls that are redundant (except when necessary for health and safety) or too restrictive will go unsupported. In fact, such controls will stimulate covert and overt opposition. Too many controls, confusing controls, and too few controls create stress and resistance. Frustration, fear, and loss of motivation and initiative can result.

Through flextime, a motivational technique introduced in Chapter 13, employees gain more control over how and when they work. Although over 40 percent of U.S. employers offer some kind of flexible work schedules, their employees perceive that a request for such an accommodation may put their careers and job security at risk. In many cases when employees seek such changes, their bosses view them as being in some kind of trouble, putting their private lives ahead of their working ones, or asking for "special" treatment at an inconvenient time. To prevent such biases from sabotaging efforts to accommodate its employees, Work/Family Directions (WFD) "does *not* ask the reason for the request, so the request is easier to approve or deny strictly on business grounds" (Bianchi, 1995). The decision is made on the basis of how the new work arrangement being requested "will benefit the company." Thus acceptance of the program by all parties is enhanced.

http://www.wfd.com

Timeliness

Controls must ensure that information reaches those who need it *when they need it;* only then can a meaningful response follow. One reason for setting deadlines is to ensure that information flows promptly. If deadlines are treated casually or unrealistically (if the manager always wants things yesterday), people will soon come to ignore them. In such a case, deadlines are totally ineffective as controls.

http://www.kmart.com

Ensuring timely flow is one goal of management information systems. Kmart employs modern technology to link its stores to headquarters and vendors. Among the sophisticated equipment the organization uses are point-of-sale devices that, via satellite, transmit merchandise information to buyers and vendors. The devices can also provide instant credit authorization to speed customer checkout. These tools saved enough money to pay for the satellite system in less than two years (Comins, 1992).

Economic Feasibility

The costs of a control system must be weighed against its benefits. If the resources expended on the controls do not return an equal or greater value, the controls are better left unimplemented. Suppose a costly security system includes highly trained personnel, sophisticated electronic surveillance equipment, and fingerprint scanning. Such a system is suitable for valuable capital equipment and facilities, but not the office supply cabinet.

Sometimes controls must be costly and redundant. Jet aircraft, nuclear power plants, hospital operating and intensive care facilities, and the space shuttle need redundant systems, or backup systems, to allow them to overcome a potentially

Though a costly control measure, NASA will not launch its space shuttle if one of the three main computers on board is malfunctioning.

http://www.nasa.gov

life-threatening failure of the primary system. NASA will not launch the space shuttle if one of the three main computers on board is malfunctioning. Redundant and expensive controls are often required to prevent problems that, if they occur, would mean irrecoverable loss or irreparable damage far more costly than the controls.

Accuracy

Information is useful if it is accurate. Accuracy relates particularly to concurrent controls used to diagnose deviations from standards. Controls that offer inaccurate assessments feed decision makers the wrong input, which causes them to give inappropriate responses. When a project manager reports that production is two weeks behind schedule because of poor team attendance, her boss begins an investigation. It turns out that, though several people have been absent, they were not key to production. The delay was actually caused by the failure to properly plan the flow of work and set meaningful deadlines.

Comprehensibility

The more complex a control becomes, the more likely it is to create confusion. The simpler the control, the easier it will be to communicate and apply. Anyone who has struggled with assembly instructions for a hobby kit knows firsthand how rare well-written instructions are. Controls in the form of instructions are often complex because more than one person created, implemented, or interpreted them. Complexity can also result when control users lose sight of the purposes of the control.

Too many controls can lead to confusion. (The notion that if one control is good, two must be better, is common but incorrect.) Refinements in reporting procedures often lead to the proliferation of controls. The result can be a profusion of data that sidetracks control efforts.

Computers are reducing complexity and confusion in many environments. Bar codes attached to inventory items or materials moving along an assembly line simplify the process of tracking. Some computer software allows voice commands—

even commands in a foreign language—to activate or access processes. Machines that use symbols rather than words further overcome language barriers. "Smart" software and a few keystrokes or flicks of a light pen can get things on track. All these innovations enhance communication by keeping it simple.

CONTROL MONITORING

Explain the steps managers can take to make controls more effective

Controls are effective as long as they do what they are intended to do, do not generate opposition, and do not result in costs greater than the benefits they provide. Changing circumstances require organizations to monitor controls to ensure that they remain effective.

Monitoring Organizational Impacts

Managers need to know the impacts of controls. Controls can generate support or antagonism. Involving employees in the design of controls can help ensure support. Controls that employees believe are equitable seldom encounter resistance. When monitoring the impact of controls, managers can use the following techniques:

- *Before-and-after comparisons.* This approach assesses the organization's environment before and after implementation of the control and notes differences that have occurred. If defects were 10 per 100 before the control and then dropped to 1 per 1,000 after the control was implemented, the organization should obviously retain the control and keep working on reducing the defects.

  Before-and-after comparison left no doubt that changes Jontee Accessories made in collection procedures were effective. The company, a manufacturer of hats and hair accessories, instituted the changes after experiencing difficulties in collecting on invoices. Instead of waiting for weeks to contact overdue customers, it began telephoning each customer whose account was overdue by ten days. Jontee set up special payment arrangements and allowed financially troubled customers to return merchandise. The results? "We had an upsurge in payments, but more important, we were able to detect problems early on," says owner Francesca Kuglen. Mutual Life Insurance Company, the U.S. Chamber of Commerce, and *Nation's Business* designated the firm as California's 1992 Blue Chip Enterprise (*Nation's Business*, 1992). Jontee Accessories was acquired by Goody Products, Inc., in 1995.

http://www.goodyproducts.com

- *Surveys of employees affected by the controls.* A manager who wants to determine the impact of a control should collect relevant data at several points in time. Multiple surveys will not only reveal perceptions, but also show when the perceptions were formed. Positive feedback indicates that controls are accepted and integrated. Negative feedback can be further analyzed to determine the causes of resistance. Factors other than controls may affect perceptions. The manager must take care to consider all the changes that have taken place between measurements.
- *Controlled experiments.* To form a sound assessment of the effect of a change, scientific practice requires a survey of the changed group as well as of a group that works without the change. The unchanged group is called the *control group*. Both groups are studied to determine significant differences in their results, norms, values, perceptions, and behaviors. The technique of the controlled experiment isolates those effects that can be specifically linked to the change.

Updating Controls

Controls are designed to deal with specific people, processes, and circumstances. When any of these variables changes, managers need to reevaluate the controls. Figure 16.3 presents a list of changes that usually call for a reexamination of an organization's controls.

FIGURE 16.3 *Typical changes that require reexamination of controls*

- **Changes to Mission**
  What is the present purpose of the organization?
  Was the recent change planned?
  If not, how much of the change was driven by controls and the control system?
  Are the changes good? How will current plans affect the mission?
  Should the mission be changed again? If so, how?
  How will changes to the mission affect controls and the control system?

- **Structural Changes**
  Have the changes altered the organization's ability to meet its goals?
  What roles did controls and the control system play in making these changes come about?
  Have efforts at controlling affected the organization's span of control, chain of command, degree of decentralization, and job definitions? If so, have the effects been positive or negative?
  Are the controls worth any difficulties they have created?
  Have structural changes made changes to controls or the control system necessary?

- **Changes in Decision Making**
  Did the control system alter the information flow required for decision making?
  Is there more decentralized decision making now than in the recent past?
  Is the quality of decisions being made today equal to that of the past?
  Is the management information system adequate?
  What roles have controls played in any of these issues?
  Do changes in decision making require changes in controls, the control process, or the control system?

- **Changes in Human Relations**
  Do people enjoy working in the organization?
  Is there an unacceptable level of waste?
  Are high costs or frequent disciplinary actions, tardiness, or absenteeism related to personnel actions?
  Have quality and productivity been affected?
  Have there been changes to group norms and cultures?
  Has the interaction between managers and their subordinates improved or worsened?
  Are controls or control systems contributing factors to improvements or declines?
  Are changes needed in either the controls or the control system?

- **Technological Changes**
  What is the effect of recent technological change on controls and the control system?
  Are any changes in technology being planned?
  What will be their impacts on controls and the control process?
  Are the controls, control process, and control system using the latest beneficial technology? Should they be?
  Are the costs of using the latest technology worth its adoption?

People tend to get comfortable with the way things are. Once controls are introduced, implemented, and yield results, people become complacent; the controls become a part of daily routine. A continual repetition of the past, however, means lost opportunities and delays in implementing needed changes. By simply relying on controls and systems that are in place, managers fail to make full use of the preventive nature of the controlling process. The instant that changes occur or are planned, managers should begin to determine if present controls will be adequate and applicable in the new situation. Invariably, changes are needed to the controlling effort as well. Controls themselves need to be controlled!

CHAPTER SUMMARY

1 Describe the relationship between controlling and the other four functions of management. Planning is part of every function. Management must create standards to govern people and operations. To prevent, identify, and correct deviations from standards, management must design controls. It must also teach people what controls are supposed to do and how to use them effectively and efficiently.

Organizing is affected by controls known as the principles of organizing. Different levels within any organization require different controls and standards. As organizations change their structures, they must eliminate, modify, or create standards and controls to accommodate the changes.

Staffing and controlling are linked because people make controls and must be taught to use them correctly. Changes in job descriptions usually mean changes in controls and controlling. Changes in personnel through such actions as downsizing, promotions, and transfers mean changes to controlling efforts as well.

Leading is linked to controlling because leaders at every level must be capable of labeling critical control points, gathering needed information, creating and modifying their controls, and overseeing those who are responsible for controlling activities.

2 List and describe the four steps in the control process. The four steps in the control process are

1. *Establishing performance standards.* Organizations create standards to help measure and monitor both productivity and quality efforts. People and processes are governed by qualitative and quantitative standards. An organization uses these standards to teach, train, and evaluate; they function as the link between planning and controlling.
2. *Measuring performance.* An organization measures actual performances of people and processes to ascertain if they are functioning according to plans and expectations. Performance can be measured (diagnosed) as it takes place (in real time) or after it has taken place. Either way, what is happening must be monitored.
3. *Comparing measured performance to established standards.* This step asks the question: Is "what is" the same or better than the "what should be"? If the answer is yes, things are going well. If the answer is no, corrective action is usually called for.
4. *Taking corrective action.* When significant deviations from established standards occur, the organization must determine the cause by identifying the nature and scope of the problem. Deviations may be caused by internal or external factors and may or may not be within the power of a controller to control. Solutions are often prescribed by procedures and policies. Some corrective actions are automatic, but even automatic controls can malfunction on occasion.

3 Describe the nature and importance of feedforward, concurrent, and feedback controls. Feedforward controls are preventive in nature. They are created to screen out possible causes of problems. Procedures and training can be preventive as well as remedial. Concurrent controls monitor ongoing operations as they occur in real time, allowing for instant reactions and the spotting of trends. Feedback controls are after-action controls. Inspecting output after an operation has been performed and soliciting customer feedback are examples of after-action control. All three types of controls are important to managers and their organizations. When designed and used properly, they can prevent, identify, and correct deviations from established standards.

4 Describe the importance of a control system. For an organization to achieve the maximum benefit from its controls, it must design all controls so they operate in harmony with one another, with no overlap or duplication of effort. A control system is composed of subsystems operating in integrated and cooperative ways. Productivity and quality controls, for example, must not impede each other's goal achievement. Controls operating in harmony will lead to increases in profitability.

Explain the characteristics of effective controls. The characteristics of effective controls are

- *Focus on critical control points.* Present in all operations, they are the most vital points at which a failure cannot be tolerated or at which the costs in time and money are the greatest. All three types of controls are needed to monitor and measure cash flow, probably the most vital, or critical, area in any organization.
- *Integration.* Controls are supported by the organization's culture and work in harmony with one another in a control system approach. Controls are coordinated and do not impede operations.
- *Acceptability.* Those who must apply, interpret, and react to controls recognize their importance, accept them, and do not resist effective use of them. Unless people are willing to enforce and live by the controls in their environments, the controls will not be effective or efficient.
- *Timeliness.* Measurements provided through controls reach the proper decision makers at the time they are needed. Only then can managers properly respond to the information provided. Deadlines are a means to guarantee timeliness in control efforts.
- *Economic feasibility.* Control costs must be measured against the benefits they provide. When benefits outweigh, in a substantial way, the costs incurred, economic feasibility exists.
- *Accuracy.* Accuracy exists when controls provide a precise enough view of what they were set up to measure. In some instances, a ballpark view is sufficient; most efforts to control people and processes require exactness and precise measures.
- *Comprehensibility.* A control is comprehensible when people understand everything they need to in relation to that control. The simpler, the better; as controls pile on top of controls or become too high-tech for their users, they lose comprehensibility.

6 **Explain the steps managers can take to make controls more effective.** An organization must continually monitor and reevaluate controls to see if they are still needed and are operating effectively and efficiently. Managers can use before-and-after comparisons to judge continued effectiveness. They can survey employees affected by controls to guarantee that employees accept and comprehend the controls. Managers can also conduct controlled experiments (for example, when judging the effects of new medications) to determine if the controls are doing what they are designed to do. When controls need to be dropped, redesigned, or created, those affected must be enlisted to help fashion them.

REVIEW QUESTIONS

1. How is planning related to controlling? In what ways will controlling be part of the other management functions?
2. What happens first in the control process? How are its Steps 1 and 3 related? What will happen in the process if no deviations from established standards are discovered?
3. Can organizations function without controls? Why or why not?
4. Why must controls be integrated into a coherent system to work most effectively?
5. To be effective, what characteristics should feedforward, concurrent, and feedback controls have?
6. What can managers do on a regular basis to increase the effectiveness of the controls they are using?

DISCUSSION QUESTIONS FOR CRITICAL THINKING

1. In this chapter's Global Applications feature, what kind of controls did Toyota use? Which control seemed to work best? Why?
2. What kind of controls do you use regularly? What areas of your life seem to be "out of control"? What can you do to bring them into control?
3. What are the critical control points in the effective and efficient operation of a motel? A fast-food restaurant?

INTERNET EXERCISES

Check the text Web site at http://plunkett.swcollege.com for updated links to the Internet Exercises.

1. GE calls Six Sigma "The Roadmap to Customer Contact." Results have exceeded GE's most optimistic predictions. Briefly list and explain the three key elements of quality. How would you set about establishing performance standards for these key elements of quality?
   http://www.ge.com/sixsigma/keyelements.html

2. What are the key concepts of Six Sigma? As a manager, would you use Six Sigma? Explain.
   http://www.ge.com/sixsigma/sixsigstrategy.html

3. What is a control chart? How would you integrate it into your management process? Explain.
   http://erc.msh.org/quality/foutools/foucgrf.cfm

APPLICATION CASE

New Broom Sweeps Clean

In 1995, after years of chronic financial deficits, mismanagement, unethical conduct, and waste, the Illinois legislature passed a reform act designed to root out systemic problems in Chicago's public schools. The city's mayor, Richard M. Daley, received sweeping new powers to gain control. He oversaw the selection of a management team, the Chicago School Reform Board of Trustees, to replace the previous school board and "restore confidence in school leadership."

Among the many problems the new board was created to deal with were a general lack of control over spending of all kinds and either a lack of policies or incoherent ones governing the conduct of the majority of school personnel. For example, there was no policy on the use of school phones, which led to hundreds of thousands of dollars being spent to pay for personal phone calls, many to 900 numbers. Waste proliferated in travel expenses for board and administrative staff and lavish decorating allowances for administrators. Much-needed school equipment, worth hundreds of thousands of dollars and purchased over several years, was found decaying in storage. The departing school board president had used her position to enrich herself and the companies she owned and was indicted for failure to pay nearly $350,000 in personal income taxes.

Until April 1995, only high-level administrators were required to report any possible conflicts of interest and their sources of outside income. In April these requirements were extended to members of the local school councils, which oversee the operations of neighborhood schools and vote on a variety of local schools' purchasing contracts. Clearly, these controls were not enough, given the scale and depth of corruption found in the public school system.

From the very beginning of the new board's operations, control was gained over spending with various freezes on accounts and a requirement that all spending be approved through board oversight. A policy was immediately instituted to control phone usage. A new ethics policy, required by the Illinois reform act, was created to cover all school employees, trustees, and contractors doing business with the school system. The new policy goes far beyond its predecessor, forbidding "city employees from accepting gifts for services or using their position to win personal favors. It also discourages employees from hiring or conducting city business with relatives." A new travel policy was formulated to prevent staff from receiving reimbursement for travel without prior authorization from the new board.

http://www.cps.k12.il.us

Questions

1. What caused the general lack of control found by the reform board, and who do you think was primarily responsible for it?
2. What type of controls did the new board propose or institute?
3. What characteristics of effective controls do the policies created by the new board have? Which do they seem to lack?

Source: Haynes, V. Dion. "Ethics Will Be Subject of First Meeting of New School Board," *Chicago Tribune*, July 26, 1995, sec. 2, p. 3.

VIDEO CASE

Organizational Control at Archway Cookies

Archway Cookies is the third largest producer of cookies in the United States, and is well known for producing products of extremely high quality. The company's philosophy of quality is an integral part of its mission statement—which is to produce the best "home style cookies from our family to yours" that is possible. The company's mission is very visible and is continually reinforced at all levels of the organization.

To produce high quality cookies, Archway stresses two important issues: quality control and cost control. In terms of quality control, over the decades Archway has developed detailed specifications that help guarantee that only the highest quality cookies are produced. As part of this process, the company carefully screens its suppliers and holds them to stringent standards. In addition, the company sends employees to visit its suppliers' facilities, to make sure that the suppliers' procedures are in line with good manufacturing practices. Archway also provides its suppliers rigid specifications for each ingredient. When an ingredient is delivered to an Archway facility, a sample of the ingredient is tested and certified before it enters Archway's production process. Once a product enters the production process, the quality of the product is in the hands of Archway's production employees. At this stage, the company relies on employee training, detailed production specifications, and its quality-oriented culture to maintain high standards. When a batch of cookies is finally ready for sale, at least two packages of each batch are kept to have available for testing if the company receives any complaints. The final test, of course, is a taste test. One of the managers in the video related his feeling that the ultimate test of the quality of a cookie is to break it in half and take a bite.

In addition to quality control, Archway also emphasizes cost control in its production process. Cost control measures include working with suppliers, training employees to eliminate downtime and scrap, and reducing employee turnover by instilling in employees the type of pride that makes them want to stay with the firm. The company involves its employees in the quality process through suggestion groups, task forces, and quality teams. The top managers of the firm also spend time interacting with production workers to solicit input. According to one manager featured in the video, many useful suggestions have resulted from these interactions. Archway also believes that there is a direct relationship between the use of quality ingredients and cost control. The use of quality ingredients not only makes for a better cookie, but also helps eliminate downtime and scrap.

Archway is well known for its high-quality cookies and a committed workforce. Maintaining these positive attributes is a primary objective of the company's approach to organizational control.

http://www.archwaycookies.com

For Discussion:

1. Is Archway Cookies' approach to organizational control consistent with its overall mission? Explain your answer.
2. To what extent does Archway Cookies set standards for performance? Does the setting of standards for performance help the company reach its ultimate objectives?
3. Describe how Archway Cookies uses feedforward control to ensure product quality.
4. Do you believe that Archway Cookies has an effective control system? If so, what part of its control system impresses you the most? Why?

Control Techniques

KEY TERMS

audit

balance sheet

budget

control technique

financial budget

financial ratio

financial responsibility center

human asset accounting

income statement

operating budget

sources and uses of funds statement

LEARNING OBJECTIVES

After studying this chapter, you should be able to

1. Describe the content of the three primary financial statements and how managers use them
2. Explain ratio analysis and four types of ratios used by managers
3. Describe the five types of financial responsibility centers and their relationships to budgeting
4. Describe the four approaches to creating budgets
5. Explain the two major types of budgets used in businesses
6. Describe the five major marketing control techniques used in businesses
7. Describe the six major human resource control techniques used in businesses

MANAGEMENT IN ACTION

Yahoo!'s Webvertising

Advertising is used to inform, persuade, and remind consumers about a seller's products or organization. "The world's television stations, radio stations, newspapers and magazines take in more than $200 billion a year for ads, and most of the people doing the buying are working on blind faith that their dollars are producing a return" (Hardy, 2000). Budgeting and measuring the results of advertising spending is difficult. However, online advertising brings advantages that traditional advertising doesn't. The online medium provides companies with the ability to target specific ads and measure their success. Yahoo!, the world's most recognized Web portal, has the tracking technology to let advertisers know who is viewing when the ad is online. "Yahoo!'s Buzz Index spots trends in a thousand separate categories as fast as they arise and alerts 13,000 online retail affiliates and Yahoo! advertisers" (Hardy, 2000).

My Yahoo! is a service that relies on Web surfers supplying their personal details and preferences to Yahoo!, which allows Yahoo! to tailor the site with news and other content so it appears as a personalized service. These personal preferences go into Yahoo!'s databases, which are made up of millions of user names, email addresses, hobbies, geographic locations, and birthdays. Also, these databases tell Yahoo! where people are going on the Internet, because they are using Yahoo! for direction. Yahoo! puts the right message in front of people at the right time. It does this by profiling and targeting [making a message relevant to a person's interest]. "Traditional media should get scared," declares Timothy A. Koogle, Yahoo!'s former CEO (Hardy, 2000).

Stanford University classmates Jerry Yang and David Filo started Yahoo! [**Y**et **A**nother **H**ierarchical **O**fficious **O**racle] in April 1994 as a way to keep track of their personal interests on the Internet. Later that year, they converted Yahoo! into a customized database and developed software to help them efficiently locate, identify, and edit material stored on the Internet (See Yahoo! Company History at http://docs.yahoo.com/info/misc/history.html).

By March 1995, Sequoia Capital (a venture capitalist) invested nearly $2 million for a 25 percent stake in Yahoo!. In May, they brought in Koogle to turn Yahoo! from a directory and search service into a business and make it profitable. He has accomplished this goal by developing a targeted ad model and acquiring and adding services to Yahoo!'s original directory and search services.

> *And what they are building, he vows, is a killer ad machine, more powerful than print or television—and able to charge far higher prices. It will offer marketers mass reach, with a customized, close-up intimacy they never had before. And it will offer instant feedback on every ad. The advertiser will know how many people saw an ad, who they are and how many reacted with a further click or a purchase (Hardy, 2000).*

The Internet is the only advertising medium that can tell you how many people actually see your ad and respond to it. With print, television, cable, and radio, you never really know. Internet research firm Jupiter forecasts that global ad spending

© REUTERS NEWMEDIA, INC./CORBIS

Since joining the company in mid-1995, Tim Koogle has led Yahoo! to its current leading position as a profitable, global Web network. Koogle will remain on Yahoo!'s board of directors after stepping down as CEO in May of 2001.

will reach $28 billion by 2005. By January 2001, Yahoo! had 12.5 percent of the online ad market with its market share growing.

Sources: Hardy, Quentin. "The Killer Ad Machine," *Forbes Global*, December 11, 2000, Forbes.com, http://www.forbes.com/global/2000/1211/0325066a.html; Trigg, Mike. "Two Do Yahoo!," *The Motley Fool*, January 24, 2001, http://www.fool.com/duelingfools/2001/duelingfools01012401.htm; and visit Yahoo! at http://www.yahoo.com.

INTRODUCTION

control technique
Device designed to measure and monitor specific aspects about the performances of an organization, its people, and its processes.

http://www.yahoo.com

Chapter 16 examined controlling as a management function. This chapter explores important **control techniques**—devices designed to measure and monitor specific aspects about the performances of an organization, its people, and its processes. Within these techniques are characteristics of feedforward, concurrent, and feedback controlling. As we present each technique, consider how it helps managers set and achieve goals and at which management level each technique would be most useful. In our opening case, Yahoo! measures advertising performance with a variety of techniques: sales volume, repeat customers, profits, and levels of customer satisfaction were but a few. Top management uses the results to provide performance data that show results.

Keep in mind that control techniques depend on the proper interpretation and understanding of both the quantitative and qualitative information they generate by those in charge of various activities and processes. Thus the types, design, and number of control techniques will vary with each level of management and with each manager and operation. As the previous chapter has pointed out, however, control techniques must be integrated into a system to promote maximum effectiveness and efficiency.

SUBSYSTEM CONTROLS

An organization needs an overall control system, as do its subsystems. A firm's strategic plan guides the creation of its overall control system; the plans of subsystems (most often functional areas or processes) do the same at or throughout their levels.

The functional subsystems that require integrated and flexible control techniques are finance, marketing, operations (production), human resources, management information systems, and other management support activities. Among management support subsystems are legal services, public relations, and centralized computer services. This chapter examines several control techniques used by finance, marketing, and human resource managers (see Figure 17.1). (Chapter 18 will discuss control techniques for operations managers; Chapter 19 will address techniques appropriate for those in charge of management information systems.)

Finance Controls

Finance managers need to gather as well as generate information about all aspects of the organization's operations to determine its current and future ability to meet its financial obligations. Based on the organization's strategic plan, financial managers measure and monitor ongoing operations and prepare their estimates and

FIGURE 17.1 *Control techniques for common functional areas of a business*

FINANCIAL CONTROL TECHNIQUES

• Plans	• Financial responsibility centers	• Ratio analysis	• Audits
• Financial statements	• Financial ratios	• Budgets	

MARKETING CONTROL TECHNIQUES

• Plans	• Test marketing	• Sales quotas	• Budgets
• Market research	• Marketing ratios	• Stockage models	• Audits

OPERATIONS CONTROL TECHNIQUES

• Plans	• Cost centers	• Inventory reordering and delivery systems	• Budgets
• Quality assurance	• Material requirements planning	• Maintenance scheduling	• Audits
• Productivity indexes	• Production scheduling and routing	• Inspection and sampling	

HUMAN RESOURCE CONTROL TECHNIQUES

• Plans	• Human asset valuation	• Attitude surveys	• Budgets
• Statistical analysis	• Performance appraisals	• Training and development programs	• Audits

MANAGEMENT INFORMATION SYSTEMS CONTROL TECHNIQUES

• Prototype and pilot testing	• Decision support systems	• Expert systems	• Budgets
• Security systems	• Networks	• Software programs	• Audits

forecasts for future sources and uses of funds. All organizational operations affect and are affected by the work of financial managers, thus close working relationships are necessary between them and all other managers. The organization must measure and monitor all processes to properly assess their financial impacts. It must gather, analyze, and disseminate the financial data generated in a timely manner. It must also establish and enforce standards in the form of limits on spending in each unit, department, and the organization as a whole.

As discussed in this chapter's Management in Action case, advertisers must determine how much of their advertising budget will be spent on the Internet. An advertiser's budget might be based on what is affordable, on a percentage of sales, on competitors' spending, or on the objectives and tasks. Advertisers must have funds before they can spend those funds to purchase Internet advertising; before deciding to spend money on new advertising, finance people have to assure top management that the money will be available when needed.

Marketing Controls

As with finance, the organization's strategic plan dictates in part the plans of marketing managers. Like finance managers, marketing managers must work closely with others—finance and operations in particular—in designing, pricing, promoting, and distributing products and services. They must gather research on the composition and location of potential as well as current customers. They must determine product and service features and performance characteristics that meet or exceed customer expectations, but they must build these in at a price consumers are willing to pay and in line with allocated funds. Projected sales will determine, in part, production scheduling.

Returning to the Management in Action case,

> *Yahoo! reaches 60% of all net users worldwide and 70% of employees in the 500 biggest companies in the U.S. It tracks the visits of 166 million users, 55 million of whom have obligingly revealed such things as their identities, home addresses and personal preferences. Yahoo! slices its huge audience into narrow, highly targeted groups as small as 17,000 like-minded souls. Each month it drills into 16 trillion bytes of data on the browsing, buying and social behavior of millions of people. From this, Yahoo! can divine that an anonymous user is a 25-year-old man in Germany with a Visa card, in need of flowers for his wife and keen to see a "click here" ad from a nearby florist (Hardy, 2000).*

The company knows its market and the number of users it reaches; the typical age, gender, and income for its users; and the number of repeat visitors it draws. "As users leave more of their personal DNA, there's more value here than in any other medium," former CEO Koogle says. "Advertisers want a personal interaction, a lead to convert—and that's what we sell" (Hardy, 2000).

Human Resource Controls

Although Chapter 11 discussed staffing functions and their various controls, a brief summary of the major human resource control techniques is in order here. The organization's strategic plan tells HR managers whether staffing requirements will increase or decrease over the short and long term. HR managers need plans to acquire or shed personnel. They must continually review existing jobs to keep the job descriptions and specifications up to date. Plans for expansion or decisions to reorganize anywhere in the organization may create new jobs and activities. HR must establish and conduct training and development programs to teach the new and different procedures and prepare people for job changes. HR managers must also periodically review each employee's morale and performance, as well as the climate and culture to determine what, if anything, needs changing.

We now turn our attention to specific functional control techniques used to some extent by every business. We begin with the area of financial controls, examining, in turn, financial statements, ratio analysis, responsibility centers, and audits. Following these we examine budget, marketing, and human resource control techniques.

One control technique of the human resource department is to conduct training and development programs for company employees.

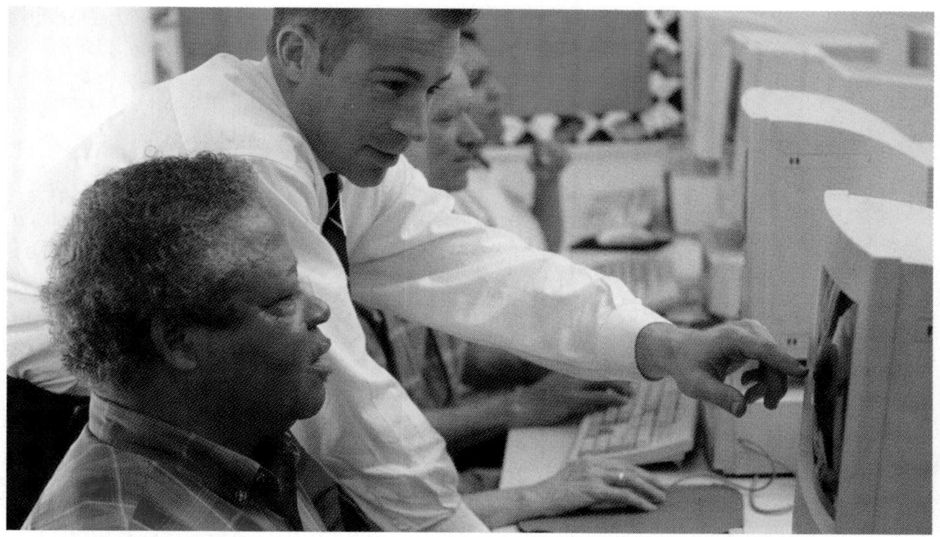

FINANCIAL CONTROLS

Describe the content of the three primary financial statements and how managers use them

Financial resources are central to management. Without control over adequate funds, an organization cannot survive. Each financial activity requires specific, relevant control techniques. Some types of organizations (banks, for instance, or the Internal Revenue Service) require unique and elaborate fiscal controls. The controls such organizations use are unlike those of manufacturers and retailers. This chapter will examine control techniques common to all types of businesses.

Financial Statements

balance sheet
A listing of the assets of a business and the owners' and outsiders' interests in them. The equation that describes the content of a balance sheet is assets = liabilities + stockholders' equity.

income statement
A report that presents the difference between an organization's income and expenses to determine whether the firm operated at a profit or a loss over a specified period.

Nearly all organizations use two primary financial statements, the balance sheet and the income statement. The **balance sheet** identifies the assets of an organization—what it owns and the nature of the ownership—at a fixed *point* in time. The **income statement** presents the difference between an organization's income and its expenses to determine whether the enterprise operated at a profit or a loss over a specified *period* of time. Each provides a measure of feedback and concurrent control over financial and related activities. Both are used to prepare budgets and other kinds of plans and controls and to monitor the organization's financial health.

Balance Sheet

Figure 17.2 presents the balance sheet of the Excel Corporation, a hypothetical medical supply company, for one full year of operations, its *fiscal* year. (Like a calendar year, a fiscal year contains 365 days. A fiscal year, however, can begin at any time. The fiscal year for the U.S. government, for example, is from October 1 to September 30.) The balance sheet presents three categories of financial data—assets, liabilities, and stockholders' equity—as they exist on a specific date. The word *balance* in the term *balance sheet* derives from the fact that the total assets must equal (balance) the sum of liabilities and stockholders' equity. Thus, the equation that describes a balance sheet is

$$\textit{Assets} = \textit{Liabilities} + \textit{Stockholders' Equity}$$

Assets are the resources owned by a business. They usually fall into one of two categories—current or fixed. *Current assets* are cash or items that are normally converted into cash within one year from the date of the balance sheet. *Fixed assets* are assets not intended for sale or conversion to cash. Fixed assets include land, buildings, and the equipment used to conduct the activities of the business.

Liabilities are what a company owes—its current and long-term debts. *Current liabilities* are debts due and payable within one year of the date of the balance sheet.

FIGURE 17.2 *Balance sheet of the Excel Corporation*

Excel Corporation
Balance Sheet
December 31, 200__

Assets			
Current Assets			
Cash	$ 17,280		
Accounts Receivable	84,280		
Inventory	41,540		
Prepaid Expenses	12,368		
Total Current Assets		$155,468	
Fixed Assets			
Building (Net)	$ 33,430		
Furniture and Fixtures (Net)	13,950		
Land	14,000		
Total Fixed Assets		61,380	
Total Assets			$216,848
Liabilities			
Current Liabilities			
Notes Payable	$ 10,000		
Trade Accounts Payable	41,288		
Salaries Payable	400		
Taxes Payable	14,000		
Total Current Liabilities		$ 65,688	
Long-Term Liabilities			
Mortgage Payable	$ 8,000		
Bonds Payable	3,280		
Total Long-Term Liabilities		11,280	
Total Liabilities		$ 76,968	
Stockholders' Equity			
Common Stock (1,000 shares at $100 par value)	$100,000		
Retained Earnings	39,880		
Total Stockholders' Equity		139,880	
Total Liabilities and Stockholders' Equity			$216,848

Long-term liabilities are those due after one year from that date. Included as liabilities are the claims by outsiders (creditors) on the assets of a business.

The difference between the value of an organization's assets and its liabilities equals the owners' interests in the assets of the business—their *equity*. Since stockholders own a corporation, its equity is called *stockholders' equity*. In a sole proprietorship or partnership, the equity portion of the balance sheet is usually called *owner's equity*. To illustrate, assume that a sole proprietor buys a delivery truck that costs $10,000. The proprietor pays $3,000 in cash for the truck and arranges to borrow $7,000. The business owner now possesses an asset worth $10,000 but also incurred a liability, or debt, of $7,000. The difference between the truck's value and the debt created to purchase it is $3,000—the amount of the proprietor's money that was used to purchase the truck. The proprietor's equity is $3,000.

Even as the balance sheet is being prepared, of course, changes occur that alter the mix of assets, liabilities, and equity. The utility of the balance sheet lies in the fact that it allows analysts to make comparisons from year to year and identify trends. In addition, the balance sheet yields information used to calculate various measures of the company's financial health and of management effectiveness. We will discuss some of these measures later in this chapter.

Income Statement

Figure 17.3 presents the Excel Corporation's income statement, which summarizes the firm's accumulated income and expenses for a one-year period. The content of an income statement, like the content of a balance sheet, can be expressed as an equation. The equation that describes an income statement is

$$\textit{Income} - \textit{Expenses} = \textit{Profit or Loss}$$

Managers use income statements as tools for reviewing the expenses and revenue of a business on an ongoing basis. They can prepare these tools to reflect any necessary time frame—a day, a week, a month, and so on. An income statement includes seven important categories:

1. Net sales, or the revenue from sales minus returns and allowances
2. Cost of goods sold, or the costs connected with making or acquiring goods that the organization has sold
3. Gross profit, or the measure of operating profits (obtained by subtracting the cost of goods sold from net sales)
4. Operating expenses, or overhead expenses (such as rent, advertising, utilities, insurance, and compensation paid to personnel not engaged in producing goods) that reduce gross profit
5. Net income (or loss) before taxes, the profit or loss of the business (obtained by subtracting operating expenses from gross profit)
6. Taxes, the percentage of net income paid to governments
7. Net income, the profit left after paying taxes (the literal "bottom line")

Like a balance sheet, an income statement yields information needed to track the health of the organization it describes. The major purpose of the income statement is to measure trends in costs and income, noting growth or decline in each category.

FIGURE 17.3 *Income statement of the Excel Corporation*

Excel Corporation
Income Statement
Year Ended December 31, 200__

Revenue			
Sales	$778,918		
(Less Returns and Allowances)	(14,872)		
Net Sales		$764,046	
Cost of Goods Sold			
Beginning Inventory, January 1	$ 37,258		
Plus Net Purchases	593,674		
Goods Available for Sale	$630,932		
(Less Ending Inventory, December 31)	(41,540)		
Cost of Goods Sold		589,392	
Gross Profit on Sales			$174,654
Operating Expenses			
Selling Expenses	$ 69,916		
General and Administrative	45,100		
Research and Development	9,970		
Total Operating Expenses			(124,986)
Net Income Before Taxes			$ 49,668
(Less Federal and State Income Taxes)			(18,315)
Net Income			$ 31,353

Sources and Uses of Funds Statement

sources and uses of funds statement
A summary of the cash flowing into an organization and how it is used over a fixed period of time. This statement is often called a cash flow statement.

A summary of the cash flowing into an organization and how it is used over a fixed period is called its **sources and uses of funds statement**. Sometimes called a *cash flow statement*, this document tracks a company's cash receipts (from sales revenue and asset disposal, for example) and payments (for such items as reducing accounts payable and interest on debt). Financial managers use it as a control technique to measure net increases or decreases in cash over a period and to spot cash flow trends through comparisons to previous cash flow statements. A sources and uses of funds statement for Excel Corporation is shown in Figure 17.4.

Using financial data generated from Excel's activities throughout one year, we can construct the statement in Figure 17.4. Note that cash flow is divided into three main groupings: operating, investment, and financing activities. Numbers shown in parentheses represent *uses* of funds—that is, decreases to cash receipts because of dollars invested or used to pay debts. All other numbers are *sources* of funds. The sources and uses of funds statement shows a net increase of $18,353 for the one-year period covered by its balance sheet and income statement. It also shows that Excel had the cash needed to acquire new inventory and fixed assets and to reduce accounts payable, notes payable, and long-term debt.

FIGURE 17.4 *Sources and uses of funds statement for the Excel Corporation*

Excel Corporation
Sources and Uses of Funds Statement
December 31, 200__

Cash Flow from Operating Activities		
Net income after tax	$31,353	
Decrease in accounts receivable	5,400	
Increase in inventory	(6,200)	
Decrease in accounts payable	(2,550)	
Cash provided by operations		$28,003
Cash Flow from Investment Activities		
Increase in gross fixed assets	$ (4,300)	
Cash used for investments		(4,300)
Cash Flow from Financing Activities		
Decrease in notes payable	$ (3,200)	
Decrease in long-term debt	(2,150)	
Cash used for financing		(5,350)
Net Increase in Cash		$18,353

Financial Ratio Analysis

2

Explain ratio analysis and four types of ratios used by managers

financial ratio
The relationship of two critical figures from financial statements—expressed in terms of a ratio, decimal, or percentage—which helps managers measure a company's financial health and its progress toward goals.

A *ratio* expresses the relationship between numbers. The fraction ½ is a ratio. Ratios can be used to express the relationship between numbers in several ways: in words (as in "one to two" or "one part of two parts"), as a percentage (50 percent), or as a decimal (0.5).

A **financial ratio** involves selecting two critical figures from a financial statement and expressing their relationship as a ratio or percentage. Financial ratios help accountants and others measure a company's progress toward goals and assess its financial health. On the surface a firm may appear to be sound, its balance sheet reflecting impressive assets. But if the ratio of current assets to current liabilities is poor (less than 2 to 1), the company may have difficulty raising enough cash to meet short-term debts. Ratios can be involved in one of two types of comparisons. First, this year's ratio can be compared with the same kind of ratio for a past year. Or, a ratio describing one company can be compared with the same kind of ratio that describes a competitor.

Figure 17.5 lists frequently used ratios, describing how they are calculated and for what purposes they are used. This chapter will focus on four of the most common types: liquidity, profitability, debt, and activity ratios.

Liquidity Ratios

To measure the ability of a firm to raise enough cash to meet short-term debts, managers use liquidity ratios. To derive the most common liquidity ratio—the *current ratio*—the manager simply divides the figure for current assets by the figure for current liabilities (both figures are available on the company's balance sheet).

FIGURE 17.5 *Commonly used financial ratios*

Ratio	Obtained by	Purpose
Current assets to current liabilities	Dividing current assets by current liabilities	To determine a firm's ability to pay its short-term liabilities
Net profits to net sales	Dividing net profits after taxes by net sales	To measure the short-run profitability of the business
Net profits to tangible net worth	Dividing net profits after taxes by tangible net worth (the difference between tangible assets and total liabilities)	To measure profitability over a relatively long period
Net profits to net working capital	Dividing net profits after taxes by net working capital (operating capital on hand)	To measure the ability of a business to carry inventory and accounts receivable and to finance day-to-day operations
Net sales to tangible net worth	Dividing net sales by the firm's tangible net worth	To measure the relative turnover of investment capital
Net sales to net working capital	Dividing net sales by net working capital	To measure how well a company uses its working capital to produce sales
Collection period (receivables to credit sales)	First, dividing annual net sales by 365 to determine daily credit sales; then, dividing notes and accounts receivable by average daily credit sales	To analyze the collectibility of receivables
Net sales to inventory	Dividing annual net sales by the value of the firm's merchandise inventory as carried on the balance sheet	To provide a yardstick for comparing the firm's stock-to-sales position with that of other companies or with industry averages
Fixed assets to tangible net worth	Dividing fixed assets (the depreciated book value of such items as buildings, machinery, furniture, physical equipment, and land) by the firm's tangible net worth	To show what proportion of a firm's tangible net worth consists of fixed assets (Generally, this ratio should not exceed 100% for a manufacturer and 75% for a wholesaler or retailer.)
Current liabilities to tangible net worth	Dividing current liabilities by the firm's tangible net worth	To measure the degree of indebtedness of the firm (Generally, a business is in financial trouble when this ratio exceeds 80%.)
Total liabilities to tangible net worth	Dividing current plus long-term liabilities by tangible net worth	To determine the financial soundness of the business (When this ratio exceeds 100%, the equity of the firm's creditors in the business exceeds that of the owners.)
Inventory to net working capital	Dividing merchandise inventory by net working capital	To determine whether a business has too much or too little working capital tied up in inventory (Generally, this ratio should not exceed 80%.)
Current liabilities to inventory	Dividing current liabilities by inventory	To determine whether a business has too little or too much current debt in relationship to its inventory (If current debt is excessive, the firm may have to dispose of inventory quickly, at unfavorable prices, to meet its obligations.)
Funded liabilities to working capital	Dividing funded liabilities (long-term obligations such as mortgages, bonds, serial notes, and other liabilities that will not mature for at least one year) by net working capital	To determine whether the firm's long-term indebtedness is in proper proportion to its net working capital (Generally, this ratio should not exceed 100%.)

Source: Adapted from *1970 Key Business Ratios*. New York: Dun & Bradstreet, 1971. Reprinted by permission of The Dun & Bradstreet Corporation.

To calculate the current ratio for the Excel Corporation by using the balance sheet shown in Figure 17.2, divide total current assets ($155,468) by total current liabilities ($65,688). The result is 2.37 to 1. This ratio means that Excel possesses $2.37 in cash (liquid assets) for each dollar incurred in current debt. Because most experts consider any ratio higher than 2 to 1 to be adequate, Excel may be considered fiscally healthy. Ratios lower than 2 to 1 indicate that a company is overburdened with short-term debt.

Profitability Ratios

Managers use profitability ratios to study a company's profits from several perspectives. To determine profits generated from sales, divide net profits after taxes by net sales. To calculate the profit generated from the owner's investment, divide net profits after taxes by tangible net worth. Using Excel's income statement, the company's profit ratio on sales ($31,353 in profit divided by $764,046 in net sales) is 0.041, which translates to 4.1 percent profit. In other words, the owners of Excel kept $4.10 for every $100 in sales their firm generated. To determine the adequacy of this ratio, Excel managers may compare it with the profitability ratios of competitors. During a recessionary period in which competitors are losing money, a 4.1 percent return on sales is probably more than adequate.

Debt Ratios

A debt ratio expresses an organization's capacity to meet its debts. To calculate a debt ratio, divide total liabilities by net worth (total stockholders' equity). In terms of the Excel Corporation, this means dividing $76,968 by $139,880 to yield a ratio of 0.55, or 55 percent. This result means that Excel is financed by 55 percent debt. If the industry average is 65 percent, Excel should be able to borrow additional funds on the commercial market. But, if the industry average is considerably below this level, borrowing may be difficult. Any banker that Excel approaches for a loan might think that Excel was overdependent on others peoples' money. Of course, when deciding to approve a loan, creditors consider other factors besides ratios—including the company's management and competitiveness.

Activity Ratios

Activity ratios shed light on a firm's key internal areas to reveal performance. If managers wish to assess inventory levels, for example, several different activity ratios are helpful: inventory to net working capital, current liabilities to inventory, and average inventory levels to total sales. These relationships indicate whether inventory levels are too high in relation to sales and whether too much money is tied up in inventories. When inventories are high, managers are often tempted to make hasty sales that yield a less-than-normal profit.

Activity ratios can monitor many important activities. The manager wishing to know how quickly orders are being processed, for example, can select a week and divide the number of orders filled by the number of orders received. By recording ratios for particular activities over extended time periods, the manager can spot trends and plan needed changes.

Financial Responsibility Centers

Describe the five types of financial responsibility centers and their relationships to budgeting

financial responsibility center
An organizational unit that contributes to an organization's costs, revenues, investments, or profits.

All management control relies on *responsibility accounting*, a simple idea: Each manager is responsible for a part of the company's total activity. A manager's unit and its related activities should contribute to the enterprise. A unit's contributions could be vital services, revenues, or the manufacturing of a product. A **financial responsibility center** is any organizational unit that contributes costs, revenues, investments, or profits. The unit manager who accepts the obligation to achieve certain goals is responsible for reporting progress toward them. The author of a respected planning handbook (Dudick, 1983) summarized the notion of fiscal control and responsibility this way:

> *Internal financial reports should follow management's lines of responsibility. Careful evaluation is necessary to determine whether present financial reports track the results that are controllable by the individual held responsible for them. Reasonable assurance should exist that reported information is reliable, that transactions are recorded appropriately, and that corporate assets are safeguarded.*

Figure 17.6 defines the principal financial responsibility centers in large businesses. Each manager's organizational unit within a firm's fiscal structure functions as a financial responsibility center. For each center, top managers must specify the specific financial objective and then decide how to measure progress toward it. Because each manager contributes to unit and company-wide cost control and profitability, selection of each objective is important. Profit, for instance, should be used as a measure of financial responsibility only when profit increases as the direct result of actions for which the manager is responsible (Vancil, 1975).

Figure 17.6 indicated that the sales manager who manages a revenue center is responsible for profit contribution generated by sales, not by cost reductions. Similarly, the production manager who leads a cost center is responsible for costs, not revenue. Only the manager of a production division, who is responsible for both revenues and costs, can be held accountable for the unit's generated profits. Identifying responsibility centers, then, focuses managers' energies on controlling those factors actually within their scope of influence.

http://www.trw.com

Joseph Gorman heads Ohio-based TRW, Inc., a major player in the auto-parts business. His focus, like that of his counterparts in every industry, is on continual growth in quality, productivity, and profitability. "We're expected [by automakers] to decrease our prices every year, through productivity, better design, better process. In most of our automotive business we're taking our costs down 5% to 6% a year" (Flint, 1995). While passing along most of the savings his cost and expense centers generate to customers in the form of lower prices, he has managed to keep TRW's profit, investment, and revenue centers busy too; together they generated a return on capital around 17 percent for 1995, an increase of about four percentage points since 1985 (Flint, 1995).

Financial Audits

audit
A formal investigation conducted to determine if records and the data on which they are based are correct and conform to policies, rules, procedures, and laws.

Financial information is only as good as the data and interpretation on which it is based. **Audits** are formal investigations conducted to determine if financial data, records, reports, and statements are correct and consistent with the organization's policies, rules, and procedures. Insiders or outsiders may conduct audits.

FIGURE 17.6 *Principal financial responsibility centers*

- **Standard cost centers.** A production department in a factory is an example of a standard cost center. In a standard cost center, the standard quantities of direct labor and materials required for each unit of output are specified. The supervisor's objective is to minimize the variance between actual costs and standard costs. In addition, he or she is usually responsible for a flexible overhead expense budget that the manager uses, once again, to minimize the variance between budgeted and actual costs.
- **Revenue centers.** A sales department in which the manager does not have authority to lower prices to increase volume is an example of a revenue center. The resources at the manager's disposal are reflected in the expense budget. The sales manager's objective is to spend no more than the budgeted amount and produce the maximum amount of sales revenue.
- **Discretionary expense centers.** Most administrative departments are discretionary expense centers. There is no practical way to establish the relationship between inputs and outputs in a legal department or information processing department, for example. Managers can only use their best judgment to set budgets. The department manager's objective is to spend the budgeted amount to produce the best (though still unmeasurable) quality of service possible.
- **Profit centers.** A profit center is a unit such as a product division in which the manager is responsible for achieving the best combination of costs and revenues. The objective is to maximize the bottom line, the profit that results from the manager's decisions. A great many variations on this theme can be achieved by defining "profit" as only those elements of cost and revenue for which the manager is responsible. Thus, a sales manager who is allowed to set prices may be responsible for gross profit (actual revenue less standard direct manufacturing costs). Profit for the marketing manager of a product line, on the other hand, might reflect deductions for budgeted factory overhead and actual sales-promotion expenses.
- **Investment centers.** An investment center is a unit in which the manager is responsible for the magnitude of assets employed. The manager makes trade-offs between current profits and investments to increase future profits. To help themselves appraise the desirability of new investments, many managers of investment centers think of their objective as maximizing return on investment or residual income (profit after a charge for the use of capital).

Source: Reprinted by permission of the *Harvard Business Review.* Adapted from "What Kind of Management Control Do You Need?" by Richard F. Vancil, March–April 1975. Copyright © 1975 by the Harvard Business School Publishing Corporation; all rights reserved.

Internal Audits

Most companies maintain controls to determine if people are handling corporate financial activities according to policy and procedural, legal, and ethical guidelines. A superior's regular appraisal of a subordinate's functions is a kind of internal audit. Most accounting systems incorporate controls to guarantee adherence to procedures, as do regular reviews by teams of internal auditors.

http://www.cps.k12.il.us

During the 1995 overhaul of the Chicago public school systems, the reform board prefaced its reengineering activities on results from the system's internal auditors. Among its findings were nearly a quarter of a million dollars worth of much needed school supplies in storage, hundreds of thousands of dollars of missing or unaccounted-for school supplies, and theft of school board property by employees. One employee was arrested in a sting operation for selling supplies to local merchants at prices well below what they cost the board.

Internal audits keep problems in-house, and they are likely to be conducted by people who know operations well. Those who conduct internal audits may lack objectivity, however, and they may also lack the power to penetrate cover-ups.

External Audits

The annual external audit is an American business tradition. An independent public accounting firm conducts an external audit. Such firms are staffed with certified public accountants (CPAs) who provide expert accounting and management services. Federal regulations require publicly traded companies to conduct certified external audits each year. The managers of many nonpublic companies choose to have their companies undergo external audits. The presumed objectivity of the audit enhances the organization's credibility with stockholders, creditors, investors, and key insiders, and such audits often uncover important information.

A certified external audit includes thorough inspection and analysis of policies, procedures, and records, and such tests as the auditors believe may be applicable to the situation. When they are satisfied, the audit team manager certifies that the financial data presented in the firm's financial reports is in keeping with generally accepted accounting practices and procedures and government regulations.

This chapter's Global Applications feature presents shareholder groups' auditing efforts in Russia. In like fashion, investment brokers and mutual and pension funds investor groups regularly request and receive the results of external auditors' findings in the companies in which these investors have a stake. They receive these findings via quarterly and annual reports, interviews with company officials, and, on occasion, through leaks to the press from other internal sources.

BUDGET CONTROLS

budget
A plan and control for the receipt and spending of income over a fixed period.

The primary financial control used to manage operating organizations is a budget. As both a plan and feedforward control, a **budget** provides estimates (projections) of revenues and expenses for a given period of time. A budget serves as the standard for measuring the firm's performance, because it allows managers to compare actual revenues and expenses to projections.

When forecasted revenue is insufficient to support projected spending (expenditures), revenue must be increased or supplemented by borrowing or the use of savings (reserves). The alternative is to reduce expenditures. Conversely, if expenditures rise more quickly than the revenue needed to support them, spending must be reduced to avoid the need to borrow or to deplete reserves.

Budgets serve managers in four important ways:

- They expedite allocation and coordination of resources for programs and projects.
- They operate as a powerful monitoring system when supplemented with periodic budget updates.
- They provide rigorous control guidelines for managers by setting limits on expenditures.
- They facilitate evaluation of individual and department performance.

GLOBAL APPLICATIONS
Russian Stockholders' Struggle for Control

With the fall of Communism in the former Soviet Union, government-owned enterprises were gradually converted to corporations and given or sold to Russian citizens and outside investors through the issuance of shares of stock. Before this privatization, all managers of these companies had to do to keep their jobs was meet the production quotas set by Communist party planning officials. It didn't matter if the goods produced were actually needed by anyone or if they met specific user needs. Many companies, such as the Zil truck factory, continued to make the same model for decades. The cab of the Zil truck looks very much like a Chevrolet truck's cab of the late 1950s, complete with a wraparound windshield.

The problem for these new owners is how to bring their companies into viable economic shape in a rapidly changing economy. Through shareholders' meetings and investment funds' pressures, the old guard is being forced to produce needed changes or leave. The Derzhava Fund has a large stake in Yaroslav Rubber Company, formerly a big supplier to the Soviet military. As that demand fell off, the company did not seek to replace its lost sales until Derzhava and a group of other investors engineered a management shakeup. "They installed a new CEO and a team of young financial experts. In three months, the company [had] signed new orders equal to [1994's] sales."

The old guard, using various techniques, has blocked efforts to make such changes in other companies however. "[These techniques] range from diluting the ownership stake of investors to such simple ploys as erasing the names of outside investors from computerized shareholder lists." When an investment group with an 18 percent interest in Zil wanted to change management and block a new offering of stock, Zil's management responded by petitioning President Boris Yeltsin to replace the investors "with more 'patriotic' ones." The future prosperity of the Russian economy depends on the struggle for shareholder rights.

Source: Galuszka, Peter, and Patricia Kranz. "Look Who's Making a Revolution: Shareholders," *Business Week*, February 20, 1995, p. 60.

Budget status reports allow managers to make timely activity adjustments. Figure 17.7 presents a sample budget status report. It includes the approved budget for certain items and actual expenditures for the first two quarters. Note that spending for long-distance telephone calls (line 5) is 25 percent over budget at the end of the second quarter. The manager of this department must take timely corrective action to avoid a shortfall during the last quarter.

Budget Development Process

4 Describe the four approaches to creating budgets

Budgeting requires (1) setting goals, (2) planning and scheduling to reach the goals, (3) identifying and pricing resources, (4) locating needed funds, and (5) adjusting goals, plans, and resources to match actual fund availability. Some organizations involve all their people in these tasks. Others involve managers only. Either way, budgets must be prepared and adhered to at each level and in each unit of an organization.

Budget preparers can follow one or more of the four standardized approaches: top-down, bottom-up, zero-based, or flexible budgeting. Following a standardized approach helps ensure consistency in the process.

FIGURE 17.7 *Sample budget status report*

Line No.	Category	Approved Budget January 1	Budget Report April 1		Budget Report July 1	
	Salary Expense	*Actual*	*Actual*	*% Used*	*Actual*	*% Used*
1	Professional	$160,000	$40,000	25%	$ 80,000	50%
2	Administrative	60,000	15,000	25%	30,000	50%
3	Clerical Support	32,000	8,000	25%	16,000	50%
	Total Salary Expenses	$252,000	$63,000	25%	$126,000	50%
	Operating Expense					
4	Basic Telephone Service	$ 2,000	$ 500	25%	$ 1,000	50%
5	Long-Distance Telephone Service	2,000	1,000	50%	1,500	75%
6	Insurance	8,000	2,000	25%	4,000	50%
7	Utilities	12,000	4,000	33%	9,000	75%
8	Printing	9,000	1,500	17%	3,000	33%
9	Copying	15,000	3,000	20%	6,000	40%
10	Software	15,000	10,000	67%	10,000	67%
11	Office Supplies	5,000	1,000	20%	2,000	40%
	Total Operating Expense	$ 68,000	$23,000	34%	$ 36,500	54%
	Total Salary and Operating Expenses	$320,000	$86,000	27%	$162,500	51%

Top-Down Budgeting

In top-down budgeting, senior managers prepare budgets and distribute them to lower levels, with or without input from below. Managers who use this method may plan and control without cooperation and knowledge of their subordinates. These managers may miss or neglect significant information about opportunities and risks—information that others could provide and that should be assessed during budget building.

Bottom-Up Budgeting

Sometimes called grassroots budgeting, the bottom-up system taps the knowledge and experiences of all organization members. The men and women closest to the planned activities contribute to building the budget that affects them. In harmonious dialogue, participants come to understand one another's priorities, limits, perspectives, and goals. They negotiate the inevitable compromises. (Few departments get all the resources their managers would like.) As input moves up the hierarchy, various views are consolidated to create an inclusive framework. A compelling advantage of this process is that it earns support for the budget from the people who will be governed by it.

Many companies today are decentralizing, forming autonomous units and divisions. Corporate headquarters provides overall guidance and goals, but the divisions set their own priorities and run their own operations. They also construct their own budgets, partly because downsized organizations no longer maintain the large staffs required for top-down budgeting.

Zero-Based Budgeting

In some companies budget preparers begin their job by looking at last year's budget and building on the numbers it contained. The preparers factor in relevant recent experience, and a new budget emerges. Some managers simply increase last year's numbers by some percentage, on the assumption that what went before should continue. Such budgeting does not force managers to examine their operations and explore more efficient ways of operating. *Zero-based budgeting* eliminates such complacency by requiring preparers to launch each new budget from a clean sheet of paper (or, more likely, a blank computer spreadsheet). The head of each financial responsibility center must justify every dollar requested in light of the coming year's strategic plans and goals, not simply explain changes from previous years.

Zero-based budgeting requires managers to list their goals for the fiscal period and then identify the people and other resources they need to achieve the goals. They must also list the costs of all resources. The managers choose priorities and create alternatives for accomplishing the unit's part in the overall strategic plan. In discussions with higher-level managers, requests and plans from each unit are studied in light of the overall availability of resources and the organization's strategic objectives. Once agreement about resource allocation is reached, the budget is created. The key to zero-based budgeting is that the process is repeated for each fiscal period.

Flexible Budgeting

All approaches to budget building can utilize *flexible budgeting*, in which set levels of expense are correlated with specified output levels. The expense levels permit managers to judge whether expenses are acceptable at a given level of output. Managers can then adjust expenses accordingly (Heyel, 1982).

Flexible budgeting sets "meet or beat" standards with which expenditures can be compared. Incentives should be provided to managers at every level to meet and beat budget targets. Unit expenses within budgeted amounts are usually permitted. Managers who exceed guidelines must present compelling reasons or face curbs on their spending.

http://www.walmart.com

Sam Walton (1992) used flexible budgeting to build his Wal-Mart empire:

> *I tried to operate on a two percent general office expense structure. In other words, two percent of sales should have been enough to carry our buying office, our general office expense, my salary, Bud's salary—and after we started adding district managers or any other officers—their salaries too. Believe it or not, we haven't changed that basic formula from five stores to two thousand stores. In fact, we are actually operating at a far lower percentage today in office overhead than we did thirty years ago.*

When asked how he arrived at his 2 percent rule, Walton admitted that he just "pulled it out of the air." Wal-Mart's success is due in no small measure to its founder's obsession with controlling costs.

Operating Budgets

Explain the two major types of budgets used in businesses

operating budget
A financial plan and control for each financial responsibility center's revenues, expenses, and profits.

http://www.sears.com

Operating budgets are financial plans and controls for each financial responsibility center's revenues, expenses, and profits.

Revenue Budgets

The organization as a whole as well as each revenue center uses revenue budgets, which forecast total revenues from all anticipated sources over a given time. Sears may forecast its revenues by store, line of merchandise, and region. States and cities forecast revenues from various taxes and fees—license and permit fees, sales tax, and property tax, for example.

Expense Budgets

Like revenue budgets, expense budgets are developed for each cost center and the whole organization. Expense budgets refer to several standard categories of costs. *Fixed costs* are facility-related expenses that an organization incurs regardless of the amount of activity in any function. Fixed costs include rent, real estate taxes, insurance premiums, wages and salaries of administrative and support personnel, interest payments, and payments on long- and short-term debts. *Variable costs* relate directly to operations and vary with revenue and production levels. The cost of utilities (typically, telephone, electricity, gas or heating oil, waste disposal, and water) is a variable cost. Other variable costs include the costs of raw materials and supplies, wages and salaries paid to people engaged in production and marketing, and advertising expenses. *Mixed costs* are costs that contain fixed and variable elements. For example, suppose a janitor maintains office and factory buildings. Part of the janitor's salary will be allocated to administration as a fixed cost and part will be allocated to production as a variable cost. Travel expenses are sometimes mixed costs. The travel expenses of administrators may be fixed expenses, whereas those of sales and production people may be variable expenses.

The cost of utilities, including natural gas, is a variable cost, which means it varies with revenue and production levels.

Profit Budgets

http://www.ibm.com

Profit budgets simply merge revenue and expense budgets to calculate derived profit for the organization and each profit center. IBM operates product and service profit centers, as do most large retailers. Commercial bank profit centers are established according to the types of loans they grant—real estate, consumer, or commercial, for example. Profit budgets are useful in gauging manager performance. In whatever the business, where profits fail to reach projected levels, the responsible manager must increase profits or risk losing his or her line, department, or division.

Financial Budgets

financial budget
The details of how a financial responsibility center will manage its cash and capital expenditures.

Financial budgets detail how each financial responsibility center will manage its cash and capital expenditures. Financial budgets include cash budgets and capital expenditures budgets.

Cash Budgets

Often called cash flow budgets, cash budgets project the amount of cash that will flow into and out of an organization and its subsystems during a fixed period. Line items include cash left over from the previous period, cash revenue from sales, and monies secured through borrowing. A cash budget also accounts for outlays—cash payments for all resources, including borrowed funds. Cash flow budgets project time frames during which managers expect expenses to outstrip revenues. Such periods call for a dip into investments or for loans. Any excess cash on hand during any period can be invested, thus yielding additional revenue.

Capital Expenditures Budgets

Managers use capital expenditures budgets to project the short- and long-term funding needed to acquire capital goods. Capital goods include machinery, office equipment, buildings, vehicles, computers, and other expensive assets that will take more than one year to pay for.

http://www.boeing.com

Only sound coordination of capital goods expenditures with ongoing expenses sustains operations. When sufficient funding cannot be found from the cash budget or from borrowing, managers may lease needed capital items. Raising capital can be an exercise in creativity. Aircraft maker Boeing helps small airlines and countries raise the capital they need to purchase airliners by giving marketing assistance to its would-be customers. Boeing representatives actively solicit U.S. buyers for the products or services its customers offer, and the representatives bring the sellers and buyers together.

MARKETING CONTROLS

Describe the five major marketing control techniques used in businesses

Under the marketing umbrella are product design, packaging, pricing, sales, distribution, and customer service. Among the control techniques marketing managers use to prevent problems and monitor operations, this chapter will examine market research, test marketing, marketing ratios, sales quotas, and stockage.

Marketing Research

Marketing research is a feedforward control technique. It consists of gathering and analyzing geographic, demographic, and psychographic data. The analysis helps planners decide what potential and current customers want and need so that the planners can design products and services to meet those needs (Bittel and Ramsey, 1985). Market researchers gather information from varied public and private sources. These sources include published materials, personal and telephone interviews, direct-mail questionnaires, and focus groups. A newer source of information is chat, the topic of this chapter's Managing Technology feature.

http://www.greatplains.com

Great Plains Software of Fargo, North Dakota, now a subsidiary of Microsoft, runs some 50 focus groups nationwide. Marketing and development staff from the company visits the groups as often as monthly to discuss current and projected needs with customers who use the company's software every day (Finegan, 1992). Combined with in-depth phone interviews with users, customer satisfaction surveys, and vendor feedback, focus group input has allowed Great Plains Software to add hundreds of new features to its accounting package.

Market research draws upon data developed by professionals in academic, government, and commercial settings. *Demographic data* refer to people's income, age, gender, occupation, marital status, or education. *Geographic data* describe where

MANAGING TECHNOLOGY
Chat

Chat is two or more people discussing online in real-time by typing messages, visible to the people in the same chat room. Chatting on the Internet is accomplished through a window or dialogue box in a chat room. The participant simply types in his or her comments and views the comments of others in the same chat room. A chat room is part of a chat network that consists of one or more network servers hosting the actual chat rooms. Chat programs on chat servers are file oriented, and all of the messages or posts are in the files. Thus, chat rooms are public. A network may have from one to many thousands of individual chat rooms, generally set up by subject in targeted chat environments.

Managers are taking advantage of chat as a real-time medium because of its timeliness to exchange information and to collaborate. They use chat to connect with employees regardless of physical location. Colleagues can connect without having to walk through the building to another office. With chat, a person can be summoned quickly. Messages are delivered instantly, on top of any open desktop window. Employees are notified when other, specified users are online and communicate instantly with them.

One-to-one chats might be two colleagues, thousands of miles from each other, viewing a Web page at the same time and *discussing* it electronically. Group chats might involve employees in different locations; all online at the same time, typing in ideas and offering their reactions to what's being *said* over the Internet. Chat can be used while doing other work. For example, one-on-one communication can take place during a conference call. People can refine their thoughts online, be aware of others online, and communicate with someone online without interrupting the conversation.

Chat can be used to recruit, develop, and maintain good employees. Prospective employees can visit an online auditorium, where executives explain the business model and field questions. Online training programs can be used to educate employees. Moderated chats, such as corporate communications, can be used to introduce new products and share business updates.

people live by region, neighborhood, or type of housing. *Psychographic data* relate to cultural origin, religion, political philosophy, and personal interests. Researchers study needs and wants and the buying habits and motives of different population segments. Possessing such knowledge about current and potential customers allows managers to tailor products, advertising, sales, and distribution systems to individuals and groups.

Market research has generated many product innovations and identified discrete target markets. Imaginative research led pet food companies to formulate dog and cat food to appeal to owners with pets of different ages. Where Henry Ford once offered only a single standard model in "any color so long as it's black," market research has spawned a dizzying array of vehicles—from Rolls-Royce limousines and zippy Miata convertibles to minivans of every description, all with an array of options.

http://www.millerbrewing.com

Wisconsin-based Miller Brewing Company, owned by Philip Morris, shocked its competitors in 1977 by introducing Miller Lite, a brew designed to capture "young adults and . . . people who were watching their calories" (Lubove, 1995). This product, which quickly increased Miller's market share, resulted from careful market research that uncovered unmet needs. Instead of one national advertising campaign to launch the new brew, "Miller launched several, each aimed at a different part of the market: twentysomethings, blacks, Hispanics, jocks, working stiffs" (Lubove, 1995). Under the leadership of a former Anheuser-Busch manager, John MacDonough, the company continued to be an innovator, introducing "16 new brands [in 1994], to Anheuser-Busch's 7" (Lubove, 1995).

Test Marketing

http://www.mcdonalds.com

http://www.3m.com/post-it

Suppose a new product or service has been conceived and a prototype developed. Planners may decide to test-market the new item—that is, introduce it to a limited market on a small scale to assess its acceptance. McDonald's launches new menu items on a limited basis through careful test marketing. First, candidate states, cities, and towns are chosen. Next, advertising and in-store displays promote the new offerings. Then, customers who try the new product are asked for their opinions. 3M Corporation began test marketing for Post-it Notes in-house. The program began with the distribution of custom-made packets of the product to managers throughout the home office. The CEO also sent samples of Post-it Notes to other CEOs of Fortune 500 companies. Soon demand outstripped 3M's capacity to supply the product; then marketing took over. This product now contributes over $400 million to 3M sales each year.

http://www.panasonic.com

http://www.motorola.com

http://www.sony.com

http://www.honda.com

One disadvantage of extensive test marketing is that it can tip a company's hand to competitors. A smaller version of the practice has become popular for companies in highly competitive industries. These firms involve small groups of users or potential users and restrict their sampling of options. Working closely with users in a controlled environment, marketing and production people assess the marketability of a new product and make decisions on the basis of the users' feedback, however limited. Managers at Panasonic, Motorola, and Sony favor this method. Honda managers consider the company's dealers and customers the most reliable source of marketing information.

No matter which test-marketing methods are employed, planners analyze the results of testing to determine if the company should proceed with manufacturing and distribution and if modifications to the new product or service are needed. Test marketing limits the risks a company faces when introducing something new, and it increases the new item's prospects for success.

Marketing Ratios

As heads of financial responsibility centers who are responsible for profitability, marketing managers must track and control their costs. Along with supervising the sales force and reviewing income statements, marketing managers regularly calculate various ratios to monitor ongoing operations and determine needs for improvement. Frequently used measures include the ratio of profit to sales, costs of selling to gross profit, sales calls to orders generated and profitability of each order, and changes in sales volume to price changes. Marketing managers also calculate the ratio of bad debts to total credit granted, and sales volume to production capacity for the entire organization and its individual product lines. In addition, market share and order turnaround time are two common measures.

In many industries, total market share ranks as the critical standard of success. Market share performance often drives a marketing manager's decision making. General Motors (GM) is driven by market share and makes decisions on brands based on market share. In 2000, GM decided to discontinue the oldest U.S. auto brand, Oldsmobile, due to poor sales.

http://www.gm.com

Japanese companies aim to dominate a market, sometimes at the cost of little or no profit. This strategy has led to charges of "dumping"—selling goods in a foreign market at less than the cost of manufacture or less than fair market value at home. America's Big Three carmakers frequently charge their Japanese rivals with dumping, and global trade negotiators wrestle with the topic in tariff negotiations.

The focus on total market share has paid off in consumer electronics, an area in which large Japanese firms have all but eliminated U.S. manufacturing. Nintendo follows this strategy in the computer games market. Its trade practices effectively keep large retailers from stocking competitors' games. A retailer who does stock competitors' products may find that he or she has trouble getting Nintendo games. Retailers who cut the price of Nintendo products find themselves stripped of their status as authorized outlets.

http://www.nintendo.com

Sales Quotas

In many organizations each salesperson operates with a sales quota—a minimum dollar amount of sales within a specific time period to justify his or her salary. Many salespeople work on a commission-only basis, earning money in direct proportion to and as a fixed percentage of the value of the goods or services they sell. If commissioned salespeople make no sales, they get no pay. Commissions and quotas stimulate salespeople to meet or exceed specific quantity goals, but they can also lead to abuses. Overly aggressive salespeople may harass customers or sell them things they cannot afford or do not want. But managers usually favor quotas. Quotas ensure that professionals try their best and feed the ambition of those who want to succeed and advance.

Stockage

The level of inventory for any item is called *stockage*. Stockage is important to business success. You cannot sell what you do not have, and you cannot produce when components are not on hand. In addition, maintaining inventories is expensive, as Figure 17.8 shows. Money tied up in inventories is unavailable for other uses. Retailers and manufacturers must track their inventories to ensure that they do not run out of needed items. They must reduce the number of slow-moving items or eliminate the items altogether. Retailers quickly learn to devote most of their best display areas to the items that yield the largest profits, either individually or by volume. By tracking stockage levels, managers can determine normal usage rates, maintain minimum levels, and set efficient reorder points.

http://www.kmart.com

Today large retailers and manufacturers endeavor to keep as little stock as possible. Many now rely upon just-in-time (JIT) inventory control—that is, they require their suppliers to deliver inventory just in time to meet production or sales demands. Wal-Mart, Kmart, and Sears maintain computer links that allow their suppliers to track sales of the items they produce, and ship items as needed to prevent stores from running out. On the manufacturing floor, JIT systems send items to each production stage as necessary. The notification to move materials along comes from operator signals or computerized inventory control processes. (Chapter 18 will discuss controlling inventories in greater detail.)

HUMAN RESOURCE CONTROLS

Describe the six major human resource control techniques used in businesses

Human resource managers employ diverse control techniques. Among the most frequently used are statistical analysis, human asset valuation, training and development, performance appraisals, attitude surveys, and management audits. Each is intended to provide information about the productivity of the workforce and the quality and quantity of individual and group performance.

Statistical Analysis

Companies need to gather and store data about the composition of their workforce, compliance with equal opportunity guidelines, employee turnover and absenteeism, and effectiveness of recruiting and compensation efforts. Companies need data about

FIGURE 17.8 *Costs of maintaining inventories*

1. Costs of producing or acquiring inventory items
2. Costs of loss to obsolescence, damage, or theft
3. Freight charges
4. Security costs (guards, alarm systems, insurance)
5. Storage costs (buildings and maintenance)
6. Administrative expenses (wages and salaries of those who run storage facilities, keep track of inventory, and inspect and move inventory)
7. Costs of computerized inventory control system
8. Costs of maintenance and operation of storage equipment
9. Costs connected with procurement and inspection of and payment for inventory items

managerial and individual effectiveness, levels of job satisfaction and motivation, and employee safety and health. Many companies create databases containing facts about employees' skills, training levels, evaluations, formal education, and job experiences. Such information facilitates recruiting, promotion, and other employment decisions. Though data in all these categories is important, this section will focus on two standard measures: turnover and absenteeism. (Workforce composition and safety will be discussed in relation to management audits.)

Turnover

The number of employees who leave an organization during a specific period of time is known as employee turnover. Some turnover occurs through attrition—retirement, resignation, illness, and death. Some turnover is seasonal and planned—farm laborers are hired to harvest a crop, and many salesclerks are hired only for the holiday shopping rush. Some turnover results from economic conditions and competitors' actions that decrease a firm's sales and its ability to support its workforce. Resulting layoffs may be permanent or temporary. Substantial turnover results from bad management. In many cases people lost to turnover must be replaced, and replacing people is costly. It is normally in a company's best interest to retain its most valuable employees for as long as possible.

The rate of turnover often serves as a measure of an organization's internal environment—its morale, stress, and managerial skill levels. Each organization, and each subsystem, needs to determine its acceptable turnover, or an acceptable number of people who must be replaced compared to the total workforce. To determine an acceptable ratio, most companies study their own past and the experiences of other companies in their industries. Some businesses, such as the fast food and hospitality industries, experience unusually high turnover rates. Managers must analyze the causes of turnover carefully and determine which among them are signs of trouble. Then managers must act to eliminate those causes.

The turnover of farm laborers hired to harvest a crop is seasonal and planned.

Absenteeism

Absenteeism is the percentage of an organization's workforce not at work on any given day. All organizations must maintain a realistic standard for absenteeism—say 5 percent. As with turnover, managers must assess the causes for absences and judge their validity. Many companies find that 90 percent of their absenteeism is caused by less than 10 percent of their workforce members. At any given time, absenteeism that exceeds the standard may or may not be a sign of trouble. Circumstances such as a widespread flu outbreak or a natural disaster that prevents people from getting to work may temporarily and legitimately raise absenteeism. Many managers try to prevent absenteeism by encouraging 100 percent attendance; they offer financial rewards and set realistic and equitable attendance policies.

Human Asset Valuation

human asset accounting
Treating employees as assets, not expenses, by recording money spent on people as increases in the value of those assets.

Various monitoring devices help managers assess the value of each employee to a company. One approach focuses on accounting. Another projects the long-range potential (promotability) of each person. **Human asset accounting** tracks the money spent to recruit, hire, train, and develop employees. This type of accounting treats each person as an asset, not an expense. Expenditures for the development of human assets are considered investments, not unlike the investments made to build an office or factory building. Managers who use human asset accounting realize that each person represents a sizable investment of company resources, and these managers tend to be committed to retaining good people. Many managers with this view keep balance sheets that list employees as assets. (These balance sheets are not for tax purposes.) When someone leaves, the corresponding investment is deducted from the total, showing a net loss of assets.

In an approach less common than human asset accounting, managers attempt to assign a dollar value to each employee's contribution to company profits. Such calculations are not easy to make. They consist of creating general categories of employees and assigning dollar amounts to each category on a percentage basis. Arbitrary as such an approach may be, it does attempt to focus attention on people as resources, not simply expenses.

Training and Development

As Chapter 11 (on staffing) has indicated, training and development (T & D) impart knowledge, skills, and attitudes necessary for successful job performance. The standards necessary for effective and efficient operations must be taught and then enforced, usually by those closest to these standards. T & D are control techniques concerned with preventing problems from arising and dealing with them quickly when they do. T & D get people ready for changes *before* those changes arrive. The subject matter or areas of training become the standards by which employees are appraised, rewarded, or punished.

With the increasing diversity found in most organizations today, training employees to value diversity has become a norm. People cannot, however, be expected to value the uniqueness they bring to a workplace if they cannot communicate with each other. Such was the case at Standard Motor Products (SMP) in Edwardsville,

Kansas, where two primary groups of employees had trouble communicating in English (Hayes, 1995). This chapter's Valuing Diversity feature describes how SMP handled this problem.

Performance Appraisals

Perhaps the most important control device employed by human resource managers is the use of a regularly scheduled legal, objective, and equitable appraisal system. The focus of such a system must be on comparing people's performances to standards established for them and then sharing the results. Appraisal standards are feedforward control devices; the appraisals themselves are concurrent and feedback devices.

http://www.dominos.com

Domino's Pizza uses a computer test to gauge employees' effectiveness and alertness before they are allowed to take on their duties. When drivers are hired they are given a hand-eye coordination test. The results are recorded as that person's standard for acceptable performance. On reporting to work each day, the driver takes the same machine-based test. The results (answers and reaction times) are compared to those for their first test. The driver who fails to meet those standards may be assigned to alternative duties for that day or given the day off. The point is to keep people away from potentially dangerous and difficult-to-operate equipment when they are not in top form.

VALUING DIVERSITY

Valuing Diversity Through Self-Directed Work Teams

"The members [of self-directed work teams] have a built-in opportunity to build the intercultural bridges that some companies are paying diversity consultants thousands to install." A consultant on work teams, Darrel Ray, notes that in such teams, members must work through their problems and difficulties face-to-face every day. They have the power to write their own schedules, evaluate their own performances, and even discipline their fellow members. Most importantly, they must share the job of leading the group.

Just how effectively self-managing teams can overcome their members' personal differences is illustrated at the Edwardsville, Kansas, plant of Standard Motor Products (SMP). Its workforce has traditionally consisted of African Americans, Asian-Americans, and Latino-Americans. Whites are in the minority. Whites and blacks rarely mixed with the others, primarily because of the language barriers. SMP routinely struggled with resolving language differences by offering voluntary English instruction; but until it made the decision (in 1992) to increase productivity by creating self-managed work teams, few employees attended the classes. Teaming changed everything.

Employees now had to communicate in a common language—English. Employees having trouble with English had to learn the language or leave. The common language encouraged interactions; and new, open relationships within and between groups formed almost immediately. No longer were workers allowed to "claim language ignorance when something doesn't get done." All could now concentrate on the job at hand—how to cut cost and boost efficiency. Productivity has improved and workers share the gains achieved—an average of $2,000 each in the first year of teaming. Worker complaints have dropped to fewer than half of what they were, morale has improved significantly, and the turnover rate has declined.

http://www.smpcorp.com

Source: Hayes, Cassandra. "The New Spin on Corporate Work Teams," *Black Enterprise* (June 1995), pp. 229–230, 232, 234.

Attitude Surveys

An attitude survey shows how employees feel about their employer. It can highlight what is going right in the workplace and where problems exist. Top managers usually hire an outside consulting firm to conduct such a survey. The fact that the polls are objective and can be answered anonymously encourages employees to respond to them.

Attitude surveys ask questions about key processes, units, and personnel in an organization, and they can be tailored to the specific unit being evaluated. Questions should help companies pinpoint areas of dissatisfaction and gather suggestions about how to improve people, procedures, and policies. Sample questions are "How well does your boss respond to your requests for assistance?" and "What are the sources of stress for you on your job?"

After the answers are collected and analyzed, the results are given to management. For best results, the results should be shared (with nothing held back) with all employees. Data gathered from the surveys—facts about employees' gender, marital status, age, and job categories—become useful for determining which programs or changes are best for which group.

Management Audits

http://www.osha.gov

http://www.eeoc.gov

The Occupational Safety and Health Administration (OSHA) and the Equal Employment Opportunity Commission (EEOC) require regular recording, reporting, and disclosure of statistics about employment. Both agencies set national standards and procedures for the workplace. In many cases, managers must also comply with state regulations about employment.

To ensure that regulations are being followed, managers should conduct regularly scheduled management audits, or compliance audits. In addition, they must continually track and record statistics about safety, health, and compliance with equal employment opportunity guidelines. Violations of government employment regulations are punishable by significant sanctions.

As the previous chapters have pointed out and Chapter 22 explores more deeply, ethics and ethical conduct are of great concern to most companies today. Companies promote and monitor ethical behavior within their environments through various methods. Some provide ethical training, others list codes of conduct, still others have ethics committees, and some make it a part of each employee's appraisal. Risk managers, human resource managers, or outsiders may handle training. Regardless of the method, all employees must be given enforceable guidelines for determining what is and what is not proper conduct. See this chapter's Ethical Management feature for reasons why some type of control technique is needed to monitor employee behavior.

COMPUTERS AND CONTROL

One of the major revolutions in the control function has been the application of computers to nearly every business process. More than two-thirds of employees now work to some degree with a computer as part of their daily routines, and all employees are affected by computer use.

ETHICAL MANAGEMENT
Ethics and Secretaries

"Unresolved ethical dilemmas in the office drain productivity and profitability," according to the president of the Minnesota-based consulting firm Executary Services. A 1995 survey of over 2,000 U.S. and Canadian secretarial employees shows that those surveyed face several similar, unresolved ethical situations; most are related to their bosses' conduct or the fear of losing their job.

For example, what would you do if your boss asked you to falsify a time sheet or an expense account? According to the survey, about 33 percent said they did the former while about 5 percent reported doing the latter. How would you handle a request from your boss to deceive others about his or her whereabouts or reason for being absent? Fifty-eight percent of those surveyed did so. Finally, how would you respond to your boss's request to destroy or remove damaging (to the company or its personnel) information from files? Ten percent reported that they complied with such requests.

Is the conduct cited here unethical? Who is accountable for such actions: the person requesting it, the person performing it, or both? How can companies deal with such issues in the workplace?

Source: Kleiman, Carol. "Should Secretary Be Fall Girl When Boss Asks for Fib?" *Chicago Tribune*, July 20, 1995, sec. 3, p. 3.

The most important contribution that computers have made to the control process is data. Computers can provide data more quickly, cheaply, and accurately than can traditional means. Computers facilitate communications throughout and among organizations and their members, placing data in the hands of anyone who needs it. Moreover, they can do so in *real time*—the time in which an event is actually happening.

Control needs served by computers include data collection; data analysis, reduction, and reporting; statistical analysis; process control; test and inspection; and systems design. The activities of data analysis, reduction, and reporting can be programmed to occur automatically as the data are collected or to occur on command. Decision rules can be employed in the program that will automatically signal the likelihood of a problem and corrective action can be taken. The collection, utilization, and dissemination of control information is best accomplished when the information is incorporated into a management information system (MIS), which maintains relationships with other activities, such as inventory control, purchasing, design, marketing, accounting, and production control.

CHAPTER SUMMARY

1 **Describe the content of the three primary financial statements and how managers use them.** The three statements are the balance sheet, income statement, and sources and uses of funds statement. The first lists the assets of an organization and points out who owns them and to what extent—the proprietors, partners, stockholders (equity), or creditors (liabilities). It is a snapshot of a company's situation at a given moment in time. The income statement lists income from all sources and the amount of money actually paid out during the time period covered by the statement. It is a historical summary. The sources and uses of funds statement is a summary for a given time of the flow of cash into and out of an organi-

zation. All statements help financial managers to make comparisons, spot trends, and forecast future financial activities.

2 Explain ratio analysis and four types of ratios used by managers. Ratio analysis takes key figures and compares them to others. The purpose of ratio calculations and comparisons is to gauge the financial health of the organization and its ability to meet its obligations. Liquidity ratios measure the ability of a firm to raise enough cash to meet its near-term debts. Profitability ratios are used to study a company's profits after taxes. They answer such questions as "What is the return on capital invested?" "What departments, products, and services return the best profits?" Debt ratios express an organization's capacity to meet its liabilities, or debts. Activity ratios help measure and monitor all internal activity areas such as inventory turnover, sales per department, and personnel costs related to human resource activities.

3 Describe the five types of financial responsibility centers and their relationships to budgeting.

- *Standard cost centers* are production units that have standard, or prescribed, quantities of direct labor and materials required for each unit of output. The unit supervisor's job is to minimize the variance between the actual costs in labor and materials and the standard costs. In addition, unit supervisors usually have to create and live within a budget for nonproduction-related expenses.
- *Revenue centers* generate income for an organization, but their managers, while charged with maximizing revenues, do not have the authority to adjust prices for goods or services sold to the firm's customers. Each center has a budget and must spend within its limits while conducting its activities. Center managers may or may not participate in the preparation of the budget.
- *Discretionary expense centers* are usually administrative service providers such as staff departments. These centers and their managers exist to serve all organization personnel with their particular expertise. These centers must prepare their own budgets, usually on the basis of past performance experiences and do their best to live within them.
- *Profit centers* generate revenues but also have the authority to manipulate pricing and offer other incentives to customers. Managers seek to obtain the best possible combination of costs and revenues. Such centers also prepare budgets and must live within their limits.
- *Investment centers* put a firm's cash to work in various ways, including short- and long-term financial instruments. The managers of such centers must struggle to maintain an appropriate balance among the firm's assets, given its immediate and future needs. The goal is to maximize the return on invested capital through the manipulation of a firm's assets. Each center prepares its budget in light of previous experience and is charged to do its best to live within it.

4 Describe the four approaches to creating budgets.

- *Top-down budgeting* is a budgeting approach in which senior managers prepare, with or without input from below, budgets for the entire organization and its various subsystems. This approach is most often the case in not-for-profit and government organizations. Such systems usually depend on large support staffs, or expense centers.
- *Bottom-up budgeting* taps into the knowledge and experience of subsystem managers and relies on them to create efficient budgets, which, when consolidated as they move to the top, will govern the firm's fiscal period. This system is based on compromise and trade-offs; priorities become the driving force.
- *Zero-based budgeting* is an approach in which managers start the budgeting process by making no assumptions and by disregarding past practices. Every dollar requested is justified in light of the coming time period, not last year's experiences. Starting with unit goals and priorities for each, managers calculate the minimum they believe they will require to achieve those goals. In defending their requests to higher-level managers, managers must adjust their requirements in line with available resources.
- *Flexible budgeting* may be used with the previous approaches to budgeting. It utilizes standard costs that can be correlated to specified output levels. The manager projects output for a unit and calculates expected expenses by using standard costs assigned to each output activity. The manager's job is to meet or beat the standards set for operations. Exceeding budgeted cost is only permitted under exceptional circumstances.

5 Explain the two major types of budgets used in businesses.

- *Operating budgets* are financial plans and control techniques for each financial responsibility center's revenues, expenses, and profits. They include revenue budgets and expense budgets. Revenue budgets are forecasts and projections of the amount of income expected from all sources over a given period. Expense budgets project the outflow of dollars for a given period.
- *Financial budgets* detail how each financial responsibility center will manage its cash and capital expenditures. Thus a cash budget and a capital expenditures budget are called for. Cash budgets are often called cash flow budgets. They predict the amount of money from all sources that will flow into and out of an organization over a fixed period. In this way they are similar to their feedback control counterpart, the sources and uses of funds statement. This document, however, represents financial reality, rather than a projection.

6 Describe the five major marketing control techniques used in businesses.

- *Marketing research* is a feedforward technique. It consists of gathering and analyzing geographic, demographic, and psychographic data. After being interpreted, these data become information needed to tailor products and services to specific market segments.
- *Test marketing* is the introduction of new products and services to a specific identifiable population group to determine their marketability. The effects of various marketing activities, such as sales promotion and advertising, can also be gauged through test marketing. By limiting what a company does to a small enough audience, test marketers can effectively measure and analyze the audience's reactions.
- *Marketing ratios* are used to measure, monitor, and project activities and trends. Frequently used ratios are profit to sales, costs of selling by department, costs of selling to gross profits, and sales calls to orders generated.
- *Sales quotas* are specified revenue targets for a given time period to be achieved by sales activities and personnel. They are often the basis for salespeople's compensation. A minimum sales volume must be met each pay period to justify the salesperson's salary or draw. Sales in excess of quota may be rewarded with bonuses or commissions in addition to salary.
- *Stockage*, or inventory, levels must be measured and monitored. Too much inventory represents waste and cash unavailable for other uses. Also, inventories must be safeguarded, housed, insured, handled, and counted. All these activities are expenses that may be excessive or unnecessary if inventories are better managed.

Describe the six major human resource control techniques used in businesses.

- *Statistical analysis* helps HR managers determine and control costs. By collecting and analyzing various data on such things as absenteeism, turnover, safety, and individuals' performances, HR managers can measure and improve the effectiveness and efficiency of the company's operations.
- *Human asset valuation* is a control technique that views people as assets, not as expenses. Money spent on recruiting, hiring, training, developing, and rewarding people is considered an investment in them. Therefore, their worth to an organization increases steadily over time, and their departure represents a considerable loss to the company. The emphasis shifts from arbitrary layoffs and downsizing to retaining valuable assets.
- *Training and development* represent a considerable expenditure for most companies, and those dollars need to be spent wisely. The best way to adjust to change and prevent problems is through training. People are given the knowledge, skills, and attitudes needed to perform to standards. The subject matter or areas of training also become the basis for appraising people. They will be expected to exhibit the skills they were taught.
- *Performance appraisals* monitor and measure how people carry out their duties. How well they do so is the basis for either rewards or punishments. Appraisals help to measure the effectiveness of all human resource activities. They are both feedback and concurrent controls.
- *Attitude surveys* show how employees feel about their employer. Attitude surveys ask questions about key processes, units, and personnel in an organization, and they can be tailored to the specific unit being evaluated. After the answers are collected and analyzed, the results are given to management. In turn, the results can highlight what is going right in the workplace and where problems exist.
- *Management audits* are performed to ensure that regulations (OSHA, EEOC) and policies (ethics) are being followed. These compliance audits provide management with data to determine how well the company is meeting established standards.

REVIEW QUESTIONS

1. What does a balance sheet tell managers? An income statement? A sources and uses of funds statement?
2. What do the four primary financial ratios measure? Why is ratio analysis used by managers?
3. What is a standard cost center? A revenue center? A discretionary expense center? A profit center? An investment center? How do all five centers enter into the budget process?
4. How does top-down budgeting work? Bottom-up budgeting? Zero-based budgeting? Flexible budgeting?
5. What are operating budgets? Financial budgets?
6. What are the five major marketing control techniques? How does each serve the needs of marketing managers?
7. What are the six major human resource control techniques? How does each serve the needs of human resource managers?

DISCUSSION QUESTIONS FOR CRITICAL THINKING

1. As the chief financial officer for a video rental store, how will this year's balance sheet, income statement, and sources and uses of funds statement help you budget for next year's operations?
2. You are the owner/manager of a neighborhood restaurant. Your chef has created what he calls "a delicious, fat-free cheesecake, capable of taking a variety of fresh fruit toppings." He wants to add his creation to the menu. Before doing so, what do you think you should do?
3. You have just received the following in a memo from your boss:

As the above numbers point out, your division ranks below average on the basis of the most recent statistics for our industry. Your employee turnover is twice the normal rate and your absenteeism has risen by 50 percent since one year ago. Finally, your department's recent injuries have been the primary cause of a 15 percent increase in our workers' compensation insurance premiums.

What control devices do you think were used to reach these conclusions? Are these increases related to one another? If so, in what ways?

INTERNET EXERCISES

Check the text Web site at http://plunkett.swcollege.com for updated links to the Internet Exercises.

1. Budgets help businesses (and individuals) manage their money. Use the Web site listed below to create your own budget. How do your budget percentages compare to those shown at the Web site that represent a typical breakdown of fixed and variable expenses? Did you find anything surprising in your budget?
   http://www.themint.org/documents/make_a_budget.htm
2. A balance sheet is a summary of what the business (and individual) owns (assets) and owes (liabilities). Prepare your own balance sheet.
   http://www.swcollege/vircomm/gita/gita10-1.html
   http://www.americancredit.org/netwrth.htm
3. As a manager, you want your customers to be satisfied. The two complementary paradigms for the measurement-analysis-understanding-acceptance-action-improvement sequence are the customer satisfaction paradigm and the customer value paradigm. What are the differing emphases of each? Which would you choose as a marketing control?
   http://www.cval.com/Intro.html

APPLICATION CASE

Kroch's Cracks, Then Crumbles

In 1995 a venerable old Chicago bookseller slipped into bankruptcy, ending nearly 90 years of service to the city and its suburbs. Founded by the Kroch and Brentano families and headed until 1993 by Carl Kroch, the son of one of the founders, Kroch's & Brentano's pioneered hardbound and paperback bookselling in suburban malls. The bookseller was a leading full-service greeting card and book chain until the discounters overwhelmed it. At its peak in the early 1980s, the company had nineteen stores.

Cracks first began to appear in the 1980s, when the large discount chains began to sell best-sellers at significant discounts, causing Kroch's sales of those books to collapse. Carl's initial reaction was a shrug of his shoulders. He and his management team held that there would always be a place for his kind of store, one that shunned the discounting fad and catered to loyal customers who were true book lovers. The stores specialized in selling scholarly works, references, and books for professionals through an "informed and personalized approach to bookselling."

Kroch's culture resisted meaningful responses to the challenges the company faced. As one recent hire put it, "Almost the entire hierarchy of the company had spent their entire careers there and many didn't understand the extent to which dramatic changes needed to be made and made quickly." The bookseller had adopted a kaizen approach when reengineering was called for. Operations were not computerized, and discounting didn't start until the company was facing financial ruin. By 1993 several outlets had been closed and the rest were barely profitable. Kroch then sold the chain to Businesship International (BI), a company specializing in business start-up kits and looking for ready outlets for their products.

Businesship International made two mistakes. It did not adequately fund its planned changes for the chain, and it made no significant alterations in the chain's management. Kroch's president was a 32-year veteran who had presided over the implosion of the company since 1988. BI initially wanted to turn the remaining stores into "learning centers," shunning the entertainment approach taken by their major rivals. In hindsight, the demise of Kroch's & Brentano's exemplified the cliché "too little, too late."

Questions

1. What were the primary causes behind this company's failure?
2. What failures linked to controlling and control techniques can you see in this case?
3. If you had been hired to turn this company around in the late 1980s, what would you have done? Why?

Source: Blades, John. "Final Chapter: Could Kroch's & Brentano's Have Righted Its Sinking Ship? Maybe," *Chicago Tribune*, July 31, 1995, sec. 5, pp. 1, 2.

VIDEO CASE

Quality Control at Bindco Corporation

The Bindco Corporation was one of the largest, independently owned software manufacturing turnkey service providers in the country. The company provided a variety of services to its clients, including (1) operations management (e.g., electronic services; manufacturing, warehousing, and inventory management; order fulfillment and distribution; and package design and manufacturing); (2) component services (e.g., printing, binding, and demand publishing; media mastering and replication; and loose-leaf products and multimedia packaging); and (3) fulfillment operations for software and related products. Founded in the Silicon Valley in 1981, the company had locations in Los Angeles, San Diego, and Redwood City, California. In 1994, the company opened its first European subsidiary in Amsterdam, Holland.

However, Bindco recently merged with ZBR Publications, Inc., to form a new company, GlobalWare Solutions. With the combined resources of both companies, GlobalWare Solutions today has annual revenues in excess of $100 million. The merger marked a major step toward creation of a worldwide, sole-source provider for the computer hardware/software and information-based industry. The company provides its customers with an "end-to-end" business solution for the global management and delivery of digital content, information, and physical products. Customers include Sun Microsystems, The Learning Company, Cannon Information Systems, and Hewlett-Packard.

GlobalWare Solutions is headquartered in Haverhill, Massachusetts, in a state-of-the-art, 300,000-square-foot facility. Its

European division is based in Amsterdam (a 50,000-square-foot facility). The West Coast division (the 250,000-square-foot Bindco facility highlighted in the video) is still at Bindco's original Redwood City, California, location.

To satisfy the needs of its clients and numerous customers, Bindco implemented a large number of control systems to ensure quality and efficiency. The company is ISO 9000 compliant and utilizes a pervasive team of quality assurance inspectors who conduct production-line investigations and generate weekly reports. Furthermore, all personnel are trained extensively in the general quality assurance methods utilized by the company.

Other more specific control measures are in place at the Bindco facility. Personnel examine each software disk for any flaws or physical defects. To combat mislabeling, employees utilize scanners to conduct bar code labeling inspections. All electronic artwork, which is generated by clients, is proofed and shown to them before it goes to press. Assembly kits are sampled, and prototype testing is based on diagrams illustrating the method by which products are to be packaged. Extremely sensitive scales are used to ensure that each product package includes the proper mix of CDs, manuals, and floppy disks.

Bindco prides itself on the ability of its control measures to keep defects to a minimum, maintain high product quality, and ensure customer satisfaction.

http://www.globalwaresolutions.com

For Discussion:

1. Is Bindco's use of "personal accountability" an effective control technique?
2. Do the organizational control measures at Bindco represent preventive controls, corrective controls, or both?

Operations Management

KEY TERMS

acceptance sampling
aggregate planning
agile manufacturing
attribute inspection
capacity planning
cellular layout
computer-aided design (CAD)
computer-aided manufacturing (CAM)
computer-integrated manufacturing (CIM)
critical path
design control
design for disassembly (DfD)
design for manufacturability and assembly (DFM/A)
detailed inspections and tests
economic order quantity (EOQ)
facilities layout
finished goods inventory
fixed-position layout
flexible manufacturing system (FMS)
Gantt chart
inventory
manufacturing resource planning (MRPII)
master schedule
materials requirement planning (MRP)
network scheduling
operations management
operations strategy
outsourcing
process control sampling
process layout
product control
product layout
program evaluation and review technique (PERT)
purchasing
qualification testing
raw materials inventory
reorder point (ROP)
robotics
soft manufacturing system (SMS)
variable inspection
work-in-process inventory

LEARNING OBJECTIVES

After studying this chapter, you should be able to

1. Discuss the nature and importance of operations strategy and operations management
2. Discuss the nature and importance of product and service design planning
3. Describe the four main strategies for facilities layout
4. Discuss the nature of process and technology planning
5. Explain the factors in facilities location planning and capacity planning
6. Describe the role of operations control in achieving quality and productivity
7. Discuss the purpose of design controls
8. Discuss the importance of managing and controlling materials purchasing
9. Explain how EOQ, MRP, MRPII, and JIT differ
10. Discuss the importance and methods of schedule controls
11. Describe the importance and methods of product control

MANAGEMENT IN ACTION

Knitting at a Record Pace

Brenda French remembers the day. "I just couldn't take my eyes off it." The "it" refers to the gleaming $80,000 used German-made Stoll knitting machine. Unlike the traditional weaver's loom, which creates fabric in long serpentine stretches, the Stoll knitting machine employs thousands of precisely angled needles to do things the old-fashioned way—one stitch at a time—while moving at a pace a stadium full of doting grandmothers could never hope to equal.

The machine's mix of new technology and timeless craft presented Brenda French, CEO of French Rags, with a dazzling possibility: mass customization. It would now be possible, she realized, to churn out custom-made garments at virtually the same speed needed to produce the cookie-cutter offerings of the industrial age. Although her 200 hand knitters produced quality custom-made products, the technology would enable French to respond immediately to customer desires. She no longer would produce hundreds of products that might or might not be sold. Instead, French could respond to trends as well as individual needs and give her customers more choices at better prices. Today, "women can order the French Rags line in a multitude of styles, 75 colors with a myriad of pattern choices, all tailored to their specific size requirements" ("About Us," http://www.frenchrags.com).

French's decision to buy the Stoll knitting machine was the first in a series of technically driven leaps that transformed the scarf-making company French founded in a spare bedroom in 1978 into a $5 million, full-line clothing manufacturer with net profits that range from 10 percent to 15 percent. "By 1983, French Rags' sales more than tripled to $5 million. By 1986, when French Rags offered a whole coordinated knit sportswear line, and sales were reaching the $8 million mark, French began to restructure the company and started merchandising directly to the consumer" ("About Us," http://www.frenchrags.com).

French Rags is a classic study in the power of technology to reinvent a company and of the rewards that accrue to those who champion technical innovation along with new ways of thinking. The key to French's success is her company's use of computer-aided design/computer-aided manufacturing (CAD/CAM) technology.

At French Rags's West Los Angeles factory, French's business partner Milé Rasic developed and integrated the manufacturing system. To supplement the software Stoll provided to run its knitting machines, Rasic designed a program that produced portable templates. The templates contain instructions about which color yarns should be loaded on which spools atop one of the knitting machines as the machine is about to knit a particular garment. The templates dramatically decrease the time it takes to go from an on-screen design to the start of production. Thanks to the Stoll–template union, an elaborate knit jacket that used to take a skilled craftsperson a day and a half to knit by hand can now be produced in less than an hour.

Rasic is also responsible for the 500 MB Silicon Graphics workstation that is the heart of the operation. The workstation (a combination of CAD

© TIM WRIGHT/CORBIS

French Rags uses the latest manufacturing technologies to convert color yarns, like the ones seen here, into individually tailored knit fashions.

and CAM) turns Brenda French's clothing sketches into full-color graphic images. Then it programs each of the eleven Stoll knitting machines to develop what the customer wants. Today, "the factory has 26 large computerized knitting machines plus hand machines that allow for incredible creativity and flexibility. French Rags stocks over 30,000 lbs. of yarn and runs its production 20 hours a day" ("About Us," http://www.frenchrags.com).

"The aim of French Rags is to produce wardrobe components that can be individualized for each and every woman" ("Brenda's Corner," http://www.frenchrags.com). The marriage with technology has made French Rags a leader in custom manufacturing of knitted clothing. French Rags sells its clothes directly to women through trunk shows. "Time-challenged women who crave personal attention when they shop for clothes are finding it in the neighborhood—at in-home trunk shows" (Winters, 1998). French Rags is an example of technology, innovation, and creativity focused on customer satisfaction. ■

Sources: Winters, Wendi. "In-Home Trunk Shows Peddle Fine Fashions Direct," *The Associated Press*, January 30, 1998, http://www.s-t.com/daily/01-98/01-30-98/b04li044.htm; Sansoni, Silvia. "Home Shopping with No TV," *Business Week*; Plotkin, Hal. "Riches from Rags," *Inc. Technology* (Summer 1995), pp. 62–68.

INTRODUCTION

http://www.frenchrags.com

http://www.stoll.de

French Rags, like many companies involved in the competitive world of business, is refining and restructuring its technology to gain the upper hand in the marketplace. The companies that are making these changes have discovered that strategic success is directly related to the efficiency and responsiveness of their production operations (Morley, 1992). In turn, these companies are going on the offensive by using their operations management strategy (as did French Rags with its computer-controlled Stoll knitting machines) as a competitive weapon to change the way they develop superior products and services.

Innovative managers don't just manage people; they also manage the technical resources and processes associated with the production of goods and services. One method of doing this is to use chat, the subject of this chapter's Managing Technology feature. This chapter is devoted to a discussion of the processes, decisions, and systems involved in manufacturing and service operations. After defining operations management, the chapter will discuss how companies plan operations. The second part of the chapter will discuss operations control.

NATURE OF OPERATIONS MANAGEMENT

Discuss the nature and importance of operations strategy and operations management

operations strategy
The element of the strategic plan that defines the role, capabilities, and expectations of operations.

Operations Strategy and Operations Management Defined

Operations strategy is the part of a strategic plan that defines the role, capabilities, and expectations of operations. **Operations management** consists of the managerial activities and techniques used to convert resources (such as raw materials and labor) into products and services (Adam and Ebert, 1989). The terms *production* and *operations* are commonly applied to manufacturing operations. Remember, however, that operations management applies to all organizations, not just manufacturers.

Every organization produces something. Some companies, such as French Rags, Allen-Bradley, Caterpillar, and Nike, produce physical goods. Others, such as Sheraton Hotels, Trans World Airlines, and the University of Michigan, produce services. Except for the fact that a service business does not produce a physical product to be

MANAGING TECHNOLOGY
Chatiquette

Successful chat requires manners. Chatiquette is etiquette rules for online chat. Chat works best for intimate dialogue, usually with groups of five or fewer. It's not as appropriate for conversations involving large groups because chat can get unruly.

- Schedule the chat for a specific time. For example, present for 20 minutes and field questions for 40 minutes.
- Focus the topic for the chat. Make topics specific, targeted to the chat audience.
- Fine-tune the agenda and distribute it in advance.
- Distribute personal information in advance.
- Allow many people to listen, but limit how many can type. The others may offer valuable comments in a discussion forum, available after the chat.
- Read the frequently asked questions (FAQ) before posting a message.
- Read what people are talking about before participating.
- Be clear when addressing a specific person, so the whole group doesn't reply.
- Wait for people to finish before typing a response. Generally a period (.) signifies the end of a response.
- Beware of the lag factor of chat and expect delays.
- Address each post to the party to whom it is intended. Posts that are not addressed to anyone often go unanswered.
- Do not repeat the same message over and over. This is known as flooding.
- Beep only to attract a person's attention.
- Remember that chat is public and participants are NOT anonymous.
- Act and speak as if everything is being recorded, because it is.
- Spellcheck before posting.
- Reply in a courteous manner.
- Use bolding and CAPS for emphasis only.

operations management
The managerial activities directed toward the processes that convert resources into products and services.

http://www.ab.com

http://www.cat.com

http://www.nike.com

http://www.sheraton.com

http://www.twa.com

http://www.umich.edu

placed in inventory, organizations that produce goods and services have similar operational problems:

- Each is concerned with converting resources into something saleable.
- Each must acquire materials or supplies to achieve that conversion.
- Each must schedule the process of conversion.
- Each must control processes and ensure quality.

With these similarities in mind, examine Figure 18.1, which illustrates the flow of operations. Notice that every organization takes inputs and transforms them into outputs, either products or services.

Importance of Operations Management

The heart of an organization is its production of goods or services to sell. Some managers, such as Brenda French at French Rags, have discovered that their success is directly related to the effectiveness of their operations strategy and operations system. In addition, managers now realize that when developing strategic plans, they must include a component that consists of an operations strategy. Without an effective operations strategy and operations management, few organizations would survive (Adam and Swamidass, 1989).

No matter the company, the goal is to squeeze the bottom line for more profits. Managers cannot increase profits if operations management is left out of strategic planning or if the goal of operations is simply to keep pace with the industry.

FIGURE 18.1 Flow of operations

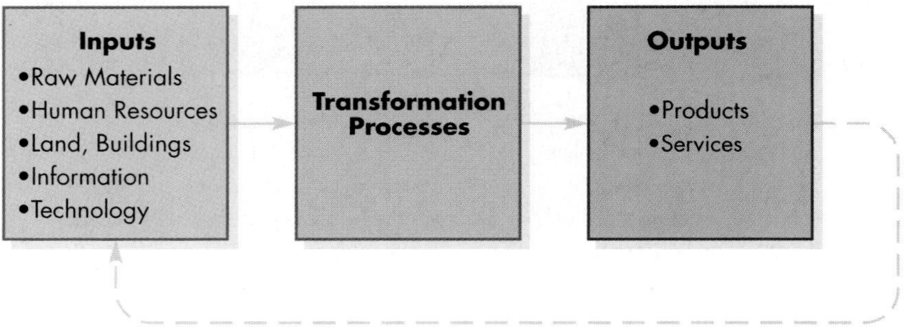

Operations management must be viewed as a competitive weapon to be used with marketing and finance. In this capacity the process of strategic management often leads to new strategic concepts (Hayes and Wheelright, 1984). The results can be (as proven by French Rags) lower prices or better quality, performance, or responsiveness to consumer demand. When operations management receives proper emphasis, marketing and financial strategies are not the only tools of competition (Hill, 1985).

Figure 18.2 illustrates the pervasive role that operations management plays in an organization. Note that operations management embraces product, facilities, and process design; implementation structure; and control processes. In all areas of operations management the focus is on improving productivity and quality.

OPERATIONS PLANNING

The starting point of any undertaking is planning. In the case of an organization's operations, the planning stage involves decisions about product or service design, facilities layout, production processes and technology, facilities location, and capacity planning.

Product or Service Design Planning

2

Discuss the nature and importance of product and service design planning

Historically product and service design has not been acknowledged as part of operations management. Managers have discovered, however, that the goals of operations management (competitiveness, response time, and production efficiency) are well served by two design concepts called *design for manufacturability and assembly (DFM/A)* and *design for disassembly (DfD)*. These concepts involve designing products for effective performance while considering how they will be manufactured, assembled, and disassembled.

Design for Manufacturability and Assembly

In the past, design engineers designed products with a complete lack of thought—some would even say with disdain—for product manufacture and assembly. Design engineers handed finished designs to manufacturing engineers. More often

FIGURE 18.2 *Role of operations strategy and operations management*

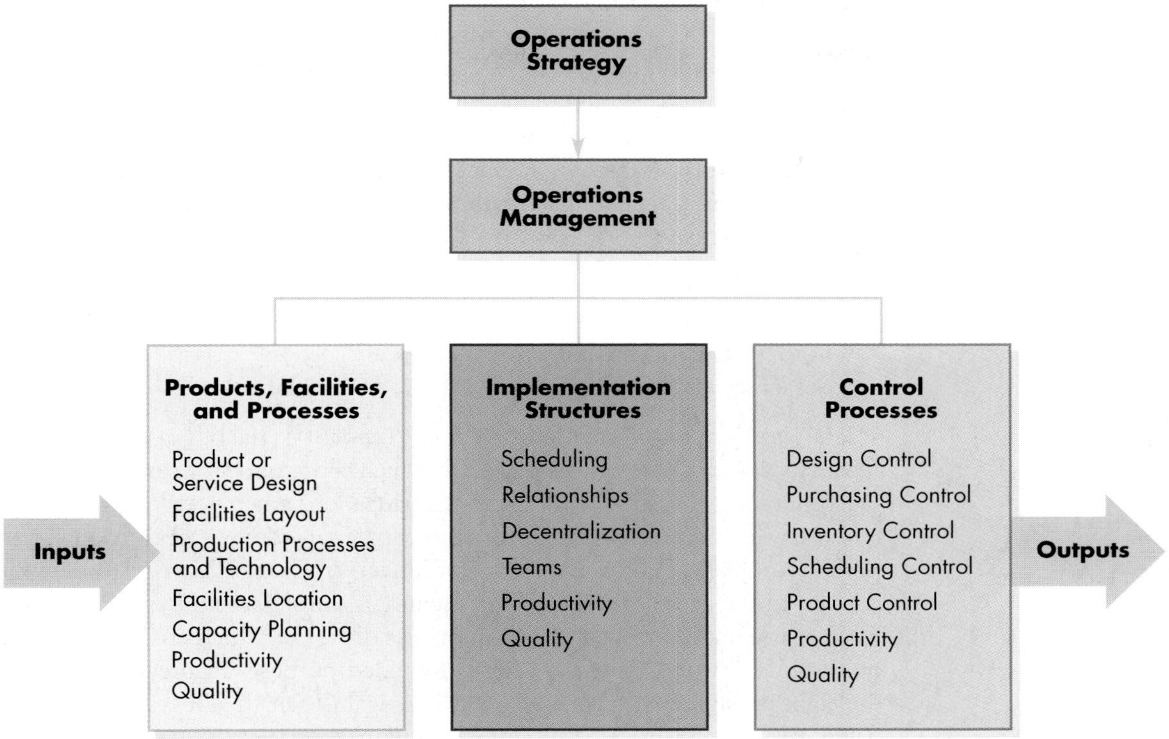

than not, the products the designs specified could not be assembled easily, and they had to be inspected for quality during production. The design-centered approach also led to products that contained a greater number of parts than necessary. "[T]he main point of DFM/A is to discover problems long before the design gets to that stage" (Greco, 2000).

design for manufacturability and assembly (DFM/A)
Considering, during the design stage, how products will be manufactured and assembled.

http://www.realitywave.com

http://www.vuent.com

http://www.thermoking.com

http://fordvehicles.com/cars/taurus

Design for manufacturability and assembly (DFM/A) calls for design teams consisting of designers, manufacturers, and assemblers. Because these specialists all have a say in product design, actual production of the product becomes more efficient. "The enormous potential of the Internet is starting to be realized, as companies such as EAI, RealityWave, Vuent (formerly Adaptive Media and recently acquired by iEngineer.com) and many others have begun making products that allow users to collaborate over the Internet through a virtual design review" (Greco, 2000). At Thermo King, product design teams include engineering, marketing, and manufacturing personnel (Morley, 1992). Another example of DFM/A is found at Ford Motor in the production of the Taurus. Team Taurus's design team included process, product, and manufacturing engineers, designers, marketers, financial experts, suppliers, and factory-floor workers. As a result of the team's work, the Taurus contains 45 percent fewer parts, and assembly has been simplified. For instance, as prototypes were built to test the ease of manufacturing, a team member noticed that he would need three different sized wrenches to tighten different fasteners on a carbon canister. Responding to this observation, engineers simplified the design by making all three bolts the same. When another worker stated that the air-bag cover had to be pounded on with a hammer, team members altered the cover so it could be pushed on by hand, saving time (Kerwin, Updike, and Naughton, 1995).

http://www.gm.com

General Motors has transformed its operations management by incorporating DFM/A. Not only have the number of parts per car been reduced, but vehicles are easier to assemble. A strategic initiative, as a result of DFM/A, is its use of common parts and the same engineering and manufacturing processes regardless of where the product is manufactured or sold. As one GM manager observed (Taylor, September 1994)

> *We now have a much more effective functional execution of car building. It makes engineering more effective. It makes materials management more effective and the assembly center more effective. That is because we are using the total technical voice of the division plus the knowledge of outside suppliers.*

DFM/A product design involves four criteria: producibility, cost, quality, and reliability. Producibility is the degree to which the product or service can be manufactured for the customer within the organization's operational capacity. The criterion of cost includes the costs of labor, materials, design, overhead, and transportation. Quality, in the eyes of the producer, is the excellence of the product or service. In the eyes of the consumer, quality is the serviceability and value gained by purchasing the product. Reliability is the degree to which customers can count on the product or service to fulfill its intended purpose. Figure 18.3 summarizes the eight possible major benefits of DFM/A against which all new designs are evaluated at General Motors. (Notice that the last three relate to operations.)

http://www.fedex.com

http://www.ups.com

Automakers are not the only companies using DFM/A. At Federal Express and UPS, teams that include members from materials handling, transportation, computer services, and customer service now make service design decisions. The results of DFM/A include fewer questions when the services begin and fewer modifications after service has been implemented for a while (Brown, 1992).

FIGURE 18.3 *Major benefits of the DFM/A approach, against which GM evaluates new designs*

Quality	Excellence of the car, including serviceability
Reliability	The degree to which the car fulfills its intended purpose
Durability	The degree to which the car withstands performance demands
Mass	The total weight of the car
Safety	The degree to which the car increases the protection of occupants
Manufacturability	The degree to which the car can be manufactured and assembled within existing operational capacity
Time to market	The time from product design until the car is ready for sale to the consumer
Total cost	The total amount of materials, labor, transportation, design, and overhaul expenses associated with the design

The criteria of producibility, cost, quality, and reliability should apply to the design of services as well as the design of products. In addition, service design calls for another criterion: timing. This criterion relates to the customer's requirements for timeliness. At Federal Express, the customer wants the package the next day, not two days later.

Design for Disassembly (DfD)

design for disassembly (DfD)
Considering, during the design stage, how products will be refurbished, reused, or disposed of at the end of the product's life cycle.

Another design technique is **design for disassembly (DfD)**. The goal of DfD is to conceive, develop, and build a product with a long-term view of how its components can be refurbished and reused—or disposed of safely—at the end of the product's life (Bylinsky, 1995). In a world where the costs of disposal are rising, ease of destruction becomes as important as ease of construction.

http://www.xerox.com

http://www.kodak.com

Xerox photocopiers and Kodak cameras are already being designed for disassembly and component reuse. By designing with fewer parts and materials as well as reusable components, companies are producing products that are more efficient to build and distribute than are conventionally built ones. This is the case because DfD meshes with today's manufacturing strategies: DFM/A and total quality.

http://www.ibm.com

http://www.hp.com

IBM and Hewlett-Packard (HP) have introduced DfD technology across the board. HP used DfD to build all twelve models of its Vectra PC. Each Vectra now contains only three screws, a construction that allows easy upgrade by users. "Our customers love it," says Gilles Bouchard, who heads Vectra's mechanical design team (Bylinsky, 1995).

http://www.interfaceinc.com

An example of a company using DfD in the service economy is Interface of Atlanta, Georgia (Hawken, Lovins, and Lovins 2000). It has evolved from a seller of carpet to a provider of floor covering services. Old carpets are filling landfills and can take up to 20,000 years to decay. Interface developed a new polymeric carpet material that can be remanufactured. Its research showed that 10 to 20 percent of a carpet has 80 to 90 percent of the wear. So they replaced carpet with carpet tiles and routinely check and replace the worn carpet tiles of all their customers. In addition, Interface determined that customers want the warmth, comfort, and beauty of a floor covering, not the covering itself. Thus, Interface offers the service of floor coverings without selling the carpets. "It maintains the ownership of its carpet through its life, repairing and upgrading the product as required. This has led to over an 80 percent saving in materials. This new service and continual recycling approach has resulted in reducing by over 30 times the resources needed to provide carpets" (Hawken, Lovins, and Lovins 2000).

3

Describe the four main strategies for facilities layout

Facilities Layout

facilities layout
The element of operations planning concerned with the physical arrangement of equipment and work flow.

After design, the next step in operations is to plan the actual production. This step involves, among other things, determining the **facilities layout**—the physical arrangement of equipment at the manufacturing site and how the work will flow. There are four main types of layouts from which to choose: process, product, cellular, and fixed position. Figure 18.4 illustrates these four options.

Process Layout

process layout
A facilities layout option in which all the equipment or machines that perform a similar task are placed together.

In a **process layout**, all the equipment or machines that perform a similar task or function are located together (see Figure 18.4a). A product is moved from process to

FIGURE 18.4 *Four options of facilities layout*

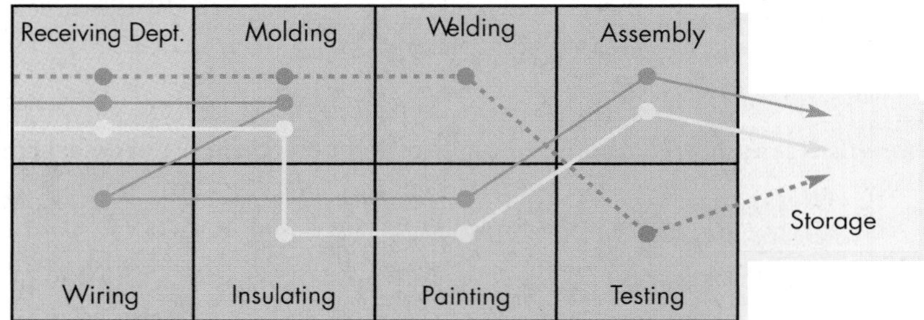

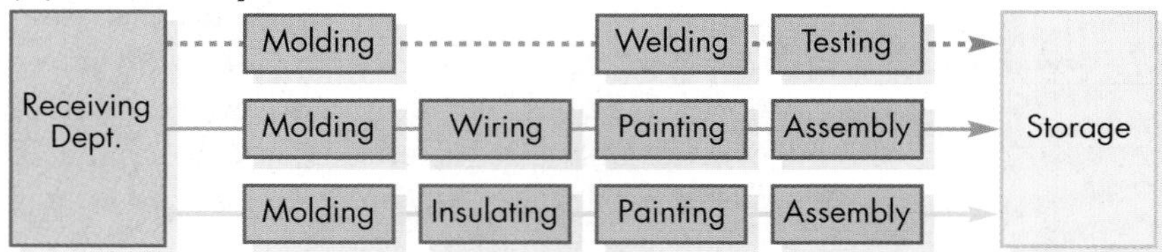

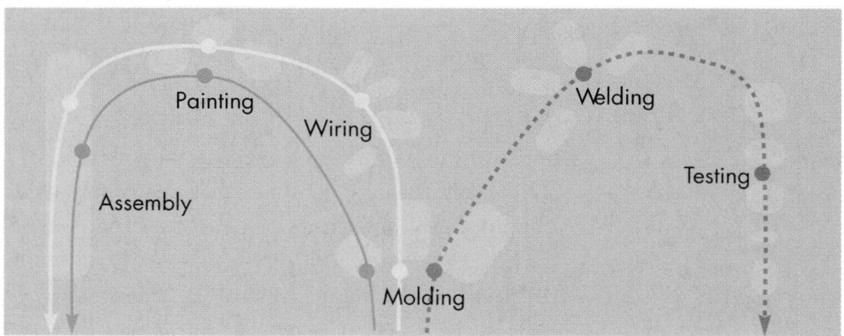

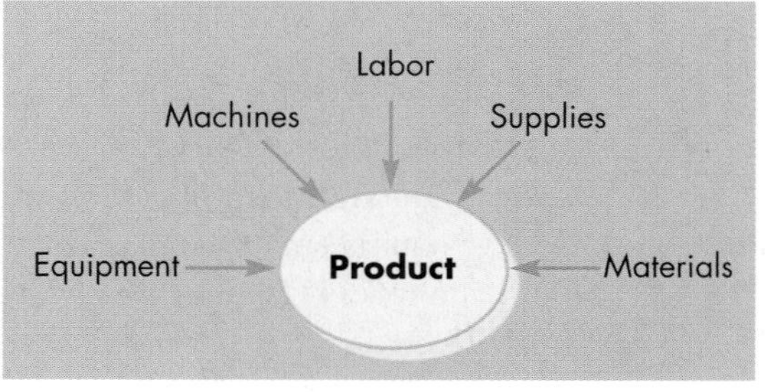

process as needed—all products may not require all processes. The major advantage of this layout is its potential for reducing costs. Because all similar work is done in one area, the process layout requires fewer people and pieces of equipment than does a decentralized arrangement. One limitation of the process layout is the need to move the product through several different processes. Each move costs time and money. In manufacturing, process layouts are used in print shops, settings in which many different products (such as business cards, color brochures, and bound books) do not require the same processes. A hospital is a service-oriented business that uses a process layout. The layout is appropriate because patients receive many different types of services.

Product Layout

product layout
A facilities layout option in which the machines and tasks are arranged according to the progressive steps by which the product is made.

In a **product layout**, machines and tasks are arranged according to the progressive steps by which the product is made (see Figure 18.4b). This layout is efficient when the business produces large volumes of identical products. Car manufacturing on an assembly line is the best-known example of a product layout. Other examples include computer manufacturing and appliance assembly. A hospital might use a product layout when doctors are undertaking a large-scale vaccination effort, for example. In this case many patients are moved through a line, each receiving the same treatment.

Cellular Layout

cellular layout
A facilities layout option in which equipment required for a sequence of operations on the same product is grouped into cells.

The **cellular layout** combines some of the characteristics of process and product layouts. In a cellular arrangement, all the equipment required for a sequence of operations on the same product is placed together in a group called a *cell* (see Figure 18.4c). The cellular groupings allow efficient handling of materials and inventory. In addition, the cellular layout facilitates teamwork; workers are physically close enough to work together to solve problems (Daft, 1994). In service settings, the cellular layout is used where many workers, as teams, see to the needs of a group. A hospital ward is an example of a cellular layout.

A hospital uses a process layout, since it provides many different types of services to patients.

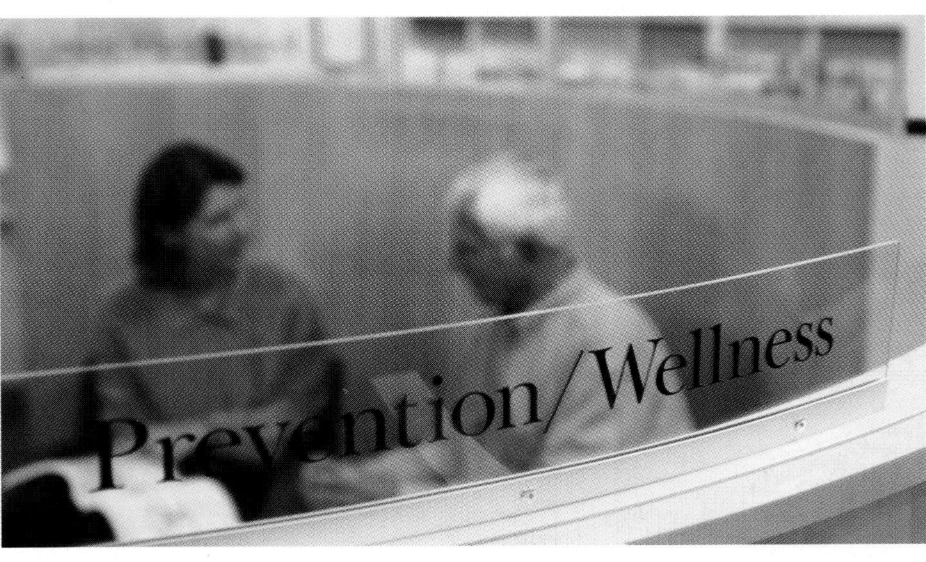

Fixed-Position Layout

fixed-position layout
A facilities layout option in which the product stays in one place and the equipment, tools, and human skills are brought to it.

Figure 18.4d shows a **fixed-position layout**. It is used when, because of size or bulk, the product remains in one location. Tools, equipment, and human skills are brought to the product. Organizations that build planes and ships use this form of layout. The fixed-position approach is sound for bulky products and custom-ordered goods, but not for high-volume manufacturing. This type of layout is used in a hospital operating room, where a number of specialists gather to work on a single patient.

Production Processes and Technology

4
Discuss the nature of process and technology planning

The challenge facing operations managers is to identify the proper blend of people and technology to use in transforming inputs into finished products and services. "The supply chain of a manufacturing enterprise is a worldwide network of suppliers, factories, warehouses, distribution centers and retailers through which raw materials are acquired, transformed and delivered to customers" (Enterprise Integration Laboratory). Supply chain management functions include capacity planning, demand forecasting, production planning, supply chain transaction automation, financial services, payment, and logistics. For any given production task, several conversion methods are available—some labor intensive, others equipment intensive. The nature of the product and the objectives and resources of the organization are critical factors in choosing one method over another.

The growing trend today is toward the use of more sophisticated technology in manufacturing. This type of manufacturing, associated with the "factory of the future," relies increasingly on equipment that works almost unaided by employees.

http://www.emc.sea.siemens.com

> *Michael Spear of Siemens Energy and Automation says the factory of the future will be developed primarily from existing facilities. This is possible by optimizing current capabilities and increasing the use of information technologies. Central to such optimization is linkage of the three primary information systems within the manufacturing environment. These include: the enterprise resource planning aspects that manage company operations, the manufacturing execution systems that handle factory processes, and the individual machine control systems. Such integration permits remote diagnostics, maintenance, and operation using the Internet (Modern Materials Handling, 2000).*

The technologies most responsible for revolutionizing manufacturing processes include robotics, CAD/CAM, flexible manufacturing systems, computer-integrated manufacturing, soft manufacturing systems, and agile manufacturing.

Robotics

robotics
The use of programmed machines to handle production.

The use of programmed machines to handle production constitutes **robotics**. The machines, or robots, are constructed to do the work of employees. They weld, deliver materials and parts, load and unload, and more. Robots provide greater precision than do humans; therefore, they enhance quality. The disadvantages of robots include capital expenditures, maintenance costs, and malfunctions.

http://www.ifr.org

"By 2003 there will be nearly 900,000 multi-purpose robots in use worldwide compared with 750,000 today, according to 'World Robotics 2000', a survey running to 350 pages published by the United Nations Economic Commission for Europe in co-operation with the International Federation of Robotics. Multi-purpose robots are those which may be reprogrammed easily to perform another task, as

http://www.robotics.org

http://www.apple.com

distinct from dedicated robots built into automated systems" (Robotics Industries Association, 2001). In 1994, there were about 45,000 robots at work at U.S. factories, up dramatically from the 6,000 in place just a dozen years before (DeMott, 1994). Once the province of giant corporations like Apple Computer and Caterpillar, robots are taking their place in the manufacturing operations of far smaller companies. One is Engineering Concepts Unlimited, a maker of electronic engine controls. Engineering Concepts has three employees, four robots, and sales of $1 million. Says CEO Adam Suchko, "It's difficult to get the same skill level that you need to assemble these kinds of products and [to find people to] do only that for a living because it's *boring. So boring.* So you use the machines to create an environment where people do other things" (DeMott, 1994).

Shimizu Corporation, the subject of this chapter's Global Applications, has revolutionized the manufacturing of buildings by incorporating robots and computers. Only two people are required to monitor the computers and robots during the construction phase.

computer-aided design (CAD)
A design technique that uses a computer monitor to display and manipulate proposed designs for the purpose of evaluating them.

computer-aided manufacturing (CAM)
A technology in which computers coordinate people, information, and processes to produce quality products efficiently.

CAD/CAM

Among the most widely adopted technologies in manufacturing today are **computer-aided design (CAD)** and **computer-aided manufacturing (CAM)**. A survey of manufacturers revealed that 60 percent employ CAD and 28 percent use CAM (Bylinsky, 1994).

CAD allows engineers and designers (such as Brenda French of French Rags) to develop new products by using a computer monitor to display and manipulate three-dimensional drawings. The assistance of the computer helped cut some engineers' design time in half. In addition, the CAD system allows the engineer to visualize the effects of any design change. Some other companies, besides French

GLOBAL APPLICATIONS
The Newest Assembly Line

Shimizu Corporation has revolutionized the process of manufacturing buildings. Shimizu's Smart System (Shimizu manufacturing system by Advanced Robotics Technology) allows a building to build itself from the ground up in a closed, climate-controlled, factory-like environment that is capable of functioning 24 hours a day. The high-rise building is assembled, not constructed.

The Smart System integrates computers, robots, and just-in-time manufacturing. The computerized systems incorporate the latest factory automation technology, including fully automated equipment for ordering and delivering bar-coded materials such as columns, beams, floor panels, exterior walls, and interior fittings—each in its proper order—to the floor under construction.

A computer-controlled overhead crane transfers the material from the delivery equipment to its precise place on the floor. Robots then weld the joints of columns and beams. Next, the crane snaps interior and exterior wall panels and floor panels into place. When one floor is completed, a built-in, hydraulic climbing system raises the entire factory assembly enclosure one story, so work on the next floor can begin. "It is reported that an Automated Construction System will cut the man-hours required in construction by 30% and reduce the volume of industrial waste by 50%" (CSE, 2000).

http://www.shimz.co.jp/english

Sources: CSE Research Bulletin No. 13. "Construction Automation in Improving Construction Productivity in Singapore," January 2000, http://www.ntu.edu.sg/cse/research/bulletin/1999_2000/pdf/CEco3.pdf; Yates, Ronald E. "U.S. Lags in Construction Technology," *Chicago Tribune*, June 13, 1994, pp. 1D, 4D.

http://www.rockwell.com

http://www.ge.com

http://www.chrysler.com

Rags, that use CAD are Rockwell International, GE, and Chrysler. Using CAD, the design engineers at Chrysler can call up on the computer screen a semitransparent view of a car door being worked on, operate the latch and run the windows up and down to check how they work, experiment with lighter materials by adjusting the underlying equations, and use the same data to direct machinery to make prototypes of the parts. The CAD unit helped Chrysler complete its Neon subcompact in a record 33 months—lopping a year off the company's usual development cycle (Bylinsky, 1994).

http://www.chaparralsteel.com

CAM involves the use of computers to guide and control manufacturing processes. The computer is programmed to direct a piece of equipment to perform a certain action, such as drilling holes or pouring steel. Compared with human control, computer control results in less waste, lower costs, higher quality, and improved safety. Chaparral Steel uses CAM throughout manufacturing. Computers monitor the temperature of liquid steel, make adjustments to each batch, control the pouring of molten steel, and direct the cutting of rods and bars (Dincen, 1992).

Flexible Manufacturing Systems

flexible manufacturing system (FMS)
A technology in which an automated production line is coordinated by computers and can produce more than one product.

A **flexible manufacturing system (FMS)** is an automated production line. Computers coordinate the machinery. The automated line controls assembly, welding, tightening, and adjusting. In addition, an FMS allows rapid adjustment of the assembly process, so the production line can produce more than one model. For example, when General Motors installed an FMS at its plant in Lordstown, Ohio, it was able to mass produce four different car models.

An FMS automates the entire production line by controlling and providing instructions to all the machines. The greatest advantage of an FMS is that through computer instructions, a single manufacturing line can be adapted to produce different products. (The adaptability of an FMS is the characteristic that distinguishes it from CAM.) The computer instructs the machines to change parts, machine specifications, and tools when a new product must be produced.

Computer-Integrated Manufacturing

Originally, computer-integrated manufacturing meant controlling machinery through a system of interconnected computers. Such a system was supposed to make human labor unnecessary. Today, however, **computer-integrated manufacturing (CIM)** is a computerized system that orchestrates people, information, and processes to produce quality outputs efficiently.

computer-integrated manufacturing (CIM)
Using computers to guide and control manufacturing processes.

Allen-Bradley's manufacturing center in Milwaukee is an example of a CIM operation. The facility embodies Allen-Bradley's Electronic Manufacturing Strategy, or EMS 1. The strategy was designed to help the company get more solid-state products to market more quickly while not compromising the company's philosophy of putting the customer first.

Using a continuous-flow assembly line, the facility can automatically assemble six or more different types of circuit boards on a single integrated line. Boards can be produced in lots as small as one, and as many as ten different types of circuit boards can be in production at one time. The facility turns out more than 1,000 panels in a 40-hour workweek. Those panels may contain more than 500,000 integrated circuits, resistors, capacitors, memory chips, and other electronic components.

In addition, the plant can move the panels with incredible efficiency. A conveyer system can carry each panel through all the process options, including surface mounting, robotics assembly, and soldering; or a panel can bypass a process that is inappropriate. The company has also incorporated in-line testing to keep defective products out of customers' hands.

Allen-Bradley has staffed the operation with four self-managed EMS 1 work teams. The teams are composed of enthusiastic veteran employees who trained under the direction of EMS 1 managers and instructors from the Milwaukee School of Engineering.

Soft Manufacturing Systems

soft manufacturing system (SMS)
A manufacturing system that relies on computer software to continuously control and adjust the manufacturing processes.

Soft manufacturing systems were designed as an answer to the struggle of businesses to respond to the demand for customized products. A **soft manufacturing system (SMS)** relies on computer software to continuously control and adjust the manufacturing processes. Rather than mammoth installations like FMS or CIM, a soft manufacturing system groups machines into smaller, more manageable cells and spreads computers literally around the plants.

http://www.motorola.com

Soft manufacturing systems bring unheard-of agility to the factory. Companies can customize products literally in quantities of one, while churning them out at mass production speeds. SMS blurs the boundaries of the traditional factory by bringing production closer to the customer. For example, at Motorola's Boynton Beach, Florida pager manufacturing plant, orders stream in from resellers and Motorola salespeople, typically via an 800 line or email. As the salesperson spells out what the customer wants, the plant digitizes the data and sends them to the assembly line. There, so-called pick-and-place robots select the proper components, and humans assemble the pagers. Often the plant completes the order within 80 minutes; and, depending on where the customer lives, he or she can have the pagers that same day or the next day.

IBM's PC Direct operation in North Carolina follows a similar pattern. Rows of sales reps answer 1-800 calls from customers—about 8,000 a day—and take orders for various models of IBM PCs. As they talk, the sales reps enter the particulars of the order on-screen and check to make sure the parts are available. Finished orders are zapped to a nearby assembly plant where computers check them every ten minutes (Bylinsky, 1994).

Agile Manufacturing

agile manufacturing
A manufacturing system incorporating ultraflexible production facilities; computer technology; alliances among suppliers, producers, and customers; and direct sales data to customize goods at the speed of mass production.

"**Agile manufacturing** is a conceptual framework for more efficient manufacturing, which is now resulting in mass customization. . . . The basic idea (in mass customization) is to get the right product to the right person, at the right time. . . . This high-quality yet flexible way of producing goods involves both the manufacturer and the customer" (Emigh, 1999). Although similar to Allen-Bradley's EMS 1, agile manufacturing facilities are smaller, with fewer but smarter machines that need only token care and that turn out a richer variety of customized goods. The customized goods are made as fast and as cheaply as mass-produced products. For example, at the Ross/Flex plant in Lavonia, Georgia, customers talk via phone with company engineers to discuss what valves they need. The plant enters the specifications into a CAD/CAM system, which designs a one-of-a-kind valve; automated machine tools then grind out the metal parts overnight. Finished valves are delivered in as little as 72 hours, at a typical cost of $3,000. That is about one-hundredth of the time and one-tenth of the cost of traditional methods (Port, 1995).

> *Agile manufacturing includes modularization and virtual manufacturing. Modularization involves building products from components chosen by customers. GE sells railroad car "components" in a choice of color combinations. Virtual manufacturing means a company doesn't do all its own manufacturing, but outsources some or all the work to subcontractors. Most car companies adhere to the virtual manufacturing model, allowing them to focus on services like product design and marketing. "Car companies have become auto assemblers, as opposed to auto manufacturers," Goldman says. DaimlerChrysler is already manufacturing less than 30% of the parts used in its cars; Volkswagen AG, less than 12%. Toyota Motor Corp. is looking at "the five-day car" and possible sales of autos over the Internet. U.S. manufacturers are feeling pressure to reduce their current production cycle of about six weeks to one week or less (Emigh, 1999).*

Computers and the Delivery of Services

Computers and the Internet have revolutionized delivery as well as manufacturing. The widespread access to information that computers and the Internet provide has allowed businesses to improve the quality of customer service. "Thanks to global networks and telecommunication capabilities, businesses can deal with customers and suppliers on an individual basis" (Emigh, 1999). For example, computerized point-of-sale terminals constantly update inventory records; the up-to-date records facilitate rapid response to customers' needs. At Schneider National, a major trucking firm, data sent from computers in the cabs of trucks allow dispatchers to monitor the load status and location of each rig. Dispatchers know which trucks are in the vicinity of a customer and when each will be empty. Computers and the Internet also enhance the ability to track orders. At UPS and Federal Express, computerized monitoring of shipments has allowed both companies to improve delivery time and quality of service.

http://www.schneider.com

Facilities Location

Explain the factors in facilities location planning and capacity planning

In considering the placement of facilities, managers must ask two important questions: Should the firm have one or two large plants, or several smaller ones? Where should the facilities be located?

The decision about the number of plants depends on the company's long-range objectives and distribution strategies, financial resources, and equipment costs. The choice regarding location depends on a number of factors: the location of the market where the product will be sold, availability of labor skills, labor costs, proximity to suppliers, tax rates, construction expenses, utility rates, and quality of life for employees (Straub and Attner, 1994). To make the decision, the company must undertake a cost-benefit analysis. When TRW chooses among two or more potential locations, it analyzes the costs of land, transportation, relocation, construction, zoning, and taxation. Then planners examine perceived benefits—proximity to customers, quality of work life for employees, and labor supply (Robbins, 1992). Finally, they divide total benefits by total costs for each potential location.

http://www.trw.com

Capacity Planning

capacity planning
An element of operations management that determines an organization's capability to produce the number of products or services necessary to meet demand.

A critical element in operations management is **capacity planning**—determining an organization's capability to produce the products or services necessary to meet demand. Capacity planning is essentially a matter of trying to convert sales forecasts into production capabilities. Decisions about capacity should be made carefully. Too little capacity means that the organization cannot match demand and that it will lose customers. The reverse—excess capacity—results in facilities and equipment that sit idle while incurring costs.

http://www.compaq.com

http://www.usx.com/corp/ussteel/index.htm

http://www.goodyear.com

http://www.dell.com

To increase capacity, companies have a number of options. They can build new facilities, create additional shifts and hire new staff, pay present staff overtime, subcontract work to outside firms, or refit existing plants. When former CEO Eric Pfeiffer mandated that Compaq transform itself from a supplier of PCs to corporations into a maker of machines for every market—from pocket communicators to home computers—the company changed to around-the-clock manufacturing to meet customer demand. Although the seven-day-a-week, 24-hour-a-day operation required changes in attitudes and logistics, it is being credited with helping Compaq more than double its share of the $35 billion a year PC and workstation market (Losee, 1994). U.S. Steel adopted the same approach at its Gary, Indiana, plant boosting production by 30 percent with no additional capital investment (Baker, 1995). Goodyear Tire and Rubber employs a different tactic. It opts to refurbish old plants when operations call for more capacity (Schiller, 1995). If a company has to decrease capacity, its options include laying off workers, reducing the hours of operation, and closing facilities. On February 15, 2001, the first time in its sixteen-year history, Dell Computer eliminated 1,700 regular full-time positions or about 4 percent of its workforce. Chairman and CEO Michael Dell said there had been a pullback in capital spending in the PC sector (WSJ.com, 2001).

Capacity is a dynamic variable in operations management. It changes from month to month as well as year to year. Producers attempt to plan capacity to avoid boom-and-bust cycles of plant expansion followed by layoffs and the reduction of operations. The key determinant in capacity planning is the demand for goods and services. (As discussed in Chapter 7, managers can determine demand by using forecasting techniques.) If a company is operating with stable demand, managers should provide plant capacity equal to the monthly demand. Suppose, however, those seasonal fluctuations, uncertain economic conditions, or other factors result in unstable demand. In this situation managers should build a small plant to meet normal demand and add extra shifts or subcontract work during peak periods (Williams, 1990).

MANAGEMENT OF OPERATIONS

Once managers have made the strategic planning decisions about design, layout, process and technology, location, and capacity, the operations management team needs to develop specific plans for the overall production activities. This involves aggregate planning, master scheduling, and structuring for operations.

Aggregate Plan

aggregate planning
An element of operations management that involves the planning of production activities and the resources needed to achieve them.

Aggregate planning involves planning production activities and the resources needed to achieve them. It draws the "road map" for operating activities for a period of time up to one year.

Aggregate planning begins with consideration of the demand forecast for products or services and study of the capacity of the operations. By examining demand and capacity, the operations management team sets production rates, inventory levels, materials requirements, and labor needs. The result of this process is a general operating (aggregate) plan. For a restaurant, such a plan would show the total number of customers to be served but not the specific meals each would consume. For a facility that makes cooking ranges, the plan would show the total number of ranges to be produced but not the color of each one. Details come later. When completed, the aggregate plan serves as the basis for the master schedule (Williams, 1990).

Master Schedule

master schedule
An element of operations management that specifies the quantity and type of each item to be produced and how, when, and where it should be produced.

The **master schedule**, derived from the aggregate plan, specifies the quantity and type of each item to be produced and how, when, and where it should be produced (Robbins, 1994). Figure 18.5 illustrates the development of a master schedule from an aggregate plan. Materials requirements are derived from the master schedule, and the schedule affects inventory levels. These two points will be discussed later in this chapter.

FIGURE 18.5 *Development of a master schedule from an aggregate plan*

Aggregate Plan (Units per Month)

	January	**February**	March	April	May
Electric Ranges	1,000	1,250	1,200	1,300	1,200
Gas Ranges	750	800	700	1,000	1,000
Total	1,750	2,050	1,900	2,300	2,200

Master Schedule for Electric Ranges (Units per Week)

	January				**February**			
	1	2	3	4	5	6	7	8
3,600	100	100	50	50	100	100	50	100
3,665	100	100	50	100	100	50	100	100
3,670	100	50	100	100	150	150	150	100

January Total 1,000

February Total 1,250

Note: Another master schedule will be developed for the gas ranges

Structure for Implementing Production

One more element of operations remains to be planned: the structure for implementing production. In this regard the operations management team must decide how to organize the department, what type of employees are needed and how they should be trained, whether and how to incorporate teams, the authority of relationships, and the extent of decentralization. The operations management team must address each one of these concepts (which were discussed in earlier chapters) in the context of operations. The desired result is an integrated, flexible organization structure that can respond to changes in the aggregate plan. If, as in the case of Eagle Bronco, this chapter's Valuing Diversity feature, an element is neglected, quality performance suffers.

CONTROLS FOR QUALITY AND PRODUCTIVITY

Describe the role of operations control in achieving quality and productivity

As discussed in Chapter 3, the driving forces in the organizations of today are productivity and quality—or quality and productivity. The order is irrelevant; the two cannot be separated.

Traditionally, managers viewed productivity in terms of greater output. They did not give much thought to whether the units of output were usable or not. Enlightened managers now realize that productivity is related to saleable, high-quality units of output, whether the outputs are products or services.

The costs associated with poor productivity relate to quality. These include the costs of scrap, repair, and downtime. Such costs are directly observable during production. Quality is also related to costs incurred before manufacturing begins. These expenses include the cost of incoming materials, purchasing, and inventory (Holt, 1991).

VALUING DIVERSITY
Training for Quality

Eagle Bronco, Inc., a 58-employee metal-casting company, faced a shortage of labor. Eagle, located in rural Lander, Wyoming, was being bombarded with orders from artists who purchased its castings. To solve the problem, Eagle hired Native Americans from the Wind River Indian Reservation.

Initially, the company pushed the workers to grasp the basics of their metal-casting jobs too quickly. As a result, quality dropped on some orders, and a few of the 20 Native American recruits left the company. Eagle managers realized the mistake they had made. People who wanted to work and who added to the work group did not have the skills to do the job.

To solve the training problem, Eagle reconsidered how it worked with new employees. A new training manual identified a checklist of skills required in each casting job; and compensation was tied to mastery of various levels of skills. In addition, Eagle managers designed a coaching program to assist the workers in acquiring the skills.

The program has been successful. Eagle plans to hire an additional half dozen Native American workers. Also, one of the original recruits has shown leadership potential and is being trained for a supervisory role.

Source: Litvan, Laura M. "Casting a Wider Employment Net," *Nation's Business* (December 1994), pp. 50–51.

All these factors fall within the purview of operations management. To achieve high quality and productivity, managers use a number of operational controls. These include control of design, materials, inventory, scheduling, and products.

Design Control

Discuss the purpose of design controls

design control
An area of operations control that involves incorporating reliability, functionality, and serviceability into product design.

The team approach to product design, discussed earlier in the chapter, provides an opportunity for designers to insert quality and performance controls before a product is produced. **Design control** focuses on creating new products engineered for reliability, functionality, and serviceability.

For example, the characteristics of materials to be used in manufacturing can be examined to ensure up front that they meet production standards. This orchestrated process should ensure a well-functioning final product. In creating the Taurus, Team Taurus included triple rubber seals and insert doors in its design plans. Both innovations were in response to customer complaints. Now the Taurus doors fit together and the interior is quieter (Kerwin, Updike and Naughton, 1995).

The team approach can be expanded to integrate marketing research specialists who can provide the connection between consumer needs and production capabilities; or the team may work directly with the consumer, as Team Taurus did. Regardless of the approach, the team can then incorporate quality, as defined by the consumer, at the design stage.

Materials Control: Purchasing

Discuss the importance of managing and controlling materials purchasing

purchasing
The acquisition of goods and services at optimal costs from competent and reliable sources.

An integral component of an operations management control system, materials control is achieved through effective purchasing. **Purchasing** is the acquisition of needed goods and services. The goal of the purchasing agent is to acquire them at optimal costs from competent and reliable sources. What an organization produces depends on the inputs—the materials and supplies. Therefore, purchasing is critical for the following reasons:

- If the materials are not on hand, nothing can be produced.
- If the right quantity of materials is not available, the organization cannot meet demand.
- If the materials are of inferior quality, producing quality products is difficult or costly.

The goal of purchasing control is to ensure the availability and acceptable quality of material while balancing costs. Maintaining relationships with reliable sources is one strategy to achieve this goal. At times, even when this is the case, unforeseen problems occur, as illustrated in this chapter's Ethical Management feature.

The advent of total quality management (see Chapter 3) has shifted the emphasis of materials purchasing control. Traditionally, controls focused on—in order of emphasis—quantity, time, and quality specifications. Now quality has the same priority as quantity.

ETHICAL MANAGEMENT
Made in the USA?

The Federal Trade Commission cracked down on New Balance, the Boston-based maker of running shoes, for what the feds insist are deceptive "made in the USA" claims. The problem lies in the shoe's imported components. Although New Balance will sew and glue the bulk of its 2.5 million pairs, it imports the soles for most of its shoes as well as some pre-sewn "uppers" from China.

Consequently, the FTC ordered New Balance to stop using ads or labels that imply that the running shoes are made wholly in the states. The applicable labeling law states that a product may be labeled and advertised as "Made in the USA" only if "all, or virtually all," of the labor and components are of U.S. origin.

The FTC maintains that its only concern is that consumers are not deceived. Said an FTC spokesperson, "All they gotta do is tell the truth." Unfortunately, companies already face a thicket of conflicting domestic-content regulations from rules imposed by the U.S. Customs Service to standards defined by NAFTA. Given the choices, whose truth prevails? A compromise offered by the FTC to New Balance is a label reading, "Made in the USA from domestic and imported components." The offer was not acceptable to New Balance.

1. Is it ethical to label products "Made in the USA" if components or labor are supplied outside the United States?
2. Does the increasing global economy make 100 percent U.S. content an unreachable goal?
3. What percent of components and labor would you propose qualify a product for a "Made in the USA" label?

http://www.ftc.gov

http://www.newbalance.com

Source: Oneal, Michael. "Does New Balance Have an American Sole?" *Business Week*, December 12, 1994, pp. 86–90.

Managers are initiating two practices to reflect this change. First, they are building long-term relationships with suppliers. This creates a partner for the producer and a sure source of sales for the supplier. The practice of building long-term relationships contrasts starkly with the traditional practice of pitting vendors against one another. The traditional practice was a short-term approach that often led to financial savings and quality reductions.

The second practice is the shifting of responsibility for quality to suppliers. Contracts are developed based on materials and equipment being preinspected and guaranteed to have minimum defects.

http://www.mcdonalds.com

http://www.osigroup.com

McDonald's global growth depends on both of these purchasing strategies (see Chapter 20's Management in Action case). It buys the majority of its food from a group of loyal suppliers. McDonald's sets not only the product specifications but also the profits for many suppliers who have an open-book relationship with McDonald's. Meat supplier OSI Industries is one of a core supplier group that has followed McDonald's overseas. It has formed joint ventures in seventeen countries, where it works with local companies making McDonald's hamburgers. One such site cranks out some 2.5 million patties a day. Computers mix ground beef to ensure that fat content meets the McDonald's world standard, 20 percent or less. Says OSI President Douglas Gullang, "Meeting McDonald's standard is a huge challenge. To some it seems insane what we do. But, we are committed to McDonald's" (Serwer, 1994).

Outsourcing

In addition to the quality movement, purchasing has been influenced by management decisions to focus on core competencies. Rather than manufacturing or assembling component parts, companies like GM, DaimlerChrysler, Dell, and General Mills are outsourcing. Companies that employ **outsourcing** as a strategy contract with suppliers to perform functions in lieu of performing the functions themselves. Outsourcing for some companies may include marketing, accounting, or shipping; but in manufacturing, outsourcing encompasses suppliers who design, engineer, manufacture, or integrate parts—or perform all these activities.

http://www.daimlerchrysler.com

http://www.generalmills.com

outsourcing
A purchasing strategy in which a company contracts with a supplier to perform functions in lieu of the company.

http://www.ford.com

http://www.lear.com

http://www.jci.com

For example, Ford sold its assembly seat-making operation; it now outsources this operation to Lear Seating. DaimlerChrysler's leather and fabric seat covers are no longer produced internally; instead, Johnson Controls is the supplier. GM has disposed of radiator caps, vacuum pumps, and 41 other lines of business; all will be made by suppliers. Of the Big Three automakers, DaimlerChrysler outsources 70 percent of its parts; Ford, 62 percent; and GM, 53 percent (Taylor, September 1994).

Outsourcing thrives in the fluid, fast-changing world of computers. Many big companies don't manufacture anything. Dell and Zeos of Minneapolis concentrate on marketing. They buy circuit boards, disc drives, and other modules—designed specifically for them from outside manufacturers—and assemble the computers in their own warehouses (Tully, 1994).

Paying someone else to handle all or part of a company's operations can reduce costs and avoid headaches. Outsourcing can be a successful option if managers take the following steps to minimize risk and maintain control (Snyder, 1995):

- Do not outsource functions critical to the company's operation. The idea is to protect the core business from delays or problems with the outside source.
- Minimize cost fluctuations by outsourcing only functions whose costs do not vary much from month to month. This way, outsourcing expenses are predictable.
- Be wary of extremely low fees. They may have been set low to get the business, then will increase dramatically next year.
- Share the risk with the vendor. Make fees contingent on meeting deadlines. Include this in the contract.
- Find out if the vendor has a heavy commitment to one large company, which signals the vendor's priorities.
- Have a backup plan that includes a list of other vendors.
- Stipulate, by contract, that all data pertaining to the business is owned by the company, not the vendor.

Inventory Control

inventory
The goods an organization keeps on hand.

The goods an organization keeps on hand are called **inventory**. Inventory control is critical to operations management because inventory represents a major investment. The aim is to get the parts in and out of the factory as fast as possible. Many of the machines used for manufacturing can communicate with one another electronically, which gives manufacturers real-time data about their inventories.

Most organizations have three types of inventory: raw materials, work-in-process, and finished goods. Each type is associated with a different stage of the production process, as Figure 18.6 shows.

FIGURE 18.6 *Three types of inventory*

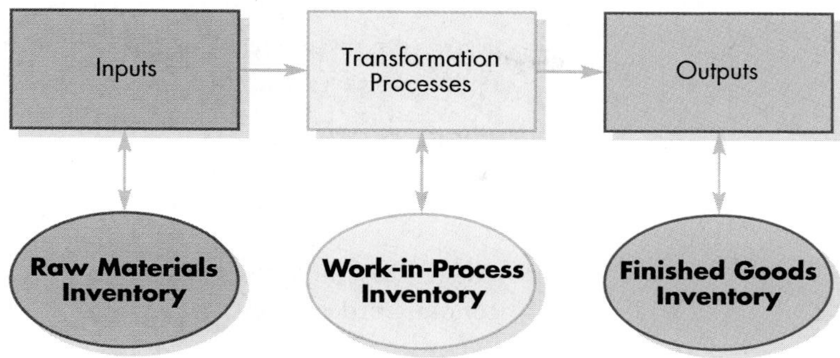

raw materials inventory
Inventory consisting of the raw materials, parts, and supplies used as inputs to production.

http://www.wendys.com

work-in-process inventory
Inventory consisting of materials and parts that have begun moving through the production process but are not yet assembled into a completed product.

finished goods inventory
Inventory consisting of products that have not been sold.

The **raw materials inventory** includes the materials, parts, and supplies an organization uses as inputs to production. The raw materials for a Hewlett-Packard laser printer include the printer engine, the circuit boards, and the power supply. At a Wendy's fast-food restaurant, the inventory includes meat patties, buns, tomatoes, and lettuce. Raw materials inventory is the least expensive type of inventory because the organization has not yet invested any labor in it. Nevertheless, an excessive raw materials inventory ties up cash unnecessarily.

Work-in-process inventory consists of the materials and parts that have begun moving through the production process but are not yet a completed product. At Hewlett-Packard, the toner and drum assembly and the shell of a laser printer are work-in-process inventory. Because labor has been expended to produce work-in-process inventory, this type of inventory represents a greater investment than raw materials inventory.

The **finished goods inventory** consists of the products that have completed the entire production process but have not yet been sold. Assembled and boxed Hewlett-Packard printers, for example, stored in a warehouse before shipping are finished goods inventory. This inventory, of course, represents the greatest investment of all three types.

Importance of Inventory Control

At one time, managers prided themselves on maintaining large inventories. Inventories were regarded as measures of wealth. Today managers realize that a large inventory can indicate wasted resources. Money not tied up in inventory can be used elsewhere. The goal of inventory control is to sustain the proper flow of materials while maintaining adequate inventory levels and minimum costs. Many companies let customers use the Web to cut the ordering time for parts. "When you let customers order on the Web with speed, you have to be able to manufacture and deliver the product with speed" (Liesman, 2001).

> *"Improvements in manufacturing have shortened production time and allowed manufacturers to respond quickly to signs of slackening demand. In fact, in its recent decision to cut its discount rate by half a percentage point, the Federal Reserve suggested the rapid slowdown in manufacturing was the result of 'new technologies' appearing to have accelerated the*

response of production and demand to high inventories. New technologies for supply-chain management and flexible manufacturing imply that businesses can perceive imbalances in inventories at a very early stage—virtually in real time," Fed Chairman Alan Greenspan told Congress Tuesday [February 13, 2001]. Quicker production means manufacturers need to keep less inventory on hand (Liesman, 2001).

With this goal in mind, organizations have four specific techniques for inventory management. They are: economic order quantity, materials requirement planning, manufacturing resource planning, and just-in-time inventory systems.

Economic Order Quantity

Explain how EOQ, MRP, MRPII, and JIT differ

economic order quantity (EOQ) *An inventory technique that helps managers determine how much material to order by minimizing the total of ordering costs and holding costs based on the organization's usage rate.*

The **economic order quantity (EOQ)** is the order quantity that minimizes ordering and holding costs based on the rate of inventory use. Ordering costs are the costs of placing the order. Ordering costs include, for example, the costs of postage, receiving, and inspections. Holding costs are the costs of keeping the inventory on hand. These expenses include the costs of storage space, financing, and taxes (Daft, 1994).

The EOQ may be derived by calculation. The formula for EOQ is

$$\sqrt{\frac{2 \times D \times C}{H}}$$

where D represents demand, or annual usage rate; C represents ordering costs; and H represents holding costs.

Suppose the manager of a small shop that manufactures valves needs to order 1-inch valve gaskets. A review of records indicates that ordering costs for the gaskets amount to \$20, the annual holding cost is \$12, and the annual demand for the gasket is 1,815. The formula to calculate the EOQ in this case is

$$\sqrt{\frac{2 \times 1{,}815 \times \$20}{\$12}} = 77.8$$

The best order quantity, then, is 78.

reorder point (ROP) *The most economical point at which an inventory item should be reordered.*

The next question facing the manager is when to order. This is determined by calculating the **reorder point (ROP)**. The formula for ROP is

$$\frac{D}{Time} \times Lead\ Time$$

Assuming that gaskets can be delivered five days after the order is placed, the manager determines the ROP by using the following calculation:

$$\frac{1{,}815}{365} \times 5 = 24.86, \text{ or } 25$$

This formula tells the manager that, because the time to receive new orders is five days, at least 25 gaskets should be in inventory at all times. Any time the number of gaskets drops to 25, a new order for 78 gaskets should be placed.

EOQ can result in substantial savings and improvement in inventory management. It forces managers to evaluate usage rates, ordering costs, and holding costs. The major disadvantage of EOQ is that it focuses on optimal order quantity while ignoring quality. Another disadvantage of EOQ is that it does not take into account supplier performance.

Materials Requirement Planning

http://www.boeing.com

materials requirement planning (MRP)
A production planning and inventory system that uses forecasts of customer orders to schedule the exact amount of materials needed for production.

EOQ is useful so long as each inventory item, as in the valve example, is independent of others. When demand for one inventory item depends on other inventory items, however, EOQ is no longer applicable. Such is the case for Boeing, for example. To produce one hundred 747s, each of which includes some three million parts, Boeing must have a vast number of discrete components on hand. One technique for managing such an inventory is **materials requirement planning (MRP)**. This production planning and inventory system uses forecasts of customer orders to schedule the exact amount of materials needed to support the manufacture of the desired number of products.

An MRP program begins with a master schedule of planned production. (Recall that a master schedule uses sales forecasts to determine the quantities of finished goods required in a specific time period.) The next step is to use a computer to analyze product design and determine all the parts and supplies needed to manufacture the finished product. This information is then merged with existing inventory records. The quantities of each item on hand are identified, and usage rates are calculated. Then the system can determine ordering times and quantities. In essence, MRP incorporates EOQ, perpetual inventory control, and statistics to provide a comprehensive system for purchasing materials and scheduling various production activities to meet projected customer orders (Daft, 1994).

MRP results in purchasing on time and according to actual needs. In most cases MRP means a reduction in inventory and fewer production stops due to lack of stock. The changes save money. The major limitation associated with MRP is the extensive organizational commitment it requires. To use MRP properly, an organization must develop adequate support systems and skilled personnel. The system cannot be implemented in a piecemeal fashion.

MRP solved Boeing's inventory problems. The system that preceded MRP at Boeing was designed to keep track of the several million parts that went into each plane, rather than following the development of the plane itself. The system worked when Boeing was building 10,000 identical planes, but it became a major problem when each airline wanted its planes to be slightly different. Moreover, the lists of parts produced by engineering for a given airplane was configured differently from the list put together by manufacturing, customer service, or other Boeing operations. So the parts list had to be broken down, converted, and recomputed as many as thirteen times during the construction of a single plane.

Today, instead of treating most airplane parts as unique, Boeing's MRP system groups them into three categories, depending on how frequently they are used. Boeing also assembled a complete parts list that every division can use without modification or tabbing. In place of defining a plane by the parts that go into it, Boeing defines the parts by the plane they are in (Taylor, 1995).

Manufacturing Resource Planning

manufacturing resource planning (MRPII)
A comprehensive planning system that controls the total resources of a firm.

An even more sophisticated system than MRP is **manufacturing resource planning (MRPII)**. MRP is used to manage inventory; MRPII, on the other hand, is a comprehensive planning system. It emphasizes planning and controlling all of a firm's resources—its finances, capital, and marketing strategies—as well as production and materials management (Migliorelli and Swan, 1988). MRPII creates a model of the overall business, allowing top managers to control production scheduling, cash flow, human resources, capacity, inventory, purchasing, and distribution. Because of its comprehensiveness, MRPII can be used effectively for strategic planning. At Stanley Works in New Britain, Connecticut, the MRPII system not only ensures that the next product is being manufactured at the right time, but it also coordinates the warehouse management system (Holt, 1991).

http://www.stanleyworks.com

The value of MRPII lies in its comprehensiveness. It is a strategic management system that links the entire organization. Because it is very expensive to implement, only large companies can afford to use it. In addition, it must be custom designed for the user, which involves a major commitment of the organization's time and human resources.

Just-in-Time Inventory Systems

Another technique for inventory control is designed to reduce inventory by coordinating supply deliveries with production. This technique, called the *just-in-time (JIT) inventory system*, originated in Japan. The JIT concept is sometimes referred to as the *kanban* system, the stockless system, or zero-inventory system.

With the JIT approach, suppliers deliver exact quantities of materials directly to manufacturers, as the manufacturers need them. There is no buffer of "safety" inventory. There is no warehousing or in-process handling. The benefits managers expect to receive from JIT include reduced inventory and setup time, better workflow, shorter manufacturing time, and less consumption of space. They often reap unexpected benefits, however. When a company changes to a JIT system, managers are often able to identify problems that were masked by inventory reserves, slack schedules, and devices that workers developed to keep up the required flow (Marenghi, 1992).

http://www.behlenmfg.com

http://www.saturnbp.com

A JIT system depends on reliable suppliers who must meet strict delivery schedules. When the system works, it works well. At Behlen Manufacturing Company, within two years from adopting a just-in-time inventory system, inventory costs were down $10 million, work flow improved, and delivery time for finished goods improved 20 percent (Greco, 1994). But when the supplier has troubles, the result is production stoppages. In the mid-1990s the Saturn plant in Lordstown, Ohio, was shut down as a result of labor strikes against suppliers.

Scheduling Control

Discuss the importance and methods of schedule controls

Another important element of operations control is schedule control—techniques for scheduling operations and tracking production. There are two basic scheduling techniques: Gantt charts and network scheduling.

Gantt Charts

An early pioneer in scientific management, Henry L. Gantt, was the first to devise a reliable method for reserving machine time for jobs in production. The method promotes the orderly flow of work from one process to the next, with a minimum of lost time or delays. His method involved a tool called a **Gantt chart**. As you can see by examining Figure 18.7, a Gantt chart tracks a project from beginning to end, comparing the time estimates for the steps involved with the actual time they require and adjusting the starting and ending times of steps if necessary.

Gantt chart
A scheduling and control tool that helps managers plan and control a sequence of events.

FIGURE 18.7 Gantt chart for a manufacturing department

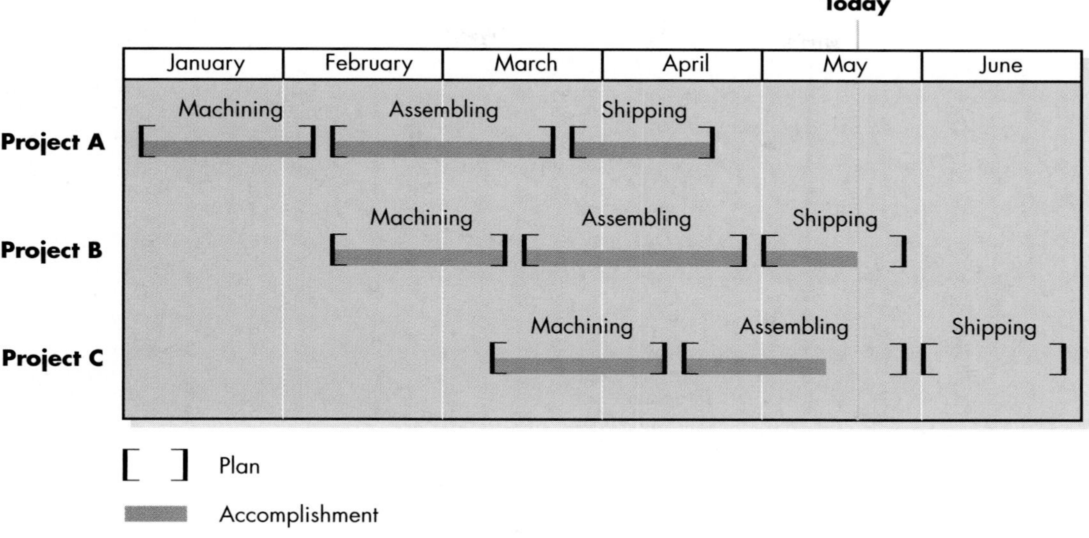

Figure 18.7 shows a Gantt chart for a manufacturing department. The processes it tracks are machining, assembling, and shipping. To aid the production manager in monitoring the progress of each process and making any required adjustments, the chart presents two sets of information: (1) the planned time for each task, represented by the area enclosed in brackets; and (2) the actual completion time, represented by a solid bar within each set of brackets. The length of the line indicates how much of the task is complete.

Gantt charts work best for scheduling and tracking sequential events, the completion times of which will determine the total time for an entire project. Gantt charts are not appropriate for highly complex projects requiring many different kinds of sequential operations that begin or run simultaneously.

Network Scheduling

network scheduling
A scheduling technique used to track projects in which events or activities are interrelated and have time estimates assigned to them.

Managers use **network scheduling** to schedule and track projects in which the events or activities are interrelated. This technique for scheduling and controlling uses events and activities that have time estimates assigned to them. Figure 18.8 presents a network diagram. Events, represented by circles, indicate the starting point of some production operation, such as delivery of materials. Activities, or processes, are represented by lines with arrows. The lines indicate the time required to complete the event.

The network diagram in Figure 18.8 shows the schedule for a project that involves fifteen events and eighteen activities. Event Number 1 marks the start of Activities A and B. The notation "A.10" means that Activity A is scheduled for 10 days. Event Number 2 marks the end of Activity A and the beginning of Activity C, which is scheduled to take 2 days. To construct this network, the managers had to list each activity, estimate the time for each, and identify the immediate predecessors

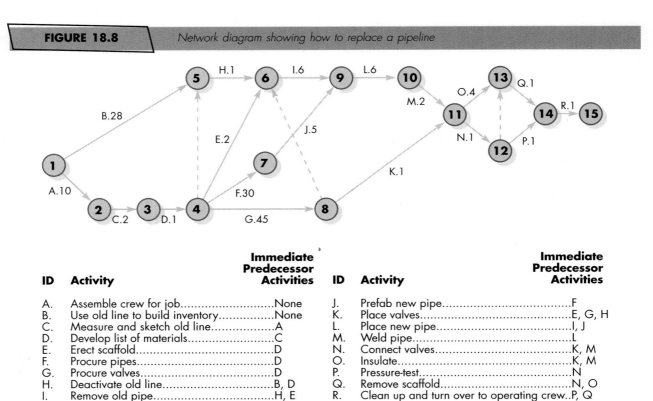

FIGURE 18.8 *Network diagram showing how to replace a pipeline*

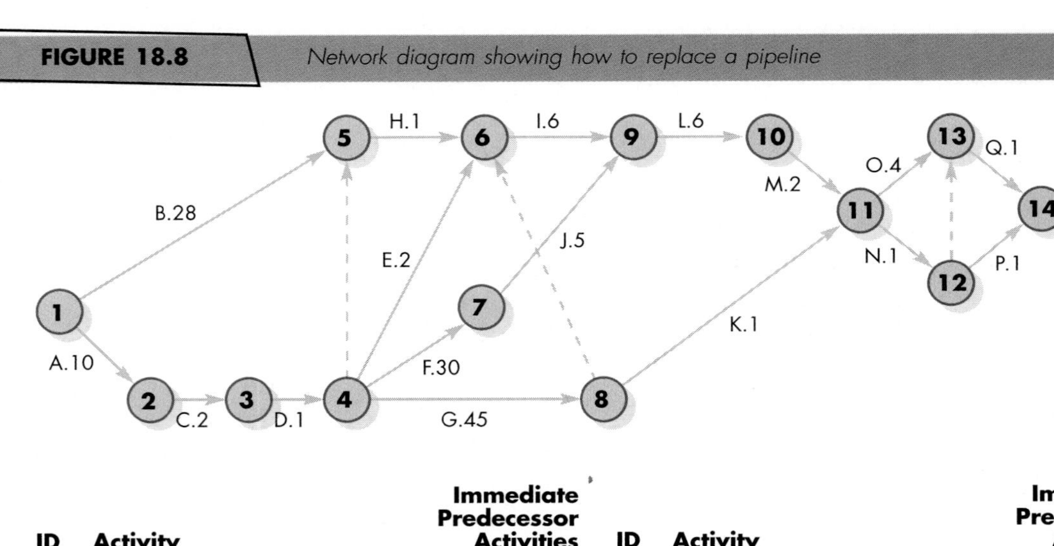

ID	Activity	Immediate Predecessor Activities	ID	Activity	Immediate Predecessor Activities
A.	Assemble crew for job	None	J.	Prefab new pipe	F
B.	Use old line to build inventory	None	K.	Place valves	E, G, H
C.	Measure and sketch old line	A	L.	Place new pipe	I, J
D.	Develop list of materials	C	M.	Weld pipe	L
E.	Erect scaffold	D	N.	Connect valves	K, M
F.	Procure pipes	D	O.	Insulate	K, M
G.	Procure valves	D	P.	Pressure-test	N
H.	Deactivate old line	B, D	Q.	Remove scaffold	N, O
I.	Remove old pipe	H, E	R.	Clean up and turn over to operating crew	P, Q

Source: Production-Inventory Systems: Planning and Control, 3rd edition by Elwood S. Buffa and Jeffery G. Miller, pp. 614, 622. Copyright Richard D. Irwin, Inc., Homewood, IL. Reprinted by permission of The McGraw-Hill Companies.

for each activity. Note that an activity cannot be started until its predecessor has been completed. Note, too, that some activities can take place simultaneously.

program evaluation and review technique (PERT) *A network scheduling technique for planning and charting the progress of a complex project in terms of the time it is expected to take—an estimate that is derived from probability analysis.*

http://www.lockheedmartin.com

The **program evaluation and review technique (PERT)**, an adaptation of network scheduling, assigns four time estimates to activities: optimistic, most likely, pessimistic, and expected. The expected time (the amount of time the manager thinks the activity will actually take) is based on a probability analysis of the other three time estimates.

The PERT method, originally devised at Lockheed Corporation for planning complex aerospace development projects, provides managers with a graphic view of the details of the project from initiation to completion. It functions as a control device by helping the manager spot trouble areas and see when a project is falling behind schedule. The manager can take corrective action before the delay becomes critical.

critical path *The longest sequence of events and activities in a network production schedule or the longest time a job could take.*

One benefit of a PERT network is that it helps managers identify the **critical path**—the longest possible path or least direct route from the beginning to the end of a network diagram. Given current time estimates the critical path shows the longest time a job could take. Figure 18.9 shows the calculations that define the critical path for the pipeline project introduced in Figure 18.8. The critical path represents the earliest possible completion time for the project—65 days—assuming that the worst combination of events occurs.

FIGURE 18.9 Calculation of the critical path

Activity		Time in Days
A		10
C		2
D		1
G		45
K		1
O		4
Q		1
R		1
Critical Path	=	65 Days

Awareness of the critical path equips a manager with the ability to really control a project. For example, a delay in the completion of Activity B by 1 day will not affect the total project's completion time. If, however, Activity G takes 47 days instead of 45, the entire project will be 2 days off schedule, unless the manager takes some corrective action. By maneuvering to ensure that the length of the critical path does not increase, the manager can maintain effective control of the project.

Product Control

11

Describe the importance and methods of product control

product control *A component of operations control that reduces the probability and costs of poor quality and unreliable products by implementing controls from purchasing to end use.*

acceptance sampling *A product control technique involving a representative group of products before a new stage of production.*

At one time, the entire concept of operations control focused on inspection of the physical product. With the advent of TQM, inspection was placed in a new perspective, as only one part of controlling. Now **product control** encompasses controls from purchasing to end use. It involves reducing the probability and costs of poor quality and unreliable products. Product controls focus on inspection and testing techniques.

Acceptance Sampling

Any inspection of a representative group of products that takes place prior to the beginning of a new phase of production constitutes **acceptance sampling**. The inspection may occur prior to the receipt of raw materials, when subassemblies are completed, after critical processes of manufacturing, and prior to shipping finished goods. The data from the sample are used to evaluate all items in the group. Organizations use acceptance sampling to make cost-effective evaluations on large numbers of items. The evaluations determine whether they accept or reject entire batches. The increase in acceptance sampling has led to the rapid development of statistical software (Daniel, 1992).

detailed inspections and tests *A product control technique in which every finished item receives an examination or performance test.*

Detailed Inspections and Tests

Rather than a sampling approach to product control, some operations conduct **detailed inspections and tests** on every finished item. Medicines, for example, are tested this way. The goal of the technique is to identify all parts not meeting standards. The inspection or test may consist of an examination of attributes or

Some operations require detailed inspections and tests on every finished item.

variables. The inspection and classification of items as acceptable or unacceptable is called **attribute inspection**. Potato chips and nail polish are evaluated this way. An inspector compares the items against a standard and rates their quality as acceptable or unacceptable. In comparison, **variable inspection** involves taking a measurement to determine how much an item varies from standards. Any item that measures within the range is accepted, and those outside are rejected. For example, Ross/Flex might test a valve to see whether a valve would hold between 300 and 350 pounds of pressure per square inch. If it did not, the valve would not meet tolerance standards.

attribute inspection
A product control technique that compares items against a standard and rates their quality as acceptable or unacceptable.

variable inspection
A product control technique that involves taking measurements to determine how much an item varies from standards and, therefore, whether it will be accepted or rejected.

Process Control Sampling

With **process control sampling** the purpose is to detect variations in production processes. The technique involves periodic tests to uncover problems with equipment, worn tools, bad parts, or personnel. When managers know about problems, they can correct them. For example, a process control procedure at Frito-Lay would be able to detect if a bagging machine was out of adjustment because it was filling 32-ounce bags with only 16 ounces of potato chips. Managers could then stop the process and adjust the machine.

process control sampling
A product control technique designed to detect variations in production processes.

http://www.fritolay.com

Qualification Testing

In **qualification testing** a sample product is checked for performance on the basis of reliability and safety. New car models are driven hundreds of thousands of miles so engineers can test the overall car and its components. Thousands of golf balls are hit by automated golf clubs so that engineers can check on the quality of the balls and the reliability of their flight. The goal of qualification testing is to ensure that a product, as a class, performs as it should. The purpose of detailed testing is to ensure that each version of the product meets established standards.

qualification testing
A product control technique in which products are tested for performance on the basis of reliability and safety.

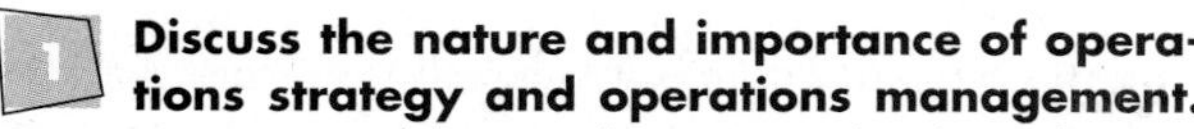

CHAPTER SUMMARY

1 **Discuss the nature and importance of operations strategy and operations management.** Operations strategy is the part of a strategic plan that defines the role, capabilities, and expectations of operations. Operations management consists of the managerial activities and techniques used to convert resources into products and services. Without an effective operations strategy and operations management, few organizations would survive. Together they are viewed as a competitive weapon to be used with marketing and finance. When this is the case, the results can be lower prices or better quality, performance, or responsiveness to consumer demand.

2 **Discuss the nature and importance of product and service design planning.** In the past, engineers designed products with a complete lack of thought for product manufacture and assembly. The products could not be assembled easily, contained a greater number of parts than necessary, and had to be inspected for quality during production. Adopting a concept called design for manufacturability and assembly (DFM/A) can eliminate the problems. DFM/A calls for design by teams consisting of designers, manufacturers, and assemblers. Because these specialists have a say in product design, actual production of the product becomes more efficient. Design for disassembly (DfD) is another design concept. Its goal is to close the production loop—that is, to conceive, develop, and build a product with a long-term view of how its components can be refurbished and reused at the end of the product's life cycle.

3 **Describe the four main strategies for facilities layout.** The four main strategies for facilities layout are

- *Process layout.* In a process layout all the equipment and machines that perform a similar task or function are located together. A product is moved from process to process as needed.
- *Product layout.* In a product layout the machines and tasks are arranged according to the progressive steps by which the product is made.
- *Cellular layout.* The cellular layout combines the characteristics of process and product layouts. In a cellular arrangement all the equipment required for a sequence of operations on the same product is placed together in a group called a cell.
- *Fixed-position layout.* A fixed-position layout is used when, because of bulk or size, the product remains in one location. Tools, equipment, and human skills are brought to the product.

4 **Discuss the nature of process and technology planning.** The challenge facing operations managers is to identify the proper blend of people and technology to use in transforming inputs into finished products or services. For any given production task, several conversion methods are available—some labor intensive, others equipment intensive. The nature of the product and the objectives and resources of the organization are critical factors in choosing one method over another. The growing trend today is toward the use of more sophisticated technology in manufacturing. The technology responsible for revolutionizing manufacturing processes includes robotics, CAD/CAM, flexible manufacturing systems, computer integrated manufacturing, soft manufacturing systems, and agile manufacturing.

5 **Explain the factors in facilities location planning and capacity planning.** In considering the location of facilities, managers must ask two important questions: Should the firm have one or two large plants or several smaller ones? Where should the facilities be located? The decision on the number of plants will depend on the company's long-range objectives and distribution strategies, financial resources, and equipment costs. The choice of locations depends on the location of the market where the product will be sold, availability of labor skills, labor costs, proximity to suppliers, tax rates, construction expenses, utility rates, and quality of life for the employees. Capacity planning is a matter of trying to convert sales forecasts into production facilities. Too little capacity means that the organization cannot match demand and that it will lose customers. The reverse results in facilities and equipment sitting idle while incurring costs.

6 **Describe the role of operations control in achieving quality and productivity.** The costs associated with poor productivity relate to quality. These include the costs of scrap, repair, and downtime. Such costs are directly observable during production. Quality is also related to costs incurred before manufacturing begins. These expenses include the cost of incoming materials, purchasing, and inventory. All of these factors fall within the purview of operations management. To achieve high quality and productivity, managers can use a number of operations controls. These include control of design, materials, inventory, scheduling, and products.

7 **Discuss the purpose of design controls.** Design control focuses on creating new products engineered for reliability, functionality, and serviceability.

8 **Discuss the importance of managing and controlling materials purchasing.** What an organization produces depends on the inputs—the materials and supplies. Therefore purchasing is critical for the following reasons:

- If the materials are not on hand, nothing can be produced.
- If the right quantity of materials is not available, demand cannot be met.
- If the materials are of inferior quality, producing quality products is difficult or costly.

The goal of purchasing control is to ensure the availability and acceptable quality of material while balancing costs.

Explain how EOQ, MRP, MRPII, and JIT differ.

- *EOQ.* The economic order quantity (EOQ) is the order quantity that minimizes ordering and building costs based on the rate of inventory use. EOQ is useful as long as each inventory item is independent of others.
- *MRP.* When the demand for one inventory item depends on other inventory items, materials requirement planning (MRP) is applicable. This production planning and inventory system uses forecasts of customer orders to schedule the exact amount of materials needed to support the manufacture of the desired number of products.
- *MRPII.* Even more sophisticated than MRP is manufacturing resource planning (MRPII). MRP is used to manage inventory; MRPII, on the other hand, is a comprehensive planning system. It emphasizes planning and controlling all of a firm's resources—its finances, capital, and marketing strategies as well as its production and materials management. MRPII creates a model of the overall business, allowing top managers to control production scheduling, cash flow, human resources, capacity, inventory, purchasing, and distribution.
- *JIT.* The just-in-time inventory system is designed to reduce inventory by coordinating supply deliveries with production. With the JIT approach, suppliers deliver exact quantities of materials directly to manufacturers as the manufacturers need them. There is no buffer of "safety" inventory or in-process handling.

10 **Discuss the importance and methods of schedule controls.** Schedule controls are techniques for scheduling operations and tracking production. There are two basic scheduling techniques: Gantt charts and network scheduling.

- A *Gantt chart* tracks a project from beginning to end, comparing the time estimates for the steps involved with the actual time they require and adjusting the starting and ending times of steps if necessary. Gantt charts work best for scheduling and tracking sequential events. Gantt charts are not appropriate for highly complex operations requiring many different kinds of sequential operations that begin or run simultaneously.
- *Network scheduling* is used to schedule and track projects in which events or activities are interrelated. This technique uses events and activities that have time estimates assigned to them. An adaptation of network scheduling is program evaluation and review technique (PERT). PERT assigns four time estimates to activities: optimistic, most likely, pessimistic, and expected. The expected time is based on probability analysis of the other three time estimates. One benefit of a PERT network is that it helps managers identify the critical path—the longest path or least direct route from beginning to the end of a network diagram. The critical path equips a manager with the ability to really control a project. By maneuvering to ensure that the length of the critical path does not increase, the manager can gain effective control of the project.

11 **Describe the importance and methods of product control.** Product control encompasses controls from purchasing to end use. It involves reducing the probability and cost of poor quality and unreliable products. There are four methods of product controls.

- *Acceptance sampling.* Any inspection of a representative group of products that takes place prior to the beginning of a new phase of production constitutes acceptance sampling. Organizations use acceptance sampling to make cost-effective evaluations of large numbers of items. The evaluations determine whether they accept or reject entire batches.
- *Detailed inspections and tests.* Rather than a sampling approach, some operations conduct detailed inspections and tests on every finished item. The inspections may consist of an examination of attributes or variables.
- *Process control sampling.* With process control sampling, the purpose is to detect variations in production processes. The technique involves periodic tests to uncover problems with equipment, worn tools, bad parts, or personnel.
- *Qualification testing.* In qualification testing, a sample product is checked for performance on the basis of reliability and safety. The goal of qualification testing is to ensure that a product, as a class, performs as it should.

REVIEW QUESTIONS

1. What is operations management? Why is operations strategy important?
2. Why is design for manufacturability and assembly important in terms of overall operations management?
3. When should a process layout be used? Why?
4. What benefits can CAD or CAM technology provide for a manufacturer?
5. What factors should managers consider when selecting a facility location? What is the role of a cost-benefit analysis in the decision?

6. What is the role of operations control in achieving quality and productivity?
7. What is the purpose of design controls?
8. Why is it important for an organization to control materials purchasing?
9. How do EOQ and JIT systems control inventory?
10. What is the purpose of a Gantt chart? What is the purpose of PERT scheduling?
11. What is the difference between acceptance sampling and process control sampling?

DISCUSSION QUESTIONS FOR CRITICAL THINKING

1. Are operations management and operations strategy most closely related to corporate-level, business-level, or functional-level strategy? Why? In what way?
2. You have been asked by the owner of a local video store to identify a possible location for a second store. How would you proceed? How would you help the store owner determine the new store's capacity?
3. Of the three types of inventory, which of these is most likely to be affected by the just-in-time inventory system? Why?
4. If you were the manager of a donut shop, what product control would be the most critical? What would be the least critical? Why?

INTERNET EXERCISES

Check the text Web site at http://plunkett.swcollege.com for updated links to the Internet Exercises.

1. Explain the relationship between bar coding and inventory control as detailed in the following Web site.
   http://www.zebra.com/about/aboutbar.htm
2. Briefly describe the Gantt chart. Who was its creator? Read about its uses and applications. Give another example of how it might be used.
   http://www.eob.org/gantt.htm
3. What is logistics? What are some other terms for logistics? How would you use logistics as a competitive advantage?
   http://www.dti.gov.uk/mbp/bpgt/m9gb00001/m9gb000012.html#toc_1

APPLICATION CASE

Outsourcing Leads to Success

When Tomina Edmark started the TopsyTail Company in 1991, she had two strong convictions. First, she believed the hair-care gadget she invented would be a smashing success, and second, no matter how big her success became, she would not end up managing some big outfit with "suits" running to and fro at her beckoning.

That second criterion stemmed from Edmark's eight years as a marketing representative at IBM. There, she chafed at the amount of time she regarded as "wasted" on office politics, personnel issues, and countless meetings. "In my own business I wanted to spend my time doing business rather than managing people," says the entrepreneur.

Edmark has been true to her convictions. "Relying on a score of vendors, from design firms to injection molders through fulfillment houses, TopsyTail has produced more than $100 million in sales at retail with only three employees (a chief financial officer, a marketing director and a general assistant)" (Harris, 1998). Her secret: outsourcing, a strategy she also learned at IBM and which she applied to the nth degree in her own business. Instead of hiring the 50 or more employees TopsyTail would need today to get its product to market, the company has set up a network of 20 outsourced vendors who handle everything from the manufacture of the products to the servicing of retail accounts.

Edmark started by farming out the tooling and injection molding of her plastic hair product, saving at least $5 million in start-up manufacturing costs. Today, Edmark's production partners include a toolmaker, two injection molders, a package designer, freelance photographers, and a printer. She also outsources packaging and shipping, television commercials to a video production company, customer mailings to a mailing firm, and publicity to a public relations firm. To sell the product, TopsyTail has exclusive agreements with four distributors that serve retailers in the company's six markets—the United States, Canada, Mexico, the Pacific Rim, Europe, and South Africa.

Despite all the outsourcing, Edmark has been careful to retain control of new product development and marketing strategy, the core competencies that form the very heart of the company. She also keeps control of her vendors by including a performance clause in virtually all contracts. The clause typically spells out minimum performance standards and time frames for deliveries. Edmark coordinates vendors' activities by faxing purchase orders to the appropriate party. Each vendor fulfills its part of the operation, faxes back the completed purchase order, and then delivers the finished work to the next outsource vendor in the chain.

http://www.topsytail.com

Questions

1. Why has Tomina Edmark been successful in using outsourcing? Cite specific examples from the case to support your answer.
2. If vendors do not perform according to their agreements, what options are available to Edmark?
3. Why do you believe Edmark retained control over product development? What would be the risks if Edmark outsourced product development?
4. In the event Edmark's packaging and shipping vendor went out of business or had employee problems, how would this impact TopsyTail, Inc.? If this happened, would you recommend that Edmark not outsource packaging and shipping? Why?

Sources: Harris, Joyce Saenz. "Dallas Inventor's TopsyTail Turned Her World Topsy-Turvy," *The Dallas Morning News*, August 16, 1998, p. 1E; Garrett, Echo Montgomery. "Innovation & Outsourcing = Big Success," *Management Review* (September 1994), pp. 17–20.

VIDEO CASE

Operations Management: World Gym

Management at the World Gym franchise in San Francisco applies operations management (OM) principles to optimize the gym's operation. Understanding the amount and nature of the services demanded—and the gym's capacity to meet demand—allows for minimizing slack and maximizing customers' experiences.

The gym employs a management information system to catalog and evaluate gym equipment, and to reconcile equipment and facility space with expected usage. As a mid-sized facility in a fairly nonautomated environment, data collection is rather rudimentary. It usually involves a visual survey of the various apparatus at the close of the working day, class rosters for all scheduled activities, and turnstile or swipe card data from the front desk.

However, opportunities for coupling information systems to customers, both to enhance operations research and to deliver services, continue to expand. In the case of World Gym, recent trends in incorporating microprocessors into gym equipment allow new means of data collection and customization. As equipment is used, a record can be obtained not just of how much it's been used, but also when and how hard. The day's reporting could include charts showing distribution of busy and idle machines for various time periods and expected times of needed replacement.

Taking data collection further, within a few years World Gym might be offering its patrons the ability to interact with the equipment themselves (digitally, that is!) by recording calories burned, miles cycled, or kilometers rowed to construct a record of activities and progress. End-user technology such as bar codes or swipe cards is already sufficiently advanced economically to make point-of-service interaction cheap and efficient. Thus, the gym could collect extremely valuable information on customer preferences and equipment use. The data could also be used to analyze customer progress and to suggest other services (e.g., to recommend a personal trainer based on observed performance). Customers would find World Gym most attentive to their individual needs.

Clearly, there's a fine line between service and surveillance. Just as the video monitor that prevents employee theft from the cash register is, to be truthful, spying on employees' actions, the more that systems record customers' activities, the greater cause they may have to be concerned. Invasions of customer privacy could lead to increased junk mail (e.g., if a gym sold customer weight and fitness data to a pharmaceutical company) and even to problems in securing a job, a loan, or insurance.

Unlike manufacturers of goods, World Gym's most important "raw materials" and "finished goods" are people. Expensive gym apparatus notwithstanding, people—in the form of trainers and other staff—are also the organization's most important asset.

Being human, both customers and staff are subject to human frailties (e.g., missed buses, schedule conflicts, or the flu). World Gym's management processes need to account for such potential problems. Like many service organizations, World Gym operators maintain rosters of substitute staff to ensure full coverage in the event of staff no-shows. If, despite forecasted demand, attendance is light, the gym might have to send staff home or reschedule duty hours on short notice.

http://www.worldgym.com

For Discussion:

1. How might service demands at World Gym change during a year?
2. Unlike a goods producer, World Gym can't put excess patrons in inventory. How might it manage to ensure a steady flow of patrons and avoid overly large crowds or lines for some gym apparatus?
3. World Gym is local, physical, and relatively low-tech. How might it make use of the Internet and World Wide Web to enhance its operations?

Information Management Systems

KEY TERMS

application program
artificial intelligence (AI)
batch processing
computerized information system (CIS)
data
data center
database
decision support system (DSS)
end-user computing
executive information system (EIS)
expert system
group decision support system (GDSS)
information
information system (IS)
information technology (IT)
knowledge management
management information system (MIS)
networking
operating system
transactional processing

LEARNING OBJECTIVES

After studying this chapter, you should be able to

1. Describe the seven characteristics of useful information
2. Describe the three functions of an effective information system (IS)
3. Describe the five guidelines for establishing an information system (IS)
4. Describe the eight basic functions of a computerized information system (CIS)
5. Describe the two basic data processing modes
6. Discuss the various methods used for linking computer systems
7. Explain the purposes of decision support systems (DSSs)
8. Discuss the four challenges that must be met by managers of an information system

MANAGEMENT IN ACTION

Managing Information at Amazon.com

Few companies better exemplify how the Internet is changing the way the world shops than Amazon.com. It was named after the world's biggest river, and Jeff Bezos—Amazon's founder, president, and chief executive officer—has the ambition for Amazon.com to have "the Earth's Biggest Selection™." He said, "The wake up call was discovering in the spring of 94 that web usage was growing at 2300 percent a year! Books were chosen as the first best product because you could build a book store on line that simply couldn't exist any other way, with ten times the selection" (Time Chat, 1999).

Amazon's origin was in selling books. The books that Amazon sells are exactly the same as the books consumers can buy in their local bookshops. Yet, Amazon is an innovator and a leader in Internet retailing and is known for its great customer service. "Amazon.com announced that cumulative customer accounts, including Auctions bidders and sellers, increased by 2.5 million during the second quarter to 22.5 million at June 30, 2000. Repeat customer orders represented 78 percent of orders during the quarter ended June 30, 2000" (FAQ, 2000). The site focuses on community, is interactive, and tailors itself to each individual shopper. Anyone, anywhere can buy almost anything, anytime they choose. Customers can get hard-to-find books, shipping updates, fast delivery, gentle reminders about holidays, newly available books, and a Web page customized with their interests. In addition, Amazon has become the reference site for the publishing industry where people search for information about books.

The Electronic Commerce Resource Center (ECRC) defines *electronic commerce* as *electronic business*. It's using the power of computers, the Internet, and shared software to send and receive product specifications and drawings; bids, purchase orders, and invoices; and any other type of data that needs to be communicated to customers, suppliers, employees and/or the public. Electronic commerce is the new, profitable way to conduct business that expands electronic transactions from point-of-sale requirements determination and production scheduling, right through to invoicing, payment, and receipt.

Electronic commerce refers to all forms of business transactions involving both organizations and individuals that are based upon the processing and transmission of digitized data, including text, sound, and visual images. The major difference between electronic commerce and traditional commerce is the tools used. Traditional business uses person-to-person contact, as well as mail, faxes, and telephone as its primary tools, whereas in electronic business, entire transactions—between businesses and consumers (known as *business to consumer*—B2C or electronic retailing—etailing) or among businesses (known as *business to business*—B2B)—rely on a computer-to-computer exchange of data. Traditionally, many transactions have been handled manually. Electronic commerce automates this process. Customers can go to a Web site to get information about a product, and then they can configure and order products, make payments, and monitor their order status, 24 hours a day, 7 days a week.

"Jeff Bezos has always been interested in anything that can be

Jeff Bezos, founder of Amazon.com, has led his company to become the Internet's number one retailer.

revolutionized by computers. . . . He graduated summa cum laude, Phi Beta Kappa in electrical engineering and computer science from Princeton University in 1986" (Management Biography, 2000). He was named *Time Magazine's* Person of the Year in 1999. Bezos opened Amazon's virtual doors in July 1995, and today, Amazon.com is the Internet's number one retailer. "Amazon.com seeks to be the world's most customer-centric company, where customers can find and discover anything they might want to buy online" (About Amazon.com, 2000). ■

Sources: Time, vol. 154, no. 26: Special Issue/Person of the Year, December 27, 1999, http://www.time.com/time/magazine/0,9263,1101991227,00.html; Time Chat Event, Jeff Bezos, *Time* 1999 Person of the Year, Transcript from Dec. 22, 1999, http://www.time.com/time/community/transcripts/1999/122299bezos.html.

INTRODUCTION

http://www.ecrc.ctc.com

Managers continually make decisions that affect and are within the framework of their organization's mission, vision, core values, policies, ethical standards, and culture. As leaders, they implement change and guarantee customer satisfaction by setting goals, monitoring progress toward them, and creating and maintaining effective and efficient work environments and workers. To do all this successfully, they must have support from a variety of sources.

information technology (IT)
Manual and electronic means for creating and handling intellectual capital and facilitating organizational communication.

information system (IS)
An organizational subsystem enabling an organization to effectively and efficiently share intellectual capital and create and maintain a working environment in which employees can exploit it.

http://www.doc.gov

This chapter examines **information technologies (IT)**—manual and electronic means for creating and handling intellectual capital and facilitating communication—as they relate to an **information system (IS)**. Information management can be done manually, but most organizations rely upon computers. Computers began as an engineering tool and later as a means of storing data. Today they are essential to business. Taking advantage of developments in technology and methodology to increase the level of decision support, the concept of an information system was introduced in the mid-1960s. An information system enables an organization to effectively and efficiently share intellectual capital and create and maintain a working environment in which employees can exploit it. In its third annual report on the economic effect of computers and the Internet, the U.S. Department of Commerce on June 5, 2000, said that the information technology industry is the number one driver of the American economy. Managers "must ensure that all employees have access to information. . . . In the information age, a company's survival depends on its ability to capture intelligence, transform it into usable knowledge, embed it as organizational learning, and diffuse it rapidly throughout the company" (Bartlett and Ghoshal, 1995).

INFORMATION AND THE MANAGER

Describe the seven characteristics of useful information

data
Unprocessed facts and figures.

information
Data that have been deliberately selected, processed, and organized to be useful to an individual manager.

Data are unprocessed facts and figures that—until they are gathered, sorted, summarized, processed, and distributed to those who need them—are of little value. Data include such things as sales figures, costs, inventory items and quantities, customer complaints, and government statistics on the performance of the economy.

Information results from processing data through information technologies. The result must have value and be useful to decision makers everywhere in an organization. "To have value, information must be linked to other information. Only then does it become a source of knowledge and the basis of organizational learning" (Bartlett and Ghoshal, 1995). For example, Tuesday's total sales figures become more valuable to a store manager when they are broken down by salesperson, department, and inventory item. To be useful, information must have value and be understandable, reliable, relevant, complete, concise, timely, and cost-effective. These characteristics are described in Figure 19.1. Examples of information include quarterly sales projections, annual budgets, daily sales summaries by inventory item, and an organization's primary financial statements. Along with its people, information is any organization's most vital resource.

Besides ensuring that information is useful, managers "must build a network through which all members of the organization can exchange information, develop ideas, and support one another. To do so, they must nurture the horizontal information flows" (Bartlett and Ghoshal, 1995). In other words, managers must practice open-book management. This form of management is essential if an organization's intellectual capital is to deliver its maximum potential. In recent years, the term **knowledge management** (KM) has been used to describe the merging of a company's human and technical knowledge assets (Thurm, 1999).

knowledge management
The merging of a company's human and technical knowledge assets.

FIGURE 19.1 *Characteristics of useful information*

- **Understandable information** is in suitable (correct) form and uses appropriate terms and symbols that the receiver will know and interpret properly. When jargon, abbreviations, shorthand notations, and acronyms are used, the person receiving the information must be able to decode them.
- **Reliable information** is accurate, consistent with fact, actual, and verifiable. The sources of the information, and the people who gather and process it, must be trustworthy. Reliable information will be as free from filtering and rephrasing as possible. Sales figures that have not been adjusted for returns and refunds are not reliable. Stating the value of a company's assets without showing the claims against them by others inaccurately portrays the real financial situation.
- **Relevant information** pertains to a manager's area of responsibility and is essential for the manager to have. Information about maintenance costs of the company's truck fleet, for example, is needed by only a few managers. Irrelevant information can waste a manager's time.
- **Complete information** contains all the facts that a manager needs to make decisions and solve problems. Nothing vital is left out. Managers with incomplete information are handicapped. Although information cannot always be complete, every reasonable effort should be made to obtain whatever information is missing.
- **Concise information** omits material that is extraneous. Just enough—no more, no less—is received by those in need. Giving managers a 200-page computer printout to wade through wastes their time. Summaries of key information, leaving out the details and supporting documents, may be all that is needed. Whenever appropriate, information should be displayed using visual devices such as charts, graphs, and tables. A standard used in the law offers a sensible guideline: Include only that which is necessary and sufficient.
- **Timely information** comes to managers when they need it. Premature information can become obsolete or be forgotten by the time it is actually needed. Information arriving after the time of need is likewise useless. Timeliness is one reason why so many managers rely on computers; they help managers to monitor events as they happen and obtain the real-time information and instant feedback necessary for spotting trends and reacting promptly to circumstances and events.
- **Cost-effective information** is gathered, processed, and disseminated at reasonable cost. A weekly detailed survey of all of a company's customers might delight the sales manager, at least until the survey costs were matched against revenues. A scientifically conducted periodic survey of consumers is likely to yield comparable results at more acceptable cost.

No single force embodies electronic transformation more than the evolving medium known as the Internet. The Internet is a transforming invention that has been adopted faster than any other technology in history. It has had a dramatic impact on the world of business. Firms can now link their systems directly to those of their suppliers and partners, can do business online around the clock, and can learn more than ever about their customers. Cisco's CEO, John Chambers, predicts dramatic growth will continue. "Internet business, in today's times—it's only in the second or third inning," Chambers said. "Think about how long it took other industries to reach $300 billion. Literally, in under a decade, we've reached a level that it took other industries 100 years to reach" (Center for Research on Electronic Commerce, 1999).

http://www.cisco.com

http://www.amazon.com

In this chapter's opening case, Amazon.com's customers can order on the Internet 24 hours a day, 7 days a week. They can track the status of their order online. Approvals can be granted instantly, enhancing the speed with which the order is created and delivered. Today, more than ever before, *speed* is the key to productivity and competitiveness. Adopting digital technologies—converting from atoms to bits—is giving companies a competitive edge. We discuss going digital in more detail later in this chapter.

Managers require a wide variety of information, depending on their positions. Functional information—about marketing, production, finance, and personnel—is needed by both line and staff managers. Information gathered or generated by staff personnel—legal, public relations, computer services, or research and development—may be useful to some line managers as well. Production managers need timely information about inventories, schedules, materials and labor costs, and the maintenance and serviceability of machines and equipment. Supervisors in marketing need sales figures (by stores, departments, and products), order-processing times, inventory levels, delivery schedules, and market-research findings. Finance and accounting managers need financial statements, payroll figures, accounts-receivable and accounts-payable numbers, asset valuations, budgets, and cost data. Regardless of the information needed, an organization's management system must provide it effectively and efficiently to those in need. Says one authority succinctly, "Information provides the substance for coordinating every aspect of the management process" (Bittel, 1989). Information can be downloaded from the Internet. See this chapter's Managing Technology feature.

Top-level managers need information on economic conditions, competitors, legal and political developments, technological innovations, customers' needs for and acceptance of the company's products and services, and progress of operational units toward the organization's goals. Middle managers need information on their particular divisions' operations, including sales, costs, production output, personnel employed, and budget status. The primary difference between what is needed at the top and what is required in the middle lies in the source of information. Much of what top management requires comes from external sources. Most of what middle managers require comes from internal sources—observations, meetings, and reports.

Lower-level managers and autonomous teams need information and feedback about daily, weekly, and monthly activities. The sales manager needs to know how the salespeople are spending their time and the results they generate. Production people need to know the figures on waste, quality, productivity gains, units pro-

MANAGING TECHNOLOGY
Downloading Files from the Internet

1. Make a place to receive the files, such as a folder on your hard drive named *Downloads*. Right-click on your desktop and select *New* and *Folder* from the pop-up menu and type *Downloads*. For Word files (.docs) you may wish to make this folder a subdirectory of your *My Documents* directory. Always write down the name of the file. This will enable you to search your hard drive should you misplace the file or want to make sure it even made it to your computer.
2. Next RIGHT mouse click on the link for the file you wish to download. You will now see a "Save As" dialog box asking how you would like the file to be handled. If you are using Netscape click on *Save File*. If you are using Microsoft Internet Explorer click on *Save to File*.
3. Navigate in the save box to your desktop and choose your newly created folder, or select the location on your hard drive (the subdirectory) or floppy disk on your "A" drive in which you wish to download. Your hard drive is simply a filing cabinet with folders and documents and files inside the folders.
4. Once the file is downloaded you can locate it with your Windows Explorer.
5. Start your word processing program (e.g., Microsoft Word) and open the file.

duced, and schedules met. Personnel may require daily and weekly figures on safety, attendance, new hires, interviews conducted, and job openings. With today's emphasis on empowering workers and staying close to the customer and suppliers, feedback from these sources is essential for quick responses to their and the organization's needs.

As the need for new information grows and as the organization evolves, so too must the ways in which the organization gathers, processes, stores, and disseminates information. The information system must be continually updated to provide what is needed.

INFORMATION MANAGEMENT SYSTEMS

management information system (MIS) *A formal collection of processes that provides managers with suitable quality information to allow them to make decisions, solve problems, and carry out their functions and operations effectively and efficiently.*

An information system exists to serve all employees and depends on each to function properly. All employees must have input to their organization's IS and be able to effectively access and use it and its outputs. A **management information system (MIS)** is a subsystem within an organization's IS designed to serve the specific information needs of all decision makers—managers as well as empowered individuals and teams. It is a formal collection of processes that provides managers with the quality of information they need to make decisions, solve problems, implement change, and create effective and efficient working environments.

Computers and the Internet make the process of gathering intelligence easier. Yet, many managers can't always get everything they need by using just one application from an MIS. Instead of one central system from which to retrieve information, it is more common to have to go to many places to get needed information. Too much data is coming into most organizations from too many directions. Hundreds of electronic sources flow into companies separately. In fact, many companies subscribe to different information products from different publishers in different formats.

Calling to mind our system model from earlier chapters, we can describe an IS or a MIS as one that

> *gathers and transmits data (input); it combines and files data (conversion); and it retrieves, formats, and displays information (output). In addition, [ISs and] MISs have managers who monitor progress and take corrective action to solve problems and keep the system[s] going (Virga, 1987).*

Information provided to managers through their MIS helps them to plan, organize, staff, lead, and control operations and properly use their resources. Information systems provide input to monitor ongoing operations as well as measure their results. Information helps to highlight actual and potential problems by keeping managers in touch with present conditions and trends. Information also gives managers the data they will need to create, and help their MIS create, forecasts and both strategic plans and operational plans. See Figure 19.2 for an example of an MIS.

Functions of an Effective Information System (IS)

2

Describe the three functions of an effective information system (IS)

ISs and MISs must be designed with their users' needs in mind. In addition to linking individuals and their subsystems, they must link an organization to all external customers, partners, and suppliers. Besides creating and providing valuable and useful information, an IS or an MIS should perform three functions:

- Assist organizations and their members in achieving their objectives; information systems should augment, enable, and facilitate, but not interfere with processes and operations.
- Facilitate information access; ideally, people in need of information should be able to obtain it directly, in person or with the assistance of appropriate technologies. When access in this manner is not possible, appropriate support personnel should provide the access.
- Facilitate information flow; the proper quantity and quality of information must flow in the fastest, most direct way to those who need it, when they need it.

Guidelines for Developing an Information System (IS)

Describe the five guidelines for establishing an information system (IS)

Developing an IS and MIS usually begins with the formation of a task force or committee that will conduct an organization-wide assessment of existing technologies and practices. An inventory is taken of equipment on hand; machine capabilities along with those of their support personnel are determined. A survey of current information practices is conducted to determine how effectively and efficiently employees are meeting their needs for information. Inefficiencies and unmet needs are recorded. Finally, the organization's culture and climate must be analyzed to determine how they support current practices and whether they may offer resistance to the implementation of any new systems. (Overcoming resistance is discussed on pages 632–633 in the "Managing Information Systems" section of this chapter.) By beginning with a knowledge of "what is," investigators can then concentrate on creating an IS and MIS in line with the three functions listed earlier.

FIGURE 19.2 *A simplified MIS for an oil company*

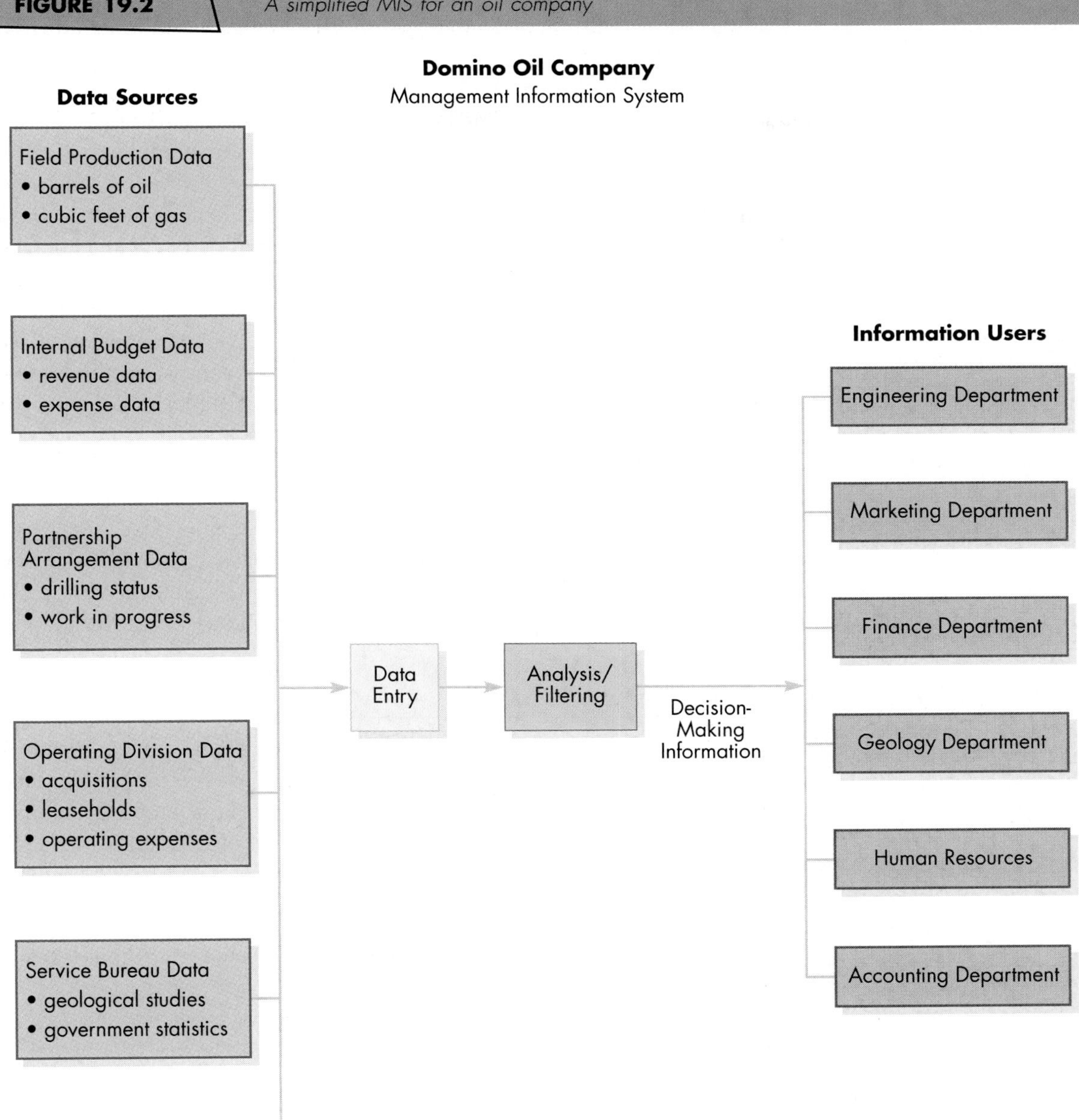

When an organization establishes or improves an IS or an MIS, the following guidelines should prove useful:

- Involve users in the system's design. Where computers will form the heart of the system, users should be consulted on choices of hardware and software. Make certain that components are user-friendly and fully compatible—able to communicate with one another. Because the information specialists (such as system-design people and IS personnel) will not be using the information they help to prepare and disseminate, they need the guidance of those they are to serve.

- Establish clear lines of authority and leadership for the IS personnel. If the group is to operate a centralized IS serving the entire organization's needs, place it under the control of a top-level manager—a chief information officer. If decentralization is chosen, establish unambiguous links and guidelines for those on lower levels to use while running their data centers; link them to the top for control, coordination, and guidance. Many firms use a standing committee for this purpose, composed of department heads, IS supervisors, or a mixture of both.
- Establish clear procedures for gathering, sorting, interpreting, displaying, storing, and distributing data and for interacting with the system. Structure reduces fear and helps to guarantee security, uniformity, quality, and productivity.
- Where technical specialists are used, ensure that both they and the people they support fully understand each specialist's function and roles. Many organizations, such as Hallmark Cards, provide *information guides*—information and technical specialists who can direct people to the proper sources and help them with access problems, thus saving time.
- Build an IS and MIS staff of sufficient quantity and with sufficient skills needed to adequately provide services. Keep personnel up-to-date with continual training and avoid under- and overstaffing; both degrade service quality.

http://www.hallmark.com

COMPUTERIZED INFORMATION SYSTEMS

Describe the eight basic functions of a computerized information system (CIS)

It is difficult to imagine how a company in any industry of any size can effectively operate without the benefits of information technology. When electronically linked to customers, suppliers, and partners, businesses can conduct operations at anytime, anywhere. The improvements in speed, accuracy, and cost of operations made possible by computers and their software are just too great for any company to do without. As authors and consultants, James R. Mensching and Dennis A. Adams (1991), report:

> *almost all forms of organizations are dependent on digital computer technology to process information. With the tremendous advances in microcomputers, office automation, robotics, telecommunications, and computer-aided manufacture and design, computer technology is affecting almost all aspects of business. . . . Computers have become so important to some firms that the successful administration of the information system can mean life or death for the organization.*

computerized information system (CIS) *An MIS built upon computer hardware and software to collect and process data and store and disseminate the resulting information.*

http://www.chrysler.com

http://www.dassault-aviation.fr

A **computerized information system (CIS)** is an IS built on computers and their related hardware (peripherals) and software. Figure 19.3 shows the basic core equipment of any CIS and its related terminology. DaimlerChrysler has teamed up with France's Dassault Aviation's systems designers to create the CIS software that will govern manufacturing designs for its next generation of automobiles. It allows "Chrysler [design and manufacturing] engineers to simulate each step of the assembly process and view it on screen before building a tool or prototype. . . . They can detect potential problems with each motion of the welding robots, for example, and redesign or change the process" (*Chicago Tribune*, 1995). According to DaimlerChrysler management, the system will save millions of dollars and about 20 percent of the time it takes to design a new car's manufacturing processes.

FIGURE 19.3 *Basic core equipment and terminology of CIS*

Glossary

Accelerator board: Speeds up your computer.

Applications: These are the programs that allow you to do work, play games, pay bills, etc.

ASCII: American Standard Code for Information Interchange, pronounced "as-kee." It allows the accurate transmission of data between different computers.

Bus: A "highway" of wires connecting one part of a computer to another.

Card: A plastic board with electronic parts and connecting circuits. It expands the computer's powers.

Coprocessor: Used to relieve the CPU from time-consuming tasks such as math calculations. Allows for faster operations.

Download: To "grab" something from another computer, generally via a modem.

E-mail: Electronic mail. Easier than the Postal Service but not as universal. Yet.

Hz: Hertz, a measure of frequency used to gauge speed. One Hz = one cycle per second. A megahertz (MHz) equals 1 million cycles per second.

Multimedia: Combining text, graphics, sound, video and/or animation in a presentation.

Operating system: Software, like MS DOS, that controls basic computer tasks.

Pixels: The tiny rectangles that compose the image on a TV screen or monitor.

Port: The location where peripherals like printers connect to the computer body.

SCSI: Small computer systems interface, pronounced "scuzzy." A connection used to transfer data at high speeds between the computer and another device, such as a printer or CD-ROM.

Setup

Speakers: Normally built in; but for better sound, external speakers are an option. These often come packaged with CD-ROM drives.

Monitor: Basically, a television for your computer. Comes in many sizes with a range of colors.

Printer: Used to output hard copies of your electronic files. An absolute necessity for those who still like paper.

CPU/hard drive: The central processing unit, a silicon chip about the size of a thumbnail, is the computer's brain. The hard disc drive acts as the permanent memory for the CPU.

Modem: Sends data over telephone lines. This is the computer's connection to the outside world.

The Basics

Floppy drive: Reads the floppy discs used to store data. Discs hold between 360 kilobytes and 1.4 megabytes of data.

The Peripherals

CD-ROM drive and discs: Uses the same technology as audio CDs to store and play data for the computer.

Mouse: Allows the user to point to and select items on the screen. Takes a little getting used to, but ultimately it's a fast and smooth way to navigate.

Scanner: Translates pictures and text into electronic form.

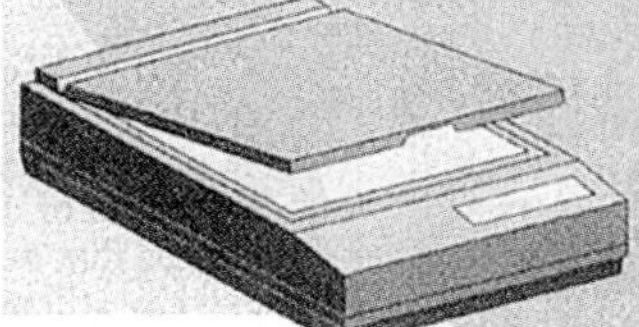

Removable disc drive and cartridge: A heavy-duty storage device using cartridges that hold as much as 200MB.

Keyboard: A typewriter with additional keys. Allows you to type commands and text into the computer.

A Guide to Memory

Memory is the most confusing aspect of computer lingo. All memory is composed of a series of on/off switches, filled or not filled, one or zero. This is called binary storage, and there are two types of usage: working memory (RAM) and storage memory (as on a hard drive).

Each binary digit is called a bit.

Eight bits make a byte. A byte represents one character (letter, number, symbol) of data.

1,024 bytes is a kilobyte or K. Most files are several K in size.

1,048,576 bytes is a megabyte or MB. Most new hard drives have at least 100MB of memory.

101101001011110010110001010100111010001101000111

RAM: Random-access memory. Temporarily stores data and instructions for the CPU. The horsepower of the computer.

ROM: Read-only memory. Memory that stores data or programs permanently.

Cache: Composed of superfast RAM chips, it holds the most recently used data for quick and easy access.

SIMM: Single in-line memory module. A small board containing additional RAM. Boosts the power of the PC.

Source: "The ABCs of Computing," in *Computers & the Family, Special Issue, Newsweek* (Fall, 1994), p. 14.

Computer technology is allowing many companies to replace human resources with automated robots, especially for performing tedious, repetitive tasks.

Computerized information systems may be centralized or decentralized. After a brief explanation of each, we examine computer operations.

The centralized CIS is under top management's direction and control, usually through the office of a chief information officer (CIO).

> *Its primary function is to assist other units of the organization to function in a more effective and efficient manner. Unless the information systems area also sells computing services to external users, it will not produce an end product or generate external revenue. Hence, it is of the utmost importance that the managers within the information systems area understand the operations of their client departments and the company as a whole (Mensching and Adams, 1991).*

data center
A unit of a decentralized CIS that operates to serve its unit's members with their own sets of hardware, software, and specialists (machine operators and programmers).

A CIS functioning both at the top and at other management levels is said to be decentralized. Each unit of a decentralized CIS is called a **data center** and operates to serve its unit's members with their own sets of hardware, software, and specialists (machine operators and programmers). The basics for operating a decentralized CIS include the following:

> *At a minimum there must be data exchange standards established so that files can be easily transferred. For the sake of economy and efficiency, many firms find it best to establish company-wide standards such as those for hardware and software compatibility. Not only does this allow for the exchange of data but, more importantly, it encourages the sharing of resources and the uniformity of reports (Mensching and Adams, 1991).*

Centralized or decentralized, a CIS must deliver the basic functions shown in Figure 19.4.

end-user computing
The use of information technology (IT) by people who are not controlled and directed by top management.

Decentralized CISs result in **end-user computing**: the use of information technology (IT) by people who are free from control by top management. Although end-user computing can stimulate innovative problem solving and decision making, it does present managers with collateral problems.

FIGURE 19.4 *The basic functions of a CIS*

Function	Description
Computer Operations	Runs the system; involves starting jobs, mounting the proper input and output volumes, and responding to problem conditions
System Programming	Installs and maintains the operating system and associated system software
Data Entry	Enters data in machine-readable form
Application Program Development	Writes new application systems
Application Program Maintenance	Corrects and updates existing application systems
Data Management	Assures data security, access, integrity, and usability
Communications Management	Configures and maintains the network
End-User Computing	Helps and educates users

Source: From *Managing an Information System* by James R. Mensching and Dennis A. Adams, p. 56. © 1991 by Prentice Hall, Inc. Reprinted by permission of Pearson Education, Inc. Upper Saddle River, NJ, 97458.

The first problem concerns control. Efforts must be made to coordinate multiple end-users' computing efforts in order to avoid duplication of work and consequent waste. Top management and other units must be encouraged to share useful approaches with one another and keep informed of projects and processes.

A second problem concerns possible duplication of expensive software and hardware. Planners must ensure that such components are fully compatible—able to efficiently share and exchange data through suitable interfaces and networks.

database
A collection of computerized data arranged for ease and speed of retrieval; sometimes called a data bank.

The third problem lies in orderly, authorized access to both the organization's systems and to its **database**—a collection of data arranged for ease and speed of retrieval. In today's business environment, employees and customers want immediate access to information. So, successful Web sites have databases, which involve the exchange and sorting of information. As long as users have a Web browser and an Internet connection they can access data via the Internet. A database might simply be a list of names and addresses to which are added all the facts the organization thinks might be relevant for communicating better with its customers. Another database might be the catalog of products offered. Databases help organizations to explore and answer questions. Users interact directly with the database to retrieve information.

Much of the selling on Amazon.com is based on the effective use of database technology. For example, repeat Amazon customers are greeted by name and are given personalized book recommendations. The technology is called *collaborative filtering*. It looks at the customer's past purchases and compares them with other customers in aggregate. It makes a reasonably insightful guess as to what other things might interest the customer.

Databases rank among some organizations' most valuable assets: loss or impairment may shut down the enterprise cold. Imagine American Express or the New York Stock Exchange or Pacific Bell with their computers down. A lack of trained users or inadequate controls over access and scheduling renders systems and components vulnerable to damage or compromise.

http://www.americanexpress.com

http://www.nyse.com

http://www.pacbell.com

Databases may be created internally, by outsiders, or both. Accessing outside databases can be useful but expensive. Because external users are commonly billed by the amount of time they are in contact with a commercial data source, one of a firm's database users may be able to acquire information and then share it with others within the organization, thus avoiding duplication in time and billing.

Among outside sources are PC Globe, whose software atlas includes digitized maps and data for some 200 countries, among them the countries of Eastern Europe, as well as the Baltic states and the nations that once composed the Soviet Union. This database contains a wealth of statistics and graphs of interest to managers dealing with the global economy (Reid and Hume, 1992). The remainder of this chapter concentrates on management information systems that are at least partially computerized and thereby qualify as full or partially computerized information systems.

Computer Operations

Computer hardware consists of input devices, a control unit, a central processing unit (CPU), storage devices, and output devices. A computer system also includes software—the programs that give the hardware the instructions for processing and storing data. Computer software encompasses two fundamental classes of programs: operating systems and application programs. An **operating system** comprises "an extensive and complex set of programs that manages the operation of a computer and the application [programs] that run on it" (Keen, 1991). In other words, it is the collection of computer programs that controls how the computer works. Computer manufacturers design their computers to run on one or more operating systems. Some 100 million personal computers (PCs)—a computer used by one person at a time—were estimated to be in use in early 1993, many in business settings. The PC was introduced by IBM in 1981 and revolutionized communication. It was built over an Intel processor (8088) and fitted to Microsoft's operating system MS-DOS. The great majority of the IBM-compatible PCs use a graphical user interface based on Microsoft's Windows. Apple Macintosh computers employ a different operating architecture altogether, and large IBM machines (mainframes and minicomputers) run on MVS and DOS/VSE operating systems.

operating system
An extensive and complex set of instructions that manages the operation of a computer and the application programs that run on it.

http://www.ibm.com

http://www.intel.com

http://www.microsoft.com

http://www.apple.com

application program
A computer program designed to execute specific sets of tasks such as word processing.

http://www.adobe.com

http://www.quicken.com

http://www.boeing.com

http://www.nscorp.com

http://www.sabre.com

Application programs are software programs designed to execute specific sets of tasks such as word processing, graphics design, accounting and finance, production operations and marketing, personnel and inventory control, and many more. Some are specially designed (and programmed) in-house, whereas others may be purchased commercially from a vast array of options. Among well-known off-the-shelf programs are Adobe Photoshop, Quicken, and Microsoft Office (Word, Excel, PowerPoint, and Access). Custom-developed programs include many of Boeing's design and engineering packages, Norfolk Southern's computer-aided reporting system, and the SABRE travel reservation system. System designers first consider the software that will meet the company's needs and then select equipment that can run that software. Care must be taken to ensure that user groups and units within the company can use all equipment and software interchangeably. In the case of the SABRE reservation system, outside users such as travel agents must be able to access it as well.

5

Describe the two basic data processing modes

batch processing
A computer procedure in which data are collected over time and entered into databases according to prescribed policies and procedures.

transactional processing
A computer procedure in which data are received about a company's ongoing operations and entered into data banks as each transaction occurs.

Data Processing Modes

Two data processing modes are commonly used in the business setting: batch processing and transactional processing. Under **batch processing**, data are collected over time and entered into data banks according to prescribed policies and procedures. For example, a clerk may collect orders from outside salespeople and enter them into the order database at the end of each week. In **transactional processing** data are received about a company's ongoing operations and entered into data banks as each transaction occurs. In order to accomplish the intended utility of transactional processing, certain kinds of information must be entered into the system in real time or as close to real time as possible. Without such immediacy, these data will be unavailable to users and managers when needed. Bank automated-teller machines (ATMs) record transactions in the computer's memory as they occur; travel agents book reservations directly into the database. Most CISs are built around transactional processing to yield the best results.

Discuss the various methods used for linking computer systems

Linking Computer Systems

In an ideal world, all companies and their employees would have identical and up-to-date computers and software and be able to communicate with one another effortlessly. The reality, however, is that companies, their customers, suppliers, and partners use a great variety of ITs, each with differing capabilities and operating standards.

Automated teller machines use transactional processing to provide real-time account information to customers.

© PATRIK GIARDINO/CORBIS

How, then, do you get hundreds of computers, made by dozens of manufacturers, operating on scores of different networks, and using many different software programs to communicate with one another? The answer lies in making them compatible through the use of *middleware*—software that creates compatibility links between asimilar networks, software programs, and their computers. In banking, for example, "middleware lets each computer—at a credit reporting agency or at a branch—continue operating independently yet, without reprogramming, cooperate intimately with the others" (Verity, 1995).

networking
The electronic linking of two or more computers.

The electronic linking of two or more computers is called **networking**. Such linkage—supported by servers, bridges, PBXs, gateways, and modems—allows computers to communicate directly—for example, by email and file sharing—through cables, wires, microwaves, cellular or radio networks, or fiber optics. Local area networks (LANs) link computers throughout a facility transmitting data at about ten million bits (megabits) per second; they can be linked through the use of a *bridge*. "Cathay Pacific Airways expects to install email capability on its entire fleet starting in spring [2001], together with access to a multitude of Web pages stored in the planes' intranet, part of a local area network (LAN) accessible only on a particular plane" (McDowell, 2001). Wide area networks (WANs) link computers and their LANs to those at remote locations, including computers linked to the Internet—a worldwide network of computers linked by phone lines. Most businesses use WANs to link their remote operations and to connect them to the operations of their customers, partners, and suppliers.

http://www.cathaypacific.com

The Internet is an open network of computers providing a worldwide means of exchanging information and communicating. A network is a group of interconnected computers, including the hardware and software used to connect them. The Internet allows people who are often significantly removed from each other in time, space, thought, and emotion to connect with others and to be contacted by others, almost anywhere and anytime. Voice, video, and data signals can be carried simultaneously over one phone line, linked to a computer and its LAN by a *gateway*, through a modem using one of two leading technologies: digital simultaneous voice and data (DSVD) or analog simultaneous voice and data (ASVD).

The Internet exists wherever devices communicate over publicly accessible networks using a protocol, called TCP/IP. Protocol is rules and standards for transferring information between computers. Some of the most common TCP/IP protocols are SMTP for email, NNTP for Usenet news groups, FTP for file transfer, and DNS for servers exchanging directions with each other. The World Wide Web is another such subset of the overall Internet, a system in which hypertext information, in a format called HTML or hypertext markup language (a standard language for creating documents), is exchanged via a protocol called HTTP or hypertext transfer protocol. TCP/IPs are also widely used to build private networks, called intranets, that may or may not be connected to the Internet.

Metcalfe's Law explains the viral growth of the Internet. It says that as more and more people connect to a system, the network of contacts gains value, enticing even more people in . . . and so on. As this text has so often pointed out, "the biggest payoff from networking comes when companies use it to do better by their customers [and suppliers]" (Arnst, 1995). In 1995 Choice Hotels International, Inc. "opened one of the first commercial World Wide Web sites that links Internet users directly to a reservations database" (Arnst, 1995). Choice Hotels offers

http://www.hotelchoice.com

true reservations services to its franchised chains—including Comfort Inn, Rodeway Inns, and Econo Lodge—through its Choice 2001. Actual reservations can be made by credit card; users are protected through the use of various security devices (Arnst, 1995). See this chapter's Ethical Management feature.

CIS Management Tools

Explain the purposes of decision support systems (DSSs)

Effective managers use every available asset to accomplish their jobs. Few assets rival the computer for sheer utility in helping managers plan, organize, staff, lead, and control. Among the great strengths of computer technology is the ability to automate the data processing that underlies a sound MIS. The power and flexibility of most computer systems is limited only by the imagination of their users. The editors of a respected management handbook, however, caution their readers to remember, "computers do not have the feelings, perceptions, or flexibility of the human mind" (Virga, 1987).

Decision Support Systems

decision support system (DSS)
A specialized variant of a CIS; an analytic model that joins a manager's experience, judgment, and intuition with the computer's data access, display, and calculation processes; allows managers to interact with linked programs and databases via the keyboard.

To harness the immense quantities of data now accessible to managers, imaginative thinkers have devised a specialized variant of a CIS, the **decision support system (DSS)**. In general, the MIS produces a standard report according to a schedule. Unlike an MIS, a decision maker can interact directly with the decision support system (DSS), which adds speed and flexibility to the decision making process. This analytic model joins the manager's experience, judgment, and intuition with the computer's data access, display, and calculation strengths (Virga, 1987). Decision makers can access databases to produce nonstandard reports that can be used on a problem-to-problem basis. Managers can analyze, manipulate, format, display, and

ETHICAL MANAGEMENT
Staying Close to Customers Can Get You Too Close

In an effort to get and stay close to their customers, companies are moving deeper into what is called database marketing—"collecting mountains of information about you, crunching it to predict how likely you are to buy a product, and using that knowledge to craft a marketing message precisely calibrated to get you to do so." After all, the more they know about you and your needs, the better they can help you to meet them. Many companies require a customized approach to meeting their needs. Off-the-shelf won't do. For this reason and others, many companies routinely practice open-book management with their suppliers and partners.

When you shop by mail, in person, or on the Internet, you distribute a lot of personal information to others—your name, address, phone number, credit card numbers, and so on. In addition, smart, aggressive salespeople are trained to ask you a lot of questions, the answers to which can be used for future sales efforts. Customer feedback of all kinds is sought and used to help improve operations, products, and services. Companies store this information in their databases and often share it with other merchants. Your state's department of motor vehicles probably sells the data on your driver's license. Credit bureaus specialize in selling your credit history.

- What privacy issues are raised here?
- What safeguards do you want businesses with information about you to exercise?
- What laws are you aware of that deal with protecting your privacy?

Source: Berry, Jonathan, et al. "Database Marketing: A Potent New Tool for Selling," *Business Week*, September 5, 1994, pp. 56–62.

output data in different ways. The DSS provides a modeling function to help interpret the information retrieved. Each DSS is developed and adapted to support a firm's own decision problems. DSS programs are available off-the-shelf or may be tailored in-house. With such a system, a marketing manager may ask the computer, "What happens to sales if we lower prices by 10 percent?" The system will manipulate the model and stored data, then present likely outcomes: production volume, sales, inventories, revenues, and costs.

expert system
A specialized end-user decision support program that stores the knowledge of a group of authorities for access by nonexperts faced with the need to make topic-related decisions.

Specialized end-user decision support programs include the **expert system**, software that stores the knowledge of a group of authorities for access by nonexperts faced with the need to make topic-related decisions (Mensching and Adams, 1991). To build such a system, information specialists study an expert's way of analyzing an issue or solving a problem; then they write a program that simulates the expert's methods and techniques.

artificial intelligence (AI)
The ability of a machine to perform those activities that are normally thought to require intelligence; giving machines the capability to learn, sense, and think for themselves.

Expert systems are a kind of **artificial intelligence (AI)**—the capability of computers to learn, sense, and think for themselves. Other branches of AI include voice-recognition systems, speech synthesis programs, computer vision, and neural networks. According to Purdue University engineering and computer technology professor Ray Eberts, "a *neural network* is a computer program modeled after the brain that can learn to perform tasks and make decisions based on past examples or experience" (Kleiman, 1995). Basic variations of expert systems using neural networks currently help to diagnose and analyze medical, legal, and mechanical problems for doctors, lawyers, and garage mechanics.

group decision support system (GDSS)
A variant decision support system that allows groups focusing on a problem to interact with one another and to exchange information, data, and ideas.

Yet another variant decision support system is the **group decision support system**, or **GDSS**. The GDSS allows a group focusing on a problem, like a product or process design team, to interact with one another and exchange information, data, and ideas. GDSSs are used in brainstorming and problem-solving sessions and to facilitate conferencing of all kinds. For example, a group of participants, assembled anonymously from terminals in their offices or in remote locations, may interact in real time under the direction of a moderator as ideas and questions are presented.

Group decision support systems are often used to facilitate videoconferences.

A GDSS requires networking and *meetingware* or *groupware* software programs. "Meetingware products support 'same time, same place' and 'same time, different place' meetings, which can be held at a single location or at several locations via videoconferencing. Groupware products like Lotus Notes let people share a workspace for discussion, message exchange, and collaboration" (Sacks and Lancione, 1995). Lotus Notes runs on a variety of computers and operating systems; but "it's a development platform that forces companies to build or buy all types of collaborative applications before users can share documents, exchange data, update databases . . . and more" (Stahl, 1995). The growing popularity and demand for network technology is just one reason why IBM bought Lotus Development Corporation for $3.5 billion in 1995.

http://www.lotus.com

It should be empasized that a DSS is an analytical *support* system, not a maker of decisions (Bittel and Ramsey, 1985). As two experts observe, a "DSS allows the manager to examine more thoroughly a problem and experiment with many different solutions. This tends to give the manager more confidence in the decision. But, due to the multitude of possibilities to explore, it usually does not make the decision process any quicker" (Mensching and Adams, 1991).

http://www.generalmills.com

General Mills utilizes a DSS by making appropriate data available to autonomous factory teams so that they can make their own decisions:

> *At some beverage plants, for example, four shifts of 20-person teams are informed of marketing plans and production costs. "They have at their fingertips all the data that would normally be held by management," says Daryl D. David, a human resources director. The self-managed teams do everything from scheduling production to rejecting products not up to quality standards, and they receive bonuses based on plant performance. Some 60% of General Mills' plants have been converted to such high-performance work systems. The approach has produced significant gains in productivity, and the company is now moving to spread it to all operations* (Business Week, *1992).*

Executive Information Systems

executive information system (EIS)
A decision support system custom designed to facilitate executive decision making; may include forecasting, strategic planning, and other elements.

An **executive information system (EIS)** is a decision support system custom designed to facilitate executive decision making. Typical executive uses include forecasting; strategic planning; performing risk and cost-benefit analyses; running business game simulations; linear programming; monitoring quality, productivity, ethics, and social responsibility efforts; and monitoring critical success factors and stakeholder expectations (Crockett, 1992). EISs and DSSs "are particularly useful when they are able to access the databases used by other organizational information systems as well" (Bittel and Ramsey, 1985).

A sophisticated EIS can integrate many levels of information and abstraction. Users may draw upon data from a division, department, function, individual employee, or discrete transaction. Moreover, the exponentially expanding resources of external databases may be accessed electronically.

For meetingware and groupware to be used most effectively, a company culture that values and rewards teams and has a horizontal process focus must exist. See this chapter's Valuing Diversity feature for a look at how networking can contribute to getting the best from diverse groups and individuals.

VALUING DIVERSITY
Meetings and Diversity

Many individuals from different cultural and ethnic backgrounds are reluctant to voice their true opinions to others, face-to-face. They have been taught to defer to their elders and to not object to or contradict their elders' ideas. Other individuals experience embarrassment when asked to speak in front of others. Still others are never asked for their opinions or ignored when they offer them. Information technology in the form of groupware can help to overcome such problems by concealing the identity of both contributors and their contributions. Examples of this software include Lotus Notes and Microsoft Exchange, both of which facilitate calendar sharing, email handling, and the replication of files across a distributed system so that all users can view the same information.

The beauty of holding meetings and interacting with others electronically is that face-to-face communications are not necessary. The exception, of course, is videoconferencing. "Participants can share ideas individually and anonymously. The platform can be free-form brainstorming, or input can be precategorized into electronic file folders. Participants are more likely to share their off-the-wall—but creative—thoughts in an anonymous forum." Examples of software for electronic "face-to-face" meetings include CU-SeeMe and Microsoft NetMeeting.

The experiences of the many companies that use this software prove that most employees will express themselves more candidly through it. Contributions can be made without fear of receiving negative feedback or contradicting others. People can step out of their cultures for the duration of a meeting, knowing that their contributions will be considered and recorded. One's concern about "saving face" and deferring to elders is effectively eliminated. Since no one really knows who contributed what, contributions must stand or fall on their own merits; thus, many will receive more serious consideration than they otherwise might.

Sources: WhatIs definition of Groupware at http://whatis.techtarget.com/WhatIs_Definition_Page/0,4152,212217,00.html; Sacks, Jeffrey D., and Frank A. Lancione. "Start Groupware at the Top," *Informationweek*, June 26, 1995, p. 152.

MANAGING INFORMATION SYSTEMS

8 Discuss the four challenges that must be met by managers of an information system

To manage an IS effectively, an organization must confront four basic challenges: overcome resistance to the new and different, enable employees to use the system, decide what operations to keep and what to outsource, and evaluate the results of the system's operations. Many companies, after merging, face the task of enabling the employees inherited to use a more advanced CIS. As a result, a company may outsource some initial training until a base of newcomers becomes technically proficient. They can then train others.

Overcoming Resistance

Getting people to use their IS or MIS effectively can be difficult. Thomas H. Davenport (1994), a professor and consultant, believes that this is so because managers "glorify information technology and ignore human psychology." They build elaborate IT systems and then wonder why people don't use them properly. What's missing is a concern for the organization's culture and "how people in organizations actually go about acquiring, sharing, and making use of information" (Davenport, 1994). Davenport further states that "research conducted since the mid-1960s shows that most managers don't rely on computer-based information to make decisions."

http://www.eds.com

Electronic Data Systems' director of client/server technical services adds another dimension: "The problem is not with the technology, but with the corporate processes. Companies must fundamentally change the way they do business, and that's hard" (Arnst, 1995). For example, a company with a traditional functional organization and vertical command structure will find it difficult to change the ways in which information is gathered and shared. Such structures impede the flow of and access to information; they have too many levels and filters for swift dissemination and use of vital facts and figures.

People fear change and often become irrational when faced with machines, technology, and terminology that they do not understand. Just as many customers are intimidated and annoyed by an organization's voice-mail system, employees react in similar fashion to technology that complicates or eliminates their established routines. ITs encourage and depend on information sharing. But all too often people have learned that information is a precious commodity and needs to be protected, especially when there are rewards attached to its generation and use. "Changing a company's information culture requires altering the basic behaviors, attitudes, values, management expectations, and incentives that relate to information" (Davenport, 1994).

Chapter 10 discussed culture and change in detail, but a few words are in order here about training employees before making changes. First, for change to be effective, those who will have to implement the change should be involved in the making of decisions. Second, people need to be kept informed and forewarned about impending changes and given time to adequately prepare for them through either training or development programs. Additional information on this issue appears later in this chapter.

Enabling Users

A study funded by the U.S. Labor Department and conducted by a consulting firm and two universities "indicates that using information technology to improve business practices brings the biggest benefits to the corporate bottom line when workers are well-trained" (McGee, 1995). What this chapter has already said about overcoming resistance applies here as well. Once those who will be served by an IS and its IT have participated in building the systems, they must be adequately trained to use its technology and support services.

http://www.fedex.com

Support personnel need constant training. FedEx, the air freight company, knows this and takes its IS training seriously. According to the company's senior manager of development services, Rick Nordtvedt (McGee, 1995):

> *FedEx IS employees and their managers are expected to regularly evaluate their training needs for upcoming and ongoing projects. . . . IS training focuses on three specific areas: technology, business, and . . . "personal process enabling" skills. . . . [IS employees] take core MBA courses as well as FedEx-specific business classes. FedEx's personal process enabling skills includes course work in project management, leadership skills, and creative thinking. . . .*

In addition to staying current in technologies, IS employees at FedEx must know what their customers know and need in order to serve them effectively.

Outsourcing

A 1995 survey by Massachusetts-based Computer Sciences Corporation of 603 North American chief information officers (CIOs) shows that the top five reasons for turning to outsiders are to better manage their PC procurement and maintenance, training and end-user support, applications software development, disaster recovery capabilities, and telecommunications and networking (Caldwell, 1995). Among the giants that furnish outsourcing services are EDS, Perot Systems, Computer Sciences Corporation, AT&T, IBM, and Unisys. These companies, and their smaller counterparts, specialize in employing the latest technologies, usually at lower costs, to all kinds of IT/IS services; thus, they offer their clients greater control and efficiency.

http://www.perotsystems.com

http://www.csc.com

http://www.att.com

http://www.unisys.com

For many companies the decision to outsource IT/IS operations in part or in total is made by asking a simple question: "Does the particular IT operation provide a strategic advantage or is it a commodity that does not differentiate us from our competitors?" (Lacity, Willcocks, and Feeny, 1995). Commodities are outsourced when more efficient providers are found; other operations are kept in-house. But research suggests that such measures should be secondary; a "company's overarching objective should be to maximize flexibility and control so that it can pursue different options as it learns more or as its circumstances change" (Lacity, Willcocks, and Feeny, 1995).

Before outsourcing an IT/IS operation, a company must know what its operations are and what IT/IS needs exist for each. It must then analyze how efficiently and effectively these needs are being met. If improvements are called for, it must then determine who is best able to provide them—in-house or outside personnel. If the answer is outsiders, could in-house staff be effectively upgraded to provide the service? If not, under what terms and conditions will service be provided by an outsider and what consequences could result if it fails to provide adequate support? Can we afford to live with those consequences? One key to outsourcing is to retain some measure of control and flexibility over the outside provider and the service it provides. Another is to recognize that all these situations and the answers to them will continually change. Constant auditing of IT/IS operations is, therefore, a necessity. See this chapter's Global Management feature for British Petroleum's approach to IT outsourcing.

Evaluating Results

The Connecticut-based consulting firm Gartner Group, Inc., has estimated that about one-half of the costs associated with owning and operating PCs in corporate America represents waste. "Companies waste money by duplicating PC equipment, providing ineffective training, losing productivity, and failing to take advantage of volume discounts" (Caldwell, 1995).

Because information technology changes so swiftly, many companies consider their desktops and laptops to be expendable equipment with a usable life of around two to three years, and they replace them nearly as often. When companies adopted Microsoft's Windows 95, for example, "it required at least twice as much memory as most corporate PCs had at that time" (Caldwell, 1995). In order to run the latest

GLOBAL APPLICATIONS
IT Outsourcing at BP

BP Exploration Operating Company Limited is a division of British Petroleum Company. In 1993 it made the decision to stop focusing on supporting business operations and start focusing on performing them. The result was the outsourcing of all IT operations and a reduction in IT personnel of nearly 1,150 people.

After some experimenting with managing multiple service providers and investigating companies using a single-provider approach, the company formulated an "outsourcing vision." It looked for companies that knew their markets and capabilities and were dedicated to innovation, a customer focus, and cost containment. The company created a list of six possible service providers by carefully screening 65. BP asked the six to create alliances that would meet BP's cost objectives and IT/IS needs. Three managed to do so to BP's satisfaction and were hired, under initial two-year contracts, to work together to provide "a single seamless service to [its] 42 businesses around the globe."

One contractor is the primary provider and coordinates the services of the others. The contractors outsource and manage whatever services they cannot themselves provide. The company's IT department, in turn, manages the primary contractor. Business units may contract with IT suppliers for customized services. BP has the right to audit suppliers and evaluates each every year. Periodically, the suppliers are benchmarked against others in the industry. Suppliers who reduce their costs below BP's targets keep one-half of the funds saved.

http://www.bp.com

Source: Cross, John. "IT Outsourcing: British Petroleum's Competitive Approach," *Harvard Business Review* (May–June 1995), pp. 94–102.

http://www.nexgen.com

http://www.informationweek.com

software and software upgrades, computer manufacturers had to include Intel's Pentium chip or NexGen's Nx chip in their new models; both of these chips were eventually made obsolete by newer models (Hof, 1995).

The results of a 1995 survey by *InformationWeek* magazine show why IT/IS costs can explode. The survey revealed that about one-half "of all PCs used in organizations were bought by the central IS department" (Violino, 1995). Managers in SBUs bought about 45 percent; individuals purchased about 8 percent. Software purchases were handled in a similar way.

Auditing by both insiders and outsiders, such as customers and consultants, will bring to light just what is and what should not be happening with both MIS and CIS operations. First, users of the system must evaluate it; they are the ones who know whether or not their needs are being met. Second, the CIO and information technology managers must perform audits as well. Their primary focus is on meeting needs effectively and efficiently—within or below their budgets. Their audits should include a periodic analysis of IT policies and the costs connected with delivering MIS/CIS services. They should also conduct an annual inventory of all personnel and equipment to determine needs and capabilities.

In line with *InformationWeek*'s survey, New York-based Home Insurance Company's CIO, Joe Campbell, had an environment in which IT costs were out of control. His company's " 'PC jockeys' were doing their own thing. If they needed some PC hardware or software, they'd buy it . . . and put it on their expense accounts" (Violino, 1995). Among the results were rapidly rising software and training costs, PCs unable to network with one another, and employees who could not use each other's machines. Campbell created a new policy that set easily understood standards designed to stop the waste (Violino, 1995):

- All PCs must be 486, 66-MHz machines that run Microsoft's Windows or IBM's OS/2 operating systems and use the Microsoft Office suite of word processing, spreadsheet, and graphics software.
- All LANs must use Novell's NetWare network operating system.
- Any deviations from the above require approval by senior information systems management.

Campbell countered initial resistance to these changes by carefully explaining the "economics of the situation" (Violino, 1995).

CHAPTER SUMMARY

1 **Describe the seven characteristics of useful information.** To be useful to decision makers, information must have value—be linked to other information—and must be

- Understandable—presented in a suitable form, using appropriate terms and symbols that a receiver will know and interpret properly
- Reliable—accurate, consistent with fact, actual, and verifiable
- Relevant—pertains to a decision maker's area of responsibility and is essential
- Complete—containing all the facts that a person or group of people needs to make decisions and solve problems
- Concise—just enough, omitting material that is not needed
- Timely—available when needed, in real time when possible
- Cost-effective—created and disseminated at a reasonable cost; this characteristic relates to most of the others as well

2 **Describe the three functions of an effective information system (IS).**

- Assisting organizations and their members in achieving their objectives
- Facilitating information access through people and technology
- Facilitating information flow by using the fastest, most direct way to disseminate and share information

3 **Describe the five guidelines for establishing an information system (IS).**

- Involve users in the system's design.
- Establish clear lines of authority and leadership for IS personnel.
- Establish clear procedures for gathering, sorting, interpreting, displaying, storing, and distributing data and for interacting with the system.
- Where technical specialists are used, ensure that both they and the people they support fully understand each specialist's function and roles.
- Build an IS staff of sufficient quality and quantity and with sufficient skills needed to adequately provide services.

4 **Describe the eight basic functions of a computerized information system (CIS).**

- *Computer operations*—Runs the system; involves starting jobs, mounting the proper input and output volumes, and responding to problem conditions
- *Systems programming*—Installs and maintains the operating system and associated system software
- *Data entry*—Enters data in machine-readable form
- *Application program development*—Writes new application systems
- *Application program maintenance*—Corrects and updates existing application systems
- *Data management*—Assures data security, access, integrity, and usability
- *Communications management*—Configures and maintains the network
- *End-user computing*—Helps and educates users

5 **Describe the two basic data processing modes.** The two most common modes are batch processing and transactional processing. Under the first, data is collected over time and entered into data banks according to prescribed policy and procedures. Under the latter, data is received about a company's ongoing operations and entered into data banks as each transaction occurs. Both cases in this chapter are about companies using transactional processing.

6 Discuss the various methods used for linking computer systems. Networking and middleware allow for computers to communicate with one another. Networks use servers, bridges, PBXs, gateways, and modems. Cable, microwaves, cellular or radio networks, and fiber optics allow for transmissions. Local and wide area networks link computers within and from within to those outside an organization. Most businesses can use their local telephone lines to simultaneously transmit voice, video, and data.

7 Explain the purposes of decision support systems (DSSs). Decision support systems are analytical models that join the manager's experience, judgment, and intuition with the computer's data access, display, and calculation strengths. They may be off-the-shelf or tailored for in-house use. DaimlerChrysler's new manufacturing software is tailored to meet its needs. The French company that developed it is now tailoring it to meet the needs of other manufacturers.

Expert systems are a kind of artificial intelligence and are specialized end-user decision support programs. Software stores the knowledge of a group of authorities for use by nonexperts faced with the need to make topic-related decisions.

Group decision support systems allow a group focusing on a problem to interact with one another and exchange information, data, and ideas. Such systems make use of both meetingware and groupware.

8 Discuss the four challenges that must be met by managers of an information system. To manage an IS effectively, an organization must confront four challenges: overcoming resistance to changes, enabling employees to use the system, deciding what operations to keep and outsource, and periodically evaluating the system's effectiveness and efficiency. The first and second challenges are usually dealt with through training and development programs and by involving users in the design of the system and the choice of its equipment. The third is made after carefully considering in-house capabilities and efficiencies; operations and functions that can be performed better by outsiders are usually outsourced. The fourth challenge is a basic element of control. All operations need periodic reviews by both insiders and outsiders. Just as conditions change, so too will the ways in which IS functions and ITs are dealt with.

REVIEW QUESTIONS

1. What makes information valuable to decision makers? Useful?
2. How can an organization decide on the effectiveness of its information systems?
3. How should an organization and its strategic business units go about establishing their information systems?
4. What basic functions must any CIS perform for its users?
5. What data processing modes would you prescribe for each of the following? (a) handling airline reservations, (b) handling total sales by department for each day of operations, (c) measuring the quality of cookies coming off an assembly line.
6. How do local area networks (LANs) operate? Wide area networks (WANs)? Why do most companies usually require both?
7. What is a decision support system (DSS)? What kinds exist?
8. How does a company usually decide if an IS or IT function should be outsourced? If they are operating effectively? If people are using them to their best advantage?

DISCUSSION QUESTIONS FOR CRITICAL THINKING

1. You are the chief information officer for a neighborhood bank that has just been absorbed into a larger one. Both banks have differing hardware and software. What must you do in order for your IS to properly network with the parent's?
2. You have been asked to build and lead a committee to evaluate your company's ISs and ITs. How would you go about selecting members for your committee? What issues should you deal with at your first meeting?
3. How do information needs differ at the various levels of management? Why should all their computers be networked to both insiders (intranet) and outsiders (Internet)?

INTERNET EXERCISES

Check the text Web site at http://plunkett.swcollege.com for updated links to the Internet Exercises.

1. Peter Drucker coined the term "knowledge workers" in a 1959 book, *Landmarks of Tomorrow*. Read "The Age of Social Transformation," as originally published in *The Atlantic Monthly*, November 1994. What is a knowledge worker? How can you become a knowledge worker? **http://www.theatlantic.com/politics/ecbig/soctrans.htm**

2. Read the Wharton School's Emerging Technologies Management Research Program report, "How Will Technology Change the Work of Managers?" from the Emerging Technologies Insight-building Event on May 19, 2000. What major trends are "technology-driven" or "technology-enabled"? **http://emertech.wharton.upenn.edu/emertech/ConfRpts_Folder/cfWorkofMgrs.html**

3. Read the Wharton School's Emerging Technologies Management Research Program February 1999 technology update, "Emerging Technologies That Could Transform YOUR Industry." What are some of the emerging technologies with the potential to change the world, as we know it? **http://emertech.wharton.upenn.edu/emertech/ET%20Tech%20Update.html**

4. Faith Popcorn, a futurist, is recognized as America's foremost trend expert. Which three trends, identified by Popcorn, do you think are most important to managers? Explain. **http://www.faithpopcorn.com**

APPLICATION CASE

Networking at VF Corporation

"VF Corporation is the largest clothing manufacturer in the world" (Overview). It sells its wares to such retail giants as Wal-Mart, J.C. Penney, and Federated Department Stores. Along with its stable of brands—Lee, Wrangler, Healthtex, Jantzen, and Vanity Fair—VF is adding to its rivals' envy because of its state-of-the-art, computer-driven distribution system. For stock on hand, VF guarantees delivery within three days of receiving an order to retail outlets on its network.

The system depends on networking with the stores being supplied. Each evening, networked stores send data gathered through their ISs to VF, which then uses it to determine stock levels and create an order for restock, all automatically. Merchandise in stock is shipped immediately; when it is not in stock, VF automatically creates an order for itself and ships within one week.

Customers love the VF system. It helps them to avoid overstocking, leads to faster inventory turns, and saves them money. Networked dealers need to invest less in inventory and have fewer clearance sales. VF is happy, too. Since 1991 the system has helped the company to increase "income and sales at a compound annual growth rate of nearly 20%." "For the full year 1999 sales reached a record $5,551.6 million" (FAQ).

While its competitors, like Levi Strauss, are struggling to catch up with VF's restocking system, VF is building its Trendsetter system to "track groups of goods—say jeans and shirts of various sizes, styles, and colors—to find sales patterns that can help retailers forecast ideal supply levels."

One downside to VF's system is that it will not work well with high-fashion, trendy merchandise. "Only 25% of shipments of Vanity Fair's constantly changing line of undergarments uses the replenishment system and 10% to 15% of VF's Healthtex, Inc. children's line."

http://www.vfc.com

Questions

1. What major advantages does VF Corporation have over its competition?
2. Why do you think the restocking system does not work well for high-fashion, trendy styles?
3. Will such a distribution system work as well for lesser-known brands made by smaller companies? Why or why not?
4. What data must be shared by retailers with VF to make the system work? How do you suppose the retailers gather these data?

Sources: Overview and FAQ at http://www.vfc.com; Weber, Joseph. "Just Get It to the Stores on Time," *Business Week*, March 6, 1995, pp. 66–67.

VIDEO CASE

Management Information Systems: A Study of Archway Cookies

Archway Cookies is the third largest producer of cookies in the United States, and is well known for its high-quality products. The company's "bake to order" system, in which cookies are baked, packaged, and sent to distributors within 48 hours, has been an important part of the company's success. As Archway has grown, so has the company's need for an advanced management information system (MIS). For many years, Archway maintained a number of stand-alone computer systems, including a general ledger system, a payables and receivables system, and an inventory management package. These systems involved a lot of manual tabulations and provided very little "real time" decision-making assistance to managers. As time went on, it became increasingly clear to the managers of Archway that the company needed a more integrated, forward-looking management information system.

Archway focused on two priorities in evaluating potential management information systems. First, the company needed a system that would tie all of the separate departments in the firm together and would facilitate the exchange of information between managers. Second, the company needed a system that would deliver information quickly and accurately and equip managers to make decisions in a timely and effective manner. The system also needed to be capable of producing different types of information for different levels in the organization. The company selected a system that met its criteria. If the full benefits of the system were realized, the company felt that it could recoup its investment in just 16 months. In addition, the company felt that it could improve its decision-making process, which could have long-lasting effects on the company's ability to produce high-quality cookie products.

In implementing the new system, Archway realized that its primary challenge was gaining user acceptance. The company overcame this challenge by convincing its employees that the system would make their jobs easier rather than more difficult, and would improve decision making at all levels within the organization. Archway was also careful to make sure that the system conformed to the company's existing culture and business practices. In support of this point, a top manager at Archway commented, "I would never allow a computer information system to dictate how we do business—it's suppose to support us, not dictate our direction." Archway now feels that its MIS is an important component of its ability to remain a major producer of cookie products. With a first-class MIS, the company now looks forward to many years of producing top-quality products.

http://www.archwaycookies.com

For Discussion:

1. Describe the way Archway Cookies managed information prior to its adoption of an MIS. Was the company's original way of managing information effective? Why or why not?

2. Evaluate Archway's criteria for selecting a new management information system. Were the criteria appropriate or inappropriate? Explain your answer.

3. Describe Archway's approach to implementing its new management information system. Do you believe that the company had a good awareness of the steps it needed to take to effectively implement its information system? Explain your answer.

4. Do you believe that Archway's new MIS will be an important component of the company's future success? Why or why not?

International Management

KEY TERMS

cross-cultural management
embargo
global structure
international division
international management
ISO 9000
multinational corporation
quota
tariff

LEARNING OBJECTIVES

After studying this chapter, you should be able to

1. Explain the primary reasons why businesses become international
2. Describe the characteristics of multinational corporations
3. Discuss the political, legal, economic, sociocultural, and technological elements of the international environment
4. Describe the major strategies for going international
5. Explain the phases a company goes through when moving from domestic operations to a multinational structure
6. Discuss the major staffing concerns for an international corporation
7. Describe the major concerns relating to leading a cross-cultural workforce
8. Discuss the major concerns relating to controlling an international corporation

MANAGEMENT IN ACTION

McDonald's Commitment to Global Expansion

"McDonald's today is arguably the most awesome service machine on the planet, and a virtual blueprint for taking a service organization global" (Serwer, 1994). McDonald's is America's most profitable fast-food retailer and the largest and best-known global foodservice retailer. It has more than 28,000 restaurants in 120 countries. In 1999, annual sales exceeded $38 billion. Jack M. Greenberg, chairman and chief executive officer, said, "We added 1,790 McDonald's restaurants in 1999, more than 90 percent of them outside the U.S. In 2000, we will continue to open restaurants at the remarkable pace of five per day—and as each day passes, the power of our brand grows stronger." Ronald McDonald is second only to Santa Claus in terms of recognition around the world. The company attributes these record increases to be primarily the result of its aggressive international expansion efforts—more than one half of its sales and operating income come from foreign operations (McDonald's Annual Report, 2000).

Ray Kroc founded McDonald's Corporation in 1955. He had never seen so many people served so quickly when he pulled up to take a look at Dick and Mac McDonald's restaurant in San Bernardino, California. Seizing the day, he pitched the idea of opening up several restaurants, convinced that he could sell eight of his Multimixers to each and every one. "Who could we get to open them for us?" Dick McDonald said. "Well," Kroc answered, "what about me?" Ray Kroc mortgaged his home and invested his entire life savings to become the exclusive distributor of a five-spindled milk shake maker called the Multimixer. He opened the first McDonald's in Des Plaines, Illinois, in 1955 (McDonald's—History, 2001).

According to Caroline Levy, a member of the consulting firm of Lehman Brothers, McDonald's possesses the two essentials to move easily across borders: a brand known to millions worldwide and a low-priced product base. In addition, McDonald's practices a collection of basic strategies that, when coupled with heavy marketing support, make it a success wherever it goes (Serwer, 1994):

- Gather your people together regularly to help them learn from each other.
- Put your people through in-depth and repetitive training, thus maximizing autonomy.
- Form strong alliances with your suppliers.
- Hire locals whenever possible.
- Tailor the menu just a bit from place to place.
- Keep pricing low to build market share; profits will flow from resulting economies of scale.

These basic strategies enable McDonald's to excel at providing quick service, cleanliness, standardized food, and smiles at each of its outlets.

A model for McDonald's expansion into a new country exists with its Polish operations. Before Tim Fenton and his team of 50 U.S. and European employees pioneered the company's expansion into Poland in 1992, eighteen months of planning were required. "Locations, real estate, construction, supply, personnel, legal, and government relations were all

© EYE UBIQUITOUS/CORBIS

More than one-half of McDonald's sales and operating income come from foreign operations.

worked out in advance" (Serwer, 1994). Over the two years that followed, seventeen restaurants were established, and Fenton's team of 50 was replaced with Polish citizens. When performing the initial staffing for McDonald's, Fenton's team discovered that there was no shortage of Poles who wanted to work at the franchises. Counter positions paid about 75 percent more than comparable jobs elsewhere in Poland ($1.70 per hour). Management jobs paid $900 per month and included a visit to Hamburger University in Illinois.

Despite their preparation, there have been a few cultural shocks for Fenton (who speaks fluent Polish) and other European representatives from McDonald's. He has had to convince more than a few Polish patrons to leave their vodka at home. Also, Fenton had to teach his Polish managers how to negotiate with suppliers and others. Finally, the menu had to be adjusted for local tastes to include black currant shakes.

McDonald's restaurants all over the world adjust their regular menus to meet the demands of the local culture. In Japan, McDonald's offers the Teriyaki McBurger, a sausage patty on a bun with teriyaki sauce. Ireland offers the Shamrock shake. Italy offers all the taste of Mediterranean flavors in fresh and tasty salads. The Netherlands offers the McKroket, a burger made of 100 percent beef ragout with a crispy layer around it, topped with a fresh mustard/mayonnaise sauce. Switzerland has a unique sandwich called the Vegi Mac, composed of a vegetable patty. The introduction of McCafe spaces in most of the Portuguese McDonald's restaurants provides the traditional "bica" (like "expresso"), served using porcelain cups rather than the regular McDonald's coffee cups. Additionally, "pasteis de nata," Portuguese-style cakes, are served alongside the McDonald's muffins and brownies (McDonald's—Countries, 2001).

As was the case in Poland, when McDonald's moves into a new country, it usually brings its suppliers along—like OSI Industries and Coca-Cola—until host-country sources can be found. This results in lower transportation costs and avoids the need for currency conversions. OSI Industries is the company's major supplier of ground beef. It has followed McDonald's to seventeen countries, setting up partnerships and enforcing McDonald's quality standards with local entrepreneurs to provide quick-frozen patties of 20 percent fat content or less. Coca-Cola has been with McDonald's from the beginning and earns about 5 percent of its U.S. sales from McDonald's outlets.

McDonald's employs a number of options to implement its global expansion. About 70 percent of McDonald's overseas outlets are franchised. In Europe most of the outlets are company owned. In Asia most are joint ventures with ownership shared equally between partners —McDonald's and host-country nationals. In Saudi Arabia the company licenses the name with strict limitations and guarantees itself an option to buy in later.

Regardless of the option selected before an owner or partner is chosen, the company screens them over a two-year period. Applicants must then go through intensive training at an outlet in the United States before being allowed to sign a 20-year agreement and pay an initial fee of $45,000. In addition to this training, McDonald's managers meet frequently by discipline and geographic region to learn from each other at various locations around the world. At its Hamburger University, 200 managers with between two to five years of experience and suppliers' representatives from over 70 countries take extensive two-week training programs on such topics as staff retention and team building. ■

Sources: The McDonald's Story, http://www.mcdonalds.com/corporate/info/history/index.html; McDonald's Chairman's Letter to Shareholders, March 15, 2000, and Annual Report, http://www.mcdonalds.com/corporate/investor/financialinfo/annualreport/online99/index.html; McDonald's Country Specific Sites, http://www.mcdonalds.com/countries/index.html; Serwer, Andrew E. "McDonald's Conquers the World," *Fortune*, October 17, 1994, pp. 103–104, 106, 108, 112, 114, 116; Morris, Betsy. "The Brand's the Thing," *Fortune*, March 4, 1996, p. 84; *Chicago Tribune*. "McDonald's Sets Its Sights on Ubiquity," January 18, 1996, sec. 3, p. 3; *Chicago Tribune*. "Expansion Boosts McDonald's; Sara Lee, Donnelley Profits Rise," January 26, 1996, sec. 3, p. 2; *Chicago Tribune*. "New Stores, Overseas Growth Drive McDonald's," April 18, 1996, sec. 3, p.1.

INTRODUCTION

American businesses are part of a global economy regardless of how large or small they may be. Most U.S. businesses have discovered that significant portions of their inputs come from other nations. Today companies need the flexibility to acquire needed inputs from sources offering the highest quality, greatest dependability, and lowest cost, whether located overseas or down the street.

http://europa.eu.int

http://europa.eu.int/euro/html/entry.html

http://www.telmex.com.mx

As probably never before in our nation's history, managers must pay attention to what is going on in economies around the globe. The world is changing more rapidly every day, and the changes are monumental. As communism lost its hold in the Soviet Union, many of its former satellite republics have become independent nations and have opened their borders to foreign investment and international trade. Soon after East Germany merged with West Germany, the republic of Czechoslovakia split into two nations. Fifteen European Communities (EC) have formed an economic union referred to as the European Union (EU) and have created a common currency, the Euro, and banking system; EU citizens will eventually carry one passport. China has opened its doors to foreign investment. Great Britain and countries in Central and South America are moving steadily away from socialist economies with the privatization of many government-owned operations. (The sale of Telmex, Mexico's telephone company, to private investors is but one example.) These events and others discussed throughout this text and chapter mean vast economic challenges and opportunities to both businesses and individual consumers around the world.

Companies in every country need the freedom and flexibility to act quickly in anticipation of or in reaction to changes taking place around the world. Communicating can be accomplished through instant messaging, the topic of this chapter's Managing Technology feature. Each day the values of countries' currencies fluctuate, offering advantages and disadvantages. As the value of the dollar falls against a foreign currency, U.S. goods and services become cheaper and more appealing to the citizens in that country. As the value of the U.S. dollar rises against that of another country's currency, that country's products and services become more appealing to U.S. consumers and companies.

MANAGING TECHNOLOGY
Instant Messaging

Instant messaging (IM) allows communication faster than email but more personal than chat. While there is typically a delay between the moments when an email message is sent and received, instant messaging permits near real-time conversations. Two or more people using compatible IM programs can connect instantly to chat, as well as send URLs; exchange files, graphics, and full-motion video; and leave messages for those who are offline. Alerts and information can be sent and then receivers can act on that information. Users store the online nicknames for friends and family in a personalized list. In a small software split-screen window on their desktops, users can see whether people on a contact list are online, and whether they're busy or away from their computers. They begin a chat by clicking the appropriate nickname to type messages, read replies, and send an instant message.

While instant messaging lets you talk to another person, it also gives you the ability to find out information about them (such as, where they are, what their status is). It's the presence of information. You can see where a person is or if they're away or working. You can add people to your buddy list to track them. Once connection speeds improve, and voice communication becomes a standard feature, the "buddy list" will become an immensely valuable telephone directory.

IM Courtesy

- Ask permission before adding a person to your buddy list.
- Announce your arrival and ask if you are intruding.
- Ask your buddy if he or she has the time to talk.
- Make visits meaningful and know when to sign off.
- Consider others. IMs, like emails, are not necessarily private.
- Send an email note of apology later, if you did not respond.

WHY BUSINESSES BECOME INTERNATIONAL

Explain the primary reasons why businesses become international

http://www.mcdonalds.com

http://www.pepsico.com

As this chapter's Management in Action case points out, companies such as McDonald's see expansion into new foreign markets as a primary strategy for survival, as well as for boosting sales and profits. McDonald's expands through various means from building company-owned outlets to licensing and partnership agreements. McDonald's is but one U.S. company that has found domestic sales slowing due to saturated domestic markets, thus leaving it little choice about how to increase earnings. PepsiCo is another U.S. company that is pursuing overseas markets to overcome a less than satisfactory 4 to 5 percent domestic sales growth. In the emerging international sectors PepsiCo has had sales growth in excess of 20 percent a year in Asia, Eastern Europe, and the Middle East (*Chicago Tribune*, April 3, 1996).

In general, companies go international for two basic sets of reasons or motives: proactive and reactive. *Proactive motives* include the search for new customers, new markets (as illustrated by the Daewoo Group, this chapter's Global Applications feature), increased market share, increased return on investments, needed raw materials and other resources, tax advantages, lower costs, and economies of scale. This last reason, economies of scale, encourages companies to find foreign partners to share the costs connected with building factories, conducting research, and expanding one's sales and presence in additional markets.

The drive to reduce costs has led to setting up operations in countries with lower wages and fewer restrictions on business. Many businesses from around the world have chosen northern Mexico for its nearness to American customers and lower wages and benefits—on average one-fourth to one-fifth those of the United States, Germany, and Japan.

Reactive motives include the desire to escape from trade barriers and other government regulations, to better serve a customer or group of customers (many Japanese auto parts suppliers, for instance, have moved to the United States to be near the Japanese companies they supply), and to remain competitive. Fear of potential trade restrictions has led U.S. automakers to expand their presence in Europe, Asia, and Latin America and has led Japanese and German automakers and their suppliers to build plants in America. Nearly every major foreign producer of automobiles has established subsidiaries in the United States to escape actual or potential American trade restrictions. One of the more recent is Mercedes-Benz with its manufacturing operations in Alabama.

http://www.mercedesbenz.com

http://www.ge.com

http://www.motorola.com

The desire to escape government regulation is not limited to automobile manufacturers. Hundreds of U.S. companies such as GE and Motorola have established their own foreign subsidiaries. Likewise, Japan's largest cosmetics maker, the Shiseido Company, entered U.S. and European markets in response to government actions. Shiseido had long enjoyed a comfortable dominance of Japan's $14 billion-a-year cosmetics market. Lax antitrust enforcement let it keep retail prices high, while import regulations insulated it from cheap foreign products. But since mid-1995, Japan has clamped down on Shiseido's business practices and deregulated cosmetics imports. Shiseido planned a number of foreign acquisitions to wean itself from the Japanese market where it did 91 percent of its sales (Shirouzu, 1996). Overseas sales data for 2000 region breakdown: Americas 29%, Europe 41%, Asia/Oceania 30%.

GLOBAL APPLICATIONS
Daewoo Eyes the World

The Daewoo Group, based in South Korea, has launched a global offensive to create new markets. Driven by a goal to become a major global player in cars and trucks, chairman and founder Kim Woo-Chong plans to invest $11 billion in target countries over the next four years and quadruple Daewoo's annual production to 2 million vehicles. The achievement of this annual production target will make Daewoo as big as DaimlerChrysler.

Woo-Chong's plan of attack is to go after two very different markets simultaneously, the developed world and the developing world. Selling successfully in the United States and Western Europe is important because doing so will give Daewoo prestige. But, the more important market is the world beyond the affluent West. Says Woo-Chong, "We have to move into big potential markets where few competitors have gone—India, China, Russia, and the Eastern European countries. So, I'm going into those places as quickly as possible to start production."

The plan is rapidly being implemented. Daewoo has built an automobile plant in Iran and is in the process of constructing a $658 million factory in Uzbekistan, a Central Asian republic that once belonged to the former Soviet Union. When completed, the Uzbekistan operation will put Daewoo's vehicles within striking distance of the huge Russian market.

In addition to these ventures, Woo-Chong has bought plants in the Czech Republic, Romania, and Poland. In the process he has practiced his own brand of trade and investment. Admits Woo-Chong, "We try to get as many incentives in as possible. It's only natural." One example is in Romania. Before taking over an idle auto plant, Woo-Chong persuaded the government to pass a law granting Daewoo tax concessions and duty-free privileges for bringing in components from Korea to assemble cars. In Poland Woo-Chong outbid General Motors for Poland's state automaker FSO (14 factories in total) by promising the Polish government that Daewoo would put $1.1 billion into FSO without laying off any of its 21,000 employees for at least three years. The deal, combined with an earlier purchase of a light-truck manufacturer, gives Daewoo a key role in a country half a world away from Korea. Daewoo will soon be the biggest direct foreign investor in Poland, the largest economy in Central Europe.

http://www.daewoous.com

Source: Kraar, Louis. "Daewoo's Daring Drive Into Europe," *Fortune,* May 13, 1996, pp. 145–152.

THE MULTINATIONAL CORPORATION

Describe the characteristics of multinational corporations

international management
The process of managing resources (people, information, funds, inventories, and technologies) across national boundaries and adapting management principles and functions to the demands of foreign competition and environments.

Many firms around the world, large and small, have become involved in international business over the past decade. The managers of these businesses conduct international trade and are engaged in **international management**—managing resources (people, information, funds, inventories, and technologies) across national boundaries and adapting management principles and functions to the demands of foreign competition and environments.

These international companies can do business in foreign countries in several ways. Some simply maintain sales offices in other lands; others only buy materials from companies in other countries. Those companies with operating facilities, not just sales offices, in one or more foreign countries are classified as **multinational corporations** (Baker, 1992).

In general, there are two kinds of multinational companies: those that market their product lines in relatively unaltered states throughout the world (*standardization*) and those that modify their products and services along with the marketing of them to appeal to specific groups of consumers in specific geographical

multinational corporation
A company with operating facilities, not just sales offices, in one or more foreign countries; management favors a global market and strategy, seeing the world as their market.

http://www.lee.com

http://www.wrigley.com

http://www.marykay.com

areas (*customization*). Products that illustrate the first group are sporting goods, soft drinks, cigarettes, chemicals, oil products, liquors, and certain types of clothing—Lee Jeans for example. Both Pepsi and Wrigley's chewing gum are sold around the world with only their packaging, promotion, and labeling altered to suit foreign requirements. Examples of customization include computer software programmed to work in foreign languages; cars manufactured to meet a country's safety, pollution, and drivers' preferences (right-hand drive for example); fast-food menus altered to cater to cultural tastes; and cosmetics formulated to complement the skin tones and coloring of different populations. McDonald's, for example, adjusts its menus and food services to suit the tastes of foreign customers (black currant shakes in Poland, salads with shrimp in Germany, veggie burgers in Switzerland); Mary Kay cosmetics are specially formulated to suit foreign preferences as well (Morris, 1996).

http://www.whirlpool.com

Customization is often the best strategy to adopt. Companies that attempt to sell the same product to different nationalities soon discover that there will be problems. With regard to laundry products, "Germans, for example, demand a product that's gentle on lakes and rivers and will pay a premium for it. Spaniards want cheaper products that get shirts white and soft. And Greeks want smaller packages that allow them to hold down the cost of each store visit" (Browning, 1992). Whirlpool Corporation has discovered in its European experience that, "Not only are kitchen appliances different from one country to another, but consumers also react differently to advertising messages from one country to the next" (Nelson, 1992).

CHARACTERISTICS OF MULTINATIONALS

Even though multinationals around the world differ in sales volumes, profits, markets serviced, and the number of their subsidiaries, they do share some common traits. One common trait is the creation of foreign affiliates, which may be wholly owned by the multinational or jointly held with one or more partners from foreign countries. Arvind Phatak (1992) describes the relationship of multinationals to their affiliates in this way:

> *The foreign affiliates are linked with the parent company and with each other by ties of common ownership and by a common global strategy to which each affiliate is responsive and committed. The parent company controls the foreign affiliates via resources that it allocates to each affiliate—capital, technology, trademarks, patents, and [people]—and through the right to approve each affiliate's long- and short-range plans and budgets.*

McDonald's, Daewoo, Whirlpool, and Motorola are examples of multinationals with affiliates in foreign countries.

Another common characteristic of multinationals is that their management operates with a global vision and strategy—viewing the world as their market. Top managers coordinate long-range plans and usually allow the foreign affiliates to work with great autonomy, leaving the day-to-day management decisions to those closest to the problems in foreign markets. Affiliates' operations are integrated and controls are exercised through management reports, frequent meetings and communications between headquarters staff and those in the affiliates, and the setting of objectives both alone and with headquarters' inputs. Foreign affiliates become

http://www.jnj.com

the training grounds for company managers as well as the sources for them. Johnson & Johnson provides managers of its far-flung empire with autonomy. Its top management believes "the people closest to the action have the best view." As CEO Ralph Larsen explains, "Decentralization is at the heart of Johnson & Johnson. With decentralization you get tremendous speed at the local level" (O'Reilly, 1994).

A third characteristic is the tendency of multinationals to choose certain types of business activities. Most multinationals are engaged in manufacturing. The rest tend to cluster around the petroleum industry, banking, agriculture, and public utilities (Heyel, 1982).

A fourth characteristic is the tendency to locate affiliates in the developed countries of the world—EU nations, Canada, South Korea, Taiwan, Japan, and the United States. "It is estimated that about two-thirds of the world's direct investments are in the developed countries" (Labich, 1992). Less-developed countries (LDCs) tend to be seen as sources for raw materials and cheap labor, and as markets for fairly inexpensive consumer products that can be mass-produced to standardized designs. Motorola's operations in China exemplify this latter category. It produces pagers and cellular phone components made to standardized designs and available to most of the citizens at a relatively modest cost.

http://www.deere.com

http://www.ford.com

http://www.att.com

A fifth characteristic is the adoption of one of three basic strategies regarding staffing. The first is to decide to adopt a "high skills strategy," in which the company exports products, not jobs. "Rather than push pay to the lowest common denominator, companies such as Deere, Ford, and Motorola are training workers to improve their skills, boost productivity [and quality]—and keep jobs at homes" (*Business Week*, 1992). The second is to "dumb down jobs" and shift the work to cheap-labor countries. This has been the choice for the majority of companies around the world. The third strategy is to mix the preceding two strategies: ". . . for every Motorola or Ford, a trendsetter such as AT&T is turning high-paying jobs into low-wage ones. Even those that upgrade worker skills, such as Ford Motor Co. and General Electric Co. . . still shift work to cheap-labor countries—thus pursuing both approaches" (*Business Week*, 1992).

INTERNATIONAL ENVIRONMENT

Discuss the political, legal, economic, sociocultural, and technological elements of the international environment

The environment in which managers in an international company function is far more complex than its domestic management settings. The key task for top management in a multinational company is to develop and maintain an in-depth understanding of the environments of every country in which it has operations, affiliates, suppliers, and customers. Five basic environments must be monitored: political, legal, economic, sociocultural, and technological (Phatak, 1992). Each environment is constantly undergoing change. Figure 20.1 summarizes the components of each environment. The discussion that follows focuses on the key issues of each.

Political Environment

Political environments can foster or hinder economic development and investment by native and foreign investors and businesses. The political philosophy and type of economic philosophy held by a nation's leaders can give rise to laws that promote domestic commerce and raise barriers to trade with the outside world. The stability of a government and its support by the people will affect decisions to seek commercial opportunities or to avoid investments in a nation. "As the fast-food industry's superpower, McDonald's is a global symbol of Western pop culture, Yankee know-how and American corporate cunning. But prominence on the world stage can be a lightning rod for trouble, and the company is often exposed to outbursts of anti-American sentiment and a myriad of political grievances" (Block, 1999).

FIGURE 20.1 *Components of the international environment*

POLITICAL ENVIRONMENT

Form of government	Social unrest
Political ideology	Political strife and insurgency
Stability of government	Governmental attitude toward foreign firms
Strength of opposition parties and groups	Foreign policy

LEGAL ENVIRONMENT

Legal tradition	Patent and trademark laws
Effectiveness of legal system	Laws affecting business firms
Treaties with foreign nations	

ECONOMIC ENVIRONMENT

Level of economic development	Membership in regional economic blocks (EU, LAFTA, CIS)
Population	Monetary and fiscal policies
Gross domestic product	Nature of competition
Per-capita income	Currency convertibility
Literacy level	Inflation
Social infrastructure	Taxation system
Natural resources	Interest rates
Climate	Wage and salary levels

SOCIOCULTURAL ENVIRONMENT

Customs, norms, values, and beliefs	Social institutions
Languages	Status symbols
Attitudes	Religions
Motivations	Demographics and psychographics

TECHNOLOGICAL ENVIRONMENT

State-of-the-art in various industries	CAD, CAM, and CIM
Research and development	Host countries' levels of acceptance and utilization
Recent innovations	Presence of educated workforce in host countries
Robotics	Potential partners around the globe

Source: From *International Dimensions of Management*, 3/e, by Arvind V. Phatak. Copyright © 1992. Reprinted with permission of South-Western College Publishing, a division of Thomson Learning. Fax 800-730-2215.

Various groups of citizens with vested interests—farmers, manufacturers, distributors, and political parties—can create civil protests and promote protectionist legislation to safeguard their particular interests. Japanese farmers have pressured their government successfully for years to keep foreign agricultural commodities such as rice out of the country. They don't want competition; they have been selling their domestic rice for six times the price of California rice for years (Ono, 1992). When the Tokyo discount liquor store chain, Kawachiya Shuhan Co., imported sake—the traditional Japanese rice wine—made in California with California rice, the chain was able to sell the wine cheaper than the Japanese product. The company soon encountered resistance from Japanese brewers. The president of the chain, Yukio Higuchi, says that "all five U.S. brewers, which are affiliates of Japanese sake makers and wholesalers, have refused to supply his stores—or any Japanese liquor store—with the U.S.-made sake." Higuchi suspects "liquor makers, fearing that the cheaper sake would threaten the high prices of Japanese sake, have joined forces against him" (Ono, 1992).

http://www.enron.com

http://www.bjp.org

http://www.shivsena.org

Enron Corporation, which builds power plants, suffered a huge blow to its global ambitions with the cancellation of a $2.9 billion power project by the Maharashtra (India) state government. Enron found itself in the middle of a power struggle between the Bharatiya Janata party (BJP) and the ruling Congress party. Long in search of a way to counter the Congress party, the BJP formed a coalition with the Shiv Sena party. After its actions crushed Enron, BJP president, L. K. Advani, delivered a nationalistic message. The party "has no objection to foreign investment as long as it doesn't compromise the nation's economic sovereignty" (Moshavi, 1995).

Legal Environment

Each country has its own unique set of laws that have an impact on commerce. Laws designed to protect the rights of individuals and labor unions differ as well. Just as managers working in America need to be certain that their actions will not violate any of the many laws bearing on commerce, so, too, must international managers in each host country.

quota
A government regulation that limits the import of a product to a specified amount per year.

tariff
A tax placed on imported goods to make them more expensive and thus less competitive in order to protect domestic producers.

embargo
A government regulation enacted to keep a product out of a country for a time or entirely.

Some countries erect trade barriers, such as quotas, tariffs, and embargoes. **Quotas** limit the import of a product to a specified amount per year. The Japanese automakers have agreed to restrict their imports into America and the EU nations to a specific number of cars each year for several years.

Tariffs are taxes placed on goods in order to make them more expensive and less competitive. Under the 1992 North American Free Trade Agreement (NAFTA) between Mexico, Canada, and the United States, Mexican tariffs on imported agricultural commodities are being phased out over a period of years. Under the terms of the treaty, the United States has fifteen years before markets will be totally open to Mexican sugar, peanuts, and frozen orange juice concentrate (Longworth, 1996). In the ongoing trade wars between the United States and China, Chinese silk apparel exports have been threatened with a 100 percent tariff. If imposed, the tariff would more than double the price of a silk blouse produced in the United States (Agins, 1996).

Embargoes keep a product out of a country for a time or entirely. "Following a five-year phase-in [under the terms of NAFTA], Mexico [can] bar U.S. exports of soybeans for three months annually, when Mexican farmers are harvesting their crops . . ." (Arndt, 1992). On the other side of the border, the United States continues to bar the import of Mexican avocados. Although the official reason for the embargo is stated as "fear of infestation from Mexican pests harbored in the avocados," Mexican growers are not convinced. Says one grower, "We buy American apples, American peaches, all kinds of American goods, every day. If we are to have free trade, then it must be in both directions" (Corchado, 1996).

Economic Environment

When companies analyze their options for going multinational, they must consider factors such as the stability of a country's currency, its infrastructure, its availability of needed raw materials and supplies, its levels of inflation and taxes, its citizens' levels of income, its closeness to customers, and its climate. When Whirlpool, a U.S. appliance maker, wanted to expand its operations overseas, it used "many factors, including ease of access, growth potential and government regulation. Europe got the green light in 1987, when the Netherlands-based conglomerate Philips N.V. made overtures about spinning off its appliance business" (Adler, 1992). In 1988 Whirlpool formed a partnership with Philips and eventually bought out its partner's interests in 1991, by which time 37.5 percent of Whirlpool's sales came from Europe, up 5.5 percent since 1988 (Adler, 1992).

http://www.philips.com

Today, the distant regions of Asia are proving irresistible to businesses. Once written off as remote, areas in rural Malaysia and Thailand are attracting major corporations because of improved infrastructure, lower costs, and fat government incentives. (For instance, Thailand has an eight-year exemption on corporate income tax and an exemption on import duties for machinery.) Seagate Technology, a California computer components manufacturer, has taken advantage of the economic environment. It has built four plants in Malaysia, the latest in Ipoh, 90 miles inland from Penang (Biers, 1996).

http://www.seagate.com

Sociocultural Environment

The sociocultural environment for the international manager includes such concerns as a people's traditions, languages, customs, values, religion, and levels of education. To accomplish the company's objectives, the international manager works daily in the cultures of different nations and regions, which differ from his or her own culture.

Understanding the host country's people and their values (and how to respond to them) has helped Amway expand its overseas operation. Capitalizing on the Hungarian population's "long-time habit of moonlighting, the government's benign view of Amway's training in free enterprise and the cachet of being a typically American import . . . ," Amway recruited 44,000 Hungarians to be its distributors (Ingram, 1992). According to Klaus Tremmel, the head of Amway Hungaria Marketing Ltd, the company is using the same appeals that have brought 150,000 former East Germans into the company's family—"namely, that in a time of growing unemployment and falling living standards, this business gives people the opportunity to influence their income. . . . success through individual initiative is our byword" (Ingram, 1992).

http://www.amway.com

Before American managers go abroad, it is imperative that they understand the cultures of countries in which they must operate and how those cultures compare to America's. To gain this understanding, the manager must first understand what makes American culture what it is. Figure 20.2 shows five dimensions of American society.

After analyzing American culture, the international manager must evaluate the cultures in the countries and regions where he or she will be doing business. One suggested approach is to use the following five dimensions (Phatak, 1992):

1. *Material Culture.* The international manager needs to evaluate the technology and the technological know-how for producing goods in a country, the manner in which the country makes use of these abilities, and the resulting economic benefits to the society.
2. *Social Institutions.* The international manager needs to analyze the influence on individuals of social institutions—schools, family, social class, religions, political parties. These strongly affect individuals' work ethics and their abilities and willingness to work in groups.

FIGURE 20.2 *Five basic dimensions of American culture pertaining to business*

- **Individualism.** The attitude of independence of people who feel that a large degree of freedom in the conduct of their personal life constitutes their individualism. The effects of individualism can be seen in self-expression and individual accomplishment. This value may not be shared in other cultures.
- **Informality.** Informality has two components. First, American culture does not place a great deal of importance on tradition, ceremony, or social rules. Second, the "style" in American culture is to be direct and not waste time in the conduct of meetings and conversation. Neither of these values may be significant when conducting business in Latin America or the Middle East.
- **Materialism.** There are two elements in American materialism. First, there is a tendency to attach status to physical objects—certain types of cars or designer clothing, for example. Second, because of vast natural resources, Americans are inclined to buy objects and then discard them while they still have a functional value. Both of these behaviors, if exhibited in other societies, may create problems for the international manager.
- **Change.** Although viewed as part of American culture, change is also perceived as something an individual can influence. That one person can bring about significant change is a fundamental tenet of American culture. In other societies, this same cultural value may not exist. Change is seen as inevitable but as a phenomenon that occurs naturally—a part of the overall evolution of people and their world. Change is accepted; it is predetermined. There is no deliberate attempt to influence it or bring it about.
- **Time orientation.** Time in American culture is seen as a scarce and precious resource. As a result, there is an emphasis on the efficient use of time. This belief dictates the practices of setting deadlines and of making and keeping appointments. But in other societies, time is often viewed as an unlimited and never-ending resource. This attitude explains why people in some cultures tend to be quite casual about keeping appointments or meeting deadlines.

Source: From *International Dimensions of Management*, 3/e, by Arvind V. Phatak. Copyright © 1992. Reprinted with permission of South-Western College Publishing, a division of Thomson Learning. Fax 800-730-2215.

© LINDSAY HEBBERD/CORBIS

International managers need to be aware of the influence of social institutions, such as religion, on individuals' work ethics and attitudes. For example, 90% of the Indonesian population is Muslim.

3. *Humans and the Universe.* The values and beliefs of people in other cultures may be influenced greatly by religion, customs, and superstitions. The international manager needs to understand that these elements are an integral part of the culture.
4. *Aesthetics.* This dimension is composed of the art, folklore, myths, music, drama, and native traditions in a culture. These factors can be important in interpreting the symbolic meanings of artistic expressions and various kinds of communications, such as gestures and visual representations. Failure to interpret these signals as the natives do is bound to cause problems.
5. *Languages.* The most difficult dimension for the international manager is languages and their various dialects. Not only does the manager need to speak the language of the host country, an international manager must also understand the interpretations and nuances of the languages as their words have more than dictionary meanings. This dimension logically extends to understanding which groups within a society are at odds with one another and which traditionally get along.

Technological Environment

This environment contains the innovations that are rapidly occurring in all types of technologies, from robotics to cellular phones. In the global environment, American technology companies (electronics, computers) are forging strategic alliances with Swiss, Japanese, and German rivals at an unprecedented rate in an effort to survive and remain competitive in the global marketplace. Forty-six percent of the nation's electronics manufacturers have alliances with domestic competitors and more than 63 percent have alliances with foreign-based firms, according to a study by the accounting firm Peat Marwick (Koretz, 1995). The name of the game in electronics [and nearly every other industry] is, according to Stephen Almassy, national director of Ernst & Young's electronics industry service division, "to achieve world-class product development and delivery. The goal is to deliver—not necessarily build—the highest-quality products and bring them to market in the shortest possible time" (Yates, 1992).

http://www.ibm.com

http://www.toshiba.com

Unless companies want to go it alone with all the expenses in money, time, and bricks and mortar that such a decision carries with it, they must join forces with others to quicken the pace and to cut the costs connected with this goal. IBM and Toshiba created a partnership to develop and manufacture flat panel television screens:

> *The joint venture, dubbed Display Technologies, Inc. (DTI), already churns out 10,000 screens per month for the two computer giants. By sharing its technology, Toshiba gained access to IBM's superior skills in computer-integrated manufacturing. Just as important for both companies, however, was the ability to share the enormous cost and risks of developing what is proving to be an extremely difficult technology to perfect (Goozner, 1992).*

The flat panel screen can be used in just about every product requiring a visual display. When its price comes down and its size increases, it will rival television cathode ray tubes.

http://www.gm.com

Regardless of the kind of business a company is in, it must choose partners and locations that have what it lacks. The best equipment and state-of-the-art technology will be wasted unless those chosen to employ it in manufacturing have the know-how and the willingness to learn how to use it properly. Many companies have chosen Mexico and Mexican partners because they find a willing and capable workforce. GM has a plant in Arizpe, Mexico, that rivals its North American ones in quality.

PLANNING AND THE INTERNATIONAL MANAGER

Regardless of whether a manager is planning for domestic or international operations, forecasts for the future depend on assumptions. Planning on an international level involves the same planning elements that we discussed earlier in this text: assessing the environment, developing assumptions, and then forecasting based on those assumptions. Although the process is the same, planning in an international company will be more difficult because many more variables and environments must be considered.

Choosing Strategies

4

Describe the major strategies for going international

There are basically four ways to get involved in overseas trade. When deciding to "go international," a company may consider any combination of the following strategies:

1. Export your product or service.
2. License others to act on your behalf (as sales agents, franchisees, or users of your processes and patents).
3. Enter into joint ventures (partnerships) for mutual benefit to produce or market or both.
4. Build or purchase facilities outside your home country to conduct your business on your own.

Most companies begin by exporting their goods through foreign distributorships that can successfully place the products on dealer shelves or in consumers' hands. Before deciding on one or another course, however, a company must choose a target market.

http://www.rei.com

In 1987 Recreational Equipment Incorporated, a small Seattle-based consumer co-op, successfully used the first strategy. REI began to find unsolicited cash flowing from Japanese consumers looking for its lines of sporting goods. It got the message and began offering its catalog (printed in English and with prices in dollars) "through ads in Japanese outdoor publications." By 1991 it had quadrupled its sales to the Japanese market and had 10,000 Japanese members (*Chicago Tribune*, 1992).

http://www.cocacola.com

http://www.harley-davidson.com

Coca-Cola Company of Atlanta is using the second strategy to expand into Central and Eastern Europe. It has invested over $1 billion with its licensed affiliates to achieve the expansion. Harley-Davidson is using strategy number three. It has formed several partnerships around the world to market its motorcycles and its line of sportswear. Its most recent venture has created theme restaurants dedicated to the world of motorcycle enthusiasts. McDonald's uses licensing, partnerships and stand-alone operations in its international operations. As noted in this chapter's Global Applications feature, Daewoo is using strategy number four to enter the European automobile market (Kraar, 1996).

Assessing the External Variables

In an international company, the managers must assess and monitor the changes in the five environments of the countries in which the company has operations to determine the presence of threats and opportunities. They must determine how these independent external environments will have an impact on and influence each other and how these impacts and influences will affect the company's internal environment—the areas for which individual managers are responsible and over which they have control. They must then choose goals and strategies and create programs to bring them to reality. In developing plans, the international manager is monitoring and assessing a set of unique external issues and problem areas, including the following (Phatak, 1992):

1. *Political Instability and Risk.* Changes in both governments and their policies can and do affect commerce, company plans and strategies, and the ability to conduct trade within and outside of the host country's borders.
2. *Currency Instability.* Changes in the exchange rates of currencies mean changes in the ways in which companies conduct their operations. Large sums are at stake because a company's earnings are in local currencies and must be spent around the globe as well as within the borders of a host country. Large multinationals are dealing with millions of dollars, yen, marks, pounds, and francs daily.
3. *Competition from National Governments.* State-owned or controlled companies and industries often operate with sizable government assistance and subsidies and are often not expected or required to earn profits. This policy places any international competitor at a great disadvantage. It gives the host country monopoly powers to use for or against both domestic and foreign competitors.

4. *Pressures from National Governments.* Companies have been and can be accused of sending unsafe or environmentally unsound technologies and products to a host country, exporting technology and jobs, and interfering with domestic industries. It's important for corporations, like individuals, to be good citizens.
5. *Nationalism.* In developing countries and developed nations, national pride creates political ideologies that can inhibit commerce, especially from foreign-owned operations. From such ideologies can come trade restrictions, local ownership restrictions, and limits on how much money can be exported.
6. *Patent and Trademark Protection.* Some countries will offer no protection and anyone's property is fair game. Others offer limited protection to foreign-owned enterprises. Some countries and industries are known for their piracy of ideas and technology as this chapter's Ethical Management feature illustrates.
7. *Intense Competition.* Lucrative markets will always exhibit intense competition from both the domestic and foreign sectors. Companies should expect competition in the best markets and most profitable product areas to increase.

http://www.iso.ch

ISO 9000
The set of five technical standards, known collectively as ISO 9000, designed to offer a uniform way of determining whether manufacturing and service organizations implement and document sound quality procedures.

A factor that will continue to expand competition is the quality of a company's products or services. In this regard, a set of quality standards is rapidly becoming the passport for success in the international marketplace. The standards were created in the late 1980s by the International Organization for Standardization. The set of five technical standards, known collectively as **ISO 9000**, was designed to offer a uniform way of determining whether manufacturing plants and service organizations implement and document sound quality procedures.

To register, a company must undergo an audit of its manufacturing and customer service processes, covering everything from how it designs, produces, and installs its goods to how it inspects, packages, and markets them. More than 50 countries, including the United States and those in the European Union (EU), have endorsed the standards.

There is no legal requirement that companies adopt the standards, but some experts say the guidelines eventually will largely determine what may be sold to and within the EU. Several EU industries—toys, construction products, gas appliances, machinery, and some medical devices—have already announced timetables for adopting ISO standards. The regulations would apply to EU companies making those goods as well as to the manufacturers that supply parts or materials to those companies (Miller, 1993).

As we can see from these variables, planning in the international marketplace is extremely complicated and surrounded by many issues and uncertainties. The consequences of inadequately assessing the variables will usually mean failures in such things as timing, selection of strategies, and financial decisions. The effectiveness of the assessment efforts depends on whether a company can decide how to (l) apportion responsibility for gathering and analyzing information between line and staff managers and between in-house personnel and outside consultants, (2) build credibility and effectiveness into the analysis so that the organization takes it seriously, and (3) bring an understanding of the importance of analysis into corporate operations, particularly capital budgeting and long-term planning (Phatak, 1992).

Assessments lead to forecasts, which managers then use to construct their plans. The aim of all the efforts at assessing, interpreting, forecasting, and creating goals,

ETHICAL MANAGEMENT
Beneath the Surface

Since 1986, China has been in negotiations to join the World Trade Organization. The United States takes a leading role in the negotions. On the surface some of the issues are complex but obvious. The government in Beijing has failed to enforce an intellectual-property rights agreement reached in February 1995. Under the terms of the agreement, China was to crack down on pirates who counterfeited American compact discs, videos, and software. Although China made progress in eliminating retailers of the pirated goods, it did little to stem the production from the factories of the counterfeiters.

Despite repeated requests from the United States to respect the treaty, the Chinese government ignored its obligations. The United States pressured the Chinese by threatening to impose sanctions on $3 billion worth of Chinese goods, including $2 billion of textile products, $500 million of electronics, and $500 million of miscellaneous consumer items. Also in the equation was the possibility that President Clinton would not recommend granting China a most-favored-nation (MFN) trade status. (The MFN grants free emigration in China.)

Thus threatened, the Chinese immediately retaliated by publishing a list of U.S. products on which they would impose tariffs (agrarian products, vehicles, telecommunications equipment, liquor, and cosmetics). The Chinese also proposed to ban all U.S. audiovisual products (movies, TV programs, tapes, discs). Finally, China stated that the government departments would stop accepting new applications from U.S. businesses seeking permission to operate in China.

Although these actions and reactions received all the attention, there was more below the surface. The counterfeiters were not fly-by-night operations run by individuals hiding in dimly lit buildings as one might suspect. Rather, the majority of factories, 34 in all, were run or backed by provincial governments, the People's Liberation Army, or the Public Security Bureau. In other words, the counterfeiters were government sponsored and financed. The government entities in turn received the benefits from the "cash cow." CDs that cost pirates $0.36 to make were then sold for $5.00 in Hong Kong.

In the United States the administration was not simply enforcing the treaty. There were other influences. The proposed sanctions on textiles would gain side benefits in heavily unionized textile states in the United States. Also, punishing China for violating copyright and trademark agreements would help the U.S. entertainment industry. Simultaneously, the administration was being pressured by the thought of U.S. companies who had invested billions in China falling out of favor with the Chinese Ministry of Foreign Trade and Economic Cooperation. It was believed that these companies would react negatively to the administration. For example, Motorola, the largest U.S. investor in China, with an estimated $1.2 billion in production facilities scheduled to go on line by the end of the 1990s, would suffer immense losses.

1. What role does personal benefit of individuals, companies, and governments play in this situation?
2. What ethical conflict of interest exists between the Chinese government's role as a treaty signee/enforcer and its role as a financial beneficiary of the counterfeiting?
3. What ethical conflict of interest might exist between the government officials' political motives and its duty as a treaty signee/enforcer?

Sources: Baranthan, Joyce. "A Pirate Under Every Rock," *Business Week*, June 17, 1996, pp. 50–51; Yates, Ronald E. "U.S. China Talk Tough But Quiet Ending Likely," *Chicago Tribune*, May 16, 1996, sec. 1, p. 1, 30; Newkirk, William. "Clinton Gives China Deadline to Reduce High-Tech Piracy," *Chicago Tribune*, May 9, 1996, sec. 1, p. 6; and Moffatt, Susan. "China's Crackdown on CD Counterfeiting: Too Little, Too Late?" *Fortune*, March 4, 1996, p. 32.

strategies, and tactics is to create a unity within management of the multinational and to be a decent corporate citizen in the host countries. Corporate strategy determines how the organization will deploy its resources in order to achieve its objectives. It will become the framework for the formulation of strategies in the affiliates around the world. Figure 20.3 highlights the major areas in which global corporate objectives are needed and the areas toward which strategies are directed.

FIGURE 20.3 *Areas to be addressed by the objectives of a multinational*

PROFITABILITY

- Level of profits
- Return on asset, investment equity, sales
- Annual profit growth
- Annual earnings per share growth

MARKETING

- Total sales volume
- Market share—worldwide, region, country
- Growth in sales volume and growth in market share
- Integration of host-country markets for marketing efficiency and effectiveness

PRODUCTION

- Ratio of foreign to domestic production volume
- Economies of scale via international production integration
- Quality and cost control
- Introduction of cost-efficient production methods

FINANCE

- Financing of foreign affiliates—retained earnings or local borrowing
- Taxation—minimizing tax burden globally
- Optimum capital structure
- Foreign exchange management—minimizing losses from foreign fluctuations

TECHNOLOGY

- Type of technology to be transferred abroad—new or old generation
- Adaptation of technology to local needs and circumstances

HOST GOVERNMENT RELATIONS

- Adapting affiliate plans to host-government developmental plans
- Adherence to local laws, customs, and ethical standards

PERSONNEL

- Development of managers with global orientation
- Management development of host-country nationals

RESEARCH AND DEVELOPMENT

- Innovation of patentable products
- Innovation of patentable production technology
- Geographic dispersion of research and development laboratories

ENVIRONMENT

- Harmony with the physical and biological environment
- Adherence to local environmental legislation

Source: From *International Dimensions of Management*, 3/e, by Arvind V. Phatak. Copyright © 1992. Reprinted with permission of South-Western College Publishing, a division of Thomson Learning. Fax 800-730-2215.

ORGANIZING AND THE INTERNATIONAL MANAGER

5

Explain the phases a company goes through when moving from domestic operations to a multinational structure

Companies develop organizational structures to achieve objectives. As the objectives of the organizations change, so too will their organizations. As companies extend their operations to host countries, their internal organization structures must evolve. The structures a firm chooses at any time in its evolution depend on the extent of the operations of these companies abroad, their locations and contributions to the parent company, and the degree of experience and competence possessed by both the parent and host-country managers. The structure chosen must be able to cope with sociocultural, political, legal, and economic differences between the host-country and parent-country operations. The structure developed to simply market a product overseas will have to change when the company moves to actually produce the product overseas. A decision about the degree of decentralization must be made and continually reexamined as time and operations unfold.

When a firm attempts to establish an international organization, it must address traditional issues, including the following:

- Achieving operational efficiencies
- Creating flexibility to respond to national and global changes
- Allowing units to share information and technology quickly
- Coordinating activities from various cultures
- Responding swiftly to changes in consumer needs and demands
- Differentiating operations by function, product, customers, or geography
- Developing management teams with common goals and shared visions

Although the organization structure utilized by a company depends on its objectives, the typical evolution for a company becoming multinational takes it through three phases: pre-international division phase, international division phase, and global structure phase (Phatak, 1992). A major point to note as we trace the evolution of these phases is that in a domestic company, a two-dimensional structure—functional and product or functional and territorial—is often used to meet objectives. In the international arena, a three-dimensional structure is eventually required. It combines functional, product, and territorial patterns to provide the functional expertise, product and technical know-how, and host-country knowledge for a company (Phatak, 1992).

Pre-International Division Phase

Companies with a unique product, a product that incorporates the latest technology, a superior product (in features, performance, or price), or a totally new product should consider themselves ready for entry into the international arena. For many companies the first strategy used to introduce the product to a new nation or nations of consumers is to find a way to export the product. The result is typically the addition of an export manager to the marketing department. Companies with a broad line of products—such as a chemical company—may establish an export manager who reports directly to the CEO and works in a staff capacity with the individual product divisions to coordinate production and marketing. The export manager will establish the methods chosen for foreign distribution and marketing —whether to place parent company employees in a host country or to work through agents (importers, distributors, or retailers) already established there. Figure 20.4 shows the addition of the export manager to an established domestic management structure.

International Division Phase

international division
A parent company's corporate unit, commonly a marketing or production operation, located in a host country offshore from the parent headquarters and whose head reports directly to the CEO.

In time, pressures may mount from host-country laws, trade restrictions, and competition, placing the company at a cost disadvantage. In such an event, the company often decides to defend and to expand its foreign market position by establishing marketing or production operations in one or more host countries. Figure 20.5 shows the establishment of an **international division** with its head reporting directly to the CEO.

FIGURE 20.4 *Organizational structures with export manager engaged in exporting to foreign markets*

A. Company with Narrow Product Line

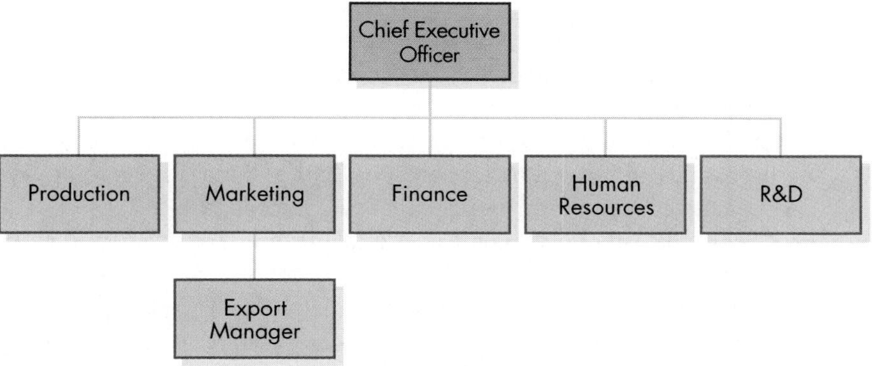

B. Company with Broad Product Line

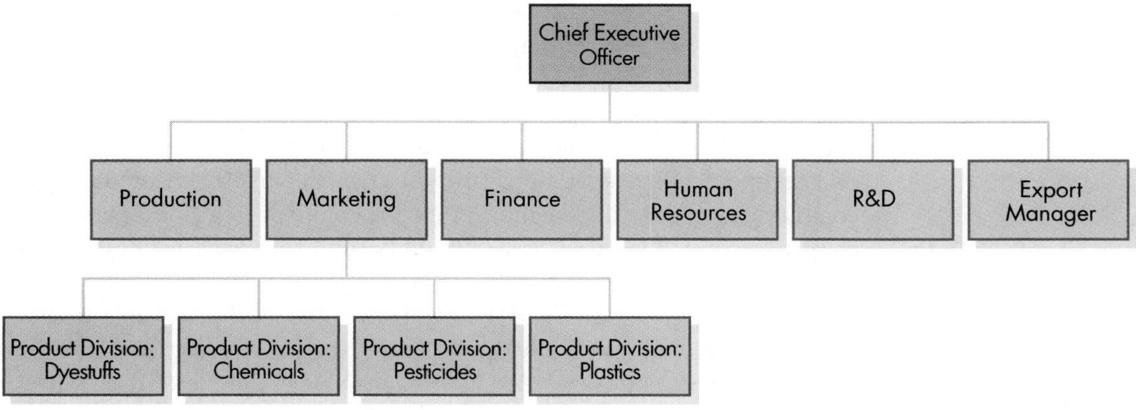

Source: From *International Dimensions of Management*, 3/e, by Arvind V. Phatak. Copyright © 1992. Reprinted with permission of South-Western College Publishing, a division of Thomson Learning. Fax 800-730-2215.

FIGURE 20.5 *International division of a company in the early stages of global involvement*

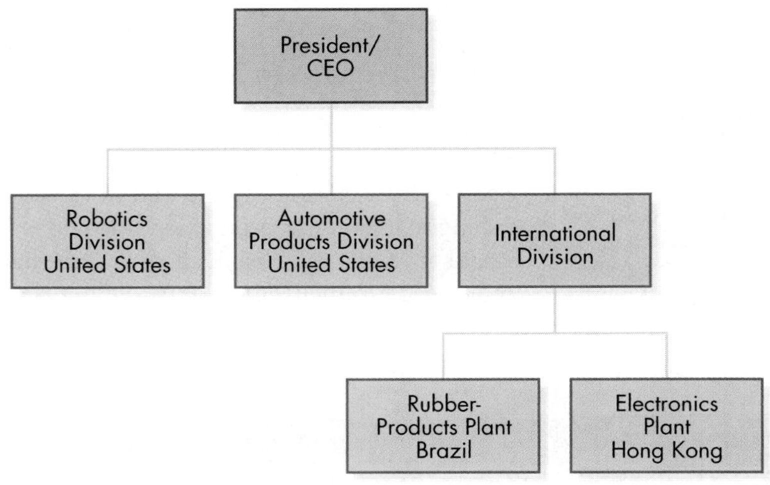

The international division structure works well for companies in the early stages of international involvement. These firms typically have certain characteristics: "limited product diversity, comparatively small sales (compared to domestic and export sales) generated by foreign subsidiaries, limited geographic diversity, and few executives with international expertise" (Phatak, 1992).

In the early stages, companies may practice centralization to keep a tight control over the establishment and staffing of the international facilities. In time, decentralization begins, giving those closest to the problems and opportunities the authority they need to respond quickly to customer, political, and economic demands and challenges. As those on site gain experience and expertise, they pass it on for future planning purposes and become trainers for those who will follow them in present or future overseas ventures. Many managers will pass through the international divisions on their way to regional and corporate headquarters jobs.

Global Structure Phase

As the international operations gain success, top management makes a greater commitment to them and begins to view the company in a global perspective. Most companies, as is the case with McDonald's, find that as their international operations expand, a greater percentage of revenues and profits begin to flow from them. With its international division, the company finds itself better able to serve many more markets than it could without them. It becomes nearly immune from most trade restrictions and is closer to its customers. It usually finds itself with an ever-increasing amount of foreign nationals on its payrolls and running its operations, both in foreign markets and in the firm's various headquarters. The company's culture begins to change as these forces for change are absorbed and take power.

According to the research done by *Business International* (1970), a company is ready to move away from an international division phase when it meets the following criteria:

- The international market is as important to it as the domestic market.
- Senior officials in the company have both foreign and domestic experience.
- International sales represent 25 to 35 percent of total sales.
- The technology used in the domestic division has far outstripped that of the international division.

global structure
The arrangement of an organization's management decision-making to efficiently and effectively operate in a multinational context; form may contain functional, product, and geographic features based on worldwide product or area units.

The shift to a **global structure** means a change in the ways in which decision making will take place. Typically, decisions that previously were made by separate and autonomous divisions will, after the shift, be made at the corporate headquarters for the total enterprise. Corporate decisions now need a total-company perspective. The final structure will contain functional, product, and geographic features and may be based on worldwide product groups, worldwide area groups, or a mixture of these two. Each group becomes a profit center with command and control passing from the president/CEO to a group vice president.

The product group structure works best for diverse and widely dispersed product lines and for those with relatively high levels of technology or research and development operations. Figure 20.6 illustrates product group structure. Johnson & Johnson has capitalized on the product group structure by organizing its 33

FIGURE 20.6 *Simplified global structure integrating worldwide product groups*

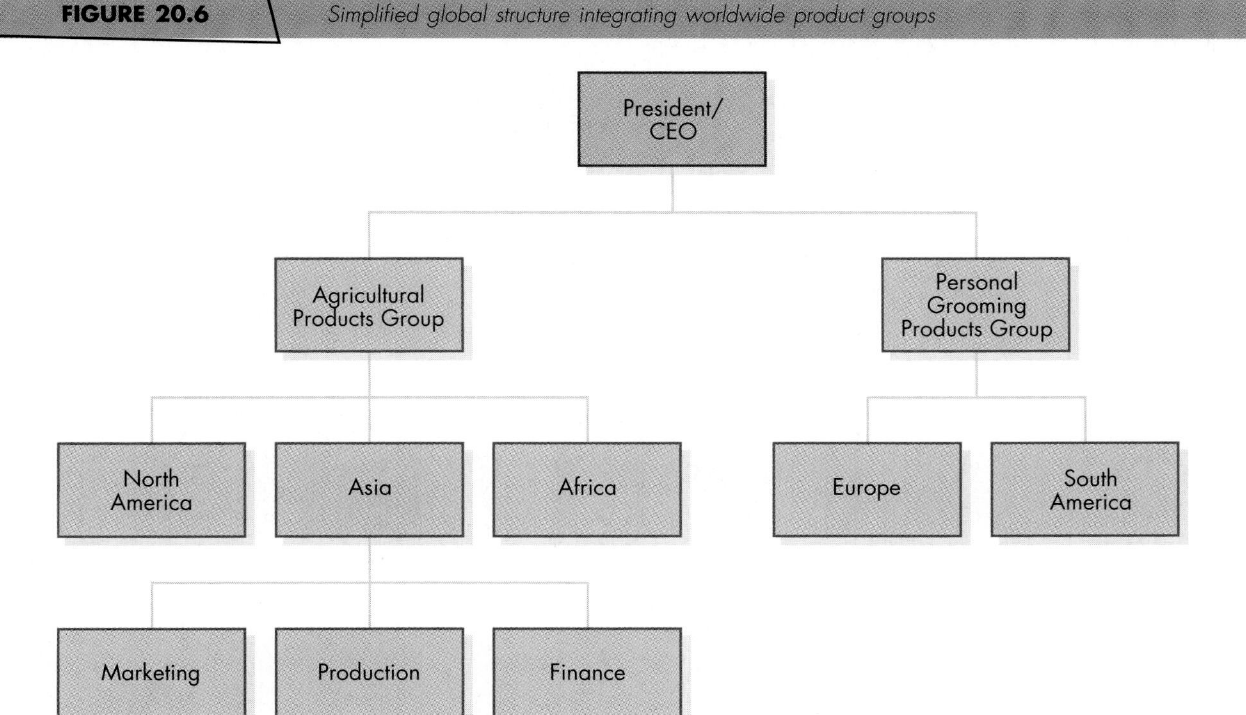

major lines of business in 53 countries into three worldwide customer product groups: pharmaceutical products, professional products, and consumer products (O'Reilly, 1994).

http://www.mobil.com

The regional or area approach works best with a narrow group of similar products and products that are closely tied to local consumer markets. Oil companies, specialty food manufacturers, and rubber products companies tend to adopt this structure. The functions of the international division are carried out by the regional managers, who report directly to the parent headquarters (see Figure 20.7). Mobil Corporation was an example of the regional approach structure when it aligned its eleven business groups, or strategic business units (SBUs), into three categories (Davidson, 1996):

- North American businesses, comprising exploration, production, refining, and marketing
- Integrated regional businesses, combining Mobil's exploration, production, refining, and marketing in four areas: Africa and the Middle East, Asia-Pacific, Europe, and South America
- Worldwide businesses that consist of chemicals, liquefied gas, and independent power projects; new exploration and production ventures; and supply trading and transportation

FIGURE 20.7 *Simplified global structure integrating regional divisions*

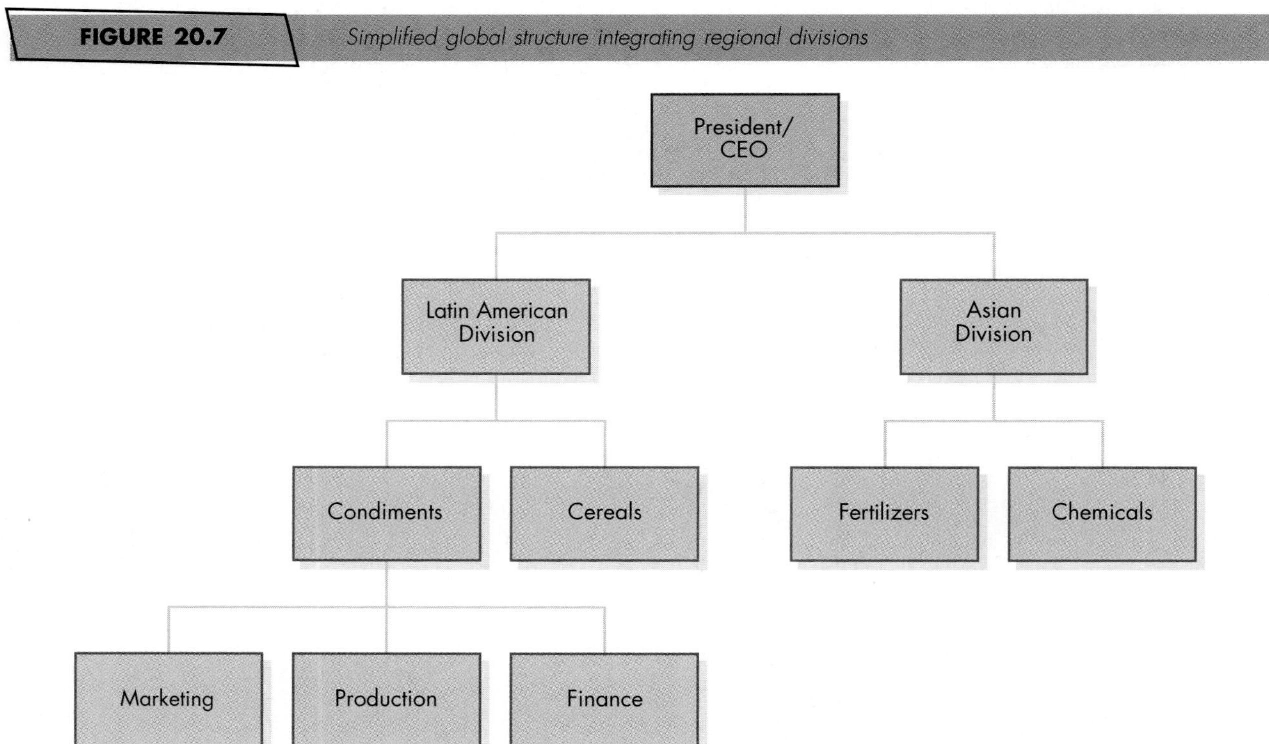

STAFFING AND THE INTERNATIONAL MANAGER

Discuss the major staffing concerns for an international corporation

The role of the staffing function in an organization is to identify and acquire qualified human resources to ensure the success of the organization. In an international company, staffing becomes far more complex because the search for talent knows no national boundaries.

Staffing Problems and Solutions

Finding qualified persons to fill jobs in host countries can be difficult, especially when a company attempts to find qualified managerial and technical people in developing or less-developed countries. In the initial stages of expansion into overseas markets, positions in host-country operations may have to be filled from those already on board in domestic operations. But, as a survey of multinational companies indicates, this is not always an adequate approach. "Only 28 percent of U.S. managers are eager for foreign duty. Executives cite family responsibilities such as children's education, spouses' careers or fears about living conditions abroad" (Weidenbaum, 1995).

Eventually, through training and development programs conducted by a company or by outsiders, host-country citizens and others can be groomed for various jobs. Local conditions are also a factor. Finding executives for U.S. and other multinational companies' operations in Mexico is particularly tough. With so many foreign companies already operating and with many more coming, "the pool of qualified Mexican executives is so thin, and the demand so great, that competent Mexican managers often command greater salaries than their counterparts in the U.S." (Moffett, 1992).

http://www.3m.com

http://www.honda.com

Different companies take different approaches to staffing their foreign operations as well as their domestic ones. Minnesota Mining & Manufacturing (3M) "brings dozens of foreigners every year from overseas units for stints at its St. Paul, Minnesota, headquarters. These 'inpatriates' become accustomed to the business climate in the U.S. and receive valuable training in corporate culture" (*Wall Street Journal*, 1992). Honda, on the other hand, sends managers from its home office to the host countries. While they are on these assignments, Honda believes that these "managers dispatched from the head office should be encouraged to become part of the community by understanding local culture and ways of thinking; to delegate authority to local personnel; and to create a sense of unity between management and labor so that everyone is working toward a common goal" (Sigiura, 1990).

http://www.pilotpen.com

Although the Japanese prefer to send a core of Japanese executives to head their foreign operations, many other multinational companies are moving toward giving host-country citizens, especially Americans, more important roles. Ronald G. Shaw is one of the new breed of Americans who serve as presidents and CEOs of Japanese subsidiaries in the United States. He is the CEO of Pilot Pen of America, a United States subsidiary of Pilot Corporation of Japan. In 1992 he achieved a major accomplishment in comparison to his American counterparts when he was appointed to the parent company's board of directors (Rosenberger, 1992).

George Varga, the former manager of General Electric's lighting manufacturing plant in Hungary, is an example of an ideal international manager. He is a veteran of overseas assignments. A native of Hungary, he left as a teenager and has worked in the United States, Spain, Holland, Switzerland, and Mexico. He speaks six languages and has Western know-how in marketing and financial management. While he was at GE Hungary one of his first decisions was to replace half the Hungarian managers with seasoned GE executives (his managers averaged over eighteen years of service). "We didn't want the young tigers. We needed people with sensitivity to perform a cultural marriage. We had the ideal team to sell our ideas to the Hungarians" (Tully, 1992).

Whereas Ronald Shaw is an American in a Japanese company and George Varga an expatriate Hungarian returned home, many foreign nationals have risen through the ranks to head up the headquarters staffs of American multinationals. Swiss national Fritz Ammann won the top job at Esprit de Corp, a U.S. sportswear manufacturer based in San Francisco. Ammann previously ran a Paris shoe company and beat out seven other candidates including four Americans. " 'In [the 1990s] and beyond, as more and more [U.S.] companies are forced to be global companies, you are going to see more mixing of nationalities' at the top," predicts Joseph Canion, founder of Compaq Computer Corp. in Houston. He ought to know. He lost his job to his second in command, Eckhard Pfeiffer, a native of Germany (Lublin, 1992).

http://www.esprit.com

http://www.compaq.com

For managers who would like to duplicate the success of Shaw, Varga, Ammann, and Pfeiffer, Kathryn A. Vegso, director of the career services center of the American Graduate School of International Management in Glendale, Arizona, has sound advice: "You need to learn the culture, speak the language, have the connections, and know how to do the job" (Kleiman, 1990). Scott A. Scanlon, an editor of the monthly newsletter *Executive Search Review*, reinforces Vegso's advice by noting that three qualities are needed to be an international manager: being able to speak the language, knowing the country's culture and business environment, and being trained in Western management techniques (Kleiman, 1990).

http://www.t-bird.edu

Compensation

Compensating host-country personnel in line with parent-company practices seldom works. Traditions, legally mandated pay scales and benefits, differing tax rates and levels of inflation, differing standards of living, the relative values of currencies, and host-country competitors all combine to make compensation a difficult issue. The American customs of rewarding individuals and groups on the basis of short-term performances and rewarding managers for their departments' or divisions' successes must be tempered with the contributions they make to the whole enterprise and the kinds of barriers they have had to overcome. Some cultures shun group compensation plans; others live by them. Some countries have strong unions (Germany for one); others have none. In addition, factors such as the value of seniority, the cost of living in a host country (Japan has the highest), and the level of status a manager has as perceived by peers must be considered and compensation plans adjusted accordingly.

A brief look at some compensation issues and numbers will give you a feeling for the pay and benefit differences that exist around the world. The average annual salaries for a marketing manager in four foreign countries are as follows: in Poland, $18,000; in Indonesia, $23,000; in France, $35,000; and in Japan, $42,000

(Weidenbaum, 1995). Perks for managers and salespeople working abroad—things provided in addition to voluntary and legally mandated benefits—include the following: In Belgium, as elsewhere in Western Europe, a car and a cellular phone along with a discretionary expense account; in Japan, a company car for executives; in Great Britain, company cars equipped with telephones; in South Korea, pickup by a car pool, graduating to a company car and driver, and a generous expense account; in Hungary, a company car for managers and salespeople and payment in hard (Western) currency. Average paid vacation days for workers in Denmark are 30; for those in France, 26; for those in Spain, 22.

LEADING AND THE INTERNATIONAL MANAGER

Describe the major concerns relating to leading a cross-cultural workforce

People are not the same around the world. They have different languages, cultures, traditions, and attitudes that affect the ways in which they work, how they want to be approached, and how they approach others. These differences make directing foreign nationals a challenge for the international manager. Managers who are not natives of the countries in which they manage need to pay particular attention to the ways they communicate and interact with foreign nationals. What should be kept in mind throughout this section is that most nations today are blends of nationalities, and their workforces reflect cross-cultural influences just as the American workforce does. Most European nations are hosts to many peoples from around the world—Turks, Arabs, and Asians—as well as other Europeans. Many Asians, particularly Koreans, work in Japan. Blending of populations can be expected to continue as European, Asian, and Latin American countries continue to attract foreign labor and as multinational businesses expand their operations to more and more nations.

The key for organizations "going international" is to recognize the diversity that exists and value the contributions this diversity will make to the organization. Companies that will be successful in the decades to come will continue to change their definition of diversity (as has Rockwell International, the subject of this chapter's Valuing Diversity feature) as they evolve.

Employee Attitudes

John E. Rehfeld has worked in an executive capacity for two major Japanese companies in the United States. He points out two differences between traditional U.S. and Japanese management attitudes. First, when something goes wrong in a Japanese company, the emphasis is on solving problems, not placing blame. Japanese managers want to know what went wrong and how to fix it. Second, when Japanese managers set a goal and achieve it, they keep going and don't wait for praise. "The Japanese simply are not interested only in absolute results; they are equally interested in the process and in how you can do it better next time. . . . [T]hey not only plan something and do it but also stop to see the result to determine how it could be done better" (Rehfeld, 1990).

When GE took over the management of the Tungsram works in Hungary, it found 18,000 workers—about as many as it had in the rest of its lighting division in the United States, which generated seven times the sales volume. "In the West

VALUING DIVERSITY
Rockwell Celebrates Its People

One might assume that a company that employs over 80,000 people in more than 35 countries and generates one-third of its total sales outside the United States would have a clear understanding of what diversity means in cultural terms. "Not really," states Earl Washington, senior vice president of communications for Rockwell International Corporation. "The definition continues to evolve, much like our evolving as a company. We now think of ourselves as a 'global company' and not as an 'export company.' We are beginning to understand what being 'global' means, and this understanding is making us all the more sensitive to the unique differences we, as individuals, possess."

Diversity at Rockwell "is viewed as a critical business issue and a key component of high-performance organizations," explains Nanette Clements, director of succession planning and corporate human resources. Former Rockwell Chairman Donald Beall underlined the importance of their workforce by stating, "valuing and promoting diversity is a business and morale imperative."

As part of his commitment, Beall chartered a task force to develop a comprehensive diversity plan that spans all of Rockwell's businesses. The Rockwell Diversity Task Force devised an overarching strategy—a template—for Rockwell's worldwide businesses to use in developing their own detailed plans. The elements of this strategy include

- Communicating to all employees how workforce diversity is linked directly to Rockwell's business goals
- Integrating diversity management into business practices
- Holding employees at all levels accountable for their behavior
- Aligning people practices with diversity goals
- Measuring the success of the strategies

Regardless of which business unit implements the strategy or in what country the business is located, the underlying philosophy is clear. As Nanette Clements explains, "We want our people to be able to grow and reach their full potential here at Rockwell, over and above anything else. In return, the Company benefits from their enhanced skills and from the unique perspective that diversity brings to solving business problems." Rockwell does not have all the answers, but it is truly attempting to understand and value its diversity in a global environment.

http://www.rockwell.com

Source: Fortune. "Rockwell International Corporation, Celebrating Its People," August 21, 1995, pp. 127–128.

There are two major differences between traditional U.S. and Japanese management attitudes. First, the Japanese emphasis is on solving problems, not placing blame. Second, when Japanese managers reach a goal, they keep going and don't wait for praise.

the solution would be huge layoffs. But the Hungarians' deep fear of joblessness [prompted] GE to take a more modest approach." It chose to reduce worker ranks by early retirements and normal attrition. Hungarians are also used to being paid in cash and few have checking accounts. GE chose to continue to keep stuffing pay envelopes with cash (Tully, 1992).

At Ahlstrom Fakop (now Foster Wheeler Energy Fakop), a boiler manufacturing facility in Poland that had 400 employees, the same attitude about job security proved a key to turning the company around. Conventional business wisdom in the West believes an effective way to motivate workers is through incentive pay. But, the incentive pay failed to revive low employee morale; so the company responded by offering to maintain staffing at current levels if sales targets were met. The result: an increase in sales and morale. Turned inside out by the transition to a market economy, the employees were more concerned with keeping their jobs than getting a bonus (Jacob, 1995).

Communication Problems

An international manager may be presented with a number of communication dilemmas. Not only words, but body language as well differs from one culture to another. For example, it is considered an insult by Arabs to cross your feet or legs or to show the bottoms of your shoes to them. In Spain, the "okay" sign using the thumb and the forefinger is considered to be a vulgar gesture. Seating yourself at a formal meeting before those of a higher rank are seated may be acceptable in American businesses, but it is viewed as disrespectful in many other cultures.

Money may even cause communication problems. The parent company may wish to transact business in English and in dollars, but it will have to adjust to Japanese, Korean, German, Spanish, and other languages and currencies. Also a manager at headquarters may be Swiss and speak German and meet with host-country managers who are Italian, German, American, and Mexican or mixtures of several nationalities. One solution used by some companies is to have all company correspondence and conversations among managers take place in one language—usually English or French in American and Western European companies, and Japanese in Japanese companies. Relying on translators can be tricky. Host-country nationals may pretend to lack understanding when it is in their interest to do so. Also, many words in one language have no direct translation into others.

Even though English is becoming more and more the language of international business, and most educated people around the world must learn it, host-country managers must have a firm grounding in their host country's language. There just is no good substitute for language fluency when it comes to directing the host-country's workforce, dealing with in-country unions and government officials, keeping abreast of local commercial and political affairs, and negotiating with suppliers and customers from several nations. Motorola, for example, gives language instruction to its managers before placing them in foreign countries.

As a final word on communications, consider the messages sent by the choice of a gift for a foreign colleague or business associate. This is an area with many potential problems. The choice of a gift can cause embarrassment or trouble for the gift giver if a country's customs and traditions are not understood. Figure 20.8 outlines a few rules for giving gifts to foreign associates.

FIGURE 20.8 *Tips on how to avoid some common pitfalls of gift giving among foreign associates*

- Don't rely on your own taste.
- Don't bring a gift to an Arab man's wife; in fact, don't ask about her at all. Bringing gifts for the children is, however, acceptable.
- In Arab countries, don't admire an object openly. The owner may feel obligated to give it to you.
- Do not bring liquor to an Arab home. For many Arabs, alcohol is forbidden by religious law.
- Don't try to out-give the Japanese. It causes great embarrassment and obligates them to reciprocate even if they cannot afford it.
- Do not insist that your Japanese counterpart open the gift in your presence. This is not their custom and can easily cause embarrassment on the part of the recipient.
- As a courtesy, hold your gift with two hands when presenting it to a Japanese businessperson, but do not make a big thing of the presentation.
- Be careful when selecting colors or deciding on the number of items. The color purple is inappropriate in Latin America because it is associated with Lent.
- Avoid giving knives and handkerchiefs in Latin America. Knives suggest the cutting off of the relationship, and handkerchiefs imply that you wish the recipient hardship. To offset the bad luck, the recipient must offer you money.
- Logos should be unobtrusive.
- In Germany, red roses imply that you are in love with the recipient. Perfume is too personal a gift for business relationships.
- In the People's Republic of China, expensive presents are not acceptable and cause great embarrassment. Give a collective gift from your company to theirs.
- In China, a banquet is acceptable, but you will insult your hosts if you give a more lavish banquet than the one given you.
- A clock is a symbol of bad luck in China.
- The most important rule is to investigate first. After all, no one laughs at gift games. True, it is the thought that counts: the thought you give to understanding the culture and the taste of the people with whom you plan to negotiate.

Source: Reprinted by permission of the *Harvard Business Review.* Excerpt from "It's The Thought That Counts," by Kathleen K. Reardon, September–October 1984.

Cross-Cultural Management

cross-cultural management
An emerging discipline focused on improving work in organizations with employee and client populations from several cultures.

Culture has been defined earlier in this text as a societal group's shared beliefs, traditions, customs, behaviors, and values. A relatively new field called **cross-cultural management** "studies the behavior of people in organizations around the world and trains people to work in organizations with employee and client populations from several cultures." It describes and compares organizational behavior within and across countries and cultures and "seeks to understand and improve the interaction of co-workers, clients, suppliers, and alliance partners from different countries and cultures" (Adler, 1991).

Managers of global enterprises interact regularly with people of differing backgrounds, educational systems, business training, and personal perspectives and biases. "Diversity exists both within and among cultures; but within a single culture, certain behaviors are favored and others repressed. The norm for a society is the most common and generally most acceptable pattern of values, attitudes, and behavior" (Adler, 1991). We have mentioned a few of these in our discussion of communication differences. In this section we look briefly at what can be said collectively about the norms that international managers must recognize and with which they must cope.

Individualism Versus Collectivism

In general, Americans and citizens of many Western countries like to think and act as individuals, preferring to gain their personal identities through personal achievements and individual efforts. Many societies, such as Japan and several Latin American countries, however, are more group oriented. From an early age, children are taught to work in groups and to obtain a large portion of their personal identity through group membership and efforts. Working with teams, especially those that need to be empowered and autonomous, may not be so easy in cultures that foster individualism.

Doing Versus Being

A *doing* orientation is an action orientation. Western culture fosters this orientation; citizens like to be rewarded for individual actions and behaviors. "Managers in doing-oriented cultures motivate employees with promotions, raises, bonuses, and other forms of public recognition" (Adler, 1991). By contrast, a *being* orientation "finds people, events, and ideas flowing spontaneously; the people stress release, indulgence of existing desires, and working for the moment . . . they will not work strictly for future rewards" (Adler, 1991).

Asian cultures foster the being orientation. Individual performance rewards are not popular. Employers are often viewed as surrogate parents and usually offer job security and collective benefits to encourage a family atmosphere and long-term commitments from employees. Progression in such companies is methodical, slow, and through the ranks, with few if any shortcuts or fast-track careers.

Value of and Focus on Time

Some cultures value time more than others. To many people in the Middle East, time is not considered a precious commodity. Many people see work as a means to support life, not as a reason for living. Some cultures promote precise timetables and deadlines; others see precise deadlines and the need to meet them as relatively unimportant. Some cultures emphasize planning for the long term; others focus on the present or the past and the following of traditions.

Masculinity Versus Femininity

Geert Hofstede defines *masculinity* as the extent to which the dominant values in a society emphasize assertiveness and the acquisition of money and things, while not emphasizing concern for people. He defines *femininity* as the extent to which the dominant values in society emphasize relationships among people, concern for others, and the overall quality of life (Hofstede, 1980). Hofstede sees the Scandinavian countries as feminine; he sees Mexico, Japan, and much of Western Europe as masculine. Societies with feminine cultures "tend to create high-tax environments, extra money often fails to strongly motivate employees. . . . Conversely, masculine societies tend to develop into lower-tax environments in which extra money or other visible signs of success effectively reward achievement (Mexico, for example)" (Adler, 1991).

Once these values, attitudes, and behaviors are identified, training can be developed. Training programs typically deal with such areas as understanding cultures, language training, managing one's family life in the host country, and career development (Sherman, Bohlander, and Snell, 1996). Motorola offers its employees and their spouses a formal, predeparture course tailored to the countries to which the people will be going. In addition, it has a worldwide network of experienced *expatriates*—home country nationals with overseas experience—to help the newcomers settle in overseas. Arthur Andersen and Company, a worldwide accounting firm, has training facilities in St. Charles, Illinois; Manila; and Geneva, Switzerland. Employees from its many locations, like those from McDonald's, regularly meet to learn from each other.

http://www.andersen.com

When employees return to their home bases from foreign assignments, the training is not necessarily over. They often require programs to help them adjust. One example for such a *repatriation* program comes from Ciba-Geigy (now Ciba Specialty Chemicals), the international chemical company. Its purposes are to reverse the effects of any culture shock for both an individual and his or her family, help the individual to adjust to the new home assignment, and facilitate the sharing of the expatriate's knowledge and experiences (Sherman, Bohlander, and Snell, 1996).

http://www.cibasc.com

CONTROLLING AND THE INTERNATIONAL MANAGER

Discuss the major concerns relating to controlling an international corporation

The management function of control involves setting standards, measuring performances, applying standards to performances, and taking corrective actions as needed. These fundamentals do not change with multinational operations but some of the specifics about controlling do. We look next at control characteristics and problems for international managers.

Characteristics of Controls

Multinationals use a variety of controls to monitor and to adjust the performances of their foreign affiliates. These controls fall into two groups: direct and indirect controls. Direct controls include the use of such devices as periodic meetings, visits by the home office top-management teams to foreign operations, and the staffing of the foreign affiliates by home-country nationals. Meetings are often held by satellite communications linkups and by teleconferencing between both foreign affiliates and the company's top management. Periodically, host-country managers are called to headquarters to give first-hand reports on strategic progress. Such is the case with McDonald's international managers.

Indirect controls include the various kinds of reports sent daily, weekly, monthly, and soon by fax and by computer linkups. The main criteria used to measure performances are the costs being experienced, the return on invested capital, the market share held by an affiliate, and the profits earned by each affiliate by product line and areas of operations. In the same family of reports are whole arrays of budgetary and financial controls that are imposed by both local and corporate headquarters managers.

Control Problems

International controlling is made difficult by everything from language to legal restrictions. Most companies rely on the following methods of controlling:

1. Regular reporting procedures and communications between affiliates and their headquarters
2. Progress reports toward goals established with local input by strategic planners
3. Regular screening of reported data by area and functional experts
4. Regular on-site inspections by a variety of corporate personnel, both staff and line

"McDonald's, for example, has a team of five [human resource] directors who travel as internal consultants. Their job is to keep local directors in over fifty countries updated on international concerns, policies, and programs" (Sherman, Bohlander, and Snell, 1996).

http://www.thomson.fr

At Thomson, S.A., a French electronics giant, controlling international operations means touching bases with key managers on a regular schedule (in much the same way that Wal-Mart keeps track of its far-flung operations). Thomson has four major product groups and operations in the United States, Canada, Central America, Europe, Australia, and the Pacific Rim of nations. Regular meetings and seminars are held in France each year involving employees from all the company's divisions.

> *The CEO of the consumer electronics division spends at least one week in the U.S. every month, plus a week in Asia every second month, plus, of course, commuting inside Europe. Two of the executive vice presidents in charge of the four world product groups are based in Indianapolis, while the other two are in Paris. They have to meet regularly as well as travel to their sales organizations (McCormick and Stone, 1990).*

A final note on controlling human resources abroad. In many countries, bonuses, pensions, holidays, and vacation days are legally required and considered by many employees to be their right. Particularly powerful unions exist in many parts of the world and their demands restrict management's freedom to operate. Many countries have laws requiring that money be paid regularly into funds to provide for employee separations and terminations. Also, it can be expensive to fire or lay off a manager in many countries, as a study by William M. Mercer, a New York–based management consulting firm has discovered. The cost of firing

> *a 45-year-old middle manager with 20 years of service and a $50,000 annual salary, for example, varies in cost from $13,000 in Ireland to $130,000 in Italy. The amount is often much more than in the United States where a comparable worker doesn't have the same statutory protection . . . in Germany, managers receive . . . six months' notice-period pay after working 12 years* (Fortune, *1992).*

CHAPTER SUMMARY

1 Explain the primary reasons why businesses become international. Companies go international for two basic sets of reasons or motives: proactive and reactive.

- Proactive motives include the search for new customers, new markets, increased market share, increased return on investments, needed raw materials and other resources, tax advantages, lower costs, and economies of scale.
- Reactive motives include the desire to escape from trade barriers and other government regulations, to better serve a customer or group of customers, and to remain competitive.

2 Describe the characteristics of multinational corporations. Multinational corporations are companies with operating facilities, not just sales offices, in one or more foreign countries. In general, there are two kinds of multinational companies: those that market their product lines in relatively unaltered states throughout the world (standardization), and those that modify their products and services along with the marketing of them to appeal to specific groups of consumers in specific geographic areas (customization).

Even though multinationals around the world differ in sales volumes, profits, markets serviced, and the number of their subsidiaries, they do share some common characteristics. These include

- Creating foreign affiliates, which may be wholly owned by the multinational or jointly held with one or more partners from foreign countries
- Viewing the world as the market
- Choosing specific types of business activities (manufacturing, petroleum, banking, agriculture, public utilities)
- Locating affiliates in the developed countries of the world
- Adopting one of three basic strategies regarding staffing: (1) a high skills strategy in which the company exports products not jobs, (2) a strategy to "dumb down jobs" and shift the work to cheap-labor countries, and (3) a strategy to mix the preceding two strategies

3 Discuss the political, legal, economic, sociocultural, and technological elements of the international environment. The five environments of the international manager are the political, legal, economic, sociocultural, and technological.

- *Political environment:* This environment can foster or hinder economic development and investment by native and foreign investors and businesses. The political philosophy and type of economic philosophy held by a nation's leaders can give rise to laws that promote domestic commerce and raise barriers to trade with the outside world. The stability of the government and its support by the people will affect decisions to seek commercial opportunities or to avoid investments in a nation.
- *Legal environment:* Each country has its own unique set of laws that have an impact on commerce. Laws designed to protect the rights of individuals and labor unions differ as well. In addition, some countries erect trade barriers, such as quotas, tariffs, and embargoes. International managers must be aware of these legal constraints.
- *Economic environment:* When companies analyze their options for going multinational they must consider such factors as the stability of a country's currency, its infrastructure, its availability of needed raw materials and supplies, levels of inflation and taxes, citizens' level of income, closeness to customers, and climate.
- *Sociocultural environment:* This environment includes such concerns as a people's traditions, languages, customs, values, religion, and levels of education. The international manager can analyze the cultures in countries following these dimensions: material culture, social institutions, humans and the universe, aesthetics, and languages.
- *Technological environment:* This environment contains all the innovations that are rapidly occurring in all types of technologies. Regardless of what kind of a business a company is in, it must choose partners and locations that have what it lacks.

4 Describe the major strategies for going international. There are basically four ways to get involved in overseas trade. These are to

1. Export your product or service
2. License others to act on your behalf (as sales agents, franchisees, or users of your processes or patents)
3. Enter into joint ventures (partnerships) for mutual benefit to produce or market or both
4. Build or purchase facilities outside your home country to conduct business on your own

5 Explain the phases a company goes through when moving from domestic operations to a multinational structure. The evolution of a company becoming multinational takes it through three phases: pre-international division phase, international division phase, and global structure phase.

- *Pre-international division phase:* The first strategy used to introduce the product to a new nation is to find a way to export it. The result is typically the addition of an export manager to the marketing department. The export manager will establish the methods for foreign distribution and marketing—whether to place parent-company employees in a host country or to work through agents (importers, distributors, or retailers).
- *International division phase:* Pressures from host-country laws, trade restrictions, and competition may place the company

at a cost disadvantage. In response, the company establishes marketing or production operations in one or more countries. This international division reports directly to the CEO.

- *Global structure phase:* As the international operations gain success, top management makes a greater commitment to them and begins to see the company in a global perspective. Decisions that previously were made by separate and autonomous divisions need a total-company perspective. The final structure will contain functional, product, and geographic features and may be based on worldwide product groups, worldwide area groups, or a mixture of these two.

6 Discuss the major staffing concerns for an international corporation. One major staffing concern for an international corporation involves finding qualified persons to fill jobs in host countries, especially finding qualified managerial and technical people in developing or less-developed countries. A second concern relates to compensating host-country personnel. Traditions, legally mandated pay scales and benefits, differing tax rates and levels of inflation, differing standards of living, the relative values of currencies, and host-country competitors all combine to make compensation a difficult issue.

7 Describe the major concerns relating to leading a cross-cultural workforce. The major concerns relating to leading a cross-cultural workforce are employee attitudes, communication problems, and cultural norms.

- *Employee attitudes:* Attitudes about work are different throughout the world. For example, when something goes wrong in a Japanese company, the emphasis is on solving problems, not placing the blame. Japanese managers want to know what went wrong and how to fix it. Second, when Japanese managers set a goal and achieve it, they keep going and don't wait for praise. Also, in both Hungary and Poland job security are prime motivators.
- *Communication problems:* An international manager may be presented with a number of communication dilemmas. Both words and body language differ from one culture to another. The decision on what language to use (English, French, Japanese) in a meeting can present problems.
- *Cultural norms:* The norm for a society is the most common and generally most acceptable pattern of values, attitudes, and behavior. International managers must recognize and cope with the following norms: individualism versus collectivism, doing versus being, value of and focus on time, masculinity versus femininity.

8 Discuss the major concerns relating to controlling an international corporation. Controlling is made difficult by everything from language to legal restrictions. As a result most companies rely on

1. Regular reporting procedures and communications between affiliates and their headquarters
2. Progress reports toward goals established with local input by strategic planners
3. Regular screening of reported data by area and functional experts
4. Regular on-site inspections by a variety of corporate personnel

An additional concern focuses on controlling human resources abroad. In many countries bonuses, pensions, holidays, and vacation days are legally required and considered by many employees to be their right. Particularly powerful unions exist in many parts of the world, and their demands restrict management's freedom to operate. Many countries have laws requiring that money be paid regularly into funds to provide for employee separations and terminations. Also, it can be quite expensive to fire or lay off a manager in many countries.

REVIEW QUESTIONS

1. What are two reasons why a company becomes international?
2. What are the major characteristics of the multinational company?
3. What are the major components of each of the following international environments: political, legal, economic, sociocultural, and technological?
4. What are the major strategies for going international?
5. What are the three organizational phases that a company passes through in going multinational?
6. What are two concerns faced when attempting to staff international affiliates?
7. What are three problems connected with directing a cross-cultural workforce?
8. What are the major control problems for a multinational corporation?

DISCUSSION QUESTIONS FOR CRITICAL THINKING

1. You are the CEO of a rapidly growing video rental company and have plans to go international in the very near future. What steps would you take to enter the international marketplace? How would you organize your company? Why?
2. Which of the four strategies for going international require the greatest commitment by management? Why? What factors should be considered when selecting a strategy? Which is the most important?
3. An organization that is seeking to expand into international operations needs to monitor several environments. What aspect of each environment has changed or will change the way in which businesses select and train managers?
4. How might the cultural norms of individualism/collectivism and masculinity/femininity affect the management process and organizational design in an international company?

INTERNET EXERCISES

Check the text Web site at http://plunkett.swcollege.com for updated links to the Internet Exercises.

1. The CIA WorldFactbook is a comprehensive resource of facts and statistics on more than 250 countries and other entities. Choose a country and provide a brief overview of how political, legal, economic, sociocultural, and technological forces might affect international operations.
   http://www.odci.gov/cia/publications/factbook/index.html
2. Business travelers must be prepared when visiting foreign countries. Prepare a list of misunderstandings that can occur when cultural lines are being crossed.
   http://www.tradeport.org/ts/trade_expert/infobase/basic/ch08.html#cult
3. Have you ever dreamed of working abroad for part of your career? Well, you will need more than a valid passport. Labour Mobility has developed a checklist for full details of what you need to work abroad. Read over the checklist. What do you need to work abroad?
   http://www.labourmobility.com/checklist.htm

APPLICATION CASE

Benetton's International Dilemmas

Benetton's international apparel empire is struggling. The global retailing giant, whose look-alike stores from Brazil, to India, to Germany make it the McDonald's of the fashion business, has a growing list of problems. Luciano Benetton, who, along with brothers Carlo and Gilberto and sister Giulianna, manage Benetton's worldwide business interests, is faced with sales that are virtually flat at $1.69 billion. In addition, operating profits have tumbled 5 percent to $245 million, and margins have slipped to 13.9 percent, well below the 14.7 percent they have averaged since 1991. The factors contributing to the downward spiral include

- A tough European recession that saw shoppers unable or unwilling to spend.
- A franchise-style operation that allowed Benetton's to grow explosively, but is now showing cracks and strains; whereas most clothing retailers, such as Gap, Inc., own their own outlets, Benetton relies on a system in which entrepreneurs put up capital for new stores. The system attracts a great number of potential storeowners. When granting the franchises, Benetton did not establish territories or service areas but, rather, encouraged too many stores to be built too close together. In the U.S. market alone, the practice resulted in 150 stores remaining from around 500 stores in the late 1980s.
- A controversial ad campaign that focused on social issues, such as AIDS, racism, and ethnic violence; in Germany the ad campaign generated dozens of lawsuits from store owners, who refused to pay for several million dollars worth of goods. The retailers claimed the ads—which featured photos of dying AIDS patients and Palestinian refugees—turned shoppers away in droves. In France and Spain, storeowners, faced with threats of consumer boycotts, are also complaining.
- A lawsuit filed by one of Italy's largest operators of Benetton shops; management for Santomo, the complainant, contended that Benetton often shipped goods late and that it lagged far behind rivals who change their product lines much more frequently.

http://www.benetton.com

Questions

1. Which management functions (planning, organizing, staffing, leading, controlling) has Benetton failed to perform successfully? Provide examples from the case to support your answer.
2. Which international environments has Benetton management failed to adequately analyze and prepare for? Provide examples from the case to support your answer.
3. What actions would you recommend to resolve each of the four factors contributing to Benetton's problems?

Source: Rossant, John. "The Faded Colors of Benetton," *Business Week*, April 10, 1995, pp. 87–90.

VIDEO CASE

Global Strategy: Enforcement Technology

Enforcement Technology, Inc. (ETEC), provides online automated parking and traffic citation management systems and services for cities, counties, states, provinces, countries, colleges, and universities in both the United States and abroad. Since its incorporation in 1986, ETEC has expanded to serve more than 450 agencies in 50 states and 8 countries. Today it is the worldwide leader in hand-held parking and traffic enforcement technology, manufacturing and servicing its own hardware and software.

The ETEC products are known worldwide as Automated Citation Management Systems (AutoCITE) and consist of two major systems. One is the Automated Citation Issuance System (AutoISSUE), the enforcement system used to issue parking and traffic citations in the field. These citations are then downloaded and compiled on a PC at a company office. The second system is the Automated Citation Processing and Collection System (AutoPROCESS), which provides all the processing and collection functions for the company's clients.

The ETEC parking enforcement service centers currently process more than 4 million parking citations a year. As part of their basic processing and collection contracts, they also provide follow-up on delinquent citations and citations issued to out-of-state vehicles. The company has been very successful in improving the collection rates (fines paid) for its clients throughout the world.

In the United States, ETEC provides all the services that a client might want because the firm has a good grasp of the U.S. market and its clients' needs. However, management knows that ETEC's continued growth and success internationally must be based on successfully serving unique markets throughout the rest of the world. This realization is reflected in its global strategies.

ETEC routinely engages in strategic alliances or partnerships when entering foreign markets. It applies a "when in Rome do as the Romans do" philosophy to its international ventures, believing that it must understand the market rather than try to change it to be more like the U.S. market. By having a local partner, ETEC gains immediate insights into the host nation's culture, laws, customs, and currency issues—all of which can have an impact on its products and how they are delivered.

ETEC practices a relatively simple global pricing strategy, whereby all prices are pegged to the U.S. dollar and all exchange rate risks are passed on to its customers. Finally, when deciding on which global markets to enter, ETEC enjoys the luxury of having potential clients approach the company. ETEC then decides which ventures best fit its overall global strategy.

For Discussion:

1. Explain why ETEC chooses local partners for its operations in other countries.
2. Explain the international business strategy options from which ETEC must choose to compete internationally. Which method(s) does it utilize most often?

Succeeding in Your Organization

KEY TERMS

burnout

career

career management

career perspective

career planning

job

mentor

networking

obsolescence

organizational politics

organizational socialization

organizational visibility

psychological contract

sponsor

stress

telecommuting

whistle-blower

LEARNING OBJECTIVES

After studying this chapter, you should be able to

1. Discuss the nature of careers
2. Describe what is meant by having a career perspective
3. Describe the changes that have occurred in the career environment
4. Identify and describe the four stages of career development
5. Identify and discuss the five steps for career planning
6. Discuss how a manager can understand his or her organization and why it is important to do so
7. Identify and describe the abilities and actions that organizations value in managers
8. Discuss the strategies associated with career advancement
9. Discuss the organizational dilemmas experienced when personal and organizational interests are in conflict

MANAGEMENT IN ACTION

Success Unlimited

To be considered eminently successful in a career, a manager needs multifaceted experiences and seeks opportunities. "Kent Sutherland talked his way into Sam Walton's office 18 years ago—and hasn't stopped relying on the legendary entrepreneur's advice ever since" (Welles, 1998). Sutherland has the skills and tenacity to succeed in today's turbulent career environment.

In 1980, Sutherland's first job out of college at age 23 was as a vendor for Becton Dickinson, a supplier of health-care products. One of his customers was Wal-Mart. Sam Walton, the legendary founder of Wal-Mart, occasionally greeted the vendors. (Becton Dickinson happened to sell a certain syringe that Walton himself used for allergy shots.) "Sutherland wanted to get into business for himself, as Walton had. He figured that if he could get the elder's ear, then perhaps he could glean some of his precious knowledge. . . . Sutherland first met Walton on his third visit to Wal-Mart, and over the next seven years Walton would grant Sutherland brief, intermittent audiences, in which he would take the younger man aside and they'd talk business, like coach and quarterback crafting a game plan" (Welles, 1998).

Sam Walton changed retailing. "His empowering management techniques were copied by businesses far beyond his own industry; his harnessing of information technology to cut costs quickly traveled upstream to all kinds of companies; and his pioneering retailing concepts paved the way for a new breed of "category killer" retailer—the Home Depots, Barnes & Nobles and Blockbusters of the world" (Huey, 2000). *Time* (2000) included him in its list of "Most Influential People of the 20th Century," as number nine in the "Builders & Titans" field of endeavor. His "business philosophy was based on the simple idea of making the customer number one. He believed that by serving the customer's needs first, his business would also serve its associates, shareholders, communities and other stakeholders" (About Wal-Mart, http://www.walmart.com/cservice/aw_index.gsp). Walton's Five and Dime opened in 1950 in Bentonville, Arkansas. "Sam Walton's dream was simple: Give people high value, low prices, and a warm welcome" (The Wal-Mart Story, http://www.walmart.com/cservice/aw_story.gsp). The first Wal-Mart opened in 1962 in Rogers, Arkansas, offering consumers the highest value at the lowest prices. By 1991 Wal-Mart surpassed Sears to become the biggest retailer in the United States. In 2001, Wal-Mart Stores, Inc., employed more than 885,000 associates in some 3,000 stores and offices across the United States. The company has expanded internationally with more than 1,000 stores located beyond U.S. borders.

In 1966, Walton realized that to grow, he would have to add computerized merchandise controls. "Wal-Mart went on to become the icon of just-in-time inventory control and sophisticated logistics—the ultimate user of information as a competitive advantage. Today Wal-Mart's computer database is second only to the Pentagon's in capacity, and though he is rarely remembered that way, Walton may have been the first true information-age CEO" (Huey, 2000).

Sam Walton, founder of Wal-Mart, was a helpful mentor to Kent Sutherland and many others in the development of their business careers.

In 1988, Kent Sutherland started selling insurance. By 1998, he had 2,000 customers. He also owns a mini-storage facility, as well as other businesses. He is a millionaire. "In Kent Sutherland's world, Sam Walton's wisdom proffers the guiding invisible hand. 'I feel that he has had a tremendous impact by motivating me to do things a different way than I might have,' says Sutherland" (Welles, 1998).

The career of Kent Sutherland illustrates three major points of career management. First, he has taken risks. Risk is associated with change. Second, he evaluated his career and position and made moves that were best for him. Third, he has been in control of his career. ■

Sources: Huey, John. "Discounting Dynamo Sam Walton, *Time*, http://www.time.com/time/time100/builder/profile/walton.html. For more on Wal-Mart, visit http://www.walmart.com. For more on mentoring, read Welles, Edward O. "The Mentors," *Inc.*, June 1, 1998, http://www.inc.com/articles/details/0,,CID943_PAG5_REG14,00.html.

INTRODUCTION

Kent Sutherland, discussed in this chapter's Management in Action feature, managed to achieve success in two areas: his jobs and his career. He is knowledgeable and gets results. Successful managers develop their own career plans by focusing on the key elements: planning, preparation, and understanding the workings of organizations.

New managers need support. They need ongoing professional development. They need a sense of belonging, of common cause, and the knowledge that over time they will make a difference not only in the lives of individual employees they manage, but in their organizations. The need for this support is the focus of career development and the mentoring process.

http://www.uoregon.edu/~joelja/odyssey.html

Mentoring is not a new idea. People have always sought the wisdom and counsel of those with more experience. In Homer's epic poem, the *Odyssey*, a wise old sea captain named Mentor gives Odysseus's son, Telemachus, guidance in coping with his father's long absence. Mentor taught Telemachus the values he would need to rule Ithaca.

Not all companies have a formal mentoring program, pairing younger managers with older managers to help the younger ones excel. Yet, each employee can develop his or her career by finding a mentor.

> *In fact, suggests Kathy Kram, an associate professor of organizational behavior at Boston University School of Management, putting all your mentor eggs in one basket can be a mistake. 'I think people really ought to think in terms of multiple mentors instead of just one,' concludes Kram, the author of* Mentoring at Work. *And they don't all have to be grizzled business veterans. 'Peers can be an excellent source of mentorship,' she says (Welles, 1998).*

This chapter is about being successful in career management. First, the chapter will examine the nature of careers and then discuss the elements of career planning. The remainder of the chapter will examine career management and some associated dilemmas.

MANAGING TO SUCCESS

1

Discuss the nature of careers

Nature of Careers

One observer of the workplace puts the matter succinctly, "Some people have jobs, others have careers—it all depends on what you want, and how you approach it"

job
A specific position a person holds in an organization.

career
The series of jobs a person holds over a lifetime and the person's attitude toward the involvement in those job experiences; includes a long-term perspective, a sequence of positions, and a psychological involvement.

(Vreeland, 1992). For some people, work is a **job**—a specific position they hold in an organization. They take pride in it and do well; but a job does not take on a long-term perspective nor imply that the person doing it extends himself or herself beyond its requirements.

A **career**, on the other hand, is the sequence of jobs a person holds over a lifetime and the person's attitude toward his or her involvement in those jobs (Feldman, 1989). A career is a person's entire life in a work setting or settings. Because it encompasses a lifetime, a career reflects a long-term perspective and includes a series of jobs (Hall, 1986). A career also denotes involvement. People who have careers are so psychologically involved in their work that they extend themselves beyond its requirements.

Career Perspective

2

Describe what is meant by having a career perspective

career perspective
A proactive strategy that involves a global view of career progress or growth over time.

Adopting a career perspective can increase an individual's probability of success in his or her career. A **career perspective**, as illustrated in Figure 21.1, is a proactive strategy that involves a global view of career progress or growth over time. It requires a person to adopt a broad vision that includes all the elements involved in a successful career: objectives, timetables, career stages, skills improvement, organizational politics, power, stress, and values. Adopting such a broad vision can be accomplished through career planning, which emphasizes the activities involved in making career decisions, and career management, which emphasizes the activities and behaviors involved in career advancement.

New Career Environment

3

Describe the changes that have occurred in the career environment

As a prerequisite for career planning, a manager must understand the new career environment. In recent years many facets of careers have radically changed. "The notion that you can work for one company and be guaranteed that you will retire from there at age 62 is not so reasonable anymore," says economist Michael

FIGURE 21.1 *Taking a career perspective*

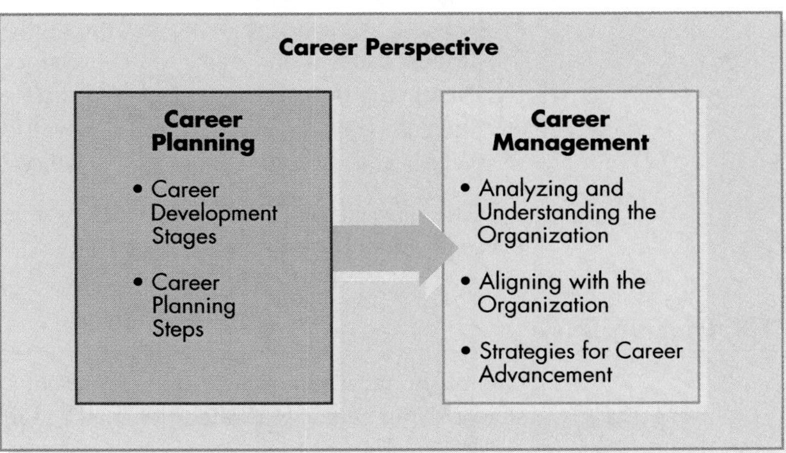

Podursky of the University of Massachusetts (Franklin, 1994). "The relationship isn't what it was. The new compact between company and worker dismisses paternalism and embraces self-reliance" (Hammonds, Kelly, and Thurston, 1994).

http://www.ibm.com

Gone are the days of "unconditional lifetime employment, even at the bluest of blue-chip companies . . . that clearly is no longer the name of the game," says Kevin Becraft, director of employee relations and resources at IBM. "Instead, it's lifetime employability." The key difference: shared responsibility. Employers have an obligation to provide opportunity for self-improvement; employees have to take charge of their careers (Hammonds, Kelly, and Thurston, 1994).

The economy and industries are changing so rapidly that no company can really know what it will be doing one or more years in the future. The emphasis now is on gaining a competitive edge. Downsizing, restructuring, empowering, telecommuting, employee leasing, teaming, decentralizing, outsourcing, and reengineering are all changing the complexion of work and the workplace. All these efforts bring sudden and often painful changes to a company's employees and careers. Reengineering has eliminated many of the old "career pathways"; the middle-manager staircase is gone in most organizations. Businesses have redrawn their boundaries as they focus on core competencies and outsource noncore work. As a result, work follows a contractor-subcontractor model, not one of vertical integration. Project-based (versus position-based) work, long the norm in industries like construction and many professional services, has changed companies with career hierarchies (Stewart, 1995).

For the career manager, the message is clear. The rules indeed have changed. Now instead of security, seek opportunity. Instead of position, chart your contribution. Careers will be defined less by companies ("I work for IBM") and more by profession ("I am a professional manager"). Harvard Business School professor John Kotter has taken a new look at success in this dynamic environment. In his book *The New Rules* (Kotter, 1995), Kotter identifies seven rules for career success:

- Do not rely on convention; career paths that were winners for most of the twentieth century are often no longer providing much success.
- Keep your eyes on globalization and its consequences. With competition and opportunity arising all over the world, success comes to the alert and agile.
- Move toward the small and entrepreneurial organization and away from the big and bureaucratic.
- Do not just manage; now you must also lead. Managers cope with change; leaders cause it and make the competition cope.
- Never stop trying to grow; lifelong learning is increasingly necessary for success.
- Increase your competitive drive. Driven people reap the greatest rewards.
- Wheel and deal if you can. Take chances and seek opportunities.

The new environment, with its new rules, makes it even more important to plan and monitor a career.

CAREER PLANNING

One of the most important principles about careers is that you alone are responsible for your career. Although you may be fortunate to work for organizations and managers who help you develop your career and help you to advance, the hard fact is that you cannot sit back and wait for that to happen. Kent Sutherland in the Management in Action case took charge of his career. It is simply not enough to work hard and be good at work. Those people who plan their careers greatly improve the chance of long-term success.

career planning
The process of developing a realistic view about how individuals want their careers to proceed and then taking steps to ensure that they follow that course.

Career planning is the process of developing a realistic view about how one wants one's career to proceed and then making plans to ensure that it follows that course. The process includes a series of activities to help make informed decisions: performing a self-assessment, identifying opportunities, matching skills to career-related activities, developing objectives and timetables, and evaluating progress. The process is important because it links personal needs and skills with career goals and opportunities.

Planning one's career is a successful process because it is systematic. Such planning involves linking long-term and short-term objectives, developing personal capabilities en route, and performing a focused analysis of progress. It is not, however, a one-time process. Career planning is ongoing; as the environment and organizations change, you need to review, update, and adjust career plans on a continuous basis (Stewart, 1995).

Stages of Career Development

4
Identify and describe the four stages of career development

To understand how to plan a career, it is helpful to view how careers unfold. Most careers go through four distinct stages, each dealing with different issues and tasks (Hall, 1986). Figure 21.2 illustrates these four stages, and Figure 21.3 lists the tasks for each stage.

FIGURE 21.2 *Four stages of career development*

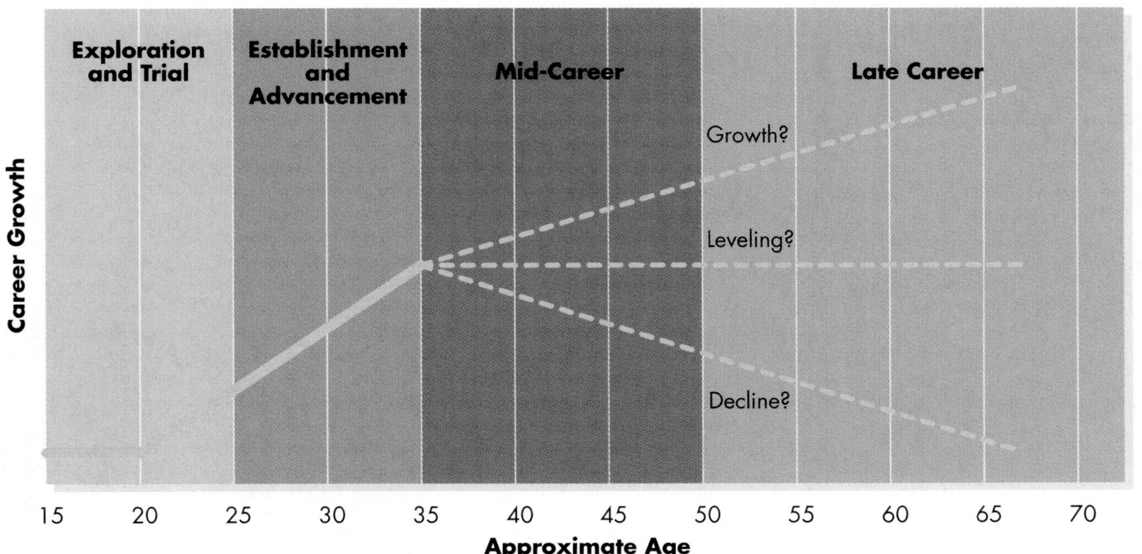

FIGURE 21.3 *Characteristics of the four stages of career development*

Stage	Task Needs
Exploration and Trial	• Varied job activities • Self-exploration
Establishment and Advancement	• Job challenge • Develop competence in a specialty area • Develop creativity and innovation • Rotate into new area after three to five years
Mid-Career	• Technical updating • Develop skills in training and coaching others (younger employees) • Rotation into new job requiring new skills • Develop broader view of work and role in organization
Late Career	• Shift from power role to one of consultation and guidance • Identify and develop successors • Begin activities outside the organization • Plan for retirement

Source: D. T. Hall and M. A. Morgan, "Career Development and Planning," *Contemporary Problems in Personnel*, revised edition. W. C. Hammer and Frank L. Schmidt, editors (Chicago: St. Clair Press), 1977.

Stage 1: Exploration and Trial

This first stage usually occurs between the ages of 15 and 25. For most people it begins with the decision to become serious about employment after having concentrated on education. This stage is a learning process as it includes many firsts—the first job interview, first part-time job, and first full-time job—and introduces the individual to the challenges associated with working. People in this stage face the issue of staying with an organization or moving to a job with another company.

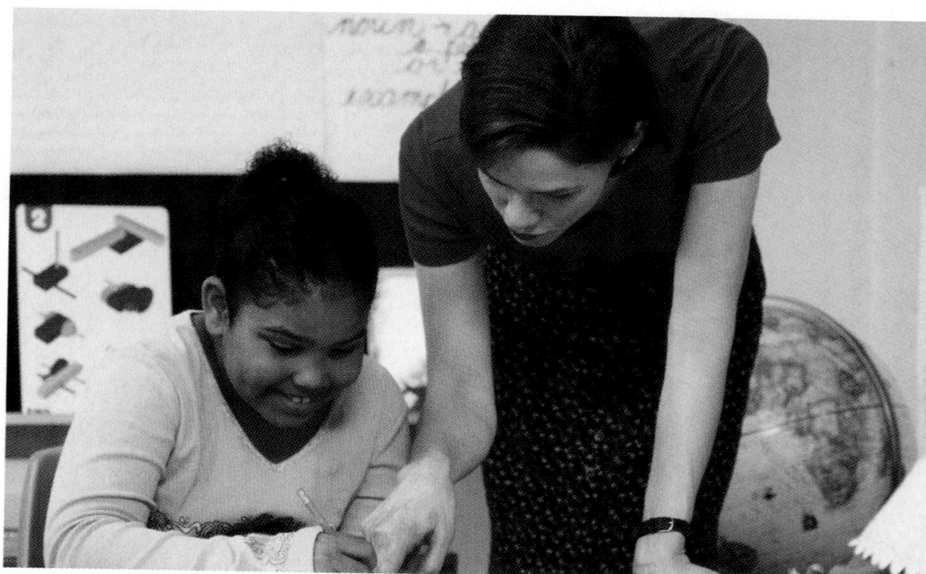

In the exploration and trial stage, young workers get their first taste of full-time work and the challenges that accompany it.

Stage 2: Establishment and Advancement

In this second stage—normally occurring between the ages of 25 and 35—people are involved in their first "real job." They experience success as well as frustrations and receive promotions and transfers. In this period most people take stock and begin to develop a career strategy—they begin to identify a field of specialization and weigh long-term success. For many, this stage includes new specialties and offers for new jobs outside the organization.

Stage 3: Mid-Career

The mid-career stage most often occurs between the ages of 35 and 50. Most people don't face their first career dilemma until they reach this stage. In the modern-day organization, a career may take one of three possible directions at this point: growth, leveling, or decline. If the direction is growth, the person is valued by the organization and is receiving promotions and increased responsibility. Career growth is the direct result of a strategy focused on enhancing skills and continual learning. If the career levels off, the individual may receive transfers but not promotions. The person may be secure, but with no growth in sight, he or she should consider the option of developing a second career. If the career is in decline, the person is seen as surplus in the eyes of the organization; he or she feels insecure and has a growing sense of failure. Tactically, such a person should try to move to a different company. Switching careers can pay off, both in money and satisfaction, as evidenced in this chapter's Global Applications feature.

Obviously, the mid-career stage is critical. In today's business environment, companies have little patience or tolerance for individuals who allow their skills and careers to level or decline. Being proactive and committed to continuous quality improvement is imperative (Stewart, 1995).

GLOBAL APPLICATIONS
Switching Careers

China's complicated politics prompted worries about whether government work was the right career for Weng Xianding. He doubted he could make a major impact as a Beijing bureaucrat. Even though he was a rising star at the State Planning Commission, Xianding switched to a business career.

Now he runs an ambitious $120 million investment company in fast-paced Shenzhen, the economic zone near Hong Kong. Among the projects of his New China Industries Investment Company: a futures and commodities trading firm, a clinic to treat nearsightedness with lasers, a raft of high-tech start-ups, a major office complex, and a sports club with racquetball courts and bowling lanes.

Xianding has managed his career well. He has parlayed ability, education, performance, and networking to reach his present position. After working at a brick factory, Xianding scored so well on a university entrance exam that he was admitted into the master's program at the Chinese Academy of Social Sciences. There, he met students who would later attain government positions and with whom he networked to build his company.

After acquiring his degree, Xianding broadened his skills by getting a second master's degree, in banking and finance, in Milan, Italy. Immediately, he set up New China Industries. Its seventeen shareholders include many of his old classmates, many provincial governments from around China, as well as his old employer, the State Planning Commission.

Source: Engardio, Pete, Dexter Roberts, and Bruce Einhorn. "From Technocrat to Tycoon," *Business Week*, June 5, 1995, p. 51.

Stage 4: Late Career

The late career stage—occurring between the ages of 50 and retirement—is marked by a peak in prestige for those who experienced growth in the prior stage. Their value to the organization lies in their judgment and experience and their ability to share this knowledge with others. Such managers become reliable trainers of the next generation of managers. Normally, plans are made to slow down, develop outside interests, and prepare for retirement.

Steps in Career Planning

Identify and discuss the five steps for career planning

A person should use the career planning model continuously in his or her employment life. Regardless of whether a person is on the outside looking in—just beginning a career—or trying to advance within an organization, the same steps apply (Plunkett, 1995). Figure 21.4 illustrates the steps in career planning.

Step 1: Self-Assessment

Performing a realistic self-assessment is the first step to career planning. A thorough data-gathering process includes evaluating your values, interests, skills, abilities, experience, and likes and dislikes. This step requires a clear and objective view of what you believe is important (values), what makes you happy at work, and what rewards you expect. Figure 21.5 provides an assessment checklist that a person can use to identify skills and values.

At the beginning of a career, this step involves identifying initial skills and interests. For an aspiring manager in today's business environment, being independent, flexible, and a team player are points against which to benchmark. The person who likes to learn, is self-reliant, and thrives on change meets the prescription for the future (Kiechel, 1994). Figure 21.6 outlines ten attributes organizations look for in filling management positions.

As a career progresses, a person should continue to undertake a self-assessment a number of times to ensure that he or she has retained his or her focus and to see what additional skills and training are needed. Avoiding obsolescence is essential.

obsolescence
A state or condition that exists when a person is no longer capable of performing up to job standards or to management's expectations.

Obsolescence exists when a person is no longer capable of performing up to job standards or management's expectations (Plunkett, 1995). A person can become obsolete in attitudes, knowledge, skills, and abilities. Obsolescence in any of these areas marks a person as a potential candidate for the scrap heap. Such a person may become too costly to maintain. Figure 21.7 provides a short quiz a person can continue to use to identify areas of obsolescence.

FIGURE 21.4 *Steps in career planning*

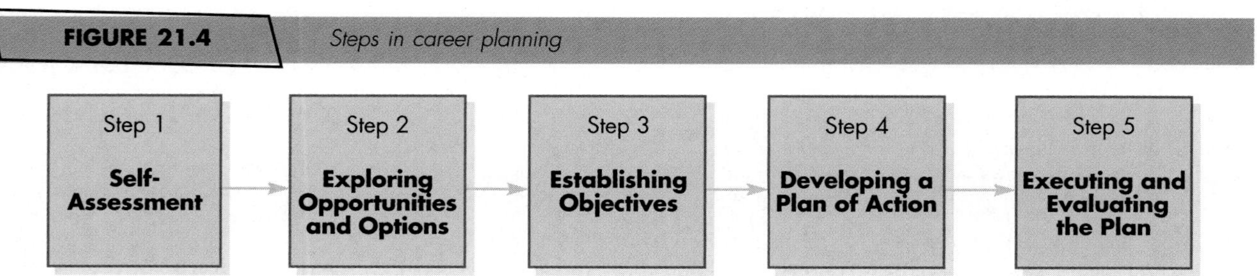

FIGURE 21.5 *Assessment checklist for identifying skills and values*

WHAT DO I DO WELL?

Check the items that apply to you:

- ❑ Organizing
- ❑ Handling details
- ❑ Making things
- ❑ Researching
- ❑ Creating
- ❑ Reasoning / logic
- ❑ Writing
- ❑ Drawing / painting
- ❑ Computing / mathematics
- ❑ Dealing with others
- ❑ Innovating
- ❑ Making decisions
- ❑ Teaching others
- ❑ Supervising
- ❑ Dressing well
- ❑ Persuading
- ❑ Communicating
- ❑ Dealing with criticism
- ❑ Coordinating activities
- ❑ Developing new skills
- ❑ Other (specify) ______________________

My five most important abilities are: ______________

______________ ______________

______________ ______________

WHAT IS IMPORTANT TO ME?

Check the items that apply to you:

- ❑ Helping others
- ❑ Working alone
- ❑ Working with others
- ❑ Making decisions
- ❑ Chance for advancement
- ❑ Monetary reward
- ❑ Physical challenge
- ❑ Power and authority
- ❑ Improving society
- ❑ Competition
- ❑ Fast pace
- ❑ Gaining knowledge
- ❑ Creativity
- ❑ Change and variety
- ❑ Security
- ❑ Recognition
- ❑ Excitement
- ❑ Independence
- ❑ Responsibility
- ❑ Intellectual challenge
- ❑ Other (specify) ______________________

My five most important abilities are: ______________

______________ ______________

______________ ______________

Source: W. Richard Plunkett. *Supervision*, 6/e, 1992, p. 39. © 1992 by Prentice Hall, Inc. Reprinted by permission of Pearson Education, Inc., Upper Saddle River, N.J. 07458.

For managers, personal obsolescence can happen quite suddenly. Reengineering that shifts a company from vertical layers of management to cross-functional teams can render an individual's performance inadequate or unnecessary. If a

FIGURE 21.6 *Ten attributes that organizations look for in applicants for management positions*

1. **Oral communication skills:** Effective expression in individual or group situations (includes gestures and nonverbal communication).
2. **Oral presentation skills:** Effective expression when presenting ideas or tasks to an individual or group when given time for presentation (includes gestures and nonverbal communication).
3. **Written communication skills:** Clear expression of ideas in writing and in correct grammatical form.
4. **Job motivation:** The extent to which activities and responsibilities available in the job correspond with activities and responsibilities that result in personal satisfaction.
5. **Initiative:** Active attempts to influence events to achieve goals; self-starting rather than passive acceptance; taking action to achieve goals beyond those called for; instigating change.
6. **Leadership:** Utilizing appropriate interpersonal styles and methods in guiding individuals (subordinates, peers, superiors) or groups toward task accomplishment.
7. **Planning and organization:** Establishing a course of action for self and/or others to accomplish a specific goal; planning proper assignments of personnel and appropriate allocation of resources.
8. **Analysis:** Relating and comparing data from different sources, identifying issues, securing relevant information, and identifying relationships.
9. **Judgment:** Developing alternative courses of action and making decisions that are based on logical assumptions and reflect factual information.
10. **Management control:** Establishing procedures to monitor and/or regulate processes, tasks, or the responsibilities of subordinates: taking action to monitor the results of delegated assignments or projects.

Source: From William C. Byham, "Starting an Assessment Center," *Personnel Administrator* (February 1980). Reprinted with the permission of *HRMagazine*, published by The Society for Human Resource Management, Alexandria, Va.

company decides to outsource, positions are eliminated. When a manager refuses to learn new technology, he or she is left standing at the train station. Avoiding obsolescence is critical in career management. Later in the chapter we will discuss strategies for avoiding obsolescence.

Step 2: Exploring Opportunities and Options

The second step in career planning requires examining the opportunities that exist in the industry and within a company. At the beginning of a career, this step involves determining the following:

- What are the future prospects for the industry?
- What career opportunities exist in the industry?
- What jobs are available?
- What jobs relate to a career path?

FIGURE 21.7 *Twenty questions to help assess the degree of personal obsolescence*

Ask yourself the following questions to determine your degree of personal obsolescence:

Attitudes

1. Is my mind free from anxiety over personal matters while I work?
2. Do I believe in myself—my knowledge, skills, and abilities—and in my associates?
3. Am I open and receptive to advice and suggestions, regardless of their sources?
4. Do I look for the pluses before looking for the minuses?
5. Am I more concerned with the cause of management's action than with its effect?

Knowledge

1. Am I curious—do I still seek the why behind actions and events?
2. Do I read something and learn something new every day?
3. Do I question the old and the routine?
4. Do I converse regularly with my subordinates, peers, and superiors?
5. Have I a definite program for increasing my knowledge?

Skills

1. Is what I am able to do still needed?
2. In light of recent trends and developments in my company and industry, will my skills be required one year from now?
3. Do I practice my skills regularly?
4. Do I regularly observe how others perform their skills?
5. Have I a concrete program for acquiring new skills?

Abilities

1. Do my subordinates, peers, and superiors consider me competent?
2. Do I consistently look for a better way of doing things?
3. Am I willing to take calculated risks?
4. Do I keep morally and physically fit?
5. Have I a specific program for improving my performance?

Source: W. Richard Plunkett. *Supervision*, 7th ed., 1995, p. 40. © 1995 by Prentice Hall, Inc. Reprinted by permission of Pearson Education, Inc., Upper Saddle River, N.J. 97458.

For a person in mid-career, the emphasis shifts to evaluating options both inside and outside the organization:

- What are the future prospects for the company?
- What positions will open up in the company?
- What skills does the company value?
- What training and development are available?
- Who is being promoted?
- When are they being promoted?
- What is the job market?

In the new business environment, which emphasizes flatter organization structures and team orientation, this step becomes even more critical. The answers to many of the questions—what opportunities exist, what jobs are important to the company, what positions will open up in a company, who is being promoted—

evolve on a day-to-day basis. For the career planner the implications are clear: research thoroughly, build in flexibility, constantly evaluate, and update. Remember, times have changed. It takes more personal energy and vigilance to see signs of career trouble and to identify opportunities. According to Richard Moran, a consultant at PricewaterhouseCoopers, "The rule used to be incremental promotions every year or two. If you missed one . . . that was a warning. You don't get the little clicks now" (Unger, 1995). Warnings are subtler; many are available to only the person, not the boss or colleagues. Warning signs include the following (Stewart, 1995):

http://www.pwcglobal.com

- Are you learning? If you can't say what you've learned in the past six months or what you expect to learn in the next, beware. Says Harvard's John Kotter, "When there is nothing you can learn where you are, you've got to move on even if they give you promotions."
- If your job was open, would you get it? Benchmark your skills regularly. Says Betsy Collard, program director at the Career Action Center, "Look at the want ads and see what they are looking for in your field."
- What would you do if your job disappeared tomorrow? The answer to the question identifies marketable skills. More and more people have to sell themselves inside the company.

Step 3: Establishing Objectives

Once the opportunities are identified, the career planner has to make short- and long-term decisions. The key is to make the long-term decisions first and then derive the short-term decisions from them. Traditionally, according to Professor Sal Davita, "The two issues of paramount importance once were: what position do you want to hold the day you retire, and in what industry do you want to make a career?" The decision on the industry is still critical for a few reasons. First, an individual's abilities and interests are more or less suited to work in different industries. Second, industries vary in their future prospects (Davita, July 1992). The decision on the final position is not as relevant as it once was because many career paths will not exist in the future. Instead, according to management consultant Michael Hammer (Stewart, 1995), the second objective is for "you to think of yourself as self-employed—think of yourself as a business. Then the next decision is to define the business' product or service: the area of expertise. This leads directly to a crucial, career-defining choice: specialist or generalist?" The answer means the person concentrates on one area of expertise or instead develops a broad range of skills.

Opinions on the best decision vary. The conventional wisdom is that generalists are better off. Says Dan Burnham of Allied-Signal, "A marketing manager can't be just a marketing manager. He needs a broader dimension of skill." (Allied-Signal merged with Honeywell and GE acquired Honeywell. See press release of October 22, 2000, http://www.honeywell.com/mediakit/page4_1_1.jsp?doc=729.) Adds headhunter Gary Knisely, "Never narrow your options. To the extent that technical expertise narrows your market, you've made a bad career decision. Companies may love you at the moment, but if you've got that good of a crystal ball, get out of a job and into investing" (Stewart, 1995). Betting your career on a specialty is like putting all your money in one stock.

http://www.honeywell.com

http://www.pepsico.com

On the other hand, says David Hatch, a human resources vice president at PepsiCo, "It's a little dangerous to be esoteric, but companies treat specialists very well—as the scarce resource they are—compared to people who are more interchangeable." One company who does is PricewaterhouseCoopers. Instead of the traditional "up or out," twelve-years-to-partner timetable, the structure creates three levels—consultant, principal consultant/director, and managing director/partner—with no clock. The purpose: to make it easier for specialists to stay (Kiechel, 1994).

Once these long-term objectives are established, other decisions follow:

- Which functional or specialty area of the organization needs to be learned about?
- What jobs and experiences will lead to the ultimate objective?
- What skills are needed to attain the objective?
- What people and other resources are necessary to achieve the objectives?
- What work assignments will be valuable?

Step 4: Developing a Plan of Action

This step provides the detailed map to accomplish the objectives. It requires thinking through specifically how to acquire the skills—whether the career planner needs formal education or whether he or she can learn the skills by seeking a special project. The plan should include establishing specific timetables for completing training, reaching a new job level, and gaining new exposure in a company. This stage also identifies potential barriers and resources to work around the barriers.

Step 5: Executing and Evaluating the Plan

Once the plan is in place, it must be put into action. In this step the career planner takes charge of his or her career, rather than waiting for things to happen. The second part of this step is to follow up and evaluate progress on the plan. As the environment changes, adjusting the plan may become necessary. The evaluation also needs to consider individual growth, career progress, new assignments—those items that were targeted by objectives and developed in the action plan. This execution phase—career management—is the next topic of discussion.

Before we move on to the topic of career management, however, let us look at Beth Randolph, who provides us with an excellent example of how the steps in career planning unfold. Randolph, a self-motivated achiever, put herself through two-year Hocking College by working in a telemarketing facility operated by Choice Hotels. "I was a sponge," says Randolph, who managed the center when her boss was away. "I love travel. I absolutely love the hospitality industry." Randolph had found her industry and the start of her career.

http://www.choicehotels.com

After graduation, Randolph worked as a travel agent. Then Choice, which operates Quality Inns and Comfort Inns, called to say that the company planned to open a large reservation center in North Dakota: would she like to manage it? She hurriedly moved to Minot and built a business from scratch. She interviewed most job candidates, trained the supervisors, and negotiated contracts for office equipment, cleaning supplies, and even food for the kitchen.

Randolph overcame early fears of supervising people older than herself. She built a cohesive team and received recognition from top management. Building on success, Randolph told Don Brockway, Choice's vice president of reservation operations, "I'm ready to be more creative and solve problems on a higher level." In response, Brockway chose Randolph over three older candidates to oversee Choice's rapidly expanding reservations system across Europe. "This was a huge decision," says Brockway, "she's a fireball who always gets the job done." Beth Randolph is in charge of her own career (Sellers, 1994).

CAREER MANAGEMENT

career management
The planning, activities, and behaviors involved in executing a career.

The key to success is to be self-reliant: to take charge and actively manage your career. **Career management** involves three elements—understanding the organization, aligning yourself with the organization, and implementing career-enhancing strategies.

Analyzing and Understanding the Organization

Discuss how a manager can understand his or her organization and why it is important to do so

As noted in Chapter 10, all organizations are unique. Each develops its own methods, values, rewards; each makes clear what it accepts and does not tolerate. Before a person can develop strategies for career growth, he or she must know the company—what abilities it values, what actions it rewards, how it compensates achievers. He or she must both accept the organization's way and be accepted by it. This critical phase has been identified by organizational psychologist Edgar H. Schein as the organizational socialization process.

Organizational Socialization

organizational socialization
A process through which new members of an organization gain exposure to its values, norms, policies, and procedures.

Regardless of whether it is a new employee's first or fifth company, he or she undergoes **organizational socialization**. In this process new members of an organization gain exposure to its values, norms, policies, and procedures. At the same time, they discover who wields power, what restrictions there are on behavior, and how to succeed and survive.

Figure 21.8 present's Schein's model for the process through which an employee becomes an accepted and conforming member of the organization. In Phase I, a job seeker forms impressions and expectations of the company. Phase II is the period of adjustment in which the new employee matches individual needs to those of the organization. Phase III marks the mutual acceptance of employee and organization. Not all employees survive these last two phases; faced with conflicts and compromises too great to overcome, employees who cannot adjust and conform may quit voluntarily or be asked to leave (Schein, 1978).

psychological contract
The unspoken contract that marks the end product of the organizational socialization process and defines what people are expected to give to the organization and what they can expect to receive.

At the end of Phase III, the employee and the organization enter into a **psychological contract**, an unspoken agreement defining what people are expected to give the organization and what they can expect to receive in return. Formed in the mind of the employee, it is based on experiences, promises, and personal observations of how the organization operates. The terms of the contract are the result of the interaction between the employee and boss, the employee and coworkers, and the employee's first-hand experience with the organization's efforts to enforce the rules and behaviors it considers essential. A sense of fairness or equity must exist between employee and employer—each must believe the other is doing his or her part and giving in proportion to what he or she expects to receive.

FIGURE 21.8 *Schein's model of the phases of organizational socialization*

PHASE I

ENTRY

- Occupational choice
- Occupational image
- Anticipatory socialization to occupation
- Entry into labor market

PHASE II

SOCIALIZATION

- Accepting the reality of the human organization
- Dealing with resistance to change
- Learning how to work: coping with too much or too little organization and too much or too little job definition
- Dealing with the boss and deciphering the reward system—learning how to get ahead
- Locating one's place in the organization and developing an identity

PHASE III

MUTUAL ACCEPTANCE: THE PSYCHOLOGICAL CONTRACT

Organizational acceptance
- Positive performance appraisal
- Pay increase
- New job
- Sharing organizational secrets
- Initiation rites
- Promotion

Individual acceptance
- Continued participation in organization
- Acceptable job performance
- High job satisfaction

Source: Edgar H. Schein, *Career Dynamics*, © 1978 by Addison-Wesley Publishing Company, Inc. Reprinted by permission of Pearson Education, Inc., Upper Saddle River, N.J. 07458.

The psychological contract today is often far different from one in the past. "In the days of the Organization Man, job security, raises, and promotions were exchanged for hard work, loyalty, and a job-first philosophy" (Penzias, 1995). In the new employer-employee contract . . . "you are responsible for your own career; we, your employer, will help provide you the experience and training to keep you marketable, but not necessarily a job forever" (Kiechel, 1994). In practice, this contract is best represented by the sentiments of William Paine, a bond salesman at Gruntal & Company: "I'm very loyal. I'll remain loyal if they supply me phones, a computer, execution, and inventory. I owe them integrity and production" (Stewart, 1995).

http://www.gruntal.com

Identify and describe the abilities and actions that organizations value in managers

Determining What Is Valued and Rewarded

Organizational socialization provides the employee with the opportunity to identify and focus on what the organization values and rewards—what abilities are associated with advancement and what actions are seen as valuable. Although it is critical to identify the abilities that a specific organization values, a survey of major organizations and leading CEOs identified a number of abilities that are associated with career success in a broad spectrum of companies (Fram, 1994):

- *Communications skills.* The ability to communicate one-to-one, in groups, and in writing
- *Interpersonal skills.* The ability to work with others, relating well to people at all levels of the organization, understanding how others feel, and establishing networks
- *Competence.* The ability to produce quality work, get results, be accountable, know the field, perform consistently, and upgrade skills
- *Conceptual skills.* The ability to focus on the big picture and understand all the interlocking pieces
- *Decision skills.* The ability to handle more and more complex problems
- *Flexibility.* The ability to adjust to rapid change, new variables, and new environments

Interviews conducted at Fortune 500 companies revealed that the actions most likely to be valued and rewarded in today's organization include (Kiechel, 1994):

- *Hard work.* Working hard means being willing to accept more responsibility, being committed, and being dedicated. It also involves working more hours than the standard workweek and producing high-quality work.
- *Risk taking.* This action includes a willingness to move into unfamiliar areas of the business, take on new assignments, and accept increases in responsibility.
- *Making contributions.* Making contributions involves focusing on the critical parts of a job—quality and innovation. It also involves looking at the company's objectives and seeing how the present position fits in and how it affects the bottom line.

Good communication skills are essential for career success.

- *Being a team player.* Being a team player means being dedicated to making the organization run more effectively rather than focusing on just a job or a department. It involves a person's being able to step back and align his or her objectives with those of others, rather than trying to dominate or isolate.

In commenting on the team player, professor Leonard Greenlaugh notes, "The action today is all about connectedness, about forming effective teams, and building strategic alliances." Robert L. Smith, of the executive search firm that bears his name, agrees:

> *In the past a lot of people looked for what I would call the equivalent of the singles tennis pro, the individual who could move mountains and catch bullets in his teeth. In the market today, not only is that no longer desired, it's shunned. We're looking for the team player because in today's environment an executive can't get the job done without support from everyone else (Harari, 1994).*

Assessment and Alignment

After individuals have identified the abilities and actions that are valued and rewarded by the organization, they need to assess both of these and possibly make a midcourse correction. Their actions and abilities must align with those the organization values. To assist this process, the individual must ask the following questions:

- How do my skills match those the organization values?
- Am I capable of the actions necessary?
- What other preparation—education or training—do I need?

Becoming committed to continuous evaluation and skill building is equally important for the employee.

STRATEGIES FOR CAREER ADVANCEMENT

Discuss the strategies associated with career advancement

Knowing and understanding the organization provide the basis on which to develop and implement strategies for career advancement. As shown in Figure 21.9, these strategies focus on committing to lifelong learning, creating visibility, developing mentor relationships, developing networks, understanding power and politics, working with the boss, and managing stress.

Committing to Lifelong Learning

"I've got people who report to me who need to learn how to type, because if they can't get on the Internet, they're going to be obsolete," states Ray-Chem CEO Robert Soldich. The key to avoiding obsolescence—and creating a successful career—is a commitment to lifelong learning. Just as corporations are reengineering themselves, managers must accept the fact that multiple career changes will become increasingly common. In the early 1990s one university president told incoming freshmen that as many as 85 percent of the jobs that would be available by 2010 have not been thought of yet. He also predicted that the students should expect to have four to five career—not job—changes during their working life (Unger, 1995).

FIGURE 21.9 *Strategies for career advancement*

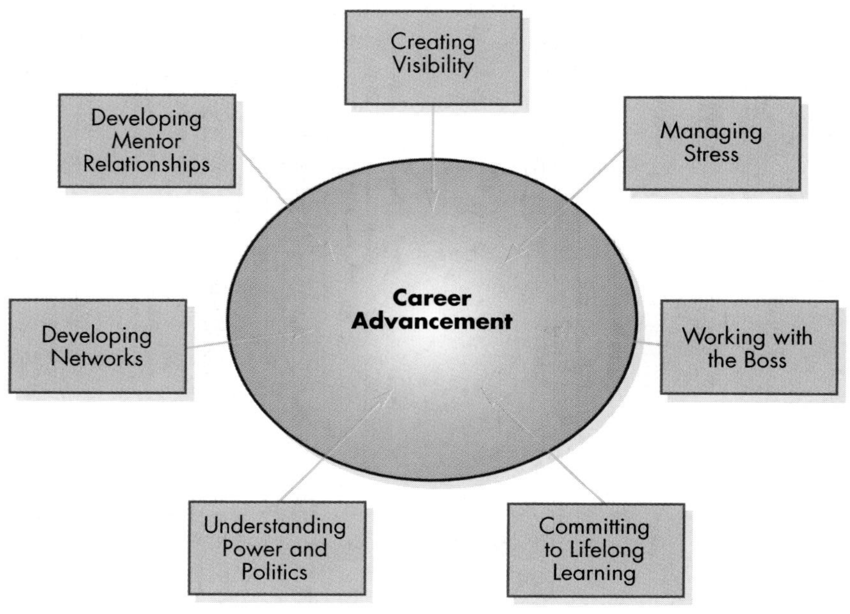

What this situation clearly indicates is the need for constant preparation, for learning new technology, and for packaging new skills. To avoid obsolescence (and resolve the generalist/specialist dilemma discussed earlier), Walter Kiechel (1994) advises that you have to be both a generalist and a specialist. "From the very first day on the job managers have to bring some special expertise to the party. In the new economy, managers will have to add content." Even as a manager you have to add value. "And as managers of technical teams, they will need to understand the different technologies and disciplines to be able to mediate among them."

http://www.bus.indiana.edu

To upgrade skills and balance the generalist-specialist scale, former Dean John Rau of Indiana University's School of Business has this advice (Kiechel, 1994):

> *[Focus] along each of three dimensions. On what [is called] traditional content: the classic choices are functions like marketing or finance, but because more companies are thinking of their businesses as processes, perhaps some focus on that—distribution, say, or customer acquisition. Then overlay a concentration on a particular industry or sector—publishing for instance, or health care. Finally, you will of course need process skills—team leadership, team membership, the ability to communicate.*

Creating Visibility

Of course, one way to create visibility on the job is to perform effectively. People who do a good job get noticed. Unfortunately, performance evaluations and recommendations for promotion may involve a substantial degree of subjectivity. To make yourself stand out, a major strategy for career advancement is creating organizational visibility (Robbins, 1994).

organizational visibility *A strategy for career advancement that involves the highlighting of a person's abilities, talents, and contributions for those people in the organization who influence promotions and advancements.*

Organizational visibility is the spotlighting and highlighting of a person's abilities, talents, and contributions for those people in the organization who influence promotion and advancement. In addition to the subjective nature of evaluation, many individuals perform jobs that have low visibility—they work in remote locations or have limited contact outside a department. For your talent to be recognized and rewarded, you must be observed. Not all employees are as fortunate in this regard as Patricia Bush. Polaroid, the subject of this chapter's Valuing Diversity feature, has supported Bush by giving her jobs with visibility. Most people must seek visibility on their own.

Documenting Contributions

http://www.battelle.org

http://www.bt.novations.com

telecommuting *The partial or total substitution of telecommunications technology (such as computers, mobile phones, fax machines, and the Internet) for the trip to and from the primary workplace. Simply put, it's moving the work to the workers, instead of the workers to work.*

Making others—your immediate supervisor and upper-level managers—aware of your accomplishments is often necessary. Therefore, an approach to gaining visibility is to document contributions. One method is to follow the example of a technician at the Battelle Memorial Institute who told Gene Dalton of the Novations Group that "he made sure he could give anyone who asked, a two-minute summary of what he did, why it mattered, and what he accomplished." Another approach is to identify accomplishments through progress reports to the boss.

Documentation is especially important for telecommuters. According to the *Smart Valley Telecommuting Guide* (http://www.svi.org/PROJECTS/TCOMMUTE/TCGUIDE/HTMLVERS/tcg1.html#intro):

> **Telecommuting** *is the partial or total substitution of telecommunications technology for the trip to and from the primary workplace along with the associated changes in policy,*

VALUING DIVERSITY
Polaroid Supports Careers

Patricia Bush is the kind of employee every company wants. She's hardworking, creative, and gets things done. An African-American project manager at Polaroid Corporation, Bush joined the Cambridge, Massachusetts, employer after college in 1979 and has moved steadily up through production, marketing, and sales. Polaroid has supported Bush and other ethnically diverse and female professionals by giving them jobs with high visibility and clout. What is more, top management gives free reign to an advocacy group of senior African-American managers that Bush helps run.

Polaroid is in the forefront of companies taking a long-term view on diversity. Unlike past efforts, Polaroid realizes that just starting a mentoring program or putting a woman on the board of directors is not enough. Rather, the company has created a host of programs to attract, develop, and retain an ethnically diverse workforce.

For example, Polaroid is building ties with ethnically diverse students as early as high school. Also, Polaroid is investing in employee organizations that monitor corporate policies on diversity and work with the community. Managers at Polaroid, as part of their performance reviews, are held accountable for developing career plans for employees. These managers are also held accountable for meeting diversity goals. Finally, Polaroid is committed to promoting ethnically diverse employees and women to decision-making positions, not so-called soft positions or staff jobs such as human resources.

http://www.polaroid.com

Source: Galen, Michele, and Ann Palmer, "Diversity: Beyond the Numbers Game," *Business Week*, August 14, 1995, pp. 60–61.

> *organization, management, and work structure. Simply put, it's moving the work to the workers, instead of the workers to work. Computers, cellular phones, fax, and advanced communications links such as ISDN and dial-up access have removed the physical barriers that once required workers to be in their offices.*

Telecommuters must often access their company's computer system through the Internet. One annoyance of this is the storage of "cookies" on their hard drives from the Web sites they visit. Cookies are the subject of this chapter's Managing Technology feature.

Volunteering for Visibility

Another approach to obtaining visibility is to volunteer for projects, task forces, and other high-profile assignments (Schlee, 1992). These assignments not only highlight talents and abilities, but also provide young executives with developmental opportunities. To reach general management responsibilities, individuals should, preferably, spend time in two of the major functions of an organization. Getting that range of experience can be accelerated through volunteering (Fiant, 1992). According to Mary Herbert, vice president and director of quality for the international operations at Motorola, "You have to go to management and say here's what I can do; here's why; let me try it" (Fischer, 1992).

http://www.motorola.com

Not every task force, project, or extra task should be targeted for volunteering. Rather, for career spotlighting, the decision to volunteer should come after you consider the following points:

- What new experience or knowledge can be gained?
- What will be the impact on your immediate boss and the boss's success?
- What will be the impact on the organization?
- What will be the exposure to multilevel management?

MANAGING TECHNOLOGY
Cookies

Most Web sites track their visitors by using cookies, small text files that are placed on your computer's hard disk so that a site will recognize your browser the next time you visit the site. Cookies contain information about you and your preferences, but only the information that you provide, or the choices you make while visiting a Web site. Cookies have advantages and disadvantages.

Advantages of Cookies. On sites with registration forms, cookies can store your responses so that you don't have to fill out the forms every time you visit. They are part of the technology that allows you to have a virtual shopping cart when shopping online and to use "express checkout" services.

Disadvantages of Cookies. Cookies can be used to collect information about you without your knowledge. They can track where you go on a site, and how much time you spend there. This information, however unwittingly supplied, may be used to target you with online advertising.

You can configure your browser so that it will not accept cookies at all, accept only some, or warn you every time a cookie is going to be sent. Visit Cookie Central to find out more about cookies and to edit your cookies in the latest browsers.

http://www.cookiecentral.com

Sponsorship

sponsor *An individual in the organization who will promote a person's talents and look out for his or her organizational welfare.*

Yet another approach for gaining visibility is to find a **sponsor**—a person who will actively promote a subordinate's talents and look out for his or her organizational welfare. A sponsor is someone in the organization who is at least one position higher than the immediate boss, is successful, and who has a promising future.

Developing Mentor Relationships

mentor *A senior employee who acts as guide, teacher, counselor, and coach for a less-experienced person in the organization.*

Another key strategy for career advancement is to find a mentor. Whereas a sponsor actively promotes the abilities of and seeks opportunities for a protégé, a **mentor** is a senior employee who acts as a guide, teacher, counselor, and coach. A mentor takes a less-experienced person under his or her wing and helps that person navigate the organization. A mentor should be someone who is successful and well thought of in the organization (Kram, 1985).

For individuals working in companies without formal mentoring programs, Joyce Lain Kennedy (1999) offers the following advice:

- *At your own company, find a leader to learn from. Ask a supervisor if you can assist or 'shadow' one with interesting projects. Or choose a hero and directly communicate your appreciation of that individual's work and talents; start informally and, if you're receiving the help you need, propose a regular mentorship, perhaps an interactive meeting at lunchtime every two weeks to take stock of your progress.*
- *At your own company and in your professional community, discover multiple mentors, each of whom excels in a different area where you need growth hormones. Florence Stone identifies examples: market knowledge, researching capability, writing skills, organizational talent and technical knowledge.*
- *Internet savvy? Look online for mentors in your field.*
- *Ask at your college alumni office, women's group or minority organization. The right headhunter can be a treasure.*

Mentor Programs

http://www.pacbell.com

http://www.hp.com

http://www.telementor.org

Mentoring is seen as so critical for success that many large organizations—like Pacific Bell, for example—have implemented formal mentoring programs. In this situation, a senior executive is formally appointed as a mentor to a few junior managers (Shea, 1994). Students will be future employees, and many companies know that they've got to recruit early and create leadership opportunities. Thus, in Hewlett-Packard's Telementor Program, HP employees volunteer as email mentors to motivate students to excel in math and science and help students improve their communication and problem-solving skills. The International Telementor Center (ITC) is built upon the success of HP's program.

> *Telementoring is an electronic version of the proven practice of mentoring, in which an older, more experienced person shares his or her experience and expertise with a younger 'protégé' in a way that helps the protégé achieve a goal or gain entry into the mentor's world. In telementoring, this exchange of information and inspiration takes place in the electronic world of e-mail and secured online discussion forums (ITC, http://www.telementor.org/itc/Overview/Telementoring/telementoring.html).*

Several key statistics have been published on the importance of mentoring:

- Over 60% of surveyed college and graduate students list mentoring as a criteria for selecting an employer after graduation (Source: MMHA).
- 77% of companies report that mentoring programs were effective in increased retention (Source: Center for Creative Leadership).
- A survey of CEOs states that one of the top-three key factors in their career was mentoring (Source: Account Temps Survey of Fortune 500).
- On 11 job essential skills, protégés increased skills by an average of 61% through a successful mentor program (Source: MMHA).
- Gains were reported in 9 of 11 generic career and life effectiveness skills after 13 months (Source: MMHA).
- 75% of overall executives said mentoring played a key role in their career (Source: ASTD).

Mentors for Women and Men

http://www.autodesk.com

http://www.women-mentors.com

The conventional model of mentoring that was created by and for men has not been as successful for women. First, there are few female senior executives, making it difficult to find a woman mentor. Second, when acting as mentors for women, men normally provide advice and information but not the emotional support needed. "It almost killed me," notes CFO Carol Bartz of Autodesk, in recalling her first mentoring experience while at Digital Equipment. Bartz tried to mimic the way she was *supposed* to act according to her male mentor, but the relationship did not work for Bartz. Without the proper support, the pressure got so bad, she said, that one day she thought she was having a heart attack (Gruner, 1994).

One solution has been to move to a dual-mentor relationship in which women identify both a male and female mentor. Rather than receiving only one type of support, the dual mentor relationship provides a balance—advice, information, and emotional support (Siegel, 1992).

Developing Networks

networking
A strategy for career advancement that involves building long-term, two-way interaction based on shared ideas, personal relationships, and common experiences.

Some managers still view networking as a short-term activity leading to a specific goal like a new job or a career change. Today, however, **networking** is viewed as a long-term, two-way interaction, based on shared ideas, personal relationships, and common experiences. Successful networking for the twenty-first century means assembling a focused, highly select group of advisers, who can help assess situations, refine strategies, make decisions, and define management style.

In today's business climate, downsizing and flattened corporate hierarchies have resulted in managers with significantly less career security. At the same time, managers often face intense pressure to make decisions and perform successfully. A network can help managers perform better in their current assignments and manage their careers more successfully.

According to Andrew Olson (1994), when developing the network, keep these qualities in mind:

- *Diversity*. Include people from a variety of industries and functions. Seek balance in ethnicity and gender.

- *Candor.* Require candor. These individuals do not necessarily have to be close friends, but they should be candid and willing to challenge assumptions.
- *Clout.* Include some individuals who might hold positions one or two levels above your own.
- *Confidentiality.* Keep the career network separate from other internal organizational relationships, to ensure confidentiality and provide a broader perspective.

Understanding Power and Politics

organizational politics *The unwritten rules of work life and informal methods of gaining power and advantage.*

In an ideal world, everybody would receive raises, promotions, and a fair share of desirable and undesirable assignments—based on merit. But in real life, many of these decisions are decided by **organizational politics**—the unwritten rules of work life and informal methods of gaining power or advantage (Siegel, 1992). The politics of any organization result from the interaction between those in positions of influence and those seeking influence. These interactions are evidenced by power being acquired, transferred, and exercised on others.

The term *politics* offends many people—organizational veterans and novices alike—because it connotes deceit and deception. But engaging in politics is simply a matter of seeking an advantage. As noted management consultant and author Tom Peters says, "If you want to escape organizational politics—forget it. Politics is life. Politics involves investing in a relationship—investing time, energy, and emotions" (Peters, 1992). Although this sentiment has probably always been true, in today's fiercely competitive corporate environment, rife with justifiable insecurity and radically shifting power bases, it is even more important. Now a person will need every bit of political moxie that he or she can master. According to Dorry Hollander in *Managerial Reality* (1995), "the newly restructured organizations of the 1990s are competitive playing fields without referees, cluttered with confusing ambiguities, and competing factions. . . . It's hard for most of us to know what's expected anymore. All this calls for greater ability to read between the lines. . . . If you don't activate your political horse sense, you might as well park your career in a time capsule."

Identifying the Power Structure

Knowing that politics are a way of life, the first strategy is to identify the power structure in the organization. Doing so means examining both the formal organizational structure and the workings of the informal organization. In this process you determine the following:

- Who are the people on whom the leaders of the organizations rely?
- What skills and knowledge do these people provide?
- Are you able to supply the same skills and knowledge?
- Could these people help you as sponsors or mentors?

Once you identify the key people, the next step is to acquire power.

Acquiring Power

From a career management viewpoint, people obtain power—the ability to influence—in four ways:

- *Developing expertise in areas critical to the company.* Knowledge and reputation in a specific area can provide the opportunity to participate in projects and lend advice. In today's marketplace expertise is valued in quality control, understanding consumer preferences, making teams successful, and working with ailing organizations to cure problems (Plunkett, 1995).

- *Developing a network of contacts.* As previously discussed, by developing a network, you can acquire information, you can gather support for new ideas, and you can make expertise for solving problems available. Being a lone wolf will not get you ahead in organizational politics.
- *Acquiring line responsibility.* The position a person holds in an organization automatically carries certain power. But line managers—those whose work is tied directly to the primary purpose of the organization—have more power than staff groups. Nicole Williams, executive vice president of worldwide operations of SPSS, a $34 million software manufacturer in Chicago, claims that moving from a staff to a line position solidified her career. "It provided exposure and responsibility" (Hellwig, 1992).
- *Solving others' problems.* Career advancement is associated with positive support from as many areas as possible. A good way to acquire power and support is to help someone else by solving his or her problems. Whether the person is a colleague, someone in another department, or a superior, the result is the same—positive reviews and endorsements (Schlee, 1992).

http://www.spss.com

Working with the Boss

A major strategy in career management involves learning to work with the boss. A career can be extinguished by not developing a positive alliance with a superior (Jensen, 1992).

Understanding the Boss

To work with the boss, you must spend time determining and understanding your boss's priorities, objectives, and negative "hot buttons." The valued subordinate is one who understands that his or her job is to relieve the boss's pressure, not add to it.

Making the Boss Successful

The second element of working with the boss is to add to his or her success. After identifying the boss's objectives and priorities, you should develop a set of subobjectives that support the accomplishment of these major objectives. Doing so will keep the objectives aligned, which is not only a good strategy for career advancement, but sound management.

Supporting Versus Bucking the Boss

No boss-subordinate relationship is ideal. An expectation in any working relationship is that there will not always be agreement, operations won't always run smoothly, and problems will inevitably surface. In such situations, the subordinate can take several approaches:

- *Provide solutions rather than register complaints.* Identifying a problem is only the first step. The people who advance are those who develop an array of alternative solutions to problems.
- *Practice constructive disagreement rather than rebellion.* This is disagreement focused on a problem—not on a person—with the aim of identifying weak-

nesses and solutions. Once the discussion is over—win done. In contrast, rebellion says "my way only." Rebellio disagreement doesn't end with the discussion—it will cor with other people.

- *Support the decision.* Once the boss makes a decision, the subordina it out with the intention of making it work. Ignoring the decision or s it by not implementing it effectively will not endear the subordinate to the manager. In situations in which the decision may counter the organization's goals or be ethically questionable, the subordinate may need to take the issue to someone other than the boss. In such a situation, having a mentor can be valuable.

Managing Stress

Another cornerstone of career management is stress management. A rapid pace, conflicting deadlines, and multiple events characterize a manager's job. In addition, all managers have responsibility for planning, organizing, and controlling the actions of their departments; and the amount of this responsibility increases as the manager moves up in an organization. Given these realities, stress is obviously a part of the job.

Nature of Stress

stress
The physiological and psychological reaction of the body as a result of demands made on it.

Stress is the physiological and psychological reaction of the body as a result of demands made on it (Beehr and Bhagat, 1985). The demands may be emotional (role conflict, fear of unemployment, sexual harassment) or environmental (noise, a lack of privacy, or improper ventilation).

People experiencing stress perceive, through their body's reactions, that the stressful situation is demanding beyond their ability to cope. People experience stress when they aren't finished with a project and the deadline looms, or when they are trying to solve a customer's problem but cannot reach a key decision maker.

Positive and Negative Stress

Although stress is always discussed in a negative context, not all stress is negative. Moderate stress is a normal part of a manager's work. A deadline—determined three months earlier—to submit the year's budget forecast for approval causes stress as the date approaches. As shown in Figure 21.10, a moderate amount of stress has a positive effect on performance, as it provides motivation.

Extreme levels of stress, on the other hand, are negative and contribute to performance decline. As shown in Figure 21.10, if the periods of high stress are extended over a long period of time the result can be **burnout**—a state of emotional exhaustion as a result of overexposure to stress (Freudenberger, 1980).

burnout
A state of emotional exhaustion as a result of overexposure to stress.

The many possible causes of negative stress for managers are summarized in Figure 21.11. For career managers the most critical include the following:

- Incongruence of values between the manager and the company
- Downsizing or layoffs that threaten security or long-range plans
- Limited opportunities for advancement
- Role ambiguity
- Incompatibility with the immediate supervisor's leadership style

FIGURE 21.10 *Manager's stress level and performance*

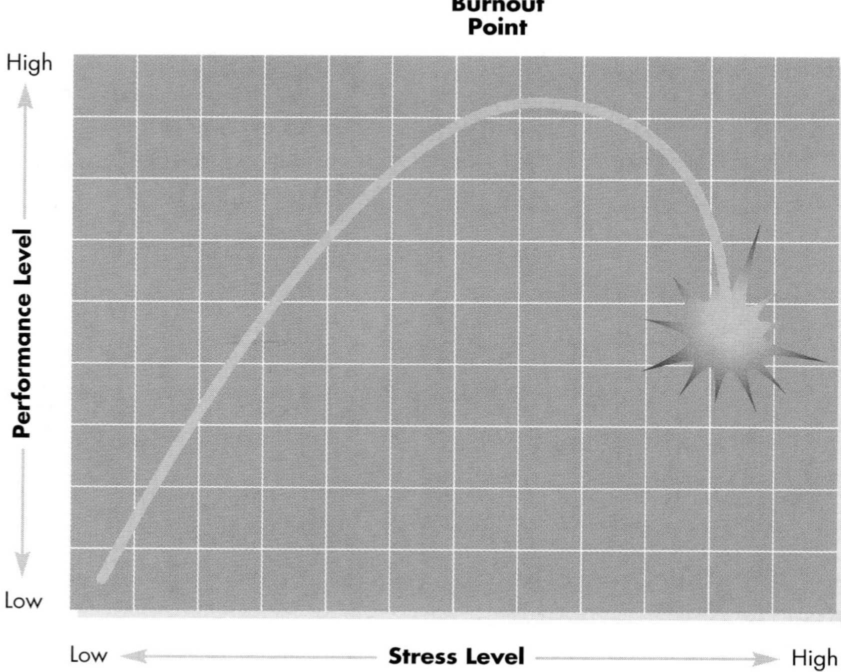

FIGURE 21.11 *Causes of negative stress for managers*

- Downsizing or other threats to security
- Limited opportunities for advancement
- Role ambiguity
- Interpersonal conflict
- Limited decision-making responsibility
- Incompatibility with immediate supervisor's leadership style
- Incongruence of values between the manager and the company
- Boredom or underutilization
- Take-home work and erratic work schedule
- Constant change
- Task or work overload
- Unrealistic deadlines
- Sexual harassment
- Physical environment: noise, lighting, privacy, climate

In addition, George Gendron (1994) reports that in today's organization one of the major causes of stress for managers is the growing complexity of business. There really is no simple business anymore. Thanks to technological change, the globalization of markets, and the rise of government regulation, even the smallest businesses have become enormously complicated. As complexity increases, so have the time and energy required to manage a company's internal functions.

This situation, in turn, has enormous consequences for managers. They are forced to focus more narrowly on their specific parts of the business process. As a result, "they feel isolated, insecure, and unsure—or [they may even question] whether they are contributing to the well-being of the business as a whole. Increased stress is the result" (Gendron, 1994).

Although the manager may be stressed by these situations, it is important to remember that he or she may in turn be the source of stress for others by causing these situations. When employees develop the following perceptions, managers are the source of stress:

- Uncertainty about the specific responsibilities of the job
- Inability to make decisions or have decisions made when needed
- Unrealistic deadlines
- Lack of control over the things that affect the person in the work environment
- Work overload

The last point, work overload, is the primary cause of employee stress in the work setting. In a survey conducted by Harris Research, more than half of the 5,300 respondents claim they have too few staff or their level of activity and responsibility has increased. In commenting on the situation, Catherine Romano (1995) states, "corporate anorexia resulting from management downsizing and restructuring seems to be producing significant numbers of overworked, and overstressed employees." The situation is such that one-third of the respondents would not choose the same career again if they had the chance. Management has caused this situation and must address it if stress is to be managed.

Symptoms of Stress

What are the signs that might indicate an excessive stress level? Common symptoms include anxiety, increased blood pressure, headache, backache, fatigue, insomnia, depression, irritability, muscular tightness, and inattention. What these signs don't indicate is the degree of wear and tear on the individual—emotionally and physically. The hidden effects can cost the organization through loss of productivity, absenteeism, and health-care expenses. Excessive stress can also cost the individual his or her health and future.

Three types of strategies available for managing stress relate to the manager's own stress, that of employees, or organization-wide stress management programs. A manager's own strategy involves developing a balanced approach to life that includes plenty of rest, good eating habits, exercise, and anticipating personal stressors. Research on stress points to the importance of relaxation, nutrition, and regular exercise as keys to stress management.

Allied Signal CFO Larry Bossidy and international public relations executive Pam Alexander score well in each category. Alexander, whose firm serves such

It is important for managers to manage stress through relaxation, good nutrition, and regular exercise.

high-tech companies as CompuServe, Hewlett Packard, and Philips Electronics, sleeps six hours; starts the day with a three- or four-mile jog; and watches her diet closely. In addition, she recently weaned herself off caffeine, swallows generous amounts of vitamin C, and goes easy on alcohol. Likewise, Bossidy rises at 5 A.M. for 45 minutes of using the treadmill and doing sit-ups and push-ups. Despite a twelve-hour workday, he maintains a regimen of six hours of sleep around a low-calorie, high-protein diet (Smith, 1994).

The other key to combating stress is to identify personal stressors. Not all people react the same way to a situation. Knowing what causes stress allows a person to develop preventive maintenance. A manager must also learn to delegate, to disagree constructively with the boss, and to try consciously to limit the hours of work (Maturi, 1992). Managers help themselves by learning to say no to workloads that are unacceptable and unrealistic.

Managers have an obligation to monitor employees and the work environment for signs of stress. A manager can minimize employees' stress by providing clear and current job descriptions and expectations, initiating timely and relevant feedback, facilitating employees' control over their own jobs, recognizing employee contributions, and encouraging work and personal support groups (Maturi, 1992).

http://www.cdc.com

http://www.jnj.com

Many companies have chosen to institute formalized stress management programs. Control Data's "Stay Well" program uses a combination of exercise, smoking cessation, hypertension screening and control, and nutrition counseling. Johnson & Johnson's "Live for Life" program emphasizes exercise, relaxation, and nutrition. Other organizations have provided the following to help manage employees' stress:

- Facilities for physical exercise, ranging from jogging tracks to full gyms with instructors and organized classes
- Quiet rooms for meditating and reading
- On-site and off-site clinical psychologists or counselors
- Courses focusing on stress reduction and coping techniques (Maturi, 1992)

ORGANIZATIONAL DILEMMAS

Discuss the organizational dilemmas experienced when personal and organizational interests are in conflict

Within career planning and management, an individual is often confronted with organizational dilemmas. The four dilemmas involve value conflicts, loyalty demands, decisions on advancement, and concerns for independence.

Conflicts Between Personal and Organizational Values

To have a successful career, a person's value system needs to fit that of the organization. Despite socialization, there are times when a person's values do come in conflict with the organization's, resulting in dissatisfaction (Davita, April 1992).

To minimize this possibility, managers need to do periodic self-analyses to determine their personal values and to select an organization that ensures a match. In addition, they should constantly analyze the demands of the organization against their values to monitor any conflict. But even when individuals are vigilant, the organization may evolve and its values may change. Or individuals may not have completely analyzed the value system and a conflict can occur (Davita, March 1992). For example, a job that initially required minimal travel now requires the manager to be out of town for two weeks each month. This change creates a conflict in the manager's values of home and family. Of course, each individual will resolve this situation differently. Some will accept the development, thriving on the travel or hoping that the situation will change again shortly; others may switch jobs, feeling that the new demands are unacceptable.

In other instances, when the values conflict touches on ethical or illegal practices, managers may opt to inform their bosses, the media, or government agencies. These managers, as in this chapter's Ethical Management feature, are referred to as **whistle-blowers** (Straub and Attner, 1994). Because circumstances do change, managers must be ready to consult their own values—and goals—in developing a response to those changes.

whistle-blower
Individuals who take action to inform their bosses, the media, or government agencies about unethical or illegal practices within their organization.

http://www.whistleblower.org

Loyalty Demands

A dilemma intimately related to a person's value system is the question of loyalty. Often, early in a career, loyalty demands are made on a person by the immediate supervisor, who may convey messages such as, "Don't make me look bad, protect me," or "Trust me, tell me about. . . ."

Both of these messages are requests for loyalty. In both cases the subordinate faces a dilemma. The first loyalty demand—don't make me look bad, protect me—may not seem so unusual. Employees should naturally try to make the boss look good by doing excellent work. Likewise, protecting the boss by keeping him or her informed—no surprises—is a sound practice. But these demands go beyond that; they may involve covering up for weak performance or holding back information that would place a superior in a bad light. In such situations the subordinate needs to acknowledge what is happening and not be drawn into that behavior. A demand for loyalty—trust me, tell me about . . .—potentially places the subordinate in the position of being an informant on someone or of violating a confidence. The superior has gained information but at the same time has caused the subordinate to compromise his or her values. Such a demand for loyalty should be recognized for what it is and avoided.

ETHICAL MANAGEMENT
A Question of Values

Values are a basis for ethical behavior. This situation is true for both individuals and organizations. Noted management consultants and writers Tom Peters and Robert Waterman assert, "Every company takes the process of value shopping seriously . . . you either buy into the company's values or you get out."

Michael Lissack did not buy in; instead he blew the whistle. As one of Smith Barney's most gifted bankers in its public finance department, Lissack made millions for the firm and millions for himself, advising municipalities on bond issues and structuring bond deals. In the process, Lissack found himself facing a dilemma. He noted, and asserted, that Smith Barney's underwriters routinely overpriced U.S. Treasury securities that they sold to issuers for bond refinancings. Smith Barney denied the practice. In 1995, Lissack filed a qui tam lawsuit brought under the False Claims Act, which permits individuals with knowledge of fraud against the government to file suit on its behalf.

For his efforts Lissack was unceremoniously fired. Since coming forward with his claims, he has suffered through a divorce, a severe depression, and an attempted suicide. In April 2000, Salomon Smith Barney Inc. agreed to pay $38 million to the federal government to settle charges that they defrauded the federal government by overpricing securities sold in connection with certain municipal bond transactions.

1. Do you believe an employee should blow the whistle on his or her employer? Why or why not?
2. Why does corporate America treat its whistle-blowers badly?
3. Why does the notion persist that it is disloyal and irresponsible to criticize one's employer, even if the company has done wrong?

http://www.tompeters.com

http://www.salomonsmithbarney.com

Sources: Fortune. "The Whistle Blower," August 7, 1995, p. 118; Ettorre, Barbara. "Whistle Blowers: Who's the Real Bad Guy?" *Management Review* (May 1994), pp. 18–23.

Advancement Decisions

Another set of dilemmas is met in regard to advancement. They fall into two categories: (1) whether to take a position when it is offered and (2) what to do when advancement does not occur.

Taking a new job offer may be problematic if it requires a person to move, uprooting a family or relocating to an undesirable location. The situation may be complicated as well by a spouse's career. The offer may come at a time when the manager believes that he or she is not really ready. In this case the manager should talk to his or her mentor to get an objective appraisal of current skills and competence in regard to the new job. Having planned a career from the start, the manager is probably not surprised by the offer; he or she should be prepared for the possibility. Still, the manager needs to make the decision and that decision can come only after a thorough discussion with his or her spouse and a complete analysis of the costs and benefits—both professionally and personally—of the alternatives.

A situation in which advancement does not occur may simply mean that the organization's timetable for advancement does not match the manager's timetable—three years between promotions. Nonadvancement may also mean that the organization believes the person is not promotable. In either case the manager is faced with a dilemma—stay and possibly lose time if a promotion is not forthcoming or leave and lose security and familiarity. Again, the best approach is a complete analysis of the costs and benefits. The manager should give consideration to his or her stage in career development. How much does he or she have invested in the organization? What are the chances of moving to another organization with immediate opportunity?

Independence and Sponsorship

A final dilemma faced by individuals is striking the balance between the need for independence and the advantages of sponsorship. The support of a sponsor sometimes carries a negative price tag; the person sponsored gives up a degree of independence to be on the team. Worse, if a sponsor is fired, the person who was sponsored may suffer similar consequences (Dubrin, 1990). A possible solution to the dilemma is to build relationships with many individuals and groups in the organization.

CHAPTER SUMMARY

1 **Discuss the nature of careers.** A career comprises the series of jobs a person holds over a lifetime and the person's attitude toward involvement in these job experiences. It includes a long-term perspective, a sequence of positions, and a psychological involvement.

2 **Describe what is meant by having a career perspective.** A career perspective is a proactive strategy that takes a global view of career progress or growth over time as it develops. It requires a person to adopt a broad vision that includes all the elements involved in a successful career—objectives, timetables, career stages, skills improvement, organizational politics, power, stress, and values.

3 **Describe the changes that have occurred in the career environment.** A person can no longer be guaranteed a career with one organization. Gone are the days of lifetime employment and paternalism. Instead, the individual can expect to have many jobs and careers in a lifetime. The person must be self-reliant, constantly update and upgrade skills, seek opportunity rather than security, and chart contributions.

4 **Identify and describe the four stages of career development.** A person's career normally evolves through four stages: exploration and trial, establishment and advancement, mid-career, and late career.

- *Exploration and trial.* This first stage usually occurs between the ages of 15 and 25. It begins with the decision to become serious about employment; this stage is a learning process.
- *Establishment and advancement.* In this stage, normally between ages 25 and 35, people are involved in their first real job. This is the stage when most people take stock and begin to develop a career strategy.
- *Mid-career.* The mid-career stage most often occurs between the ages of 35 and 50. There are three possible directions a career may take at this point: growth, leveling, or decline.
- *Late career.* The late career stage—between the ages of 50 and retirement—is marked by a peak prestige for those who experienced growth in the prior stage. These people become trainers for the next generation of managers. In addition, plans are made to slow down, develop outside interests, and prepare for retirement.

5 **Identify and discuss the five steps for career planning.** Career planning involves five steps: self-assessment, exploring opportunities and options, establishing objectives, developing a plan of action, and executing and evaluating the plan.

- *Self-assessment.* Performing a realistic self-assessment involves gathering and analyzing data on your values, interests, skills, abilities, experiences, and likes and dislikes. This step is not only critical for an aspiring manager but should be done on a continuous basis to avoid obsolescence.
- *Exploring opportunities and options.* This step requires examining the opportunities that exist in the industry and a company.
- *Establishing objectives.* Once the opportunities are identified, the career planner has to make short- and long-term decisions. The first decision involves selecting an industry. The next major decision is to choose between being a specialist or generalist. Once that decision is made other decisions involve identifying needed skills, resources, assignments, training, and experiences that will help accomplish the objectives.
- *Developing a plan of action.* This step provides the detailed map to accomplish the objectives. The plan should include establishing specific timetables for training, reaching a new

job level, and gaining new exposure in a company. This stage also identifies potential barriers and the resources to work around the barriers.

- *Executing and evaluating the plan.* Once the plan is in place, it must be put into action. This is a matter of taking charge of your career, rather than waiting for things to happen. The second part of this action is to follow-up and evaluate progress. You may need to adjust the plan as the environment changes and there is individual growth, career progress, and new assignments.

6 **Discuss how a manager can understand his or her organization and why it is important to do so.** All organizations are unique. Each develops its own methods, values, rewards; each makes clear what it accepts and does not tolerate. Before a person can develop strategies for career growth, he or she must know the company—what abilities it values, what actions it rewards, how it compensates its achievers; he or she must both accept the organization and be accepted by it.

The process by which this mutual acceptance is accomplished is known as organizational socialization. In this process new members of an organization gain exposure to its values, norms, policies, and procedures. At the same time, they discover who wields power, what restrictions there are on behavior, and how to succeed and survive. Eventually, through this process an employee either becomes an accepted and conforming member of the organization or leaves the organization.

7 **Identify and describe the abilities and actions that organizations value in managers.** The abilities organizations value in managers include communication, interpersonal, conceptual, and decision skills; competence; and flexibility. Organizations also value individuals who make contributions, take risks, work hard, and are team players.

8 **Discuss the strategies associated with career advancement.** To advance in an organization an individual must develop and implement strategies that focus on committing to lifelong learning, creating visibility, developing mentor relationships, developing networks, understanding power and politics, working with the boss, and managing stress.

- Committing to lifelong learning is the key to avoiding obsolescence. Managers must reengineer themselves through constant preparation, learning new technology, and packaging new skills.
- Creating organizational visibility involves the spotlighting and highlighting of a person's abilities, talents, and contributions for those in the organization who influence promotion and advancement. Organizational visibility can be obtained by documenting contributions, volunteering, and finding a sponsor.
- By developing a mentor relationship a person has available a senior employee who acts as a guide, teacher, counselor, and coach. The mentor helps the person navigate the organization.
- Developing a network involves assembling a focused, highly select group of advisers. These advisers help assess situations, refine strategies, make decisions, and refine management style.
- Understanding power and politics is necessary for career success. Organizational politics are the unwritten rules of work life and informal methods of gaining power and influence. Individuals need to not only understand politics but also become adept at it. The first strategy is to identify the power structure; the next is to acquire power.
- Working with the boss is a major strategy in career management. Three elements of the strategy involve understanding the boss, making the boss successful, and supporting the boss.
- Managing stress is another cornerstone of career management. Stress, the physiological and psychological reaction of the body as a result of demands made on it, is a part of all managers' jobs. Managers must learn the causes and symptoms of stress as well as strategies for managing it.

9 **Discuss the organizational dilemmas experienced when personal and organizational interests are in conflict.** There are four organizational dilemmas experienced when personal and organizational interests are in conflict. The four dilemmas involve value conflicts, loyalty demands, decisions on advancement, and concerns for independence.

- *Conflicts between personal and organizational values.* There are times when a person's values come in conflict with the organization, resulting in dissatisfaction. When this situation occurs, some will accept the development hoping the situation will change shortly; others may switch jobs, feeling that the new demands are unacceptable. In other instances in which the values conflict touches on ethics or illegality, managers may opt to become whistle-blowers and inform their bosses, the media, or government agencies.
- *Loyalty demands.* Often loyalty demands are made on a person by the immediate supervisor. Requests for loyalty take the form of "Don't make me look bad, protect me" or "Trust me; tell me about. . . ." Each creates a dilemma for the manager.
- *Advancement decisions.* These dilemmas fall into two categories: (1) whether to take a position when it is offered and (2) what to do when advancement does not occur.
- *Independence and sponsorship.* Many individuals face a dilemma caused by trying to strike a balance between the need for independence and the advantages of sponsorship.

REVIEW QUESTIONS

1. What is the difference between a job and a career?
2. What is meant by the statement "A manager should have a career perspective"?
3. What changes have occurred in the career environment? How do the changes affect career planning and management?
4. What are the four stages of career development?
5. What are the five steps involved in career planning?
6. Why is it important for a manager to understand his or her organization?
7. What abilities do organizations typically value in managers seeking advancement?
8. What is the importance of organizational visibility? How can it be achieved?
9. How does a decision on advancement present an organizational dilemma?

DISCUSSION QUESTIONS FOR CRITICAL THINKING

1. What satisfaction might come from having a career rather than a job?
2. Although you are responsible for your career, what obligation does the organization have for a plateaued employee whose skills have become obsolescent?
3. What career planning steps have you taken? What additional steps will you take based on educational progress or career progress?
4. Which two of the strategies suggested for career advancement are the most valuable to you? Why?

INTERNET EXERCISES

Check the text Web site at http://plunkett.swcollege.com for updated links to the Internet Exercises.

1. *Mentor, in Greek mythology, was the friend of Odysseus to whom Odysseus entrusted the care of his son Telemachus when he went off to fight in the Trojan wars. Telemachus eventually leaves the wise Mentor to go in search of his father, but the Mentor persona and role continue as Athena appears in the wise old man's guise to both Odysseus and Telemachus.*

   How would you define mentoring? What kinds of challenges will you face in taking on the role of guide, friend, listener, cheerleader, confidant, coach, and tutor for your mentee employee?
   http://www.mentoringworks.org/about_mentoring

2. During the Industrial Revolution, people moved to the cities to be near their work. This led to the centralization of work and the growth of large organizations and cities. Before the Industrial Revolution, crafts people worked from their homes or cottages and had a certain control over their working hours. Today we could be witnessing the opposite, as telecommuters begin to operate from their homes. Telecommuters may choose to live away from the cities, with all their noise, pollution, and traffic. They work on their computers from their homes or electronic cottages and send the work to their employers by modem.

   How might telecommuting transform your management career? What advantages do you see in telecommuting for the employee and the manager?

   How Managers Can Successfully Supervise Telecommuters by Robert Moskowitz
   http://www.smartbiz.com/sbs/arts/mos52.htm

   Smart Valley Telecommuting Guide
   http://www.svi.org/PROJECTS/TCOMMUTE/TCGUIDE/HTMLVERS/tcg1.html

3. What is locus of control? What is its relationship to your career advancement? Assess your locus of control and report your score. What does your score mean?
   http://www.ncrel.org/sdrs/areas/issues/students/learning/lr2locus.htm

   http://www.queendom.com/tests/personality/lc.html

APPLICATION CASE

Career Growth Through Feedback

Managers at Stride Rite have a new tool to help in career development: a 360-degree feedback program. This approach calls for managers to be reviewed by a constellation of business contacts, including supervisors, peers, employees, customers, and even the employees in the mailroom.

At Stride Rite a human resources professional distributes performance evaluation questionnaires to the chosen respondents. The surveys are completed anonymously. Then composite feedback sheets are created from the respondents' answers by an experienced outside consultant. Any information that would suggest the source is removed to preserve anonymity.

Next, the manager receiving the 360-degree feedback is given the written composite evaluation to read; then the manager discusses it with his or her immediate supervisor. The manager is then scheduled for a session with either a human resource professional or an outside consultant to process the feedback or to facilitate follow-up group sessions with staff or supervisors.

In addition, at Stride Rite the manager is assisted in completing an individual development plan. The process requires the manager to select three problem areas that have surfaced in the review. Next, steps and timetables are designed to address the problem areas.

There are four kinds of data a manager may receive: feedback that is positive and expected, positive and unexpected, negative and expected, and negative and unexpected. Managers often find the last category hard to accept. For example, if the manager is unexpectedly told that he or she is a "bad listener" or "untrustworthy," his or her ego is severely jolted.

http://www.striderite.com

Questions

1. As it relates to career development, what is the value of the 360-degree feedback program? Explain your answer.
2. Should a 360-degree feedback program be used to determine evaluations, pay, or promotions? Why or why not?
3. What specific dangers could be involved with the 360-degree feedback program?
4. Would you recommend that a company adopt the program? Why or why not?

Sources: Snyder, Adam. "Executive Coaching: The New Solution," *Management Review* (March 1995), pp. 29–32; O'Reilly, Brian. "360 Feedback Can Change Your Life," *Fortune*, October 17, 1994, pp. 93–100.

VIDEO CASE

Career Management: LaBelle Management

In 1948, Norm LaBelle opened his first restaurant in the small town of Mt. Pleasant, Michigan. Since then, his two sons, Bart and Doug LaBelle, have grown the business into a very successful enterprise known as LaBelle Management. LaBelle Management operates over thirty restaurants and hotels throughout the Midwest, including Bennigans, Big Boy, Ponderosa, and Italian Oven restaurants, and Comfort Inn and Fairfield Inn motels.

A distinctive attribute of LaBelle is its career management system. A persistent challenge in the hospitality management industry is finding and retaining qualified employees. To meet this challenge, LaBelle has put into place a comprehensive career management system that has reduced turnover and has made LaBelle an attractive employer. LaBelle's career management system is based on two objectives:

- Employee retention
- Helping employees achieve their personal goals

To increase employee retention, the company has adopted a number of specific programs. For example, the company has implemented a "critical entry period" program that is directed toward new hires. This program is designed to retain new employees, and to make sure that they receive the training and attention they need during their first few weeks on the job. (Historically, the company had lost about 45% of its new employees during their first 90 days.) For more experienced employees, the company has an expressed policy of promoting from within and rotates its personnel among its different concepts (i.e., casual-dining restaurants, fast-food restaurants, and motels) to avoid burnout and to provide employees a variety of experiences.

In terms of helping employees achieve their personal goals, the company is very focused on providing employees the tools they need to be successful. As evidence of this, the company has a formalized "tier management" program that allows an employee to enter management with a clear path to upper management provided that certain milestones are accomplished. The company also has an innovative "adopt a manager" program. Each management team in the company's thirty restaurants and hotels is responsible for selecting and training one aspiring manager per year. That way, the company has a cadre of thirty new potential upper-level managers available each year (that graduate from the program), which reduces the need to go outside the company to find managerial talent.

Over the years, LaBelle Management has developed a career management program that meets the needs of the company and its employees. Its career management program will continue to be an important factor in LaBelle's future growth.

http://www.labellemgt.com

For Discussion:

1. Are you impressed with LaBelle's career management program? If so, why?
2. Identify how LaBelle emphasizes the five steps for career planning in its career management practices. Provide at least one example from the video of how each of the five steps for career planning is emphasized in a positive manner.
2. Although not specifically discussed in the video, do you believe that delegation is an important part of LaBelle's career management program? Why or why not?

Management Ethics and Social Responsibility

KEY TERMS

business ethics
ethical dilemma
green products
morality
proactive approach
reactive approach
resistance approach
social audit
social responsibility

LEARNING OBJECTIVES

After studying this chapter, you should be able to

1. Describe the two broad categories of ethical theories
2. Explain what individuals need in order to act ethically
3. Describe the organizational influences on ethical conduct
4. Discuss three primary ways in which businesses can promote ethical conduct
5. Describe the relationship between law and ethics
6. Explain the concept of an ethical dilemma
7. Discuss the guidelines for acting ethically
8. Explain the three approaches by businesses to social responsibility
9. Explain the responsibilities businesses have to stakeholders
10. Describe government's role in promoting socially responsible conduct by businesses
11. Discuss the ways in which businesses can promote socially responsible conduct

MANAGEMENT IN ACTION

Ben & Jerry's: Social Responsibility

Ben & Jerry's Homemade, Inc. —a manufacturer of super premium ice cream, frozen yogurt, and sorbet —was founded in 1978 by childhood friends Ben Cohen and Jerry Greenfield. (Super premium ice cream has greater richness and density than other kinds of ice cream.) The company has grown from one ice cream parlor located in a renovated gas station in Burlington, Vermont, to sales of over $237 million in 1999.

Ben & Jerry's strives to integrate into its day-to-day business decisions a concern for the community and to seek ways to lead with its values. In 1985, Ben Cohen contributed a portion of his stock to begin the Ben & Jerry's Foundation, Inc., a charitable organization. These funds were used as an endowment. In addition, the company makes cash contributions equal to 7.5% of its pretax profits to philanthropy through The Ben & Jerry's Foundation, Community Action Teams (employee led groups from each of its five Vermont sites), and through corporate grants. For 1999, the 7.5% amounted to approximately $1,120,000. The Ben & Jerry's Foundation, Inc. targets its grants to small grassroots social change organizations (Ben & Jerry's 10-K).

"Grassroots organizing" implies activism from the ground up as opposed to top down decision making. "Social change" addresses the root causes of problems, addressing whole communities, systems, and institutions. "Grant applicants need to demonstrate that their projects will: lead to societal, institutional, and/or environmental change; address the root causes of social or environmental problems; lead to new ways of thinking and acting. Projects must: help ameliorate an unjust or destructive situation by empowering constituents; facilitate leadership development and strengthen the self-empowerment efforts of those who have traditionally been disenfranchised in our society; support movement building and collective action" (The Ben & Jerry's Foundation, Guidelines).

In 1988 Ben & Jerry's created a document called the "Statement of Mission," dedicating the company to a new corporate concept of linked prosperity. The company operates under a tri-part mission to produce the finest quality all-natural ice cream and related products, to operate profitably so that shareholder values continue to grow and employees enjoy career opportunities and financial rewards, and to be socially conscious and improve the quality of life of a broad community. Since 1988, Ben & Jerry's Annual Report to Stockholders has contained a "social report" on its performance during the year.

A 1999 Harris Interactive Poll regarding public perceptions of corporate reputability ranked Ben & Jerry's fifth overall, and first in the "social responsibility" category. The results of the survey were published in *The Wall Street Journal*. The Harris-Fombrun Reputation Quotient was used as an assessment tool to measure a company's reputation, based upon several key areas—social responsibility, emotional appeal, products and services, vision and leadership, workplace environment, and financial performance. The Harris-Fombrun Reputation Quotient develops a

© RICHARD T. NOWITZ/CORBIS

Ben & Jerry's is known for its philanthropic and socially responsible initiatives.

company's rating among competitors based on 20 attributes comprising the six dimensions of reputation.

- **Emotional Appeal**
  Have a good feeling about the company.
  Admire and respect the company.
  Trust the company a great deal.
- **Products & Services**
  Stands behind its products and services.
  Develops innovative products and services.
  Offers high quality products and services.
  Offers products and services that are a good value for the money.
- **Financial Performance**
  Has a strong record of profitability.
  Looks like a low-risk investment.
  Looks like a company with strong prospects for future growth.
  Tends to out-perform its competitors.
- **Vision & Leadership**
  Has excellent leadership.
  Has a clear vision for its future.
  Recognizes and takes advantage of market opportunities.
- **Workplace Environment**
  Is well-managed.
  Looks like a good company to work for.
  Looks like a company that would have good employees.
- **Social Responsibility**
  Supports good causes.
  Is an environmentally responsible company.
  Treats people well.

On November 20, 2000, Ben & Jerry's Homemade, Inc. appointed Yves Couette, a native of France, as its new Chief Executive Officer. Continuing Ben & Jerry's social mission is important to Couette. "Working in countries like Mexico and Indonesia, I have seen first hand the glaring social problems people face everyday. This has strengthened my belief that business has an important role to play in achieving social progress. In Guadalajara, Mexico, for example we established an ice cream shop, run by a non-profit organization, to support disabled children. This is very much in keeping with Ben & Jerry's three-part—product, economic and social—mission" (Ben & Jerry's press release, November 20, 2000). ■

Sources: Form 10-K405 filed March 22, 2000, http://lib.benjerry.com/fin/1999/10K.html; "Ben & Jerry's Appoints Yves Couette as Chief Executive Officer," November 20, 2000, http://lib.benjerry.com/pressrel/press1120.html; The Ben & Jerry's Foundation, Guidelines, http://www.benjerry.com/foundation/guidelines.html; *The Wall Street Journal.* "The Best Corporate Reputations in America: Just as in Politics, Trust, Reliability Pay Off Over Time," Sept. 23, 1999; Harris Interactive and the Reputation Institute publish results of nationwide public perceptions studies. Read more about Harris Interactive and the Harris-Fombrun Reputation Quotient at http://www.harrisinteractive.com/pop_up/rq. Twenty attributes reprinted courtesy of Harris Interactive.

INTRODUCTION

http://www.benjerry.com/mission.html

This chapter examines the responsibilities that businesses and their employees bear to themselves and to others. It concentrates on what is best for all of an organization's and an individual's constituents, including the recipients of their outputs—their customers. One assumption here is that the best decisions maximize achievement of legitimate goals, conform to high standards of legal and ethical behavior, and promote good corporate citizenship. This chapter examines basic principles and methods through which managers and their organizations can strengthen their personal and institutional capacities to act in both an ethical and socially responsible manner.

MANAGING ETHICALLY

Ethics, you will recall from Chapter 1, is the branch of philosophy concerned with human values and conduct, moral duty, and obligation. Specifically, ethics is concerned with what constitutes right and wrong human conduct, values, beliefs, and attitudes in light of a specific set of circumstances. The best time for individuals to consider the ethics of their behavior is while they are selecting a course of action and *before* they actually take the action. Thus they can identify any possible negative consequences and avoid or, at the very least, consider them before any harm is done.

Describe the two broad categories of ethical theories

According to authors Daniel Davidson et al. (1990):

> *There are two broad categories of ethical theories. Ethical theories may be based on consequential principles or nonconsequential principles.* Consequential *principles judge the ethics of a particular situation by the consequences of that action. Consequential ethics determines the "rightness" or "wrongness" of any action by determining the ratio of good to evil that the action will produce. The "right" action is that action that produces the greatest ratio of good to evil of any of the available alternatives. . . .*
>
> Nonconsequential *principles tend to focus on the concept of duty. Under the nonconsequential approach, a person acts ethically if that person is faithful regardless of the consequences that follow from being faithful to that duty. If a person carries out his or her duties, the greatest good occurs* because *the duty of the individual is carried out. If each individual carries out his or her duty, society knows what to expect from each individual in any given situation.*

business ethics
The rules or standards governing the conduct of persons or members of organizations in the field of commerce.

Business ethics addresses the applications of the preceding theories within the context of for-profit organizations and is the primary focus of this chapter. Our main concern is to look at how individuals and their organizations can, in any situation, avoid wrongdoing and do the right thing.

Robert C. Solomon and Kristine R. Hanson (1985), business consultants on ethical issues, have discovered that

> *Good business begins with ethics. The most successful people and companies are those that take ethics seriously. This is not surprising, since ethical attitudes largely determine how one treats employees, suppliers, stockholders, and consumers as well as how one treats competitors and other members of the community. Inevitably, this affects how one is treated in return. Ethical managers and ethical businesses tend to be more trusted and better treated and to suffer less resentment, inefficiency, litigation, and government interference. Ethics is just good business.*

Managers must continually strive to balance diverse and sometimes contradictory demands of multiple constituencies—employees, owners, customers, suppliers, and their communities (local and regional)—while allocating and managing limited resources. Near the arrival of the twenty-first century, two powerful factors imperil the balance.

First, never have so many conflicting demands been made so insistently on those who manage institutions and hold power; the construction industry, cigarette companies, the military, environmentalists, nuclear-power advocates, teachers, school boards, the Baby Boomers. The list of powerful special interests is matched only by the list of less powerful general interests: children, the poor and homeless, disadvantaged minorities, the undereducated, and the elderly.

Second, the consequences of management decisions affect far more people and environments—and more profoundly—than ever before. Whether directing a medical research laboratory at work on cancer or AIDS, maintaining a fleet of 747s, commanding transoceanic supertankers, supervising a nuclear reactor at Chernobyl

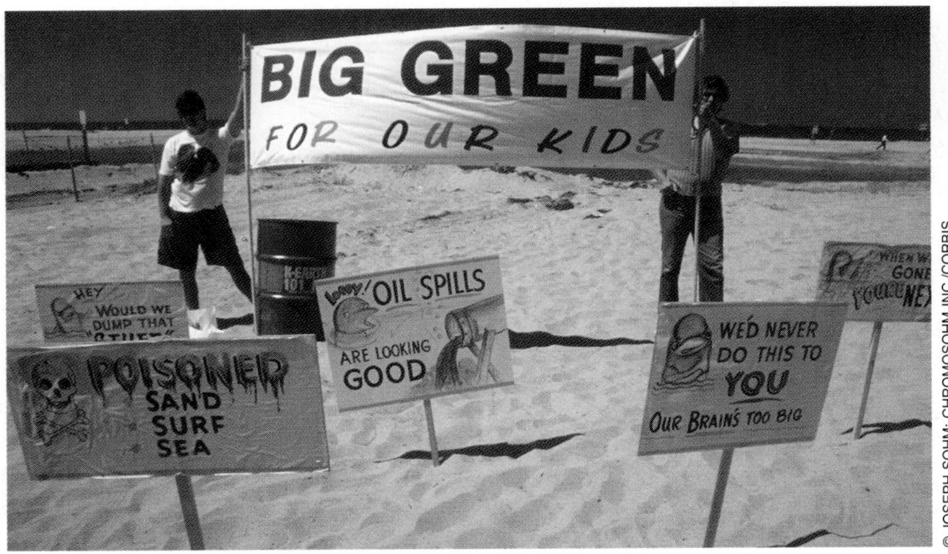

Environmentalists are insisting that companies take steps to becoming more socially responsible.

or an insecticide plant in Bhopal, leading the police department in Los Angeles, or plotting the future of General Motors, today's managers wield unprecedented influence over the world of today and tomorrow.

With the accelerating rate of change in our society and the explosion of information and technology, the pace of real events approaches that of a video game—with relentless hazards surfacing almost too fast to manage. Pressures to improve quality of products and operations, to increase productivity, to stay close to suppliers and customers, to value diversity, and to react swiftly to global changes all combine to compress the time managers and their organizations can take to make decisions and choose courses of action. Managers need guidelines to help them to cope with these pressures.

Individuals and Ethical Conduct

Explain what individuals need in order to act ethically

Few individuals and organizations would openly endorse cheating, stealing, telling lies, breaking laws, and threatening the physical well-being of others. Each of these actions is a violation of commonly held standards in most societies, under most circumstances. Yet, as too many of today's newspaper headlines indicate, people and businesses are accused and convicted of doing these things every day. After a brief look at ethics and individuals, we turn our attention to the organizational influences that affect the ethical conduct of institutions and their members.

morality
Core values and beliefs that act as a guide (i.e., conscience) when individuals formulate courses of action.

A person's ethics are influenced by his or her **morality**—core values and beliefs (i.e., principles and philosophy) that act as a guide (i.e., conscience) when formulating courses of action; once they are formulated, a person chooses or rejects a course of action based on the action's anticipated effects on both the person doing the selecting and others. "Religious beliefs and training, educational background, political and economic philosophy, socialization through family and peer group influences and work experience all come together to produce a personal moral code of ethical values with associated attitudes" (Dunfee, 1984). All these factors are usually referred to as an individual's code of ethics, or moral code, and are the primary control device used by individuals to judge and regulate conduct—their own and that of others.

Consider the results of two 1995 polls concerning just one area that affects employees and their organizations on a daily basis—absenteeism. A poll by CCH Inc., an Illinois-based business information firm, shows that "unscheduled absenteeism by employees at U.S. firms rose 3.46 percent from [1994] . . . up 4.1 [percent] since 1992" (*Chicago Tribune*, "Absenteeism," 1995). Unscheduled costs for this increased absenteeism amount to an average per employee of $505 a year. "Companies with fewer than 100 employees are hardest hit, currently paying upward of $662 an employee" (*Chicago Tribune*, "Absenteeism," 1995). A Gallup Poll shows that 10 percent of employees "called in sick when they really weren't" (*Daily Herald*, 1995). This poll also discovered that workers consider themselves "productive" only about 32 hours out of every 40 they work.

Human behavior derives from discernible causes or motives that can be identified, acknowledged, and modified. For this reason wise individuals cultivate a continuous awareness of their personal priorities, goals, values, needs, beliefs, attitudes, and assumptions. Such awareness allows individuals to realistically assess the motivation that underlies their personal choices and actions. All of us must continuously strive to identify the influences on and causes for our motivations and those of our leaders.

Leaders' Ethics

How a leader treats employees influences employee loyalty. A national employee survey by the nonprofit Hudson Institute and Walker Information, an Indianapolis research company, found that only 47 percent of employees believed their companys' leaders were people of high integrity. "And here's the kicker: Only 9 percent of employees who believed they were led by less-than-ethical executives were loyal to the company—as measured by the employees' inclination to stay with the company. Conversely, 55 percent of workers with ethical leaders wanted to remain. Of employees who were neutral, only 24 percent were loyal" (Kunde, 1999).

In his study of leadership, business writer Danny Cox compiled a list of ten characteristics common to great leaders. The first is "cultivating a high standard of personal ethics" (Cox and Hoover, 1992). Cox feels that "at the core of any high standard of personal ethics is the declaration of personal responsibility. A person who refuses to accept responsibility lacks the ethical armor to stand against temptation" (Cox and Hoover, 1992).

http://www.honda.com

Consider the case of American Honda Motor Company's former top sales executive, Stanley Cardiges. Throughout the 1980s this corporate executive solicited and received millions of dollars from Honda dealers who were anxious to get as many of the company's best-selling models as possible. The more each dealer "contributed" to Cardiges, the more vehicles that dealership received. In 1992 Cardiges resigned; in 1995 he pled guilty to federal charges of racketeering, mail fraud, and conspiracy and was sentenced to five years in jail (*Chicago Tribune*, "Former," 1995).

Author Verne E. Henderson (1992) adds, "Managers and executives who are . . . unaware of what motivates them are ethical accidents searching for a place to happen." Henderson suggests that when colleagues—including a boss—recommend a course of action, we must consider their motives as well as our own. As reasons unfold, watch for rationalizations (self-satisfying but incorrect justifications for one's behaviors) that excuse and bury subtle warnings from our conscience.

In our opening case, Ben Cohen and Jerry Greenfield exemplify leaders with a strong personal code of ethics. They believe in winning but doing so in the right way. Each "walks his talk" as an example and model for their teams to follow. Each has the ethical armor needed to evaluate his choices and balance the competing demands from his constituents.

Organizational Influences on Ethical Conduct

3

Describe the organizational influences on ethical conduct

Professors and authors Peter J. Frost, Vance F. Mitchell, and Walter R. Nord (1995) believe that organizations can have a negative impact on an individual's ability to act ethically: "[A]s organizations become especially central to people, people face strong temptations to do what they perceive to be good for the organization even when it means they act inconsistently with the standards of ethical behavior."

Professor Saul W. Gellerman (1992) points out that organizations can encourage (overtly or covertly) unethical behavior in employees in several ways:

- Offering unusually high rewards. "Huge bonuses and commissions can distort one's values, in much the same way that too much power can corrupt one's standards of decency. You can motivate people without corrupting them simply by keeping their rewards within the bounds of reason."
- Threatening unusually severe punishments. "If people are desperate to avoid what they regard as a calamity, they will go to whatever lengths they must to avoid it. One's conscience will be anesthetized by terror, so the dirty business can be done."
- Emphasizing results and avoiding concern for the means employed by subordinates to achieve those results.

In their capacity of setting an example for subordinates, managers teach more about ethics through their actions than they do through their words or what is written in a company's ethics code. An employee who is expected to turn a blind eye to a superior's unethical behavior receives the message loud and clear that ends are more important than means.

Ethics professor at Harvard Business School, Lynn Sharp Paine (1994) connects unethical behavior to corporate culture as well. She believes that

> *unethical business practice involves the tacit, if not explicit, cooperation of others and reflects the values, attitudes, beliefs, language, and behavioral patterns that define an organization's operating culture. Ethics, then, is as much an organizational as a personal issue. Managers who fail to provide proper leadership and to institute systems that facilitate ethical conduct share responsibility with those who conceive, execute, and knowingly benefit from corporate misdeeds.*

Just as organizations can exert negative influences, they can also exert positive ones.

Importance of Organizational Controls

4

Discuss three primary ways in which businesses can promote ethical conduct

Corporate cultures promote values and beliefs that govern the ways in which people interact with others. Several subcultures exist in most organizations, reflecting different work groups or discrete ethnic groups that arise from the workforce. Although these subcultures may display differing sets of values and perceptions, they can achieve a unity of viewpoint: "In a pluralistic society, business is the one place where different cultures and personal values are forced to cooperate and compromise. It is the one place where a single and unifying ethic is essential" (Henderson, 1992). To achieve this unified view, organizations rely on the commitment of top management, codes of ethics, and compliance programs.

Commitment of Top Management

It is top management's job to ensure that its organization's cultures support ethical conduct and social responsibility. To do this, top management must make organizational integrity a core value. Ethics professor Paine (1994) provides the following explanation of this concept:

> *[O]rganizational integrity is based on the concept of self-governance in accordance with a set of guiding principles. From the perspective of integrity, the task of ethics management is to define and give life to an organization's guiding values, to create an environment that supports ethically sound behavior, and to instill a sense of shared accountability among employees.*

To determine if a corporate culture and its subcultures support or oppose ethical conduct, see Figure 22.1. It is a checklist for examining a company's culture. Every "no" response indicates that some change is necessary to foster ethical as well as socially responsible behavior.

Gellerman (1992) asserts that the "first line of defense against unethical conduct is each individual's conscience." Managers "have to do everything [they] can to keep it awake. The second line of defense is to eliminate or minimize the circumstances that can overwhelm a conscience, or deceive it, or put it to sleep." He recommends three steps that top managers can take to discourage unethical behavior in their areas of responsibility:

- "Draw a clean line between the behavior you'll tolerate and the behavior you'll have to punish." This step means establishing a code of ethics or conduct that management is willing to commit to and enforce.
- "Invest the time and money in making sure that those distinctions are understood and remembered." This step requires training, constant oversight, and the establishment of rewards for ethical behavior.
- "Put the fear of God into would-be violators by conspicuously raising the risk of exposure." This step means punishing wrongdoers fairly and swiftly. People will learn from each example of misbehavior and how it is handled by management.

Codes of Ethics

http://www.conference-board.org

Although there is no generic code of ethics for business, individual organizations often find such codes useful. In 1992 the Conference Board, a business-funded

FIGURE 22.1 *Checklist for determining if a corporate culture supports ethical behavior and social responsibility*

Is the company:	Yes	No
1. Concerned about quality in its services, products, and operations?	❑	❑
2. Concerned about its employees' quality of life?	❑	❑
3. Proud of its reputation in the industry?	❑	❑
4. Proud of its reputation in the community?	❑	❑
5. Focused on the needs of its customers?	❑	❑
6. Honest in its dealings with you?	❑	❑
7. Honest in its dealings with customers?	❑	❑
8. Honest in its dealings with others?	❑	❑
9. Fair and equitable in the ways in which it decides on promotions?	❑	❑
10. Fair and equitable in the ways in which it compensates employees?	❑	❑
11. Open in its communications?	❑	❑
12. Trusting in its relationships with employees?	❑	❑
13. Concerned with developing and keeping its employees?	❑	❑
14. Actively promoting ethical conduct in all its operations and employees?	❑	❑
15. Actively searching for ways to better serve its stakeholders?	❑	❑
16. Carefully monitoring how decisions are made and checking them for their concern for ethical behavior?	❑	❑

research group, reported, "company codes of conduct are becoming increasingly sophisticated [and] nearly one-third of the 264 chief executives surveyed had issued a personal statement or [engaged in a] formal discussion of ethics issues in [1991]" (Widder, 1992). To be effective and influential in an organization's culture and command structure, codes of ethics must be specific enough to give concrete guidance and must be reinforced by the examples set by key corporate figures. They must be written in such a way as to develop a clear understanding of a company's values and commitment to ethical behavior, both inside the organization and in relation to key outside stakeholders. Codes should deal directly with situations known by a company to have been problematic in the past.

Authors Solomon and Hanson (1985) outline the following characteristics for codes of ethics:

- They are visible guidelines for behavior at all levels.
- They are an unchallengeable basis for firing an unethical employee, even when his or her action is not, strictly speaking, against either the law or the specific terms of the job.
- They protect all personnel from the pressures of the market, which tend to incite desperation and unethical behavior.
- They remind employees to look beyond the bottom line, and they provide a touchstone for appeals through the hierarchy.

Compliance Programs

http://www.lcl.cmu.edu

Without some means to communicate and enforce codes of ethics and conduct, they will be just words on paper. Peter Madsen, executive director at Carnegie Mellon University's Center for the Advancement of Applied Ethics, separates ethics training into two areas:

- Compliance training that alerts people to policies, regulations, and laws that establish acceptable behavior within a company; and
- Cognitive thinking exercises that develop skills to allow people to think through various "moral mazes" with which they may be confronted in the workplace (*Human Resources Management*, 1992).

http://www.championpaper.com

http://www.brtable.org

According to Andrew D. Sigler of Champion International, "You need a culture and peer pressure that spells out what is acceptable and isn't and why [and a program] involving training, education, and follow-up" (Byrne, 1988). To make such a program effective, the Business Roundtable, an advisory and research group comprising the chief executives of two hundred major corporations, recommends that top management devote a greater commitment to ethics programs, boldly assert management's expectations through clearly written and communicated codes, and conduct surveys to monitor compliance (Byrne, 1988).

> *Measuring something makes it important even if it wasn't before. In the U.S. Army, the phrase is "don't expect what you don't inspect." The corporate equivalent is, "what the boss watches well gets done well." The same principle applies to the ethical side of enterprise. It only becomes important if and when it's measured (Henderson, 1992).*

See this chapter's Global Applications feature for an article about an illegal clothing factory supplying garments to major retailers.

http://www.gm.com

http://www.lockheedmartin.com

Several trends are in evidence today. A growing number of corporate boards of directors have ethics committees. The majority of large companies have ethics officers who are members of top management or report directly to a member. Companies like General Motors have employee hot lines through which any employee can report wrongdoing anonymously or request ethical assistance in resolving an issue. The large aerospace and military contractor, Martin Marietta Corporation (now part of Lockheed Martin), uses a corporate ethics office and ethics representatives at its major locations to administer its "integrity-based ethics program" which contains "a code of conduct, an ethics training program, and procedures for reporting and investigating ethical concerns within the company. It also includes a system for disclosing violations of federal procurement law to the government" (Paine, 1994).

http://www.citicorp.com

http://www.ge.com

http://www.ti.com

Ethics programs can be creative. Citicorp uses "an ethics board game, which teams of employees use to solve hypothetical quandaries. General Electric employees can tap into specially designed interactive software on their personal computers to get answers to ethical questions. At Texas Instruments, employees are treated to a weekly column on ethics over an international electronic news service" (Labich, 1992).

Professor Dupuy at LaGrange College has developed a condensed version of Friedrich Dürrenmatt's renowned 1956 play, *The Visit*, in which a wealthy woman returns to her hometown to take revenge on a person who hurt her when she was

GLOBAL APPLICATIONS
Thais Run a Sweatshop in Los Angeles

In the summer of 1995, a federal grand jury indicted nine Thai nationals for allegedly enslaving 70 illegal Thai immigrants—many of them since 1992—in a makeshift clothing factory (run by SK Fashions and D & R Fashions) in El Monte, California. The illegals were recruited in Thailand, smuggled into the United States, and forced to work to pay the cost of their transport by laboring for up to 22 hours per day for wages that amounted to an average of $1.60 per hour. The operators of the facility violated numerous state and federal laws.

The merchandise seized in the August 2 raid was destined for some of America's largest, most prestigious retailers. According to Victoria Bradshaw, California's former labor commissioner, boxes of merchandise addressed to Mervyn's, Montgomery Ward, Macy's, Hecht's, and Filene's, among others, were found in the factory. Former U.S. Secretary of Labor, Robert Reich, claimed that as many as eighteen major retailers may have received goods from the illegal operation. Sixteen different clothing makers were subpoenaed in the ongoing investigation.

Practices in the garment industry usually put a middleman between the retailer and the manufacturer. The store chain makes an agreement with a contractor who all too often subcontracts the work to a sweatshop. There is joint liability for any damages between the illegal firm and those contracting with it. Investigators focus on a paper trail between manufacturers and retailers and their middlemen.

The retailers that were contacted all stated that they have policies against doing business with illegal firms. Most claimed to be investigating on their own for any possible links to illegal operations. Montgomery Ward responded by suing one of its suppliers, claiming it had damaged the retailer's reputation. It removed merchandise made by the illegals from its shelves.

Sources: Buck, Genevieve. " 'Prison Camp' Sweatshop Probe Widens," *Chicago Tribune*, August 10, 1995, sec. 3, pp. 1, 3; *Chicago Tribune*. "16 Apparel Firms Subpoenaed in Sweatshop Investigation," August 16, 1995, sec. 3, pp. 1, 4.

young. After buying the town's factories and shutting them down to cause a local depression, she offers $1 million to any person who agrees to kill the man who wronged her. After some soul-searching among the characters, a mob kills the man. After the performance, audience members participate with the cast to explore their values and ethics in relation to one another's. "Such self-discovery should be invaluable to participants when they confront ethical issues on the job," says Dupuy (Bell, 1992).

Legal Constraints

5 Describe the relationship between law and ethics

Competent managers cultivate an informed awareness of the role of the law in organizational and individual conduct. Because ours is a nation of laws, certain presumptions influence decision making at several levels. From the broadest context of constitutional rights to the most minute municipal regulation, companies and their managers are witting and unwitting creatures of the law. One group of business law experts view the relationship of the law to ethics in this way:

> *There is a basic problem facing any business in its efforts to be "ethical": there are no fixed guidelines to follow, no formal codes of ethics to set the standards. The legal profession has a Code of Professional Responsibility; the medical profession has its Hippocratic Oath; the accounting profession has a code of ethics; the real-estate industry has a code of conduct; other professions have codes to guide them. But business has no 'road map' of ethical conduct.*

> *The closest thing business has is the law. If a business obeys the law, it is acting legally, and it is seemingly meeting its minimum social requirements* (Davidson et al., 1990).

Those minimum requirements offer only a structure, however, void of content and context. Says Peter Madsen,

> *Laws and policies form an ethical foundation. But the law is a moral minimum. And no law or policy is going to cover every situation. Sooner or later organizations will have to rely on people to make choices when there is no on-point law or policy to follow. The best ethics training goes beyond legal compliance* (Human Resources Management, 1992).

Author Vincent Barry adds,

> *Although useful in alerting us to moral issues and informing us of our rights and responsibilities, law cannot be taken as an adequate standard of moral conduct. Conformity with law is neither requisite nor sufficient for determining moral behavior, any more than conformity to rule[s] of etiquette is. By the same token, nonconformity with law is not necessarily immoral, for the law disobeyed may be unjust* (Barry, 1986).

http://www.eeoc.gov

http://www.senate.gov

http://www.dellabs.com

Every leader should understand by now that sexual harassment is illegal and is governed by strict Equal Employment Opportunity Commission (EEOC) guidelines. But day after day we read about people in positions of power who harass employees. Senator Robert Packwood of Oregon is one highly visible example. In 1995 he resigned from the United States Senate after a Senate Ethic's Committee decision that he be censured. In the same year, "cosmetics-maker [Del Labs] agreed to pay nearly $1.2 million to settle a sexual harassment complaint brought against its chief executive by 15 women workers" (*Chicago Tribune*, "Del," 1995). It appears that in spite of the losses Dan K. Wassong has caused to his company, he remains, as of December 31, 2000, as chief executive with an annual compensation of over $1 million per year; he owns 35 percent of the company's outstanding shares of stock.

http://www.supremecourtus.gov

Legal sanctions against individual and corporate criminal behavior can be significant. Since 1909 when the U.S. Supreme Court held that corporations can be "held liable, as individuals can be, for crimes involving intent," corporate liability has translated into fines and jail terms for corporate officials. More than half of the 50 states now have some form of corporate criminal liability law under which business owners can be prosecuted for criminal negligence. According to New York attorney Steven Alan Reiss, during the past ten years the trend has been toward escalating criminal penalties that "can be drastically reduced if the company can show it has in place [a legal] compliance program" (Widder, 1992).

In November 1991 the trend toward harsh penalties for white-collar crime continued, as new federal guidelines went into effect. They "cover many offenses that can be committed by employees without a business owner's knowledge. Some of the new penalties [base fines range from $5,000 to $72.5 million] may be enough to destroy a small company" (Jacobs, 1992). Heavy penalties for a variety of offenses "including serious misrepresentation of a product by a salesperson and bribery of a public official by a subcontractor" are included. "If high-level managers were not involved in the crime and [they] have taken steps to ensure employees' compliance with the law, a firm could pay as little as 5% of the base fine."

On the other hand, if senior managers "have encouraged or taken part in the law breaking, fines can reach 400% of the base rate" (Jacobs, 1992).

http://www.ussc.gov/guidelin.htm

In the adoption of the laws called Federal Sentencing Guidelines, "the U.S. government codified fines and penalties for corporate wrongdoing. It also laid out how leniency would be granted to companies with concrete internal programs to detect and prevent illegal acts" (McCarthy, 1999). Thus, managers see self-regulation as a way to avoid legislative or judicial intrusions into their operations. Ethics codes also help promote tolerance of diverse practices and customs while doing business abroad.

Figure 22.2 is a simple grid with four quadrants representing the four possible combinations when balancing ethical issues with the law or the absence of a law. Position 1 (upper left) shows a legal and ethical position for the issue in question—smoking in the workplace. Position 4 (lower right) shows an illegal and unethical treatment of the issue. The other two positions represent ethical or legal concerns to a manager.

Ethical Dilemmas

6

Explain the concept of an ethical dilemma

Ethics is not prescriptive. No simple set of rules tells us how to behave morally or ethically in all situations. Codes of conduct—when they are documented—are written in the manner of company policies—as brief, general guidelines. Interpretation varies from one individual to the next. Like policies, codes are meant to give freedom of action within certain boundaries and require interpretation. Saul W. Gellerman, dean of the University of Dallas Graduate School of Management, queries and replies:

> *How can you tell if a rule "really" applies to what you are doing? How can you avoid crossing a line that is almost never defined precisely? The only safe answer is not even to*

FIGURE 22.2 *Legal/ethical behavior model applied to the issue of smoking in the workplace*

1. Ethical/Legal	**2. Ethical/Illegal**
A decision to allow employees to smoke on the job with no secondhand smoke affecting others	A decision to allow smoking on the job with no secondhand smoke affecting others but in violation of laws
3. Unethical/Legal	**4. Unethical/Illegal**
A decision to allow secondhand smoke to affect others without violation of laws	A decision to allow secondhand smoke to affect others in violation of laws

move in the direction of the line. Here is where the real *ethical dilemma begins to emerge, however. Because if you constantly played it safe, and never tested the limits of what you could and couldn't get away with, you'd risk being considered inefficient, or even gutless, by your superiors (Gellerman, 1992).*

ethical dilemma
A situation that arises when all courses of action open to a decision maker are judged to be unethical.

Managers constantly face dilemmas—situations that require a choice between options that are or seem equally unfavorable or mutually exclusive. Dilemmas involve uncertainty and risk over the rightness or wrongness of actions. Besides uncertainty about which course of action is ethical, an **ethical dilemma** also arises when all courses of action open to a manager are judged to be unethical. For example, a company's plant is simply unable to bring work in at a profit. Managers are considering three possible alternatives: (1) shut the plant down and outsource the work to subcontractors who will give the firm the costs it needs, (2) invest in computerization that will eliminate half the jobs but make the plant productive enough to continue to operate, or (3) seek wage and benefit concessions from all employees to bring costs into line. Any of these choices will impose immediate hardship on the employees of the plant and those who depend on them—families, local merchants, and others.

Because of technology's central role in business, opportunities, and innovation, the role of technology managers has become more critical in setting and enforcing ethical standards. In an *InformationWeek Newsletter*, Stephanie Stahl (2001) poses several ethical dilemmas:

It's Monday morning, and you're studying up on a large-scale project that your company intends to bid on. You're well into the details when you realize the company issuing the request for proposals has accidentally included confidential information that could give you a serious leg up on your competitors. What do you do? Pretend you didn't see it? Take advantage of it and act on it? Alert the company to the mistake and remove yourself from the negotiations?

You find out an employee has been circulating pornographic files via the company email system. Do you ignore it? Give the employee a warning? Fire the employee?

One of your business partners offers to pay you big bucks for access to your customer data. You've assured customers that such data will remain confidential, but your company is cash-hungry. Do you sell it? Keep your promise to customers?

When managers face such gray areas, Professor Gellerman (1986) offers the following suggestions:

- When in doubt, don't.
- Don't try to find out "how far is too far."
- Superiors who push you to do things better, faster, cheaper will turn on you when you cross the line between right and wrong.

Gellerman offers this practical, concrete stratagem:

When what you might or might not do is questionable, let the burden of the decision rest on someone who is paid to make the tough decisions. Make your boss earn his [or her] pay. You can't openly condone what policy prohibits. Neither can your boss. That's why bringing the question into the open keeps both of you honest (Gellerman, 1992).

Guidelines for Acting Ethically

Discuss the guidelines for acting ethically

Someone struggling with a decision, torn between one or another course of action, may well be confronting an issue that involves ethics. The time to consider the ethical dimensions of an act is before acting. Companies and individuals must strive to make ethics a priority in the processes by which they make their decisions. Different people and groups invoke different criteria for determining if an intended action (or inaction) is the ethical course to follow. The Golden Rule states that we should treat others as we ourselves want to be treated. A variation is to do to others what they want you to do to them. Both work well if the people involved are moral and aware of prevailing social conventions. The utilitarian standard of the greatest good for the greatest number of people provides another ethical test, which works well if the consequences and circumstances surrounding the intended act are fully foreseen and understood.

Authors Solomon and Hanson (1985) offer the following rules for contemplating the ethical implications of intended actions:

- Consider other people's well-being, including the well-being of nonparticipants.
- Think as a member of the business community and not as an isolated individual.
- Obey, but do not depend solely on, the law.
- Think of yourself—and your company—as part of society.
- Obey moral rules.
- Think objectively.
- Ask the question, "What sort of person would do such a thing?"
- Respect the customs of others, but not at the expense of your own ethics.

These rules remind us that we are all part of a larger community and that our actions affect others, whose interests must be considered. Keeping these rules in mind can help managers analyze the consequences of their actions before they take any steps. When an individual makes decisions without a moral and ethical base, he or she is adrift and may rely solely on self-interest and economics. People lacking a moral foundation put themselves, their organizations, and others at great risk. Risk taking shows up in most managers' job descriptions. "[T]hey are paid to know which risks are worth taking. One risk that is definitely not worth taking is the risk of ruining the rest of your career" (Gellerman, 1992).

Management professor Kenneth Blanchard and noted cleric Norman Vincent Peale (author of *The Power of Positive Thinking*) have written a cogent book, *The Power of Ethical Management*. In it they offer a simple sequence of three tests for determining the ethical implications of intended actions (Blanchard and Peale, 1988):

- Is it legal? Will I be violating either civil law or company policy?
- Is it balanced? Is it fair to all concerned in the short term as well as the long term? Does it promote win-win relationships?
- How will it make me feel about myself? Will it make me proud? Would I feel good if my decision were published in a newspaper? Would I feel good if my family knew about it?

With these inquiries a manager can examine his or her intentions in private and with complete objectivity. When judging the ethical facets of a decision, a person must take ample quiet time, away from pressures and the biases of others, for unhurried reflection on the facts and implications of the decision.

NATURE OF SOCIAL RESPONSIBILITY

social responsibility
The notion that, in addition to their business interests, individuals and organizations have certain obligations to protect and benefit other individuals and society and to avoid actions that could harm them.

The notion that individuals and organizations have certain obligations, in addition to their business interests, to protect and benefit others and to avoid actions that could harm them is what constitutes **social responsibility** (Davis, 1975). One reason for the prevalence of this belief in the developed countries of the world is that societies have given businesses tremendous power and rely on them to meet various individual and societal needs.

Businesses are open systems, and most of what they do generates direct benefits and costs for their societies. At one time businesses did only what they had to do. Today society demands that businesses join in the urgent task of solving societies' problems. Corporations must nourish cultures that promote ethical conduct, and their owners and employees must act with an ethical perspective in order to be socially responsible. Being socially responsible does not mean making everyone happy. Businesses face conflicting demands, and at times a socially responsible action puts the needs of one group of stakeholders ahead of the needs of others—such as donating money to charity rather than paying stockholders higher dividends or giving employees higher raises. Such issues require managers to consider their duty (the course of action required of them by their position or by law) and the priorities of their specific obligations.

Author Rogene A. Buchholz expresses the need for businesses to act in a socially responsible way: "Corporations are more than economic institutions and have a responsibility to devote some of their resources to helping to solve some of the pressing social problems, many of which corporations helped to create" (Buchholz, 1989). Benjamin Franklin may have been the first American businessman to advocate such responsible conduct for businesses. Franklin believed that "public service and philanthropy were legitimate concerns . . . because it is good business to improve the health of the communities from which wealth is derived and because public problems can benefit from private solutions" (Watson, 1991).

http://www.levistrauss.com

Robert D. Haas, president and CEO of Levi Strauss, persuasively argues the case for businesses to cultivate social responsibility:

> *Corporations can be short-sighted and worry only about our mission, products, and competitive standing. But we do it at our peril. The day will come when corporations will discover the price we pay for our indifference. We must realize that by ignoring the needs of others, we are actually ignoring our own needs in the long run. We may need the goodwill of a neighborhood to enlarge a corner store. We may need well-funded institutions of higher learning to turn out the skilled technical employees we require. We may need adequate community health care to curb absenteeism in our plants. Or we may need fair tax treatment for an industry to be able to compete in the world economy. However small or large our enterprise, we cannot isolate our business from the society around us. Nor can we function without its goodwill (Haas, 1984).*

Approaches to Social Responsibility

8

Explain the three approaches by businesses to social responsibility

American businesses adopt different approaches to the demands made on them. Some businesses eagerly seek ways to accommodate societal needs, whereas others vehemently resist external obligations. Businesses can adopt any of three primary strategies to manage the issue of social responsibility: to resist, to react, and to anticipate.

Resistance Approach

resistance approach
A social responsibility strategy in which businesses actively fight to eliminate, delay, or fend off demands being made on them.

Companies adopt the **resistance approach** when they actively fight to eliminate, delay, or fend off the demands being made on them. In the earliest days of the Industrial Revolution, businesses were relatively unaffected by government regulation. Labor was cheap and plentiful. Businesses behaved pretty much as they wanted, exerting tremendous influence over their towns, industries, and governments. Resistance to government interference and active opposition to demands from both insiders and outsiders marked this early phase of business history. The emphasis was on maximizing profits and the self-interests of owners. The prevailing attitude was that managers owed their allegiance to owners, a view reinforced by the courts. In a 1919 decision, a Michigan court refused to let Henry Ford divert stockholder dividend payments to "certain socially beneficial programs." The court held that directors had an obligation to stockholders and could not renege on that duty (Davidson et al., 1990). Regulatory agencies were virtually nonexistent. No laws protected consumers or the environment, and both suffered as a consequence.

Even in today's regulatory environment and with so many of society's needs vividly apparent, some businesses persist in doing as little as possible—only what the law demands—and even that they do reluctantly. Previous chapters have cited examples of corporate efforts to resist stockholders' demands. Another example occurred in 1992, when Toyota Motor Corporation encountered problems with its 1987 to 1991 Camry models—some 890,000 vehicles. The automatic door locks "could jam, and lock owners out of the car or trap occupants inside the vehicle." Toyota cooperated with the investigation by the National Highway Traffic Safety Administration, but the company (although admitting that some locks were faulty) maintained that a recall wasn't warranted. Both the Center for Auto Safety (a consumer group) and *Consumer Reports* magazine wrote about the problem, and the Center recommended a recall (Mitchell, 1992).

http://www.toyota.com

http://www.nhtsa.dot.gov

http://www.consumerreports.org

Reactive Approach

reactive approach
A social responsibility strategy in which businesses wait for demands to be made and then react to them, choosing a response by evaluating alternatives.

Businesses taking a **reactive approach** wait for demands to be made on them and then respond to those demands by weighing their options. In 1995 fashion designer and clothing maker Calvin Klein ran a national jeans ad campaign featuring scantily clad young models in provocative poses. Although the company claimed that all models were over eighteen years of age, various community and religious groups alleged the ads bordered on child pornography. Some groups "sent letters to 50 of the country's biggest retailers" threatening to boycott and picket their stores (Millman, 1995). Several weeks following the public outcry, the Federal Bureau of Investigation launched a probe, and Calvin Klein bowed to public pressure by announcing the withdrawal of the ads.

http://www.fbi.gov

Proactive Approach

proactive approach *A social responsibility strategy in which businesses continually look to the needs of constituents and try to find ways to meet those needs.*

http://www.patagonia.com

http://www.unitedway.org

http://www.aafrc.org

Companies taking the **proactive approach** continually look to the needs of their constituents, constantly staying in touch, sensing their needs, and trying to find ways to meet them. Many companies have a variety of programs to help their communities. Some, like the small California sportswear producer Patagonia, encourage their employees to give of their talents in a variety of ways, such as community cleanups, tutoring local schools' students, and sponsoring fund-raisers to assist local environmental groups. Most companies support the national United Way campaigns and other community-based charitable drives. Some of America's small and most of its largest businesses have established funds or foundations that donate money to worthy causes such as education, the arts, environmental and ecology groups, and various communities' human services agencies. According to the American Association of Fundraising Counsel (AAFRC) Trust for Philanthropy's 1999 estimates of charitable giving in the United States, total giving was $190.16 billion. Of this total, individuals contributed $143.71 billion to charitable causes, whereas total corporate giving reached $11.02 billion.

A new trend, called "strategic philanthropy" and "financially sound goodwill" by the Conference Board (a U.S. industry research association), however, is emerging (Schwartz and Smart, 1995). Corporate donations must, in some way, provide a return to the giver. Dollars given must support specific efforts, and the results must be monitored. The Conference Board's research indicates that when companies adopt this approach they gain "a better image, increased employee loyalty, and improved customer ties" (Schwartz and Smart, 1995).

http://www.ge.com

http://www.rand.org

http://www.nike.com

One example is General Electric's GE Fund, which has a "$20 million College Bound Program at high schools in 14 cities to help increase the number of students going on to college. It gauges the program's success by how many students go to college and has hired Rand Corp. to conduct an independent evaluation" (Schwartz and Smart, 1995). Nike, a sports products manufacturer, sponsors student sporting events and showcases the students in its advertising.

This chapter's Valuing Diversity feature is an open letter from Douglas Whitley, the president of Ameritech Illinois, a division of Ameritech, which is the primary provider of local phone services to the Midwest. Whitley's letter links a proactive approach to valuing diversity with being socially responsible.

Responsibilities to Stakeholders

Explain the responsibilities businesses have to stakeholders

Stakeholders are those who have an interest in or who are affected by how a business conducts its operations. In general, the stakeholders in most businesses include their owners and stockholders, employees, customers, suppliers, and communities. Society as a whole can be considered a stakeholder, as well, if the business is large enough to affect people and environments beyond its physical location.

Owners and Stockholders

A business and its employees owe their best efforts to owners. Assets must be conserved and used effectively and efficiently. Employees must do their best to maximize the return on invested capital and to generate a reasonable profit. Owners and employers should have the right to hire, train, reward, promote, discipline,

VALUING DIVERSITY
Diversity's Link to Social Responsibility: An Open Letter to the Citizens of the Chicago Metropolitan Area

CHICAGO—In Congress, civil-rights organizations and corporate offices, everyone is discussing affirmative action. Regardless of what happens to specific government programs, however, we as corporate leaders must continue to promote the message that diversity works.

It is not solely a social issue. At Ameritech, we are convinced that diversity contributes to good business decisions and is vitally important to the economy.

Diversity differs from affirmative action because it is more than a black and white or male and female issue. It is an inclusionary process that makes us more productive and a stronger team. A corporate culture sensitive to diversity goals creates a spirit of cooperation and draws on a wider spectrum of ideas to meet and exceed our objectives.

As corporate leaders, we must point out the business advantages to others who would prefer to bury the issue. An inclusive economy is fundamental to social, political and community issues. Urban centers such as Chicago that are culturally diverse are incubators for new businesses, which, in turn, help to furnish economic security for everyone.

The city's economic development should reflect the nation's growing diversity. In the future, women, Latinos, African-Americans and other minorities will make up a greater percentage of our workforce and customers. Let's not allow the debate and scrutiny of government affirmative-action programs to distract us from a constructive business agenda that invites everyone into the workplace.

Last year alone, Ameritech spent more than $100 million with small and developing businesses, including minority and women suppliers, in our five-state region. We expect to exceed that in 1995. We are also major supporters of many organizations that provide financial and management assistance to help developing businesses in all types of industries.

In furthering our commitment to diversity, we contracted with the Chicago Urban League to help develop opportunities for small businesses in the construction of the Ameritech corporate center in Hoffman Estates. As a result, millions of dollars of contracts were awarded to those businesses on that project.

By partnering small businesses, including minority and women suppliers, we meet our internal needs while providing economic growth opportunities to the community. At the same time, the creation of new jobs represents increased business revenue and additional residential customers.

On the hiring front, one quarter of the Ameritech workforce is minority. One in five managers is minority. There are members of minority groups at every level. Our focus now is to reach wider in our recruitment efforts and to continue to set the example by promoting diversity from the top down.

The business community locally and nationally has a responsibility to be visible promoters of diversity. Given this reality, it makes sense to seize the opportunity to build a climate of cooperation and inclusion throughout the Chicago metropolitan area.

Douglas Whitley
President, Ameritech Illinois
Vice chairman, Economic
Development Committee
Chicago United

http://www.ameritech.com

Source: Chicago Tribune. "Voice of the People: Diversity Is Good for Business," August 19, 1995, sec. 1, p. 20. Reproduced by permission from the author.

and remove employees in accordance with ethical, moral, and legal restraints. Owners and employers should have the right to expect ethical, moral, and legal conduct from their employees.

Employees

Employees should enjoy equal access to the rights, responsibilities, and privileges afforded by employers. Employees need to receive fair and equitable compensation, to be dismissed only for just cause, and to be treated without discrimination.

Employees should experience a quality of work life that provides satisfying jobs. They should receive competent guidance and direction in their work and be accorded due process in disputes.

Employees hold certain rights to freedom of expression, safety, adequate information, and privacy and confidentiality in regard to personal concerns. A growing trend in several areas of the country is to fire employees for their consumption of alcohol or tobacco (both on and off the job), and for working a second job (moonlighting). Several states, including Illinois, have addressed these privacy issues. Since July 1992, no employer in Illinois can fire an employee for engaging in a lawful activity away from work (Vitale, 1992). Numerous laws have been enacted on the local, state, and federal level to protect the health, privacy, and welfare of employees.

Customers

Businesses and their employees owe fair and honest representation of their products and services to their customers. Such products and services should encompass quality of design, manufacture, distribution, and sales. Consumers have a right to be warned of any hazards they may encounter while using a product or receiving a service. In short, customers have a right to be treated fairly and with respect. Many laws have been passed to protect consumers; government inspection of food, drugs, and cosmetics is one result of such consumer protection legislation. Credit laws are another example. A 1992 case suggests the scope of these laws:

> *Three companies that sell consumer credit data nationwide settled federal charges that they released such information without determining whether their customers were using the sensitive information legally [a violation of the federal Fair Credit Reporting Act]. Under the settlement, the companies agreed to undertake periodic audits to ensure that their customers are requesting and using the information for legitimate purposes* (Saddler, 1992).

Suppliers

Suppliers and businesses should build relationships based on mutual trust. Suppliers deserve to receive needed information in time to render quality service and supplies. They, like all parties to business contracts, have the legal right to be treated according to the terms of their agreements.

http://www.gm.com

In July 1992 General Motors made a startling announcement:

> *GM would provide suppliers [worldwide through September 1993] not only with paid workers but also with leased factories for them to build parts. GM would benefit in that a portion of any savings its suppliers realized in plant and production costs could be returned to GM to help it reduce costs* (Mateja, 1992).

http://www.uaw.org

The offer came because, according to its contract with the United Auto Workers, GM pays laid-off workers 95 percent of their pay for 36 weeks. In the 37th week they join a job bank from which they may be assigned any position by a plant's Jobs Committee while they earn 100 percent of their pay.

Communities

Those environments and their governments that are affected by a company's operations constitute its community. The quality of life in a community; its air, land,

and water quality; and its specific needs all come into play. All its constituents, many of whom may be customers, deserve ethical, legal, and moral treatment. A suburban restaurant owner got complaints from neighbors about food-packaging debris on lawns and streets. He now employs a person full-time to patrol the neighborhood and pick up all litter within a square mile of the restaurant.

green products
Those products with reduced energy and pollution connected with their manufacture and disposal.

Pollution is a growing concern around the world, with mounting pressure to produce **green products**—those that minimize energy consumption and pollutive by-products connected with their manufacture and disposal. Automakers have developed more fuel-efficient and cleaner-burning engines, encouraged in no small measure by California's tough environmental laws and the Clean Air Act of 1990 (*Wall Street Journal*, 1992).

http://www.mcdonalds.com

The music-recording industry has bowed to pressures from several sources and agreed to phase out its "long box" packaging for compact disks (CDs). In a practice initiated in 1993, most CDs are now sold in simple plastic "jewel boxes"; the only waste is plastic shrink-wrap to prevent tampering (Cox, 1992). McDonald's reduced its packaging for similar reasons in the late 1980s. The fast-food chain has also made attempts to help individuals with vision, hearing, and speech impairments by adding Braille menus in 1979 and picture menus in 1988 (Ryan, 1992).

Government Regulation: Pros and Cons

Describe government's role in promoting socially responsible conduct by businesses

Corporations have committed acts that harm the environment, consumers, communities, and society as a whole. Laws now in existence were brought about largely by these abuses. When society can't depend on the perpetrators to act appropriately, it must compel such action. But the enforcement of many laws depends more on individuals' commitments to social responsibility than it does on government agencies. Governments simply do not have enough money or people to adequately enforce their regulations. Society's best protection rests in an informed citizenry and a formed conscience in each and every owner and employee.

http://www.whistleblowers.org

As noted in Chapter 21, concerned employees who bring company wrongdoing to the attention of authorities who can do something about it are called *whistle-blowers*. Research shows that people become whistle-blowers for a variety of reasons. Some blow the whistle because of their strong moral and ethical codes. Some do so because they feel a strong obligation to protect others and their communities. Some are participants in the wrongdoing and may blow the whistle out of fear that disclosure may be made by others (Yates, 1995). Many whistle-blowers believe that their superiors, like themselves, do not want to let their companies or customers be harmed by unethical or illegal conduct and will take action to stop the wrongdoing.

According to Stephen M. Kohn, chairman of the Washington, D.C.–based National Whistle-blower Center, "There are 20 federal laws that protect whistle-blowing in certain areas and there are now about 40 states with laws to protect whistle-blowers" (Yates, 1995). Unfortunately, all too often the bearer of bad news becomes a victim of retaliation by those individuals and companies that suffer from his or her disclosures. Research shows that they are often isolated, verbally denigrated, harassed, demoted, and even fired (Yates, 1995). Because these things occur, Mike Cavallo, a commodities trader from Boston, established the Cavallo

Foundation. Every year since 1988 its nine-member board has selected three significant whistle-blowers and awarded them $10,000 each (Yates, 1995).

http://www.benjerry.com

http://www.fda.gov

Ben & Jerry's has taken a stand against the use of a genetically engineered bovine growth hormone. The U.S. Food & Drug Administration has approved the hormone, but many consumers are concerned about its possible long-term effects on the safety of dairy products and their users' health. Although it contends that the hormones are perfectly safe, the dairy industry has resisted efforts to label which of its products are ones produced by cows that are given the hormone. Thus consumers who wish to avoid these products must rely on their neighborhood food retailers to inform them as to which products do and do not come from such cows.

In 1995 the FDA gave poultry producers approval for the limited use of a new synthetic antibiotic (sarafloxacin) to kill bacteria that harm poultry but not people (Hansen, 1995). The potential problem here is that the new antibiotic—the only weapon against several virulent strains of dysentery and typhoid fever—may allow these bacteria to develop a resistance to the whole class of synthetic antibiotics called fluoroquinolones. To determine if this potential problem is a real possibility, the FDA has agreed to very limited use of the drug while it carefully monitors the drug's effects "and [will] halt its use if resistance develops" (Hansen, 1995).

http://www.aqmd.gov/rules/html/tofc20.htm

One final case illustrating government's role involves California's Regional Clean Air Incentives Market (RECLAIM). In line with federal guidelines from the 1990 Clean Air Act, RECLAIM gives the 400 highest polluters in Southern California "increasingly tighter annual limits on emissions through [the year] 2003. . . . [C]ompanies that reduce their pollutant discharges below their annual maximums can sell excess emissions rights to other local manufacturers" (Litvan, 1995). The program focuses on allowing companies to determine the best ways for reducing two key smog-producing pollutants: nitrogen and sulfur oxides. In 1996 RECLAIM expanded to include the reduction of reactive organic compounds—those produced when manufacturing solvents and paints—and about 1,000 additional businesses. Although some environmental groups claim that RECLAIM's methods are an inferior approach to controlling pollution, the South Coast Air Quality Management District, which oversees the program, estimates that RECLAIM "will cost industry an estimated $81 million annually . . . or about 42 percent less than it would have cost under the [preexisting system]" (Litvan, 1995).

http://www.epa.gov

The costs of regulation are high and getting higher. Businesses spend billions of dollars and millions of hours reporting to governments and complying with legal mandates. In 1992 the federal Environmental Protection Agency estimated that the chemical industry "will spend $347 million in capital costs and $182 million a year in operating expenses to meet [1992's] new technology requirements for cutting . . . cancer-causing emissions" (Rosewicz, 1992). Although regulations, many argue, have made the United States less competitive around the world, they have also brought about needed reforms. It must be remembered that society grants businesses the right to operate. In return, society retains the right to proper treatment and a clean environment. When these fundamental rights are abused, we all suffer.

Unfortunately, after their products are produced and sold, too many businesses do not consider the costs placed on society. Such costs include cleanups of all kinds and the pressing need to recycle. Our nation has created a Superfund to

Too many businesses do not consider their responsibilities to the environment, resulting in costly cleanups and sometimes irreparable damage.

clean up the worst cases of toxic waste; in fact, it spends hundreds of millions of dollars each year to right the wrongs of irresponsible businesses and individuals. Some environmental damage can never be repaired, or will take more than money to make right. Cleaning up such environmental hazards as nuclear waste, toxic dumps, and oil spills will take years of commitment by dedicated individuals willing to invest the energy and talent required to remedy what has been done. All of us bear the costs through taxes.

Times, however, are changing. A growing number of individuals and corporations are moving from a reactive to a proactive approach and becoming more socially responsible. These people are redesigning processes and products, recycling and repackaging for reduced waste, anticipating needs, and facing problems up front. Businesses are finding that being good citizens pays off, with dividends that contribute to corporate bottom lines. Many companies have found that pollution prevention is better than pollution control. These organizations have made profits through their efforts to both prevent and reduce pollution. In addition, a growing number of consumers are showing their willingness to pay a premium for products that are environmentally friendly.

MANAGING FOR SOCIAL RESPONSIBILITY

Discuss the ways in which businesses can promote socially responsible conduct

Managers today must anticipate society's concerns and actively forecast and plan to meet its needs. They must make social responsibility a priority and, as with ethics, build a concern for it as a priority in their cultures and employees as well.

Top-Management Commitment

Executives in top management must commit the time and money necessary to make their organization socially responsible. They need to act as well as talk. They set the tone for their entire operation and establish its priorities. Authors Christopher B. Hunt and Ellen R. Auster (1990) recommend the following key elements to top managers who want to make their organizations proactive:

- Top-level commitment and support
- Corporate policies that integrate environmental issues
- Effective interfaces between corporate and business-unit staff
- High degree of employee awareness and training
- Strong auditing programs
- Establishment of responsibility for identifying and dealing with real and potential environmental problems

Figure 22.3 provides a checklist for implementing the proactive environmental management program.

Many organizations have built in a variety of safeguards to promote social responsibility. They usually start with the commitment in words and deeds of top management. Policies are written or revised to include concerns for social responsibility as well as ethics. They create programs for promoting an active role for their organizations in meeting societal needs. It is important for companies to write ethical policies for conducting electronic commerce, the subject of this chapter's Managing Technology feature. Training is given to employees, emphasizing

FIGURE 22.3 *Checklist for implementing a proactive environmental management program*

- Secure top-level commitment and long-term funding.
- Develop a corporate environmental policy statement.
- Assign a senior executive to champion the program.
- Assess areas of environmental exposure (i.e., conduct environmental audits and legal reviews).
- Appoint a manager with superior managerial skills and influence within the organization.
- Prioritize program goals and objectives.
- Revise corporate organizational structure to maximize the program's visibility, accessibility, and effectiveness.
- Develop formal reporting relationships within the department and across divisions.
- Identify key individuals in other divisions to serve as liaisons with the environmental department.
- Develop streamlined yet comprehensive management information and record-keeping systems.
- Develop formalized inspection programs.
- Develop training and education programs for environmental staff and key individuals in other divisions.
- Establish a career track for environmental professionals.
- Continually reevaluate program needs and design.

Source: Reprinted from "Proactive Management: Avoiding the Toxic Trap," by Christopher B. Hunt and Ellen R. Auster, *MIT Sloan Management Review*, 1990, p. 24, by permission of the publisher.

MANAGING TECHNOLOGY
Electronic Commerce Ethics

Clinton Wilder, editor at large of *InformationWeek*, provides the following list so that you can make sure your company considers ethics in conducting electronic commerce:

- Be proactive. It's not enough to have a great ethics policy that sits on a shelf with the corporate mission statement. Institute regular ethics training and awareness programs. Move ethics away from "rules to be followed" to becoming a way of doing business.
- Information Technology (IT)-related ethics must be cross-functional. Work with marketing, human resources, and other departments to determine proper ethical standards.
- Link ethics policies to real-world scenarios that your employees may face. Establish clear procedures about who employees should contact with ethics-related questions when questionable situations arise.
- Identify areas where IT management can take the lead in establishing new ethics guidelines. For example, IT executives at Praxair Technology Inc. and Aventis Pharmaceuticals Inc. have led the charge to establish policies for employees' safe use of cell phones and wireless devices while driving.
- Make clear that your standards of ethical behavior also apply to third-party contractors and on-site consultants working in your company.
- If your company doesn't already have one, push for a publicly displayed privacy policy regarding customer data. And pay attention to how that data is shared within the company, as well as with outsiders.
- Above all, emphasize that good ethics makes good business sense. Sacrificing ethics for short-term gain is sure to lose customers and partners in the long run. Ethics is not just a matter of moral correctness—it also means business success.

Source: Wilder, Clinton. "Business Ethics for IT Managers—What You Can Do," *Information Week.com News*, February 19, 2001, http://www.informationweek.com/825/ethics_side.htm.

how they can contribute. They encourage people to participate in their communities by granting time off and other incentives. Managers on leave, whose salaries are paid by their business employer, for instance, staff most United Way campaigns. General Electric has had a public policy committee staffed by members of its board of directors since 1970. It seeks to create social programs and keep track of their progress and achievements (Steiner, 1975). The larger the enterprise, the more likely it is to have a separate department to plan for and oversee organizational efforts to be socially responsible and to see to it that environmental, fair employment, and safety and health regulations are followed (Buehler and Shetty, 1976).

Managers are the key to making ethics and social responsibility realities in their organizations. They need fully formed consciences based on sound values. They need to understand the motives that support their decisions and those of others. They need principles, rewards, examples, and other forms of guidance and support to keep their commitments to ethical and socially responsible actions. See this chapter's Ethical Management feature for an example of ethical leadership by Bob Holland, former CEO of Ben & Jerry's. When an organization is truly committed to meeting its social responsibilities, it reflects this commitment in routine management decision making and ongoing planning efforts; and it monitors those efforts to ensure compliance.

ETHICAL MANAGEMENT
Bob Holland, Ethical Leader

Ben & Jerry's former CEO Bob Holland pleas for an end to the hatred behind the burning of African-American churches at the annual shareholders' meeting on June 22, 1996. Excerpts from his speech are as follows:

A law professor at the University of Pennsylvania, Lani Guinier, who many of you know her name, effectively used a parable about the miner's canary, which I would like to apply here. First of all, for many of you who know that story, canaries have a low tolerance to oxygen deprivation, and the miners took them in the mines with them to warn them that conditions were becoming unsafe, a signal of dire consequences for the inhabitants unless they did something.

The seemingly mindless act of burning a church goes at the heart of the notion of freedom in this country, the right to worship, the freedom of which was the driving force behind the settlement of the new world. These burnings . . . I do not believe are the products of some grand conspiracy. I am afraid, though, that they are the product of a more dangerous and insidious source. It's the source called an era of permissive intolerance.

I can recall perhaps a brighter time a few years ago when friends, my friends were very sensitive to being viewed as insensitive to minority issues, and in fact they'd always use the rejoinder for the slip-ups that, "some of my best friends are black." We've gone from that period to a period of "no need to be insensitive" to a period where it is perfectly acceptable to not only be anti-black, but to also be downright hostile to any notion of rights with respect to any minority, and to act out those hostilities.

These acts of violent intolerance are becoming as seductive in our society, yet as blightful and as harmless as graffiti. It's a form of freedom of expression. Some people might consider it to be an American art. I speak out from here not because . . . maybe because I am personally fearful of what it means. I'm fearful for my family, I'm fearful for my friends, I'm fearful for myself. But I also speak out because I'm fearful that too many of my fellow non-African American Americans don't see the danger to themselves of what is ostensibly a remote act.

I ask you, no I beseech you to think as a new church burns that this is another canary dying. This stands as a signal that something more significant is in imminent peril. What larger and more important treasure is next? This is not an issue of small consequence to all of us, it is a major issue to any of us. Do not remain silent.

Source: Transcript Excerpts—CEO's Remarks from the Ben & Jerry's Annual Shareholders' Meeting 1995, June 22, 1996, http://lib.benjerry.com/fin/anmtgtrans-bob.html. Excerpt reproduced by permission.

Social Audit

To be truly effective, social responsibility needs the backing of all owners, managers, and employees. It must be a consideration in daily decisions, not secondary to those decisions. Managers and owners need to know what is being done to meet social obligations, what will be expected in the future, and what past results and contributions have been.

social audit
A report on the social performance of a business.

The **social audit** is a report on the social performance of a business. No uniform format currently exists, but most proactive firms have devised some method for auditing their efforts and for disclosing the results to both insiders and outsiders. Such an audit usually summarizes corporate activities under the following headings: charitable contributions, support of local community groups and activities, employment of protected groups, political contributions, pollution control and cleanup, health and safety measures, and efforts to improve the quality of work life for employees.

Progress may be stated in terms of goals set and met, in monetary terms, or both. Those who benefit are clearly labeled, and the extent to which they benefit is quantified when possible. A company should share the results of the social audit with all constituents and stakeholders so that it can reinforce awareness of and commitment to the programs. Management should continue programs that have been successful, expand them if the need still persists, and eliminate programs that yield few positive results so that it may institute more productive ones. Finally, management should cite and reward people who contribute to successes.

CHAPTER SUMMARY

1 **Describe the two broad categories of ethical theories.** Ethical theories can be grouped under two main headings: consequential and nonconsequential. The first deals with the ratio of good to evil flowing from an action. The "right" course is the one that yields the highest good to evil ratio.

The nonconsequential theories deal with the obligation to do one's duty to the best of his or her ability. If one is faithful to one's duty, the greatest good occurs because the duty of the individual is carried out.

2 **Explain what individuals need in order to act ethically.** Individuals need a personal moral and ethical code. Morality provides a set of core values and beliefs that act as a guide for evaluating intended actions. This code is acquired through life experiences. In addition, individuals must be able to cultivate a continuous awareness of their personal priorities, goals, values, needs, beliefs, attitudes, and assumptions and how these influence their personal choices.

3 **Describe the organizational influences on ethical conduct.** In addition to individuals' moral and ethical codes, environmental influences affect their choices within the context of their organizational affiliations. An organization's culture, the person's superiors, and the core values and working climate send value messages as to what is essential to survive. Individuals are tempted to place the good of the organization above their personal ethics and the interests of other stakeholders. Ethics, thus, becomes as much an organizational issue as a personal one.

4 **Discuss three primary ways in which businesses can promote ethical conduct.** Organizational controls on employee behaviors and practices can be summarized as a commitment of top management to promote an ethical culture based on organizational integrity through the establishment of codes of ethics and compliance programs. Training, "walking the talk," providing rewards as well as punishments, and establishing clear guidelines and limits are all part of an ethical culture. A variety of mechanisms are used by companies, including hot lines, committees, ethics officers, and the encouragement of whistle-blowing.

5 **Describe the relationship between law and ethics.** The law is an ethical and moral minimum. Individuals must take care to think beyond the law to what is best for all concerned and the effects of their actions. Conforming to the law cannot guarantee ethical conduct. Some laws may be immoral or unjust. No law may exist to forbid an action that can result in unethical behavior.

6 **Explain the concept of an ethical dilemma.** An ethical dilemma exists when people are required to make a choice between options that are or seem equally unfavorable or mutually exclusive. An ethical dilemma also arises when all courses of action open to a manager are judged to be unethical.

7 **Discuss the guidelines for acting ethically.** Many ethical tests exist. Most rely on an individual's personal morals and on a focus beyond the individual or organization. People must think as members of a broad community. They need to recognize that actions can affect many in subtle and not so subtle ways. Consideration for others' welfare is a must. Start with the law and move beyond it. Respect your moral code and those of others. Ask yourself, "What sort of person would take the action I intend to take?" Consider balance: Is there a win-win situation? Finally, ask yourself if you would be willing to tell those you love and the public in general about your intended actions.

8 **Explain the three approaches by businesses to social responsibility.** The three approaches are resistance, being reactive, and being proactive. In the resistance approach, an organization fights to eliminate, delay, or fend off the demands being made on it. In the reactive approach, organizations wait for demands to be made and then respond to them by evaluating their alternatives. The proactive approach leads organizations to actively seek ways to be socially re-

sponsible. They continually look at their operations for ways in which to make them more environmentally friendly. They encourage their employees to be active in community causes. They look at the needs of constituents, constantly staying in touch, sensing their needs, and trying to find ways to meet them. An emerging trend, called "strategic philanthropy" or "financially sound goodwill," encourages businesses to get something in return for what they give.

9 **Explain the responsibilities businesses have to stakeholders.** Stakeholders are owners, employees, external customers, suppliers, and the communities affected by business operations. To owners, a business owes its most effective and efficient use of resources and an adequate return on owners' investments. To employees, it owes respect for their legal rights, fair and equitable treatment, competent guidance, and due process. To external customers, a business owes quality and safe products and services, honest dealings, warnings about any hazards, and fair and equitable treatment. To suppliers, a business owes relationships built on integrity and mutual trust, conformance to the law governing business dealings, and honest conformance to all contractual obligations. Finally, to the communities on which it has an impact, a business owes socially responsible behavior and ethical conduct. It must, at a minimum, obey all laws affecting its interactions.

10 **Describe government's role in promoting socially responsible conduct by businesses.** Businesses exist because government allows them to. Government is the referee in a capitalist society, setting rules and boundaries for economic activity. It must seek a balance between the rights of the individual and those of the various groups in the society it represents. For its laws to be effective, governments depend on individuals throughout society to know and obey them and assist in their enforcement. Additionally, it must put in place various sanctions that will encourage compliance.

11 **Discuss the ways in which businesses can promote socially responsible conduct.** As with ethical conduct, businesses must have leadership at the top that makes socially responsible behavior a core value. If top management is committed, then awareness training, auditing, and rewards for those who act on the core value will follow. Quality of working life will improve, and the company will reap the benefits that result from being a good corporate citizen.

REVIEW QUESTIONS

1. How can simply doing your duty be considered to be acting ethically?
2. In what ways are a person's morals and ethics linked? Can an individual's moral code be an ethical code as well?
3. How can an organization's culture influence the ethics of its members?
4. What can organizations do to promote ethical conduct from their members?
5. What, if anything, is wrong with this statement: "If it's legal, it's ethical."
6. You have been ordered to reduce your ten-person staff, all of whom are quite competent, by two people. What are the possible ethical dilemmas you may face?
7. What guidelines do you use to determine if an intended action is ethical?
8. When a company hires lawyers to find ways around a new environmental law, what approach to social responsibility is it exhibiting?
9. Who are a company's stakeholders? What obligations does the company have to each?
10. How does government promote socially responsible conduct on the part of businesses?
11. How can a business ensure its socially responsible conduct?

DISCUSSION QUESTIONS FOR CRITICAL THINKING

1. A car wash in your neighborhood has decided to increase its business by showcasing bikini-clad ladies drying cars as the cars exit the washing operations. The company proposes to begin offering the new process next week. As a neighborhood resident, what are the ethical and social responsibility issues here? As an alderman in the city government that must approve the proposed change, would you give it your approval? Why or why not?

2. A city ordinance has been proposed for your community. It would require that all sales of alcoholic beverages take place no closer to churches or schools than two city blocks. If it is enacted into law, six businesses (restaurants and taverns) would be forced to relocate or cease doing business. The ordinance is a response to calls for action by church-sponsored community groups and parent-teacher associations. What are the ethical and social responsibility issues here?

3. For both ethical and socially responsible behavior to take place within organizations, their top management must commit to making this happen. Why is top management's commitment essential?

4. Your boss has asked you to alter your time sheets so that more of your time can be allocated to a government project and less of it allocated to business customers. What will you do in response to this request?

INTERNET EXERCISES

Check the text Web site at http://plunkett.swcollege.com for updated links to the Internet Exercises.

1. In a confidential employee survey at TDIndustries (a mechanical contracting and service company), 94 percent of employees agreed with the statement "management is honest and ethical in its business practices." TDIndustries garners that sort of loyalty with a management philosophy of "servant leadership," which emphasizes the leader's role in helping employees develop their careers. Are you a servant leader? Give examples of your servant leadership. How can you become a servant leader?
http://www.tdindustries.com/About/values.asp

2. Many businesses have their own standards—sometimes they're written, sometimes they're just understood. Sometimes they're followed; sometimes they're ignored. And sometimes it comes down to your own personal standards. Read several codes of ethics. Prepare your own personal code of ethics.
http://www.ethics.ubc.ca/resources/business/codes.html
http://csep.iit.edu/codes/business.html

3. Describe an ethical dilemma that you might encounter in the classroom. Use the "TI Ethics Quick Test" to make your decision. Be sure to share your responses to each question.
http://www.ti.com/corp/docs/company/citizen/ethics/quicktest.shtml

APPLICATION CASE

Columbia/HCA's Hospitals: Does Getting Lean Mean Getting Mean?

Columbia-HCA Healthcare Corporation grew to become the largest U.S. health-care provider in 1995 by acquiring nonprofit health-care providers and turning them into profit centers. "By bringing to health care the sort of hard-nosed deal making, consolidating, and cost-cutting tactics that have made other U.S. industries lean, agile, and profitable, Columbia's former chief executive, Richard L. Scott, created a $15 billion juggernaut in just eight short years." For 1995 the company had earnings growth of 27 percent and profit margins of 22 percent. Although Columbia's stockholders and managers were happy, many of its nonprofit competitors believed the company's tactics ignored what was best for patients and their communities.

When Columbia-HCA decided to enter a geographic area, it typically purchased two or more health-care providers, consolidated their services, pooled their talent, and reduced their costs. One tactic for improving efficiency was to replace high-skilled jobholders, such as registered nurses, with lesser skilled and lower paid nurse's aides. Because of its enormous size—326 hospitals and over 100 outpatient facilities—Columbia negotiated price concessions from many of its suppliers, saving it millions each year. The company's efficiencies put pressure on competing facilities to lower their costs, and insurers reported paying less for their policyholders' care in areas where Columbia's facilities were operating. When the company proposed cuts to nursing staff at an El Paso facility, however, physicians objected on the grounds that patient care would be compromised. As a result, the proposal was dropped.

Columbia gives some of its physicians a share in ownership of its facilities, thus enlisting their help in and commitment to generating revenues. Such physicians have been accused of sending indigent cases to nonprofit institutions and steering those who can pay or who are insured to their company's facilities. Columbia denied this accusation.

When Columbia-HCA tried to purchase the not-for-profit South Miami Hospital and prevent it from merging with Baptist Health Systems, South Miami's board rejected the offer. "These were not the sort of people we wanted to do business with in the long term," said Dr. Melvin A. Mackler, chairman of South Miami's board.

http://www.hcahealthcare.com

Questions

1. In what ways might Columbia-HCA's drive for increasing efficiency and profits place patient care in its communities in jeopardy?
2. What ethical issues do you see in this case? [In October 1997, HCA announced the development of its Ethics, Compliance and Corporate Responsibility Department (EC Department), http://www.hcahealthcare.com/ethics/default.htm]
3. What issues relating to social responsibility exist for Columbia-HCA and its nonprofit rivals?

Source: Schiller, Zachary, et al. "Balance Sheets That Get Well Soon," *Business Week*, September 4, 1995, pp. 80–81, 84.

VIDEO CASE

Social Responsibility: Ben & Jerry's

Ben & Jerry's Homemade, Inc., was purchased by the consumer giant Unilever in the summer of 2000. Despite this acquisition, Ben & Jerry's remains a major competitor in the ice cream and frozen yogurt industries by not straying far from its humble beginnings and dedication to social responsibility.

The company's founders are childhood friends Ben Cohen and Jerry Greenfield. Armed with only $12,000 ($4,000 of which was borrowed), a $5 correspondence course on ice cream making, and an old-fashioned rock salt ice cream maker, the two opened their company in 1978 in a renovated gas station in Burlington, Vermont. Their business soon began to prosper, and they became known for their innovative flavors made from fresh Vermont milk and cream. The company grew and diversified until today it makes and distributes ice cream, low-fat ice cream, frozen yogurt, sorbet, and novelty products nationwide and in selected foreign countries. Retailers that handle its products include supermarkets, grocery stores, convenience stores, franchised Ben & Jerry scoop shops, and restaurants.

For the first ten years the company operated as a village culture, whereby the values of the company were passed on orally rather than as a formal written document. However, in 1988, as the company began to grow rapidly, the founders and employees decided to write a formal mission statement for the company. This statement explains what the company stands for and has three interrelated parts, addressing product, economic, and social concerns. Ben & Jerry's is committed to making quality products, achieving economic rewards for its shareholders, and meeting its social mission by having a commitment to its community. All three parts are viewed as working in harmony to achieve the company's goals.

One example of how Ben & Jerry's attempts to achieve the social aspect of the company's mission is through its philanthropic efforts. It annually gives 7.5 percent of its pretax earnings to three beneficiaries: the Ben & Jerry's Foundation, employee community action teams at five Vermont locations, and projects supported by corporate grants made by its director of social mission development. These support projects are models for social change and exhibit creative problem solving and give hope to many people. The foundation, for example, is managed by nine employees who consider proposals relating to children and families, disadvantaged groups, and the environment.

Cohen and Greenfield believe that the company enjoys its current position in the marketplace by "brand equity" generated by its foundation work and other socially responsible actions. Brand equity is manifested by consumers who choose Ben & Jerry's, are brand loyal in their continuing purchases, and buy shares of stock in the company. Being socially responsible is viewed by everyone at Ben & Jerry's as fulfilling its mission, not as a drain on its resources.

http://www.benjerry.com

For Discussion:

1. Describe and give examples of how Ben & Jerry's actions reflect the company's mission.
2. Is Ben & Jerry's argument that "brand equity" is responsible for the company's continued success valid? Explain.

Recommended Reading

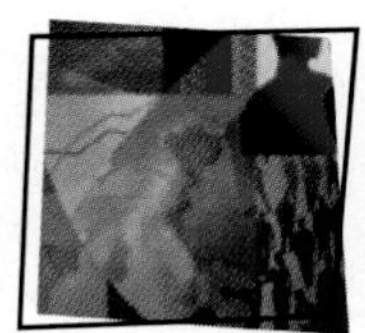

CHAPTER 1

Blanchard, Kenneth V., Sheldon M. Bowles, Don Carew, and eParisi-Carew. *High Five! The Magic of Working Together*, William Morrow & Co., 2000.

Buckingham, Marcus, and Curt Coffman. *First, Break All the Rules: What the World's Greatest Managers Do Differently*, Simon & Schuster, 1999.

Fried, Lisa. "The Worst Boss in the World," *Management Review* (December 1994), pp. 24–25.

Graham, John R. "Ten Trends That Will Shape Business and Careers," *Management Review* (April 1995), p. 3.

Hutt, Michael D., Beth A. Walker, and Gary L. Frankwick. "Hurdle the Cross-Functional Barriers to Strategic Change," *Sloan Management Review* (Spring 1995), pp. 22–30.

Jennings, Jason, and Laurence Haughton. *It's Not the Big that Eat the Small . . . It's the Fast that Eat the Slow*, HarperCollins, 2001.

Jones, Thomas, and W. Earl Sasser, Jr. "Why Satisfied Customers Defect," *Harvard Business Review* (November–December 1995), pp. 88–107.

Kotter, John P. "Leading Change: Why Transformation Efforts Fail," *Harvard Business Review* (March–April 1995), pp. 59–67.

Lee, William G. "Southwest Airlines' Herb Kelleher: Unorthodoxy At Work," *Management Review* (January 1995), pp. 9–12.

Morris, Betsy. "Roberto Goizueta and Jack Welch: The Wealth Builders," *Fortune*, December 11, 1995, pp. 80–84, 88, 90, 94.

Paine, Lynn Sharp. "Managing for Organizational Integrity," *Harvard Business Review* (March–April 1994), pp. 106–117.

CHAPTER 2

Bartlett, Christopher A., and Sumantra Ghoshal. "Changing the Role of Top Management: Beyond Systems to People," *Harvard Business Review* (May–June 1995), pp. 132–142.

Champy, James. *Reengineering Management: The Mandate for New Leadership*. New York: HarperBusiness, 1995.

Colenso, Michael. *Kaizen Strategies for Successful Organizational Change: Evolution and Revolution in the Organization*. Financial Times Prentice Hall Publishing, 2000.

Collins, James C., and Jerry I. Porras. *Built to Last*. HarperBusiness, 1997.

Davenport, Thomas H. "The Fad That Forgot People," *Fast Company*, November 1995, p. 70, <http://www.fastcompany.com/online/01/reengin.html>.

Feigenbaum, Armand V. "Total Quality Control," *Harvard Business Review* (November–December 1956), pp. 95–98.

Ghoshal, Sumantra, and Christopher A. Bartlett. *The Individualized Corporation: A Fundamentally New Approach to Management*, HarperBusiness, 1999.

Hamel, Gary, and C. K. Prahalad. *Competing for the Future*. Boston: Harvard Business School Press, 1994.

Hammer, Michael, and James Champy. *Reengineering the Corporation*, New York: HarperBusiness, 1993, pp. 32–33.

Hammer, Michael, and Steven A. Stanton. *The Reengineering Revolution: A Handbook*. New York: HarperBusiness, 1995.

Hymowitz, Carol, "Great Plains Software CEO Studies Past to Learn Future," *The Wall Street Journal Interactive Edition*, November 21, 2000, <http://interactive.wsj.com/archive/retrieve.cgi?id=SB974762012632265786.djm>.

Maslow, Abraham, Deborah C. Stephens, and Gary Heil. *Maslow on Management*, Wiley, 1998.

Sellers, Patricia. "To Avoid a Trampling, Get Ahead of the Mass," *Fortune*, May 15, 1995, p. 201.

Weber, Max. *Theory of Social and Economic Organization*. New York: Free Press, 1947.

Wren, Daniel A. *The Evolution of Management Thought*, 3rd ed. New York: Wiley, 1987.

CHAPTER 3

A Business Week Guide. The Quality Imperative, eds. of *Business Week*. New York: McGraw-Hill, 1994.

Cox, Jeff (Contributor) and William C. Byham (Preface). *Zapp!: The Lightning of Empowerment: How to Improve Quality, Productivity, and Employee Satisfaction*. Fawcett Books, 1998.

Crego, Edwin T., Jr., and Peter D. Schiffrin. *Customer-Centered Reengineering: Remapping for Total Customer Value*. New York: Irwin, 1995.

Dean, James W., Jr., and James R. Evans. *Total Quality: Management, Organization, and Strategy*. New York: West, 1994.

Dubrin, Andrew J. *Reengineering Survival Guide: Managing and Succeeding in the Changing Workplace*. Cincinnati, Ohio: Thomson Executive Press, 1996.

Hamel, Gary, and C. K. Prahalad. *Competing for the Future*. Boston: Harvard Business School Press, 1994.

Harry, Mikel J. and Richard Schroeder. *Six Sigma, The Breakthrough Management Strategy Revolutionizing The World's Top Corporations*. Doubleday, 1999.

Heil, Gary, Tom Parker, and Rick Tate. *Leadership and the Customer Revolution*. New York: Van Nostrand Reinhold, 1995.

Johansson, Henry J., Patrick McHugh, A. John Pendlebury, William A. Wheeler III. *Business Process Reengineering: Breakpoint Strategies for Market Dominance*. New York: Wiley, 1993.

Juran, Joseph M. (Editor), A. Blanton Godfrey (Editor), A. Blanford Godfrey. *Juran's Quality Handbook*, 5th Ed. McGraw-Hill Book Company, 1999.

Naumann, Earl. *Creating Customer Value: The Path to Sustainable Competitive Advantage*. Cincinnati, Ohio: Thomson Executive Press, 1995.

Nauman, Earl, and Kathleen Giel. *Customer Satisfaction Measurement and Management*. Cincinnati, Ohio: Thomson Executive Press, 1995.

Pande, Peter S. et al, Robert P. Neuman, Roland R. Cavanagh. *The Six Sigma Way: How GE, Motorola, and Other Top Companies are Honing Their Performance*. McGraw-Hill Professional Publishing, 2000.

Peppers, Don, and Martha Rogers. *The One to One Manager: Real-World Lessons in Customer Relationship Management*, Currency/Doubleday, 2000.

Peters, Tom. *The Pursuit of Wow!*. New York: Vintage Books, 1994.

Treacy, Michael, and Fred Wiersema. *The Discipline of Market Leaders: Choose Your Customers, Narrow Your Focus, Dominate Your Market*. Perseus Press, 1997.

Walther, George R. *Upside-Down Marketing: Turning Your Ex-Customer into Your Best Customers*. New York: McGraw-Hill, 1994.

CHAPTER 4

Bartlett, Christopher A., and Sumantra Ghoshal. "Changing the Role of Top Management: Beyond Systems to People," *Harvard Business Review* (May–June 1995), pp. 132–142.

Bates, Anthony W. *Managing Technological Change*. Jossey-Bass, 1999.

Buzzell, Robert D., and Gwen Ortmeyer. "Channel Partnerships Streamline Distribution," *Sloan Management Review* (Spring 1995), pp. 85–96.

Case, John. "The Open-Book Revolution," *Inc.* (June 1995), pp. 26–30, 32, 43, 36, 38–40, 43.

Davidow, William H., and Michael S. Malone. *The Virtual Corporation*. New York: HarperBusiness, 1992.

Frost, Peter J., Vance F. Mitchell, and Walter R. Nord. *Managerial Reality: Balancing Technique, Practice and Values*, 2nd ed. New York: HarperCollins, 1995.

Haywood, Martha. *Managing Virtual Teams: Practical Techniques for High-Technology Project Managers*. Artech House Professional Development Library, 1998.

Jacob, Rahul. "The Struggle to Create an Organization for the 21st Century," *Fortune*, April 3, 1995, pp. 90–92, 94, 96, 98–99.

Joël de Rosnay. *The Macroscope*. Originally published in 1979 by Harper & Row (New York), http://pespmc1.vub.ac.be/MACRBOOK.html. This book is an excellent easy-to-read introduction to cybernetics and systems thinking, with applications to living organisms, the economy, and the world as a whole. The main theme is that the complex systems which govern our life should be looked at as a whole, rather than be taken apart into their constituents. The different systems, processes, and mechanisms are beautifully illustrated with examples and pictures. Although the text is over 20 years old, this visionary document is still highly relevant to our present situation and state of knowledge. It is particularly recommended to people who wish to get an understanding of the basic concepts and applications of systems theory and cybernetics. The chapters can be read independently of each other.

Labich, Kenneth. "Why Companies Fail," *Fortune*, November 14, 1994, pp. 52–54, 58, 60, 64, 68.

Peters, Tom. *The Tom Peters Seminar*. New York: Vintage Books, 1994.

Senge, Peter M. *The Fifth Discipline: The Art & Practice of the Learning Organization*. New York: Currency Doubleday, 1994.

Tidd, Joseph, Keith Pavitt (Contributor), Joe Tidd, and J. R. Bessant. *Managing Innovation: Integrating Technological, Market and Organizational Change*. John Wiley & Sons, 1997.

Tully, Shawn. "Purchasing's New Muscle," *Fortune*, February 20, 1995, pp. 75–76, 78–79, 82–83.

CHAPTER 5

Byrne, John A. "Hired Guns Packing Hired-Powered Knowhow," *Business Week*, January 17, 1995, pp. 92–96.

DeMott, John S. "New Mission," *Nation's Business* (November 1994), pp. 20–27.

Ettorre, Barbara. "A Strategy Session with C. K. Prahalad," *Management Review* (April 1995), pp. 50–52.

Finegan, Jay, "Everything According to Plan," *Inc.* (March 1995), pp. 78–85.

Hamel, Gary. *Leading the Revolution*. Harvard Business School Press, 2000.

Hamel, Gary, and C. K. Prahalad. "Seeing the Future First," *Fortune*, September 5, 1994, pp. 64–70.

Harari, Oren. "Beyond the Vision Thing," *Management Review* (November 1994), pp. 29–31.

Henkoff, Ronald. "Keeping Motorola on a Roll," *Fortune*, April 18, 1994, pp. 68–78.

Jacob, Rabul. "Corporate Reputations," *Fortune*, March 6, 1995, pp. 54–64.

Kaplan, Robert S., and David P. Norton. *The Strategy-Focused Organization: How Balanced Scorecard Companies Thrive in the New Business Environment*. Harvard Business School, 2000.

Labich, Kenneth. "Why Companies Fail," *Fortune*, November 14, 1994, pp. 52–68.

McGrath, Rita Gunther, and Ian MacMillan. *The Entrepreneurial Mindset*. Harvard Business School Press, 2000.

Zellner, Wendy. "Go-Go Goliaths," *Business Week*, February 13, 1995, pp. 64–75.

CHAPTER 6

Axelrod, Alan, George Steinbrenner III (Preface), and William A. Cohen. *Patton on Leadership: Strategic Lessons for Corporate Warfare*. Prentice Hall Press, 1999.

Bhide, Amar. "How Entrepreneurs Craft Strategies That Work," *Harvard Business Review* (March–April 1994), pp. 150–161.

Dudik, Evan Matthew. *Strategic Renaissance: New Thinking and Innovative Tools to Create Great Corporate Strategies Using Insights from History and Science*. AMACOM, 2000.

Fierman, Jaclyn. "When Genteel Rivals Become Mortal Enemies," *Fortune*, May 15, 1995, pp. 90–100.

Garvin, David A. "Leveraging Processes for Strategic Advantage," *Harvard Business Review* (September–October 1995), pp. 77–90.

Gault, Robert F. "Large Companies Are You Listening," *Management Review* (September 1994), pp. 42–44.

Gertz, Dwight. "The Dynamics of Corporate Growth," *Management Review* (January 1995), pp. 46–48.

Langley, Ann. "Between 'Paralysis by Analysis' and 'Extinction by Instinct,'" *Sloan Management Review* (Spring 1995), pp. 63–76.

Lesley, Elizabeth. "Hot Growth Companies," *Business Week*, May 22, 1995, pp. 68–80.

Mamis, Robert. "Crash Course," *Inc.* (February 1995), pp. 54–63.

McCune, Jenny C. "In the Shadow of Wal-Mart," *Management Review* (December 1994), pp. 11–16.

Symonds, William C., and Paula Dwyer. "A Third Front Is the Cola Wars," *Business Week*, December 12, 1994, pp. 66–68.

Threadgill, John. "Expansion Strategies," *Inc.* (December 1994), pp. 37–46.

Wells, Stuart. *Choosing the Future, The Power of Strategic Thinking*. Butterworth-Heinemann, 1997.

CHAPTER 7

Balle, Michael. *Managing with Systems Thinking: Making Dynamics Work for You in Business Decision Making*. New York: McGraw-Hill, 1994.

Bartlett, Christopher A., and Sumantra Goshal. "Executive Decision Models," *Harvard Business Review* (November–December 1994), pp. 79–89.

Baverman, Jerome D. *Management Decision Making: A Formal-Intuitive Approach*. New York: Wiley, 1994.

Bursk, Edward C., and John Chapman. *New Decision Making Tools for Managers*. Westport, Conn.: Greenwood Publishing Group, 1994.

Driver, Michael. *Dynamic Decision Maker: Five Decision Styles for Executives*. San Francisco: Jossey-Bass, 1994.

Ellis, Donald G., and Mary B. Aubrey. *Small Group Decision Making: The Group Processes*. New York: McGraw-Hill, 1994.

Heller, Robert, and Tim Hindle. *Essential Managers: Making Decisions*. Dk Pub Merchandise, 1999.

Hickson, David J. *Strategic Decision-Making in Organizations*. San Francisco: Jossey-Bass, 1994.

Hoenig, Christopher W. *The Problem Solving Journey: Your Guide for Making Decisions and Getting Results*. Perseus Press, 2000.

Klein, Gary. *Sources of Power: How People Make Decisions*. MIT Press, 1999.

Mandel, Michael. "How Game Theory Rewrote All the Rules," *Business Week*, October 24, 1994, p. 44.

OxenFeld, T. *Cost-Benefit Analysis for Executive Decision Making*. New York: McGraw-Hill, 1994.

Sims, Ronald R. *Organizational Decision Making*. Westport, Conn.: Greenwood Publishing Group, 1994.

CHAPTER 8

Belasco, James A., and Ralph C. Stayer. "Why Empowerment Doesn't Empower: The Bankruptcy of Current Paradigms," *Business Horizons* (March–April 1994), pp. 29–42.

Blanchard, Kenneth H. (Preface), John P. Carlos (Preface), Alan Randolph, and Ken Blanchard. *The 3 Keys to Empowerment: Release the Power Within People for Astonishing Results*. Berrett-Koehler Publishers, Inc., 1999.

Caudron, Shari. "Delegate for Results," *Industry Week*, February 6, 1995, pp. 27–30.

Hise, Phaedra, "Making A Clean Break: Delegating," *Inc.* (June 1994), p. 111.

Kanter, Rosabeth Moss. *Evolve!: Succeeding in the Digital Culture of Tomorrow*. Harvard Business School Press, 2001.

March, James, and Herbert Simon. *Organizations*, 2nd ed. Cambridge, Mass.: Blackwell, 1994.

Marshall, Robert. "Keeping Employees Focused During A Reorganization," *Nation's Business* (March 1995), p. 12.

McGinty, Sarah Myers. *Power Talk: Using Language to Build Authority and Influence*. Warner Books, 2001.

Pinchot, Gifford, and Elizabeth Pinchot. *The End of Bureaucracy and the Rise of Intelligent Organizations*. San Francisco, Calif.: Berret-Koehler, 1994.

Redding, John C., and Ralph Catalanello. *Strategic Readiness: The Making of a Learning Organization*. San Francisco, Calif.: Jossey-Bass, 1994.

Riggs, Joy. "Empowering Workers by Setting Goals," *Nation's Business* (January 1995), p. 6.

Roebuck, Chris. *Effective Delegation*. AMACOM, 1999.

Sentell, Gerald D. *Fast, Focused, and Flexible: Bold New High Performance Organizations*. Knoxville, Tenn.: Pressmark International, 1994.

Stone, Florence. "How Do You Rate As a Delegator?" *Management Review* (May 1994), p. 2.

CHAPTER 9

Ackoff, Russell Lincoln. *Re-Creating the Corporation: A Design of Organizations for the 21st Century*. Oxford University Press, 1999.

Beer, Michael (Editor), and Nitin Nohria (Editor). *Breaking the Code of Change*. Harvard Business School Press, 2000.

Bottoms, David. "Back to the Future: Revisiting the Promise of the 'Virtual Corporation,'" *Industry Week*, October 3, 1994, pp. 61–64.

Curtis, Keith A. *From Management Goal Setting to Organizational Results: Transforming Strategies into Action*. Westport, Conn.: Greenwood Publishing Group, 1994.

Davis, Margaret R., David A. Weckler, and Janis Paris. *A Practical Guide to Organization Design*. Crisp Publications, 1996.

Ettorre, Barbara. "Reengineering Tales from the Front," *Management Review* (January 1995), pp. 13–18.

Galbraith, Jay. *Competing with Flexible Lateral Organizations*, 2nd ed. Reading, Mass.: Addison-Wesley, 1994.

Goldstein, Jeffrey. *The Unshackled Organization: Facing the Challenge of Unpredictability Through Reorganization*. Fort Lauderdale, Fla.: Pro Publishing, 1994.

Greising, David. *I'd Like the World to Buy a Coke: The Life and Leadership of Roberto Goizueta*, John Wiley & Sons, Inc., 1998.

Jergens, Elliott. "When Slimming Is Not Enough," *The Economist*, September 3, 1994, pp. 59–61.

Kimberly, John. *The Organizational Life Cycle: Issues in the Creation, Transformation, and Decline of Organizations*. Ann Arbor, Mich.: Books On Demand, 1994.

Merron, Arthur. *Architecting Your Organization*. New York: Van Nostrand Reinhold, 1994.

Morevec, Milan. "The Right Way to Downsize: 10 Mistakes Companies Make in Downsizing," *Industry Week*, September 5, 1994, p. 46.

Schmenner, Roger, and Charles Lackey. "Slash and Burn Doesn't Kill Weeds: Other Ways to Downsize the Manufacturing Organization," *Business Horizons* (July–August 1994), pp. 80–88.

Tushman, Michael L (Contributor), Mark B. Nadler, and David A. Nadler. *Competing by Design: The Power of Organizational Architecture*. Oxford University Press, 1997.

CHAPTER 10

Anthony, Peter. *Managing Culture*. Washington, D.C.: Taylor & Francis, Inc., 1994.

Bate, Paul. *Strategies for Cultural Change*. Newton, Mass.: Butterworth-Heinemann, 1994.

Connors, Roger, and Thomas Smith. *Journey to the Emerald City: Achieve A Competitive Edge by Creating A Culture of Accountability*. Prentice Hall Press, 1999.

Crane, Thomas G. *The Heart of Coaching: Using Transformational Coaching to Create a High-Performance Culture*. F T A Press, 1998.

Egan, Gerard. "Cultivate Your Culture," *Management Today* (April 1994), pp. 38–43.

Fairholm, Gilbert W. *Leadership and the Culture of Trust*. Westport, Conn.: Praeger, 1994.

Farquhar, Katherine. "The Myth of the Forever Leader: Cultural Recovery from Broken Leadership," *Business Horizons* (September–October 1994), pp. 42–51.

Hammer, Michael. "Hammer Defends Reengineering," *The Economist*, November 5, 1994, p. 11.

LaBarre, Polly. "The Cultural Revolution," *Industry Week*, March 16, 1994, pp. 12–18.

Neuhauser, Peg, C. Ray Bender, and Kirk L. Stromberg. *Culture.com: Building Corporate Culture in the Connected Workplace*. John Wiley & Sons, 2000.

Schneider, William E. *Zeroing in on Success: How to Focus the Corporate Culture*. San Francisco, Calif.: Jossey-Bass, 1994.

Shaughnessey, Haydn. *Collaboration Management: Cultural Issues and Priorities*. New York: Wiley, 1994.

Spiker, Barry K. "Making Change Stick," *Industry Week*, March 7, 1994, p. 45.

Zwell, Ph.D. Michael, *Creating a Culture of Competence*. John Wiley & Sons, 2000.

CHAPTER 11

Allen, Jeffrey G. *Complying with the ADA: A Small Business Guide to Hiring and Employing the Disabled*. New York: Wiley, 1993.

Caruth, Donald L. and Gail D. Handlogten. *Staffing the Contemporary Organization*. Quorum Books, 1997.

Davis, Robert, Susan Rosegrant, and Michael Watkins. "Managing the Link Between Measurement and Compensation," *Quality Progress* (February 1995), pp. 101–106.

Flynn, Julia, and Farah Nayeri. "Continental Divide over Executive Pay," *Business Week*, June 3, 1995, pp. 40–41.

Galen, Michele, and Ann Palmer. "White, Male, and Worried," *Business Week*, January 31, 1994, pp. 50–55.

Gordon, Edward E., Ronald R. Morgan, and Judith A. Ponticell. *Future Work—The Revolution Reshaping American Business*. New York: Praeger, 1995.

Klimas, Molly. "How to Recruit a Smart Team," *Nation's Business* (May 1995), pp. 26–27.

McKirchy, Karen. *Powerful Performance Appraisals: How to Set Expectations and Work Together to Improve Performance*. Career Press, 1998.

Outlaw, Wayne. *Smart Staffing*. Upstart Publishing Co., 1998.

Sonnenberg, Frank. *Managing with a Conscience*. New York: McGraw-Hill, 1994.

Thorne, J. D. "How to Head Off Termination Suits," *Nation's Business* (May 1995), pp. 28–29.

Tully, Shawn. "America's Healthiest Companies," *Fortune*, June 12, 1995, pp. 98–100, 104, 106.

Tully, Shawn. "Are Your Paid Enough?" *Fortune*, June 26, 1995, pp. 66–69, 72, 76.

CHAPTER 12

Buzzell, Robert D., and Gwen Ortmeyer. "Channel Partnerships Streamline Distribution," *Sloan Management Review* (Spring 1995), pp. 85–95.

Case, John. "The Open-Book Revolution," *Inc.* (June 1995), pp. 26–30, 32, 34, 36, 38–43.

Dumaine, Brian. "The Trouble with Teams," *Fortune*, September 5, 1994, p. 92.

Kegan, Robert, and Lisa Laskow Lahey. *How the Way We Talk Can Change the Way We Work: Seven Languages for Transformation*. San Francisco, Calif.: Jossey-Bass, 2000.

Lacity, Mary C., Leslie P. Willcocks, and David F. Feeny. "IT Outsourcing: Maximize Flexibility and Control," *Harvard Business Review* (May–June 1995), pp. 84–93.

Lichtenberg, Ronna. *It's Not Business, It's Personal*. Hyperion, 2001.

Maremont, Mark. "Digital's Turnaround: Time for Phase Two," *Business Week*, June 19, 1995, pp. 130, 132, 134–135.

Mateja, Jim. "J. D. Power Speaks; Chrysler Listens," *Chicago Tribune*, August 21, 1994, sec. 4, p. 7.

Maynard, Roberta. "The Growing Appeal of Telecommuting," *Nation's Business* (August 1994), pp. 61–62.

Senge, Peter M. *The Fifth Discipline: The Art and Practice of the Learning Organization*. Currency/Doubleday, 1994.

Sprout, Alison L. "Reality Boost," *Fortune*, March 21, 1994, p. 93.

Tetzeli, Rick. "Surviving Information Overload," *Fortune*, July 11, 1994, p. 61.

CHAPTER 13

Atkinson, John W. *Motivation and Achievement*. Glenview, Ill.: Praeger, 1994.

Bailey, Debra. "Aligning Work and Rewards," *Management Review* (February 1995), pp. 19–24.

Beck, Robert C. *Motivation: Theories and Principles*. Prentice Hall, 1999.

Cronin, Michael P. "Motivation the Old-Fashioned Way," *Inc.* (November 1994), p. 134.

Fierman, Jaclyn. "The Perilous New World of Fair Pay," *Fortune*, June 13, 1994, pp. 57–62.

Franken, Robert E. *Human Motivation*, 3rd ed. Pacific Grove, Calif.: Brooks/Cole, 1994.

Kinni, Theodore. "The Empowered Work Force," *Industry Week*, September 14, 1994, pp. 37–40.

Madsden, K. B. *Theories of Motivation: A Comparative Study of Modern Theories of Motivation*. San Francisco, Calif.: Jossey-Bass, 1994.

McClelland, David C., and David H. Burnham. "Power Is the Great Motivator," *Harvard Business Review* (January–February 1995), pp. 126–136.

O'Neil, Harold, and Michael Drillings. *Motivation: Theory and Research*. Hillsdale, N.J.: Erlbaum, Lawrence Associates, 1994.

Pinder, Craig C. *Work Motivation in Organizational Behavior*. Prentice Hall College Division, 1997.

Rheem, Helen. "Effective Leadership: The Pygmalion Effect," *Harvard Business Review* (May–June 1995), p. 14.

Thomas, Kenneth W. *Intrinsic Motivation at Work: Building Energy & Commitment*. Berrett-Koehler Publishing, 2000.

CHAPTER 14

Caminiti, Susan. "What Team Leaders Need to Know," *Fortune*, February 20, 1995, pp. 93–94, 98, 100.

Covey, Stephen R., A. Roger Merrill, and Rebecca R. Merrill. *First Things First*. New York: Simon & Schuster, 1994.

Covey, Stephen R., A. Roger Merrill, and Rebecca R. Merrill. *First Things First: To Live, to Love, to Learn, to Leave a Legacy*. Fireside, 1996.

Davidow, William H., and Michael S. Malone. *The Virtual Corporation: Lessons from the World's Most Advanced Companies*. New York: HarperBusiness, 1993.

Fisher, Anne B. "Making Change Stick," *Fortune*, April 17, 1995, pp. 121–122, 124, 128–131.

Hamel, Gary, and C. K. Prahalad. "Seeing the Future First," *Fortune*, September 5, 1994, pp. 64–67, 70.

Henkoff, Ronald. "Finding, Training, & Keeping the Best Service Workers," *Fortune*, October 3, 1994, pp. 110–111, 114, 116, 118, 120, 122.

Huey, John, "The New Post-Heroic Leadership," *Fortune*, February 21, 1994, pp. 42–44, 48, 50.

Kotter (Editor), John P. *John P. Kotter on What Leaders Really Do*. Harvard Business School, 1999.

Kotter, John P. "Leading Change: Why Transformation Efforts Fail," *Harvard Business Review* (March–April 1995), pp. 59–67.

Langley, Ann. "Between 'Paralysis by Analysis' and 'Extinction by Instinct,'" *Sloan Management Review* (Spring 1995), pp. 63–76.

Pacetta, Frank, with Roger Gittines. *Don't Fire Them, Fire Them Up*. New York: Simon & Schuster, 1994.

Pacetta, Frank, with Roger Gittines. *Don't Fire Them, Fire Them Up: Motivate Yourself and Your Team*. Fireside, 1995.

Pound, John. "The Promise of the Governed Corporation," *Harvard Business Review* (March–April 1995), pp. 89–98.

Ulrich, David, Jack Zenger, Norman Smallwood. *Results-Based Leadership*. Harvard Business School Press, 1999.

CHAPTER 15

Cornyn-Selby, Alyce P. *Teamwork & Team Sabotage*. Portland, Ore.: Beynch Press, 1994.

Crawley, John. *Constructive Conflict Management: Managing to Make a Difference*. Nicholas Brealey, 1997.

Crawley, John. *Constructive Conflict Management: Managing to Make a Difference*. San Diego, Calif.: Pfeiffer & Company, 1994.

Deegan, Denise. *Managing Activism: A Guide to Dealing with Activists and Pressure Groups*. Kogan Page Ltd., 2001.

Elledge, Robin, and Steve Phillips. *Team Building for the Future: Beyond the Basics*. San Diego, Calif.: Pfeiffer & Company, 1994.

Fisher, Kimball. *Leading Self-Directed Work Teams: A Guide to Developing New Team Leadership Skills*. McGraw-Hill Professional Publishing, 1999.

Frohman, Mark A. "Do Teams . . . But Do Them Right," *Industry Week*, April 3, 1995, pp. 21–24.

Harper, Ann, and Bob Harper. *Team Barriers: Actions for Overcoming the Barriers to Empowerment, Involvement, and High-Performance*. Mohegan Lake, N.Y.: MW Corporation, 1994.

Kindler, Herbert S., and Kay Keppler (Editor). *Managing Disagreement Constructively: Conflict Management in Organizations*. Crisp Publications, 1997.

Meyer, Christopher. "How the Right Measures Help Teams Excel," *Harvard Business Review* (May-June 1994), pp. 95–104.

Rabin, M. Afzalur, and Albert Blum. *Perspectives on Organizational Conflict*. Glenview, Ill.: Greenwood Publishing Group, 1994.

Thompson, Leigh L. *Making the Team: A Guide for Managers*. Prentice Hall, 2000.

Van Horn, Eric. "The Trouble with Teams," *The Economist*, January 14, 1995, p. 61.

Wellauer, Suzy. "The Team That Wasn't: With a Group of Talented Hard-Working People, Why Isn't This Team Working?" *Harvard Business Review* (November–December 1994), pp. 22–33.

Yeattis, Dale E., Martha Hipskind, and Debra Barnes. "Lessons Learned from Self-Managed Work Teams," *Business Horizons* (July–August 1994), pp. 11–19.

CHAPTER 16

Bianchi, Alessandra. "The Strictly Business Flextime Request Form," *Inc.* (May 1995), p. 79.

Johnson, Michael D., and Anders Gustafsson. *Improving Customer Satisfaction, Loyalty, and Profit: An Integrated Measurement and Management System*. San Francisco, Calif.: Jossey-Bass, 2000.

Keen, Peter G. W., and Mark McDonald. *The eProcess Edge: Creating Customer Value & Business in the Internet Era*. Computing McGraw-Hill, 2000.

Kelly, Kevin. "Deere's Surprising Harvest in Health Care," *Business Week*, July 11, 1994, pp. 107, 111.

Loeb, Marshall. "Leadership Lost—and Regained," *Fortune*, April 17, 1995, pp. 217–218.

Macht, Joshua D. "How Has Technology Changed the Way You Do Your Job?" *Inc. Technology* (July 1995), p. 37.

Naumann, Earl. *Creating Customer Value: The Path to Sustainable Competitive Advantage*. Cincinnati, Ohio: Thomson Executive Press, 1995.

Naumann, Earl, and Kathleen Giel. *Customer Satisfaction Measurement and Management*. Cincinnati, Ohio: Thomson Executive Press, 1995.

Smith, Timothy K. "Why Air Travel Doesn't Work," *Fortune*, April 3, 1995, pp. 42–46, 50, 52, 56.

Treacy, Michael, and Fred Wiersema. *The Discipline of Market Leaders*. New York: Addison-Wesley, 1995.

Treacy, Michael, and Fred Wiersema. *The Discipline of Market Leaders*. Perseus Press, 1997.

Tully, Shawn. "Purchasing's New Muscle," *Fortune*, February 20, 1995, pp. 75–76, 78–79, 82–83.

Zweig, Phillip L. "Prudential: Making It Rock-Solid Again," *Business Week*, October 31, 1994, p. 96.

Zweig, Phillip L., et al. "Managing Risk," *Business Week*, October 31, 1994, pp. 86–90, 92.

CHAPTER 17

Breyfogle III, Forrest W., James M. Cupello, and Becki Meadows. *Managing Six Sigma: A Practical Guide to Understanding, Assessing, and Implementing the Strategy That Yields Bottom-Line Success*. John Wiley & Sons, 2000.

Chabow, Eric R. "The Training Payoff," *Informationweek*, July 10, 1995, pp. 36–38, 40, 42, 46.

Conlin, Elizabeth. "Pieces of Advice," *Inc.* (May 1995), pp. 57–60, 61.

Harvard Business Review on Measuring Corporate Performance. Harvard Business School Press, 1998.

Hodgetts, Richard M. *Measures of Quality and High Performance: Simple Tools and Lessons Learned from America's Most Successful Corporations*. AMACOM, 1998.

Hof, Robert D. "Intel: Far Beyond the Pentium," *Business Week*, February 20, 1995, pp. 88–90.

Huey, John. "Eisner Explains Everything," *Fortune*, April 17, 1995, pp. 44–48, 52, 56, 58–60, 64, 68.

Huey, John. "The New Post-Heroic Leadership," *Fortune*, February 21, 1994, pp. 42–44, 48, 50.

Kaydos, W. J. *Operational Performance Measurement: Increasing Total Productivity*. CRC Press—St. Lucie Press, 1998.

Lacity, Mary C., Leslie P. Willcocks, and David F. Feeny. "IT Outsourcing: Maximize Flexibility and Control," *Harvard Business Review* (May–June 1995), pp. 84–93.

Lubove, Seth. "Get 'em Before They Get You," *Forbes*, July 31, 1995, pp. 88–93.

Mamis, Robert A. "Master of Bootstrapping Administration," *Inc.* (August 1995), pp. 40–42, 45.

Paine, Lynn Sharp. "Managing for Organizational Integrity," *Harvard Business Review* (March–April 1994), pp. 106–117.

Taylor III, Alex. "Boeing: Sleepy in Seattle," *Fortune*, August 7, 1995, pp. 92–94, 96, 98.

Verity, John W., and Russell Mitchell. "A Trillion-Byte Weapon," *Business Week*, July 31, 1995, pp. 80–81.

CHAPTER 18

Brandimarte, Brandon. *Advanced Models: Manufacturing Systems Management*. Elkins Park, Penn.: Franklin Book Co., 1995.

Bushnell, P. Timothy. *Transformation of the American Manufacturing Paradigm*. New York: Garland, 1994.

Darlin, Damon. "Automating the Automators," *Forbes*, February 14, 1994, pp. 156–157.

Davis, John W., and Steven Ott (Contributor). *Fast Track to Waste-Free Manufacturing: Straight Talk from a Plant Manager (Manufacturing and Production)*. Productivity Press, 1999.

Dorf, Richard C., and Andrew Kusiak. *Manufacturing Systems and Automation*. New York: Wiley, 1994.

Duncan, William. *Manufacturing Two Thousand*. New York: AMACOM, 1994.

Eaton, B. Curtis, and Nicholas Schmitt. "Flexible Manufacturing and Market Structure," *American Economic Review* (September 1994), pp. 87–101.

Groover, Mikell P. *Automation, Production Systems, and Computer-Integrated Manufacturing*. Prentice Hall, 2000.

Harrison, Bennett. "The Dark Side of Flexible Production," *Technology Review* (May–June 1994), pp. 38–46.

Kempfer, Lisa. "Speeding Along to Manufacturing," *Industry Week*, July 18, 1994, pp. 24–28.

Laraia, Anthony C., Patricia E. Moody, and Robert W. Hall. *The Kaizen Blitz: Accelerating Breakthroughs in Productivity and Performance*. John Wiley & Sons, 1999.

Reese, Sue. "Sharpen Your Competitive Edge: Scheduling Systems Help Manufacturing Companies Stay Competitive," *Industry Week*, December 5, 1994, p. 26.

Todd, Jim. *World Class Manufacturing*. New York: McGraw-Hill, 1994.

CHAPTER 19

Arnst, Catherine. "The Networked Corporation," *Business Week*, June 26, 1995, pp. 86–89.

Bartlett, Christopher A., and Sumantra Ghoshal. "Changing the Role of Top Management: Beyond Systems to People," *Harvard Business Review* (May–June 1995), pp. 132–142.

Berry, Jonathan, John Verity, and Gail DeGeorge. "Database Marketing: a Potent New Tool for Selling," *Business Week*, September 5, 1994, pp. 56–62.

Chabrow, Eric. "The Training Payoff," *Informationweek*, July 10, 1995, pp. 36–38, 40, 42, 46.

Cortese, Amy, et al. "Cyberspace: Crafting Software That Will Let You Build a Business Out There," *Business Week*, February 27, 1995, pp. 78–82, 84, 86.

Davenport, Thomas H. "Saving IT's Soul: Human-Centered Information Management," *Harvard Business Review* (March–April 1994), pp. 119–131.

Dixon, Nancy M. *Common Knowledge: How Companies Thrive by Sharing What They Know*. Harvard Business School Press, 2000.

Evans, Philip, and Thomas S. Wurster. *Blown to Bits: How the New Economics of Information Transforms Strategy*. Harvard Business School Press, 1999.

Gross, Neil, Peter Coy, and Otis Port. "The Technology Paradox: How Companies Can Thrive as Prices Dive," *Business Week*, March 6, 1995, pp. 76–80, 84.

Hotch, Ripley, and Jon Pepper. "How to Buy Business Software," *Nation's Business* (June 1994), pp. 20–22, 24, 26–28.

Jennings, Jason, and Laurence Haughton. "It's Not the Big that Eat the Small . . . It's the Fast that Eat the Slow," *HarperBusiness*, 2001.

Lacity, Mary C., Leslie P. Willcocks, and David F. Feeny. "IT Outsourcing: Maximize Flexibility and Control," *Harvard Business Review* (May–June 1995), pp. 84–93.

Locke, Christopher. *The Cluetrain Manifesto: The End of Business as Usual*. Perseus, 2000, http://www.cluetrain.com/.

Shapiro, Carl, Hal R. Varian, and Carol Shapiro. *Information Rules: A Strategic Guide to the Network Economy*. Harvard Business School Press, 1998.

Wilder, Clinton. "Advertising a Commitment." *Informationweek*, June 26, 1995. pp. 70, 74.

CHAPTER 20

Chilton, Kenneth. "How American Manufacturers Are Facing the Global Marketplace," *Business Horizons* (July–August 1995), pp. 10–20.

Deresky, Helen. *International Management: Managing Across Borders and Cultures*. Glenview, Ill.: HarperCollins, 1994.

Elashmawi, Farid, and Philip R. Harris. *Multicultural Management 2000: Essential Culture Insights for Global Business Success*. Gulf Professional Publishing Company, 1998.

Greenlaw, Harold J. "Advocacy: Supporting U.S. Jobs in Global Competition," *Business America* (October 1995), pp. 65–90.

Hodgetts, Richard M., and Fred Luthans. *International Management*, 2nd ed. New York: McGraw-Hill, 1994.

Lonnroth, Juhani. "Global Employment Issues in the Year 2000," *Monthly Labor Review* (September 1985), pp. 5–16.

Mead, Richard. *International Management: Cross Cultural Dimensions*. Cambridge, Mass.: Blackwell, 1994.

Neff, Robert, et al. "Tearing Up Today's Organization Chart," *Business Week*, November 18, 1994.

Ricks, David A. *Blunders in International Business*. Blackwell Publishing, 2000.

Trompenaars, Alfons, Charles Hampden-Turner, and Fons Trompenaars. *Riding the Waves of Culture: Understanding Cultural Diversity in Global Business*. Irwin Professional Publishing, 1998.

Tung, Rosalie. *International Management*. Brookfield, Vt.: Ashgate, 1994.

Zukerman, Amy. "ISO 9000's Worth," *Industry Week*, February 5, 1996, p. 11.

Zukerman, Amy. "One Size Doesn't Fit All: U.S. Multinationals Alter ISO 9000 to Meet Their Needs," *Industry Week*, January 9, 1995, pp. 37–39.

CHAPTER 21

Allen, David. *Getting Things Done: The Art of Stress-Free Productivity*. Viking Press, 2001.

Baskerville, Dawn. "Get a Mentor: The Right Way to Choose a Savvy Career Advisor," *Black Enterprise* (May 1994), p. 44.

Bolles, Richard N. *What Color Is Your Parachute?* Berkeley, Calif.: Ten Speed Press, 1994.

Bolles, Richard Nelson. *What Color Is Your Parachute? 2001: A Practical Manual for Job-Hunters and Career-Changers*. Ten Speed Press, 2000.

Borchard, David. "Planning for Career and Life," *The Futurist* (January–February 1995), pp. 8–13.

Bruce, Robert C. *Job Search Strategies: The Guide to Career Transition*. Lincolnwood, Ill.: NTC Publishing Group, 1994.

Caldwell, Brian J., and Earl M. Cater. *The Return of the Mentor: Strategies for Workplace Learning*. Washington, D.C.: Taylor & Francis, Inc., 1994.

Clarke, Carolyn V. "Taking the Right Career Risks: Advancing Your Career Means Taking Chances," *Black Enterprise* (February 1995), pp. 72–85.

Connelly, Julie. "How to Choose Your Next Career," *Fortune*, February 6, 1995, pp. 145–146.

Delisser, Peter. *Be Your Own Executive Coach: Master High-Impact Communications Skills for Dealing With Difficult People, Improving Your Personal Image, Learning How*. Chandler House Press, 1999.

Fierman, Jaclyn. "Are Companies Less Family-Friendly?" *Fortune*, March 21, 1994, pp. 64–67.

Glassner, Barry. *Career Crash: The End of America's Love Affair with Work*. New York: Simon & Schuster, 1994.

Prugh, Charles C. *How to Jump Start a Stalled Career*. Lincolnwood, Ill.: NTC Publishing Group, 1994.

Simonsen, Peggy. *Career Compass*. Davies-Black Publishing, 2000.

Simonsen, Peggy. *Promoting a Development Culture in Your Organization: Using Career Development As a Change Agent*. Davies-Black Publishing, 1997.

Stone, Florence M. *Coaching, Counseling, & Mentoring: How to Choose & Use the Right Tool to Boost Employee Performance*, AMACOM, 1998.

Weeks, Dan. "21st-Century Mentoring," *World Traveller Magazine*, http://www.menttium.com/news_wt1.htm.

CHAPTER 22

Andrews, Kenneth R., ed. *Ethics in Practice*. Boston: Harvard Business School Press, 1989.

Barry, Vincent. *Moral Issues in Business*, 3rd ed. Belmont, Calif.: Wadsworth, 1986.

Blanchard, Kenneth, and Norman Vincent Peale. *The Power of Ethical Management*. New York: Morrow, 1988.

Chakraborty, S. K. (Editor), and Pradip Bhattacharya (Editor). *Leadership and Power: Ethical Explorations*. Oxford University Press, 2001.

Demars, Nan. *You Want Me to Do What?: When, Where, and How to Draw the Line at Work*. Fireside, 1998.

Frost, Peter J., Vance F. Mitchell, and Walter R. Nord, eds. *Managerial Reality: Balancing Technique, Practice, and Values*. New York: HarperCollins, 1995.

Gellerman, Saul W. *Motivation in the Real World*. New York: Dutton, 1992.

Gellerman, Saul W. *Motivation in the Real World*. Plume, 1993.

Gouillart, Francis J., and James N. Kelly. *Transforming the Organization*. New York: McGraw-Hill, 1995.

Henderson, Verne E. *What's Ethical in Business?* New York: McGraw-Hill, 1992.

Hunt, Christopher B., and Ellen R. Auster. "Proactive Environmental Management: Avoiding the Toxic Trap," *The Best of MIT's Sloan Management Review* (Winter 1990), pp. 7–18.

Linden, Dan Wechsler, Robert Lenzer, and Frank Wolfe. "The Cosseted Director," *Forbes*, May 22, 1995, pp. 168–173.

Madsen, Peter, and Jay M. Shafritz, eds. *Essentials of Business Ethics*. New York: Meridian, 1990.

Paine, Lynn Sharp. "Managing for Organizational Integrity," *Harvard Business Review* (March–April 1994), pp. 106–117.

Richman, Tom. "What Does Business Really Want from Government?" *Inc., Special Issue*, May 16, 1995, pp. 92–94, 96, 98–103.

Whitacre, Mark, and Ronald Henkoff. "My Life as a Corporate Mole for the FBI," *Fortune*, September 4, 1995, pp. 52–56, 60, 62.

References

CHAPTER 1

Austin, Nancy K. "The Skills Every Manager Must Master," *Working Woman* (May 1995), pp. 29–30.

Caminiti, Susan. "What Team Leaders Need to Know," *Fortune*, February 20, 1995, pp. 93–94, 98, 100.

Case, John. "Games Companies Play," *Inc.* (October 1994), p. 56.

Chicago Tribune. "Rude Awakenings Come Early," November 20, 1995, sec. 4, p. 3.

Chicago Tribune. "U.S. Overwork Habit Spreads Overseas," November 13, 1995, sec. 4, p. 6.

Cox, Danny, with John Hoover. *Leadership When the Heat's On*. New York: McGraw-Hill, 1992. p. 23.

Dunfee, Thomas W. "Employee Ethical Attitudes and Business Firm Productivity," *The Wharton Annual*, University of Pennsylvania, Pergamon Press, 1984, p. 76.

Erez, M., and P. C. Earley. *Culture, Self-Identity and Work*. New York: Oxford University Press, 1993.

Fagiano, David. "Coping with the Global Village," *Management Review* (May 1995), p. 5.

Federal Trade Commission, "Spread the Word about Telemarketing Fraud," http://www.ftc.gov/bcp/conline/edcams/telemarketing/index.html.

Finegan, Jay. "Unconventional Wisdom," *Inc.* (December 1994), pp. 45–46, 49–50, 52, 54, 56.

Fins, Antonio, and Jane Taner. "Has Paul Kahn Lost His Midas Touch?" *Business Week* (12 June 1995), pp. 90–91.

Harari, Oren. "The Missing Link in Performance," *Management Review* (March 1995), p. 21.

Harari, Oren. "When Intelligence Rules, the Manager's Job Changes," *Management Review* (July 1994), pp. 33–35.

Huey, John. "The New Post-Heroic Leadership," *Fortune*, February 21, 1994, pp. 42–44, 48, 50.

Jacobson, Gary. "MIT Prof Advocates Love in the Workplace," *The Dallas Morning News* (17 July 1994), p. 2H.

Johnson, Mike. "Drucker Speaks His Mind," American Management Association (October 1995), pp. 10–14.

Johnson, Ross, and William O. Winchell. *Management and Quality*. Milwaukee: ASQC Press, 1989.

Katz, Robert L. "Skills of an Effective Administrator," *Harvard Business Review* (September–October 1974), pp. 90–102.

Kleiman, Carol. "Making Diversity Work," *Chicago Tribune*, May 1, 1994, sec. 8, p. 1.

Kunde, Diana. "Middle Managers Broaden Expertise to Win Positions," *Dallas Morning News*, August 2, 1995, sec. D, pp. 1, 3.

Longenecker, Clinton O., and Dennis A. Gioia, "Ten Myths of Managing Managers," *Sloan Management Review*, vol. 33, no. 1 (1991), pp. 81–90.

Macht, Joshua D. "Will Your Next Big Technology Investment Pay Off?" *Inc.* (Summer 1995), pp. 70–76.

Maremont, Mark. "Kodak's New Focus," *Business Week*, January 30, 1995, pp. 62–63.

Mercado, Gus. "CEO Profile: Herb Kelleher," *Business Horizons* (December–January–February 1995), pp. 42–44, 46–47, 65.

Mintzberg, Henry. "The Manager's Job: Folklore and Fact," *Harvard Business Review* (July–August 1975), pp. 49–61.

Plunkett, W. Richard. *Supervision: Diversity and Teams in the Workplace*. Englewood Cliffs, N.J.: Prentice-Hall, 1996.

Romano, Catherine. "AMA Research: Managing Change, Diversity and Emotions," *American Management Association* (July 1995), pp. 6–7.

Sherman, Stratford. "How Tomorrow's Best Leaders Are Learning Their Stuff," *Fortune*, November 27, 1995, pp. 90–93, 96, 100.

Stoner, James A. F., and R. Edward Freeman. *Management*. Englewood Cliffs, N.J.: Prentice-Hall, 1992, p. 704.

Sullivan, Barbara. "Sure, Telemarketing Grates, But Lots of Folks Are Buying," *Chicago Tribune* (18 February 1995), sec. 1, pp. 1, 6.

Weber, Thomas E. "Net's Explosive Growth Spurs Need to Build Efficient Links," *The Wall Street Journal* (4 December 2000), http://interactive.wsj.com/archive/retrieve.cgi?id=SB975887242522775859.djm; Google, http://www.google.com.

Woodruff, David. "Talk About Life in the Fast Lane," *Business Week*, October 17, 1994, pp. 155–166.

Yates, Ronald E. "Structural Weakness from Re-engineering," *Chicago Tribune*, November 24, 1995, sec. 3, pp. 1, 4.

CHAPTER 2

Barrett, Thomas M., and Richard J. Kilonski. *Business Ethics*, 2nd ed. Englewood Cliffs, N.J.: Prentice-Hall, 1986.

Bartlett, Christopher A., and Sumantra Ghoshal. "Changing the Role of Top Management: Beyond Systems to People," *Harvard Business Review*, (May–June 1995), p. 134.

Bittel, Lester R., and Jackson E. Ramsey, eds. *Handbook for Professional Managers*. New York: McGraw-Hill, 1985, p. 634.

Campbell, Jeremy. *Grammatical Man: Information, Entropy, Language, and Life*. New York: Simon & Schuster, 1982, pp. 15–31.

Collins, James C., and Jerry I. Porras. *Built to Last: Successful Habits of Visionary Companies*. New York: HarperBusiness, 1994, pp. 150–168.

Davenport, Thomas H. "The Fad That Forgot People," *Fast Company* (November 1995), p. 70, <http://www.fast company.com/online/01/reengin.html>.

Dumaine, Brian. "Distilled Wisdom: Buddy, Can You Paradigm?" *Fortune*, May 15, 1995, pp. 205–206.

Feigenbaum, Armand V. "Total Quality Control," *Harvard Business Review* (November–December 1956), pp. 95–98.

Gabor, Andrea. *The Man Who Discovered Quality*. New York: Penguin, 1990, pp. 47–48, 126–127.

Garvin, David A. *Managing Quality: The Strategic and Competitive Edge*. New York: Free Press, 1988, p. 5.

Goodman, David. "One Step at a Time," *Inc.* (August 1995), pp. 64–66, 68, 70.

Graham, Rex. "Evolving Business, with a Santa Fe Institute Twist," *Bulletin of the Santa Fe Institute* (Winter 1998), Vol. 13, No. 1, http://www.santafe.edu/sfi/publications/Bulletins/bulletin-winter98/feature.html.

Griffith, Victoria. "Emergent Leadership: Bringing Free-Market Risks and Rewards to Commands-and-Control Corporations," *Strategy & Business*, Fourth Quarter, 1998, p. 3.

Haigh, Christopher, ed. *The Cambridge Historical Encyclopedia of Great Britain and Ireland* (Cambridge, England: Cambridge University Press, 1990), p. 269.

Hammer, Michael, and James Champy. *Reengineering the Corporation*. New York: HarperBusiness, 1993, pp. 32–33.

Hart, Christopher W. L., and Christopher E. Bogan. *The Baldrige: What It Is, How It's Won, How to Use It to Improve Quality in Your Company*. New York: McGraw-Hill, 1992, pp. 5, 8, 77, 96.

Hymowitz, Carol. "Software Maker Studies the Past to Learn How to Face the Future," *The Wall Street Journal* (21 November 2000), p. B1.

Jones, Del. "Reengineering and Rescuing a Legacy's Distorted Image," *USA Today*, February 19, 1999, p. 12B.

Maslow, Abraham with Deborah C. Stephens and Gary Heil. *Maslow on Management* (Wiley, 1998).

Matteson, Michael T., and John M. Ivancevich, eds. *Management Classics*, 3d ed. (Santa Monica, Calif., Business Publications, 1986), pp. 18, 156, 232, 280.

Mayo, Elton. *The Human Problems of an Industrial Civilization*. New York: Macmillan, 1933.

McGregor, Douglas. *The Human Side of Enterprise*. New York: McGraw-Hill, 1960, pp. 33–48.

Merrill, Harwood F., ed. *Classics in Management*, rev. ed. New York: American Management Association, 1970, pp. 10, 56, 188.

Ouchi, William G. *Theory Z: How American Business Can Meet the Japanese Challenge*. Reading, Mass.: Addison-Wesley, 1981.

Peters, Thomas J., and Robert H. Waterman. *In Search of Excellence: Lessons from America's Best-Run Companies*. New York: Harper & Row, 1982.

Roberts, Paul. "John Deere Runs on Chaos." *Fast Company* (November 1998), p. 164, http://www.fastcompany.com/online/19/deere.html.

Sellers, Patricia. "To Avoid a Trampling, Get Ahead of the Mass," *Fortune*, May 15, 1995, p. 201.

Senge, Peter. *The Fifth Discipline: The Art and Practice of the Learning Organization* (Currency/Doubleday, 1994).

Verespej, Michael A. "To Lead or Not to Lead?" *Industry Week*, January 9, 1995, p. 17.

Widder, Pat, "More Corporations Learning That Ethics Are a Bottom Line Issue," *Chicago Tribune*, June 7, 1992, sec. 7, pp. 1, 6.

CHAPTER 3

Akao, Yoji., ed. *Quality Function Deployment* (Productivity Press, 1990).

American Customer Satisfaction Index (ASCI) <http://www .bus.umich.edu/research/nqrc/asci.html>.

ASQ "American Society for Quality." Glossary of Terms, http://www.asq.org/info/glossary/definition.html#b.

Barrier, Michael. "Re-engineering Revisited," *Nation's Business* (May 1995), p. 36.

Barry, Thomas J. *Management Excellence Through Quality*. Milwaukee: ASQC Press, 1991, pp. ix, 3, 7, 19.

Business Week (Special Quality Issue 1991). "A QFD Snapshot," pp. 22–23; "A Tighter Focus for R&D," p. 170.

Byrne, John A. "Management Meccas: Everyone Seems to Be Studying U.S. Corporate Stars," *Business Week*, September 18, 1995, pp. 122–126, 128, 132.

Case, John. "The Open-Book Revolution," *Inc.* (June 1995), pp. 26–30, 32, 34, 36, 38–43.

Caudron, Shari. "Ten Steps to Employee Involvement EMPOWER THE PEOPLE," *IW Growing Companies* (June 1998), http://www.cast-fab.com/news/6_98IW.html.

CFI Group <http://www.cfigroup.com/overview.html>.

Chicago Tribune. "Japan a Study in Productivity," November 13, 1994, sec. 17, p. 11.

Chicago Tribune. "Toyota Rates on Efficiency," May 28, 1995, sec. 17, p. 11.

Collins, James C. "Change Is Good—But First, Know What Should Never Change," *Fortune*, May 29, 1995, p. 141.

Crosby, Philip B. *Quality Without Tears*. New York: Plume, 1984, pp. 59–63, 99–100, 106–107.

Dean, Edwin B. *Design for Quality from the Perspective of Competitive Advantage* (1998). <http://akao.larc.nasa.gov/dfc/dfqual.html> 980714.

Deming, W. Edwards. *Out of the Crisis*. Cambridge, Mass.: Massachusetts Institute of Technology, Center for Advanced Engineering Study, 1986, pp. 167–169.

Gabor, Andrea. *The Man Who Discovered Quality*. New York: Penguin, 1990, pp. 47–48, 126–127.

Greising, David. "Quality: How to Make It Pay," *Business Week*, August 8, 1994, pp. 54–59.

Hart, Christopher W. L., and Christopher E. Bogan. *The Baldrige: What It Is, How It's Won, How to Use It to Improve Quality in Your Company*. New York: McGraw-Hill, 1992, pp. 5, 8, 77, 96, 128–130.

Hunt, Daniel V. *Quality in America* (Homewood, Ill.: Business One Irwin, 1992), pp. 23, 43, 64–76, 268–269, 286.

Hunt, Daniel V. *Quality in America: How to Implement a Competitive Quality Program* (Irwin Professional Publlishers, 1995).

Ishikawa, Kaoru. *What Is Total Quality Control?* David J. Lu, trans. Englewood, Cliffs, N.J.: Prentice-Hall, 1985, pp. 44–45, 98, 125–128, 186.

Jones, Patricia, and Larry Kahaner. *Say It & Live It: 50 Corporate Mission Statements That Hit the Mark*. New York: Doubleday, 1995, pp. ix–xii, 33.

Juran, Joseph M., and A. Blanton Godfrey, eds. *Juran's Quality Handbook*, 5th ed. (McGraw-Hill Book Company 1999).

Kraar, Louis. "Korea's Automakers Take on the World (Again)," *Fortune* (6 March 1995), pp. 154, 158.

Loeb, Marshall. "How to Grow a New Product Every Day," *Fortune*, November 14, 1994, pp. 269–270.

Longworth, R. C. "Downsizing Craze Turns Out to Be Profitless Folly," *Chicago Tribune*, April 23, 1995, sec. 4, pp. 1, 4.

Mizuno, Shigeru, and Yoji Akao editors. *QFD: The Customer-Driven Approach to Quality Planning and Development*, Asian Productivity Organization, Tokyo, Japan.

Nation's Business. "Avoiding the Pitfalls of Outsourcing" (May 1995), p. 12.

Performance. "The 'Discoverer' of Reengineering Pounds His Critics, But Michael Hammer Still Has a Few Details to Nail Down" (March 1995), pp. 25–28.

Petersen, Donald E., and John Hillkirk. *A Better Idea: Redefining the Way Americans Work*. Boston: Houghton Mifflin, 1991, pp. 6–11.

Pine II, Joseph B., Don Peppers, and Martha Rogers. "Do You Want to Keep Your Customers Forever?" *Harvard Business Review* (March–April 1995), pp. 103–114.

Pritchett, Price. *New Work Habits for a Radically Changing World: 13 Ground Rules for Job Success in the Information Age* (Dallas, Texas: Pritchett & Associates, 1994), pp. 2–6.

Richman, Louis S. "The New Work Force Builds Itself," *Fortune*, June 27, 1994, pp. 68–70, 74, 76.

Sewell, Carl, and Paul B. Brown. *Customers for Life: How to Turn That One-Time Buyer into a Lifelong Customer* (Pocket Books, 1998).

Shewhart, Walter A. *Statistical Method from the Viewpoint of Quality Control*. Washington, D.C.: Graduate School of the Department of Agriculture, 1939, pp. 2–4.

Stern, Aimee L. "How to Build Customer Loyalty," *Your Company* (Spring 1995), pp. 36–37.

Storck, Bob. "2000 Hyundai Accent: Accent Proves That Korean Car Industry Has Arrived," *2000 WOMAN MOTORIST*, http://www.womanmotorist.com/review/hyundai/bs-hyundai-accent-2k-01.shtml.

Townsend, Patrick L., and Joan E. Gebhardt. *Quality in Action*. New York: Wiley, 1992, p. 17.

Treacy, Michael, and Fred Wiersema. *The Discipline of Market Leaders: Choose Your Customers, Narrow Your Focus, Dominate Your Market* (Perseus Press, 1997).

Tully, Shawn. "Why to Go for Stretch Targets," *Fortune*, November 14, 1994, pp. 145–146, 148, 150, 154, 158.

Van, Jon. "Firms Tool Up with Information," *Chicago Tribune*, November 5, 1991, sec. 1, p. 12.

Verespej, Michael A. "To Lead or Not to Lead?" Industry Week, *January 9, 1995, pp. 17–18.*

Walton, Mary. *The Deming Management Method at Work*. New York: Perigee, 1986, pp. 19–20, 25–26, 72.

CHAPTER 4

Ady, Robert M. "Why BMW Cruised into Spartanburg," *Wall Street Journal*, July 6, 1992, p. 8.

Ashley, William C., and James L. Morrison. *Anticipatory Management: 10 Power Tools for Achieving Excellence into the 21st Century* (Issue Action Publications, 1995).

Associated Press. "Amazon Emphasizes Efficiency," November 26, 2000.

Beck, Rachel. "Toys 'R' Us Makes Improvements," *Associated Press*, June 12, 1999, http://wire.ap.org.

Bertalanffy, L. von, "The Theory of Open Systems in Physics and Biology," *Science*, 111 (13 January 1950), pp. 23–29.

Bittel, Lester R. *The McGraw-Hill 36-Hour Management Course*. New York: McGraw-Hill, 1989, pp. 31–34, 179, 184–185.

Bridis, Ted. "Study: Internet Impact Put at $301B," *Associated Press*, (10 June 1999), http://wire.ap.org/.

Buck, Genevieve. "Warm Winter Melts Evans Profits," *Chicago Tribune*, sec. 2, p. 3.

Chandler, Clay, and Joseph B. White. "It's Hello Dollies at Nissan's New 'Dream Factory,' " *Wall Street Journal*, July 6, 1992, p. B11.

Chicago Tribune. "Measure for Measure, EU Rules Irk British," October 1, 1995, sec. 1, p. 13.

Chicago Tribune. "Disney Surrenders, Won't Build Theme Park Near Civil War Site," sec. 1, p. 3.

Churchman, W., *The Systems Approach* (New York: Delacorte Press, 1968).

Clark, Kenneth R. " 'Cola Wars' Forming on College Campuses," *Chicago Tribune*, November 6, 1994, sec. 1, pp. 23–25.

Conard, Wes. "Toys 'R' Us Plans Online Challenge," *Bloomberg News*, June 9, 1999.

Garvin, D. A., "Building a Learning Organization," *Business Credit*, 96 (1) (1993), pp. 19–28.

Goldstein, Alan. "America OnLine Overcomes Obstacles to Outpace Rivals," *The Dallas Morning News*, April 27, 1998.

Fuchsberg, Gilbert. " 'Visioning' Mission Becomes Its Own Mission," *The Wall Street Journal*, 7 January 1994, pp. B1, 3.

Labich, Kenneth. "Why Companies Fail," *Fortune*, November 14, 1994, pp. 52–54, 58, 60, 64, 68.

Loeb, Marshall. "Ten Commandments for Managing Creative People," *Fortune*, January 16, 1995, pp. 135–136.

Menaker, Drusilla. "Doing Worse by Doing Good?" *Business Week*, June 12, 1995, pp. 50–51.

Peters, Tom. *The Pursuit of Wow!* New York: Vintage Books, 1994, pp. 219–241.

Rose, Frederick. "Chevron Develops Diesel-Fuel Formula That Meets California's New Standard," *Wall Street Journal*, March 27, 1992, p. B5.

Schoderbek, C. G., Schoderbek, P. P., and Kefalas, A. G., *Management Systems: Conceptual Considerations* (Business Publications, 2d. 1980), pp. 169–90.

Senge, P. M. "The laws of the fifth discipline," *The Fifth Discipline* (New York: Currency Doubleday, 1994a), pp. 57–67.

Senge, P. M. "The leader's new work," *Executive Excellence*, 11 (11) 1994b, pp. 8–9.

Smart, Tim. "A Lot of the Weaknesses Carbide Had Are Behind It," *Business Week*, January 23, 1995, pp. 83–84.

Tessler, Joelle. "As Imitators Proliferate, AOL Stakes Bigger Claim on the Web," *Dow Jones Newswires*, January 22, 1998.

Warner, David. "How Do Federal Regulations Affect You?" *Nation's Business* (May 1992), p. 56.

Yates, Ronald E. "Foreign Firms Flock to Suburbs," *Chicago Tribune*, July 13, 1992, sec. 4, pp. 1, 2.

Yates, Ronald E. "Intellectual Capital a Downsizing Casualty," *Chicago Tribune*, June 4, 1995, sec. 7, p. 2.

CHAPTER 5

Bukro, Casey. "Morton Buying into De-Inking Business," *Chicago Tribune*, December 13, 1995, sec. 3, pp. 1, 4.

Chicago Tribune. "Amoco Increases Capital Outlays," December 20, 1995, sec. 3, p. 1.

Chicago Tribune. "Coke Targets Bigger Slice of Market," December 16, 1995, sec. 2, p. 1.

Chicago Tribune. "Polaroid to Cut 1,300 Jobs, Reducing Work Force by 11%," December 20, 1995, sec. 3, p. 2.

Collins, James C., and Jerry Porras. *Built to Last*. New York: Harper/Collins, 1994, pp. 91–114.

deLosa, Patty. "What Business Am I In," *Fortune*, November 14, 1994, p. 54.

Drucker, Peter F. The Practice of Management. New York: Harper & Row, 1954, pp. 49–61, 65–83.

Dupuy, John. "Learning to Manage World Class Strategy," *Management Review* (March 1992), pp. 40–43.

Green, Heather. "Margaret C. Whitman" section in Steve Hamm. "The e.biz 25: Masters of the Web Universe," *Businessweek Online*, September 27, 1999, http://www.businessweek.com/1999/99_39/b3648001.htm.

Gruber, William. "Tenneco Auto-Parts Unit Taking Road to Worldwide Growth," *Chicago Tribune*, Dec. 18, 1995, sec. 4, p. 3.

Gutman, Roberta. "Changing the Face of Management," *Working Woman* (November 1994), pp. 21–23.

Jacobs, Deborah L. "Are You Guilty of Electronic Trespassing?" *Management Review* (April 1994), pp. 21–25.

Jones, Patricia, and Larry Kahaner. *Say It and Live It: The 50 Best Corporate Mission Statements That Hit Their Mark*. New York: Currency-Doubleday, 1995, pp. 33–35.

Kendall, Peter, and Christi Parsons. "Listen Up: Bosses May Be on the Line," *Chicago Tribune*, December 18, 1995, sec. 1, pp. 1, 12.

Lamb, Sara, and Sherri Chunn. "Mercedes Rolls in with New Age," *Chicago Tribune*, December 3, 1995, sec. 12, p. 7.

Lienert, Anita. "What Do You Think?" *Chicago Tribune*, December 10, 1995, sec. 12, pp. 1, 5.

Lorange, P. *Strategic Planning And Control*. Cambridge, Mass.: Blackwell, 1993.

Mangelsdorf, Martha E. "Plan of Attack," *Inc.* (January 1996), pp. 41–44.

Mateja, Jim. "Improved Caddy Catera No Show Job," *Chicago Tribune*, December 10, 1995, sec. 12, p. 1.

Pitta, Julie. "Webb Master," *Forbes Magazine*, December 13, 1999, http://www.forbes.com/forbes/1999/1213/6414322a.html.

Rebello, Kathy. "Apple's Assault," *Business Week*, June 12, 1995, pp. 98–99.

Saporito, Bill. "The Eclipse of Mars," *Fortune*, November 28, 1994, pp. 82–92.

Tully, Shawn. "Why to Go for Stretch Targets," *Fortune*, November 14, 1994, p. 145.

Ward, John, and Craig Aronoff. "Passion and Its Place in Business," *Nation's Business* (March 1995), pp. 50–51.

CHAPTER 6

Berss, Marcia. "The Zhen-uine Article," *Forbes*, June 5, 1995, pp. 104–105.

Bolfert, Thomas C. *The Big Book of Harley-Davidson*. Milwaukee, Wis.: Harley-Davidson, Inc., 1991.

Buss, Dale. "Hitching Your Wagon to a Retail Star," *Nation's Business* (November 1994), pp. 33–38.

Chandler, Susan. "Can Hallmark Get Well Soon?", *Business Week*, June 19, 1995, pp. 62–63.

Daft, Richard L. *Management*, 3rd ed. Homewood, Ill.: Dryden Press, 1994, p. 220.

Ehrenfeld, Tom. "The Demise of Mom and Pop," *Inc.* (January 1995), pp. 46–48.

Ehrenfeld, Tom. "The New and Improved American Small Business," *Inc.* (January 1995), p. 36.

Galbraith, Jay R., and Robert Kazanjian. *Strategy Implementation: Structure, Systems, and Process*, 2nd ed. St. Paul, Minn.: West, 1986.

Garvin, David. "Leveraging Processes for Strategic Advantage," *Harvard Business Review* (September–October 1995), pp. 77–90.

Gnoffe, Anthony, Jr. "Taking Flight Simulators for a Ride," *Philadelphia Inquirer*, August 20, 1992, pp. D1, D7.

Goldstein, Alan. "Microsoft and Intel gearing up for change," *The Dallas Morning News* (15 October 1999).

Greising, David. "It Hurts So Good at Delta," *Business Week*, December 11, 1995, pp. 106–107.

Gupta, Anil K., and V. Govindarajan. "Business Unit Strategy, Managerial Characteristics, and Business Unit Effectiveness at Strategy Implementation," *Academy of Management Journal* 29 (March 1984), pp. 25–41.

Hammonds, Keith A. "Tandy Cleans Out Its Closets," *Business Week*, January 16, 1995, p. 38.

Hanks, Vince. "Harley-Davidson Rides High," *The Motley Fool*, August 22, 2000, http://www.fool.com/dripport/2000/dripport000822.htm.

Henshaw, Peter. *Harley-Davidson*. Stamford, Conn.: Regency House Publishing, 1994.

Hill, Charles W. L., and Gareth R. Jones. *Strategic Management: An Analytical Approach*. Boston: Houghton Mifflin, 1989.

Holt, David H. *Management: Principles and Practices*, 2nd ed. Englewood Cliffs, N.J.: Prentice-Hall, 1990, p. 174.

Lienert, Anita. "Going Whole Hog," *Chicago Tribune*, December 31, 1995, sec. 12, pp. 1, 5.

Litvan, Laura M. "Casting a Wider Employment Net." *Nations Business* (December 1994), p. 49.

Loeb, Marshall. "Where Leaders Come From," *Fortune*, September 19, 1994, p. 241.

Miles, Raymond E., and Charles E. Snow. *Organizational Strategy, Structure, and Process*. New York: McGraw-Hill, 1978.

Miller, Robert. "Cashing In at Southwest," *Dallas Morning News*, May 3, 1995, p. 3D.

Oliver, Suzanne, "I Love These Brands," *Forbes*, September 25, 1995, pp. 94, 96.

O'Neal, Michael, Ronald Grover, and William L. Symonds. "The Mogul," *Business Week*, April 24, 1995, pp. 122–125.

Porter, Michael E. *Competitive Strategy: Techniques for Analyzing Industries and Competitors* (Free Press, 1998).

Porter, Michael E. *Competitive Strategy: Techniques for Analyzing Industries and Competitors*. New York: Free Press, 1980, pp. 36–46.

Prescott, John E. "Environment: As the Moderator of the Relationship Between Strategy and Performance," *Academy of Management Journal* 29 (March 1986), pp. 329–346.

Schonfeld, Erick. "Betting on the Boomers," *Fortune*, December 25, 1995, pp. 78–80, 84, 86–87.

Serwer, Andrew E. "McDonald's Conquers the World," *Fortune*, October 17, 1994, pp. 103–116.

Symonds, William C., and Linda Bernier. "A Belgian Brewer's Plans Come to a Head." *Business Week*, June 19, 1995, p. 56.

Treacy, Michael, and Fred Wiersema. "How Market Leaders Keep Their Edge," *Fortune*, February 6, 1995, pp. 88–89.

Turner, James. "Dr. Pepper Is Cadbury's Prescription for Greater Strength in Soft Drinks," *Dallas Morning News*, January 24, 1995, pp. 1D, 8D.

Wiegand, Virginia S. "Quaker State Departure a Bitter Blow to Oil City," *Dallas Morning News*, June 6, 1995, pp. 1D, 16D.

Woodruff, David. "Who's Afraid of J & J and 3M?" *Business Week*, December 5, 1994, p. 66.

Yang, Dori Jones. "The Starbucks Enterprise Shifts into Warp Speed," *Business Week*, October 24, 1994, pp. 76, 78–79.

Young, David. "No Discounting in 'Newellization,' " *Chicago Tribune*, August 15, 1994, sec. 4, pp. 1–2.

Zimmerman, Martin. "Little Caesars to Start Delivering Pizza! Pizza!" *Dallas Morning News*, June 13, 1995, p. 8D.

CHAPTER 7

Bazerman, Max H. *Judgement in Managerial Decision Making*. New York: Wiley, 1986, p. 42.

Berss, Marcia. "The Zhen-uine Article," *Forbes*, June 5, 1995, pp. 104–105.

Bloomberg News. "Kings of Commerce," December 25, 1999.

Briggins, Angela. "Win-Win Initiatives for Women," *Management Review* (June 1995), p. 6.

Buss, Dale D. "Hitching Your Wagon to a Retailing Star," *Nation's Business* (November 1994), p. 34.

Carlton, Jim. "They Coulda Been a Contender," *Wired*, November 11, 1997.

Cohen, Charles. "Managing Older Workers," *Working Woman* (November 1994), pp. 61–62.

Daft, Richard L. *Management*, 3rd ed. Fort Worth, Tex.: Dryden Press, 1994, p. 250.

Drucker, Peter F. *The Practice of Management*. New York: Harper & Row, 1954, p. 351.

Edmonson, Gail. "Grabbing Markets from the Giants," *Business Week*, January 9, 1995, p. 156.

Eilon, Samuel. "Structuring Unstructured Decisions," *Management Science* 33 (1987), pp. 121–123.

Ettling, Jennifer T., and Arthur G. Jago. "Participation Under Conditions of Conflict: More on the Vroom-Yetton Model," *Journal of Management Studies* 25 (1988), pp. 73–83.

Etorre, Barbara. "Breaking the Glass . . . or Just Window Dressing," *Management Review* (March 1992), p. 16.

Etzioni, Amitai. "Humble Decision Making," *Harvard Business Review* (July–August 1989), pp. 122–126.

Grover, Edward L. "Group Decision Making: Approaches to Problem Solving," *Small Business Reports* (July 1988), pp. 30–33.

Harkey, Del. "Food Lion Under Attack Once Again," *Dallas Morning News*, May 4, 1995, p. 2D.

Helm, Leslie. "Playing to Win," *Dallas Morning News*, October 22, 1994, p. 1F.

Holt, David H. *Management: Principles and Practices*, 2nd ed. Englewood Cliffs, N.J.: Prentice-Hall, 1990, p. 100.

Howard, Ronald A. "Decision Analysis: Practice and Promise," *Management Science* 34 (1988), pp. 679–695.

Ireland, R. Duane, Michael A. Hill, and J. Clifton Williams. "Self-Confidence and Decisiveness: Prerequisites for Effective Management in the 1990s," *Business Horizons* (January–February 1992), pp. 36–42.

Jackson, Susan, and Jane E. Dutton. "Discerning Threats and Opportunities," *Administrative Science Quarterly* 33 (1988), pp. 370–375.

Kepner, C., and B. Tregoe. *The Rational Manager*. New York: McGraw-Hill, 1965.

McCaffery, Richard. "Nokia Grabs Market Share," *The Motley Fool*, October 24, 2000, http://www.fool.com/portfolios/rulemaker/2000/rulemaker001024.htm.

Mondy, R. Wayne, and Shane R. Premeaux. *Management: Concepts, Practices, and Skills*, 7th ed. Englewood Cliffs, N.J.: Prentice-Hall, 1995, p. 120.

Peters, Tom. "Time-Obsessed Competition," *Management Review* (September 1990), pp. 17–18.

Rousell, Philip A. "Cutting Down the Guess Work in R & D," *Harvard Business Review* (September–October 1983), pp. 154–157.

Shermach, Kelly. "Sheraton Adds Staff, Laptops to Improve Satisfaction," *Marketing News*, April 24, 1995, p. 14.

Simon, Herbert A. *The New Science of Management*. Englewood Cliffs, N.J.: Prentice-Hall, 1977, p. 47.

Steel, Charles R. "The Starbucks Enterprise Shifts into Warp Speed," *Business Week*, October 24, 1994, p. 76.

Steele, Bob. "ABC and Food Lion: The Ethics Questions," *RTNDA Communicator* (April 1997), p. 56, http://www.poynter.org/research/me/me_abc-fl.htm.

Stewart, Thomas A. "Mapping Corporate Brainpower," *Fortune*, October 30, 1995, pp. 209–211.

Turner, James L. "Dr. Pepper Is Cadbury's Prescription for Greater Strength in Soft Drinks," *Dallas Morning News*, January 24, 1995, pp. 1D, 8D.

Verespej, Michael A. "Tough Times, Tough Decisions," *Industry Week*, February 17, 1992, pp. 27–28.

Vroom, Victor H., and Phillip Yetton. "A New Look at Managerial Decision Making," *Organizational Dynamics* (Spring 1973), p. 67.

Whyte, Glenn. "Decision Failures: Why They Occur and How to Prevent Them," *Academy of Management Executive* 5, no. 3 (1991), pp. 23–31.

Whyte, Glenn. "Groupthink Reconsidered," *Academy of Management Review* 14 (1989), pp. 40–56.

Zellner, Wendy. "Why Continental's CEO Fell to Earth," *Business Week*, November 7, 1994, p. 32.

CHAPTER 8

Ayers-Williams, Roz. "Mastering the Fine Art of Delegation," *Black Enterprise* (April 1992), pp. 91–93.

Child, John. *Organization: A Guide to Problems and Practices*, 2nd ed. London: Harper & Row, 1984.

Daft, Richard L. *Management*, 3rd ed. Fort Worth, Tex.: Dryden Press, 1994, p. 291.

Davis, Keith, and John Newstrom. *Human Behavior at Work: Organizational Behavior*, 8th ed. New York: McGraw-Hill, 1989, p. 262.

Davis, Ralph C. *Fundamentals of Top Management*. New York: Harper & Row, 1951.

Dilley, John. "Honda Tacitly Ok'd Payoffs," *Dallas Morning News*, May 13, 1995, p. 3F.

Drucker, Peter. "Management's New Paradigms," *Forbes* (5 October 1998), http://www.forbes.com/forbes/98/1005/6207152a.htm.

Etorre, Barbara. "Reengineering Tales from the Front," *Management Review* (January 1995), pp. 13–18.

Evans, Charles. "Digital's Turnaround: Time for Phase Two," *Business Week*, June 19, 1995, pp. 130–133.

Fenn, Donna. "Out to Lunch," *Inc.* (June 1995), p. 89.

Hammonds, Keith H. "Rethinking Work," *Business Week*, October 17, 1994, p. 87.

Harmon, Theo, and William B. Scott. *Management in the Modern Organization*. Boston: Houghton Mifflin, 1970, p. 452.

Hellman, Paul. "Delegating Is Easy, Deputizing a Posse Is Tough," *Management Review* (June 1992), p. 58.

Jacob, Raul. "How One Red Hot Retailer Wins Customer Loyalty," *Fortune*, July 10, 1995, pp. 77–80.

Jones, Thomas M. "Ethical Decision Making by Individuals in Organizations," *Academy of Management Review* (April 1988), pp. 366–390.

Kent, Carolyn. "The Technical and Administrative Staff of the Future," *Work Teams Newsletter* (Summer 1997), http://www.workteams.unt.edu/newsletter/Archive/v7-2.html.

Kountz, Harold, and Cyril O'Donnel. *Management*. New York: McGraw-Hill, 1976, p. 375.

Lawrence, Paul R., and Jay W. Lorsch. *Organization and Environment*. Homewood, Ill.: Irwin, 1967.

McNealy, Scott. "The Future of the Net—Why We Don't Want You to Buy Our Software," *The Wall Street Journal*, September 1, 1999.

Miller, Karen Lowrey. "Siemens Shapes Up," *Business Week*, May 1, 1995, pp. 52–53.

Miner, Anne S. "Idiosyncratic Jobs in Formal Organizations," *Administrative Science Quarterly* (September 1987), pp. 327–351.

Moskal, Brian S. "The Buck Doesn't Stop Here," *Industry Week*, July 15, 1992, pp. 29–30.

O'Reilly, Brian. "Johnson & Johnson Is on a Roll," *Fortune*, December 26, 1994, p. 190.

Saul, Michael. "Lockheed Martin to Trim 12,000 Jobs, Close Plants," *Dallas Morning News*, June 27, 1995, pp. 1D, 15D.

Smart, Tim. "Global Mission," *Business Week*, May 1, 1995, pp. 132–136.

Smith, Adam. *The Wealth of Nations*. New York: Modern Library, 1937.

Spertus, Philip. "It's Easy to Fool the Boss," *Management Review* (May 1992), p. 28.

Stodghill, Ron. "A Mea Culpa—And a Comeback?" *Business Week*, July 3, 1995, p. 33.

Taylor, Alex. "Chrysler's Next Boss Speaks," *Fortune*, July 27, 1992, pp. 82–83.

Twomey, Daniel, Frederick C. Scherer, and Walter S. Hunt. "Configuration of a Functional Department: A Study of Contextual and Structural Variables," *Journal of Organizational Behavior*, vol. 9 (1988), pp. 61–75.

Van Fleet, David. "Span of Management Research and Issues," *Academy of Management Journal* (September 1983), pp. 546–552.

CHAPTER 9

Astley, W. Graham. "Organization Size and Bureaucratic Structure," *Organization Studies* 6 (1985), pp. 201–228.

Burns, Lawton R. "Matrix Management in Hospitals: Testing Theories of Matrix Structure and Development," *Administrative Science Quarterly* 34 (1989), pp. 349–368.

Burns, Tom, and G. M. Stalker. *The Management of Innovation*. London: Taristock, 1961.

Charan, Ram. "Managing To Be the Best: The Century's Smartest Bosses Have Influence Beyond Their Companies," *Time* (7 December 1998), http://www.ge.com/news/welch/articles/t1298.htm.

Connor, Michael. "Coke Chairman Robert Goizueta Hospitalized," *Reuters* (14 October 1997), http://198.62.75.1/www2/fcf/cokechairhospitalized101497.html.

Daft, Richard L. *Management*, 3rd ed. Fort Worth, Tex.: Dryden Press, 1994, p. 292.

Flynn, Julia. "An Ever-Quicker Trip from R & D to Customer," *Business Week*, January 10, 1995, p. 88.

Greising, David. "I'd Like the World to Buy a Coke: The Life and Leadership of Roberto Goizueta," *Business Week Online*, April 13, 1998, http://www.businessweek.com/1998/15/b3573108.htm.

Hays, Constance L. "Learning to Think Smaller at Coke," *The New York Times* (6 February 2000), http://www.lincoln.ac.nz/comm/subjects/bmkt326/coke.htm.

Jacob, Rahul. "The Struggle to Create an Organization for the 21st Century," *Fortune*, April 3, 1995, p. 92.

Kerwin, Kathleen. "Vapor Lock at GM," *Business Week*, November 7, 1994, pp. 28–29.

Kerwin, Kathleen, and James B. Treece. "GM Is Meaner but Hardly Leaner," *Business Week*, October 19, 1992, pp. 30–31.

Kirk, Randy W. "It's About Control," *Inc.* (August 1994), pp. 25–26.

Koloday, Harvey F. "Managing in a Matrix," *Business Horizons* (March–April 1981), pp. 17–24.

Kunde, Diana. "Minorities and Women: Steps to the Top," *Dallas Morning News*, May 7, 1995, pp. 1H–2H.

Lammers, Teri. "The New Improved Organization Chart," *Inc.* (October 1992), pp. 147–149.

Lawrence, Paul R., and Jay W. Lorsch. *Organization and Environment*. Homewood, Ill.: Irwin, 1969.

Miles, Raymond E. "Adapting to Technology and Competition: A New Industrial Relation System for the 21st Century," *California Management Review* (Winter 1989), pp. 9–28.

Miles, Raymond E., and Charles C. Snow. *Organizational Strategy, Structure, and Process*. New York: McGraw-Hill, 1978.

Mitchell, Jim, and Jennifer Files. "Challenging the Imagination," *Dallas Morning News*, May 17, 1992, p. 18K.

Nemetz, Patricia L., and Louis W. Fry. "Flexible Manufacturing Organizations: Implications for Strategy Formulation and Organization Design," *Academy of Management Review* (October 1988), pp. 627–638.

Newsweek, November 9, 1992, pp. 54–57.

O'Reilly, Brian. "J & J Is on a Roll," *Fortune*, December 26, 1994, p. 180.

Quinn, Robert E., and Kim Cameron. "Organizational Life Cycles and Shifting Criteria of Effectiveness: Some Preliminary Evidence," *Management Science* 29 (1983), pp. 33–51.

Porter, Michael E. *Competitive Strategy*. New York: Free Press, 1980, pp. 36–46.

Rammrath, Herbert G. "Globalization Isn't for Whiners," *Wall Street Journal*, April 6, 1992, p. C27.

Reese, Jennifer. "The Big and the Bloated," *Fortune*, July 27, 1992, p. 49.

Robbins, Stephen P. *Management*, 4th ed. Englewood Cliffs, N.J.: Prentice-Hall, 1994, p. 281.

Saul, Michael. "Lockheed Martin to Trim 12,000 Jobs, Close Plants," *Dallas Morning News*, June 27, 1995, pp. 1D, 15D.

Simnacher, Joe. "Boardroom Rumblings," *Dallas Morning News*, April 8, 1992, pp. 18–20.

Stewart, Thomas A. "The Search for the Organization of Tomorrow," *Fortune*, May 18, 1992, pp. 93–94.

Taylor, Alex. "Can GM Remodel," *Fortune*, January 13, 1992, pp. 26–28.

Templeman, John, and David Woodruff. "Mercedes Can't Shift into Cruise Control Yet," *Business Week*, November 21, 1994, p. 85.

Van Fleet, David D. *Contemporary Management*, 2nd ed. Boston: Houghton Mifflin, 1991, p. 250.

Verespej, Michael A. "Stern Hand," *Industry Week*, February 17, 1992, p. 25.

Verity, John. "A Company That Is 100% Virtual," *Business Week*, November 21, 1994, p. 85.

Weber, Joseph. "For DuPont, Christmas in April," *Business Week*, April 24, 1995, pp. 128–130.

Womack, James P., Daniel T. Jones, and Daniel Roos. *The Machine That Changed the World: The Story of Lean Production*. New York: Harper Perennial, 1991, pp. 43–45.

Woodward, Joan. *Industrial Organization: Theory and Practice*. London: Oxford University Press, 1965.

CHAPTER 10

Argyris, Chris, and Don Schon. *Organizational Learning: A Theory of Action Perspective*. Reading, Mass.: Addison-Wesley, 1978.

Barnes, Louis B. "Managing the Paradox of Organizational Trust," *Harvard Business Review* (March–April 1981), pp. 107–118.

Brenner, Jo-el Glenn. "The World According to the Planet Mars," *Dallas Morning News*, April 19, 1992, pp. 1H, 2H, 7H.

Briggins, Angela. "Win-Win Iniatives for Women," *Management Review* (June 1995), p. 6.

Burton, Gene E. "Organizational Development—A Systematic Process," *Management World* (March 1976).

Collins, James C. "Building Companies to Last," *Inc.* (January 1995), pp. 83–85.

Collins, James C. "Change Is Good—But First Know What Should Never Change," *Fortune*, May 29, 1995, p. 141.

Collins, James C., and Jerry I. Porras. *Built to Last*. New York: HarperBusiness, 1994, pp. 3, 117–118, 132, 134.

Dallas Morning News. "Executive Fired After Caring for Ill Wife Sues Perelman," July 6, 1995, p. 2D.

Deal, Terrence E., and Allan A. Kennedy. *Corporate Cultures: The Rites and Rituals of Corporate Life*. Reading, Mass.: Addison-Wesley, 1982, p. 25.

Deutsch, Claudia H. "At Corning, Ideas Now Match Markets," *The New York Times* (7 January 2001).

Dubrin, Andrew J. *Fundamentals of Organizational Behavior*. New York: Pergamon Press, 1974, pp. 331–361.

Elmer, Vickie. "Kmart Risks New Approaches," *Dallas Morning News*, April 30, 1995, p. 8H.

Executive Management Forum. "Transformational Wizards: Leaders Who Create Change," *Management Review* (June 1995), p. 4.

Fisher, Anne B. "Making Change Stick," *Fortune*, April 17, 1995, pp. 122–131.

Fishman, Charles. "Creative Tension," *Fast Company* (November 2000), http://www.fastcompany.com/online/40/corning.html.

Greiner, Larry. "Evolution and Revolution as Organizations Grow," *Harvard Business Review* (July–August 1972), pp. 55–64.

Greiner, Larry. "Patterns of Organizational Change," *Harvard Business Review* (May–June 1967), pp. 119–130.

Hammer, Michael, and James Champy. *Reengineering the Corporation*. New York: HarperBusiness, 1993, pp. 32–33.

Hodgetts, Richard M., and Steven Altman. *Organizational Behavior*. Philadelphia: Saunders, 1979, pp. 353–355.

Jacobson, Gary. "Kodak's CEO Sees His Role as Standard Bearer," *Dallas Morning News*, May 10, 1995, p. 4D.

Kotter, John P. *Organizational Dynamics: Diagnosis and Intervention*. Reading, Mass.: Addison-Wesley, 1978.

Kotter, John P., and James Heskett. *Corporate Culture and Performance*. New York: Free Press, 1992, p. 11.

Lammers, Terry. "The New Improved Organization Chart," *Inc.* (October 1992), pp. 147–149.

Lawlor, Julia. "Executive Exodos," *Working Woman* (November 1994), pp. 39–41, 80–87.

Lewin, Kurt. "Frontiers in Group Dynamics: Concept, Method, and Reality in Social Science," *Human Relations* (1947), pp. 5–41.

Loeb, Marshall. "Ten Commandments for Managing Creative People," *Fortune*, January 16, 1995, pp. 135–136.

Manganelli, Raymond, and Mark Klein. "A Framework for Reengineering," *Management Review* (June 1994), pp. 9–16.

Manganelli, Raymond, and Mark Klein. "Your Engineering Toolkit," *Management Review* (August 1994), pp. 26–30.

Maremont, Mark. "Kodak's New Focus," *Business Week*, January 30, 1995, pp. 62–68.

McCracken, Douglas M. "Best Practice—Winning the Talent War for Women: Sometimes It Takes a Revolution," *Harvard Business Review* (November–December, 2000), http://www.us.deloitte.com/us/news/00Dec/hbr.htm.

Mitchell, Jim. "Dunlap's Math: 1 + 1 = 3," *Dallas Morning News*, July 18, 1995, pp. 1D, 4D.

Musits, Bela L. "When Big Changes Happen to Small Companies," *Inc.* (August 1994), pp. 27–28.

Nadler, David A. "The Fine Art of Managing Change," *New York Times*, November 29, 1987, p. F3.

Nakarami, Laxmi. "Goldstar Is Burning Bright," *Business Week*, September 26, 1994, pp. 129–130.

Nakarami, Laxmi. "Will Lucky Goldstar Reach Its Peak with Zenith?" *Business Week*, August 7, 1994, p. 40.

Peters, Thomas J., and Robert H. Waterman, Jr. *In Search of Excellence: Lessons from America's Best-Run Companies*. New York: Harper & Row, 1982, p. 173.

Sherman, Stratford. "Is He Too Cautious to Save IBM," *Fortune*, October 3, 1994, pp. 78–90.

Tichy, Noel M., and Stratford Sherman. *Control Your Destiny or Someone Else Will*. New York: Doubleday Currency, 1993, pp. 245–246.

USA Today. "Happy Boss's Day From Each of Your 16,000 Employees at Southwest Airlines," October 14, 1994, p. 9A.

CHAPTER 11

Amend, Patricia. "Job References Hard to Come by These Days," *USA Today*, February 2, 1990, p. 4B.

The Auto Channel. "Conyers-Riverside Ford Auto Dealer Receives National Business Award," February 11, 2000, http:www.theautochannel.com/news/press/date/20000211/press007745.html.

Beck, Joan. "Matching the Workplace to the Work Force," *Chicago Tribune*, March 9, 1992, sec. 1, p. 15.

Bennett, Amanda. "Executive Pay: A Little Pain and a Lot to Gain," *Wall Street Journal*, April 22, 1992, p. R1.

Bravo, Ellen, and Ellen Cassedy. *The 9 to 5 Guide to Combating Sexual Harassment*. New York: Wiley, 1992.

Brown, Tom. "Manage with a Conscience," *Industry Week*, January 9, 1995, pp. 20–22, 25.

Bulkeley, William M. "Computer Use by Illiterates Grows at Work," *Wall Street Journal*, June 9, 1992, p. B1.

Chicago Tribune. "Workers Lack Three R's, Hurting Small Firms, Study Says," June 5, 1992, sec. 3, p. 3.

The Dallas Morning News. "Employment Success Story, September 3, 2000.

The Detroit News. "Conyers Honored by Ford Motor," May 15, 1998, http://detnews.com/1998/biz/9805/15/05150126.htm.

Federal Register. "Uniform Guidelines on Employee Selection Procedures," 43, #156 (August 1978), pp. 38, 295–238, 309.

Fenn, Donna, ed. "Check My References—Please!," *Inc.* (April 1995), p. 111.

Fingleton, Eamonn. "Jobs for Life: Why Japan Won't Give Them Up," *Fortune*, March 20, 1995, pp. 119–120, 122–123, 125.

Fisher, Anne B. "Getting Comfortable with Couples in the Workplace," *Fortune*, October 3, 1994, pp. 138–142, 144.

Fortune. "America's Top Employers" (January 2001), http://www.fortune.com/bestcompanies.

Fraser, Jill. " 'Tis Better to Give and Receive," *Inc.* (February 1995), pp. 84–86, 88, 90.

Fuchsberg, Gilbert. "Study Says Women Face Glass Walls as Well as Ceilings," *Wall Street Journal*, March 3, 1992, pp. B1, B8.

Gill, Jennifer. "Bigwigs Rake in Ever Bigger Bucks," *Business Week Online* (30 November 2000), http://www.businessweek.com/careers/content/nov2000/ca20001130_879.htm.

Hammonds, Keith H., Kevin Kelly, and Karen Thurston. "The New World of Work," *Business Week*, October 17, 1994, pp. 76–77, 80–81, 84–87.

Hoerr, John, et al. "Privacy," *Business Week*, March 28, 1988, pp. 61, 65.

Holly, Dan. "Heads, We Win," *Black Enterprise* (June 1995), pp. 134–136, 140.

Inc. "Healthy Workers Cost Less," (May 1995), p. 37.

JAMA: *Journal of the American Medical Association* 266(13): (2 October 1991), 1827–1830; Letters.

JAMA: *Journal of the American Medical Association* 267(9): (4 March 1992), 1207–1208.

Kleiman, Carol. "Are You in the Market for Some Advice?" *Chicago Tribune*, June 28, 1995, sec. 6, p. 5.

Kleiman, Carol. "Employee Reviews Merit Close Attention," *Chicago Tribune*, February 2, 1992, sec. 8, p. 1.

Kleiman, Carol. "Employer-Based Training Is a Growing Job Source," *Chicago Tribune*, January 12, 1992, sec. 8, p. 1.

Kleiman, Carol. "From Genetics to Honesty, Firms Expand Employee Tests, Screening," *Chicago Tribune*, February 9, 1992, sec. 8, p. 1.

Kleiman, Carol. "In Brief, This Interview Technique Is a Plus," *Chicago Tribune*, December 14, 1994, sec. 6, p. 5.

Kleiman, Carol. "Making Diversity Work," *Chicago Tribune*, May 1, 1994, sec. 8, p. 1.

Kleiman, Carol. "Some Firms Breaking Glass Ceiling," *Chicago Tribune*, April 13, 1992, sec. 4, p. 7.

Kleiman, Carol. "Worker Skepticism Aside, Firms Like Exit Interviews," *Chicago Tribune*, October 13, 1991, sec. 8, p. 1.

Klimas, Molly. "How to Recruit a Smart Team," *Nation's Business* (May 1995), pp. 26–27.

Larimer, Tim. "Great News: No More Jobs for Life," *Time Asia*, November 1, 1999, http://www.time.com/time/asia/magazine/99/1101/japan.nissan.html.

Mohrman, Allan, Jr., Susan Resnick-West, and E. E. Lawler III. *Designing Performance Appraisal Systems: Aligning Appraisals and Organizational Realities*. San Francisco: Jossey-Bass, 1989.

Moskal, Brian S. "Sexual Harassment '80s Style," *Industry Week*, July 2, 1989, p. 24.

Nulty, Peter. "Serial Entrepreneur: Tips from a Man Who Started 28 Businesses," *Fortune*, July 10, 1995, p. 182.

Rigdon, Joan E. "Using Lateral Moves to Spur Employees," *Wall Street Journal*, May 26, 1992, pp. B1, B5.

Schuler, Randall R. *Managing Human Resources*, 5th ed. New York: West, 1995, pp. 261–262.

Steinert-Threlkeld, Ton. "Computer Revenge a Growing Threat," *Chicago Tribune*, March 9, 1992, sec. 4, p. 3.

Stodghill, Ron. "Managing AIDS," *Business Week*, February 1, 1993, pp. 48–52.

U.S. Congress. Senate. Subcommittee on Labor of the Committee on Labor and Public Welfare. *Equal Employment Opportunity Act of 1972* (March 1972), p. 3.

Wallace, Elizabeth. "Rhode Island Enacts Gay Civil Rights Law," *Windy City Times*, May 25, 1995, pp. 1, 6.

Wilke, John R. "Digital's Offer to Employees Proves Popular," *Wall Street Journal*, June 1, 1992, p. B6.

CHAPTER 12

Barua, Anitesh, Prabhuder, Andrew Whinston, and Fang Yin. "Making E-Business Pay: Eight Key Drivers for Operational Success," *IEEE IT Professional* (November/December 2000), http://crec.bus.utexas.edu.

Burns, Greg. "A Froot Loop by Any Other Name . . .," *Business Week*, June 26, 1995, pp. 72, 76.

Comins, Frederic M., Jr. "Renewal at Kmart," a letter to the editor of *Harvard Business Review* (September–October 1992), p. 176.

Davis, Keith. *Human Behavior at Work: Organizational Behavior*. New York: McGraw-Hill, 1989.

Deutschman, Alan. "The CEO's Secret of Managing Time," *Fortune*, June 1, 1992, pp. 136, 140, 144, 146.

Dodge, John. "Dell's Internet-Based Plant Keeps Production Efficient," *The Wall Street Journal*, September 26, 2000, WSJ.COM.

Dumaine, Brian. "The Trouble with Teams," *Fortune*, September 5, 1994, p. 92.

Fisher, Anne B. "CEOs Think That Morale Is Dandy," *Fortune*, November 18, 1991, pp. 83–84.

Freeman, Diane. "Offices: To Wall or Not to Wall?" *Boulder County Business Report*, 1998, http://www.bcbr.com/dec98/cubicle2.htm.

Gabarro, John J. "Retrospective Commentary," *Harvard Business Review* (November–December 1991), p. 108.

Garza, Melita Marie. "Language Barrier," *Chicago Tribune*, June 15, 1995, sec. 5, pp. 1–2.

Huber, Janean. "The Big Picture: Learning from Big Business," *Entrepreneur* (June 1992), pp. 186–187.

Kenney, Charles C. *Riding the Runaway Horse*. New York: Little, Brown, 1992.

Kirkpatrick, David. "Here Comes the Payoff from PCs," *Fortune*, March 23, 1992, pp. 93, 96, 100.

Mateja, Jim. "J. D. Power Speaks; Chrysler Listens," *Chicago Tribune*, August 21, 1994, sec. 4, p. 7.

Miller, Donald. "Alcoa Corporate Center: A Triumph Over Pretension," *Post-Gazette*, September 18, 1998, http://www.post-gazette.com/regionstate/19980918alcoa5.asp.

Mintzberg, Henry. *The Nature of Managerial Work*. New York: Harper & Row, 1973.

Peters, Tom. "Steps to Turn Workers into Business People," *Chicago Tribune*, November 25, 1991, sec. 4, p. 4.

Pitney Bowes Workplace Study. "Messaging for Innovation: Building the Innovation Infrastructure Through Messaging Practices," (28 August 2000), http://www.pb.com.

Plunkett, Lorne C., and Robert Fournier. *Participative Management*. New York: Wiley, 1991, pp. 123–124, 126–127.

Ramirez, Roberto R. "The Hispanic Population in the United States," (March 1999), http://www.census.gov/prod/2000pubs/p20-527.pdf.

Ryan, Nancy. "Interaction on the Way for Offices," *Chicago Tribune*, June 9, 1992, sec. 3, p. 1.

Sayles, Leonard R., and George Strauss. *Human Behavior in Organizations*. (Englewood Cliffs, N.J.: Prentice-Hall), 1966, pp. 93–94, 238–246.

Spragins, Ellen E. "An Employee Newsletter with Zing," *Inc.* (April 1992), p. 121.

Sprout, Alison L. "Reality Boost," *Fortune*, March 21, 1994, p. 93.

Taylor, William. "Message and Muscle: An Interview with Swatch Titan Nicolas Hayek," *Harvard Business Review* (March–April 1993).

Tetzeli, Rick. "Surviving Information Overload," *Fortune*, July 11, 1994, p. 61.

Walton, Sam, with John Huey. *Sam Walton: Made in America*. New York: Doubleday, 1992, pp. 247–248.

CHAPTER 13

ABC News 20/20. "Making Millionaires," May 26, 2000, http://more.abcnews.go.com/onair/2020/2020_000526_millionaires.html.

Adams, J. Stacy. "Toward an Understanding of Equity," *Journal of Abnormal and Social Psychology* (November 1963), pp. 422–436.

Alderfer, Clayton. *Existence, Relatedness, and Growth: Human Needs in Organizational Settings*. New York: Free Press, 1972.

Argyris, Chris. *Personality and Organization*. New York: Harper & Bros., 1957.

Austin, Nancy K. "How Managers Manage Flexibility," *Management Review* (August 1994), pp. 19–20.

Barrier, Michael. "Re-Engineering Revisited," *Nation's Business*, May 19, 1995, p. 36.

Case, John. "Collective Effort," *Inc.* (January 1992), pp. 32–43.

Case, John. "The Open-Book Revolution," *Inc.* (June 1995), pp. 26–40.

Cohen, Sharon. "One In a Million: Boss Rewards Workers by Splitting 9-Figure Fortune," *Associated Press*, September 12, 1999, http://www.dallasnews.com/national/0912nat2thanks.htm.

Collins, James C., and Jerry I. Porras. *Built to Last*. New York: HarperBusiness, 1993, pp. 156–158.

Daft, Richard L. *Management*, 3rd ed. Fort Worth, Tex.: Dryden Press, 1994, pp. 515–521.

Dallas Morning News. "They Didn't Expect a Pink Slip for Daughter's Day at Work," May 5, 1995, p. 1D.

Davis, Keith, and John W. Newstrom. *Human Behavior at Work: Organizational Behavior*, 9th ed. New York: McGraw-Hill, 1992, p. 105.

Deutschman, Alan. "The Managing Wisdom of High-Tech Superstars," *Fortune*, October 17, 1994, pp. 203–204.

Dumaine, Brian. "Why Do We Work?" *Fortune*, December 26, 1994, pp. 196–198.

Etorre, Barbara. "Breaking the Glass . . . or Just Window Dressing," *Management Review* (March 1992), p. 17.

Executive Management Forum. "Job Sharing Is Family Friendly," *Management Review* (April 1995), p. 2.

Fenn, Donna. "More Than Just Affirmative Action," *Inc.* (July 1995), p. 93.

Fierman, Jaclyn. "Winning Ideas from Maverick Managers," *Fortune*, February 6, 1995, pp. 66–80.

Files, Jennifer. "Incentive for Everyone," *Dallas Morning News*, July 25, 1992, pp. 1D, 4D.

Finegan, Jay. "Pipe Dreams," *Inc.* (August 1994), pp. 64–70.

Fleming, Peter C. "Empowerment Strengthens the Rock," *Management Review* (March 1992), pp. 34–37.

Gleckman, Howard. "Bonus Pay: Buzzword or Bonanza," *Business Week*, November 14, 1994, pp. 62–64.

Goodman Paul S., and Abraham Fredman. "An Examination of Adam's Theory of Inequity," *Administrative Science Quarterly* (December 1971), pp. 271–288.

Hall, Cheryl. "The Brinker Touch," *Dallas Morning News*, March 3, 1992, p. 23H.

Hall, Sheri. "Shrewdness, Humanity Blend to Make Corporate Benefactor," *The Detroit News*, July 25, 1999, http://detnews.com/1999/biz19907/25/07250046.htm.

Hamner, W. C. "Reinforcement Theory and Contingency Management in Organizational Settings," *Organizational Behavior and Management: A Contingency Approach*, H. L. Tosi and W. C. Hamner, eds. New York: Wiley, 1974, pp. 86–112.

Herzberg, Frederick. "One More Time: How Do You Motivate Employees?" *Business Classics: Fifteen Key Concepts for Management Success*. Cambridge, Mass.: Harvard Business Review, 1975, pp. 16–17.

Hyatt, Joshua. "Real-World Re-Engineering," *Inc.* (April 1995), pp. 40–53.

Krizan, William G. "Award of Excellence," *Engineering News-Record*. April 17, 2000, http://www.enr.com/new/c41700.asp.

Kuratko, Donald F., and Richard M. Hodgetts. *Entrapreneurship: A Contemporary Approach*. Chicago: Dryden Press, 1989.

McClelland, David C. *The Achieving Society*. New York: Van Nostrand Reinhold, 1971.

McClelland, David C., and David Burnham. "Power Is the Great Motivator," *Harvard Business Review* (March–April 1976) pp. 100–110.

McGregor, Douglas. *The Human Side of Enterprise*. New York: McGraw-Hill, 1960, pp. 23–27.

Maslow, Abraham H. "A Theory of Human Motivation," *Psychological Review* 50 (1943), pp. 370–396.

Mills, D. Quinn, and Mark D. Cannon. "Managing the New Work Force," *Management Review* (June 1992), p. 38.

Oliver, Joyce Ann. "Mattel Chief Followed Her Vision," *Marketing News*, March 16, 1992, p. 15.

Peters, Tom. "Time-Obsessed Competition," *Management Review* (September 1990), p. 18.

Pinchot, Gifford. *Entrepreneuring*. New York: Harper & Row, 1985.

Porter, Lawrence W., and Edward E. Lawler. *Managerial Attitudes and Performance*. Homewood, Ill.: Irwin, 1968.

Robbins, Stephen P. *Organizational Behavior: Concepts, Controversies, and Applications*, 5th ed. Englewood Cliffs, N.J.: Prentice-Hall, 1991, p. 209.

Schlossberg, Howard. "Internal Marketing Helps Companies Understand Culturally Diverse Markets," *Marketing News*, January 21, 1991, pp. 7, 9.

Schuler, Randall S. *Personnel and Human Resource Management*, 3rd ed. St. Paul, Minn.: West, 1987, pp. 41–43.

Semler, Ricardo. *Maverick: The Success Story Behind the World's Most Unusual Workplace*. Warner Books, 1995.

Single, John L. "The Power of Expectations: Productivity and the Self-Fulfilling Prophecy," *Management World* (November, 1980), pp. 19, 37–38.

Skinner, B. F. *Contingencies of Reinforcement*. New York: Appleton-Century-Crofts, 1969.

Steers, Richard M., and Lyman W. Porter, eds. *Motivation and Work Behavior*, 4th ed. New York: McGraw-Hill, 1987, pp. 3–4.

Stewart, Thomas A. "How to Lead a Revolution," *Fortune*, November 28, 1994, pp. 48–61.

Straub, Joseph T., and Raymond Attner. *Introduction to Business*, 5th ed. Boston: PWS-KENT, 1994, p. 182.

Tarpy, R. M. *Basic Principles of Learning*. Glenview, Ill.: Scott, Foresman, 1974, pp. 71–79.

Trimble, Vance H. *Sam Walton: The Inside Story of America's Richest Man*. New York: Signet, 1992, p. 109.

Van Fleet, David D. *Contemporary Management*, 2nd ed. Boston: Houghton Mifflin, 1991, p. 371.

Vroom, Victor H. *Work and Motivation*. New York: Wiley, 1964.

Whitford, David. "The Trouble with Harry," *Inc.* (April 1995), pp. 64–73.

Wilson, Larry. "Creating the Best Work Culture: How Managers Can Avoid the Trap of Ignoring the 'People' Skills in Dealing with Their Employees," *Nation's Business* (April 1992), p. 38.

Winters, Terry E., and Donald L. Murfin. "Venture Capital Investing for Corporate Development Objectives," *Journal of Business Venturing* (Summer 1988), p. 207.

CHAPTER 14

Boyett, Joseph H. and Henry P. Conn. *Workplace 2000*. New York: Plume, 1991, pp. 330–331.

Cooper, Helen. "Carpet Firm Sets Up an In-House School to Stay Competitive," *Wall Street Journal*, October 5, 1992, pp. A1, A5.

Davis, Keith, and John Newstrom. *Human Behavior at Work: Organizational Behavior*. 8th ed. New York: McGraw-Hill, 1989, pp. 213, 215.

Erdman, Andrew. "Staying Ahead of 800 Competitors," *Fortune*, June 1, 1992, p. 111.

Fiedler, Fred E. "The Contingency Model—New Directions for Leadership Utilization," *Journal of Contemporary Business* 3, no. 4 (Autumn 1974), pp. 65–80.

Fisher, Anne B. "Making Change Stick," *Fortune*, April 17, 1995, pp. 121–122, 124, 128–131.

Franklin, Stephen. "Aggressive Describes ADM," *Chicago Tribune*, July 11, 1995, sec. 3, pp. 1, 5.

Gruner, Stephanie. "The Team-Building Peer Review," *Inc.* (July 1995), pp. 63–65.

Gunset, George, and Michael Tackett. "Controversy May Have High Cost for ADM," *Chicago Tribune*, July 11, 1995, sec. l, pp. 1, 12.

Henkoff, Ronald. "Finding, Training, & Keeping the Best Service Workers," *Fortune*, October 3, 1994, pp. 110–111, 114, 116, 118, 120, 122.

Hersey, Paul, and Kenneth H. Blanchard. *Management of Organizational Behavior*, 4th ed. Englewood Cliffs, N.J.: Prentice-Hall, 1982.

House, Robert J. "A Path-Goal Theory of Leader Effectiveness," *Administrative Science Quarterly* 16 (1971), pp. 321–338.

House, Robert J., and Terrence R. Mitchell. "Path-Goal Theory of Leadership," *Journal of Contemporary Business* 3, no. 4 (Autumn 1974), pp. 81–97.

Inc. "Managing People" (October 1992), p. 33.

Keller, Robert, and Andrew Szilagyi. "A Longitudinal Study of Leader Reward Behavior, Subordinate Expectations, and Satisfaction," *Personnel Psychology* (Spring 1978), pp. 119–129.

Kiechell, Walter, III. "The Leader As Servant," Fortune, May 4, 1992, pp. 121, 122.

Kleiman, Carol. "1990s Will See Opportunity for New Breed of Manager," *Chicago Tribune*, March 22, 1992, sec. 8, p. 1.

Kleiman, Carol. "Male, Female Leadership: A Study In Contrasts," *Chicago Tribune*, July 20, 1992, sec. 4, p. 3.

Konrad, Walecia, and Andrea Rothman. "Can Wayne Calloway Handle the Pepsi Challenge?" *Business Week*, January 27, 1992, pp. 90, 91, 92.

Kotter, John P. "Leading Change: Why Transformation Efforts Fail," *Harvard Business Review* (March–April 1995), pp. 59–67.

Kotter, John P., and James L. Heskett. *Corporate Culture and Performance*. New York: Free Press, 1992, pp. 94–96.

Lancaster, Hal. "Kelleher's Main Strategy: Treat All Employees Well," *The Wall Street Journal*, August 31, 1999.

Lienert, Paul. "Jac the Knife," *Automobile* (April 1995), pp. 87–88, 92–93.

Likert, Rensis. "From Production- and Employee-Centeredness to Systems 1–4," *Journal of Management* 5 (1979), pp. 147–156.

Likert, Rensis. *The Human Organization*. New York: McGraw-Hill, 1976.

Losee, Stephanie. "Revolution from Within," *Fortune*, June 1, 1992, p. 112.

Mateja, Jim. "Scary Wakeup Calls Worked for Olds," *Chicago Tribune*, July 10, 1995, sec. 4, p. 5.

Miller, Jim. "It's the End of the Road for Olds," *The Detroit News*, December 12, 2000, http://detnews.com/2000/autos/0012/12/901-161212.htm.

Nation's Business. "Women Entrepreneurs: A Pretty Big Game," (August 1992), p. 53

Nulty, Peter. "How to Live by Your Wits," *Fortune*, April 20, 1992, p. 119.

Peace, William H. "The Hard Work of Being a Soft Manager," *Harvard Business Review* (November–December 1991), pp. 40–47.

Rosener, Judy B. "Ways Women Lead," *Harvard Business Review* (November–December 1990), pp. 119–125.

Schriesheim, C. A., and B. J. Bird. "Contributions of the Ohio State Studies to the Field of Leadership," *Journal of Management* 5 (1979), pp. 135–145.

Sullivan, Barbara. "Despite New, Expanded Horizons, Women's Businesses Face Old Boundaries," *Chicago Tribune*, July 5, 1995, sec. 3, pp. 1, 2.

Walton, Sam, with John Huey. *Sam Walton: Made in America*. New York: Doubleday, 1992, p. 169.

Wright, Richard A. "Oldsmobile was America's Oldest Surviving Nameplate," *The Detroit News*, November 6, 2000, http://detnews.com/joyrides/2000/oldsmobile/oldsmobile.htm.

Yukl, Gary A. *Leadership in Organizations*. Englewood Cliffs, N.J.: Prentice-Hall, 1981, p. 70, 121–125.

Yung, Katherine. "From David to Goliath," *The Dallas Morning News*, December 26, 1999.

CHAPTER 15

Albanese, Robert, and David D. Van Fleet. "Rational Behavior in Groups: The Free-Riding Tendency," *Academy of Management Review* 10 (1985), pp. 244–255.

Anderson, K. Jackson. "The Best of Times," *Herald Net*, March 9, 1997, http://www.heraldnet.com/Stories/97/3/9/boeing.htm.

Brown, Tom. "Want to Be a Real Team," *Industry Week*, July 20, 1992, p. 17.

Byham, William C. "Self-Directed Work Team Magic," *Boardroom Reports*, June 15, 1992, pp. 1–8.

Caminiti, Susan. "What Team Leaders Need to Know," *Fortune*, February 20, 1995, pp. 93–100.

Cartright, Dorwin, and Alvin Zandler. *Group Dynamics: Research and Theory*, 3rd ed. New York: Harper & Row, 1968.

Case, John. "Collective Effort," *Inc.* (January 1992), p. 35.

Case, John. "The Open Book Revolution," *Inc.* (June 1995), pp. 26–40.

Cox, Allan. "The Homework Behind Teamwork," *Industry Week*, January 7, 1992, p. 21.

Cronin, Michael P. "Asking Workers What They Want," *Inc.* (August 1994), p. 103.

Daft, Richard L. *Management*, 3rd ed. Forth Worth, Tex.: Dryden Press, 1994, p. 585.

Deutschman, Alan. "The Managing Wisdom of High-Tech Superstars," *Fortune*, October 17, 1994, p. 200.

Dumaine, Brian. "The Trouble with Teams," *Fortune*, September 5, 1994, pp. 86–92.

Dumaine, Brian. "Unleash Workers and Cut Costs," *Fortune*, May 18, 1992, p. 88.

Etorre, Barbara. "Retooling People and Processes," *Management Review* (June 1995), pp. 19–23.

Executive Management Forum. "Customer-Focused Teams (CFTeams) on The Start," *Management Review* (September 1994), p. 2.

Executive Management Forum. "Teaming a Cornerstone at Reengineered Taco Bell," *Management Review* (December 1994), p. 2.

Executive Management Forum. "The Facts of Life About Teambuilding," *Management Review* (February 1995), p. 4.

Fisher, Kimball, Maureen Duncan Fisher, Mareen D. Fisher, *The Distributed Mind: Achieving High Performance Through the Collective Intelligence of Knowledge Work Teams*, AMACOM, 1997.

Gersick, Connie J. G. "Marking Time: Predictable Transitions in Task Groups," *Academy of Management Journal* (June 1989), pp. 274–309.

Gleckman, Howard. "Bonus Pay: Buzzword or Bonanza?" *Business Week*, November 14, 1994, pp. 62–64.

Greenwald, John. "Is Mr. Nice Guy Back," *Time*, January 27, 1992, pp. 42–44.

Gunn, Eileen P. "Empowerment That Pays Off," *Fortune*, March 20, 1995, pp. 145–146.

Huey, John. "The New Post-Heroic Leadership," *Fortune*, February 21, 1994, p. 48.

Jacob, Rahul. "The Struggle to Create an Organization for the 21st Century," *Fortune*, April 3, 1995, pp. 98–99.

Kerwin, Kathleen, Edith Updike, and Keith Naughton. "The Shape of a New Machine," *Business Week*, July 24, 1995, pp. 60–66.

Labich, Kenneth. "Boeing's New Dream Machine," *Fortune*, February 19, 1996, http://www.fortune.com/fortune/magazine/1996/960219/boeing.html.

Larson, Carl E., and Frank M. J. LaFasto. *TeamWork*. Newbury Park, Calif.: Sage, 1989.

Litvan, Laura M. "Casting a Wider Employment Net," *Nation's Business* (December 1994), pp. 49–51.

McKee, Bradford. "Turn Your Workers into a Team," *Nation's Business* (July 1992), p. 36.

Murphy, Anne. "The Enemy Within," *Inc.* (March 1994), pp. 58–69.

Owens, Thomas. "Business Teams," *Small Business Report* (January 1989), pp. 50–58.

Parker, Glenn. *Team Players and Teamwork*. San Francisco: Jossey-Bass, 1990.

Prince, George. "Recognizing Genuine Teamwork," *Supervisory Management* (April 1989), pp. 25–36.

Reynolds, Larry. "Quality Circles," *Management Review* (January 1992), pp. 53–54.

Robbins, Stephen. *Managing Organizational Conflict*, 3rd ed. Englewood Cliffs, N.J.: Prentice-Hall, 1986, p. 321.

Sager, Ida. "The Butterfly: From a Little Girl's Building Blocks," *Business Week*, July 24, 1995, p. 72.

Schein, Edgar. *Process Consultation*. Reading, Mass.: Addison-Wesley, 1969, pp. 42–43.

Shaw, M. E. *Group Dynamics*, 3rd ed. New York: McGraw-Hill, 1985.

Singer, Merv, and Susan Lazar. "Who's in Charge Here?" *Nation's Business* (January 1995), p. 37.

Stewart, Thomas A. "How to Lead a Revolution," *Fortune*, September 28, 1994, pp. 48–61.

Stoner, James A. F. *Management*, 3rd ed. Englewood Cliffs, N.J.: Prentice-Hall, 1986, p. 85.

Thomas, Kenneth W. "Conflict and Conflict Management," *Handbook of Industrial and Organizational Psychology*, Marvin Donnette, ed. Chicago: Rand McNally, 1976, pp. 889–935.

Tuckman, B. W. "Developmental Sequence in Small Groups," *Psychological Bulletin*, 63 (1965), pp. 384–389.

Uris, Auren. *Techniques of Leadership*. New York: McGraw-Hill, 1964, p. 58.

Verespej, Michael A. "When Workers Get New Roles," *Industry Week*, February 3, 1992, p. 11.

Yang, Dori Jones. "Nordstrom's Gang of Four," *Business Week*, June 15, 1992, pp. 122–123.

Zellner, Wendy. "Team Player: No More 'Same-ol-Same ol'," *Business Week*, October 17, 1994, pp. 95–96.

CHAPTER 16

Barry, Thomas J. *Management Excellence Through Quality*. Milwaukee: ASQC Press, 1991, pp. 5, 6.

Bianchi, Alessandra. "The Strictly Business Flextime Request Form," *Inc.* (May 1995), p. 79.

Bittel, Lester R. *The McGraw-Hill 36-Hour Management Course*. New York: McGraw-Hill, 1989, pp. 179, 184, 185.

Bittel, Lester R., and Jackson E. Ramsey, eds. *Handbook for Professional Managers*. New York: McGraw-Hill, 1985, pp. 194, 196.

Business Week. "Equifax Vows to Get It Right," July 13, 1992, p. 38.

Business Week. "This Inspector Gets Under a Plane's Skin," November 18, 1991, p. 69.

Comins, Frederic M., Jr. "Renewal at Kmart," a letter to the editor of *Harvard Business Review* (September–October 1992), p. 176.

Del Valle, Christina, and Larry Armstrong. "33 Crashes: Design Flaw or Pilot Error?" *Business Week*, June 12, 1995, p. 40.

Garcia, Olivia Reyes. "Powerful Latino Bloc to be Heard," *The Bakersfield Californian*, November 5, 2000, http://www.bakersfield.com/top/Story/243499p-232175c.html.

Guth, Rob. "Restructuring a Behemoth: How Mr. Nishimuro Reinvented Toshiba," *The Wall Street Journal*, December 27, 2000.

Haynes, V. Dion. "Ethics Will Be Subject of First Meeting of New School Board," *Chicago Tribune*, July 26, 1995, sec. 2, p. 3.

Heraud, Daniel. "Test Drive," *MSN CarPoint Reviews*, http://carpoint.msn.com/Vip/Heraud/Toyota/Camry/2000O.asp.

Industry Search. "Quality Control Plan Hoped to Save Toshiba 130 Billion Yen in FY2000," July 11, 2000, http://www.industrysearch.com.au/news/viewrecord.asp?ID=3921.

Kelly, Kevin. "Deere's Surprising Harvest in Health Care," *Business Week*, July 11, 1994, pp. 107, 111.

Loeb, Marshall. "Leadership Lost—and Regained," *Fortune*, April 17, 1995, pp. 217–218.

Macht, Joshua D. "How Has Technology Changed the Way You Do Your Job?" *Inc. Technology* (July 1995), p. 37.

Melcher, Richard A. "Why Hyatt Is Toning Down the Glitz," *Business Week*, February 27, 1995, pp. 92, 94.

Nation's Business. "Getting What They Owe You" (August 1992), p. 53.

Naughton, Keith and Edith Hill Updike. "Will Less Be More for Toyota's Camry?" *Business Week*, July 24, 1995, p. 66.

Odiorne, George, Heinz Weihrich, and Jack Mendelson. *Executive Skills: A Management by Objectives Approach*. Dubuque, Iowa: Brown, 1980, pp. 26–28.

Pyzdek, Thomas. "Motorola's Six Sigma Program," *Quality Digest* (December 1997), http://www.qualitydigest.com/dec97/html/motsix.html.

Schine, Eric. "California's Latino Backlash," *Business Week*, December 26, 1994, p. 67.

Walton, Richard E. "From Control to Commitment in the Workplace," *Harvard Business Review* (March–April 1985), pp. 76–84.

Zweig, Phillip L. "Prudential: Making It Rock-Solid Again," *Business Week*, October 31, 1994, p. 96.

Zweig, Phillip L., et al. "Managing Risk," *Business Week*, October 31, 1994, pp. 86–90, 92.

CHAPTER 17

Bittel, Lester R., and Jackson E. Ramsey, eds. *Handbook for Professional Managers*. New York: McGraw-Hill, 1985, p. 550.

Blades, John. "Final Chapter: Could Kroch's & Brentano's Have Righted Its Sinking Ship? Maybe," *Chicago Tribune*, July 31, 1995, sec. 5, pp. 1, 2.

Dudick, Thomas S., ed. *Handbook of Business Planning and Budgeting*. New York: Van Nostrand Reinhold, 1983, pp. 22, 74.

Finegan, Jay. "Taking Names," *Inc.* (September 1992), p. 129.

Flint, Jerry. "The TRW Way," *Forbes*, July 31, 1995, pp. 45, 46.

Galuszka, Peter and Patricia Kranz. "Look Who's Making a Revolution: Shareholders," *Business Week*, February 20, 1995, p. 60.

Hardy, Quentin. "The Killer Ad Machine," *Forbes Global*, December 11, 2000, http://www.forbes.com/global/2000/1211/0325066a.html.

Hayes, Cassandra. "The New Spin on Corporate Work Teams," *Black Enterprise* (June 1995), pp. 229–230, 232, 234.

Heyel, Carl, ed. *The Encyclopedia of Management*, 3rd ed. New York: Van Nostrand Reinhold, 1982, p. 328.

Kleiman, Carol. "Should Secretary Be Fall Girl When Boss Asks for Fib?" *Chicago Tribune*, July 20, 1995, sec. 3, p. 3.

Lubove, Seth. "Get 'em Before They Get You," *Forbes*, July 31, 1995, pp. 88–93.

Therrien, Lois. "Thomson Needs a Hit, and It's Up to Nipper to Go Fetch," *Business Week*, July 6, 1992, p. 80.

Trigg, Mike. "Two Do Yahoo!" *The Motley Fool*, January 24, 2001, http://www.fool.com/duelingfools/2001/duelingfools01012401.htm.

Vancil, Richard F. "What Kind of Management Control Do You Need?" *Harvard Business Review on Management*. New York: Harper & Row, 1975, p. 481.

Walton, Sam, with John Huey. *Sam Walton: Made in America*. New York: Doubleday, 1992, p. 231.

CHAPTER 18

Adam, Everett E., Jr., and Ronald J. Ebert. *Production and Operations Management*, 4th ed. Englewood Cliffs, N.J.: Prentice-Hall, 1989.

Adam, Everett E., Jr., and Paul M. Swamidass. "Assessing Operations Management from a Strategic Objective," *Journal of Management* (June 1989), pp. 181–204.

Baker, Stephen. "A Real Stealman For USX," *Business Week*, May 15, 1995, p. 47.

Brown, Tom. "Managing for Quality," *Industry Week*, July 20, 1992, p. 28.

Bylinsky, Gene. "The Digital Factory," *Fortune*, November 14, 1994, pp. 92–110.

Bylinsky, Gene. "Manufacturing for Reuse," *Fortune*, February 6, 1995, pp. 102–112.

CSE Research Bulletin No. 13. "Construction Automation in Improving Construction Productivity in Singapore," January 2000, http://www.ntu.edu.sg/cse/research/bulletin/1999_2000/pdf/CEco3.pdf.

Daft, Richard L. *Management*, 3rd ed. Fort Worth, Tex.: Dryden Press, 1994, pp. 723, 730–731.

Daniel, Mel. "Statistical Software Rings in Quality," *Computerworld*, January 6, 1992, p. 64.

DeMott, John S. "Look, World, No Hands!" *Nation's Business* (June 1994), p. 41.

Dincen, Steve. "Can American Steel Find Quality," *Industry Week*, January 26, 1992, pp. 37–39.

Emigh, Jaqueline. "Agile Manufacturing," *Computerworld*, August 30, 1999, http://www.computerworld.com/cwi/story/0,1199,NAV63-128-231-235_STO36805,00.html.

Enterprise Integration Laboratory. "The Integrated Supply Chain Management Project," http://www.eil.utoronto.ca/iscm-descr.html.

Garrett, Echo Montgomery. "Innovation & Outsourcing = Big Success," *Management Review* (September 1994), pp. 17–20.

Greco, Joe. "Design for Manufacturability and Assembly," *CADENCE Magazine* (March 2000), http://www.cadenceweb.com/2000/0300/issuefocus0300.html.

Greco, Susan. "The Decade-Long Overnight Success," *Inc.* (December 1994), pp. 73–79.

Harris, Joyce Saenz. "Dallas Inventor's Topsy Tail Turned Her World Topsy-Turvy," *The Dallas Morning News*, August 16, 1998, p. 1E.

Hawken, Paul, Amory Lovins, L. Hunter Lovins. *Natural Capitalism: Creating the Next Industrial Revolution*, Back Bay Books, 2000, pp. 139–144, http://www.interfaceinc.com.

Hayes, R. H., and S. C. Wheelright. *Restoring Our Competitive Edge: Competing Through Manufacturing*. New York: Wiley, 1984.

Hill, T. *Manufacturing Strategy: The Strategic Management of the Manufacturing Function*. London: Macmillan, 1985.

Holt, David. *Management: Principles and Practices*, 2nd ed. Englewood Cliffs, N.J.: Prentice-Hall, 1991, p. 550.

Kerwin, Kathleen, Edith Updike, and Keith Naughton. "The Shape of a New Machine," *Business Week*, July 24, 1995, pp. 60–66.

Liesman, Steve. "High-Tech Devices Speed Manufacturing, And May Play Larger Role in Economy," *The Wall Street Journal*, February 15, 2001, http://interactive.wsj.com/articles/SB982187508898449347.htm.

Litvan, Laura M. "Casting a Wider Employment Net," *Nation's Business* (December 1994), pp. 50–51.

Losee, Stephanie. "How Compaq Keeps the Magic Going," *Business Week*, February 21, 1994, pp. 88–92.

Marenghi, Catherine. "Stanley Hammers on Quality," *Computerworld*, February 6, 1992, p. 62.

Migliorelli, Marcia, and Robert T. Swan. "MRP and Aggregate Planning—A Problem Solution," *Production and Inventory Management Journal* 29, No. 2 (1988), pp. 42–44.

Modern Materials Handling. "A Look at the Factory of the Future," July 1, 2000, http://www.manufacturing.net/magazine/mmh/archives/2000/mmh0701.00/0701news2.htm.

Morley, Brad. "Management's Competitive Weapon," *Industry Week*, May 18, 1992, p. 44.

Oneal, Michael. "Does New Balance Have an American Sole?" *Business Week*, December 12, 1994, pp. 86–90.

Plotkin, Hal. "Riches from Rags," *Inc. Technology* (Summer 1995), pp. 62–68.

Port, Otis. "Customer-Made Direct from the Plant," *Business Week*, January 10, 1995, pp. 158–159.

Robbins, John. "TRW Relocation on the Horizon," *Dallas Morning News*, February 14, 1992, p. C1.

Robbins, Stephen P. *Management*, 4th ed. Englewood Cliffs, N.J.: Prentice-Hall, 1994, p. 638.

Robotic Industries Association. "World Survey Reports Boom in Robot Investment," 2001, http://www.robotics.org.

Sansoni, Silvia. "Home Shopping with No TV," *Business Week*, November 20, 1995.

Schiller, Zachary. "And Fix That Flat Before You Go, Stanley," *Business Week*, January 16, 1995, p. 35.

Serwer, Andrew. "McDonald's Conquers the World," *Fortune*, October 17, 1994, pp. 103–114.

Snyder, Gary T. "Avoiding the Pitfalls of Outsourcing," *Nation's Business* (May 1995), p. 12.

Straub, Joseph, and Raymond Attner. *Introduction to Business*, 5th ed. Boston: PWS-KENT, 1994, pp. 241–244.

Taylor, Alex. "The Auto Industry Meets the New Economy," *Fortune*, September 5, 1994, pp. 52–60.

Taylor, Alex. "Boeing: Sleeping in Seattle," *Fortune*, August 7, 1995, pp. 97–98.

Tully, Shawn. "You'll Never Guess Who Really Makes . . ." *Fortune*, October 3, 1994, pp. 124–128.

Williams, Frederick P. *Production/Operations Management*. Boston: Houghton Mifflin, 1990, p. 32.

Winters, Wendi. "In-Home Trunk Shows Peddle Fine Fashions Direct," *The Associated Press*, January 30, 1998, http://www.s-t.com/daily/01-98/01-30-98/b04li044.htm.

WSJ.com. "Dell's Revenue Climbs 28% But Net Income Remains Flat," February 15, 2001, http://interactive.wsj.com/articles/SB982255428790108216.htm.

Yates, Ronald E. "U.S. Lags in Construction Technology," *Chicago Tribune*, June 13, 1994, pp. 1D, 4D.

CHAPTER 19

Arnst, Catherine. "The Networked Corporation," *Business Week*, June 26, 1995, pp. 86–89.

Bartlett, Christopher A., and Sumantra Ghoshal. "Changing the Role of Top Management: Beyond Systems to People," *Harvard Business Review* (May-June 1995), pp. 132–142.

Berry, Jonathan, et al. "Database Marketing: A Potent New Tool for Selling," *Business Week*, September 5, 1994, pp. 56–62.

Bittel, Lester R. *The McGraw-Hill 36-Hour Management Course.* New York: McGraw-Hill, 1989, p. 229.

Bittel, Lester R., and Jackson E. Ramsey, eds. *Handbook for Professional Managers.* New York: McGraw-Hill, 1985, pp. 220, 222.

Business Week. "Management's New Gurus," August 31, 1992, p. 50.

Caldwell, Bruce. "Keep Them or Outsource Them?" *Informationweek*, June 26, 1995, pp. 36–37.

Center for Research on Electronic Commerce, University of Texas at Austin. "Internet Indicators Coverage," (June 1999), http://www.cism.bus.utexas.edu.

Chicago Tribune. "Chrysler to Put It All on Computer," August 13, 1995, sec. 17, p. 11.

Crockett, Fess. "Revitalizing Executive Information Systems," *Sloan Management Review* (Summer 1992), p. 41.

Cross, John. "IT Outsourcing: British Petroleum's Competitive Approach," *Harvard Business Review* (May–June 1995), pp. 94–102.

Davenport, Thomas H. "Saving IT's Soul: Human-Centered Information Management," *Harvard Business Review* (March–April 1994), pp. 119–131.

Hof, Robert D. "Intel: Far Beyond the Pentium," *Business Week*, February 20, 1995, pp. 88–90.

Keen, Peter G. W. *Every Manager's Guide to Information Technology: A Glossary of Key Terms and Concepts for Today's Business Leader.* Boston: Harvard Business School Press, 1991, pp. 156–157.

Kleiman, Carol. "Top Executives Are Different from Other Bosses," *Chicago Tribune*, August 9, 1995, sec. 6, p. 5.

Lacity, Mary C., Leslie P. Willcocks, and David F. Feeny. "IT Outsourcing: Maximize Flexibility and Control," *Harvard Business Review* (May–June 1995), pp. 84–93.

McDowell, Edwin. "Web Access Taking Flight," *New York Times News Service*, February 18, 2001, http://www.dallas news.com/travel2/archive/288314_webfiller_00tr.html.

McGee, Marianne K., ed. "Show Workers the Way to Go," *Informationweek*, June 26, 1995, p. 124.

Mensching, James R., and Dennis A. Adams. *Managing an Information System.* Englewood Cliffs, N.J.: Prentice-Hall, 1991, pp. 1–2, 19, 54, 295, 296.

Reid, T. R., and Brit Hume. "PC Globe's Software Atlas Will Bring the World to Your Computer Keyboard," *Chicago Tribune*, May 31, 1992, sec. 7, p. 6.

Sacks, Jeffrey D., and Frank A. Lancione. "Start Groupware at the Top," *Informationweek*, June 26, 1995, p. 152.

Stahl, Stephanie. "Is Notes Worth It?" *Informationweek*, June 26, 1995, pp. 14–16, 18.

Thurm, Scott. "What Do You Know?," *The Wall Street Journal*, June 21, 1999.

Time, vol. 154, no. 26: Special Issue/Person of the Year, http://www.com/time/magazine/0.9263,1101991227,00 .html.

Verity, John W. "Cyber-Networks Need a Lot of Spackle," *Business Week*, June 26, 1995, pp. 92–93.

Violino, Bob. "Reigning in the 'PC Jockeys,' " *Informationweek*, June 26, 1995, pp. 41, 44.

Virga, Patricia H., ed. *The NMA Handbook for Managers*, Englewood Cliffs, N.J.: Prentice-Hall, 1987, p. 312.

Weber, Joseph. "Just Get It to the Stores on Time," *Business Week*, March 6, 1995, pp. 66–67.

CHAPTER 20

Adler, Alan L. "Whirlpool Puts Its Brand on Europe," *Chicago Tribune*, March 30, 1992, sec. 4, p. 5.

Adler, Nancy J. *International Dimensions of Organizational Behavior.* Boston: PWS-KENT, 1991, pp. 10–11.

Agins, Teri. "Silk Importers Feel a Tariff Would Spell Ruin," *Wall Street Journal*, June 5, 1996, p. B1.

Arndt, Michael. "Key Issues Remain in North American Trade Talks," *Chicago Tribune*, August 11, 1992, sec. 3, p. 3.

Baker, Stephen. "Along the Border, Free Trade Is Becoming a Fact of Life," *Business Week*, June 18, 1992, p. 41.

Baranthan, Joyce. "A Pirate Under Every Rock," *Business Week*, June 17, 1996, pp. 50–51.

Biers, Dan. "More of Asia's Hinterlands Benefiting from Investors," *Wall Street Journal*, February 5, 1996, p. A10.

Block, Robert. "How Big Mac Kept From Becoming a Serb Archenemy," *Wall Street Journal*, September 3, 1999, p. B1.

Browning, E. S. "In Pursuit of the Euroconsumer," *Wall Street Journal*, April 23, 1992, p. B1.

Business Week. "The Global Economy: Who Gets Hurt," August 10, 1992, p. 50.

Chicago Tribune. "Co-Op Hits the Jackpot in Japan," June 21, 1992, sec. 7, p. 8C.

Chicago Tribune. "McDonald's Sets Its Sights on Ubiquity," January 18, 1996, sec. 3, p. 3.

Chicago Tribune. "Expansion Boosts McDonald's; Sara Lee, Donnelley Profits Rise," January 26, 1996, sec. 3, p. 2.

Chicago Tribune. "Pepsi Tries for More Fizz Overseas," April 3, 1996, sec. 3, p. 3.

Chicago Tribune. "New Stores, Overseas Growth Drive McDonald's," April 18, 1996, sec. 3, p. 1.

Corchado, Alfredo. "Avocado Ban Pits Mexican Exporters Against U.S.," *Dallas Morning News*, June 16, 1996, pp. 1H, 3H, 4H.

Davidson, Dale. "Mobil Realigns Operations into 11 Business Groups," *Dallas Morning News*, June 4, 1996, p. 7D.

Fortune. "Goodbyes Can Cost Plenty in Europe," April 6, 1992, p. 16.

Fortune. "Rockwell International Corporation, Celebrating Its People," August 21, 1995, pp. 127–128.

Goozner, Merrill. "Venture Tilts Flat-Screen Technology Japan's Way," *Chicago Tribune*, April 29, 1992, sec. 7, pp. 1, 4.

Heyel, Carl, ed. *The Encyclopedia of Management*, 3rd ed. New York: Van Nostrand Reinhold, 1982, p. 495.

Hofstede, Geert. "Motivation, Leadership, and Organizations: Do American Theories Apply Abroad?" *Organizational Dynamics* (Summer 1980), pp. 42–63.

Ingram, Judith. "Amway Sells a Piece of the American Dream in Hungary," *Chicago Tribune*, November 21, 1992, sec. 3, pp. 1, 2.

Jacob, Raul. "Secure Jobs Trump Higher Pay," *Fortune*, March 20, 1995, p. 24.

Kleiman, Carol. "Planning, Not Dreaming, Will Land That Foreign Job," *Chicago Tribune*, November 4, 1990, sec. 8, p. 1.

Koretz, Gene. "Borders Are for Crossing," *Business Week*, February 13, 1995, p. 28.

Kraar, Louis. "Daewoo's Daring Drive into Europe," *Fortune*, May 13, 1996, pp. 145–152.

Labich, Kenneth. "Airbus Takes Off," *Fortune*, June 1, 1992, p. 102.

Longworth, R. C. "Opponents Say NAFTA Is Raw Deal for Workers," *Chicago Tribune*, April 15, 1996, sec. 4, pp. 1, 4.

Lublin, Joann S. "Foreign Accents Proliferate in Top Ranks as U.S. Companies Find Talent Abroad," *Wall Street Journal*, May 21, 1992, p. B1.

McCormick, Janice, and Nan Stone. "From National Champion to Global Competitor: An Interview with Thomson's Alain Gomez," *Harvard Business Review* (May–June 1990), p. 135.

Miller, Cyndee. "U.S. Firms Lag in Meeting Global Quality Standards," *Marketing News*, February 15, 1993, p. 16.

Moffatt, Susan. "China's Crackdown on CD Counterfeiting: Too Little, Too Late?" *Fortune*, March 4, 1996, p. 32.

Moffett, Matt. "White-Collar Migrants Head Into Mexico," *Wall Street Journal*, February 24, 1992, p. B1.

Morris, Betsy. "The Brand's the Thing," *Fortune*, May 4, 1996, p. 84.

Moshavi, Sharon. "India's Pols May Be Turning Against Foreign Business," *Business Week*, August 21, 1995, p. 44.

Nelson, Mark M. "Whirlpool Gives Pan-European Approach a Spin," *Wall Street Journal*, April 23, 1992, p. B1.

Newkirk, William. "Clinton Gives China Deadline to Reduce High-Tech Piracy," *Chicago Tribune*, May 9, 1996, sec. 1, p. 6.

Ono, Umiko. "Japanese Liquor Dealer Imports Sake Made in United States, Igniting a Controversy," *Wall Street Journal*, February 28, 1992, p. D3.

O'Reilly, Brian. "Johnson & Johnson Is on a Roll," *Fortune*, December 21, 1994, pp. 178–192.

Phatak, Arvind. *International Dimensions of Management.* Boston: PWS-KENT, 1992, p. 5.

Rehfeld, John. "What Working for a Japanese Company Taught Me," *Harvard Business Review* (November–December 1990), p. 169.

Rosenberger, Jane Ellen. "Japanese Firm Opens Door to Executive at U.S. Unit with Board Appointment," *Wall Street Journal*, March 27, 1992, p. B5A.

Rossant, John. "The Faded Colors of Benetton," *Business Week*, April 10, 1995, pp. 87–90.

Serwer, Andrew E. "McDonald's Conquers the World," *Fortune*, October 17, 1994, pp. 103–104, 106, 108, 112, 114, 116.

Sherman, Arthur, George Bohlander, and Scott Snell. *Managing Human Resources*, 10th ed. Cincinnati: South-Western, 1996, pp. 695–706.

Shirouzu, Norihiko. "Deregulation Jolts Shiseido's Foundation," *Wall Street Journal*, June 14, 1996, p. A7.

Sigiura, Hideo. "How Honda Localizes Its Global Strategy," *Sloan Management Review* (Fall 1990), p. 78.

Tully, Shawn. "GE in Hungary: Let There Be Light," *Fortune*, October 22, 1992, p. 37.

Wall Street Journal, "3M Tries to Scotch Inpatriate Problems," June 16, 1992, p. B1.

Weidenbaum, Murray. "Isolationism in a Global Economy," *Management Review* (December 1995), p. 43.

Yates, Ronald. "Going Abroad for Allies," *Chicago Tribune*, April 26, 1992, sec. 7, p. 1.

Yates, Ronald E. "U.S. China Talk Tough But Quiet Ending Likely," *Chicago Tribune*, May 16, 1996, sec. 1, p. 1, 30.

CHAPTER 21

Beehr, T. A., and R. S. Bhagat. *Human Stress and Cognition in Organizations: An Integrated Perspective.* New York: Wiley, 1985.

Davita, Sal. "Personal Values Affect Your Career Satisfaction," *Marketing News*, April 13, 1992, p. 16.

Davita, Sal. "The Two Most Important Decisions in Career Designing," *Marketing News*, July 6, 1992, p. 16.

Davita, Sal. "Value System Can Make or Break Your Career," *Marketing News*, March 16, 1992, p. 16.

Dubrin, Andrew. *Winning Office Politics: Dubrin's Guide for the 90's.* Englewood Cliffs, N.J.: Prentice-Hall, 1990, p. 167.

Engardio, Pete, Dexter Roberts, and Bruce Einhorn. "From Technocrat to Tycoon," *Business Week*, June 5, 1995, p. 51.

Ettorre, Barbara. "Whistle Blowers: Who's the Real Bad Guy?" *Management Review* (May 1994), pp. 18–23.

Feldman, Daniel C. "Careers in Organizations: Recent Trends and Future Directions," *Journal of Management* 15 (1989), pp. 135–156.

Fiant, Ray J. "Leadership Training for Long-Term Results," *Management Review* (July 1992), pp. 50–53.

Fischer, Anne B. "When Will Women Get to the Top," *Fortune*, September 21, 1992, p. 56.

Fortune. "The Whistle Blower," August 7, 1995, p. 118.

Fram, Eugene. "Today's Mercurial Career Path," *Management Review* (November 1994), pp. 40–44.

Franklin, Stephen. "Shifting Sands of Job Stability," *Chicago Tribune* (September 15, 1994), Sect 3, 12.

Freudenberger, Herbert J. *Burnout: The High Cost of High Achievement.* Garden City, N.Y.: Anchor Press, 1980, p. 13.

Galen, Michele, and Ann Palmer. "Diversity: Beyond the Numbers Game," *Business Week*, August 14, 1995, pp. 60–61.

Gendron, George. "Working Twice As Hard for the Same Results (and How to Stop)," *Inc.* (November 1994), p. 11.

Gruner, Stephanie. "Providing a Mentor Mismatch," *Inc.* (October 1994), pp. 66–68.

Hall, Douglas T. *Career Development in Organizations.* San Francisco: Jossey-Bass, 1986.

Hammonds, Keith, Kevin Kelly, and Karen Thurston. "Beyond the New World of Work," *Business Week*, October 17, 1994, pp. 76–77.

Harari, Oren. "An Open Letter to Job Seekers," *Management Review* (December 1994), pp. 38–42.

Hellwig, Basia. "Who Succeeds, Who Doesn't," *Working Woman* (May 1992), pp. 108–112.

Hollander, Dorry. *Managerial Reality.* New York: HarperCollins, 1995, p. 130.

Huey, John. "Discounting Dynamo Sam Walton," *Time*, January 19, 2000, http://www.time.com/time/time/00/builder/profile/walton.html.

Jensen, Blair. "How to Figure Out What Others Expect of You," *Computerworld*, January 20, 1992, p. 1.

Kennedy, Joyce Lain. "Forgotten Art of Mentoring Can Put New Zip in Your Career," *The Dallas Morning News*, February 7, 1999, sec. D, p. 1.

Kiechel, Walter. "A Manager's Career in the New Economy," *Fortune*, April 4, 1994, pp. 68–72.

Kotter, John P. *The New Rules.* New York: Free Press, 1995.

Kram, Kathy E. *Mentoring at Work: Developmental Relationships in Organizational Life.* Glenview, Ill.: Scott, Foresman, 1985.

Maturi, Richard. "Stress Can Be Beaten," *Industry Week*, July 20, 1992, pp. 23–26.

Olson, Andrew. "Long-Term Networking, A Strategy for Career Success," *Management Review* (April 1994), pp. 33–35.

O'Reilly, Brian. "360 Feedback Can Change Your Life," *Fortune*, October 17, 1994, pp. 93–100.

Penzias, Arno. *Harmony.* New York: HarperCollins, 1995, p. 30.

Peters, Tom. "If You Want to Escape Office Politics—Forget It," *Chicago Tribune*, July 27, 1992, Section 4, p. 7.

Plunkett, W. Richard. *Supervision*, 7th ed. Englewood Cliffs, N.J.: Prentice-Hall, 1995, pp. 38, 44.

Robbins, Stephen P. *Management*, 4th ed. Englewood Cliffs, N.J.: Prentice-Hall, 1994, p. 364.

Romano, Catherine. "Too Much Work Causes Stress," *Management Review* (March 1995), p. 6.

Schein, Edgar H. *Career Dynamics.* Reading, Mass.: Addison-Wesley, 1978.

Schlee, Adele. "Feeling Invisible? Here's How to Get Clout," *Working Woman* (February 1992), pp. 36–37.

Sellers, Patricia. "Don't Call Me Slacker," *Fortune*, December 12, 1994, pp. 182–187.

Shea, Gordon F. *Mentoring: Helping Employees Reach Their Potential.* New York: American Management Association, 1994, p. 29.

Siegel, Alexander. "Making the Most of Mentors: Yours Differs from His," *Working Woman* (May 1992), p. 26.

Smith, Lee. "Stamina: Who Has It, Why You Need It, How You Get It," *Fortune*, November 28, 1994, pp. 127–139.

Snyder, Adam. "Executive Coaching: The New Solution," *Management Review* (March 1995), pp. 29–32.

Stewart, Thomas A. "Planning a Career in a World Without Managers," *Fortune*, March 20, 1995, pp. 72–80.

Straub, Joseph, and Raymond Attner. *Introduction to Business*, 5th ed. Belmont, Calif.: Wadsworth, 1994, p. 58.

Unger, Paul. "Culture Shock: Tips for Transitioners," *Management Review* (June 1995), pp. 44–47.

Vreeland, Leslie. "Managing the Risks," *Working Woman* (April 1992), pp. 61–63.

Welles, Edward O. "The Mentors," *Inc.*, June 1, 1998, http://www.inc.com/articles/details/0,,CID943_PAG5_REG14,00.html.

CHAPTER 22

Barry, Vincent. *Moral Issues in Business*, 3rd ed. Belmont, Calif.: Wadsworth, 1986, pp. 5, 9–10, 156.

Bell, David. "Stage Set for Ethics in Business," *Chicago Tribune*, June 21, 1992, sec. 7, p. 8B.

Blanchard, Kenneth, and Norman Vincent Peale. *The Power of Ethical Management.* New York: Morrow, 1988, p. 27.

Buchholz, Rogene A. *Fundamental Concepts and Problems in Business Ethics.* Englewood Cliffs, N.J.: Prentice-Hall, 1989, p. 5.

Buck, Genevieve. "Prison Camp' Sweatshop Probe Widens," *Chicago Tribune*, August 10, 1995, sec. 3, pp. 1, 3.

Buehler, Vernon M., and Y. K. Shetty. "Managerial Response to Social Responsibility Challenge," *Academy of Management Journal* (March 1976), p. 69.

Byrne, John A. "Businesses Are Signing Up for Ethics 101," *Business Week*, February 15, 1988, pp. 56–57.

Chicago Tribune. "Absenteeism on Rise at $505 an Employee," August 29, 1995, sec. 3, p. 3.

Chicago Tribune. "Del Labs Settles Case Against Top Executive," August 4, 1995, sec. 3, p. 3.

Chicago Tribune. "Former Top Honda Exec Sentenced," August 26, 1995, sec. 2, p. 1.

Chicago Tribune. "16 Apparel Firms Subpoenaed in Sweatshop Investigation," August 16, 1995, sec. 3, pp. 1, 4.

Chicago Tribune. "Voice of the People: Diversity Is Good for Business," August 19, 1995, sec. 1, p. 20.

Cox, Danny, with John Hoover, *Leadership When the Heat's On.* New York: McGraw-Hill, 1992, p. 23.

Cox, Meg. "CD Marketers Will Eliminate Paper Packaging," *Wall Street Journal*, February 28, 1992, p. B1.

Daily Herald. "They Work to Keep the Streak Alive," September 6, 1995, sec. 1, p. 9.

Davidson, Daniel V., et al. *Business Law: Principles and Cases*, 3rd ed. Boston: PWS-KENT, 1990, pp. 107, 111, 112.

Davis, Keith. "Five Propositions for Social Responsibility," *Business Horizons* 18, no. 3 (June 1975). Adapted from article reprinted in Barry, 1986, p. 156.

Dunfee, Thomas W. "Employee Ethical Attitudes and Business Firm Productivity," *The Wharton Annual.* University of Pennsylvania: Pergamon Press, 1984, p. 76.

Frost, Peter J., Vance F. Mitchell, and Walter R. Nord. *Managerial Reality: Balancing Technique, Practice, and Values.* New York: HarperCollins, 1995, pp. 307–309.

Gellerman, Saul W. *Motivation in the Real World.* New York: Dutton, 1992, pp. 265, 266–267, 269–271, 273–274.

Gellerman, Saul W. "Why 'Good' Managers Make Bad Ethical Choices," *Harvard Business Review* (July–August 1986), pp. 88–89.

Haas, Robert D. Acceptance speech, Lawrence A. Wein Prize in Corporate Social Responsibility, Columbia University, New York, November 19, 1984, as recorded in Watson, 1991, pp. 321–322.

Hansen, Lars. "Will Healthier Birds Mean Sicker People?" *Business Week*, September 4, 1995, p. 34.

Henderson, Verne E. *What's Ethical in Business?* New York: McGraw-Hill, 1992, pp. 62, 74–75, 202, 205.

Human Resources Management: Ideas & Trends in Personnel 273, April 15, 1992. "The best ethics training goes beyond legal compliance by giving people skills needed to make value-based decisions," an interview with Dr. Peter Madsen (Chicago: Commerce Clearing House), p. 60.

Hunt, Christopher B., and Ellen R. Auster. "Proactive Environmental Management: Avoiding the Toxic Trap," *The Best of MIT's Sloan Management Review* (Winter 1990), pp. 7–18.

Jacobs, Deborah L. "Stiff New Penalties: Companies Can Be Fined For Workers' Misdeeds," *Your Company* (Winter 1992), p. 12.

Kunde, Diana. "Corporate Integrity Tied to Loyalty, Survey Finds," *Dallas Morning News*, October 20, 1999.

Labich, Kenneth. "The New Crisis in Business Ethics," *Fortune*, April 20, 1992, pp. 167, 168, 172, 176.

Litvan, Laura M. "A Breath of Fresh Air," *Nation's Business* (May 1995), pp. 50–51.

Mateja, Jim. "GM Offers Workers Free to Parts Suppliers," *Chicago Tribune*, July 18, 1992, sec. 1, pp. 1, 6.

McCarthy, Michael J. "Ex-Divinity Student Works To Find Corporate Soul," *Wall Street Journal*, June 18, 1999.

Millman, Nancy. "FBI Examines Klein Jeans Ads," *Chicago Tribune*, September 9, 1995, sec. 2, pp. 1–2.

Mitchell, Jacqueline. "Toyota Finds Itself in Jam on Door Locks," *Wall Street Journal*, August 19, 1992, p. B1.

Paine, Lynn Sharp. "Managing for Organizational Integrity," *Harvard Business Review* (March–April 1994), pp. 106–117.

Rosewicz, Barbara. "EPA Acts to Cut Toxic Emissions, Draws Criticism," *Wall Street Journal*, October 30, 1992, p. A5.

Ryan, Nancy. "McDonald's Update for Special Menus," *Chicago Tribune*, March 12, 1992, sec. 3, p. 3.

Saddler, Jeanne. "Three Credit Data Firms Agree to Try to Keep Clients from Misusing Reports," *Wall Street Journal*, August 19, 1992, p. C9.

Schiller, Zachary, et al. "Balance Sheets That Get Well Soon," *Business Week*, September 4, 1995, pp. 80–81, 84.

Schwartz, Nelson, and Tim Smart. "Giving—and Getting Something Back," *Business Week*, August 28, 1995, p. 81.

Solomon, Robert C., and Kristine R. Hanson. *It's Good Business.* New York: Athenaeum, 1985, pp. xiii–xiv, 20–21, 46–49, 146–148.

Stahl, Stephanie. "IT Takes the Lead in Enforcing Ethics," *InformationWeek Newsletter*, February 23, 2001, http://www.informationweek.com/magazine.

Steiner, George. "Institutionalizing Corporate Social Decisions," *Business Horizons* (December 1975), p. 18.

Vitale, Robert. "If It's Legal, Law Says Workers May Do It on Their Own Time," *Chicago Tribune*, July 1, 1992, sec. 2, p. 2.

Wall Street Journal. "The Best Corporate Reputations in America: Just as in Politics, Trust, Reliability Pay Off Over Time," September 23, 1999.

Wall Street Journal. "'Green' Cars Struggle to Gain Acceptance," November 3, 1992, p. B1.

Watson, Charles E. *Managing with Integrity, Insights from America's CEOs.* New York: Praeger, 1991, p. 321.

Widder, Pat. "More Corporations Learning That Ethics Are Bottomline Issue," *Chicago Tribune*, June 7, 1992, sec. 7, pp. 1, 6.

Wilder, Clinton. "Business Ethics for IT Managers—What You Can Do," *InformationWeek.com News*, February 19, 2001, http://www.informationweek.com/825/ethics_side.htm.

Yates, Ronald E. "Whistle-Blowers Pay Dearly for Heroics," *Chicago Tribune*, July 23, 1995, sec. 7, pp. 1–2.

Glossary

A

acceptance sampling A product control technique involving a representative group of products before a new stage of production.

accountability The need to answer to someone for your actions. It means accepting the consequences—either credit or blame—of these actions.

affirmative action A plan to give members of specific groups priority in hiring or promotion.

aggregate planning An element of operations management that involves the planning of production activities and the resources needed to achieve them.

agile manufacturing A manufacturing system incorporating ultraflexible production facilities; computer technology; alliances among suppliers, producers, and customers; and direct sales data to customize goods at the speed of mass production.

alternatives Potential solutions to the problem.

analyzer strategy An attempt to maintain the current market share while innovating in some markets.

application program A computer program designed to execute specific sets of tasks such as word processing.

artificial intelligence (AI) The ability of a machine to perform those activities that are normally thought to require intelligence; giving machines the capability to learn, sense, and think for themselves.

assessment center A place where candidates are screened for managerial positions, which usually involves extensive testing and hands-on exercises.

attribute inspection A product control technique that compares items against a standard and rates their quality as acceptable or unacceptable.

audit A formal investigation conducted to determine if records and the data on which they are based are correct and conform to policies, rules, procedures, and laws.

authority The formal and legitimate right of a manager to make decisions, give orders, and allocate resources.

autocratic style A leadership approach in which a manager does not share decision-making authority with subordinates.

avoidance A conflict strategy in which a manager ignores the conflict situation.

B

balance sheet A listing of the assets of a business and the owners' and outsiders' interests in them. The equation that describes the content of a balance sheet is *assets* = *liabilities* + *stockholders' equity*.

batch processing A computer procedure in which data are collected over time and entered into databases according to prescribed policies and procedures.

behavioral school Recognized employees as individuals with concrete human needs, as parts of work groups, and as members of a larger society.

benchmark The product to meet or beat in terms of design, manufacture, performance, and service.

benefit Legally required or voluntary compensation provided to employees in addition to their salaries or wages.

Boston Consulting Group (BCG) Growth Share Matrix A technique often employed by organizations to help them evaluate their portfolios.

boundary spanning The surveillance of outside areas and factors that can influence plans, forecasts, decisions, and organizations. Sometimes called **environmental scanning**.

boundaryless organization An organization not defined or limited by horizontal, vertical, or external boundaries imposed by a predetermined structure.

brainstorming A group effort at generating ideas and alternatives that can help a manager solve a problem or seize an opportunity.

budget A single-use plan that predicts sources and amounts of income that will be available over a fixed period of time and how those funds will be used.

bureaucracy A rational organization based on the control of knowledge.

burnout A state of emotional exhaustion as a result of overexposure to stress.

business ethics The rules or standards governing the conduct of persons or members of organizations in the field of commerce.

business-level strategy Answers the question, "How do we compete?" It focuses on how each product line or business unit within an organization competes for customers.

C

capacity planning An element of operations management that determines an organization's capability to produce the number of products or services to meet demand.

career The series of jobs a person holds over a lifetime and the person's attitude toward the involvement in those job experiences; includes a long-term perspective, a sequence of positions, and a psychological involvement.

career management The planning, activities, and behaviors involved in executing a career.

career perspective A proactive strategy that involves a global view of career progress or growth over time.

career planning The process of developing a realistic view about how individuals want their careers to proceed and then taking steps to ensure that they follow that course.

cellular layout A facilities layout option in which equipment required for a sequence of operations on the same product is grouped into cells.

centralization A philosophy of organization and management that focuses on systematically retaining authority in the hands of higher level managers.

chain of command The unbroken line of reporting relationships from the bottom to the top of the organization.

change Any alteration in the current work environment.

change agent A person who implements planned change.

chaos theory The mathematical study of complex, unstable systems.

classical administrative school Emphasized the flow of information and how organizations should operate.

classical management theory A theory that focused on finding the "one best way" to perform and manage tasks.

classical scientific school Focused on the manufacturing environment and getting work done on the factory floor.

coercive power The power dependent on fear of the negative results that may happen if one fails to comply.

cohesion A strong attachment to the group and a closeness measured by a singleness of purpose and a high degree of cooperation.

collaboration A conflict strategy in which the manager focuses on mutual problem solving by both parties.

collective bargaining Negotiation between a union and an employer in regard to wages, benefits, hours, rules, and working conditions.

committee A horizontal team—either ad hoc or permanent—designed to focus on one objective; members represent functional areas of expertise.

communication The transmission of information and understanding from one person or group to another.

compensation All forms of financial payments to employees. Compensation includes salaries, wages, and benefits.

complexity theory A theory that emphasizes the ways in which a factory resembles an ecosystem, responding to natural laws to find the best possible solutions to problems.

compressed workweek A schedule that allows employees to fulfill weekly time obligations in fewer days than the traditional five-day workweek.

compromise A conflict-resolution strategy in which each party gives up something.

computer-aided design (CAD) A design technique that uses a computer monitor to display and manipulate proposed designs for the purpose of evaluating them.

computer-aided manufacturing (CAM) A technology in which computers coordinate people, information, and processes to produce quality products efficiently.

computer-integrated manufacturing (CIM) Using computers to guide and control manufacturing processes.

computerized information system (CIS) An MIS built upon computer hardware and software to collect and process data and store and disseminate the resulting information.

conceptual skills The mental capacity to conceive and manipulate ideas and abstract relationships.

concurrent control A control that applies to processes as they are happening.

conflict A disagreement between two or more organizational members or teams.

confrontation A conflict strategy that forces parties to verbalize their positions and area of disagreement.

content theories A group of motivation theories emphasizing the needs that motivate people.

contingency model A leadership theory stating that a manager should focus on either tasks or employees, depending on the interaction of three variables—leader-member relations, task structure, and leader position power.

contingency plan An alternative goal and course or courses of action to reach that goal if and when circumstances and assumptions change so drastically as to make an original plan unusable.

contingency school A theory based on the premise that managers' preferred actions or approaches depend on the variables of the situations they face.

continuous-process production A technology in which the entire conversion process is completed through a series of mechanical or chemical processes.

control process A four-step process that consists of establishing performance standards, measuring performance, comparing measured performance to established standards, and taking corrective action.

control system A system in which feedforward, concurrent, and feedback controls operate in harmony to ensure that standards are enforced, goals are reached, and resources are used effectively and efficiently.

control technique Device designed to measure and monitor specific aspects about the performances of an organization, its people, and its processes.

controlling The process through which standards for the performance of people and processes are set, communicated, and applied.

core competencies What an organization knows and does best.

core values Values that should never change; bedrock principles.

corporate-level strategy Answers the questions: "What business are we in?" and "What business should we be in?"

cost-leadership strategy A strategy focused on keeping costs as low as possible through efficient operations and tight controls.

critical control point An area of operations that directly affects the survival of a firm and the success of its most essential activities.

critical path The longest sequence of events and activities in a network production schedule or the longest time a job could take.

cross-cultural management An emerging discipline focused on improving work in organizations with employee and client populations from several cultures.

cross-functional team A team with an undefined life span designed to bring together the knowledge of various functional areas to work on solutions to operational problems.

customer Any person or group, both inside and outside an organization, who uses or consumes outputs from an organization or its members.

customer departmentalization Grouping activities and responsibilities in departments based on the needs of specific customer groups.

D

data Unprocessed facts and figures.

data center A unit of a decentralized CIS that operates to serve its unit's members with their own sets of hardware, software, and specialists (machine operators and programmers).

database A collection of computerized data arranged for ease and speed of retrieval; sometimes called data bank.

decentralization A philosophy of organization and management that focuses on systematically delegating authority throughout the organization to middle- and lower-level managers.

decision A choice made from available alternatives.

decision making The process of identifying problems and opportunities, developing alternative solutions, choosing an alternative, and implementing it.

decision support systems (DSS) A specialized variant of a CIS; an analytic model that joins a manager's experience, judgment, and intuition with the computer's data access, display, and calculation processes; allows managers to interact with linked programs and databases via the keyboard.

decision tree A graphical representation of the actions a manager can take and how these actions relate to other events.

defender strategy A strategy based on holding current market share or even retrenching.

delegation The downward transfer of formal authority from one person to another.

Delphi technique Group decision making conducted by a group leader through the use of written questionnaires; it provides a structure, leads to consensus, and emphasizes equal participation.

demotion A reduction in an employee's status, pay, and responsibility.

departmentalization The basic organizational format or departmental structure for the company.

design control An area of operations control that involves incorporating reliability, functionality, and serviceability into product design.

design for disassembly (DfD) Considering, during the design stage, how products will be refurbished, reused, or disposed of at the end of the product's life cycle.

design for manufacturability and assembly (DFM/A) Considering, during the design stage, how products will be manufactured and assembled.

detailed inspection and test A product control technique in which every finished item receives an examination or performance test.

development Efforts to acquire the knowledge, skills, and attitudes needed to move to a job with greater authority and responsibility.

diction The choice and use of words in speech and writing.

differentiation strategy An organization's attempts to set its products or services apart from those of other companies.

directly interactive forces An organization's owners, customers, suppliers and partners, competitors, and external labor pool.

discrimination Using illegal criteria when making employment decisions. Discrimination results in an adverse impact on members of protected groups.

disparate impact The result of using employment criteria that have a significantly greater negative effect on some groups than on others.

distinctive competitive advantage A unique position in relationship to its competition.

diversification strategy A strategy adopted if the company wants to move into new products or markets; normally achieved through the acquisition of other businesses and their brands.

diversity Includes people from differing age groups, genders, ethnic and racial backgrounds, cultural and national origins, and mental and physical capabilities.

division of labor *See* **specialization of labor**.

divisional structure An organizational design that groups departments based on organizational outputs; these divisions are self-contained strategic business units that produce a single product.

downsizing Also known as **rightsizing**, it calls for shrinking both the size of the company and the number of employees.

dysfunctional conflict Conflict that limits the organization's ability to achieve its objectives.

E

economic forces Conditions in an economy that influence management decisions and the costs and availability of resources.

economic order quantity (EOQ) An inventory technique that helps managers determine how much material to order by minimizing the total of ordering costs and holding costs based on the organization's usage rate.

embargo A government regulation enacted to keep a product out of a country for a time or entirely.

empowerment The sharing of information and decision making.

end-user computing The use of information technology (IT) by people who are not controlled and directed by top management.

environmental scanning The process of collecting information about the external environment to identify and analyze trends.

equal employment opportunity Legislation designed to protect individuals and groups from discrimination.

equity theory A motivation theory stating that comparisons of relative input-outcome ratios influence behavior choices.

ERG theory A motivation theory establishing three categories of human needs: existence needs, relatedness needs, and growth needs.

ethical dilemma A situation that arises when all courses of action open to a decision maker are judged to be unethical.

ethics The branch of philosophy concerned with what constitutes right and wrong human conduct, including values and actions, in a given set of circumstances.

evolutionary change The incremental steps taken to bring about progress and change.

executive information systems (EIS) A decision support system custom designed to facilitate executive decision making; may include forecasting, strategic planning, and other elements.

executive team A team consisting of two or more people to do the job traditionally held by one upper-level manager.

expectancy theory A motivation theory stating that three factors influence behavior: the value of rewards, the relationship of rewards to the necessary performance, and the effort required for performance.

expert power Influence due to abilities, skills, knowledge, or experience.

expert system A specialized end-user decision support program that stores the knowledge of a group of authorities for access by nonexperts faced with the need to make topic-related decisions.

external environment Includes all the forces outside an organization's borders that interact directly or indirectly with it.

F

facilities layout The element of operations planning concerned with the physical arrangement of equipment and work flow.

feedback Information about the receiver's perception of the sender's message.

feedback control A control that focuses on the outputs or results of operations.

feedforward control A control that prevents defects and deviations from standards.

financial budget The details of how a financial responsibility center will manage its cash and capital expenditures.

financial ratio The relationship of two critical figures from financial statements—expressed in terms of a ratio, decimal, or percentage—which helps managers measure a company's financial health and its progress toward goals.

financial responsibility center An organizational unit that contributes to an organization's costs, revenues, investments, or profits.

finished goods inventory Inventory consisting of products that have not been sold.

first-line management Supervisors, team leaders, and team facilitators who oversee the work of nonmanagement people, often called operating employees, associates, or team members.

fixed-position layout A facilities layout option in which the product stays in one place and the equipment, tools, and human skills are brought to it.

flexible manufacturing systems (FMS) The automating and integrating of manufacturing elements such as product design, production equipment, robotics, and performance analysis.

flextime An employment alternative allowing employees to decide, within a certain range, when to begin and end each workday.

focus strategy When the managers of a firm target a specific market—a particular region or group of potential customers.

force field analysis A technique to implement change by determining which forces drive change and which forces resist it.

forecasting A planning technique used by an organization's managers to concentrate on developing predictions about the future.

formal communication channels Management-designated pipelines—running up, down, and across the organizational structure—used for official communication efforts.

formal communication network An electronic link between people and their equipment and between people and databases.

formal organization The official organizational structure that top management conceives and builds.

formal team A team created by managers to function as part of the organizational structure.

forming stage The phase of team development in which team members are becoming acquainted.

free rider A person who receives the benefit of team membership but does not do a proportionate share of work.

free-rein style A leadership approach in which a manager shares decision-making authority with subordinates, empowering them to function without direct involvement from managers to whom they report.

functional authority The authority that permits staff managers to make decisions about specific activities performed by employees within other departments.

functional conflict Conflict that supports the objectives of the organization.

functional definition The activities to be performed determine the type and quantity of authority necessary.

functional departmentalization Creating departments on the basis of the specialized activities of the business—finance, production, marketing, human resources.

functional-level strategy Focuses on the major activities of the company: human resources management, research and development, marketing, finance, and production.

functional manager Manager whose expertise lies primarily in one or another of the specialty areas.

functional structure An organizational design that groups positions into departments based on similar skills, expertise, and resources.

G

game theory Attempts to predict how people or organizations will behave in competitive situations.

Gantt chart A scheduling and control tool that helps managers plan and control a sequence of events.

geographical departmentalization Grouping activities and responsibilities according to territory.

global structure The arrangement of an organization's management decision making to efficiently and effectively operate in a multinational context; form may contain functional, product, and geographic features based on worldwide product or area units.

goal An outcome to be achieved or a destination to be reached over a period of time through the exercise of management functions and the expenditure of resources.

goal-setting theory A motivation theory stating that behavior is influenced by goals, which tell employees what they need to do and how much effort they need to expend.

grand strategy The overall framework or plan of action developed at the corporate level to achieve an organization's objectives. There are five basic grand strategies —growth, integration, diversification, retrenchment, or stability.

grapevine An informal communication channel.

green products Those products with reduced energy and pollution connected with their manufacture and disposal.

group decision support system (GDSS) A variant decision support system that allows groups focusing on a problem to interact with one another and to exchange information, data, and ideas.

groupthink Group members becoming so committed to the group that they become reluctant to disagree.

growth strategy A strategy achieved internally by investing or externally by acquiring additional business units.

H

horizontal integration A strategy to consolidate competition by acquiring similar products or services.

horizontal team A team composed of members drawn from different departments.

human asset accounting Treating employees as assets, not expenses, by recording money spent on people as increases in the value of those assets.

human resource manager also called **personnel manager**; a manager who fulfills one or more personnel, or human resource, functions.

human skills The abilities to interact and communicate successfully with other persons.

hygiene factors Maintenance factors (such as salary, status, working conditions) that do not relate directly to a person's actual work activity, but when of low quality are the cause of unhappiness on the job.

I

income statement A report that presents the difference between an organization's income and expenses to determine whether the firm operated at a profit or a loss over a specified period.

indirectly interactive forces Domestic and foreign economic, legal/political, sociocultural, technological, and natural forces.

influence The power to sway people to one's will or views.

informal communication channels The informal networks, existing outside the formal channels, that are used to transmit casual, personal, and social messages at work.

informal organization A network of personal and social relationships that arise spontaneously as people associate with one another in a work environment.

information Processed data that is useful to the receiver.

information system (IS) An organizational subsystem enabling an organization to effectively and efficiently share intellectual capital and create and maintain a working environment in which employees can exploit it.

information technology (IT) Manual and electronic means for creating and handling intellectual capital and facilitating organizational communication.

integration strategy A strategy adopted when the business sees a need (1) to stabilize its supply line or reduce costs or (2) to consolidate competition.

intellectual capital An organization's collective experiences, wisdom, knowledge, and expertise.

interaction chart A diagram that aids in identifying the informal organization structure by spotlighting the informal interactions people have with one another.

internal environment Composed of elements within an organization's borders that managers create, acquire, and utilize, including the organization's mission, vision, core values, core competencies, leadership, culture, climate, structure, and available resources.

international division A parent company's corporate unit, commonly a marketing or production operation, located in a host country offshore from the parent headquarters and whose head reports directly to the CEO.

international management The process of managing resources (people, information, funds, inventories, and technologies) across national boundaries and adapting management principles and functions to the demands of foreign competition and environments.

interpersonal communication Face-to-face or voice-to-voice (telephone) conversations that take place in real time and allow instant feedback.

intrapreneur An employee who thinks and acts like an owner.

intrapreneurship Entrepreneurship within an organization, allowing employees flexibility and authority in pursuing and developing new ideas.

inventory The goods an organization keeps on hand.

ISO 9000 The set of five technical standards, known collectively as ISO 9000, designed to offer a uniform way of determining whether manufacturing and service organizations implement and document sound quality procedures.

J

jargon The specialized or technical language of a trade, profession, subculture, or other group.

job A specific position a person holds in an organization.

job analysis A study that determines the duties associated with a job and the human qualities needed to perform it.

job depth An element of job redesign referring to the degree of discretion an employee has to alter the job.

job enlargement Increasing the variety or the number of tasks a job includes, not the quality or the challenge of those tasks.

job enrichment Designing a job to provide more responsibility, control, feedback, and authority for decision making.

job evaluation A study that determines the worth of a job in terms of its value to an organization.

job redesign The application of motivational theories to the structure of work, to increase output and satisfaction.

job rotation Temporarily assigning people to different jobs, or tasks, on a rotating basis.

job scope An element of job redesign that refers to the variety of tasks incorporated into a job.

job sharing A technique to provide flexibility by permitting two part-time workers to divide one full-time job.

just-in-time inventory Delivery of raw materials or other kinds of normal inventories to correspond to production schedules, leading to the elimination of the need to warehouse items.

K

kaizen A Japanese term used in business to mean incremental, continuous improvement for people, products, and processes.

knowledge management The merging of a company's human and technical knowledge assets.

L

large batch technology Also called **mass production technology**; a type of technology that produces a large volume of standardized products.

leadership The process of influencing individuals and groups to set and achieve goals.

Leadership Grid® Blake and Mouton's two-dimensional model for visualizing the extent to which a manager focuses on tasks, employees, or both.

leadership style The perceived approaches and behaviors a manager uses to influence others.

learning organization A process whereby groups and individuals within the organization challenge existing models of behavior and learn to rapidly and creatively adapt to a changing environment.

legal/political forces The general framework of statutes enacted by legislatures; precedents established by court decisions; regulations and rulings created by various federal, state, and local regulatory agencies; and agreements between and among governments and companies from different nations.

legitimate power The power possessed by managers and derived from the positions they occupy in the formal organization.

life-cycle theory A view of management that asserts that a leader's behavior toward a subordinate should relate to the subordinate's maturity level. The focus on tasks and relationships should vary as the subordinate matures.

limiting factors Those constraints that rule out certain alternative solutions. One common limitation is time.

line authority The relationship between superior and subordinate. Any manager who supervises operating employees—or other managers—has line authority.

line departments The departments established to meet the major objectives of the business and directly influence the success (profitability) of a business.

M

management One or more managers individually and collectively setting and achieving goals by exercising related functions (planning, organizing, staffing, leading, and controlling) and coordinating various resources (information, materials, money, and people).

management by objectives (MBO) A technique that emphasizes collaborative objective setting by managers and their subordinates.

management by reaction A management method that does not anticipate change but merely reacts to it.

management hierarchy The top, middle, and first-line levels of management.

management information system (MIS) A formal collection of processes that provides managers with suitable quality information to allow them to make decisions, solve problems, and carry out their functions and operations effectively and efficiently.

management science The study of complex systems of people, money, equipment, and procedures, with the goal of understanding them and improving their effectiveness.

manager A person who allocates and oversees the use of resources.

manufacturing resource planning (MRPII) A comprehensive planning system that controls the total resources of a firm.

mass production technology *See* **large batch technology**.

master schedule An element of operations management that specifies the quantity and type of each item to be produced and how, when, and where it should be produced.

materials requirement planning (MRP) A production planning and inventory system that uses forecasts of customer orders to schedule the exact amount of materials needed for production.

matrix structure An organizational design that utilizes functional and divisional chains of command simultaneously in the same part of the organization.

maximize Managers' want to make the perfect decisions.

mechanistic structure A tight organizational structure characterized by rigidly defined tasks, formalization, many rules and regulations, and centralized decision making.

medium The means by which a sender transmits a message.

mentor A senior employee who acts as guide, teacher, counselor, and coach for a less-experienced person in the organization.

message The information that the sender wants to transmit.

middle management Includes managers below the rank of vice president but above the supervisory level.

mission A clear, concise, written declaration of an organization's central and common purpose, its reason for existence.

mission statement When a mission is formalized in writing and communicated to all organizational members.

morale The attitude or feelings workers have about the organization and their total work life.

morality Core values and beliefs that act as a guide (i.e., conscience) when individuals formulate courses of action.

motivation The result of the interaction of a person's internal needs and external influences—involving perceptions of equity, expectancy, previous conditioning, and goal setting—that determine behavior.

motivation factors The conditions, intrinsic to the job, that can lead to an individual's job satisfaction.

multinational corporation A company with operating facilities, not just sales offices, in one or more foreign countries; management favors a global market and strategy, seeing the world as their market.

mutual trust The ability of individuals to rely on each other based on their character, ability, and truthfulness.

N

natural forces Forces such as climate, weather, geography, and geology that affect how businesses operate and locate their operations.

needs Physical or psychological conditions in humans that act as stimuli for behavior.

network scheduling A scheduling technique used to track projects in which events or activities are interrelated and have time estimates assigned to them.

network structure An organizational design option in which a small central organization relies on other organizations to perform manufacturing, marketing, engineering, or other critical functions on a contract basis.

networking A strategy for career advancement that involves building long-term, two-way interaction based on shared ideas, personal relationships, and common experiences.

noise Anything in the environment of a communication that interferes with the sending and receiving of messages.

nominal group technique Creating a structure to provide for equal—but independent—participation by all members.

nonprogrammed decisions Decisions made in response to problems and opportunities that have unique circumstances, unpredictable results, and important consequences for the company.

nonverbal communication Images, actions, and behaviors that transmit messages.

norming stage The phase of team development in which disagreement and conflict have been resolved and team members enjoy unity and focus.

norms Values or attitudes that employees as a group accept as standards of behavior and that serve as guidelines of behavior and an internal control device on members.

O

obsolescence A state or condition that exists when a person is no longer capable of performing up to job standards or to management's expectations.

open-book management Commits organizations and their people to continual learning and requires that well-trained people be allowed to apply, without fear, what they learn.

open system A system that regularly affects and is affected by various and constantly changing forces (elements and components) outside itself.

operating budget A financial plan and control for each financial responsibility center's revenues, expenses, and profits.

operating system An extensive and complex set of instructions that manages the operation of a computer and the application programs that run on it.

operational objectives The specific results expected from first-level managers, work groups, and individuals.

operational plan The first-line manager's tool for executing daily, weekly, and monthly activities. Operational plans fall into two major categories: single-use and standing plans.

operations management The branch of management science that applies to manufacturing or service industries.

operations research An area of management science that commonly uses models, simulations, and games.

operations strategy The element of the strategic plan that defines the role, capabilities, and expectations of operations.

opportunity A chance, occasion, event, or breakthrough that requires a decision to be made.

OR/MS Operations research (OR) and the management sciences (MS) are the professional disciplines that deal with the application of information technology for informed decision making.

organic structure A flexible, free-flowing organizational structure that has few rules and regulations and decentralizes decision making right down to the employees performing the job.

organization An entity managed by one or more persons to achieve stated goals.

organization chart The complete organizational structure shown visually.

organizational climate An outgrowth of a corporation's culture showing how employees feel about working there.

organizational culture A dynamic system of shared values, beliefs, philosophies, experiences, customs, and norms of behavior that gives an organization its distinctive character.

organizational design The creation of or change to an organization's structure.

organizational development (OD) A process of conducting a thorough analysis of an organization's problems and then implementing long-term solutions to solve them.

organizational learning The ability to integrate new ideas into an organization's established systems to produce better ways of doing things.

organizational life cycle The stages an organization goes through: birth, youth, midlife, and maturity. Each stage involves changes in the overall structure.

organizational politics The unwritten rules of work life and informal methods of gaining power and advantage.

organizational socialization A process through which new members of an organization gain exposure to its values, norms, policies, and procedures.

organizational visibility A strategy for career advancement that involves highlighting a person's abilities, talents, and contributions for those people in the organization who influence promotions and advancements.

organizing The management function that establishes relationships between activity and authority.

orientation Introducing new employees to the organization by explaining their duties, helping them meet their coworkers, and acclimating them to their work environment.

outside-the-box thinking To adopt a new perspective and see it work; not get caught up in the old ways.

outsourcing A purchasing strategy in which a company contracts with a supplier to perform functions in lieu of the company.

P

participative style A leadership approach in which a manager shares decision-making authority with subordinates.

path-goal theory A view of management asserting that subordinates' behaviors and motivations are influenced by the behaviors managers exhibit toward them.

payback analysis A technique that ranks alternatives according to how long each takes to pay back its initial cost.

perceptions Ways in which people observe and the bases for their judgments about the stimuli they experience.

performance appraisal A formal, structured comparison between employee performance and established quantity and quality standards.

performing stage The phase of team development in which team members progress toward team objectives, handle problems, coordinate work, and confront each other if necessary.

perk A payment or benefit received in addition to a regular wage or salary.

personnel manager *See* **human resource manager**.

philosophy of management A manager's attitude about work and the people who perform it, which influences the motivation approaches he or she selects.

plan The end result of the planning effort—commits individuals, departments, entire organizations, and the resources of each to specific courses of action for days, months, and years into the future.

planned change Trying to anticipate what changes will occur in both the external and internal environments and then developing a response that will maximize the organization's success.

planning Preparing for tomorrow, today.

policy A broad guide for organizational members to follow when dealing with important and recurring areas of decision making. They set limits and provide boundaries for decision makers.

portfolio strategy Determines the mix of business units and product lines that will provide a maximum competitive advantage.

power The ability to exert influence in the organization. Power is personal.

proactive approach A social responsibility strategy in which businesses continually look to the needs of constituents and try to find ways to meet those needs.

problem The difference between the current and desired performance or situation.

procedure A set of step-by-step directions for carrying out activities or tasks.

process control sampling A product control technique designed to detect variations in production processes.

process improvement team A team made up of members who are involved with a process. They meet to analyze how they can improve the process.

process layout A facilities layout option in which all the equipment or machines that perform a similar task are placed together.

process team A team that groups members who perform and refine the organization's major processes.

process theories A group of theories that explain how employees choose behaviors to meet their needs and how they determine whether their choices were successful.

product control A component of operations control that reduces the probability and costs of poor quality and unreliable products by implementing controls from purchasing to end use.

product departmentalization Assembling the activities of creating, producing, and marketing each product into a separate department.

product development team A team organized to create new products.

product layout A facilities layout option in which the machines and tasks are arranged according to the progressive steps by which the product is made.

productivity The relationship between the amount of input needed to produce a given amount of output and the output itself; usually expressed as a ratio.

program A single-use plan for an operation from its beginning to its end.

program evaluation and review technique (PERT) A network scheduling technique for planning and charting the progress of a complex project in terms of the time it is expected to take—an estimate that is derived from probability analysis.

programmed decisions Decisions that involve problems or situations that have occurred often enough that both the circumstances and solutions are predictable; made in response to recurring organizational problems.

project improvement team A team usually composed of a group of people involved in the same project. They determine how to make the project better.

project team A team organized to complete a specific task in the organization.

promotion A job change that results in increased status, compensation, and responsibility.

prospector strategy A strategy based on innovation, taking risks, seeking out opportunities, and expansion.

psychological contract The unspoken contract that marks the end product of the organizational socialization process and defines what people are expected to give to the organization and what they can expect to receive.

purchasing The acquisition of goods and services at optimal costs from competent and reliable sources.

Q

qualification testing A product control technique in which products are tested for performance on the basis of reliability and safety.

quality The totality of features and characteristics of a product or service that bear on its ability to satisfy stated or implied requirements of those who use or consume them.

quality assurance team A team created to guarantee the quality of services and products, contact customers, and work with vendors.

quality audit Determines if customer requirements are being met.

quality circle A temporary team consisting primarily of workers who share a problem. It meets regularly until the problem is solved.

quality control audit A check of quality control efforts that asks two questions: How are we doing? and What are the problems?

quality function deployment (QFD) A disciplined approach to solving quality problems before the design phase of a product.

quality improvement team Usually a group of people from all the functional areas of a company. The group meets regularly to assess progress toward goals, identify and solve common problems, and cooperate in planning for the future.

quality of work life (QWL) Factors in the work environment contributing positively or negatively to workers' physical and emotional well-being and job satisfaction.

quality school The essence of the quality of any output is its ability to meet the needs of the person or group.

quantitative school Emphasized mathematical approaches to management problems.

queueing model A model that helps managers decide what length of waiting line or queue would be optimal.

quota A government regulation that limits the import of a product to a specified amount per year.

R

raw materials inventory Inventory consisting of the raw materials, parts, and supplies used as inputs to production.

reactive approach A social responsibility strategy in which businesses wait for demands to be made and then react to them, choosing a response by evaluating alternatives.

reactor strategy An organization adopting this strategy could be said to have no strategy; it responds to environmental threats as they occur and has no clear sense of internal direction.

receiver The person or group for whom a communication effort is intended.

recruiting Efforts to find qualified people and encourage them to apply for positions that need to be filled.

reengineering The fundamental rethinking and radical redesign of business processes to achieve dramatic improvements in critical, contemporary measures of performance, such as cost, quality, service, and speed.

referent power The power that is based on the kind of personality or charisma an individual has and how others perceive it.

reinforcement theory A motivation theory that states a supervisor's reactions and past rewards and penalties affect employees' behavior.

reorder point (ROP) The most economical point at which an inventory item should be reordered.

research and development (R&D) Projects that uncover information useful to create a variety of new materials, processes, and products.

resistance approach A social responsibility strategy in which businesses actively fight to eliminate, delay, or fend off demands being made on them.

resource deployment Defines how the company intends to allocate its resources —material, financial, and human—to achieve its strategic goals.

responsibility The obligation to carry out one's assigned duties to the best of one's ability.

retrenchment strategy A strategy used to reduce the size or scope of a firm's activities by cutting back in some areas or eliminating entire businesses.

revolutionary change Bold, discontinuous advances that bring about dramatic transformations in organizational strategies and structure.

reward power The power that comes from the ability to promise or grant rewards.

rightsizing *See* **downsizing**.

risk manager A high-level person in charge of planning for and overseeing efforts to control the management of all the risks an organization faces.

robotics The use of programmed machines to handle production.

role A set of expectations for a manager's behavior.

rule An ongoing, specific guide for human behavior and conduct at work. Rules are usually "do" and "do not" statements established to promote employee safety, ensure the uniform treatment of employees, and regulate civil behavior.

S

sanctions Rewards or penalties used by an informal group to persuade its members to conform to its norms.

satisfice To make the best decision possible with the time, resources, and information available.

scoreboarding A technique that routinely keeps employees aware of changes in the critical numbers used to measure a company's processes.

selection Evaluating applicants and finding those best qualified to perform a job and most likely to fit into the culture of the organization.

self-managed work team A team, fully responsible for its own work, that sets goals, creates its own schedules, prepares its own budgets, and coordinates its work with other departments.

semantics The study of the meanings of words.

sender The person or group that initiates the communication process.

separation The voluntary or involuntary departure of employees from a company.

sexual harassment Unwelcome verbal or physical conduct of a sexual nature that implies, directly or indirectly, that sexual compliance is a condition of employment or advancement or that interferes with an employee's work performance.

simulation A model of a real activity or process.

single-use plan A plan used for a one-time activity—an activity that does not recur. Two examples of single-use plans are programs and budgets.

situation analysis A search for strengths and weaknesses and opportunities and threats.

Six Sigma A highly disciplined process that helps companies focus on developing and delivering near-perfect products and services.

small batch technology Also called **unit production technology**; a type of technology that produces goods in small quantities designed to customer specifications.

smoothing A conflict strategy in which the manager diplomatically acknowledges that conflict exists but downplays its importance.

social audit A report on the social performance of a business.

social responsibility The notion that, in addition to their business interests, individuals and organizations have certain obligations to protect and benefit other individuals and society and to avoid actions that could harm them.

sociocultural forces The influences and contributions from diverse groups outside an organization.

soft manufacturing system (SMS) A manufacturing system that relies on computer software to continuously control and adjust to the manufacturing processes.

sources and uses of funds statement A summary of the cash flowing into an organization and how it is used over a fixed period of time; often called a **cash flow statement**.

span of control The number of subordinates under the direction of a manager.

specialization of labor Breaks a potentially complex job down into simpler tasks or activities.

sponsor An individual in the organization who will promote a person's talents and look out for his or her organizational welfare.

stability strategy A strategy used when the organization wants to remain the same.

staff authority The authority to serve in an advisory capacity; it flows upward to the decision maker.

staff departments The departments—including legal, human resources, computer services, and public relations—that provide assistance to the line departments and to each other, making money indirectly for the company through advice, service, and assistance.

staffing Efforts designed to attract, hire, train, develop, reward, and retain the people needed to accomplish an organization's goals and promote job satisfaction.

stakeholders Groups directly or indirectly affected by the ways in which business is conducted and managers conduct themselves. Stakeholders include owners, employees, customers, suppliers, and society.

standard Any established rule or basis of comparison used to measure capacity, quantity, content, value, cost, quality, or performance.

standing plan Specifies how to handle continuing or recurring activities, such as hiring, granting credit, and maintaining equipment. Examples of standing plans include policies, procedures, and rules.

statistical process control (SPC) The use of SQC to establish boundaries that determine if a process is in control (predictable) or out of control (unpredictable).

statistical quality control (SQC) The use of statistical tools and methods to determine the quality of a product or service.

stereotype Predetermined belief about a group of people.

storming stage The phase of team development characterized by disagreement and conflict as individual roles and personalities emerge.

strategic business units (SBUs) Autonomous businesses with their own identities but operating within the framework of one organization.

strategic goals Long-term, company-wide goals set by top-management strategic planning efforts. They focus on the changes desired in productivity, product innovation, and responsibilities to stakeholders.

strategic management A responsibility of top management, it defines the firm's position, formulates strategies, and guides the execution of long-term organizational functions and processes.

strategic plan Contains the answers to the who, what, when, where, how, and how much for achieving strategic goals—long-term, company-wide goals established by top management.

strategic planning The process of creating or rewriting an organization's mission, identifying and evaluating the long-term goals and strategies to reach those goals, and determining the required resources.

strategy A course of action created to achieve a long-term goal.

strategy formulation The planning and decision making that goes into developing the company's strategic goals and plans, including assessing the environments, analyzing core competencies, and creating goals and plans.

strategy implementation The means associated with executing the strategic plan. These include creating teams, adapting new technologies, focusing on processes rather than functions, facilitating communications, offering incentives, and making structural changes.

stress The physiological and psychological reaction of the body as a result of demands made on it.

stretch goals Goal that requires great leaps forward on such measures as product development time, return on investment, sales growth, quality improvement, and reduction of manufacturing cycle times.

subculture A unit within an organization that is based on the shared values, norms, and beliefs of its members.

superordinate objective An objective that overshadows personal interests, to which a manager can appeal as a strategy for resolving conflict.

symptom A signal that something is wrong and draws the manager's attention to finding the cause—that is, the problem.

synergy The increased effectiveness that results from combined action or cooperation.

system A set of interrelated parts that work together to achieve stated goals or to function according to a plan or design.

systems school The theory that an organization comprises various parts (subsystems) that must perform tasks necessary for the survival and proper functioning of the system as a whole.

T

tactic A course of action designed to achieve a short-term goal—an objective.

tactical objectives Short-term goals set by middle managers that must be achieved in order to reach top management's strategic goals and the short- and long-term goals of middle managers.

tactical plan Developed by middle managers, this plan has more details, shorter time frames, and narrower scopes than a strategic plan; it usually spans one year or less.

tariff A tax placed on imported goods to make them more expensive and thus less competitive in order to protect domestic producers.

task force A horizontal team composed of employees from different departments designed to accomplish a limited number of objectives and existing only until it has met the objectives.

team A group of two or more people who interact regularly and coordinate their work to accomplish a common objective.

team structure An organizational design that places separate functions or processes into a group according to one overall objective.

technical skills The abilities to use the processes, practices, techniques, and tools of the speciality area a manager supervises.

technological forces The combined effects of processes, materials, knowledge, and other discoveries resulting from research and development activities.

technology The knowledge, machinery, work procedures, and materials that transform the inputs into outputs.

telecommuting The partial or total substitution of telecommunications technology (such as computers, mobile phones, fax machines, and the Internet) for the trip to and from the primary workplace. Simply put, it's moving the work to the workers, instead of the workers to the work.

test Any criterion or performance measure used as a basis for an employment decision.

theory Part of an art or science that attempts to explain the relationships between and among its underlying principles.

Theory X A philosophy of management with a negative perception of subordinates' potential for and attitudes toward work.

Theory Y A philosophy of management with a positive perception of subordinates' potential for and attitudes toward work.

three-step approach A technique of behavior modification to change attitudes in a lasting way; it consists of three phases: unfreezing, change, and refreezing.

top management The chief executive officer (CEO) and/or president and his, her, or their immediate subordinates, usually called vice presidents.

total quality management (TQM) A strategy for continuously improving performance at every level, and in all areas of responsibility.

training Giving employees the knowledge, skills, and attitudes needed to perform their jobs.

transactional processing A computer procedure in which data are received about a company's ongoing operations and entered into data banks as each transaction occurs.
transfer Moving an employee to a job with similar levels of status, compensation, and responsibility.
tunnel vision Having a narrow viewpoint.

U

understanding The situation that exists when all senders and receivers agree about the meaning and intent of a message.
unit production technology *See* **small batch technology**.
unity of command The organizing principle that states that each person within an organization should take orders from and report to only one person.
unity of direction The establishment of one authority figure for each designated task of the organization.

V

variable inspection A product control technique that involves taking measurements to determine how much an item varies from standards and, therefore, whether it will be accepted or rejected.
vertical integration Gaining ownership of resources, suppliers, or distribution systems that relate to a company's business.
vertical team A team composed of a manager and subordinates.
virtual team A team where members primarily interact electronically because they are physically separated (by time and/or space).
vision A clear statement as to where an organization wants to be in the future.
Vroom and Yetton decision tree A series of questions that guide the manager to the appropriate option.

W

waiting line model *See* **queueing model**.
whistle-blowers Individuals who take action to inform their bosses, the media, or government agencies about unethical or illegal practices within their organization.
work team A team, composed of multi-skilled workers, that does all the tasks previously done by individual members in a functional department or departments.
work-in-process inventory Inventory consisting of materials and parts that have begun moving through the production process but are not yet assembled into a completed product.

Index

A

Absenteeism, 571
Acceptability, 536
Acceptance sampling, 607
Accountability, 246
Accuracy, 537
Ackerman, Roger, 314
Activities, classifying and grouping, 234–237
Activity ratios, 557
Adaptability, 318–319
Adaptive strategies, 180
Advancement decisions, 710–711
Affiliator, 424
Affirmative action, 340
Aggregate plan, 596
Agile manufacturing, 593–594
Ahlman, Kaj, 4
AIDS, and drug testing, 344
Akao, Yoji, 70
Albertson, Bruce, 4
Alcoa, 397
Alderfer, Clayton, 424
Alderfer's ERG Theory, 424–426
Allaire, Paul, 172
Allen-Bradley, 582, 592, 593
Allen, Paul, 191
Allen, Ronald W., 175
Allied-Signal, 692, 707
Alpine Banks, 185
AltaVista, 199
Alternative, selecting the best, 201
Alternatives, 199
  analyzing the, 200–201
  evaluating, 145
  identifying, 145
Amazon.com, 4, 615
America OnLine, 99, 102, 104, 109
American Airlines, 166, 267, 274, 278
American Express, 626
American Honda Motor Company, 72, 247, 267, 567, 721
American Management Association, 12
American Motors, 273
Ameritech, 733
Amgen, 127, 175
Analyzer strategy, 181
Andrews, Nigel, 4
Anheuser-Busch, 181, 344, 567
Apple Computer, 134, 191, 486, 490
Application form, 352
Application program, 626
Appraisal methods, 362–364
Appraisal systems, components of, 361–362
Appraisals, legality of, 364
Archway Cookie Company, 65
Argyris, Chris, 435
Argyris's Maturity Theory, 435–436
Arthur Andersen and Company, 672
Artificial intelligence (AI), 630
Asea-Brown Boveri, 283
Assessment, 42–44
  alignment and, 697
  contingency management theory, 54–55
  of behavioral school, 48–49
  of classical administrative school, 48
Assessment center, 355
Assumptions, improving the quality of, 147–148
AT&T, 75, 99, 236, 306, 433, 437, 453, 492, 634, 649
Attitude surveys, 573
Attribute inspection, 608
Audit, 558
Audits, 85–86
Authority, 239–240
  delegating, 237
  tips for successful delegation of, 247
  types of, 240–241
Autocratic style, 464–465
Avoidance, 511
Avon Corporation, 104

B

Babbage, Charles, 41
Balance sheet, 551–553
Ballmer, Steve, 172
Bank of America, 178
Barad, Jill, 437
Barnard, Chester, 44
Barnes & Noble, 181, 206, 215, 681
Bartlett, Christopher A., 42
Basham, Robert D., 14
Batch processing, 627
Bechtel, 106
Behavioral management theory, 46–49
Behavioral school, 46
  proponents, 46–48
Bell Atlantic, 486, 506
Ben & Jerry's Homemade, Inc., 339, 717–718, 740, 741
Benchmark, 70
Benefits, 370–371
Bennett, Stephen, 4
Bethlehem Steel, 41
Bittel, Lester, 49
Blanchard, Kenneth, 474
Blockbusters, 681
Blue Cross Blue Shield, 215
BMW, 12, 70, 107
Boeing, 294, 393, 485, 487, 490, 491, 502
Borders, 387
Boss, working with the, 704–705
Boston Consulting Group (BCG) Growth-Share Matrix, 178
Bottom-up budgeting, 562–563
Boundary spanning, 116
Boundaryless organization, 106
Brainstorming, 212
British Petroleum Company, 12, 635
BRW, 439
Bryant, J. D., 15
Budget, 137, 560
Budget controls, 560–565
Budget development process, 561–562
Bureaucracies, 44
Burger King, 174, 208
Burgum, Doug, 38
Burke, Jim, 250
Burnout, 705
Business ethics, 719
Business Wire, 334
Businesses, why they become international, 646–647
Business-level strategy, 167
  formulating, 180–183
Butterfield & Butterfield, 125

C

CAD/CAM, 591–592
Cadbury, 176–177, 210
Calloway, Wayne, 472
Calvin Klein, 732
Campbell's Soup, 267
Capacity planning, 595
Capital expenditures budgets, 565
Career advancement, strategies for, 697–708
Career development, stages of, 685–688
Career environment, new, 683–684
Career management, 694–697
Career perspective, 683
Career planning, 684–694
  steps in, 688–694
Career, 683
Careers, nature of, 682–683
Carey, Chris, 455
Carrabba's Italian Grills, 14
Case, Steve, 99
Cash budget, 565
Caterpillar, 582
CBS, 110
Cellular layout, 589
Centralization, relationship to span of control, 251–252
  versus decentralization, 249–252
Ceremonies, 300
Chain of command, 230
Chambers, John, 114
Champion International, 725
Champy, James, 56, 57, 60, 79, 83
Change agent, 314
Change, 398
  how to manage, 313–317
  implementation of, 319–323
  management and, 313
  methods of effecting, 321–323

nature of, 307–313
qualities promoting, 317–319
rates of, 310–313
resistance to, 319–320
responding to, 267–268
sources of, 307–308
types of, 308–310
why efforts fail, 320–321
Chaos theory, 37–38
Chase Manhattan Bank, 513
Chevrolet, 128
Chevron Chemical Company, 116
Chevron, 531
Chili's, 410–411, 438
Chrysler Corporation, 14, 72, 76, 90, 110, 185, 267, 273, 274, 393, 490, 504, 527, 592
Cin-Made Corporation, 87, 442
CIS management tools, 629–632
Cisco Systems, Inc., 114, 618
Citicorp, 488, 725
Classical administrative school, 44–46
assessment, 46
early contributors, 44–46
Classical management theory, 40–46
Classical scientific school, 41–44
Climate, 301–302
Coca-Cola, 111, 114, 131, 177, 208, 210, 265–268, 271, 276, 656
Coercive power, 244
Cohen, Ben, 717, 722
Coherence, 306
Cohesion, 255
Collaboration, 511
Collective bargaining, 345
Collins, James C., 6, 80
Collins, Robert, 4
Comfort Inn, 629
Commitment, 505
Commitments
at the bottom, 86–87
at the middle, 84–86
at the top, 80–82
external, 88–90
Committee, 489
Communication problems, 669–670
Communication process, 378–379
Communication, 378
and teams, 385–386
breakdowns in, 510
improvement of, 399–403
interpersonal, 384–389
mediums of, 380–384
nonverbal, 382–384
organizational, 389–399
ten commandments of, 403
verbal, 380–382
Communities, 735–736
Compaq, 236, 523, 595
Compensation, 368–371, 666–667
executive, 371
Competition, 508
Competitive strategies, 182–183
Competitors, 110
Complexity theory, 37–38
Compliance programs, 725–726
Comprehensibility, 537
Compressed workweek, 444
Compromise, 511
CompuServe, 99, 104, 109, 708
Computer City, 162
Computer monitoring, 364
Computer operations, 626–627
Computer Sciences Corporation, 634
Computer systems, linking, 627–629
Computer-aided design (CAD), 591
Computer-aided manufacturing (CAM), 591
Computer-integrated manufacturing (CIM), 592
Computerized information systems, 622–632
Computers
and control, 573–574
and delivery of services, 594
Conceptual skills, 26
Concurrent controls, 533–534
Conflict situation, analysis of the, 510
Conflict stimulation, 512–514
Conflicts
between personal and organizational values, 709
sources of, 508–510
strategies for managing, 510–514
team and individual, 507–510
views of, 507–508
Confrontation, 511
Connelly, Jo Ann, 275
Conseco, 4
Content theories, 415, 416–426
Contingency management theory, 54–55
Contingency model, 469–471
Contingency plans, 141–142
Contingency school, 54
Continuous-process production, 277
Contributions, documenting, 699–700
Control monitoring, 538–540
Control process, 525–530
Control system, establishing a, 202–203
Control systems, 534
and information, 174–175
types of, 530–534
Control technique, 548
Control
and computers, 573–574
problems, 673
Controlling variables, overemphasis on, 151
Controlling, 20, 522
and the international manager, 672–673
and the other management functions, 524–525
Controls
characteristics of, 672–673
for quality and productivity, 597–608
types of, 530–534
updating, 539–540
Cook, Michael, 296
Coors, 277
Core competencies, 104
Core values, 80
Corning, 293, 299, 308, 314
Corporate-level strategy, 165
formulating, 175–180
Corrective action, taking, 530
Cost-effective quality, 75
Costello, Robert, 73
Cost-leadership strategy, 183
Costs
power-realignment, 505
team-training, 505
Cote, David, 4
Cox, Danny, 9
Creativity, 211
Critical control point, 535
Critical path, 606
Critical points, focus on, 535
Crosby, Philip B., 60, 73, 75
Cross-cultural management, 670–672
Cross-functional team, 489
Cultural diversity, 342
Culture
creation of, 302–307
factors contributing to effectiveness of, 305–307
factors shaping, 295–298
manifestations of, 298–302
Customer departmentalization, 236
Customer satisfaction, hypothetical model, 69
Customers, 7, 109, 118, 735
Cypress Semiconductor, 486

D

Daewoo Group, 647, 648
Daft, Douglas, 265
Daimler-Chrysler, 281, 600, 622, 647
Data, 616
Data center, 624
Data processing modes, 627
Database, 625
Datatec, 465
De Mar Plumbing, 274
Debt ratios, 557
Decentralization
guidelines for judging, 250–251
versus centralization, 249–252
Decision, 192
implementing the, 201–202
Decision making approaches, personal, 209
Decision making,
approaches to, 193–194
creating environment for effective, 219–220
environmental influences on, 203–209
group, 211–215
in the five management functions, 194
influence of managerial style on, 209–211
universality, 193
what it is, 192–196
Decision support system (DSS), 629
Decision trees, 215–216
Decisional roles, 23–24
Decision-making process, seven-step, 196–203
Decision-making styles, 464–466
Decision-making techniques, quantitative, 215–219
Decisions
commitment to previous, 211
timing of, 210
Deere & Company, 37, 49, 527, 532, 649
Deere, John, 37
Defender strategy, 181
Degree of certainty, 203–204
Delegation, 245–246
Delegation process, 246
Dell Computer Corporation, 272, 310, 377–378, 381, 595, 600
Dell, Michael, 310, 377
Deloitte & Touche, 212, 296
Delphi technique, 213–214
Delta Air Lines, 104, 109, 110, 175

Deming, W. Edwards, 59, 60, 73, 76, 77, 81
Deming's chain reaction, 78
Deming's fourteen points, for improving quality, 82
Demotions, 365–366
Departmentalization, 235
Design control, 598
Design for disassembly (DfD), 587
Design for manufacturability and assembly (DFM/A), 585
Detailed inspections and tests, 607–608
Development
  and training, 357–360
  purposes of, 360
  techniques of, 360
Diction, 386
Differentiation strategy, 183
Dippenaar, Andre, 8
Directly interactive forces, 109–112
Discrimination, 336
Disney World, 67, 301, 304, 306, 339
Disney, Walt, 303
Disparate impact, 339
Distinctive competitive advantage, 163–164
Diversification strategy, 177
Diversity, 10–11
  recognizing and valuing, 438
Division of labor, 233
Divisional structure, 279–281
Dominant coalition, 296
Domino's, 167, 208, 215, 216, 572
Dow Chemical, 283
Downsizing, 229
Drucker, Peter, 5, 149
Dunlap, Albert, 313, 314
DuPont, 269, 274, 276, 279
Dysfunctional conflict, 508

E

E. W. Blanch, 4
Eastman Chemical Company, 527, 528
Eastman Kodak, 303, 308, 311, 392, 513, 587
eBay, 125, 127, 129, 130, 132, 141, 147
Econo Lodge, 629
Economic environment, 652
Economic feasibility, 536–537
Economic forces, 112
Economic order quantity (EOQ), 602
EDS Corporation, 11, 634
Effective controls, characteristics of, 535–538
Electronic Data Systems (EDS), 110
Electronic noise, 399
Embargo, 651
Emotions, 389
Employee attitudes, 667–669
Employees, 117, 734–735
  empowering, 438–440
  role of, 304–305
Employment decisions, implementation of, 364–367
Employment, offer of, 357
Empowerment, 83
End-user computing, 624
Enrico, Roger, 276
Enron Corporation, 651
Enterprise Rent-A-Car Company, 73
Environment, 272–274
  analyzing and evaluating, 143–145
  internal, 205–208
Environmental scanning, 100
Environments
  and management, 115–119
  influencing, 116
  sensing and adapting to, 116
Equal employment opportunity, 336–338
Equipment, and machinery, 108
Equity theory, 432–433
ERG theory, 425
Ernst & Young, 654
Estée Lauder, 180
Ethical conduct
  and individuals, 720–721
  organizational influences on, 722
Ethical dilemmas, 728–729
Ethics, 9–10
  codes of, 723–724
  leaders', 721–722
Evaluation system, establishing, 202–203
Evolutionary change, 310
Excel Corporation, 553–558
Executive compensation, 371
Executive information systems (EIS), 631–632
Executive team, 495
Exit interviews, 367
Expectancy theory, 427–429
Expectations, development of, 436
Expense budgets, 564
Expert power, 244–245
Expert system, 630
External audits, 560
External commitments, 88–90
External environment, 102, 109–115, 208–209, 298
  adaptability to, 306–307
  analyzing, 169–172
External influences, 91–92
External sources, of change, 307–308
External threats, and opportunities, 171
External variables, assessing the, 656–659
ExxonMobil, 181, 267, 274, 277

F

Facilities layout, 587–590
Facilities location, 594
Facilities, and infrastructure, 107
Fagiano, David, 12
Fayol, Henri, 44, 53
Feasibility, assessing, 496
FedEx, 19, 117, 163, 183, 486, 633
Feedback, 379
  360-degree, 364
  initiating, 403
  seeking and giving, 401
Feedback controls, 534
Feedforward control, 532–533
Feigenbaum, Armand V., 60
Ferguson, Dan, 162
Ferro Corporation, 240
Fiat Spa, 4
Fiedler, Fred, 469
Fiedler's Contingency Model, 469–471
Filene's, 726
Filo, David, 547
Filtering, by levels, 395
Finance controls, 548–549
Finance managers, 16
Finances, 108–109
Financial audits, 558–559
Financial budgets, 565
Financial controls, 551–560
Financial ratio analysis, 55
Financial ratio, 555
Financial responsibility center, 558
Financial statements, 551–554
Financial strategy, 184
Finished goods inventory, 601
First-line management, 15, 22
Fisher, George, 303, 311, 312, 313, 314
Fixed-position layout, 590
Fleming, Peter C., 438
Flexibility, 505
  creating, 444
Flexible budgeting, 563
Flexible manufacturing systems (FMS), 277, 592
Flextime, 444
Focus strategy, 183
Follett, Mary Parker, 44, 47
Food Lion, 194, 196
Force field analysis, 322
Forces
  natural, 115
  sociocultural, 114
  technological, 114
Ford Motor Company, 14, 61, 81, 110, 128, 147, 232, 267, 268, 273, 274, 281, 284, 461, 477, 512, 600, 649
Forecast comparison, and inventory, 350
Forecasting, 148
Forecasts, improving the quality of, 147–148
Formal communication channels, 389
Formal communication networks, 393–394
Formal downward channels, 390–391
Formal horizontal channels, 391–392
Formal organization, 228
Formal team, 487
Formal upward channels, 392–394
Forming stage, 500
Forte, Mary, 275
Fortune Brands, 178
Fox Inc., 339
Free riders, 506
Free-rein style, 466
Free-riding costs, 506
Fresca, Paolo, 4
Frey, Robert, 87
Frito-Lay, 181, 184, 274, 276, 280, 492
Fuji Xerox, 13
Functional authority, 241
Functional conflict, 508
Functional definition, 237
Functional departmentalization, 235
Functional managers, 16–18
Functional structure, 278–279
Functional-level strategy, 167, 183–185

G

Game theory, 218
Gannon, J. Timothy, 14
Gantt chart, 604
Gantt, Henry, 41
Gates, Bill, 191–194, 351
GE Medical Systems, 270

General Dynamics, 490
General Electric, 3–4, 5, 106, 108, 131, 178, 219, 229, 284, 311, 486, 586, 592, 649, 665, 667, 669, 692, 733, 740
General Mills, 600, 631
General Motors, 19, 88, 90, 108, 110, 147, 151, 185, 236, 267, 273, 274, 276, 281, 306, 568, 600, 647, 720, 725, 735
Genetic screening, 344–345
Geographical departmentalization, 235
Gerstner, Louis V., Jr., 26, 314
Ghoshal, Sumantra, 42
Gilbreth, Frank, 41
Gilbreth, Lillian, 41
Gioia, Dennis, 30
Glass ceilings, 342–343
Glass walls, 342–343
GlaxoSmithKline, 172
Global challenges, coping with, 12–13
Global structure phase, 662–664
Global structure, 663
Goal, 5
Goals, 129–130
  reviewing, 230–232
  strategic, 134–135
  unified hierarchy of, 141
Goal-setting theory, 433
Goizueta, Roberto, 265–266, 271
Goldstar Company, 310–311
Goodyear Tire and Rubber Company, 108, 505, 595
Google, 199, 258
Government regulation, pros and cons, 736–738
Grand strategy, 176
Grapevine, 394
Great Plains Software, 38, 566
Green products, 736
Greenberg, Jack, 643
Greenfield, Jerry, 722
Grievance processing, 345–346
Group decision making, 211–215
  advantages and disadvantages of, 214–215
Group decision support system (GDSS), 630
Groupthink, 214
Grove, Andrew S., 6
Growth strategy, 176
Growth, five phases of, 314–316
GTE, 506
Guidelines, for acting ethically, 730–731
Gutman, Bobbi, 135

H

H&R Block, 99
Haas, Robert D., 731
Hammer, Michael, 56, 60
Harley-Davidson, 159–164, 475, 656
Hayek, Nicolas, 380
Hecht's, 726
Heritage Insurance Group, 173
Heroes, 300
Hersey and Blanchard's life cycle theory, 474–475
Hersey, Paul, 474
Herzberg, Frederick, 420
Herzberg's two-factor theory, 420–423
Hewlett-Packard, 8, 80, 293, 339, 587, 708
Hierarchy of relationships, designing a, 237–239
High achiever, 423
History
  ancient, 39
  value of, 39
Home Depot, 3, 181, 681
Honeywell, 692
Horizontal integration, 176
Horizontal team, 488
House and Mitchell's path-goal theory, 471–473
House, Robert, 471
Human asset accounting, 571
Human asset valuation, 571
Human resource controls, 550–551, 569–573
Human resource forecasting, 348–350
Human resource inventory, 347–348
Human resource manager, 335
Human resource managers, 17–18
Human resource planning, 346–350
Human resources strategy, 184
Human resources, 174
Human skills, 26
Hyatt Hotels Corporation, 524
Hygiene factors, 420
Hyundai, 72

I

IBM, 77, 99, 110, 164, 191, 192, 293, 306, 314, 504, 565, 587, 593, 626, 631, 634, 684
IDEX Corp., 4
IDS, 486
Impact
  negative, 258–259
  positive, 257
Income statement, 551–554
Incredible Universe, 162
Independence, and sponsorship, 711
Independent work teams, 494–495
In-depth interview, 355
Indirectly interactive forces, 112–115
Individual approaches, disagreements about, 510
Individuals, treating people as, 436–437
Influence, 452
Informal organization, 252–259
  defined, 253
  emergence of, 254–255
  impact of, 257–259
  structure of the, 255–256
  working with the, 257
Informal organizations, compared to formal, 253–254
Information communication channels, 394–395
Information management systems, 619–622
Information system (IS), 616
  functions of an effective, 620
  guidelines for developing, 620–622
  managing, 632–636
Information technology (IT), 616
Information, 107, 379, 616
  and control systems, 174–175
  and the manager, 616–619
  inferior, 151
  sources of, 169
Informational roles, 22
Infrastructure, and facilities, 107
Integrated motivation model, 413–415
Integration strategy, 176
Integration, 535
Intellectual capital, 104
Intent, being certain of, 399
Interaction chart, 255
Interbrew, 176
Internal audits, 559–560
Internal environment, 102–109, 205–208
  analyzing, 169–172
Internal influences, 90–91
Internal sources, of change, 308
International division, 661
International division phase, 661–662
International environment, 649–655
International management, 647
International manager
  and controlling, 672–673
  and leading, 667–672
  and organizing, 660–664
  and staffing, 665–667
Internet Capital Group, 4
Interpersonal communication, 384–389
  barriers to, 386–389
Interpersonal roles, 22
Intrapreneurs, 83
Intrapreneurship, promoting, 442–443
Intuit, 4
Intuitive decision model, 209
Inventory control, 600–601
  importance of, 601–602
Inventory, 600
  and forecast comparison, 350
Iomega, 4
ISO 9000, 657
ITT Sheraton, 214
Ivester, Douglas, 266

J

J. C. Penney, 281
Jaguar, 70
Jargon, 387
Jeep, 128
Jenson, Warren, 4
JIAN, 65
Job analysis, 346–347
Job, 683
  depth, 441
  enlargement, 441
  enrichment, 442
  evaluation, 368
  redesign, 440–441
  rotation, 441
  scope, 441
  sharing, 444
John Greenberg & Associates, 314
John Labatt, Ltd., 176
Johnson & Johnson, 181, 236, 240, 250, 272, 280, 281, 294, 310, 344, 649, 708
Johnson Controls, 600
Johnson, Robert Wood, 250
Jostens, 129
Juran, Joseph M., 59, 60, 68, 73, 78
Just-in-time inventory systems, 604

K

Kaizen approach, 55–56
Kaizen, 55
Katz, Robert, 25
Kelleher, Herb, 27, 300, 451, 462
Kemper, 128
Kmart, 138, 183, 218, 313, 314, 569

Knowledge management, 617
Kobayashi, Yotaro, 13
Kofman, Fred, 11
KPMG Peat Marwick, 107
Kroc, Ray, 643
Kroger Grocery, 184
Kvasnica, Jean, 8

L

L. M. Ericsson Corporation, 283
Labor force, 111
Lands' End, 164
Large batch technology, 277
Larsen, Ralph, 250
Layoffs, 366–367
Leaders, challenges facing, 475–477
Leadership, 105, 173, 452–460
  and power, 460–462
  and rapid response, 476
  management versus, 457–460
  need to provide, 8–9
  of the group, 255–256
  throughout an organization, 475–476
Leadership and tough decisions, 476–477
Leadership behaviors, 455–457, 472–473
Leadership Grid, 468
Leadership skills, 454–455
Leadership styles, 463–469
Leadership traits, 453–454
Leading, 20
  and the international manager, 667–672
Learning organization, 37, 39, 106
Lee Jeans, 648
Lee Roy Selmon's, 14
Leffell, Dan, 11
Legal constraints, 726–728
Legal environment, 336–341, 651–652
Legal/political forces, 113–114
Legitimate power, 244
Lehman Brothers, 643
Leschly, Jan, 172
Levi Strauss, 339, 486, 731
LG Electronics Inc., 59, 310–311
Life-cycle theory, 474
Lifelong learning, committing to, 697–698
Limiting factors, 198–199
Line authority, 240
Line departments, 241–243
Linear programming, 150
Liquidity ratios, 555–557
Listening, actively, 401
Little Caesars Pizza, 167, 208, 215, 216
Lockheed Martin Corporation, 229, 239, 268, 606
Lokey, Lorry, 334, 370
Long term, lack of focus on, 151
Longenecker, Clinton, 30
Loose, John, 293
Loyalty demands, 709–710

M

MacAndrews and Forbes Group, Inc., 303
Machinery, and equipment, 108
Macy's, 275, 726
Management, 5
  and change, 313
  and environments, 115–119
  and managers, 5
  by objectives, 363
  first-line, 15, 22
  functions and the levels of, 20–21
  Henri Fayol's general principles of, 45
  history and theory of, 39–40
  leadership versus, 457–460
  levels of, 13
  middle, 14, 21
  of team processes, 500–504
  open-book, 82–83
  skills and levels of, 26–29
  three levels, 17
  top, 14, 21
Management audits, 573
Management by objectives (MBO), 149–150
Management by reaction, 313
Management functions, 18–22
Management hierarchy
  definition of, 13
  pyramid, 14
Management information system (MIS), 50, 619
Management myths, and realities, 29–30
Management of operations, 595–597
Management roles, 22–25
  Mintzberg's ten, 23
Management science, 49–50
Management skills, 25–29
Management theory
  behavioral, 46–49
  contingency, 54–55
  quality, 55–61
  quantitative, 49–51
  systems, 51–53
Manager
  collateral demands on, 25
  evaluating performance of, 30–31
Manager's universe, 6–13
Managers, 5
  becoming better leaders, 477–478
  finance, 16
  functional, 16–18
  human resource, 17–18
  implications for, 419, 422–426, 428–429, 431, 433
  marketing, 16
  operations, 16
  role of, 302–304
Managers' interpretations, 398
Managing
  ethically, 718–731
  for social responsibility, 738–742
  information systems, 632–636
  to success, 682–684
Manufacturability, design for, 584–585
Manufacturing resource planning (MRPII), 603–604
Marketing controls, 550, 565–569
Marketing managers, 16
Marketing ratios, 568
Marketing research, 566–567
Marketing strategy, 184
Marmot Mountain, 56
Martin Marietta Corporation, 725
Mary Kay Cosmetics, 104, 300, 648
Maslow, Abraham H., 47, 416
Maslow's hierarchy of needs, 416–420
Mass production technology, 277
MassMutual, 128
Master schedule, 596
Materials control, purchasing, 598–600
Materials requirement planning (MRP), 603
Materials, and supplies, 109
Matrix structure, 282–284
Matsushita, 267
Mattel USA, 437
Maximize, 205
Mayo, Elton, 47
Mazda, 183
McClelland, and the need for achievement, 423–424
McClelland, David, 423
McDonald's, 91, 103, 104, 162, 166, 175, 176, 183, 208, 215, 232, 281, 294, 567, 599, 643–644, 646, 648, 650, 662, 672–673, 736
McDonnell Douglas Corporation, 208, 485
McDonnell, John, 208
McDuff, 162
McGregor, Douglas, 47
McNealy, Scott, 227
McNerney, James, 3
Measured performance, comparing to established standards, 528–529
Measurements, 86
Mechanistic structure, 269
Medium, 379
  indicating an appropriate, 402
Member roles, 499
Mentor, 701
Mentor programs, 701–702
Mentor relationships, developing, 701–702
Mentors, for women and men, 702
Mercedes, 70, 148
Merwyn's, 726
Message, 379
Metcalf, Henry, 41
Michelin, 12
Microsoft, 77, 80, 99, 127, 172, 191–194, 339
Middle management, 14, 21
Midvale Steel, 41
Miles, Raymond, 180
Miller Brewing Company, 567
Minnesota Mining & Manufacturing (3M), 3, 53, 71, 73, 79, 83, 90, 105, 180, 294, 302, 318, 567, 665
Mintzberg, Henry, 29
Mission statement, 126–129
  creating a, 167–169
  reassessing, 171–172
Mission, 80
  defining, 496
Mitchell, Terrence, 471
Monsanto, 283, 440
Montgomery Ward, 726
Morale, 410
Morality, 720
Morton International, 148
Motel 6, 183
Motivation factors, 420–421
Motivation model, 412–413
Motivation theories
  focusing on behaviors, 427–433
  focusing on needs, 416
Motivation
  basics of, 412
  challenge of, 410–415
  managing for, 436–444

Motorola, 61, 78, 87, 135, 294, 303, 310, 567, 593, 649, 658
Multinational corporation, 647–648
Multinationals, characteristics of, 648–649
Mutual trust, 317–318

N

Nardelli, Robert, 3
Nasser, Jacques A., 461
Natural forces, 115
NBC, 110
Needs, 412
  five levels of, 416–418
Negative motivation, versus positive, 463–464
Net2Phone, 384
Network scheduling, 605–607
Network structure, 285–287
Networking, 628, 702
Networks, developing, 702–703
New Balance, 599
New Jersey Bell Telephone Company, 44
Newell Company, 162
Nike, 582, 733
Nishimuro, Taizo, 521
Nissan, 14, 76, 107, 183
Noise, 389
Nokia, 201, 202
Nominal group technique, 212–213
Nonleader roles, for members, 256
Nonprogrammed decisions, 194–196
Nonverbal communication, 382–384
Nordstrom's, 180, 193, 294, 410–411, 495
Norming stage, 501
Norms, 255
Nortel Networks, 267
Northern Telecom, 267
Nynex, 486

O

Objectives
  defining, 496
  differences in, 508–509
  operational, 140
  setting, 142–143
Obsolescence, 688
Ohio State University Studies, 467
Okamura, Tadashi, 521
Ollila, Jorma, 202
Omidyar, Pierre, 125
Opel, 232
Open system, 101
Open-book management, 82–83
Openness, lack of, 397
Operating budgets, 564–565
Operating system, 626
Operational objectives, 140
Operational plans, 136–141
Operations management, 50
  importance of, 583–584
  nature of, 582–584
Operations managers, 16
Operations planning, 584–595
Operations research, 49
Operations strategy, 582
Operations, management of, 595–597
Opportunity, 193
  defining the, 196–198
OR/MS, 50
Organic structure, 269
Organization chart, 238
Organization, 5
  age of the, 274
  as a system, 100–102
  size of the, 274
Organizational arrangements, formal, 297
Organizational climate, 105
Organizational communication, 389–399
  barriers to, 395–399
Organizational concepts, major, 239–252
Organizational controls, importance of, 723–726
Organizational culture, 104–105, 294–298
Organizational design outcomes, range of, 269–271
Organizational design
  contingency factors affecting, 271–277
  defined, 266–267
  objectives of, 267–269
  structural options in, 278–287
Organizational development, 323–326
Organizational dilemmas, 709–711
Organizational impacts, monitoring, 538
Organizational learning, 318
Organizational life cycle, 274
Organizational politics, 703–704
Organizational processes, key, 295–296
Organizational socialization, 694–695
Organizational structure, 105–106, 173
Organizational structures, designing, 266–269
Organizational systems, 208
Organizational visibility, 699
Organizing process, 229–230
  five-step, 230–239
  in action, 231
Organizing, 19–20, 229
  and the international manager, 660–664
  benefits of, 230
Orientation, 351–357
Orientation, task versus people, 466–469
Outback Steakhouse, 14, 16, 20, 22
Outside-the-box thinking, 211
Outsourcing, 600, 634
Overload, 395
Owen, Robert, 46
Owners, 109, 117
  and stockholders, 733–734

P

Pace, 183
Pacific Bell, 626, 701
Pan Am, 108
Panasonic, 567
Participative style, 465–466
Partners, and suppliers, 110
Patagonia, 733
Path-goal theory, 471
Payback analysis, 217
Payne, P. L., 40
Peace, William, 454
Pearce, Richard A., 383
Peat Marwick, 654
Penske Corporation, 13
Penske, Roger, 13
People-centered change, 310
PepsiCo, 111, 114, 164, 173, 177, 208, 210, 265, 276, 280, 472, 646, 648
Perceptions, 388
Performance appraisal, 360–364, 572
Performance standards, establishing, 525–528
Performance, measuring, 528
Performing stage, 501–502
Perk, 371
Perot Systems, 634
Perot, Ross, 110
Personnel manager, 335
Pervasiveness, and depth, 306
Peters, Thomas J., 60
PetsMart, 71, 88
Pfeiffer, Eckhard, 523
Philip Morris, 177, 567
Philips Electronics, 708
Philosophy of management, building a, 434–436
Physical environment, 302
Physical exam, 356
Pittsburgh Plate Glass, 108
Pizza Hut, 167, 208, 215
Plan
  implementing, 146
  inability to, 150
Planned change, 313
  steps in, 316–317
Planning department, overreliance on, 151
Planning process
  basic, 142–146
  lack of commitment to, 150
  steps in, 143
Planning tools, 149–150
Planning, 18
  and the international manager, 655–659
  barriers to, 150–151
  defined, 126–133
  duration and scope of, 18–19
  flexibility in, 19
  for development time, 497–498
  for feedback, 497–498
  for training needs, 497
  influences on, 19
  relationship between organizing and, 229
  to empower, 497
Plans, 130
  contingency, 141–142
  making effective, 146–150
  operational, 136–141
  reviewing, 230–232
  single-use, 136–137
  standing, 137–140
  strategic, 134
  tactical, 135–136
  types of, 133–142
Polaris Industries, 4
Polaroid Corporation, 133, 699
Policy, 137
Political environment, 649–651
Politics, understanding, 703–704
Portfolio strategy, 178–180
Positive motivation, versus negative, 463–464
Potential alternatives, developing, 199–200
Power, 243–245
  and leadership, 460–462
  coercive, 460

expert, 461
legitimate, 460
referent, 462
reward, 461
understanding, 703–704
Power-motivated person, 423
PPG Industries, 267, 278
Predisposed decision model, 209
Pre-international division phase, 660–661
Preliminary interview, 352–354
PricewaterhouseCoopers, 3, 211
Primedia, 4
Principle, statements of, 298–299
Priorities
ability to set, 209–210
identifying, 496
Proactive approach, 733
Problem, 193
defining the, 196–198
funnel approach to defining, 198
Procedure, 137
Process control sampling, 608
Process improvement team, 85
Process layout, 587–589
Process teams, 492
Process theories, 415, 427–433
Process-oriented change, 309–310
Procter & Gamble, 219, 284, 296, 440
Prodigy, 99
Product control, 607
Product departmentalization, 236
Product development team, 489
Product layout, 589
Product planning, 584–587
Production processes, and technology, 590–594
Production strategy, 184
Production, structure for implementing, 597
Productivity, 75–76, 527
controls for, 597–608
improving quality and, 77–90
internal and external influences on, 90–92
lost, 506
quality, and profitability, 68–77
Profit budgets, 565
Profitability ratios, 557
Profitability, quality and productivity, 68–77
Program evaluation and review technique (PERT), 606
Program, 137
Programmed decisions, 194–196
Project improvement team, 85
Project team, 490–491
Promotions, 365
Prospector strategy, 180
Protected groups, 338–340
Prudential Insurance Company, 438, 533
Psychological contract, 694
Purchasing, 598

Q

Quaker State Corporation, 173
Qualification testing, 608
Quality, 7, 527–528
controls for, 597–608
improving productivity and, 77–90
internal and external influences on, 90–92
productivity, and profitability, 68–77
Quality assurance team, 492
Quality audit, 85
Quality circle, 87
Quality control audit, 85
Quality function deployment (QFD), 70–73
Quality improvement team, 84
Quality management theory, 55–61
Quality management, major contributors to, 57
Quality of work life, 410–411
Quality school, 55
Quality teams, 492
Quality-productivity-profitability link, 76
Quantitative decision-making techniques, 215–219
Quantitative management theory, 49–51
Quantitative school, 49
Queueing models, 218
Quilmes Industrial, 176
Quota, 651

R

Radford, G. S., 60
RadioShack, 162
Raff, Beryl, 275
Ralcorp Holdings, Inc., 383
Ramquist, Lars, 283
Ramsey, Jackson, 49
Rand Corporation, 733
Rank, status in the company or, 398
Rating scales, behaviorally anchored, 363
Rational/logical decision model, 209
Raw materials inventory, 601
Ray-Chem, 697
Reactive approach, 732
Reactor strategy, 182
Receiver, 379
Recruiting, strategies for, 351–352
Recruitment, 351–357
Reengineering approach, 9, 56–57
Reengineering, 56
Reference checks, 355–356
Referent power, 244
Reinforcement theory, 429–431
Reinforcement, types of, 429–431
Reorder point (ROP), 602
Research and development (R&D), 90
Research and development strategy, 184–185
Research, operations, 49
Resistance approach, 732
Resistance, overcoming, 632–633
Resource deployment, 163
Resource requirements, determining, 132–133
Resources, 106–107
imperfect, 205
Responsibilities
of senders, 399–401
receivers of, 401–403
Responsibility, 246
Results
controlling and evaluating, 146
evaluating, 634–636
monitoring, 175
Retrenchment strategy, 177
Revenue budgets, 564
Revlon Cosmetics, 103, 180, 303
Revolutionary change, 311
Revson, Charles, 103
Reward power, 244
Reward system, providing an effective, 440
Reynolds Aluminum, 88
Rightsizing, 229
Risk International, 459
Risk manager, 523
RJR Nabisco, 531
Robotics, 590–591
Rockwell International Corporation, 592, 669
Rodeway Inns, 629
Rogers, Tom, 4
Role requirements, disagreements about, 509
Roles, 22
and managerial functions, 24
and the expectations of others, 24
decisional, 23–24
informational, 22
interpersonal, 22
Royal Dutch/Shell, 181
Rubbermaid Inc., 71, 72, 162
Rule, 138

S

Salaries, and wages, 368
Sales quotas, 568
Sam's Wholesale Clubs, 183
Satisfice, 205
Scheduling control, 604–607
School
classical administrative, 41–46
classical scientific, 41–44
contingency, 54
quality, 55
systems, 51–52
Schultz, Howard, 174
Scope, 162
Scoreboarding, 83
Scott Paper Company, 312–314, 513
Scott Technologies, 4
Scottish Inns, 183
Seagram, 177, 178
Sears & Roebuck, 99, 267, 281, 302, 306, 569
Selection, 351–357
Self-managed work team, 494
Semantics, 386
Semco, 412
Semler, Ricardo, 412
Sender, 379
Separations, 366–367
Service design planning, 584–587
Sewell Automotive Company, 67–68
Sexual harassment, 340–341
Sheraton Hotels, 582
Shewhart, Walter A., 60
Siemens, 232
Silicon Graphics, Inc., 426
Simonds Rolling Machine, 41
Simulations, 217–219
Single-use plans, 136–137
Situation analysis, 169
Situational factors, 473
Situational leadership, theories of, 469–475

Six Sigma, 522
Skills
conceptual, 26
human, 26
management, 25–29
technical, 26
Skinner, B. F., 429
Slogans, 299
Small batch technology, 277
Smith Barney, 710
Smith, Jack, 267, 274
SmithKline Beecham, 164, 172
Smoothing, 511
Snow, Charles, 180
Social audit, 741–742
Social responsibility
managing for, 738–742
nature of, 731–738
Social system, 297
Society, 118
Sociocultural environment, 342–345, 652–654
Sociocultural forces, 114
Soft manufacturing systems (SMS), 593
Solution, selecting the best, 145–146
Sony, 232, 567
Sources and uses of funds statement, 554
South African Airways, 8
Southwest Airlines, 27, 110, 132, 166, 175, 300, 410–411, 451, 460
Span of control, 238, 246–249
inappropriate, 398
proper, 249
wide and narrow, 248–249
Specialization of labor, 233
Spindler, Michael, 134
Sponsor, 701
Sponsorship, and independence, 711
Stability strategy, 177–178
Staff authority, 241
Staff departments, 241–243
Staffing environments, 336–346
Staffing problems, and solutions, 665–666
Staffing process, 335–336
Staffing, 20, 334
and the international manager, 665–667
responsibility for, 334–335
Stakeholders, 116
meeting responsibilities to, 116–117
responsibilities to, 733–736
Standard Motor Products, 571–572
Standard, 522
Standing plans, 137–140
Stanley Works, 4, 604
Staples, 251
Starbucks Corporation, 127, 174, 176, 210
Starwood Hotels & Resorts Worldwide, Inc., 214
State Farm Insurance, 343
Statistical analysis, 569–570
Statistical process control (SPC), 86
Statistical quality control (SQC), 86
Stead, Jere, 433, 437
Stegemeier, Richard, 201
Stephens, Deborah C., 47
Steppenwolf Theater, 10
Stereotype, 388
Stockage, 569
Stockholders, and owners, 733–734
Stories, 299
Storming stage, 501
Strategic business units (SBUs), 178
Strategic change, 308
Strategic goals, 134–135
Strategic management, 161
nature of, 161–167
Strategic managers, characteristics of successful, 165
Strategic plan, 134
Strategic planning process, 167–175
Strategic planning, 161, 164–165
elements of, 162–164
nature of, 161–167
Strategies
choosing, 655–656
for managing conflict, 510–514
formulating, 172
implementing, 172
Strategy formulation, versus strategy implementation, 165
Strategy implementation principles, 174
Strategy implementation, versus strategy formulation, 165
Strategy, 131, 271–272
analyzer, 181
cost-leadership, 183
defender, 181
development of a, 511
differentiation, 183
diversification, 177
financial, 184
focus, 183
functional-level, 183–185
grand, 176
growth, 176
human resources, 184
integration, 176
levels of, 165–167
marketing, 184
portfolio, 178–180
production, 184
prospector, 180
reactor, 182
research and development, 184–185
retrenchment, 177
stability, 177–178
Stress
managing, 705
symptoms of, 707–708
Stretch goals, 131
Structural change, 308–309
Subaru, 128
Subculture, 305
Subordinate involvement, five levels of, 206
Subordinates, 205–208
Subsystem controls, 548–551
Sullivan, Chris T., 14
Sun Microsystems, 227, 228, 232
Sunbeam, 303
Sunshine Cleaning, 65
SuperCuts, 184
Superiors, 205
Superordinate objective, 511
Suppliers, 118, 735
and materials, 109
and partners, 110
Support, providing, 437–438
Sutherland, Kent, 681–682, 685
Swiss Corporation for Microelectronics and Watchmaking, 380
SWOT analysis chart, 170
Symbols, 301
Symptom, 196
Synergy, 52, 164, 504
cumulative energy of, 52–53
systems and, 52
System, 51
the organization as a, 52
Systems management theory, 51–53
Systems school, 51–52

T

Taco Bell, 174, 215
Tactic, 131
Tactical objectives, 136
Tactical plans, 135–136
Taiwan Aerospace, 208
Tandy Corporation, 162
Target, 183, 313
Tariff, 651
Task force, 489
Taylor, Frederick W., 41
Team building
eliminating barriers to, 496–497
process of, 495–498
Team cohesiveness, 502
Team development, stages of, 500–502
Team effectiveness, measurements of, 504–506
Team leadership, 500
Team management, philosophical issues of, 489–495
Team norms, 502–503
Team organization, establishment of, 495–500
Team personality, 503–504
Team size, 498
Team structure, 284–285
Team, benefits of, 504–505
Team-building considerations, 498–500
Teams, 84–85
and communication, 385–386
characteristics of effective, 487
closely controlled by management, 494
costs of, 505–506
how much independence to give, 493–495
how to use, 489–493
nature of, 487–489
types of, 487–489
with moderate independence, 494
Technical skills, 26
Technological environment, 654–655
Technological forces, 114
Technology, 276–277, 298
and production processes, 590–594
Telecommuting, 699
Tellep, Daniel, 229, 239
Tenneco Inc., 147, 151
Test marketing, 567–568
Test, 355
Testing, 355
Texas Instruments, 490, 505, 725
Textron, 501
TGI Fridays, 215
The Container Store, 333

The Dow Chemical Corporation, 112
Theory, 39
Theory X, 434–435
Theory Y, 434–435
Third party, decisions by a, 512
Thompson, Robert M., 409
Thompson-McCully Company, 409–411
Thomson, S. A., 673
Three-step approach, 322
Tiller, Thomas, 4
Timeliness, 536
Timing, 397
Tony's Café, 274
Top management, 14, 21
Top-down budgeting, 562
Top-management commitment, 738–741
Toshiba, 110, 521–522
Total quality management (TQM), 73
Toyota, 12, 70, 72, 76, 110, 523, 732
Toys 'R' Us, 104, 181
TQM, the seven step model, 74
Training
  and development, 357–360, 571–572
  challenges of, 358–359
  purposes of, 358
  techniques of, 359–360
Trani, John, 4
Trans World Airlines, 582
Transactional processing, 627
Transfers, 365
Transmission, timing the, 401
Tribune Company, 176
Tropicana, 280
Trust, lack of, 397
TRW, Inc., 4, 558, 594
Tunnel vision, 211
Turnover, 570

U

Understanding, 379
Union Carbide, 112
Union environment, 345
Unisys, 634
Unit production technology, 277
United Airlines, 52, 491
United States Surgical Corporation, 392
United Technologies, 239, 454
Unity of command, 243
Unity of direction, 230
Universal Studios, 177
University of Michigan Studies, 467
Unocal, 201
UPS, 70–71
USAA, 164
Users, enabling, 633
USX, 278

V

Valujet, 175
Variable inspection, 608
Variables, overemphasis on controlling, 151
Verbal communication, 380–382
Veridian, 166
Vertical integration, 176
Vertical team, 488
Video Concepts, 162
View
  behavioral, 507–508
  interactionist, 508
  traditional, 507
Virtual team, 491
Visibility
  creating, 698–701
  volunteering for, 700
Vision, 80
Volkswagen, 57, 58
Von Pierer, Heinrich, 232
Vroom and Yetton decision tree, 206–207
Vroom, Victor, 206

W

Wages, and salaries, 368
Waiting line models, 218
Wal-Mart, 50, 71, 164, 194, 218, 294, 299, 306, 313, 378, 563, 569, 681
Walt Disney Company, 103, 114, 294, 531
Walton, Sam, 299, 303, 378, 476, 563, 681
Waltz, Frank, 270
Weatherup, Craig, 173
Webb, Maynard, 141, 147
Weber, Max, 44
Welch, Jack, 3, 106, 131, 311
Wendt, Gary, 4
Wendy's, 208
Western Electric, 47
Westinghouse, 454
Whirlpool, 648
Whistle-blowers, 709
Whitman, Margaret C., 125, 127, 129, 134, 147
Williams, Dennis, 4
Woolard, Edgar, 279, 281
Woolworth, 527
Work activities
  determining, 233
  disagreements about, 510
Work specialization, disadvantages of, 234
Work team, 492
Work, assigning, 237
Workers, loss of productive, 506
Work-in-process inventory, 601
Wrigley's, 648
Wyatt Company, 79

X

Xerox, 61, 73, 75, 164, 172, 177, 358, 438, 486, 490, 495, 587

Y

Yahoo!, 199, 547–548
Yang, Jerry, 547
Yaroslav Rubber Company, 561
Yetton, Phillip, 206

Z

Zale Corporation, 275
Zazarac, 14
Zenith, 59
Zero-based budgeting, 563
Zhen Cosmetics, 193, 274